La Geste Francor

Edition of the
Chansons de geste
of MS. Marc. Fr. XIII (=256)

Medieval and Renaissance
Texts and Studies
Volume 348

La Geste Francor

Edition of the
Chansons de geste
of MS. Marc. Fr. XIII (=256)

With glossary, introduction and notes by

Leslie Zarker Morgan

ACMRS
(Arizona Center for Medieval and Renaissance Studies)
Tempe, Arizona
2009

© Copyright 2009
Arizona Board of Regents for Arizona State University

Library of Congress Cataloging-in-Publication Data

Geste francor di Venezia.
  La Geste francor : edition of chansons de geste of MS. Marc. Fr. XIII (=256) / with glossary, introduction and notes by Leslie Zarker Morgan.
    p. cm. -- (Medieval and Renaissance texts and studies ; v. 348-)
  Includes bibliographical references and index.
  ISBN 978-0-86698-396-9 (alk. paper)
  1. Doon de Mayence (Legendary character)--Romances. 2. Charlemagne, Emperor, 742-814--Romances. 3. Dialect literature, French--Italy--Venice. 4. Geste francor di Venezia. I. Morgan, Leslie Zarker. II. Title.
  PQ1463.G53 2008
  841'.1--dc22

2008030886

∞
This book is made to last.
It is set in Adobe Caslon Pro,
smyth-sewn and printed on acid-free paper
to library specifications.
Printed in the United States of America

Table of Contents

VOLUME I

List of Illustrations and Charts	*xiii*
Acknowledgments	*xv*
Preface	*xvii*
Abbreviations	*xix*

1.0 General Introduction	1
1.1 Description of the Manuscript.	2
1.2 Handwriting.	5
1.2.1 Text Handwriting.	5
1.2.2 Rubrics.	6
1.3 Illuminations.	7
1.4 History of the manuscript.	13
2.0 Language: Franco-Italian and the Franco-Italian of V^{13}	17
2.1 Franco-Italian.	17
2.1.1 Arrival of the French Language in Italy.	17
2.1.2 The Franco-Italian Language in general.	19
2.2 The Franco-Italian of V^{13}	22
2.2.1 Franco-Italian of V^{13}: Earlier Treatments and Approach Here.	24
2.2.2 The Franco-Italian of V^{13}: Hypothesis.	26
2.2.2.1 Phonology.	26
2.2.2.2 Morphology.	30
2.2.2.2.1 Nouns.	30
2.2.2.2.2 Definite article.	37
2.2.2.2.3 Verbs.	38
2.2.2.2.4 Verbal Syntax.	43

2.2.2.2.5 Subject pronouns.	44
2.2.2.2.6 The role of rhyme in deviant forms.	46
2.3 Conclusions: Language of V.^{13}	51
3.0 Versification and Metrics	53
3.1 Rhymes.	53
3.2 Syllable count.	57
4.0 The literary contents of V^{13}	73
4.1 *Bovo (I and II)*.	76
4.1.1 V^{13} *Bovo*.	77
4.1.2 Other Italian versions.	77
4.1.2.1 The *Laurenziano*.	78
4.1.2.2 The *Udinese*.	78
4.1.2.3 The prose *Toscano*.	79
4.1.2.4 *I Reali di Francia*.	79
4.1.3 French Versions.	82
4.1.3.1 Anglo-Norman.	82
4.1.3.2 French "Continental" versions: Continental I.	85
4.1.3.3 Continental II.	86
4.1.3.4 Continental III.	90
4.1.4.5 *Daurel et Beton*.	92
4.1.4 Spanish texts.	94
4.1.5 German versions.	95
4.1.6 Scandinavian version.	95
4.1.7 Dutch version.	95
4.1.8 British Isles.	96
4.1.8.1 English version.	96
4.1.8.2 Irish version.	97
4.1.8.3 Welsh version.	97
4.1.9 Discussion.	97
4.2 *Berta da li pe grant*.	106
4.2.1 V^{13} *Berta*.	108
4.2.2 Other Italian versions.	108

4.2.2.1 *I Reali di Francia*.	109
4.2.2.2 *Aspramonte*.	111
4.2.2.3 *Aquilon de Bavière*.	111
4.2.2.4 Later Italian works.	112
4.2.2.5 Other references.	112
4.2.3 French versions.	114
4.2.3.1 *Chronique santongeaise*.	114
4.2.3.2 Philippe Mousket.	115
4.2.3.3 Girard d'Amiens.	115
4.2.3.4 *Miracle de Berte*.	116
4.2.3.5 *Chronique de France* / BN 5003.	116
4.2.3.6 *Valentine et Orson*.	117
4.2.3.7 *Histoire de la Reine Berte et du Roy Pepin*.	118
4.2.3.8 *Adenet le Rois*.	119
4.2.4 Iberian Versions.	122
4.2.4.1 *Gran conquista de Ultramar*.	122
4.2.4.2 *Noches de invierno*.	123
4.2.4.3 Catalan versions.	124
4.2.5 German texts.	124
4.2.5.1 Stricker.	125
4.2.5.2 *Weihenstephan Chronik*.	126
4.2.5.3 Wolter.	126
4.2.5.4 World histories.	127
4.2.5.5 Hohenmut.	128
4.2.6 Scandinavian versions.	129
4.2.7 Dutch version.	130
4.2.8 English versions.	131
4.2.9 Discussion.	131
4.2.9.1 Mythological symbolism.	132
4.2.9.2 Fairy tale sources.	132
4.2.9.3 Stemma creation.	134
4.2.9.4 Genre definition.	135
4.2.9.5 Socio-political analysis.	135

4.3 *Karleto*.	139
4.3.0 Mentions: *Pseudo-Turpin*.	139
4.3.1 V^{13} version.	140
4.3.2 Other Italian versions.	140
4.3.2.1 Andrea da Barberino.	140
4.3.2.2 *Aquilon de Bavière*.	142
4.3.3 French versions.	143
4.3.3.1 Fragments.	143
4.3.3.2 Girard d'Amiens.	144
4.3.3.3 Jean d'Outremeuse.	147
4.3.3.4 David Aubert.	148
4.3.4. Spanish versions.	149
4.3.4.1 *Primera crónica*.	149
4.3.4.2 *Gran conquista de Ultramar*.	150
4.3.5 German versions.	151
4.3.5.1 *Karl der Grosse*.	151
4.3.5.2 *Weihenstephan Chronik*.	152
4.3.5.3 Hohenmut.	152
4.3.5.4 *Karl Meinet*.	153
4.3.5.5 Füetrer.	154
4.3.6. Scandinavian versions.	155
4.3.7 Dutch versions.	156
4.3.8 English versions.	156
4.3.9 Discussion.	156
4.3.9.1 Historical considerations.	157
4.3.9.2 *Enfances* and the *chanson de geste*.	159
4.4 *Uggieri il Danese: Enfances* and *Chevalerie*.	167
4.4.1 V^{13} plot.	167
4.4.2 Other Italian versions.	167
4.4.2.1 *I Reali di Francia*.	168
4.4.2.2 *Rinaldo*.	168
4.4.2.3 *Aquilon de Bavière*.	171
4.4.2.4 Versions of *Ogier le Danois* in Italy.	171
4.4.2.5 Later Italian references to *Uggieri*.	172

4.4.3 French versions.	172
4.4.3.1 Raimbert de Paris.	172
4.4.3.2 Adenet le Rois.	175
4.4.3.3 Girard d'Amiens.	177
4.4.3.4 Philippe Mousket.	178
4.4.3.5 Jean d'Outremeuse.	178
4.4.3.6 Unedited French versions.	180
4.4.3.7 David Aubert.	180
4.4.3.8 Printed editions.	182
4.4.4 Iberian versions.	182
4.4.5 German versions.	183
4.4.6 Scandinavian versions.	183
4.4.7 Dutch versions.	186
4.4.8 English versions.	186
4.4.9 Discussion.	186
4.5 *Berta e Milone, Orlandino*.	194
4.5.1 V^{13} version.	194
4.5.2 Other Italian versions.	196
4.5.2.1 *I Reali di Francia*.	197
4.5.2.2 Relation of *cantari* and *I Reali*.	199
4.5.2.3 Pulci's *Morgante*.	200
4.5.2.4 *Aquilon de Bavière*.	200
4.5.2.5 Folengo's *Orlandino*.	200
4.5.2.6 Aretino's *Orlandino*.	201
4.5.3 French versions.	202
4.5.4 Spanish versions.	203
4.5.5 German versions.	203
4.5.6 Scandinavian version.	203
4.5.7 Dutch versions.	203
4.5.8 English versions.	203
4.5.9 Discussion.	204
4.5.9.1 Charlemagne's Sin.	204
4.5.9.2 Italian tradition.	206
4.5.9.3 St. Gilles.	208

4.5.9.4 French tradition.	209
4.5.9.4.1 Fourteenth century.	209
4.5.9.4.2 Fifteenth century.	210
4.5.9.5 Provençal.	210
4.5.9.6 Spanish.	211
4.5.9.7 German.	211
4.5.9.8 Scandinavian.	212
4.5.9.9 Art as evidence.	213
4.5.9.10 Historical details.	214
4.5.9.11 Literary repercussions.	215
4.5.9.12 V^{13} version's significance.	216
4.6 *Macario*.	219
4.6.1 V^{13} version.	219
4.6.2 The tradition.	221
4.6.2.1 Other Italian versions.	221
4.6.2.2 *I Fatti di Spagna*.	222
4.6.2.3 *Spagna in rima*.	223
4.6.3 French versions.	223
4.6.3.1 Albéric des Trois-Fontaines.	223
4.6.3.2 Fragments.	224
4.6.3.3 Arsenal 3351 (*Garin de Monglane*).	225
4.6.3.4 *Chronique de France* / BN 5003.	226
4.6.3.5 Jean d'Outremeuse.	226
4.6.4 Spanish versions.	227
4.6.4.1 *Gran conquista de Ultramar*.	227
4.6.4.2 *Noble cuento*.	228
4.6.5 German versions.	230
4.6.5.1 *Karl Meinet*.	230
4.6.5.2 World histories.	231
4.6.5.3 Schondoch and Sachs.	231
4.6.6 Scandinavian versions.	232
4.6.7 Dutch versions.	232

4.6.8 English versions.	233
4.6.9 Discussion.	234
4.7 Conclusions	242
5.0 Works Cited	255
5.1 Manuscripts Consulted.	255
5.2 Reference Works.	255
5.3 Modern Editions and Criticism Cited.	257
6.0 Edition, V^{13}: Introduction	289
6.1 Editorial Norms.	289
6.2 Equivalency to Other Editions.	290
6.3 Line Numbering and Rubric Positioning.	292
6.4 Lexeme Division.	293
6.5 Orthography.	294
6.6 Abbreviations.	295
6.7 Emendations.	298
6.8 Accents.	299
6.9 Semivowels.	303
6.10 Capitalization.	304
7.0 Texts of MS. Marc. 13, the *Geste Francor*	305
7.1 *Enfances Bovo*.	305
7.2 *Berta da li pe grant*.	345
7.3 *Chevalerie Bovo*.	411
7.4 *Karleto*.	506
7.5 *Berta e Milone*.	637
7.6 *Enfances Ogier le Danois*.	656
7.7 *Orlandino*.	708

VOLUME II

7.8 *Chevalerie Ogier le Danois.*	728
7.9 *Macario.*	804
8.0 Endnotes to Edition	941
8.1 Endnotes to *Enfances Bovo.*	941
8.2 Endnotes to *Berta da li pe grant.*	959
8.3 Endnotes to *Chevalerie Bovo.*	983
8.4 Endnotes to *Karleto.*	1009
8.5 Endnotes to *Berta e Milone.*	1044
8.6 Endnotes to *Enfances Ogier le Danois.*	1052
8.7 Endnotes to *Orlandino.*	1070
8.8 Endnotes to *Chevalerie Ogier le Danois.*	1077
8.9 Endnotes to *Macario.*	1111
9.0 Glossary	1139
9.1 Introduction and explanation of procedure.	1139
9.2 Proper Nouns.	1141
9.3 Lexical anomalies.	1142
9.4 Abbreviations used in the Glossary.	1142
9.5 Reference works cited by abbreviation.	1143
Glossary: V^{13} (*Geste Francor*)	1145
Glossary: Proper Nouns V^{13}	1436
Index of Proper Names	1461
Index of Subjexts	1475
Index of Titles	1479

List of Illustrations and Charts

Section 2

    Map of Italy, including relevant cities for manuscript   23
and for literary description

    Forms of *dama*

    Forms of *fema*   31

    Forms of *sir(e) / signor(s) /segnor(s)*   34

    The definite article   37

    Definite article use examples   37

    The verb "to have" in all tenses   39

    The subject pronoun   45

    Verbs in rhyme: Effects of rhyme on infinitive endings

        Chart 1: Variation of *-oir* and other endings at rhyme position   49

        Chart 2: Variation in first conjugation Latin reflex infinitive   49
endings (-ARE) at rhyme position and not

        Chart 3. Variation of conjugation: Verb stems with an *-ir(e)*   50
compared to an *-er* ending and their appearance at rhyme position

        Chart 4. Variation of conjugation: with and without final *-e*,   51
verbs with *-er* and *-ir* stems at rhyme position

Section 3

    Total rhymes and percentages of total lines   53

    Complete summary, laisse by laisse, of rhymes and variations   58

Section 4

4.0 Charlemagne's Family: V[13]   75

    4.1 *Bovo, Enfances* and *Chevalerie*

        A: Proper Names in V[13] *Bovo* compared to other versions   99

        B: Selected versions of *Bovo d'Antona / Beuve d'Hamstone*   104

    4.2 Versions of *Berta da li pe grant*   138

4.3 *Karleto*

    A: Versions of *Enfances Charlemagne / Karleto*: characters — 163

    B: Versions of *Enfances Charlemagne* — 166

4.4 *Uggieri il danese / Ogier le danois*

    A: Versions of *Ogier* (*Enfances* and *Chevalerie*) by country/date until 1599 — 189

    B: Proper names in selected versions of *Ogier le Danois* — 192

4.6 *Macario*

    A: Versions of *Macaire / Macario / Reine Sibille* — 235

    B: Character names in representative versions of *Macaire / Macario / Reine Sibille* — 237

    C: Major plot elements in different versions of *Macaire / Macario / Reine Sibille* — 239

    D: Episodes of *Macaire / Macario / Reine Sibille* absent from V^{13} — 241

4.7 Conclusions

    A: Collections of Charlemagne tales — 251

    B: V^{13} (*Geste Francor*) plot interactions — 252

    C: *Enfances* plots in V^{13} — 253

    D: *Chevalerie* plots in V^{13} — 254

    E: Female *enfances* in V^{13} — 254

Section 6

6.2 Equivalency with earlier editions of the *Geste Francor* and *chansons de geste* in it — 290

Acknowledgments

Thanks are due to many who have helped me complete this edition and encouraged progress toward completion over the years. Over twenty-eight years, my list is long indeed. Emilio Faccioli of the Magistero in Florence inspired my desire to know of Ariosto's predecessors. Professor Braccini in Filologia Romanza at the University of Florence started me on my way with bibliography for the study of Franco-Italian. My doctorate thesis directors, Howard Garey, Paolo Valesio, and Rufus Hendon, of Yale University, guided me from 1978 through 1983 to complete my initial edition and concordance of the *Chevalerie Ogier* in Franco-Italian; Howard Garey, in particular, read and reread my work, asking the hard questions. Special thanks go to Mt. Holyoke College for the Hannum-Warner Travel Grant for the summer of 1984 which enabled me to go to Venice to compare my microfilm reading with the manuscript. The Biblioteca Marciana allowed me access to V^{13} and V^{21} during my stay that summer, and the library assistants were very patient and helpful with someone unfamiliar with their system.

This work would have been impossible without the State University of New York at Stony Brook Library and Loyola-Notre Dame Library, and most especially their Interlibrary Loan Offices, for their valiant efforts to obtain out-of-print and obscure items. The extensive collection of Eisenhower Library of The Johns Hopkins University has played an important role over the last twelve years, together with its circulation assistants, both at the circulation desk and at the remote sites, who were always kind and helpful in person and via e-mail. The computer center staff at the State University of New York at Stony Brook and at Loyola College in Maryland provided invaluable help initially in purchasing and installing mainframe computer programs for text analysis.

Numerous colleagues have provided me with copies of their own unpublished materials: Gloria Allaire of *Rinaldo*; Daniel Métraux of Girard d'Amiens's *Charlemagne*, Annalee Rejhon, Hans van Dijk, and others, copies of conference papers. Geert Claassens generously provided summaries of Dutch materials and read and commented portions of the introduction. Günter Holtus invited me to the first Franco-Italian Symposium in Bad Homburg in 1987, thus introducing me to the world of Franco-Italianists, and has continued to provide an excellent example with his precise work; Robert F. Cook has given me a computerized version of his edition of V^4 and Joseph Duggan of his edition of V^7 and Châteauroux, for use in glossarial work. Edward Heinemann and John McLucas both also read and commented upon portions of the introduction, catching many errors and making numerous helpful suggestions. And finally, thanks to Gloria Allaire for going above and beyond in her indexing, catching with her careful close reading many infelicities of style and errors before the work went to press. Any errors, of course, remain my own.

The staff of MRTS has been unfailingly helpful and understanding in producing these volumes. I thank editors and staff for their assistance through this lengthy project, from the anonymous reviewers through the director (Robert Bjork), managing editor (Roy Rukkila), design and production manager (Todd Halvorsen), editorial assistant (Leslie MacCoull) and student workers (William E. Bolton and Stephanie Volf), all have been helpful and professional through the process, whether via email, in person at the International Medieval Conference, in the offices at the Arizona State University, or by phone. I apologize in advance if I have omitted anyone, and appreciate all their effort and time expended on this publication.

I also thank the Department of Modern Languages and Literatures of Loyola College in Maryland for their continuing belief in the importance of my project and the Dean's office of the College of Arts and Sciences, which has supported travel to numerous professional conferences in order for me to share my work and learn of other projects in progress. Colleagues too numerous to mention here have assisted by gentle criticism as well as by example. Finally, I especially acknowledge my husband's encouragement of my research since 1976; he is as eager as I to see this finished. I thank them all.

Preface

Biblioteca Nazionale Manoscritto marciano fondo francese XIII (=256) of Venice [National Library of St. Mark French Manuscript 13, new call number 256], usually abbreviated V^{13}, is a text frequently cited in critical literature about early Italian and late Old French language and literary tradition. It has been studied by scholars since 1839 and published in photofacsimile as well as in editions of various eras, primarily in scholarly journals. Most recently Aldo Rosellini published the complete text.[1] He includes a very complete summary of discussion on the nature of Franco-Italian, an exhaustive bibliography of the field, and a complete plot summary of the entire manuscript. However, it is marred by typographical errors and lacks a complete glossary; furthermore, the bibliography is ordered by date of publication, which makes it difficult to consult.

This new edition seeks to fulfill several needs; it does not reproduce Rosellini's work, but expands upon it, including knowledge and techniques not available at that time and incorporating commentary upon his edition. This new edition presents all the *chansons de geste* in a single format, for a reliable interpretative edition of the entire text, and will have a greater distribution than earlier separate *chansons* and be more available to the Anglophone world. It also provides further materials for study in the several areas of interest into which this manuscript falls, including literary precedents and later versions of individual *chansons*, and a complete glossary of the lexicon unavailable in previous editions (thanks in part to computer techniques). Finally, because the text is in digital format, it is possible to make analyses and studies not feasible earlier due to the manuscript's length, so that where editorial intervention is contemplated, other forms in the text have been closely scrutinized to maintain a similar linguistic patina throughout the edition.

Though the primary object of this edition of V^{13} is scholarly—providing an accessible complete version accurately transcribed and annotated—it is hoped that this somewhat unusual text will receive a wider audience, from students of Old French to students of the oral epic and Italian dialects, in this country and elsewhere.

---

[1] A. Rosellini, ed., *La Geste Francor di Venezia. Edizione integrale del Codice XIII del Fondo francese della Marciana* (Brescia: La Scuola, 1986).

Abbreviations

OF	Old French (Ancien français)
MF	Middle French (Moyen français)
MSF	Modern Standard French (Français moderne)
OI	Old Italian
MSI	Modern Standard Italian
adj	adjective
adv	adverb
conj	conjunction
CR	object case (cas régime)
CS	subject case (cas sujet)
dir obj	direct object
excl	exclamation (interjection)
f	feminine
FP	feminine plural
FS	feminine singular
I	Italian
ind obj	indirect object
inf	infinitive
interj	interjection
m	masculine
MP	masculine plural
MS	masculine singular
N	noun
obj	object
OC	object case (FR. cas régime)
P	plural

part	present participle
ppart	past participle
prep	preposition
pro	pronoun
S	singular
subj	subject
SC	subject cast (Fr. cas sujet)
V	verb
Ven	Venetian
<	derives from
>	becomes
*	hypothetical
[	closed syllable (ends in consonant)
]	open syllable

1.0
GENERAL INTRODUCTION

Venice, Biblioteca marciana fondo francese manuscript XIII (= 256), usually referred to as V^{13}, is the earliest known northern Italian production (that is, original work) of *chansons de geste*. It is anonymous, and its precise date is unknown. The existence of *chansons de geste*, written and oral, in Italy, is attested in numerous documents, personal letters, and artistic manifestations from the twelfth century on.[1] The phenomenon presents an unusual intersection of oral and written tradition. The Franco-Italian "language" in which V^{13} is written is unlike any modern-day language, which remains difficult to define, though its syntactic and lexical basis has been examined in specific texts and in general.[2]

This introduction describes the manuscript, gives its history, discusses rhyme and meter, and outlines the problem of Franco-Italian language as seen in V^{13}. The linguistic study is based upon computational analysis of the entire text and is completed by the glossary following the edition. The length of the text, 17,067 lines, precludes a complete analysis of the language here.

---

[1] A. Viscardi cites various examples of French literature in Italy ("Arthurian Influence on Italian Literature from 1200–1500," in *Arthurian Literature*, ed. R. S. Loomis [Oxford: Clarendon Press, 1959], 419–29), as does D. Delcorno Branca (*L'Orlando Furioso e il romanzo cavalleresco medievale* [Florence: Olschki, 1973]). The most famous, of course, is Lovato de' Lovati's letter in C. Foligno, "Epistole inedite di Lovato de' Lovati e d'altri a lui," *Studi medievali* 2 (1906): 49. For art specifically related to *chansons de geste*, see R. Lejeune and J. Stiennon, *La Légende de Roland dans l'art du Moyen Age* (Brussels: Arcade, 1967). The manuscript is in Venice, Biblioteca Nazionale Marciana MS. Fr. Z. 13.

[2] G. Holtus summarizes the discussion about the name "Franco-Italian" effectively, ending the dispute once and for all: Franco-Italian is neither a language nor a dialect, in "Ist das Franko-italienische eine Sprache oder eine Dialekte?" in *Beiträge zum romanischen Mittelalter*, ed. Kurt Baldinger, Sonderband zum 100 Jährigen Bestehen, *Zeitschrift für romanische Philologie* (Tübingen: Niemeyer, 1977), 79–97. His subsequent publications further develop the description of Franco-Italian. See "Language" (section 2.0) for a discussion of the nature of Franco-Italian in relation to V^{13}.

1.1 Description of the manuscript.

Manoscritto marciano fondo francese XIII (= 256) is an undated Franco-Italian text which contains no direct reference to place of origin. An approximate dating can be made by examining the handwriting and miniatures.[3] Rajna, following Còggiola, states that the manuscript is a palimpsest; however, earlier writing is not visible to the naked eye.[4]

The support is vellum. When perfect, the pages measure approximately 318 mm. by 217 mm.[5] There are 95 folios, bound hairside to hairside and flesh to flesh. There are two sets of numbers on the pages. One set is in pencil in the center of the lower margin, by page, added after the writing of the manuscript; the other

---

[3] Much of this manuscript description is drawn from my earlier dissertation, L. K. Z. Morgan, "Between French and Italian: Ogier le Danois (Ms. marc. fr. 13=254)," Ph. D. diss., Yale University, 1983, xxiv–xxxv (Ann Arbor, MI: UMI, 1984). The manuscript was originally examined in the Biblioteca San Marco, Venice, in May 1980. The complete transcription from microfilm was verified with the manuscript from May to June 1984, thanks to a Hannum-Warner Travel Fellowship from Mt. Holyoke College. More recent re-examination has relied upon the microfilm purchased from the Biblioteca Marciana in Venice and the photofacsimile of V^{13} available at the New York Public Library (P. Rajna, *Geste Francor* [Milan: Bestetti e Tuminelli, n.d. but 1925 or 1926]).

[4] Rajna (*Geste Francor*, 21–22) cites Giulio Còggiola, the librarian of the Biblioteca Marciana, as does Rosellini (*Geste Francor*, 15–16). Neither cites a published work; rather this is Rajna reporting personal discussion in his introduction, which is then quoted by Rosellini. Rajna states that from reading what is discernible of the original text, it appears to be derived from several sources, primarily books of statutes, and other archival records: acts, protocols, or registers (*Geste Francor*, 22). Again, according to Rajna, most of the previous writing is carefully scraped off; where it is visible, it is perpendicular to the present writing. Again according to Rajna, the original text was not divided into columns, and ran across the full width of the page; he saw different line lengths by different hands. The best examples of the previous writing, according to Rajna, are on fols. 2^v, 3^v, 13^v, 21^r, 60^r, 60^v (*Geste Francor*, 22). The column of writing on fols. 2^v and 7^r is much narrower than that of fol. 13^v. This would suggest different origins for the sheets of parchment. To the naked eye, while some folios are darker and more imperfect, there was little writing visible at the time of my examination of the manuscript; only undistinguishable writing on fols. 3^v, 21^v, 60^r, 80^v was visible. S. Bisson, who offers the most recent description, says the MS. is entirely palimpsest. The parchment was originally used for a notarial register from the Bologna area ("I manoscritti di epica carolingia a Venezia," in *L'épopée romane*, Actes du XVe Congrès international Rencesvals, Poitiers, 21–27 août 2000, ed. Gabriel Bianciotto et al. [Poitiers: CESCM, 2002], 741–48).

[5] Rajna (*Geste Francor*, 21); Rosellini (*Geste Francor*, 11) gives 330 mm. by 222 mm, following G. E. Ferrari (*Documenti marciani e principale letteratura sui codici veneti di epopea carolingia* [Venice: Biblioteca nazionale marciana, 1961], 4). Folios vary in size, and Rajna's figures fall within the most frequent range of those which I measured.

set, by folio, occasionally not visible, is in a brownish ink in the upper right-hand corner of each recto. Folio 1ʳ also has a number "135" in the top center. This has excited some comment, but seems most probably to be a label for the location (shelf mark) from some point in its career.[6]

All evidence points to the physical unity of the manuscript, though the sheets appear to be of different origins and are of different sizes and variable quality. The incipit of the manuscript is missing; the first *chanson* begins *in medias res*. The first folio is torn and faded. The first signature is complete, so the total number of missing initial folios is not known. There are eleven signatures of eight folios each, and, at the end, one signature of seven folios. The end of the manuscript is on fol. 95ʳ, which includes the *explicit*. The Biblioteca San Marco has added two guard sheets, one in front and one in back. Catchwords end each signature, at fols. 8ᵛ, 16ᵛ, 24ᵛ, 32ᵛ, 40ᵛ, 48ᵛ, 56ᵛ, 64ᵛ, 72ᵛ, 80ᵛ, 88ᵛ, in the center of the lower margin, for the first seven signatures, each decorated with pen flourishes. Since the final signature ends the text, a catchword was not necessary. The catchwords all correspond to the succeeding line and there are no interruptions in rhyme or assonance between folios. The manuscript is bound in a single volume, in an eighteenth-century binding of brown calfskin with a lion imprint, the symbol of St. Mark, on its cover.[7] It is stamped "DOON DE MAY./ ROM" on the spine. On the first guard sheet are glued several lines from a printed text, as follows (where ʃ stands for the long *s*):

cod xiii
in foglio, di carta pecora, di fogli 95
doone, ovvero doolino di magonza, romanzo in verʃi
manca in principio
questo romanzo trovaʃi stampato in parigi nel mdlxxxxiv, in
4. a bonfons.
il signore della MONNOYE, nelle sue note al Verdier, *crede che*
poʃʃa eʃer ʃtato compoʃto dal re adenes.

Through the glued-on portion, the other side of the page can be read: "CARLOM/E' diverso altri due di sopra/ CODICE XIX. [embossed]/ in foglio." This glued-in piece of paper is an excerpt from a copy of Zannetti's catalogue, who lists it so.[8]

---

[6] Rajna, *Geste Francor*, 25–27.

[7] The binding information comes from Rajna, *Geste Francor*, 21. It is also quoted also by others, e.g., M. Zorzi, ed., *Biblioteca Marciana, Venezia: Le grandi biblioteche d'Italia* (Florence: Nardini Editore. Centro Internazionale del Libro, 1988), 119.

[8] A. Zannetti, *Latina et Italica D. Marci Biblioteca Codicum Manu Scriptorum: Per titulos digesta* (Venice: Simone Occhi, 1741), 258–59. The St. Mark's copy of Zanetti's volume has "Sec XIV" handwritten in the left margin of page 258 in modern handwriting (probably end of the nineteenth century).

The manuscript is in fair condition. The first sheet is practically illegible, as it is faded and torn; a central portion of the page is missing. There are many holes (some of which were present when the manuscript was written, since the scribe avoided them) and patches, some sewn on with hide. The binding has come apart. Many pages are torn at the bottom or are rough. The manuscript also smells strongly of a chemical used on the pages to discourage bookworms. Folio 92 is folded, and the creases make the writing more difficult to read. It has been suggested that the manuscript began similarly to the *Reali di Francia*, with *Gisberto*, *Ottaviano*, *Fioravante*, *Fiovo*, and *Ugo d'Alvernia*.[9]

The text is normally in two columns of forty-nine lines each in brown-black ink.[10] The folios are lined, with the lining occasionally visible. There are the forty-nine lines necessary for the text, with a fiftieth at the top, with approximately .625 cm (1/4 inch) between the lines. There are also six vertical lines: two separate each column of verse-initial capitals from the text, and a third vertical line marks the end of the column of text.[11] Similarly, the second column begins with two vertical lines that define the location of laisse-initials beginning that column; the sixth marks the margin at the right side of the page. The vertical lines are often not straight (for example, on fol. 17^r). The depth of the lines makes them at times quite visible; they were evidently ruled with lead. No pricking is visible, but lead and scratching out are visible. A guide letter appears before each line of text to inform the rubricator which initial to write and rubricate. There are fourteen illuminations, all of two-column width, each of which reduce the number of text lines on those folios.

There is no specific division between the *chansons de geste*. The text is continuous throughout, though there are larger and smaller spaces left for rubrics.

---

[9] Rajna, *Geste Francor*, 27–33.

[10] For an exhaustive list of exceptions, see Rosellini, *Geste Francor*, 12.

[11] The separation of the first letters was a convention for classical and other poetry that seems to have started in the eighth century (if not earlier) and continued through early printers into the fifteenth and sixteenth centuries (D. Miner, V. I. Carlson, and P.W. Filby, comps., *2,000 Years of Calligraphy: A Three-Part Exhibition Organized by the Baltimore Museum of Art, the Peabody Institute Library and the Walters Gallery*, June 6–July 18, 1965 [Meriden, CT: Meriden Gravure, 1965], 39).

1.2 Handwriting.

There are at least two hands: that of the rubricator (or rubricators) and that of the text scribe.

1.2.1 Text Handwriting.

The text ink is brown-black, varying in darkness throughout the manuscript. The first letter of each text line is an initial, set apart from the text. The first line of each laisse begins with a larger initial with a red stroke through it; the second letter in that line is the size of capitals which begin the following lines. In the rest of the laisse, the initial capital stands apart from the line and has a red line through it. Capitalization, other than verse initial, is arbitrary. Occasionally a capital standing alone, as the abbreviation of a proper name, will also receive a red stroke; R, N, or K are the most common. It is clear that the text was given to the rubricator after having been completed, since a small letter in the text hand, in the text ink, to the left of the line, shows what letter was to be initialed at the beginning of each verse.

The handwriting itself is a rounded Italian gothic bookhand. It differs from northern gothics both in the spacing of the letters (which is much wider than in northern manuscripts) and in the roundness of the letters themselves.[12] The forms of the *a*s and *e*s, as well as the use of both kinds of *s* are gothic characteristics (the long *s* and the short cursive *s*). There are few abbreviations: the ones present are primarily for the letter *n*, in a few cases for *r*, or for proper names (for a complete list, see below). Two types of *r* are present (both the gothic and the connected cursive). One peculiarity of the script is the use of the cedillaed *c* (*ç*) for *z*, which developed from the gothic form of *z*: an upper arching line, a second line reduced to a dash, and a third in the opposite direction from the first. This letter is characteristic of Italian gothic from the last years of the thirteenth century through the whole fourteenth century.[13] Two types of *d* are also present: one is a capital *d* (e.g., fol. 72[va]) with the minuscule form; the rest are standard capitals.

Some of the initials are more elaborate than others. On fol. 25[r], for example, there is extra decoration of three capitals: *a*, *l*, *c*.[14] On fol. 33[r], *S* and *Q* are more elaborately decorated. On fol. 31[r] there are seven lines of text, three of rubric, and

---

[12] Miner et al., *2,000 Years*, 49, speaks of the differences between Italian and northern Gothics.

[13] G. Battelli, *Lezioni di paleografia*, 3ª ed. (Rome: Società Arti Grafiche e Fotomeccaniche Sansaini, 1949), 225.

[14] This is also mentioned by S. M. Cingolani, "Innovazione e Parodia nel Marciano XIII (*Geste Francor*)," *Romanistisches Jahrbuch* 38 (1987): 62–64, who discusses the meaning of such differences for the text.

a huge *S*. The catchwords are also encircled with elaborate red pen flourishes on fols. 64^v and 72^v, at the ends of those signatures. The function of these differences is not clear. Did the scribe or redactor wish to indicate a new *chanson* beginning on 31^r and on 33^r? Or is the decoration purely arbitrary?

From the characteristics of the handwriting, therefore, the manuscript is of the gothic period. Because the end of the fourteenth century was dominated by the humanistic reform in Italy, that would constitute a *terminus ante quem* for the manuscript. At the end of the thirteenth century these gothic forms, especially the use of *c* with a cedilla (ç), were just coming into use. Thus, from the handwriting, the manuscript would be datable to between the very end of the thirteenth century and the last portion of the fourteenth century.[15]

1.2.2 Rubrics.

V^{13} is rubricated throughout. That is, each laisse is preceded by a rubric or space for a rubric. In this it differs from other Franco-Italian manuscripts: neither of the versions of the *Chanson de Roland* from San Marco (V^4, V^7) is rubricated; the *Entrée d'Espagne* is not rubricated; *Aliscans* is not rubricated. The procedure obviously created technical problems for its creator.

The overall rubric handwriting style, gothic, is similar to that of the text, but there are peculiar problems associated with the rubrics. As Rajna points out, the rubrics differ from each other as well as the text. Those in fols. 1^r–8^v (the first signature) are elegant and regular; from fol. 9 through the first part of fol. 10, the form is similar but somewhat smaller; and from fol. 10 on the rubrics are irregular and full of malformed letters (*Geste Francor*, 23). The rubrics contain an unusual form of initial capital from fol. 10^r on; the first letter of a rubric always begins with a rounded sigma-shaped curve. The *a* and *r* capital forms of the rubrics differ from those used in the text. In the text they are half-open and uncial-like; in the rubrics, a simple cursive (Rajna, *Geste Francor*, 23). The nib of the pen used in the rubrics was broader than that used for the text; the strokes of the letters are less clear. The rubricator uses abbreviations similar to those found in the text, primarily for *r* and *n* (for a complete list, see section 6.6).

Inconsistencies in the rubrication indicate that the scribe copied from another source. A varying amount of space is left for the rubricator, from one to five lines, with no evident planning. The rubrics themselves are from one to four lines long. Four spaces left for the rubricator are blank (fols. 8ra, 13vb–14ra, 39rb, 85vb). Two rubrics, at fols. 24va and 26va respectively, are omitted (that is, two seem to

---

[15] Others have suggested different dates; e.g., Ferrari says end of the twelfth, beginning of the thirteenth century (*Documenti marciani*, 4). However, I am speaking specifically of the manuscript and handwriting, not the contents.

have been skipped from the "original," probably written, copy of the rubrics). The scribe catches up on fol. 25ra (Rubric 116, after line 4414), so that subsequently the rubrics agree with the following text. Therefore, there is no rubric for laisse 22 (at the top of fol. 8rb, line 1345); from laisse 23 (Rubric 22, following line 1371) through laisse 52 (after line 2378), the rubrics describe the previous laisse; there is no rubric for laisse 53; then from laisse 55 (Rubric 54, after line 2438) through 116 (through line 4414), the rubrics describe the action two laisses back. The space for the first two lines of rubric 116, which precedes laisse 117, is heavily scraped, and the rubricator includes two rubrics. From that point on, the rubrics agree with the following laisses. It is impossible to know if the rubricator deliberately compensated for copying errors, but the scraping would seem to indicate that this is what happened.[16]

1.3 ILLUMINATIONS.

There are fourteen illuminations, each of two-column width. They are on fols. 38^r, 38^v, 40^r, 40^v, 42^v, 51^r, 51^v, 55^r (under which Rajna says he can distinguish handwriting, possibly directing the illuminator as to subject [*Geste Francor*, 24]), 62^r, 64^v, 70^r, 73^v, 80^v, and 90^v. They take up varying amounts of space, from seventeen to twenty-five lines total. They are pen and ink drawings, sketches with light water-color-like washes on them. Certain colors predominate: blue, brownish, yellow, one shade of green, one grey, one flesh color, and one shade of orange-red. They are all water-color tones, not intense or heavy.[17] The illuminations are not evenly distributed throughout the manuscript, as is clear from this list.

I shall briefly describe each of the illuminations. Rosellini gives names to many of them, using rubrics as titles; these therefore are Franco-Italian, close to Old French. The first is on fol. 38^r, at the top, with twenty-four lines below in each of the usual two columns across the page. It is in the *Karleto* portion of the text and portrays part of a battle scene: a man on horseback leads forces on

---

[16] Rajna notes variation in the rubrics, dividing them into three sections by handwriting. The three sections are from fols. 1 to 8; from fols. 9 to the beginning of 10; and finally, from fols. 10 to 95. In the second section, the characters are smaller than in the first, but otherwise similar. According to Rajna, the third section differs substantially from the other two (*Geste Francor*, 23); but these distinctions are difficult to make, given the poor quality overall of the rubrication.

[17] P. Toesca speaks of Venetian miniatures, the status of craftsmen, and related arguments (*Monumenti e studi per la storia della miniatura italiana* [Milan: Ulrico Hoepli, 1930], 35–36). P. D'Ancona says Venetian miniatures are uninteresting, without a "caractère propre" (*La miniature italienne du Xe au XVIe siècle*, trans. M. P. Poirier [Paris: Van Oest, 1925], 26).

the left, his horse covered with a fleur-de-lys drapery; on the right are opposing forces with a pennon visible and whose leader sports a different type of armor. In the foreground, alone, is an arm holding a sword on the ground. This would seem to depict Karleto and the Christians versus the pagans, with Florian's arm on the ground. ("Coment Florian s'en fuit ver l'oste et Karloeto li oit trençé li braço cun li spee," Rosellini, *Geste Francor*, 12.)

On fol. 38^v, at the top, again with twenty-four lines in each of the two columns at the bottom of the page, is a further battle scene ("una battaglia di Braibante," Rosellini, *Geste Francor*, 12). This would seem to be Galafrio and his men versus Braibant and his forces. There is a horse with a fleur-de-lys covering on the left, and on the right a pennon with a small design, possibly a dog. Both this and the previous illumination have the same face looking right with a visor up on the right half of the illumination, though at a slightly different angle.

On fol. 40^r, at the top of the folio, with eighteen lines in each column at the bottom, there are two single combat scenes: the fighter on the left wears the fleur-de-lys on his horse's caparison, and on the right the warrior wears a winged helmet. In the upper scene, they fight with lances; in the lower, with swords. This seems to be Karleto's single combat against Braibant. I disagree with Rosellini here; he calls it "il ferimento di re Galafrio . . . da parte di Braibante," referring to fols. 40^r–40^v (Rosellini, *Geste Francor*, 12).

The illumination on fol. 40^v is again in the upper portion of the page, with eighteen lines in each column below, and is again a double scene. Above, the knight on the left with the fleur-de-lys is hitting the combatant on the right, whose sword lies on the ground, with a sword at the neck. In the lower scene, the combatant on the left is on foot, sword high, with his opponent on his knees (with a winged helmet), with three mounted men and rocks on the right, in the background. Each of the three men behind bears a distinctive shield and helmet: one with what seem to be wings, one with horns, and a third with a ball. This must be Karleto's defeat of Maradras perhaps witnessed by the three brothers, Marsilio, Falsiron, and Balugant, followed by Danabrun offering his arms to Karleto.

On fol. 42^v, again the illumination is in two panes (upper and lower) with eighteen lines in each column below. Above, there is a foot soldier and a horseman with a dragon helmet (no fleur-de-lys); below, there are two scenes. On the left, a horseman with the winged-helmed head fights a combatant with a dragonhead, touching his left shoulder with a sword; on the right, the left figure wears the helmet with a dragon and holds the helmet with wings; the man to the right (in armor), with a sword in the first horse's croup, reaches for the helmet with wings. A man lies on the ground with no helmet or sword. There are rocks to the left. This seems to reflect ll. 7427–7430, 7450–7451, and 7462–7466, where Karleto gives Morando the helmet and sword. Rosellini states, "il ferito è Carlot [sic], al quale viene ucciso da Braibante anche il cavallo" (Rosellini, *Geste Francor*,

12). That is possible, though no mention is made of Karleto's being without sword and helmet; in fact Karleto goes on to slice Braibant with Çoiosa.

On fol. 51ʳ, the illumination is on the lower portion of the page, with twenty-seven lines in each column above. It is a city scene, with a gate on the left, a group of soldiers with one man bound in front of them (who wears a *capuchon*). To the right, four bearded men seem to lecture in front of a tower which reaches to the top of the page in the margin. Three of the men wear hats: perhaps these are Karleto's advisors, Naimes, Morando, and Guarner d'Aviçon or Bernard? This must be Lanfroi and Landris judged by Charlemagne with his councilors, dressed as "doctors of law," ll. 8934–8974 ("Coment .K. tenoit grant corte à Paris," Rosellini, *Geste Francor*, 12).

Folio 51ᵛ again has an illumination at the bottom of the page, with twenty-seven lines in each column at the top of the page. There is a city to the left with a gateway; two horsemen are in the center; and a giant tree (which looks like a mushroom) is to the right. Two blindfolded men with their hands tied in front of them are below the tree; a soldier with a spear over his shoulder and two men on horseback with *capuchons* are in the center. This would be the punishment of Lanfroi and Landris (ll. 9003–9004) ("Coment K. tenoit grant corti et ot asenblé tota soa baronie," Rosellini, *Geste Francor*, 12).

The illumination on fol. 55ʳ is also at the bottom of the page, here with thirty lines of text above in each of the two columns and a castle below. The tower rises into the right margin and there are two scenes, one on the right, above, and one on the left, in the lower corner. In the first, five men, four with crowns and one with the *capuchon*, face the king on a throne. Below, to the left, a scribe is sitting with parchment, pen, and inkwell, facing four men, two with a crown, two with *capuchon*; one is in the back and not very visible. This would seem to portray first, the council after Charlemagne's dream (ll. 9644–9688) and second, having the letter written according to the barons' advice (ll. 9688–9691) ("Coment li rois fo en Paris," Rosellini, *Geste Francor*, 12).

On fol. 62ʳ, the illumination is at the bottom of the page, with thirty-three lines of text in each column at the top. This is a table scene. At the top, five men are standing; at the left, the crowned king is seated on his throne. He has his hand out, with his left index finger raised, as if giving an order. In the front, a boy in a *giubotto*, not fully dressed, with no head covering (and somewhat plump) stands near the king on the left. To the right, are two men standing and a peasant with a cane, all three wearing the *capuchon*. This illustrates ll. 10930–10939 (*Orlandino*), with the raised finger of ll. 10938–10939 ("varî personaggi intorno a una mensa imbandita," Rosellini, *Geste Francor*, 12).

Fol. 64ʳ bears an illumination at the top, with twenty-nine lines of text in each column below. At the top is the crowned king in the center. Women to the left wear garlands; men to the right wear mostly *capuchons*. A woman with a crown is being united with a man by the king: he is holding their hands toward each other, and the man is holding a large ring. On the far right is an unhooded character, possibly Roland. There are two possibilities here: this could be the "wedding" of Berta and Milone which occurs on fol. 64rb in the text (ll. 11316–11320), but which mentions two rings (l. 11317), or Naimes's daughter and the Dane, which occurs on fol. 64vb (ll. 11385–11386) ("Coment Milon sposò Berte si fo facto çivaler et avec lui cento autres," Rosellini, *Geste Francor*, 12).

At the bottom of fol. 70^r, under thirty lines of text in each column, are two scenes side-by-side. On the left is a king to the left with his left arm up. Another king and others, including two women at the edge, are in the scene. In the second, right-hand scene, there are two kings (evidently the same two as in the first scene) and a boy kneeling, looking down, holding something up, perhaps a letter. This could be first, Braer and his council (ll. 12323–12369) and second, Braer giving or accepting a message (ll. 12370–12397). These events take place on fols. 69^v–70^r, so the placement is appropriate ("Coment li rois parole al mesaçer," Rosellini, *Geste Francor*, 12).

On fol. 73^v, below thirty lines of text in each column, are the Dane and Braer. An army led by a man with a horned helmet and banner is outside a tower which reaches into the top of the page (in the right margin). One knight has a hawk helmet and shield. The tower is filled with people watching events (ll. 13059–13061). It would seem to depict the Dane challenging Braer (ll. 13052–13070) on fol. 74ra ("Coment li Danois feri .K. sor li heume e Coment se parole e senbre," Rosellini, *Geste Francor*, 12).

The last two illuminations are also at the bottom of folios. On fol. 80^v there are thirty-two lines of text above in each column. The illumination is a table scene, in great detail, with food, drink, knives, a candlestick, and what seem to be rolls. On the upper side, we see the king, a hatted man, Macario, and another hatted man. To the left is a standing man, with no hat and his arms crossed. To the right are two hatless men standing with their arms crossed. In front of Macario, a huge dog has his front legs on the table, with teeth showing. This would illustrate ll. 14305–14311 on fol. 80va, where Alberis's dog comes after Macario ("quattro personaggi dietro una tavola imbandita più alcuni paggi ai lati e 'li can' che *vait sovra Macario*," Rosellini, *Geste Francor*, 12–13).

The final illumination, on fol. 90^v, is below thirty-one double lines of text and, unlike previous illuminations, has no frame. It is in two panes; to the left is a battle scene: a knight with a feathered helm and a ball on his helmet encounters a man with a horned helmet. In front is a man with a lance and a horse with a man falling off, and two men lying dead with two swords. This must be the French versus Blançiflor's father and men. This may reflect line 16168, where Varocher holds the lance and knocks the Dane off his horse, but Ogier is not hurt (ll. 16179–16180). To the right of the illumination, in a second scene not separated from the first, there is a tent camp. Within a small tent, there is a knight on his knees holding a book; a body; and a lady with a book (sitting, and perhaps reading?) on a stool. Curtains are drawn around the edge of the tent. This would seem to illustrate Bernardo kneeling before Blançiflor (ll. 16221–16224) ("Coment fu grande la bataille," Rosellini, *Geste Francor*, 13).

The illuminations tend to center on certain types of events: battles (mêlées); duels; table scenes; councils. The size of each is predictable, and the format has few variations. The backdrops are limited to rocks on one side and city towers. Clothing is predictable: crowns indicate kings; *capuchons* seem to indicate nobility in non-fighting moments or *doctores;* and one cannot sit in the presence of the king or queen — one must either stand or kneel. The use of heraldry to distinguish Christian and Saracen, friend and foe, would certainly bear further examination. The fact that Blançiflor is depicted as reading in the last scene is also interesting for possible cultural information. It is odd, however, that all illuminations are in fols. 38–90. Why are there none from fols. 1–37? One wonders if the plan of the manuscript changed during the writing.

A black frame encloses each of the drawings except the last, but no background is used; portions of the scenes are not within the framework. Towers extend into the margins several times (fols. 51^r, 51^v, 73^v, 90^v). There are, on occasion, several consecutive incidents within one frame. The scenes shown include specific details (a shield, a hat) but there is little or no perspective. The illuminator clearly knows the text and is illustrating specific events near the spot of the illumination. The illuminator or whoever gave instructions to him succeeded very well.

The few critics who have examined specifically the illuminations of V[13] — Frati, D'Ancona, Toesca, Salmi, Lejeune and Stiennon, D'Arcais, and Antonioni — have not been favorable to the illuminations, judging them generally inferior.[18] Frati, the first to mention them, calls them "rozze miniature (o meglio disegni acquerellati)" (Frati, "Recenti pubblicazioni," 231), suggesting that they be used to date the text. D'Ancona, Toesca, and Salmi, like many art historians, are primarily

---

[18] C. Frati, "Di alcune recenti pubblicazioni tratte dal Cod. Franc. XIII della Biblioteca Marciana," *Nuovo archivio veneto* n. s. 21 (1911): 223–31; D'Ancona, *La Miniature italienne*; P. Toesca, *Monumenti e studi* and idem, *La Pittura e la miniatura nella Lombardia: Dai più antichi monumenti alla metà del Quattrocento* (Turin: Einaudi, 1966); M. Salmi, *La miniatura italiana* (Milan: Electra editrice, 1956); Lejeune and Stiennon, *La Légende de Roland*; F. D'Arcais, "Les Illustrations des manuscrits français des Gonzague à la Bibliothèque de Saint-Marc," in *Essor et fortune de la chanson de geste dans l'Europe et l'Orient latin*, Actes du IXe Congrès international de la Société Rencesvals (Padoue-Venise, 29 août–4 septembre 1982), ed. A. Limentani et al. (Modena: Mucchi, 1984), 585–616; and A. Antonioni, "Tav. LXIII. ROMANZI diversi del ciclo carolingio [sic]," in *Biblioteca Marciana: Venezia*, ed. Zorzi, 119.

interested in the *Entrée d'Espagne*; Toesca also calls V^{13}'s illuminations "rozze miniature," dates them to the middle of the fourteenth century, and characterizes them as Lombard, from northern Italy (*Monumenti e studi*, 165, n. 3). Lejeune and Stiennon note that V^{13}'s illuminations are of "qualité fort médiocre" (*La légende de Roland*, 259) and date them to ca. 1200 (illustrations 135 and 137).

The figures in V^{13} are stiff, but with no background; colors are light and the drawings sketchy. Salmi mentions in passing that this sort of drawing spread throughout the Veneto during the fourteenth century (*La miniatura italiana*, 38).[19] Treviso has a *loggia* decorated with subjects from romances from the thirteenth and fourteenth centuries in what is described as a similar style. Among the examples Salmi gives of the style are a *Divine Comedy* from the late part of the fourteenth century and the *Entrée d'Espagne* that dates to 1320–1340 (*La miniatura italiana*, 38).

Upon examination, only a small portion of the miniatures in the *Entrée d'Espagne* (fols. 29^v–84^v) are of the watercolor wash type found in V^{13}. The other illuminations of the *Entrée d'Espagne* have a dark contrasting background, and are much more formal. There is a definite French influence (possibly through Lombardy) in the manner of drawing clothes, faces, and hair in V^{13}. There is little information available on this style other than that provided by Salmi (at least partly in error, as here demonstrated).

D'Arcais is the only critic to discuss specifically the illuminations of V^{13}. In examining the entire Franco-Italian collection of the Biblioteca Marciana, she suggests that, as a group, they run from the end of the thirteenth through the end of the fourteenth century ("Les Illustrations," 586). For V^{13}, she suggests mid-fourteenth, basing herself on the gothic elements in the architecture (593–94). She finds one parallel, an *Ovide moralisé* in Latin, dating to the second half of the fourteenth century, attributed to a Northern Italian illuminator (594). She compares V^{13}'s miniatures to others of the Marciana collection, noting the "ton popularisant" (587) and similar colors in the series of twenty manuscripts, and later, specifically of V^{13}, "de dessins . . . assez frustres et populaires" (594). She also suggests it is probably from the "région vénitienne," without offering specific evidence.

Later critics generally follow D'Arcais. Rosellini calls the illuminations "rozze" (*Geste Francor*, 12). Antonioni, as others, follows D'Arcais on the provenance and the "gusto popolare," but dates the miniatures to the second half of the fourteenth century, perhaps following up on her parallel with the *Ovide moralisé* ("Tav. LXIII. ROMANZI," 119).

---

[19] Of course, manuscripts are not always illuminated at the same time they are written, so the dating of illuminations alone is an imprecise indication of manuscript date.

It is interesting to note that the Franco-Italian manuscripts at St. Mark's are in general classified as Venetian art, especially since it is now generally agreed that the manuscript is only "Venetian" by virtue of its location in St. Mark's Library.[20] All available information on V[13]'s illumination describes it as "Venetian." Of course Venice was larger in the fourteenth century than now, and borders were not as clear. But Lombard miniatures were closely tied to northern European (especially French) work, so it is surprising that there has been no work on the Franco-Italian miniatures from that point of view. There was little miniature work done in Venice (city) during the Middle Ages and it was used mainly to illustrate official documents for the doges and government in general. Those illuminations are very Byzantine and formal, not at all like these.[21]

The combination of handwriting and illuminations in V[13] points to the first seventy years of the fourteenth century as a date. The origin is northern Italy, possibly near Treviso, with French influence. The exact geographical origin and date remain unknown, but it is to be hoped that with further investigation of the illuminations and the entire manuscript more information will come to light.

1.4 HISTORY OF THE MANUSCRIPT.

The history of the manuscript itself is not completely known, but the history of the codex as it now exists begins in 1407. On 14 March, after the death of Francesco Gonzaga, the fourth captain of Mantua, two inventories were made of his books.[22] The *Capitulum librorum in lingua francigena* (now Archivio Gonzaga, D.V. 4.I) lists 67 books in French (French and Franco-Italian are not distinguished). Number 44 reads:

---

[20] See G. Holtus, *Lexicalische Untersuchungen zur Interferenz: die franko-italienische "Entrée d'Espagne,"* Beihefte zur *Zeitschrift für romanische Philologie* 170 (Tübingen: Niemeyer, 1979), 11ff, and idem, "Plan- und Kunstsprachen auf romanischer Basis IV. Franko-Italienisch/Langues artificielles à base romane IV. Le franco-italien," in *Lexikon der romanistichen Linguistik*, ed. idem et al. (Tübingen: M. Niemeyer, 1998), 7: 705–56, here 705, for discussions of "Franco-Venetian" versus "Franco-Italian," but also here p. 21.

[21] See R. Bratti, "Miniatori veneziani," *Nuovo archivio veneto* 2nd ser. 1 (1901): 72–74, for specific information on miniatures from the city of Venice.

[22] The original publication of the inventory is in W. Braghirolli, G. Paris, and P. Meyer, "Inventaire des manuscrits en langue française possédés par Francesco Gonzaga I, capitaine de Mantoue, mort en 1407," *Romania* 9 (1880): 497–514. There are two inventories; the second was published by F. Novati, "I codici francesi de' Gonzagi secondo nuovi documenti," *Romania* 19 (1890): 161–200. Since V[13] is not mentioned in the second publication, it has no bearing on our discussion here (on that subject see also G. G. Ferrero, *Poemi cavallereschi del Trecento* [Turin: UTET, 1965], 13).

44. Item. KAROLUS MAGNUS. Incipit: *Segnur barons deu vos sia in gua rant.* Et finit: *da qui auant se noua la canzun.* Continet cart. 218. (Braghirolli et al., "Inventaire," 511).

Several objections can be raised against identifying this item in the inventory with our manuscript: the number of fols. does not correspond; the beginning of V^{13} is missing, so we cannot compare it; and finally, V^{13} ends:

> Da qui avanti se nova la cançon.
> E Deo vos beneie qe sofrì pasion.
> Explicit liber Deo gracias. ame*n*. ame*n*.

Rajna answered these objections: the "E deo . . ." is crossed out in red, "Explicit" is in red; both are in the rubricator's hand. In general, the scribe making the inventory takes the last words of the text and not an added explicit, so V^{13} could be this manuscript 44 (Rajna, *Geste Francor*, 27). Secondly, because the beginning folios of V^{13} are missing, it is impossible to verify the first line of the text. A number of folios must be missing, since there are only ninety-five, as the original would have had 218 according to the inventory. The original beginning of V^{13} can now be only a matter of conjecture; there is nothing quite like this text to which we can compare it. Rajna offers two possible solutions, basing himself on the *Reali di Francia*: first, *Bovo* "would have been preceded by (I follow retrograde order) *Gisberto, Ottaviano, Fioravant, Fiovo*" (my translation; Rajna, *Geste Francor*, 29). In that case, Rajna comes up with 123 folios for a total of the 218 indicated (*Geste Francor*, 30). Or there may have been a *Ugo d'Alvernia* which preceded it, but in that case there would have been still twenty-two blank folios. He concludes by leaving it to the reader to decide upon the merits of various arguments, concluding that V^{13} is clearly number 44 of the inventory. The method of elimination (that is, many of the other manuscripts in the inventory have been identified at San Marco) and the proven inaccuracy of the inventory scribe (there are errors in folio numbers and in transcribing lines in known manuscripts) are the most positive evidence that can be offered for identification of V^{13} with number 44. Rajna and others after him conclude that manuscript 44 of the Gonzagan inventory is V^{13}.

In 1708, at the death of Duke Ferdinand-Carl IV, the books of the house of Gonzaga were sold in Venice. J. B. Recanati bought many of them. On 12 November 1734, when Recanati died, he left most of his library (approximately 200 volumes) to the Republic of Venice (Braghirolli et al., "Inventaire," 499). Antonio Maria Zannetti made a catalogue of those books in 1741. He states that until the discovery of the Gonzagan inventory, V^{13} was thought to have belonged to the Duke of Nevers (256–57). Zannetti's appendix to the catalogue includes a list of books purportedly in Old French (256–61), all but the last two of which had been part of the Recanati collection. V^{13} is listed as Recanati X, and given the title *Doone*, etc., as listed in our "description of the manuscript" above, since that excerpt describing V¹³ is glued into the first of the guard sheets bound into the volume by the library.

There was no public interest in the manuscript until the nineteenth century. Paul Lacroix (under the pseudonym P. L. Jacob, Bibliophile) first published a report on the manuscript. Adelbert von Keller, in Italy 1840–1841, stopped in Venice on his way back to Germany; he includes V¹³ in the chapter "San Marco in Venedig," where he transcribes 172 lines and all the rubrics, mentioning that Jacob gives it the title of *Doone de Maganza*.²³ He calls it *Dodo de Magance* himself, and refers to the *Reali di Francia* for comparison. Thus a further selection from the manuscript came to print.

In 1880 W. Braghirolli sent the Gonzagan inventory to the journal *Romania*. Paul Meyer and Gaston Paris realized its importance and, in publishing it, commented upon it and first identified no. 44 with V¹³ (Braghirolli et al., "Inventaire," 502, 511–12). Though he was hindered by wartime difficulties, Pio Rajna ultimately published the photofacsimile of V¹³ with an extensive introduction in 1925 or 1926 (the volume is undated, but preceded by an "Avvertenza" in which he explains the various vicissitudes involved, giving a date of 1914 as when he submitted the proofs), with the title *Geste Francor*. Multiple publications since have made portions of V¹³ available in journals.²⁴ Until Rosellini's publication in 1986, however, the entire text was not available in a single volume in a modern

---

²³ P. Lacroix, "Sur les manuscrits relatifs à l'histoire de France et à la littérature française conservés dans les bibliothèques d'Italie," *Dissertations sur quelques points curieux de l'histoire de France et de l'histoire littéraire* (Paris: Techener, 1839), 7: 147–89, repr. in J.-J. Champollion-Figeac, *Documents historiques inédits* (Paris: Firmin Didot, 1847), 3: 345–76. A. v. Keller, "San Marco in Venedig," *Romvart: Beiträge zur mittelalterlicher Dichtung aus italienischen Bibliotheken* (Mannheim: Basserman, 1844), 42–77.

²⁴ A. Mussafia, ed., *Macaire. Ein altfranzösisches Gedicht*, Altfranzösische Gedichte aus venezianischen Handschriften 2 (Vienna: Carl Gerold's Sohn, 1864); F. Guessard, ed., *Macaire, chanson de geste*, les anciens poëtes de France (Paris: Librarie A. Franck, 1864); A. Mussafia, ed., "Berta de li gran pié," *Romania* 3 (1874): 339–64, 4 (1875): 91–107; Idem, "Berta e Milone —Orlandino," *Romania* 14 (1885): 177–206; J. Subak, "Die frankoitalienische Version des *Enfances Ogier* nach dem Codex Marcianus XIII," *Zeitschrift für romanische Philologie* 33 (1909): 536–70; B. Cerf, "The Franco-Italian *Chevalerie Ogier*," *Modern Philology* 8 (1910–1911): 187–216, 335–61, 511–25; V. F. Chichmaref, "Di alcune enfances dell'epopea francese: il *Karleto* del Codice XIII della Marciana," *Zapiski Neofilologicheskago obshchestva pri Imperatorskom Petrogradskom Universitete* 5 (1911): 194–237; J. Reinhold, "Die franko-italienische Version des Bovo d'Antone," *Zeitschrift für romanische Philologie* 35 (1911): 555–607, 683–714; 36 (1911): 1–32; 36 (1912): 512. idem, "Karleto," *Zeitschrift für romanische Philologie* 37 (1913): 27–56; 145–76, 287–312, 641–78; C. Cremonesi, *Berte da li pè grandi: Codice marciano XIII* (Milan: Varese, 1966); eadem, *Berta e Milon, Rolandin: Codice Marciano XIII* (Milan: La Goliardica, 1973); eadem, *Le Danois Oger: Enfances–Chevalerie: Codice Marciano XIII* (Milan: Cisalpino-Goliardica, 1977).

edition; and Rajna's photofacsimile (*Geste Francor*) was available in only a limited number of libraries.

Now, more than twenty years after Rosellini's work, numerous reviews of it have appeared. Many reviewers note that older editions are still not surpassed. They express the need for elucidation of obscure passages, a detailed glossary, and correction of typographical errors: some reviewers provide multiple pages of readings that need verification.[25] Furthermore, there is "no literary analysis, examination of the extent of poetic unity, or comparison with analogous French texts where appropriate" so the *chansons* seem "arbitrarily or fortuitously selected."[26] Therefore, Rosellini's readings need to be checked against the manuscript, the glossary expanded (especially to assist a non-Italophone reader), equivalencies with earlier editions by line number should be provided, and a literary component added to tie the *chansons* to French (and other) versions.

Part four of this introduction examines each of the *chansons* in their European context and their role in V^{13}. The final *Glossary* includes all words within V^{13}, lemmatized and cross-referenced by different spellings. I have verified the questioned readings against V^{13}, and noted earlier editors' readings as well as reviewers' corrections in footnotes on each page of the edition itself. Since Rosellini's publication in 1986, computer use has become more widespread and programs available to assist textual analysis are simpler and more readily usable. With the help of a digital edition (that is, the transcription is word-processed), making a glossary and linguistic analyses are no longer matters for many notecards. Difficulties, however, remain; the editor must still make many decisions in rendering the text readable, in classifying graphically different forms of the same word and in representing the word on the page for readers accustomed to different editorial traditions for Old French and Italian. In the next section, we will examine some of the difficulties involved in V^{13}'s language, their derivation, and what they mean to comprehension.

---

[25] For example, M. G. Capusso, review of *Geste Francor*, ed. Rosellini, *Studi mediolatini e volgari* 34 (1988): 183–207; M. Plouzeau, review of Rosellini, *Revue de langues modernes* 93 (1989): 171–83; L. Morini, review of Rosellini, *Romance Philology* 45 (1992): 547–54. More reviews are cited in the endnotes to the edition to comment upon specific textual difficulties.

[26] L. C. Brook, review of Rosellini, *French Studies* 43 (1990): 201–2.

2.0
LANGUAGE: FRANCO-ITALIAN AND THE FRANCO-ITALIAN OF V¹³

It is traditional to include a section on the language of the manuscript in the introduction to an edition. However, here "language" is more complicated than usual for a medieval text owing to the mixture of French and Italian. Because of the complexities deriving from the mixed nature of the language in this manuscript, rather than a complete analysis of the language, I present here a brief summary of the origins of this mixed language, a survey of scholarly analysis of its nature, and an outline of previous examinations of Franco-Italian in the manuscript together with a sample of some of the difficulties it presents.

2.1 FRANCO-ITALIAN

The name of the "language" and its status remain subjects of contention among scholars. Italian scholars usually call it *franco-veneto*, a name with a venerable tradition in Italian scholarship, while German and more recent American researchers tend to use the term "Franco-Italian." The reasons for these usages become evident through the history of its development.

2.1.1 Arrival of the French Language in Italy.

Knowledge of the *langue d'oïl* (Northern French) and its literature arrived in Northern Italy by two routes: oral and written.[1] The Italian peninsula was not only a pilgrimage destination in itself (to Rome) but also a port of departure for pilgrimage to the Holy Land, via either Genoa or Venice. Thus pilgrims arrived and passed through Northern Italy, especially Emilia, Lombardy, and Venice (via Treviso, Verona, Modena, and Vicenza; the main roads from northern Europe to Venice have changed little over the centuries). Oral entertainers accompanied them, spreading stories of Roland and Oliver.

---

[1] I will refer to the Italian peninsula and Italy interchangeably in order to simplify expression, though of course "Italy" as a national concept did not exist in the era.

Legal documents and art testify to knowledge of Roland and Oliver in the Italian peninsula before they appear in literature, and documents in Latin cite Arthurian names in Italy from the beginning of the twelfth century. At Rome, there are frescoes illustrating stories about Charlemagne in Santa Maria in Cosmedin, ca. 1120. In Verona, the cathedral portal bears sculptures of Roland and Oliver dated to ca. 1139; Modena and Fidenza offer similar testimony.[2] Odofredo, a jurist who died in 1265, speaks about singers of *Rolando et Oliviero*.[3] Lovato de' Lovati (d. 1309) speaks of street entertainers distorting French songs to the pleasure of public listeners. Laws on the books in cities try to discourage such public singers from blocking the way.[4]

Thus we know that French stories arrived in Italy by oral routes. But we also know that French manuscripts were imported into Northern Italy. By the end of the twelfth century, the seignorial courts established in Liguria, Lombardy, and Venice acted as magnets for French culture and encouraged its spread. During the thirteenth, fourteenth, and fifteenth centuries, the lords of these courts collected manuscripts both by copying loaned manuscripts and by purchasing manuscripts. Inventories now in Mantua from the Gonzaga family, for example, list many French manuscripts; these inventories date to 1407, 1437, 1467, 1480, and 1488.[5] Braghirolli also cites a letter of 1389 from Francesco Gonzaga who was in France accompanying Valentina Galeazzo to marry Louis of Valois, Duke of Orléans, brother to Charles VI. On 18 September, he wrote to Modena to ask for a letter of exchange for 5,000 ducats to purchase "both honorable and useful things"; it is suspected that among these purchases were manuscripts.[6] Francesco

---

[2] See R. Lejeune, "La Légende de Roland dans l'art italien du Moyen Âge," in *La Poesia epica e la sua formazione*, Atti del Convegno internazionale (Roma, 28 marzo–3 aprile 1969), Problemi attuali di scienza e di cultura, Accademia Nazionale dei Lincei 367 (Rome: Accademia Nazionale dei Lincei, 1970), 299–314, here 300–3, 308–10; D. Delcorno Branca, *Il Romanzo cavalleresco medievale* (Florence: Sansoni, 1974), 2–7.

[3] P. Meyer, "De l'expansion de la langue française en Italie pendant le Moyen Age," in *Atti del Congresso Internazionale di scienze storiche*, 4: *Atti della sessione III: Storia della letteratura*, Roma, 1–9 aprile 1903 (Rome: Salviucci, 1904), 61–104, here 69.

[4] L. A. Muratori, *Antiquitates Italicae Medii Aevi* (Milan: Palatinae, 1739), 2, column 844; year 1341. P. Rajna addresses some of the issues raised by Muratori in "Il Teatro di Milano e i canti intorno ad Orlando e Ulivieri," *Archivio Storico Lombardo* 14 (1887): 6–28, but notes that there are problems with Muratori's data; for example, he does not always include a date for a specific example, and has thus misled some readers.

[5] The inventories have been published, some of them a number of times: P. Rajna, "Ricordi di codici francesi posseduti dagli Estensi nel secolo XV," *Romania* 2 (1873): 49–58; see also Braghirolli, "Inventaire," and Novati, "I codici francesi."

[6] For a negative comment to this presumption, see Novati ("I codici francesi," 163), who cites documents proving that many of the volumes were held long before 1407, probably from the days of Francesco. He quotes a letter of 30 May 1366, about *Meliadus* and *Guillaume d'Orange* (164), another about *Aspramonte* probably from 1371 (171), and so on.

Gonzaga maintained ties with Paris, sending a servant of his, Antonio della Paga, to purchase numerous items. On Francesco's death the first Gonzagan inventory, that of 1407, was made. Sixty-seven entries of the seventy-seven manuscripts are "French."[7]

Franco-Italian manuscript texts date to the period between the middle of the thirteenth century and the early fifteenth century, documenting approximately two centuries of French influence in Northern Italian literature. It is not clear whether the manuscripts are copies of originals or themselves the originals, nor whether the texts were read individually or aloud to groups. Thus there are multiple levels of language to consider: from "author" through redactor and scribe. The possibility for various linguistic layers makes the search for an archetype an impossibility in many cases, especially where only one witness of a tradition exists.

2.1.2 The Franco-Italian Language in general.

Critics examining the arrival of Charlemagne stories and Northern French material into Northern Italy have suggested two, three, even four phases.[8] P. Meyer, for example, divides the phases into: 1. knowledge of French and its literature; 2. transcription of French works in Italy; and 3. Italians writing French ("De l'expansion," 68). This last, in turn, Meyer divides into Italians writing French and those writing Franco-Italian, and, in the case of Carolingian epic, into those writing poems following French models closely versus those writing original poems (89). Antonio Viscardi, arguably the best-known and most frequently cited authority on Franco-Italian until recently, divides the phases of productions which we know into

1. copies of French originals (more or less contaminated with Italian) still known today;
2. elaborate rewrites (often quite free) of French originals; and
3. completely original works.[9]

---

[7] Braghirolli, "Inventaire," 498–99. Braghirolli's count of the French MSS. is on p. 498.

[8] Holtus, "Plan- und Kunstsprachen," summarizes the discussions (708–11).

[9] A. Viscardi, *Letteratura franco-italiana*, Istituto di filologia romanza della R. Università di Roma, Testi e manuali 21 (Modena: Società tipografica modenese, 1941), 37–38. A. Rosellini's lengthy article in two parts ("Il cosiddetto franco-veneto: Retrospettive e prospettive," *Filologia moderna* 2 [1977]: 219–303; 4 [1980]: 221–61) reviews the major critics in chronological order up to the time of his publication, with extensive quotes from relevant critics (unfortunately marred by typographical errors). Holtus, "Plan- und Kunstsprachen" offers an excellent and useful overview of the entire field, including the concepts of register and communication, and the major discussions about Franco-Italian, replete with examples.

Günter Holtus, the modern authority on Franco-Italian, has most recently divided the phases into 1. French texts slightly italianized deriving from written tradition; 2. French texts noticeably italianized, deriving from a knowledge of contemporary French and written later; 3. Franco-Italian texts in the strictest sense, that is, those which are an artificial literary product consciously produced by authors playing with language; and 4. Franco-Italian texts without a conscious attempt at creating a mixture.[10] His list of texts falling into category number three, which interests us here, contains sixty-five items, of which those numbered eight to fifteen are from the *Geste Francor* ("L'État actuel," 150–60; "Plan- und Kunstsprachen," 711–16). His list classifies these works by level of italianization alone, rather than by date. Manuscripts of different dates are italianized in varying proportions, and dating medieval texts is always difficult in the absence of dates within the text itself. It must be emphasized that the division of text types is not chronological by any means: copies were made at different levels of italianization near the same time. We have many fourteenth-century manuscripts in different stages of italianization, that is, with a greater or lesser degree of Italian in the French.

A major difficulty in defining Franco-Italian text-types is that authorial intentions are not always clear, and are not normally stated. This has long been a point of discussion among literary critics studying these texts in mixed French and Italian. Did authors consciously know they were not writing good French? Were they using a locally spoken language or a literary koiné? Though Holtus would seem to have laid to rest forever the possibility of Franco-Italian being a language or a dialect,[11] that is the first question that normally arises upon encountering a Franco-Italian text, one disproved by the phonological inconsistency. The second is whether or not the language is consistent through all of V^{13}, that is, whether or not it is all by one author, or whether one can distinguish differences from *chanson* to *chanson*. It *is* consistent through V^{13} in that similar formulae appear throughout, though the orthography and verbal reflexes (that is, parallel forms deriving from the same, usually Latin, ancestor) in the formulae may differ.

Rajna's contention that an author "volle e non seppe" compose in *lingua d'oïl* became a touchstone of the whole issue: thus Ruggieri responds, "i nostri autori vollero e seppero scrivere la *Mischsprache*."[12] The role of comprehension on

---

[10] G. Holtus, "L'État actuel des recherches sur le franco-italien: corpus de textes et description linguistique," in *La Chanson de Geste: Écriture, Intertextualités, Translations*, ed. François Suard, Cahiers du département de français, Littérales 14 (Nanterre: Service 10FFUSION [sic], 1994), 147–71, here 149; compare idem, "Plan- und Kunstsprachen," 711.

[11] G. Holtus, "Ist das Franko-italienische eine Sprache oder eine Dialekte?" in *Beiträge zum romanischen Mittelalter*, ed. Kurt Baldinger (Tübingen: Niemeyer, 1977), 79–97.

[12] P. Rajna, "La rotta di Roncisvalle nella letteratura cavalleresca italiana," *Il Propugnatore* 3.2 (1870): 384–409, here 396; R. Ruggieri, "Origine, struttura e caratteri del

the part of a Northern Italian public, the prestige of French culture, the traditional form of the *chanson de geste*, and the traditional *scripta* used for Latin, rather than for the vernacular language, all play a part in the written Franco-Italian texts we now have. Furthermore, regional and dialect standards also play a part. Rosellini emphasizes rightly that during the thirteenth and fourteenth centuries Old French was changing too, and that we should not compare our texts with twelfth-century standards ("Il cosiddetto franco-veneto," Part 1, 293–94). Early analyses condemned the works for their authors' lack of French skills (e.g., "l'affreuse corruption du langage dans lequel est écrite cette compilation").[13] Ascoli pointed out that many of the so-called Venetian forms in fact coincided with French forms.[14] Attempts to localize specific manuscripts have not succeeded overall, and, as Contini states, "È ovvio che francoitaliano non signifchi restrittivamente francoveneto, troppa diffusa equazione mentale dovuta alla presenza in Marciana della massa dei codici gonzagheschi . . ."[15] Thus, most scholars today speak of "Franco-Italian" in order to cover the range of linguistic productions, since it is clear that there is a gradation between extremely deliberate mixture or editing (e.g., *Attila*), and attempts at writing in French. The exact cutoff point between writing literary Old French and Italian is unclear, and there are numerous points along that continuum.[16]

Critics' approaches to this "mixed language," *Mischsprache*, as Mussafia called it, have been varied.[17] Initially, mere transcriptions were produced. Then early

---

Franco-veneto," in *Saggi di linguistica italiana e italo-romanza* (Florence: L. S. Olschki, 1962), 159–68, here 163.

[13] F. Guessard, "Notes sur un manuscrit français de la Bibliothèque de S. Marc," *Bibliothèque de l'école des chartes* 4th ser. 4 (1857): 393–414, here 395.

[14] G. Ascoli, "Saggi ladini," *Archivio Glottologico Italiano* 1 (1873): 1–537, here 451–53.

[15] G. Contini, "La canzone della Mort Charlemagne," in *Mélanges Maurice Delbouille*, ed. Jean Renson (Gembloux: Duculot, 1964) 2: 105–26, here 112; also quoted in part in Holtus, "Plan- und Kunstsprachen," 705.

[16] Some of this discussion appears in my earlier exposition on Franco-Italian in ORB (L. Z. Morgan, "Franco-Italian Epic: The *Geste Francor* [anonymous]," in *On-Line Reference Book for Medieval Studies (Encyclopedia)*, http://www.the-orb.net/encyclop/culture/lit/Italian/morgan-a.html (18 August 2002 update). Further discussion of the nature of Franco-Italian can also be found there. Since this chapter was written, several studies have appeared that address this issue. Of particular intrest is C. Segre, "La letteratura franco-veneta," Chapter VI in Volume I of *Storia della letteratura italiana* (Roma: Salerno, 1995), 631-47.

[17] A. Mussafia, "Handschriftliche Studien II. Zu den altfranzösischen Handschriften der Markus-Bibliothek in Venedig," *Sitzungsberichte der K[aiserlichen] Akademie der Wissenschaften* [Vienna], *Philosophisch-Historische Classe* 42 (1863): 276–326, here 276–77. For German sources, I give translations into English, where for French and Italian sources I give the original text. Where the German original is a longer quote, I give the original in a note.

critics produced synchronic descriptions of the language of a given Franco-Italian text, primarily the morphology (e.g., for V^{13}, Mussafia, *Macaire*; Reinhold, "Bovo d'Antone"). Others have been interested in the phonological aspects and some scholars have examined the graphemic reality: what the alphabetic symbols mean in relation to the sound that would be produced.[18] There is a mixture of multiple language areas in Franco-Italian. In Italy, the northwestern and north central Italian dialect area is Gallo-Italian, and as such is close to French dialects; the Venetian area was and is nearer to Tuscan than to the Gallo-Italian dialects. Recently, all have acknowledged, and Holtus has examined at length for the *Entrée d'Espagne* (*Lexicalische Untersuchungen*), the importance of lexicon in Franco-Italian texts. The language used in Franco-Italian texts has garnered the lion's share of critical interest in comparison with the literary content, though characterization of Franco-Italian as a whole still remains sketchy.

It is now generally accepted that the degree of mixture between Old French and other linguistic components in a given Franco-Italian text derives from a series of considerations. These include the redactor's linguistic knowledge and abilities (that is, competence and performance); his need to be understood by the public; and possibly his desire to nobilize the language or to parodize or ironize the literary tradition (see, for example, Rosellini, "Il cosiddetto franco-veneto," Part 2, 244, and idem, *Geste Francor*, 56–57). These considerations come into play in editing V^{13} as in all Franco-Italian texts: what is truly an error and what is intended? Where could these lexemes come from, and in using them together what did the poet hope to accomplish?

2.2 THE FRANCO-ITALIAN OF V^{13}.

This manuscript, like the others in the Gonzagan inventory, was known to have been in Mantua, near the edge of the Venetian *terraferma* and in the Gallo-Italian area (what is now Emilia-Romagna; see the chapter map for geographical references). Known influences on V^{13}'s language thus include Old French, Northern Italian (both Gallo-Italian and Venetian), as well as Tuscan and Latin

---

[18] For the phonological aspects, see L. Renzi, "Per la lingua dell'*Entrée d'Espagne*," *Cultura neolatina* 30 (1970): 59–87; G. Pellegrini, "Osservazioni sulla lingua franco-veneta di V4," in *Atti dell'8 congresso internazionale di Studi Romanzi* (Firenze, 3–8 aprile 1956) (Florence: Sansoni, 1960), 707–17. For the graphemic reality, and especially ç/z, see Rosellini, "Il cosidetto franco-veneto," Part 1, 286–92, and idem, *Geste Francor*, 34–39. See also P. Wunderli, "Un luogo di 'interferenze': Il franco-italiano," in *La cultura dell'Italia padana e la presenza francese nei secoli XIII–XV* (Pavia, 11–14 settembre 1994), ed. Luigina Morini (Alessandria: Edizioni dell'Orso, 2001), 55–66.

2.1 Franco-Italian.

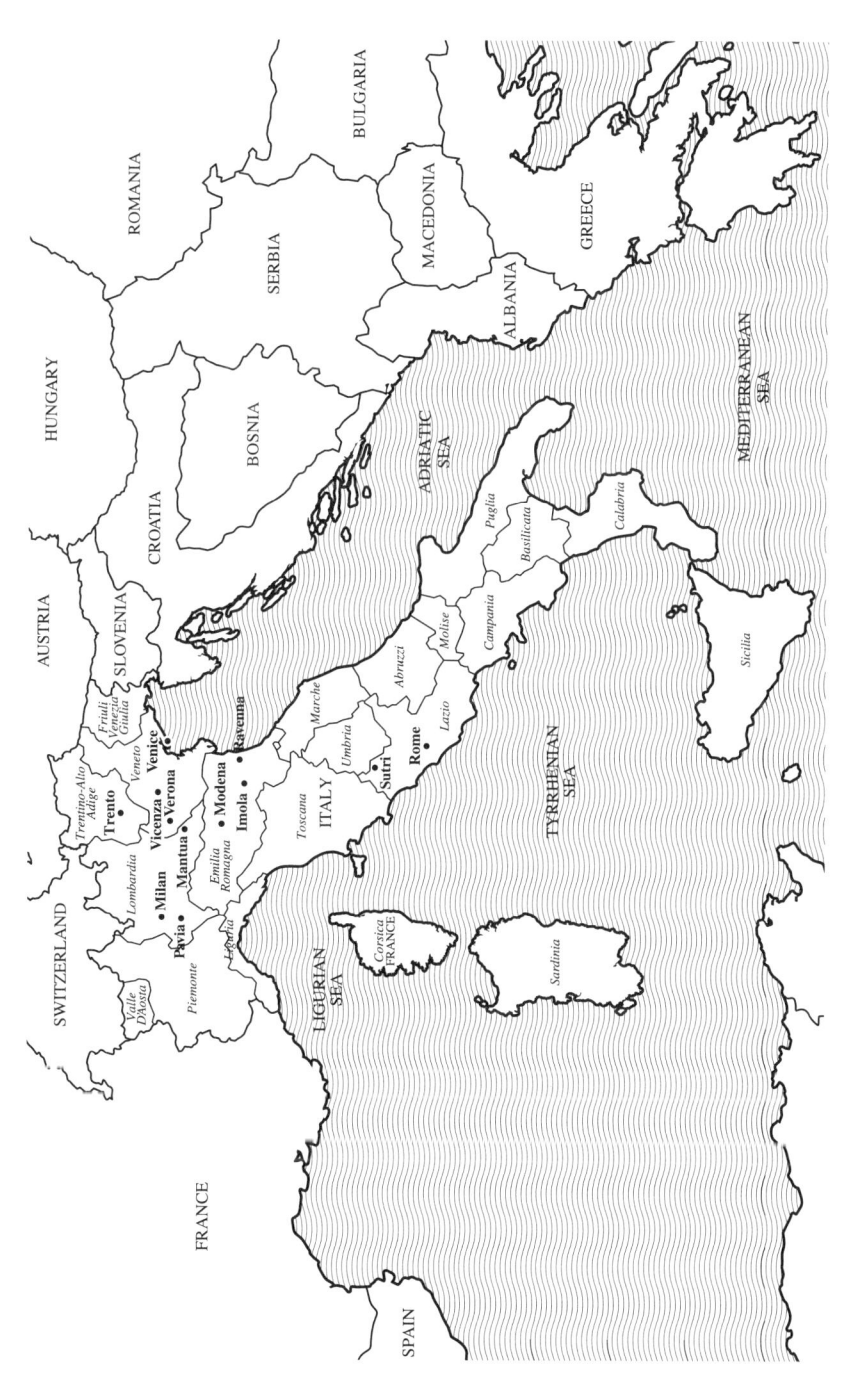

Map of Italy, including relevant cities for manuscript and for literary description

traditions.[19] The Carolingian *chanson de geste* form and characters were of Old French origin; the public (for books or for oral performance), as well as possibly the redactor, was Northern Italian; possible Dantean quotations in V[13] attest to the growing influence of Tuscan;[20] and, of course, scribes were trained in Latin.

Holtus places V[13] in category 3, "les textes franco-italiens au sens strict qui peuvent être considérés comme étant le produit artificiel et littéraire d'auteurs jouant consciemment avec la langue pour en faire une langue artificielle stylisée et très littéraire" ("Plan- und Kunstsprachen," 711).[21] The language is the same throughout, as is the handwriting and the illumination: we find similar linguistic constructions through a series of procedures related to both French and Italian language development. That "language," however, is not one used for communication between people for their daily needs; rather, it is artificial and varies from that used in other Franco-Italian manuscripts.

2.2.1 Franco-Italian of V[13]: Earlier Treatments and Approach Here.[22]

The linguistic composition of V[13] has never been entirely treated. Earlier editors have given lists of forms or treated certain aspects of the language. A complete treatment of the language of V[13] would require at least one separate volume. Therefore, I will briefly survey earlier analyses and commentary of V[13]'s language, analyze samples of representative forms, and finally discuss the effects of overlapping linguistic traditions on comprehension. At the end of the edition, a lemmatized glossary completes the analysis.

---

[19] For information on different dialect areas, see G. Devoto and G. Giacomelli, *I dialetti delle regioni d'Italia* (Florence: Sansoni, 1972); modern Veneto includes Treviso (30–32); Lombardy includes Brescia (20–22); Emilia-Romagna includes Mantua (54–55). Each section also offers a brief historical overview.

[20] See C. Cremonesi for discussion of specific passages that sound Dantean ("A proposito del Codice marciano fr. XIII," in *Mélanges offerts à Mme. Rita Lejeune, Prof. à l'Université de Liège* [Gembloux: J. Duculot, 1969], 2: 747–55, esp. 749; and eadem, ed., *Berta e Milon*, 28–31). To these can be added l. 2203; see text line below and endnote.

[21] Cf. R. F. Cook, "Was Venice-Four Roland Comprehensible?", paper read at the Medieval Congress at Western Michigan University, May 1997: "Perhaps the joy of making the marginal mixture that is Franco-Italian come clear as a vehicle of meaning was a phenomenon co-existing with and counterbalancing the pleasures of the bemused but happy Trevisan crowd." I thank Professor Cook for making his paper available to me.

[22] After this volume went to press, in 2007, Wunderli's analysis of *Aquilon de Bavière's* language appeared: P. Wunderli, *Raffaele da Verona. Aquilon de Bavière: roman franco-italien en prose (1379–1407)*. Volume 3: *Commentaire*. Beihefte zur Zeitschrift für romanische Philologie 337 (Tübingen: Niemeyer, 2007).

2.2 The Franco-Italian of V¹³

Those who examine the language of V¹³ explicitly are only five, and a sixth weighs in briefly. Mussafia reviews the linguistic system as seen in *Macaire*, emphasizing the non-Frenchness of V¹³'s language (*Macaire*, v–xvi); Reinhold follows Mussafia's example, giving the most important sound changes and listing non-French verb forms ("Bovo d'Antone," 558–59). His *Karleto* refers to his earlier discussion with a few additions (656–59). D. E. Frierson did not edit V¹³ or any portion of it; rather, he produced an historical study of the language of V¹³ based upon sampling the entire text.[23] Cremonesi explicitly avoids a linguistic analysis before having edited the entire text, though she mentions a few characteristics of the language of V¹³ in her three editions (*Berte*, *Berta e Milon*, *Danois Oger*). Rosellini treats several aspects of *Macaire* in one article ("Il cosiddetto franco-veneto," Part 2, 245–52), and touches upon selected linguistic issues in the introduction to his edition of the entire poem (*Geste Francor*, 34–58).

Certain questions return for discussion in each examination of a portion of V¹³'s language: phonologically, the inconsistency can be seen in historical terms (that is, multiple developments of one Latin sound appear throughout the manuscript); morphologically, the inconsistency of verbal forms (multiple ending and stem types, deriving from Latin via different routes, appear throughout the manuscript); syntactically, multiple constructions appear for a given structure (e.g., the future tense). Critics also regularly note that rhyme seems to play a significant role in the appearance of "deviant" word forms.

Since earlier analyses were completed before the advent of personal computers–Frierson, for example, wrote in 1937–critics surely used notecards for analyses. Frierson relied upon different editors' work for various portions of one manuscript, which means that they did not always treat a given phenomenon in the same way, from the resolution of abbreviations to inclusion of rubrics (which he does not discuss). With a single set of editorial guidelines, and the entire text available in a database, it is simpler to verify critical statements, though perhaps at least as difficult, if not more so, to produce generalizations or to synthesize results, given the overwhelming number of variants.[24] I will use that database to examine chosen problems in phonology, morphology, and syntax, guided in part by precedents set in the nineteenth and twentieth centuries. Here we will examine

---

[23] D. E. Frierson, "A Historical Study of the Language of 'Venice XIII,' Franco-Italian Manuscript of the Fourteenth Century" (Ph.D. diss., University of North Carolina-Chapel Hill, 1937).

[24] R. G. Potter says, very aptly, ". . . the fundamental problem for the literary critic turned computer text analyst, like the fundamental problem for research scientists in general, remains the wealth of gathered data that goes unreported" ("Literary Criticism and Literary Computing: The Difficulties of a Synthesis," *Computers and the Humanities* 22 [1988]: 91–97, here 95–96).

samples from the entire text in order to provide a structure for argument, rather than attempt to cover all phonological and morphological forms in selected portions of the text as Frierson ("Historical Study"), Mussafia (*Macaire*), Reinhold ("Bovo d'Antone," "Karleto") and Rosellini ("Il cosiddetto franco-veneto"; *Geste Francor*) have done.[25]

2.2.2 The Franco-Italian of V^{13}: Hypothesis.

The writer of V^{13} takes advantage of the many possible forms at his disposition according to his needs at the moment. Though word endings are important to comprehension, it is rather context that is most essential to understanding a given word; a word in isolation can at times not be disambiguated by number or gender in the case of a noun, pronoun, or adjective; or by tense or person, in the case of a verb. This does not mean that the text of V^{13} is incomprehensible; rather, it is comprehensible but not within the expected parameters of Old French or Italian and its dialects alone. Frierson contends in his historical study of the phonology that there are "harmonious rules" at the basis of V^{13}'s Franco-Italian ("Historical Study," 31), while Rosellini says, ". . . alla base di tutte queste trasformazioni che conferiscono alla nuova parola (nuova e per rapporto all'afr. [sic] e per rapporto all'it. antico) un suo *status* particolarissimo, non è possibile ipotizzare una qualsiasi norma" (*Geste Francor*, 45). Let us therefore begin at the level of phonology: do norms in fact exist in the Franco-Italian of V^{13}?

2.2.2.1 Phonology.

Earlier critics have all cited the rarity of diphthongs typical of Old French in V^{13}. Thus Mussafia notes that diphthongs are rare, though one finds *voir* as well as *vor*. We find *nose, nosa* (for OF *noise*), *froser, cortos, tros* (Mussafia, *Macaire*, vi–vii); Reinhold similarly notes *cros, frosent, veor, vora, vos* (OF *voix*) ("Bovo d'Antone," 558). Cremonesi too mentions the general lack of diphthongs, but also the existence of pairs such as *vor* and *voir* (*Berte*, 45). Frierson mentions that free closed *e* usually becomes *oi* though it may remain *e*, and suggests that words with *oi* < *e* (< Latin Ē[or Ĭ[) are "wholesale importations"; thus words such as *boir, fois, avoir* in comparison with *dever, pelo* ("Historical Study," 43).[26] Other examples which critics cite for the lack of diphthong are from closed *e* in a stressed open syllable

---

[25] Rosellini gives long lists of forms without distinguishing the process he is exemplifying, "lasciando all'attento lettore la fatica di conferire ad ognuno di essi [gli esempi] il suo proprio peso" (*Geste Francor*, 35–36, 40–45, here 40). In "Il cosiddetto franco-veneto," Part 2, he specifically discusses *Macaire*.

[26] I use the conventions of [to designate open syllable,] closed syllable, capital letters for Latin etymons, > for becomes, < for derives from.

or of closed *o* in a stressed open syllable (< Latin Ŭ[or Ō[). In Italian the standard developments are, respectively, closed *e* and closed *o*. In Old French, Latin Ē[or Ĭ[> closed *e* > *ei*, which by the mid-twelfth century had become *oi*; similarly, Latin Ŭ[or Ō[> closed *o* > *ou* > *eu*. Spelling did not necessarily change to reflect changing pronunciation, of course. Searching our text, we find 6450 words, or "tokens" (443 different forms, or "types") out of 128,505 words (8502 types) with any of the four diphthongs *ei, oi, ou, eu*, a bare 5%. There are twelve types (seventy-seven tokens) in V^{13} that contain *ou*; thirty-seven types (182 tokens) that contain *eu*; fifty-five types (246 tokens) that contain *ei*; 339 types (5545 tokens) that contain *oi*. Of the words with the diphthong *ou*, all are verb forms: *conou, coupé, couper, doust, loué, poumes, pousés, poust, pout, reconou, trouver*. Of these, a number derive from OL (COLP-), nine total, leaving sixty-eight verb forms containing a *ou* not derived from OL. Of the forms with *eu*, most are verbs. A number of the non-verb forms derive from EL (HELMO; HELMONT; FELTRE-, MELT-), fifty-seven total; there is one pronoun, *eus* (cf. MSF "eux"). All the rest are verbs, 125 total tokens. Of *ei* forms, 139 tokens (nineteen types) are not verbs; there are nouns (e.g., *leit, leito*); adverbs (*mei*); adjectives (*bei*); prepositions (*deveir*); pronouns (*lei*); etc., leaving 107 verb tokens (thirty-six types). Thus for *ei*, while there are more types that are verbs, there are fewer actual verb tokens than tokens of other parts of speech with an *ei* diphthong. The largest of the three groups of diphthongs examined, *oi* forms, have representatives in all parts of speech (listed as types/tokens): adverbs (25/163), nouns (38/1405), adjectives (20/136), conjunctions (13/53), pronouns (5/290), exclamations (1/10), and proper names (21/371), for a total of 121 types (2428 tokens), leaving 3117 tokens that are verb forms (there are some types that have multiple meanings; thus an infinitive can be a noun, such as *avoir*, as well as a verb). So all four Old French diphthongs appear, but some are more frequent than others, and those which are part of verb forms—in particular the imperfect and conditional endings -*oi*- typical of French—occur frequently.

If we examine words developing through the normal Italian derivation process from Latin, we frequently find forms without a diphthong parallel to French forms with a diphthong. For example, if we look at the noun types (38) with an *oi* (the *oi* forms with which I begin are italicized; other forms are not, so some alternative spellings to the base diphthongized form appear unitalicized): *arnois* (1): arnise (4); *avoir* (72); avoire (1); avor (3); *bois* (43); boscho (14); boschaje (1); boschi (1); boschon (1); bosco (2); *broilo* (2): broili (2); broli (1); *burgois* (2)—no other form; *çoie* (24) : çoja (81); çoya (1); joie (1) [= joy].[27] çoie (2) [= jewel(s)]—no other form; *droit* (6): droito (2)—no non-diphthonged noun form, though they

---

[27] For an explanation of spelling differences, see below, "Editorial Norms," section 6. Usage is partially in relation to syllable count in the line.

exist for adjective and adverb forms; *droiture* (2): dritura (1); *fois* (28): fogo (8); foço (1); *foi* (11) : fo (1); fois (4) [= faith; note the spelling for OF *foi* < Latin FĪDE(M)]; *fois* (27) [= time, occasion]—no equivalent without diphthong; *loi* (20): lo (17); loe (1); lois (6); *lois* [= place] (15): logo (4); *mois* (16): mesi (1); *noit* (39): note (1); *oile/i* : ocli (12); oile (1); oili (1); olz (1); *palafroi* (45); palafro (7); *poi* (12): po (6); pois (3); *poine/a:* pena (27); pene (19); poina (2); poine (19); *poir* (1): pooir (1); *proie* (2): proja (4); *restoi* (1): restojo (2); *roi:* rege (1); rois (1093); roi (17); roy (1); roys (2); ros (1); *roine* (1): raine (220); ragina (1); raina (66); rayna (1); rayne (6); reine (1); *sarcoil* (1); sarcol (1) (in this particular example both are equally frequent, a hapax; this is an unusual word: Italian would use *sarcofago*); *soir/e/a*: sira (1); soir (4); soira (1); soire (2): the diphthonged form is the more popular one; *voie* (8): via (9); vi (1) vie (16); voja (1): the diphthonged form is not the most used; *voloir* (35) voler (5); volor (3); volore (1). Certain lexemes are overwhelmingly represented by the diphthonged form: *roi/s* for example.

In order to explain the variation in diphthong distribution, we must resort to sociocultural criticism, looking at the contents of the text. There is no clear linguistic reason for variation in diphthong distribution. But, Charlemagne, the king of France, is the center of the Carolingian cycle from France, and is closely associated with it, so using predominantly a French form for "king" makes sense. It is interesting to note that Italian forms for "pain and suffering" are more than double the number of the French forms; perhaps this is of particular meaning to the Italian poet.[28] Other usages are equally balanced between French and Italian forms, usually where there are few appearances of a given word or expression. Interesting is the predominance of *raine/a*; it is a form found in writing also in Old French, but the pronunciation of which was strongly affected by that of *roi* and the desire to avoid confusion with *raine* (< RANA), "frog."[29]

Another phonological group frequently discussed by editors is the development of Latin AU, which corresponds to V^{13}'s *ol* in many cases: *colsa, loldar, olde, olsava, olsé, repolser, golta* (Mussafia, *Macaire*, vii); as Reinhold clarifies, specifically before a consonant ("Bovo d'Antone," 558). Frierson suggests that Northern Italians diphthongized an open *o* in the stressed syllable and then the semi-vowel *u* developed to *l*, though normally the reverse is the case ("Historical Study," 67). If we look at examples of *ol* in pre-consonantal position in V^{13}, we find that most

---

[28] For sociological analysis, see the discussion below about Krauss's theories (H. Krauss, *Epica feudale e pubblico borghese: Per la storia poetica di Carlomagno in Italia*, trans. F. Brugnolo, A. Fassò, and M. Mancini, Ydioma Tripharium 6 [Padua: Liviana, 1980]).

[29] M. K. Pope, *From Latin to Modern French with Especial Consideration of Anglo-Norman Phonology and Morphology* (Manchester: Manchester University Press, 1934), 111, ¶ 246.

are etymological: *ascolter* and its forms, *coltra*, *molt*, for example. Only five lexical families that contain derivations from -AU- appear as *ol*:

- *colsa* (76) and *colse* (37);
- *loldar* (2) and related forms *loldason* (1), *lolder* (2);
- *oldir* (13) and related forms *olda* (2), *oldando* (1), *olde* (71), *oldeç* (1), *oldent* (7), *olderen* (1), *olderés* (2), *olderì* (3), *olderia* (1), *oldés* (4), *oldì* (1), *oldì* (53), *oldie* (1), *oldirà* (2), *oldire* (1), *oldiré* (5), *oldirent* (2), *oldirés* (23), *oldirò* (1), *oldiron* (1), *oldisi* (1), *oldist* (2), *oldo* (5), *oldò* (2), *oldrie* (1), *oldu* (2), *oldua* (1), *olldu* (1);
- *olsa* (7) and related forms *olsas* (1), *olsase* (5), *olsast* (4), *olsava* (4), *olsé* (3), *olsent* (2), *olso* (3), *olsò* (4), *olsoit* (2);
- *repolser* (4) and its forms *repolsa* (1), *repolse* (1), *repolsé* (7); cf. *polser* (9), *polsé* (6).

These derive from Latin CAUSA; LAUDARE; AUDIRE; *AUSARE (AUDERE); (RE)PAUSARE. For two, there are also versions without *l*: *loer*, etc., and *oir*; but for the others there are no alternatives. These forms appear throughout Franco-Italian texts; in V⁴ we find the forms of *lloer*, **oldir*, **oser*, *polsé*, *repolser*.[30] Rohlfs cites the *ol* spelling as typical of Old Milanese, Old Lombard, Trentino, etc.: e.g., *olcire*, *oldire*, *olsá*, *colse*.[31] There are examples of Latinate AU in V¹³, specifically in forms of *laudar*, *staurer*, and *autor*; the context of these forms is appropriate to such Latinisms. For example, l. 14015, "En laudent Deo" forms a liturgical refrain and thus the Latin spelling fits the sociocultural context. Otherwise, *au* reflects the normal OF development of *al* (e.g., *auba*, *hauberg*, *daumaçe*) or the result of lenition typical of Gallo-Italian areas: *amaura; deschaue; paure; sau*, etc.[32]

---

[30] C. Beretta, ed., *Testo assonanzato franco-italiano della Chanson de Roland: cod. Marciano fr. IV (=225)* (Pavia: Tipografia Commerciale Pavese, 1995), 530, 559, 563, 580, 599.

[31] G. Rohlfs, *Grammatica Storica della lingua italiana e dei suoi dialetti*, 3 vols., trans. S. Persichino (Turin: Einaudi, 1966), ¶¶ 42, 143. One of Fieberg's criteria (#16) for the identification of Franco-Italian is the development of stressed Latin -AU- > -ou-, as in *chouse, pouvres* (W. Fieberg, *Das "Livre d'Enanchet" nach der einzigen Handschrift 2585 der Wiener Nationalbibliothek* [Jena: Gronau, 1938], xxxvi ff., cited in Holtus, *Lexicalische Untersuchungen*, 19–20). The representation of vowel + *l* and vowel + *u* can alternate in a given text, as here for *ultr-/autr-*, so his criterion could be generalized to apply to V¹³ in this case.

[32] Lenition is the process typical of northern Italy (and found in Romance areas in general) in which intervocalic occlusives become weakened, even to the point of being lost (e.g., *ria* < Latin RIPA). They are voiced, then spirantized and lost. Not all occlusives in every region undergo the entire process. Lepschy and Lepschy define the process, "a change from voiceless and tense to voiced and lax, . . . a form of weakening and it is related to spirantization (as in [p] > [v]) and to complete disappearance (particularly for [t]>[d]>∅) . . ." (A. L. Lepschy and G. Lepschy, *The Italian Language Today* [London: Routledge, 1988], 52).

There is no logical reason that particular words are represented with *ol*. Cultural reasons—local influence and *scripta* (for *ol*) together with Latinate influence (for *laudar, autor*)—must account for some of the variation.

While earlier editors thus correctly identified phenomena of diphthongization and its development, the availability of the entire V[13] text allows finer distinctions in the appearance of diphthongs. The predominance of diphthongs in verbal forms and in key words related to the Charlemagne cycle (*rois, foi, loi*, etc.) help us identify what gave a patina of "Frenchness" to the compiler of V[13] and his public, and goes beyond the history of phonological development.

Phonological variation at the morphological level results in a French patina in some tenses and persons: paradigms do not have the familiar constant form of modern languages or even slightly varied paradigms possible in some individual medieval authors or texts. A few samples of each of the usual morphological paradigms given with a medieval text will demonstrate the degree of constant variation through the text and how variation affects comprehension: morphology alone does not suffice to explain some of the variation. Historical development and lexical fields clarify the meaning of alternate forms in certain situations.

2.2.2.2 Morphology.

As representative samples, we will examine two nouns deriving from the Latin first declension; two from the third declension; two imparisyllabics; the definite article; the verb "to have"; and subject pronouns. Since the topic of rhyme has so frequently been brought into question, we will include in our considerations the line position of words discussed, to see whether in fact line-position is a defining formal characteristic.

2.2.2.2.1 Nouns.

First declension

Feminine nouns deriving from the Latin first declension would seem to be least problematic, since there was no two-case system for them in either Old French or Italian. Frierson, in his sample analysis of one hundred words, says, "the singular form in -*a* is preferred to -*e* by three to one. In the plural the form in -*e* occurs about twice as often as that in -*es*" ("Historical Study," 69). These figures would indicate the avoidance of final -*s* as a flexional symbol and suggest the need for methods other than desinence for distinguishing number in feminine nouns. The difference between the French and Italian systems for marking number, a final -*e* frequently marking the singular in French and the plural in Italian, gives rise to uncertainties.

1. **dama** < Latin DOMINA(M): lady; woman.³³ (348 total appearances)
dama (221 appearances): FS, no rhyme position
dame (124 appearances): FS and FP, context needed to distinguish; no rhyme
dames (2 appearances): FP, no rhyme
dan (1 appearance): FS, at rhyme position

2. **fema** < Lat. FEMINA(M): woman. (19 total appearances)

fema 1 FS	*femena* 5 FS
feme 10 FS?	*femene* 1 FS

femes 2, (1/2 in a rubric) FP: appears linked with *homes* in both cases

These two nouns, both originating in the Latin first declension and overlapping in meaning, have a very different distribution; *dama* is much more frequent than *fema* and shows different proportions of forms in different positions. *Dama* is clearly feminine singular, and *dames* is clearly plural. *Dame* can be either singular or plural. Similarly *fema/femena* is clearly singular, as *femes* is clearly plural.³⁴ The number of appearances of forms with a final *-e* in each case is not inconsiderable. In certain contexts, the meaning can be entirely different if the noun is plural or singular. Looking at *dama* and its forms, where the article *la* is present, there is no problem in distinguishing number (e.g., in ll. 283, 287); but this occurs in only forty-two appearances. Similarly, other adjectives can clarify number (e.g., *cesta* l. 279). However, we also find contexts such as "Le dame . . ." (l. 1022), "Dame e polçele . . ." (l. 9064). Examining context closely, we find that of the 125 appearances of *dame*, forty-two are clearly singular by the article; eighty-seven are clearly singular because of another adjective form indicated with a final *-a*; but there are also twenty-four with only a modifier in *-e* and fourteen with no modifier or with an unmarked modifier (e.g., final *-l*). A number of these are clearly singular, as they refer to a clear antecedent or because, in one case, it is a title (Rubric 100, line

---

³³ I will use standard abbreviations throughout this section: FS for "feminine singular," FP for "feminine plural," MS, MP for "masculine singular" and "masculine plural," distinguishing OC and SC if necessary for "object case" and "subject case." Where "?" appears after a listing, it indicates that the designation is unsure or could in fact represent another number, case, or gender. * derives from computational usage and designates a "wild card"; that is, any letter or group of letters can follow. It thus works well to designate a stem end. *Dame* appears once as "checkers" and therefore is not included in this discussion.

³⁴ The only difference in the two is in the syllable count for the line, which is one more in *femen** forms.

2); others are clearly plural, as the example in l. 9064 cited above. Several examples require more than one line to disambiguate—thus *dame* in l. 7728 "Qi donc oldist quelle dame plurer" must be plural because it refers to the women imprisoned in a tower whom Karleto rescued in the preceding laisse.

The meaning of the text can depend upon this context around the *dame* form. For example, in lines 9373 and 9418, the number of "Petit(e) dame . . ." is not immediately clear, especially when the following verbs are singular. In line 9373, the meaning is important—did Berta have "a little woman" helping her give birth or "a few women"? Line 9418 clarifies the plural meaning, since "there were few X in the world who were wiser than Berta" is possible where "there was a small X in the world who . . ." makes little sense. In all, in spite of other forms nearby, there remain seventeen appearances that need a much larger context for disambiguation. Out of one hundred and twenty-five, that is a small percentage (13.6%). The only form at rhyme position (*dan*) is unique and a hapax legomenon.

The situation for *feme* is somewhat different. As for *dama*, for eleven forms of *feme* we must rely upon context—adjectives (e.g., articles and possessives) or verbs—to distinguish number. So, for example, we rely upon the verb or other markers, as in lines 1987 (*alast*), 14738 (*sa*). Yet verbs as well do not always distinguish between singular and plural, especially in the third person. However the immediate context, one line of verse, of all ten forms of *feme*, immediately reveals that all are singular. Rhyme here plays no role at all.

We might ask why there are so many more forms of *dame* than of *feme* though many have the same number of syllables, and both mean "woman / women," and that there is no difficulty disambiguating the forms of *feme* where there is for *dame*. There is the distinction of *dame* as a title, accepted in both language areas; but there is also the fact that *feme* is not generally used in Northern Italian dialect areas. It is a Gallo-Italian word in its meaning of "female" specifically of the human species. In Modern Standard Italian (MSI), *donna* is the word for a grown woman. This, added to the use of the form as a title, "Lady," we might expect to find more appearances of a Latin reflex in *d-* than otherwise. In order to understand the choices made, therefore, we need to know more than endings and immediate syntactic position: we need the context of the poem segment (at least several lines), a knowledge of lexical fields and historical developments of phonemes in both Northern Italy and Gallo-Italian areas. This need for multiple approaches is true in other nouns as well.[35]

---

[35] In K. Jaberg and J. Jud, *Sprach- und Sachatlas Italiens und der Südschweiz*, Band 8, II. Teil: Einzelsätze, Konjugationstabellen, Ergänzungsmaterialien (Zofingen: Ringier AG, 1940), map 1678, "Questa donna non mi piace" [I don't like this woman]: above the Po River there are many responses using reflexes of FEMINA(M), as there are in the southern part of the Italian peninsula. For the general category of male and female

2.2 The Franco-Italian of V^3

Nouns deriving from the Latin third declension: imparisyllabics

For nouns deriving from the third declension, not only number but also gender can be unclear. In the French and Italian areas some of these nouns diverged in gender, and our author takes advantage of all possible configurations as he needs them. We will examine the forms of four imparisyllabics, together with their apparent gender and number by context in the text as well as, again, note any variations at the rhyme position.

3. **flor / flors** (< Latin FLOS, FLORIS): flower. (12 appearances)
flor (11) nine appearances at rhyme position; masculine or feminine, singular or plural:
  un flor, le flor, la flor
flors (1), at rhyme position

Without further knowledge, either historical or otherwise, one cannot predict the number or gender of *flor*. *Flor* is feminine in French both Old and Modern, but masculine in Italian, and varies in gender in V^{13}. Without a modifier, the gender is unclear. Of eleven appearances, nine are at rhyme position. It is clearly feminine four times through its modifiers (*la flor; tota flor; una flor; la flor*); once it is clearly masculine (*un flor*) and the other appearances are all without gender markers: *a flor* (4 times), *qe flor* (once); the one appearance of *flors* is *a flors* and is at the rhyme position. So, at rhyme position, the expressions *a flor/ a flors* vary freely with no distinction of gender or number, but samples are few.

4. **dent** (< Latin DENS, DENTIS): tooth, teeth. (11 appearances)
dent (5) : always *li dent*; none at rhyme position; all examples seem plural
dente (3): *le* (2), *li* (1); none at rhyme position; all seem plural
denti (3) *li denti*: none at rhyme position; all seem plural

Nine forms of *dent* appear in a fixed expression, *tros* or *trosqu'a* or *trosqua in* + article + a form of *dent* + either *e/i*. The remaining two appear in the fixed expression *cun li denti*. So all are object of a preposition, requiring the object case if such exists. Only three appear with an adjective, *cler* (6530), or *agu* (14506, 14510); in each case, these three adjectives are at rhyme position.

---

of animals, Volume 6, map 1078, "maschio e femmina" are the universal choices. In very few cases in the north is a cognate of "dama" given, volume 1 (1928), map 49. The situation of the fourteenth century and "literary" language is of course more complex, since it reflected Tuscan usage frequently in combination with Veneto usage, where we find again reflexes of DOMINA(M) (see 376, 385, etc., on map 1678). For a discussion of the history of the terms and their development in Italian, see E. Passera, "The Semantic Evolution of the Latin Terms *Domina, Femina*, and *Mulier*," *Quaderni d'Italianistica* 19 (1998): 105–25.

Dent would be feminine in French, but in Italian masculine. (There was also fluctuation of gender in certain classes of nouns in French during the twelfth century; among these is *dent*, which changes gender from masculine to feminine under the analogy of *gent* [Pope, *From Latin to Modern French*, 305, ¶ 777].) Here, *li dent* is an example of subject case masculine plural, but in object position, after a preposition; we also find *le dente* and *li dente* in the same construction (one would expect *les denz* or something similar for either masculine or feminine object case plural in French style). And finally, *li denti* is also object of prepositions (*a, cun*), seemingly a masculine plural Italian style. Gender and case are unclear from this variety of forms, leading us to believe that the distinction was unessential, especially when meaning is clear. Unless the person were prematurely toothless, one would be striking through to the <u>teeth</u>, not just one tooth.[36]

Imparisyllabic nouns, continued: masculine forms

The masculine imparisyllabic forms generally have two stems: the subject and object case stems are different. In French, the two were sometimes disassociated to become two separate lexemes, as for example, *sir(e)*, which remained as a title, versus *seigneur*, which was used as "lord."

5. **abes, abé** (< Latin *ABBATE): abbot (imparisyllabic).[37] (31 appearances)
abes 30, everywhere except at rhyme position, including rubrics;
abé 1, at rhyme position

6. **sir(e) / signor(s) / segnor(s)** (< Latin SENIOR, SENIOREM): lord, lords; sir.

142 appearances, total	211 appearances, total
segnor 110; 10 at rhyme position (S/P??)	*signor* 3, 1 at rhyme position
segnors 3 clearly P, never at rhyme pos.	*signore* 1 (R)
segnur 90, never at rhyme pos. (S/P??)	*signur* 1 P
segnurs P, 3 never at rhyme pos.	
ser 4, all at rhyme position, S	*sir* 22, never at rhyme position, S/P?
	sire, never at rhyme position, 116 S/P?

In the case of *abé, abes*, rhyme position keeps the correct Old French form; elsewhere *abes* has been generalized. In Old French, *abes* was subject case singular, *abé(t)* object case singular. All the forms here are singular, and all appear in the last segment of V[13], *Macario*, where they refer either to the abbot who confesses

---

[36] It should be noted that in Northern Italy, noun endings are frequently derived by analogy. See Rohlfs, *Grammatica storica*, ¶ 362, ¶ 365, ¶ 366.

[37] For development in Old French, see Pope, *From Latin to Modern French*, 312, ¶ 800.

Queen Blançiflor accused of adultery or the abbot who baptizes her son, Leoys. The one example at rhyme position is direct address (which is object case in parallel with the rest of the sentence, "I beg of you . . ."); the rest are all *abes*, for whatever function: subject case masculine, object of preposition, direct object, within a line or a rubric—and none are at rhyme position. *-és* is a relatively frequent rhyme and no forms appear at rhyme position; so it would seem that *abes* is recognized as a paroxytone form versus *abé*, an oxytone form. The assumption of *abes* being paroxytone can be documented in one case where the final *-es* is uncounted in caesura (l. 14049) to obtain a syllable count of 3 + 7. Given the overlap of *-é, -és, -er* at rhyme position and of *-é, -er* on occasion within the line, it is legitimate to wonder whether **abés*, an oxytone pronunciation, might be possible. In line 16311, for example, the final *-es* must be counted in caesura to obtain a syllable count of 4 + 6. With the variation of syllable count in caesura, however, and the fact that all forms of the word are singular, a paroxytone form seems most likely.

For the forms of *sire*, we have a variety of phonological as well as of case forms. The Old French and Old Italian overlap in various ways, in part also because Italian adapted the word from French. In Old French, *sire* would be subject case singular, *seignour* subject case plural and objet case singular, *seignours* object case plural. *Ser* is the Italian proclitic form, used as a title (cf. Rohlfs, *Grammatica Storica*, ¶ 316); *sire* also exists as a Gallicism (¶ 344). *Signore* is the Standard Italian derivation for the noun "lord, ruler."[38] So in Old French one subject case form appears in Italian as a title. *Ser* appears four times, always at rhyme position, meaning "ruler, lord"; one is a predicate nominative, the other three objects of prepositions. *Sir* appears predominantly as direct address, but also as object of a preposition (l. 6382, 10289, etc.). It is never at rhyme position. *Sire* appears predominantly in direct address and as a title, though also as object of a preposition. *Segnor*, which should be object case singular or subject case plural, appears as direct address for the plural, object of a preposition, both singular and plural, as does *segnur*. The three appearances of *segnurs* are for direct address, and are plural. Even though these forms are not at the rhyme position, the writer does not follow the "rules." *Segnor* falls in the rhyme position, where it is used as a object case plural (direct object) rather than Old French object singular or subject plural, in order to fit the rhyme. Its other two appearances are as a subject and as a predicate nominative, both singular and therefore correct. The *-ors* forms, technically object

---

[38] The initial pretonic vowel in *signore* exhibits anaphonesis, a characteristic of Tuscan dialects, including Florentine, in which pretonic Ē or Ĭ before the palatal *l*, palatal *n* (n + k or g) and *skj*, remain *i* and *u* respectively, instead of closed *e* and closed *o*: thus, "famiglia," "lingua," "ischia" instead of *fameglia, *lengua, and *eschio (Rohlfs, *Grammatica Storica*, ¶ 49) and Ō or Ŭ before n + k or g or before ñ becomes a *u* instead of a closed *o*; thus, "ungere," "fungo," instead of *ongere, *fongo (¶ 70).

case plural, appear only in three examples, as direct address within the line. *-or* is a relatively frequent rhyme: it appears in 410 lines, for 2.4% of the total, eighth in overall frequency, whereas an occasional ending *-ors* appears only as an assonance in *-os* laisses. So in this manuscript, there are many more *-or* endings than *-ors*, yet overall the non-rhyme position appearances of *segnor* are not substantially more correct than those in the rhyme position. Final *-s* is clearly not popular, and a final *-r* is frequently without a final vowel, typical of Northern Italy (both Gallo-Italian and Venetian).[39] So a series of events prevents the use of appropriate distinctive subject and object case singular and plural forms of this imparisyllabic noun. First, during the twelfth century, alternation of imparisyllabic radicals began to falter in France. By the end of the thirteenth century, case distinctions were already disappearing in Old French in the central area of France, and they were gone at the end of the fourteenth century (Pope, *From Latin to Modern French*, 313–14, ¶ 805.2–806), thus the degeneracy of the two-case system for an alternating radical in a manuscript from the first half of the fourteenth century can be expected. Secondly, loss of the final vowel following final *-r* in Northern Italy was typical; and together with the unpopularity of final *-s* in the Italian peninsula both lead to an expected *-r* final form over an *-rs* form.

After examining these samples, while we might not go so far as to say with Mussafia, "We cannot even begin to think of a rule for declension,"[40] it is clear that for feminine nouns the *-e* ending is problematic while the meanings of final *-a* and *-s* are evident. For masculine imparisyllabics, the original subject case form has, in some cases, been detached to form a separate lexeme, a title. One finds similar examples in *ber/barons*.[41] Similarly, we should find *enfes*, contrasted with *enfant/enfant/enfanz*, but do not. Nor do parisyllabic masculine nouns necessarily show case; *mur*, for example, appears nine times, to one time for *murs*, and all are objects of a preposition (*dentro, en, a, por*) and none are at rhyme position. We find *dos mur grant* (1105), the only case of a clear plural (thanks to modifiers); we find *li/le mur*, and *celle mur* (2 times), where surprisingly, the adjective *celle* appears feminine (like MSI *le mura*). However, number (and gender) in this case is not essential to sense. If Blondoja is walled in, does it matter if it is inside one wall or between two? *a le murs ne se voit a 'pojer* (6450) would seem to be singular, but the noun would be object case plural in the standard Old French declension—one

---

[39] Of twenty-five rhymes, only six, among which the most rare, bear final *-s*: *-és, -os, -is, -uç, -iç/iz, -uz* (allowing z, ç to stand for *-ts* or *-ds*). This too testifies to the unpopularity of the final *-s*.

[40] "An eine DECLENATIONSREGEL ist nicht zu denken [sic] . . ." (*Macaire*, viii).

[41] See also L. Foulet, *Petite syntaxe de l'ancien français*, 3rd ed. rev., Les Classiques Français du Moyen Âge, 2e série: Manuels (Paris: Honoré Champion, 1966), 5, ¶ 9.

2.2 The Franco-Italian of V³

leans with difficulty on more than one wall—and it is paralleled in l. 13244, *a li mur apoçé*, so *a le murs* would seem to be a synonym for *a li mur*.⁴²

2.2.2.2.2 Definite article.

We have mentioned *la, cella*, and other forms as possible disambiguators for nouns of unclear gender or number. However, the definite articles do not necessarily assist in disambiguation of a noun. The forms *l', lo, la, ·lla, e, el, ·lli* are are clearly singular and *les, ili* are clearly plural. Again, subject and object case are not distinctive features: we find *li* in both cases and numbers as a masculine, *le* as both cases and numbers for the feminine and masculine. Thus there is also frequently no distinction by gender in the definite article.

	singular	plural
M Subj	*li, le, lo, l'/·l, e, el*	*le, les, li, ili*
M Obj	*li, le, l'/·l, lo, (·u?), ·lli* (R)	*le, les, li, i, ·s*
F Subj	*la, le, l'*	*le, les*
F Obj	*la, le, l', ·lla* (R)	*le, les*

We find *l* in two positions, before a vowel and combined with a preposition, clearly singular in form. In the masculine singular, we find also *le* and *li*. I do not give examples of the *l* form as they are relatively straightforward. Here are a few examples of other overlapping forms and possible misapprehensions.

Masculine singular:

Subject	Object
Li porter se partì . . . (402)	Feru l'averoit con li brant d'açer (6849)
	Fora de li leto l'oit tiré (2630)
Cum fait le lion quand . . . (137)	Le scu li speçe, l'auberg li oit falsé (218)

Masculine plural:

Tot les autres qe son (de) sa masné (10087)	Davant les oile le font inbinder (OP) (8997)
	En Paganie tot les autres avançc (DO) (12645)
Le parenti taites . . . (57) ?	Por le çavi ela l'oit pié (2627)
	Veste l'aubers e calça le ganber (4993)

---

⁴² Rosellini too discusses the loss of the case system as related to phonological changes in French, but not just in V¹³ ("Il cosiddetto franco-veneto").

Li cento soldaer ferì . . . (22)	Quant Uberto l'inte*n*t a <u>li pe</u> . . . (447)
Tante so dolçi <u>i versi</u> e·l çanter . . . ? (633)	. . . <u>d·i Persant</u> (101) (OP)
Quant <u>ili mesaçi</u> s'en retornò . . . (12119)	
Feminine singular:	
<u>Le tronbe</u> fu sonée . . . (999) s/p?	A·l donojer, et a <u>le cortesie</u> grant (7797)
	Le ben e·l mal s'atrova en <u>le cité</u> (766) s/p?
<u>La spea</u> torna qe ferì en canton (8)	Dist Teris, "Sire est de <u>la contré</u> (195)
Feminine plural:	
Quand <u>le aste</u> son frate . . . (156)	Grant oit l'inforchaure e por <u>le spale</u> les (1740)
Qe tot <u>les spales</u> e lo çevo . . . (4853)	Prendent <u>les armes</u>, . . . (16139)

Les is relatively infrequent (22 appearances only), and appears as MP OC except for two examples, ll. 4853 and 16139. *Le* appears throughout the paradigms, making distinction of number (and gender) at times difficult. From what we have seen of nouns, then, we can add the evidence of definite articles: the language of V[13] does not distinguish between subject and object cases; other than *e* (which appears only once) and *·u* (which appears only eleven times as part of the name of *Girardo Aufraite/Au Fraite*, and is an issue of word division), and a few *el*, the forms for masculine and for feminine each work in both subject and object position. *i* appears almost entirely as object of a preposition; it may be a creation of interpreting *di* as *d* + *i* like *·s* and, in the singular, *·l*. (See also section 6.4 below.)

The writer takes advantage of having a number of substantive forms at his disposition, nouns and adjectives, and uses them all, both French and Italian, to fit into rhyme, syllable count, and meter.

2.2.2.2.3 Verbs.

With verbs, the text does the same as with nouns, combining possible stems and endings from French and Italian. Again, the context usually clarifies tense or person where there is an overlap, but not always. The verb "to have" is one of the most frequently used verbs and therefore will give a good sample of the variety extant in verb forms and how the stems combine and co-exist with endings, as well as demonstrate how forms work with rhyme.

8: **"To have"** †: form is found at rhyme position; –: the form is lacking; ? whether the form in this tense/number is unsure; (R) found in Rubrics only. For frequencies, see Glossary.

2.2 The Franco-Italian of V³

		Infinitive: avoir, aver, avoire, avor	**past participle:** eut†, euet†, au
		present indicative:	
		Singular	*Plural*
1		aço, ò, oe, ai	avont†, aon, avemo, aven, avont†
2		ai, ais, as, a	ajés, avét†, aveçt†, avez, avì
3		àt†, ait, oit, ont†	aient, avont, on, ont
		present subjunctive:	
1		–	açamo
2		–	aça, açét†, açeet†, ajést†, ajez
3		abia, açe, aça	aient
		imperative:	
2		aça	aça, ajeç
		future:	
1		averai, averò, avrò (R)	averemo, averen, averon, averemo
2		averà	arés, avereç, averés, avrì, avrez, avrés, averez, averà, averéet†, averì
3		averà, avrà, averò	averont, averà, averont†
		conditional:	
1		averoie, averia	averesemo
2		–	averisi
3		averia, averoie, averoit	–
		imperfect:	
1		avoie, avea, avì?	–
2		–	avisi?
3		avit?, avoi, avoit, avoja, avot?, oit?, oi, ayt, avè, avea, avoie, avoient	avoient
		imperfect subjunctive:	
1		avese, aust	aumes?
2		–	ausés, austes, avesés
3		aust, avese, ast	ausent, austes
		simple past (perfect):	
1		avì?	aumes?
2		–	avisi
3		avè, avì, avit?, avot?, oi?, oit	arent[43]

---

[43] I have checked these listings against those who have similar analyses: Frierson, "Historical Study"; Mussafia, *Macaire*; Reinhold, "Bovo d'Antone"; Reinhold, "Karleto."

There are phonological oddities to be noted, such as the frequency of French forms: *oi* and *au* are frequent in spite of an overall rarity of diphthongs in V¹³ (see above, 2.2.2.1). There are eighty-three types in the forms of "to have" (that is, graphically different forms), and a total of 3007 appearances (tokens) of forms of the verb "to have" in V¹³. Among these, the numbers of certain forms are overwhelming. Thus, among the most freqent types are *oit*, with 1278 tokens; *avoit*, with 253 tokens; *à* with 233; *ont* with 170; *ò* with 129. In the past tenses, especially the imperfect, the diphthongs make a very French-seeming form.[44] In the present tense, in first and third persons, "to have" is very Italian. Looking at the entire present indicative paradigm, however, the plural appears largely French in contrast to the singular Italian forms. This is an example of the variation between forms in given tenses. Similarly, in the future and conditional, both the syncopated and unsyncopated forms appear (*averoie* compared to *avrà*), but none of the forms is frequent enough to draw a firm conclusion as to the more popular form.

To go beyond the mere listing of forms for a moment in an attempt to explain the variation we see, one interesting etymological note is the multiple derivations of the conditional, which explain the variety of endings. There are not just two variations, expected in Old Italian, but three. In most of the Romance area, the conditional was formed using the infinitive + the imperfect of Latin "to have" (HABEBAM); that area includes France and, in part, Italy. However, what has become the MSI form for the conditional derives from the infinitive + the perfect of Latin "to have" (HABUIT). In older texts, one finds "avría" (derived from the imperfect) together with "avrei/avrebbe" (derived from the perfect). In Northern Italian, the form derived from the Latin imperfect was used largely in the first and third persons, thus it is no surprise to find it so used here (Rohlfs, *Grammatica Storica*, ¶ 595).[45] However, the forms we find here in the plural conditional,

---

[44] Cremonesi discusses the possible pronunciation of *oi* and *ai* (in French by the end of the twelfth century oi>oe/ue). She offers a line from the V⁴ *Chanson de Roland* (2537) as proof that it was pronounced as spelled, for example, *lo-ý* since it is in a laisse with -*i* assonance. She suggests that errors in V¹³ such as *vor* in her *Rolandin*, 170, raise more questions than answers — is this oral or written in origin? She suggests, "Le deformazioni sono più numerose e clamorose in rima, il che rivelerebbe l'arbitraria e voluta trascuratezza del rispetto della lingua" (C. Cremonesi, "Note di franco-veneto. I. Francoveneto, franco-italiano, franco-lombardo; II. L'oste: un motivo ricorrente," in *Studi di lingua e letteratura lombarda offerti a Maurizio Vitale* [Pisa: Giardini, 1983], 1: 5–21, here 12, n. 27).

[45] There is some disagreement about the origin of the infinitive + imperfect in Italian, whether it is of Northern or Southern origin, or perhaps even due to external influences. It is found in the earliest lyric, from the Sicilian School, as well as in Northern Italian writings and in Tuscan. Rohlfs suggests that as far as actual phonological development is concerned, it would be possible only in the extreme south of Italy, where the romance language development of infinitive + HABERE was unknown. Whether it came

averesemo and *averisi*, are closely related to Old Paduan forms, probably derived through analogy with the imperfect subjunctive forms, though an interrogative form with postposed subject may also have contributed in some areas (Rohlfs, *Grammatica Storica*, ¶ 598). Frierson derives these from the infinitive plus pluperfect subjunctive ("Historical Study," 106). There are thus three different types of forms here in the conditional: those we would expect from French, Northern Italian (or Italian poetic language), and Old Paduan.

Looking at the forms of "to have," it is clear that, at the morphological level, verb form cannot alone determine the person, as it frequently does in Modern Italian or French (the second through a stated subject). Furthermore, as with nouns, the immediate context does not always assist in disambiguating which form is intended, though a larger segment usually does. The overlap of personal forms within a given tense, as well as overlap between tenses, is very clear. Thus, *ai* appears both as first and second person singular (though this more rarely): e.g., 1829 vs. 10702; *-on* appears as third person singular and plural form: 3880 vs. 11413, like *ont* (2065 could be singular); *à* is third person singular but also second person singular (e.g., ll. 12241, 14009, etc.). Another example of an overlapping form is *aust*, used as a plural (14365). Similarly, *oit* serves for third person singular (e.g., 4226, 4336, etc.), but is also used for impersonal expressions which at first glance seem plural; e.g., l. 6067. For this reason, I did not separate different persons of the verb in the glossary.

The difficulty of distinguishing between singular and plural is not limited to the third person singular and plural. Distinction between *tu* and *vous* forms is confused by frequent switching within a single conversation; thus, for example, in Bovo's speech to his half-brother he switches between *tu* and *vu* (ll. 1135–1153): first he says, "Tu è un çovençel" (1137) then "Sì vu ça venir . . ." (1140).[46] Thus one wonders if *ensì* in line 1146 is second person singular (*ensì*) or plural

---

through Provençal influence on the Sicilian School or through Northern Italy to Tuscany is unclear (Rohlfs, *Grammatica Storica*, ¶¶ 593–96).

[46] Foulet speaks of the ease with which characters switch from *tu* to *vous* and the reverse, through in general the uses of the two seem parallel to modern usage (*Petite syntaxe*, 198–201, ¶¶ 287–89). A number of studies have addressed specific texts in Old French and their usage of *tu/vous*, as for example, E. Kennedy, who also makes an argument for the rational use of *tu* and *vous* ("The Use of *Tu* and *Vous* in the First Part of the Old French Prose *Lancelot*," in *History and Structure of French: Essays in Honour of Professor T. B. W. Reid*, ed. F. J. Barnett et al. [Totowa, NJ: Rowman and Littlefield, 1972], 135–49). F. Lebsanft is more general and points out that the phenomenon is found in other medieval languages as well ("Le Problème du mélange du 'tu' et du 'vous' en ancien français," *Romania* 108 [1987]: 1–19, here 3). Among his examples is Italian, which brings him to compare contemporary examples of *tu / vous* mixture with medieval usage. He argues that the effect of mixture is partially a type of "poetic licence" and partially a result of "certaines habitudes graphiques, mais aussi certaines évolutions proprement

because there is no nearby personal pronoun or other indication of *tu* or *vu*. The meaning is clear, but the actual position in the paradigm is not. Where an unusual use is found, there is sometimes a personal pronoun subject form to disambiguate: as the forms of *avì* are normally second plural, disambiguation through pronouns may occur where they are first person: for example, we find *eo* (e.g., ll. 2128, 11304, 14989); or where they are third person: for example, we find *ello* (15784). Many times even with the second person plural there is also the pronoun subject *vu* (e.g., 2253, 2625, etc.).

Different tense stems also overlap. The present subjunctive forms, used for first and third person singular, are the same as the imperative, *aça*. This is not entirely unexpected since in both Old French and Italian the present subjunctive and the imperative share the same stems. But Mussafia comments on the difficulty of distinguishing the tense of *oit*: is it present or perfect? As Mussafia notes, "Phonologically it corresponds best to *ha[b]uit*, and so it is in some spots . . . the perfect is not to be mistaken. In other spots one can be in doubt whether it designates a perfect or a present; most of the time this form can only be understood as a present."[47] For some of the verbal forms, earlier editors may disagree. Frierson includes *açé* among imperatives, second plural; *avit*, *avot*, and *oie* as preterit; *aumes* as simple past. As mentioned, Mussafia lists *oit* as both present and perfect; Reinhold ("Bovo d'Antone," 562; "Karleto," 659) as only present; Frierson, as both present and preterit (= perfect) ("Historical Study," 247). On the basis of pronunciation and the Italian precedent, one might wonder whether or not it was understood as imperfect, with the common *-oit* ending of the imperfect, since Italian forms the *trapassato prossimo* (pluperfect I) with the imperfect + the past participle (see Rohlfs, *Grammatica Storica*, ¶ 674). Of course the entire text of V[13] was not available to any one of the grammatical commentators so, in their defense, no single one included all the forms listed here.

Thus, in verb forms, it is not always possible to know, in the absence of an identifying subject pronoun, which person is intended. For third person singular and plural, the presence of a subject or a pronoun can clarify the situation. For first person, the use of the "royal we" as well as "I" makes number more clear than in other persons. Yet the overlap of stems of different verbs and endings between different persons renders parsing isolated forms difficult. In other words, the

---

linguistiques" ("Le problème du mélange," 19). Such evolution would be comparable to the semi-deliberate mixture found in Franco-Italian.

[47] "Lautlich stimmt sie am besten zu *ha[b]uit*, auch ist an einingen Stellen, . . . die Perfectbedeutung nicht zu verkennen. An andren Orten kann man im Zweifel sein, ob ein Perfect oder ein Præsens vorliegt; in den meisten Fällen jedoch kann diese Form nur als Præsens gefasst werden" (*Macaire*, xiii).

morphology of verbs, like that of nouns, relies upon context rather than on fixed morphological form for comprehension and disambiguation.

2.2.2.2.4 Verbal Syntax.

A number of unique syntactical constructions mark V^{13}. Both Frierson ("Historical Study," 104) and Mussafia (*Macaire*, xiv) mention one that does not exist in either source language, the "double future": that is, the use of the future of *avere* with the infinitive of the verb in question. It should be noted that a double verb form occurs not only with the future (cf. 7009, 12908; 13741; etc.), but also with other tenses. In the present subjunctive, for example, we find "Non v'aça merveler," (2653; cf. 9899, etc.), "don't be surprised" with a subjunctive of *avoir* followed by the infinitive. In the imperfect subjunctive, we have "Sença bataile s'aumes acorder," (5007), "Without combat we could/should come to agreement." For the perfect, see also lines 6980, 11902, etc.; for the conditional, 16586.

The use of *aver* with reflexive verbs also stands out. In both Modern French and Modern Italian, "to be" is used as the auxiliary verb in reflexive constructions. V^{13} uses both "to have" and "to be" in this position. Use of "to have" as reflexive auxiliary is not unheard of in the Romance area; Spanish, for example, does exactly that. In Old Italian, too, it was frequent—e.g., in the *Decameron* (Rohlfs, *Grammatica Storica*, ¶ 731). Rohlfs notes that Standard Italian abandoned such use only in the seventeenth century, but that it still exists in parts of the Veneto (¶ 731). In Old French as well, one finds "to have" as auxiliary for reflexives.[48] Of the sixteen appearances of *s'* + the verb "to have," in fifteen *s'* is the reflexive pronoun (lines 818, 2345, 6980, 7586, 9328, 10506, 10717, 11744, 11902, 13310, 13641, 13714, 15693, 16073, 16592) and in only one is it the conjunction "if" (line 6926). We find, for example, "El s'à pris en seno a covoter" (10971); "Da ora avanti el s'à fato apriser," (16802), etc.

A further source of difficulties with the third person reflexive and *avoir* is that in V^{13} we find that reflexive forms coincide with forms of the verb "to know," especially in the perfect form *s'avè*: "Da nu s'avè sevrer" (6980) [From us he had to leave]; this could also be *"Da nu savè sevrer" [From us he knew to leave/he had to leave]. Similarly, "E cun un osto s'avè a conseler" (11744) [And with a host he had to consult], could also be *"E cun un osto save a conseler" [And with a host wise at counselling], for example. There are five of these, but *save* as an adjective does not appear, though forms of "to know" with the *sav* stem do appear: *save, savé,* etc. These are clearly verbs by the morphology; for example, Rubric 8, "Coment Bovo oit recovré sa cité; e de Drixiana / Ni de ses filz non <u>save</u> niant; e coment / Braidamont li mandoit mesaçer."

---

[48] See J. Anglade for examples (*Grammaire élémentaire de l'ancien français* [Paris: Armand Colin, 1965], 182).

Avoir is also used instead of *deber*, "to ought to" in the construction *aver + a +* infinitive: for example, line 4715, "No li lasò si l'avè a strangoler" [He (the king's son, Falcon) did not let him (Bovo's horse) go, and he (the horse) had to kill him (Folcon)].There are historical reasons for this, of course; in the history of the romance languages, the use of "to have" and the infinitive in various combinations forms both analytic and synthetic tenses. As Rohlfs outlines, these constructions originated in an element of "have to" or "must," a modal usage (*Grammatica Storica*, ¶ ¶ 675–677).

Avoir can create a further lexical confusion with homonyms in *oir*, "to hear." Thus *oi, oit*, etc., in their simple tenses need to be disambiguated. *oie* appears at rhyme position only as a form of "to hear," yet Frierson misconstrues it as the perfect of "to have" ("Historical Study," 247; cf. my line 1336). *oi* appears only twice as an auxiliary; the other five are past participles of "to hear." In context, there is no confusing the forms; it is only in seeing them written out of context that they could be mistaken.

Finally, the role of rhyme in choice of forms is one we will further investigate. It is worth noting for now, however, that certain endings are favored at rhyme position, and that therefore only verb forms with that ending will appear. Thus certain tenses and persons are favored: for example, imperatives appear frequently at rhyme position. The few others appear once only, like *à/a, on*, etc. Since "to have" is an auxiliary verb, because of syntactical considerations, few forms will appear at the rhyme position, whereas past participles lend themselves to that position.

As the highly irregular verb *avere* demonstrates in V^{13}, morphological forms overlap in persons, moods, and tenses. Conjugated verb forms vary in agreement patterns with their subjects. Singular and plural verbs do not always agree with the subject; verb forms are used loosely and do not necessarily indicate the person. There are also possible lexical homonyms that could cause momentary confusion, but usually syntax and context easily disambiguate such a passage. Yet the text remains comprehensible overall, because action in context carries the meaning.

2.2.2.2.5 Subject pronouns.

We have seen that subject pronoun forms may disambiguate verb forms when morphological endings do not. Yet among subject pronouns, as among nouns and verbs, there is much overlapping of forms, partially because of different etymological developments in French and Italian tradition and in part to the Northern Italian usage of using third person singular pronouns also in the plural.The lack of distinction lies primarily with the third person singular and third person plural. When stated, the other persons are generally clear, with the possible exception of *i*, in one unique case (lines 15157–15158). The feminine third person forms are distinctive; it is the masculine forms that overlap not only in the third person singular and plural but also in case. As Mussafia has remarked and was quoted by Reinhold ("Bovo d'Antone," 559), *li* and *le* are used without distinction as direct and indirect object third person forms (*Macaire*, viii).[49] In spite of various overlapping forms, the text is comprehensible, again through a larger context.

	Singular	**Plural**
First person	je, eo, e, jo, i	nos, nu
Second person	tu	vos, vu, vue, vui
Third person (masc)	e, ello, elo, il, i, ·l, el, lo	i, ille, ili
Third person (fem)	ela, ella, elle, ila, la, illa, le	ele

Beyond the form of the pronouns themselves is the fact that at times it is unclear whether or not a pronoun is present; for instance, when the subject follows the verb, as in interrogative phrases. There are a number of examples where the verb ending could be followed by the first person *je*. There are two types in particular, written in the manuscript *doie* and *voie*. Are these in fact *vo·je* and *do·je*? There are four appearances of *doie,* each of which is first person: "Qe vos doie li plais plus alonçer" (1799, 6321, 9001) [. . . should I lengthen the matter/story further] and, closely related, "Qe vos doie li plais plus çir avant" (8097) [. . . should I make the matter/story go on longer (for you)], thus clearly a formula. There is also one form *deie* in a similar situation (10956). There are three examples of *voie* as a verb where there is no stated subject: "Or voie ben la nostra destrucion" (9148) [Now I clearly see our destruction], "E lui voie ao(r)er e projer"(11477) [And him I want to adore and pray (to)], "Dist li rois, 'Questo non voie mie'" (15941) [Said the king, 'This I don't want at all'].[50] In each case, either another expression begins the line, and thus could cause the postposition of the subject pronoun, or there is a rhetorical question. The case may seem perfectly clear thinking in French terms, as *doie* and *voie*. Yet, in each case, the subject is first person, and, given the forms we normally find for the first person pronoun, could therefore be construed *do·je* or *vo·je*. The forms *do* and *vo* appear in the text. However, we note that those examples are parallalled by *doja* (twelve tokens) and *voja* (thirty-five tokens) with similar expressions. A triphthong is necessary to keep one syllable in *voic* and *doic* as is the semivowel before the final *a* for a second syllable in the lines containing *doja* and *voja*. The frequency of the *-oie* ending argues for that interpretation here.

---

[49] Frierson includes a complete list of pronouns, subject and object, so I do not go into the argument here ("Historical Study," 78–79).

[50] These are obviously from two different verbs, "to see" and "to want." I do not include the noun "voie" (MSI *via*, MF *voie*) in the discussion here.

Another similar case is *oe*: is this *ò* + *e* (first person pronoun in Old Northern Italian, *e'*, see Rohlfs, *Grammatica Storica*, ¶ 444) or *oe*, for the present tense of "to have," [I have]? A possible source for the final *e* could be to make the form paroxytonic (cf. Modern Florentine *sì-e* for *sì*) or analogical, related to the Old Italian *ae* attested for the third person (Rohlfs, *Grammatica Storica*, ¶ 541). Mussafia interprets the form as *oe*; it does not appear in Reinhold's editions; Frierson also interprets *oe*, as does Rosellini, without comment. There are only two appearances, in lines 2425 and 2429, and there are only seven of the earlier v*oie/doie* conundrum, so the comprehension issue is small.

2.2.2.2.6 The role of rhyme in deviant forms.

It is frequently contended that rhyme causes many of the deviant forms in V^{13} (Cremonesi, "Note di franco-veneto," 12, n. 27; Rosellini, *Geste Francor*, 47) or in other medieval texts.[51] There are several ways we can examine this: the total number of hapax legomena and the percentage that appear at rhyme position should demonstrate the frequency of totally unique creations at rhyme position. Comparison of specific forms at the rhyme position, even if not hapax legomena, with synonymous forms within the line, can give an idea of the extent to which the poet stretches his resources. In order to have a large enough sample, we will look at alternate infinitive forms at the rhyme position compared to those within the line.

First, to examine the total number of hapax legomena: there are 3882 hapax legomena in V^{13}. Of those, 1690, or about 43.5%, are at rhyme position, less than one-half. This is less than 10% of all rhyme words, which is, in fact, a smaller percentage of hapax use than we find in the total rubric vocabulary. In the rubrics, 590 hapax legomena are present, or approximately 15.2 % of all hapax legomena in V^{13}, for 12% of the rubric vocabulary.[52] Clearly, rubrics were problematic for

---

[51] Discussed, for example, in W. van Emden, "Quelques hapax de mes connaissances," in *Ce nous dist li escris... che est la verite: Études de littérature médiévale offertes à André Moisan*, ed. Miren Lacassagne, Sénéfiance 45 (Aix-en-Provence: CUER MA, 2000), 289–303.

[52] These figures are based on my lexeme division, of course, which gives 128,505 tokens (individual "word" appearances) for the entire text, 5,030 tokens for the rubrics. It is a very rough estimate, since some of the hapax legomena are merely graphic variants. A more precise analysis would be necessary to respond to the many comments on the subject. Ruggieri says, "molti vocaboli italianizzati o comunque storpiati posti soprattutto in fine di verso a causa appunto dell'assonanza, della rima o per altre ragioni metriche, ricompaiono poi, nell'interno di altri versi, scritti in francese passabile se non proprio ottimo, e che un buon numero di essi implica una indubbia conoscenza della sua fonetica e del suo lessico" ("Origine, struttura, caratteri del francoveneto," 164–65). Rosellini, in the introduction to his edition, says, "Insistere sulla natura della rima come punto

2.2 The Franco-Italian of V^{13}

the manuscript writers and more likely to produce deviant (not to mention illegible) forms than the rhyme position (see also section 1.2.2, above, for further details on the problematic nature of the rubrics).

The most popular rhyme is *-er*, which, among other uses, is the infinitive ending for the first conjugation in French, deriving from Latin -ARE. *-é*, for which it is occasionally exchanged, is also quite popular. Many verbal forms never appear at all at rhyme position; in the infinitives in V^{13}, most variation is in the stem; e.g., double letters (*coler* vs. *coller*) or variations of prefix (*enbraçer / ambraçer*; *enbinder / inbinder*). The most frequent variation in all conjugation endings is between the *-r/re* ending (thirty infinitives, chart 4 below). Other variations are consonant + *-ere* vs. consonant + *-re* (syncope) (7); *-oir* vs. *-er/ir* (7) and *-ar/er* (26), documented in chart 1. Variation between *-re* and *-r* does not occur because of rhyme except for in cases of *-are* vs. *-er*; thus *-r/-re* seem to be free variants.

There are twenty-seven verbs with both an *-ar* and *-er* ending (see chart 2 below); of those, twenty-four *-er* forms appear at rhyme position, and no *-ar* forms. There are a total of sixty *-ar* tokens total, and 544 *-er*. But of the 544, only 229 appear at rhyme position, a little under one-half. Few are variations of conjugation; of 551 verbs which appear in the infinitive form, only sixty-eight infinitives vary in their form. Where *-ar* and *-er* alternate, only the *-er* is at rhyme position; it <u>does not have to</u> be at rhyme position, however. Thus, looking closely at chart 2, we can see that neither *amendar* nor *amender* is at rhyme position. *Paser* appears five out of twelve times at rhyme position, and *pasar* appears three times, only within a line. Similarly, looking at chart 4, *-er* instead of *-ere* appears both within the line and at rhyme position. In only four of eight instances does the *-er* alternate for *-ere* appear at rhyme position, and even then, not necessarily in every situation. Where *-ir* and *-er* endings alternate it is not always the *-er* that is found at rhyme position (see *courir*), and even so, the numbers at rhyme position are rarely large in contrast to those not at rhyme position. One example of alternation is *sevelir/er*, where one form is at rhyme position and one is not. Where there is an alternation *-ere / -ire* with *-er / -ir*, forty-four have a final *-e* (are paroxytone),

---

cruciale in cui avvengono le trasformazioni lessicali più profonde e più impensate, può sembrare atteggiamento dettato più da pigrizia mentale che da autentica preoccupazione di ricercare il *perché* delle cose. Ma non è così . . ." (*Geste Francor*, 47). In a more general context, van Emden, speaking about several interesting hapax legomena, says, "Il est fort à craindre que nous n'ayons là [à la rime] en fin de compte la clef de beaucoup de hapax qui nous préoccupent dans nos éditions de textes, sans doute même la majorité" ("Quelques hapax," 302). While certain hapax legomena here (e.g., *borfolu*) are at rhyme position, it is less than one-half, as is clear by the percentages. I hope to return to this discussion at a later date for a closer analysis. For more on *borfolu*, see L. Z. Morgan, "A Franco-Italian Etymological Note: *Borfolu*," *Neophilologus* 85 (2001): 529–34.

145 do not, yet only thirty-five (less than one-quarter) of the -*r* forms appear at rhyme position. The tonic syllable of the historical infinitive does not seem to matter either; MÉTTERE > *meter* at rhyme position; *NÁSCERE (for classical NASCI) > *naser*, not at rhyme position. Again, the vowel + *r* infinitive form and the vowel + *re* infinitive form appear to be in free variation outside of rhyme position, though only -*er* (and rarely -*ir*) is possible at rhyme position. It should also be noted that, as a result of the desire for sight rhyme, the infinitive "form" can hide the past participle, since in the first conjugation the sound would be the same. Occasionally one finds the infinitive as past participle within the line, but graphic alteration is predominantly a rhyme-position phenomenon. So, at least in the case of the infinitives, an oxytone form is more popular (in keeping with both Northern Italian and French phonology) but does not necessarily mean that the form is at rhyme position.[53]

It is clear that in verb formation the redactor selects among French, Northern Italian, and Italian forms in relation to not just rhyme but also other considerations, such as syllable count and stylistic needs. Among infinitives, the redactor uses the endings descending from Latin -*are*, -*ére*, -*ere* and -*ire* endings in free variation within the poetic line; at rhyme position, generally -*er* is preferred, with a few -*ir* endings.[54] The result is a preponderance of verbs deriving from the Latin first conjugation. The rhyme use explains also, in part, the rarity of second and third conjugation infinitives: fourteen and sixty-one of each, respectively, including the -*oir* variant, in comparison to 632 -*er* infinitives. Below are four charts, comparing alternatives to the -*er* infinitive ending at rhyme position in comparison with within the poetic line.

---

[53] One of the characteristics of the Veneto region which makes it more similar to Tuscan is the frequency of dropping a final vowel (-*e*/-*o*) after nasals and liquids. See Rohlfs, *Grammatica Storica*, ¶¶ 143, 145, 146, and Devoto and Giacomelli, *I dialetti*, 33.

[54] The only exception is in Laisse 85, where the rhyme is in -*ir*: *soffrir, morir*, etc. for only twenty-two lines total in the entire poem. It should be noted that the greatest number of verbs in the modern languages are first conjugation verbs, and that it and the third (-*ir[e]*) are the only living conjugations. That is, new verbs generally come into the first conjugation, except for certain types of lexical items like adjectives and colors, which tend to go into the third, or -*ir(e)* conjugation.

Effects of rhyme on Infinitive endings: Contrastive Charts and Summative comments

CHART 1: Variation of -*oir* and other endings at rhyme position in the same verb stem (underlined forms are at the rhyme)

Verb	# appearances	rhyme?	alternative form(s)	# appearances	rhyme?
aler	182	<u>yes (98)</u>	alere, alloir	1, 1	no
aver	8	no	avoire, avor, avoir	1, 1, 59	no
banir	3	no	banoir	2	<u>yes (2)</u>
fuçir	1	no	fuir, foir	1, 14	no
renegar	1	no	renoiar, <u>renoier</u>	1, <u>7</u>	no, yes (6)
veer	2	yes (2)	veoir, voir	47, 45	no
voler	1	no	volir, voloir	1, 3	no

In those verbs deriving from -ER(E), normally the form with an *-er* appears at rhyme position. The only exception is *banoir*, which appears twice, both times at rhyme position, in contrast to *banir*.

CHART 2: Variation in first conjugation Latin reflex infinitive endings (-ARE) at rhyme position and not

Verb	# appearances	rhyme?	alternative form(s)	# appearances	at rhyme position?
amendar	1	no	amender	4	no
çelar	2	no	celer, çeler	1, 25	yes
çetar	1	no	çiter	3	yes (2)
començar	2	no	comencer	11	yes (9)
contrastar	1	no	contraster	20	yes (14)
çostrar	1	no	çostrer	41	yes (12)
demorar	1	no	demorer	37	yes (13)
donar	6	no	doner	63	yes (12)
dotar	1	no	doter	29	yes (7)
entrare/intrar	11	no	entrer/intrer	30, 7	yes (12, 7)
laʒar	5	no	laʒer/laʒere	20, 1	yes, no (10, 0)
levar	2	no	lever	17	yes (15)
loldar	2	no	lolder	2	yes (2)
mandar	2	no	mander	3	yes (3)
montar	4	no	monter	31	yes (25)
orar	1	no	orer	12	yes (9)
paʃar	3	no	paʃer	12	yes (5)

portar	1	no	porter	30	yes (11)
relevar	1	no	relever	4	yes (1)
renegar	1	no	renojer	7	yes (6)
renojar	3				
retornar	1	no	retorner	18	yes (10)
seçornar	1	no	seçorner	10	yes (10)
stratornar	1	no	stratorner	7	yes (6)
tornar	7	no	torner	15	yes (12)
trençar	5	no	trençer	25	no
trovar	1	no	trover	58	yes (15)
usar	1	no	user	1	yes (1)
totals: 27 stems	60 tokens in -ar		# of tokens in -er:	544	229 tokens in -er at rhyme position

Though no -ar forms appear at rhyme position, not all -er forms do either. In general there are fewer -ar forms than -er forms of a given stem, though that form is not necessary for rhyme. -re infinitive endings are extremely rare—only one appears at all as an alternative in these infinitives, out of 604—as might be expected in the Veneto region, where vowels after -r and -n are frequently dropped, to an extent greater than in Standard Italian.

CHART 3: Variation of conjugation: verb stems with an -ir(e) compared to an -er ending and their appearance at rhyme position

Verb	# appearances	at rhyme position?	alternative form	# appearances	at rhyme position?
cair	17	yes (2)	caire	1	no
courir	1	yes (1)	corer	4	no
sevelir	1	no	seveler	1	yes (1)

The data here are few. There are three tokens of -ir verbs at rhyme position, but for the first, only two of eighteen total tokens from that stem in the infinitive form are at the rhyme (cair), so it is not a big surprise. Alternating courir at rhyme position and corer is perhaps more surprising, though the numbers, again, are low. Other variations are not too surprising: the -er variation at rhyme position and the -re not at rhyme position could have been predicted from earlier data.

CHART 4: Variation of conjugation: with and without final -*e*, verbs with -*er* and -*ir* stems* at rhyme position

Verb	# appearances	at rhyme position?	alternative form	# appearances	at rhyme position?
aparilere	1	no (R)	apariler	7	no
apelere	1	no (R)	apeler	16	yes (10)
bandere	1	no	bander	3	yes (2)
bandire	1	no (R)	bandir	9	no
dormire	1	no	dormir	1	no
metere	5	no	meter	1	yes (1)
nasere	2	no	naser	1	no
ocire	1	no	ocir	1	no
oldire	1	no	oldir	13	no
oncire	1	no	oncir	20	no
prendere	24	no	prender	34	no
rispondere	1	no	responder	1	no
revenire	1	no	revenir	2	no
spendere	1	no	espenser, spender, spenser	1, 6, 8	no, no, yes (7)
tençere	1	no	tençer	21	yes (15)
Totals:	43			145	35

* (R) = appears in a rubric

No verbs with forms both in -*ir*/-*ire* and -*er* have -*ir*/*ire* at rhyme position; no verbs with infinitives both in -*ir*/*ire* and -*ere* have -*ere* appear at rhyme position. The infinitive ending -*er* is preferred at rhyme position.

2.3 CONCLUSIONS: LANGUAGE OF V¹³.

The redactor of V¹³ is not writing archaic Old French, his variations in the case system are current with his time, the early fourteenth century. While using traditional elements from the *chanson de geste* structure, he is also taking advantage of the poetic morphological system to his benefit, adopting forms as needed. Frierson's hope for certain "harmonious rules" working in "a symmetrical manner" ("Historical Study," 31) is answered but not in the same way (totally consistent orthography and morphology) as in a modern literary language.

We can conclude that, though vestiges of the Old French case system are visible because we see representations of both subject and object case forms, it is not followed in the Franco-Italian of V[13]. Subject and object are not distinguished by desinence, and masculine and feminine are frequently also not distinguished. When disambiguation of a noun is necessary, the reader must rely upon modifying adjectives, the verb, or other contextual evidence, if not on knowledge of the two contributing languages. Similarly, the verb is not clearly distinguished by desinence or a subject pronoun. Most particularly third person, but also occasionally second person, do not distinguish between singular and plural. While we find these phenomena throughout the text, there are not fixed "paradigms" into which we can fit given nouns or verbs, saying "in the singular the ending is X, in the plural, the ending is Y," or "second person singular ends in -*i* while second person plural ends in -*és*."

As examples of possible misapprehension—or possibilities for deliberately created misapprehension—arise, these will be noted in the endnotes to the edition, whatever their source.

3.0
Versification and Metrics

Certain rhymes predominate throughout the entire manuscript. That fact creates stylistic effects as well as the difficulties seen in the previous section in apprehending morphology and lexicon.

3.1 Rhymes.

French is an oxytone language while Italian is a paroxytone language. Verse lengths in Italian are usually an odd number of syllables rather than even (the standard literary length is the hendecasyllable), and stress patterns differ. The combination of the two produces a problematic metrical system. V^{13} is primarily rhymed decasyllables. The following is a chart of rhymes together with number of lines total for each rhyme (or assonance, in some cases) and the percentage of the total. (For a complete listing of laisses and numbers of lines, see the end of section 3.)

Total rhymes and percentages of total lines

Rhyme ending	Number of laisses	# lines total	Percentage of total
-er	112 laisses	5148 lines*	30.2%
-é	78	3729 lines*	21.85%
-ant	81	3027 lines**	17.74%
-on	60	1774	10.4%
-ent	21	641 ***	3.76%
-ie	22	486†	2.85
-u	19	457††	2.68
-or	21	410†††	2.4
-an	11	309⁺	1.81
-és	9	304	1.78
-ée	6	205	1.2
-ançe	8	108	.63
-a	3	84	.49
-os	5	83⁺⁺	.49
-is/iz	3	58⁺⁺⁺	.34

Rhyme ending	Number of laisses	# lines total	Percentage of total
-al	3	43	.25
-ue	3	41	.24
-as	1	31	.18
-in	2	30	.18
-el(l)e	2	26††††	.15
-uç/-uz	2	23	.13
-ir	1	22	.13
-i	1	17	.1
unreadable		10	.06
TOTAL (25 rhymes)	474 laisses	17067 lines	100%*

*Laisses 362 and 398 change from -é to -er and from -er to -é respectively. I include the -é lines with the -é lines and -er with -er but do not increase the number of laisses. Also, we find *boscher* in an -é laisse, line 9470.

**There are many assonances among the -ant lines: *anc, banc, blanc, canp, destranç, entranb, fianç, flanc, franc, Franc, Franç, gran, guanto, guando, ireament, Jovan, lanc, lanç, Maganç, Maganc, Moral, penetanç, pietanç, Proanç, sang, soldo, tanp, vanp, viçanç, viltanç*

***Assonances: *ensemant, tenp*

† *ramue* for *ramie*

†† *Valbrun* in assonance

††† *ancon* for *ancor*

†††† assonance of *tere* with -el(l)e rhymes

⁺ Assonances: *avant, enfant, caroiant*

⁺⁺Assonances: many words in -rs: *amors, arbors, colors, contors, desenors, dolors, estors, flors, intors, ires, Marsilions, milors, milsolders, milsoldors, mons, ors, parentors, pecaors, perdons, secors, sejors, tençons, tors, traitor, traitors, uxors, vigors*

⁺⁺⁺ Alternate spelling: *pensiç*

The role of rhyme in this manuscript must be examined from several points of view; earlier (section 2.2), we saw that, of the hapax legomena found in V[13], less than half are found in rhyme position. Thus, words found at the end of the line are not necessarily invented words. Many of the rhymes are sight rhymes, words which appear with several spellings depending upon the laisse rhyme. Thus, *-ant/-ent*, for example, obviously have the same value to the redactor though both spellings occur.[1] It is clear that the infinitive, the past participle, and second person plural of first conjugation verbs sounded alike, as those are frequent rhymes and are even interchangeable; witness the examples of *-er* endings for the past participle (e.g., line 15076) and *-é* endings on infinitives (e.g., 2465).

---

[1] This is not surprising, as the sounds fell together in Old French by the end of the eleventh century; see Pope, *From Latin to Modern French*, 347, ¶ 921.

The length of laisses with the most frequent assonance, and the low number of possible rhymes are the most striking features of metrics in V^{13}. 17,067 lines, 474 laisses, have only twenty-five rhymes total, for an average of nearly nineteen laisses per rhyme. Furthermore, the average laisse length is long in comparison to other Franco-Italian texts: the average number of lines per laisse in V^{13} is thirty-six. To compare with other Franco-Italian texts of the same era, DiNinni, for example, in her analysis of the three works of Niccolò da Verona, finds seventy-one rhymes for 338 laisses in 10,276 lines; this would be an average laisse length of thirty lines.[2] In the *Entrée d'Espagne*, with 681 laisses in 15,805 lines, A. Thomas finds eighty-four rhymes, which would produce an average of twenty-three lines per laisse.[3] *Huon d'Auvergne*, in the Berlin manuscript, is 12,225 lines long in 452 laisses, for an average of twenty-seven lines per laisse.[4] The Franco-Italian *Aliscans*, 7772 lines in 148 laisses, 38 rhymes, averages slightly over fifty-two lines per laisse, and thus also has quite long laisses on an average, but must be seen in relation to other versions, unlike the previously-cited texts.[5]

---

[2] F. DiNinni, ed., *Niccolò da Verona: Opere* (Venice: Marsilio Editori, 1992), 43–55.

[3] A. Thomas, *L'Entrée d'Espagne: Chanson de geste franco-italienne*, Société des anciens textes français (Paris: Firmin Didot et Cie, 1913), cxxvii–cxxxvi; cf. A. Limentani, "Problemi dell'epica franco-italiana, appunti sulla tecnica della lassa e della rima," in *Alberto Limentani: L'«Entrée d'Espagne» e i signori d'Italia*, ed. M. Infurna and F. Zambon (Padua: Antenori, 1992), 226–42, here 229.

[4] Berlin, Kupferstichkabinett 78 D 8 (olim MS. Hamilton 337), is not yet edited, though Holtus and Vitale-Brovarone are working on an edition (A. Vitale-Brovarone, "De la Chanson de *Huon d'Auvergne* à la *Storia di Ugone d'Avernia* d'Andrea da Barberino: techniques et méthodes de la traduction et de l'élaboration," in *Charlemagne et épopée romane*: Actes du VIIe Congrès international de la Société Rencesvals (Liège 28 août–4 septembre 1976), ed. M. Tyssens and C. Thiry [Paris: Les Belles Lettres, 1978], 393–403, here 393; Holtus, "L'État actuel des recherches," 155), as, according to A. F. Labie-Leurquin, "Huon d'Auvergne," in *Le Moyen Age*, *Dictionnaire des lettres françaises* (Paris: Fayard, 1994), 1: 702, is Möhren; however, by personal communication (2003), he is not. For the one section which I have examined carefully, 1364 lines (fols. 33^r–41^v), there are forty-one different rhymes, fifty-seven laisses, for an average of just over twenty-three lines per laisse; see L. Z. Morgan, "The Passion of Ynide: Ynide's Defense in *Huon d'Auvergne* (Berlin, Staatsbibliothek, Hamilton 337) (I)," *Medioevo Romanzo* 27 (2003): 67–85.

[5] G. Holtus, ed., *La versione franco-italiana della "Bataille d'Aliscans": Codice Marcianus fr. VIII (= 252). Testo con introduzione, note e glossario* (Tübingen: Niemeyer, 1985). See Limentani for similar discussions about the *Entrée d'Espagne* and the *Prise de Pampelune* (= *Continuazione dell'Entrée* in DiNinni's edition). He also gives many more comparisons of laisse size and structure in other Franco-Italian *chansons de geste*. For example, *Gui de Nanteuil* with 210 laisses, in 3338 lines, would average fifteen and nine-tenths lines per laisse (Limentani, "Problemi dell'epica franco-italiana," 229–30).

In fact there are even fewer rhymes in V¹³ than suggested in the chart. The varieties of *-é* (*-er, -és, -ée*) encompass 9386 lines, or 55% of all the lines; varieties of *-ant* (*-an, -ent*) rhyme total 3977 lines, or a little under 37%. Together, this makes 92% of all lines! It is hardly surprising that early critics believed the poet less than skilled. Looking then at those laisses with the two most frequent rhymes, those with *-é* encompass 205 laisses, so would have a forty-six-line average length, and those in *-ant* encompass 113 laisses, so have an average thirty-five-line length. The longest laisse in V¹³ is 144 lines (laisse 11), rhyming in *-é*; the shortest (laisse 228) is eight lines, rhyming in *-anço*.⁶ The shortest *-ant* laisse (295) is sixteen lines long; the shortest /ę/ (*-er*, laisse 175) is seventeen lines long. Of laisses greater than 100 lines long, one is in *-ant* (laisse 7, 119 lines); the other three are in *-é* (the longest of all, just mentioned, and laisses 4 [111 lines] and 8 [104 lines]). The shorter laisses are dominated by the rarer and more problematic rhymes. As a further example, in V¹³ there are only six feminine rhymes (*-ie, -ée, -anço, -ue, -elle*) for forty-one laisses, 866 lines total, a bare 5%.⁷ The consequence of this fact is that the same sound recurs frequently at short distances. The effect links laisses in spite of rubrics in between. Unlike the *Entrée*, for example, where Limentani argues a strong sense of individuality for each laisse because of the carefully designed rhymes, here the work is a united piece. Limentani says, referring to the *Entrée*, ". . . si tratta di un senso vigoroso dell'autonomia della singola lassa e della forza che essa trae dall'essere lavorata come tale, in continua opposizione con la precedente e la successiva . . ." ("Problemi dell'epica franco-italiana," 232).

---

⁶ This does not include the two partial laisses, 362a in *-é* which becomes *-er* (only 7 lines) and 398a in *-er*, which becomes *-é*, only 6 lines.

⁷ Limentani suggests that the *Entrée d'Espagne* poet may have known V¹³, and that the poet used earlier texts as sources, repeating rhymes. However, the *Entrée*'s variety of rhymes, self-reference, and avoidance of repeating words in rhyme is totally foreign to V¹³ (Limentani, "Problemi dell'epica franco-italiana," 239). The total lack of classical references in V¹³ in contrast to their frequency in the *Entrée* further demonstrates the very different goals and interests of the two poets. For a discussion of classical references, see also G. Allaire, "Considerations on *Huon d'Auvergne / Ugo d'Alvernia*," *Viator* 32 (2001): 185–203, on *Huon d'Auvergne*, and L. C. Brook, "Allusions à l'antiquité gréco-latine dans l'*Entrée d'Espagne*," *Zeitschrift für romanische Philologie* 118 (2002): 573–86, for the *Entrée d'Espagne*. Since this volume went to press, J.-C. Vallecalle also has written of classical influences in "Roland sénateur de Rome dans *L'Entrée d'Espangne*," in *Romans d'antiquité et littérature du Nord. Mélanges, offerts à Aimé Petit*, eds. Sarah Baudelle-Michels et al. (Paris: Champion, 2007), 769-99.

3.2 Syllable count.

The lines are based on the decasyllable, with much variation. Giving every benefit of the doubt, it is possible to bring 10,585 lines, approximately 62%, into decasyllables. Nearly half of those have the classic caesura of 4 + 6 (46%); the next most frequent in 5 + 5 (11%); then 3 + 7 (2.6%), with 6 + 4, 7 + 3, and 2 + 8, each having a minuscule number. Of the non-decasyllables, 4936, or about 30% of the total, are greater than ten syllables, and 1497, or nearly 9%, are less than ten syllables.[8]

Early poetry is known in general to be irregular in its metrical schemes, so variation in rhyme (especially since the genre was originally assonanced) is not a surprise. Hills suggests further that exact syllable count was not necessary in epic, that approximate count was enough.[9] Comprehension may have been more important than meter (Hills, "Irregular Epic Metres," 776). It could also be that the number of stresses was important rather than the number of syllables per se. Of course, because of the nature of Franco-Italian, and the fact that editions of Franco-Italian texts are frequently of a single manuscript, editors emend very little in order to preserve the linguistic patina, whatever its difficulties. Thus metrical imperfections are immediately evident. A line such as 2823 where two lines are written together into the column margin can be divided, but those such as 552, of six syllables, cannot be easily rectified without the possibility of recourse to other manuscripts that might offer alternatives to the missing part of the line. In our manuscript, the majority of short lines are of nine syllables (1345); only 152 lines are shorter than nine syllables, and of those 142 are of eight syllables, eleven are of seven,[10] and one of six.[11] Many eight-syllable lines could be brought to nine by dieresis of, for example, *oit* or *rois*. There does not seem to be a true standard to which the editor should adhere. Just over 60% of the lines are decasyllables, by playing with the system of syllable counting—allowing both Italian elision of final vowel and initial vowel—and French epic caesura. Dieresis is therefore not marked in this edition.

---

[8] These numbers were given in an earlier article, which unfortunately truncated some of the numbers. Table 2 should have read 4936 for greater than ten syllables, and the final line should have ended (of the total 17029 analyzable lines) (L. Z. Morgan, "Meter and Rhyme in Franco-Italian Ms. 13 [The *Geste Francor*]," *Italian Culture* 11 [1993]: 13–29, here 26).

[9] F. C. Hills, "Irregular Epic Metres. A Comparative Study of the Metre of the Poem of the Cid and of Certain Anglo-Norman, Franco-Italian and Venetian Epic Poems," in *Homenaje a Menéndez Pidal* (Madrid: Libreria y casa editional Hernando, 1925), 1: 759–77; the discussion here relates to page 776.

[10] Lines 1441, 2568, 4660, 5443, 10041, 10972, 12266, 13122, 13335, 14127, 15995. Some of these could be brought to nine by dieresis: e.g., 1441, mais; 2568, Fait; 5443, plais; 10041, lasoit; 10972, poit; 15995, lui (as in Italian).

[11] "Q'el aust son per vencé": this could be seven if *aust* is two syllables.

Complete Summary, laisse by laisse, of rhymes and variations

Rhyme	laisse	number of lines	exceptions to rhyme	line numbers of laisse
-a	24	27		1405-1431
-a	96	20		3768-3787
-a	348	37		12024-12060
Total -a		84		
-al	188	21		6553-6573
-al	235	13		8119-8131
-al	306	9		10432-10440
Total -al		43		
-an	133	27		4915-4941
-an	163	25		5724-5748
-an	297	17		10093-10109
-an	319	32		10896-10927
-an	331	28		11396-11423
-an	382	45		13433-13477
-an	387	31	enfant	13647-13677
-an	412	38		14552-14589
-an	430	22		15334-15355
-an	439	22		15646-15667
-an	472	22		16979-17000
Total -an		309		
-ançe	105	17		4046-4062
-ançe	119	13		4479-4491
-ançe	160	16		5642-5657
-ançe	228	8		7924-7931
-ançe	285	13		9710-9722
-ançe	334	15		11480-11494
-ançe	363	10		12640-12649
-ançe	428	16		15267-15282
Total -ançe		108		
-ant	3	74	74 total; includes tanp, canp, soldo (not incl. in rhyme #)	77-150
-ant	7	119	anc; flanc; tanp; canp; Maganc	368-486
-ant	9	53	franc	591-643

Rhyme	laisse	number of lines	exceptions to rhyme	line numbers of laisse
-ant	13	67	franc, Franc	957-1023
-ant	16	30	canp, tanp	1094-1123
-ant	17	40	franc, Franc	1124-1163
-ant	20	32		1278-1309
-ant	28	44	Franc, banc	1523-1566
-ant	30	68	flanc, canp, tanp, anc	1610-1677
-ant	39	25	flanc	1960-1984
-ant	45	22		2158-2179
-ant	51	26		2318-2343
-ant	63	37		2715-2751
-ant	66	37	2823-24 written as one line; tanp	2823-2859
-ant	71	23	Magançs,	3006-3028
-ant	78	25		3257-3281
-ant	81	30		3348-3377
-ant	84	25	canp	3494-3518
-ant	88	37	canp, sang	3565-3601
-ant	97	42	Maganc	3788-3829
-ant	103	39	Franc, canp	3987-4025
-ant	106	26		4063-4088
-ant	111	29	Magançs	4214-4242
-ant	115	27		4370-4396
-ant	120	19	pietanç	4492-4510
-ant	124	33	tanp, viltanç	4616-4648
-ant	127	30	tanp	4738-4767
-ant	131	31		4848-4878
-ant	134	23	canp	4942-4964
-ant	143	51	tanp	5181-5231
-ant	147	21	vanp	5312-5332
-ant	153	16	canp, tanp	5475-5490
-ant	157	25		5555-5579
-ant	164	38		5749-5786
-ant	170	51		5990-6040
-ant	182	64	lanç	6347-6410
-ant	192	52	Moral, canp	6644-6695
-ant	196	10		6783-6792
-ant	201	53	blanc, canp	7010-7062

Rhyme	laisse	number of lines	exceptions to rhyme	line numbers of laisse
-ant	205	28	canp	7182-7209
-ant	213	25	blanc	7386-7410
-ant	218	24	canp	7513-7536
-ant	221	58	flanc	7610-7667
-ant	225	41	banc, destranç	7793-7833
-ant	233	35	canp, gran	8065-8099
-ant	238	21	Magançc, tanp	8185-8205
-ant	244	22	tanp, Franc	8406-8427
-ant	252	36	Magançc, lançc, tanp, canp	8612-8647
-ant	265	31	tanp	9104-9134
-ant	270	45		9255-9299
-ant	275	38		9412-9449
-ant	280	26	Jovan	9560-9585
-ant	284	18		9692-9709
-ant	288	32	canp	9799-9830
-ant	292	34	canp	9913-9946
-ant	295	16	destranç, Viçanç, canp	10027-10042
-ant	300	37	Franc, canp, Proanç	10176-10212
-ant	302	34		10267-10300
-ant	305	48	canp, fiançc	10384-10431
-ant	309	23	Franc	10518-10540
-ant	312	38	canp	10637-10674
-ant	321	66	anc, entranb	10996-11061
-ant	326	27		11177-11203
-ant	346	25		11956-11980
-ant	351	43		12135-12177
-ant	356	38	guando, Franc, tanp	12356-12393
-ant	360	42	canp, franc	12498-12539
-ant	375	48	blanc	13124-13171
-ant	380	47	canp	13358-13404
-ant	388	32		13678-13709
-ant	396	49		13971-14019
-ant	401	49		14181-14229
-ant	414	54		14640-14693
-ant	419	37		14857-14893

3.2 Syllable Count

Rhyme	laisse	number of lines	exceptions to rhyme	line numbers of laisse
-ant	422	38		15027-15064
-ant	425	33		15128-15160
-ant	441	21		15678-15698
-ant	452	51	Franç	16012-16062
-ant	456	45	tanp, Franç	16232-16276
-ant	461	38		16523-16560
-ant	467	40		16806-16845
Total -ant		3027		
-as	148	31	lais for (las)	5333-5363
-as		31		
Total -as				
-é	4	111		151-261
-é	8	104		487-590
-é	11	144		735-878
-é	14	27		1024-1050
-é	23	33		1372-1404
-é	26	40		1455-1494
-é	29	43		1567-1609
-é	38	41		1919-1959
-é	42	52		2044-2095
-é	49	46		2241-2286
-é	55	35		2439-2473
-é	60	70		2579-2648
-é	65	56		2767-2822
-é	70	63		2943-3005
-é	77	33		3224-3256
-é	95	32		3736-3767
-é	101	38		3913-3950
-é	110	25		4189-4213
-é	112	30		4243-4272
-é	114	47		4323-4369
-é	123	51		4565-4615
-é	129	33		4788-4820
-é	140	37		5089-5125
-é	150	37		5392-5428
-é	161	33		5658-5690
-é	169	49		5941-5989
-é	174	36		6128-6163

Rhyme	laisse	number of lines	exceptions to rhyme	line numbers of laisse
-é	177	28		6197-6224
-é	180	33		6274-6306
-é	186	28		6493-6520
-é	195	40		6743-6782
-é	198	55		6876-6930
-é	202	57		7063-7119
-é	216	43		7460-7502
-é	222	58		7668-7725
-é	226	27		7834-7860
-é	232	51		8014-8064
-é	240	61		8242-8302
-é	245	35		8428-8462
-é	248	21		8511-8531
-é	251	49		8563-8611
-é	253	39		8648-8686
-é	257	49		8803-8851
-é	260	36		8927-8962
-é	264	34		9070-9103
-é	269	42		9213-9254
-é	276	21	boscher	9450-9470
-é	281	57		9586-9642
-é	286	38		9723-9760
-é	296	50		10043-10092
-é	303	33		10301-10333
-é	310	46		10541-10586
-é	317	31		10830-10860
-é	327	56		11204-11259
-é	330	60		11336-11395
-é	338	57		11613-11669
-é	343	63		11785-11847
-é	347	43		11981-12023
-é	352	60		12178-12237
-é	359	47		12451-12497
-é	362a	7		12587-12593
-é	364	53		12650-12702
-é	368	53		12843-12895
-é	377	52		13218-13269

3.2 Syllable Count

Rhyme	laisse	number of lines	exceptions to rhyme	line numbers of laisse
-é	385	34		13556-13589
-é	390	57		13761-13817
-é	395	27		13944-13970
-é	398b	52		14038-14089
-é	404	62		14289-14350
-é	408	36		14446-14481
-é	413	50		14590-14639
-é	418	48		14809-14856
-é	421	47		14980-15026
-é	427	48		15219-15266
-é	433	46		15442-15487
-é	453	56		16063-16118
-é	457	91		16277-16367
-é	464	62		16646-16707
-é	473	54		17001-17054
Total -é		3729		
-ée	50	31		2287-2317
-ée	67	36		2860-2895
-ée	82	43		3378-3420
-ée	102	36		3951-3986
-ée	137	26		5027-5052
-ée	162	33		5691-5723
Total -ée		205		
-el(l)e	62	16	tere	2699-2714
-elle	463	10		16636-16645
Total -elle		26		
-ent	35	22		1823-1844
-ent	59	32		2547-2578
-ent	166	28		5822-5849
-ent	178	24		6225-6248
-ent	194	27		6716-6742
-ent	209	26		7283-7308
-ent	230	19		7953-7971
-ent	237	35		8150-8184
-ent	247	20		8491-8510
-ent	277	25		9471-9495
-ent	314	39		10712-10750

Rhyme	laisse	number of lines	exceptions to rhyme	line numbers of laisse
-ent	339	30		11670-11699
-ent	353	32	tenp	12238-12269
-ent	366	44		12755-12798
-ent	371	31		12953-12983
-ent	391	31		13818-13848
-ent	416	39		14727-14765
-ent	438	23		15623-15645
-ent	446	26		15829-15854
-ent	465	52		16708-16759
-ent	471	36		16943-16978
Total -ent		641		
-er	2	26	again, many unreadable; 36 in my text total	41-76
-er	6	81		287-367
-er	10	91		644-734
-er	12	78		879-956
-er	15	43		1051-1093
-er	19	78		1200-1277
-er	27	28		1495-1522
-er	31	40		1678-1717
-er	34	50		1773-1822
-er	37	63		1856-1918
-er	40	42		1985-2026
-er	47	29		2197-2225
-er	52	35		2344-2378
-er	54	37		2402-2438
-er	61	50		2649-2698
-er	72	67		3029-3095
-er	75	51		3147-3197
-er	80	42		3306-3347
-er	83	73		3421-3493
-er	89	21		3602-3622
-er	93	27		3685-3711
-er	100	29		3884-3912
-er	104	20		4026-4045
-er	107	20		4089-4108

3.2 Syllable Count

Rhyme	laisse	number of lines	exceptions to rhyme	line numbers of laisse
-er	109	45		4144-4188
-er	113	50		4273-4322
-er	117	32		4415-4446
-er	121	36		4511-4546
-er	126	55		4683-4737
-er	130	27		4821-4847
-er	135	53		4965-5017
-er	142	21		5160-5180
-er	145	40		5248-5287
-er	151	33		5429-5461
-er	156	26		5529-5554
-er	159	31		5611-5641
-er	165	35		5787-5821
-er	167	57		5850-5906
-er	171	30		6041-6070
-er	175	17		6164-6180
-er	181	40		6307-6346
-er	183	41		6411-6451
-er	187	32		6521-6552
-er	191	26		6618-6643
-er	197	83		6793-6875
-er	200	58		6952-7009
-er	203	37		7120-7156
-er	208	28		7255-7282
-er	215	22		7438-7459
-er	219	56		7537-7592
-er	223	33		7726-7758
-er	227	63		7861-7923
-er	231	42		7972-8013
-er	239	36		8206-8241
-er	242	60		8318-8377
-er	254	61		8687-8747
-er	258	40		8852-8891
-er	267	33		9158-9190
-er	271	46		9300-9345
-er	273	28		9357-9384
-er	279	39		9521-9559

Rhyme	laisse	number of lines	exceptions to rhyme	line numbers of laisse
-er	282	38		9643-9680
-er	287	38		9761-9798
-er	291	36		9877-9912
-er	294	55		9972-10026
-er	298	41		10110-10150
-er	301	54		10213-10266
-er	304	50		10334-10383
-er	308	48		10470-10517
-er	311	50		10587-10636
-er	316	54		10776-10829
-er	320	68		10928-10995
-er	325	43		11134-11176
-er	329	33		11303-11335
-er	333	41		11439-11479
-er	336	58		11516-11573
-er	340	47		11700-11746
-er	344	59		11848-11906
-er	350	54		12081-12134
-er	354	52		12270-12321
-er	357	35		12394-12428
-er	362b	46		12594-12639
-er	365	52		12703-12754
-er	369	36		12896-12931
-er	373	84		13018-13101
-er	376	46		13172-13217
-er	379	57		13301-13357
-er	384	59		13497-13555
-er	386	57		13590-13646
-er	389	51		13710-13760
-er	393	37		13892-13928
-er	398a	6		14032-14037
-er	400	60		14121-14180
-er	402	40		14230-14269
-er	406	51		14382-14432
-er	411	24		14528-14551
-er	415	33		14694-14726
-er	420	86		14894-14979

3.2 Syllable Count

Rhyme	laisse	number of lines	exceptions to rhyme	line numbers of laisse
-er	423	41		15065-15105
-er	426	58		15161-15218
-er	429	51		15283-15333
-er	432	64		15378-15441
-er	435	40		15526-15565
-er	437	40		15583-15622
-er	440	10		15668-15677
-er	445	65		15764-15828
-er	448	49		15881-15929
-er	451	35		15977-16011
-er	458	69		16368-16436
-er	462	75		16561-16635
-er	466	46		16760-16805
-er	469	35		16881-16915
-er	545	78		16154-16231
Total -er		5148		
-és	33	36		1737-1772
-és	44	45		2113-2157
-és	68	22		2896-2917
-és	125	34		4649-4682
-és	212	21		7365-7385
-és	246	28		8463-8490
-és	255	23		8748-8770
-és	261	64		8963-9026
-és	399	31		14090-14120
Total -és		304		
-i	220	17		7593-7609
Total -i		17		
-ie	21	35		1310-1344
-ie	53	23		2379-2401
-ie	58	31		2516-2546
-ie	74	18	aje X 2	3129-3146
-ie	92	21		3664-3684
-ie	98	23		3830-3852
-ie	116	18		4397-4414
-ie	139	11		5078-5088
-ie	155	21		5508-5528

Rhyme	laisse	number of lines	exceptions to rhyme	line numbers of laisse
-ie	168	34		5907-5940
-ie	176	16		6181-6196
-ie	189	23		6574-6596
-ie	229	21		7932-7952
-ie	268	22	ramue for -ie	9191-9212
-ie	335	21		11495-11515
-ie	342	19		11766-11784
-ie	355	34		12322-12355
-ie	372	34		12984-13017
-ie	394	15		13929-13943
-ie	407	13		14433-14445
-ie	443	19		15725-15743
-ie	449	14		15930-15943
Total -ie		486		
-in	283	11		9681-9691
-in	323	19		11079-11097
Total -in		30		
-ir	85	22		3519-3540
Total -ir		22		
-is	32	19		1718-1736
-is	210	28		7309-7336
Total -is		47		
-iz	272	11	pensiç	9346-9356
Total -iz/-is		58 (-is + -iz)		
-on	1	39	many lines missing; 40 lines in my text total	1-40
-on	5	25		262-286
-on	18	36		1164-1199
-on	22	27		1345-1371
-on	41	17		2027-2043
-on	48	15		2226-2240
-on	57	26		2490-2515
-on	69	25		2918-2942
-on	73	33		3096-3128
-on	76	26		3198-3223
-on	79	24		3282-3305
-on	90	30		3623-3652

3.2 Syllable Count

Rhyme	laisse	number of lines	exceptions to rhyme	line numbers of laisse
-on	99	31		3853-3883
-on	108	35		4109-4143
-on	118	32		4447-4478
-on	132	36		4879-4914
-on	141	34		5126-5159
-on	146	24		5288-5311
-on	149	28		5364-5391
-on	154	17		5491-5507
-on	158	31		5580-5610
-on	179	25		6249-6273
-on	185	17		6476-6492
-on	190-	21		6597-6617
-on	199	21		6931-6951
-on	207	32		7223-7254
-on	214	27		7411-7437
-on	224	34		7759-7792
-on	243	28		8378-8405
-on	256	32		8771-8802
-on	259	35		8892-8926
-on	262	28		9027-9054
-on	266	23		9135-9157
-on	274	27		9385-9411
-on	278	25		9496-9520
-on	289	29		9831-9859
-on	299	25		10151-10175
-on	313	37		10675-10711
-on	318	35		10861-10895
-on	324	36		11098-11133
-on	328	43		11260-11302
-on	337	39		11574-11612
-on	341	19		11747-11765
-on	345	49		11907-11955
-on	358	22		12429-12450
-on	361	47		12540-12586
-on	370	21		12932-12952
-on	381	28		13405-13432
-on	392	43		13849-13891
-on	405	31		14351-14381

Rhyme	laisse	number of lines	exceptions to rhyme	line numbers of laisse
-on	409	23		14482-14504
-on	431	22		15356-15377
-on	434	38		15488-15525
-on	444	20		15744-15763
-on	450	33		15944-15976
-on	454	35		16119-16153
-on	459	58		16437-16494
-on	468	35		16846-16880
-on	470	27		16916-16942
-on	474	13		17055-17067
Total -on		1774		
-or	25	23		1432-1454
-or	36	11		1845-1855
-or	43	17	anco(r) for ancon	2096-2112
-or	56	16		2474-2489
-or	94	24		3712-3735
-or	122	18		4547-4564
-or	173	29		6099-6127
-or	193	20		6696-6715
-or	211	28		7337-7364
-or	234	19		8100-8118
-or	241	15		8303-8317
-or	249	17		8532-8548
-or	263	15		9055-9069
-or	315	25		10751-10775
-or	332	15		11424-11438
-or	349	20		12061-12080
-or	383	19		13478-13496
-or	397	12		14020-14031
-or	403	19		14270-14288
-or	424	22		15106-15127
-or	442	26		15699-15724
Total -or		410		
-os	87	11	estors, milsoldors	3554-3564
-os	128	20	secors, traitor; ir(os) for ires; pecaors	4768-4787
-os	136	9	milseldors, ors, colors, tors	5018-5026

3.2 Syllable Count

Rhyme	laisse	number of lines	exceptions to rhyme	line numbers of laisse
-os	290	17	milors, intors, estors, sejors, vigors, flors, arbors, uxors	9860-9876
-os	447	26	desenors, contors, estors, dolors, traitors, amors, parentors, milors, Marsilions, tençons, perdons, mons	15855-15880
Total -os		83		
-u	64	15		2752-2766
-u	138	25		5053-5077
-u	144	16		5232-5247
-u	152	13		5462-5474
-u	172	28		6071-6098
-u	184	24		6452-6475
-u	204	25		7157-7181
-u	236	18		8132-8149
-u	250	14		8549-8562
-u	293	25	Valbrun	9947-9971
-u	307	29		10441-10469
-u	322	17		11062-11078
-u	367	44		12799-12842
-u	374	22		13102-13123
-u	378	31		13270-13300
-u	410	23		14505-14527
-u	417	43		14766-14808
-u	436	17		15566-15582
-u	460	28		16495-16522
Total -u		457		
-uç	86	13		3541-3553
Total -uç		13		
-ue	46	17		2180-2196
-ue	91	11		3653-3663
-ue	206	13		7210-7222
Total -ue		41		
-uz	217	10		7503-7512
Total -uz/-uç		23 (-uz + -uç)		

4.0
THE LITERARY CONTENTS OF V¹³

The *chansons de geste* in the manuscript, in the order in which they appear, can be called (since there are no titles in the manuscript): *Bovo d'Antona, Enfances* (fols. 1^(ra)–7^(rb), lines 1–1163); *Berta da li pe grant* (fols. 7^(rb)–16^(vb), lines 1164–2917); *Bovo d'Antona, Chevalerie* (16^(vb)–31^(ra), lines 2918–5490); *Karleto* (fols. 31^(ra)–51^(vb), lines 5491–9026); *Berta e Milone* (fols. 51^(vb)–54^(rb), lines 9027–9495); *Uggieri il Danese, Enfances* (fols. 54^(rb)–61^(vb), lines 9496–10895); *Orlandino* (fols. 61^(vb)–64^(rb), lines 10896–11335); *Uggieri il Danese, Chevalerie* (fols. 64^(rb)–76^(ra), lines 11336–13477); and *Macario* (fols. 76^(ra)–95^(rb), lines 13478–17066). (Here I have used primarily the Italian names; I use both the French and Italian throughout this commentary—*Beuve d'Hanstone, Berte aux grands pieds*, etc.). I also break the *chansons* at the end of a laisse, and so differ slightly in the labeling from that of other editors.[1]

The *chansons* in V¹³ belong to European tradition; they are not exclusively Italian in content, though certain details are Italian. The "cycle" idea—combining a group of *chansons* with a common interest—occurs also in France; compare the proverbial division of Bertrand de Bar-sur-Aube's *Girart de Vienne* (ca. 1180):

> N'ot que trois gestes en France la garnie;
> Dou roi de France est la plus seignorie . . .
> Et l'autre apres, bien est drois que jeu die,
> Fu de Doon a la barbe florie,
> Cil de Maience qui molt ot baronnie

---

[1] Naming Franco-Italian texts, as any medieval works, is difficult. Note DiNinni's choice in her edition of Niccolò da Verona's *Opere*; she renamed what Mussafia called the *Prise de Pampelune* (A. Mussafia, ed., *Prise de Pampelune. Ein altfranzösisches Gedicht* [Vienna: Carl Gerold, 1864]) the *Continuazione all'Entrée d'Espagne* in order to portray the work more accurately (F. DiNinni, ed., *Niccolò da Verona: Opere*). There is no title on the manuscript, of course. Between the early commentators, the French and the Italian schools, there is frequently a choice between names. Particularly difficult has been trying to give a name to the equivalent of *Berte aux grands pieds*. Finally, because of the four times the name appears in its entirety, two are "da li pe grant", a third is "a li pe grant" (but the reading here is somewhat unsure), and a fourth "da li pe grandi," I decided to go with the most frequent of the forms, Berta (for the distribution of "Berte" and "Berta" see the glossary) and "da li pe grant" though I have earlier called it otherwise.

> El sien lingnaje ot gent fiere et hardie.
> De tote France eusent seignorie . . .
> Se il ne fusent plain d'orgueil et d'envie . . .
> La tierce geste, qui molt fist a preiseir,
> Fu de Garin de Monglenne au vis fier.
> De son lignaje puis je bien tesmoignier
> Que il n'i ot coart ne lannier
> Ne traitor ne vilein losangier (11–50). [2]

Similar cyclification occurs throughout European tradition in various guises. One of the most common techniques in creating a cycle is the amplification of a hero's life, describing his childhood, knighthood, and old age (becoming a monk), that is, *Enfances*, *Chevalerie*, *Moniage*. The redactor of V^{13} has crafted originally separate tales into a cyclic manuscript which includes the youth and knightly deeds of Carolingian royalty, of selected members of the nobility, and of their womenfolk. Examining the *chansons* in this manuscript one by one, it is clear that some portions of the tale are better represented than others within Europe, France, or Italy.

In this introduction, I will first examine one by one the individual *chansons* of V^{13}, with later versions in the Italian peninsula, and their European counterparts. After examining all the individual *chansons*, I will examine the compilation as a whole, how it is united by structures common to cyclical texts: family relations of characters, repeated motifs, linking characters, and other textual strategies. These structures create the overall narrative content of V^{13}, both didactic and parodying within social and literary structures inherent to literature about Charlemagne's lineage.

For each segment of this introduction, the subdivisions are numbered in the same way so as to permit readers to follow a specific line of national interest: thus, for each section, where "x" stands for the *chanson* number (e.g., *Bovo* = 1): 4.x.1 summarizes the V^{13} version; 4.x.2 are the other Italian versions; 4.x.3 are French versions; 4.x.4 are Iberian versions; 4.x.5 are German versions; 4.x.6 are Scandinavian versions; 4.x.7 are Dutch versions; 4.x.8 are English (and others from the British domain: Welsh, etc.); and finally, 4.x.9 are discussion and conclusions about the V^{13} segment in question. This means that some segments will have no entries under a given subheading because there are no related versions in that language group.

---

[2] F. G. Yeadle, ed., *Girart de Vienne* (New York: Columbia University Press, 1930), 13–14.

4.0 The Literary Contents of V^{13}

CHART 4.0: Charlemagne's Family: V^{13}

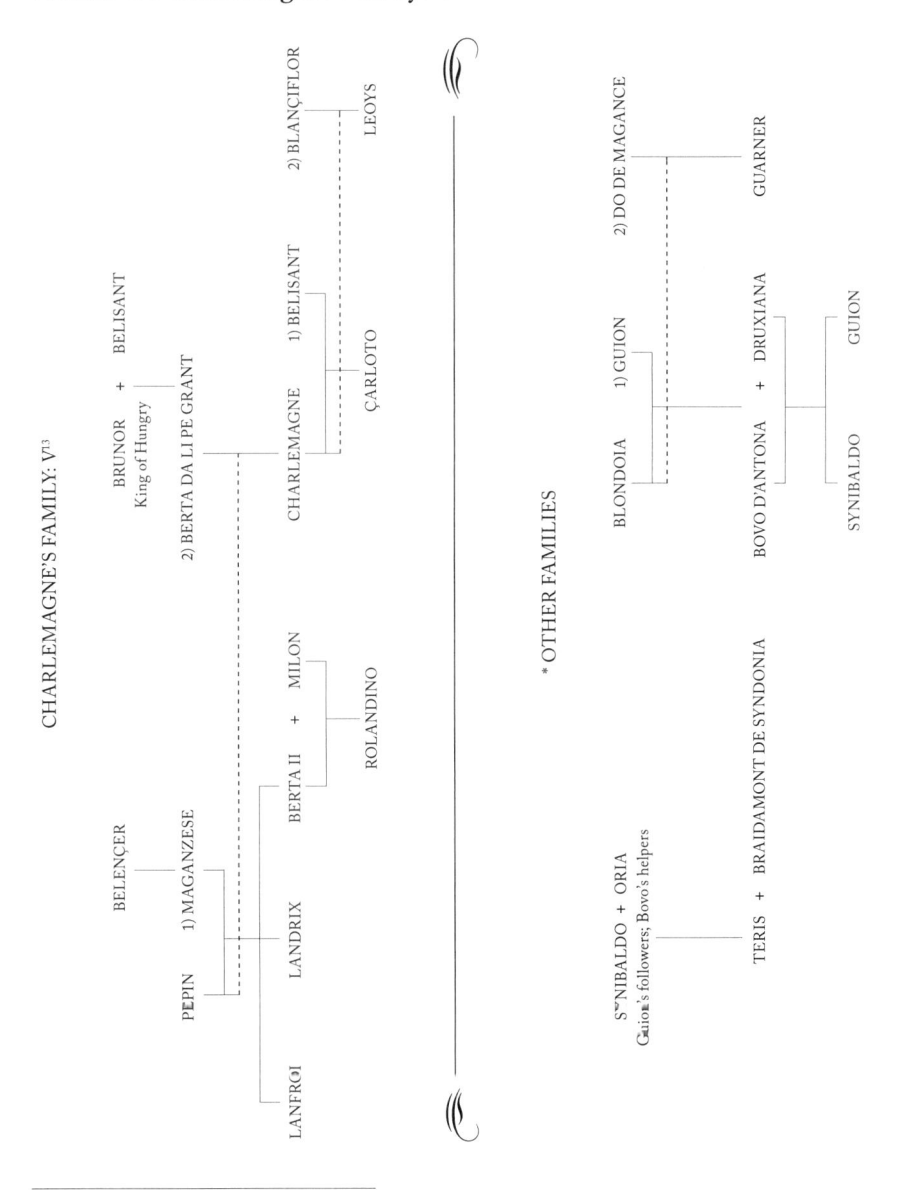

CHARLEMAGNE'S FAMILY: V^{13}

```
                            BRUNOR    +    BELISANT
                          King of Hungry
                         2) BERTA DA LI PE GRANT
                                  |
       BELENÇER                   |                      2) BLANÇIFLOR
                                  |                            |
PEPIN      1) MAGANZESE      CHARLEMAGNE    1) BELISANT      LEOYS
                                  |
LANDRIX    BERTA II  +  MILON   ÇARLOTO
                |
            ROLANDINO
                |
            LANFROI
```

*OTHER FAMILIES

```
                                                   2) DO DE MAGANCE
  BLONDOIA    1) GUION                                      |
                                                          GUARNER
          BOVO D'ANTONA  +  DRUXIANA
                        |
                     SYNIBALDO        GUION

S"NIBALDO + ORIA
Guion's followers; Bovo's helpers

TERIS + BRAIDAMONT DE SYNDONIA
```

---

*Originally in L. Z. Morgan, "Ogier le danois in *Geste Francor* (V^{13}): *Chevaleries*, the Maganzesi and Incompetent Kings," in *L'Épopée romane au moyen âge er aux temps modernes*, ed. Salvatore Luongo (Naples: Fridericiana, 2001) 3005–51, here 348.

4.1 Bovo (I and II).

The *Bovo* story exists in Old French, Scandinavian languages, Anglo-Norman, Middle English, Welsh, and Irish, as well as continuing in Italian tradition in the *Reali di Francia* and through Italian to Russian, Yiddish, and Romanian. Stimming and his students did exhaustive studies of the manuscript tradition, publishing and analyzing the relationship of the Anglo-Norman and three Continental French versions, concluding that the third Continental version is the Italian versions' closest relative.[3] Krauss lists seventeen versions: Anglo-Norman (which passed into Welsh, Scandinavian, and Middle English), four; continental Old French, three; Irish, one; Dutch, one; Italian, six; and one each in Russian/Yiddish deriving from the Italian (*Epica feudale*, 25). For a list of versions, see chart 4.1B.

Critics of the last century have divided the *Bovo* story into twenty-two "Chapters" which help us to compare the episodes present and the order of episodes. These are: 1. Bovo's childhood; 2. first heroic deeds; 3. Bovo and fiancée-to-be; 4. message to Braidimont ("Uriah's letter" motif); 5. fiancée's marriage to someone else; 6. Bovo's deliverance from prison; 7. Bovo's meeting with fiancée; 8. the abduction; 9. from Cologne to Hantone; 10. meeting with Soibaut (= Sinibaldo); 11. fiancée's need (attempted marriage) and deliverance; 12. Do's defeat and death: a. battle before Hantone; b. indictment; c. trial; 13. Bovo and

---

[3] A. Stimming, ed., *Der anglonormannische Boeve de Haumtone*, Biblioteca normannica 7 (Halle: Max Niemeyer, 1899); idem, ed., *Der festländische Bueve de Hantone, Fassung I*, Gesellschaft für romanische Literatur 25 (Dresden: Max Niemeyer, 1911); idem, ed., *Der festländische Bueve de Hantone IIa*, Gesellschaft für romanische Literatur 30.1 (Dresden: Niemeyer, 1912); idem, ed., *Der festländische Bueve de Hantone, Fassung III*, 1, Gesellschaft für romanische Literatur 34 (Dresden: Max Niemeyer, 1914); idem, ed., *Der festländische Bueve de Hantone, Fassung II*, Gesellschaft für romanische Literatur 41 (Dresden: Niemeyer, 1918); idem, ed., *Der festländische Bueve de Hantone, Fassung III, 2*, Gesellschaft für romanische Literatur 42 (Dresden: Niemeyer, 1920). F. Oeckel, *Ort und Zeit der Entstehung der Fassung II des festländischen Boeve von Hantone* (Göttingen: Dieterichschen Universitäts-Buchdruckerei, 1911); G. Sander, "Die Fassung T des festländischen Bueve de Hantone" (Diss. Universität Göttingen, 1912); L. Behrens, *Ort und Zeit der Entstehung der Fassung I des festländischen Bueve de Hantone* (Göttingen: Dieterichschen Universitäts Buchdruckerei-W. Fr. Kaestner, 1913); H. G. W. H. Paetz, *Ueber die gegenseitige Verhältnis der venetianischen, der franko-italienische* [sic] *und der französischen gereimten Fassungen d*es Beuve de Hantone, Beihefte zur *Zeitschrift für romanische Philologie* 50 (Halle: Niemeyer, 1913); J. Meiners, *Die Handschriften P [R, W] = Fassung II des festländischen Bueve de Hantone* (Göttingen: Friedrich Haensch, 1914); H. Kühl, "Das gegenseitige Verhältnis der Handschriften der Fassung II des festländischen Bueve de Hantone" (Diss. Universität Göttingen, 1915); L. Dingerling, "Das gegenseitige Verhältnis der Handschriften der Fassung III des festländischen Bueve de Hantone" (Diss. Universität Göttingen, 1917).

fiancée at home; 14. to London; 15. the race; 16. exile; 17. wife's giving birth and seizure by previous husband; 18. Soibaut finds wife; 19. at Simile; 20. Bovo and wife reunited; 21. death of former husband; 22. end.[4]

4.1.1 V[13] Bovo.

V[13] *Bovo* begins the series of paired narrations characteristic of V[13]: the second part of *Bovo* follows *Berta da li pe grant*, but both portions are discussed here because there is not a clear separation in action, and other versions of *Bovo* follow a similar plot but in a different order, with no division.

At the beginning of the V[13] version (the initial portion of the manuscript is missing, so we are truly *in medias res*), Bovo is trying to regain his father's city, Antona. He has returned incognito and is staying with one of his father's men, Siginbaldo. Siginbaldo is at war with Do (also called Dodo, both here and in other manuscripts) of Magance, Bovo's stepfather. Bovo assists in the fight. Siginbaldo's wife, Oria, is suspicious of Bovo and discovers his identity by recognizing a birthmark when she tricks him into taking a bath. Together Bovo and Siginbaldo's men recover the city of Antona.

In the second portion of *Bovo*, following *Berta da li pe grant* in V[13], Do's family, the Maganzesi, has bribed King Pepin to fight Bovo in order to retrieve Antona. King Pepin and his nobles are defeated and imprisoned, but Drusiana, Bovo's wife, persuades Pepin of Bovo's right to Antona. Pepin agrees to support Bovo forever against those from Magance (Mainz), the Maganzesi.

4.1.2 Other Italian versions.

D. Delcorno Branca has investigated the extensive printed history of *Bovo d'Antona* in Emilia, bringing to light especially the different versions of 1480 and 1497.[5] However, for our date and text, the Italian versions of interest are five:

---

[4] Compare A. Wolf, "Das gegenseitige Verhältnis der gereimten Fassungen des festländischen Bueve de Hantone" (Diss. Universität Göttingen, 1912); note that I have relabeled in some cases to avoid using a specific name, since Bovo's wife's name differs between versions, as do other names.

[5] D. Delcorno Branca, "Note sull'editoria bolognese nell'età dei Bentivoglio," *Schede umanistiche* 2 (1988): 19–32; eadem, "Vicende editoriali di due poemi cavallereschi: *Buovo d'Antona* e *Innamoramento di Galvano*," in *Tipografie e romanzi in Val Padana fra Quattro e Cinquecento*, ed. R. Bruscagli and A. Quondam (Modena: Panini, 1988), 75–83; eadem, "Fortuna e trasformazioni del *Buovo d'Antona*," in *Testi, cotesti e contesti del franco-italiano*, Atti del 1° simposio franco-italiano (Bad Homburg, 13–16 aprile 1987), ed. G. Holtus et al. (Tübingen: Niemeyer, 1989), 285–306; eadem, "Un nuovo testimone del *Buovo d'Antona* in ottava rima," *Italianistica* 21 (1992): 705–13.

Bovo udinese; Bovo veneto;[6] *Bovo laurenziano*;[7] the *Toscano*, in Tuscan prose;[8] and *Reali di Francia*.[9] The versions in octaves are believed to derive from the *Reali*. Among Italian versions, only the *Reali* is complete; the others are fragmentary, but fortunately at different places from V^{13}'s version, so that the fragments help fill in the plot.

In the first part of V^{13}, the damaged *Bovo* part I, V^{13} contains "chapters" 9, 10, 12 (in variant form), 19, and 20; also recounted are 17 and 18 which must have occurred during the initial lost portion (they are retold in Drusiana's song); then, in the second part of *Bovo*, "chapters" 14, 15, and 16 appear. To give an idea of the variety in detail and presence of episodes, multiple other versions are summarized below.

4.1.2.1 The *Laurenziano*.

The *Laurenziano*, a rhymed version,[10] is dated to the thirteenth or possibly the fourteenth century by Rajna (*Ricerche intorno ai "Reali"*, 145). It covers Blondoia's message to Dodo, Bovo's flight to Arminia, Drusiana's falling in love with him, his saving her from Marcabrun (who wishes to marry her), his betrayal by Ugolin to the Soldan, and Malgaria's falling in love with him. He finds Drusiana with Marcabrun, untouched, and they flee; she gives birth to twins in the forest, then they are separated; he regains Antona with Sinibaldo's help; Malgaria requests his help against invasion, and offers to marry him. Drusiana arrives, with their sons, and the two ladies meet—thus ends the manuscript.

4.1.2.2 The *Udinese*.

The *Udinese* is dated late fourteenth century (Rajna, "Frammenti" [1887], 153). It covers the period after Do of Magance's taking Antona (where he asks for Bovo's death), Bovo's flight to Arminia, Drusiana's falling in love with him, and Bovo's fight with Marcabrun; finally, it includes his return to Monbrando and attempts to contact Drusiana.

---

[6] C. Boje, *Über den altfranzösischen Roman von Beuve de Hamtone* (Halle: Niemeyer, 1909).

[7] L. Jordan, *Über Boeve de Hanstone* (Halle: M. Niemeyer, 1908).

[8] P. Rajna, "Frammenti di redazioni italiane del Buovo d'Antona," *Zeitschrift für romanische Philologie* 15 (1891): 47–87.

[9] A. Roncaglia and F. Beggiato, *Andrea da Barbarino*: *I Reali di Francia*, Storia e documenti (Brugherio-Milan: Gherardo Casini Editore, 1987). See Paetz, *Ueber die gegenseitige Verhältnis der venetianischen* . . . , for commentary on textual relationships.

[10] In P. Rajna's edition, in *decasillabo tronco* (*Ricerche intorno ai "Reali di Francia"* [Bologna: Gaetano Romagnoli, 1872], 125).

4.1.2.3 The prose *Toscano*.

Dates given elsewhere in the same manuscript inform us that the prose *Toscano* version is post-1458 (Rajna, "Frammenti" [1888], 465). In ninety-seven short prose sections, it includes a genealogy including Guido's father, and Guido's vendetta with Maganza. Here we learn the beginning of Brandoria's desire for Dodo (V^{13}'s Do), her plot to have Guido killed, and her attempt to poison Bovo. Bovo flees to Erminia (cf. the Anglo-Norman version below), where he is bought by the King, and Drusiana, the King's daughter, falls in love with Bovo. He saves her from Marcabruno, and there the fragment ends.

4.1.2.4 *Reali di Francia*.

Andrea da Barberino's *Reali* dates to the late fourteenth or early fifteenth century and covers the entire story, but with interesting differences from V^{13} that Rajna attributes to a mixing of sources, which must be V^{13} plus the ottava rima tradition (Rajna, *Ricerche intorno ai "Reali"*, 179). Book 4 of the *Reali* is "Buovo d'Antona" and consists of 80 chapters (I will use V^{13}'s names for the major characters in order to assist in following plot parallels; see Chart 4.1A at the end of this section for actual names). Preceding books in the *Reali* detail the family relationship of Bovo with the French king: his family derives from a parallel genealogical line. In Book 5, Andrea also adds Bovo's death at the hands of Gailone, his half-brother, and a new book on the vengeance taken by Bovo's sons against Gailone's family. In Book 4, as in other versions, Brandoria (his stepmother and old Guido's wife) sets her husband, Bovo's father, up to be killed by Do. Sinibaldo, who had brought up Bovo with his wife, tries to rescue Bovo, but Bovo's horse loses a shoe and he is taken. Bovo's mother tries to poison him, but a maid tells him and allows him to flee. Brandoria tells Do that Bovo is poisoned. Bovo takes the name Agostino and is picked up by merchants, who take him to Erminia, the city of Erminias ruled by King Erminione. The King buys him from the merchants (again, see the Anglo-Norman and Continental versions). Erminione's daughter, Drusiana, sees Bovo and falls in love with him; she arranges to have him serve at a private party, but she embarrasses him and then he avoids her. Marcabruno di Polonia comes seeking Drusiana as a bride, but Bovo defeats him. Lucafero of Buldras then shows up and defeats both Erminione and Marcabruno. Here too Bovo saves the day, this time after he is knighted and armed by Drusiana. They betroth themselves, and he reveals his identity. Ugolino and Marcabruno plot to get rid of Bovo, which they do by sending him to Sinella, Buldras's city, with a letter identifying him as the killer of Lucafero (the "Uriah's letter" motif). He is saved from death by Margaria and is instead put in prison. He eventually escapes, but meanwhile Drusiana has been married to Marcabruno. She has kept her chastity, however, by making Marcabruno wait for a year after marriage (note that no magic is used here);[11] Bovo appears just as the year is ending, the day before the ceremony marking its end. Bovo contacts Drusiana through her servants (including the maid who had saved him from poisoning) and they flee to a nearby castle owned by an enemy of Marcabruno. Marcabruno sends Pulicane out after the fugitives, but they persuade Pulicane to help them. Marcabruno besieges the castle, takes the owner (Canoro), and forces him to give in. Pulicane kills Canoro and again the group flees. During the flight, Drusiana gives birth; Bovo goes to find help. Lions attack and kill Pulicane (not Bonefoy as in the Continental versions), but Drusiana flees with their twin sons. Bovo returns to find the dead Pulicane and lots of blood, and thinks that all have died. Drusiana finds a ship and flees home, where she stays with her father, her identity unknown.

Bovo takes another boat, which turns out to be Terigi's (Terigi is his faithful retainer), and returns to Antona to reconquer his lands. (Here begin parallels with V[13]'s story.) Sinibaldo's wife believes she recognizes Bovo while medicating wounds, and tricks him into a bath with Sinibaldo where she sees the cross which identifies him. Bovo and Terigi enter Antona as doctors; they stay with Ruberto (not Uberto) della Croce, Sinibaldo's brother, and plan a coup for the next day. When Bovo and Terigi go to visit Do, ostensibly to medicate him, they seize him and his family. However, they let Do go, since he is ill, together with Gailone, his son, and Alberigo, his brother. Meanwhile, King Agnolo dies and Pepin becomes King. Do goes to him and swears fealty; Pepin sends an army to Antona. Do and King Pepin fight Bovo and his armies; Do and his brother Alberigo are killed. Brandoria is immured with only her head visible at the foot of the stairs. Bovo arranges for Pepin to sentence Brandoria, who is quartered.

After five years of ruling Antona, Bovo receives a message from Margaria of Sinella requesting help; she has been invaded by Druano di Soria. Bovo goes to help; Terigi acts as messenger, and he wants to fight, so he foments a war by misrepresenting messages. Bovo and his men win; Margaria and her people are converted. Bovo will not yet marry her though it has been twelve years since Drusiana was lost. He returns to Antona and proclaims a tournament three years hence. Word reaches Erminia, where Drusiana hears the news and decides to go. She goes to the court where she sings of Drusiana, Pulicane, and Bovo. This leads to a reunion. Margaria is married to Terigi; Bovo and Drusiana have eight

---

[11] See J.-P. Martin for this particular narrative motif, 5.A.4 (*Les motifs dans la chanson de geste: Définition et utilisation*, Discours de l'épopée médiévale 1 [Lille: Université de Lille III, Centre d'Études Médiévales et Dialectales, 1992], 351). On the meaning of the belt, Josiane's defense in some versions, see R. Wolf, "Nouer l'amour, nouer la mort: la ceinture sarrassine dans *Beuve de Hantone*," in « *Si a parlé par moult ruiste vertu*»: *Mélanges de littérature médiévale offerts à Jean Subrenat*, ed. J. Dufournet (Paris: Champion, 2000), 551–71.

more children, five boys and three girls (who die), for a total of ten before Guglielmo, who will eventually become king of England. Terigi goes to Hungary to rule with Margaria.

The next incident is essential to the Italian versions of Bovo and placing them in relation to others. King Guglielmo of England invites Bovo to come to his son's knighting (Antona is specifically stated to be in England). Drusiana and Sinibaldo go with him. Rondello wins a horse race, and Fiore, the king's son, asks for the horse. A Maganzese encourages Fiore to take the horse. Servants are killed, as is Fiore, the heir. The king hears the story and wants the horse and the horse's guard, who has fled. Bovo pulls his sword, and is exiled from England and Antona. He has fifteen days to leave. He leaves Drusiana in charge of Antona, and goes to Sinella where he fights Margaria's battles. Terigi and Sinibaldo are killed, leaving Sicurans, Terigi's son, in charge. Guido and Sinibaldo, Bovo's own sons, help; one of the enemies, Arbaul, insults them: "Voi non sapete di chi voi siate figliuoli," since their mother was alone for a long time and had left her husband, Marcabruno (Roncaglia, *Reali*, 512).[12] Bovo stays fifteen years, gaining three realms. In England, the king of Langle dies, naming Guido as heir; Erminione dies, leaving his land to Sinibaldo. After fifteen years, the king of England dies, and his godson, Bovo's son, is heir. Drusiana sends a message to Bovo, who returns. Guido has a son Chiaramonte, who dies at sixteen; Guido names a castle in his honor. Bernardo is born later in that same castle, so is known as Bernardo di Chiaramonte, giving the line its name. Meanwhile, Gailone, Bovo's half-brother, is mocked for not having avenged his father. He goes to Antona where he kills Bovo with a knife in the back while he is in church praying. Drusiana lives fifteen days after her husband and then dies too. The fifth book of nine chapters details the vendetta of Bovo's sons: they decide to kill Gailone and all six of his sons. Since this is not present in other versions, it will not be further discussed here.

For the differences in names between the Italian versions, see Chart 4.1A which accompanies this section. Other differences between versions lie in small details; the overall plot is the same where it is clear: first the murder of Guido, then the attempted killing of Bovo; his flight to Erminia/Arminia; his betrothal to Drusiana; his being tricked to go to Sinella/Syndonia where a second woman wishes to marry him; his flight and retrieval of Drusiana, their joining and twin

---

[12] This is a favorite insult in Barberino's work; Carlomagno is insulted similarly. Guerrino says to Charles: "O come puoi tu essere figliuolo di Pipino, che fusti generato in un bosco, e non sai di chi si sia tuo padre? . . . " (Roncaglia, *Reali*, 640). Oldrigi says to him, "Tu di' che se' figliuolo di Pipino, e fusti generato d'uno ribaldo cacciatore" (Roncaglia, *Reali*, 643), both from Barberino's *Reali di Francia*. Compare below (4.3), the discussion of *Karleto*.

sons and losing each other again. Bovo regains Antona, is confronted by both women, marries off the second to his faithful retainer, and lives happily with his wife until the return of the Maganzesi with Pepin. Pepin is conquered and Bovo gains various rights. He then goes to the English court where the heir attempts to steal his horse and is killed, and Bovo is exiled. These are the points in common. The Yiddish, Russian, and Rumanian are literary versions derived from these so we shall not examine them here.[13]

4.1.3 French Versions.

4.1.3.1 Anglo-Norman.
The Anglo-Norman version (3850 lines) is the source for English versions (beginning with *Sir Beves of Hamtoun*), an Irish prose version (fifteenth century), the Scandinavian *Bevers saga* in prose (fourteenth century), and the Welsh version *Bowno Hamtwn* (thirteenth century) of *Bovo*. In the Anglo-Norman version (3850 lines total), dated to the first half of the thirteenth century (Stimming, *Der anglonormannische Boeve*, lviii), Bovo's (Boef, in this version) mother loves the emperor of Germany, to whom she sends a message after Bovo's birth. She pretends to be ill; Gui will help her by seeking a boar, but the emperor kills him during the hunt. Bovo accuses his mother of killing Gui; she slaps him to the ground, and Sabot, a faithful retainer, takes him home where he has Bovo work as a shepherd. Though Bovo's mother makes Sabot promise to kill Bovo, he does not, killing a pig and bloodying Bovo's clothes instead. But while herding, Bovo sees a festival in the palace, breaks in, wounds the emperor, and flees. His mother comes looking for him; he gives himself up and she gives him to knights to sell

---

[13] Dates given for the Yiddish version differ, but seem to fall into the first decade of the sixteenth century for the translation and the mid-sixteenth century for publication. According to C. Hogetoorn, the translation was done in Venice in 1501, and it was first published in 1547 ("Bevis of Hampton," in *Cyclification: The Development of Narrative Cycles in the Chansons de Geste and the Arthurian Romances*, Proceedings of the Colloquium, Amsterdam, 17–18 December 1992, ed. Bart Besamusca et al., Koninklijke Nederlandse Akademie van Wetenschappen, Verhandelingen, Afd. Letterkunde, Nieuwe Reeks 159 [Amsterdam: North-Holland, 1994], 62–64, here 63); M.-R. Jung gives a date of 1507 for translation without specifying whether that means "publication" or not ("Beuve d'Hamtone," in *Enzyklopädie des Märchens. Handwörterbuch zur historischen und vergleichenden Erzählforschung*, ed. Kurt Ranke et al. [Berlin: de Gruyter, 1979], 2: 270–74, here 273). Smith states that it was written in Northern Italy in 1507, and first published in Isny, Germany, in 1541 (J. C. Smith, "Elia Levita's 'Bovo-Buch': A Yiddish Romance of the Early 16th Century" [Ph.D. diss., Cornell University, 1968], v). For the Russian and Rumanian versions, scholars agree in calling these derived from the Italian; see, for example, Jung, "Beuve d'Hamtone," 274.

in port. (Notice that she is never named!) The merchants who buy him take him to Egypt, where King Hermyne has a daughter Josiane (= V^{13} Drusiana, Druxiana). Bovo reveals his identity and refuses to convert, but is nonetheless kept in a high position. At fifteen, he goes to kill a boar in the forest; ten foresters who have sworn his death because they are jealous of him hunt him. He kills six and the other four flee. Josiane has been watching and is in love with him.

Brademund, king of Damascle, besieges the city. He demands Josiane. She asks the king to knight Bovo so he can defend her, telling about the foresters. Bovo receives his sword, Murgleie, and his horse, Arundel. When he succeeds in battle, Josiane declares her love, but Bovo refuses her because he is a poor knight. After a battle in which he participates, she goes to him and offers to convert. However, two knights delivered by Bovo from Brademund accuse Bovo of abusing Josiane. They counsel sending Bovo with the "Uriah's letter" to Brademund.

En route, Bovo meets a palmer who feeds him. It is Sabot's son, seeking Bovo. Bovo (pretending to be someone else) claims that Bovo was hanged. When Bovo arrives at Brademund's court, Brademund feeds him and then has him thrown in prison, tied by neck and feet. Bovo must use a stick to kill serpents and vermin in the prison. Meanwhile, King Hermyne lies to Josiane, saying that Bovo has returned to England. She takes care of his horse and sword. Yvori of Munbraunt asks for Josiane's hand. Her father gives her, but she uses a magic belt to keep her virginity.[14] She also takes Arundel with her. When Yvori tries to ride him, he is bucked off, injuring his head.

Bovo is in prison for seven years. The guards attack, and Bovo kills them but then has no food. He has to climb fifteen feet to get out. In the middle of the night, he finds arms and clothes, but no food. He takes a horse, goes to the gate, and leaves. He arrives at Damascle, but is starving. Graunder, Brademund's nephew, goes to the prison to check on Bovo. When they see he is gone, they seek and find him, but he will not give up. He fights and kills Brademund and Graunder. He reaches the sea where he must leap or turn back. His horse swims over. He gets food from a lady after killing her giant husband (brother of Graunder).

Bovo goes to Monbraunt, where he hears Josiane weeping for him. He persuades her of his identity by Arundel's recognition; she persuades him that she is still a *pucele*. They flee with the help of her man Bonefey. However, lions kill Bonefey while Bovo is out seeking food, and then they are confronted by Escopart (a monster). They subvert Escopart who then helps them take a ship, and they go to Colonie (Cologne). The bishop there is Bovo's uncle; he baptizes Josiane and Escopart. Bovo, calling himself Gyraut, leaves alone for Hampton, where he first meets Do (called Doun), the emperor. Do gives Bovo men and provisions, and Bovo goes over to Sabaoth.

---

[14] See note 11 above.

Josiane meanwhile is courted by Miles, another knight. When Escopart is entrapped, she agrees to marry Miles, then hangs him on their wedding night. Bovo and Escopart arrive to save her from being burned. They return to Hampton.

Bovo defeats Do, whose men pay homage to Bovo. Bovo's mother receives the news, kills the messenger, and jumps from the tower to kill herself. Bovo takes the city, marries Josiane, and engenders two sons, Miles and Guion.

After half a year, he goes to London where the horse-race incident takes place. Three men stand up for Bovo and he is exiled rather than killed. Bovo, Terri (Sabaoth's son), and Josiane ride off. En route, Josiane gives birth to their twins; Saracens show up, take her, and leave the twins. Bovo and Terri return to look for her, but cannot find her. Sabaoth has a dream that Bovo is assaulted; his wife, Eneborc, interprets the dream, and Sabaoth dresses as a pilgrim to find Josiane. He rescues her from the pagans; she darkens her skin and dresses as a man to travel. The boys, meanwhile, have been entrusted to a forester and a fisherman. Bovo and Terri go to Civile.[15]

Bovo wins the ruler there, a *pucele*, through combat, and she wishes to marry him. He refuses, but they make an agreement, that if Josiane does not return in seven years, she will marry him; otherwise she will marry Terri. Josiane does arrive with Sabaoth, and the female ruler's marriage with Terri proceeds. There is another run-in with Yvori. Hermyne becomes ill and calls for Gui to be crowned. Miles is made duke. Sabaoth leaves to go home to his wife via a pilgrimage route. Bovo's horse is stolen, but Sabaoth, warned by another dream, returns to save Arundel. Yvori is finally conquered, and Bovo and Josiane are crowned rulers of Monbrant.

News arrives that Sabaoth's son Robant has been disinherited; Bovo goes to help. At London, King Edgar makes peace with Bovo and Sabaoth by giving his daughter to Bovo's son Miles. Miles is crowned as heir to the country.

Bovo goes to Rome; Morant becomes archbishop of his kingdom. He goes to Monbrant, where queen Josiane is dying. His horse dies in the stable, and Bovo returns to expire in Josiane's arms. They are buried together in the church of St. Laurent. Gui becomes king, so all his children are rulers.

In this version, important differing details are that Bovo is sold as a child. His mother, never named, is the daughter of the king of Scotland. Bovo identifies himself to Hermyne (he is not disguised or using another name). He kills the wild boar as a proof of his strength and courage, and the ten foresters are a further part of that proof. Two knights at court, not a relative of Josiane's (his wife), suggest

---

[15] Knowing the other versions of the story, it seems that something is missing here: how do Bovo and Terri know to go to Civile? They clearly go with a purpose in mind; perhaps there was a message which was removed by the redactor, or was it lost in this part of the tradition?

the Uriah's letter. The lions kill only Bonefey, not Josiane or the boys, nor does it seem that they kill anyone else. Bovo's mother kills herself; Josiane has many suitors; Bovo and Josiane marry after reconquering Hampton. In England, the king gives the city to Bovo without demur. Josiane is disguised as a man when they are separated; the boys are raised by others; the lady of Civile has no name; at Civile, Bovo and Josiane's daughter, Beatrix, is born, as well as Bovon, one of Teris's sons. Sabaoth's dreams are an essential element of the later plot. For the family tree for the Anglo-Norman version, see Chart 4.1, "Other Families."

4.1.3.2 French "Continental" versions: Continental I.
The three Continental versions are in some ways quite similar. The title, given by Stimming, is in some ways deceptive, since his editions are of Old French texts though he includes the Franco-Italian version as part of version three, in agreement with Paetz (Stimming, *Fassung III*, 2: 336). In version one, 10,614 lines (dated to ca. 1200 by Stimming [*Fassung I*, xxix]), Gui's wife invites Do to kill Gui. Bovo is sold, falls in love with the king's daughter, and fights other knights. He is sent to the enemy whom he has defeated and escapes. Upon his return he finds Josiane and they flee. Açopart appears after they fight the lions, and they continue to Cologne. Bovo goes to Hanstone while Josiane stays in Cologne. There Miles attempts to marry her, but is saved in the nick of time by Bovo and Açopart. All go to Hantone and thence to London. There Bovo's problem is placed before the king, and Bovo and Do fight a judicial duel. Do organizes an ambush, but his men are killed, he loses and is hanged by the king. Shortly afterward the horse race takes place; the king's son is egged on by Rohart, related to the Maience clan. When Bovo is exiled, Josiane volunteers to come though she is pregnant. They take a ship to Monbranc, where they land and Josiane gives birth shortly thereafter (with the help of Bovo who is blindfolded).[16] Yvorin's men find them; they capture Josiane and the two sons, but Bovo escapes to Simile.

---

[16] See also version three, below. A birth scene occurs in all versions, but differs in length and details. Here (ll. 7009–7114), Bovo is blindfolded with a torn silk *bliaut* for the birth; he stays in the shelter with Josiane who holds onto him, and passes the twins out to Terri to wash, etc. In continental version three (Stimming, ed., *Fassung III*, 1. 328–33), lines 8700–8803, many of the same expressions and words appear; Bovo does not want to see or hear her labor. He is blindfolded with a silk cloth, and again he has the golden *boucler* with him, and passes the children out to Thierry as they are born. Bovo's expressions of dismay at being caught in this job are interesting too—he'd rather be fighting two men single-handed than have to do this.

In version two (Stimming, ed., *Bueve de Hantone IIa*), Bovo just holds her while she gives birth; the scene lasts only five lines. In the Anglo-Norman (Stimming, *Der anglo-normannische Boeve*), she forbids Bovo to stay, saying it is not proper for men to see or hear, and in the English (E. Kölbing, *The Romance of Sir Beues of Hamtoun* [London: Early

Bovo there must marry an (unnamed) queen while Josiane is held for four years by Yvorin. Sobaut has bad dreams and comes in search of Bovo. He finds Josiane first; she is disguised as a musician and they go together to find Bovo. All leave together (except Teris [spelled "Tierri" here; see chart 4.1 A], who marries the queen of Simile and stays) for London. There the twin boys are baptized and made heirs of the thrones of England and Scotland (there is a prevailing relationship of some kind for Gui's wife with Scotland, the exact nature of which varies from text to text). During seven years at Hantone, Josiane and Bovo have two more sons. Then Bovo is recalled to Hermin (= Arminia, Josiane's home) to relieve a siege. One son is designated heir. Bovo continues to the Holy Sepulcher, where a crisis in kingship makes him king. Bovo then returns to England and Scotland, leaving the sons designated as heirs there in place; Sobaut is made duke of Hantone. Bovo finally returns to the Holy Land where he works hard and the fourth son inherits his position.

In this continental version, the king of England certainly has greater power and integrity than in the V^{13} version.[17] He settles the dispute and ensures succession both of his lands and Bovo's. No women other than Josiane are named: the emphasis is clearly on the male line. Though Sobaut's wife takes part in the action, helps with Bovo, and is long-suffering during her husband's travels, and though Bovo's mother starts the action, both are without names, as is the queen of Simile who so long holds Bovo in her power.

4.1.3.3 Continental II.

Continental version two is by far the longest at 19,127 lines, with many summaries of future actions and other additions or expansions. The laisses are by far the longest also, extending over several pages, especially during battle scenes. Gui marries the daughter of Renier. She tries to persuade the cook to poison him, but he refuses and is beaten and thrown in prison as a reward. Finally her clerk Salemon writes a letter to Do, offering him her love and the opportunity

---

English Text Society, 1885], 171) again there is a short scene, just a few lines. There Bovo and Thierry prepare a shelter for Josiane and she sends them away so that they cannot hear her. The "childbirth in the woods" motif appears elsewhere in various romance epics; compare Dickson on *Valentine and Orson* (Arthur Dickson, ed., *Valentine and Orson*, trans. Henry Watson, EETS [London: Oxford University Press, 1937], 168–69). For recent commentary on this, see P McCracken, *The Curse of Eve, the Wound of the Hero: Blood, Gender, and Medieval Literature* (Philadelphia: University of Pennsylvania Press, 2003), 84–91, which includes translations of some of the scenes.

[17] See Vitullo for a discussion of the king's role in resolving disputes in different editions, and the possible sociocultural meanings of those differences (J. M. Vitullo, *Constructing an Urban Mythology: The Chivalric Epic in Medieval Italy* [Gainesville: University Press of Florida, 2000], 17–20).

to avenge his father and uncle, both killed by Gui. She feigns a sick headache caused by the trout prepared by the cook; she needs a raw, fresh deer heart to cure her. Similar to other versions, Fromont and Hate are used to seek out and finally to sell Bovo. The abbot Savari gives Bovo a pine cone to protect him from his enemies (not just from poison).

Bovo is at Aubefort with king Hermin; when teased about "playing" in his country, he sets up a joust and injures several of them, exciting Josiane's admiration. He saves Gonsselin and Fourré in the battle with Danebruns, but they ultimately betray him to the king. Bovo is sent to Braidimont and ends up in prison. Josiane is married to Yvorin, but she uses spells so that he cannot sleep with her, and he is furious about this (the only version in which the reader knows he is aware of what he is missing). Bovo flees; fights the giant Ysoré; fights ten criminals in the woods; and goes to Jerusalem. He returns to Monbranc, sees and takes Josiane (there is no ploy here to get away; they just flee). During the flight, the two lions appear and kill Bonnefoi, seizing Josiane. Açopart appears, they subvert him, and he helps them leave the country.

They take a ship to Cologne; on the way they are attacked and must fight off a ship from Yvorin. They see an old man who tells of Soibaut fighting Do de Maience. Amaurri, the archbishop of Cologne, is Bovo's uncle. He decides to leave Josiane and Açopart with the archbishop while he returns to Hantone. After a baptism ceremony, he goes directly to Soibaut saying he's Girard de Digon. They go to Do to fight. Do is upset and is convinced that "Girard" must be Bovo; his wife says he is wrong and Do beats her. She sends a spy to find out; but the spy concludes that Bovo is not Bovo. Aelis, Soibaut's wife (the only Continental version in which she is named), is also convinced that this is Bovo and wants to see the cross on his shoulder. Soibaut and his wife prepare a private dinner and get Bovo to admit his identity; Soibaut urges him to go get Josiane and marry her. As they are leaving, Do takes advantage and attacks his fortress. Aelis, Soibaut's wife, plays a very active role in the defense.

At Cologne, one of the archbishop's nephews, Huidemer, wants Josiane and arranges to trick the archbishop and Açopart. As Huidemer and his men are trying to force her to marry, Soibaut hears her cries and he and Bovo rescue her. They leave by sea, run into a storm, and land at a hostile city where they must fight. (This is an extra incident not present in other texts.) When they return they burn the town and take the animals, forcing Do to flee to London to complain about Bovo. Do does not succeed in getting the king's attention until Rohart, his relative, assists, on his third appeal. Meanwhile, Bovo and Soibaut take Hantone. Bovo's mother comes out barefoot and asks for mercy for her sins. They then depart for London to complain about Do.

At first the king refuses to act; but Soibaut has his sons seal off the palace, and says men do not have to serve an unjust king. Finally, Bovo's challenge is accepted and the next day Do and Bovo will fight. Bovo kills Do by cutting off his head; Do's body is hanged separately and burned. Bovo takes Do's position of gonfaloniere and all proceed to Hantone for the wedding. Fromon and Hate are punished. Bovo stays seven months at Hantone, and then leaves for London. There Bovo encourages a young knight in a similar position to his own, Maxin, so that he can regain his lands (this is a completely new incident). The horse race proceeds as usual, though Josiane suggests that Bovo is covetous to participate. Rohart and the king's son go for Arondel and the prince is killed. The king wishes to kill Bovo; but Maxin shows up and confronts the king, which no one else had dared to do. So Bovo is exiled. They depart by sea, and once on land, Josiane gives birth, held by Bovo.

While Bovo and Tierri seek food, Yvorin's men take Josiane and one son, leaving the other behind. When Bovo returns, he laments and places the child in a small boat on the sea. Yvorin's men end up at St. Gille because of bad weather; Soibaut hears a tale of St. Gille and Josiane and comes to the rescue. A fisherman rescues the other child, who calls him Gui after himself. They return to Hantone where Soibaut is sick for a long time.

Bovo and Tierri end up at Simile, where they help Vencadousse against her enemies. She forces him to marry her, and initially he has nothing to do with her. Soon he tells her a story that he has been castrated, but can be made whole by a virgin. She obliges and they have a son together. Note that, in this version, it is only Bovo who is unfaithful, and for reasons that are unclear.

Josiane and Soibaut leave after Soibaut is healed. She wears poor clothing and uses an herb to darken her skin. They arrive in Simile; Josiane sings a song of their adventures (Bovo thinks she is a man). The host works with Josiane to procure clothing, etc., and they appear at court. Bovo gives Vencadousse to Tierri and leaves. They depart via Herminie, where they help the king fight Yvorin. This involves Josiane fighting first with a *baston*, then in full armor (13813–13816).[18] A whole series of events—traitorous guards, etc.—follows, with Bovo eventually winning and converting Yvorin. Bovo and his retinue continue to Aubefort where King Hermin is dying. He crowns Bovo king. They then respond to a call for help from Yvorin, and Bovo's newly knighted son, Beuvonnet, participates in the action.

The other son, meanwhile, has been raised by the fisherman (Gui), who thinks it is time to apprentice him. He sends the boy, named Gui after him, to a

---

[18] Fighting with an inappropriate weapon and by an inappropriate person are both typical comic motifs (see L. Z. Morgan, "What's so Funny About Roland? (O)Roland(o)'s Life and Works in the Northern Italian Tradition," in *L'Épopée Romane: Actes du XV*^{e} *Congrès international Rencesvals*, Poitiers, 21–27 août 2000, ed. G. Bianciotto and C. Galderisi [Poitiers: Université de Poitiers, Centre d'Études supérieures de civilisation médiévale, 2002], 377–92).

furrier to be trained (16392), but the young Gui refuses to obey; he buys a horse instead of the goods.[19] On the way home, a host notices the boy's resemblance to Bovo and knows that the king is seeking Bovo because the king of England is dead and Bovo is heir. The host gives him his daughter in marriage and Gui goes to seek his father. Gui proceeds to Simile, where he sees Tierri and meets his half-brother. Gui helps defeat a pagan host, then goes with his half-brother to Simile, to his father. Josiane and Bovo meet him and notice the physical resemblance. Buevonnet, the other son, hears the news also and comes from Monbranc. Gui delivers the king of France's news. Gui is made king of Aubefort; Bovo, Josiane, and Soibaut head for Paris. On the way, there is a battle with a pagan; then they continue to Rome, then Lyon, and finally Paris. He is welcomed and made king. Rohart and Amaurri try to prevent this, but they are hanged for their crimes. Upon their return, Soibaut receives Hantone as a fief, and dies shortly thereafter (his wife was already dead upon his return).

After five years in London, Josiane dies. Bovo leaves the court after making Vencadousse's son king after him, called *Li Restorés*. Bovo stays in a hermitage for five years, where his sons visit him shortly before he dies. The writer identifies himself at the end and asks to be prayed for.

Continental version two was rewritten in prose in the mid-fifteenth century and published by Vérard. A new edition came out in 1984 with complete commentaries.[20] There are variations in names and episodes in the prose. Episodes vary even between the prose manuscripts and printed manuscripts which the editor documents in her introduction (Ival, *Beufves*, xix–xxii). She carefully documents the processes involved when a manuscript becomes a printed text, from the re-introduction of episodes from the poetic version to the accentuation of various prose traits, such as the suppression of detail and addition of certain types of episodes (xxiv–xxv). She notes in particular the addition of psychological commentary and moral judgments, and the suppression of dialogue and proverbs. Ceremony and *bon ton* mark the Vérard version (xxxvii). A few interesting plot points may be mentioned: the use of spies by Do and Sobaut; the fact that Sobaut's wife figures out who Bovo is and asks to see the cross on his shoulder (as in the Italian version), since Bovo has been operating under a false name, Girart de Bourgogne. Bovo conquers Do in England, where Bovo finally marries Josiane; Achoppart goes back to his former owner and tells Ygnorin what has been happening, so that he attacks Arminie, Josiane's home. The horse race is organized by Rohart, one of the king's enemies. The queen of Cyrelle is named Vaudoce. Josiane becomes

---

[19] As has been commented, this motif is also found in *Hervis de Metz* and other *chansons de geste* (Boje, *Über den altfranzösischen Roman*, 126).

[20] M. Ival, ed., *Beufves de Hantonne: version en prose*, Sénéfiance 14 (Aix-en-Provence: CUER MA, 1984).

a fierce warrior with an armored suit to free Sebault ("et ja estoit armee d'ung haulbert qui tout le corps luy couvroit jusques aux genoux et en son chief une coiffe de fin acier avoit mise" [Ival, *Beufves*, 240]). Bovo becomes heir to Hermin; Beufvonnet (Bovo's son) is crowned after him and Bovo returns to France. Guion becomes king of Armenie. Bovo becomes a hermit. The boys return to France, warned by a dream, and go to the forest where Bovo dies in their presence. A number of elements are quite different: the holy end (*moniage*-style) as well as the stronger and named female characters are immediately evident.[21]

4.1.3.4 Continental III.

In Continental version three (16,391 lines), there are slight differences from version two. Gui's wife is Count Renier's daughter. She looks at herself in a mirror from Persia to decide that she is too pretty and young for Gui (compare the Irish version). An abbot warns Bovo that he will be poisoned, and gives him a *pume* against poisons. After a year, Bovo is given a meal which he wonders about, so he gives it to a dog which dies on the spot. Gui's wife has given pledges for Bovo's health. Soibaut threatens her when he hears that Bovo is gone, but the wife says he has gone to Oudart, her brother, to learn chivalry. When Bovo arrives at Aubefort, he tells his name and story to King Hermin. Josiane falls in love; Bovo fights bravely; Gonces and Fourré are jealous and lie, forcing the Uriah's letter, which here is Hermin's idea. During a nap along the way, after his meal with the pilgrim, Bovo dreams of three lions and prison.

In version three, Josiane uses an herb to remain pure during her marriage to Yvorin de Monbranc. The names of various nephews and characters vary in the episode of his flight; the giant's home on the other side of the water is Esmeré. Bovo is attacked by four thieves on his way to Jerusalem, where he is cleansed of snake venom (from his imprisonment) in the river Jordan. When Bovo arrives in Monbranc and meets Josiane, he stays one month to recover. Josiane arranges a false letter from Yvorin's uncle to draw him away, and gives an herbed drink to Garsiles to have him sleep through their escape. During their flight, the two lions eat all of Bonnefoi except his hands and feet. Açopart assists their flight to Cologne.

At Cologne, Archbishop Meuron assists Bovo and Josiane, baptizing Josiane and Açopart, and marries Bovo and Josiane. Josiane has a bad dream and does not want to stay behind, but Bovo goes without her to retake Hantone. Do is checking out all new arrivals, and has Bovo followed by a *jugleor*, Jolipin. Bovo persuades him with gifts that he is in fact safe, but the next day leaves with his host and Do's gifts for Soibaut (calling himself Miles/Millon).

---

[21] On *moniages*, see N. L. Bard, Jr., *Changing Orders: The Poetics of the Old French Epic Moniages* [Ann Arbor: UMI, 1998].

Back in Cologne, Widemers wants Josiane and manages by a false witness (a pilgrim) to persuade the archbishop that Bovo is dead.[22] He also imprisons Açopart. Bovo dreams that Josiane is taken by two bears in Cologne, and rushes to save her, having to identify himself to Soibaut in order to carry out his mission. He returns with Josiane, and fights further with Do. Do sends for reinforcements from Germany, but meanwhile Bovo has captured the two traitors who had sold him: they are hanged and burned. Do's men kill Açopart. Soibaut at this point leaves for London to appeal Bovo's case. He enlists all their friends and allies to stand as pledges for Bovo. Do too ensures pledges. The two fight a judicial duel on an island, watched by Josiane from a tower. Do is defeated, confesses, and is hanged. Bovo is given Antone by King Guillaume, and would have burned his mother, but she is saved by Josiane.

Josiane is pregnant; Bovo goes to London with Thierri and Rodoart. The incident of the King's son, Huon, occurs; Rohart, Ertaut, and Novelet urge the boy to take the horse (Rohart is related to Do). Bovo's three hundred relatives in court stand up for him, so he is exiled instead of killed. He goes home, and Josiane insists on accompanying him abroad. When they alight from the ship and are traveling overland, near Monbranc, Josiane must deliver their children, and a comic scene ensues during which Bovo blindfolds himself so he can stay with Josiane during the birth (cf. version one); he passes the children out of the cave to Thierry, who bathes them. Thierry goes into town for horse fodder and then to look for food for them. Four foresters see him, follow him, and finally lead Yvorin to Josiane. Bovo cannot fight the number of men there, and flees, ending up in Sivele as a soldier. He assists in defending the city so well that the queen (never named, though Aiglentine, her niece and confidante, is) insists on marrying him. He will not sleep with her, giving a rather extended story on why not, though he then recants and they have a son (who is never again mentioned). Thus in this version, as in Continental two, Bovo is unfaithful after initial protests, while Josiane remains steadfast in protecting her honor.

Yvorin, meanwhile, has Hermin judge his daughter. He decides to imprison her and her sons. Soibaut and another relative are out seeking Bovo and Josiane;

---

[22] For this trick of persuading a people that a ruler is dead in order to be able to marry his wife, compare some versions of *Macaire*, especially the *Fatti di Spagna* (R. M. Ruggieri, ed., *Li Fatti di Spagna. Testo settentrionale trecentesco già detto "Viaggio di Carlo Magno in Ispagna"* [Modena: Società tipografica modenese, 1951]), *La Spagna* (M. Catalano, ed., *La Spagna: Poema cavalleresco del secolo XIV*, 3 vols. Collezione di opere inedite o rare [Bologna: Commissione per i testi di lingua, Casa Carducci, 1939], 4.6.2), and also the German versions: the chronicles of Enikel (P. Strauch, ed., *Jansen Enikels Werke* [Hannover: Hahnsche Buchhandlung, 1900]) and Weihenstephan (O. Freitag, *Die sogenannte Chronik von Weihenstephan. Ein Beitrag zur Karlssage* [1904; repr. Tübingen: Niemeyer, 1972], ¶4.6.5.2).

they find her and they sneak away back to Hantone. They all go together to the king of England to persuade him to baptize the boys and forgive Bovo. He agrees; Soibaut and Josiane disguise themselves and go seeking Bovo. They hear of Bovo and the queen of Simile, and go there. Josiane sings a song of their doings, and Bovo recognizes her.[23] Bovo has his men and the archbishop who married him and Josiane witness that they were indeed married before; the queen of Simile then settles for Thierry instead. Bovo and family head for home. Bovo goes to London to see the king, who asks Bovo's help against King Brian of Ireland. Bovo conquers Brian and takes David back to England. In seven more years, Bovo is at home and has two more sons. Bovo embarks on one final voyage to Jerusalem; he stops to visit Thierri and then Hermin, whom he saves from Yvorin and Açopart (whom he and we had thought to be dead). He asks Hermin for a punishment for treachery, then identifies himself. Gonce and Fourré must fight a judicial duel with Bovo, since they say that they had seen the two sleeping together before they were married. Bovo and Josiane (who comes for the occasion) maintain the contrary. The traitors lose, and are disarmed and stoned to death. Yvorin and his men are baptized.

Bovo continues to Jerusalem, where he is crowned after a long battle. King William of England calls for Bovo to make his son the heir; Hermin comes too, leaving Herminet, another of Bovo's sons, as his heir. All of Europe gives itself to Bovo as he passes: Limesol (Cyprus), Rome, Germany, and so on. All of Bovo's sons are settled in kingdoms, as are his men. At the end, both Bovo and Josiane die.

4.1.4.5 *Daurel et Beton.*

A text related to the French versions is *Daurel et Beton*. Arthur S. Kimmel, its most recent editor, notes, "By using famous names, the author is echoing a respected but vaguely conceived tradition."[24] *Daurel et Beton* is a Provençal epic of 2184 lines which has been linked to *Bovo* since Gautier.[25] Riquer and scholastic

---

[23] The role of Josiane here is noted in M. V. Coldwell, "*Jougleresses* and *Trobairitz*: Secular Musicians in Medieval France," in *Women Making Music: The Western Art Tradition, 1150–1950*, ed. J. Bowers and J. Tick (Urbana: University of Illinois Press, 1986), 39–61, here 44. She compares the music of women in literature to documentary and iconographic evidence, and mentions several Old French romances in which a noblewoman disguises herself and travels as a *jougleresse*.

[24] A. S. Kimmel, *A Critical Edition of the Old Provençal Epic "Daurel et Beton" with Notes and Prolegomena* (Chapel Hill: University of North Carolina Press, 1971), 125.

[25] L. Gautier, *Les Épopées françaises: Étude sur les origines et l'histoire de la littérature nationale*, 2ᵉ éd. (Paris: Société générale de librarie catholique, 1880–1892).

manuals in general have called it an imitation of *Beuve de Hantone*.²⁶ There are, however, questions of dating, since the continental versions are dated to 1200 at the earliest and *Daurel* dates to 1150–1168 (though the single manuscript in which it is found dates to the fourteenth century [Kimmel, *Critical Edition*, 13; 34–36]). Kimmel believes that it is to this epic that Provençal and Catalan troubadours refer when they use variations on the name "Boeve" and "Hantone" (*Critical Edition*, 36–46). Whichever came first, the two, *Bovo d'Antona*, or *Daurel*, the two share names, plots, and themes typical o romans d'aniquite de litterature du nord f so-called "feudal epics": " . . . but there is no evidence indicating any close relationship between them" (*Critical Edition*, 45). The Provençal poem is linked with the *geste du roi* through Charlemagne: Bove of Antone, sworn companion to Guy (an impoverished count), marries Ermenjart, Charlemagne's sister. Guy is evil, acquiring wealth and desiring Bove's wife while Bove serves. Guy kills Bove in a boar hunt after Beton is born. Guy deceives Charlemagne and marries Ermenjart (who is not deceived). Daurel takes Beton away, sacrificing his own son to save his former lord's son. Daurel and Beton wander the East, where a pagan princess courts Daurel and is betrothed to him when she agrees to convert. Her father gives Beton men to reconquer his own land. Beton returns, and kills Guy and his supporters. He attempts to gain revenge from Charlemagne for Ermenjart's dishonor, but she advises him to avoid fighting the emperor. Charlemagne in fact laughs at them and the manuscript ends.

Many names are similar, though used for different characters: Guy is now the enemy, Beatrix is the retainer's wife (who kills herself when her own son is killed). Similarities with other *enfances* narratives are also present; the exiles flee an evil stepfather, accompanied by a faithful retainer. The hero is brought up in a foreign court, and he is betrothed to the pagan ruler's daughter, where his nobility is proved by his not accepting money. He eventually returns to regain his kingdom. But the traitorous friend, victimized wife, and singer-companion all differ. Furthermore, Bove is identified as the son of Ogier, which had wide influence in Catalan and Castilian versions typical of the *Daurel* type. *Ogier* in the Old French version had no direct influence on *Daurel* (Kimmel, *Critical Edition*, 127–28), but the linking of the two is of interest in connection with the Italian tradition, considering that both Bovo and Ogier are linked to the French royal family. We therefore leave this poem as a note to the overall composition, not as

---

²⁶ M. de Riquer, "Cantares de gesta francoitalianos y persistencia de epopeya francesa en Italia," in *Las cantares de gesta franceses: Sus problemas, su relación con España* (Madrid: Editorial Gredos, 1952), 346–50.

a close congener. There are too many question marks to include it definitively as a version of the *Bovo* story.[27]

4.1.4 Spanish texts.

In the Spanish area, there are echoes of the *malmariée* motif in both in the *Romance de Celinos y la Adúltera* and in a version of it in the *Romancero sefardí* (dated to the eighteenth to nineteenth centuries).[28] In this story, the young wife invites her lover to kill her husband, but the husband fights the lover. Here, however, the husband wins, which, according to Armistead and Silverman, reflects a moral judgment on the importance of marriage.[29] The fact that the wife feigns pregnancy to persuade her husband to go hunting resembles the Italian versions, which are the only others where this is her excuse (elsewhere she is only ill). Menéndez-Pidal originally compared the episodes with *Bovo*, but since they reflect only the initial episode and actually do not involve the child Bovo, the objective, theme, and result are entirely different, and again do not interest us here.[30] Heintze suggests that the *romance* of Gaiferos derives from Continental versions two and three of *Bueve de Hantone*, as do the two previous *romances* ("*Beuve de Hantone en Espagne*," 929–31).[31] The *Condesa traidora* has also been suggested as a parallel;

---

[27] A. Adler offers an interesting perspective, suggesting the *chansons de geste* as a chess game, with different characters playing different roles (*Rückzug in Epischen Parade: Studien zur "Les quatre fils Aymon," "La Chevalerie Ogier de Danemarche," "Garin le Loherenc," "Aliscans," "Huon de Bordeaux"* [Frankfurt: Vittorio Klostermann, 1963], 164–65). Since the same names do reappear in different versions as different characters—or even objects—such an exercise is tempting.

[28] Hogetoorn, "Bevis of Hampton," 63–64. Heintze is currently working on these pieces as well; his thesis is that they are in fact linked to *Bovo* (personal communication, 15 Nov. 1998; and now "*Bueve de Hantone* en Espagne. À propos des romances sur Gaiferos," in *L'épopée romane au Moyen Âge et aux temps modernes, Actes du XIV Congrès International de la Société Rencesvals pour l'étude des Épopées Romanes (Naples, 24–30 juillet 1997)*, ed. S. Luongo [Naples: Fridericiana Editrice Universitaria, 2001], 929–31). Modern sources usually cite the Spanish *romances* as dating to the late fourteenth and early fifteenth centuries (see, for example, *Britannica Online* <http://www.eb.com:180/cgi-bin/g?DocF = micro/509/24.html>, s.v. "romancero").

[29] S. G. Armistead and G. H. Silverman, "El Romance de Celinos y la adúltera," *Anuario de Letras* 2 (1962): 5–14, here 14.

[30] R. Menéndez-Pidal, *Romancero Hispánico (hispano-portugués, americano y sefardí)*, 2 vols., in idem, *Obras completas* 9–10 (1953; repr. Madrid: Espasa-Calpe, 1968), 1: 261 and 2: 406, quoted in Armistead and Silverman, "El Romance," 8, n. 7.

[31] The *romance* of Gaiferos is from F. J. Wolf and C. Hofmann, *Primavera y flor de romances ó coleccion de los mas viejos y mas populares romances castellanos* (Berlin: A. Asher, 1856), 248–50.

however, we will accept Horrent's conclusion that "les deux œuvres traitent indépendamment l'une de l'autre le thème général de la femme qui, pour des raisons sentimentales variées, tue son mari et tente de tuer son fils."[32]

4.1.5 German versions.
None.

4.1.6 Scandinavian version.
The Scandinavian version consists of the Icelandic *Bevers Saga* (fourteenth century), which follows the Anglo-Norman version so closely that modern editors examine it for translation errors made by the Icelandic scribe.[33] This will not be examined further.

Occasionally mentioned as having the same initial motif is the Faroese Bovo story, *Bevusar taettir* (written down in 1848 [Jung, "Beuve d'Hamtone," 274]). This may be an episode from the Scandinavian *Bevers Saga* passed through oral tradition (Hogetoorn, "Bevis of Hampton," 63), but critics differ on the issue, and again, this is not a version one can consult.

4.1.7 Dutch version.
The Dutch version, as frequently the case for Dutch epic materials, is fragmentary. A Middle Dutch fragment (Düsseldorf) dates to the first half of the fourteenth century, and is 118 lines related to the Continental version three (there, ll. 5385–9491). There is also a 1504 Dutch *Volksbuch* that derives directly from Continental version two. As research still continues on these pieces, and Dutch materials are under serious study, we will leave further conclusions to the experts in that area.[34]

---

[32] Jacques Horrent, "*Bueve de Hantone* et la *Condesa traidora*," *Les Lettres romanes* 36 (1982): 41–58, esp. 57–58.

[33] S. Hunt, "Further Translation Errors in *Bevers Saga*," *Notes and Queries* 230 (1985): 455–56.

[34] H. Beckers, "*Boeve van Hamtone*. Ein neuentdecktes Düsseldorfer Bruchstuck einer bisher unbekannten mittelniederländischen Versarbeitung des altfranzösischen *Bueve de Hantone*. Dem Andenken an Theodor Frings," in *200 Jahre Landes- und Stadtbibliothek Düsseldorf*, Veröffentlichungen 6 (Düsseldorf: Landes- und Stadtbibliothek Düsseldorf, 1970), 75–98, discusses the Düsseldorf Middle Dutch fragment and its relation to Continental version three (81). He discusses the Dutch *Volksbuch* on page 82.

4.1.8 British Isles.

4.1.8.1 English version.

The English version, *Beves of Hampton*, closely follows the Anglo-Norman; seven manuscripts survive to demonstrate its popularity.[35] The earliest manuscripts date to the fourteenth century (Kölbing, *The Romance of Sir Beues*, vii–viii). Five of these are stanzaic, two in couplets. The similarities have been closely examined; Baugh compares the Anglo-Norman with the English quite carefully ("The Making of *Beves*"). There are three additions: a Christmas day incident among the Saracens, where Bovo defends himself against their jeers (ll. 585–738); a fight with a dragon which has both religious and legendary significance (ll. 2597–2910); and a fight with the citizens of London which demonstrates an excellent geographical knowledge of the town (ll. 4287–4538). Jacobs points out similarities between *Beves* and other romances in its manuscript, especially *Degarré* in having a fight with dragons;[36] Weiss suggests that the incidents were consciously added in English interests, since they demonstrate a hostility to Rome together with a growth of patriotic sentiment found in other English adaptations of the same time.[37] Mehl notes, "It may be coincidence that *Sir Beves of Hamtoun* stands next to poems like *Arthour and Merlin* (in A), *Athelstan* (in E) and *Richard Coeur de Lion* (in S) in some of the manuscripts, but it could also indicate that the novel was felt to be some kind of family chronicle or at least a tale from England's past which had some important bearing on the present."[38] Mehl compares exemplary and moralizing tendencies in *Beves* to other Middle English romances. These, he notes, make the plot "far more coherent and meaningful than is generally admitted" (*Middle English Romances*, 253). Clearly, similarities exist with V[13] in these factors and also in the use of burlesque.[39] Some try to claim the *Bovo* is insular

---

[35] A. C. Baugh, "The Making of *Beves of Hampton*," in *Bibliographical Studies in Honor of Rudolf Hirsch*, ed. W. E. Miller and T. G. Waldman with N. D. Terrell, special issue of *Library Chronicle* 40 (1975): 15–37. The number of manuscripts is listed on page 35.

[36] N. Jacobs, "*Sir Degarré, Lay Le Freine, Beves of Hamtoun* and the 'Auchinleck Bookshop'," *Notes and Queries* 227 (1982): 294–301.

[37] J. Weiss, "The Major Interpolations in *Sir Beues of Hamtoun*," *Medium Aevum* 48 (1979): 71–76, here 75.

[38] D. Mehl, *The Middle English Romances of the Thirteenth and Fourteenth Centuries* (New York: Barnes and Noble, Inc., 1969), 211.

[39] On the seriousness and lack of seriousness of the tale, see M.-G. Grossel and C.-T. Cemo, "Le Burlesque et son évolution dans les trois versions continentales de la chanson de *Beuve de Hanstone*," in *Burlesque et dérision dans les épopées de l'occident médiéval*, Actes du Colloque international des Rencontres Européennes de Strasbourg et de la Société Internationale Rencesvals (Section française), Strasbourg, 16–18 septembre 1993, ed. Bernard Guidot (Paris: Les Belles Lettres, 1995), 255–68.

(= British) material in origin, related to *Havelock*, *Horn*, and *Guy of Warwick*, but given its widespread distribution (as we see here) this seems unlikely.[40]

4.1.8.2 Irish version.

There is a fifteenth-century Irish fragment analyzed and translated into English by Robinson.[41] He suggests that its source is a free redaction of lost English versions. He lists seven points of difference: 1. Bovo's (Bevis's) mother is in love with the son of the emperor; 2. she decides to marry her lover upon seeing her own beauty in the bath (compare Continental version three); 3. Bovo is sent to tend swine, not sheep; 4. there is no conversation elsewhere compelling him to avenge his father's murder; 5. he goes to India and Rhodes rather than Jerusalem and / or Egypt; 6. Sisian and Yvor appear much later here; 7. during the dragon fight, Bovo is inundated with four waves of vomit. There are a few other differing details (such as Bovo being up to his neck in the sea twice a day while in prison; Bovo marrying the daughter of the king of England, Mirmidonia). The general plot, insofar as critics can tell from the fragment, is the same.

4.1.8.3 Welsh version.

The Welsh version (*Bowno Hantown*), according to Stimming, also derives from this branch, but serious questions have been raised about that relationship.[42] Believed to date to the early thirteenth century, it exists in four manuscripts. The earliest manuscript is from the late thirteenth century, and the best-known editions were, for a long time, not critical editions (Watkin, "Albert Stimming's *Welsche Fassung*," 372). The many errors in English translations led Stimming astray in his commentary. However, as a text related to the Anglo-Norman and not any closer to the Italian versions, we shall not examine it further.

4.1.9 Discussion.

The differences between the Italian version and Continental versions lie in the names of the characters; in Bovo's relationships (married or not to a second woman); in whether or not he has progeny, and if so, how many. The plot is basically the same: Bovo's mother had killed her husband for Do, Bovo's stepfather. Do leads Pepin to fight Bovo. Bovo finally succeeds in obtaining Antona to pass on to his children. The two major plot differences between the Italian and other

---

[40] P. C. Hoyt, "The Home of the Beves Saga," n.p., n.d. (1904?), makes such a claim.

[41] F. N. Robinson, "The Irish Lives of Guy of Warwick and Bevis of Hampton," *Zeitschrift für celtische Philologie* 6 (1908) : 9–180, 273–338.

[42] See M. Watkin, "Albert Stimming's *Welsche Fassung* in the *Anglonormannische Boeve de Haumtone*: An Examination of a Critique," in *Studies in French Language and Literature Presented to Mildred K. Pope* (Manchester: Manchester University Press, 1939), 371–79.

versions are, first, the point at which Bovo and Drusiana marry—in the Continental and others, it is after Bovo reconquers Antona and before the horse race, where in V^{13} it is clearly before conquering Antona, since Drusiana appears with their sons at the festivities to celebrate a second marriage after the city is reconquered. Thus the children in Continental versions are born during the flight *after* regaining Antona rather than before. Secondly, the concluding visit to the Holy Land appears both in V^{13} and in Andrea da Barberino's *Reali*; rather than form a portion of Bovo's adventures before his final settling in Antona, it follows both sets of wanderings, unlike in other Continental versions.

The differences between Italian and non-Italian versions as well as between Italian versions themselves have been attributed to recall of oral presentations.[43] However, the positivistic researchers of *stemmata* ignored the fact that *Bovo* is here integrated into a cyclical text. The redactor sought to tie the characters and chronology to the Charlemagne cycle. In V^{13}, Pepin, Charlemagne's ancestor, is shown in action. The development of the Bovo story demonstrates that it became an exemplar of what a good father should do and how a noble family should behave: the father should hold (or if necessary regain) his lands, increase them, and ensure positions of at least equal nobility for his offspring. Seriousness in exemplarity of the tale varies through the different versions, since high seriousness is broken by the comic element (for example, Açopart, which is lacking here due to missing folios). Similar questions and elements reappear throughout V^{13} — seriousness and desire for exemplarity—as each of the tales reappears in varied reincarnations throughout Europe and as well as in other V^{13} texts. It should be noted that the other versions "localize" the story too; the British dragon example is unique.

Bovo is a hero story which appears as part of longer texts, as far as is currently known, only in Italy: in V^{13} and the *Reali*. V^{13} and the *Reali* differ from each other and from all other versions in the order of episodes; particularly of note is the V^{13} division of *Bovo* into two parts which could be designated *enfances* and *chevalerie*, unlike any other version. Bovo regains his home in the first part after youthful wanderings (not fully documented here, due to the loss of initial folios) and, after *Berta da li pe grant*, he must defend first his home, then his (and his horse's) honor against the traitors. As such, *Bovo* in V^{13} follows a late epic thematic tradition, rather than the characteristic romance form. It also sets the pattern for the following alternations of *enfances* and *chevaleries* that characterize V^{13}.

---

[43] See, for example, C. Dionisotti, "Appunti su cantari e romanzi," *Italia medioevale e umanistica* 32 (1989): 227–61.

CHART 4.1A: Proper Names in V¹³ *Bovo* compared to other versions

V¹³	*Bovo veneto*, Florence, Laur. MS. Med. Pal. XC.III	*I Reali di Francia*, Andrea da Barberino	*Bovo udinese*	*Bovo toscano*, Florence, Ricc. MS. 1030	*Boeve de Haumtone* (Anglo-Nor)	Continental I	Cont. II	Cont. III	Role in text
Antona/e	Anton(i)a	Antona	Antona	Antonia	Haumtone	Hantonne	Hantonne	Hantone	Bovo's city
Ari/eminion di Arminia/e	Arminion di Arminia	Erminione d'Erminia	Arminiun di Arminia	Erminia	Hermyne of Hermonie	Hermin of Herminie	Hermin of Aubefort, Biaufort	Hermin of Aubefort	Drusiana's city and father
Bernard(o) de Clermon and Morando/Morant de River									Bovo's allies at court
Blondoja/e or Blionda	Blondoia	Brandoria	Blondoia	Brandoria	daughter of King of Escoce	Beatris	Renier daughter, unnamed	Renier's daughter, unnamed	Gui's wife
Bovo	Bovo	Buovo	Bovo	Bovetto/Buovo	Boefs	Bueves	Bueves	Bueve	Protagonist
Braidamont	Malgaria	Margaria						Vencadouse	Drusiana's rival: Soldan's daughter
Clarença/e	Chiarenza/Chiarença	Chiarenza	Clarença		Murgleie				Bovo's sword
Corcher de Baldras; Corche(s)									Pagan in Holy Land conquered by Bovo

V13	Bovo veneto, Florence, Laur. MS. Med. Pal. XC.III	I Reali di Francia, Andrea da Barberino	Bovo udinese	Bovo toscano, Florence, Ricc. MS. 1030	Boeve de Haumtone (Anglo-Nor)	Continental I	Cont. II	Cont. III	Role in text
Do de Magançe; Dodo; Does, Doo, Doon; Duo, Duon	Dodon	Duodo di Maganza	Dodon	Duodo di Maganza	Emperor of Germany (Duon)	Do(on) de Maienche	Doon de Maienche	Doon de Maience	Enemy; Bovo's stepfather
Drus/xiana/e	Drus/xiana	Drusiana	Drusiana	Drusiana	Josiane	Josienne	Josienne	Josiane	Bovo's wife
Folcone		Fiore				Hues	Hugone		Son of English King
G(u)arner		Gailone							Bovo's stepbrother
Gui, Gujon	Guidon	Guido	Guidon	Guido	Guioun	Guis/Guion	Guion	Guion de Hantoune	Bovo's father
Guielme; Gui		Guglielmo			Edegar	Guillaume	Guillaume		English king
Gujon and Sinibaldo	Guidon and Sinibaldo	Guidone and Sinibaldo			Guion and Miles; Beatrix	Guillaume, Guion, Hermin, Sinibaldo	Buevon Guillaume, Guionnet, Hermin	Beuve, Gui; Tierri is son with Venca	Bovo's offspring
Luchafer	Lucafer(o) di Baldras	Lucafero di Buldras	Lucafer						other woman's brother
Machabrun	Marchabrun	Marcabruno di Polonia	Marchabrun ... Polonia	Marcabruno di (Ap)polonia	Yvori of Munbrant	Yvorin	Yvorin de Monbronc	Yvorin de Monbranc	Wants to marry Drusiana; does so without consummation of marriage
Oria		Aluzia/Luzia		Aulitia	Eneborc			Aelis	Wife of seneschal

Pulican(t)	Pulican(t)	Pulicane		Escopart	Açopart	Achoupart	Açopart	Half-dog, half-man; assists Bovo and Drusiana
Rondel(o)	Rondelo	Fordello	Rondel	Arundel	Arondel/Arondiaus	Arondel	Arondel	Bovo's horse
San Si/ymon d'Ariant	San Symon	Focca a San Simone	San Simon		Neve Freté	Noeve Freté		Seneschal's location
Si/ynibaldo, Siginbaldo; Latro	Synibaldo	Sinibaldo	Sinibaldo	Sab(a)ot	Sobaut	Soybaut	Soibaut	Loyoal seneschal
Sy/indonia/e or Sindon		Sinella		Civile	Siviele	Sivele	Sivele	Where the other woman is from
Teris	Teris	Tergi/Teris		Terri, Robeant	Teri/Tierri	Thierri, Rodoars	Tierri, Roboet	Sinibaldo's son; Bovo's ally, second woman's husband
Uberto da la Cros	Cilberto (Sinibaldo's brother)	Ruberto della Croce			Davis (Sobaut's nephew)			Bovo's ally in Antona
	(H)Orio (wife is Drusiana's cousin)	Cantoro						Marcabrun's enemy
	Abrayn and Troncati			Graunder				Soldan's nephews; they pursue escaped Bovo
	Angossos/zo	Agostino	Agostino	Gerraud	Aimers de Hongherie (to Doon)	Miles/Millon (to Sobaut)	Gerars de Digon (le Bourguigon)	Bovo's pseudonym in exile

V13	Bovo veneto, Florence, Laur. MS. Med. Pal. XC.III	I Reali di Francia, Andrea da Barberino	Bovo udinese	Bovo toscano, Florence, Ricc. MS. 1030	Boeve de Haumtone (Anglo-Nor)	Continental I	Cont. II	Cont. III	Role in text
	Foresta di Sclaravena			Selva Bruna		Ardane	Ardene	Ardene; Monfaucon; Argonne	Where Guido, Bovo's father, was killed
	Gutifer and Rizardo	C and Riccardo di Conturbia							Bovo and Sinibaldo's allies
	Monbrand	Polonia	Monbrando		Munbrant	Monbranc	Monbranc	Monbrant	Yvorin or Marcabrun's city
	Passamonte d'Ongaria	Druano di Soria					Escorfaus		Enemy attacking Sindonia
	Rizardo	Antonio (Guascon)		Antonio			Salemon		Messenger to Do of Magance
	Soldan(o) di Sadonia	Ba/uldras di Sinella (in Schiavonia or Ungheria)	Soldan di Sandonia				Ottrans li vius de Monferrant and Disdier de Portingal (uncles); Josserant		Father of other woman
	Ugolin	Ugolino (brother of Erminione)	Ugolino						Gonfalonier of Arminion; Drusiana's jealous brother / uncle

	Rohart	Rohart, Ertaut, Novele	Rohart	Do's nephew; steals horse
Brademund of Damascus	Brademund	Bradmont	Braidimont	Hermyne's enemy, King of Damascus
	Morins	Meuron	Amaurri	Archbishop of Cologne, Bovo's uncle
Bonefoy/Bonefas	Boinefoi	Bonefoi	Bonefoi(s)	Bovo's wife's seneschal
Miles	Audemars	Widemer	Huidemers (nephew of the Archbishop)	Knight who marries / wants to marry Bovo's wife at Cologne
				Oudart
	Froimont and Hastes; Gouses and Fouré	Fromont and Haton; Gonces and Forrez	Fromont and Haton; Gonsselin and Fourré	Traitors, Queen's henchmen
Garcie	Garsile	Garsile		Bovo's wife's guard while Yvorin leaves
	Danemons de Persia	Danebruns de Perse	Danebus de Perse	Pagan enemy; uncle of Braidamont

CHART 4.1B: Selected Versions of *Bovo d'Antona/Beuve d'Hamstone*:

Italian

– *Franco-Italian*
1. V^{13} *Bovo*, first half fourteenth century
2. Florence, Laur. MS. Med. Pal. XC.III, *Bovo veneto* (Rajna, *Ricerche*, *493–566*), second half fourteenth or first half fifteenth century (*Ricerche*, 125–6); composed 1250–1330 (*Ricerche*, 145).
3. Udine, Archivio capitolare; "Udinese fragments" (Rajna, "Frammenti" [*Zeitschrift für romanische Philologie* 11 (1887), 162–84]), late fourteenth century (8 folios); rhymed laisses

– *Tuscan*
1. Florence, Ricc. MS. 1030; *Buovo toscano* (Rajna, "Frammenti" [1891, 55–87]), fifteenth-century prose fragment ("Frammenti" [1888, 465])
2. *I Reali di Francia* by Andrea da Barberino, late fourteenth-early fifteenth century
3. Florence, Ricc. MS. 2080, v. 2 (*ottave*), early fifteenth century (Delcorno Branca, "Fortuna," 290)
4. Florence, Bibl. Nazionale Centrale, Magl. Cl. VII, palch. 10, cod. 1202 (Rajna, *Ricerche*, 202)/ MS. Magl. VII. 1202 (Delcorno Branca, "Fortuna," 289–90), "di Gherardo" (*ottave*), fifteenth century

– *Emilian* (printed texts)
1. *Buovo* (Bologna), 1480; 20 *canti (*Delcorno Branca, "Fortuna," 290)
2. *Buovo* (Bologna), 1497; 22 *canti (*Delcorno Branca, "Fortuna," 290)

Derived From Italian:
1. Yiddish, early sixteenth century
2. Slavic versions, sixteenth century

Outside Italy:
1. Anglo-Norman, first half of thirteenth century (Stimming, *Der anglonormannische Boeve de Haumtone*, lviii)
2. English, fourteenth century (date from Kölbing, *The Romance of Sir Beues of Hamtoun*, v)
3. Continental I, ca. 1200 (date from Stimming, *Der festländische Bueve de Hantone, Fassung I*, xix)
4. Continental II, ca. 1225 (date from Stimming, *Der festländische Bueve de Hantone Fassung II*, 65)
5. Continental III, before 1220 (date from Stimming, *Der festländische Bueve de Hantone, Fassung III*, Vol. 2, 68)

6. Irish, fifteenth century
7. Dutch fragment, first half of fourteenth century; *Volksbuch* 1504
8. Icelandic/Norwegian *Bevers Saga*, fourteenth century
9. Welsh, thirteenth century
10. Faroese, *Bevusar taettir*, 1848
11. Spanish *Celinos y la Adúltera* (Sephardic version), eighteenth-nineteenth centuries
12. Spanish *Gaiferos*, fifteenth century

4.2 Berta da li pe grant

With *Berta*, Charlemagne's mother, begins the true "story" or "history" of Charlemagne in this manuscript. It is followed by the story of Charlemagne's youth, and all the subsequent pieces either concern Charlemagne specifically or are during his reign.

From the earliest publication and discovery of *chansons de geste*, the historical basis of events recounted therein has been of interest. In the case of *Berta*, editors and historians have pursued many leads. Noting the variation in origin for Berta and the long time spent in the woods, plus the naming differences between versions, critics have attempted to identify any central point of historical fact in the account. The search is closely identified with the overall positivistic slant toward debate on the origin of the epic: traditionalists versus individualists. Those who argue conscious composition tend to argue deliberate creation of propaganda at a specific date, imposing current situation on earlier hazy history.[1] The search has been largely fruitless since the details—an accused and threatened wife exiled or removed, later found again—do not match those of any early French king. There have been four candidates suggested for Pepin: Pepin (of Herstal); Pepin (the Short); Robert the Pious; and Philip I.[2] Pepin of Herstal (680–714) is a popular candidate, since he had two wives, Alpaïs and Plectrude, and there was disagreement between them. Pepin the Short (741–768) was married to Bertrade, daughter of Charibert, Count of Laon. The interest here is that Charlemagne was seven or eight years old when she was crowned, making him technically a bastard legitimized after the fact. Robert the Pious (996–1031) caused ecclesiastical scandal by repudiating his first wife (Bertha, daughter of the count of Friesland) and marrying the wife of a vassal, Bertrade of Montfort, near the forest of Mans. The second evidently persecuted Louis, son of the first.[3] Philip I (1060–1108) had two wives, Berthe and Bertrade. Gautier already states that there is no relation between the *chanson* and Pepin of Herstal and Alpaïs / Plectrude (Gautier, *Épopées françaises*, 3: 11). Green suggests that Philip I is the most likely candidate, since he lived at the time that the *chansons de geste* were appearing in the form with which we are familiar (Green, "The Pépin-Bertha Saga," 918–19). (This subject will be touched upon again below in discussing *Karleto*, since the identity of Charlemagne is closely tied to the identity of Pepin.) Charlemagne

---

[1] On this subject, see G. Duby, *The Knight, the Lady and the Priest: The Making of Modern Marriage in Medieval France*, trans. Barbara Bray (New York: Pantheon Books, 1983).

[2] The source of historical dates here is C. W. Hollister, *Medieval Europe: A Short History*, 6th ed. (New York: McGraw-Hill, 1990), 356, 358.

[3] H. J. Green, "The Pépin-Bertha Saga and Philip I of France," *PMLA* 58 (1943): 911–19, here 916.

and Charles Martel were often confused as well.[4] The lack of historical congruence has been explained by recourse to traditional motifs, either mythological or from folktales; these will be discussed after the different versions of the *chanson de geste*, at the end of the chapter.

There are many versions of the *Berta* story, twenty-eight including V[13].[5] The story enjoyed a wide popularity throughout western Europe from the twelfth through the nineteenth century. The total of twenty-eight includes versions through the sixteenth century. These are discussed in the following order: V[13] and other Italian (3 versions); references and Latin mentions (6 total); French versions (8 total); German (6 versions); Dutch (1 only); Spanish versions (2); and finally, Catalan (2). This chapter is particularly difficult to organize, as Adenet le

---

[4] M. Rumpf, "Berta," in *Enzyklopädie des Märchens*, 2: 156–62, here 158; R. Folz, *Le Souvenir et la légende de Charlemagne dans l'Empire germanique médiéval* (Paris: Les Belles Lettres, 1950) 11, 137; R. Morrissey, *Charlemagne and France: A Thousand Years of Mythology*, trans. C. Tihanyi (Notre Dame: University of Notre Dame Press, 2003), 95.

[5] Critics count the versions differently; some include the brief references, others include only a relatively complete account. More versions have been discovered through the early years of this century as well. Thus, Gautier cites thirteen (*Epopées françaises*, 3: 12 ff); A. Feist cites thirteen (*Zur Kritik der Bertasage* [Marburg: N.G. Elwert'sche Verlagsbuchhandlung, 1886], 3–4); Arfert eight (P. Arfert, *Das Motiv von der unterschobenen Braut in der internationalen Erzählungslitteratur mit einem Anhang: Über den Ursprung und die Entwicklung der Bertasaga* [Schwerin: Bärensprungschen Hofbuchdruckerei, 1897], 59), though he mentions other shorter pieces which he does not include in his primary list as well; Paris seven (G. Paris, *Histoire poétique de Charlemagne* [Paris: Bouillon, 1905; repr., Geneva: Slatkine, 1974], 234); Reinhold cites twenty (J. Reinhold, "Über die verschiedenen Fassungen der Bertasage," *Zeitschrift für romanische Philologie* 35 [1911]: 1–30, 129–52), though he also mentions two others in passing, mere references, which he does not include in his *Stammbaum*; Memmer twenty literary versions (A. Memmer, *Die altfranzösische Bertasage und das Volksmärchen* [Halle (Saale): Niemeyer, 1935]); Henry mentions twenty (A. Henry, "*Berta da li gran pié* et la *Berte* d'Adenet," in *Atti del 2º in Congresso internazionale della 'Société Rencesvals'*, special issue of *Cultura Neolatina* 21 [1961]: 135–40); Colliot says there are eighteen important ones (R. Colliot, *Adenet le roi, Berte aus grans piés: Etude littéraire générale*, 2 vols. [Paris: Picard, 1970], 7) but cites twenty-five total (*Adenet le roi*, 11–12); Krauss follows Reinhold, giving twenty (*Epica feudale*, 71). I have included all here. I have attempted to check all references against available editions; unfortunately not all are available, or are unedited and therefore only in manuscript. Feist and Paris each print selections from different texts in question. I note where my knowledge comes from other critics. Particularly lamentable until recently was the lack of an edition of *Charlemagne* by Girard d'Amiens, a lack corrected while this edition is in press with Daniel Métraux's recent edition, Daniel Métraux, ed., *A Critical Edition of Girart d'Amiens' L'istoire le Roy Charlemaine: poème épique du XIVe siècle* (New York: Mellen, 2003).

Rois's version, a later French rendering, was extremely important for all following authors. Thus, there are influences across chronological and linguistic lines forcing us to anticipate sections; we ask the reader to bear with us. Within each language section the texts are arranged in chronological order.

4.2.1 V[13] Berta.

King Pepin takes the daughter of the King of Hungary as a wife. On the way to Paris, she befriends a daughter of Belençer of Magance (I use this form throughout; a "Maganzese" [plural "Maganzesi"] is someone from Magance, that is, Mainz) who could be her twin. Their resemblance is so close that when the procession arrives in Paris, Berta (I use this form of her name throughout except where referring specifically to the title of another work or when quoting) asks the Maganzese to substitute for her in Pepin's bed because she herself is exhausted from the long ride. The girl (never named) does so. The replacement decides that she likes being queen and attempts to have Berta killed. She has her men take Berta into the forest, but one henchman, Teris, allows Berta to go free if she will never return. Berta flees and must hide in the forest with a widower and his family (Sinibaldo and his two daughters) until her mother, Blançiflor, queen of Hungary, becomes suspicious of the lack of news from Paris. Queen Blançiflor visits Pepin, finds the impostor, and forces Pepin to find Berta. The impostor is burned but her sons remain at court, where they will cause trouble. Her daughter, Berta, also remains at court under Berta's care.

4.2.2 Other Italian versions.

In Italy, beyond V[13], the story exists in three other versions and perhaps in one lost version: Andrea da Barberino's *Reali di Francia*, book 6 (Roncaglia and Beggiato, eds., *I Reali di Francia*, 540–72; late fourteenth- early fifteenth century); his *Aspramonte*, which also includes a reference that implies knowledge of the story (Book 3, 137: 5–7);[6] *Aquilon de Bavière* (completed 1407);[7] and it seems that there was a short poem, *Il padiglione del re Pepino*, which Rajna says is no longer available.[8]

---

[6] M. Boni, ed., *Andrea da Barberino: L'Aspramonte. Romanzo cavalleresco inedito* (Bologna: Antiquaria Palmaverde, 1951), 270.

[7] P. Wunderli, ed., *Raffaele da Verona, Aquilon de Bavière: Roman franco-italien en prose (1379–1407)* (Tübingen: Max Niemeyer Verlag, 1982).

[8] Rajna, *Ricerche intorno ai Reali*, 226. Gloria Allaire clarifies that Rajna's MS. citation is erroneous, that it should be Med. Palat. 101. t. IV, fol. 3r–v, where it is called "Il padiglione di Filidoro" (personal communication, Sept. 2008) . It is a widespread topic, and she describes two main variants. Her examples are from the fifteenth century, but she offers proof

Note that I use the names as given in each version so as to distinguish V^{13}'s from others, unless otherwise noted, except "Berta," who is throughout this discussion the heroine.

4.2.2.1 *I Reali di Francia*.

Andrea da Barberino's *Reali*, in book 6, chapters 1–17, differs notably from the Franco-Italian in some respects. It is extremely detailed, allowing the author much leeway for additions. 1. Pepin is old and has never married; 2. Filippo of Hungary has a daughter with 3. one foot bigger than the other, but otherwise beautiful and 4. an excellent horsewoman. 5. Falisetta is Berta's good friend, daughter of the count of Magance, and looks like her except for the feet. 6. Falisetta was born in Hungary, since her father had escaped from prison in France (so she is not met on the way back to France). Pepin's men ask for her hand in marriage for Pepin, and her father, the king of Hungary, reveals her large foot, showing them to the ambassadors but 7. swearing them to secrecy. The men marry her by proxy for Pepin; 8. Berta's mother (unnamed) tells her that Pepin is old, but not 9. that he is little. Falisetta will accompany Berta, together with two of her clansmen, though 10. the queen worries about the reputation of the Maganzesi. When Berta sees Pepin, 11. she is upset; she asks Falisetta to take her place. Falisetta consults with the others of her clan; 12. they persuade her to marry Pepin and go to bed with him. 13. Falisetta's two men tell four boys that Falisetta (= Berta) is meeting a boy in the garden and that they are to take her into the Mans wood and cut her throat for shaming them. All goes as planned, except Berta tells her story to the four men and they 14. tie her to a tree. The men 15. take her dress and put dog's blood on it as proof that they have killed her. The Maganzesi kill the assassins. Falisetta and Pepin have two sons, 16. Lanfroy and Oldrigi. 17. A hunter, Lamberto, finds Berta; he has a wife and 18. four daughters. Berta invents a story and they call her 19. Falisetta. She teaches the girls to sew in order to build up a dowry. (She writes instructions for Lamberto, what to get at the fair, etc.) He sells the goods in Paris and no longer needs to hunt. She hears of Pepin's two boys and 20. decides to get her own back. She makes a special decorated tent for Lamberto to sell with her story woven on it. Grifon of

---

that such a poem existed before Andrea da Barberino's death ("Un manoscritto del «Cantare»," 15). This is of interest because in Andrea da Barberino's *Reali* Berta sews a pavilion telling her story and has her host sell it in hopes that she will be rescued. In German versions as well Berta is a talented seamstress. Ferrario mentions a manuscript at the Biblioteca di San Lorenzo in Florence, "Il Padiglione del Re Pipino detto il Padiglione di Giaccio." However he gives no date (Ferrario, *Storia ed analisi degli antichi romanzi di cavalleria e dei poemi romanzeschi d'Italia* [Milan: Dalla tipografia dell'autore, 1928–1929], 2: 174–75).

Magance buys and burns it. In the meantime, Berta's parents are worried about her. A spy has told them that it is Falisetta ruling. 21. They both go to France. The false Berta takes ill. The queen of Hungary pushes her way in, and recognizes Falisetta. 22. Filippo and his wife want to leave, but Pepin insists on taking Filippo hunting. King Pepin is separated from the others while hunting a deer; he runs into Lamberto and stays with him. The girls serve Pepin; 23. he notices Berta's similarity to his wife. 24. He propositions her and she agrees (Lamberto makes a point of asking if she really wants to). 25. The whole hunting group arrives and dines there. Lamberto and his wife are upset at Berta. 26. Berta reveals herself to Pepin that night, and he insists on finding out whether or not she is a virgin. The next morning, Filippo sees Berta and recognizes her. Pepin has her recount the whole story to everyone. The party returns to Paris; Filippo tells his wife what has happened. The king's men move against the Maganzesi in town. 27. Pepin takes Falisetta out by her hair and wants to kill her, but Bernardo will not allow it. Many Maganzesi are killed. Falisetta is burned, but the boys are saved. Pepin calls for Berta. 28. The Maganzesi remember the pavilion and also ride out for her. 29. The Maganzesi meet with the king's men as they return; Berta helps in the fight and kills a man herself with a lance. All return to an emotional reunion. One month later, Filippo and his wife return to Hungary. "Carro Magno" [Big Cart] is the name of the son born nine months later for the cart in which he was conceived. Morando di Riviera is to take care of him. Twelve years later, Berta has a daughter (unnamed).

Andrea's version is clearly much elaborated, but related to V^{13}. Rajna believes that the author is repeating a story that he has heard rather than copying it, as in the case of *Bovo* (*Ricerche intorno ai "Reali"*, 226). The variations between the Italian and French tradition are not consistent; various French versions seem to be conflated here. In both part of the French tradition and the Franco-Italian, Berta herself asks the look-alike to take her place.[9] It is unlike Adenet's version in that Berta sleeps with Pepin on a *carro* before recognition,[10] though she tells her story as in the *Saintonge* chronicle.[11] The forceful female characters are more like the Franco-Italian, unlike Adenet, yet their names seem to reflect knowledge of a version like Adenet's: Aliste could easily become Alisetta, and by analogy and comparison with Italian "falso," her daughter, Falisetta; the forest is named

---

[9] Specifically, in Philippe Mousket's *Chronicle* (Baron de Reiffenberg, ed., *Chronique rimée de Philippe Mouskes* [Brussels: M. Hayez, 1836–1838]; see below, paragraph 4.2.3.2).

[10] A. Henry, ed., *Berte as grans piés* (Geneva: Droz, 1982); see below, paragraph 4.2.3.8.

[11] F. W. Bourdillon, ed., *Tote listoire de France (Chronique Saintongeaise)* (London: David Nutt, 1897); see below, paragraph 4.2.3.1.

Magno (= "Maine"). In Andrea da Barberino, as in the Franco-Italian version, the deception is blamed on the Maganzesi; here, though, the men lead Falisetta astray, where in the Franco-Italian the impostor (never named) invents the deception herself. The *padiglione* concept is different from the French, as is the fearful reaction of Berta's parents.[12]

4.2.2.2 *Aspramonte*.
Andrea da Barberino refers to the story further in his *Aspramonte*, in calling Charlemagne a bastard (Gherardo da Fratta, a descendant of Buovo d'Antona, speaks):

> Voi vedete che Iddio ci è contro e la fortuna, ed à tolto a fare singnore questo bastardo di Carlo, che non si sa di cui figliuolo si sia. Egli si chiama figliuolo di Pipino, e io so per vero ch'egli è figliuolo d'uno mandriano e cacciatore di Pipino, el quale si tenne la madre nel bosco del Mangno molto tempo, e fece morire Lanfroi e Oldris che erano figliuoli di Pipino.... (Book 3: 137. 5–7; Boni, *Andrea da Barberino: L'Aspramonte*, 270)

4.2.2.3 *Aquilon de Bavière*.
Aquilon de Bavière contains an otherworldly, Dantean story. 1. Gaiete is an ancestor of Aquilon, the impostor. She is telling her story after her death. She is 2. the king of Corvatie's daughter. She went with Berta to be her private maid. (So we are hearing the story from the impostor's point of view.) 3. Pepin spoke with her before the wedding, saying that if he had known Gaiete was so attractive he would have married her. (Since Berta and she had arrived together just before the wedding, and he had never met either of them, he did not know this in advance.) So Gaiete had Berta taken away and married Pepin. Pepin found Berta while hunting, conveniently 4. when his mother-in-law was supposed to be arriving. He saw Berta, 5. he tried to force her, and 6. she told him of the plot. They shared the cart near the Maine river and she conceived Charlemagne; Pepin returned to court 7. to find the queen, his mother-in-law, there. Gaiete was forced to tell all, and Pepin had her burned. Here the queen (Berta's mother) has lost most of her role, and again Berta revealed herself instead of concealing her identity. [13]

---

[12] Rajna compares the names used, including Adenet, V[13], and the *Reali* (*Ricerche*, 240, n. 2).

[13] A. Thomas, "Aquilon de Bavière. Roman franco-italien inconnu," *Romania* 11 (1882): 538–69; text paraphrased, 557–61; Wunderli, *Raffaele da Verona. Aquilon de Bavière*, 1: 389–97.

4.2.2.4 Later Italian works.
Berta is mentioned in later Italian works as well; Pulci refers to her as Eraclio's (Heraclius's) daughter so her genealogical position as an heir and blood continuance of the Byzantine Empire becomes a given in later Italian Carolingian epic.[14]

4.2.2.5 Other references.
Miscellaneous references to Berta appear in vernacular and Latin versions. The first record of the Berta story is at the end of the twelfth century in a Latin manuscript: "Per quoque, per certe, per cetera juro, Roberte, / Perque pedem Berte, quia tu versificaris aperte, . . . " nothing more than a reference.[15] Godfrey of Viterbo († 1192) mentions her in Latin verse: Berta is Hungarian, but her mother is the daughter of Heraclius Caesar, a genealogical attribution which returns in other later versions, as in Pulci, mentioned above.[16] In the French-speaking area, there is an allusion in *Anseis de Mes* (second half of the twelfth century) in a version quite different from ours or any other; she is a baptized schismatic, Batheheut baptized with the name Berte (cited in Colliot, *Adenet le roi*, 11; Feist, *Zur Kritik der Bertasage*, 42).[17] In *Floire et Blanchefleur* (second half of the twelfth century), the poet, while introducing his subject, refers to Berta in presenting Blancheflor:

> Ce est du roy Floire l'enfant
> Et de Blancheflor la vaillant,
> De cui Berte aus granz piez fu nee,
> Puis fu en France coronnee;

---

[14] G. Fatini, ed., *Il Morgante di Luigi Pulci*, Classici italiani UTET (1948; repr. Turin: UTET, 1984), 28, 127.

[15] E. Faral, "Pour l'histoire de *Berte au grand pied* et de *Marcoul et Salomon*," *Romania* 40 (1911): 93–96, here 94.

[16] . . . sponsa fuit regi grandis pede nomine Berta
Venit ab Ungaria, sed Graeca matre reperta
Caesaris Heraclii filia namque fuit (G. Waitz, ed., *Gotifredi Viterbiensis Speculum Regum*, Monumenta Germaniae Historica (Series ed. Georgius Heinricus Pertz), Scriptorium 22 [Hannover: Hahn, 1872], 92); both Arfert, *Das Motiv von der unterschobenen Braut*, 66, and Colliot, *Adenet le roi. Berte aus grans pies*, 11, cite from the same edition though with slight errors in the copy. Note that Blançiflor, Charlemagne's queen in *Macario*, is here daughter of the Emperor of Constantinople, here named Cleramon.

[17] A Saint Denis la lievent au mostier,
Par droit non la font Betain huchier.
Pepin l'espouse et d'argant et d'or mier.
Puis fist ses noces sus au palais plenier.
Grant tenz vesqui avec celle moillier.
Et si en ot de li maint hiretier.

Fame fu au gentill baron,
Pepin le roy, pere Charlon.
Berte fu mere Charlemainne
Que puis tint et France et le Mainne (ll. 7–14).[18]

Vincent of Beauvais mentions her in his *Speculum historiale*, chapter 23 (ca. 1250): there too she is the daughter of Heraclius Caesar, and thus she and Charlemagne unite Greeks, Romans, and Germans (Colliot, *Adenet le roi*, 12). Pseudo-Turpin and texts deriving from it contain neither *Berta* nor *Enfances Charlemagne* (also known as *Karleto*, or *Mainet*). The *Grandes Chroniques* (referred to as the *Chronicles of St. Denis* by Primat, the first translator), in the portion that contains the death of Berta and Charles sharing the realm with his brother Carloman without dissension, make reference only once in passing to Berta.[19] The various versions of *Mainet*, the childhood of Charlemagne, mention Charlemagne's birth (cf. *Karleto*, which follows in V[13]). In the French version (twelfth century):

A veu de Karlot com on l'ot fait mener,
Et con li serf le fisent fors de France geter,
Et Pepin le bon roi orent fait enherber
Et Bertain sa moillier od le viaier *cler*;
Lui vaurent il mourdrir et par *engien tuer* . . . (ll. 89–93)[20]

Ne mais ançois qu'eüst celle moillier
Ot deus cens anz, si con j'oï noncier.
De ceste dame dont je ci vos devis
Ainq qu'il morust out il des enfans sis.

Charles li chaus en fu premiers nasquis (ll. 14545–55: H. J. Green, ed., *Anseÿs de Mes, According to Ms. N. (Bibliothèque de l'Arsenal 3143)* [Paris: Les Presses Modernes, 1939], 428).

[18] M. M. Pelan, ed. *Floire et Blancheflor*, Edition du MS. 1447 du fonds français avec notes, variantes et glossaire (Paris: Les Belles Lettres, 1956).

[19] For Primat, see R. Levine, ed., *A Thirteenth-Century Life of Charlemagne* (New York and London: Garland Publishing, Inc., 1991), 25 for the death of Charlemagne; 20 for Charles sharing the realm with his brother. For Bertha as the wife of Pepin the Short (referred to as the second Pepin), see R. Levine, ed., *France Before Charlemagne: A Translation from the "Grandes Chroniques"* (Lewiston, New York: Edwin Mellen Press, 1990), 286. This corresponds to J. Viard, ed., *Les Grandes Chroniques de France* (Paris: Société de l'histoire de France, 1922), 2: 257–58. On Primat and its reliability in general, see also Morrissey, *Charlemagne and France*, 90–95.

[20] G. Paris, "*Mainet*: fragments d'une chanson de geste du XIIe siècle," *Romania* 4 (1875): 305–37, here 333. The French version of *Mainet* is very fragmentary. There are clearly other points where references to the Berta story were made; e.g., fol. VI a, v. 8 begins "Alistes et . . . " which could be a reference to the daughter of the nurse (Paris, *Histoire poétique*, 334).

4.2.3 French versions.

The first French work to tell Berta's story, in however abbreviated a form, is the *Chronique saintongeaise* (early thirteenth century), followed by Philippe Mousket (finished ca. 1243). Other French versions or mentions are found in: Girard d'Amiens's *Charlemagne* (between 1285–1314); the *Miracles de Notre Dame* (ca. 1373); BN 5003 (late fourteenth– early fifteenth century); *Valentin et Orson* (1489); the Berlin prose version (MS. Gall. 130, fifteenth century) and Adenet le Rois's *Berte aus grans piés* (ca. 1272–1274); this last is placed at the end of the discussion, out of chronological order, because of its supreme importance in the *Berta* tradition and of the extensive discussion necessary.

4.2.3.1 *Chronique santongeaise*.

The *Chronique saintongeaise* account is quite brief.[21] (The differences between it and the Franco-Italian version are noted with numbers in the following account.) It recounts only that Pepin was counseled to marry. 1. Floire, king of Hungary, sends his daughter Berta to France. The nurse (unnamed) has her daughter sleep with Pepin in Berta's place, and says that Berta has cut the impostor with a knife. The hired men refuse to kill Berta. 2. Pepin's cowherd finds Berta in the forest. He and 3. Constance, his wife, keep her for 4. four years as their maid. Pepin meanwhile has two sons, 5. Remfri and Audri, with the impostor. Berta's mother (6. unnamed) hears how horrible the queen of France is and comes to see. The girl feigns illness; the queen of Hungary, however, 7. orders candles and reveals the imposture by the lack of big feet. The girl must tell her story. Pepin goes to hunt afterward, gets lost in the forest, and goes to the cowherd's home for lodging. He sees Berta and asks to sleep with her, which 8. the cowherd grants. 9. She reveals who she is and why she is there, while they sleep on a *char*. Pepin returns to Paris, where he reveals that he has found Berta. He then goes to battle against the Lorrains. 10. When he returns, Magniez is born. Pepin and Berta have two boys and 11. two girls; Magniez will be king next and is to be guarded by 12. "Rollant de laubara/loubare,"[22] duke of Brittany. This version is quite short. The characters' names differ from the Franco-Italian (and sometimes are missing); the profession of Berta's savior is different; and her personality is totally undeveloped. There is also no overt development of the etymology of Charlemagne's name, though the elements are present.

---

[21] I consult the Bourdillon edition (*Tote listoire de France*, 53–55).
[22] Could this be *Lonbare* or *Lonbara*, for "Lombardy"?

4.2.3.2 Philippe Mousket.

Philippe Mousket's version is also short; it cuts all description between events.[23] 1. Rois Flore sends Pepin's prospective wife with a maid and a servant, her mother, to Paris. In the evening, from sources unknown, 2. the girl is afraid and has the maid go in her place to Pepin.[24] Pepin believes the servant that Berta harbors ill will against her and sends the real Berta to be killed. A forester finds her; 3. she serves him and his wife well. Meanwhile, Pepin has two sons, 4. Raienfroit and Heldri, with the impostor. Pepin later comes into the woods, runs into the forester, and gets his wife back. There is no mention of any servants' names, the king or queen of Hungary having any concern about their daughter, or even Berta's big feet.[25]

4.2.3.3 Girard d'Amiens.

Girard d'Amiens's *Charlemagne* has now been edited; until recently, readers had to rely upon G. Paris's *Histoire poétique* (Appendix IV, 471), which includes little of the actual text. Reinhold summarizes it briefly also ("Über die verschiedenen Fassungen," 142–43).[26] Memmer too summarizes Girard, but more thoroughly. In Book I, Charles' family background is given; a short genealogical sketch includes Berta's story. The servant had two sons with Pepin (ll. 41–48). He will tell the correct story of Charlemagne, as treated in Latin (Memmer, *Die altfranzösische Bertasage*, 53). Pepin suffers the servant for a long time; he finally finds the real Berta in the forest with Simon the *voier*. With her he has two sons and two daughters. The older daughter is Gylain, whom Pepin would give to Mile

---

[23] The edition used is Reiffenberg, *Chronique rimée*. For general background about Mousket and his work, see also Morrissey, *Charlemagne and France*, 86–90.

[24] "La dame ki foment douta / Pepin por çou que grant vit a" (Reiffenberg, *Chronique Rimée*, 81–92), a concept which Gautier calls "obscène" (*Les Épopées françaises*, 3: 12). Memmer notes that Gröber calls *vit* an error for *pied* (*Die altfranzösische Bertasage*, 122 n. 2, quoting G. Gröber, *Grundriss der romanischen philologie* [Strasbourg: Trübner, 1902], 2.1: 783).

[25] However, in ll. 2334–2339, we find "Bierte ... fille au roi Florie / Et Blanceflor ... Bierte as grans-piés," so that the characteristic is used as a surname; it does not play any role in the plot (Reiffenberg, *Chronique rimée*).

[26] For a summary, see also Pelan, *Floire et Blancheflor*. See note 18, above. G. J. Brault announced that he was working on an edition ("The Legend of Charlemagne's Sin in Girart d'Amiens," *Romance Notes* 4 [1962]: 72–75, here 74), but it seems to have not been completed. J. R. Allen had also been working on Girard; he kindly put me in touch with Daniel Métraux, who sent me a copy of Book I of his edition in progress on diskette, as well as his summary of the entire text. It has now appeared in print, D. Métraux, *A Critical Edition of Girart D'Amiens: L'Istoire Le Roy Charlemaine,* Studies in French Literature 72 (Lewiston, NY: Mellen, 2003).

d'Ayglent as a wife, and who would become Roland's mother. The other daughter is Constance who becomes queen of Hungary. Both sons are called Carl; the older one is raised for twelve years by his grandfather Floire; the other, who stayed in France, is Charlemagne. Girart returns to the two sons born of the servant, and the *Enfances Charlemagne* follow (ll. 123ff).

4.2.3.4 *Miracle de Berte*.

The *Miracle of Berte* is a play.[27] The main characters among the thirty-two who appear are Floire, Blancheflour, Berta, the servant (Maliste), Thibert, and Aliste. The primary source is Adenet's *Berte*.[28] It lacks the similarity between Berta and Aliste; the hermit; and Adenet's scenes with the robbers and with a bear. It adds specific geographic details of the trip between France and Hungary and also the intervention of the Virgin Mary. It changes *Margiste* to *Maliste* (cf. "mal"); Maliste warns Berta that she might die from lying with Pepin; Berta's heart is replaced with that of a *pourcel*. Her story to her rescuer is that she is fleeing an abusive parent (*marrastre*). Queen Blanchefleur of Hungary comes alone to France, as in the Franco-Italian; the impostor is recognized since she will not hug her mother. Blanchefleur returns to Hungary without any satisfaction on the state of her daughter. Berta meanwhile stays with Simon (I use this form throughout, though it is spelled differently in different texts and even within a single text) and his family for nine and a half years, when Pepin becomes lost in the forest. He sees Berta at the chapel and asks for directions; then he attempts to seduce her. She must avow her real name in order to deter him. When they arrive at Simon's house, Pepin asks for information about her, but Simon knows nothing. She denies everything she has said once Pepin has left. Pepin writes to Hungary; Blanchefleur and Fleur come and recognize Berta, and eight days' festival is held at Mans.

4.2.3.5 *Chronique de France* / BN 5003.

BN 5003, fols. 91ᵛ–123ʳ, which Guessard calls the *Chroniques de France* and which G. Paris calls "une autre chronique" (*Histoire poétique*, 104), are also unedited, but again, G. Paris includes a summary of it in his Appendix V (*Histoire poétique*, 483); Guessard includes an excerpt relating to *Macario* in his appendix (*Macaire*,

---

[27] G. Paris and U. Robert, eds., "Miracle de Berte," in *Miracles de Nostre Dame par personnages* (Paris: Firmin Didot, 1880), 5: 154–255.

[28] A. Henry, "Note sur le *Miracle de Berthe*," in *Mélanges de linguistique et de littérature romanes à la mémoire d'István Frank, offerts par ses anciens maitres, ses amis et ses collègues de France et de l'étranger* (Saarbrücken: Universität des Saarlandes, 1957), 250–61, here 252, 256.

315–16); Feist gives the relevant excerpt (*Zur Kritik*, 40–41) and Memmer a summary (*Die altfranzösische Bertasage*, 132–33).[29] G. Paris calls it a *Histoire de Berte d'après Adenès*. Berta is Hungarian; the nurse has a pretty daughter who looks like Berta. Since the version (in the excerpt) is so short, much is glossed over. Where the substitution takes place is not clear: "Et quant Berthe volt dire qu'elle estoit celle qui devoit estre femme du roy, nul ne luy tesmoigna" (Feist, *Zur Kritik*, 40). One of the conspirators is inspired by God that anyone who kills Berta will himself die, so he will not allow her to be killed. She stays near Mans with a forester, "Simon le voyer." Meanwhile, Pepin has numerous children with the impostor. The plot is discovered through God's will. When the king comes to the forest Berta recognizes him but pretends not to. Simon's two daughters are not mentioned until he recounts to Pepin how he met Berta. Berta's parents play no role. The impostor is placed in a cloister. Charlemagne brings his men to the forest, takes Berta back to court, and marries her. They then have two sons, both named Charles.

4.2.3.6 *Valentine et Orson.*

Valentine et Orson is also unedited, but Feist includes the relevant text (*Zur Kritik*, 42). It is a prose version based on an earlier verse romance. The English version, a sixteenth-century translation, has been edited (Dickson, *Valentine and Orson*). Both contain a brief summary of the Berta story in Chapter 1 (Dickson, *Valentine and Orson*, 11–13). Neither the servant (here an old woman) nor the daughter are named (though the resemblance with Berta is marked in the Middle English—not in the French excerpt), but Hauffroy / Haufray and Henry (who "were came to put the Quene Berthe in exile"), as well as Charlemagne, are named, and the text includes a brief account of Charlemagne's being exiled by them. Valentine and Orson are the sons of Pepin's sister, Bellyssant, and Alexander, the Emperour [sic] of Constantinople, so Berta's story provides background—and foreshadowing—for the tale.

---

[29] I have not been able to find any publication of this MS. It is not Jules Viard's edition of *Les Grandes Chroniques de France*, Tome première. Société de l'histoire de France 395 (Paris. Société de l'histoire de France, 1920), for which he gives the shelf-mark St. Geneviève 782, anc. Lf (dated post-1250, because largely modeled on a Latin MS. of that date: *Grandes Chroniques*, xii–xiv). In any case, there is no Berta story there; she is mentioned only as Charlemagne's mother (volumes 2 and 3), including her death. Nor is it *Croniques [sic] et Conquestes de Charlemaine* perhaps by Primat, ed. R. Guiette (*Croniques et Conquestes de Charlemagne*, Académie royale de Belgique, Classe des Lettres et des Sciences Morales et Politiques. Collection des Anciens Auteurs Belges (Brussels: Palais des académies, 1940–1951), which publishes MSS. 9066, 9067, 9068 of the Royal Library of Belgium.

4.2.3.7 *Histoire de la Reine Berte et du Roy Pepin*.

The Berlin prose version, on the other hand, is available in a dissertation from 1933 and an edition from 2001.[30] Portions are also cited in Feist (*Zur Kritik*, 33–40). Florens/Florant and Blanchefleur's daughter Berta is suggested as Pepin's second wife. Berta agrees to the match. 1. Margiste is French, in the Hungarian court with her daughter Aliste and cousin Thibault. When the group arrives in Paris, 2. Margiste frightens Berta that whoever sleeps with the king on the first night risks death.[31] Margiste and the king have two sons and a daughter. Berta is taken to the forest of Mans and abandoned. 3. She hides in a robbers' den where 4. she resolves to keep her virginity under any conditions. The two robbers return and kill each other fighting over her. She runs away and finds a hermit who sends her to Simon the Voier (a local justice official) and his wife 5. Constance. Berta 6. invents an incredible story to explain her presence in the forest, and stays with them. The two daughters of the house, 7. Aiglante and Ysabel, learn to work silk with her and make a good dowry. Many offer to marry her but she refuses. Simon calls her his niece. Meanwhile, the queen of Hungary has been hearing stories about how evil her daughter is. She goes to Paris, to find the impostor sick in bed. The queen meets 8. Rainfroi and Hauldry, the impostor's two sons with Pepin. Finally she manages to slip into the girl's room, decides that this is not her daughter, and tears down the window coverings to reveal the girl's feet (9. this is the first reference to her feet). Blanchefleur drags her out by the hair. The king's council decides the fate of the impostor and her two children. Afterward, 10. Morant tells what had happened in the forest. The king's men search the forest of Maine. 11. Aliste and the two boys live since they were forced to their action by Aliste's mother. 12. Blanchefleur returns to Hungary. 13. Simon hears talk and wonders about Berta, especially since she holds the same name. She denies being the real queen. Pepin goes hunting in the Mans forest after he has given up ever finding her. Berta is in a chapel near Simon's house when the king is lost. He asks her the way to Mans; she directs him and 14. he tries to force her, eventually even

---

[30] G. M. Dorsey, "HISTOIRE DE LA ROYNE BERTE ET DU ROY PEPIN [sic] (Ms. Berlin Staatsbibliothek, 130)" (Ph.D. diss., The Johns Hopkins University, 1933), cited in B. Woledge, *Bibliographie des romans et nouvelles en prose française antérieurs à 1500* (Geneva: Droz, 1975), 106, # 138. The dissertation is available for consultation through Special Collections at The Johns Hopkins University Eisenhower Library. Recently, as this edition is nearing completion, the text has also been re-edited and published: P. Tylus, *Histoire de la Reine Berthe et du roy Pepin: Mise en Prose d'une chanson de geste* (Geneva: Droz, 2001).

[31] No specific reason is given. One cannot help wondering if the Mousket solution, typical of later interpolations and folktale motifs, might have been the implication in the earlier versions and others of this storyline as well.

throwing her to the ground. She tells him she is the queen, when Simon arrives. Pepin investigates her claim, but Simon and his wife know nothing. 15. They arrange for Pepin to hide behind a curtain while they interview Berta; she sticks to her story, she is not the queen. Pepin is still convinced that this is Berta. 16. He writes to Fleur and Blanchefleur to come in order to identify her. There is an emotional reunion; 17. they are married at Simon's house, and Berta is put to bed by Constance and Blanchefleur under Pepin's eyes, so that he will not be tricked again. 18. Gille, the mother of Roland, is engendered that night.

There are quite a number of differences between this version and V^{13}. Berta is described as having one foot bigger than the other. The legend of Charlemagne being engendered in a *char* is mentioned, but he is not the child born of the first night. Many of the differences here are typical to the French versions: the girl's mother plots to replace Berta, and the reason is hers, not Berta's. Robbers are added (as we shall see, this is typical of Adenet derivatives); Berta's story to Simon is quite complicated, and her stay with him and his family is quite lengthy and detailed. Her beauty, which causes her to turn down suitors, is also a new emphasis. Her decision (though not specifically religious) to maintain her virginity differs from the Franco-Italian, as does Pepin's forceful assault on her person. The names of characters are given throughout, and differ at points from the Franco-Italian.

4.2.3.8 Adenet le Rois.
Adenet le Rois's French version is the most famous. It dates to the end of the thirteenth century (Henry, *Les Œuvres*). There have been multiple editions printed, and it has continued in popularity through the centuries; for example, Brandin published an adapted version in 1924.[32] Gautier remarks, ". . . c'était LA PREMIÈRE DE NOS CHANSONS DE GESTE FRANÇAISES [sic] qui recevait en notre siècle l'honneur de l'impression" (*Les Épopées françaises*, 3: 9).

Adenet says he consulted the real historical source at St. Denis to get the true story. One day, Charles Martel is in Paris eating in his garden. A lion escapes from a cage, terrifying the guests. Pepin, only five and one-half feet tall, kills the beast. Pepin had married a girl named Blanchefleur as a first wife, but had no heirs. The barons therefore propose a new wife: the daughter of the king of

---

[32] In order by date of publication: P. Paris, ed., *Li Romans de Berte aus grans piés*, Romans des douze pairs de France 1 (Paris: Techener, 1832); A. Scheler, ed., *Li Roumans de Berte aus grans piés par Adenés le Rois* (Brussels: Comptoir Universel / C. Muquardt, 1874); A. Henry, ed., *Les Œuvres d'Adenet le Rois: Berte aus grans piés*, 1963; A. Henry, ed., *Berte as grans piés*, 1982); and finally, L. Brandin, ed., *Berthe au grand pied: D'après deux romans en vers du XIIIe siècle* (Paris: Boivin & Cie, 1924), is in modern French with ink illustrations.

Hungary. Pepin sends an envoy and escort; King Fleur and Queen Blanchefleur agree and send their daughter back with Pepin's men. Berta's mother sends Margiste, her daughter Aliste (who resembles Berta), and their cousin Tibert to help her.[33] In Paris, Margiste informs Berta of the danger in sleeping with Pepin and offers to send her own daughter instead. Berta enters the next morning to take Margiste's place, but Aliste cuts herself with a knife and accuses Berta. Pepin allows them to punish her. Three men take Berta into the forest of Mans to kill her. Moran, however, hesitates, and persuades them to let her go. Berta spends an agonizing night in the forest; two thieves find her and kill each other fighting over her. She swears not to tell anyone who she is unless she must to save her virginity. She follows a path to a hermit, who refuses to let her in, but gives her bread, and directs her to Simon and Constance.

After escaping a bear, Berta finds Simon. She tells him she has fled a stepmother who beat her. She gives her name as Berta, and stays nine and a half years, teaching the two girls sewing. Meanwhile, in Paris, Aliste and Pepin have two sons, Rainfroi and Heudri. The French hate her because of heavy taxes. The king and queen of Hungary in the meantime have lost their other two children; only Berta is left. The king decides to ask for Heudri to stay with them to assure the succession to the Hungarian throne. He sends a messenger, but is refused by Aliste. Blanchefleur has bad dreams about Berta and decides that she must go to France. She hears people malign the queen. A messenger alerts the court to Queen Blanchefleur's arrival, and the traitors arrange for Aliste's illness. Pepin goes to meet Blanchefleur. Finally, after numerous frustrations, Blanchefleur breaks into the sickroom and discovers no big feet! Margiste and the cousin die; Aliste is sent to the cloister, and Blanchefleur goes back to Hungary.

A search for Berta is unsuccessful. Simon and Constance keep asking Berta about her past without finding anything out. Pepin goes hunting in the forest of Mans, gets lost, and meets Berta coming out of a chapel near Simon's home. He asks her the way, and becomes increasingly insistent in asking her favors. She identifies herself. Once home, however, she denies it. Pepin listens from behind a curtain as Simon and Constance question her again. Pepin decides to send for her parents. Fleur and Blanchefleur leave for Paris immediately; after one night there, they accompany Pepin to Mans. As soon as Berta and Blanchefleur meet, they fall into each other's arms. They all rest at Simon's for three days. The first night, Gille is conceived, future mother of Roland. Pepin knights Simon and his two sons, and makes gifts to Constance and the two girls. After a few days of festival, all return to Paris. A month later, Fleur and Blanchefleur return to Hun-

---

[33] I will continue using the name "Berta" throughout in order make the connections between the heroines of different versions clear, though Adenet usually writes "Berthe."

gary. They will have another daughter, whom they will name Constance in honor of Berta's hostess. Charlemagne will be born afterwards to Pepin and Berta.

Adenet le Rois's version has evoked many studies and much commentary. Though he uses more characters and elaborates the plot in a more Christian manner (e.g., no extramarital affair between Berta and king Pepin), the plot is much the same and has been discussed at length and from all conceivable critical stances: philological, mythological, psychological, and historical. We will examine these more specifically in relation to V^{13} at the end of the discussion of differing versions. Adenet's version is extremely influential, appearing in many later versions, as is clear from the plot summary in relation to the Berlin manuscript, the Middle Dutch version, and others.

Whether or not the compiler of V^{13} was familiar with Adenet's work or whether Adenet was familiar with Italian tradition is unclear. Adenet lived and worked at the end of the thirteenth century in the Flanders area; our last reference to him is in 1297 (Henry, *Berte as grans piés*, 19). He went on a crusade with Gui de Flandre, and passed from Palermo (1270) through Italy and southern France to return home, passing through Sutri, Rome, Orvieto, Arezzo, Prato, Bologna, Modena, Milan, and Aosta.[34] That Adenet writes and V^{13} contains *Berta* and an *Enfances Ogier* is a striking coincidence. Henry suggests that V^{13} and Adenet both derive their *Enfances Ogier* from the same lost source (*Les Œuvres* [1963]: 20 ff). He is convinced, "Quelle qu'ait été la source du jongleur «franco-italien» de V XIII, son *rifacimento* est indépendant de toutes les autres versions connues" (40). Cremonesi carefully contrasts Adenet's version of both *Berta* and *Enfances Ogier* with the Franco-Italian versions. About *Berta*, she says, "Di tutte le versioni che conosciamo l'unica che permetta un confronto con la versione di V XIII è quella di Adenet, anche se si tengano presenti tutti gli aspetti negativi di tale confronto."[35] She argues that the compiler edits to his liking and needs. In comparing the two versions of *Ogier*, Cremonesi finds similarities of expression and plot development. In comparing the two with Raimbert's earlier text, she asks whether two different writers would be likely to develop a preceding poem in the same way.[36] She says, "Anch'io penso [referring to Rajna] . . . a confusioni mnemoniche, ma di uno che conosce il testo non solo per averlo udito, ma per averlo recitato o letto e che poi ha voluto rifare a modo suo . . . " including emphasizing Italy and Italian events (*Le Danois Oger*, liii). Though there are no solid

---

[34] A. Henry, ed., *Les Œuvres d'Adenet le Roi* (Brussels: Presses Universitaires de Bruxelles, 1951), 1: 23–29.

[35] C. Cremonesi, ed., *Berte da li pè grandi: Codice marciano XIII* (Milan: Varese, 1966), 32–33.

[36] C. Cremonesi, ed., *Le Danois Oger. Enfances–Chevalerie: Codice Marciano XIII* (Milan: Cisalpino-Goliardica, 1977), xliv.

proofs of any specific connection between Adenet le Rois and V[13], the compiler of V[13] recycles (pun intended) material that is circulating in the thirteenth and fourteenth centuries that is common also to Adenet le Rois in the case of both *Berta* and *Enfances Ogier.*

The differences in French stories from V[13]'s version of *Berta* lie in 1. names of people and places which are given; 2. the active role of the servant and the presence of her mother; 3. the length and development of various sections: a. Pepin's decision to marry; b. the marriage ceremony; c. time Berta spends with Simon and family; d. profession and family state of "Simon"; e. persistence of Queen Blanchefleur, depending upon the redactor; 4. the story—and its existence—which Berta gives for her presence in the forest; 5. the number of times the Hungarian queen (or king and queen) come to France; 6. the "blood will tell" concept: the evil Maganzesi twin overtaxes and is hated.

4.2.4 Iberian Versions.

4.2.4.1 *Gran conquista de Ultramar.*

In Spain, the *Gran conquista de Ultramar* (late thirteenth–early fourteenth century) also recounts Berta's story, but in a different context (Book 2, 43).[37] It is cited as part of the background of a combatant, Folquer Ubert de Chartres. There are numerous differences of detail here too. Berta is the daughter of 1. king Flores and queen Blancaflor of Almeria, Spain (cf. the *Volksbuch*). The beginning of the story is quite short; in a summary we learn that the nurse has her daughter take Berta's place because 2. Berta fears to die. Berta is accused of attempted harm. She is taken to the forest, 3. tied to a tree in only her shirt 4. in January. The impostor and Pepin have two sons, 5. Manfre and Carlon. Pepin's forest-keeper saves her after he hears her (unspecified) story. He hosts her for 6. three years, calling her 7. his daughter. Pepin comes hunting and orders the girl brought to his bed. 8. She is brought (there is no discussion). 9. "Cárlos Mainete el Bueno" is conceived (no *char* or similar name derivation). The forester is to take care of Berta. 10. Berta's father, Flores, dies; Blancaflor is sad and comes to see her daughter. The queen, as elsewhere, must penetrate the façade of illness; she is quite suspicious and when she checks Berta over, finds normal feet, not 11. joined toes. She drags Berta out of her room by her hair. The girl and her mother must tell Pepin

---

[37] Don P. de Gayangos, ed., *La Gran conquista de ultramar que mandó escribir el rey Don Alfonso el Sabio* (Madrid: M. Rivadeneyra, 1858). H. Goldberg, *Motif-Index of Medieval Spanish Folk Narratives* (Tempe, AZ: MRTS, 1998), 46 (H50), 107 (K1911), includes this version under the motifs of "Recognition by bodily marks or physical attributes" and "The false bride."

the truth. Pepin has a search made, and calls the forester. 12. The forester will talk only to Pepin himself, and he includes Cárlos, now six years old, in his account. Pepin calls for Berta and tells her mother. When they meet, the mother Blancaflor wants revenge; the impostor's mother is killed; 13. the daughter is allowed to give birth to the child she is now expecting and then will be immured and live on bread and water only. 14. Morante and Mayugot are assigned to help Cárlos. 15. Queen Blancaflor is extravagant in her weeping, yelling, etc., to the extent that, in joy or anguish, courtiers want to lock her up. Here too, the motivation for substitution of the bride, the names, time spans, and dates, and the story length are different. The Spanish version here, in fact, is different from all other versions in certain aspects and is the first Spanish version known.[38]

4.2.4.2 *Noches de invierno.*

Noches de invierno is mentioned by both G. Paris and Gautier, who summarize it as part of the tradition. Antonio de Eslava seems to have been born ca. 1570.[39] He was much influenced by Italian literature. Aliste offers to take Berta's place while Berta flees with another (Dudon) whom she loved before (*Les Épopées françaises*, 3: 13), an account which we can compare with Aliste's story about Berta in the *Reali*. Memmer (*Die altfranzösische Bertasage*, 151–52) and Colliot (*Adenet le roi*) summarize it at length. Berta is accompanied by the count of Burgundy to Pepin's residence where she is to be his third wife. Fiameta is her physical twin, from the house of Magance, in her escort. Berta reveals her disgust at Pepin's physical form, especially since she loves Dudon of Lis. She suggests the change of role. Fiameta agrees and soon conceives of the idea of killing Berta; she communicates with her relatives, who assist her. Fiameta goes to Pepin and tells Berta to go to the gallery near the garden; the Maganzesi take her from the garden. Especially in the use of the garden, this version quite resembles the Italian *Reali*. Berta stays near Magno with a knight named Lipulo and his wife Sintia, who are childless, for two years until Pepin finds her.

---

[38] A. Rey, "Las Leyendas del ciclo carolingio en la *Gran conquista de ultramar*," *Romance Philology* 3 (1949–1950): 172–81, here 174.

[39] J. Barella Vigal, ed. *Antonio de Eslava. Noches de Invierno* (Pamplona: Gobierno de Navarra, 1986), 13.

4.2.4.3 Catalan versions.

Recently, A. M. Mussons has called attention to two versions in Catalan:[40] the *Libre de les nobleses dels reys* dated to the fifteenth century, and an untitled genealogy of the kings of France dating to the end of the fourteenth century. She suggests that there are further copies in other genealogical manuscripts.[41] The *Libre* contains eight chapters recounting the Berta story (Mussons, "Berthe ou le labyrinthe," 44). This is similar to the German versions such as *Weihenstephan* (see below), in that a count substitutes his own daughter before arriving in Paris. The usual events occur (though she stays with two young men in the woods), and Berta returns in victory to Paris after her mother has revealed the impostor. The impostor retires to a convent. The names are different: Blanchaflor is Pepin's mother; the royal couple's first child is Lotary; Berta is the daughter of the king of Germany. According to Mussons's summary, there is no mention of Berta's feet, which would be consonant with those versions having a substitution before arrival at Paris. In the second text, Berta's story is not complete. It would seem to follow the same lines as the first.[42]

4.2.5 German texts.

In Germany, several texts contain Berta's story or references to it. Earlier texts seem to have not known the details; thus there is a reference to Berta in the *Kaiserchronik* (ca. 1150) but no story.[43] The story appears briefly in Stricker's *Karl der*

---

[40] A. M. Mussons [Freixas], "La Història del rei Pipí i la filla de l'emperador d'Alemanya," in *Actes du XIe Congrès international de la Société Rencesvals (Barcelone, 22–27 août 1988)*, spec. issue of *Boletín de la Real Academia de Buenas Letras de Barcelona* 21–22 (1990): 297–312. See also A. G. Elliot, "The Emperor's Daughter: A Catalan Account of Charlemagne's Mother," *Romance Philology* 34 (1981): 398–416.

[41] A. M. Mussons [Freixas], "Berthe ou le labyrinthe généalogique," *Revue des langues romanes* 94 (1990): 39–59; for genealogical commentary, see 47.

[42] I do not dwell on these versions as I have not been able to consult the text and must rely on Mussons's summaries. As presented in her article, the lack of female names would seem to indicate a patriarchal genealogical survey, which is only a portion of the Italian (Mussons, "Berthe ou le labyrinthe").

[43] For the references to Berta, see Folz, *Le Souvenir et la légende*, 162; H. F. Massman, ed., *Der keiser und der kunige buoch oder die sogennante Kaiserchronik, Gedicht des zwölften Jahrhunderts* (Quedlinburg and Leipzig: Gottfr. Basse, 1849), 378. The reference is: "Karl der Pippînnes sun / der sæligen Berhtun" (ll. 14831–32) [Karl the son of Pepin / of the blessed Berta]. (The more recent edition, E. Schröder, ed., *Die Kaiserchronik eines Regensburger geistlichen* [Hannover: Hahnsche, 1852], differs only offering the form "Perhtun"; the passage there is ll. 14815–16, 349.) Folz says that at that time, "les légendes relatives à cette mystérieuse personne n'ont pas encore pénétré en Allemagne" (Folz, *Le Souvenir et la légende*, 162).

Grosse (ca. 1230–1235),[44] and in Henry of Munich's *Chronik* (early fourteenth century, unedited), basically copied from Stricker, and is elaborated in various later chronicles, for example the prose *Weihenstephan Chronik* (fifteenth century), Wolter's Latin *Chronica Bremensis* (ca. 1475), Füetrer's *Bayerische Chronik* (fifteenth century), as well as the Zurich *Volksbücher* by Georg Hohenmut (manuscript date 1475).[45] There are other chronicles based on these. Unfortunately, Henry of Munich's *Chronik* is as yet unedited, though Massman (*Der keiser und der kunige buoch*, 977), Reinhold ("Über die verschiedenen Fassungen," 8) and Memmer (*Die altfranzösische Bertasage*, 155) include the relevant lines; other texts are difficult to obtain. We will therefore briefly examine Stricker, *Weihenstephan* in its summary (Reinhold, "Über die verschiedenen Fassungen," 9–18; Freitag, *Die sogenannte Chronik*, esp. 45–57), Wolter, and then Füetrer's and Hohenmut's versions. It is frequently necessary to rely on Folz and Gautier for supporting information.

4.2.5.1 Stricker.
Stricker's *Karl der Grosse* contains a brief introduction (ll. 124–142) that leads into an account of Charlemagne's youth. The eighteen lines mention that Pepin's wife was lost (because exchanged), that he found her again later, that they had a daughter, Gertrude, and a son, Karl, and that Pepin died shortly thereafter. The poet comments "daz wære ze sagene ze lanc, / wie daz dinc allez ergie" [it's too long to tell how the whole thing went] (Bartsch, *Karl der Grosse*, 4 [ll. 132–133]). There is too little information to discuss any differences here, other than the name of a daughter, Gertrude, a name not present in the Italian or French versions of *Berta* (cf. Memmer, *Die altfranzösische Bertasage*, 154–55). Henry of Munich (ca. 1320–1325) follows Stricker almost word for word, so the same limitations apply (Massman, *Der keiser und der kunige buoch*, 977; Reinhold, "Über die verschiedenen Fassungen," 8; Memmer, *Die altfranzösische Bertasage*, 155).

---

[44] K. Bartsch, ed., *Karl der Grosse von dem Stricker* (Quedlinburg and Leipzig: Gottfr. Basse, 1857; Berlin: W. de Gruyter, 1965), gives the date of Stricker. In general, unless specified otherwise, dates of German materials here are drawn from Folz. Modern critics seem to agree on dating in most cases, but Folz is careful to explain whence disagreements arise, and therefore I follow his dates for texts.

[45] Other chronicles contain related stories but not close enough to include here. For example, in Enikel (last quarter of thirteenth century), which derives its version from the *Kaiserchronik*, a rumor that Charlemagne is dead forces him to return rapidly to avoid Berta's remarrying (Folz, *Le Souvenir et la légende*, 325). I abbreviate the *Chronik von Weihenstephan* throughout this commentary as *Weihenstephan Chronik* or *Weihenstephan* as do other critics.

4.2.5.2 *Weihenstephan Weltchronik.*

Weihenstephan Chronik has Berta as a daughter of the king of Britaia [sic: Reinhold, "Über die verschiedenen Fassungen," 10], from Kerlingen. They exchange pictures in light of a proposed betrothal. The head of the intrigue is the *Hofmeister*, who takes charge of the affair. He goes to examine visually the prospective bride. He contrives together with his wife to replace her with their youngest daughter, who resembles Berta. He and his three sons escort Berta from Kerlingen, but they take her goods, and he sends her with two henchmen to be killed. She begs for mercy, and is released. Berta stays with a miller. Pepin marries the chamberlain's daughter, and they have three sons, Leo, Weneman, and Rapot, and a daughter, Agnes. Seven years later, Pepin goes hunting and gets lost in the company of an astrologer; a charcoal-maker directs him to the miller. The astrologer predicts that if he sleeps with his true wife he will have an important son, ruler of Christendom. The miller brings forth his two daughters, then finally Berta. Berta accepts Pepin and shows him her ring to identify herself. She stays a number of years with the miller. Berta and Pepin's son is named Karl. Karl is brought to court to be trained with his stepbrothers; he reveals the truth. Pepin takes counsel from the barons: the chamberlain is killed, his wife cloistered.[46]

4.2.5.3 Wolter.

Wolter's Latin *Chronik* section including Berta is summarized by Massman (*Der keiser und der kunige buoch*, 976–77), Reinhold ("Über die verschiedenen Fassungen," 18–19), and Memmer (*Die altfranzösische Bertasage*, 158–59).[47] It is quite similar to the *Weihenstephan*, in contrast with the romance-language versions. Pepin's messengers (here there are three instead of one) are supposed to bring him his new bride, the daughter of king Theodoric of Swabia, Bavaria, and Austria. They decide to eliminate her *en route*. One of the henchmen does not want to kill her, so they leave her alone. She comes upon a miller and his daughter in the evening. She stays with them. They sell her remaining costly things in the next town in order to help pay for food. Pepin marries the daughter of a councilor instead of Berta; together they have a son and daughter. One day Pepin is hunting in that same wood, gets lost, and comes upon the miller. He asks for lodging overnight. When he sees the miller's (supposed) two daughters, he asks for one as a bedfellow for the night. Berta goes, and conceives a king (n.b. it is not clear

---

[46] Reinhold ("Über die verschiedenen Fassungen," 10–12), Memmer (*Die altfranzösische Bertasage*, 155–58), and Freitag (*Die sogenannte Chronik*) summarize the text (Freitag also includes excerpts); Krämer's edition includes only the "world history" portion, since Freitag discussed the Charlemagne story (*Die sogennante Weihenstephaner*, 10, 173).

[47] The source for Heinrich Wolter is H. Meibom Jr., ed., *Rerum Germanicarum 2, Historicos Germanicos* (Helmstedt : G.W. Hamm, 1688), 19–23.

whether or not she reveals the truth of who she is). He leaves her behind, telling the miller to come to him with a distaff if a girl is born, or a bow and arrow if a boy. It is a boy, and when the miller comes to court, the queen cries out to remove the ugly "kerl"; thus the king names the boy "Karl." After the boy grows up, Pepin takes him with his own sons, which upsets the queen, so Pepin sends him to Theoderic. Berta reveals her identity to her son during his frequent visits. He, in turn, tells his grandmother about her. Berta's mother then goes to France and finds the impostor in Berta's place. She reveals the true situation; the traitors are condemned to death (except for the one who had saved Berta). Karl brings his mother, whom his grandmother (Berta's mother) immediately recognizes. Berta becomes queen, and Karl king, of France. The specific courtiers who replace her with a daughter of theirs are not named; the names of Pepin's children with the impostor are not given. There is no stargazer or astrologer with Pepin when he finds the miller, as there is in other German versions.

4.2.5.4 World histories.
The many fifteenth-century world histories which tie the local lords to nobility include the Carolingian empire. Füetrer's *Bayerische Chronik* contains a lengthy and interesting version of Berta.[48] Here an evil steward arranges to substitute his daughter for the daughter of the king of Kerlingen, whom Pepin has never seen. His own daughter had been kept by relatives away from town, and thus had never been seen by anyone at court. He arranges to be the messenger to Kerlingen, and brings a picture of the prospective bride—his own daughter! (Note that there is thus no need for close resemblance between the impostor and prospective bride.) While escorting the bride-to-be through the woods, the steward orders her killed. The men show her mercy; she thus wanders through the woods, until she comes to a mill (there is no hermit or other guide). She says only that she has lost her way. She gives him a ring and a piece of clothing to sell in the market, with instructions as to their worth, to buy what she needs. She sews beautiful bags. Meanwhile, Pepin and the impostor have three sons and a daughter, Rapot, Wineman, Marchona, and Leo (who would become pope). Pepin, with his astrologer, loses his way through the wood one day. The king admires the beautiful clothwork, and hears the whole story from the miller (as he knows it). The king

---

[48] R. Spiller, ed., *Ulrich Füetrer. Bayerische Chronik*, Quellen und Erörterungen zur bayerischen und deutschen Geschichte (1909; repr. Aalen: Scientia Verlag, 1969), 83–98 (paragraphs 119–40); compare Memmer, *Die altfranzösische Bertasage*, 161–62. According to Spiller, Füetrer did not use the *Weihenstephan Chronik* or any oral version, but rather the written precedents of the *Weihenstephan Chronik* (Spiller, *Ulrich Füetrer*, lv). Spiller's introduction discusses the sources at length, including the *Bertasage*, where it came from and what it became.

wishes to see the girl who had made the cloth. When he asks for the whole story, she says she has sworn not to tell. The philosopher interrupts to tell Pepin that he must lie with his real wife that night. So Berta (here, Perchta) tells all, including her promise. That night she and Pepin sleep together and Charles is conceived. Pepin returns to court, and calls for the two youths who were to put her to death, for confirmation of her story. He sends them to the miller. The king calls his court together; he tells of the crime and asks the steward what the punishment should be. He refuses to answer. The steward is condemned to death and his wife is immured. The queen becomes very ill because of her father's shameful death and her mother's imprisonment, and dies soon after. Perchta is then brought back and crowned as queen. So much time had passed that she had given birth to their child Karolus at the miller's. Many details are missing here — for example, the miller's family and condemnation of the impostor — so many details of Adenet's story as well as of the Franco-Italian are not present.

4.2.5.5 Hohenmut.

Hohenmut's Zurich *Volksbuch* contains the Berta story;[49] it is also summarized in Modern German in a 1929 version of the Charlemagne tale; Reinhold ("Über die verschiedenen Fassungen," 19–20) and Memmer (*Die altfranzösische Bertasage*, 159–61) include summaries as well. Berta's parents are Florus and P(l)antschiflur of Spain. When she is fifteen years old, she is married to Pepin, king of France. Pepin is big and fat (!), rich and powerful. His first wife, with whom he had had two sons, Wineman and Rappote, dies. When she dies, he marries Berta. She is brought to him with her maid, a young girl. The king rides forth to meet them, and Berta sees that he is big and tall and is afraid. So she asks her maid to take her place. The king knows no better, and the two have a son, Leo, who will become pope. All the while, Berta is with a miller at a mill. This miller has many daughters. Once when Pepin is out riding, he ends up at the mill for the night. His astrologer points out the stars to Pepin and says that he should lie with his real wife that night to have a son who would be a blessing to Christendom. Pepin rejects this as impossible, but that, God willing, it might at least occur with another willing maid. He asks the miller to send him each of his daughters with a loaf of bread. They each toss the loaf at him. He notices that Berta is not participating. The king says that she too must come. She takes off her kerchief, wraps it around the bread, and kneels to the king to offer it. Pepin likes this and asks her to join him. They sleep together on the "karren" and she becomes pregnant. She

---

[49] A. Bachmann and S. Singer, eds., *Deutsche Volksbücher aus einer Zürcher Handschrift des fünfzehnten Jahrhunderts* (Tübingen: Litterarischer Verein, 1889), is the edition of the *Volksbuch* used here; see 15–17 for the reference. P. Zaunert, ed., *Das deutsche Volksbuch von Karl dem Grossen (Das Buch vom heiligen Karl)* (Jena: Eugen Diederichs, 1929), 67–69, contains the modern German version.

tells him her whole story, and Pepin is happy at finding his true wife. He returns and has the other woman tell the truth, assuring her that no evil will happen to her. Pepin arranges things for her and her son. Pepin takes Berta as his true wife; when their son is born, he calls him "Karlus" since the child was conceived on a cart. Berta then also had a daughter named Gertrut. Shortly afterward, Pepin dies. Reinhold suggests that the author here knew both the Germanic and Romance versions, since the noble friend is asked to take Berta's place.

We notice here several differences between the German and French/Franco-Italian versions. The names are different, as are the distribution of children—which are the children of which wife. The national origin of the wife is also varied: Kerlingen or Spain, not Hungary. Furthermore, there are no big feet! Her main physical feature, and her sharing her general physical characteristics with the impostor, have both disappeared. A miller instead of a forester helps her. The agency of Berta herself is also quite noticeable. As Folz says, "la fiancée légitime de Pépin porte personellement la responsabilité de son destin" (*Le Souvenir et la légende*, 472). That is, though Pepin's councilors may remove her, she, not a servant or friend, supports herself personally via her sewing. When Pepin comes to the forest, she chooses actions that make her stand out and force Pepin to choose her as a bedmate.[50]

4.2.6 Scandinavian versions.

Scandinavia lacks references to Berta's history; the *Karlamagnús Saga* contains only the fact that Pepin was married to a queen Berta "who was called Bertha the Big-footed," "et était surnommée Berta au(x) grand(s) pied(s)"—so the number of big feet is not clear.[51]

---

[50] The edition by Zaunert, which the author bases on Johann Christoph Aretin's *Älteste Sage über die Geburt und Jugend Karls des Großen. Zum erstenmale bekannt gemacht und erläutert* (Munich: J. Schererschen Kunst, 1803), differs even further. The daughter is from Britannien (cf. *Weihenstephan*). Berta sees smoke in the woods, and a coal-maker (whom she thinks is the devil) gives her bread and water, then leads her to the miller. The miller sells her items of value at Augsburg, where he then buys silk and thread for her to make more items to support herself. The miller becomes rich from her work. Pepin and his astrologer come by the wood, the miller has only two daughters and Berta. Pepin must sleep with a woman, but the astrology says that neither daughter is the right one. Berta reveals her story, and they lie together. Again, the miller is to bring a bow and an arrow for a boy, a distaff for a girl. Berta asks him not to come until the child is born. Pepin is away at war for many years, and finally she is willing to have him back with her. The steward is punished by the words of his own sons.

[51] The citations are from the following editions: English, from C. Hieatt, trans., *Karlamagnús Saga: The Saga of Charlemagne and his Heroes*, 1 [Parts I–III], Mediaeval Sources in Translation 17 (Toronto: Pontifical Institute of Mediaeval Studies, 1975), 54. The

4.2.7 Dutch version.

There exists a fragment in Middle Dutch, *Beerte metten breden voeten*, in extremely damaged condition.[52] It dates to the end of the fourteenth or early fifteenth century.[53] The beginning is entirely missing; the fragment begins with Pippijn hearing how Symoen (= Simon) met Beerte in the forest. He tells all he knows about her: he met her 1. fifteen years ago and 2. they have called her their niece to protect her. (It is unclear whether they actually know that she is the king's wife.) 3. Symoen had heard six years ago that a woman was lost. 4. Beerte says that she claimed to be queen just to preserve her virginity (143–160). There are illegible segments around this section (119–142; 161–200) and there is a lacuna afterward. (One cannot help wondering whether or not Pippijn hides behind the curtain to overhear a more private interview between Symoen and Constance here as he does in the Adenet and Berlin versions.) 5. Florijs and Blancefloer go to France to help Peppijn identify Beerte. After many damaged lines, Pippijn meets with Symoen, who leads Beerte to Blanceflor. Blanceflor asks how Symoen found her, and we again hear his tale. Notable here are also 6. the lack of any mention of big feet; the time frame (fifteen years!); 7. missing references to Charlemagne; and 8. Beerte's striking beauty (again, compare the Berlin version, where she has many suitors). However, since the piece is so fragmentary, it is difficult to make much of it. It is related to Adenet's *Berthe* and to the Berlin fragment as well.[54] There

---

French translation is K. Togeby and P. Halleux, eds., *Karlamagnús Saga. Branches 1, 3, 7 et 9*, Texte norrois édité par Agnete Loth, Traduction français par Annette Patron-Godefroit, avec une étude par Povl Skårup (Copenhagen: C.A. Reitzels Boghandel [La Société pour l'étude de la langue et de la littérature danoises], 1980), 2.

[52] A summary appears in Memmer (*Die altfranzösische Bertasage*, 152–54), and Besamusca also summarizes the plot quite effectively ("Beerte metten breden voeten," *Olifant* 19 [1994–1995]: 145–53).

[53] I would like to thank Geert Claassens for providing me with a precise summary of the Dutch version in English, together with notes about its dating and background. The numbers in this outline refer to his summary by line numbers (personal communication 1996).

[54] Compare B. Besamusca, "'Beerte metten breden voeten'. Diplomatische uitgave van het enig overgeleverde fragment," *Tijdschrift voor Nederlandse Taal- en Letterkunde* 102 (1986): 1–20. G. Claassens says, "Though it is evident that Adenet's *Berte* was the source, this does not imply that the translation was necessarily a slavish one" (personal communication, 1996). As I do not read Dutch fluently, I will not attempt further analysis. I can see that Besamusca cites the Berlin version, and that there are certain undeniable similarities. Memmer says that it is derived from Adenet (*Die altfranzösische Bertasage*, 235). Recently B. Besamusca edited and translated the fragment and commented upon it: "Berte metten breden voeten," *Olifant* 23.1 (2004): 14–25.

are other shorter references in Dutch, as in French. The Middle Dutch *Floris ende Blancefloer* also contains a reference to Berta, similar to that in the French ("Baerte hietsi metten breden voeten, (. . .), Die nam te wive die coninc Puppijn, Een gheweldich coninc, ende wan an hare Een kint, daer vele af te segghen ware, Dat was die coninc Kaerle van Vrankerike, (...)," ll. 3961–3966 [(A daughter had he by his wife,) Baerte she was called, with big feet . . . Whom king Pepin took to wife, A mighty king, and begot on her A child, about whom much could be told, That was king Charles of France].[55]

4.2.8 English versions.
There are no medieval English versions.

4.2.9 Discussion.
Memmer effectively divides the story into five parts in order to discuss the differences: first, Berta's origin, character, and betrothal; second, Berta's voyage and the events en route; third, Berta's life and difficulties until the betrayal is discovered; fourth, Berta's return to the palace and the punishment of the traitors; and finally, the death of Berta and Pepin and Charlemagne's youth. This last will be covered at greater length in the next section of the introduction (4.3). Memmer's divisions can clarify the points of difference: Berta is designated as a royal daughter, but from different kingdoms in different versions; her betrothal, in some cases, is through pictures, in others through direct personal approval of advisors. Berta's voyage can be through hostile lands or can be rerouted by hostile court personnel; in German versions, the false bride is substituted en route. In all versions, Berta lives a life of hardship, in some contributing to her own living, in others acting as a servant, but in any case living beneath her station. The amount of time she remains in the forest and her behavior when approached by Pepin, her rightful husband, differ. She does return to the court, and the impostor and any relatives implicated in the plot are punished either with death or with banishment to a nunnery.

This overwhelming collection of stories from different countries and in many variations has been examined in the light of prevailing literary critical tendencies of the times since they have first come to light. The most important of these

---

[55] J. J. Mak, ed. *Floris ende Blancefloer van Diederic van Assenede* (Zwolle: Tjeenk Willink, 1960), 170–71. I thank G. Claassens for this reference (2002). Unfortunately, Dutch versions of Old French texts are little known and less available than many others, and remain beyond the linguistic competence of many. It is to be hoped that this will be remedied in the near future; a series of translations are scheduled for publication in *Olifant*. The first portion appeared in the 23, 1 (2004) volume, as mentioned above, see note 54.

are historical, mythological, folkloric, philological, psychological, and socioeconomic. We have already touched upon the historical traces at the beginning of this chapter; let us examine the other possibilities here.

4.2.9.1 Mythological Symbolism.
One of the first attempts to explain the story and its frequency was that of the mythological symbolism embodied in the story. The three proposals are 1. Berta is the bride of the sun, lost to her people during the winter (G. Paris, *Histoire poétique*, 432); 2. she is Perchta / Perhta, a German wood nymph, who wanders through the woods with a foot big from use on the spinning wheel; or, finally, 3. she is the Germanic Frau Holle/Hullda, as seen in a fourteenth-century Icelandic saga, Odin's girlfriend (not wife) who stayed in the woods with two daughters (Feist, *Zur Kritik*, 22–25). Critics have generally denied these possibilities because of the lack of connections between Germanic and Romance tradition. The Germanic versions of *Berta*, as we have seen, do not have big feet or a big foot; furthermore, the spinning wheel did not exist until the fifteenth century, so is unlikely to have passed thence into French *chansons*. Hulda seems to be a later derivation as well, and part of Epiphany celebrations (Arfert, *Das Motiv von der unterschobenen Braut*, 70).

4.2.9.2 Fairy tale sources.
The similarity of many of the events in the *Berta* story with fairy tales has not gone unremarked. A number of themes reappear within this compilation as well as elsewhere, such as the repudiated queen lost in the woods. The substituted bride has been a regular subject of analysis.[56] Arfert in 1897 includes a separate section on the origin and development of the Berta story (*Das Motiv von der unterschobenen Braut*, 59–71). He admits that the late date of the first appearance of *Berta* makes linking the story to mythical-folkloric motifs difficult. He points out the similarities to the tales he has collected, especially the mutilated bride, the woman lost in the wilderness, executioners who forgive the victim, and her long wanderings (62). The motif of the rejected and then restored bride is found in much medieval literature as well as the oldest Indian collections, the Greek novels, and the newest fairy tales. He compares Berta with Sibilla, Genoveva,

---

[56] Arfert (*Das Motiv von der unterschobenen Braut*); Margaret Schlauch (*Chaucer's Constance and Accused Queens* [New York: New York University Press, 1927]); Memmer (*Die altfranzösische Bertasage*); Riquer (*Los cantares de gestas francesas*); Colliot (*Adenet le roi*); and K. Wais ("Märchen und Chanson de geste: Themengeschichtliches zu Robert le Diable, Berte aus grans piés, Loher und Maller," in *Festgabe Julius Wilhelm zum 80. Geburtstag*, ed. Hugo Laitenberger [Wiesbaden: Steiner, 1977], 120–38, 314–34) are the primary critics to examine these themes, surveying earlier criticism as well.

and others.[57] Particularly interesting is that many of the fairy tales' heroines seek to escape unnatural marriage with their fathers (Pepin's supposed age and deformity/ies would make him fit into an "unnatural" category, perhaps). Weaving in a hut in the woods is a feature of the story (63), but women are frequently shown as supporting themselves by weaving or sewing.[58] So how did what is clearly an extension of the folk-story come to be associated with Berta? Pepin probably had a concubine (or possibly more than one); but history tells us nothing. Einhard says he will tell nothing of Charlemagne's youth; people will make things up about famous people to fill the blanks. Stories grow with time. How far the poet (and he specifies that he thinks an individual poet is the case here) used the underlying legend is unclear; but that he found material to build with is clear (65). The developments must have been quite early, since Berta is already from Hungary and the half-siblings who will torment Charlemagne are already found in the first documents. Arfert points out the influence of *Tristan and Iseut* in the Brangwein-like switch, and says that the German versions could precede the French, which were influenced by *Tristan*. This is then a tale "aus historisch-anecdotenhaften Ueberlieferungen, aus dem Märchen von der unterschobenen Braut und dem internationalem Novellenmotiv von der verläumdeten und wiederhergestellten Frau" [from historical-anecdotal developments, from the fairy tales of the substituted bride and the international novella-motif of the falsely-accused and restored wife] which underwent many changes as it came into the literary sphere (69). Her big feet and her sewing things to pay for her expenses go together too: they should be connected with swan maidens and the Germanic goddess Freyja. When and why they were added to the tale can only be conjectured (70). The connection with Berta and Hollen is impossible because of the time factor (70–71). Schlauch (*Chaucer's Constance*) is most interested in Chaucer's Constance, but includes many international versions of the falsely accused spouse, and will be of more interest in discussing *Macaire* (below, section 4.6). Memmer in 1935 gives summaries of all the versions he knows, attempts to figure out the original form from that information (after having divided it into various pieces: the parents of the heroine; the heroine herself and her character;

---

[57] Sibilla is Charlemagne's queen whom we shall see as Blançiflor in *Macaire*, the last poem of V[13]. Geneviève of Brabant is the heroine of a popular medieval legend (first in the *Golden Legend*) who was accused of adultery by Seneschal Golo who had tried to seduce her. Her husband, Siegfried, believes the accusation. She escapes death thanks to the servants who were to kill her. Her husband discovers her innocence much later, after she had suffered so much that she soon died (*Grand Dictionnaire Encyclopédique* [Paris: Larousse, 1962], s.v. "Geneviève de Brabant.").

[58] Thus, for example, D. Herlihy's *Opera muliebria: Women and Work in Medieval Europe* (New York: McGraw-Hill, 1990), 56–59 on the subject of literary references to sewing and similar work.

her homeland and her trip to court; the happenings on the trip; the betrayal; her reinstatement and the punishment of traitors). He too says that people fill in with folk-tales where they do not know or understand history (*Die altfranzösische Bertasage*, 224). He maintains that the work was done in a wide circle, not just by one poet. He agrees with Rajna that the *Mainet* (= *Karleto*) story came first, and that there was confusion especially with Charles Martel's illegitimate birth. He says that this is a folk development that mixes "den namen einer historischen persönlichkeit mit einem weitverbreiteten märchenstoff [sic]" [the name of an historical person with a widespread fairy-tale motif] (225). As a result, he argues that the poem was originally brought from the Germanic homeland, reworked during the ninth century in Pepin's homeland area (Herstal, Landen, Vlamenland) with historical elements, and then developed into two separate lines, the French and the German (241–42). Riquer and Colliot point out these earlier studies and call our attention to the folk-themes and discussions about them: Riquer discusses the "goose-foot" (*pédauque / pedes aucae*) (*Los cantares de gestas francesas*, 213) and Colliot further analyzes how Adenet specifically uses them ("Synthèse de thèmes romanesques," in *Adenet le rois*, 77–161) though she calls them "romance" themes. Wais ("Märchen und Chanson de geste") examines the folk-tales in three epics, among them *Berta*. His web is wider; he compares Berta's story to the goose maiden's and the "big foot" with the stories embodying physical transformation. He is most specifically interested in the problematic of epic and folktale relations. Berta merits a place in the *Enzyklopädie des Märchens* for all the motifs present (Rumpf, "Berta," 158).

4.2.9.3 Stemma creation.

As more and more of the versions of *Berta* were found, it was natural to attempt to establish the relationship among them. Thus critics attempted to create a stemma of relationships among the widely-dispersed versions of *Berta*. That construction was altered and corrected as more versions came to light. Feist in 1886 first established a tree with seven missing manuscripts, listing V^{13} as a separate witness deriving directly from the lost original (*Zur Kritik der Bertasage*). Rajna in 1872 was more specifically interested in the Italian versions, and derived the *Reali* from a combination of Adenet and V^{13}, allowing for Andrea da Barberino's changes as well (*Ricerche intorno ai "Reali"*). Reinhold in 1911 simplified the family tree to only six originals derived from the lost original (Stricker, *Saintonge*, Mousket, *Gran Conquista*, V^{13}, and Adenet) ("Über die verschiedenen Fassungen"). All other texts would then derive from these. Jordan, in a review of Reinhold, basically agrees with him.[59] Memmer lists five romance sources from the *Urtext*, as

---

[59] L. Jordan, *Litteraturblatt für germanische und romanische Philologie* 33 (1912): columns 402–4.

does Reinhold (Memmer, *Die altfranzösische Bertasage*). Holmes in 1946 follows Memmer.[60] That is the current state of manuscript relationship studies.

4.2.9.4 Genre definition.

Beyond stemmata, however, it must also be recognized that the dividing line between genres—epic, romance, chronicle, and folktale—is often fuzzy. Different versions of *Berta* extend beyond the border of any single genre. Psychological analysis of characters has been used to distinguish between epic and romance as well as in attempts to make aesthetic judgements. The development of Berta's character appeals to some sensibilities in a way that Roland's deeds do not. Thus Adenet's version which shows Berta's personal suffering has been greatly valued (e.g. Colliot, *Adenet le roi*). But epic in general is for action, so psychological analysis is not usually part of the genre. Horrent remarks of Adenet: "Il éveille surtout l'émotion par l'évocation humaine de mille souffrances de Berte . . . Berte, c'est l'innocence maltraitée et finalement vengée et triomphante. C'est aussi l'exemple. Une belle image morale, donc, plutôt qu'un portrait psychologique, chargé d'illustrer une leçon, celle des vertus et de l'indéfectible confiance en Dieu et de la fidelité à un vœu solennel."[61]

4.2.9.5 Socio-political analysis.

During the middle of the twentieth century, socio-economic analysis was popular, though even early critics comparing Adenet and V^{13} felt that social differences between France and Italy affected the tales; Reinhold notes "le respect d'une éthique sociale" in Adenet, but not in V^{13} ("Über die verschiedenen Fassungen," 44). A. Adler says, "A good many references in the FI [sic; = Franco-Italian] version to money and monetary values might determine the impression that, whereas Adenet was catering to aristocrats, the *çubler* [of V^{13}] sang for lower classes in the towns."[62] Furthermore, this is a bourgeois "whose goal is not yet a middle class goal as an end in itself, but the ability of the bourgeois to live with *gentilezza*" (Adler, "Structural Meaning," 108). Henry, commenting on Adler, says, "Le remanieur de V^{13}, lui, est un jongleur populaire, qui travaille pour le peuple" and

---

[60] U. T. Holmes, Jr., ed., *Adenet le Roi's "Berte aus grans pies," Edited with an Introduction, Variants and Glossary* (Chapel Hill: University of North Carolina Press, 1946).

[61] Jules Horrent, "Chanson de Roland et geste de Charlemagne (Partie documentaire)," in *Les Épopées romanes*, ed. Rita Lejeune, Jeanne Wathelet-Willem, and Hennig Krauss, Vol. 1, fascicle 2A.I.1, 1–51. Grundriss der romanischen Literaturen des Mittelalters 3 (Heidelberg: Carl Winter Universitätsverlag, 1981), here 18.

[62] A. Adler, "The Structural Meaning of *Berta da li pe grandi*," *Italica* 17 (1940): 101–8, here 102.

notes the relationship of style to audience, suggesting, "Le récit de V^{13} a parfois quelque chose de brutal, de primitif, de presque barbare et de cru."[63]

Krauss most recently (1980) has analyzed V^{13} specifically in light of the "bourgeois" differences between Italy and France resulting in different themes and plot. He assumes the independence of V^{13}'s *Berta* from Adenet's version, yet speaks as if the compiler knew Adenet, to omit or alter certain episodes or characteristics (e.g., "la rinuncia al personaggio di Margiste" [*Epica feudale*, 80]; "eliminare i vincoli dalla gerarchia feudale" [89]). He points out that Adenet effectively develops Berta's psychological growth where V^{13} is more interested in action; Berta is there reduced to an interchangeable female figure. He also argues that wealth and gentility are equal in Adenet, as are poverty and evil, whereas in V^{13} it is genealogy that defines good (= Carolingian) and evil (= Maganzese). Belisant as an expression of free will based on independent means (and the strength of character) is the center of his argument of bourgeois accumulation as the key to choice. He emphasizes that these *chansons de geste* date to the thirteenth century, though the compilation manuscript is of the fourteenth.

Yet it is the nature of V^{13} as a compilation that is key to understanding *Berta* as well as V^{13}. It contains multiple points of view; since we have nothing like it earlier in Italy, we cannot presume anything about an *Urtext*: we have no way of knowing what changes the redactor made to adapt *Berta* to his history in verse. That the redactor emphasizes action over psychological growth is a characteristic of the genre (Krauss, *Epica feudale*, 88). But Berta is not an interchangeable figure; she is the personification of nobility precisely because of her behavior when removed from the court: she rolls up her sleeves and finds a place for herself where she can contribute to the common good—here, teaching the girls to sew (compare the German versions, where she actually supports herself, and in some cases, her host). She puts herself and her abilities at the disposal of the household. Berta's mother, Belisant, also chooses her way, and it is noble: she gives to those who assist and accompany her. Rather than defeating his own purpose in joining "la concezione borghese del guadagno e la liberalità feudale" in one person (Krauss, *Epica feudale*, 99), the compiler has united the best of two worlds: the evils of aristocracy (e.g., Pepin going against his marriage vows, Sinibaldo stretching the truth to Berta about Pepin's threats) and the evils of lower status (poverty, Maganzese grasping for wealth through stealth) are both avoided, and Belisant, Berta's mother, is the best of both worlds. Here, as in other *chansons* in the compilation, the redactor laughs at *chanson de geste* convention in creating

---

[63] A. Henry, "*Berta da li gran pié* et la *Berte* d'Adenet," in *Atti del 2° Congresso internazionale della 'Société Rencesvals'*, special issue of *Cultura Neolatina* 21 (1961): 135–40, here 137, 138.

Belisant's harridan performance with the impostor (present also in other versions), yet accepts the reality of power structures—what would indeed have happened if Sinibaldo had not been able to persuade Berta? (In other versions he does not even ask, or else she offers herself.) He thus plays to both audiences—the struggling but deserving bourgeois and the aristocratic—but the second wins in the end, with the girl, money, and heir. And, finally, it is in fact genealogy that is important: the impostor non-queen is not of high enough rank, and her children cannot inherit the kingdom. They also do not know how to rule: the impostors' mother made the people hate her.

Berta is echoed in *Berta e Milone* and *Macaire*, each of which also continues the *Charlemagne* story. Each features a queen in the woods, though for different reasons, in variations on the theme. In each segment, a woman has a child in exile. In this it also continues a theme from *Bovo* where Drusiana bore Bovo's twins in the woods, though she was not the central character of that *chanson*. Here the woman is tricked out of matrimony; in *Berta e Milone*, she has her child (outside of marriage); in *Macaire*, as a firmly established queen, Blançiflor is exiled by the accusation of adultery though pregnant with the royal heir, Louis. *Berta e Milone* is a sequel to *Karleto*; *Macario* ends the V[13] compilation. Noble women in trouble frame and structure the compilation from beginning to end, paralleling noble *enfants* in their need to regain their positions. The Maganzesi and their evil ways link *Bovo* and *Berta*; in both, Pepin is deceived (as also noted by Krauss, *Epica feudale*, 77). Pepin's personality too parallels that of his son, Charlemagne, who begins life contending with the Maganzesi in the form of his half-brothers assisted only by loyal retainers. The plot action of *Berta da li pe grant* would be directly followed by Charlemagne's youth, *Karleto*. But the next manuscript section is *Ogier le Danois*, which is woven into the Charlemagne story in order to prepare chronologically the action in Charlemagne's court and as a parallel to *Bovo* and to Roland's *Enfances*.

CHART 4.2: Versions of *Berta da li pe grant*

Italian and Franco-Italian (where not otherwised indicated, the dating derives from the editor or editors)
1. V¹³ *Berta da li pe grant*, first half fourteenth century
2. *I Reali di Francia*, Book 6, by Andrea da Barberino, late fourteenth-early fifteenth century
3. *Aquilon de Bavière* by Raffaele da Verona, completed 1407

French
1. *Chronique Saintongeaise*, first half thirteenth century
2. *Chronique rimée* by Philippe Mousket, before 1240
3. *Berte aus grans piés* by Adenet le Rois, ca. 1272-1274
4. *Charlemagne* by Girard d'Amiens, 1285-1314
5. *Chronique de France*, Book 6, Paris, BnF MS. 5003, late fourteenth-early fifteenth century
6. *Miracle de Berte*, ca. 1373
7. Berlin prose, fifteenth century (now Krakow Poland, Biblioteka Jagiellońska, Ms. Gall. Fol. 130)
8. *Valentin et Orson*, ca. 1475-1489
9. Nineteenth-century reworkings, Brandin et al.

German
1. *Karl der Grosse* by Stricker, ca. 1230-1250
2. *Chronik* by Henry of Munich, ca. 1320-1325
3. *Weihenstephan Chronik*, ca. 1435
4. *Chronica Bremensis* by Henry Wolter, ca. 1460-1475 (in Latin)
5. Hohenmut, *Volksbuch* from Zurich, MS. dates to 1475
6. *Bayerische Chronik b*y Ulrich Füetrer, 1477-1481
7. Nineteenth century reworking, Karl Simrock

Dutch
1. *Berte metten breeden voeten*, late fourteenth-early fifteenth century

Spanish
1. *Gran conquista de Ultramar*, Book 2, Chapter 43, late thirteenth-early fourteenth century
2. *Noches de invierno* by Antonio de Eslava, 1609, 1610

Catalan
1. *Libre de les nobleses dels reys*
2. Mussons summary, untitled

4.3 Karleto

The discussion and analysis of *Karleto* is much simplified by the work of Jacques Horrent, Jules Horrent, and John Robin Allen.[1] In a series of articles over the past thirty years, they have identified and discussed all known versions of the story and numerous references to it. Allen's dissertation (*Genealogy and Structure*) includes summaries, analyses, and some translations of all versions. Jacques Horrent's book (*Les Versions françaises*) summarizes and analyzes all known versions in relation to one another. As is the case for *Berta*, which *Karleto* can be considered to complete, there are Italian, French, Spanish, German, Dutch, and Scandinavian versions, but the first mention is in Latin.

4.3.0 Mentions: Pseudo-Turpin.

The first reference to the childhood of Charlemagne is found in the Pseudo-Turpin chronicle, from the first half of the twelfth century. There we find two references: first, to the fact that Charlemagne knew Arabic because of his stay in Spain; second, to the daughter of Galafre and battle against Braimant (179, lines 1–14).[2] For other mentions as opposed to specific versions of the story, see Allen (*Genealogy and Structure*, 4–11) and Jacques Horrent (*Les Versions françaises*, 71–73).

---

[1] Jacques Horrent, "L'Allusion à la chanson de *Mainet* contenue dans le *Roncesvalles*," *Hommage des romanistes liégeois à la mémoire de Ramón Menéndez Pidal*, special issue of *Marche romane, Cahiers de l'A. R. U. Lg.* 20 (1970): 85–92; idem, "Un Récit peu connu de la légende de Mainet," *Mediaevalia 76: Marche romane, Cahiers de l'A. R. U. Lg.* 26 (1976): 87–96; and idem, *Les Versions françaises et étrangères des Enfances de Charlemagne* (Brussels: Palais des Academies, 1979). Jules Horrent, "Mainet," in *Le Moyen Age, Dictionnaire des lettres françaises* 1 (1964; repr. Paris: Fayard, 1994), 978–80; idem, "Chanson de Roland et geste de Charlemagne"; J. R. Allen, *The Genealogy and Structure of a Medieval Historic Legend: Mainet in French, Spanish, Italian, German and Scandinavian Literature* (Ann Arbor: UMI, 1969), and idem, "Les Structures de *Mainet*," in *Charlemagne et l'épopée romane*, Actes du VIIe Congrès international de la Société Rencesvals (Liège 28 août–4 septembre 1976), ed. M. Tyssens and C. Thiry (Paris: Les Belles Lettres, 1978), 2: 405–14.

[2] C. Meredith-Jones, *Historia Karli Magni et Rotholandi ou Chronique du Pseudo-Turpin: Textes revus et publiés d'après 49 manuscrits* (Paris: La Faculté des Lettres: Droz, 1936), 131, lines 7–9. The reference to Galafre's daughter and battle against Braimant is at 179. See also Morrissey, *Charlemagne and France*, 51–57.

4.3.1 V¹³ VERSION.

(1) Lanfroi (frequently mis-written Çofroi in the manuscript) and Landris (sons of Pepin's Maganzese impostor bride) and Pepin remain at court, well-treated but unhappy. (2) These two sons poison Berta and Pepin simultaneously to gain the throne, eventually (3) forcing the legitimate son, Charles (the future Charlemagne), to flee. (4) Charles, aided by Morando of River, flees south; after a (5) run-in with local bandits, (6) he arrives in Spain and marries king Galafre's daughter; (7) he must combat pagan rulers in order to save the realm. (8) Eventually, the jealousy of her brothers (Marsile and Falsiron; Balugant, the third brother, informs on the other two to their mother) forces Charles and Belisent to flee to Rome. (9) There, the pope is an ally of Charles's Maganzese half-brothers. A price which the pope places on Charles's head leads his innkeeper to betray them. (10) Charles and his wife are saved, however, by Berta's (Charles's mother's) relatives. (11) Charles returns and reconquers his realm, (12) executing his half-brothers, much against his will, and placing his half-sister, Bertella, under the guidance of his wife.

4.3.2 Other Italian versions.

In Italian, after V¹³'s *Karleto*, versions of Charlemagne's childhood are found in the *Reali di Francia* and *Aquilon de Bavière*.

4.3.2.1 Andrea da Barberino.

The *Reali* version, book 6, chapters 17–51, from the late fourteenth– early fifteenth century; I will use the names from *Reali* here) is quite lengthy and explicit.[3] The imposter Berta has been burned; Oldrigi (not Landris) and Lanfroy first poison Berta and then kill Pepin with knives while he sleeps, a scene Charles witnesses by chance. Charles flees, changes his clothes with a shepherd, and goes to St. Omer to become a monk. The abbot there protects him, giving him a suit of armor to wear once he recognizes Charles. Morando searches four and a half years for Charles, and, upon identifying himself to the abbot, is allowed to take Charles to Saragozza, Spain, to Galafro's court. Galeanna, Galafro's daughter, is ten, and falls in love with him. She arranges for him to serve her instead of an old man. After five years, there is a tournament for her hand; Charles wishes to fight but finds that he has grown so much that his arms are too small for him. Galeanna's confidante overhears him cursing and arranges for Galeanna to give him arms for the tournament. Charles wins the tournament but leaves before Galafro can learn his name. Morando, however, has recognized him. Galeanna makes a hole in the wall to listen to the two talking, and finds out also. She has Morando baptize her

---

[3] All references to the *Reali* follow Roncaglia and Beggato, eds., *I Reali di Francia*.

and marries Charles secretly. Meanwhile, Bramante, a king of Africa, has heard from Ulieno how pretty she is, and comes to wage battle for her hand; but she will marry only the "unknown" knight. Bramante conquers Galeanna's three brothers—Marsilio, Balugante, Falserone—and then Morando. Charles offers to go to Galeanna's defense, so she knights him in order to make him Bramante's equal.

On the second day, Polinoro, who owns Durindarda, accuses Charles of defending a *puttana*, and Charles kills him. Charles then fights Bramante; the fight lasts all day, and they put off more fighting until the next day. Bramante sends Morando to offer Charles to join him. Morando, as a prisoner, has seen Bramante disarm, and knows that he is poorly armed around the neck; he informs Charles of this fact during his ostensible mission as a messenger. The next day, Charles kills Bramante. Agolante, Bramante's brother, goads Gualfediano into continuing the war. Gualfediano's son, Ogier, becomes Charles's good friend when he is given to Charles at his father's defeat.

Galafro's sons, meanwhile, become progressively more jealous of Charles. With their mother's connivance, they plan to do away with him. However, Ogier (Uggieri) has infiltrated the group and he reveals the plan to Charles. Charles, Ogier, Morant, and Galeanna flee. She dresses as a boy, and brings jewels to assist the effort. The brothers pursue them, but the refugees arrive safely at Rome. There Cardinal Leone, son of Bernardo of Clermont, is Pepin's friend and willing to assist Charles. The Franks wait three months in Rome, then with Leone's money are able to cross the Alps and return home. Staying with Namo, they discover the popular hatred for Charles's half-brothers and gather an army which fights against the half-brothers and Gherardo da Fratta. One of the brothers, Lanfroy, is killed in battle, and Oldrigi is taken prisoner; Gherardo flees. Paris is taken; Charles kills Oldrigi. There is an emotional reunion of Charles and Berta, here his *full* sister, who is now seventeen. At the coronation, Cardinal Leone comes to Paris. Ogier is baptized and Charles becomes emperor.

Barberino appeals greatly to the emotions: the reunion of Charles and Berta, the scenes of Galeanna and Charles, are all gauged for effect. The importance of bloodline is greater than in V^{13}: Berta is Charles's full sister, making Roland (yet to come) conveniently and completely without stain of bastardy in his family history. The greatest insult is to be of unidentified parentage: Guerrino says to Charles: "O come puoi tu essere figliuolo di Pipino, che fusti generato in un bosco, e non sai di chi si sia tuo padre? . . ." (Roncaglia and Beggiato, 640). Oldrigi says to him, "Tu di' che se' figliuolo di Pipino, e fusti generato d'uno ribaldo cacciatore" (643). Though Charles says Oldrigi is "figliuolo del dimonio" (643), he himself cuts off Oldrigi's head so that "nessuno non mettesse mano nel sangue reale" (648): Oldrigi's father was King Pepin, so only another king can kill him without committing regicide. Gherardo does not want peace because Charles is a bastard. Thus genealogy is crucial in determining right to rule.

Barberino also reuses details of the *Karleto* story in his *Aspramonte*:[4] in the Introduction to the first book, Lanfroi e Oldris are called the "bastardi di Pepino"; Charles's finding of Orlandino at Rome and recalling of Milone from exile is mentioned, and the fact that he made Orlando his "figliuolo adottivo" (Boni, *Andrea da Barberino: L'Aspramonte*, 3). Agolante's forgiveness and assistance with regaining France because of Charles's marrying his daughter is also mentioned (12), and the origin of Durindarda recalled when Orlandino is knighted (175–80). Gherardo continues to question Charles's ancestry as well, calling him "questo bastardo di Carlo . . . figliuolo d'uno mandriano" (137).

4.3.2.2 *Aquilon de Bavière.*

Aquilon (manuscript completed 1407)[5] tells the story through Berta's substitute, Gaiete, as mentioned above in the discussion of *Berta* (Book 5).[6] Lanfroi and Lodris are the two half-brothers. When Pepin dies, Charles is only seven years old, and under the protection of Bernard de Clermont, Aquilon de Bavière, Quintin de Normandie, Grifon de Altefoile, and Morant de Rivière. The half-brothers succeed through bribery in getting the allegiance of most of the nobles, and begin to plan Charles's death. Morant arranges to bring Charles to Galafre in Spain. Galafre has heard of Charles's flight, and has all borders guarded. Charles and his party are seized and brought to Saragoze. Morant and the group pretend at first to be just horse traders (cf. *Karleto*), but Galafre suspects the truth. He orders them to tell the truth or be killed. They do, and Galafre is delighted. He gives them all they need to live there, and they stay until Mainet (= Charles) is fifteen years old. Braimant in the meantime is making war on Galafre. (Why is not stated.) Galion, Braibant's nephew, captures Galafre's sons and three Frenchmen. Galienne is here Galafre's wife; she arms Charles, and he captures the sword Zogioxe (= Çoiose) from king Brunador. Later, he kills Braimant and captures Durendarte (= Durendarda). At the end, the return to France is not described. For this narrative, the story of the sword is the most important aspect.[7]

---

[4] The edition of *Aspramonte* cited is Boni, ed., *Andrea da Barberino: L'Aspramonte*.

[5] Thomas, "Aquilon de Bavière," 561–64; Wunderli, *Raffaele da Verona: Aquilon de Bavière*, 2: 538–40.

[6] Wunderli, *Raffaele da Verona: Aquilon de Bavière*, 2: 538–40.

[7] There are later pieces based on portions of the Charlemagne story; for example, *Carlo Mainetto*, a fourteenth-century *cantare* that really does not treat Charlemagne at all; it is an incomplete version of a battle between Pepin and a Saracen, Giustamonte. It ends in the middle of a version of the lion story: the lion bows and accedes to Pepin, but then returns. Pepin captures it again, when it bows to him; Pepin threatens him with the swipe of a sword, but the lion flees. It is here that the *cantare* ends. For the importance of lions and royalty, cf. *Bovo* (above), and the *Reali* on the subject.

While the Italian versions share many points in common, they are not identical. Some of the differences derive from different emphasis placed by author or compiler; others may be differences in source. That Charles's identity is known in Spain (here Saragossa, not Toledo), and going to meet friends in Rome instead of going to free it from a Saracen invasion, are the major differences between Italian versions and others. The unique *Reali* integration of Ogier the Dane into *Karleto* is also touched upon the section on *Ogier le Danois* (4.4, below).

4.3.3 French versions.

Complete French versions of *Mainet* (named for "Maine" = "big" plus the diminutive suffix; compare English "Charlemagne"), with few exceptions, are portions of other texts rather than stand-alone *chansons de geste*. The versions of some length are: a stand-alone set of twelfth-century fragments, just three folios; Philippe Mousket (pre-1240); Girard d'Amiens (late thirteenth to early fourteenth century); Jean d'Outremeuse (mid to second half of the fourteenth century); David Aubert (second half fifteenth century); and Dresden 0.81, *Chroniques de Charlemagne* (late fifteenth century).[8] All these versions are now available for examination. Thanks to Allen, we can discard Dresden 0.81 from the list as a *remaniement* of David Aubert (Allen, *Genealogy and Structure*, 17 and 133–36).

4.3.3.1 Fragments.

The *Fragments* are just that; they are three sheets, back and front, from a version of *Enfances Charlemagne*. G. Paris attempts to fill the gaps using Girard d'Amiens and *Karl Meinet* ("*Mainet*: fragments"). As the text stands, Hainfroi and Heudri, the half-brothers, have poisoned Berta and Pepin; the two have taken over the country for themselves. David (Esmeré while in Spain; similar to Morando in Italian versions) flees with Charles to Tudele in Spain. They go to Galafre, the king, who takes them in to fight for him at Monfrin against Braimant. After a gap, we find our Christians near a body of water; Mainet challenges an opponent, wins, and returns with a horse for Maingoy, making references to the incident of the peacock on the spit, which caused his departure from France. They return to camp. At the fight the next day, Charles again does well, and the Christian side wins. Charles sends half the booty to Galafre. Morant announces the news to Galafre and tells of Charles's prowess. We pick up again

---

[8] Editions used are as follows. For the fragments, G. Paris, "*Mainet*: fragments d'une chanson de geste du XIIe siècle"; Reiffenberg, *Chronique rimée de Philippe Mouskes*; Métraux, *Girard d'Amiens's Charlemagne*; A. Borgnet, *Ly Myreur des Histors: Chronique de Jean des Preis dit d'Outremeuse*, Corps des chroniques liégeoises (Brussels: M. Hayez, 1864–1880); Guiette, *Croniques et Conquestes*.

in Galienne's apartments, where she is avowing her love for Charles to Blanchandrine, who is trying to calm her down. Galafre says he will give her to Charles, with money, if he brings back Braimant's head (III c. 114; G. Paris, *Mainet*, 326). Charles keeps his own sword, Joieuse, and departs for his mission. The last page finds the Christians in the midst of battle; Charles's protectors worry about him since they have been separated. Maines (= Charles) has killed Braimant and has thus conquered Braimant's shield and sword, Durendal. There is a reference to Roland regaining the shield at Aspremont when he kills Eaumont (Almonte). They compliment Charles. The pagans are so impressed that they ask for baptism, which is done. Mainet takes over Braimant's tents. Marsile is irritated at the favor Charles is receiving and tries to interest Baligant in doing something about Charles, who Galienne believes will rule Spain. She tattles her brothers' plot to Galafre. Galienne goes to Charles in bed, but he refuses her. The pagans are meanwhile working on Galafre against Charles, accusing him of plotting to take over Spain and his daughter. Galienne knows magic, reads the stars, and thus finds out about Charles's heritage and the plot that Marsile has hatched for him. She goes to Morant and David to warn them; they arm and she helps Charles to arm. On the recto of the final page, much is unreadable; Charles's ships meet Saracen ships at the Tiber; the Christians win much booty. With the siege lifted, Saracens run to fight again, and those inside of Rome are delighted; and that is the end of the Fragments. Recapturing Paris and punishment of the criminal half-brothers is not included.

4.3.3.2 Girard d'Amiens.

Girard d'Amiens's version is longer; the first of the three books in his *Charlemagne* is Charlemagne's childhood. It is summarized by G. Paris (*Histoire poétique*, 471–82); Bartsch (*Über Karlmeinet*, 9–12); Gautier (*Les Épopées françaises*, 3: 41–52); Memmer (*Die altfranzösische Bertasage*, 210); Allen (*Genealogy and Structure*, 13–16); and Jacques Horrent (*Les Versions françaises*, 52–68) — though this last is in comparison with the *Fragments*, not a complete summary in itself; and the entire text appears in an edition by Daniel Métraux.[9] First Berta and later Pepin are poisoned by the sons of the first wife, Rainfroi and Heudri (not both at once). After a year, they begin to plan Charles's death as well. David arranges to have Charles taken to Anjou, to stay with Milon and Gilles, Charles's sister. Heudri and Rainfroi try to make arrangements for Charles to be crowned at Reims at Pentecost, so he will be in their power. Charles's men agree but,

---

[9] Again I thank Daniel Métraux for his kindness in making available to me his edition of Book I, together with notes and summary. The edition has now appeared, as mentioned above, p. 115 n. 26.

thanks to Milon's foresight, also arrange to have armed friends on hand in case of need. The half-brothers persuade the barons to put off the crowning for a year, since Charles is just fifteen. The half-brothers are thrilled, since they can certainly arrange a poisoning within another year. Rainfroi asks Charles to serve him at the table, but only with pheasant; Charles is upset but agrees; he alerts his men for a fight. Charles is courteous to all but his half-brothers; he goes to the kitchen where he gets a peacock still on the spit in juice, which he then tosses in Rainfroi's face. The half-brothers flee and meet with their fellow conspirators. Charles holes up in a fort outside Reims, and his men march to meet Rainfroi's. The duke of Dijon speaks with both sides in order to stop the fighting. An agreement is reached whereby Charles will be crowned in a year, but he must stay in his land—that is, near the half-brothers. David leaves Charles in a safe place, then goes to the half-brothers to persuade them that he has switched sides. He is so convincing that he learns of the plan to poison Charles. He writes Hugues and Henri, Charles's other protectors; they meet and decide to flee. The brothers are upset and seize many of Charles's men and the country.

Charles and his protectors go to Spain. They pass through Pampelune, change their names, and are given Morant, a Turk, by king Menjue. They go to Toledo with an interpreter and offer their services to the king. The king accepts them and they do great deeds. But Mainet (Charles's *nom d'exil*) laments at being alone and not allowed to fight. Galafre then sends Morant and the others against Bruiant, king of Aragon and Bascle, at Monfrin. Morant will not allow Charles to fight, so Charles assembles 100 other bacheliers of his age and follows. Morant is losing when Charles arrives and saves the day, cutting off Bruiant's head. On their return, Morant tells of Mainet's bravery and pulls Bruiant's head out of a box (!). Galafre rewards Charles with a horse and knighthood; David gives him two things from his father: a white hauberk and Joyeuse, the sword. Galafre suspects Charles's identity and offers his help to Morant: together they can regain France. He furthermore offers Charles his daughter in marriage. Morant promises to look into it; he speaks with Hugues of Auvergne, who makes him promise to tell only Galafre in order to preserve Charles's safety.

Braimant now threatens, and Charles offers to fight him (for Monfrin and Galienne). Galienne encourages him. Marsile hears of this and hates Charles even more. Mainet wins and divides the spoils with his men. Galafre reveals Charles's identity to his daughter, who is now completely taken with Charles. She sends a messenger to him with jewels and other rewards. After eight days, Braimant marches away, followed by Charles and his men. Braimant offers single combat for Galienne; Charles wants to accept but his advisors will not allow him to. Braimant is forced to do all-out battle. The Saracens finally must flee; Charles follows Braimant and they fight. Braimant asks his identity, and Charles reveals it, saying he had come to Spain for love of Galienne.[10] Mainet kills Braimant. Morant is so amazed in finding him over Braimant dead that he asks to convert. They return to the army. Mainet rests and heals; he has Braimant's head sent to Galafre. Morant, Charles's messenger, is affianced to Galienne in Mainet's name. He alerts her to Marsile's hatred. He goes to Mainet, who in the meantime has learned of Saracens menacing the pope at Rome and plans to go save the pope as soon as he has married Galienne. As soon as he is well, Mainet goes to Galafre and sees Galienne as well. Galafre announces that Galienne will return to Monfrin with Morant, receive baptism, and receive a kingdom from him. Mainet asks permission to return to Monfrin, and Galafre grants it.

The French decide to retake France at this point. Marsile plans a trap for Charles on the way, but Charles is forewarned and takes a different route. Marsile follows them to fight anyway. The French win. At Monfrin, Galienne, Morant and friends are baptized. Galienne and Mainet are married. Galafre and all concerned decide that, for his own safety, Mainet must leave; they go to Rome first. They arrive to find Corsuble's fleet blocking the city. They take the fleet and Mainet sends messengers into the city to announce his success. Corsuble attacks Charles at night, but again, forewarned, Charles is ready. His men pillage Corsuble's camp while he is away; he attacks the French anyway. Corsuble is wounded and taken; Charles goes to the pope to announce his victory. Charles stays long enough to heal and to receive the thanks of the pope in person. He then leaves Rome for France. Rumors fly along the way. Charles arrives in Lyon; he sends out messengers to his allies and family. When his army arrives near Soissons, the half-brothers hear the news and cannot believe it. Heudri disguises himself as a pilgrim and enters Charles's camp. He is arrested and recognized. They find poison on him and Charles orders him held safely. Messages reach Rainfroi with a few faithful (most of his men had already switched sides); he flees to Dinant. Rainfroi then marches out to meet Charles's army on the way to Paris. He is taken prisoner and the two are judged. They are condemned to be hanged and quartered, but Charles commutes it to beheading.[11] Charlemagne

---

[10] This is an important point for the establishment of the stemma for some critics. For example, Jules Horrent divides Spanish accounts by Charles's reason(s) for coming to Spain by it (Jules Horrent, *Roncesvalles: Etude sur le fragment de cantar de gesta conservé à l'Archivo de Navarra (Pampelune)*, Bibliothèque de la Faculté de Philosophie et Lettres de l'Université de Liège [Paris: Les Belles Lettres, 1951], 181–85).

[11] Earlier critics were not in agreement about the fate of the half-brothers in Girard d'Amiens's version. Memmer: "Die bastarde [sic] werden verbrannt" (*Die altfranzösische Bertasage*, 210) [the bastards were burnt]. But Riebe has "enhaupten" [beheaded] at Namur (P. Riebe, *Über die verschiedenen Fassungen der Mainetsage. Nebst Textprobe aus Girart's von Amiens Charlemagne* [Greifswald: Hans Adler, 1906], 23); Paris: "A Namur,

rights wrongs throughout the country; Galienne dies with her child; Charles's older brother is crowned at Soissons; at his brother's crowning Charles changes his name to "Charlemagne." Eventually Charlemagne marries the daughter of Desier, king of Lombardy.

4.3.3.3 Jean d'Outremeuse.

Jean d'Outremeuse (1338–1400) wrote both the *Geste de Liège*, a verse chronicle, and *Ly Myreur des Histors*, a longer prose chronicle. The *Geste* includes a brief reference to Charles's struggles with his bastard brothers after Pepin is taken prisoner. He kills Rainfroi and Alpais is burned (Borgnet, *Ly Myreur* [1869], 2: 632–38, strophe 371). The prose chronicle's treatment is more extensive (2: 472–84). Pepin is imprisoned (year 733) and his men think him dead; therefore Charlemagne is crowned king of Austrie, while Ranfrois and Hondris become duke of Orlins and count of Savoy. Charles-Pepin, the other legitimate heir with Charles Mainet, is killed in battle in 737.[12] Charlemagne should get his lands, but Griffon d'Aultrefuelhe works with Ranfrois and Hondris to take possession of the realm. Emperor Constantine of Rome, Charles's uncle, must assist Charlemagne. Doon finds Pepin in Saxony; Pepin hears the whole story and goes to

---

Charles fait décapiter les serfs . . ." (*Histoire poétique*, 478); Bartsch says Heudri's head was cut off when he was found out disguised as a pilgrim in Charles's camp, and Reinfroy was captured later and beheaded as his brother (Bartsch, *Über Karlmeinet*, 11–12). However, the situation is clear from the text: their heads were cut off to avoid disfiguring their bodies!

    La fu jugié Rainfr*oi* et son frere Heudris,
     et fussent lors penduz et detrés a ronci[n]s
    ne fust ce que Pepin les ot engenuïs;
    pour quoi le roy ne volt que nus d'els fust laidis
    que des testes couper, don't pris ne fu respis.
    Ainz furent amenez et l'un lez l'autre assis;
    la furent de leur fez vilainement repris,
    puis leur <u>trancha les chiés</u> le pendierre Tierris
    qui de tele oevre s'iert mainte fois entremis;
    et fu cascun des cors a Namur enfouïs.
    (6890–6899; emphasis added, courtesy of D. Métraux)

    [12] As Michel notes, Jean d'Outremeuse construes *mainnet* as "puis-né" [after-born], not as MAGNU(S) > maine (L. Michel, *Les Légendes epiques carolingiennes dans l'œuvre de Jean d'Outremeuse* [Brussels: Palais des Académies, 1935], 733). Note also the lack of the *Berta* story here; the background is thus not entirely clear (Michel, *Les Légendes épiques*, 160). The localization is around Namur; Girard d'Amiens and others narrate the execution of the half-brothers at Namur. The popularity of the tale in Northern Europe and in Italy, away from the central Carolingian realm, is interesting.

Paris where he arranges to kill all Charles's enemies. The brothers are killed at Namur. Pepin finds Charlemagne in Spain at Galafre's court by necromancy. Charlemagne loves Gloriande (note the name), Galafre's daughter; they go to Paris, where she is baptized and they are married.

In this version, Pepin is still alive at the time of the betrayal. Allen also points out that a very similar story is told of Charles Martel in the same volume by the same author (*Genealogy and Structure*, 52; Borgnet, *Ly Myreur* [1869], 2: 356). Here genealogical legitimacy is again important: the role of the legitimate heirs over the bastards is emphasized.

4.3.3.4 David Aubert.

David Aubert's version (second half of the fifteenth century; Guiette, *Croniques et Conquestes*, 1: 15–17) begins with a short recapitulation: Charles suffered much, since he was left an orphan with two traitors in France. These two conspired against Berta, Charlemagne, and his brother Charles. Charlemagne had to leave the realm; he went to Tholette (= Toledo) and served at the court of King Galafre. All the lords there watched him grow in strength and beauty; Galafre approved of him too and knighted him. Braymant, a terrible and marvelous giant, is currently fighting Galafre; Charlemagne offers himself in battle with the giant and is accepted. Charlemagne wins, of course. Galafre had hoped to keep Charlemagne with him, but Charlemagne is worried about his mother Berta and his older brother. So he returns to France, recovers his realm, and judges the traitors and their allies to the general rejoicing of his mother and of the realm. There is no mention of any female relative of Galafre or Charles's marriage to her. Here Berta is still alive, and Charlemagne has no Spanish wife. The punishment of the traitors is not specified.

There is a slight difference in the names within the French tradition as a whole, but it is interesting that generally the initial consonant is the same and differs from the Italian versions. Furthermore, Galafre is king of Toledo, not Saragossa. Thus in French versions, differences from the Italian are in proper names, the chronology of Berta and Pepin's deaths in relation to Charlemagne's disputes with the half-brothers, and the presence or absence of a trip to Italy. If the trip to Rome is present, the reason is also different: to save the pope from a Saracen invasion or merely to save himself. The presence of Galafre's daughter and Charles's attraction and marriage or not to her is also appearing as an issue, one which appears in examining further versions.

4.3.4. Spanish versions.

The Spanish versions appear in the *Primera crónica* (PC) and the *Gran Conquista de Ultramar* (GC).[13] Only in Spanish versions does Charlemagne flee his father because of disagreements with him. There are also a number of texts in Latin from Spanish soil, and fragments relevant to the account of Charlemagne's youth. *De rebus Hispaniae* by Rodrigo Jiménez de Rada (el Toledano) was completed by 1243; Juan Gil de Zamora's *De Preconiis Hispaniae* (1241?–post 1318), and the fragments of *Roncesvalles* (Jules Horrent, *Roncesvalles*, lines 54–62) offer pieces of the story, but the *Crónicas* are the most complete witnesses.[14]

4.3.4.1 *Primera crónica*.

The *Primera crónica* dates to 1270–1289 (Menéndez-Pidal, *Primera crónica*, 340–43). There are no half-brothers and no trip to Rome. Charles is angry with his father about injustices committed, and flees to Spain. There Morant is a Spanish nobleman who must explain Charles's not bowing to the Infanta Galeana. Shortly after his arrival in Toledo, Bramant contends with Galafre because Galafre will not allow Galeana to marry him. There is a siege in Val Somorian and "Mainet" is left behind.[15] He awakes alone, and laments his fate; Galeana goes

---

[13] R. Menéndez-Pidal, ed., *Primera crónica general de España que mandó componer Alfonso el Sabio y se continuaba bajo Sancho IV en 1289*, 2 vols. (Madrid: Editorial Gredos, 1955) and Gayangos, *La Gran conquista de Ultramar*, are the editions consulted.

[14] J. Gibbs, "Las Mocedades de Mainete," in *Guillaume d'Orange and the Chanson de geste: Essays Presented to Duncan McMillan in Celebration of his Seventieth Birthday by his Friends and Colleagues of the Société Rencesvals*, ed. W. van Emden and P. E. Bennett (Reading: Reading University Press, 1984), 33–42, and Jacques Horrent, *Les Versions françaises*, 159–62, both dicuss the *Roncesvalles* information. For complete analyses of the Spanish versions, their relation to each other, and to the tradition, see Rey ("Las Leyendas del ciclo carolingio"), who argues that the PC is intermediate between the French *Fragments* and the PC, and that the *Roncesvalles* offers a version similar to PC (for a more recent treatment, see Jacques Horrent, *Les Versions françaises*). Recently, F. Bautista ("La tradición épica de las *Enfances* de Carlomagno y el *Cantar de Mainete* perdido," *Romance Philology* 56 [2003]: 217–44), has proposed that there must have been a *Mainet* in Spanish at the end of the twelfth or the beginning of the thirteenth century. This would have formed the base of Spanish versions. However, no fragments or physical proof exists, so the hypothesis does not affect this discussion directly.

[15] The identity of Val Somorian, and its reading in the manuscript, is a vexed point: see R. Menéndez-Pidal, "«Galiene la belle» y los palacios de Galiana en Toledo," in idem, *Poesía árabe y poesía europea* (Buenos Aires: Espasa-Calpe Argentina, S.A., 1941), 71–92, here 87–88; Jules Horrent, *Roncesvalles*, 449–50; Jacques Horrent, "«Mainet» est-il né à Tolède?" *Le Moyen Age* 74, 4th ser. 23 (1968): 439–58, here 449–50; and idem, *Les Versions françaises*, 144.

to see him and will give him what he wants (horse and armor) if he will promise to take her back to France and baptize and marry her. He agrees and goes to save the day. Bramant has been in his tent; he hears of the unknown warrior's bravery. Bramant goes out and sees Charles riding the horse he had given Galeana as a gift. They fight; Charles cuts off Bramant's sword arm sword and all, picks up Durendal, and, with a sword in each hand, kills Bramant. He takes Bramant's head to Galeana. The next year, news of Pepin's death reaches Spain; the French want to return, but are afraid that Galafre will not allow them to. They plan to go hunting with the horses shod backwards and thus attain the border with France. The plan works; Morant is sent back to get Galeana. She is baptized, they are married, and Charlemagne shares the kingdom with his brother Charles. As Gibbs points out, this version "appears to avoid introducing superfluous details into its more sober account of its material" ("Las Mocedades," 40).

4.3.4.2 *Gran conquista de Ultramar*.

The *Gran conquista de Ultramar* (late thirteenth– early fourteenth century), on the other hand, is much more extensive (Gayangos, *La Gran conquista de Ultramar*, 178–85 [Book 2, Chap. 43]). Morant and Mayugot de Paris are Charles's companions/guards appointed by Pepin before he dies. Manfre and Carlon (175, col. 1) or Eldois (180, col. 2), sons of Berta's servant's daughter, take the throne when Pepin dies, and bribe the nobles to accept them. Charles then serves like any other boy (179). Morant goes through France seeking support for Charles, while Mayugot stays with Charles. The brothers try to humiliate Charles by holding a "round table" ceremony, supposedly originated in France, where a young girl serves a cooked peacock on a silver platter to the men of the court. Charles is to be the girl. He is upset but agrees and arranges for friends to stand by. He uses a spit instead of a silver platter and throws the peacock at Eldois. The brothers berate him, but he says that this is how traitors should be served. Charles then knocks Eldois out with the spit. He is forced to flee to Spain. He and his supporters stay at Bordeaux to fight the Moors. The king of Toledo, Hixem, invites them through Halaf (= Galafre) to come help fight Abrahin of Zaragoza and Abdalla of Cordoba for Halia (= Galienne). The French arrive, go to fight, and leave Charles asleep—at which point we have the same scene as in the PC. Halía overhears Charles cursing his family; she offers him arms and horse in exchange for marriage, and he rides to join the battle. He duels with Abrahin (cf. Braimant) and obtains Durendarte. Mayugot discovers what Charlemagne has done and is angry; he is then both pleased at Charles's deeds and concerned about Halía's love for him. Charles needs to return in France to regain his throne, but can do that only with money. Halía agrees to provide her father's wealth if Charles will marry her. He agrees, and Charles and Halía kiss to seal their bargain. Charles and his men hear of the count of Burgundy being taken and other atrocities and decide to return to France; Morant is to return for Halía. The two brothers hear of Charles's return and try to negotiate, but Charles, wealthy from his exploits in Spain, buys off many men and the traitorous brothers are defeated. Morant retrieves Halía, using the same ruse of the horses shod backwards (184, col. 2). Halía is baptized, renamed Sevilla, and she and Charles are married. At first Halía's father is unhappy, but since she is his only daughter, he leaves his lands to her.

The GC differs from the PC on a number of counts. The "arabization" of the names and forms of *Mainet* names in general is one; the two brothers in France and the peacock episode are related to French versions, but the "round table" is different. Morant / Morando is in one a Turk, the other a faithful knight (as in the Franco-Italian).[16] There are similarities among the Spanish versions, Girard d'Amiens, and the German *Karl Meinet*, the last of which has caused much comment and speculation.

4.3.5 German versions.

In Germany, versions of Charlemagne's childhood are found within various chronicles, like the *Berta* story, of which they form a part: *Karl der Grosse* by Stricker (1230–1235); Hohenmut's *Zuricher Volksbücher* (manuscript of the fifteenth century); *Karl Meinet* (first quarter of the fourteenth century); the so-called *Weihenstephan Chronik* (ca. 1435); and Henry of Munich (fourteenth century), who basically follows Stricker and Füetrer's *Bayerische Chronik* (1477–1481). (Wolter's *Chronica Bremensis* [ca. 1460] does not include the *Enfances* portion though it does include the Berta story.)

4.3.5.1 *Karl der Grosse*.

The *Karl der Grosse* version is quite short; it follows the (also short) version of *Berta* (ed. Bartsch, *Karl der Grosse*, 4–8). Wineman and Rapot are Charles's half-brothers. With twelve barons, they attempt to kill Charles. Diepolt, count of Troyes, is the faithful friend (= Morando; David) who flees with Charles to Spain, to the court of king Marsilie. They change their names and go into the king's service. At eighteen, Charles is a very courageous knight who wins all his battles. Marsilie's sister is in love with him, she asks him to leave his God and marry her. Charles is afraid for his life and beliefs, so he tells Count Diepolt, who reaches an agreement with the Lord of Kerlingen: the same will help form an army for the rightful heir with Marsilie's knights. They all go to Kerlingen. His brothers submit to him and beg for mercy; they serve him and are remorseful for

---

[16] For the Arabic names, see F. M. Warren, "The Arabic Origin of *Galafre*, *Galienne*, and *Orable*," *Modern Philology* 27 (1929–1930): 23–26.

their earlier plans to kill him. Charles is a wise and prudent king, who does not kill them but forgives them and makes them rich (cf. Memmer, *Die altfranzösische Bertasage*, 154–55, 212).

4.3.5.2 Weihenstephan Chronik.

The *Weihenstephan Chronik* is related to Stricker but more detailed (cf. Freitag, *Die sogenannte Chronik*, 59–68).[17] Seven years after Charles's birth, Pepin dies leaving Charles and Karelmonio, his children with Berta. Wenemann, Rappolt, twelve nobles, and the son of the seneschal attempt to kill Charles. Count Diepolt of Troyes takes Charles with him first to his grandfather and then to the heathen king Marsilie, while Berta and Karlemonio (the second son) remain with Charles's maternal grandfather near Kärlingen. Diepolt and Charles help him against a heathen king. Wenemann and Rappolt must flee from Germany to France before Bohemians and Saxons; when Marsilie hears this, he wants to expel the two half-brothers from France, but Charles pleads with him to save Kärlingen. Diepolt sends messages to France that everyone should flee to Kärlingen. In the battle, Rappolt is taken and given to Charles as a prisoner. Charles frees him, and he goes to Wenneman, saying how powerful and generous Charles is. They change their ways. Charles allows Marsilie to take Hungary. Marsilie's sister gains Charles's love and sleeps with him, but when the message arrives from Kärlingen, Charles returns to France without taking her along.[18] According to critics, this is an extended version of Stricker (Freitag, *Die sogenannte Chronik*, 64).

4.3.5.3 Hohenmut.

The *Zuricher Volksbuch* has Pepin die soon after the second child's (Gertrude's) birth (Bachmann and Singer, *Deutsche Volksbücher*, 15–19). The bastards Wineman and Rapote, afraid of being disinherited, want to kill Charles. A count flees with Charles to the heathen king Marsilie (who has an excellent reputation in spite of being a heathen); they change their names. Marsilie's sister loves Charles; she begs him to leave his belief and marry her. He is afraid of her beauty, that she will lead him astray, so he asks the count's advice. The count sends messengers to Kerlingen in France, to Charles's brothers, friends and countrymen, announcing that he, the count, is returning with the true heir to the throne. He also gives the reason for their flight and that Charles is considered one of the best knights in the world; he should be welcomed with honor. Charles has been considered dead, so all are delighted. The count and Charles return to Kerlingen; Charles is welcomed

---

[17] The original source is again Aretin, *Älteste Sage über die Geburt und Jugend Karls des Großen*.

[18] This segment also outlined by Memmer, *Die altfranzösische Bertasage*, 157–58, 212; and Allen, *Genealogy and Structure*, 37–39, 137–42.

with honor and crowned king. At this point, Charles is twenty-five years old. The brothers humble themselves and beg forgiveness when they see Charles's strength. Charles makes them rich.[19] Many lines are the same as Stricker, word for word.

4.3.5.4 *Karl Meinet*.

Karl Meinet relates a different story, and, like Füetrer, bears a resemblance to Spanish texts in parts.[20] There are two brothers (whose genealogy is unclear; there is no false wife for Pepin in this text), Hoderich and Haenfrait, who live near Paris at Balduch. A dwarf reveals a treasure to them. They use the treasure to build a house near Paris; they become rich and famous through usury. Pepin appoints them regents for twelve-year-old Charles at his death. They use their wealth, however, to ensure their own position and prevent his becoming king. He is forced to work in the kitchen as a servant. Pepin had assigned David to help Charles; David promises the brothers to help with a plot to poison Charles while in fact delaying it. David travels around France to help find faithful nobles to help while leaving another servant to protect Charles. David suggests the immediate knighting and coronation of Charles. He makes the brothers wait to try poisoning him until a certain plant blooms. At the coronation, Charles is turning a peacock on a spit in the kitchen; other boys are to be knighted at the same time. The parents see the boys imitating Charles (in the kitchen!) and decide to wait a year. Charles throws the spit in Hoderich's face rather than serve him; there is a general melee which forces David to decide that Charles needs protection. They go to Spain to serve Galaffer, who is already at war with Bremunt. Three days later they are in Spain, and Hoderich crowns himself king of France. The French ask for protection when they arrive, and it is granted. Galya, Galaffer's daughter, falls in love with Charles. The heroes fight Bremunt and win. One year later, Bremunt is back again with his nephew Kayphas, a giant. Charles (at sixteen years old) wants to help, but needs to be knighted. Galya asks her father to grant his wish, and he does, giving him the sword Galosevele and the horse Affeleir. That evening Charles sees her at the banquet and falls in love with her too.

Charles cannot sleep, so he goes out riding. He is challenged by Kayphas. They duel, Charles wins, and fastens Kayphas's head to the saddle. He wins the sword Durendarde from Kayphas. He returns to glory, finding David seeking him. Galya tells her confidante of plans to convert and asks to meet with Charles. Through a hole in the wall, they speak that evening. She promises him treasure;

---

[19] Again, Memmer, *Die altfranzösische Bertasage*, 159–61, 213, as well as Allen, *Genealogy and Structure*, 35, 143–44, outline this segment.

[20] A. v. Keller, ed., *Karl Meinet*, Bibliothek des literarischen Vereins in Stuttgart (Stuttgart: Litterarischer Verein, 1858), 834–42 (ll. 1–325).

he goes to fight in the morning. At Val Morial, Charles fights with the French and others against Bremunt, and they win. Galaffer will help Charles regain France; Charles will return for Galya later.

Upon the return to France, adventures are slightly different from any encountered in other versions. The lands of Gerfein, a baron loyal to Charles, are invaded. There is a recognition scene. The two brothers are captured; Charles is crowned and the brothers are executed. Galaffer returns to Spain. Dederich, David, and Charles return to Toledo in disguise. They protect a girl in the forest from another man's advances. Charles and Galya spend time together in a city ruled by a cousin of hers, Orias. He makes advances to Galya, but she screams. Charles and his party write letters home, and French barons come to accompany them back to Paris. Galya is baptized and marries Charles. (There are further details here omitted.) Morant is accused of adultery with Galya on the voyage back; parts of that same story that also occurs in the *Gran conquista* (cf. Allen, *Genealogy and Structure*, 39–44).

4.3.5.5 Füetrer.

Füetrer's *Bayerische Chronik* is based largely on *Weihenstephan* (cf. Paris, *Histoire poétique*, 502 and Allen, *Genealogy and Structure*, 44).[21] Charles is raised with his half-brothers, Wineman and Rapot. They are jealous of his abilities, and speak to Pepin against him. He complains to Pepin, which only makes Pepin harder of heart to Charles. Thus Charles decides to go away for a while until Pepin changes his mind, a decision supported entirely by Pepin. Donatus of Troyes and other friends accompany him to Tholeta in Spain. There Calastrus, Marsilies, and Galian welcome them. The French agree to help against Bromant. Bromant is defeated, but prepares for another battle. The stronger second force makes a surprise attack on Galafre and his men; Charles is left sleeping while they go out to fight. The same scene we have seen before—Charles berating fate and his family, thinking himself betrayed—is played out, with Galienne who arms him in return for betrothal. Charles joins the fight and does much damage against Braimant who fights with Dürrndart. Charles wins the sword by killing him. Galafre and his men rout the others; there is much treasure in Braimant's tent, and glory for Charles. Meanwhile, a message from France arrives: Pepin is dead, Charles should return. Galienne asks to be taken away and baptized. With the parents' blessings and jewels, Galienne accompanies Charles, and is baptized and married in France. She dies shortly thereafter (Spiller, *Ulrich Füetrer*, 99–105; cf. Allen, *Genealogy and Structure*, 44).

---

[21]Text is found in Spiller, *Ulrich Füetrer*, 99–105.

In the German versions, the names of the half-brothers are different from the Italian, as are others, those of Charles's faithful companions. The number of plotters varies (twelve in Stricker; just two brothers elsewhere, with their followers). The pagan king is Marsilie or Galafre, but definitely in Toledo. Whether or not Galafre's daughter converts and marries Charles varies; there can be a relationship only (*Weihenstephan*) or merely interest (Stricker). Other differences are the existence of a sibling—a brother appears in *Weihenstephan*; or the geographical center: Kä/erlingen is an important site, home of Berta's relative(s); there is no trip to Rome (Stricker; *Weihenstephan*; *Karl Meinet*; *Volksbuch*); the half-brothers are forgiven and become faithful liegemen. The appearance of a dwarf in one version betrays the interference of legends and possibly of courtly literature. Otherwise, expansion or condensing result in more or less plot detail. The number of battles fought for the Spanish king can be multiplied, using various techniques seen in other *chansons de geste* in V^{13}: doubling; the nephew of the opponent being killed; other pagan attacks drawn by the girl's reputation for beauty. Miscellaneous good knightly deeds are interspersed—thus, in *Karl Meinet*, protecting females from male advances. Pepin's being alive or dead at the time of the attempts on Charles is another variable (in Füetrer, Pepin is alive). The reason for Charles's flight also varies; in Füetrer, again, we find a difference: his half-brothers' dislike, not death threats.

4.3.6. Scandinavian versions.

Scandinavian versions of this tale appear in the *Karlamagnús Saga* and its derivatives. Whether or not these should be included in a discussion of the *Mainet* story may be questioned. Jacques Horrent (*Les Versions françaises*, 73–75) says they do not interest the argument because they take place when Charlemagne is not young, but a grown man. The *Karlamagnús Saga* (ca. 1240–1250) in Branch One contains the story of a plot against Karl by the two brothers Renfrei and Heldri (Togeby and Halleux, *Karlamagnús Saga*, 2–52; Hieatt, *Karlamagnús Saga* [1975], 54–102). Charles, who is thirty-two years old when Pepin dies, is warned by an angel to flee to the Ardenne and to take the name Magnus (perhaps the writer is aware of the etymology of *Maine*?). He is to work with a thief, Basin; Namlun (Naimes) assists in arrangements. While robbing, he hears Renfrei telling his wife of a plot by twelve men against him. Renfrei himself is to become king. He lists the participants to her, including Heldri, his brother. She reproves her husband and he hits her.[22] Charles collects the blood from her wounds (she holds her face over the side of the bed to avoid soiling the sheets) in his right

---

[22]Note that her reproof to her husband concerns family: "you and your offspring shall pay for this" (Hieatt, *Karlamagnús Saga* [1975], 59).

glove as evidence. Charles invites many lords to his consecration at Aix, including the plotters. Among those to be present are Milon, the pope, and well-armed Romans. Karlamagnus then plans with his faithful men to have the conspirators taken as they come to the consecration. They are taken, confess all, and are beheaded.

The circumstances—Charles's age, type of plot—are quite different, yet the same names and some of the same circumstances occur. The two brothers (though it is never stated that they are also brothers of Charles) are major plotters; Milon is the pope and an ally; Gelim is Charles's sister who helps in the plot. Thierry (here Drefia) is a faithful knight in the Ardennes; and Charles must maintain anonymity during the period of exile (cf. Allen, *Genealogy and Structure*, 45). The whole is also related to Dutch (thirteenth century) and German pieces, *Charles and Elegast*, where Elegast plays a similar role to Basin. The Scandinavian tradition is thus quite different, for whatever reasons—the compiler's additions and changes, many intermediaries now lost.[23]

4.3.7 Dutch versions.
None.

4.3.8 English versions.
None.

4.3.9 Discussion.
Differences found between German versions can be compared to the differences found in European versions. Names, motivations, and number and type of episodes vary. The one common factor is the plot woven against a prince, Charles, particularly by two brothers, with or without help. Even Charles's age and whether his father is still alive or not varies.

Very early, critics divided *Karleto* versions into two groups: those with the trip to Rome and those without (e.g., G. Paris, "*Mainet*: fragments"). Later critics divide the texts by those where Charlemagne flees home because of difficulties

---

[23] For more on the Scandinavian tradition—problems in dating, relationship between the *Karlamagnús Saga* and the Danish (fifteenth and sixteenth centuries) and Swedish (fifteenth century) versions, etc.—see Hieatt's introduction, where she gives the date of the original translation as 1217–1263, under Hakon IV (*Karlamagnús Saga* [1975], 11–52); P. Skårup ("Contenu, sources, rédactions," in *Karlamagnús saga*, ed. Togeby and Halleux, 331–55, here 333–55) and A. Loth ("Les manuscrits norrois," in *Karlamagnús saga*, ed. Togeby and Halleux, 356–78, here 359–78) also provide further precision in dating the texts.

with his father vs. those where he must flee his evil half-brothers (Riebe, *Über die verschiedenen Fassungen*; Jacques Horrent, *Les Versions françaises*). However, since we are not trying to create a stemma here, but rather to place the story in the context of V^{13}, two points are of particular interest: 1. the historicity of the story and 2. the *enfances* or childhood *chanson de geste* and its place in tradition and in this compilation.

4.3.9.1 Historical considerations.

There is no factual historical background for the events as narrated in *Karleto*. Historical accounts such as the *Grandes Chroniques de France* recount neither the *Berta* story nor the childhood of Charlemagne. There are, however, several points of intersection with history: the names of the so-called half-brothers and the Spanish adventures.

The only historical basis found for the *Enfances* was by Pio Rajna,[24] followed by G. Paris (*Histoire poétique*, 438–40), who noted that Charles Martel, a bastard, at Pepin of Heristal's death had to contend with Chilperic II and the palace official, Raginfreid. They suggested that popular songs would have been created at the time and have spread through oral routes, only to be confused with later legends about another Charles and Pepin. "Heudri" and "Rainfroi" then would derive from "Chilpericus" and "Raginfridus." Bédier gives an eleventh-century Stavelot document (a saint's life) as a possible source of the story. It recounts Charles Martel's victory over the two usurpers Raginfridus and Helpricus; this could then have been confused with Charlemagne, and the names gallicized to Rainfroi and Helpri (later Heudri).[25] But did the epic influence the poem, or vice versa? Lejeune suggests rather that epic legends in Latin or vulgar Latin celebrated Charlemagne first.[26] As Horrent points out, the names of the brothers in the oldest versions do not correspond with the French forms; "Heudri" cannot derive regularly from "Chilpericus" or vulgar Latin "Helpricus"; we would expect "Helpri(c)," with a "p" not a "d" (*Les Versions françaises*, 251–53). These are unknown in any French versions and, in fact, in any version of *Mainet*. "Rainfroi" does not derive regularly either. The "R" form appears only in secondary texts where it replaced the "H" form. Thus Horrent contends "la chanson est née dans la première moitié du XIIe siècle, sans attache au passé" (*Les Versions françaises*, 252). However, the *Ausnahmslösigkeit* [exceptionlessness] of phonological

---

[24] P. Rajna, *Le origini dell'epopea francese* (Florence: Sansoni, 1884), 204.

[25] J. Bédier, *Les Légendes épiques: Recherches sur la formation des chansons de geste*, 2e éd. (Paris: Champion, 1913), 3: 3–38.

[26] R. Lejeune, *Recherches sur le Thème: Les Chansons de Geste et l'Histoire* (Liège: Faculté de Philosophie et Lettres, 1948), 24.

development has long since been recognized as fallible. Furthermore, name-pairs are subject to mutual influence; the tendency to assonance, especially initially, is notable elsewhere in literature (*Erec et Enide*; *Amis et Amile*, etc.), so the presence of a non-etymological initial "H" in one name is not surprising; the middle occlusive may well have undergone analogical influence as well. Thus it seems safer here to indicate the possibility of influence from the Charles Martel story. Allen points out that all earlier critics had sought a single source for the story, "as if the latter were similar to a long river which can be traced back to a single point of origin . . .the essential elements of *Mainet* are a part of all heroic legends and simply cannot be traced to any particular source" (*Genealogy and Structure*, 70).

That the source might be Spanish was first suggested by Menéndez-Pidal ("«Galiene la belle»," 76). Alfonso VI, exiled by Sancho II, went to Toledo in 1072 accompanied by a faithful servant and companions. The Muslim king Mamun received him well and Alfonso served against Muslim enemies. When Sancho died, Alfonso was afraid of conditions being placed upon his departure, so he left Toledo secretly to go home and receive his inheritance. In 1090 he married Zaida, the king of Seville's daughter, who had been his lover in a Toledan castle, and who brought with her part of Toledo as a dowry. This resembles the Spanish version of Charlemagne's youth: no half-brothers, in returning to his realm after the death of the ruler. The name Galeana also seems to come from Spain; a road as well as buildings in Spain and Southern France bear the name. "Val Somorial" may be a place once in existence near Toledo (Menéndez-Pidal, "«Galiene la belle»," 87); shoeing horses backwards is also mentioned, along with a lot of smaller details which resemble *Enfances Charlemagne* (see discussion in Allen, *Genealogy and Structure*, 72–73). The attachment to local interest and legends is illustrated clearly in the different versions: as Becker pointed out in 1913, local interests played a strong role in encouraging the *chanson de geste*: "ein gut Teil ist unter dem Patronat der interessierten Kultstätten entstanden und gesungen worden" [a major part was sponsored and sung under the patronage of the interested cult places],[27] but the whole life of the times ("das ganze Leben der Zeit") is in play: thus the need for history in Liège made d'Outremeuse an accepted historical source through the eighteenth century.[28] Sholod's 1966 work focuses on local interest in Spain, departing from Menéndez-Pidal's traditionalistic

---

[27] P. A. Becker, review of *Les légendes épiques*: Recherches sur la formation des chansons de geste.—III. La légende des 'Enfances' de Chalemagne et l'histoire de Charles Martel, by Joseph Bedier [sic], professeur au Collège de France, *Literaturblatt für germanische und romanische Philologie* 34 (1913): 370–75, here 374.

[28] As Michel argues in *Légendes epiques carolingiennes*, 6.

theoretical basis infused with oral research derived from Lord and Parry. He suggests that the rise of Carolingian epic derives from French jongleurs in Spain, a source for Spanish information in *Mainet*.[29]

That various historical events—Charles Martel and his fight for power, or Alfonso VI and his exile—may have influenced some versions, however indirectly, is possible.[30] Clerks wrote, read, and copied. Each clerk had personal interests in his specific area: Spain, Germany, Scandinavia, the Italian peninsula. Each genre has certain motifs and a characteristic style, but, as we have seen, the same basic plot can cross generic boundaries: saints' lives, chronicles, *chansons de geste* all narrate versions of Charlemagne's story. If they share the story, they may also share motifs. Sources, oral and written, that redactors used in the Middle Ages are lacking today; we cannot trace all details.

4.3.9.2 *Enfances* and the *chanson de geste*.

One of the primary motifs of the later *chanson de geste* is the creation of *enfances*, the childhood of a hero. Shen suggests that *chansons de geste* after 1175 tend to follow a biographical format instead of focusing on events, and the *enfances* are part of that trend.[31] As Carney has said, where the adult existed first, that fact may form the child.[32] However, Allen notes that *Karleto*, unlike other *enfances*, is not written to describe the youth of a hero made famous in other epic poems (*Genealogy and Structure*, ii). In fact, Einhard had avoided telling of Charlemagne's youth, and the *Chanson de Roland*—which in some form existed at the Battle of Hastings in 1066—is the background against which Charlemagne is depicted.

Readers and critics have become too involved in the possibly historic background to regard the Italian version in its own context. The interest is not only

---

[29] B. Sholod, *Charlemagne in Spain: The Cultural Legacy of Roncesvalles* (Geneva: Droz, 1966), 228.

[30] Here is not the place for an extended discussion of *chanson de geste* origins. Bédier argued for a twelfth-century date, against others who argued a continual derivation from the eighth century. A combined learned and popular influence could be the source, but specific dates and contents are unidentifiable. That discussion is a part of ongoing debate on the development of the French *chanson de geste*, unsolvable and therefore undiscussed here.

[31] L. S. Shen, *The Old-French 'Enfances' Epics and their Audience* (Ann Arbor: UMI, 1982), 2.

[32] A. P. Carney, "Portrait of the Hero as a Young Child: Guillaume, Roland, Girard, and Gui," *Olifant* 18 (1993–1994): 238–77, here 239. This is now almost a truism; cf. S. Sturm-Maddox and D. Maddox, eds., *Transtextualities: Of Cycles and Cyclicity in Medieval French Literature*, MRTS 149 (Binghamton: Medieval and Renaissance Texts and Studies, 1995), 8.

genealogical, but also exemplary and scholarly. In all versions, Charles must gain credibility as a king—honor and finances being the primary prerequisites (cf. Allen, *Genealogy and Structure*, 110). "Duty . . . to lineage" is family salvation, first secular, then ecclesiastical.[33] It is urgent to establish the family territory before going on crusade. The writer establishes the hero's origins (here the French royal family's), justifying each generation and its right to the land. Here, as in Bédier's contention, the lineage never exceeds three generations.[34] But instead of the conflict deriving from a choice between conflicting responsibilities (as Vine Durling suggests), in V^{13} the conflict is to regain lost land or a missing genealogical link.

Though Wolfzettel's analysis of *Enfances* has been criticized for being too rigid because of his archetypal approach (Shen, *The Old-French 'Enfances'*, 5), there is a striking similarity between the *Enfances* in V^{13} and Wolfzettel's summary—treachery forces the hero into exile; his prowess makes possible his triumphant return and the punishment of the traitors (compare Vine Durling, *Permutations in Genealogy*, 5); it works for both *Bovo* and *Karleto*.[35] A hero's (or heroine's) misfortunes may include bastardy; parents murdered by usurpers; or reduction to servitude. Shen summarizes the general characteristics of the plot: the child must flee with his tutor or other household member; his noble birth is visible in his appearance and instinctive skills; he masters skills precociously (cf. *Orlandino*, ll. 9458 ff); he has a tendency to haughty and violent behavior toward traitors and those who impede him and his followers; only the hero stands up to the increasingly-high-handed usurpers; he must flee for support before he can attack them; he wins fortune in a foreign court; marries a foreign [if not Saracen] princess and thus attains a higher rank. Jealous opponents at the court, frequently the princess's brother(s), oppose him; he is reunited with his parents, reconciled with the king, wins back family lands, and punishes the traitors. He frequently then has new troubles from the remaining traitors (or their relatives) and must kill every last one (Shen, *The Old-French 'Enfances'*, 201–9; my comments added).

Krauss has suggested that the *enfances* provide a model for the rising bourgeoisie (*Epica feudale*, 129), because they represent ability, not fame from historical

---

[33] Quote from N. Vine Durling, *Permutations in Genealogy: A Study of Kinship Structure in Old French Hagiography, Chansons de Geste and Romance* (Ann Arbor: UMI, 1981), 3.

[34] J. Bédier, "L'origine lignagère des chansons de geste. Lettre inédite de J. Bédier écrite en 1913," *Romanic Review* 33 (1942): 319–35, here 323.

[35] F. Wolfzettel, "Zur Stellung und Bedeutung der *Enfances* in der altfranzösischen Epik I, II," *Zeitschrift für französische Sprache und Literatur* 83 (1972): 317–48, 84 (1974): 1–32.

deeds, as important.³⁶ However, the role of family and territory argue a different story. As Vine Durling says, "Often, as in the case of the *enfances* epics, literature presents an idealized model for a particular social group" (*Permutations in Genealogy*, 8). It is not just a reflection, but also a projection of the *desiderata* of life, a model also for nobles to return to glory. Duby suggests that this genealogical urge is the "Vulgarisation progressive d'un modèle royal, celui du lignage par qui s'effectue le passage de la noblesse fluide des IXe et Xe siècles à la noblesse fixée de l'époque féodale, afermissement de la conscience familiale, qui d'abord s'attache à l'hérédité d'un titre et d'un patrimoine, mais qui peu à peu devient plus attentive à la valeur morale des aïeux et aux exemples de comportement qu'ils proposent . . .".³⁷ He also suggests that the further back the ancestors, the later the genealogy (Duby, "Remarques," 296), as Bloch also states: "The earlier a character or event can be situated chronologically within the global cycle, the later, generally speaking, the date of its addition to the whole."³⁸ This historical genealogical tendency provides confirmation of the lateness of the V¹³ compilation, but also of a broad audience: the up-and-coming bourgeoisie as well as the nobles would be interested.³⁹

In V¹³, *Karleto* is the first generally recognized *enfances*. However, if we re-examine *Bovo* and its bipartite division, we can see that it too is divided into *Enfances* and *Chevalerie*. Using the criteria mentioned above, *Bovo* was exiled and returned to take his land, and he had to exterminate the family of his enemy (one branch of Maganzesi) similarly to Charlemagne. At the end of the second half of *Bovo*, there is no end: Bovo settles in to age with Drusiana. *Bovo* sets the mold for V¹³ and the series of *Enfances* to come, a mold which *Karleto* follows. At the end

---

³⁶ "La tradizionale poesia della *Enfances*, volta a legittimare le pretese esclusivitiche della nobiltá di sangue come *classe de droit*, è sottoposta a un tale rovesciamento di valori che il giovane eroe svincolato dalla propria posizione sociale ereditaria può ora esser visto dalla borghesia italiana emergente come figura di identificazione" (Krauss, *Epica feudale*, 129).

³⁷ G. Duby, "Remarques sur la littérature généalogique en France," in idem, *Hommes et structures du moyen âge: Recueil d'articles* (Paris-La Haye: Mouton, 1967), 287–98, here 297.

³⁸ R. H. Bloch, *Etymologies and Genealogies: A Literary Anthropology of the French Middle Ages* (Chicago: University of Chicago Press, 1983), 94. This may be relevant to making Blanchefleur the daughter of the Byzantine emperor Heraclius (d. 641).

³⁹ For a recent article about different interpretations of different audiences, see C. Kramsch, "The Privilege of the Nonnative Speaker," *PMLA* 112 (1997): 359–69, esp. 360–61, where non-native French speakers interpret an advertisement referring to the *Ancien Régime* differently. One might presume, similarly, that different classes would interpret a text differently.

of *Karleto*, Charles is changing: he shows signs that he too, like Pepin (as shown in part two of *Bovo*), is weak before moral imperatives such as judging evil-doers. The moral consistency of rulers is an issue which returns throughout V^{13} as a part of the parallelism in plot and character typical of late *chansons de geste*, as part of the belief in consistency of family or blood.

CHART 4.3A: Versions of *Enfances Charlemagne/Karleto*: characters

V13	*I Reali di Francia*, Andrea da Barberino	*Aquilon de Bavière*, Raffaele da Verona	*Primera crónica general*	*Gran conquista de Ultramar*	Role in text
Lanfroi, Landris	Oldrigi, Lanfroy	Lanfroi, Lodris	n/a	Manfre, Eldois	Traitor brothers
Aquilon de Baiver, Bernard de Clermon, Morando da River	Morando	Aquilon de Baiver, Bernard de Clermont, Morand de Rivere	Don Morant	Morante de Rivera, Mayugot de Paris	Allies and helpers
Galafrio	Galafro	Galafrie	Galafre	King Hixen	Saracen king of Spain
Belisant	Galeanna	Galiane**	Galiana	Halía > Sevilla	Galafre's daughter ** Galafre's wife
Braibant	Bramante	Braibant	Bramant	Abrahin of Zaragoza	Galafre's enemy
Falsiron, Marsilio and Balugant	Falsirone, Marsilio and Balugante	Falsiron, Marsilie and Balugant	n/a	n/a	Galafre's sons
Cardinal Blançe	Cardinal Leone (Bernardo of Clermont's son)	n/a	n/a	n/a	Charles's ally in Rome
Berte(l)la	Berta	n/a	n/a	n/a	Charles's half-sister
Durendart (from Braibant)	Durincarda (from Polinoro)	Durindarde (from Braibant)	Durendart (from Bramant)	Durendart (from Abrahin)	Sword (received from defeated enemy)
Saragoça	Saragossa	Saragoze	Toledo	Toldeo	Charles's refuge
Karleto	Charles	Mainet	Maynet	Maynete	Charles's nickname / alias

French Fragments	Charlemagne, Girard d'Amiens	Ly Myreur des Histors, Jean d'Outremeuse	Croniques et Conquestes, David Aubert	Role in text
Hainfroi, Heudri	Rainfroi, Heudri	Ranfrois, Hondris	no names given	Traitor brothers
David (Esmeré), Maiengot, Tierri, Hugues, Henri	David, Hugues l'Auvergnat, Henri	n/a	n/a	Allies and helpers
Galafre	Galafre	Galafre	Galafre	Saracen king of Spain
Galienne	Galienne	Gloriande	n/a	Galafre's daughter
Braimant	Braimant	n/a	Braymant	Galafre's enemy
Marsile, Baligant	Marsile, Baligant	n/a	n/a	Galafre's sons
n/a	n/a	n/a	n/a	Charles's ally in Rome
n/a	Gille	Berthe	na/	Charles's half-sister
Durendal (from Braimant)	(unnamed) (from Braimant)	Durendal (source unknown)	n/a	Sword (from defeated enemy)
Toulete	Toledo	Spain, not further specified	Tholette	Charles's refuge
Maines	Mainet	Mainnes	n/a	Charles's nickname/alias

Karlamagnús Saga	Karl der Grosse, Stricker	Zurich Volksbuch, Hohenmut	Karl Meinet	Weihenstephan Chronik	Bayerische Chronik, Ulrich Füetrer	Role in text
Reinfrei, Heldri (not Charles's brothers)	Wineman, Rapote	Wineman, Rapote	Hoderich, Haenfrait	Winemann, Rapol	Winemann, Rapot	Traitor brothers
Namlun, Basin, Drefia et al.	Diepolt of Troyes	count; unnamed	David	Count Deipolt of Troyes	Donatus of Troyes	Allies and helpers
n/a	King Marsilie	King Marsilius	Galaffer	Marsilies	Calastrus	Saracen king of Spain
n/a	sister; unnamed	(sister)	Galya	sister; unnamed	Galiana	Galafre's daughter
n/a	n/a	n/a	Bremunt	n/a	Bramandis	Galafre's enemy
n/a	n/a	n/a	n/a	n/a	Marsilie (one son)	Galafre's sons
Pope Milon and Archbishop Rozer	n/a	n/a	n/a	n/a	n/a	Charles's ally in Rome
Gelim and Belisent (sisters)	n/a	Gertrud	n/a	n/a	n/a	Charles's half-sister
n/a	n/a	n/a	Durendart (from Bremunt)	n/a	Dürrndart (from Bramand)	Sword (from defeated enemy)
n/a	Spanje	n/a	Toledo	Yspaniam	Tholeta	Charles's refuge
Magnus	n/a	n/a	n/a	unnamed	n/a	Charles's nickname/alias

CHART 4.3B: Versions of *Enfances Charlemagne*

Italian and Franco-Italian
1. *V¹³ Karleto*, first half fourteenth century
2. *Aquilon de Bavière* by Raffaele da Verona, completed 1407
3. *I Reali di Francia* by Andrea da Barberino, late fourteenth-early fifteenth century

French
1. *Mainet*, twelfth century (surviving fragments)
2. *Chronique rimée* by Philippe Mousket, before ca. 1240
3. *Charlemagne* by Girard d'Amiens, 1285–1314
4. Ly *Myreur des Histors* by Jean d'Outremeuse, mid- to second half fourteenth century
5. *Croniques et Conquestes* by David Aubert, second half fifteenth century
6. *Chroniques de Charlemaine* (Dresden MS. 0.81; heavily damaged 1948, "Kriegverlost," Oct. 2008, personal communication, Sächsische Landesbibliothek -Staats- und Universitätsbibliothek Dresden), late fifteenth century

German
1. *Karl der Grosse by* Stricker, ca. 1230–1350
2. *Chronik* by Henry of Munich, ca. 1320–1325
3. *Karl Meinet*, first quarter fourteenth century
4. *Weihenstephan Chronik*, ca. 1435
5. Hohenmut, *Volksbuch*, Zurich MS., dated 1475
6. *Bayerische Chronik*, Ulrich Füetrer, 1477–1481

Spanish
1. *Primera crónica general*, 1270–1289
2. *Gran conquista de Ultramar*, late thirteenth-early fourteenth century

Scandinavian
1. *Karlamagnús Saga*, ca. 1230–1250

4.4 UGGIERI IL DANESE: *ENFANCES* AND *CHEVALERIE*

Ogier the Dane is one of the most studied epic characters of the Old French tradition. As one of the twelve *pairs* [peers], his name appears frequently in Old French *chansons de geste*. His nationality, clearly stated (he is called "le Danois" more frequently than by his actual name), has generated much interest on the part of Scandinavians as well as French. Versions of his adventures exist in French, Spanish, Italian, German, Dutch, and Scandinavian languages.

4.4.1 V[13] PLOT.

The plot is simple: during a battle outside Rome, Ogier saves the day, and is knighted. However, in so doing, he has taken the glory from Charlemagne's son, and thus made an enemy for life. Later, back at the court, the Dane (Ogier/Uggieri) is tricked into going to the unfriendly city of Marmora to demand tribute in a scene similar to that of Ganelon's tricking Roland into rearguard duty. However, the Dane, contrary to all expectations, succeeds with the help of friendly inhabitants and returns to find his son dead by the hand of Charles's son, Carleto. Ogier's son's death was the result of Ogier's bravery outside Rome, which had eclipsed Carleto's in the *Enfances Ogier*. Ogier finally kills Carleto in response to a threat over a chess game. Roland assists the Dane in staying alive, persuading Charlemagne to imprison him instead of killing him, and providing food. Ogier is ultimately released to save the kingdom (and Paris in particular) from a pagan invader, Braier.[1] Ogier insists on taking revenge on Charlemagne before he will fight, though, and strikes Charlemagne (who wears many coats of armor) three times lightly. Note that here too I keep the names of the characters in the versions discussed except for Ogier, unless otherwise noted.

4.4.2 Other Italian versions.

After V[13], Ogier's adventures appear in the *Reali di Francia* by Andrea da Barberino, the prose *Rinaldo* (unpublished), several "Books of the Dane" (1498, 1544), and in fifteenth-century prose and rhymed versions. Other than the *Reali*, none are available outside of their original manuscripts; I was fortunate in the opportunity to see a transcription of the fifteenth-century prose *Rinaldo*. However, Rajna describes all of the texts.

---

[1] See Cremonesi on not translating the name (*Le Danois Oger*, xxiii, n. 56). Rosellini cites her as well (*Geste Francor*, 125, n. 45).

4.4.2.1 *I Reali di Francia*.

The *Reali* (late fourteenth or early fifteenth century), book 6, chaps. 34–37, tells a highly different version of Ogier's story (Roncaglia and Beggiato, *I Reali di Francia*). It is a part of the *Enfances Charlemagne* segment: Charlemagne is in Spain, having just killed Bramante and liberated Galeana's family (Galafro, Morando, and Marsilio). Agolante sends King Gualfedriano to help Bramante with troops and his son. Gualfedriano hears of Bramante's death and sends messengers to Charles, among whom is his son, Uggieri. Uggieri stays for the three days of the embassy, and wishes to remain longer. Uggieri stays as a hostage while his father fights Charles (here called "Mainetto," from the French "Mainet" < Latin MAGNU(S); see the discussion in the section on *Karleto*, 4.3). Charles makes a deal with Gualfedriano that Gualfedriano will return to Africa and Uggieri will be freed. Uggieri begs to stay, and eventually prevails. Gualfedriano returns home and dies shortly thereafter; Agolante takes over his realm.

Uggieri wants to become a Christian; Charles and Morando baptize him, and he is designated standard-bearer. He infiltrates the group of Galafro's sons to make sure Charles is safe (compare David's role in the German version of *Enfances Charlemagne, Karl Meinet*). Uggieri hears of the brothers' plot against Charles, and informs Galeana, who in turn informs Morando and Charles. Morando and Charles steal the keys and money with Galeana's assistance, and all four go to Rome, then continue on to France. Thus, in the *Reali*, Uggieri is assumed into the story in roles played by other characters in other versions: that of David in the German version, infiltrating Charlemagne's brothers-in-law to-be; and that of Açopart in *Bovo*, assisting in flight from an enemy stronghold, not to mention the role of faithful converted pagan.

4.4.2.2 *Rinaldo*.

Gloria Allaire argues that the anonymous fifteenth-century *Rinaldo* is also by Andrea da Barberino.[2] Rajna discusses Books 3 and 5.[3] In Book 3, we find Ogier (here usually "el Danese" or "Ugg(i)eri") at court, and his son Baldovino and Carleto are great friends (51ʳ). Gano causes difficulties because king Massimione of Verona has not paid his tribute for ten years and all the messengers sent to

---

[2] G. Allaire, *Andrea da Barberino and the Language of Chivalry* (Gainesville, FL: University Press of Florida, 1997), 65–92.

[3] For the confusion of "book 5," see Pio Rajna, "Uggeri il danese nella letteratura romanzesca degl'Italiani," *Romania* 2 (1873): 153–69; 3 (1874): 31–77; 4 (1875): 198–436 (for this argument in particular, [1875]: 399), and Allaire, *Andrea da Barberino and the Language of Chivalry*, 66–67. I would like to thank Gloria Allaire for a copy of her transcription of MS. Laur. Plut. 42, codex 32, *Storie di Rinaldo* in prose, Book Three, which enabled me to verify the storyline and the confusion surrounding it.

claim tribute have been killed. When Ogier volunteers to go, Gano encourages Charlemagne to accept him. Hermellina, Namo's daughter and Ogier's wife, wants Ogier to stay because of their son Baldovino. Before leaving, Charlemagne gives a sealed letter to Ogier for the king of Verona, and promises to keep Baldovino with his own son. Berlingieri accompanies Ogier. During their trip, they are attacked; Ogier helps a fairy who promises to help him in return in the future. When Berlingieri and Ogier manage to reach King Massimione, he offers a deal: either Ogier is to strike him three blows, and if Ogier doesn't win, he will be hanged; otherwise Massimione will send his tribute:[4] alternatively, Ogier can receive three blows with the same agreement. Ogier's first two blows have no result, but his prayers bring help with the third: a knight in white with a red cross helps with the blow that cuts Massimione in two.[5] Only Luchano, Massimione's brother-in-law, sees the white knight, as does Ogier. Luchano is thus converted together with 10,000 knights to help him, in honor of St. George, and Ogier conquers Verona. Then Luchano takes six cities (Brescia, Padova, Vicenza, Treviso, Mantua, Cremona) and 200 castles. Berlinghieri marries Luchano's sister. A messenger sent to Charlemagne tells of Ogier's victories and greets all but Gano.

Gano is offended, and goes to Carloto to start a rumor that Charlemagne has promised the crown to Baldovino when he (Charlemagne) dies and that Carloto will be killed. Gano and Carloto plot a joust, where Gano has Ansuigi of Maganza urge Baldovino to joust first. Ansuigi and Carloto change outfits, and Ansuigi gives Carloto the sword to cut off Baldovino's head. Carloto then flees to Pontieri where Gano aids him. Roland and Rinaldo are very upset and leave Paris. Charlemagne hears of Baldovino's death and promises a vendetta. Two days later, Ogier returns with Luchano and Desiderio, and they lie to Ogier, saying that Baldovino is in the forest hunting. Hermellina tells him the truth and he faints. When he tries to get Charlemagne to avenge Baldovino, Gano and Carloto go also and accuse him of being pagan and trying to kill Charlemagne; they attack him, but he defends himself and kills Carloto. Charlemagne orders Ogier killed. Charlemagne sends for Rinaldo and Roland; Hermellina hears and comes, persuading Ogier to give up. Roland puts Ogier in prison, and Gano suggests to Charlemagne starving him. No one can mention Ogier's name to Charlemagne. Roland arranges the delivery of quantities of food, though, so that

---

[4] One cannot help remembering *Sir Gawain and the Green Knight* in English. The three blows are clearly a part of the Dane story also.

[5] This sounds like a Templar insignia; given the date of Andrea's text, that is possible, but is not mentioned in the text itself. According to D. A. Trotter, the red cross was the French insignia during the Third Crusade (*Medieval French Literature and the Crusades (1100–1300)* [Geneva: Droz, 1988], 79).

Ogier will not starve; and his horse is with him with plenty of fodder. He can walk the horse once a month and see his wife four times a month.

King Bravieri of Nubia goes to Marsilio and demonstrates his 300 demons who make so much noise that no one can stand before him. Marsilio is convinced, and gives him 200,000 Saracens. Bravieri challenges Charlemagne, and conquers a series of knights, including Roland, Rinaldo (but Baiardo will not fight because of the demons), and Charlemagne himself. Charlemagne is in prison for forty-five days; Bravieri demands the keys to Paris, or else he will hang all the prisoners and attack the city. It takes twenty days to find a champion; Charlemagne sends to the pope and the queen for help. On the nineteenth day, Hermellina asks the queen to let Ogier fight. The queen consults the pope, who agrees. Hermellina frees Ogier and tells him of recent events, but he does not want to go help Charlemagne. In the morning St. George appears to him, as does the lady in white (whom he had helped earlier at Verona), and tells him to block his ears and his horse's ears while fighting Bravieri. Ogier goes to Paris, reports for duty, and stops his ears. After testing his hearing with music, he uses a hat to cover and hold in the ear stuffing, then goes to fight.[6] Ogier kills Bravieri. The demons shriek and carry off his soul; the corpse stinks.

Ogier enters the city, removes the stuffing from his ears, and attacks the Saracens. Marsilio, realizing that he is in trouble, goes to Charlemagne and offers to leave if permitted. Charlemagne demands a tribute as was given to Pepin. Marsilio agrees, then frees Charlemagne and Namo. Namo goes to Ogier to bring him up to date. Ogier goes to Charlemagne with his helmet on, and kneels. Charlemagne does not know who it is, but Ogier will not rise until he is forgiven, so Charlemagne forgives him. Ogier takes off his helmet, rises, and identifies himself; Charlemagne is delighted. Marsilio meets with his sister, Galerana (the queen of France), and the amount of tribute is set. Galerana kneels and asks pardon for leaving Spain with Charlemagne (a reference to *Enfances Charlemagne*), which Marsilio gives. There is a tournament to celebrate the end of hostilities three days later.

In Book 5, the portion concerning Ogier begins where Orlando, worried about his companions, leaves with Ogier, Ulivieri, and Rinaldo in search of Astolfo and Riccardo di Normandia (Rajna reads "d'Ormandia") who had been taken by Marsilio when Charlemagne had sent for his tribute (fol. 116ʳ: Allaire, transcription of MS. Laur. Plut. 42, codex 32). The main character, however, is

---

[6] K. Togeby, *Ogier le danois dans les littératures européennes*, Det danske Sprog- og Litteraturselskab (Copenhagen: Munksgaard, 1969), 212, comments on Machiavelli's *Mandragola*, where Nicia (Scene 7, act 3) says, "... m'impeciassi gli orecchi comme el Danese ... ," and wonders where it comes from ("Mais nulle part dans ces romans de chevalerie on ne trouve un incident pareil")—this is the answer.

Rinaldo. The group undertakes many adventures along the way, then arrives at Tancia where the gallows to hang the two messengers are ready. With the help of Braidamonte,[7] the Christians gain the city and kill the major Saracen figures. The citizens are persuaded by a miracle to convert to Christianity, including Guliasso, the ruler, who thus keeps his kingdom. The French return home. At this point, the manuscript ends. In the printed versions, after a series of adventures involving a challenge by a pagan which Rinaldo and his group (not including Ogier) take care of, Ogier and Orlando go to pagan lands. Baiardo takes part in a horse race and wins; Orlando and Ogier are imprisoned, then liberated by Rinaldo and Ricciardetto. They turn toward France, passing through Arna where they pursue a vendetta for a friend of theirs whom they believe dead, Gismonda and her two children. However, Gismonda is in fact alive, and a griffon and an eagle kidnap her children. One is carried to Marsilio, the other to the emperor of Constantinople. In honor of their kidnappers, they are called Aquilone and Grifone. They are eventually brought back together again, but there is no further involvement by Ogier.[8]

4.4.2.3 *Aquilon de Bavière*.

"Li Danois Uzer" appears in *Aquilon de Bavière*, where he speaks the *lingue africane*, since he was born a Saracen; he is married to Armeline, Naime's daughter, and works with Naime and his four brothers-in-law in battle (Wunderli, *Raffaele da Verona: Aquilon de Bavière*, 125 ff; 135–36).[9]

4.4.2.4 Versions of the *Ogier le Danois* in Italy.

Ferrario summarizes several versions of the *Danois* tale in Italy, beginning with the *Reali di Francia*. He also summarizes a poem (*Uggieri il Danese, poema in ottava rima, Storia ed analisi degli antichi romanzi*, 3: 16–17) dating to 1511 (4: 12–13). Uggieri is the son of Gualfedriano, king of Getulia of Sarais and the mountains on the border of Nubia. He becomes good friends with Charlemagne while Charlemagne is in exile in Spain. Uggieri fights by Charles's side until he regains France, then is converted by pope Leon and is married to Hermellina,

---

[7] This is the daughter of the Soldano and sister of Aquilante, whom readers of Renaissance epic will recognize from Ariosto's *Orlando Furioso*.

[8] I follow Rajna in editing the names to make the summary comprehensible ("Uggeri il danese," 401).

[9] P. H. Coronedi ("L'Aquilon de Baviere'," [sic] *Archivum Romanicum* 19 [1935]: 237–304, here 282) was not familiar with V^{13}, as he states that the knowledge of Ogier's marriage to Armeline (= Ermellina) was not familiar to Franco-Italian poems. While the name is different in V^{13} (it is Floriamont), Ogier's wife (Naimes's daughter) urges Ogier to avenge their son's death (ll. 11910, 11939).

daughter of Naimes of Baveria. Here Uggieri's name is derived from a letter he receives from Africa once he is baptized, saying he is "tu es damnés de l'alma" (Ferrario, *Storia ed analisi*, 4: 16). Ferrario also outlines the *Fiore de' cavalieri francesi* or the *Fiore della battaglia* 3: 284–320), followed by the story of Mervain, his son (3: 320–29). This is the French romance involving the Dane's gifts from the six fairies, Ogier's position as hostage and his role outside Rome, Charlot's jealousy taken out on Ogier's son, Ogier's imprisonment under Turpin, and his victory over Brahier. He stays with Morgana, returns briefly to France for a victory and then is retaken by Morgana.[10]

4.4.2.5 Later Italian references to *Uggieri*.
Later Italian poems treat other parts of the Dane's life: *La Morte del Danese* by Cassio da Narni, published in Ferrara in 1521, and the *Danese Uggieri* by Girolamo Tromba da Nocera, published in Venice in 1599, are based on Adenet's poem according to Ferrario (*Storia ed analisi*, 2: 179).[11]

4.4.3 French versions.

4.4.3.1 Raimbert de Paris.
In French, the first document containing Ogier's adventures is the *Chevalerie d'Ogier de Danemarche*, supposedly by Raimbert de Paris, dating to the end of the twelfth century or beginning of the thirteenth.[12] It is generally divided into twelve

---

[10] Ferrario's work is difficult to use because of its date; bibliographical requirements have changed greatly since 1828–1829. It is unclear which of the specific texts Ferrario summarizes, or whether he combines stories to make one narration. Therefore my comments here are very brief.

[11] I was unable to consult these; though a copy of the *Morte* is at Harvard University, there was no microfilm available, and as the subject is peripheral to V[13], it was not necessary.

[12] For details on dating, see F. Lot, "A quelle époque remonte la connaissance de la légende d'Ogier le Danois?" *Romania* 66 (1940–1941): 238–53, here 241. A. Henry (ed., *Les Œuvres d'Adenet le Roi. Tome III: Les Enfances Ogier*, Rijksuniversiteit te Gent, Werken uitgegeven door de Faculteit van de Letteren en Wijsbegeerte, 121 Aflevering [Brugge: De Tempel, 1956], 28), suggests the first half of the thirteenth century. Togeby places it 1200–1215, suggesting that the *Enfances* portion was known by 1195, and that the *Chevalerie* dates to the early thirteenth century, at the latest after 1210 (*Ogier le danois dans les littératures européennes*, 38, 45–71). There are two editions of *Chevalerie Ogier*: J. B. J. Barrois, *Ogier de Danemarche par Raimbert de Paris: Poëme du XII*[e] *siècle* (Paris: Techner, 1842), now outdated, and M. Eusebi, *La Chevalerie d'Ogier de Danemarche, canzone di gesta*, Testi e documenti di letteratura moderna 6 (Milan: Cisalpino, 1962). I follow Eusebi here.

"branches": I, Enfances; II, Chess game; III, War in Lombardy (the revolt is II–III); IV–VIII, Castelfort; IX–XII, War of Saxons (Brahier).[13] The French versions belong to the *baron révolté* cycles because of Ogier's long resistance against Charlemagne. The tale begins when Charlemagne's messengers return from Gaufroi of Denmark shorn; Charlemagne, angry, wishes to avenge himself on Ogier, a hostage, son of Gaufroi. He gives Ogier to Guimer of St. Omer to guard. Guimer's daughter falls in love with Ogier; they produce Bauduinet. Ogier is to die for his father's errors (in fact, his stepmother Belissent's, who seeks to get Denmark for her son, away from Ogier, son of a previous wife). However, messengers from Rome interrupt Charlemagne's plans to attack Gaufroi: these ask for help against the Saracens invading Rome. God helps Charlemagne's march: a white hart shows him the way across the Alps. At Sutri, plans for the attack are set; while the French army attacks, Naimes is in charge of Ogier and the other youths.

The Emir Corsuble's son, Danemon, leads troops out of Rome; Alori holds the Christian insignia, but becomes frightened and flees. Ogier and the other youths come down the hill, seize the insignia from Alori, and go forth to save the Christian cause. Charlemagne knights Ogier then and there. Ogier is challenged by Caraheu's messenger (Caraheu is the fiancé of Corsuble's daughter, Gloriande). Charlot (Charlemagne's son) is desperate to fight and rushes out with just 2,000 men against Corsuble's 10,000. Ogier rescues Charlot; Charlemagne is furious with his son. When the challenge is made to Ogier, Charlot wants to fight too; so a double duel is planned, Caraheu and Sandone versus the two Christians. It is to be held on an island in the middle of the Tiber. In the middle of the fight, Danemon arrives with thirty men to take the Christians by treachery. The Dane is taken and given into Gloriande's keeping. Caraheu is upset with the betrayal, and goes to the Christians to give himself up. Caraheu arranges a raid against the pagans, who must flee back to the city.

Brunamon and his men arrive to reinforce the pagan army. Brunamon is excited at the prospect of marrying Gloriande. Gloriande, however, loves Caraheu, so Ogier speaks to the Emir on her behalf, accusing Brunamon of disloyalty for taking Gloriande from Caraheu. Brunamon defies Ogier for the possession of Rome. A new duel on the island is planned, in the presence of Caraheu, who gives Ogier Curtain, his sword. Ogier wins; the Saracens flee and the Christians follow. Caraheu is offered baptism, but refuses it and is allowed to leave.

(II III) Bauduinet (= Baldovino) has come to court and is playing chess with Charlot. Bauduinet wins, and Charlot, angry, hits Bauduinet on the head, killing him. Ogier cries vendetta, demanding Charlot. Charlemagne, however, hides

---

[13] The originator of the twelve episodes was C. Voretzsch, *Über die Sage von Ogier dem Dänen und die Entstehung der Chevalerie Ogier: Ein Beitrag zur Entwicklung des altfranzösischen Heldenepos* (Halle: Niemeyer, 1891).

his son. Ogier then attacks Charlemagne; he kills Lohier, the queen's nephew, and many others. Ogier does not succeed in harming Charlemagne in person; he leaves France. He goes to Italy to Desiderio's court, where Desiderio accepts his service, giving him two cities. Charlemagne sends Bertran, son of Naimes, as a messenger to Ogier. Bertran tries to start a fight in Pavia, but is stopped. Desiderio challenges Charlemagne; Ogier bears his message to Charlemagne. Charlemagne accepts the challenge and comes with his army to St. Ajose. Battle is joined; Ogier kills Bertran. Ogier gets away, medicates himself, and goes to sleep; he would have been taken by Charlemagne and his men if his horse had not awoken him. He flees, killing many. Desiderio will not let him into Pavia, so he continues his flight.

(IV–VII) Ogier flees, killing Amis and Amile from Rome. He manages to find a castle he can take where he can rest and feed his horse Broiefort. He sees that he cannot make it there, and leaves again for Castelforte. His squire Benoit (Benedetto) with 300 men is there and Ogier arrives safely. The siege lasts five years. There are various sorties, etc. Ogier and ten men (among whom are two traitors, Hardré and Gautier) hold the castle. The traitors persuade the others to help turn over Ogier, but an angel awakens him before they can. He fights his way into the castle, alone with his horse. Ogier makes wooden dolls which he places on the crenellations to defend the castle. Charlot goes to the walls to speak with Ogier, but Ogier says he wants to kill Charlot before he himself dies. Charlot asks pardon, but Ogier has every intention of killing him in his bed and says so. Charlot, however, wisely sleeps elsewhere; Ogier throws a spear into Charlot's bed, then flees. Charlemagne then leaves the castle and the siege. Eventually, when Ogier thinks all is well, he undresses and lies down to sleep, but Archbishop Turpin finds him.

(VIII–X) Turpin takes Ogier's arms and leads him to Reims under protest. Charlemagne is told and demands Ogier. Turpin and the peers persuade him to keep Ogier imprisoned but to let him starve to death. Turpin sees to it that Ogier receives sufficient food while he spends seven years in prison. Charlemagne will not even allow Ogier's name to be spoken in his presence.

Brahier, meanwhile, has heard that Ogier is dead. He goes to France; all the barons know that they need Ogier. So 300 squires call his name in a meeting. Charlemagne goes to Reims to find Ogier, who demands Charlot. The archangel Michael saves Charlot just before Ogier can cut off his head. So Ogier slaps him well instead. Ogier wins a duel against Brahier, gaining as well his unguent to cure all ills. (Note that the king's heir is not killed in this version.)

(XI–XII) While Ogier is resting, he hears a woman sobbing. The king of England's daughter is held by Saracens. He saves her, and she falls in love with him. Ogier is without a horse, and has many enemies, so he sends her for help. Charlemagne dreams of danger, and the girl arrives to confirm it. Charlemagne arrives to help Ogier, and defeats Ogier's pagan enemies. Various exploits occur, including killing a giant and many other Saracens. Ogier marries the girl and goes to the royal court where Charlemagne gives him land. Ogier is praised and upon his death is buried at Meaux with Benoit. This last section is different from all other versions.

4.4.3.2 Adenet le Rois.
Adenet le Rois's *Enfances Ogier*, dating to the end of the thirteenth century, is based on Raimbert's version, most critics agree. It takes only the first branch, making that into the first half of his tale, however, omitting the rest, and adding a second portion not in Raimbert (Henry, *Enfances Ogier*). Upon Charlemagne's return from Spain, the Danish are fighting Constance in Hungary. Gaufroi of Denmark submits to Charlemagne upon the urging of Daimon de Bavière, his brother-in-law, and gives his son, Ogier, as a hostage. Ogier is kept by the chatelaine of Saint-Omer, whose daughter, Mahout, and Ogier fall in love. Baud(o)uyn is their son.

Charlemagne then demands tribute from Gaufroi, but he is remarried, and Ogier's stepmother receives the messengers and commits an outrage on them, hoping that Ogier will be killed and thereby make her son heir. Charlemagne convokes his army at Loon (= Laon) and has Ogier come along; Mahout dies of worry, but Naimes saves Ogier. Meanwhile, messengers arrive from Rome, where the pope is threatened by Saracens. Corsuble is there. Alori, a Lombard, has the royal insignia, and the army goes to Sustre (= Sutri). Charlemagne fights Danemon outside Rome, and Alori flees. Brunamon arrives on his horse Broiefort with 20,000 Turks to help the Saracens. Ogier and the squires see Alori and the Lombards; they chase them, seize the standard, arms, and horses, and go to save Charlemagne. Charlemagne knights Ogier, and the French return to Sustre victorious. Charlot and Thierry, his "master," arrive with reinforcements. (Note Thierry's role here, similar to that of the Thierry in *Bovo*, as a second to the ruler.) Carahuel, Gloriande's fiancé, arrives at the Saracen camp, and hears of Ogier. Charlot and his men go to fight the Saracens; they meet Carahuel and his men, and must be saved by Ogier. Carahuel sends a message to Charlemagne: convert and live! He offers to combat the best Frenchman with Gloriande as the prize. Ogier agrees but Charlot wants to fight, so they add a duel of Charlot with Sadoine.

At the double duel, Danemon, Corsuble's son, lies in wait with thirty Saracens. When the Saracens seem to be losing, Danemon comes out; Carahuel tries to help the French, and they manage to allow Charlot to flee, but cannot save Ogier. Ogier is held honorably by Gloriande. Carahuel goes to Charlemagne to offer himself as prisoner. Naimes holds him in honor.

Brunamon challenges Carahuel's faith; Gloriande informs Ogier who champions Carahuel's cause. They send messengers to Charlemagne in order to let Carahuel know what is going on. Carahuel is allowed to return to defend himself. Ogier wins and takes Broiefort, Carahuel's horse, as a symbol of his victory. He goes to Gloriande's tent; Carahuel gives Ogier his sword Curtain and returns him to Charlemagne. Carahuel returns to Rome the next day.

At the pitched battle the next day, the Christians win. They follow the pagans back to Rome. Ogier saves Carahuel and Gloriande, and the Christians take over allowing them safe-conduct. Pope Desier and his churchmen try to convert Carahuel unsuccessfully; Charlemagne allows the survivors to return home, and Carahuel swears never to bear arms against Charlemagne. Rome's churches are resanctified, Saracens return home to bury the honored dead, and Charlemagne and his army return to Paris. Ogier receives the fief of Beauvaisis in thanks, and learns that his stepmother was the source of his problems. The poem ends with a series of tactical marriages: Constance of Hungary with Gaufroi of Denmark, and her young son Henri to Gaufroi's daughter. Everyone returns home, and Ogier stays with Charlemagne's court.

These two texts, the "Raimbert" and Adenet versions, are the best known and are the usual comparisons for V^{13}. Ogier's feud with Charlemagne places the French versions within the "rebel baron" cycle. In them the heir to the French throne is not killed; Ogier is not married to Balduin's mother; and Roland does not play the role of saving Ogier (Turpin does). The humorous aspects of V^{13} are also absent; though the food description is exaggerated, it is an angel who saves Charlemagne's son from Ogier (not Ogier's courtesy, mediated by Naimes). Ogier's vengeance in V^{13} is twice exercised: once on Charlot, and then on Charlemagne, though the offending heir is already dead.[14] It should be noted that Adenet le Rois's *Enfances Ogier* is linked to his *Berte aux grands pieds* by the double marriage of Gaufroi de Danemark, Ogier's father, with Constance of Hungary (Berte's sister) and that of Flandrine, Ogier's sister, with Henry, Constance's son (Henry, *Œuvres: Les Enfances Ogier*, ll. 8062–8173).[15]

---

[14] On humor in *Ogier*, see N. Lioce, "Burlesque et dérision dans *Ogier le Dannoys* (remaniement en prose du XVᵉ siècle)," in *Burlesque et dérision*, ed. Guidot, 281–96, and E. Hoyer-Poulain, "Ridicules d'Ogier: vacillements du héros dans les remaniements de la chanson d'Ogier le Danois," 49–58, both of whom speak more of the fifteenth-century versions in French than the Franco-Italian which directly interests us here. They are also more interested in the fantastic episodes—the faery horse and his antics, Ogier losing the ring which prevents aging and having to fight an aging woman for it—than in non-fantastic humor such as Charlemagne's quaking before Ogier.

[15] A. Henry is also cited on this subject in M. Heintze, "La mort de Baldovino: un épisode du *Cantar de Sansueña* à la lumière d'un romance méconnu sur Baldovinos," in *Lirica, Drammatica, Narrativa* (Bologna: Pàtron, 1994), 47–98, here 53. Both *Berta da li pe grant* and *Ogier le Danois* exist in versions by Adenet. No connection between Italy and Adenet or V^{13} has ever been successfully established.

4.4.3.3 Girard d'Amiens.

Girard d'Amiens wrote his *Charlemagne* in the late thirteenth– early fourteenth century.[16] Granzow has edited the relevant section for the Dane.[17] It can be divided into two parts: Ogier's stay at St. Omer together with his love for the chatelain's daughter, and secondly his freedom from imprisonment and expedition into Italy against Corsuble. Granzow suggests that the source for content only is Adenet's *Enfances*; in fact, no portion of the "rebel baron" story is included. Charlemagne returns home from a battle with the Saxons to Paris for the winter. In the spring Godefroi de Danemarche had promised to send fealty and tribute, and given Ogier, his oldest son, as hostage for these. Ogier's mother, the duke of Bavière's sister, is dead, however, and the stepmother had given Ogier as hostage. He is soon led to Saint Omer; the chatelaine is noble and good to Ogier, and his daughter is young and pretty. The two love each other.

Corsuble wants to conquer France. He goes to Sezile (Sicily) with seven other kings and moves on Rome. The pope sends a message to Charlemagne to come to Rome. Charlemagne passes by St. Omer where Ogier asks to see Naimes, his relative. Naimes takes Ogier with him. The chatelain's daughter weeps and kisses Ogier because she is pregnant and does not want to see Ogier go. Corsuble has spies along the way who inform him of Charlemagne's passage through Lombardy. Corsuble's nephew Danemont is with him; Naimes and Danemont fight; Ogier acquits himself well. During the fighting, Ogier kills Cornufle de Nuble, one of Danemont's special friends. The Christians win the field thanks to Ogier's bravery. Naimes goes to Charlemagne and recounts the whole story; Charlemagne is impressed with Ogier's exploits. Corsuble is enraged that Danemont is wounded; he will allow no one to fight unless he personally orders the battle. Charlemagne, meanwhile, gets word to the pope to reinforce the French forces.

Corsuble sends a message to Charlemagne to convert, and Charlemagne responds with a challenge to fight him or to designate substitutes for a duel (note that the initiative here is on the part of the Christians, not the pagans). Corsuble thinks to surprise Charlemagne with a battle, but Charlemagne's spy informs him of the approaching fight. Ogier leads the first of seven ranks in a battle that leaves only two of the seven pagan kings alive. Charlemagne fights Corsuble finally, and Corsuble is killed. The Saracens flee in a fight in which Ogier

---

[16] A. Saly, "La Date du *Charlemagne* de Girart d'Amiens," in *Au Carrefour des routes d'Europe: La Chanson de Geste*, Xe Congrès international de la Société Rencesvals pour l'étude des épopées romanes, Strasbourg 1985, Sénéfiance 20–21 (Aix-en-Provence: CUER MA, 1987), 2: 975–81, gives the beginning of the fourteenth century.

[17] W. Granzow, "Die Ogier-Episode im 'Charlemagne' des Girart d'Amiens: Nebst vollständigem Namenverzeichnis der gesamten Dichtung" (Ph. D. diss., Universität Greifswald, 1908), 34–65.

triumphs. The Christians re-enter Rome the next day; Pope Lyons weeps and thanks Charlemagne, who stays just long enough for his men to heal. The pope accompanies Charlemagne one day's ride out of Rome, and then Charlemagne returns to Paris.

Clearly, Girard's version is greatly changed from earlier French versions: Ogier's role, though heroic, is subordinated to Charlemagne's. As hero of the poem, Charlemagne duels and defeats the pagan hero, and Ogier's personal life is of less interest than in poems treating him exclusively.

4.4.3.4 Philippe Mousket.
Mousket's *Chronique rimée* (mid-thirteenth century; Reiffenberg, *Chronique rimée*) finds in Ogier a minor figure, mentioned as "preus et légiers" in a list of warriors at Aspremont, where he is unhorsed (ll. 4471–4476). Ogier is also included in a review of his battles, ll. 4644–4655, as son of Gaufrois and hostage who served Charlemagne so well that he was placed among the twelve *pairs*, though his entire story is not recounted. Subsequently his duel with Ferragus (ll. 5778) is mentioned, and Charlemagne mourns his death at Roncesvalles (ll. 7648–7682).

4.4.3.5 Jean d'Outremeuse.
Jean d'Outremeuse (born 1338, d. 1400) in his *Myreur des Histors* (second half of the fourteenth century) includes Ogier throughout.[18] Ogier is also included in d'Outremeuse's *Geste*, lines 13080–13110. Whether or not there was a separate *Geste d'Ogier* is unclear; d'Outremeuse mentions it as one of his works, but it has been suggested that what was intended is the *Myreur* itself (Michel, *Les Légendes epiques carolingiennes*, 130). Goosse and his followers suggest *Ogier* as the source of the *Myreur*, with the original lost because it was "déjà veillot" as a genre when written. In any case, in the *Myreur*, as Michel in his volume indicates, Charlemagne has ceded his place to the "héros de prédilection: Ogier le Danois" (15), and d'Outremeuse continually cites the "précellence de la famille d'Ogier parmi les autres lignages épiques," including Ogier's ancestors and his marvelous story (16). In book 2, beginning in the year 794 (the *Myreur* is prose arranged as a history, by date), d'Outremeuse includes the story as we know it: Gaufroi and Beatrice (daughter of the king of Hungary) marry and engender Ogier. Ogier's mother dies, and Gaufroi remarries when Ogier is ten years old. Ogier is taken to Paris ostensibly to study, but ends up being a hostage. When Gaufroi refuses

---

[18] D'Outremeuse's dates come from G. Doutrepont, *Les Mises en prose des épopées et des romans chevaleresques du XIVe au XVIe siècles* (1939; repr. Geneva: Slatkine Reprints, 1969), 162. Ogier appears in Borgnet, ed., *Ly Myreur des Histors*, 3: 25–41 (*Enfances*); 189–314 (*Chevalerie*); and A. Goosse, *Ly Myreur des histors: Fragment du second livre (Années 794–826)* (Gembloux: J. Duculot, 1965), 13, 99.

to give tribute, a war ensues. Ogier is kept at St. Omer where he falls in love with Agnes, the chatelain's daughter. They have Bauduinet (ll. 1086–1180).

Messengers from Rome arrive; the army raised includes Ogier. Aloris meets the army and gives details; Ogier here too must save Charlemagne. Sadoine from the pagan army proposes a duel by King Carahus of Fagolesme, which the Danois accepts. Charlot is jealous, and is knighted by Ganelon. Charlot ventures out at night, alone, and is saved by Ogier. Carahus proposes the duel to Ogier himself, and Ogier agrees, though Charlot is unhappy. So Sadoine and Charlot will fight as well. Danemont arrives with 30,000 men; Charlot goes for help and Ogier is imprisoned. Ogier defends Carahus' rights to Gloriande against Brunamont, as elsewhere; Carahus gives Ogier Courtain, and Ogier takes Joyeuse from Brunamont and gives it to Charlemagne. Ogier returns with Charlemagne, and is made constable of France, lord of Meaux, count of Looz, and *avoué* of Liège.[19]

Ogier engages in many building projects in Liège. He rebuilds Tongres which had been destroyed by the Huns. Charlemagne and Ogier go to Rome to help the pope. Ogier conquers many cities in the East. Charlemagne decides to free Spain from the Saracens. There is much jealousy of Ogier on the part of Roland. Eventually Ogier goes on a pilgrimage and saves Queen Sibille (see *Macario*, in section 4.6 below). Ogier returns, renounces his rights to Denmark, and leaves for the Holy Land. He goes to India, Java, and the Earthly Paradise, where he is taken in by Morgan, magically staying thirty years old. D'Outremeuse will not say whether or not Ogier and she have children. He eventually must return to France to save the country because Charlemagne is too old to fight. He joins forces with the French, and the forces meet at Aspremont. The Lanson family becomes a problem again. Ogier attacks with Liegeois troops; Jean is taken, and Ogier beheads him. The Lanson family is banished. Ogier returns to Liège where he goes into the hermitage of Mont-Odile.

Clearly, d'Outremeuse has other interests than just Charlemagne's family and reign. He interweaves Liège and the Liège area throughout his version of the Ogier story. As Michel says, "Jean d'Outremeuse a réuni des narrations épiques antérieurement distinctes et les a insérées, en résumé, dans la trame de la merveilleuse 'vita' d'Ogier qu'il écrivait à manière: en attribuant toujours à son héros le rôle principal" (*Les Légendes épiques carolingiennes*, 107).

---

[19] The county of Looz is a French form of the Middle Dutch "Loon," a small town between the duchy of Brabant and the principality of Liège, on the eastern border of the Dutch area. In 1361 it was annexed by Liège (Claassens, personal communication, 2002).

4.4.3.6 Unedited French versions.

Fourteenth-century renditions of interest are two: one in decasyllables (early fourteenth) and one in alexandrines (mid-fourteenth). Both are still unedited, though summaries and discussions of them have been published. Suard notes that one can divide the poem into three parts: the first, about half the text, is approximately the Raimbert material. The second consists of the exploits of Ogier in Outremer; and the third, about a seventh of the text, consists of Ogier in the land of Faerie and his return to the earth.[20] These seek, as Suard says, "de ne rien laisser dans l'ombre, de tout expliquer" ("Ogier le danois au XIVe et XVe siècles," 58). A similar process is documented in Doutrepont, who lists "episodes ajoutés" (*Les Mises en prose*, 498); "elements religieux ajoutés" (522); "le merveilleux developpé" (530) among the typical characteristics of later elaborations of the *chanson de geste*. Doutrepont's final discussion, prose texts which seek to be chronicles, is clearly exemplified by d'Outremeuse's *Myreur* and David Aubert's *Croniques et Conquestes*.

4.4.3.7 David Aubert.

David Aubert completed his *Croniques et Conquestes de Charlemagne* in 1458; the work is primarily about Charlemagne, so the segment on Ogier is short, included in Book 1 (Guiette, *Croniques et Conquestes*, 1: 154–220). Ogier is given as hostage to Charlemagne on his second wife's advice. The nobles in Charles's court point out that Gaufroy, oldest son of Doon de Maience, is the only noble not to pay homage and tribute, and that he has not done so for ten years. Charlemagne raises an army and goes to Gaufroy, who promises to come to court the next Easter to pay homage and tribute. Ogier is about twelve years old, and stays with Bertran (Naimes's son) and Charlot and other noble children. Hardré and his family (son of Griffon, of Ganelon's line) do not love Ogier. At Easter, Gaufroy does not appear; Charlemagne is enraged, but the other nobles try to excuse him. Charles sends Ogier to Guimer to have him imprisoned at St. Omer.

Messengers reach Gaufroy at Beauffort. His second wife gives the bad advice not to worry about Ogier; they have the messengers taken, their ears, noses, and lips cut off, and sent home without a drink. Charlemagne does not recognize them at first; then, enraged, threatens to have Ogier killed. The chastelain is surprised; Ogier loves Belissent, his daughter, and in fact they are together parents of Bauduin. Ogier throws himself at Charles's feet, asking for mercy; he says that Denmark is his through his mother and that he will do homage for it. He promises to amend the situation if he lives to attain knighthood. Charles refuses.

---

[20] F. Suard, "Ogier le danois au XIVe et XVe siècles," in *Société Roncesvalles*, 4e Congrès international (Heidelberg 1967), Studia Romanica 14 (Heidelberg: A.C. Winter, 1969), 54–62, here 55.

However, between the prayers of the nobles and a message from the pope asking for help, Ogier is spared. Corsuble, the sultan, and Danemont, his son, with sixteen kings, are in Lombardy, together with Caraheu from India with 60,000 pagans, and Brunamont, king of Egypt, engaged to the sultan's daughter. Naimes persuades Charles not to kill Ogier, since his father would ravage France during the army's absence. Charles gives Ogier to Naimes to take care of; Belissent is quite preoccupied with Ogier's imminent departure because of her pregnancy.

Charlemagne goes to Rome to help the pope; Ogier comes with Charlot, Charles's son. They assemble at Sutri, where the pope is sheltered. Danemont has spies among the Christians who report to him. Naimes and his men go toward Rome; they are attacked and a few men escape to gain help from Charlemagne. Alory de Mélan, Charlemagne and his men come to aid. Danemont's nephew is killed, and Danemont is therefore upset. He attacks Charles, and Alory (the standard-bearer) flees. Ogier and the squires are watching from a hill; they organize and take the standard, arms, and horses from Alory and his men. Ogier and his squires enter the fray and save Charlemagne and the French army. Charlemagne recognizes Ogier and forgives him, then knights him.

Ogier re-enters the battle as a freshly-made knight, and does valorous deeds. Charlot shows up in camp with reinforcements. He hears of Ogier's deeds, and is not happy. He and his men attack the Saracens, and, because of pagan spies, they are overwhelmed. Ogier saves Charlot and his men. Caraheu is shown Ogier's standard and pauses in his flight to challenge him to a duel. Charlemagne reproaches Charlot upon his return. A duel is arranged between Christians (represented by Ogier and Charlot) and pagans (represented by Caraheu and Sadoine). Gloriande is the prize, together with Rome and Western Europe. (Charlot has insisted on fighting, though the challenge was from Caraheu to Ogier.) As elsewhere, the fight is to be on an island in the Tiber; the pagans betray Ogier, he is taken, and Charlot gets away. Gloriande holds Ogier as prisoner. Caraheu gives himself up to the Christians.

Brunamont, king of Egypt, arrives at Rome and accuses Caraheu of treason and of having converted to Christianity. Danemont agrees to marry him to Gloriande if he takes Rome and France. Gloriande refuses; Caraheu throws a golden cup at her face. Brunamont wants to test the Christians; he goes to find a battle, wins a short fight, and returns to slander Caraheu, supposedly with information furnished by the Christians. Danemont attacks Gloriande, who must be removed by other pagan barons. Ogier offers to fight for her honor and Caraheu's; Caraheu is to be a pledge, and is sent for. The next day, Caraheu gives Ogier his sword. This time Charlemagne secures routes to the island during the duel.

Ogier fights Brunamont and wins, taking his horse, Broiefort. Charlemagne's men, already mounted and ready to go, leave for Rome with Ogier to receive the hostages. Brunamont's Saracens decide to leave since their lord is killed; the Saracens who want to stay fight them. The Christians arrive; Ogier kills Danemont and Charlemagne kills Corsuble. The pagans flee. Ogier goes to Caraheu and his men, leads them before Charlemagne, feeds them dinner, and invites them to convert. After a polite refusal, the pagans return home by ship. On the way, Ogier tries to convert Gloriande as well, with no success. The Romans, including Pope Clement, return to their city. Charlemagne and his men return to France.

4.4.3.8 Printed editions.

The first French printed edition of *Ogier le danois* of which we have a record appeared in 1496, though it seems to be an edition of what was originally a manuscript (Togeby, *Ogier le danois dans les littératures européennes*, 221). There are two copies in existence, and a microfilm in Paris. Better known is Vérard's 1498 edition, of which six copies survive. Other editions followed in 1525; 1536; 1583; etc. A facsimile of the Turin copy has been published.[21] There are fifty-seven chapters of the prose based on the poem in alexandrines, with what Togeby characterizes as stylistic changes (223). There are changes in names and the episode with the king of England's daughter is reduced. The popularity of the Dane clearly continues through the sixteenth century in France, based largely on this edition.

4.4.4 Iberian versions.

In the Iberian peninsula, Ogier is found in Spanish, Portuguese, and Catalan. *Otger Cathaló* appears ca. 1415, and various Spanish *romances* include him and / or his son, Baldovinos. Cervantes (1604) and Lope de Vega (1604) both write of Ogier, as does Balthasar Diás. The first attributes the name "Catalonia" to *Augerius*, calquing the name *Otger Cathaló* on *Augerius Danesus* (Togeby, *Ogier le danois*, 181). The reason for the form of the name has never been resolved. Italian literary influence was strong in the peninsula during the sixteenth century, and the *Danés Urgel* appears, borrowed from Italian epics. There are three *romances* which together make up more than 1000 octosyllables telling of Baldovino's death at Carloto's hand, and the death of the murderer. Urgel or Urgero, marquis of Mantua, is married to Ermelina, the daughter of Naimes; his son is married to Sevilla, daugher of the king of Sansueno. Baldovino is Urgel's nephew. Carloto is infatuated with Baldovino's wife and wounds Baldovino during a hunt. Urgel finds Baldovino and vows to avenge him. The emperor orders Carloto to be killed. The first *romance* contains Baldovino's complaint and Urgel's promise

---

[21] K. Togeby, ed., *Ogier le Dannoys. Roman en prose du XVe siècle*, Det danske Sprog- og Litteraturselskab (Copenhagen: Munksgaard, 1967).

of vengeance. The second contains Urgel's call to Paris for justice, and Carloto's imprisonment. Urgel and Don Renaldos encamp outside Paris. In the third *romance*, judges condemn Carloto to be beheaded, and he is. Urgel is also mentioned in *Bernardo del Carpio*, as being defeated by him. *Don Quixote* contains a mention of Urgel, marquis of Mantua (Part I, chap. 5). Lope de Vega wrote the *Tragicomedia famosa de El Marqués de Mantua*, a dramatization of the *romances*. As in Italy, individual events are dramatized. Mentions of the character or his name are more frequent than accounts of his story. In Portugal, Balthasar Dias wrote a short play of which only one sheet is known from a *pliego suelto* of 1665, so the original date is uncertain (Togeby, *Ogier le danois*, 219).

4.4.5 German versions.

No German medieval versions are available. See below, under "Dutch," 4.4.7.

4.4.6 Scandinavian versions.

In the Scandinavian tradition, branch 3 of the *Karlamagnús Saga* tells the story of Oddgeir the Dane. The Scandinavian tradition is of particular interest since it recounts both Ogier's *Enfances* and *Chevalerie* and separates them, as does the Italian. Togeby (following Voretzsch) suggested that the Norwegian translation and the *Chevalerie* derive from the same source (Togeby, *Ogier le danois*, 92–93). According to Skårup too, it seems most probable that the Norwegian does not derive directly from the *Chevalerie* ("Contenu, sources, rédactions," 353).[22] Oddgeir (= Ogier) is the son of King Jofrey of Denmark, and his son is Ballduini. Belisent is Oddgeir's stepmother, and Guenelun his guardian. King Jofrey, after breaking numerous agreements with Charlemagne, agrees to leave his son Oddgeir with Charlemagne as surety for the future. As soon as Charlemagne leaves, though, Jofrey has Charlemagne's men arrested and killed. Charlemagne has Oddgeir brought before him and the court, together with Guenelon his guardian, and announces that Oddgeir will be cut apart. No one is able to obtain mercy. At that moment, messengers arrive from Rome with news of the attack by Amiral, king

---

[22] The *Karlamagnús Saga* dates to about the mid-thirteenth century. There are two sets of manuscripts, classed as Aa and Bb, and a Danish abridgement. The ending is different in the two different groups of manuscripts, the A family and the B family. The B family is related to the Danish *Karl Magnus Krønike* (Hieatt, *Karlamagnús Saga* [1975], 234). The relationships between Scandinavian texts are further explained in Skårup ("Contenu, sources, rédactions," in *Karlamagnús Saga. Branches 1, 3, 7 et 9*, ed. Togeby and Halleux, 331–55). Skårup also quotes Togeby disproving Henry's theory (*Les Enfances Ogier*, 33) that the Norwegian is derived from the French ("Contenu, sources, rédactions," 352–53).

of Babylon, and Pope Milon's request for help. Charlemagne calls for troops, and they depart for Rome. A deer shows Charlemagne the way over the mountains. Charlemagne calls Oddgeir and announces that his life is safe during the campaign. Alori brings word that Amiral and Danamunt (his son) are near and have taken hostages. Milon meets them outside of Rome and Naimes asks for the loan of Oddgeir as his squire. Battle is engaged, and Alori flees as elsewhere; Oddgeir sees the action and suggests going to Alori, taking his arms and horse. Oddgeir and his 1000 squires meet the fleeing Lombards, take their arms and horses, and enter the battle. They free the prisoners by killing the pagan capturers and save Charlemagne and his men. Charlemagne makes Oddgeir his standard-bearer. A pagan chief, Sadome, asks his name and defies him in the name of King Karvel. The French return to the town, Frustra. Karlot (= Charlot, Carlotto), Charlemagne's son, and his men arrive.

That night, Karlot sets up a raid and refuses to invite Oddgeir. A spy sees them before they reach the pagans, and the pagans are ready. Charlemagne dreams of trouble, and awakes to ask about his son. Oddgeir is sent after Karlot and saves the day. He meets Karvel at the battle and challenges him for Gloriande, the king's daughter. Oddgeir will return to Charlemagne to ask permission for the battle. Karvel returns to his king, Amiral, and prepares to go challenge Charlemagne and offer single combat to Oddgeir. When Karlot tries to stop the single combat, Karvel offers a second knight, Sodome, to fight Karlot as well. The combat is agreed. Danamunt arranges the betrayal, and the combat takes place on the island in the Tiber river.

When Danamunt comes out of the woods, Karvel and Sodome put down their arms and refuse to be a part to the betrayal. Karlot tries to withdraw; his horse swims the river and he is able to return to Charlemagne. Oddgeir is then outnumbered forty to one. Karlot reports to the Christians; Oddgeir is taken to Rome. Karvel arrives and begs King Amiral to let Oddgeir go. Amiral refuses to go, regardless of Karvel's threats. Gloriande speaks up for him too, and arranges with the guards to take good care of him. The next morning, Karvel again asks for Oddgeir's freedom; again Amiral refuses.

Karvel goes to Charlemagne and offers himself as Oddgeir's hostage. Karvel suggests that Charlemagne attack the pagans. Karlot and his men attack the pagans. Gloriande sees the action and recognizes Karvel's suggestion. She speaks to Karlot, and warns him of the arrival of more pagans. As the pagans flee, the embassy from the reinforcements arrives: Burnament (= Brunamon[t]) and his men join the pagans. Naimes and other Christians are returning from hunting when Burnament goes after them; he takes Jofrey's horse. (Burnament has a horse full of demons.) When Burnament returns with the horse, Amiral awards him Gloriande. Gloriande and Oddgeir are playing chess when they receive the news. When Oddgeir asks, she agrees to arrange for him to speak with her father, and does. Oddgeir challenges Burnament in Karvel's name, and sends a messenger to Karvel with the information. Karvel returns immediately. Karvel arms Oddgeir with Kurtein (Curtana); Oddgeir goes to the island to fight Burnament. This time Charlemagne puts his own men in the woods to make sure that Oddgeir is not betrayed. Burnament is defeated; Oddgeir presents the head to Karvel and Gloriande. Karvel goes to Amiral and says that they should leave. Karvel will help in any endeavor but those against Charlemagne. Karvel makes arrangements, giving gifts to Charlemagne and his army. This is the end of one branch. In the other (B), the story continues: Karvel returns with Oddgeir when Oddgeir goes back to Charlemagne, and the pope tries to convert him. A messenger from Gloriande arrives before Karvel is able to leave and while he is still with the Christians, preparing to depart. Feridan, king of Cordes, is attacking. Oddgeir and Karlot swear to help, and Charlemagne offers the entire army; but Karvel refuses the Christian army, and takes just the two men with him. They fight, win over the enemies, and free Gloriande. Gloriande and Karvel give generous gifts to Karlot and Oddgeir, who then return to Paris with Charlemagne. As Hieatt points out, this ending is unparalleled elsewhere.[23]

Book 8 of the *Karl Magnus Krønike* includes the futher career of Oddgeir, his quarrel with Karlot, and Karlot's death at Oddgeir's hand. Unfortunately, the *Krønike* is not available in translation, and I was therefore unable to consult it. Togeby also mentions the *Karl Magnus Krønike* and the fight of Amarus, an African king, in Italy against Karlot and Udger Danske (Togeby, *Ogier le danois*, 105–6, 192–97). Hieatt comments, "There is . . . no way of telling whether the division of the Ogier story into two parts was made by the compiler of the saga or by his source" (*Karlamagnús Saga* [1975], 235; cf. eadem, "Ogier the Dane in Old Norse," 36). It is interesting to note that both the Scandinavian and the Franco-Italian divide Ogier's life in two, separating the parts possibly because of chronology, perhaps for other reasons unknown. It is unclear why there should be such a parallel between Italy and Scandinavia.

The Ogier tradition in Scandinavia continues into modern times: it stretches from the end of the thirteenth century (a fragment *Oddgeirs Þáttr*, part of the *Karlamagnús Saga*) to a Danish ballad *Holger Danske og Burmand* (ca. 1480) and through to Hans Christian Andersen and to World War II, when Ogier was seen as a symbol of the resistance (Togeby, *Ogier le danois*, 292–93).

---

[23] C. B. Hieatt, "Ogier the Dane in Old Norse," *Scandinavian Studies* 45 (1973): 27–37, here 28.

4.4.7 Dutch versions.

In Dutch, there are seven brief fragments in fourteenth-century manuscripts.[24] Four of these tell the *Enfances* section of Charlemagne's life. The origin of these, whether they are an exact translation of a French original or not, is unclear (van Dijk, "Ogier le Danois," 528–29). There is a German version of the Dutch at the University of Heidelberg Library, dating to ca. 1460. Unfortunately there is no edition of the text available, though one is planned. Becker stated that it is a word-for-word translation of the Dutch, though van Dijk demonstrates otherwise ("Ogier le Danois," 530–31). The German version continues where Raimbert leaves off, sending Ogier to the Orient to chase Saracens. The most recently discovered fragments, E and F, have no counterpart in the German version, recounting action in the Orient. However, since that portion of the story is not included in the Italian version at all, we need not concern ourselves with it. Because of the unavailability of the texts, suffice it to say that the Dutch and the translations of them into German are further testimony of the popularity of the *Ogier* story.[25]

4.4.8 English versions.
None.

4.4.9 Discussion.

A primary literary concern in V[13] is that these two *chansons*—the *Enfances* and the *Chevalerie*—are the only ones *not* included in the Maganzese cycle in V[13]. The evil done in the *Enfances* derives from Carleto, Charlemagne's son, who acts like a spoiled coward and wishes to avenge himself on the Dane for saving the battle outside of Rome. Krauss suggests that the primary function of *Ogier* within V[13] is further destruction of the Charlemagne myth and removal of the role of "God's elect" and "defender of the Christian faith" (*Epica feudale*, 182). According to Krauss, the lack of the Longobard wars (set off by Ogier in rebellion in Raimbert's version) derives from the differing social situation in Italy, the lack of a noble class to rebel against a feudal system. He furthermore notes the desire to cater to a bourgeois audience accustomed to moralizing, didactic literature (172). One can argue,

---

[24] H. van Dijk, "Ogier le Danois," in *L'épopée romane au Moyen Âge et aux temps modernes*, ed. Luongo, 1: 525–34, here 527.

[25] G. Claassens notes that the German version is usually described as an "'Umschreibung,' actually a copy of a Middle Dutch version in which the language more or less is adapted to the new audience. There have been [some changes] made, but in general you can see the Middle Dutch 'shine through' the German" (personal correspondence, 2002).

however, that *all* audiences would respond to moralizing, typical of all types of literature in the thirteenth century (cf. Doutrepont, and Arthurian literature).

Ogier's role at the beginning of the *Chevalerie* is similar to that of Ganelon in the *Chanson de Roland*: he must go to a hostile city to demand tribute. But the results are different: Ogier follows moral behavior and is a model of how a mission to a foreign potentate should be handled. It is rather Charlemagne who does not exhibit exemplary behavior, because he does not control his son's rancor toward Ogier's son, and subsequently does not avenge Ogier's loss immediately. Furthermore, Roland's role in V^{13}'s *Ogier* is much increased, as it is throughout the manuscript (as Cremonesi also remarks [*Le Danois Oger*, xliv]). In fact, Roland acts in many ways as a mentor toward Ogier in the V^{13} *Chevalerie*, teaching him court ways and enabling him to get around Charlemagne, lessons which Ogier puts to use later in *Macario* where he arranges for the queen's return long after Roland's death.

In both the *Enfances Ogier* and *Chevalerie*, there is no Maganzese evil, only Carleto, Charlemagne's son, seeking revenge for his humiliation. In both parts, Italian place names and references are clear. "Marmora" is Verona (Cremonesi, *Le Danois Oger*, liii–liv) and Besgora is Brescia or Mantua (Cremonesi, "Note di franco-veneto," 9, and Bertolini, review of Cremonesi, 8–9); and the city of Rome is clearly the start of Carleto's need for revenge. Cremonesi suggests that the compiler has omitted or deleted anything from plots which is not of interest to Italy, such as Gloriande and her story (*Le Danois Oger*, liv). Togeby suggests, speaking of V^{13}, "Tout s'explique peut-être si l'on pense que le manuscrit XIII entier est un poème sur la famille de Charlemagne. C'est donc au fond Charlemagne et son fils qui sont au centre de l'intérêt, et Ogier ne sert qu'à mettre leur conflit en relief" (*Ogier le danois*, 127). Togeby attributes the interest in the royal family's "vie privée" and "vie morale" in V^{13} to a lack of a feudal system: "Il perd le grand souffle épique pour se réduire à un conte ou une nouvelle se concentrant autour d'une situation" (123). Upon examining all of V^{13}, one finds such a contention untenable, though it is true in Italy as in the rest of Europe that individual episodes become popular and are repeatedly developed in other forms. Though there is not an evil Maganzese class, the importance of blood and family remains.

Many similarities link *Ogier* with the rest of V^{13}. Naimes and Aquilon are essential in guiding Carleto, then Charlemagne, through the bipartite story, as elsewhere in V^{13}. Krauss notes Naimes's role here: "È nel riconoscimento di necessità oggettive e nell'invito a considerare questa realtà che consistono le qualità salienti del *milor conseler*"; Naimes is the voice of conscience: "voce della coscienza, anzi voce del profitto" (*Epica feudale*, 175). Profit, as Krauss admits, is exagerated as a term, but helps focus on Naimes's real role: accepting reality and making the most of it. Both Namo and Uggieri have lost their family line when

Baldovino dies, an important consideration. Similarly, Bovo seemed to have lost his sons until Drusiana appeared; and Charlemagne seems to have lost his heirs in this *chanson*. True, Charlemagne and his family are not the main characters here, as they are not in *Bovo*; and the Dane is not here specifically linked to the royal family (as he is in some other versions). But the issues of genealogy, protection of the clan and its property, are central, here as in *Bovo*. These themes link the *Ogier* segments with the first (remaining) *chanson* of the manuscript, *Bovo*, and the last, *Macaire*, in which Charlemagne's original heir, Carleto, is replaced by Leoys through the mediation of Ogier.

CHART 4.4A: Versions of *Ogier* (*Enfances* and *Chevalerie*) by country/date until 1599

France	Italy	Germany	Scandinavia	Netherlands
Late twelfth–early thirteenth century/ *La Chevalerie d'Ogier de Danemarche* attributed to Raimbert de Paris				
Before ca. 1240 *Chronique rimée*, Philippe Mousket			ca. 1230–1250 *Karlamagnús Saga* (Branch III, *Les Enfances d'Ogier, Oddgeirs þáttr danska*); Norwegian prose	
Late thirteenth century *Enfances Ogier*, Adenet le Rois				
1285–1340 *Charlemagne* (Bk. 2), Girard d'Amiens				Fragments (8) in Middle Dutch (subsequently translated; Heidelberg Pal. ger. MS.)
Early fourteenth century *L'Istoire d'Ogier le redouté*, Paris, BnF f. fr. 1583 in decasyllables[1]	ca. 1300–1350 V[13] *Enfances, Chevalerie*			

[1] From 1996–2005 (published 2007), T. Kruke Salberg published a series of studies on this MS. See his "Prolégomènes pour une édition de L'istoire d'Ogier le redouté (B.N. f.fr. 1583). III L'assonance problématique a oral / a nasal dans *La chanson de Roland et ailleurs*," Olifant 24.2 (2005), 9–42, which includes a bibliography. The dating of this manuscript is controversial: ca. 1310, DLF and Togeby; fifteenth century, Longpérier, fourteenth century, Suard.

France	Italy	Germany	Scandinavia	Netherlands
Mid-fourteenth century *Le Roman d'Ogier en alexandrins*. Three MSS.: Paris, Arsenal 2985; London, British Museum MS. Royal 15E.VI; Turin, BN L.IV.2				
ca. 1375–1385 *Geste de Liège*, Jean d'Outremeuse (verse) mid– late fourteenth century *Ly Myreur des Histors*, Jean d'Outremeuse (prose)	1371–1431 *I Reali di Francia*, Andrea da Barberino, prose		ca. 1420 *Krønike* (Swedish); perhaps a translation of Raimbert; Four MSS. (Togeby, *Ogier*, 188)	
	ca. 1455 *Uggeri il Danese* (Florence, Laur. Med. Cl. XCV and Florence, Magl. Pal. II. cod. 31 Strozziano), *ottava rima*		ca. 1450–80 *Karl Magnus Krønike*; MS. of 1480 and publ. Ghenen, 1509, see below (Togeby, *Ogier… littératures*, 192) (Danish)	
ca. 1458 *Croniques et Conquestes de Charlemagne*, David Aubert prose		1479 *Ogier von Dänemark* Heidelberg Pal. germ. 363,[2] attributed to Johann der Clerick		
	1480 *Danese Ugieri editio princeps*, Florence (Beer, *Romanzi di cavalleria*, 149)		1480 *Holger Danske og Burmand* ('folkevise'); 3 MSS. from second half of the sixteenth century (Togeby, *Ogier… littératures*, 200)	
1496 *Le Fait d'Ogier le Danois* first published exemplar, from Jean de Vingle de Lyon	1498 *Il Libro del danese*, attributed to Girolamo Tromba di Gualdo di Nocera, *ottava rima* (Togeby, *Ogier*, 206)			

1498 *Ogier le Dannoys*, publ. Antoine Vérard, prose based on version in alexandrines (surviving *editio princeps*)	Fifteenth century *Storie di Rinaldo*, Books 3 and 5 Laur. Pl. XLII, 37 and Laur. Pl. LXXXIX inf. 64 (bk 3) (Rajna, *Uggieri* 1872, 155) attributed to Andrea da Barberino, prose		
	1511 *Ugieri Danese*, printed, Venice, no publisher listed (Beer, *Romanzi*, 150)	1509 *Keyser Karlls Magnus Kronike*, publ. Ghenen	
1525 on: Various reworkings, reprints of Vérard edition	1521 *La Morte del Danese*, printed Ferrara by Lorenzo de' Rossi Cassio da Narni (rpt. 1522, Milan; 1534 Venice)	1534 *Keyser Karlls magnus Kronicke*, re-ed., and *Kong Olger Danske Kroenike*, Hans Pedersen	
		1571 *Kronike Denmarkische Historien*, Conrad Egenberger (Translation from Danish)	1548–83 *Holger Danske* (Danish); Many reprints of Pedersen's *Olger Danskes Krønike* (Togeby, *Ogier le danois . . . littératures*, 240)
			1630 Swedish version

Three Spanish romances about Ogier the Dane appeared in the fifteenth and sixteenth centuries (*Primavera y flor de romances*; Togeby, *Ogier le Danois dans la littérature*, 214–20). In the seventeenth century, Lope de Vega published in 1604 (*El Marqués de Mantua*); Cáncery Velasco in 1651 (*La Muerte de Baldovinos*), and Balthasar Diás in 1665 published in Portuguese.

---

[2] Now edited by H. Weddige, J. A. Broers and H. van Dijk, *Ogier von Dänemark: nach der Heidelberger Handschrift Cpg 363* (Berlin: Akademie, 2002).

CHART 4.4B: Proper Names in selected versions of *Ogier le Danois*

V13	*Chevalerie d'Ogier de Danemarche*, Raimbert de Paris	*Ogier le danois*, Adenet le Rois	*Charlemagne*, Girard d'Amiens	*Croniques et Conquestes*, David Aubert	*Karlamagnús Saga*	Role in text
	Belissant, Gaufroi	Gaufroi of Denmark	Godefroy	Gauffroy, Belissant	Gauffroy, Belisent	Ogier's father and stepmother
Uggieri/Ogier	Ogier	Ogier	Ogier	Ogier	Oddgeir	Protagonist
Naimes	Naimes	Huon de Saint Omer	Naimes	"maître"	Naimes	King Charles's advisor
		Thierry				Charlemagne's "master"
Carloto	Charlot	Charlot		Charlot	Karlot	Charlemagne's son
Alori	Aleris	Alori		Alory	Alori	Lombard standard bearer
Karoer	C/Karaheu	Caraheul		Caraheu d'Inde	Karvel	Gloriande's fiancé, Ogier's opponent
	Brunamond/t	Brunamon		Brunamont d'Egipte	Burnament	Gloriande's suitor
	Gloriande	Gloriande		Gloriande	Gloriand(e)	Danemon's daughter
Ysoré	Corsuble	Corsuble	Corsuble	Corsuble	Amiral	Sultan of Danemont; attacking Rome
Sandonio	Sandone	Sadoine		Sadoine	Sodome	Charlot's pagan opponent in the double combat
	Danemon	Danemon	Danemont	Danemont	Danamund/t	Son or nephew of Sultan (Danemont/Amiral)
Marmora						City that defies King Charles
Massimo Çudé						King of Marmora
Milon	Desier	Desier	Lyons	Clement	Milon	Pope
Besgora						City near Marmora

Baldoin	Bauduinet	Baudouyn		Bauduin	Ballduini	Ogier's son
Floriamon		Mahout	(Châtelain of St. Omer's daughter)	Belissent		Mother of Ogier's natural son
Roland	Turpin	Turpin			Rodan	Cares for Ogier in prison
Braier	Brahier				(Burnament)	Defeated by Ogier in single combat

4.5 *Berta e Milone, Orlandino*

It is difficult to separate *Berta e Milone* from *Orlandino* in a discussion of literary characteristics. Critics generally include the two in one section, and most editions of the two include them as part of one entity. Later versions of the story join the two as one plot. However, in V[13], they are separated by the *Enfances Ogier*, an important consideration for the overall meaning and structure of V[13]. In this section, we will examine the plot of *Berta e Milone*; the plot of *Orlandino*; other versions of the story (primarily later and Italian texts, including the *Reali di Francia* [by Andrea da Barberino, d. 1439], anonymous *cantari*, Pulci's *Morgante* [end of the fifteenth century], Folengo's [1526] and Aretino's *Orlandino* [1566]); the relationship between Charlemagne and his sister, "Berta"; art historical evidence of that relationship; and the historicity of "Berta." As Moisan says, "Berta e Milone n'a pas d'antecedent français connu," so there are no French versions to consider here.[1]

4.5.1 V[13] version.

Charles's half-sister (half-Maganzese, daughter of the impostor who had married Pepin in Berta's place) falls in love with, and becomes involved with, Milon, the son of Naimes, at the French court. When she becomes pregnant, they must flee. Charles has them pursued; when he cannot get them back, he banishes them. The couple ends up in Italy, where Orlando (= Roland) is born. The fugitive couple brings him up in the woods in great poverty. Meanwhile, back in Paris, Charles is called by God in a dream to save Rome from the pagans; he goes to do so. The freeing of Rome with the help of Ogier the Dane thus divides *Berta e Milone* from its plot successor, *Orlandino* [Childhood of Roland], and the following *chanson de geste*, *Enfances Ogier le Danois*.

Orlandino (also called *Rolandin* or *Enfances Roland*) begins during Charlemagne's return from Rome. The army stops at Sotrio where Charlemagne and his court recruit Orlando; they force Charlemagne to forgive Orlando's parents and wed them.[2] Certain comic features common to both the French *enfances* genre

---

[1] A. Moisan, *Répertoire des noms propres de personnes et de lieux cités dans les chansons de geste françaises et les oeuvres étrangères dérivées* (Geneva: Massot, 1986), 2.3: 54.

[2] It should be noted that Berta the Younger had committed lèse-majesté by marrying without Charles's consent. Note too that some summaries contain errors, perhaps owing to the fact that correct editions were difficult to come by until recently. Voigt, for example, says that Charlemagne ties a napkin around Orlandino's neck with the leftovers for his parents and that Orlandino bites Charlemagne to prevent his acting against Berta (F. Theodore A. Voigt, *Roland-Orlando dans l'épopée française et italienne* [Leiden: E. J. Brill, 1938], 89–90)! For an English translation of both *Berta e Milone* and *Orlandino*, see Morgan, "Franco-Italian Epic: The *Geste Francor* (anonymous)."

of the *chanson de geste* and later Italian romances appear: Orlando is huge and extremely intelligent; he knows more than the schoolmaster in short order; he also has a phenomenal appetite. It is his appetite, parallel to his enormous physical strength, which ultimately brings him to court. His antics remind the reader of those of Morgante and later giants, though Orlando's traits are not as exaggerated here as Morgante's (and other later giants') are.[3] *Orlandino* is the second poem in the *Geste Francor* which illustrates specifically the birth and childhood of a hero (as far as we know; *Bovo* resembles an *enfances* from what remains, but is not certain, so not counted). The first was *Karleto*, Charlemagne's youth. Carney remarks, " . . . whether or not the child is an original invention or a pre-existing hero is important in determining how the character development is approached" ("Portrait of the Hero," 239). Here Roland's childhood is modeled on his adult persona and the ideals of a heroic childhood.[4] This poem is paired with *Berta e Milone*, since, as Carney again remarks, " ... family relationships are also an essential element in each story of young heroes, since it is during childhood that immediate family ties are strongest" (273). However, Roland's conception and childhood are not always an optimum case for this last argument. Mythological conventions suggest problematic conception and transgressive childhood behavior as typical, as will be seen in the section below entitled "Charlemagne's Sin."

Orlandino is an Italian poem; there is nothing similar in any other tradition. Zambon says, "La sostanziale originalità delle parti dedicate a *Berta e Milon* e a *Rolandin* sembra confermata anche dal fatto che il nucleo principale della

---

[3] For Orlandino's appetite, see L. Bartolucci-Chiecchi, "Quelques notes sur Rolandin du manuscrit V[13] de la Bibliothèque de Saint-Marc," in *Essor et fortune de la chanson de geste dans l'Europe et l'Orient latin*, Actes du IXe Congrès international de la Société Rencesvals (Padoue-Venise, 29 août-4 septembre 1982), ed. A. Limentani et al. (Modena: Mucchi, 1984), 647–53. For comic features of *enfances* in general, see Ménard ("Le Rire dans les chansons de geste du XIIe siècle," in *Le Rire et le sourire dans le roman courtois en France au Moyen Âge* (1150–1250) [Geneva: Droz, 1969], 19–144), and Theodor (*Die komischen Elemente der altfranzösischen chansons de geste* [Halle: Max Niemeyer, 1913]). From the time of Theodor, the treatments of humor on the part of youth have increased; see for example the Taylor article ("Comic Incongruity in Medieval French Enfances," *Romance Quarterly* 35 [1988]: 3–10), and M. B. Predelli, "Les Bûches et la faim: relents de pauvreté dans la littérature chevaleresque franco-vénitienne," in *Le Petit peuple dans l'Occident médiéval: terminologies, perceptions, réalités*, Actes du congrès international tenu à l'Université de Montréal (Paris: Publications de la Sorbonne, 2002), 123–34, here 130–31.

[4] See Bloch, *Etymologies and Genealogies*, on the backwards development of the *chanson* in cycle form, esp. 94–96, though all of Chapter Three is relevant to Roland. Bloch argues that, as the ultimate justification for the "right meaning" of a word was its etymology, so the "right meaning" for a hero lay in his ancestors. Roland's spiritual ancestry could be traced back to Adam (105).

vicenda si svolge in Italia, e che, in particolare, è localizzata in Italia la nascita di Orlando."[5] There are different versions in tradition of Roland's first coming to the battlefield: first, in the *Karlamagnús Saga*, he fights at the siege of Vienna against Duke Girard; in *Renaut de Montauban*, he fights in Saxony against Amidan (Thomas, *Renaut de Montauban*, 251, 276 ff; laisses 119; 131–180);[6] finally, and the most frequently cited version, in the *Chanson d'Aspremont*, after leading his cohorts out of Turpin's prison in Laon, where he is held at the behest of Charlemagne, he fights against and kills Eaumont (Almonte) at Aspremont.[7] This is the version recounted by Philippe Mousket (*Chronique rimée*, 1: 178–81; ll. 4429–4495, pre-1240); Girard d'Amiens (late thirteenth- early fourteenth, end of Book II);[8] and David Aubert (Guiette, *Croniques et Conquestes*, 299–301 [reference to event, 359]; second half of the fifteenth century). In V[13], however, Roland's childhood only, not his youth and coming to arms, appears.

4.5.2 Other Italian versions.

In V[13], *Berta e Milone* are Italian: the couple settles in Italy and Roland is born there. The story is consistently popular in Italy through the following centuries. It reappears in Book 6 of the *Reali di Francia*, and later, *cantari* (originally oral poems presented in the marketplace, of Tuscan origin, in *ottava rima*, usually dating to the fifteenth and sixteenth centuries) pick up the tale. It is also found in Pulci's *Morgante* (reference only); *Aquilon de Bavière* (reference); Folengo's *Orlandino*, Aretino's *Orlandino*, and Dolce's *Le prime imprese del conte Orlando*.

---

[5] F. Zambon, "La «materia di Francia» nella letteratura franco-veneta," in *Sulle orme di Orlando: leggende e luoghi carolingi in Italia: i paladini di Francia nelle tradizioni italiane: una proposta storico-antropologica*, ed. A. I. Galletti and R. Roda (Padua: Interbooks, 1987), 53–64, here 55.

[6] Atant es .i. vaslet descendu au perron,
O lui .xxx. danzeauz de mult gente façon,
N'i a celui qui ait ne barbe ne grenon . . . ll. 4636–4638 (J. Thomas, ed., *Renaut de Montauban* [Geneva: Droz, 1989], 251).

[7] Gautier, *Les Épopées françaises*, 3: 65; G. Paris, *Histoire poétique*, 413; L. Brandin, ed., *La Chanson d'Aspremont*, Les Classiques français du Moyen Age (Paris: Honoré Champion, 1923), 192–94, ll. 6004–6070; cf. M. A. Newth, *The Song of Aspremont* (*La Chanson d'Aspremont*) (New York: Garland Publishing, Inc., 1989), 145–46.

[8] H. Damman, *Über das verlorene Epos 'Enfances Roland' nebst Textabdruck der Rollandin-Episode aus dem 'Charlemagne' des Girart d'Amiens* (Greifswald: Puff & Panzig, 1907), 60–79.

4.5.2.1 *I Reali di Francia.*

Charlemagne and Berta are not half-siblings; Charlemagne notices Berta's interest in Milone and increases his surveillance; Berta, however, takes the initiative and arranges for Milone to sneak into her bedroom.[9] Namo (Naimes) arranges for their marriage before they are exiled. Roland is born in a cave. Among the differences between the *Reali* version of *Orlandino* and that of the *Geste Francor* are: Rolandin is born in a cave at Sutri, not Imola. His name derived from "rolling" because that is what he does when Milone comes in; Milone leaves Berta and the child in order to fight, leaving Roland to support himself and his mother by begging. Roland becomes the town bully, much admired and able to beat other children at any game. They feel sorry for his not having any clothes, and together beg enough money for four pieces of fabric which they sew together, giving him the "quartering" which is never explained in the *Geste Francor*. When Charlemagne's court comes to Sutri, Roland goes only because he can beg nothing when the court is in town. He grabs food from under the king's nose three times. Before the third, Charlemagne has a dream about being saved from a dragon by a lion; his men interpret the lion as being Roland. Namo follows Roland, and finally succeeds in slowing him down by giving him a glass of wine to carry, thus making it possible for Namo and others to find Roland's home by following him (at his slowed pace). Namo arranges a reconciliation between brother and sister; Charlemagne kicks his sister, who agrees that she deserves it, preventing any uproar. Roland does not lay a hand on Charlemagne, as he does in the *Geste Francor*. Charlemagne is married to Galeanne, not Berta or Belisant. Milone never appears at the court in Sutri. (Rajna suggests that this is in order to unite the *Reali* with *Aspramonte* [*Ricerche intorno ai "Reali*," 259].)

The lèse-majesté of V[13] is missing from Andrea's version. Andrea also over-explains some phenomena, a characteristic of later texts (as for example the quartering of Orlando's clothing, above). However, the position of the story in Andrea's compilation helps us understand the place of Roland in Italian tradition. When Charlemagne relents, Andrea makes a point of saying that he loved him *like* a son: Book 6, Chap. 70, "Carlo lo amava tanto, che lo teneva per suo figliuolo adottivo, e sempre Carlo lo chiamava figliuolo il più delle volte; e però si disse volgarmente che Orlandino era figliuolo di Carlo; ma egli era figliuolo

---

[9] The edition used for the *Reali di Francia* throughout is Roncaglia and Beggiato, eds., *Reali di Francia*. The events narrated are in Book 6, chaps. 52–70 (655–690). As this volume goes to press, I have received a copy of S. Bisson's "La leggenda dell'infanzia di Rolando a Sutri," in *Sutri nel Medioevo. Storia, insediamento urbano e territorio (secoli X–XIV)*, ed. Marco Venditelli (Rome: Viella, 2008), 241–314, demonstrating the ongoing appeal of this tale to Italian scholarship.

di buono amore, ma non di peccato originale" [Charles loved him so much, that he kept him as his adoptive son, and Charles called him son most of the time; and thus it was commonly said that Orlandino was Charles's son; but he was a son of good (that is, virtuous, married or legitimate) love, but not of original sin (outside of marriage)] (Roncaglia and Beggiato, *I Reali di Francia*, 689–90; my interpretation in rounded parentheses). This would seem to suggest that the legend of the "carnal sin" was not unknown in Italy, but that it was not accepted. Artistic evidence seems to support Andrea's story as well. Lejeune and Stiennon discuss the cathedral at Borgo San Donato (Fidenza) which has scenes from the youth of Roland, and have difficulty explaining the lion (*La Légende de Roland dans l'art*, 156–58). Charlemagne's dream of the lion saving him from a dragon on the battlefield as seen in Andrea da Barberino's version may explain the appearance of the lion in this context, not, as Cremonesi suggests, Pepin's childhood bravery.[10] We should also note that some later versions of Charlemagne stories use the lion as Roland's emblem (Conrad's *Rolandslied*).[11] It should be added that Andrea begins his *Aspramonte* with a quick summary of Charlemagne's difficulties with his bastard brothers (*Karleto*) and finding Orlandino:

> ...Carlo andò a Roma, nel quale viaggio ritrovò Orlandino, figliuolo di Milon d'Angrante e di madonna Berta sorella carnale di Carlo; e menonne a Parigi la madre e 'l figliuolo, e fece ribandire Milon d'Angrante, e rendé a Orlandino Angrante e Brava; e fece Orlando suo figliuolo adottivo, e grande amore gli portava (Boni, *Aspramonte*, 3)

Note that again it is clearly stated that Orlandino is adopted by Charlemagne. Milone's delight at seeing Orlandino again is unmistakable. Charlemagne forgives him, has him marry Berta immediately, and arranges feasting throughout the kingdom (Boni, *Aspramonte*, 6–7). In *Aspramonte*, as in the French versions, Roland demands to be knighted for his work at Aspramonte after having been held by Turpin at Monlione and escaping (Boni, *Aspramonte*, 68–175).

---

[10] C. Cremonesi, *Berta e Milon, Rolandin: Codice Marciano XIII* (Milan: La Goliardica, 1973), 24.

[11] That example could, however, have had to do with local politics; Henry the Lion was supposed to model himself / be modeled on Roland (Folz, *Le Souvenir et la légende*, 243–50).

4.5.2.2 Relation of *cantari* and *I Reali*.

Franceschetti has proved that the *cantari* are based on the *Reali*, and not vice versa.[12] There are two well-known *cantari* (which date to the end of the fourteenth and early fifteenth century respectively, according to Rajna). The first, *La Storia di Milone e Berta e del Nascimento d'Orlando*, is in 100 octaves, for a total of 800 lines.[13] Berta is here the main mover of the love affair between herself and Milon. She arranges for Milon to come visit her dressed as a woman. When Berta becomes pregnant, and Charlemagne realizes the problem, he imprisons both of them. Namo arranges their marriage and helps them flee. The two are banished and excommunicated. They settle at Sutri, in a cave. Berta gives birth to "Rotolando" while Milon is away; the name, again, derives from his rolling. Milon supports the family by begging. When Rolandin is three years old, Milon leaves to seek his fortune. Roland helps support his mother by begging. He gets into a fight with the town boys and wins; he is thought of as a leader. For Carnaval, they buy two colors of fabric and have an outfit in quarters made for him. Charlemagne returns from being crowned by the pope via Sutri, where he becomes ill. Charlemagne always gives to the poor, so while he is in Sutri, it is arranged for all local citizens to attend Charlemagne's court for food. Roland goes several times, grabbing food and upsetting his mother upon his return home. After Charlemagne has a dream in which he is saved from a dragon by a lion, interpreted as Roland by the court, Namo decides to follow Roland. The fourth time that Roland comes, Namo gives him wine so that Roland must go slowly, in order not to spill it. Namo and three others arrive at the cave behind Roland. Berta identifies herself and says that Milon has been gone for three years. Namo promises to set all right with Charlemagne, which he does, much as in the *Geste Francor*. Milon is recalled from Babilonia with his men, where he has enjoyed great success, and, the poet informs us, "la virtù al fin vince ogni cosa" [virtue at the end conquers all] (Barini, *Cantàri cavallereschi*, 78, octave 100: 2).

The second *cantare*, *L'Innamoramento di Melone e Berta*, is 160 octaves long (Barini, *Cantàri cavallereschi*, 207–60), and contains many of the same wordings as the *Reali*; as Rajna says, these are literary and "abbondano i ragionamenti morali, i lamenti, le allusioni mitologiche e tante altre cose aliene all'uso schiettamente popolare" (*Ricerche intorno ai "Reali,"* 262). Both Rajna (*Ricerche intorno ai "Reali,"* 262–63) and Gautier (*Épopées françaises*, 3: 64–70) relate other versions of the two *cantari*.

---

[12] A. Franceschetti, "Appunti sui cantari di Milone e Berta e della nascita di Orlando," *Giornale storico della letteratura italiana* 152 (1975): 387–99.

[13] G. Barini, *Cantàri cavallereschi dei secoli* XV e XVI (Bologna: Romagnoli dall'Acqua, 1905), 46–78.

4.5.2.3 Pulci's *Morgante*.

Throughout *Morgante*, Orlando is called "figliuol di Milone/Mellone" thirteen times; various other knights are identified by the same type of patronymic form. This is a common confusion of "father" and authority figure, in Italian tradition. Here, Orlando speaks of Charlemagne to Alda:

> ". . . Ch'egli è pur vecchio e mio padre e signore,"
> Cosí diceva; "e fa' che sia segreto."
> Vedi s'Orlando nostro era discreto! [14]

However, this is an isolated appearance of such words in the *Morgante*, which leads one to believe that here it is meant in a paternalistic rather than literal form; see also section 4.5.9.1 where "Charlemagne's sin" and his calling Orlando "son" are discussed.

4.5.2.4 *Aquilon de Bavière*.

As noted in section 4.2.2.3, *Aquilon de Bavière* contains an unusual version of *Berta da li pe grant*. We also hear of Milone's exile from Paris (for unspecified reasons) and a period during which he lived in Sutri (Wunderli, *Raffaele da Verona: Aquilon de Bavière*, 770).[15] The story of Roland's birth is not recounted.

4.5.2.5 Folengo's *Orlandino*.

Folengo, writing as Limerno Pitocco in 1526, produced his poem *Orlandino*, following many of the conventions established by Boiardo, Pulci, and other epic writers of the time.[16] He introduces it with a sonnet of dedication to Federico II Gonzaga; following are eight *capitoli* (chapters) of varying numbers of octaves (65; 71; 83; 77; 81; 58; 70; 93), each constructed with typical current epic prologues and closings. It is full of anti-clerical venom and illustrations; in fact, more ink is spent on that than on Orlando himself. Folengo recounts Berta and Milon falling in love from a distance; each agonizing over the situation; and each finding a reliable confidant(e) to arrange a meeting. On the occasion of a feast, Berta's maid dances with Milon and leads him to her room; a mutual friend dances with Berta and tells her of Milon's distress, then escorts her to her

---

[14] Fatini, *Il Morgante*, 1: 341 (Canto 11: 118. 6–8).

[15] The text in Wunderli's edition reads "E verent a Blavie, ce est Florenze, o il furent molt bien receus e honorés da li Florentins, por coi le amerent de bon amor, che a lor paroit ch'il fust de lor nacion. Che segond che dist li contes, quand li dus Millon fu in band de Paris, il demora asutri in cil pais . . ." (*Raffaele da Verona: Aquilon de Bavière*, 2: 770). "asutri" must be *"a Sutri."

[16] M. Chiesa, ed., *Teofolo Folengo: Orlandino* (Padua: Editrice Antenore, 1991), is the edition consulted here.

room. Circumstances force the two companions to leave, and Berta and Milon celebrate the occasion—as a result of which Berta is pregnant. The two find it difficult, if not impossible, to meet. Milon fights with other knights and is banished; he sneaks into Berta's room and takes her with him. They travel by ship, and a storm comes up. The two are separated, and Berta is shipwrecked. Upon Berta's arrival on shore, she makes her way to Sutri, where a shepherd takes pity on her and lets her stay in his cave and hut while she gives birth to Orlando and recovers. When Orlando is born, wolves come out into the open and howl (*urlare*, "to howl"; Urlando, "howling"), giving him his name. For seven years she brings Orlando up alone with the help of the shepherd; Orlando appears twelve years old, but is only seven. He gets into fights with the Sutri children, and will not give in and yet is not hurt. Orlando beats up Olivero, son of Ranier, and robs an abbot. When brought before Ranier, Orlando identifies himself as Milon's son; Ranier recognizes Milon in him and lets him go. A whole section is dedicated to a farce about the abbot from whom Orlando has stolen; then Folengo summarizes Turpin's plot: Milon appears and is delighted with his family; they travel to find his brother Amone with Rinaldino and all ends well.

Clearly, the religious element in Orlando's life (his parents' legal marriage; Orlando's role as savior of Christianity) is not Folengo's main interest. Rather, Folengo is using the story as a vehicle to mock the church and court.[17] Desole discusses how *Berta e Milone* is related to Folengo's *Orlandino*.[18]

4.5.2.6 Aretino's *Orlandino*.

Aretino is even further from the *Geste Francor* version.[19] None of the story we know is in his two canti, the first of fifty octaves, the second of six, for a total of 448 lines, called the *Orlandino*. It opens with insulting language directed toward his predecessors, "ser Turpin prete poltrone," and the various characters of the classic Carolingian epic through Ariosto: Sacripante, Rodomonte, Carlo Magno, etc. The actual events begin in 1.14, at Charlemagne's court on Pentecost. Astolfo starts a fight with Rinaldo, which becomes a free-for-all. The feast and smells are

---

[17] On Folengo and the church, see C. F. Goffis, "Limerno, Pitocco evangelico," *Esperienze letterarie* 17 (1992): 3–16.

[18] C. Desole, *Repertorio ragionato dei personaggi citati nei principali Cantari cavallereschi italiani* (Alessandria: Edizioni dell'Orso, 1995), 61ff.

[19] The text consulted is G. Romagnoli, ed., *L'Orlandino, Canti due di Messer Pietro Aretino, Scelta di curiosità letterarie inedite o rare dal secolo XIII al XIX*. In appendice alla Collezione di Opere inedite o rare. Dispensa XCV (1868; repr. Bologna: Commissione per i testi di lingua, 1968); the citation is from p. 11 [Canto I, 2:1]). This reprint of Romagnoli's 1868 edition reads "1975" on the cover and "1968" on the front page. The final page reads "Finito di stampare . . . . 1975 presso la Arnaldo Forni Editore . . ."

described. Terigi (Teris), Orlando's page, is to bring Orlando all the best (1. 31). The sound of a horn interrupts the feast (1.31:8). Charlemagne tells Orlando to fight the challenger. Orlando, white as a sheet and obviously ill, says he will go take care of a couple of things first, and then puts on his armor. Astolfo meanwhile arms himself and struts through the court; Charlemagne sends him off to fight. Astolfo confesses to Turpin, then sneaks off to hide himself (1.40; 42). Rinaldo cannot go because his arms are in hock at his inn (1.42). Charlemagne yells at Astolfo, shaming him into facing the challenger (1.50).

In the second canto, the introduction speaks of how Astolfo is neither noble nor courtly, and how princes in general, like Charlemagne, choose ever more incapable, lazy men. Astolfo is knocked from his horse, and asks for mercy (2.5:7–8). He identifies himself to Cardo, the foreign knight, blaming his horse for his defeat. Cardo sends him home on foot. This is the end, so designated by a printed "IL FINE. / Stampato nella stampa, pel mastro/ della stampa, dentro dalla / Citta [sic], in casa e non di/ fuora, nel mille/ uallo cerca. The poem therefore includes little of Orlando, and seems unfinished.

4.5.3 French versions.

Not all versions which contain "ancestry and childhood of Roland" accounts are the same; names differ significantly. In *Aiquin* the story differs greatly from V[13] and Italian versions. There, Tiori de Vannes dies, and Charlemagne laments him, saying that he had given Tiori his sister "Baquehert la gentis" and that they are the parents of Roland (G. Paris, *Histoire poétique*, 408). There is no extended Old French tradition around Roland's birth and mother.

However, Sicari calls the *Chanson d'Aspremont* an *enfances* for Orlando.[20] Roland, kept under lock and key, escapes with several other *bacheliers* and saves the day for Charlemagne and the French forces. Texts which follow *Aspremont* recount a similar story: Philippe Mousket (Reiffenberg, *Chronique rimée*, 178 [ll. 4429ff]; G. Paris, *Histoire poétique*, 415) and David Aubert (Guiette, *Croniques et Conquestes*, 1: 293–301). In Girard d'Amiens, Charlemagne comes to Milon's home, Viene, near Paris, to announce Milon's death in a battle at Esclavonie. Charlemagne wishes to break the news to his sister gently (and he already knows of Roland). He and his men go hunting in the forest before seeing her, however, and therefore have an earlier run-in with Roland than anticipated (Damman, *Über das verlorene Epos 'Enfances Roland'*).[21]

---

[20] C. Sicari, *La Canzone d'Aspromonte: Poema Epico del XV secolo. Antologia con prefazione e note* (Vibo Valentia: QUALECULTURA [sic], 1991), 8.

[21] Damman argues that the version of Girard as it stands is not entirely coherent, that it was clearly adapted to fit into his plan (*Über das verlorene Epos 'Enfances Roland'*).

4.5.4 Spanish versions.

This particular story enjoyed popularity in Spain as well, where the "Historia del nacimiento y primeras empresas del conde Orlando," by Enriquez de Calatayud (Valladolid, 1585, 1594) and "Los Amores de Milon de Anglante y el nacimiento de Roldan y sus niñerias" by Antonio de Eslava derive from the octave versions (G. Paris, *Histoire poétique*, 412–13).[22]

4.5.5 German versions.

These versions do not all follow the same plot. In Füetrer (1477–1481), Baquehert marries Tiori de Vannes (G. Paris, *Histoire poétique*, 408); there Pepin and the false Berta have a daughter, Martona, who marries the prince of Cornwall to produce Roland (G. Paris, *Histoire poétique*, 502, Appendix 13). Compare with *Aiquin*, above.

4.5.6 Scandinavian version.

In the *Karlamagnús Saga,* Roland has been in the care of the canons of the abbot Ligger, being taken care of and taught to read. He has four nurses. At seven, Charlemagne calls Roland to court at Eiss, and asks if Roland knows him. The boy says yes, that he is his mother's brother. Charlemagne has Milon and Gilein (his sister's name here, like Gille) come to court, holds a great feast, then allows Roland to depart with them for Brittany (Hieatt, *Karlamagnús Saga* [1975], 117–21; Loth, "Les manuscrits norrois," 66–73). His first battle is at the siege of Viena, against Duke Girard (G. Paris, *Histoire poétique*, 415; Hieatt, *Karlamagnús Saga* [1975], 127–31; Togeby, *Ogier le danois*, 80–88).

4.5.7 Dutch versions.
There are no Dutch versions.

4.5.8 English versions.
There are no English versions.

---

[22] I was unable to locate any modern edition. Therefore I do not analyze the differences here. G. Paris contends they are practically identical to the Italian *cantari* (*Histoire poétique*, 411–12).

4.5.9 Discussion.

The story has fascinated numerous readers through the years. Ludwig Uhland (1787–1862) wrote "Klein Roland" and "Roland Schildträger" among his Carolingian poems. The first contains Berta's lament over Roland's hard life, her meeting with Charlemagne, and their reconciliation; the second recounts how Roland takes a gem from a giant with his father's arms while his father sleeps.[23] The German *Das deutsche Volksbuch von Karl dem Grossen*, published in 1929, includes the story of Charles's (unidentified) sin, Egidius (St. Gilles) and the letter from heaven (Zaunert, *Das deutsche Volksbuch*), which are all part of the legends surrounding "Charlemagne's sin," as explained below. Over forty years ago, a book club created a "Geste de Roland," including a close translation of the Franco-Italian "Berta e Milone" and "Orlandino."[24] The story and character of young Roland clearly caught the imagination of the European public and continued to be a part of tradition over many years. In the English tradition as well, we find later references to Roland: Shakespeare in his *As You Like It* includes Sir Rowland de Boys and his sons Oliver and Orlando, and Virginia Woolf's *Orlando* continually transforms himself over time.

In these two segments of V^{13}, the younger Berta displays her inherited Maganzesi tendencies in disobeying morality and her half-brother's wishes.[25] Her Maganzesi genes (derived from her mother, the here-unnamed Maganzese *donçella*) run true. Charlemagne had planned to marry her off well and to cement alliances through her marriage. The story in V^{13} is unique in that the major part of it takes place in Italy. However, the idea—that Charlemagne has an unusual relationship with his (half-)sister—is common to several traditions. In V^{13}, of course, she is merely a half-sister through their father.

4.5.9.1 Charlemagne's Sin.

Legends of an incestuous relationship between Charlemagne and his sister exist throughout Europe: in Old French tradition, Scandinavian, Latin, and German. These legends are not generally expressed or are specifically denied in Italian

---

[23] H.-R. Schwab, ed., *Ludwig Uhland, Werke: Gedichte Dramen Versepik und Prosa* (Frankfurt am Main: Insel Verlag, 1983), 152–56, 185–91, 201–4. There are a number of translations available, e.g., W. T. Hewett, *Poems of Uhland* (New York: Macmillan, 1896) and W.W. Skeat, *The Songs and Ballads of Uhland, Translated from the German* (London: Williams and Norgate, 1864).

[24] Marcel Thomas, trans., *La Geste de Roland: Textes épiques choisis, présentés et traduits* (N.p.: Firmin Didot, 1961). The bibliography included with the book is, however, archaic even for the date at which it was published, dating V^{13} to the thirteenth century (and the poems to the twelfth).

[25] See also L. Z. Morgan, "*Berta ai piedi grandi:* Historical Figure and Literary Symbol," *Olifant* 19 (1994–1995): 37–56, for more on the exemplary, didactic nature of this story.

texts. Hints of Charlemagne's sensual misdeeds also exist beyond specific incest. Literary critics list a series of standard sources, from Gautier who proclaims the incest to be a "conte trop odieux pour être antique" (*Épopées françaises*, 3: 66) to Lejeune and Stiennon who proclaim the story of Berta and Milon's premarital affair an attempt "pour laver du soupçon d'inceste la naissance mystérieuse de Roland" (*Légende de Roland dans l'art*, 157).

The documents generally cited to suggest Roland as Charlemagne's son fall into several groups: some do not specify Charlemagne's sin; they merely state that he did have a great (and in some cases unconfessed) sin. A second group accuses him of sensuality more or less directly; and the third specifically documents the sin as incest with his sister, named Gille (= Modern French Gisèle; English Giselle) or Berta. Einhard's *Life* (dated ca. 829–836) merely mentions scandals at court; there is no mention of Charlemagne's specific sin(s), but whiffs of scandal around his daughters.[26] Gaiffier documents the first appearances of this legend in Latin texts of the ninth century; a number of Latin visions of the ninth and tenth centuries indicate that Charlemagne is in Purgatory for unspecified reasons.[27] The *Visio Wetti* (mid-ninth century) shows Charlemagne in Purgatory because of his sensuality; it alone specifies, though indirectly in the form of "an animal 'perpetually gnawing the guilty member'," the type of Charlemagne's sin.[28] Pseudo-Turpin (ca. 1139), whose account of Carolingian events is perhaps the best known and which certainly is the most widespread, with many manuscripts surviving in Europe, notes that a band of demons try to take Charlemagne's soul,

---

[26] Several critics ask why Einhard was so careful to avoid documenting Charlemagne's youth. They question whether or not this is indirect proof of his early misdeeds (B. Sholod, "Charlemagne and Roland: A Mysterious Relationship?" in *III Congreso internacional de la Société Rencesvals*, special issue of *Boletín de la Real Academia de Buenas Letras de Barcelona* 31 [1965–1966]: 313–19, here 313). However, if one examines the genre of biographical literature (compare, for example, Thorpe on Einhard's *Life of Charlemagne* being modeled on the life of Caesar [L. Thorpe, trans., *Einhard and Notker the Stammerer: Two Lives of Charlemagne* (Harmondsworth, Middlesex [UK]: Penguin, 1969, 19–21)]), the *enfances* tradition is a medieval one, not a classical one. Einhard's information on Charles' daughters (Book III, "Private Life") is the center of discussion for Charlemagne's court behavior. The translation of Einhard on Charlemagne's daughters has caused some discussion: see, for example, H. Nosow ("The Double Image of Charlemagne" [Ph.D. Diss., New York University, 1985], 170 ff).

[27] B. de Gaiffier, "La Légende de Charlemagne: Le péché de l'empereur et son pardon," in *Recueil de Travaux offert à M. Clovis Brunel* (Paris: Société de l'école des Chartes, 1955), 1: 490–503, here, 490–92; cf. Lejeune and Stiennon, *La Légende de Roland dans l'art*.

[28] Nosow, "The Double Image of Charlemagne," 181. See also Sholod, "Charlemagne and Roland," esp. 313–14; and further discussion on the type of sin in Nosow, "The Double Image of Charlemagne," 179–81.

but that St. James saves him.[29] There is no reference to any specific sin. Other texts based upon the Pseudo-Turpin, such as Primat's *Chronicles of St. Denis*, follow that reading.[30]

4.5.9.2 Italian tradition.

In Italy, there is evidence that the legend of Roland's questionable birth was known.[31] In the *Spagna in rima* (fourteenth century), Charlemagne calls Roland "nepote e figliuolo" (Catalano, *La Spagna*, 3: 122 [octave 4, 1–2]), but then says specifically:

> Maladetta sia l'ora che tuo padre
> t'ingenerò con giusto matrimonio
> e maladetta l'ora che tua madre
> partorí te, incarnato demonio! . . .
> E così sopra il corpo del nepote . . . [32] (122; octaves 6–7)

Thus "figliuolo" here seems to be a term of affection. In Pulci's *Morgante* (1480s), Charlemagne seems to praise Roland's father specifically (Fatini, *Morgante*, 2: 500 [Canto 27, 203], "benedico il seme del tuo padre") and though he calls Roland "figliuol mio" (Canto 27, 205), in the context it can be taken in a metaphorical sense. Furthermore, Charlemagne also calls Rinaldo "figliuol mio diletto" (Fatini, *Morgante*, 513; Canto 27, 253), which clearly demonstrates the non-literal nature of the epithet. In a general description of Charlemagne there is no mention of any sin (Fatini, *Morgante*, 560 [Canto 28, 115 ff]). In *Li Fatti di Spagna* (1350–1360), Charlemagne calls Roland "fiollo myo": "Ay, fiollo myo, Dio abia mercede dell'anima tova . . ." (Ruggieri, *Li Fatti di Spagna*, 143).[33] However,

---

[29] A. Roncaglia, "Rolando e il peccato di Carlomagno," in *Symposium in honorem Prof. M. de Riquer* (Barcelona: Universitat-Quaderns Crema, 1984), 315–47; for St. James's role, see 323. See also Gaiffier, "La Légende de Charlemagne," 495; Meredith-Jones, *Historia Karoli Magni*, 228–31 (chap. xxxii); R. N. Walpole, ed., *Le Turpin français, dit le Turpin I* (Toronto: University of Toronto Press, 1985), 48–49; A. Demoulin, "Charlemagne, la légende de son peché et le choix de Ganelon pour l'ambassade," *Marche romane: Cahiers de l'A. R. U. Lg.* 25 (1975): 105–26; and Morrissey, *Charlemagne and France* (51) on the intent to glorify the shrine of St. James.

[30] Primat in Levine, *A Thirteenth-Century Life of Charlemagne*, 133–34.

[31] But not in V[13]. Capusso's note about 7567–68 is an erroneous reading (Capusso, review of *Geste Francor*, ed. Rosellini, 202); compare Rosellini on ll. 7564 ff (*Geste Francor*, 771). The lines must be read in context.

[32] Editions used: *Spagna in rima*: Catalano; *Li Fatti di Spagna*: Ruggieri; Pulci: Fatini; *La Rotta di Roncisvalle*: Catalano, in *La Spagna*, 3: 227–332.

[33] H.-E. Keller also cites this as part of his evidence, "Le Péché de Charlemagne," in *L'Imaginaire courtois et son double, Actes du VIeme Congrès triennal de la Société internationale

this testimony is considerably weakened by the fact that Charlemagne also calls Oliviero "fiollo myo," and similarly says to him, "Caro fiollo myo, quanto se abassa lo honore myo . . ." (136). That this is intended and not an error is clear from the immediately following rebuke by Naymo to leave the mourning for Oliviero's father, Raynere. Various other times in the same text he uses "son" as an appellative: e.g., "Fiolo myo" to Olivero (25, line 9). In *La Rotta di Roncisvalle* (end of the fourteenth century), we find Charlemagne saying: "Orlando, figliuol mio, tu se' nel cielo ed io son qui col rio" (Catalano, *La Spagna*, 3: 324 [octave 17, ll. 7–8]).[34] However, in one manuscript of the *Rotta*, Charlemagne calls Ulivieri "charo figliuolo" and specifically says "perduto io aggio nipote e ancho figlo [sic]" (MS. C; Catalano, *La Spagna*, 3: 320, 323). Because of the double use of "son" as an affectionate term and the absence of any other more specific reference, the modern reader must reserve judgement in Italian texts. In other Franco-Italian pieces, there is no evidence of any sin. In the *Entrée d'Espagne* (fourteenth-century manuscript), Roland cites his parentage as the son of Charlemagne's sister:

> —Cel roi de France», fait Rollant le gerer,
> «Une suer ot, que douna a muiler
> «Peppin le roi au duch Mille d'Angler;
> «Uns fils en ot, que l'ons fait appeler
> «Rollant: jel sui, de Rome justiser
> «Et chanppion et maitre tresorer.»
> (Laisse DLX, ll. 13112–13117)[35]

In *Aquilon de Bavière* (completed 1407) we find reference to "Rolland, fil al dux Millon d'Anglant et de dame Berte, fille a li roi Pepine e sorelle a li roi de France" (Wunderli, *Raffaele da Verona: Aquilon de Bavière*, 1: 7).[36] Milon is also listed as son of Bernard and father of Roland: "Cest Bernard avoit cinque fil: li prime avoit nom Millon e cist fu pere di Roland; ..." (A. Thomas, "Aquilon de Bavière," 562). However, the *Aquilon* version is unique in a number of ways. As Coronedi points out, 1. the name Gaiete is completely new; 2. the birth of Roland is legitimated as much as possible with an effort not known to other texts [this is through the legitimization of Berta's birth]; 3. there is no substitution of another woman; 4. Pepin and Berta recognize each immediately, 5. the suffering of Gaiete, from

---

de littérature courtoise (ICLS), Fisciano (Salerno), 24–28 juillet 1989, ed. G. Angeli and L. Formisano (Naples: Edizioni scientifiche italiane, 1991), 39–54, here 51.

[34] This too is quoted by Keller, "Le Péché de Charlemagne," 52.

[35] A. Thomas, ed. *L'Entrée d'Espagne: Chanson de geste franco-italienne* (Paris: Firmin Didot et Cie, 1913), 2: 187.

[36] Compare A. Thomas, "Aquilon de Bavière: Roman franco-italien inconnu," *Romania* 11 (1882): 538–69, here 548.

which she is liberated by Roland, is unique; 6. Gaiete is not attached to the Maganzesi, and her name is unlike the mother's name in any other Italian version ("L'Aquilon de Bavière'," 277–79).

In the *Reali di Francia*, Charlemagne is particularly fond of Roland, and Andrea says, "Carlo lo amava tanto, che lo teneva per suo figliuolo adottivo, e sempre Carlo lo chiamava figliuolo il più delle volte; e però si disse volgarmente che Orlandino era figliuolo di Carlo; ma egli era figliuolo di buono amore, ma non di peccato originale" (Roncaglia and Beggiato, *Reali di Francia*, 689–90 [Cap. LXX]). This may be an explanation for the relationship expressed or suspected.[37] In Andrea's *Aspramonte*, Gherardo da Fratta, who seems to know and relate all rumors about everyone, refers to that "bastardo d'Orlando" (Boni, *Aspramonte*, Book 3, 137. 9). There is no reference in V[13] to any such tradition.

4.5.9.3 St. Gilles.

In many texts we find a St. Gilles (Latin "Aegidius") associated with Charlemagne's sin and repentance. Although the real Aegidius's life was much too early, his literary afterlife is extensive.[38] Our knowledge of it is aided by Paris and Bos's edition of Guillaume de Berneville's *Vie de Saint Gilles* and its carefully documented introduction, used as a source by all later commentators for the question of Charlemagne's sin. Guillaume de Berneville's *Vie* dates to the twelfth century. It cites a scroll given by an angel to the saint which reveals Charlemagne's sin and forgives it—without telling the reader what that sin is (lines 3020–3080; Gaiffier, "La Légende de Charlemagne," 496–99).[39]

---

[37] There are three chapters of Andrea's *Reali di Francia* where the reader cannot help thinking that Andrea protests a bit much. First he says, upon finding out who Rolando is, "Questo infante non sarà figliuolo di Milon, ma sarà mio; e così voglio ch'egli sia mio figliuolo" (Roncaglia and Beggiato, *Reali di Francia*, 686, chap. 68). Then, the author comments shortly afterwards, "E sempre Carlo voleva Orlandino dinanzi a sé, e tanto l'amò, che s'egli fusse figliuolo nato del suo corpo, non l'arebbe potuto più amare" (688, chap. 69). And finally, the quote from chap. 70 as given in the text of the chapter. Andrea is definitely concerned with giving the correct explanation, but carefully omits the reason for it!

[38] The edition used here is G. Paris and A. Bos, eds., *La Vie de Saint Gilles par Guillaume de Berneville: Poème du XIIe siècle* (Paris: Firmin Didot et Cie, 1881). For the problems of dating the saint, see lxv, n. 2, and lxxii for a summary of the known historical dates regarding Aegidius.

[39] As G. Paris points out, there are difficulties in deriving the name Gilles from an etymon Aegidius (G. Paris and Bos, *Vie de Saint Gilles*, lxxiii), though the *Vie de Saint Gilles* and *Vita Sancti Aegidii* share the same story.

4.5.9.4 French tradition.

The sin continues to appear through the following centuries, both in direct narrative and in references in non-Carolingian texts in French. In *Huon de Bordeaux*, Charlemagne is forbidden to drink from Auberon's magic cup because of a "pecié mortel," which is, again, unspecified.[40] One cannot help but think of Ariosto's cup which spills on those whose wives have committed adultery in Canto 43 of the *Orlando Furioso*. *Huon* is dated to 1229 or later (Ruelle, *Huon de Bordeaux*, 93). Philippe Mousket's *Chronique rimée*, already mentioned in other sections of this introduction, also includes the story of the magic paper and St. Gilles, but there the sin itself not specified (ed. Reiffenberg, *Chronique rimée*, 1: 159 [ll. 3988–4019]).

4.5.9.4.1 Fourteenth century.

Through the fourteenth century, references to the sin multiply in French-language texts. Girard d'Amiens (end of the thirteenth–beginning of the fourteenth century) used Primat's *Grandes Chroniques de France* to form Book 3 of his epic *Charlemagne*. It contains Charlemagne's confession, here to Turpin, a confession of sins against chastity. There is no mention of incest. Brault suggests that at the time of the writing the legend would have been familiar to all, and that Girard could therefore be discreet, a similar possibility of discretion for the redactor of the *Chanson de Roland*.[41] *Tristan de Nanteuil* (fourteenth century), on the other hand, is quite specific: "Le peché fut orribles, on ne le sot neant; / Mais ly aucun esponent, et tous ly plus sachant / Que ce fut le peché quant engendra Rolant / En sa sereur germaine . . ."[42] In the northern range of French-speaking territories, there is the *Myreur des histors* by Jean d'Outremeuse, self-styled des Pres (1338–1400). He includes two references: one in book 2 (for the year 799):[43] on Palm Sunday at Orléans, St. Gilles receives the confession "chu veut-on dire, qu'il avoit cognut sa seurour Bertaine charnellement," with no mention of Roland (Borgnet, *Ly Myreur des Histors, Chronique de Jean des Preis dit d'Outremeuse*,

---

[40] P. Ruelle, ed., *Huon de Bordeaux* (Brussels: Presses Universitaires de Bruxelles, 1960), 384–85 (ll. 10268–10277).

[41] G. J. Brault, "The Legend of Charlemagne's Sin in Girart d'Amiens," *Romance Notes* 4 (1962): 72–75, here 73.

[42] K. V. Sinclair, ed., *Tristan de Nanteuil, chanson de geste inédite* (Assen: Van Gorcum, 1971), 691 (ll. 21705–21708).

[43] Cf. A. Goosse, ed., *Ly Myreur des histors. Fragment du second livre (Années 794–826)* (Gembloux: J. Duculot, 1965); the manuscript used is Brussels, Bib. Roy., II.3030: "ce veult on dire, qu'il avoit eyut cognoissance sa seure Bertaine charniellement." There is a confusion between Berthe, wife of Milon, sister of Charlemagne, and Berthe, daughter of Charlemagne. Berthe is married to Milon and is mother of "Rollant le preux."

Tome III, 5).⁴⁴ St. Gilles demands that Charlemagne confess and ask for absolution before absolving him. Secondly, during the war between Charlemagne and Girard de Fraite, Girard's son addresses Roland as "Rollans, niers ou fis Charle" (volume III, 107); shortly afterwards, another son calls Roland "faux awoutrons" (volume III, 108). Neither, however, elaborates upon how this may be so.

4.5.9.4.2 Fifteenth century.
The tradition continues through the next century, but not unequivocally. In Jehan Bagnyon's *Fierabras* (ca. 1478, Lausanne), Roland says, "Je suis nommé Roland, filz au duc Millon, et suis nepveu a Charles, filz de sa propre seur."⁴⁵ Keller argues that Roland says he is "said" to be son of Duke Milon and that this is thus a reference to the sin ("Le Péché de Charlemagne," 53). *Berta aus grans piés* (Berlin, Staatsbibliothek, MS. 130; fifteenth century) states "d'icelle Gille vinst le noble combatant Raoulant, qui tant fut noble guerroyer . . . Et veulent racompter les histoires que Charlemaigne, qui aussi fut filz au roy Pepin, et qu'il engendra en la noble Berthe apres l'engendra celuy Raoulant en icelle sa seur Gille . . ." (Dorsey, "HISTOIRE DE LA ROYNE BERTE [sic]," 125–26).⁴⁶ In David Aubert's *Croniques et conquestes de Charlemagne* (finished 1458), Charlemagne's soul is weighed and he is delivered from the pains of hell thanks to the churches he has built, and also thanks to help from St. James, though the actual transgressions which required the weighing are not revealed (Guiette, *Croniques et Conquestes*, 3: 294–95; cf. Nosow, "The Double Image of Charlemagne," 185).⁴⁷ French-language texts mentioning Charlemagne's sin, therefore, appear in the thirteenth century and thereafter.

4.5.9.5 Provençal.
Later texts mentioning Charlemagne's sin are also the rule in Provençal. Two texts indicate knowledge of the legend of Charlemagne's sin: first, *Ronsasvals* (second half of the fourteenth century) reads "Bel neps, yeu vos ac per lo mieu

---

⁴⁴ Michel notes that in most manuscripts of Jean d'Outremeuse, St. Gilles cannot forgive the sins without confession: "Peut-être on peut inférer que le texte qui a inspiré Jean d'Outremeuse portait la marque d'un auteur préoccupé de théologie et n'acceptant pas la non-orthodoxie de cette [= allowing forgiveness without confession] croyance" (*Les Légendes epiques carolingiennes*, 171).

⁴⁵ H.-E. Keller, ed., *L'Histoire de Charlemagne (parfois dite Roman de Fierabras) de Jehan Bagnyon* (Geneva: Droz, 1992), 95.

⁴⁶ A complete new edition of the Berlin MS. appeared recently: P. Tylus, ed., *Histoire de la Reine Berthe et du Roy Pepin: Mise en prose d'une chanson de geste* (Geneva: Droz, 2001). Here see 254, ll. 4230–4235.

⁴⁷ This is true of all texts which then follow the Pseudo-Turpin.

peccat gran / De ma seror e per mon falhimant, / Qu'ieu soy tos payres, tos oncles eyssamant, / E vos, car senher, mon neps e mon enfant," ll. 1323–1326; there is no reference to St. Gilles here or in the other part of the text (Keller, "Le Péché de Charlemagne," 50). As Nosow says, the impact is great since the confession "proceeds from the Emperor's own lips"; besides which there is no indication of remission ("The Double Image of Charlemagne," 197–98). The second is *Roland à Saragosse*, the manuscript of which dates to 1398.[48] Charlemagne says, "Aras say que perdut ay Rollan, / Per lo fol(l)és e say mon ensiant" (ll. 11–12), his folly being the incest, committed knowingly (Keller,"Le Péché de Charlemagne," 51; and idem, *Autour de Roland*, 339–40).

4.5.9.6 Spanish.

Spanish texts seem uninterested in Charlemagne's sin; in *Roncesvalles* (second half of the thirteenth century), Charlemagne says: "Naçjestes mi sobrjno . . ." (Jules Horrent, *Roncesvalles*, 67 [ll. 67–68]) and *sobrino*—in various orthographic variants—is the repeated form of address: lines 39, 44, 50, etc. From the fragment of 100 lines, Horrent is able to extract much information, but of greatest interest here is the emphatic statement of Roland's birth, as Charlemagne's nephew: "comme la tradition rolandienne, *Roncesvalles* déclare Roland neveu de Charlemagne et repousse formellement la tradition trouble de l'inceste: Roland né de Charles et de sa soeur Gilain" (*Roncesvalles*, 194). This is in spite of the French inspiration of the poem as demonstrated by lexemes used (*barba*, 141) and the date of the fragment (*Roncesvalles*, 194–96). Of course, "You were born as my nephew" does not necessarily mean that Roland was not conceived as Charles's own son, who as son of his sister would also be his nephew. The fragment is too short for a conclusive decision. No reference is made to the sin in the *Primera crónaca general* or *Conquista de Ultramar*.

4.5.9.7 German.

The German tradition on Charlemagne's sin of the twelfth and thirteenth centuries is plentiful. The *Kaiserchronik* (ca. 1150), ll. 15015–15068 (ed. Massman, 149; Book III, 1017–1028; E. Schröder, ed., *Kaiserchronik*, same line numbers, 353–54) speaks of St. Gilles, the scroll and absolution;[49] this is the first reference

---

[48] H.-E. Keller, *Autour de Roland: Recherches sur la chanson de geste* (Paris-Geneva: Slatkine, 1989), 346.

[49] In references to German texts, I follow Folz's dates. Here I rely largely on other critics because of the old German; the critics agree on textual details though not necessarily on dates. Folz summarizes the critical discussion of dates; for this reason I have followed his dates. Unfortunately, translations of these old German texts are not available, though summaries in Modern Standard German or in French are for some of them.

in German tradition.⁵⁰ Folz suggests that the story, the creation of "Charlemagne's sin," is "due à l'inconduite et à la politique anti-ecclésiastique de Charles Martel et à la vieillesse non irréprochable de son petit-fils" (*Le Souvenir et la légende*, 168). He traces further developments of the story to Stricker (318–23). Conrad, in his translation / rewrite of the *Chanson de Roland*, the *Rolandslied* (also known as *Ruolandes Liet*) ca. 1131–32, mentions a sin and St. Gilles's role in its forgiveness, but is not specific about the sin (242–43). Stricker rewrites Conrad's *Rolandslied* in his *Karl* (1230–35) and includes St. Gilles as well, but in an odd fashion. St. Gilles receives the story of Roncevaux from an angel and passes information on to Charlemagne (Keller, "Le Péché de Charlemagne," 44–5; Folz, *Le Souvenir et la légende*, 318–19). Furthermore, there is a German legend of necrophilia, unknown to the French tradition;⁵¹ in *Karl Meinet* (ca. 1300–1320),⁵² the sin is linked with Charlemagne's love for the corpse of his dead wife, that being the unmentionable sin.⁵³ Enikel (last quarter of the thirteenth century) also includes that story in its most expanded form (Folz, *Le Souvenir et la légende*, 327). Henry of Munich as well includes the Karl story (323–28). A number of German contemporary and later local chronicles and compilations recount versions of the sin story. Even Meibom, the seventeenth-century editor of Wolter's *Chronicle* (fifteenth century), mentions Wolter's free recounting of legends ("liberaliter narrare") of Charlemagne's "peccatum sodomiticum" (84–85).

4.5.9.8 Scandinavian.
Scandinavian tradition is very explicit; *Karlamagnús Saga* (ca. 1230–1250) names Charlemagne's sin: illicit relations with his sister Gille. It is, furthermore, the first reference chronologically to the sin. After absolution by Saint Egidius / Gilles, Charlemagne arranges her marriage with Milon d'Angers, and in seven months a son is born (Hieatt, *Karlamagnús Saga*, 1: 117–19; Togeby and Halleux, *Karlamagnús Saga*, 66–69).

Keller suggests that the Scandinavian, Occitan, and Italian texts reflect an incomprehension of the Germanic civilization of the Franks, and notes that this

---

⁵⁰ In Latin, the *Vita S. Caroli*, ca. 1150, ll. 14282–15091, is the first.

⁵¹ R. Lejeune, "Le péché de Charlemagne et la Chanson de Roland," in *III Congreso internacional de la Société Rencesvals*, 339–71; Keller, "Le Péché de Charlemagne."

⁵² A. v. Keller originally dated it to 1190–1210; G. Paris cites the poor philology involved, and says that it cannot predate 1305, the date of a previous poet quoted (*Histoire poétique*, 128). In the edition of *Vie de St. Gilles*, Paris and Bos misquote the page numbers on which the passage is found; it should read 492, not 392 (*Vie de St. Gilles*, cxii).

⁵³ G. Paris, "La Karlmagnus-Saga, Histoire islandaise de Charlemagne," *Bibliothèque de l'École des chartes* 5 (1864): 89–123, 6 (1865): 1–42; idem, *Histoire poétique*, 384, 489; H.-E. Keller, *Autour de Roland*, 487–92, 843; Folz, *Le Souvenir et la légende*, 326–27.

fact is reinforced by "des insinuations politiques méchantes de la politique des Plantagenêt" ("Le Péché de Charlemagne," 54). He concludes that "l'inceste de Charlemagne n'existe que dans l'imagination de quelques auteurs peu au courant de la légende carolingienne, qui remontait, après tout, à la tradition germanique" (54). Cremonesi suggests that the story of incest "non penetra in Italia" (*Berta e Milon, Rolandin*, 21). As we have seen, the sin is not expressed at all in the Italian tradition, with the possible exception of the *Rotta di Roncesvalle*, though there seems to be a polemic against that interpretation which that argues it was known. Furthermore, French texts (e.g., *Tristan de Nanteuil*) do contain the notion of Charlemagne's sin.

4.5.9.9 Art as evidence.
My comments so far have concentrated upon literary texts; there is another set of evidence centering around artistic artifacts. Lejeune and colleagues have examined evidence for knowledge of Charlemagne's sin in art. Among the exhibits they cite is the stained glass at Chartres dating to the early thirteenth century (cf. Sholod, "Charlemagne and Roland," 315; Gaiffier, "La Légende de Charlemagne," 502); Charlemagne's reliquary, again, early thirteenth century;[54] and frescoes in the Loire-Inférieure also dated to the beginning of the thirteenth century (Lejeune and Escholier, "Roland était le fils de Charlemagne," 2; Lejeune and Stiennon, *La Légende de Roland dans l'art*, 145–48). In Italy, the façade of San Donino in Fidenza, early thirteenth century, portrays Charlemagne and possibly the story of *Berta e Milone* and *Orlandino*, rather than a version of Charlemagne's sin (Lejeune and Stiennon, *La Légende de Roland dans l'art*, 158).[55] There have, however, been questions about Lejeune and Stiennon's interpretations. Labande-Mailfert points out that the illustration at Loire Bottereau is not of Milon's marriage, but of the preceding episode, Charlemagne's confession to St. Gilles, with

---

[54] R. Lejeune and R. Escholier, "Roland était le fils de Charlemagne," *Les nouvelles littéraires* 7 décembre 1961: 1–2, here 1; Folz, *Le Souvenir et la légende*, 280–82 also discusses this.

[55] There are a number of difficulties with the Lejeune and Stiennon volume (*La Légende de Roland dans l'art*). *Orlandino* does not follow immediately after *Berta e Milone* (as stated on page 156); the food is put in not a "sac de toile" but a napkin at Charlemagne's court (160, n. 17); and the placement in the manuscript is not folios 52^r–64^r, but 61^v–63^r (160, n. 15); 52^r–54^r is *Berta e Milone*, which is followed by *Enfances Ogier*. One is therefore skeptical of other details as well. The story of the lions would seem particularly questionable; Pepin's debut in fighting the lion as recounted in other versions of the *Geste Francor* (cf. *Reali*), or Charlemagne's dream of a lion at Sutri (interpreted as Roland, 4.5.2.1) seem far more likely, but one would need to see the entire frieze before being able to comment.

Milon and Gisèle following like pilgrims.[56] The Chartres window shows no "Enfances of Roland," just Charlemagne's sin (and the medallion on the subject is out of order).[57] Maines notes further difficulties with some of Lejeune and Stiennon's interpretations ("The Charlemagne Window," 809–10, n. 30). Of course, more artistic evidence has been found since Lejeune and Stiennon's book, especially about the scene of St. Gilles and the scroll, though not in Italy.[58]

4.5.9.10 Historical details.

Earlier attempts to trace possible historical details behind the story have not enjoyed success.[59] We know that Charlemagne's sister Gille entered the church; much else is unknown.[60] Roncaglia has recently tried to resurrect the possibility of historical truth behind her story, though (as he too admits) there are many holes in his arguments ("Rolando e il peccato di Carlomagno"). However, silence in chronicles and in literature has been read as significant to literary history. For example, Sholod suggests that Einhard omitted details of the Spanish invasion because of their embarassing, personal nature: the loss of a son ("Charlemagne and Roland: A Mysterious Relationship?", 317).

The discussion of Roland's parentage and birth is of particular interest in relation to the best-known and most studied representative of the Charlemagne tradition, the *Chanson de Roland*. Lines 2095–2098 refer to a *charte* and St. Gilles.[61]

---

[56] V. Labande-Mailfert, review of Lejeune and Stiennon, *La légende de Roland dans l'art du Moyen âge*, *Cahiers de Civilisation Médiévale* 9 (1966): 417–21, here 420.

[57] See C. Maines, "The Charlemagne Window at Chartres Cathedral: New Considerations on Text and Image," *Speculum* 52 (1977): 801–23; and I. Rolland, "Le Mythe carolingien et l'art du vitrail. Sur le choix et l'ordre des épisodes dans le vitrail de Charlemagne a la cathédrale de Chartres," in *La Chanson de geste et le mythe carolingien: Mélanges René Louis publiés par ses collègues, ses amis et ses élèves à l'occasion de son 75ᵉ anniversaire* (Saint-Père-Sous-Vézelay: Musée Archéologique Régional, 1982), 255–77, esp. 270–71; and Morrissey, *Charlemagne and France*, 90–91.

[58] See also G. Demaux, "Une Fresque inédite du XIIIᵉ siècle en l'abbaye d'Aiguevive (Loir-et-Cher): Saint Gilles remettant à Charlemagne la 'charte' apportée par un ange," in *La Chanson de geste: Mélanges René Louis*, 279–92; also Morrissey, *Charlemagne and France*, 55.

[59] For example, Duby, *The Knight, the Lady and the Priest*, 41–43; P. Aebischer, *Textes norrois et littérature française du Moyen Age* 1 (Geneva: Droz, 1954), 51–67.

[60] See *Two Lives of Charlemagne*, trans. Thorpe: "Gisela was Abbess of the convent of Chelles, Seine-et-Marne" (185, n. 49).

[61] J. J. Duggan, "Legitimation and the Hero's Exemplary Function in the *Cantar de mio Cid* and the *Chanson de Roland*," in *Oral Traditional Literature*, ed. John Miles Foley (Columbus, OH: Slavica Publishers, Inc., 1981), 226–31. Many editions of the *Chanson de Roland* comment upon the crux; see, for example, G. Moignet, ed., *La Chanson de Roland* (New York: Larousse, 1969), 160.

Its meaning is unclear: is it St. Gilles who authored the account of Roncevaux and sent it to Charlemagne? Or is this a reference to Charlemagne's sin and its remission through the angel and St. Gilles? Though there is no unequivocal reference in the *Chanson de Roland* to any relationship other than uncle-nephew, there has been much speculation on the mysterious closeness of the two. Lejeune, followed by Demoulin, suggests that the reason behind Charlemagne's inability to stand up to Roland's choice of Ganelon for the message in the *Chanson de Roland* is because both he and Ganelon are aware of Roland's parentage, but that Roland himself is not.[62] It is these discussions which Roncaglia follows and supports with historical data ("Rolando e il peccato di Carlomagno").

4.5.9.11 Literary repercussions.

Various interpretations of the interpolated "Charlemagne's sin" have been proposed. In the light of such a sin, Charlemagne's loss of Spain—and of Roland—looks much like the "wages of sin" and "expurgation for the same," whatever the exact nature of the sin.[63] A religious interpretation might suggest that Roland could not succeed any more than Charlemagne, in a genre that "sanctifie la guerre, laisse l'acier de Durandal oblitérer la Croix, confond le sang des batailles avec celui des martyrs."[64] That is, Planche argues that rather than because of the sin of an individual, the partial failure of heroes is because of Original Sin: paradise cannot be gained by the sword. This is surely a more modern interpretation than one accepted in a time of crusade.

Among the moral considerations, the parallel of Charlemagne's sin in fathering Roland with Arthur's in fathering Modred has not gone unnoticed: Micha suggests that the *Mort Artu* has deliberately adopted an epic theme appropriate to a crusader.[65] As he also points out, incest is frequently a characteristic of a hero, from Oedipus through modern times. Frappier, too, suggests that the motif of incestuous birth of Modred was borrowed from epic tradition, specifically that

---

[62] R. Lejeune, "Le Péché de Charlemagne," 356–61; Demoulin, "Charlemagne, la légende," 107–8, 121; mentioned also by Duggan, "Legitimation and the Hero's Exemplary Function," 231.

[63] See for example, Sholod, "Charlemagne and Roland"; J. J. Duggan,"El juicio de Ganelón y el mito del pecado de Carlomagno en la versión de Oxford de la *Chanson de Roland*," in *Mythopoesis: Literatura, totalidad, ideología*, ed. J. R. Resina (Barcelona: Anthropos, 1992), 53–64; and L. Z. Morgan, "*Berta ai piedi grandi.*"

[64] A. Planche, "Roland fils de personne: Les structures de la parenté du héros dans le manuscrit d'Oxford," in *Charlemagne et l'épopée romane*, ed. Tyssens and Thiry, 2: 595–604, here 604.

[65] A. Micha, "Deux sources de la 'Mort Artu'," *Zeitschrift für romanische Philologie* 66 (1950): 369–72, here 372.

of Charlemagne.[66] Archer Taylor demonstrates that traditional narrative shares a common pattern in the development of a hero, a development initially suggested by Lord Raglan: "4. The circumstances of his conception are unusual."[67] Duggan compares Roland and the Cid in their illegitimacy, together with legendary parallels ("Legitimation and the Hero's Exemplary Function"). Chocheyras compares the Nordic legends to the same tradition, saying, "le héros le plus grand et le dernier de sa race est probablement aussi le fruit d'un inceste."[68]

4.5.9.12 V[13] version's significance.

The Italian history of Roland's birth is mundane: he is the child of Berta and Milon.[69] The *Berta e Milone*, *Orlandino* stories are different from the stereotypical *chanson de geste* in that they involve the lives of a woman and child as well as a love story. The redactor has used these deliberately to form heavy scriptural parallels. Berta and Milone are like Mary and Joseph fleeing Herod (ll. 9195–9197). Milone works with wood, like Joseph. The parents hold Orlandino in their arms for the official marriage at the end of the story, like a "Holy Family" pose. When Roland is born, it is in a rude environment (ll. 9390–9394), a cave, and the redactor compares it to that of Jesus ("A Jesu *Christ*o nu li asomilon, . . .").

Krauss, like most critics, discusses the two portions of V[13], *Berta e Milone* and *Orlandino*, in one chapter. He believes that since Italian texts do not document St. Gilles and the sin, and, in fact, the V[7] *Chanson de Roland* changes St. Gilles to St. William, the story did not reach Italy. "È inevitabile dunque concludere che la leggenda dell'incesto di Carlo Magno non era giunta in Italia e che di conseguenza anche la funzione di discolpa assegnata al poema di *Berta e Milon* non era stata

---

[66] J. Frappier, ed., *La Mort Le Roi Artu: Roman du XIIIe Siècle*, Textes littéraires français (Geneva: Droz, 1954), xvi.

[67] F. R. R. S. Raglan, *The Hero: A Study in Tradition, Myth, and Drama* (1956; repr. Westport, CT: Greenwood Press, 1975), 174–75, quoted in A. Taylor, "The Biographical Pattern in Traditional Narrative," *Journal of the Folklore Institute* 1 (1964): 114–29; here 118.

[68] J. Chocheyras, "Les Légendes épiques du Danemark (VIIIe–IXe siècles) et les origines de la chanson de geste," *Olifant* 18 (1993–1994): 289–99, here 295. Perhaps the most interesting parallel in the Spanish tradition is that with Bernardo del Carpio: a sort of Spanish Roland, son of the king's sister and growing up in difficult circumstances to ally himself with the Saracens in order to fight Charlemagne and ultimately defeat Roland. See, for example, Gautier, *Les Épopées françaises*, 2: 331–32. On incest and punishments for it, see H. Goldberg, *Motif Index of Medieval Spanish Folk Narratives*, (Tempe, AZ: MRTS 16, 1998), T 400–499 (165) and Q 240 (140).

[69] F. Gabotto compares *Berta e Milone* to the story of Alerain in Jacopo d'Aquino under the Emperor Otto ("Les Légendes carolingiennes dans le *Chronicon Ymaginis Mundi* di Frate Jacopo d'Aqui," *Revue des langues romanes* 37, 4th ser. 7 [1893–1894]: 356–73, here 358).

capita dal compilatore" (*Epica feudale*, 132). However, there are serious problems with this argument, as there are with the origins of the story: where was the manuscript or text written, in Italy or France? As the specific purpose of the tale (that is, whether or not it was written for the disculpation of Charlemagne), that of this anecdote is a problem, so is whether or not the redactor understood such a purpose.

Krauss's argument about class relations in this poem must also be contested. He suggests that the middle class wishes to court the "strati inferiori" as allies against the aristocracy. In order to accomplish this, they use emotion as a sop (stereotyping emotion as a lower-class literary perspective). He further states, "La rinuncia di Milone a reclamare la propria reintegrazione come diritto spettante alla sua origine nobile, può essere intesa come una presa di posizione teorica del compilatore contro l'ideologia della nobiltà di nascita" (142). Krauss adds that if Milone returns to his position not through his own abilities or help from God, this is a reflections of the genre of the *chanson de geste* and social reality: "la realtà del tempo, la quale di fatto a un lavoratore che possa garantirsi solo la pura sussistenza non permette di elevarsi socialmente mediante una prestazione che produca accumulazione di capitale" (143). These two stories would thus demonstrate the division between employers and workers, as seen by a scholar in Europe at a time when just this was a major social question.

Krauss's *prise de position* neglects, however, the primary basis of the *chanson de geste*: lineage. Both Berta and Milone are of aristocratic birth, tied to specific lands; "blood will tell" as the proverb has it. Though in this case it is Roland who redeems them, he is of their blood, both royal and aristocratic. Kay's concept of multiple threads in the *chanson de geste* holds true here:[70] there is a reaction against the mercenary nature of bourgeois society (Charlemagne is shown as the great giver, l. 10919: "Qe asa averont pan, vino e provan"); but in order to survive, Milone "Si le (= legne) donoit por diner d'argent" (l. 9477), must give wood for silver money. Nobles will work if necessary, as will royalty (compare Berta in *Berta da li pe grant*). As Jones demonstrates, one can see the late epics from the point of view of either class in a given literary piece: the bourgeois sees a noble using his way of living to survive (thus validating it, not disdaining it), but the aristocrat sees his way winning at the end.[71] Milone is thrilled at the opportunity to eat

---

[70] S. Kay, *The Chanson de Geste in the Age of Romance: Political Fictions* (Oxford: Clarendon Press, 1995), esp. 74–78.

[71] C. M. Jones, *The Noble Merchant: Problems of Genre and Lineage in "Hervis de Mes"* (Chapel Hill: University of North Carolina Press, 1993), 21–22. Mine is a simplistic rendition of her very sophisticated argument. Hervis de Mes, she argues and demonstrates quite effectively, is quite different in its two different parts. However, her point about the "delicate and controversial problem" (22) of the relationship of text to social reality is very important and relevant here.

the rich food of Charlemagne's court (ll. 11025–11026: "Quando vi quela colse, molto se fe çojant, / Qe uso non ert de mançer tel provant"). He does not forbid Roland from returning to the court; he stays at home, delighted not to have to go out to work (ll. 11042–11043). When he is legally given Berta, he makes a point of telling Charlemagne how difficult his life has been (ll. 11303–11313): fighting pagans will be much easier than cutting wood for a living! The subject of suffering is dropped rapidly with Charlemagne's victory march home. *Sofferenza* is a part of the didactic and moral function: it is the repayment for a sin and treason, trespass against God and king, and, as it should be, has been hard work much deserved. That implication might not be lost on the aristocracy.

4.6 MACARIO

Macario, or *Macaire*, is one of the better-known and more cited pieces in V^{13}, perhaps in part because it is generally included among "French" *chansons*. Moisan, for example, includes it in the volume "Textes français," Tome 1, volume 1 (as *Mac1*; *Répertoire des noms propres*, 53), but does not include there *Berta*, *Berta e Milone*, *Bovo*, *Enfances Ogier*, *Chevalerie Ogier*, *Karleto (Mainet)*, or *Orlandino*, which appear instead with the *Textes Étrangers*. Furthermore, it was edited twice in a very short period of time by two important philologists, Mussafia and Guessard. It is thus honored like *Ogier* (with three editions), *Berta da li pe grant* (with two editions), and *Berta e Milone-Orlandino* (also with two). Of the nine segments in V^{13}, in some ways it stands alone: it is not paired with any surviving poem in the manuscript in the *Enfances-Chevalerie* sequence, and it takes place after Roland's death. In other ways, it is closely linked: motifs, characters, and moral lessons tie it to the preceding *chansons*.

There are many versions of the story, and these have been studied by Besamusca and his colleagues in relation to the Dutch version,[1] and Chicoy-Daban particularly in relation to the Spanish versions.[2] Tiemann has greatly facilitated comparative study by providing an accessible edition of three of the major texts in the tradition.[3]

4.6.1 V^{13} version.

This last *chanson* in V^{13} tells of Macario, a Maganzese who desires the queen of France (Charlemagne's wife), Blançiflor. (1) There is a dwarf at Charlemagne's court (origin unstated) who frequently attends the queen. (2) Although we do not find this out right away, Queen Blançiflor is the daughter of the Emperor of Constantinople (ll. 13882–13884), who is here named Cleramon (l. 15972). (3) Macario, identified as a traitor from the Maganzese family, decides to shame Charlemagne by making advances to his wife, Blançiflor. When she vigorously

---

[1] B. Besamusca et al., eds, *Sibilla: een zestiende-eeuwse Karelroman in proza* (Muiderberg: Dick Coutinho, 1988); B. Besamusca, "Willem Vorsterman's *Sibilla*: The Dutch Story of Charlemagne's Repudiated Wife," in *L'Imaginaire courtois et son double*: Actes du VIème Congrès triennal de la Société internationale de littérature courtoise (ICLS), Fisciano (Salerno), 24–28 juillet 1989, ed. G. Angeli and L. Formisano (Naples: Edizioni scientifiche italiane, 1991), 245–54.

[2] J. I. Chicoy-Daban, "A Study of the Spanish 'Queen Sibilla' and Related Themes in European Medieval and Renaissance Periods" (Ph.D. Diss., University of Toronto, 1974).

[3] H. Tiemann, *Der Roman von der Königin Sibille in drei Prosafassungen des 14. und 15. Jahrhunderts*, mit Benutzung der nachgelassenen Materialien von Fritz Burg (Hamburg: Dr. Ernst Hauswedell, Verlag, 1977).

turns down his proposition, Macario sends the dwarf to plead for him. Blançiflor rebuffs the dwarf as well, knocking him downstairs and breaking several teeth. The dwarf decides to avenge himself. At Macario's instigation, he sneaks into bed with her one morning while Charlemagne is at mass. (4) Charlemagne returns to find them in bed together, and brings in numerous nobles as witnesses. Blançiflor is exiled rather than burned because she is already pregnant. (5) Alberis, a nobleman attending court, accompanies her into exile with his dog. Macario follows her and kills Alberis, but Blançiflor escapes, and (6) is aided by a woodsman, Varocher. (7) She bears the king's child (who has a white cross on his right shoulder to identify him as a royal scion) in exile. (8) Alberis's dog vindicates his master and Blançiflor by biting Macario in the presence of Charlemagne's court and subsequently defeating him in a judicial combat.[4] (9) Varocher and Blançiflor go to Constantinople, her father's court. (10) There is extensive negotiation between Charlemagne and the emperor over compensation for the missing Blançiflor (whom Charlemagne does not know is in Constantinople). (11) Blançiflor returns with her father and an army to regain her position as queen of France. (12) The Dane fights and pretends to lose so that Blançiflor can return. Varocher is appropriately rewarded for his part in Blançiflor's survival and return. This tale specifically takes place long after the others, after Roland and the twelve *pairs* are dead. It thus is a coda to the Charlemagne story.

Maganzese evil appears in Macario's lust and the devices necessary to attain its object, the queen. Many varied characters appear, perhaps more than in any of the other V^{13} *chansons*. The development of Varocher, the "madman in the woods," and his growth into a valiant knight in the queen's service is particularly noteworthy. Though he reminds the reader of Perceval, Varocher is only and has been only, as far as the reader is informed, of lowly birth. His rise is attributed not to intellectual or spiritual growth, but only to his own strength, cleverness, and devotion to the queen. The importance of intelligence, not just strength or religion, in this character of V^{13} is worthy of note; a similar case occurs for

---

[4] This portion of *Macario* became quite famous also as a separate tale, generating a play specifically about the incident. See Guessard, *Macaire*, xx–lxiij; J. Viscardi, *Le Chien de Montargis: Etude de folklore juridique*, Etudes de sociologie et d'ethnologie juridiques 9 (Paris: Domat-Montchrestien, 1932); J. Subrenat, "Un Héros épique atypique: le chien d'Auberi dans *Macaire*," in *Studies in Honor of Hans-Erich Keller: Medieval French and Occitan Literature and Romance Linguistics*, ed. Rupert T. Pickens (Kalamazoo: Medieval Institute Publications, 1993), 81–96; and most recently, D. Collomp, "*Mucho leal es el amor del can, esto oy prouar* (à propos du chien d'Auberi dans *Le Roman de la Reine Sibille*)," in «*Si a parlé par moult ruiste vertu*»*: Mélanges de littérature médiévale offerts à Jean Subrenat*, ed. Jean Dufournet (Paris: Champion, 2000), 136–46. Note that the segments 7–8 appear in differing order in different versions.

Orlandino, the infant Orlando (Krauss, *Epica feudale*, 214–15). There, however, the boy is of noble origin, so there nobility of bloodline plays a role.

4.6.2 The tradition.

There are versions of this story, usually known as the *Reine Sebile* story, not only in Italy, but throughout Western Europe: in France, Spain, Germany, the Netherlands, Scandinavia, and England. According to recent critics (e.g., Chicoy-Daban, "A Study of the Spanish 'Queen Sibilla'"), V^{13} and German versions derive from a different prototype than the others. We shall examine the Italian versions, then the French, presumably the source of the Sebile story, followed by each of the other national groups to verify Chicoy-Daban's survey. There are three different plots: one follows the V^{13} version; a second follows the *Berta* story (that is, the *Enfances Charlemagne*, or *Karleto*) story closely. In the second, when Charles gains honor and followers enough to return to France, he leaves his fiancée, the daughter of a Spanish king, behind. He later sends Morant to accompany her to his court. She and Morant are alone, leading to accusations of adultery during the trip. The third version is similar to the ending of one version of the Arthur story, where Modred forges letters saying that Arthur is dead, and wishes to marry Guinevere, with varying success (e.g, Malory, *Morte d'Arthur*).[5] The first and last are found in Italy; the second only in Spain and in Germany.

4.6.2.1 Other Italian versions.

In Italy, versions appear in Andrea da Barberino's *Le Storie Nerbonesi* (late fourteenth- early fifteenth century); the prose *I Fatti di Spagna*, also known as *Il Viaggio di Carlomagno in Spagna* (fourteenth century, according to Ruggieri); and *La Spagna* (fourteenth century). *I Nerbonesi* retells the story but in a different framework.[6] There, an account of Amerigo of Nerbona and his family's feats opens the tale. Namo and the court decide that Charlemagne should marry because of his age and lack of heirs. (2) He marries Belistante, daughter of the emperor of Constantinople. She becomes pregnant within three months, and the Maganzesi, who would inherit if Charlemagne were without heirs, want to get rid of the competition. (3) Rinicri arranges with a dwarf, one of the queen's servants, to play (he says),

---

[5] K. Baines, trans., *Malory, Le Morte d'Arthur: King Arthur and the Legends of the Round Table* (New York: Mentor [New American Library], 1962), 495 ff.

[6] The edition consulted is I. G. Isola, ed., *Le Storie Nerbonesi: Romanzo cavalleresco del secolo XIV: Andrea da Barberino* (1877; repr. Bologna: Romagnoli-Dall'Acqua, 1887). Andrea da Barberino's works are long and generally were edited at the end of the nineteenth or beginning of the twentieth century. There have been no new editions in many years, until recently an edition came out of *Il Guerrin Meschino*, edited by Mauro Cursietti (Rome: Antenore, 2005).

a joke on Charlemagne. In fact, (4) he accuses Belistante of adultery with the dwarf who is in her bed. The king kills the dwarf, and (5) the queen flees accompanied by Almieri di Spagna. She stays with a *carbonaio*, a charcoal–maker (one who makes charcoal), (6) Ispinardo, in the forest for seven years. Meanwhile, the Maganzesi rule Charlemagne though Rinieri's plot is discovered and he is hanged (because of Almieri's dog's reappearance just once). The Nerbonesi rescue Charlemagne (there are long sections on family quarrels which interrupt the queen's story; Mattaini reduces the tale to twenty-six pages from Isola's seventy-six by giving only the portions relevant to the *Macario* story).[7] After Charlemagne's rescue, (10) a messenger arrives from Hungary, where the king of the country has found Belistante and rescued her. He challenges the Maganzesi with his own and the pope's support. (11) King, queen, and son are reunited; (12) the Nerbonesi are rewarded.

The primary differences between the *Storie Nerbonesi* and the V[13] version are: 1. Maganzese motivation. There is no physical desire expressed at all on the part of the traitor, just a desire for property. 2. The queen flees, she is not banished; 3. she stays with the charcoal–maker and his family specifically for seven years, not with an innkeeper, whence she departs to meet with her father; 4. the means of revealing her identity: the king of Hungary has one of his men harass her, the charcoal–maker kills him, and she must reveal her identity to save her protector (this is more similar to versions of the Berta story). 5. Rinieri is hanged and there is no judicial combat with a dog; 6. the pope declares a crusade against the Maganzesi; it is not Charlemagne's fault at all here: he is passive and almost uninvolved. The plot is the Maganzesi vs. the Nerbonesi. The concerns of family remain paramount, but in this case Charlemagne's family is in the background and it is rather the seven Nerbonesi sons and their exploits which interest the narrator.

4.6.2.2 *I Fatti di Spagna*.

I Fatti di Spagna, chapters 39–40, recount that Ansuyxe de Maganza, Gayno's relative, has had himself crowned king of France during Charlemagne's absence in Spain.[8] He also is about to marry the queen. Roland learns this from a spirit (a *folletto*), and he then reports the information to Charlemagne. The spirit takes Charlemagne to Paris, where he arrives just as the court is waiting for Ansuyxe to go sleep with the queen. Charlemagne sits on the throne while the people wonder. A boy who knows him arrives and asks forgiveness, as do many others. The boy says that they thought he was dead. The queen hears the news and goes to welcome him; he insults her, saying that for seven years he and his army

---

[7] A. Mattaini, ed., *I Romanzi dei Reali di Francia* (Milan: Rizzoli, 1957), 967–1084.

[8] Ruggieri, *Li Fatti di Spagna*; originally A. Ceruti, ed., *Il Viaggio di Carlo Magno in Ispagna* (Bologna: Gaetano Romagnoli, 1871).

have been without food and supplies! Ansuyxe flees, and Charlemagne leaves Algirone in charge, returning to Spain via the spirit. Roland, upon hearing the story, swears to punish the Maganzesi for their crimes. This is very different from the *Macaire* of V[13]; it resembles rather German versions of Charlemagne's life (Enikel, last quarter of the thirteenth century, and his followers; see Folz, *Le Souvenir et la légende*, 325ff.), and is similar to the ending of one version of the Arthur story where Modred forges letters saying that Arthur is dead, and wishes to marry Guinevere, with varying success (e.g, Malory, *Morte d'Arthur* [Baines, *Le Morte d'Arthur*, 495 ff.]). The *Spagna* version is even closer to those versions.

4.6.2.3 *Spagna in rima*.
The *Spagna*, cantari 21–24, recounts that Macario of Maganza, nephew of Gano, is nominated as regent during Charlemagne's absence.[9] Similarly to the *Fatti di Spagna* version, Roland casts a spell for news of France. He learns that Macario has shown false letters to the queen saying that the king is dead. Their wedding is scheduled for the next day. The devil cannot stop the wedding, but can take him there in one evening. Roland tells Charlemagne, who is then carried to Paris. Charlemagne goes to the kitchen, where Ghione saves him from a beating. A cat recognizes Charlemagne and licks his feet. The queen believes him upon seeing his wedding ring and the cross on his shoulder. Ghione organizes a group to take over; its members station themselves in the palace. Ghione accompanies the queen to the church at the time of the wedding. She asks for a wedding gift: to be permitted to hold the wedding ceremony in the palace. Once the wedding party arrives there, Charlemagne and Ghione's men, armed, demand the crown and rule back. The Maganzesi are defeated, but Macario flees through the city. Ghione becomes the new regent and Charlemagne returns to Spain with the devil.

Thus there are two Italian versions: one similar to the "falsely accused queen" plot and a second version more like the Arthurian and, as we shall see, German tale.

4.6.3 French versions.
French versions, though in fragmentary condition, tell a more unitary tale.

4.6.3.1 Albéric des Trois-Fontaines.
It is necessary to begin with Albéric des Trois-Fontaines (1200–1250), who wrote in Latin, providing the earliest summary of Sebile's story, then proceed to the various fragments, and finally to later French-language versions. The Latin is

---

[9] Catalano, *La Spagna*.

generally dated to the second quarter of the thirteenth century.[10] In his version, the story is already complete: Charlemagne married the daughter of Desiderius and repudiated her after one year. He then married Hildegard and had three sons and three daughters with her. She is called "Sibilia" by Gallic singers, and they tell a fable about her (the numbers are the parallel episodes in V[13]) concerning a (1) dwarf because of whom the queen was exiled; of (5) Albrico of Mont Desidier who was to accompany her, killed by Machario; and about (8) Albrico's hunting dog which defeated Machario in a duel before Charlemagne. Balerano and Macario are killed. (9) Varochero, a muleteer, miraculously led the queen home to her country, and they found the famous thief, Grimoardo, along the way. They also tell of a hermit and his brother Richero, emperor of Constantinople, who is the queen's father. (11) The emperor leads an expedition into France with the Greeks, whom Charlemagne must fight. Sibilie's son Ludovicus married Naimes's daughter Blanchefleur, and Charlemagne was reconciled with his wife. Six of Ganelon's men were killed. This includes all the basic elements, including the thief, hermit, and invasion by Greeks seen in the later developed versions.

4.6.3.2 Fragments.
Three sets of Old French alexandrine fragments all date to the thirteenth century: Mons, 126 lines; Loveday Library, 66 lines and 71 lines, respectively; and Sion, 168 lines.[11] The first set (Mons) contains five segments according to Scheler (the recto and verso of two non-sequential sheets, four pages). In the first segment, (7) Varocher takes his "son" to the godfather for training; one of the innkeeper's daughters declares her love for Loys; the queen recovers and (9) the group departs for Constantinople. The second segment begins with Grimoart, saved alone from robbers, telling them of Richiers and his two children while leading the

---

[10] P. Scheffer-Boichorst, ed., *Chronica Albrici monaci Trium Fontium a monacho novi monasterii Hoiensis interpolata*, Monumenta Germaniae Historica, Scriptores 23 (Hannover: Hahn, 1874), 712–13.

[11] All have been edited. 1. The Mons fragments: Reiffenberg, ed., *Chronique rimée* [1836]; Guessard, "Notes sur un manuscrit français," 315–18; and A. Scheler, "Fragments uniques d'un roman du XIIIième siècle sur la reine Sebile, restitués, complétés et annotés d'après le manuscrit original récemment acquis par la Bibliothèque royale de Bruxelles," *Bulletin de l'Académie de Belgique*, 2e série, 39 (1875): 404–23, repr. in Tiemann, *Der Roman von der Königin Sibille*, 313–18. The Loveday Library fragment: A.T. Baker and Mario Roques, "Nouveaux fragments de la chanson de *La Reine Sibille*," *Romania* 44 (1915–1917): 1–13, repr. in Tiemann, *Der Roman von der Königin Sibille*, 319–23. The Sion fragment: P. Aebischer, ed., "Fragments de la *Chanson de la Reine Sebile* et du roman de *Florence de Rome* conservés aux Archives cantonales de Sion," *Zeitschrift für romanische Philologie* 66 (1941): 385–408, repr. in Tiemann, *Der Roman von der Königin Sibille*, 323–28.

party to a hermit who finally allows them to enter upon hearing that the thieves are dead. In the third segment, he hears Sibylle's tale and identification. The fourth segment shows Grimoart loaded down with food; he takes a donkey from a peasant by putting him to sleep with magic words. He returns to the hermitage where they eat well. Of the last segment in these first fragments, only the initial hemistiches are readable, where (11) the group plans to return home.

The Loveday fragments are in English handwriting. Baker and Roques believe these fragments to come from the same redaction as the Mons fragments, and furthermore, that the Arsenal version in prose probably also derives from the same version in alexandrines (13). The Loveday fragments were guard papers from another manuscript and bear two episodes: first, (8) the dog's appearance at court and Macer's indignation at the accusations levelled at him. The second consists of Nemes' suggestion of the judicial combat between Macer and the dog up to the point where he is given a stick to fight against the dog (11).

The Sion fragments contain Varocher returning from Charlemagne's camp with Grimoart, Charlemagne's fury against the thief Grimoart, and his enchantment that allowed him to take Warochier out of prison. Ogier goes for help, and when he arrives back at Charlemagne's camp with the Normans, the pope stops battle with a truce till dawn.

MSS. Arsenal 3351 and BN 5003 also contain versions of the Sebile story.

4.6.3.3 Arsenal 3351 (*Garin de Monglane*).

Arsenal 3351 is a lengthy treatment of the same story (Tiemann, *Der Roman von der Königin Sibille*, 187–95; fifteenth century). It develops certain points, such as the dog's behavior and the queen's anxiety. (2) Charlemagne courts Sebile, the daughter of Richier, the king of Greece, when his first wife, Galienne of Spain, dies without an heir. Sometime after Sebile arrives, (1) a dwarf, Segonçon, arrives. While Charlemagne is hunting, and Sebile, already pregnant, is in bed, her ladies leave to gather flowers and (3) Segonçon enters her bedroom. She punches him when she awakens, putting out four teeth. He swears revenge. That night the dwarf sneaks into her room, and, the next morning when Charlemagne leaves for mass, undresses and climbs into bed with her. Charlemagne finds them thus. Ultimately Naymes, Ogier, Aymery, and Aubery succeed in saving the queen from death. (5) Aubery is designated to accompany her. Macaire follows; Aubery is killed; the dog accuses Macaire. (6) Meanwhile, Sebile is aided by a *charbonnier* (charcoal-maker), Varroquier, who leads her to Hungary. (8) Naymes helps Aubery's dog, which fights Macaire. The whole arrangement is quite elaborate. Macaire is taken and confesses; the emperor orders his men to "trainer et pendre" the traitor. (7) Sebile's child Loys is born, and she is ill for 10 years afterwards. The king of Hungary stands as godfather to the child, and takes him in to be trained ten years later. (9) Ultimately, Sebile is cured and they leave for Greece. The attack in the woods again comes to pass; they visit the hermit Lucaire,

Sebile's uncle; Grimoart steals goods in town; they go to Rome, convince the pope to help, and then continue to Constantinople. (11) Richier and his army go to France; Aymery of Narbonne and his family encounter the army on the move, and get the story from Loys. The army continues to Paris; Guillaume d'Orange offers his daughter, Blanchefleur, to Loys. Varroquier goes to see his wife, tests her fidelity, and continues to Paris, where he takes the horse Falcon from Charlemagne. The events proceed as in the Spanish version. The two traitors who follow Grimoart are killed; Varroquier is rescued by Naymes and Ogier, then spirited out of Hautefeuille by Grimoart. The pope eventually arranges for peace, as Sebile and her party beg Charlemagne's forgiveness and the pope orders Charlemagne to take her back. The tale ends with Loys's marriage to Blanchefleur. The piece is lengthy (108 pages of prose in Tiemann's edition) and quite detailed.

4.6.3.4 *Chronique de France* / BN 5003.
BN 5003 (published in Guessard, *Macaire*, Appendix III; fifteenth century) contains a very short summary of the Sebile story, attributing the ill will and evildoing entirely to Maquaire. (3) When he "requist la royne Sebille" and she turned him down, he decided to avenge himself by arranging for the dwarf to sleep in her bed without her knowing it. (4) The king exiles his pregnant wife, (5) defended by Auberi de Mondidier, who is killed in the Forest of Bondis where we still find the "fontaine Aubery." (7) The queen was hosted for a long time there in the woods by the woodsman Verroquier where she bore Loys. (8) Meanwhile, Auberi's dog comes often to court to eat, and people begin to wonder about Auberi's absence, so they follow the dog and find Auberi's corpse. After investigation, the dog and traitor fight, the dog wins, and the traitor confesses. He is punished by the king. The writer notes that the story is long and that thus he must abridge it. In the segment published there is no mention of the king and queen's reconciliation; the emphasis is rather on the moral issue of justice and punishment of the envious.

4.6.3.5 Jean d'Outremeuse.
D'Outremeuse (mid to second half, fourteenth century) also includes a version of the story in *Ly Myreur des Histors* (Borgnet, *Ly Myreur des Histors, Tome III*, 42–50). The historical time frame is different, since Roland is present, unlike other versions. (1) The king of Persia sends an elephant with a dwarf rider as part of his homage to Charlemagne.[12] The dwarf (3) desires the queen, who did not like him from the start. She knocks him down when he tries to kiss her, and he takes his revenge by getting into bed with her while the king is at mass. (4) The

---

[12] This echoes the gift of an elephant by the Abbasid caliph of Baghdad to Charlemagne recorded in Einhard's *Life of Charlemagne*, trans. Thorpe (London: Penguin, 1969), 70.

king finds them, and Gennulhon and his family persuade the dwarf to say that the queen had invited him. Ogier the Dane is her cousin, though, and he saves her from death, getting the dwarf to confess who had put him up to the lie. Ogier tosses the dwarf into the fire. But Sibilhe [sic] is still banished. Ogier persuades Charlemagne to agree to an escort for her, at least: (5) Albris de Mondesdier, a squire, who is not to return until she is safely out of his territory. Machar, son of Luchnois, Gennulhon's sister, follows the two, and Albris is killed. (6) The vilain (one of Ogier's liege men) helps her and they arrive at Ligny, where the son Loys is born and held at baptism by Loys, king or duke of Bohemia. (8) Albris's dog meanwhile vindicates his owner. Loys at eight years old goes to his father's court and is well seen but gets into a fight to defend his mother. He returns home and they decide (9) to go to Constantinople for help from her father. The robbers arrive; only Grimoaldins, who knows magic, is saved. Grimoart plays all kinds of tricks to get food and drink and ultimately rescues Warocher from Charlemagne's men when he is captured. (11) Names and Ogier arrange for peace, and the queen is forgiven. The whole party—Loys, king, and men—appear in chemise before Charlemagne to ask for forgiveness. D'Outremeuse carefully ties up loose ends, (12) making the queen ensure rewards for all her assistants.

4.6.4 Spanish versions.

Spanish versions are many and varied, and have been closely studied. According to Chicoy-Daban ("A Study of the Spanish 'Queen Sibilla'"), one version is possibly a Spanish translation of the French original. The versions are found in the *Gran conquista de Ultramar* (thirteenth century); the *Historia de la reyna Sebilla* (1498 or 1500; 1532; 1553 and many following editions); *Noble cuento del emperador Cárlos Maynes* . . . (MS. h-I-13) (second half of the fourteenth century; the title varies according to editor). It is this last which Chicoy-Daban argues is an accurate translation of the Old French poem. Arsenal 3351 (section 4.6.3.3) in Paris is quite similar to the *Cuento*, outlined above. Spanish versions were produced as late as 1757 (*Los Carboneros de Francia y reina Sevilla, comedia famosa*) and 1846 (*Reina Sebilla, drama comico original*, three acts, by Ramón de Villadares y Saavedra in Madrid).[13]

4.6.4.1 *Gran conquista de Ultramar.*

The *Gran conquista de Ultramar* version is quite different from our V[13]. Morante brings Halía, daughter of the king of Toledo, to France. They must go alone through great difficulties, and rumors circulate that Halía's great affection for

---

[13] Chicoy-Daban's chapter 2 discusses the relationships among the Spanish versions ("A Study of the Spanish 'Queen Sibilla'," 60–92).

Morante is because she slept with him. She changes her name to Sevilla when she is baptized, which is the link with the "Queen Sebile / Seville" story (Gayangos, *La Gran conquista de Ultramar*, 185 [Cap. 43]). This should be compared to the *Berta* story (section 4.2).

4.6.4.2 *Noble cuento.*
Critics agree that the *Noble cuento* is the source of the *Historia* and most subsequent versions, including the Dutch. Chicoy-Daban uses the *Noble cuento* as the basis for the *Reine Sebile* analysis ("A Study of the Spanish 'Queen Sibilla'").[14] The *Cuento* (1) begins with a dwarf who arrives at Charlemagne's court and is given a place there. One day while the queen's handmaidens are out gathering flowers, the dwarf enters the queen's bedchamber and wants to kiss her. (2) The queen here is the daughter of the emperor of Constantinople, as in V^{13}. (3) She awakens, and when the dwarf declares his love, punches him, breaking two teeth. He swears vengeance. That same night, the dwarf sneaks into the bedchamber (n.b., of his own volition), and when the king leaves for church the next morning, the dwarf gets into bed with her. But the queen is turned the other way and he does not dare touch her. (4) The plot proceeds as elsewhere: the traitors urge that she be burned. Here, the good Nerbonesi arrive and urge exile instead. The identity of the queen's savior(s) varies according to the author's goals. The dwarf, when asked, says that she called him. (5) A trusted knight, Aubery de Mondisder, is to accompany the queen to Rome, where she can confess her sins to the pope and do penance (the location of exile is thus very specific).

Macario sees an opportunity to have his way with the queen. He follows the queen and kills Aubery, but the queen escapes. (6) She meets the peasant Barroquer (V^{13}'s Varocher), who leaves his family to accompany her: he sends his mule loaded with wood home by itself. (8) Meanwhile, back at court, Aubery's dog leads Charlemagne's court to the body; Ogier must protect the dog from death at Macario's men's hands. When followed at Ogier's instigation, Aubery's body is found. Macario is accused of malfeasance and must fight the dog. He loses; he confesses and is dragged to death with his kinsman who attempted to save him.[15]

---

[14] There are four editions of the *Noble Cuento*. All are based on MS. h-j-13 of the Escorial Library; I use Tiemann, *Der Roman von der Königin Sibille*, for the convenience of having the three versions of the text — the German, Middle and Old French as well — all in one volume.

[15] In V^{13}: ll. 14696–14698: "Macharios fait pier tot en primer, / E a çivals elo lo fait trainer, / Par tot Paris e davant e darer . . . /"; ll. 14707–14709: "Quant à ço fato, retorna a li plaçer; / Ilec fait un gran fois alumer, / Ilec le fi et arder e bruxer" [He had Macharios taken first / And by horses he had him dragged / Though all of Paris, back and forth . . . / When he had done that, he returned to the square; / There he had a huge fire lit, / There he had him roasted and burned. (my trans.)].

(7) The queen meanwhile gives birth to a boy with a red cross on his shoulder.[16] The king of Hungary happens to be passing by when Barroquer and the host are taking the baby to be baptized; he offers to be the godfather and to teach the boy courtly manners when he is old enough. Here the queen is ill for ten years after the birth. Finally, her host presents the youth at the Hungarian court; the host's daughter falls in love with him and proposes, but he refuses her.[17] (9) When the queen finally recovers, she, Barroquer, and her son go to Constantinople. Barroquer sings loudly and badly en route, attracting the attention of a band of twelve robbers in the woods. Sebile's party kills all but one, Grimoart, who is a magician.[18]

Grimoart leads them to a hermit, who turns out to be the queen's uncle. He goes with them to the pope in Rome for help and then on to Constantinople. Grimoart procures food and supplies in the questionable manner of stealing from the richest man in town and then putting a man leading a donkey to sleep so he can load up the beast with his loot. Upon their return from Constantinople, Barroquer visits his wife in disguise and tests her fidelity. There is a happy reunion. Barroquer then goes to Paris to listen to rumors. Traitors are urging Charlemagne not to take Sevilla back. Barroquer speaks up for her and Loys. Charles asks Barroquer his profession; he says he is an excellent horseman. A horse is brought and Barroquer rides it in spite of its bucking. He identifies himself and rides off on the horse, with the court in hot pursuit. Two traitors follow too closely and are imprisoned and dragged through the streets by the Greeks. (11) Battle begins. Charles's army attacks the queen's men by night from Altafoia (Hautefeuille), where he and

---

[16] In V^{13}: l. 14887 "Desor la spala droit le vis una cros blant" [On his right shoulder he saw a white cross (my trans.)]. Cf. l. 308 "Ço fo una cros qe Deo li volse segner" [That was a cross (with) which God wanted to sign him (my trans.)], describing Bovo.

[17] This can be compared to the *Enfances Charlemagne* episode where the king of Saragoça's daughter proposes to young Charlemagne (compare Roncaglia and Beggiato, *Reali di Francia*, 370–75 [Book 4, Chaps. 10–12]). Similarly, in Bovo's *Enfances*, he is propositioned by the daughter of the king who has saved him; see, for example, *Reali di Francia*, Book 6, Chaps. 22–24 (Roncaglia and Beggiato, *Reali di Francia*, 580–87). However, there a class difference makes Jocerant's daughter's proposal a parody. This is an example of variation on a plot; though the beginning of *Bovo* is missing in V^{13}, his wife is a king's daughter who comes to court when word goes out that he is about to marry another ruler's (host's) daughter. Charlemagne in V^{13} marries his host's (the king's) daughter, so the "host's daughter" is a common motif normally resulting in marriage. Ogier's story is related as well in French versions; Balduyn is the result of a love affair with his prison-keeper's daughter. For related motifs, see J.-P. Martin, *Les Motifs dans la chanson de geste: Définition et utilisation* (Lille: Université de Lille III, Centre d'Études Médiévales et Dialectales, 1992), 4.A.1 and 5.C.1; H. Goldberg, *Motif-Index of Folk Narratives in the Pan-Hispanic Romancero*, (Tempe, AZ: MRTS 206, 2000), 115 (R162).

[18] The episode is reminiscent of *Moniage Guillaume*, where Guillaume fights for his *braies*; a comic character fights in a non-traditional manner for a not-very-worthy cause.

his army have taken refuge, and Barroquer is taken. After Barroquer's capture, Orguel (V[13]'s Ogier) and Aymeri are sympathetic to him upon hearing his story and keep him from being hanged for having stolen Charlemagne's horse.

Loys weeps at Barroquer's absence. Grimoart wishes to please Loys, so he enters Altafoia with the help of a sleep spell. There he liberates *Joliosa* (Charlemagne's sword) as well as Barroquer. Orguel arrives with reinforcements for Charles's army, and finds combat in progress. The battle ceases when the pope arrives, bringing a truce. The next day mass is celebrated, and the pope calls to him the Greek emperor, Sevilla (V[13]'s Blançiflor), and Loys. He suggests that they all go before Charlemagne in their shifts ("paños menores") to ask for mercy. (12) All are forgiven, and Barroquer is rewarded financially. The host is granted a reward, and the emperor and pope leave after blessing Charlemagne and his empire. The *Historia* is quite similar, differing primarily in details.[19]

4.6.5 German versions.

There are a number of German versions: Enikel, *Weltchronik* (end thirteenth century); *Weihenstephan Chronik* (ca. 1435); *Karl Meinet* (first quarter of the fourteenth century); *Die künigin von Frankrich und der ungetriuwe marschalk* (Schondoch, fourteenth century); Elisabeth von Nassau-Saarbrücken, *Die unschuldige Königin von Frankreich* (lived 1395–1456; ca. 1430); *Meisterlied*, 15 strophes (first half of sixteenth century); Hans Sachs, *Die königin auß Franckreich mit dem falschen marschalck* (ca. 1551). These represent three different plots.

4.6.5.1 *Karl Meinet*.

In *Karl Meinet* (Sections 215–290; A. v. Keller, *Karl Meinet*, 324–444), the first part follows the Berta story, that is, *Enfances Charlemagne*, very closely. While Charlemagne is still a child, his half-brothers by a false queen kill Pepin and the true queen, taking power for themselves (see 4.2, *Berta da li pe grant*). Charlemagne must flee, accompanied by a faithful courtier, most frequently Morant of River.[20]

---

[19] For full information on the *Cuento* and *Historia* relationship, see Chicoy-Daban ("A Study of the Spanish 'Queen Sibilla'") and A. Benaim de Lasry, ed., *"Carlos Maynes" and "La enperatris de Roma": Critical Edition and Study of Two Medieval Spanish Romances* (Newark, DE: Juan de la Cuesta, 1982), whose edition leaves much to be desired, however.

[20] In some versions, David. See the "Chart of Names" accompanying section, 4.2, *Berta da li pe grant*. The editions used are the following: F. H. van der Hagen, ed., *Gesammtabenteur, Hundert altdeutsche Erzählungen: Ritter- und Pfaffen-Mären; Stadt- und Dorfgeschichten; Schwänke, Wundersagen und Legenden*, 2 vols. (Stuttgart and Tübingen: J.G. Cotta'scher, 1850), 1: civ–cxii; 2: 165–87, which also contains information about the Schondoch story as well as the story itself. A. v. Keller, ed., Hans Sachs: "Ein comedi, mit dreyzehen personen, die königin auß Franckreich mit dem falschen marschalck, hat

When Charles gains honor and followers enough to return to France, he leaves his fiancée, the daughter of a Spanish king, behind.[21] He later sends Morant to accompany her to his court. She and Morant are alone, leading to accusations of adultery during the trip. Eventually Morant is vindicated and returns, and Sevilla is never exiled, though Morant has stayed away.[22]

4.6.5.2 World histories.

Enikel and *Weihenstephan* follow the variation on "Charlemagne's falsely accused wife" that is closely related to versions of the Arthur legend, where Modred forges documents that Arthur is dead while he is campaigning on the Continent and attempts to marry Guinevere. During a war (in Enikel (lines 25673–26180 [Strauch, *Jansen Enikels Werke*, 504–15]) and *Weihenstephan* (21c–24b [Freitag, *Die sogenannte Chronik von Weihenstephan*, 168–74]), in Hungary), the regent from the traitorous house forges letters or otherwise convinces the court that Charlemagne is dead and tries to marry the queen. He is stopped by Charlemagne's magic arrival in the nick of time. A new regent loyal to the king is installed and Charlemagne returns to war (this is also the *Nerbonesi* story).

4.6.5.3 Schondoch and Sachs.

The Schondoch and Sachs versions follow the *Macaire* story in that the queen is falsely accused because of a dwarf. They are alike in lacking (9) the detailed trip to Rome and Constantinople, as well as the war against the king (husband of the falsely accused queen), section (11). In Schondoch, Hans Sachs, and *Meisterlied* versions, it is the traitor who is after the queen and who instigates the dwarf's actions, as in V[13]. In those versions, the Marshal places the sleeping dwarf in the queen's arms; the dwarf is in no way party to the deception. The traitor, furthermore, calls attention to the "betrayal" by specifically calling in the king, which does not happen in the Franco-Italian and French versions (though in V[13], Macario does encourage Charlemagne saying that "bad songs" will be sung about him if he does not punish her). In Nassau-Saarbrücken, on the other hand, the French versions are followed very closely: there the dwarf approaches the queen himself, and the voyage to Rome and Constantinople is made with Warakir.

---

fünff actus," in *Hans Sachs Werke* (Tübingen: H. Laupp, 1874), 8: 54–80, for the Hans Sachs play; and H. Heintz, ed., *Schondochs Gedichte*, Germanistische Abhandlungen 30 (Breslau: M. & H. Marcus, 1908), for the *Meisterlied*.

[21] This is true only in some versions. In V[13], there is a trip to Italy, where she accompanies him.

[22] Compare *Berte aux grands pieds* in the *Kaiserkronik* (Massmann, *Der keiser und der kunige buoch*) and in Enikel (Strauch, *Jansen Enikels Werke*; commented on by Folz, *Le Souvenir et la légende*, 325).

4.6.6 Scandinavian versions.

The Scandinavian (Norwegian) version is quite different from the "Spanish" versions and seems related to the German versions. *Thidrekssaga* tells of King Sigmund and Queen Sisibe in Tarlungaland.[23] The king is away at war, and one of his regents, Artvin, tries to seduce the queen. When she refuses, he enlists his fellow regent, Hermann, to help urge his cause. She continues to refuse. They anticipate her reaction at the king's return by denouncing her for sleeping with an attractive servant, and suggest abandoning her in a forest instead of killing her. The two disagree once in the forest, Artvin wanting to do more than abandon her, to cut out her tongue to take back. Queen Sisibe, who had been pregnant, gives birth during their argument. She puts the boy in a glass vessel, which Artvin kicks into the nearby river as he dies (Hermann cuts his head off). The second traitor is exiled when he returns to King Sigmund. The queen dies, and there is no faithful dog. The son is Siegfried, according to Krappe the only example where this hero is a son of the "falsely accused queen" ("Une Version norroise," 586). The attempted seduction of the queen and the same traitor's subsequent pursuit is more like the Franco-Italian, but there are so many points of difference it cannot be closely related (see also Richthofen, "Seuilla-Sebile-Sisbe, Sigelint," for more about similarities between Sevilla / Sisibe stories).

4.6.7 Dutch versions.

For the Dutch Willem Vorsterman version of 1538, *Sibilla*, I rely upon Besamusca's summary and analysis that it is a translation from the Spanish *Hystoria de la reyna Sevilla*, following in the tradition of printed narrative tradition in the Low Countries ("Willem Vorsterman's *Sibilla*," 247). (1) The dwarf is in love with Sibilla, tries to kiss her in her bedroom, and she knocks his teeth out. (3) He plots his revenge and is assisted by the traitors. The dwarf is burned. (5) Auberijn of Mondiser is to escort Sibilla to the border with his greyhound, but Macharis attacks en route. Sibilla escapes, (6) meets Baroquel, and they together go to Hungary. (7) Loys is born and they stay twelve years at Josaran's inn. (8) Auberijn's dog, meanwhile, on the fifth day of guarding his master, avenges him by attacking Macharis and leading the court to Auberijn's body. Macharis undergoes the judicial duel, confesses, and is killed. Loys is at his godfather's court, and Belisarte, one of the innkeeper's daughters, proposes to him. He refuses, feeling responsible

---

[23] E. R. Haymes, trans., *The Saga of Thidrek of Bern* (New York: Garland Publishing Inc., 1988), 101–8. The story is also summarized in A. H. Krappe, "Une Version norroise de la *Reine Sibille*," *Romania* 56 (1930): 585–88, and E. v. Richthofen, "Seuilla-Sebile-Sisbe, Sigelint (*Mainete, Sebile/Macaire, Thidrekssaga/Nibelungen)," in *Mélanges de philologie romane dédiés à la mémoire de Jean Boutière (1899–1967)*, ed. I. Cluzel and F. Pirot (Liège: Editions Soledi, 1971), 1: 501–6.

for his mother. (9) He, his mother, and Baroquel eventually leave for Constantinople, and fight brigands in the woods, of whom only Guimar survives. He leads them to the hermit, Sibilla's uncle, who counsels them to travel to Rome first to complain. They do so and continue to Constantinople. (11) Sibilla's father invades France. Baroquel steals the king's horse for Loys. Eventually the remaining traitors are caught, the pope arranges peace between Charlemagne and Sibilla, and the court returns to Paris. This is clearly close to the "Spanish" versions.

4.6.8 English versions.

The English *Sir Triamour* dates to the early sixteenth century, or possibly very late fifteenth.[24] King Aradas of Aragon and his wife Margaret are childless. The king decides to go to the Holy Land. The night before his departure, she conceives. He leaves the steward Marrock in charge. (3) He develops a passion for the queen; after numerous rejections, he asks for forgiveness but decides to ruin her. When the king returns home, she is still pregnant. (4) Marrock accuses her of adultery, saying he had found her in the arms of a knight whom he had killed. The queen then supposedly had tried to seduce him. Aradas believes the story and condemns her to burn. Marrock, however, counsels exile. (5) Old Sir Roger is ordered to accompany her with his greyhound. Meanwhile, Marrock and eighteen men set an ambush for her. As elsewhere, she escapes while her guard is killed. The greyhound digs a pit, buries his master, and covers him with leaves, protecting the body from wild animals. (6) The queen makes her way to Hungary where she gives birth to a boy in the forest. A Hungarian knight (7) awakens her and offers help, which she accepts. He carries her to the nearby castle, where the boy is baptized Triamour. (8) Meanwhile, the greyhound is getting hungry since there is not much prey near his master's grave. After seven years, the dog returns to court twice to seek food. The king orders him to be followed. The third time, Marrock is there for the first time, and the dog bites him and kills him. It then leads the court

---

[24] G. Ellis, ed., "Sir Triamour," in *Specimens of Early English Metrical Romances*, ed J. O. Halliwell (London: Henry G. Bohn, 1848), 491–505. Thanks to Bett Miller, librarian at the Eisenhower Library of the Johns Hopkins University, who tracked down the earliest printed versions of *Sir Triamour*. She located two possibly "first" Triamours: one at Cambridge, and one at the Huntington Library, both without dates, but according to the dates of activity of their printers can be listed to late fifteenth or early sixteenth century. The version I used other than Ellis is the uncertainly dated Eisenhower Library microfilm, *Sir Tryamour*, Series Early English Books, 1475–1640; 1804:22 (Publisher: R. Pynson?, 1503? Repr. Ann Arbor: UMI, 1984), copied from the Huntington Library, the date of which corresponds to Ms. Miller's finding.

to his master's grave. They return with the king. When the grave is opened, they find Sir Roger in a perfectly preserved state, but no trace of the queen.

Triamour is well educated in Hungary by Sir Bernard, until he is fourteen years old. The king of Hungary dies; his fifteen-year-old daughter is the heir, and is seeking a husband. Triamour goes to try his strength at the three-day tournament with Sir Bernard. He does well, but on the last day Aradas (his father) is there as well as Sir James of Germany, son of the Emperor, who plots against Triamour. Triamour is wounded; James is killed. Triamour flees back to Margaret to heal the wound in his thigh. On the last day, the heiress asks for Triamour as winner but he cannot be found. She will wait for a year and a day. James's father seeks his son's murderer in the meantime as well. He marches on Aradas as an accessory to the murder. To resolve the conflict, a personal combat is to be fought by Marradas and Aradas's champion. The search for Triamour continues. One day, healed, he is hunting for pleasure in the woods when he is attacked by thirteen foresters. Triamour kills them all and his deer. Aradas is in a manor in the same woods, hears the horn blast, and sends three knights for Triamour. He comes, recognizes his helper from the earlier battle, and is happy to return his assistance. Aradas knights him, and together they go to Hungary. A palmer advises Triamour to avoid two giants, but Triamour goes anyway. It turns out that they are two of Marradas' brothers, trying to prevent his arrival. Another brother, Burlang, is besieging the princess in Hungary. He kills them, goes to the capital of Hungary, fights Burlong, and defeats him by cutting off his head. He is welcomed by the princess Helen.

Margaret is summoned to witness the marriage. There she tells the story of his birth. Aradas is invited to the coronation and takes his wife back. He is rewarded for all his past sufferings by the recovery of his faithful wife Margaret.

4.6.9 Discussion.

There are three versions of the *Reine Sebile* tale: first, Morant returning from Spain accused of adultery; second, the treachery of a steward or regent during the king's absence; and third, the story related to V^{13}, with a dwarf, a traitor, a pregnant queen exiled because of false accusations, and a helpful peasant. Some of these include a trip to the queen's father to obtain assistance and to the pope for support; some also include the "good robber" and the hermit-brother of the king of Constantinople, the queen's uncle. V^{13}'s version is closest to the French, which was subsequently translated into Spanish, German (by Nassau-Saarbrücken), and Dutch, but it lacks the adventures after the French heir's birth as well as the adventures on the way to Constantinople with the robber and uncle. It blames the traitor, Macario, for the whole problem, and does not attribute planning evil to the dwarf (who is only executing Macario's plan). While Blançiflor is subject to evil plots by the king's enemies, she is herself resourceful: she does not allow herself to be ruined by circumstances. She seeks allies and through them regains her position.

The "queen in exile" closes V[13] as part of the female-structured plot elements in the manuscript: at the beginning of V[13], in *Bovo*, Drusiana had produced Bovo's heirs in the woods during exile; Berta da li pe grant gives birth to Charlemagne in the woods with the assistance of the woodsman and his daughters; Berta, daughter of the false Berta, gives birth to and raises Roland in the woods in penury; and Belisant's son Loys follows the family tradition, born in exile though not in want.

CHART 4.6A: Versions of *Macaire/Macario/Reine Sibille*

Italian and Franco-Italian
  1. V[13] *Macario*, first half fourteenth century
  2. *Le Storie Nerbonesi* by Andrea da Barberino, late fourteenth or early fifteenth century
  3. *Li Fatti di Spagna*, also known as *Il Viaggio di Carlomagno*, 1370–1380
  4. *La Spagna*, fourteenth century

French
  1. *Chronica* by Albéric des Trois-Fontaines, first half of the thirteenth century
  2. Fragments: thirteenth century
      a. Anglo-Norman Loveday Library, thirteenth century
      b. Mons, thirteenth century
      c. Sion, thirteenth century
  3. *Garin de Monglane*, Paris, Arsenal MS. 3351, fifteenth century
  4. *Chronique de France,* Paris, BnF MS. 5003, fifteenth century
  5. *Ly Myreur des Histors* by Jean d'Outremeuse, composed mid- to second half fourteenth century; MS. dates to fifteenth century
  6. *Tristan de Nanteuil*, fifteenth century

Spanish
  1. *Gran conquista de Ultramar*, late thirteenth–early fourteenth century
  2. *Noble Cuento del enperador Carlos Maynes de Roma et de la buena enperatris Seuilla su mugier* (Madrid , El Escorial, MS. h-I-13), late fourteenth or early fifteenth century
  3. *Hystoria de la Reyna Sebilla* (abridged version of *Noble*) 1498/1500, 1532, 1551, 1553, 1585, 1623
  4. *Los Carboneros de Francia y la Reina Sevilla*, by Francisco de Rojas, 1757
  5. *La Reina Sebila, drama comico* by Ramón de Valladosares y Saavedra, Madrid 1846

German
1. *Weltchronik* by Enikel, late thirteenth century
2. *Weihenstephan Chronik*, ca. 1435
3. *Karl Meinet*, first quarter fourteenth century
4. *Die künigin von Frankrich und der ungetriuwe Marschalk* by Schondoch, early fourteenth century
5. *Die unschuldige Königen von Frankreich* by Elisabeth von Nassau-Saarbrücken (b. 1395–d. 1456)
6. *Meisterlied*, first half sixteenth century
7. *Die königin auß Franckreich mit dem falschen marschalck* by Hans Sachs, ca. 1551

Dutch/Flemish
1. *Sibilla* (Antwerp: Willem Vorsterman), first half sixteenth century

Scandinavian
1. *Thidrekssaga, composed* thirteenth century; MS. dates to fourteenth century

English
1. *Sir Triamour, not before* 1490, probably early sixteenth century

CHART 4.6B: Character names in representative versions of *Macaire / Macario / Reine Sibille*

V13	*Le Storie Nerbonesi*, Andrea da Barberino	*La Spagna / I Fatti di Spagna*	*Ly Myreur des Histors*, Jean d'Outremeuse	*Sir Triamour*	*Chronica*, Albéric des trois fontaines	*Noble cuento*	French Fragments	*Die küniginn von Frankrich und ungetriuwe marschalk*, Schondoch
Queen Blançiflor	Belistante	reina/Regina	Sibilhe	Margaret	Sibili	Sevilla	Sebile	n/a
Charlemagne	Carlo Magno	Carlo Mano/K.	Charles	Aradas of Aragon	Karolus	Carlos Maynes de rRoma [sic]	Challe-maine	n/a
Macario and/or dwarf (traitor)	Rinieri and dwarf	Macario / Ansuixe de Maganza	Machar (chamberlain) and Habadu (dwarf)	Marrock (steward)	Machario and dwarf	Macaire and Segon (dwarf)	Macer	Marshal and dwarf
Bernardo and Ogiera (queen's defenders)	Namo di Baviera	n/a	Ogier (Sibilhe's cousin), Nalme, et al.	n/a	n/a	Almerique de Narbona and Guyllemer de Escocia and Gaufer de Ultramer	Nemes de Beivere and Ogier de Danemarche	Duke Leopold of Austria
Albaris (Queen's escort)	Almieri	n/a	Albris de Mondesdier	Old Sir Roger	Albrico Montis Desideri	Aubery de Mondisder	Aubri de Mondidier	n/a
n/a	n/a	n/a	Grimoiart / Grimoaldins, queen's helper	n/a	Grimoaldo	Griomoart	Griomoart	n/a

V^{13}	Le Storie Nerbonesi, Andrea da Barberino	La Spagna / I Fatti di Spagna	Ly Myreur des Histors, Jean d'Outremeuse	Sir Triamour	Chronica, Albéric des trois fontaines	Noble cuento	French Fragments	Die küningin von Frankrich und ungetriuwe marschalk, Schondoch
Son's name: Leoys (baptismal name King of Hungary)	Aloigi / Luigi (Andossene)	n/a	Loys (batismal name for King of Bohemia)	Triamo(u)r	Ludowico	Loys (baptismal name for King of Hungary)	Looy / Loï (baptismal name for King of Hungary)	n/a
Varocher, peasant who helps queen	Ispinardo	n/a	Warocquier	n/a	Warothero	Barroquer	Varochier	wood-carrier, unnamed
Primeran, queen's host and family	collier	n/a	Johan and Emelienne; daughters Florentine and Froissan (host and family)	Sir Bernard, Hungarian knight and trainer (queen's host)	n/a	Joserant and wife, daughters Elifanta and unnamed; Elynant at court (trainer)	Joscerant; Elinant	n/a
Macario's kinsman (unnamed)	n/a	n/a	n/a	n/a	Gallerano of Bacaire	Galeran of Belcaire	n/a	n/a
Emperor of Constantinople (queen's father)	Emperor of Constantinople	n/a	Richier	n/a	Richero	Richarte	Richiers	n/a

CHART 4.6c: Major plot elements in different versions of *Macaire* / *Macario* / *Reine Sibille*

Plot elements	V[13]	Le Storie Nerbonesi, Andrea da Barberino	Chronica, Albéric des trois-fontaines	Garin de Monglane, Arsenal MS. 3351	Ly Myreur des Histors, Jean d'Outre-meuse	Noble Cuento	Die küningin von Frankrich und der ungetriuwe marschalk, Schondoch	Die unschuldige Königin von Frankreich, Nassau-Saarbrücken
1. dwarf's origin	unknown	Rinieri's	unknown	arrives	gift from Persia	arrives	unknown	arrives (not stated)
2. queen's origin	Constantinople	sought from Constantinople	Desiderius's daughter	sought from Constantinople	Constantinople	Constantinople	unknown	Constantinople
3. would-be seducer	Macario	Rinieri	Macharío	dwarf	dwarf	dwarf	Marshalk	dwarf
4. queen's defender	Naimes	n/a	n/a	Naymes	Ogier the Dane	Almeric et al.	Liupolt	Nymo, Otger, et al.
5. first exile companion	Morant de River	n/a	n/a	n/a	n/a	n/a	n/a	n/a
6. traitor's punishment	dragged and hanged	hanged	hanged	dragged and hanged	hanged	dragged and hanged	thrown into wall	hanged
7. dwarf's punishment	burned by Macario	not given	n/a	n/a	burned (by Ogier)	to be burned		killed
8. Queen's child's birthplace?	Hungary	Ispinardo's		Armoise	Ligny	Urmesa	Gryman	Vngern
how long a stay?	1 mo. +/-	7 yrs.	n/a	14 yrs.	12 yrs.	10 yrs.	4½ yrs.	10 yrs.
new male suitor?	no	no	yes	yes	no	yes	no	yes
visit to Charles?	no	no	yes	yes	yes	no	no	no
9. Trip to Constantinople: robbers?	n/a	n/a	n/a	yes	yes	yes	n/a	yes
hermit?		yes	yes	yes	yes	yes		yes
Grimoart's adventures?		yes	yes	yes	yes	yes		yes
detour to Rome?		no	no	yes	no	yes		yes

Plot elements	V¹³	Le Storie Nerbonesi, Andrea da Barberino	Chronica, Albéric des trois-fontaines	Garin de Monglane, Arsenal MS. 3351	Ly Myreur des Histors, Jean d'Outremeuse	Noble Cuento	Die künigin von Frankrich und der ungetriuwe marschalk, Schondoch	Die unschuldige Königin von Frankreich, Nassau-Saarbrücken
10-11. Negotiations and return								
Varocher: wife test?	no	n/a	n/a	yes	yes	yes	n/a	yes
Maganzesi killed, how many? reconcile: whose idea?	no / Dane + Varocher		yes, six / n/a	yes, two / Aymeri + Pope	yes / Ogier	yes, two / Pope	n/a	yes, two / Pope
Varocher in prison?	no	n/a	n/a	yes	yes	yes	n/a	yes
12. Rewards:								
—Varocher	goods, lands daughter married	n/a	n/a	enriched	meynie married two counts	mayordomo > 100 marks married counts	godfather land	forgiveness
—host and family	n/a	n/a	n/a	n/a	bishop then cardinal	n/a	n/a	n/a
—hermit	n/a	n/a	n/a	n/a	porter	n/a	n/a	n/a
—robber	n/a	n/a	n/a	n/a	n/a	cupholder	n/a	n/a
—Loys	n/a	marriage to Amerigo's daughter	marriage to Naimes's daughter	marriage to Aymeri's daughter	n/a	marriage to Almerique's daughter	n/a	marriage to Aymeri's daughter

Chart 4.6d: Episodes of *Macaire / Macario / Reine Sibille* absent from V^{13}

Absent from V^{13}
   a. Morant returns with Charlemagne's wife-to-be from Spain and they are accused of adultery
Gran conquista de Ultramar
Karl Meinet

   b. Court steward attempts marriage to queen during Charles's absence
I Fatti di Spagna
La Spagna
Le Storie Nerbonesi by Andrea da Barberino
Thidrekssaga

Noteworthy variations
   1. Queen's exile in local forest only
Die künigin von Frankrich und der ungetriuwe marschalk by Schondoch
Die königin auß Franckreich mit dem falschen marschalck by Hans Sachs
Sir Triamour
Chronique de France, Paris, BnF MS. fr 5003, concludes with dog's duel

   2. Queen's exile and trip to Constantinople; no robber or hermit
V^{13}
Tristan de Nanteuil

   3. Exile and trip to Rome / Constantinople; include robber and hermit
Chronica by Albéric des Trois-Fontaines
Ly Myreur des Histors by Jean d'Outremeuse
Noble Cuento; *Hystoria*; Dutch *Historie*
Die unschuldige Königen von Frankreich by Elisabeth von Nassau-Saarbrücken
Garin de Monglane, Paris, Arsenal MS. 3351

4.7 Conclusions

V^{13} is a cyclical manuscript: it fulfills all the requirements outlined by research on compilation and textualization of individual tales, both *chansons de geste* and romances. In the case of V^{13}, Cingolani has already given relevant philological evidence, but only begins sketching narrative evidence ("Innovazione e Parodia"). Krauss has advanced socio-historical theories as a unifying factor (*Epica feudale*). Outdated judgments of nineteenth-century and early twentieth-century critics still stand widely accepted on the nature of V^{13}. Viscardi originally stated, "Un po' a sé veramente, sentiamo stare le vicende di Bovo e di Uggeri; ma tutto il resto della vasta e complessa narrazione riguarda, veramente, la storia dei *Reali di Francia:* e, precisiamolo, la storia famigliare, privata dei carolingi" *(Letteratura franco-italiana,* 24). Cremonesi originally suggested that there were two different periods of composition for the manuscript: " . . . si dovrebbero espungere dalla compilazione il *Bovo,* la seconda parte dell'*Uggeri* (che corrisponde alla *Chevalerie Ogier*) e, credo, anche il *Macario,* che è, come si sa, un rimaneggiamento della *Reine Sebile,* e che nulla rilega al resto della compilazione se non la presenza d'un traditore maganzese" ("A proposito del Codice marciano fr. XIII," 755).[1]

Since Cingolani and Krauss are the only two to have spoken in defense of V^{13}'s unity (though others mention it in passing), we review their evidence. We then return to the text itself, and re-examine together the points raised in each individual section that can only lead to a conclusion of redactorially-created unity in a cyclical manuscript.

Cingolani compares the reorganization of French works in the Guillaume cycle and the *Narbonnais* to those in Italy done later by Andrea da Barberino and created around Rinaldo da Montalbano, suggesting that V^{13} is the only Franco-Italian text in the fourteenth century to attempt such reorganization ("Innovazione e Parodia"). He examines whether or not the V^{13} texts should be read as autonomous works like northern collections, or whether there is a unity in the text ("Innovazione e Parodia," 62). He notes the paleographical evidence: there are no larger initials to indicate new texts, nor illuminations to break the text; these are all placed at the external edges of the pages. He notes the practically seamless divisions between *chansons*, with no appeals to the audience, and with no easily defined cut-off point. This is, then "una sintesi assolutamente nuova" a century before Andrea da Barberino (66).

Cingolani seeks the metanarrative over the episodes centered on typical heroes, and points out the genealogical nature of the text. The terminology used, *roman, çanter, cançon,* etc., both for episodes and for the entire work, refers to

---

[1] In fairness, it must be noted that Cremonesi changed her ideas over time; " . . . l'esame a cui sono venuta sottoponendo i singoli testi . . . mi ha pienamente convinta della unitarietà di composizione di V^{13}" ("Note di franco-veneto," 16).

events thousands of lines away. He suggests that the changes in roles and the alteration of subject matter ("ridistribuzione della materia," 68) reinterpret the traditional epic world. With the addition and expansion of the importance of Italy, he sees in it a destabilization of the epic world. Romance characters and episodes add to the negative commentary on the traditional epic, creating a new form which includes "romanzo 'realista', novella, canzone, parodia" (69). He finds a simplified character structure of good and evil, and parody in frequent references to specific texts, like the *Chanson de Roland*. Well-known characters exercise their known professions to excess—Naimes's advice "più che una virtù è un vizio" (73). For Cingolani, this is a "prova del tentativo di introdurre una letteratura 'comica' nel Nord dell'Italia" (77).

Cingolani bases his arguments on Krauss, whose 1980 volume examines each of the *canzoni di gesta* separately, comparing them to the best-known other versions. Krauss's chapter nine addresses the unity of the manuscript. After summarizing earlier critics, he points out the need to subsume "vicende private" into the good of the Christian world as well (*Epica feudale*, 206). He especially treats the integration of Bovo and Uggieri (Ogier) into V^{13}, since it is these that Viscardi and Cremonesi had suggested did not belong. He notes the chronological sequences and the fact that Pepin's same councilors, Aquilone di Baviera, Bernardo di Clermont, and Morando de River, appear in both *Bovo* and *Berta da li pe grant*; furthermore, they continue in the same role through *Karleto, Berta e Milone,* and *Orlandino* (206). He notes the different name of young Charles's advisor (David) in the French, and believes that the redactor of V^{13} altered the text in this way to unify it further. Krauss also notes the differences between Bovo's sons and Pepin's, the good and the bad, which he suggests is a shared motif. He further notes that the fight at Rome by *Karleto* had to have been planned so as to avoid repetitions of episodes in the Dane's *Enfances*, which involved relieving the siege of Rome (208). The introduction of Roland into Uggieri's story is truly unique.

As an overarching argument, Krauss notes the development of the crusade ideology (209). Bovo goes to Jerusalem only to fulfill a vow. Similarly, in *Karleto* in Spain, Galafrio hedges his bets by using all the gods (210). However, the attitude toward crusades varies in the different V^{13} poems, though Krauss seems to suggest that a somewhat cavalier attitude here exemplified is typical of Northern Italy of the thirteenth century.

In V^{13}, the Charlemagne myth, according to Krauss (following Bender), is progressively destroyed and thus demonstrates a developed argument.[2] He argues that the Italian version is different from and stronger than the French, because

---

[2] K. H. Bender's original article is "Les Métamorphoses de la royauté de Charlemagne dans les premières épopées franco-italiennes," in *Atti del 2° Congresso internazionale della 'Société Rencesvals'*, special issue of *Cultura Neolatina* 21 (1961): 164–74.

Charlemagne is seen as the German emperor, a threat to Northern Italy (212). That point of view would derive from a Guelf, emerging communal bourgeoisie. He illustrates specific points of that argument, and then proposes that V^{13} is therefore not just "una semplice successione, rispondente a una cronologia puramente esteriore, di avvenimenti in sé equivalenti che si ripetono più o meno nel senso del ritorno dell'eternamente uguale" but rather an attempt at a new social order. Krauss argues therefore that V^{13} is held together by a coherent political polemic.

Cingolani's paleographical and narratological commentary and Krauss's socio-political arguments are not the only factors that link the plots in V^{13}. Other literary considerations force the modern reader to consider them as a whole, a single text, rather than an arbitrarily mixed collection of *chansons de geste*. This is a challenge to the long-standing "one-hero / one-text rule" that has sidelined V^{13} from the canonic sweepstakes in comparison to works like the *Entrée d'Espagne*.[3] Yet V^{13} holds these factors in common with many later cyclic manuscripts throughout Europe. Some of the uniting factors were raised as part of the discussion of individual *chansons*; beyond those, however, lie the interwoven, repeating structures of multiple *canzoni*.

Motifs, events, characters, and names are repeated and re-used. Their re-use is the more noticeable for differences between V^{13} versions and those found in other versions of the same *chansons*. Recent discussions of cyclification typical of many *remaniements* have centered on the dichotomy of linear, chronological time versus repetition over time.[4] Ryding's definition of repetition with variation within a chronological "historical" frame describes V^{13} perfectly, with discontinuous didactic and parodying lines patterned upon the cycles' various elements (Staines, "Cycle: The Misreading of a Trope," 110).[5]

In reading the many versions of each V^{13} segment, we notice the return of certain compilations from specific geographic areas that contain the same or related stories, and use similar techniques: Spanish chronicles, Scandinavian sagas,

---

[3] C. Altman, "Medieval Narrative vs. Modern Assumptions: Revising Inadequate Typology," *Diacritics* 4 (1974): 12–19, here 13.

[4] See, for example, D. Staines, "Cycle: The Misreading of a Trope," in *Cyclification: The Development of Narrative Cycles in the Chansons de Geste and the Arthurian Romances*, Proceedings of the Colloquium, Amsterdam, 17–18 December 1992, ed. B. Besamusca et al. (Amsterdam: North-Holland, 1994), 108–10.

[5] W. W. Ryding, *Structure in Medieval Narrative* (The Hague-Paris: Mouton, 1971), 33, for the definition of repetition with variation. The term "discontinuous didactic and parodying" lines is calqued on Murrin's term, "discontinuous allegory" (M. Murrin, *The Allegorical Epic: Essays on Its Rise and Decline* [Chicago: University of Chicago Press, 1980], 53 ff.) as advocated also by Franceschetti (in "Schede bibliografiche boiardesche," *Quaderni d'Italianistica* 15 [1994]: 157–72), though he does not use the same term.

German world histories (see Chart 4.7 A). They even play similar word games, for example, giving popular etymologies of Charlemagne's name, in both romance and Germanic languages. But the form of most of these collections is prose (with the exception of d'Outremeuse's *Geste* that parallels in condensed form his *Myreur*), and the context as well as plot line differs in significant ways from V^{13}. The absence or presence of *Bovo* and *Ogier*, for example, who in general appear in individual hero-centered poems, is a much-noted variation. The prime continuer of the V^{13} tradition in Italy, Andrea da Barberino, writes in prose; he either further integrates episodes from V^{13} into his *Reali di Francia*, rearranges them into another poem (e.g., the *Nerbonesi*), or eliminates them. However, there are also smaller poems (*cantari*) in octaves that treat an individual event from the narration, rather than the entire story (e.g., the *Innamoramento de Melone*).

Looking at the entire compilation under close examination, the plots of V^{13} could be divided into three types: *enfances, chevaleries*, and female *enfances* or "falsely accused queens" (see Chart 4.7 B). Each member of the groups shares motifs across the group. Thus, for example, in the *enfances*, each child has food problems: the parents are poisoned or the child is starving.[6] Someone else is ruling in the rightful heir's place (except in the case of Orlandino, who does not have his own kingdom or fiefdom). The exiled protagonist works for someone other than himself—Bovo and Karleto for other kings, Milone for his family. Some member(s) of the court/nobility take(s) an interest and assist(s) the protagonist in regaining his rightful position. *Bovo, Karleto,* and *Orlandino* vary slightly from the others and treat different classes—noble, landowner, and knight— which partially explains difference in motif use. Bovo is a minor ruler, Karleto is young Charlemagne (heir to France), and Orlandino is the nephew of the king of France. All are related to kings: Bovo's uncle is the king of England; Karleto is the future king; and Orlando is the nephew of the king (for the patterns of *enfances*, see Chart 4.7 C).

The *chevaleries* are three; two, *Bovo* and *Ogier*, follow a similar pattern. Each has a doubled plot: in their *Enfances* there is one main crisis, but in their *Chevaleries* there are two (Chart 4.7 D). Bovo holds his own city, Antona, having conquered it in his *Enfances*, and Ogier conquers Marmora. Uberto assists Bovo in Antona; the unnamed host assists Ogier in Marmora. In his *Chevalerie*, Bovo's

---

[6] See Bartolucci-Chiecchi for the hungry Roland (Bartolucci-Chiecchi, "Quelques notes sur *Rolandin*," and eadem, "«De tous mes ont asés . . . »: Cibo e poemi epici," *Quaderni di Lingue e Letterature* 16 [1991]: 269–78), as well as S. E. Farrier on "hungry heroes" in general, an *enfances* motif ("Hungry Heroes in Medieval Literature," in *Food in the Middle Ages: A Book of Essays*, ed. Melitta Weiss Adamson [New York: Garland Publishing, Inc, 1995], 145–59), as well as the recent Predelli, "Les Bûches et la faim."

horse kills the king of England's son as Ogier kills the king of France's son. Bovo goes into exile in the Holy Land to expiate his horse's error; Ogier goes into isolation in prison for Çarloto's error.[7] Corcher, a pagan giant whom Bovo converts, assists him in conquering cities in the Holy Land; Ogier redeems his city, Paris, after punishing the king. The second portion of *Chevalerie Ogier* is thus in some ways parallel also to the first part of *Chevalerie Bovo*, and vice versa: the keeping of the city being the emphasis here, where conquering cities and getting tribute is the emphasis in the second pair, accomplished with the help of local assistance.

Jean-Paul Martin has suggested a grammar of narrative motifs, each of which is a narrative sequence (*Les Motifs dans la chanson de geste*). The author of V^{13} has a recurring number of motifs which he persists in deploying in varying order. Among the motifs which appear throughout V^{13} are the host; the self-governed woman; the cross birthmark; the child as peacemaker; the falsely accused queen; giving birth in a forest; the messenger / ambassador.[8] The omnipresence of the host in V^{13} has been remarked both by Cremonesi ("Note di franco-veneto") and Cingolani ("Innovazione e Parodia").[9]

The order *Enfances-Chevalerie* of V^{13} is not just binary (as suggested as typical for a medieval literary work [Ryding, *Structure in Medieval Narrative*, 25]), but tertiary, in that the binary *Enfances* are paired with tripartite *Chevaleries*. Furthermore, there are three alternating groups: the third group are the "falsely accused queen" sequences, what could be called "female *enfances*" (Chart 4.7 E). Berta Big-Foot (Pepin's wife), Berta the younger (daughter of the false Berta and half-sister of Charlemagne, wife of Milone and mother of Roland), and Blançiflor (Charlemagne's second wife), are all in some way cast out from the court. Each bears a male child who helps return his mother to her position. The two classic examples in V^{13}, of which there are many parallel versions in other regions,

---

[7] Ogier kills Çarloto for threatening to kill him as he had killed Ogier's son, Balduin. Ogier had saved Çarloto outside of Rome in the *Enfances Ogier* and Çarloto never forgave him.

[8] For the motif of the messenger and message, see also J. Merceron, *Le Message et sa fiction: La communication par messager dans la littérature française des XIIe et XIIIe siècles* (Berkeley: University of California Press, 1998), which cites *Macaire* among its examples, and, again just published, J. –C. Vallecalle, *Messages et ambassades dans l'épopée française médiévale: l'illusion du dialogue* (Paris: Champion, 2006).

[9] Claude Roussel, "Le Mélange des genres dans les chansons de geste tardives" (XVIe Congrès International de la Société Rencesvals, Granada, 21–25 juillet 2003, *Les Chansons de geste*, ed. Carlos Alvar and Juan Paredes [Granada: Universidad de Granada, 2005], 65–85, here 76), speaks of the "bourgeois ou de petites gens" who are most often the most faithful servants. While he does not specifically cite hosts here, they clearly are a part of the group.

Berta and Blançiflor (= Sebile), bracket a comic example, Berta the younger, of which V[13] is one of the earliest examples.[10]

While this is a cyclical manuscript, in that the compiler has integrated Bovo and Ogier into the Carolingian cycle in parallel construction, it is also closely related to the universal histories of the Germanic tradition. The chronological concerns such as inserting Roland at the right moment to be able to save Ogier in his moment of need (as mentioned also by Cremonesi, *Le Danois Oger*, xvii), and carefully pacing out the time frame (in the introduction to *Macario*, "Poisqe fo mort Oliver e Rolan," 13456), demonstrate a historical impulse.

But it is not only related to history. The congener "history" text by Jean d'Outremeuse is the *Myreur des Hystors*. The "mirror" genre is a training tool for nobility: it offers lessons. V[13] too, offers lessons: the false Bertha dies for impersonating the queen, Charlemagne suffers for having allowed Çarleto to kill Balduyn. Roland is a savior figure, born in a stable to poor parents, as the compiler of V[13] is careful to tell us. An angel appears to Charlemagne to warn him of the siege of Rome where Ogier will earn his spurs as well as the everlasting hatred of Çarleto. In this way an element of hagiography also appears.[11]

The choice of motifs in a given position can produce a comic effect. Varocher is clearly intended to be comic, yet *Macario* is not a farce. Were he a hermit instead of a married woodsman who tells his wife not to expect him till he walks through the door, his wild hair and sturdy walking stick would be expected. Were Roland bringing Ogier a normal amount of food instead of enough wine to make any man drunk, his act would be kindness. The incongruity created by the juxtaposition of motifs placed in unexpected ways creates humor.[12]

---

[10] On comic aspects, see L. Z. Morgan, "A Preliminary Examination of Humor in Northern Italian Tradition: The Franco-Italian Epic," *Humor* 15 (2002): 129–53, and eadem, "What's so Funny About Roland? (O)Roland(o)'s Life and Works in the Northern Italian Tradition"; on *enfances* and links with "falsely accused queens" see eadem, "Female *enfances*: At the Intersection of Romance and Epic," in *The Court Reconvenes: Courtly Literature Across the Disciplines*, Selected Acts of the International Courtly Literature Society (Vancouver, 1998), ed. B. K. Altmann and C. W. Carroll (Cambridge: D. S. Brewer, 2003), 141–49. I do not go into female *enfances* extensively here, as I have treated the subject there.

[11] For more on the didactic tendencies of late epic, see S. E. Farrier, "*Das Rolandslied* and the *Song of Roulond* as Moralizing Adaptations of the *Chanson de Roland*," *Olifant* 16 (1991): 61–76, and S. C. Obergfell, "The Problem of Didacticism in the Romance Epic: *Aiol*," *Olifant* 6 (1978): 21–33 and eadem, "The Father-Son Combat Motif as Didactic Theme in Old French Literature," *Kentucky Romance Quarterly* 26 (1979): 333–48.

[12] See A. E. Cobby's precisely-argued chapter on the *Pelèrinage Charlemagne* for specific examples of how formulae set up expectations which, when in an unconventional setting, create humor (*Ambivalent Conventions: Formula and Parody in Old French*

The earliest commentators noted a Maganzese link through the V^{13} manuscript: that is, all evil in the Carolingian portions of V^{13} is committed by Ganelon's tribe. The critics therefore wondered at *Ogier* not being so linked. In fact, each of the *chansons* has an "evil" clan. In *Bovo* that role is played by Do (a Maganzese) and his family; but in *Ogier,* by the royal family. The similarity of Ogier's task in going to Marmora to Ganelon's in the *Chanson de Roland* (he is sent to Marsilie to demand tribute), and to *Huon d'Auvergne* (where the protagonist is sent to Hell for tribute by king Charles Martel), two cases where the protagonist is sent on a fruitless or impossible errand, cannot be missed. *Huon d'Auvergne* existed at the same time period (our first manuscript is also from the Gonzaga library and dates to 1341); and the *Chanson de Roland* was recopied in Italy throughout the thirteenth and fourteenth centuries.

The similarity to fairy tales too has been much remarked: the younger son who is sent to prove himself, the young girl who is taken advantage of.[13] Particularly for *Berta da li pe grant,* the possible origin of the woman relates closely to traditional tales. Martin lists it as a standard epic motif: "5.A.6. femme persécutée" (*Les Motifs dans la chanson de geste,* 351). Ryding too notes the role of "identifiable folklore motifs" in creating episodes in medieval narrative (*Structure in Medieval Narrative,* 33), as does Goldberg in her two indices.

V^{13}'s narrative, in its series of divided tales, is a hybrid like the language in which it is written. The compiler-author not only rearranges French and Italian lexicon and morphemes; he also reconstrues narratives. Thus Ogier is not a rebel baron, and does not merely threaten to kill the heir to the French throne. He suppresses his discontent (and his wife's) until confronted by Çarleto.[14] But Çarleto's killing Balduyn is the same technique that Blondoja had used on old Count Gui: he is killed during a hunt in the forest.[15] The "falsely accused queen" is not that far removed from Drusiana's wandering in the forest with newborn twins, when she is separated from Bovo. Like Blançiflor, she makes her way to her

---

[Amsterdam: Rodopi, 1995]). See also Morgan ("A Preliminary Examination of Humor in Northern Italian Tradition," and "What's so Funny About Roland? (O)Roland(o)'s Life and Works in the Northern Italian Tradition") for an examination of specific humorous episodes in V^{13} and the *Entrée d'Espagne.*

[13] See F. Wolfzettel, review of *Les Versions françaises et étrangères des Enfances de Charlemagne,* by Jacques Horrent, *Zeitschrift für romanische Philologie* 99 (1983): 168-71, for a discussion of the motif.

[14] H. Krauss, "Refoulement et hierarchie féodale: Essai de psychanalyser le comportement d'Ogier le Danois dans la version francoitalienne," in *VIII Congreso de la Société Rencesvalls* (Huarte-Pamplona: Institución Principe de Viana, 1981), 263–66 suggests memory repression as a psychological explanation of the Dane's action.

[15] This portion is lost from V^{13}, but is attested by Bovo's narrating events (e.g., ll. 198–202) and in other versions of the story.

father's court until she can return to her rightful place. So too, the redactor can send Bovo to the Holy Land after he has regained Antona instead of before (the order of other versions) so that the plot parallels that of *Ogier*. The compiler uses rhyme and assonance, ten-, eleven-, and twelve-syllable lines; so too a woodsman (or pack-carrier or charcoal maker), a *çivaler* (2142) or heir to one of the best families in France (Milone) can guide a lady lost in the woods. Characters, plots, and details echo one other throughout the compilation.

Though there are nine segments, the division is not truly even, with a division of four *enfances*, two *chevaleries*, and three "falsely accused queens." Ogier's *enfances* is quite different from that of Bovo or Karleto. *Berta e Milone* partakes both of the "falsely accused queen" and the *enfances* mode. What is really missing is a third *chevalerie*, which makes us wonder what preceded *Enfances Bovo* at the beginning of the manuscript. Rajna, followed by Thomas and others, speculated from the number of folios listed in the Braghirolli catalogue. From examining the narrative content, it appears that the plot line is chronological, and it seems to follow Carolingian history, beginning with Pepin in *Bovo*. Charles Martel has been proposed as a subject, in the form of *Huon d'Auvergne*; *Fioravante* has also been suggested, upon examination of the *Reali di Francia* by Andrea da Barberino (Rajna, *Geste Francor*, 28–34, for a summary of the discussion; see also diagram 4.7 A, that outlines the levels and parallels). Whatever may have begun the manuscript, it assuredly would have consisted of several segments with interwoven plots. But maybe the beginning was just the initial portion of *Bovo*, and it is only Roland's prowess at Roncevaux that is the implied third *chevalerie*. Roncevaux is indeed a parallel plot: Roland was sent into an impossible situation, like Bovo and Ogier. Where Ogier went out a first time and then suffered imprisonment before redeeming himself, Bovo first defended his city and then went to the Holy Land to redeem his horse; at that point Ganelon first went to Saragossa to confront King Marsilie, and then Roland fought the traitors in mountain passes, dying and eventually "redeemed" by Charlemagne, in that Charlemagne avenged Roland's death as Ogier avenged the deaths of two preceding messengers and Bovo avenged the death of the king of England's son. In that (implied) third variant of the *enfances* narrative, Roland did not return and finish out his life happily at home.

V^{13} plays upon two late-epic types of continuations: the individual hero-poem and the cyclic composition. In combining pre-existing stories and story elements, the redactor modified extant plots, names, and chronology so as to create an eschatological structure running from Pepin's time to Leoys with the internal interweaving cycles of childhood-knighthood of noble family members. The individual internal cycles reinforce traditional values (the strength of lineage and its genetic characteristics) and slyly undercut those same values by demoting nobility and royalty to working for a living. As a final ultimate variant, a poor woodcutter becomes ennobled; yet, within the chronological frame of history, nobles and royalty return to their positions, affording entertainment for all classes of an audience.[16] V[13] thus embodies both didactic and comic elements from medieval tradition by grafting motifs selectively in different ways upon a different stem, much as it grafts an Italian ending onto a French verb, or a French prefix onto an Italian noun, and comes up with something entirely different: Franco-Italian language and literature, with recognizable, though sometimes maddeningly varied patterns not reducible into modern regular paradigms.

---

[16] See G. Allaire on readers of all classes for fifteenth-century texts ("A Fifteenth-Century Florentine Community of Readers and the Romances of Chivalry," *Essays in Medieval Studies* 15 [1999]: 1–8). Similarly, J. E. Everson, *The Italian Romance Epic in the Age of Humanism: The Matter of Italy and the World of Rome* (Oxford: Oxford University Press, 2001), in her chapter II.5 (127–60), presents a convincing picture for knowledge of a variety of texts among different classes. Braghirolli's inventory ("Inventaire des manuscrits") argues similarly, at least for the Gonzagas: they held a variety of "popular" and more learned texts.

Chart 4.7a: Collections of Charlemagne tales

"Italian"	French	"German"	Spanish	Scandinavian
	Pseudo-Turpin, possibly first half 12th century	Kaiserkronik, ca. 1150		
	Chronique rimée, Philippe Mouskes, before 1240	Karl der Grosse, Stricker, ca. 1230–1250	Primera crónica general, 1270–1289	Karlmagnús Saga, ca. 1230–1250
	Charlemagne, Girard d'Amiens, 1285–1314	Weltchronik, Enikel, late 13th century		
		Karl Meinet, first quarter 14th century	Gran Conquista de Ultramar, late 13th–early 14th century	
V^{13}, first half 14th century	Ly Myreur des Histors, Jean d'Outremeuse, second half 14th century	Chronik, Henry of Munich, ca. 1320–1325		
Aquilon de Bavière, Raffaele da Verona, completed 1407				
	Chroniques de France, Paris, BnF 5003, late 14th or early 15th century			
I Reali di Francia and Le Storie Nerbonesi, Andrea da Barberino, late 14th to early 15th centuries	Croniques et conquestes de Charlemagne, David Aubert, second half 15th century	Weihenstephan Chronik, ca. 1435		
		Chronica Bremensis, Wolter, ca. 1460–1475 (Latin)		
		Volksbuch (Zurich MS.), Georg Hohenmut, 1475		
		Bayerische Chronik, Ulrich Füetrer, ca. 1477–1481		

CHART 4.7B: V¹³ (*Geste Francor*) plot interactions

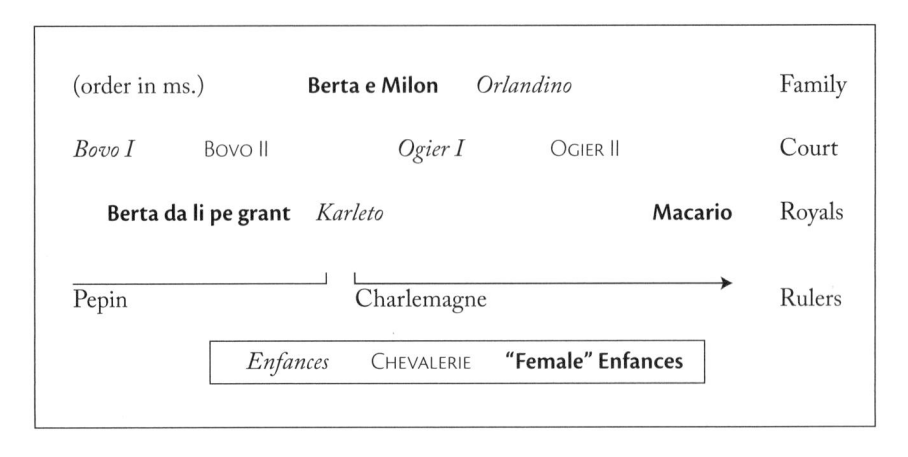

(order in ms.)		**Berta e Milon**	*Orlandino*			Family
Bovo I	Bovo II		*Ogier I*	Ogier II		Court
Berta da li pe grant		*Karleto*			**Macario**	Royals
Pepin		Charlemagne			→	Rulers
		Enfances	Chevalerie	**"Female" Enfances**		

Appeared initially in L. Z. Morgan, "Ogier le danois in the *Geste Francor* (V¹³)," in *L'Epopée romane au moyen âge et aux temps modernes*, ed. S. Luongo (Naples: Fridericiana, 335–51, here 346.

Chart 4.7c: *Enfances* plots in V[13]

Bovo	Karleto	Orlandino
(missing) Father killed; mother tries poison own son	4. Parents poisoned; protagonist banished to kitchen	7. Parents exiled
Maganzese (Do) takes over	Maganzese half-brothers take over	
Protagonist flees to Erminia	Protagonist flees to Spain	They flee to Italy
Protagonist works for King Erminion	Protagonist works for King Galafre	Protagonist's father works as woodgatherer
King's daughter falls in love with protagonist	Same	n/a
King's daughter arms protagonist	Same	n/a
Engagement/betrothal of protagonist	Same	n/a
Protagonist sent to Sivilla by brothers	Protagonist sent to Rome because of brothers-in-law	Protagonist goes to Charles's court
Betrayal: Uriah's letter	Betrayal by innkeeper	n/a
Daughter of King interested: freedom from prison	Cardinal's interest: money and freedom	Namo's interest: clothing and forgiveness
1. Return to Antona: home retaken	Return to France: country retaken	Return to France
Doon sent away	Bertella kept by Queen	Milon, Bertella married
Braidamont appears; Drusiana and sons appear. Possible happy outcome.	Half-brothers executed	n/a

Numbers (1, 4, 7) mark the beginning of V[13] plot segment, and the number of that segment in the whole:1. *Enfances Bovo d'Antona*; 2. *Berta da li pe grant*; 3. *Chevalerie Bovo*; 4. *Karleto*; 5. *Berta e Milone*; 6. *Enfances Ogier*; 7. *Orlandino*; 8. *Chevalerie Ogier*; 9. *Macario*.

Chart 4.7d: *Chevalerie* plots in V[13]

Chevalerie Bovo	*Chevalerie Ogier*
a. City of Antona attacked by Dodo and Pepin	a. protagonist sent to Marmora for tribute
b. protagonist defeats French with help of Teris and Braidamant	b. protagonist conquers city and tribute with help of the host with whom he lodges
c. the story ends well	c. returns home, finds his son dead
a. protagonist's horse kills son of King of England; he must go into exile	a. protagonist kills the son of the King of France and is imprisoned
b. protagonist conquers Saracens, cities, and Jerusalem	b. Braier attacks Paris and is magic: only protagonist, Ogier the Dane, can save his comrades-in-arms and the city
c. protagonist accomplishes miscellaneous feats; serpent, etc.	c. protagonist, Ogier the Dane, punishes the king and defeats Braier
d. he returns home, the story ends well	d. the story ends well

Chart 4.7e: Female *enfances* plots in V[13]

Berta ai piedi grandi	*Berta e Milone*	*Macario*
2. Maganzese betrayal	5. Berta is a Maganzese; she is in love with Milone and she betrays Charlemagne	9. Maganzese betrayal
Exiled: in forest	(Self-) exile in forest	Exile in forest
Stays with forester; tutors daughters (work)	In cave; Milon, her beloved, works as woodman	[In father's court]
Found by Pepin; they have a child	Have a child (Roland) in the wilderness	Has child (Leoys) in exile
	7. Child finds Charles	
Redemption by Berta's mother	Redemptions by Orlandino (son) (Milone no longer a woodsman)	Redemption by Leoys (son) and Varocher (woodsman)
Position as queen regained. Son Charles, to become king	Nobility regained, positions as nobles	Position regained as queen

Numbers mark the beginning of V[13] plot segment, and the number of that segment in the whole: 1. *Enfances Bovo d'Antona*; 2. *Berta da li pe grant*; 3. *Chevalerie Bovo*; 4. *Karleto*; 5. *Berta e Milone*; 6. *Enfances Ogier*; 7. *Orlandino*; 8. *Chevalerie Ogier*; 9. *Macario*.

5.0
Works Cited

5.1 Manuscripts Consulted
Venice, Biblioteca Nazionale Marciana, MS. Fr. Z. 13 (= 256), *La Geste Francor*.
Berlin, Kupferstichkabinett 78 D 8 (olim MS. Hamilton 337), *Huon d'Auvergne*.
Padua, Biblioteca del Seminario Vescovile MS. 32, *Huon d'Auvergne*.
Venice, Biblioteca Nazionale Marciana, MS. Fr. Z. 21 (= 257), *L'Entrée d'Espagne*.

5.2 Reference Works
Anglade, Joseph. *Grammaire élémentaire de l'ancien français.* Paris: Armand Colin, 1965.
Battelli, Giulio. *Lezioni di paleografia.* 3ª ed. Rome: Società Arti Grafiche e Fotomecchaniche Sansaini, 1949.
Battisti, Carlo, and Giovanni Alessio. *Dizionario etimologico italiano.* Florence: G. Barbera, 1950–1957.
Bloch, Oscar, and Walther von Wartburg. *Dictionnaire étymologique de la langue française.* 5th ed. Paris: Presses Universitaires de France, 1968.
Cortelazzo, Manlio, and Paolo Zolli. *Dizionario etimologico della lingua italiana.* Bologna: Zanichelli, 1979–1985.
Dauzat, A[lbert]. *Dictionnaire étymologique.* Paris: Larousse, 1939.
Desole, Corinna. *Repertorio ragionato dei personaggi citati nei principali cantari cavallereschi italiani.* Pluteus, Testi 4. Alessandria: Edizioni dell'Orso, 1995.
Devoto, Giacomo, and Gabriella Giacomelli. *I dialetti delle regioni d'Italia.* Florence: Sansoni, 1972.
FIOLA. Leslie Zarker Morgan with Christian Dupont and David Bénéteau. 2002 Update. ItalNet Consortium. <http://www.italnet.nd.edu/fiola/>.

Flutre, Ferdinand. *Table des noms propres avec toutes leurs variantes, figurant dans les romans du Moyen Age écrits en français ou en provençal et actuellement publiés ou analysés*. Publications du C.E.S.C.M. 2. Poitiers: CESCM, 1962.

Foulet, Lucien. *Petite syntaxe de l'ancien français*. 3rd ed. rev. Les Classiques Français du Moyen Âge, 2e série: Manuels. Paris: Honoré Champion, 1966.

Godefroy, Frédéric. *Dictionnaire de la langue française et de tous ses dialectes du IXe au XVIe siècle*. 1880–1902. Repr. Vaduz: Kraus, 1965.

———. *Lexique de l'ancien français*. Ed. J. and Am. Salmon Bonnard. Paris: Honoré Champion, 1982.

Greimas, A[lagirdas] J[ulien]. *Dictionnaire de l'ancien français jusqu'au milieu du XIVe siècle*. Paris: Larousse, 1968.

Henry, Albert. *Chrestomathie de la littérature en ancien français. I. Textes*. 4e éd. Berne: Editions A. Francke, 1967.

Hindley, Alan, et al. *Old French-English Dictionary*. Cambridge: Cambridge University Press, 2000.

Jaberg, Karl, and J[akob] Jud. *Sprach- und Sachatlas Italiens und der Südschweiz*. 8 vols. Zofingen: Ringier, 1928–1940.

Langlois, Ernest. *Table des Noms Propres de toute nature compris dans les chansons de geste imprimées*. Paris: Bouillon, 1904.

Lepschy, Anna Laura, and Giulio Lepschy. *The Italian Language Today*. London: Routledge, 1988.

Meyer-Lübke, Wilhelm. *Romanisches etymologisches Wörterbuch*. 4th ed. Heidelberg: Carl Winter, 1968.

Moisan, André. *Répertoire des noms propres de personnes et de lieux cités dans les chansons de geste françaises et le oeuvres étrangères dérivées*. 5 vols. Publications romanes et françaises 173. Geneva: Massot, 1986.

Mussafia, Adolfo. *Beitrag zur Kunde der Norditalienischen Mundarten im XV. Jahrhunderte*. 1873. Photorepr. Bologna: Arnaldo Forni, 1964.

Pope, Mildred K. *From Latin to Modern French with Especial Consideration of Anglo-Norman Phonology and Morphology*. Manchester: Manchester University Press, 1934.

Rohlfs, Gerhard. *Grammatica storica della lingua italiana e dei suoi dialetti*. 3 vols. Trans. S. Persichino. Turin: Einaudi, 1966.

Tobler, Adolf, and Erhardt Lommatzsch. *Altfranzösisches Wörterbuch*. Wiesbaden: Franz Steiner Verlag, 1954–1963.

Togeby, Knud. *Précis historique de grammaire française*. Copenhagen: Akademisk Forlag, 1974.

Wartburg, Walther von. *Französisches etymologisches Wörterbuch. Eine Darstellung des galloromanischen Sprachschatzes*. Bonn: Fritz Klopp Verlag, 1928–1961.

Wiese, Berthold. *Altitalienisches Elementarbuch*. Heidelberg: Carl Winters Universitätsbuchhandlung, 1904.

Woledge, Brian. *Bibliographie des romans et nouvelles en prose française antérieurs à 1500*. Société de publications romanes et françaises 42. Geneva: Droz, 1975.

5.3 Modern Editions and Criticism Cited

Adler, Alfred. *Rückzug in Epischen Parade. Studien zur "Les quatre fils Aymon," "La Chevalerie Ogier de Danemarche," "Garin le Loherenc," "Aliscans," "Huon de Bordeaux."* Frankfurt: Vittorio Klosterman, 1963.

———. "The Structural Meaning of *Berta da li pe grandi*." *Italica* 17 (1940): 101–8.

Aebischer, Paul. "Fragments de la *Chanson de la Reine Sebile* et du roman de *Florence de Rome* conservés aux Archives cantonales de Sion." *Zeitschrift für romanische Philologie* 66 (1941): 385–408.

———. *Textes norrois et littérature française du Moyen Age. I. Recherches sur les traditions épiques antérieures à la Chanson de Roland d'après les données de la première branche de la Karlamagnús saga*. Société de publications romanes et françaises 44. Geneva: Droz, 1954.

Allaire, Gloria. *Andrea da Barberino and the Language of Chivalry*. Gainesville: University Press of Florida, 1997.

———. "Considerations on *Huon d'Auvergne / Ugo d'Alvernia*." *Viator* 32 (2001): 185–203.

———. "A Fifteenth-Century Florentine Community of Readers and the Romances of Chivalry." *Essays in Medieval Studies* 15 (1999): 1–8.

———. "Un manoscritto del «Cantare del padiglione» (Cod. Riccardiano 1717)." *Studi mediolatini e volgari* 37 (1991): 9–30.

———. "An Unknown Fragment of the *Cantare del padiglione* found in Codex C.256 of the Biblioteca Marucelliana in Florence." *Medioevo Romanzo* 28 (1993): 277–92.

Allen, John Robin. *The Genealogy and Structure of a Medieval Historic Legend: Mainet in French, Spanish, Italian, German and Scandinavian Literature*. Ann Arbor: UMI, 1969.

———. "Les Structures de *Mainet*." In *Charlemagne et l'épopée romane*, ed. M. Tyssens and C. Thiry, 2: 405–14. Paris: Les Belles Lettres, 1978.

Altman, Charles. "Medieval Narrative vs. Modern Assumptions: Revising Inadequate Typology." *Diacritics* 4 (1974): 12–19.

Antonioni, Antonio. "Tav. LXIII. ROMANZI diversi del ciclo carolingio." In *Biblioteca Marciana*, ed. M. Zorzi, 119. Florence: Nardini, 1988.

Arfert, Paul. *Das Motiv von der unterschobenen Braut in der internationalen Erzählungslitteratur mit einem Anhang: Über den Ursprung und die Entwicklung der Bertasaga*. Schwerin: Bärensprungschen Hofbuchdruckerei, 1897.

Armistead, S[amuel] G., and G. H. Silverman. "El Romance de Celinos y la adultera." *Anuario de Letras* 2 (1962): 5–14.

Ascoli, Graziadio. "Saggi ladini." *Archivio Glottologico Italiano* 1 (1873): 1–537.

Au Carrefour des routes d'Europe: La Chanson de Geste. Xe Congrès international de la Société Rencesvals pour l'étude des épopées romanes, Strasbourg 1985. Sénéfiance 20–21. Aix-en-Provence: CUER MA, 1987.

Auerbach, Erich. *Mimesis: The Representation of Reality in Western Literature*. Trans. Willard R. Trask. Princeton: Princeton University Press, 1953.

Bachmann, Albert, and Samuel Singer, eds. *Deutsche Volksbücher aus einer Zürcher Handschrift des fünfzehnten Jahrhunderts*. Bibliothek des litterarischen Vereins in Stuttgart 185. Tübingen: Litterarischer Verein, 1889.

Baines, Keith, trans. *Malory: Le Morte d'Arthur. King Arthur and the Legends of the Round Table*. New York: Mentor (New American Library), 1962.

Baker, A. T., and M. Roques. "Nouveaux fragments de la chanson de *La Reine Sibille*." *Romania* 44 (1915–1917): 1–13.

Baker, Julie A. *The Childhood of the Epic Hero: A Study of the Old French Enfances Texts of Epic Cycles*. Ann Arbor: UMI, 2002.

Bard, Norval Lee, Jr. *Changing Orders: The Poetics of the Old French Epic Moniages*. Ann Arbor: UMI, 1998.

Barini, Giorgio, ed. *Cantàri cavallereschi dei secoli XV e XVI*. Bologna: Romagnoli dall'Acqua, 1905.

Barrois, Jean Baptiste Joseph, ed. *Ogier de Danemarche par Raimbert de Paris: Poëme du XIIe siècle*. Paris: Techner, 1842.

Bartoli, Adolfo. *I primi due secoli della letteratura italiana*. Milan: Vallardi, 1880.

———. *La poesia italiana nel periodo delle origini*. Storia della letteratura italiana 2. Florence: G. C. Sansoni, 1879.

Bartolucci-Chiecchi, Lidia. "Quelques notes sur *Rolandin* du manuscrit V^{13} de la Bibliothèque de Saint-Marc." In *Essor et fortune de la chanson de geste dans l'Europe et l'Orient latin*: Actes du IXe Congrès international de la Société Rencesvals (Padoue-Venise, 29 août-4 septembre 1982), ed. Alberto

Limentani, Maria Luisa Meneghetti, Rosanna Brusegan, Luigi Milone, Gianfelice Peron, and Francesco Zambon, 647–53. Modena: Mucchi, 1984.

———. "«De tous mes ont asés . . . »: Cibo e poemi epici." *Quaderni di Lingue e Letterature* 16 (1991): 269–78.

Bartsch, Karl, ed. *Karl der Grosse von dem Stricker*. Bibliothek der gesammten deutschen National-Literatur 35. Quedlinburg & Leipzig: Gottfr. Basse, 1857. Facsimile reprint with an afterword by Dieter Kartschoke. Deutsche Neudrucke. Reihe: Texte des Mittelalters. Berlin: W. de Gruyter, 1965. Page references are the same in both editions for the edited text.

———. *Über Karlmeinet*. Nürnberg: Bauer & Raspe, 1861.

Baugh, Albert C. "The Making of *Beves of Hampton*." In *Bibliographical Studies in Honor of Rudolf Hirsch*, ed. William E. Miller and Thomas G. Waldman with Natalie D. Terrell, special issue of *Library Chronicle* 40 (1975): 15–37.

Bautista, Francisco. "La tradición épica de las *Enfances* de Carlomagno y el *Cantar de Mainete* perdido." *Romance Philology* 56 (2003): 217–44.

Becker, Philipp August. Review of *Les légendes épiques: Recherches sur la formation des chansons de geste.*—III. *La légende des 'Enfances' de Charlemagne et l'histoire de Charles Martel*, by Joseph Bedier [sic], professeur au Collège de France. *Literaturblatt für germanische und romanische Philologie* 34 (1913): 370–75.

———. "Ogier von Dänemark." *Zeitschrift für französische Sprache und Literatur* 64 (1942): 67–88.

Beckers, Hartmut. "*Boeve van Hamtone*. Ein neuentdecktes Düsseldorfer Bruchstück einer bisher unbekannten mittelniederländischen Versarbeitung des altfranzösischen *Bueve de Hantone*. Dem Andenken an Theodor Frings." In *200 Jahre Landes- und Stadtbibliothek Düsseldorf*, 75–98. Veröffentlichungen 6. Düsseldorf: Landes- und Stadtbibliothek Düsseldorf, 1970.

Bédier, Joseph. *Les Légendes épiques: Recherches sur la formation des chansons de geste*. 4 vols. Paris: Champion, 1908–1913.

———. "L'origine lignagère des chansons de geste. Lettre inédite de J. Bédier écrite en 1913." *Romanic Review* 33 (1942): 319–35.

Behrens, Leopold. *Ort und Zeit der Entstehung der Fassung I des festlandischen Bueve de Hantone*. Göttingen: Dieterichschen Universitäts-Buchdruckerei-W. Fr. Kaestner, 1913.

Benaim de Lasry, Anita, ed. *"Carlos Maynes" and "La enperatris de Roma": Critical Edition and Study of Two Medieval Spanish Romances*. Newark, DE: Juan de la Cuesta, 1982.

Bender, Karl-Heinz. "Les Métamorphoses de la royauté de Charlemagne dans les premières épopées franco-italiennes." In *Atti del 2° Congresso internazionale della 'Société Rencesvals'*, special issue of *Cultura Neolatina* 21 (1961): 164–74.

Beretta, Carlo, ed. *Il Testo Assonanzato franco-italiano della Chanson de Roland: cod. Marciano fr. IV (= 225)*. Università degli Studi di Pavia, Dipartimento di Scienza della Letteratura e dell'Arte medioevale e moderna, Testi 2. Pavia: Tipografia Commerciale Pavese, 1995.

Bertolini, Virginio. "Uggieri il Danese a Verona (Dal codice marc. fran. XIII)." *Atti e memorie dell'Accademia di agricoltura, scienze e lettere di Verona* 17.143 (1968): 407–18.

———. Review of *Le Danois Oger*, ed. C. Cremonesi. *Quaderni di lingue e letterature* 2 (1977): 289–91.

Besamusca, Bart. "'Beerte metten breden voeten'. Diplomatische uitgave van het enig overgeleverde fragment." *Tijdschrift voor Nederlandse Taal- en Letterkunde* 102 (1986): 1–20.

———. "Willem Vorsterman's *Sibilla*: The Dutch Story of Charlemagne's Repudiated Wife." In *L'Imaginaire courtois et son double*: Actes du VIème Congrès triennal de la Société internationale de littérature courtoise (ICLS), Fisciano (Salerno), 24–28 juillet 1989, ed. Giovanna Angeli and Luciano Formisano, 245–54. Pubblicazioni dell'Università degli studi di Salerno, Sezione Atti, Convegni, miscellanee 35. Naples: Edizioni scientifiche italiane, 1991.

———. "Beerte metten breden voeten." *Olifant* 19 (1994–1995): 45–53.

———, Willem P. Gerritsen, Corry Hogetoorn, and Orlanda S. H. Lie, eds. *Cyclification: The Development of Narrative Cycles in the Chansons de Geste and the Arthurian Romances*. Proceedings of the Colloquium, Amsterdam, 17–18 December 1992. Koninklijke Nederlandse Akademie van Wetenschappen, Verhandelingen, Afd. Letterkunde, Nieuwe Reeks 159. Amsterdam: North-Holland, 1994.

———, W. Kuiper, and R. Resoort, eds. *Sibilla, een zestiende-eeuwse Karelroman in proza*. Populaire Literatuur 5. Muiderberg: Dick Coutinho, 1988.

Bisson, Sebastiano. "I manoscritti di epica carolingia a Venezia." In *L'Épopée romane*: Actes du XVe Congrès international Rencesvals, Poitiers, 21–27 août 2000, ed. Gabriel Bianciotto, Claudio Galderisi, foreword by Bernard Guidot, 741–48. Civilisation Médiévale 12–13. Poitiers: Centre d'Études Supérieures de Civilisation médievale, Université de Poitiers, 2002.

Bloch, R. Howard. *Etymologies and Genealogies: A Literary Anthropology of the French Middle Ages*. Chicago: University of Chicago Press, 1983.

Bober, Phyllis Pray. *Art, Culture & Cuisine: Ancient & Medieval Gastronomy*. Chicago: University of Chicago Press, 1999.

Boje, Christian. *Über den altfranzösischen Roman von Beuve de Hamtone*. Beihefte zur *Zeitschrift für romanische Philologie* 19. Halle: Niemeyer, 1909.

Boni, Marco, ed. *Andrea da Barberino: L'Aspramonte. Romanzo cavalleresco inedito*. Collezione di opere inedite o rare, nuova serie. Bologna: Antiquaria Palmaverde, 1951.

Borgnet, Adolphe, ed. *Ly Myreur des Histors, Chronique de Jean des Preis dit d'Outremeuse, Tome V*. Corps des chroniques liégeoises. Brussels: M. Hayez, 1867.

———. *Ly Myreur des Histors, Chronique de Jean des Preis dit d'Outremeuse, Tome II*. Corps des chroniques liégeoises. Brussels: M. Hayez, 1869.

———. *Ly Myreur des Histors, Chronique de Jean des Preis dit d'Outremeuse, Tome III*. Corps des chroniques liégeoises. Brussels: M. Hayez, 1873.

Bormans, Stanislaus, ed. *Ly Myreur des Histors, Chronique de Jean des Preis dit d'Outremeuse, Tome IV*. Brussels: M. Hayez, 1877.

Bourdillon, Francis William, ed. *Tote listoire de France (Chronique Saintongeaise)*. London: David Nutt, 1897.

Braghirolli, Willelmo, Gaston Paris, and Paul Meyer. "Inventaire des manuscrits en langue française possédés par Francesco Gonzaga I, capitaine de Mantoue, mort en 1407." *Romania* 9 (1880): 497–514.

Brandin, Louis, ed. *Berthe au grand pied. D'après deux romans en vers du XIIIe siècle*. Paris: Boivin & Cie, 1924.

———, ed. *La Chanson d'Aspremont*. 2 vols. Les Classiques français du Moyen Age. Paris: Honoré Champion, 1923.

Bratti, R. "Miniatori veneziani." *Nuovo archivio veneto* 2nd ser. 1 (1901): 70–93.

Brault, Gerard J. "The Legend of Charlemagne's Sin in Girart d'Amiens." *Romance Notes* 4 (1962): 72–75.

Brook, Leslie C. Review of *La Geste Francor*, ed. Aldo Rosellini. *French Studies* 43 (1990): 201–2.

———. "Allusions à l'antiquité gréco-latine dans l'*Entrée d'Espagne*." *Zeitschrift für romanische Philologie* 118 (2002): 573–86.

Capusso, Maria Grazia. Review of *La Geste Francor*, ed. Aldo Rosellini. *Studi mediolatini e volgari* 34 (1988): 183–207.

Carney, Anna P. "Portrait of the Hero as a Young Child: Guillaume, Roland, Girard, and Gui." *Olifant* 18 (1993–1994): 238–77.

Catalano, Michele, ed. *La Spagna: Poema cavalleresco del secolo XIV*. 3 vols. Collezione di opere inedite o rare. Bologna: Commissione per i testi di lingua Casa Carducci, 1939.

Cerf, Barry, ed. "The Franco-Italian *Chevalerie Ogier*." *Modern Philology* 8 (1910–1911): 187–216, 335–61, 511–25.

Ceruti, Antonio, ed. *Il Viaggio di Carlo Magno in Ispagna*. Bologna: Gaetano Romagnoli, 1871.

La Chanson de geste et le mythe carolingien: Mélanges René Louis publiés par ses collègues, ses amis et ses élèves à l'occasion de son 75ᵉ anniversaire. Saint-Père-Sous-Vézelay: Musée Archéologique Régional, 1982.

Les Chansons de geste. Actes du XVIᵉ Congrès International de la Société Rencesvals, pour l'Étude des Épopées Romanes, Granada, 21–25 juillet 2003, ed., Carlos Alvar and Juan Paredes. Granada: Universidad de Granada, 2005.

Chichmarev, V[ladimir Fedorovich], ed. "Di alcune enfances dell'epopea francese; il *Karleto* del Codice XIII della Marciana." *Zapiski Neofilologicheskago obshchestva pri Imperatorskom Petrogradskom Universitete* 5 (1911): 194–237.

Chicoy-Daban, José Ignacio. "A Study of the Spanish 'Queen Sibilla' and Related Themes in European Medieval and Renaissance Periods." Ph.D. Diss., University of Toronto, 1974.

Chiesa, Mario, ed. *Teofolo Folengo: Orlandino*. Medioevo e umanesimo 79. Padua: Editrice Antenore, 1991.

Chocheyras, Jacques. "Les Légendes épiques du Danemark (VIIIᵉ–IXᵉ siècles) et les origines de la chanson de geste." *Olifant* 18 (1993–1994): 289–99.

Cingolani, Stefano Maria. "Innovazione e Parodia nel Marciano XIII (*Geste Francor*)." *Romanistisches Jahrbuch* 38 (1987): 61–77.

Cobby, Anne Elizabeth. *Ambivalent Conventions: Formula and Parody in Old French*. Faux Titre: Etudes de langue et littérature françaises 101. Amsterdam: Rodopi, 1995.

Coldwell, Maria V. "*Jougleresses* and *Trobairitz*: Secular Musicians in Medieval France." In *Women Making Music: The Western Art Tradition, 1150–1950*, ed. Jane Bowers and Judith Tick, 39–61. Urbana: University of Illinois Press, 1986.

Colliot, Régine. *Adenet le Roi. Berte aus grans pies. Etude littéraire générale*. 2 vols. Paris: Picard, 1970.

Collomp, Denis. "Le Motif du pape combattant dans l'épopée." In *Le Clerc au Moyen Âge*, 91–112. Sénéfiance 37 [sic]. Aix-en-Provence: CUER MA (Centre Universitaire d'Études et de Recherches Médiévales d'Aix), 1995.

——. "*Mucho leal es el amor del can, esto oy prouar* (à propos du chien d'Auberi dans *Le Roman de la Reine Sibille*)." In «*Si a parlé par moult ruiste vertu*»: *Mélanges de littérature médiévale offerts à Jean Subrenat*, ed. Jean Dufournet, 136–46. Paris: Champion, 2000.

Contini, Gianfranco. "La canzone della *Mort Charlemagne*." In *Mélanges de linguistique romane et de philologie médiévale offerts à Maurice Delbouille*, ed. Jean Renson, 2:105–26. Gembloux: Duculot, 1964.

Cook, Robert F. "Was Venice-Four *Roland* Comprehensible?" Paper presented at the Medieval Conference at Western Michigan University, Kalamazoo. May, 1997.

Coronedi, P. H. "L'Aquilon de Baviere'" [sic]. *Archivum Romanicum* 19 (1935): 237–304.

Cremonesi, Carla. "A proposito del Codice marciano fr. XIII." In *Mélanges offerts à Mme. Rita Lejeune, Prof. à l'Université de Liège*, 2: 747–55. Gembloux: Duculot, 1969.

——, ed. *Berta e Milon, Rolandin: Codice Marciano XIII*. Milan: La Goliardica, 1973.

——, ed. *Berte da li pè grandi: Codice marciano XIII*. Milan: Varese, 1966.

——, ed. *Le Danois Oger. Enfances–Chevalerie. Codice Marciano XIII*. Milan: Cisalpino-Goliardica, 1977.

——. "Note di franco-veneto. I. Franco-veneto, franco-italiano, franco-lombardo; II. L'oste: un motivo ricorrente." In *Studi di lingua e letteratura lombarda offerti a Maurizio Vitale*, 1: 5–21. Pisa: Giardini, 1983.

Dammann, Hans. *Über das verlorene Epos 'Enfances Roland' nebst Textabdruck der Rollandin-Episode aus dem 'Charlemagne' des Girart d'Amiens*. Greifswald: Puff & Panzig, 1907.

D'Ancona, Alessandro. "Tradizioni carolingie in Italia." *Rendiconti della Reale Accademia dei Lincei, classe di scienze morali, storiche e filologiche* 286, 4th ser. 5 (1889): 420–27.

D'Ancona, Paolo. *La Miniature italienne du X{e} au XVIe siècle*. Trans. M. P. Porrier. Paris: G. Van Oest, 1925.

D'Arcais, Francesca. "Les Illustrations des manuscrits français des Gonzague à la Bibliothèque de Saint-Marc." In *Essor et fortune de la chanson de geste*, ed. Limentani et al., 2: 585–616.

Delcorno Branca, Daniela. "Fortuna e trasformazioni del *Buovo d'Antona*." In *Testi, cotesti e contesti del franco-italiano*, Atti del 1° simposio franco-italiano (Bad Homburg, 13–16 aprile 1987), ed. G. Holtus et al., 285–306. Tübingen: Niemeyer, 1989.

———. "Note sull'editoria bolognese nell'età dei Bentivoglio." *Schede umanistiche* 2 (1988): 19–32.

———. "Un Nuovo testimone del *Buovo d'Antona* in ottava rima." *Italianistica* 21 (1992): 705–13.

———. *L'Orlando Furioso e il romanzo cavalleresco medievale*. Florence: Olschki, 1973.

———. *Il Romanzo cavalleresco medievale*. Florence: Sansoni, 1974.

———. "Vicende editoriali di due poemi cavallereschi: *Buovo d'Antona* e *Innamoramento di Galvano*." In *Tipografie e romanzi in Val Padana fra Quattro e Cinquecento*, ed. Riccardo Bruscagli and Amedeo Quondam, 75–83. Modena: Panini, 1988.

Demaux, Germaine. "Une Fresque inédite du XIIIe siècle en l'abbaye d'Aiguevive (Loir-et-Cher): Saint Gilles remettant à Charlemagne la 'charte' apportée par un ange." In *La Chanson de geste. Mélanges René Louis*, 279–92.

Demoulin, Auguste. "Charlemagne, la légende de son peché et le choix de Ganelon pour l'ambassade." *La Chanson de geste. Marche romane: Cahiers de l'A. R. U. Lg.* 25 (1975): 105–26.

Dickson, Arthur, ed. *Valentine and Orson*. Trans. Henry Watson. Early English Text Society, original series 204. London: Oxford University Press, 1937.

Dingerling, Lothar. "Das gegenseitige Verhältnis der Handschriften der Fassung III des festländischen Bueve de Hantone." Diss., Universität Göttingen, 1917.

DiNinni, Franca. "Memorie di città e luoghi d'Italia nella *Geste Francor* di Venezia." In *Il Viaggio in Italia: modelli, stili, lingue. Atti del convegno, Venezia, 3–4 dicembre 1997*, ed. Ilaria Crotti, 17–28. Naples: Edizioni scientifiche italiane, 1999.

———, ed. *Niccolò da Verona: Opere*. Venice: Marsilio Editori, 1992.

Dionisotti, Carlo. "Appunti su cantari e romanzi." *Italia medioevale e umanistica* 32 (1989): 227–61.

Dorsey, Gladys Madeline. "HISTOIRE DE LA ROYNE BERTE ED DU ROY PEPIN (Ms. Berlin Staatsbibliothek, 130) [sic]." Ph.D. diss., The Johns Hopkins University, 1933.

Doutrepont, Georges. *Les Mises en prose des épopées et des romans chevaleresques du xive au xvie siècles*. 1939; repr. Geneva: Slatkine Reprints, 1969.

Duby, Georges. *The Knight, the Lady and the Priest: The Making of Modern Marriage in Medieval France*. Trans. Barbara Bray. New York: Pantheon Books, 1983.

———. "Remarques sur la littérature généalogique en France." In idem, *Hommes et structures du moyen âge: Recueil d'articles*, 287–98. Paris-La Haye: Mouton, 1967.

———. "Structures de parenté et noblesse dans la France du Nord aux XIe et XIIe siècles." In idem, *Hommes et structures du moyen âge*, 267–85.

Duggan, Joseph J. "Legitimation and the Hero's Exemplary Function in the *Cantar de mio Cid* and the *Chanson de Roland*." In *Oral Traditional Literature*, ed. John Miles Foley, 217–34. Columbus, OH: Slavica Publishers, Inc., 1981.

———. "El juicio de Ganelón y el mito del pecado de Carlomagno en la versión de Oxford de la *Chanson de Roland*." In *Mythopoesis: Literatura, totalidad, ideología*, ed. Joan Ramon Resina, 53–64. Ambitos Literarios/Ensayo. Barcelona: Anthropos, 1992.

Elliott, Alison Goddard. "The Emperor's Daughter: A Catalan Account of Charlemagne's Mother." *Romance Philology* 34 (1981): 398–416.

Ellis, George, ed. "Sir Triamour." In *Specimens of Early English Metrical Romances*, ed. J. O. Halliwell, 491–505. London: Henry G. Bohn, 1848.

Eusebi, Mario, ed. *La Chevalerie d'Ogier de Danemarche, canzone di gesta*. Testi e documenti di letteratura moderna 6. Milan: Cisalpino, 1962.

Everson, Jane E. *The Italian Romance Epic in the Age of Humanism: The Matter of Italy and the World of Rome*. Oxford: Oxford University Press, 2001.

Faral, Edmond. "Pour l'histoire de *Berte au grand pied* et de *Marcoul et Salomon*." *Romania* 40 (1911): 93–96.

Farrier, Susan E. "*Das Rolandslied* and the *Song of Roulond* as Moralizing Adaptations of the *Chanson de Roland*." *Olifant* 16 (1991): 61–76.

———. "Hungry Heroes in Medieval Literature." In *Food in the Middle Ages: A Book of Essays*, ed. Melitta Weiss Adamson, 145–59. New York: Garland Publishing, Inc., 1995.

Fatini, Giuseppe, ed. *Il Morgante di Luigi Pulci*. Classici italiani UTET. 1948; repr. Turin: Unione tipografico-editrice torinese, 1984.

Feist, Alfred. *Zur Kritik der Bertasage*. Ausgaben und Abhandlungen aus dem Gebiete der romanischen Philologie 59. Marburg: N.G. Elwert'sche Verlagsbuchhandlung, 1886.

Ferrari, Giorgio Emanuel, ed. *Documenti marciani e principale letteratura sui codici veneti di epopea carolingia*. Venice: Biblioteca Nazionale Marciana, 1961.

Ferrario, Giulio. *Storia ed analisi degli antichi romanzi di cavalleria e dei poemi romanzeschi d'Italia*. 4 vols. Milan: Dalla tipografia dell'autore, 1928–1929.

Ferrero, Giuseppe Guido. "Astolfo (Storia di un personaggio)" [sic]. *Convivium* 24 (1961): 513–30.

———, ed. *Poemi cavallereschi del Trecento*. Turin: UTET, 1965.

Fieberg, Werner. *Das "Livre d'Enanchet" nach der einzigen handschrift 2585 der Wiener Nationalbibliothek*. Jena: Gronau, 1938.

Foligno, Cesare. "Epistole inedite di Lovato de' Lovati e d'altri a lui." *Studi medievali* 2 (1906): 49–51.

Folz, Robert. *Le Souvenir et la légende de Charlemagne dans l'Empire germanique médiéval*. Publications de l'Université de Dijon. Paris: Les Belles Lettres, 1950.

Franceschetti, Antonio. "Rassegna di studi sui cantari." *Lettere italiane* 25 (1973): 556–74.

———. "Appunti sui cantari di Milone e Berta e della nascita di Orlando." *Giornale storico della letteratura italiana* 152 (1975): 387–99.

———. "Schede bibliografiche boiardesche." *Quaderni d'Italianistica* 15 (1994): 157–72.

Frappier, Jean, ed. *La Mort Le Roi Artu. Roman du XIIIe Siècle*. Textes littéraires français. Geneva: Droz, 1954.

Frati, Carlo. "Di alcune recenti pubblicazioni tratte dal Cod. Franc. XIII della Biblioteca Marciana." *Nuovo archivio veneto* n. s. 21 (1911): 223–31.

Freitag, Otto. *Die sogenannte Chronik von Weihenstephan. Ein Beitrag zur Karlssage*. Diss., Universität Halle-Wittenberg, 1904. Repr. as *Die sogennante Chronik von Weihenstephan. Ein Beitrag zur Karlssage*. Hermaea: Ausgewählte Arbeiten aus dem germanischen Seminar zu Halle 1. Tübingen: Niemeyer, 1972.

Frierson, David E. "A Historical Study of the Language of 'Venice XIII,' Franco-Italian Manuscript of the Fourteenth Century." Ph.D. diss., University of North Carolina-Chapel Hill, 1937.

Gabotto, Ferdinando. "Les Légendes carolingiennes dans le *Chronicon Ymaginis Mundi* di Frate Jacopo d'Aqui." *Revue des langues romanes* 37, 4th ser. 7 (1893–1894): 356–73.

Gaiffier, Baudouin de. "La Légende de Charlemagne: Le péché de l'empereur et son pardon." In *Recueil de Travaux offert à M. Clovis Brunel*, 1: 490–503. Mémoires et documents publiés par la Société de l'École des Chartes 12. Paris: Société de l'École des Chartes, 1955.

Gasca Queirazza, Giuliano, ed. *La "Chanson de Roland" nel testo assonanzato franco-italiano*. Turin: Rosenberg e Sellier, 1955.

Gautier, Léon. *Les Épopées françaises: Étude sur les origines et l'histoire de la littérature nationale*. 2e éd. Paris: Société générale de librarie catholique, 1880–1892.

Gayangos, Don Pascual de, ed. *La Gran conquista de Ultramar que mandó escribir el rey Don Alfonso el Sabio*. Biblioteca de autores españoles. Madrid: M. Rivadeneyra, 1858.

Gibbs, J[ack]. "Las Mocedades de Mainete." In *Guillaume d'Orange and the Chanson de geste*, ed. W. van Emden and P. E. Bennett, 33–42. Reading: Reading University Press, 1984.

Goffis, Cesare Federico. "Limerno, Pitocco evangelico." *Esperienze letterarie* 17 (1992): 3–16.

Goldberg, Harriet. *Motif-Index of Folk Narratives in the Pan-Hispanic Romancero*. Medieval and Renaissance Texts and Studies 206. Tempe, AZ: MRTS, 2000.

———. *Motif-Index of Medieval Spanish Folk Narratives*. Medieval and Renaissance Texts and Studies 162. Tempe, AZ: MRTS, 1998.

Goosse, André, ed. *Ly Myreur des histors. Fragment du second livre (Années 794–826)*. Académie royale de Belgique. Classe des Lettres et des Sciences Morales et Politiques; Collection des Anciens Auteurs Belges Nouvelle Série 6. Gembloux: J. Duculot, 1965.

Granzow, Willi. "Die Ogier-Episode im 'Charlemagne' des Girart d'Amiens. Nebst vollständigem Namenverzeichnis der gesamten Dichtung." Diss., Universität Greifswald, 1908.

Green, Herman J. "The Pépin-Bertha Saga and Philip I of France." *PMLA* 58 (1943): 911–19.

———, ed. *Anseÿs de Mes, According to Ms. N. (Bibliothèque de l'Arsenal 3143)*. Paris: Les Presses Modernes, 1939.

Gröber, Gustav. *Grundriss der romanischen philologie*. 2. Band, 1. Abteilung. Strassburg: Trübner, 1902.

Grossel, M.-G., and C.-T. Cemo. "Le Burlesque et son évolution dans les trois versions continentales de la chanson de *Beuve de Hanstone*." In *Burlesque et dérision dans les épopées de l'occident médiéval*. Actes du Colloque international des Rencontres Européennes de Strasbourg et de la Société Internationale Rencesvals (Section française), Strasbourg, 16–18 septembre 1993, ed. Bernard Guidot, 255–68. Paris: Les Belles Lettres, 1995.

Guessard, François. "Notes sur un manuscrit français de la Bibliothèque de S. Marc." *Bibliothèque de l'école des chartes* 4th ser. 4 (1857): 393–414.

———, ed. *Macaire, chanson de geste*. Les anciens poëtes de France. Paris: Librairie A. Franck, 1864.

Guidot, Bernard, ed. *Burlesque et dérision dans les épopées de l'occident médiéval*. Actes du Colloque international des Rencontres Européennes de Strasbourg et de la Société Internationale Rencesvals (Section française), Strasbourg, 16–18 septembre 1993. Littéraires 3. Annales littéraires de l'Université de Besançon 558. Paris: Les Belles Lettres, 1995.

Guiette, Robert, ed. *Croniques* [sic] *et Conquestes de Charlemagne*. 2 vols. Académie royale de Belgique. Classe des Lettres et des Sciences Morales et Politiques, Collection des Anciens Auteurs Belges, Nouvelle Série 3. Brussels: Palais des académies, 1940–1951.

Haymes, Edward R., trans. *The Saga of Thidrek of Bern*. Garland Library of Medieval Literature B 56. New York and London: Garland Publishing Inc., 1988.

Heintz, Heinrich, ed. *Schondochs Gedichte*. Germanistische Abhandlungen 30. Breslau: Verlag von M. & H. Marcus, 1908.

Heintze, Michael. "*Bueve de Hantone* en Espagne. À propos des romances sur Gaiferos." In *L'épopée romane au Moyen Âge*, ed. Luongo, 2: 929–31.

———. "La mort de Baldovino: un épisode du *Cantar de Sansueña* à la lumière d'un romance méconnu sur Baldovinos." In *Lirica, Drammatica, Narrativa*, 47–98. Quaderni di filologia romanza della Facoltà di lettere e filosofia dell'Università di Bologna 11. Bologna: Pàtron, 1994.

Henry, Albert. "*Berta da li gran pié* et la *Berte* d'Adenet." In *Atti del 2º Congresso internazionale della 'Société Rencesvals'*, special issue of *Cultura Neolatina* 21 (1961): 135–40.

———. "Note sur le *Miracle de Berthe*." In *Mélanges de linguistique et de littérature romanes à la mémoire d'István Frank, offerts par ses anciens maîtres, ses amis et ses collègues de France et de l'étranger*, 250–61. Annales Universitatis Saraviensis 6. Saarbrücken: Universität des Saarlandes, 1957.

———, ed. *Les Œuvres d'Adenet le Roi*. 4 vols. Brussels: Presses Universitaires de Bruxelles, 1951–1963.

———, ed. *Les Œuvres d'Adenet le Roi. Tome III: Les Enfances Ogier*. Rijksuniversiteit te Gent, Werken uitgegeven door de Faculteit van de Letteren en Wijsbegeerte, 121 Aflevering. Brugge: De Tempel, 1956.

———, ed. *Les Œuvres d'Adenet le Roi. Tome IV: Berte aus grans piés*. Bruges: PUB, 1963.

———, ed. *Berte as grans piés* [sic]. Geneva: Droz, 1982.

Herlihy, David. *Opera muliebria: Women and Work in Medieval Europe*. New York: McGraw-Hill, 1990.

Hewett, Waterman T., ed. and trans. *Poems of Uhland*. New York: Macmillan, 1896.

Hieatt, Constance B. "Ogier the Dane in Old Norse." *Scandinavian Studies* 45 (1973): 27–37.

———, trans. *Karlamagnús Saga. The Saga of Charlemagne and his Heroes*. Volume One [Parts I–III]. Mediaeval Sources in Translation 17. Toronto: Pontifical Institute of Mediaeval Studies, 1975.

Hills, Elijah Clarence. "Irregular Epic Metres: A Comparative Study of the Metre of the Poem of the Cid and of Certain Anglo-Norman, Franco-Italian and Venetian Epic Poems." In *Homenaje a Menéndez Pidal*, 1: 759–77. Madrid: Libreria y casa editorial Hernando, 1925.

Höfler, Manfred. Review of *Berta da li pè grandi. Codice Marciano XIII*, ed. Cremonesi. *Zeitschrift für romanische Philologie* 84 (1968): 179–81.

Hogetoorn, C. "Bevis of Hampton." In Besamusca, *Cyclification*, 62–64.

Holden, A. J. Review of *La "Geste francor" di Venezia*, ed. Rosellini. *Romania* 108 (1987): 562–67.

Hollister, C. Warren. *Medieval Europe: A Short History*. 6th ed. New York: McGraw-Hill, 1990.

Holmes, Urban T., Jr., ed. *Adenet le Roi's "Berte aus grans pies." Edited with an Introduction, Variants and Glossary*. University of North Carolina Studies in the Romance Languages and Literatures 6. Chapel Hill: University of North Carolina Press, 1946.

Holtus, Günter. "L'État actuel des recherches sur le franco-italien: corpus de textes et description linguistique." In *La Chanson de Geste: Écriture, Intertextualités, Translations*, ed. François Suard, 147–71. Cahiers du département de français, Littérales 14. Nanterre: Service 10FFUSION [sic], 1994.

———. "Ist das Franko-italienische eine Sprache oder eine Dialekte?" In *Beiträge zum romanischen Mittelalter*, ed. Kurt Baldinger, 79–97. Sonderband zum 100 Jährigen Bestehen [sic] *Zeitschrift für romanische Philologie*. Tübingen: Niemeyer, 1977.

———. *Lexicalische Untersuchungen zur Interferenz: die franko-italienische "Entrée d'Espagne."* Beihefte zur *Zeitschrift für romanische Philologie* 170. Tübingen: Niemeyer, 1979.

———. "Plan und Kunstsprachen auf romanischer Basis IV. Franko-Italienisch/ Langues artificielles à base romane IV. Le franco-italien." In *LRL* 7: 705–56.

———. "Les Problèmes posés par l'édition de textes franco italiens. A propos de quelques leçons problematiques de V4, V8 et d'autres manuscrits." In *Au Carrefour des routes d'Europe*, 2: 675–96.

———. Review of *Berta e Milon. Rolandin. Codice Marciano XIII*, ed. Cremonesi. *Zeitschrift für romanische Philologie* 91 (1975): 199–208.

———. Review of *La Geste Francor*, ed. Rosellini. *Zeitschrift für romanische Philologie* 106 (1990): 519–21.

———. Review of *Le Danois Oger. Enfances—Chevalerie. Codice Marciano XIII*, ed. Cremonesi. *Zeitschrift für romanische Philologie* 95 (1979): 442–48.

———. "Sulla posizione del franco-italiano nella dialettologia italiana." In *Scritti linguistici in onore di Giovan Battisti Pellegrini*, 63–71. Pisa: Pacini, 1983.

———, ed. *La versione franco-italiana della "Bataille d'Aliscans": Codice Marcianus fr. VIII (= 252). Testo con introduzione, note e glossario*. Beihefte zur *Zeitschrift für romanische Philologie*. Tübingen: Niemeyer, 1985.

Hope, T. E. *Lexical Borrowing in the Romance Languages*. 2 vols. Oxford: B. Blackwell, 1971.

Horrent, Jacques. "L'Allusion à la chanson de *Mainet* contenue dans le *Roncesvalles*." In *Hommage des romanistes liégeois à la mémoire de Ramón Menéndez Pidal*, special issue of *Marche romane,Cahiers de l'A. R.U. Lg.* 20 (1970): 85–92.

———. "*Bueve de Hantone* et la *Condesa traidora*." *Les Lettres romanes* 36 (1982): 41–57.

———. "«Mainet» est-il né à Tolède?" *Le Moyen Age* 74, 4th ser. 23 (1968): 439–58.

———. "Un Récit peu connu de la légende de Mainet." *Mediaevalia 76: Marche romane, Cahiers de l'A. R. U. Lg.* 26 (1976): 87–96.

———. *Les Versions françaises et étrangères des Enfances de Charlemagne*. Académie Royale de Belgique, Mémoires de la Classe des Lettres, 2nd ser. 64. Brussels: Palais des Académies, 1979.

Horrent, Jules. *Roncesvalles. Etude sur le fragment de cantar de gesta conservé à l'Archivo de Navarra (Pampelune)*. Bibliothèque de la Faculté de Philosophie et Lettres de l'Université de Liège. Paris: Les Belles Lettres, 1951.

———. "Mainet." In *Le Moyen Age*, 978–80. *Dictionnaire des lettres françaises* 1. 1964, repr. Paris: Fayard, 1994.

———. "Chanson de Roland et geste de Charlemagne (Partie documentaire)." In *Les Épopées Romanes*, ed. Rita Lejeune, Jeanne Wathelet-Willem, and Hennig Krauss. Vol. 1, fasc. 2A I.1, 1–51. Grundriss der romanischen Literaturen des Mittelalters 3. Heidelberg: Carl Winter Universitätsverlag, 1981.

Hoyer-Poulain, Emmanuelle. "Ridicules d'Ogier: vacillements du héros dans les remaniements de la chanson d'Ogier le Danois." In *Burlesque et dérision*, ed. Guidot, 49–58.

Hoyt, Prentiss C[heney]. "The Home of the Beves Saga." n.p., n.d. (1904?).

Hunt, Stephen. "Further Translation Errors in *Bevers Saga*." *Notes and Queries* 230 (1985): 455–56.

Isola, I. G., ed. *Le Storie Nerbonesi: Romanzo cavalleresco del secolo XIV.* Andrea da Barberino. Bologna: Romagnoli-Dall'Acqua, 1877–1887.

Ival, Madeleine, ed. *Beufves de Hantonne: version en prose.* Sénéfiance 14. Aix-en-Provence: CUER MA (Centre Universitaire d'Études et de Recherches Médiévales d'Aix), 1984.

Jacob, L., Pseud. See Lacroix, P.

Jacobs, Nicolas. "*Sir Degarré, Lay Le Freine, Beves of Hamtoun* and the 'Auchinleck Bookshop'." *Notes and Queries* 227 (1982): 294–301.

Jones, Catherine M. *The Noble Merchant: Problems of Genre and Lineage in "Hervis de Mes."* North Carolina Studies in the Romance Languages and Literatures 241. Chapel Hill: University of North Carolina Press, 1993.

Jordan, Leo. *Über Boeve de Hanstone.* Beihefte zur *Zeitschrift für romanische Philologie* 14. Halle: M. Niemeyer, 1908.

———. Review of *Über die verschiedenen Fassungen der Bertasage.* Sonderabdruck aus *Zeitschrift für romanische Philologie* 35 (1911): 1–30, 129–52. *Literaturblatt für germanische und romanische Philologie* 12 (1912): columns 402–4.

Jung, Marc-René. "Beuve d'Hamtone." In *Enzyklopädie des Märchens: Handwörterbuch zur historischen und vergleichenden Erzählforschung*, ed. Kurt Ranke et al. 2: 270–74. 10 vols. to date. Berlin: de Gruyter, 1977–.

Kay, Sarah. *The Chanson de Geste in the Age of Romance: Political Fictions.* Oxford: Clarendon Press, 1995.

Keller, Adelbert von. *Romvart: Beitræge zur Kunde mittelalterlicher Dichtung aus italiænischen Bibliotheken* [sic]. Mannheim: Basserman, 1844.

———, ed. *Karl Meinet.* Bibliothek des Litterarischen Vereins in Stuttgart. Stuttgart: Litterarischer Verein, 1858.

———, ed. Hans Sachs. "Ein comedi, mit dreyzehen personen, die königin auß Franckreich mit dem falschen marschalck, hat fünff actus." In *Hans Sachs Werke*, 8: 54–80. Bibliothek des Litterarischen Vereins in Stuttgart 121. Tübingen: H. Laupp, 1874.

Keller, Hans-Erich. *Autour de Roland: Recherches sur la chanson de geste.* Nouvelle Bibliothèque du Moyen Age 14. Paris-Geneva: Slatkine, 1989.

———. "Le Peche de Charlemagne." In *L'Imaginaire courtois et son double*: Actes du VIème Congrès triennal de la Société internationale de littérature courtoise (ICLS), Fisciano (Salerno), 24–28 juillet 1989, ed. Giovanna Angeli and Luciano Formisano, 39–54. Pubblicazioni dell'Università degli studi di Salerno, Sezione Atti, convegni, miscellanee 35. Naples: Edizioni scientifiche italiane, 1991.

———, ed. *L'Histoire de Charlemagne (parfois dite Roman de Fierabras) de Jehan Bagnyon*. Textes littéraires françaises. Geneva: Droz, 1992.

Kennedy, Elspeth. "The Use of *Tu* and *Vous* in the First Part of the Old French Prose *Lancelot*." In *History and Structure of French: Essays in Honour of Professor T. B. W. Reid*, ed. F. J. Barnett et al., 135–49. Totowa, NJ: Rowman and Littlefield, 1972.

Kimmel, Arthur S., ed. *A Critical Edition of the Old Provençal Epic "Daurel et Beton" with Notes and Prolegomena*. University of North Carolina Studies in the Romance Languages and Literatures 108. Chapel Hill: University of North Carolina Press, 1971.

Kölbing, Eugen, ed. *The Romance of Sir Beues of Hamtoun*. Early English Text Society, Extra Series 46. London: N. Trübner, 1885.

Kramsch, Claire. "The Privilege of the Nonnative Speaker." *PMLA* 112 (1997): 359–69.

Krappe, Alexander Haggerty. "Une Version norroise de la *Reine Sibille*." *Romania* 56 (1930): 585–88.

Krauss, Henning. *Epica feudale e pubblico borghese. Per la storia poetica di Carlomagno in Italia*. Trans. F. Brugnolo, A. Fassò, and M. Mancini. Ydioma Tripharium 6. Padua: Liviana, 1980.

———. "Refoulement et hierarchie féodale: Essai de psychanalyser le comportement d'Ogier le Danois dans la version francoitalienne." In *VIII Congreso de la Société Rencesvalls* [sic], 263–66. Huarte-Pamplona: Institución Principe de Viana, 1981.

Kühl, Hans. "Das gegenseitige Verhältnis der Handschriften der Fassung II des festländischen Bueve de Hantone." Diss. Universität Göttingen, 1915.

Labande-Mailfert, V. Review of *La légende de Roland dans l'art du Moyen âge*, by Rita Lejeune and Jacques Stiennon. *Cahiers de Civilisation Médiévale* 9 (1966): 417–21.

Labie-Leurquin, Anne Françoise. "Huon d'Auvergne." In *Le Moyen Age*, 1: 702–3. *Dictionnaire des lettres françaises* 1, ed. Geneviève Hasenohr and Michel Zink. 4 vols. Paris: Fayard, 1994.

Lacroix, Paul (pseud. P. L. Jacob, Bibliophile). "Sur les MSS. . . . conservés dans les bibliothèques d'Italie." In *Dissertations sur quelques points curieux de l'histoire de France et de l'histoire littéraire, 7: Sur les MSS. conservés dans les bibliothèques d'Italie*, 147–89. Paris: Techener, 1839. Repr. in Jacques-Joseph Champollion-Figeac, *Documents historiques inédits tirés des collections manuscrites de la Bibliothèque Royale et des archives ou des bibliothèques des Départements*, 3: 345–76. Paris: Firmin Didot, 1847.

Lazzeri, G. "Orlandino." In *L'influsso francese in Italia nel Medioevo*, Corso di filologia romanza, 1968–69, ed. R. M. Ruggieri, 233–52. Roma: DeSanctis, n.d.

Lebsanft, Franz. "Le Problème du mélange du 'tu' et du 'vous' en ancien français." *Romania* 108 (1987): 1–19.

Lejeune, Rita. "La Légende de Roland dans l'art italien du Moyen Âge." In *La Poesia epica e la sua formazione*, Atti del Convegno internazionale (Roma, 28 marzo–3 aprile 1969), 299–314. Problemi attuali di scienza e di cultura, Accademia Nazionale dei Lincei 367. Roma: Accademia Nazionale dei Lincei, 1970.

———."Le Péché de Charlemagne et la *Chanson de Roland*." In *III Congreso internacional de la Société Rencesvals*, special issue of *Boletín de la Real Academia de Buenas Letras de Barcelona* 31 (1965–1966): 339–71.

———. *Recherches sur le Thème: Les Chansons de Geste et l'Histoire*. Bibliothèque de la Faculté de philosophie et lettres de l'Université de Liège 108. Liège: Faculté de Philosophie et Lettres, 1948.

———. "Technique formulaire et chansons de geste." *Le Moyen Âge* 60; 4ᵉ s. 10 (1954): 311–54.

———, and Robert Escholier. "Roland était le fils de Charlemagne." *Les nouvelles littéraires* 7 décembre 1961: 1–2.

———, and Jacques Stiennon. *La Légende de Roland dans l'art du Moyen Age*. Brussels: Arcade, 1967.

Levine, Robert, ed. *France Before Charlemagne: A Translation from the "Grandes Chroniques."* Lewiston, NY: Edwin Mellen Press, 1990.

———, ed. *A Thirteenth-Century Life of Charlemagne*. Garland Library of Medieval Literature B 80. New York and London: Garland Publishing, Inc., 1991.

Levy, Raphael. "The Etymology of Franco-Italian *çubler*." *Italica* 29 (1952): 49–52.

Limentani, Alberto. "Problemi dell'epica franco-italiana: appunti sulla tecnica della lassa e della rima." In *Alberto Limentani: L'«Entrée d'Espagne» e i signori d'Italia*, ed. Marco Infurna and Francesco Zambon, 226–42. Padua: Antenori, 1992. First published in *Atti e memorie dell'Accademia patavina di Scienze, Lettere ed Arti* 95 (1982–1983): 155–74.

———, Maria Luisa Meneghetti, Rosanna Brusegan, Luigi Milone, Gianfelice Peron, and Francesco Zambon, eds. *Essor et fortune de la chanson de geste dans l'Europe et l'Orient latin*: Actes du IXᵉ Congrès international de la Société Rencesvals (Padoue-Venise, 29 août-4 septembre 1982). Modena: Mucchi, 1984.

Lioce, Nico. "Burlesque et dérision dans *Ogier le Dannoys* (remaniement en prose du XVe siècle)." In *Burlesque et dérision*, ed. Guidot, 281–96.

Lot, Ferdinand. "A quelle époque remonte la connaissance de la légende d'Ogier le Danois?" *Romania* 66 (1940–1941): 238–53.

Loth, Agnete. "Les manuscrits norrois." In *Karlamagnús Saga*, ed. K. Togeby et al., 356–78. Copenhagen: Reitzel, 1980.

Louis, René. *De l'histoire à la légende*. 3 vols. Auxerre: Imprimerie Moderne, 1946–1947.

Luongo, Salvatore, ed. *L'épopée romane au Moyen Âge et aux temps modernes: Actes du XIVe Congrès International de la Société Rencesvals pour l'étude des Épopées Romanes (Naples, 24–30 juillet 1997)*. 2 vols. Naples: Fridericiana Editrice Universitaria, 2001.

Maines, Clark. "The Charlemagne Window at Chartres Cathedral: New Considerations on Text and Image." *Speculum* 52 (1977): 801–23.

Mak, Jacobus Johannes, ed. *Floris ende Blancefloer van Diederic van Assenede*. Zwolle: Tjeenk Willink, 1960. Quoted by Geert Claassens, personal communication, 2002.

Marnette, Sophie. *Narrateur et points de vue dans la littérature française médiévale: une approche linguistique*. New York: P. Lang, 1998.

Martin, Jean-Pierre. *Les Motifs dans la chanson de geste: Définition et utilisation*. Discours de l'épopée médiévale 1. Lille: Université de Lille III, Centre d'Études Médiévales et Dialectales, 1992.

———. Review of *La «Geste Francor» di Venezia*, ed. Rosellini. *Lettres romanes* 45 (1991): 126–31.

Massmann, Hans Ferd[inand], ed. *Der keiser und der kunige buoch oder die sogennante Kaiserchronik, Gedicht des zwölften Jahrhunderts*. Bibliothek der gesammten deutschen National-Literatur von der ältesten bis auf die neuere Zeit. Vierten Bandes zweite Abtheilung. Zweiter Theil. Quedlinburg and Leipzig: Gottfr. Basse, 1849.

Matsumura, Takeshi. Review of *Old French-English Dictionary*, ed. Alan Hindley et al. *Revue de Linguistique Romane* 65 (2001): 272.

Mattaini, Adelaide, ed. *I Romanzi dei Reali di Francia*. Milan: Rizzoli, 1957.

McCormack, James R., ed. *Gui de Nanteuil: chanson de geste*. Geneva: Droz, 1970.

McCracken, Peggy. *The Curse of Eve, The Wound of the Hero: Blood, Gender, and Medieval Literature*. Philadelphia: University of Pennsylvania Press, 2003.

Mehl, Dieter. *The Middle English Romances of the Thirteenth and Fourteenth Centuries*. New York: Barnes and Noble, Inc., 1969.

Meibom, Heinrich, Jr., ed. *Henrici Wolteri Canonici S. Anscharii Bremensis Archiepiscopatus Bremensis Chronicon*. In *Rerum Germanicarum Scriptores Germanici* 2. Helmæstadii: Georgii Wolffgangi Hammii, 1688. [Wolter's Chronicle]

Meiners, Johannes. *Die Handschriften P [R, W] = Fassung II des festländischen Bueve de Hantone*. Göttingen: Friedrich Haensch, 1914.

Memmer, Adolf. *Die altfranzösische Bertasage und das Volksmärchen*. Romanistische Arbeiten 20. Halle (Saale): Niemeyer, 1935.

Ménard, Philippe. *Le rire et le sourire dans le roman courtois en France au Moyen Âge (1150–1250)*. Publications romanes et françaises 105. Geneva: Droz, 1969.

Menéndez-Pidal, Ramón. "«Galiene la belle» y los palacios de Galiana en Toledo." In idem, *Poesía árabe y poesía europea*, 71–92. Buenos Aires: Espasa-Calpe Argentina, S.A., 1941. First published in *Anales de la Universidad de Madrid* 1 (1933): 1–14.

———, ed. *Primera crónica general de España que mandó componer Alfonso el Sabio y se continuaba bajo Sancho IV en 1289*. 2 vols. Madrid: Editorial Gredos, 1955.

———. *Romancero Hispánico (hispano-portugués, americano y sefardí)*. 2 vols. In idem, *Obras completas* 9–10. Madrid: Espasa-Calpe, 1953.

Merceron, Jacques. *Le Message et sa fiction. La communication par messager dans la littérature française des XIIe et XIIIe siècles*. University of California Publications in Modern Philology 128. Berkeley: University of California Press, 1998.

Meredith-Jones, Cyril, ed. *Historia Karoli Magni et Rotholandi ou Chronique du Pseudo-Turpin: Textes revus et publiés d'après 49 manuscrits*. Paris: Droz, 1936.

Métraux, Daniel, ed. *A Critical Edition of L'istoire le Roy Charlemaine: poème épique du XIVe siècle*. 3 vols. Lewiston: E. Mellen Press, 2003. [Seen in computer script, 2000].

Meyer, Paul. "De l'expansion de la langue française en Italie pendant le Moyen Age." In *Atti del Congresso Internazionale di scienze storiche, 4: Atti della sessione III: Storia della letteratura*, 61–104. Rome: Salviucci, 1904.

Micha, Alexandre. "Deux sources de la 'Mort Artu'." *Zeitschrift für romanische Philologie* 66 (1950): 369–72.

Michel, Louis. *Les Légendes epiques carolingiennes dans l'œuvre de Jean d'Outremeuse*. Académie Royale de Langue et de Littérature françaises de Belgique, Mémoire 10. Brussels: Palais des Académies, 1935.

Millardet, G. Review of 'The Franco-italian [sic] *Chevalerie Ogier,*' ed. Cerf. *Revue des langues romanes* 55 (1912): 134–36.

Miner, Dorothy, Victor I. Carlson, and P. W. Filby, comp. *2,000 Years of Calligraphy: A Three-Part Exhibition Organized by the Baltimore Museum of Art, the Peabody Institute Library and the Walters Art Gallery,* June 6–July 18, 1965. Meriden, CT: Meriden Gravure, 1965.

Moignet, Gérard, ed. *La Chanson de Roland.* Bibliothèque Bordas. New York: Larousse, 1969.

Monaci, Ernesto. 1889. *Crestomazia italiana dei primi secoli. Con prospetto delle flessioni grammaticali e glossario.* Città di Castello: S. Lapi, 1955.

Morgan, Leslie [Katherine] Zarker. "Between French and Italian: Ogier le Danois (Ms. marc. fr. 13 = 254)." Ph. D. Diss., Yale University, 1983.

———. "Berta ai piedi grandi: Historical Figure and Literary Symbol." *Olifant* 19 (1994–1995): 37–56.

———. "Evidence of Oral Interference in Franco-Italian." *Canadian Journal of Linguistics/Revue Canadienne de Linguistique* 30 (1985): 407–14.

———. "Female *enfances*: At the Intersection of Romance and Epic." In *The Court Reconvenes: Courtly Literature Across the Disciplines,* ed. Barbara K. Altmann and Carleton W. Carroll, 141–49. Cambridge: D. S. Brewer, 2003.

———. "Franco-Italian Epic: The *Geste Francor* (anonymous)." In *On-Line Reference Book for Medieval Studies (Encyclopedia)* http://www.the-orb.net/encyclop/culture/lit/Italian/morgan-a.html. 18 August 2002 update.

———. "A Franco-Italian Etymological Note: *Borfolu.*" *Neophilologus* 85 (2001): 529–34.

———. "Franco-Italian Lexicon: Problems with *l*'s." Unpublished paper, International Medieval Conference, Kalamazoo, MI, May 1998.

———. "Meter and Rhyme in Franco-Italian Ms. 13 (The *Geste Francor*)." *Italian Culture* 11 (1993): 13–29.

———."The Passion of Ynide: Ynide's Defense in *Huon d'Auvergne* (Berlin, Staatsbibliothek, Hamilton 337)." *Medioevo Romanzo* 27 (2003): 67–85, 425–62.

———. "A Preliminary Examination of Humor in Northern Italian Tradition: The Franco-Italian Epic." *Humor* 15 (2002): 129–53.

———. Review of *La Geste francor,* ed. Rosellini. *Forum Italicum* 22 (1988): 294–98.

———. "What's so Funny About Roland? (O)Roland(o)'s Life and Works in the Northern Italian Tradition." In *L'Épopée romane: Actes du XVe Congrès international Rencesvals,* Poitiers, 21–27 août 2000, ed. Gabriel Bianciotto and

Claudio Galderisi, 1: 377–92. Poitiers: Université de Poitiers, Centre d'Études supérieures de civilisation médiévale, 2002.

Morini, Luigina. Review of *La "Geste Francor" di Venezia*, ed. Rosellini. *Romance Philology* 45 (1992): 547–54.

Morrissey, R. *Charlemagne and France: A Thousand Years of Mythology*, trans. C. Tihanyi. Notre Dame: University of Notre Dame Press, 2003.

Muratori, Ludovico Antonio. *Antiquitates Italicae Medii Aevi, etc.* Milan: Palatinae, 1739.

Murrin, Michael. *The Allegorical Epic*: *Essays on Its Rise and Decline*. Chicago: University of Chicago Press, 1980.

Mussafia, Adolfo. "Handschriftliche Studien II. Zu den altfranzösischen Handschriften der Markus-Bibliothek in Venedig." *Sitzungsberichte der K[aiserlichen] Akademie der Wissenschaften [Vienna], Philosophisch-Historische Classe* 42 (1863): 276–326.

———, ed. "Berta de li gran pié." *Romania* 3 (1874): 339–64; 4 (1875): 91–107.

———, ed. "Berta e Milone–Orlandino." *Romania* 14 (1885): 177–206.

———, ed. *Macaire. Ein altfranzösisches Gedicht*. Altfranzösische Gedichte aus venezianischen Handschriften 2. Vienna: Carl Gerold's Sohn, 1864.

———, ed. *La Prise de Pampelune. Ein altfranzösisches Gedicht*. Altfranzösische Gedichte aus venezianischen Handschriften 1. Vienna: Carl Gerold, 1864.

Mussons [Freixas], Anna Maria. "Berthe ou le labyrinthe généalogique." *Revue des langues romanes* 94 (1990): 39–59.

———. "La Història del rei Pipí i la filla de l'emperador d'Alemanya." In *Actes du XIe Congrès international de la Société Rencesvals (Barcelona, 22–27 août 1988)*, special issue of *Boletín de la Real Academia de Buenas Letras de Barcelona* 21–22 (1990): 297–312.

Newth, Michael A., trans. *The Song of Aspremont (La Chanson d'Aspremont)*. Garland Library of Medieval Literature B 61. New York and London: Garland Publishing, Inc., 1989.

Nosow, Harold. "The Double Image of Charlemagne." Ph.D. Diss., New York University, 1985.

Novati, Francesco. "I codici francesi de' Gonzagi secondo nuovi documenti." *Romania* 19 (1890): 161–200.

Obergfell, Sandra Cheshire. "The Problem of Didacticism in the Romance Epic: *Aiol*." *Olifant* 6 (1978): 21–33.

———. "The Father-Son Combat Motif as Didactic Theme in Old French Literature." *Kentucky Romance Quarterly* 26 (1979): 333–48.

Oeckel, Fritz. *Ort und Zeit der Entstehung der Fassung II des festländischen Boeve von Hantone*. Diss. Universität Göttingen, 1911; Göttingen: Dieterich'schen Universitäts-Buchdruckerei, 1911.

Paetz, Hermann G. W. H. *Ueber die gegenseitige Verhältnis der venetianischen, der franko-italienischen und der französischen gereimten Fassungen des Beuve de Hantone*. Beihefte zur *Zeitschrift für romanische Philologie* 50. Halle: Niemeyer, 1913.

Paris, Gaston. *Histoire poétique de Charlemagne*. 1905. Repr. Geneva: Slatkine, 1974.

———. "La Karlmagnus-Saga, Histoire islandaise de Charlemagne." *Bibliothèque de l'École des chartes* 5 (1864): 89–123, 6 (1865): 1–42.

———. "*Mainet*: fragments d'une chanson de geste du XIIe siècle." *Romania* 4 (1875): 305–37.

———, and Alphonse Bos, eds. *La Vie de Saint Gilles par Guillaume de Berneville. Poème du XIIe siècle*. Société des anciens textes français. Paris: Firmin Didot, 1881.

———, and Ulysse Robert, eds. "Miracle de Berte." In *Miracles de Nostre Dame par personnages*, 5: 154–255. Société des anciens textes français. Paris: Firmin Didot, 1880.

Paris, Paulin. *Li Romans de Berte aus grans piés*. Romans des douze pairs de France 1. Paris: Techener, 1832.

Passera, Elsa. "The Semantic Evolution of the Latin Terms *Domina*, *Femina*, and *Mulier*." *Quaderni d'italianistica* 19 (1998): 105–25.

Pelan, Margaret M., ed. *Floire et Blancheflor. Edition du ms. 1447 du fonds français avec notes, variantes et glossaire*. Publications de la Faculté des Lettres de l'Université de Strasbourg, Textes d'étude. Paris: Les Belles Lettres, 1956.

Pellegrini, Giambattista. "Franco-veneto e veneto antico." *Filologia romanza* 3 (1956): 122–40.

———. "Osservazioni sulla lingua franco-veneta di V4." In *Atti dell'8º congresso internazionale di Studi Romanzi*, Firenze, 3 – 8 aprile 1956, 707–17. Florence: Sansoni, 1960.

Picherit, Jean-Louis. "L'«Apostoile» dans l'épopée." *Olifant* 9 (1982): 113–28.

Planche, Alice. "Roland fils de personne: Les structures de la parenté du héros dans le manuscrit d'Oxford." In *Charlemagne et l'épopée romane*, ed. Tyssens and Thiry, 2: 595–604.

Plouzeau, May. Review of *La Geste Francor*, ed. Rosellini. *Revue de langues modernes* 93 (1989): 171–83.

Potter, Roseanne G. "Literary Criticism and Literary Computing: The Difficulties of a Synthesis." *Computers and the Humanities* 22 (1988): 91–97.

Predelli, Maria Bendinelli. "Les Bûches et la faim: relents de pauvreté dans la littérature chevaleresque franco-vénitienne." In *Le Petit peuple dans l'occident médiéval: terminologies, perceptions, réalités*. Actes du congrès international tenu à l'Université de Montréal, 123–34. Paris: Publications de la Sorbonne, 2002.

Querzuola, Osea. "La Letteratura franco-italiana: la figura di Uggeri il Danese nel manoscritto marciano XIII di Venezia." Diss. di laurea, Università degli Studi "Ca' Foscari" di Venezia, 2001. (Electronic form, without fixed page numbers.)

Raglan, Fitz Roy Richard Somerset. *The Hero: A Study in Tradition, Myth, and Drama*. 1956. Repr. Westport, CT: Greenwood Press, 1975.

Rajna, Pio. "Frammenti di redazioni italiane del Buovo d'Antona." *Zeitschrift für romanische Philologie* 11 (1887): 153–84, 12 (1888): 463–510, 15 (1891): 47–87.

———. *Geste Francor* (photofacsimile). Milan: Bestetti e Tuminelli, n.d. [but 1925 or 1926].

———. *Le origini dell'epopea francese*. Florence: Sansoni, 1884.

———. *Ricerche intorno ai "Reali di Francia."* Bologna: Gaetano Romagnoli, 1872.

———. "Ricordi di codici francesi posseduti dagli Estensi nel secolo XV." *Romania* 2 (1873): 49–58.

———. "La rotta di Roncisvalle nella letteratura cavalleresca italiana." *Il Propugnatore* 3.2 (1870): 384–409, 4.1 (1872): 52–78, 333–90, 4.2 (1872): 53–133.

———. "Il Teatro di Milano e i canti intorno ad Orlando e Ulivieri." *Archivio Storico Lombardo* 14 (1887): 6–28.

———. "Uggeri il danese nella letteratura romanzesca degl'Italiani." *Romania* 2 (1873): 153–69; 3 (1874): 31–77; 4 (1875): 398–436.

Reiffenberg, Baron de, ed. *Chronique rimée de Philippe Mouskes*. Bound with Supplément and Supplément 1845. Brussels: M. Hayez, 1836–1838.

Reinhold, Joachim. Review of *Di alcune Enfances dell'epopea francese*, ed. Chichmaref. *Literaturblatt für germanische und romanische Philologie* 33 (1912): 246–50.

———. Review of *The Franco-Italian Chevalerie Ogier*, ed. Cerf. *Literaturblatt für germanische und romanische Philologie* 33 (1912): 23–25.

———. Review of *The Franco-Italian Chevalerie Ogier*, ed. Cerf. *Zeitschrift für romanische Philologie* 36 (1912): 244–48.

———. Review of *Die franko-italienische Version der Enfances Ogier nach dem Codex Macianus XIII* [sic], ed. Jul. Subak. *Literaturblatt für germanische und romanische Philologie* 33 (1912): 19–23.

———. "Über die verschiedenen Fassungen der Bertasage." *Zeitschrift für romanische Philologie* 35 (1911): 1–30, 129–52.

———, ed. "Die franko-italienische Version des Bovo d'Antone." *Zeitschrift für romanische Philologie* 35 (1911): 555–607, 683–714; 36 (1912): 1–32, 512.

———, ed. "Karleto." *Zeitschrift für romanische Philologie* 37 (1913): 27–56, 145–76, 287–312, 641–78.

Renzi, Lorenzo. "Per la lingua dell'*Entrée d'Espagne*." *Cultura neolatina* 30 (1970): 59–87.

Rey, Agapito. "Las Leyendas del ciclo carolingio en la *Gran conquista de ultramar*." *Romance Philology* 3 (1949–1950): 172–81.

Richthofen, Erich von. "Seuilla-Sebile-Sisbe, Sigelint (*Mainete, Sebile/Macaire, Thidrekssaga/Nibelungen)." In *Mélanges de philologie romane dédiés à la mémoire de Jean Boutière (1899–1967)*, ed. Irénée Cluzel and François Pirot, 1: 501–6. Liège: Editions Soledi, 1971.

Riebe, Paul. *Über die verschiedenen Fassungen der Mainetsage. Nebst Textprobe aus Girart's von Amiens Charlemagne*. Greifswald: Hans Adler, 1906.

Riquer, Martín de. "Cantares de gesta francoitalianos y persistencia de epopeya francesa en Italia." In *Los cantares de gestas francesas: Sus problemas, su relación con España*, 346–50. Biblioteca romanica hispanica 3. Madrid: Editorial Gredos, 1952.

Robinson, F[red] N[orris]. "The Irish Lives of Guy of Warwick and Bevis of Hampton." *Zeitschrift für celtische Philologie* 6 (1908): 9–180, 273–338.

Rolland, Isabelle. "Le Mythe carolingien et l'art du vitrail. Sur le choix et l'ordre des épisodes dans le vitrail de Charlemagne a la cathédrale de Chartres." In *La chanson de geste. Mélanges René Louis*, n. ed., 255–77.

Romagnoli, Gaetano, ed. *L'Orlandino. Canti due di Messer Pietro Aretino*. Scelta di curiosità letterarie inedite o rare dal secolo XIII al XIX. In appendice alla Collezione di Opere inedite o rare. Dispensa 95. 1868. Repr. Bologna: Commissione per i testi di lingua, 1968 or 1975 (two dates in volume).

Roncaglia, Aurelio. "Rolando e il peccato di Carlomagno." In *Symposium in honorem Prof. M. de Riquer*, 315–47. Barcelona: Universitat-Quaderns Crema, 1984.

―――, and Fabrizio Beggiato, eds. *Andrea da Barberino: I Reali di Francia*. Storia e documenti. Brugherio-Milan: Gherardo Casini Editore, 1987.

Roques, Gilles. Review of *La Geste Francor*, ed. Rosellini. *Revue de linguistique romane* 51 (1987): 641–43.

Rosellini, Aldo. "Il cosiddetto franco-veneto: Retrospettive e prospettive." *Filologia moderna* 2 (1977): 219–303; 4 (1980): 221–61.

―――. "Iterazione sinonimica nel cod. XIII del fondo francese della Marciana." In *Diacronia, sincronia e cultura: Saggi linguistici in onore di Luigi Heilmann*, 421–37. Pubblicazioni del Centro di linguistica dell'Università cattolica, Saggi e monografie 4. Brescia: La Scuola, 1984.

―――, ed. *La Geste Francor di Venezia. Edizione integrale del Codice XIII del Fondo francese della Marciana*. Saggi e monografie 6. Pubblicazioni del centro di linguistica dell'Università cattolica. Brescia: La Scuola, 1986.

Roussel, Claude. "Le Mélange des genres dans les chansons de gestes tardives." In *Les Chansons de Geste*, ed. Carlos Alvar and Juan Paredes, 65–85. Granada: Universidad de Granada, 2005.

Ruelle, Pierre, ed. *Huon de Bordeaux*. Université Libre de Bruxelles, Travaux de la Faculté de Philosophie et Lettres 20. Brussels: Presses Universitaires de Bruxelles, 1960.

Ruggieri, Ruggero M., ed. *Li Fatti di Spagna. Testo settentrionale trecentesco già detto "Viaggio di Carlo Magno in Ispagna."* Istituto di Filologia Romanza della Università di Roma, Studi e testi 1. Modena: Società tipografica modenese, 1951.

―――. "Origine, struttura e caratteri del Franco-veneto." *Orbis* 10 (1961): 20–30. Repr. in idem, ed., *L'influsso francese in Italia nel Medioevo*, 113–35 and in idem, ed., *Saggi di linguistica italiana e italo romanza*, 159–68.

―――, ed. *L'influsso francese in Italia nel Medioevo*. Corso di filologia romanza, 1968–1969. Rome: DeSanctis, n.d. [1970?].

―――, ed. *Saggi di linguistica italiana e italo romanza* [sic]. Biblioteca dell'«Archivum Romanicum» Serie II: Linguistica 29. Florence. Olschki, 1962.

Rumpf, Marianne. "Berta." In *Enzyklopädie des Märchens*, ed. Ranke et al., 2: 156–62.

Ryding, William W. *Structure in Medieval Narrative*. The Hague-Paris: Mouton, 1971.

Salmi, Mario. *La miniatura italiana*. Milan: Electra editrice, 1956.

Saly, Antoinette. "La Date du *Charlemagne* de Girart d'Amiens." In *Au Carrefour des routes d'Europe*, 2: 975–81.

Sander, Gustav. "Die Fassung T des festländischen Bueve de Hantone." Diss. Universität Göttingen, 1912.

Scheffer-Boichorst, Paulus, ed. *Chronica Albrici monaci Trium Fontium a monacho novi monasterii Hoiensis interpolata.* Monumenta Germaniae Historica, Scriptores 23. Hannover: Hahn, 1874. Repr. New York: Kraus Reprint, 1963.

Scheler, August. "Fragments uniques d'un roman du XIIIme siècle sur la reine Sebile, restitués, complétés et annotés d'après le manuscrit original récemment acquis par la Bibliothèque royale de Bruxelles." *Bulletin de l'Académie de Belgique,* 2e série, 39 (1875): 404–23.

———, ed. *Li Roumans de Berte aus grans piés par Adenés le Rois.* Brussels: Comptoir Universel/C. Muquardt, 1874.

Schlauch, Margaret. *Chaucer's Constance and Accused Queens.* New York: New York Unversity Press, 1927.

Schröder, Edward. *Die Kaiserchronik eines Regensburger geistlichen.* MGH Vernaculara Lingua Tomi 1. Pars 1. Hannover: Hahn, 1892.

Schwab, Hans-Rüdiger, ed. *Ludwig Uhland. Werke. Gedichte Dramen Versepik und Prosa.* Frankfurt am Main: Insel Verlag, 1983.

Shen, Lucia Simpson. *The Old-French 'Enfances' Epics and their Audience.* Ann Arbor: UMI, 1982.

Sholod, Barton. "Charlemagne and Roland. A Mysterious Relationship?" In *III Congreso internacional de la Société Rencesvals,* special issue of *Boletín de la Real Academia de Buenas Letras de Barcelona* 31 (1965–1966): 313–19.

———. *Charlemagne in Spain: The Cultural Legacy of Roncesvalles.* Geneva: Droz, 1966.

Short, Ian, ed. and trans. *La Chanson de Roland.* Paris: Le livre de poche, 1990.

Sicari, Carmelina. *La Canzone d'Aspromonte: Poema epico del XV secolo. Antologia con prefazione e note.* Vibo Valentia: QUALECULTURA, 1991.

Sinclair, Keith V., ed. *Tristan de Nanteuil: chanson de geste inédite.* Assen: Van Gorcum, 1971.

Skårup, Povl. "Contenu, sources, rédactions." In *Karlamagnús Saga,* ed. Togeby et al., 331–55.

Skeat, W. W., trans. *The Songs and Ballads of Uhland. Translated from the German.* London: Williams and Norgate, 1864.

Smith, Jerry Christopher. "Elia Levita's 'Bovo-Buch': A Yiddish Romance of the Early 16th Century." Ph.D. Diss., Cornell University, 1968.

Smith, Marc H. "Conseils pour l'édition des documents en langue italienne (XIVe–XVIIe siècle)." *Bibliothèque de l'école des chartes* 159 (2001): 541–78.

Spiller, Reinhold, ed. *Ulrich Füetrer. Bayerische Chronik.* Quellen und Erörterungen zur bayerischen und deutschen Geschichte, N. F. 2. Abt. 2. 1909. Repr. Aalen: Scientia Verlag, 1969.

Staines, David. "Cycle: The Misreading of a Trope." In *Cyclification*, ed. Besamusca, 108–10.

Stendardo, Guido, ed. *Niccolò da Casola. La Guerra d'Attila: Poema franco-italiano.* 2 vols. Modena: Società tipografica modenese, 1941.

Stimming, Albert, ed. *Der anglonormannische Boeve de Haumtone.* Biblioteca normannica 7. Halle: Max Niemeyer, 1899.

———, ed. *Der festländische Bueve de Hantone, Fassung I.* Gesellschaft für romanische Literatur 25. Dresden: Max Niemeyer, 1911.

———, ed. *Der festländische Bueve de Hantone, Fassung II.* Gesellschaft für romanische Literatur 41. Dresden: Niemeyer, 1918.

———, ed. *Der festländische Bueve de Hantone, Fassung II*, 1. Gesellschaft für romanische Literatur 30. Dresden: Niemeyer, 1912.

———, ed. *Der festländische Bueve de Hantone, Fassung III*, 1. Gesellschaft für romanische Literatur 34. Dresden: Max Niemeyer, 1914.

———, ed. *Der festländische Bueve de Hantone, Fassung III*, 2. Gesellschaft für romanische Literatur 42. Dresden: Niemeyer, 1920.

Strauch, Philipp, ed. *Jansen Enikels Werke.* Monumenta Germaniae Historica, Deutsche Chroniken. Hannover: Hahnsche Buchhandlung, 1900.

Sturm-Maddox, Sara, and Donald Maddox, eds. *Transtextualities: Of Cycles and Cyclicity in Medieval French Literature.* MRTS 149. Binghamton: Medieval and Renaissance Texts and Studies, 1995.

Suard, François. "Ogier le danois au XIVe et XVe siècles." In *Société Roncesvalles*, 4e Congrès international (Heidelberg 1967), 54–62. Studia Romanica 14. Heidelberg: A. C. Winter, 1969.

Subak, Julius, ed. "Die franko-italienische Version des *Enfances Ogier* nach dem Codex Marcianus XIII." *Zeitschrift für romanische Philologie* 33 (1909): 536–70.

———. Review of *Die franko-italienische Version des 'Bovo d'Antona'*, ed. Joachim Reinhold. *Literaturblatt für germanische und romanische Philologie* 34 (1913): 405–8.

Subrenat, Jean. "Un Héros épique atypique: le chien d'Auberi dans *Macaire*." In *Studies in Honor of Hans-Erich Keller: Medieval French and Occitan Literature and Romance Linguistics*, ed. Rupert T. Pickens, 81–96. Kalamazoo: Medieval Institute Publications, 1993.

Taylor, Archer. "The Biographical Pattern in Traditional Narrative." *Journal of the Folklore Institute* 1 (1964): 114–29.

Taylor, Steven M. "Comic Incongruity in Medieval French *Enfances*." *Romance Quarterly* 35 (1988): 3–10.

Theodor, Hugo. *Die komischen Elemente der altfranzösischen chansons de geste*. Beihefte zur *Zeitschrift zur romanische Philologie* 48. Halle a. S.: Niemeyer, 1913.

Thomas, Antoine. "Aquilon de Bavière. Roman franco-italien inconnu." *Romania* 11 (1882): 538–69.

———, ed. *L'Entrée d'Espagne. Chanson de geste franco-italienne*. 2 vols. Société des anciens textes français. Paris: Firmin Didot, 1913.

Thomas, Jacques, ed. *Renaut de Montauban*. Geneva: Droz, 1989.

Thomas, Marcel, trans. *La Geste de Roland: Textes épiques choisis, présentés et traduits*. N.p.: Firmin Didot, 1961.

Thorpe, Lewis, trans. *Einhard and Notker the Stammerer: Two Lives of Charlemagne*. Harmondsworth: Penguin, 1969.

Tiemann, Hermann, ed. *Der Roman von der Königin Sibille in drei Prosafassungen des 14. und 15. Jahrhunderts*. Mit Benutzung der nachgelassenen Materialien von Fritz Burg. Hamburg: Dr. Ernst Hauswedell Verlag, 1977.

Toesca, Pietro. *Monumenti e studi per la storia della miniatura italiana*. Milan: Ulrico Hoepli, 1930.

———. *La Pittura e la miniatura nella Lombardia. Dai più antichi monumenti alla metà del Quattrocento*. Turin: Einaudi, 1966.

Togeby, Knud. *Ogier le danois dans les littératures européennes*. Det danske Sprog- og Litteraturselskab. Copenhagen: Munksgaard, 1969.

———, ed. *Ogier le Dannoys. Roman en prose du XVe siècle*. Det danske Sprog- og Litteraturselskab. Copenhagen: Munksgaard, 1967.

———, and Pierre Halleux, eds. *Karlamagnús Saga. Branches I, III, VII et IX*. Texte norrois édité par Agnete Loth. Traduction français par Annette Patron-Godefroit. Avec une étude par Povl Skårup. Copenhagen: C.A. Reitzels Boghandel (La Société pour l'étude de la langue et de la littérature danoises), 1980.

Trotter, D. A. *Medieval French Literature and the Crusades (1100–1300)*. Geneva: Droz, 1988.

Sir Tryamour. Series Early English books, 1475–1640, 1804:22. Publisher: R. Pynson?, 1503? Repr. Ann Arbor: UMI, 1984.

Tylus, Piotr, ed. *Histoire de la Reine Berthe et du Roy Pepin. Mise en prose d'une chanson de geste*. Textes littéraires français. Geneva: Droz, 2001.

Tyssens, Madeleine, and Claude Thiry, eds. *Charlemagne et l'épopée romane*: Actes du VIIe Congrès international de la Société Rencesvals (Liège 28 août – 4 septembre 1976). Bibliothèque de la Faculté de Philosophie et Lettres de l'Université de Liège 225. Les Congrès et Colloques de l'Université de Liège 76. Paris: Les Belles Lettres, 1978.

van der Hagen, Friedrich Heinrich, ed. *Gesammtabenteur. Hundert altdeutsche Erzählungen: Ritter- und Pfaffen-Mären; Stadt- und Dorfgeschichten; Schwänke, Wundersagen und Legenden*. 2 vols. Stuttgart—Tübingen: J.G. Cotta'scher Verlag, 1850.

van Dijk, Hans."Ogier le Danois." In *L'épopée romane au Moyen Âge*, ed. S. Luongo, 1: 525–34. Naples: Fridericiana Editrice Universitaria, 2001.

van Emden, Wolfgang G. "Quelques hapax de mes connaissances." In *Ce nous dist li escris... che est la verite. Études de littérature médiévale offertes à André Moisan*, ed. Miren Lacassagne, 289–303. Sénéfiance 45. Aix-en-Provence: CUER MA (Centre Universitaire d'Études et de Recherches Médiévales d'Aix), 2000.

———, and Philip E. Bennett, eds. *Guillaume d'Orange and the Chanson de geste: Essays Presented to Duncan McMillan in Celebration of his Seventieth Birthday by his Friends and Colleagues of the Société Rencesvals*. Reading: Reading University Press, 1984.

Veillard, Françoise, and Olivier Guyotjeannine, coord. *Conseils pour l'édition des textes médiévaux*. Fascicule I: *Conseils généraux*. Paris: Comité des travaux historiques et scientifiques, École nationale de Chartes, 2001.

Viard, Jules, ed. *Les Grandes Chroniques de France*. 3 vols. Société de l'histoire de France 395, 401, 404. Paris: Société de l'histoire de France, 1920–1923.

Vidal, Julia Barella, ed. *Antonio de Eslava. Noches de Invierno*. Literatura y filologia, 24. Pamplona: Gobierno de Navarra. Departmento de Educación y Cultura, 1986.

Vine Durling, Nancy. *Permutations in Genealogy: A Study of Kinship Structure in Old French Hagiography, Chansons de Geste and Romance*. Ann Arbor: UMI, 1981.

Viscardi, Antonio. "Arthurian Influence on Italian Literature from 1200–1500." In *Arthurian Literature in the Middle Ages: A Collaborative History*, ed. R. S. Loomis, 419–29. Oxford: Clarendon Press, 1959.

———. *Letteratura franco-italiana*. Istituto di filologia romanza della R. Università di Roma, Testi e manuali 21. Modena: Società tipografica modenese, 1941.

Viscardi, Jean. *Le Chien de Montargis. Etude de folklore juridique*. Etudes de sociologie et d'ethnologie juridiques 9. Paris: Domat-Montchresten, 1932.

Vitale-Brovarone, Alessandro. "De la Chanson de *Huon d'Auvergne* à la *Storia di Ugone d'Avernia* d'Andrea da Barberino: techniques et méthodes de la traduction et de l'élaboration." In *Charlemagne et l'épopée romane*, ed. Tyssens and Thiry, 2: 393–403.

Vitullo, Juliann Marie. *Constructing an Urban Mythology: The Chivalric Epic in Medieval Italy*. Gainesville: University Press of Florida, 2000.

Voigt, F. Theodore A. *Roland-Orlando dans l'épopée française et italienne*. Leiden: E. J. Brill, 1938.

Voretzsch, Carl. *Über die Sage von Ogier dem Dänen und die Entstehung der Chevalerie Ogier: Ein Beitrag zur Entwicklung des altfranzösischen Heldenepos*. Halle: Niemeyer, 1891.

Wagner, Robert-Léon. *Les Phrases hypothétiques commençant par "si" dans la langue française, des origines à la fin du 16e siècle*. Paris: Droz, 1939.

Wais, Kurt. "Märchen und Chanson de geste: Themengeschichtliches zu *Robert le Diable, Berte aus grans piés, Loher und Maller*." In *Festgabe Julius Wilhelm zum 80. Geburtstag*, ed. Hugo Laitenberger, special issue, *Zeitschrift für französische Sprache und Literatur*, Beiheft, n. s. 5: 120–38, 314–34. Wiesbaden: Steiner, 1977.

Waitz, Giorgio, ed. *Gotifredi Viterbiensis Speculum Regum*. Monumenta Germaniae Historica, Scriptores 22. Hannover: Hahn, 1872.

Walpole, Ronald N., ed. *Le Turpin français, dit le Turpin I*. Toronto Medieval Texts and Translations. Toronto: University of Toronto Press, 1985.

Warren, F[rederick] M[orris]. "The Arabic Origin of *Galafre, Galienne*, and *Orable*." *Modern Philology* 27 (1929–1930): 23–26.

Watkin, Morgan. "Albert Stimming's *Welsche Fassung* in the *Anglonormannische Boeve de Haumtone*: An Examination of a Critique." In *Studies in French Language and Literature Presented to Mildred K. Pope*, 371–79. Manchester: Manchester University Press, 1939.

Weiss, Judith. "The Major Interpolations in *Sir Beues of Hamtoun*." *Medium Aevum* 48 (1979): 71–76.

Wolf, Adolf. "Das gegenseitige Verhältnis der gereimten Fassungen des festländischen Bueve de Hantone." Diss. Universität Göttingen, 1912.

Wolf, Fernando José, and Conrado Hofmann. *Primavera y flor de romances ó coleccion de los mas viejos y mas populares romances castellanos*. Berlin: A. Asher, 1856.

Wolf, Romaine. "Nouer l'amour, nouer la mort: la ceinture sarrassine dans *Beuve de Hantone*." In *« Si a parlé par moult ruiste vertu»: Mélanges de littérature médiévale offerts à Jean Subrenat*, ed. Jean Dufournet, 551–71. Paris: Champion, 2000.

Wolfzettel, Friedrich. "Zur Stellung und Bedeutung der *Enfances* in der altfranzösischen Epik I, II." *Zeitschrift für französische Sprache und Literatur* 83 (1972): 317–48; 84 (1974): 1–32.

———. Review of *Les Versions françaises et étrangères des Enfances de Charlemagne*, by Jacques Horrent. *Zeitschrift für romanische Philologie* 99 (1983): 168–71.

Wunderli, Peter. "Interferenze in franco-italiano. L'esempio dell'« Aquilon de Bavière»." *Vox Romanica* 59 (1999): 142–44.

———. "Un luogo di 'interferenze': Il franco-italiano." In *La Cultura dell'Italia padana e la presenza francese nei secoli XIII–XV* (Pavia, 11–14 settembre 1994), ed. Luigina Morini, 55–66. Alessandria: Edizioni dell'Orso, 2001.

———, ed. *Raffaele da Verona. Aquilon de Bavière. Roman franco-italien en prose (1379–1407)*. 2 vols. Beihefte zur *Zeitschrift für romanische Philologie* 188, 189. Tübingen: Max Niemeyer Verlag, 1982.

Yeadle, Frederic George, ed. *Girart de Vienne*. New York: Columbia University Press, 1930.

Zambon, Francesco. "La «materia di Francia» nella letteratura franco-veneta." In *Sulle orme di Orlando: Leggende e luoghi carolingi in Italia: i paladini di Francia nelle tradizioni italiane, una proposta storico-antropologica*, ed. A. I. Galletti and R. Roda, 53–64. Padua: Interbooks, 1987.

Zannetti, Antonio M. *Latina et Italica D. Marci Biblioteca Codicum Manu Scriptorum. Per titulos digesta*. Venezia: Simone Occhi, 1741.

Zaunert, Paul, ed. *Das deutsche Volksbuch von Karl dem Grossen (Das Buch vom heiligen Karl)*. Jena: Eugen Diederichs, 1929.

Zorzi, Marino, ed. *Biblioteca Marciana, Venezia*. Le grandi biblioteche d'Italia. Florence: Nardini Editore, Centro Internazionale del Libro, 1988.

6.0
Edition, V¹³: Introduction

6.1 Editorial Norms

In preparing this edition, two criteria have been followed: ease of use for the modern reader and closeness to the manuscript reading. "Ease of use" means a text that is readable yet responsible, without too many distractions while still making clear to the reader where editorial decisions have influenced the appearance of the text. "Closeness to the manuscript reading" means following the scribe unless the meaning is incomprehensible or there is clearly a lacuna. Lacunae are annotated, along with the proposed emendations, both mine and those of other editors. Footnotes on the same page as the text give alternative readings — the manuscript reading where the printed text is emended or otherwise differs from it — as well as earlier editors' readings.

I note only once, at the first occurrence in a *chanson*, any differences between a previous editor's conventions and my own, in the endnotes. Differing punctuation in various editions is not noted unless it conveys a difference in meaning, as, for example, in the use of quotations. In several cases previous editors deviate from their normal usage in one or two places; these are mentioned in the endnotes.

An asterisk at the end of a line in the text refers to an endnote. Following the entire text, the endnotes comment on meanings, differing readings, and literary aspects of the text. The endnotes for each *chanson* also list previous editors and the conventions of their editions. Meaning is discussed where relevant, and possible translations of difficult passages offered. I also discuss manuscript imperfections, scribal errors and / or corrections, and any issues about punctuation. Though footnotes give other editors' readings, it is also sometimes necessary to elaborate upon my choice of reading, and in that case, again, explanations appear in the endnotes. References to previous portions of the story line, inconsistencies with previous events, motifs of note in relation to other texts, and interesting points about specific characters are among the plot elements which also appear in the endnotes.

The manuscript itself contains no punctuation other than a period at the end of a line and periods (usually, but not consistently) around roman numerals and abbreviations to distinguish them from text. I have included those around roman numerals and made them consistent. I have used modern punctuation to aid comprehension. Each verse begins with a capital, which is kept here conventionally. Other capitals have been added, for adjectives referring to nationalities or regions, and to proper names of people or of geographical regions. For use of the apostrophe and raised period, see below in the section on accents.

6.2 Equivalency to Other Editions

The line numbers of earlier, partial editions are noted in parentheses after the text in relevant sections, as explained in the endnotes at the beginning of each *chanson* segment. To show the line number and division differences, here, in outline form, is the list of editions and line numbers. In the chart below, italicized numbers indicate line number differences between editions. Square brackets [] indicate the equivalent line numbers in one edition for another edition's beginning or end; the number without brackets is therefore the edition which begins or ends at that line. Thus, for example, all editors begin *Berta da li pe grant* at the same point, but I end it at line 2917 where others end at the equivalent of my 2912. For each segment of the manuscript, the earlier editor(s)' line numbers are in parentheses after the lines to facilitate comparison.

Bovo 1[1]

fol.	line # (this edition)	Rosellini	Others
1[ra]	1	1	Reinhold 1
	33	33	33
	34	37	37
	58	—	—
	59	61	61
	69	—	—
1[va]	70	71	71
7rb	1163	1164	1164

Berta da li pe grant[2]

7rb	1164	1165	Mussafia/Cremonesi 1/1
	2823	2824	1660–61/1660–6
[16vb	2912]	2913	1750/1750
16vb	2917	[2918]	[—/—]

---

[1] Editions of *Bovo*, Parts I and II: J. Reinhold, ed., "Die franko-italienische Version des *Bovo d'Antone*," *Zeitschrift für romanische Philologie* 35 (1911): 555–607, 683–714; 36 (1912): 1–32, 512; Rosellini, *Geste Francor*, "Bovo d'Antona," 199–233, 293–373.

[2] Editions of *Berta da li pe grant*: A. Mussafia, ed., "Berta de li gran pié," *Romania* 3 (1874): 339–64; 4 (1875): 91–107; C. Cremonesi, ed., *Berta da li pè grandi: Codice marciano XIII* (Milan: Varese, 1966); Rosellini, *Geste Francor*, "Berta da li pe grandi," 237–90.

Bovo 2

[16vb	2913]	2914	Reinhold 1165
16vb	2918	[2919]	[1170]
31ra	5490	5491	3742

Karleto[3]

31ra	5491	5492	Chichmaref/Reinhold 1/1
[31vb	5641]	[5642]	151/[151]
[33vb	5990]	[5991]	152/[500]
[43va	7536]	[7537]	1703/[2046]
51vb	9026	9027	[—]/3535

Berta e Milone[4]

51vb	9027	9028	Mussafia/Cremonesi [—/—]
[52ra	9055]	[9056]	1/1
54rb	9495	9496	441/441 (442–453)

Enfances Ogier[5]

54rb	9496	9497	Cremonesi/Subak 1/1
61vb	10895	[10896]	[1400/1400]
[62ra	10906]	10907	1411/1411

Orlandino

61vb	10896	[10897]	Cremonesi/Mussafia [—]/[—]
[62ra	10907]	10908	1/1
64rb	11335	[11336]	[430/429*] *error, 429 given as 430
[64vb	11381]	11382]	476/475* (see above)

---

[3] Editions of *Karleto*: V. F. Chichmaref, ed., "Di alcune enfances dell'epopea francese; il *Karleto* del Codice XIII della Marciana," *Zapiski Neofilologicheskago obshchestva pri Imperatorskom Petrogradskom Universitete* 5 (1911): 194–237; J. Reinhold, ed., "Karleto," *Zeitschrift für romanische Philologie* 37 (1913): 27–56, 145–76, 287–312, 641–78; Rosellini, *Geste Francor*, "Karleto," 377–485.

[4] Editions of *Berta e Milone* and *Orlandino/Rolandin*: A. Mussafia, ed., "Berta e Milone. — Orlandino," *Romania* 14 (1885): 177–206; C. Cremonesi, ed., *Berta e Milon, Rolandin: Codice Marciano XIII* (Milan: La Goliardica, 1973); Rosellini, *Geste Francor*, "Berta e Milon," 489–503; "Rolandin," 553–67.

[5] Editions of *Ogier*: J. Subak, ed., "Die franko-italienische Version des *Enfances Ogier* nach dem Codex Marcianus XIII," *Zeitschrift für romanische Philologie* 33 (1909): 536–70; C. Cremonesi, ed., *Le Danois Oger. Enfances — Chevalerie. Codice Marciano XIII* (Milan: Cisalpino-Goliardica, 1977); Rosellini, *Geste Francor*, "Enfances Ogier," 507–49; "Chevalerie Ogier," 571–634.

Chevalerie Ogier[6]

65rb	11336	[11337]		Cremonesi/Cerf [–]/[–]
[64[vb]	11382]	11383		1412/1
70[va]	12456	—		—
[76[ra]	13456]	[13456]		3485/[2074]
76[ra]	13477	[13477]		[—/2083]
[76[rb]	13500]	13500		[—]/2118

Macario[7]

[76[ra]	13454]	[13454]		Guessard/Mussafia 1/[—]
76[rb]	13478	[13478]		[25]/[–]
[76[rb]	13501]	13501		[48]/1
96[vb]	17067	17067		3615/3566

6.3 Line Numbering and Rubric Positioning

The beginning of the manuscript is missing and the initial fol. is in very poor condition. It is torn and damaged. Lines 12–15, 33–47, 56–63, 65–70 are not easily readable. On the verso, ll. 101–117 are similarly damaged. Rosellini has included unreadable lines (his numbers 34, 35, 36, and 68) in his count (*Geste Francor*, 200). He omits my line 58; there is no note or annotation to indicate why. Line 12456 may be an error of anticipation, which all earlier editors omit; it is repeated three lines later. I have included it since it might be possible that the nervous Saracen asks a question twice. One line, 2823, is quite long, though written on a single line. I and Rosellini agree on counting it as one line. Rosellini does not divide it physically, but I do. Mussafia ("Berta de li gran pié") and Cremonesi (*Berte da li pè grandi*) count it as two lines, but only Mussafia prints it on two lines.

More complicated is the issue of rubric order. The rubricator writes in a different hand from the text hand. He is clearly copying after the text was written; a small letter distinguishable in the margin before the first initial of each laisse, to be rubricated, was intended to give him a key to what was supposed to go there. However, the spaces left for rubrics are not consistent and the rubricator becomes confused at the top and bottom of pages. From the bottom of fol. 8[ra],

---

[6] For the *Chevalerie Ogier*, in addition to those editions noted in note 5, above, see also B. Cerf, ed., "The Franco-Italian *Chevalerie Ogier*," *Modern Philology* 8 (1910–1911): 187–216, 335–61, 511–25.

[7] Editions of *Macaire / Macario*: F. Guessard, ed., *Macaire, chanson de geste*, Les anciens poëtes de France (Paris: Librarie A. Franck, 1864); A. Mussafia, ed., *Macaire: Ein altfranzösisches Gedicht*, Altfranzösische Gedichte aus venezianischen Handschriften 2 (Vienna: Carl Gerold's Sohn, 1864); Rosellini, *Geste Francor*, "Macaire," 637–744.

he skips one and is therefore behind by one rubric; he loses a further rubric at fol. 13vb and does not recoup until 25ra. In the interests of comprehension, I have moved the rubrics to the laisse which they describe, but placed them in square brackets and italicized the entire rubric where out of place. For these rubrics, resolved abbreviations are *not* italicized, but in plain text to contrast with the rubrics as printed. Cremonesi (*Berte da li pè grandi*), Reinhold ("Bovo d'Antone"), and Rosellini (*Geste Francor*) keep the original order, and Mussafia ("Berta de li gran pié") omits rubrics entirely. The numbering of rubrics is therefore sequential here, but their position is altered for the segment of the text from ll. 1344–4397. Rubrics are prose and therefore multiple lines are printed together separated by a slash (/) where they can be accomodated together. A slash is not used where the rubric line ends at the end of a line.

6.4 Lexeme Division

I have followed modern usage in lexeme division, that is, standard Old French and Old Italian editing practices, where possible. However, the two languages differ in orthographical practice for lexeme division in certain cases. Preposition and conjunction are written together following Italian practice (e.g., *Porqe*). Preposition and definite article are written joined by a raised dot (e.g., *de·l canp*) before a consonant, but separately and with an apostrophe before a vowel (e.g., *a l'ami*). *Au*, the velarized form of *a* and *l*, in line 9424, the only occurrence, is also written with the raised dot. *Qele* and *dele*, the conjunction or preposition followed by a feminine object pronoun form, I have given as *Qe le* and *De le* respectively, following the Italian forms (instead of French *Q'ele* or *D'ele*, which would also be possible).[8] For palatal vowels following a consonant and preceding *s impura* (e.g., *sestoit*) I have given *se stoit* (instead of *s'estoit*; cf. *a esperon* vs. *Le speron*) where there is only one vowel, since Italian use of epenthetic palatal is relatively infrequent. For *aler*, *andar(e)*, *venir(e)* and their various forms, where there is an *a* present following the verb, I have presumed that it is a prepositional *a* before a dependent infinitive, in an attempt to minimize the alternation between lexemes with and without the *a-* prefix (e.g., *aloit a prender*). For proper place names beginning with an *A*, or verbs with an initial *a-* I presume that vowel to have been elided when missing, and represent it with an apostrophe (e.g., *a 'Ntone* = "a Antone"; *a 'Leris* = "a Aleris"; *a 'coler* = *a acoler*). For *di*, where the *i* could be a definite article, I have written the two joined by the raised dot (*d·i enfant* (l. 633) = "of the children"); otherwise I do not separate them. Similar other uses of the raised dot are discussed with written accents, below.

---

[8] See also M. Plouzeau, review of *La Geste Francor*, ed. Rosellini, *Revue de langues modernes* 93 (1989): 171–83, who discusses *ele* vs. *le* in editing line 15303 (178).

Other word frontier issues involve the division of prepositional expressions: *trosq(u)a* versus *trosq(u)'a*; division of *en* from negative; of subject pronoun from conjunctions (*qi, si* vs. *q'i, s'i*). Where possible, the division is made, thus *trosq(u)' a* + noun phrase or adverb (23 times). *Trosq(u)a/e* remains however before *a* or *i/ en* (31 times), before *i saveroit* (13887) and *el fo* (10900), the only cases in which it precedes a subject pronoun and verb. *Trosque* remains before *Saragoçe* (6617).

Another difference between the two language conventions is larger numbers. Standard modern Italian usage is to combine through the thousands into a single word, thus "quattrocento" for "four hundred." Since, however, numbers are also partially abbreviated—e.g., .V. mil—I have followed rather French standards and written each element separately.

Word division in the manuscript is not consistent, so it cannot be used as a guide for appropriate representation of lexemes. For example, the initial capital of each line is written at a distance away from the rest of the line though it may begin a word. The *a-* is written at times together with a following verb, at times apart (e.g., *apresenter* vs. *a presenter*). This is the rationale for using modern editing standards rather than the original text.

Particularly problematic on occasion is verb tense, distinguishing between the present perfect and the simple perfect (that is, between a compound or a simple tense). I have attempted to adhere to context; i.e., if other past tense forms are in the context, I have kept to the same tense as much as possible. Thus, for example, where clearly *passato prossimo / passé composé* forms are in the context, I have used the present perfect; where clearly *passato remoto / passé simple* forms are in the context, I have used the same for the unclear forms. For example, in Rubric 53, *Coment li rois d'Ongarie aconplì li voloir / de la raine, si·lle donò parole de aler in F[r]ançe*. Here, we could have either *à conpli*, the present perfect, or *aconplì*, the simple past. Since the second line is clearly simple past, so is the first. These points are annotated, so that the editor's role here is clear. The text frequently jumps from present to past in the same sentence, typical of medieval literature in general. The distinction between present and irregular perfect can also be unclear; again, any such questions are mentioned in the endnotes.

6.5 Orthography

I have kept the orthography used by the scribe, as this is of linguistic interest. The variability between certain graphic representations has been noted before, especially between *ç* and *z*, for example.

It is worth noting that *h* is rarely used. It appears with *ch* forms occasionally and in Latinisms (e.g., *hom*), and in a few cases in weapon names of Germanic origin (e.g., *hauberk, helmi*). *K* is rarely an alternative to *ch* or *c*, but primarily found in the name of Charlemagne, abbreviated *k*. Even his son, *Çarloto*, is normally represented as *Carloto / Çarloto* or *Carleto / Çarleto*.

Double consonants are also rare. In northern Italy, both in Gallo-Italic and Venetian areas, historical double consonants are generally simplified (Rohlfs, *Grammatica storica*, 321–24 [¶ 229]). Here, we find *ll* in reflexes of the Latin ILLU(M); e.g., 13079. Note that many of these, however, are in the rubrics, not within the *chansons*; ten of twelve appear in rubrics (both definite articles and pronouns). The only double letters that we find with any regularity are *l*s: *belle, selle, celle, stalle, novelle, nulle, mille, bataille, mervelle, graille*, etc. These are words of French origin, where the double *l* does not stand for a lengthened consonant, but rather a palatal. Otherwise, we find *enn* four times and *inn* once as prepositions; *nn* once and *nne* once as the pronoun (MSF *en*, MSI *ne*). There are a few other cases of double *n*: *ennavré, ennemis, ennojament/ent*, etc. A few isolated examples of double consonants of French origin appear (graphic conventions) — *arriverent; passion; tott ora*. But in the rareness of double consonants, the two speech areas, the French and Northern Italian, agree, and thus logically double consonants appear rarely in V[13]. *-ij* at the end of words (*sij, malvasij*) is a scribal convention and as such is rendered *-ii* following standard editing practice.[9]

6.6 ABBREVIATIONS

Resolutions of abbreviations are in *italics* so that the reader can clearly tell where the resolution has been made. In footnotes and endnotes I have attempted to reduplicate the original editors' formats. I have resolved following the most frequent form found unabbreviated, unless there were excellent reasons for doing otherwise, in each case noted in the text.

7: is always resolved as *et* except in three cases (lines 17, twice in 15041) where *e* allows for one less syllable in the line to keep a total of ten syllables, since in Italian two vowels coming together in a line count as one syllable. (In the following discussion, the resolutions are printed in square brackets [] where the text is italicized.) Line 17 reads *Morto l'abate, sença nosa [e] tencon*: the first hemistich, with the epic caesura is four syllables, the second six, with *nosa-e* as two syllables. Line 15041, *Cun li çivaler vait [e] arer [e] avant*, is two hemistichs of five syllables each, with *e-arer* and *e-avant* each counting as two syllables. There are only ninety-eight total examples of the abbreviation, of which eighty-two are in the text and sixteen in the rubrics. *Berta da li pe grant, Berta e Milone*, and *Chevalerie Ogier* have a somewhat fewer appearances of this abbreviation per line than other poems; it is difficult to see any pattern in its use, however.

---

[9] F. Veillard, and O. Guyotjeannin (coord.), *Conseils pour l'édition des textes médiévaux*, Fascicule I: *Conseils généraux* (Paris: Comité des travaux historiques et scientifiques, École nationale des chartes, 2001), 24.

titulus: The titulus is usually found over the preceding vowel where the nasal is missing. For the resolution of nasals, I have examined the forms present in the text, and finding an overwhelming number of *n*s, regardless of following consonant, have always resolved the nasal abbreviation into *n*, even before labials. For example, *hon* (once *hom*, l. 2501*)* is the normal form deriving from Latin HOMINEM for all appearances at rhyme position. *Home, homo* appear where there is no rhyme. Since the abbreviation is *ho*, I have resolved as *ho[n]*. The titulus also appears for *[en]*, but only in the rubrics (e.g., *Com[en]t* in Rubric 23).

[r]: Resolutions are primarily of *r*, and, like the titulus, the abbreviation mark is normally over the preceding letter. But we do also find, among others, *m[er], m[er]velos, P[er]sant, p[re]sant, p[ri]mer, p[ri]memant, p[ri]nçer, p[ri]s, p[ri]sé, s[er]pant, v[er]gognie* for a total of twenty *[er]*, five *[re]*, seventeen *[ri]* compared to fifty-five *[r]*. In the case of *p*, the stroke below the line is crossed for the abbreviation, while there is a line over the *m* for *m[er]*. Again, there are very few examples of abbreviation: a total of seventy-six, where forty-five are for *r* (of which twenty-two in rubrics, twenty-three in the text), sixteen of *r* + vowel (of which four in rubrics), fifteen of vowel + *r* (of which five in rubrics). The many abbreviations in rubrics in comparison to the text (there are 17,067 lines of text but only 738 of rubrics) further emphasizes the difficulty the workshop or scribe had with the rubrics. One in a rubric is for a word-initial *r*, where the abbreviation is on a following vowel, in rubric 38 (originally after line 1984): *[r]ois.*

ē: for *e[st]* appears eight times, in lines 640, 14102, 14126, 16344, 16671, 16713, 16732, and 16818.

Jesu x̂ρo appears once, in 9390, for *Jesu [Christ]o.*

s̄tē appears once, in 6187, for *s[an]te.*

Proper names are abbreviated, in general, for the most frequent protagonists only.

.K. is used frequently for Charlemagne. Of eighty-five full forms, there are eight variants: *Karle, Karloete,* and *Karo* each appear once (in a rubric); *Karles* and *Karloto* each appear once in the text. *Karleto* appears sixty-four times, but only within the segment of *Karleto*; *Karlon* appears written out eight times, always at the end of a line, at rhyme position; thirty-six occurrences of the abbreviation at the rhyme require this form. *Karlo* appears eight times, both initially (2338, 9027, 9681, 9692, 9761) and within the line (1244, 1275, 2314). Therefore, within *Karleto* (ll. 5491–9026), all resolutions are to *K[arleto]* except where rhyme requires *K[arlon]*. Elsewhere, I have used *K[arlo]*, again unless rhyme requires *K[arlon]*. *Karleto* appears as subject and object, as does *Karlo*. *Karlon* and *K[arlon]* at rhyme position are both subject and object form, but are usually object forms, since the subject does not normally end a line. For example, as subject, we find "ço dist li

rois Karlon" (12429) and "Quant la novela soit li rois K*arlon*" (11935) but frequently we find the noun as object of a preposition ("Or lasaren de l'inperer K*arlon*" [15498]) or the direct object ("Naimes apella l'inperaor Karlon" [14351]).

.N. for *Naimes* also appears frequently. *Namo* appears once (in a rubric); *Naymon* (at rhyme position) and *Naimeto* also each appear once; *Naymes* appears twice. The normal unabbreviated forms are *Naimes* (thirty-two appearances) or *Naimon* (twenty-four appearances). The second form is the only possibility at rhyme position (twenty-one appearances and eleven abbreviations which must be this form because of rhyme), but also appears three times in other positions in the line. Of interest is that both more frequent forms are written out for the first few appearances: fifteen times for *Naimes* and seven for *Naimon*. Here, as with *Karles* and *Karlon*, there is no distinction between subject and object case. *Naimes* appears as both (e.g., "Per fu de Naimes qe sor tot fu la flor," 1848; "Naimes le vi, forment fo irascu," 9963) as does *Naimon*, so this is not the distinguishing factor (e.g., "E questo fe fare li bon dux Naimon," 11113; "K*arlo* le vi, si n'apellò Naimon," 16489). *Naimon* does tend to appear at the end of the line, and never begins it; *Naymon* is only at rhyme position. *Naimes* is the only form to begin a line, and generally appears in the first hemistich, as does its parallel, *Naymes*. The editor is left therefore with a choice easily made at rhyme position but less so elsewhere. Since *Naimes* appears thirty-two times, *Naimon* twenty-four, I have given N[*aimes*] as the standard resolution, except at rhyme position.

.R. (.*Ro.*, in Rubrics 530, 580, 581, 585, 617) is the abbreviation for Roland. Four forms appear in the text in full: *Rolan* (three, all at rhyme position); *Rolandin* (seven, where one is at rhyme position); *Rolando* (seven); and *Rolant* (eight and two abbreviations which must be thus resolved because at rhyme position). Within *Orlandino*, *Rolandin* is clearly the form of choice, so all abbreviations are so resolved within that segment unless the rhyme requires otherwise. In the few references before *Orlandino* (lines 9393, 9480, and 9498) the meter requires three syllables and the context refers to Roland as a child, so these too are resolved R[*olandin*]. After *Orlandino*, however, R[*olando*] is used for three syllables, and R[*olant*] for two syllables and the rubrics, unless, again, the rhyme requires otherwise. There is no differentiation between subject and object case; one finds all forms, *Rolandin*, *Rolant*, and *Rolando*, as subject and object.

.B. for B[*erte*] appears once, in Rubric 40, the only abbreviation of a woman's name.

.B. for B[*ra*]*er* appears once, in Rubric 363 (after 12649), thus disproving Rosellini's comment that only Christians' names are abbreviated (*Geste Francor*, 162); we can say, however, that only main character names are abbreviated.

.G. appears for G*[uier]* (Rubric 112, after 4272).

.M. appears twice for M*[acario]* (Rubrics 411 and 413).

.O. for O*[liver]* appears once (Rubric 631), an easy resolution since *Oliver* is found everywhere (forty appearances) except in one case (Rubric 632) where we find *Olivers*.

6.7 EMENDATIONS

Editorial additions, emendations, and deletions are in parentheses ( ). They are discussed in the endnotes. Angle brackets < > indicate other editors' readings which are not clear in the manuscript but plausible and reasonable. These are attributed to their source(s) in the notes. Where I have followed other editors' emendations those are between parentheses, like all emendations. Missing words and letters are immediately evident from the footnotes, which give the manuscript reading as well as other editors' versions. The endnote will expand, as necessary, upon reasons for the choice(s) made.

As noted by editors of other Franco-Italian texts, certain letters are characteristically difficult to distinguish: e/o; c/t; i/u/m/n; s/f (see, for example, Holtus, *Bataille d'Aliscans*, xxxv–xxxvi). Where I have added lexemes, I have where possible used the most frequent form, or at least a form that appears in V^{13}, and discussed that choice in the endnotes. I have minimized emendations of specific words (e.g., adding *l*s, *n*s etc.) in order to preserve the patina of the original. However, in cases where a hapax legomenon presents itself and where no other attestations exist, I have made changes or offered possible explanations in the endnotes in order to make the text comprehensible to the reader. In all there are 545 emendations (note that this is a strict interpretation: where a letter is indistinguishable it has been marked as an emendation) of which 178, or just under 33%, are in rubrics. The emendations fall predominantly into the following categories: distribution of minims between possible letters (e.g., *u* vs. *n*, 87; *n* written for *r*, perhaps in anticipation of following *n*, 6); *c* with or without a cedilla (12); distinguishing *e, c,* and *o* (28); metatheses (22); distinguishing *s* from *f* (23); possible missing abbreviations (123; e.g., for *n* or for *r*). Many of these are typical of other manuscripts of the same era. One particular category of unusual difficulties is the use of *l* (40 cases total). Among the examples of problems: it is confused with *b, h, s* and other letters with a longer upstroke; in several cases *li* looks like *u*; *pu* and *pus* appear for *plu(s)* (982, 1096); we find *fasités* (2127) and *mesée* (3420) with missing *l*s. There are also unique errors such as confusing the names of two protagonists (e.g., *Lanfroi* replaced by *Godefroy* in *Karleto*, passim; *Bernardo* and *Morando* reversed in 7921). Other emendations are for missing words or to help comprehension. These are discussed in the endnotes as they appear. It should be noted that a total of 303 lines are emended, for less than 2% of lines (this does not, however, include rubrics or the placement of rubrics).

The rubrics are particularly problematic. As noted above, they are out of order from lines 1344–4397 (fols. 8ra to 25ra), where the scribe was clearly having difficulty writing. (This is not counted in itself as an emendation, though those rubrics are moved.) Furthermore, many of the errors would seem to derive from miscopying (e.g., *baso*, Rubric 60) or from problems with the nib of the pen. Another such example is rubric 277, at the beginning of *Enfances Ogier*, where a portion of the rubric is overwritten without the original having been erased, and *li* is inserted above the line. Many rubrics are missing words; there are letter shapes difficult to distinguish, and variant word forms not found elsewhere in the text.

6.8 Accents

The mixture of French and Italian presents particular difficulties in the use of accents. In an edition of an Old French text, one expects certain usages; in an Old Italian text, there are others. In the original text, we find only ç. There are no other accents. French is an oxytone language and does not therefore generally use a written accent to designate the word-final stress. Italian, however, is paroxytone, and conventionally uses written accents only on the final syllable for oxytone words. Italian also conventionally marks certain stressed single-syllable words with a written accent to distinguish them from atonic homonyms in all cases, not just where the words could syntactically be confused. Some lexemes here are from the Italian system, others the French, and some are composites. Thus the editor is forced to make a composite as well. At times the interest in minimizing intervention runs contrary to ease (and habits) of reading. No single satisfactory solution has thus far been proposed, because each Franco-Italian text has varying proportions of French and Italian. I here follow standards set by recent editions of other Franco-Italian texts, keeping in mind that V^{13} is more heavily Italianized than some, less than others.

•a. **c with cedilla** Ç has been left where found and not added where none was present in the manuscript; a characteristic of early northern Italian texts, its appearance is of linguistic and paleographical interest. The scribe is very inconsistent in using it before a palatal vowel, and therefore emending might seem unnecessary. However, in order to distinguish between forms that otherwise seem the same or to consolidate a few forms to an overwhelming majority, I have emended a total of twelve times: for the verb forms of *çuçer* (deriving from JUDICARE) and related lexemes, in lines 2824 (*çu(ç)ement*), Rubric 121 (*(ç)uçé*), 11652 (*(ç)uçé*), 14730 (*(ç)u(ç)ement*), 15345 (*çu(ç)ement*), since out of seventy-eight forms only five are missing cedillas. Earlier editors read cedillas with two of these in the manuscript.[10] I also emend in line 4824 *(ç)onto* (Ital. "giunto") (from forms of Latin JUNGERE), since all other forms of that lexeme also contain the initial cedillaed *c*. *(ç)u(b)ler* (830) is a correction of metathesis (but see note on this), the manuscript reads *bulçer*; *(ç)ura* (4560) from JURARE distinguishes it from forms of *curer*, derived from CURARE, "to care for"; *(ço)strer* (897) and *(ç)ostraren* (13117) are emended to follow other forms of *çostrer*; an unnecessary cedilla is removed from in *(c)oment* (Rubric 388, after line 13677); *(ç)ant* (Rubric 451, after 16011) agrees with other forms derived from GENTE(M).

Added editorial accents:
- **b. acute accent** is used only on an *-e*.
    i. It appears on past participles (reflexes of, or analogues to, reflexes of past participles from the first Latin conjugation, -ARE) in *-é*, to distinguish them from third person singular/plural forms of the present tense where this is clear; where it is not, there is no written accent and the difficulty is noted.
    ii. The acute is also used on the second person plural indicative or imperative forms from the first conjugation like *alé* and *alés*, but not in *-ez/-eç*.
    iii. Similarly, words stressed on the final syllable of the same structure: *malvés; jamés; aprés; palés*. However, where the stressed syllable is unclear—like *demanes*—there is no written accent (Italian *dománi* or Old French *demanois*).
    iv. A few single-syllable words also bear the acute to distinguish them from other single-syllable words: *Dé* (<DEUM, like *Damnedé* [<DOMINUS DEUS]); *né* (< NATUM); *lé* (MSI *lieto*); *mé* (MF *mais*). This does not avoid all confusion; for example, *ne* still could be the negative particle and "nor." Similarly, *le* could still mean "wide" as well as "her" object of a preposition. But between positional variance (*le* as a noun is generally in rhyme position) and context, comprehension is facilitated.
- **c. grave accent** is added to final vowels *a, e, i, o*.
    i. On third person singular/plural simple past (perfect) forms of regular verbs ending in *-o*, reflexes or analogies from the first Latin conjugation, in -ARE (e.g., *trovò*), to distinguish it from the first person singular present tense. Where it is not clear whether the verb is present tense or a strong or weak stem, such as *pote*, I do not write an accent. There are two laisses ending with rhyme on the final *a*; this is problematic, as the tense of several verbs is thus called into question. (Normal third person singular present tense forms

---

[10] On ꝯ, see G. Holtus, review of *Le Danois Oger. Enfances—Chevalerie. Codice Marciano XIII*, ed. Cremonesi, *Zeitschrift für romanische Philologie* 95 (1979): 442–48, esp. 444–45.

of the first conjugation are stem-stressed, not ending-stressed. The rhymed forms appear to be ending-stressed, thus making their form unclear.) These are noted as they occur.

ii. It appears on the future endings of *-è, -ò, -à* (e.g., *farà*), following the Italian formation.

iii. On oxytone noun forms like *verità* (290), following Italian usage.

iv. On final *-i* where it is the second person plural ending (= *és*); e.g., *condurì, avì*. This includes the imperative.

v. Furthermore, the grave distinguishes between apparent homonyms and in some cases verb tenses: *ò* ("I have") vs. *o* ("where"); *à* ("he has") from *a* (preposition); *è* ("he/she/it is") vs. *e* ("and"); *dè* ("he/she/I gave"; "he/she/it must") from *de* (preposition); *dà* (from *dare*, "he/she/it gives," the imperative "give!") from *da* (preposition and past participle); *dì* (verb—only the imperative from *dire*) from *di* (preposition); *fà* (imperative) from *fa* (indicative); *sì* ("you are") from *si* ("if"; "and"; "yes"); *sè* (from *"sapere"*) and *se* (pronoun and conjunction); *lì, là* ("there") from *li, la* ("them, her"). Where an accent distinguishes lexemes, if possible, the accented form is the verb. There are cases where a third lexeme or more exist; for example, *e* also means "I," the first person subject pronoun; but I have avoided marking this in any way to avoid adding too much to the text.[11]

vi. The grave is also used on *-e* and *-i* where they are perfect tense forms (e.g., *avì, trovè*). There is, of course, no accent on strong forms of the simple past, since they are stem-stressed.

This written accentuation system is not perfect; one can still confuse *da* the preposition and the past participle, *e* "I" and "and," but context should assist in these cases.

c. **diereses:** I have avoided using these since syllable count is so variable and easily manipulated between the Italian and French systems.

d. **apostrophe:** is used to designate the elision of a vowel. Since it is frequently unclear in which direction an elision has occurred (e.g., *elo*: is it *e* < EGO + l < ILLU + o < HABEO? Or is it *el* < ILLU + o < HABEO?), I have limited use of the apostrophe to:

i. conjunction plus subject pronoun: *q'il; s'i*

ii. article plus following adjective or noun beginning with a vowel: *L'uno*

iii. negative adverbs followed by verb form or object pronoun beginning with vowel: *n'en; n'amo*

---

[11] Beretta gives nearly four pages of distinctions between lexemes by apostrophe and written accent (*Testo assonanzato*, xxviii–xxxi). Since apostrophes and accents can be distracting and overuse has been criticized, I have avoided using apostrophes as much as possible.

iv. object pronoun followed by verb beginning with vowel, or followed by another pronoun also beginning with a vowel: *l'à, s'en*

v. *a* before another lexeme also beginning with an *a*; e.g., *a 'Ntone*, for *a [A]ntone*; this is a special case, where it is the second word designated as "losing" an initial vowel; in fact, it is unclear which of the two vowels has been lost in the elision, unlike below. There is one example of *a* before another vowel (either *e* or *i* that is similarly treated, l. 10627: *Lasa 'n*, where the apostrophe stands for the initial vowel of *en* or *in* (both occur in the text).

e. **raised dot**: is used for the combination of two lexemes where the second begins with a consonant.[12]

i. preposition + article: *a·l, de·l*; exception here is *a·u*, which appears only once (l. 9424), since it represents the velarization of the consonant *l*, which appears frequently (1783 times);

ii. verb + following unstressed pronoun: *Fa·la, à·l*, etc. Because of the Tobler-Mussafia Law in Old Italian, that object pronouns do not precede a verb at the beginning of a line or phrase (Rohlfs, *Grammatica storica*, 170–72 [¶469]), this happens with relative frequency in older Italian texts. The raised dot also appears frequently with imperatives, infinitives, and the oxytone future. Stressed pronouns (*moi, nos, vos*) are not so treated;

iii. subject pronoun + object pronoun: e.g., *ela·l, ele·l, ge·l* for MSI "lei lo" or "lei la," "glielo" or "gliela";

iv. conjunction + object pronoun: *qi·l, si·l* for MSI "che lo," "se lo";

v. in a few cases where it occurs, verbs and following subject pronouns beginning with a consonant: *è·lo, è·la, fo·lo*, etc.;

vi. in cases of assimilation: a nasal to the following word beginning with a nasal; for example, *i·me* for *in + me*, "in the middle of" (10447); *co·la*, for *con + la*, "with the" (10877); a conjunction to a following subject pronoun, *e·l*, "et il" (e.g., l. 10690), *e·s*, "et les" (l. 16344), etc.; and similarly, the negative adverb plus following object pronoun, where the final nasal is assimilated to the *l*: *no·l*, MSI "non lo."

---

[12] In MSI, the equivalent is frequently an assimilation resulting in a doubled consonant: *alla, nella*, etc. Of course, *es* existed in Old French as well, and is still found in fixed expressions today: *ès lettres*. Beretta uses the raised dot "per segnalare le enclisi, quando la particella enclitica non abbia valore sillabica. È impiegato anche per indicare lo scempiamento di due *l* originarie contingue, l'una finale, l'altra iniziale iniziale di parola" (*Testo assonanzato*, xxxi). Holtus says, "Il punto in alto si trova nei pronomi enclitici, che formano un'unità grafica con la parola precedente . . . Fanno eccezione i casi in cui la parola che precede ha mutato la sua vocale a causa del pronome enclitico (*no·l oncie* . . . .*)*" (*Bataille d'Aliscans*, xxviii–xxix). Just as I am finishing this edition for print, an excellent article has appeared, directed primarily at historians, by Marc H. Smith, "Conseils pour l'édition

6.9 Semivowels

The manuscript uses *u* for both *u* and *v*, *i* for *i* and *j*. In the manuscript, *j* appears as the second in two *i*'s in a plural (e.g., *palij*) and in numbers (e.g., *xij*). It is difficult to decide how to use *j* instead of *i*, since *j* is associated with multiple phonemes in tradition. In French, the letter *j* represents (IPA) /ʒ/, whereas (IPA) /j/ is a voiced palatal, usually called a semivowel in Italian tradition.[13] I have followed French usage for resolving *i* to *j* where French forms occur (since the letter *j* is not used in Italian) and have NOT noted these changes within the text. This means that *j* appears both as a semivowel and as a fricative.

J appears under the following conditions:

    i. where it represents the modern Italian /ʤ/, the modern French /ʒ/: e.g., *jent, jant, jorno, je* (= "gente / gens, giorno / jour, –/je")

    ii. where it represents /j/: e.g., *çoja, nojer* (= "gioia, noia")

    iii. where it represents the modern Italian /ʎ/: e.g., *mujer* (= "moglie")

It represents, therefore, a consonantal value in contrast to the vowel *i* that appears either by itself or with others in a diphthong or triphthong. Thus, where there are French-style verb endings in *-oie, -oient* (/we/), these remain unaltered. There are many rhymes of infinitives and past participles in *-jé, -jer* where conjugated verb forms appear without the semiconsonant (e.g., *projer; renojer; convojer*; etc. vs. *preie, proie; renoie; convoie, convoient*). However, the relatively frequent rhyme *-ie* causes *preie* to be two syllables, *pre-ie* (l. 13933). Spelling doublets remain; *çoie* ("jewels") must be one syllable in each appearance to keep the lines ten syllables; *çoja / çoya* ("joy") are two, but *çoie* (cf. MSF *joie*) is one syllable.

---

des documents en langue italienne (XIVᵉ–XVIIᵉ siècle)," *Bibliothèque de l'école des chartes* 159 (2001): 541–78, which includes a whole section on "emploi du point en haut," 555–56. He includes my usages under b., "simplification de double consonne" and "autre assimilation avec simplification" (556).

[13] Recent editors of Franco-Italian texts have not necessarily stated their criteria for using *j*; e.g., Beretta says, "Ho realizzato tale distinzione ovunque se ne presentasse la necessità," noting that the scribe of V⁴ rarely uses it (*Testo assonanzato*, xxii). Rosellini says, "Nella riproduzione grafica del testo mi sono attenuto a quegli accorgimenti adottati dalla grande maggioranza degli editori risolvendo a) la grafia *i* del manoscritto con *j* quando il fonema ha valore palatale, b) sostituendo *u* on *v* dove occorrresse" (*Geste Francor*, 162). Others are more specific; thus, Holtus: "Per *u* e *i* valgono in generale i criteri moderni, cioè, *u* sta per la vocale, *v* per la consonante (le forme del futuro e del condizionale di alcuni verbi—*avoir, devoir, savoir, boire*—conservano nella grafia la *u* vocalica o semivocalica); in generale *i* rappresenta la forma vocalica, *j* quella consonantica solo all'inizio di parola (ad eccezione delle forme di *estre*); all'interno di parola, in particolare dopo prefissi, viene gereralmente mantenuta la *i* vocalica o semivocalica" (*Bataille d'Aliscans*, xxix-xxx). "IPA" refers to the International Phonetic Alphabet, of which the recent versions can be found in any linguistics textbook.

There are fewer problems with the use of *v*. In V¹³, *v* appears only in cardinal numbers (roman numerals). In the manuscript we find *saura, aura* and similar forms of the verbs "to know" and "to have," which I have represented as *savrà* and *avrà* because forms with the semivowel predominate: there are 243 forms of future and conditional in *-ver-* and only fourteen in *-ur/vr-* for *avoir*; similarly, there are twenty-two future and conditional forms in *-ver-* and eight in *-ur/vr-* for *savoir*. Elsewhere I have standardized the use of *u* for the vowel and *v* for the semivowel according to modern usage: thus *salver/saluer* represent respectively, "to save" (<SALVARE) and "to greet" (< SALUTARE).

6.10 Capitalization

Names are capitalized in this final edition according to modern romance language usage. In the manuscript, they are usually slashed in red by the rubricator, rarely capitalized. I also capitalize epithets and places of origin (e.g., *Çudé, Apostoile, Ascler*).

I began this edition with plans to regularize representations such as use of apostrophe and raised dot; needless to say, and as any editor can testify, especially in editing the single witness to a textual tradition, it is not possible to standardize the appearance of a medieval text, and most especially not a mixed-language text, to modern standards. I hope that my choices are clear for those using this edition and desiring to examine the language, and the text readable for those who are not so much interested in the language as in the content.

7.0
Texts of MS. Marc. 13, the Geste Francor

7.1 Enfances Bovo
Laisse 1

    Sor tot les autres fu de major renon.*   1ra
    Bovo no le querì ni merçé ni perdon:
    Ver lui s'en voit cosi fer cun lion,
    E ten (Clarença), chi à a or li pon,*
5   Qe li donò Druxiana a·l çevo blon.
    Gran colpo fer deso(r) son elmo en(s)on,*
    Qe flor e pere n'abatì a foson.
    La spea torna qe ferì en canton,
    De l'aubergo trença davanti li giron;
10 Le brando desis sovra li aragon,
    Le çevo li trençe, quel caì a·l sablon.*

---

   1 Bartoli: antres . . . maior
   2 Jacob: quer ni . . . merce; Keller: Bouo; Bartoli, Rosellini: queri, abati, etc. Guessard: merce.
   3 Jacob: cos'irez cun lion; Keller: sen uoit cosi irez; Bartoli: Vers . . . cosi irex . . . ; Guessard: Vers s'en voit . . . irez sun lion; Reinhold: i*rez* (for *fer*)
   4 MS.: claren clarença; Jacob: Et en claren clarença: "Chi a hai li pon . . ." ; Keller: Et en claren clarença chi a nor; Bartoli: a à or; Guessard: E ten claren Clarença . . . a à or; Rosellini, MS.: chia a nor li pon
   5 Keller: çeuo; Bartoli: al
   6 MS.: enfon; Reinhold: elme en son (emend for *de fon*); Keller: fer de son elmo enson; Bartoli: de son elmo en son; Guessard: de son elmo en son; Mussafia: desor son . . . en son (emend for *deson*); Rosellini, MS.: de son son elmo, (emend, son elmo) . . . enson
   7 Keller: nabaci; Bartoli: abaci; Guessard: n'abati
   8 Keller: La spee . . . qe feu en cancon; Guessard: spea . . . feri en canton
   9 Keller: O laubergo; Guessard: De l'aubergo; Reinhold: D*e* l'au . . .
   10 Keller: Le biando de sis soura (n.b.: Rosellini's typo of Keller's reading, "suora"); Guessard: brando desis; Bartoli, Guessard: Aragon
   11 Bartoli, Guessard: qu'el caï . . . ; Rosellini: trença

E Bovo escrie, "Munçoja sunon!"*
Ai, fel traites de mala legion,
Questo fino donè (anbi) de Gujon!" *
15 Celu d'Antone, qe tenpo fo p(r)o(d)on, *
E Teris fer un altro ses conpagnon;
Morto l'abate, sença nosa e tencon.
Bovo le vi, si le mis por rason:
"Bel dolçe frere, no·l tenez a perdon;
20 E mo e nos, se bon soldi me denon,*
Nu seremo freri e conpagnon."
Li cento soldaer ferì tot a bandon;
Çascun abate li so a·l sablon.*
Grande fu la bataile defora <li doj>on; *
25 E li so çivaler son ve<nu a Du>on
E si le fa monter sovra li aragon.*
E quando Dodo fu monté en arçon,
Elo dist a sa jent, "Lì retornarè non."
Sor<venu> e<rt una grant legi>on;
30 Uno trovi qe po<rta li> on.*
Deo <li maldie> qe <sofrì pasi>on!
"Tel colpo me donò sor <mon elme enson>,

---

12 Reinhold: escrie . . . ; Rosellini: "A! reux de fiz, vil hon"
14 Reinhold: Questo fu . . . doné . . . de Guion; Rosellini: furo doné da Bovos de Goion
15 MS.: ponon; Reinhold: Celu d'Antone qe . . . fo prodon; Rosellini: qe vinçe roi prodon
16 Rosellini: compagnon
17 Rosellini: l'abate (sic; cf. Plouzeau)
19 Rosellini: pardon
20 Reinhold: E mo e vos, se bon soldo me donon; Rosellini: E mo e vos
22 Rosellini: toti a
23 Rosellini: li sol al
24 Reinhold: . . . li dojon
25 Rosellini: so venu
26 Reinhold:, Rosellini: sovra un
27 Reinhold: monte; Reinhold, Rosellini: in arçon
28 Reinhold: li retornar e . . . ; Rosellini: Lì retornar evon (so always for accentuation of li)
29 Reinhold: Sorvenu n'ert una grant legion; Rosellini: n'ert
30 Reinhold: Uno li dist qe por . . . lion; Rosellini: Uno li dist qe po or roilion
31 Reinhold: sofrì pasion
32 Reinhold: mon elme en son; Rosellini: elmo enson

Enfances Bovo 307

      Fendu m'averon trosqu'a < >.* <3 lines missing>
      Qi me donast <tot li> or <de·l mon>, (37)
35   Un altro colpo . . . <desor> li g<iron>
      Si me resenbla eser un garçon."
      Lor se <partent e lasent> la tençon, (40)
      E lasent de <morti plus de cento> on
      Qe <mais non verent li doj>on;
40   Si <d>elasò tende e pavilon.*

Rubric 1
Coment Do de Magança retorne / a 'Ntone cun soa jent.
Laisse 2

      <Do de Magançe fu retorné arer>*
      <E lasa ato . . . er >* (45)
      . . . facer . . . siter
      . . . çivaler*
45   Ven a 'Ntone, entra sens entarder,*   1rb
      E quando f(u) dedens, prist Deo a 'orer,*
      Qi li oit delivré da cele soldaer: (50)
      El g'era vis <qe il> le fust darer.*
      Dama Blionda le prist a derasner:
50   "Avez preso li çastel <de·l malfer>?"
      "Dama," fait il, "No me fai enraçer!*

---

    33 Reinhold, Rosellini: m'averoit. Reinhold: tros *qua*; Rosellini: trosqe . . . reon
    36 Reinhold: *garçon*
    37 Reinhold: se part*ent*e lasent la ten*ç*on
    38 Reinhold: de *morti* plus de cento . . . ; Rosellini: cento peon
    39 Reinhold: mais no*n verent* . . . li *do*jon; Rosellini: no veront mie
    40 Reinhold: *Si* . . . *e pa*vilon; Rosellini: si delasò
    Rubric 1 (after 40) Keller: antone cun soa ient; Reinhold: *Co*ment.. /[A] *A*ntone; Rosellini: Antone cun soa jent
    41 Reinhold: *Do de Maga*nçe; Rosellini: fo retorné
    42 Reinhold: E lasa . . . [rest is blank]; Rosellini: E lasa solamente . . . [rest is blank]
    43 Rosellini: . . . so . . . con . . . frer
    45 Reinhold, Rosellini: Ven Antone
    46 MS.: fer; Reinhold: fu dedens (uses italics for all abbreviation resolutions; not remarked any further); Reinhold, Rosellini: aorer
    47 Rosellini: Ki li . . .
    48 Reinhold: El gera vis*q*e ille; Rosellini: El g'er'avis
    49 Reinhold, Rosellini: à derasner; Rosellini: Blondoia
    51 Reinhold: fa*i e*n raçer; Rosellini: far enraçer

```
         A li castel ai eu engonbler, (55)
         Qe in> ma <vie> ne <dever>ò <obli>er *
         <Venu lì sont, no è li> soldaer.
55       <Un est perigolo>so e fer;*
         S'ele no fust . . . l projer
         <Le parenti faites da> (60) *
         Qe poit ver . . .*
         <Fendu m'averoit tros> li ba<udr>er *
60       . . . . li uno dona <fo> França e Baiver
         Un altro colpo <ne li averoie> . . ."
         <Dist la dama, "Deo ne poso graci>er,
         . . . <vos ç . . . > (65)*
         <Qe de . . . >
65       <Un . . . >
         <Fost . . . >
         <Quando . . . >
         Et a (70)
         France li* [24 lines missing here]
70       XX. milia son arma, tot a destrer,                    1ᵛᵃ
         E altretant furent li peoner;
         Segurament poent çivalçer.
         Synibaldo no à cent da l'incontrer,*
         Ma la mercé de Deo e de·l bon soldaer (75)
```

---

   52 Reinhold, Rosellini: çastel
   53 Reinhold: *ne dever*ò o*b*lier; Rosellini: ne'l averò
   54 Reinhold: Ve*nu* li so*nt* no . . . e li soldaer; Rosellini: Venu li sont norie li
   55 Reinhold: *p*erigoloso; Rosellini: Un sol est piaricoloso erer
   56 Reinhold: Q'*e*le no*n fust . . . pr*oier; Rosellini: Q'ele no fust la preson por proier
   57 Reinhold: *L*e par*enti* faites da . . . ; Rosellini: Le partaçi faites da . . . faiter
   59 Reinhold: *t*ros li ba*u*dr*e*r; Rosellini: baidrer
   60 Reinhold: Qi me *d*onas*t* e França e Baiver; Rosellini: Qi me donasa e França e Baiver
   61 Reinhold: av*e*r*oie*; Rosellini: averoie apiçer
   63 Reinhold: Deo ne p*oso*; Rosellini: Vos . . . deio . . . fosi
   64 Rosellini: Qe vorò . . . inbrier
   65 Rosellini: Un son . . .
   66 Rosellini: [blank line]
   67 Rosellini: Quando rece . . .
   68 Rosellini: Et al nies li . . .
   70 Reinhold, Rosellini: .XX. milia son armà tot à destrer.
   73 Reinhold: no a çent da
   74 Rosellini: soldier

| 75 | Le farà si malame*n*t retornar arer |
| | Q'elo no atenderà lo fiolo lo per.* |

Rubric 2
Come*n*t Do fi bandire oste / E vene a san Simon.
Laisse 3

	Dodo çivalçe cun soa oste grant,*
	Por li çamin i s'en vont erant,*
	Tantq'i furent a san Symon d'Ariant. (80)
80	E (s)i le venent una doman por tanp
	Bovo era levé a l'aube aparisant,
	E reguardò fora por me li canp.
	Vi loçe tendere e pavilon tirant;
	Quela grant oste elo vi lì davant. (85)
85	Quando la vi no se smaiò niant,
	Q'el vi Synibaldo si li dist en ojant:
	"Porqe me donés vos vestre soldo, *
	A moi e a quisti altri qe vos sir(v)e pro be(s)ant?*
	E no son soldaer por star seré çadant;* (90)
90	Anci son soldaer por aler a li canp.
	Ne no son preste ni çapelant,
	Qi de soldo serve, mete sa (vi)ta por niant!
	Fà·me avrir la porte alo demantenant,

Rubric 2 (after 76) line 2: Jacob: Cuene à; Keller: euene

77 Jacob: çivalce cun son oste; Keller: son oste

78 Jacob: camin; Keller: sen (as always)

79 Jacob: Tant qi furent à San Symon davant; Keller: Tant qi ... davant; Reinhold, Rosellini: Tant q'i ... Symon davant

80 MS.: E fi; Keller, Jacob: E si ... portanp. Rosellini: venet

81 Keller: a laube (as always)

82 Jacob: por me li camp

83 Jacob: vi loce tendere

84 Jacob: Oue la grant oste, e lo vi; Keller: Que la ... e lo

85 Keller: sesmaio

86 Jacob: De lui s'ymbaldo; Keller: Del ui symbaldo; Reinhold: O' el vi; Rosellini: O el vi

87 Jacob: Por qe me donés-vos vostre; Reinhold: Por qe ... vestre ... ; Rosellini: [or et arçant]

88 MS.: sire. Reinhold: s*er*ve probebant; Rosellini: qe vos fue protejant?

89 Rosellini: seié ça dant

91 Reinhold, Rosellini: Me (but Reinhold p. 512: Meno)

> Colsa como no, li çoncé vos demant." (95)
95 Synibaldo li responde, "Bel fils, or m'entant;
> Tu po ben fora ensir a salvamant.*
> Gran perigolo est aler contra cotant
> <Sor> un de nos i sont plus de ça<nt>."
> <E dist> Bovo, "de ço son plu çojant;
100 ... por en mi canp*
> ... d·i Persant
> ... e sarçant
> ... c'a li Deo comant
> ... n li sant
105 ... co*n* tradimant
> ... te farò li to comant
> <... tos>to *et* isnelemant."
> ... monta en auferant
> ... armarent tre çant
110 ... (s)i ne fu molto çojant
> ... e*nt* amuniscant
> ... u ten <dos> mile a <ta>ant
> <... u>er colpo davant
> ... <a>lirò por li canp
115 a l<e en> avant
> ... or nen vo<s doté> niant;
> Qe anchoi seron toti riche e manant.   1vb
> E se vos me verés aler malemant,

96 Reinhold: tu po' ben; Rosellini: Tu po ben
98 Reinhold: S*or* ... çant; Rosellini: de çant
99 Reinhold: *E dist* Bovo ... ; Rosellini: ... Bovo: 'De ço so io plu çoiant.'
100 Reinhold: onor en mi canp; Rosellini: onor en mi canp
101 Reinhold: ... *do p*enant; Rosellini: du penant
103 Reinhold: a li Deo comant; Rosellini: ... à li Deo ameant
104 Reinhold: m li sant; Rosellini: ni li sant
105 Reinhold: co*n tu por* niant. Rosellini: contro Drusi[a]nt
106 Reinhold, Rosellini: ... farò li to comant
107 Reinhold: *tos*to *et* isnelamant; Rosellini: ... sto et isnelamant
109 Reinhold, Rosellini: tre çant
110 MS.: fi ne fu; Rosellini: ir si ne ...
111 Reinhold: ... *ent* à muniscant; Rosellini: et amuniscant
112 Rosellini: ... u ten dos mil talant
113 Reinhold: *u*er colpo davant; Rosellini: uer colpo davant
114 Reinhold: *a*lirò por li canp; Rosellini: alirò por li canp
115 Reinhold: le *en avant*; Rosellini: ... alere ci davant
116 Reinhold: ... nen *vos doté* niant; Rosellini: alirum nen voz doté niant

	Qe ço caist de sella en avant,*
120	E qe de bataile eo fuse recreant,
	E fose pris da cele male jant,
	Segurament nen vos tardés niant.
	Vu averés retorner a guarant
	En le çastel a vestre salvamant.
125	Ne vos so altro dir; a Jesu vos comant,*
	Qe naque de Marie là jos en Beniant."
	E qui li respondent, "Non parlez pluss avant;*
	Nu vos tenon por sire e por guarant,
	Ne vos faliron por le menbres perdant."*
130	La porte fu averté e li ponte atant;
	E Bovo ese defors con cele poche çant
	E por amor de Bovo, Teris ensì ensemant.
	E Bovo si fo pro, si le fi saçamant;
	Avantiqe qui de l'oste montese en auferant,
135	Ne aust preso arme ni guarnimant.
	Bovo si li asalì si vigorosamant
	Cum fait le lion quant s(o)a caça prant.*
	Qui de l'oste stava seguremant,
	De qui dedens ne se dotava niant.
140	Nen cuitoit mie par nesun convenant
	Qe cellé dedens fust gent tant
	Qe avec lor i venise a·l canp,
	Ne qe casu fose defors a li torniamant.
	E Bove li asalì mantenent destant,
145	E morti n'abatì tanti e de sanglant
	Qe cuverta n'era la verde erba de·l canp.
	L'oste si fu scremie e darer e davant;*
	⟨Çascun⟩ prende arme, monta en auferant.

---

119 Reinhold, Rosellini: Qe eo
125 Reinhold: sò
127 Rosellini: E quili; MS.:, Reinhold, Rosellini: pluss avant
129 Reinhold, Rosellini: le menbres perdant
130 Reinhold, Rosellini: averte (Reinhold, 512: à tant)
133 Reinhold: le fe
136 Rosellini: asalí
137 MS.: sea; Reinhold: se à caça prant; Rosellini: sea caça
141 Reinhold, Rosellini: celle
143 Reinhold, Rosellini: ensu fose
144 Rosellini: Bovo
147 Rosellini: e dare e
148 Reinhold, Rosellini: Çascun prende arme

    Lor se començe la bataile si grant,*
150 <Q>e (I)deo tonast: non olderia hon vivant.*

Rubric 3
Coment Bovo con ses cunpagnon si s'en voe<nt>*
En la bataile, e con Do <de> Magançe se ferì con Bovo.
Laisse 4

    Do de Magançe fo en cival monté,
    E tota sa jent avec lui aroté;
    Lora verisi comencer gran meslé.
    Bovo va pur davanti, li soldaer va dre;
155 E li prode Ter(is), tuta or a son costé,*
    Quant le aste son frate, mete man a le spe.
    Cu il consegue, son morti e delivré.
    En Do de Magançe Bovo se fu encontré;
    Do le ferì de un dardo amolé.
160 Grant colpo li donè, si le oit li scu frapé;
    Tota la tarça fendu en do mité.
    L'auberg fo <roto>, da mort li oit tansé;*
    <La spea> fu fraita, li troncon vola a·l pié.*
    Bovo par lui non fu d'arçon plojé,   2ra
165 E Bovo fer lui cum li brant amolé.
    Nen fust qe Dodo se çitò a li pre,
    Fendu l'averoit jusqua no de·l baudré. *
    Ma noportant, tosto fo redriçé
    Monta a çival, si oit t(r)ata la spe,*
170 E ferì Bovo desor l'eume çemé.
    E quel fo bon, non trença una deré;
    La spea torne, ne l'oit ren dalmacé.
    Adoncha verisi començar gran meslé:
    Teris e Bovo sonto molto aprisé.
175 Cu i consegue, ont morti çité.

---

  149 Reinhold, Rosellini: començe
  150 Reinhold: Qe à Deo . . . olderia; Rosellini: Qe Ideo tonast . . . olderia
  Rubric 3 (after line 150) Keller: sen/vent; . . . com do; Reinhold: s'e[n] voent/Do de *Magançe*; Rosellini: vont
  154 Reinhold: dré
  155 MS.: pro de terre; Reinhold: prode Teri[s] è; Rosellini: prode Teri è (emend for *Terre*)
  163 Reinhold: al pre; Rosellini: al pré
  169 Reinhold, Rosellini: si oit t[r]ata

Enfances Bovo

	Bovo va avanti, e Teris va dre,
	Ma la çent de Dodo sento si enforçé*
	Qe nostri çivaler ont reduti aré,
	Plus d'una arçée ver li çastel torné.
180	Quando Bovo li vi, oit un cri çité,
	"Arestés vos, me çivaler prisé,
	Aprés de moi venés tot aroté!"
	E cil le font volunter e de gre,
	Ne le fo nul qe fust desghiré.*
185	E Bovo guardò fora por la caré,
	E si vi Dodo da li altri delunçé.
	A gran mervele el fo ben armé,
	E son cor fu molto ben açesmé.*
	Bovo oit Teris queri e demandé,
190	"Qi est quel, qi mena tel ferté,
	Ses armes a bicor pituré?*
	Sor tot les autres, el par eser doté.
	Est el cont, o grant amiré?
	Gran colpo me donò de sa spe."
195	Dist Teris, "Sire est de la contré,
	Et è colu qe à l'oste ça mené;
	Do de Magançe el est apelé.
	Elo oncis men segnor, donde fi gran peçé,*
	(E un son filz oit desarité;
200	Petit enfant, Bovo era apelé).
	Por una feme, qe in malor fu né,
	Fo quel tradimento fato et ordené;
	E qi de lui en fust delivré,
	Q'el fose morto oncis e detrençé.
205	Nen dotaresemo li altri una poma poré;*

176 MS.: bovo q va
177 MS.: sento? Reinhold, Rosellini: sonto enforçé
181 Reinhold, Rosellini: Arestes
189 Rajna (*Ricerche intorno ai Reali*, 180). queri
190 Rajna (*Ricerche intorno ai Reali*, 180): Qi . . . tal ferté (no quotes)
191 Reinhold: a li cor; Rosellini: a bitor
194 Rajna (*Ricerche intorno ai Reali*, 180): Grant colpo
195 Reinhold: Tiris
196 Rajna (*Ricerche intorno ai Reali*, 180): colui
198 Reinhold, Rosellini: mon segnor; Reinhold: dond'è si gran peçe; Rajna (*Ricerche intorno ai Reali*, 180): dond' è si gran peçé; Rosellini: dond è si
201 Reinhold, Rosellini: mal or
202 MS.: 7 for *et*

Par lui avemo guera, e d'inverno e d'esté."
E dist Bovo, "Eo le conoso asé.
Quando da moi el serà desevré,
El porà ben loldar Damenedé.
210 Doncha est il cil qe fe quel gran peçé,
Contra que(l) dux qe fu si engané!"
Bovo oit pris una lança feré,
Qe un de sa gent li avoit presenté.   2ʳᵇ
Bovo prist la lançe a li fer amolé,
215 Davant da soi oit la tarça çité;*
E punçe Rondel de li speron doré
E va a ferir Dodo sor la tarça doré.
Le scu li speçe, l'auberg li oit falsé;
Ne li valse la bruine un diner moené.*
220 Entro li flanco oit li dardo fiçé,
Siq'elo l'oit durament ennavré.
O voja o no, l'oit abatu a·l pre,
E questo fu voluntà de Dé,
Qe se l'aust plu de·l canpo pié*
225 Por me li cors fu li dardo alé;
E s'el fust alore mort e delivré*
Nen fust l'ovre cosi ben alé.
Como il alò si cum vos e·l dirè,*
Et en tal mo fo presa la çité
230 Qe non seria en tota quela ste.
E Bovo trapase fora, por me li pre;
El cre q'el sia morto, e son pere vençé;
E Dodo stava reverso i·me li pre,*
E quando se ne fu desevré,
235 Sa jent li ven sovra, si l'oit suso levé. *
Quando vivo le trovent, si n'oit Deo aoré;
I descenderent, si l'ont reconforté.
A çival li tornent, e si l'ont via mené.

---

206 Rosellini: d'inverno (cf. Plouzeau)

211 MS.: que; Reinhold, Rosellini: que[l]

223 Rajna (*Ricerche intorno ai Reali*, 147): de dé

224 Reinhold: Qe se l'arat; Rajna (*Ricerche intorno ai Reali*, 147): Qe s' el aust . . . del . . .

225 Rajna (*Ricerche intorno ai Reali*, 147): Por me' (cf. 229, *mo'*)

226 Reinhold: alor e

227 Rajna (*Ricerche intorno ai Reali*, 147): Non fust . . . così

228 Reinhold, Rosellini: vos oldiré; Rajna (*Ricerche intorno ai Reali*, 147): vos el diré

233 MS.: ime li pre; Reinhold i[n] me'; Rosellini: i[n] me

```
              Da cele ora en avanti, si remis la meslé;
      240     E por quel colpo fo l'oste sbaraté.
              Ne se ge ferì plus de lança ni de spe,*
              Ni tuto mejo po, fuçe ver la cité,
              Non atendoit li fiolo li pe.
              Quelo davanti era çojant e lé;
      245     Nen voroit eser por l'or d'una cité
              Eser darer atrové.*
              E Bovo oit cun li brant açaré*
              Alé darer, donando gran colé,
              E avec lui, Teris cun li soldaé.
      250     La merçé de Deo, la vora majesté,
              Bovo oit la proja guaagné.*
              A ses conpagni l'oit partia e delivré;
              Grant fu la çoja qe qui ont mené:
              Çascun oit plu r(ob)a qe ne oit demandé,*
      255     Donde furent richament ostalé.
              En le çastel i furent retorné,
              A salvamento tuti çojant e lé,*
              E Synibaldo li fo encontra alé,
              E tot li altri qe in le çastel era torné.*
      260     Si ont çoja, or non m'en demandé,
              Quando . . . da cile ost è de(l)ivré.*
```

Rubric 4
Coment Bovo fo in lo castel Siginbaldo   2ᵛᵃ
E con la mulier Synibaldo gardoit Bovo.
Laisse 5

```
              En le çastel s'en retornò Bovon;
              A salvamento conduse ses baron,
              E Sinibaldo cun tot ses conpagnon.
```

---

242 Reinhold: Qi tuto. Rosellini: ve rla (Noted by Plouzeau also.)
254 Reinhold, Rosellini: oit plu rica qe
257 MS.: çolat; Reinhold: sa*lv*amento
258 Reinhold: *a*lé
259 Reinhold: *tot* . . . era *resté*; Rosellini: era resté
260 Reinhold: . . . *or* no m'en
261 MS.: cile oste de . . . ; Reinhold: Quando . . . *cele* oste del*iv*ré; Rosellini: Quando cil ont cele ost delivré

Rubric 4 (after 261) line 2: Keller: com la mulier siginbaldo; Reinhold, Rosellini: mulier Siginbaldo

265	Ne le remist veilardo ni garçon;*
	Asa ont guaagné robe e pavilon,
	Çival et armes, or coito e macon.*
	De quela robe oit a si gran foson,
	Qe plus non demandent per nule cason.
270	Synibaldo oit una muler de gran renon,
	E pro e saça e Oria oit non,
	Qe bailì Bovo quando fu petit garcon,
	E si le alatò cun fust ses façon,*
	E plus l'amava de tot ren de·l mon;
275	E si fasoit li son per Gujon.
	E quant fu morto, qe fu pris li garçon,
	De lu avoit si gran conpasion
	Major ne la poroit avoir en tot li mon.
	E cesta dame qe oit benecion
280	Sovento guardava Bovo por la façon,
	E de lu oit senpre sospicion
	Qe non fust li son fantin Bovon.
	E porço, la dame si le asaçon;*
	Sovente fois li metoit por rason,
285	Donde estoit e de qual legion;
	Sempre Bovo si çelava ses non.

Rubric 5
Coment la dama de Synibaldo conoit Bovo / En le bagno e si ne fe grande çoja.
Laisse 6

	La çentil dame, qe tanto fo pro e ber,
	Quant ela vit Bovo ses nome çeler,*
	Ne por losenge ne por projer
290	Da lui non poit la verità trover,
	Qe droitament se volust palenter,
	Dont se porpense d'altrament asaçer:
	Un bagno fe fare en una çanbra a·l çeler,*

---

268 Reinhold: à un gran; Rosellini: asi gran
270 Rajna (*Ricerche intorno ai Reali*, 147): grant renon
273 Rajna (*Ricerche intorno ai Reali*, 180): cum fust ses fa[n]çon
281 Rajna (*Ricerche intorno ai Reali*, 180): de lui . . . sospiçion
282 Rajna (*Ricerche intorno ai Reali*, 180): fus li
283 Reinhold, Rosellini: por ço
Rubric 5 (after 286) Keller: siginbaldo . . . esine; Reinhold: Siginbaldo

Enfances Bovo

Bovo apela: "Veneç avanti, frer,*
295 Vu (s)ì tot camufés por le arme porter,*
E por li gran colpi reçever e doner.
Entrés in bagno, si vos averés laver;
El vos farà tot quanto refrescher."
E Bovo lì entre de greç e volunter;
300 Quant fu en le bagno, q'el se cuita repolser,*
E quela si le voit a freger;*
Donde Bovo s'en prist a vergogner.
"Dama," dist il, "por Deo, tra vos arer!"
Dist la dama, "No te diça nojer."*
305 E como ela prist por lo peito a laver,*
Desor la spala droita ela le p<ris guarder>;*
Ella vi li segno qe li lasò sa mer, 2ᵛᵇ
Ço fo una cros qe Deo li volse segner;
Por gran miracolo qe in lu volse mostrer.
310 E quella dama qe tanto fo pro e ber,
A quel segno lo prist ad aviser.
Non fi mia la dame cun femena forsoner;*
Ela prist Synibaldo a clamer,
Nean Teris nen volse oblier.
315 Qi donc veist la dama cella cros baser,
E tuto Bovo e davant e darer,
"Bel filz," dist ila, "Cun te posi çeler,
A moi, e a celu qe doit eser ton per,
Qe averì dura par toi tanta pena *et* engonbrer,
320 Ne se poroit dire ni aconter?"
"Deo," dist Bovo, "Laseç star li noser;
Q'(el) no·l sa nul hon qe soit né de mer
Se no Synibaldo, e Teris mon frer,
Qe avec lor me vorò conseler,
325 Como nu poron nos ennemis mater."
E quela li dist, "De grez e volunter."
Atanto ven Synibaldo fora por le soler,
La dama li foit in la çanbra entrer,

---

295 MS.: si tot
296 Reinhold, Rosellini: recever
301 Reinhold: afreger; Rosellini: à freger
314 Reinhold: Ne an
317 Reinhold: po' si; Rosellini: <<Bel filz<<
319 Reinhold, Rosellini: aven; MS. 7 for *et*.
322 MS.: Qelel nolsa

E quant conoit Bovo, se voit a çenoler,
330 E durament el prist a larm(o)jer*
Por la gran çoja q'el oit de·l baçaler,
E por la mort la quale si fe son per.
Elo li voit le janbes a 'braçer,
Baser li volse li pe, quant cil le foit lever.
335 "Pere," ço dist Bovo, "ben vos devés penser
Quant me volun avec vos mener.
Mon çival me caì en meço la river,
Donde in Antona i me torno arer
Et a ma mer me dè por presoner.
340 Quela malvés, qe Deo doni engonbrer,
La qual cun un paon me volse atoseger,
Eo m'en foçì; Deo m'à volu aider.
Se vos dovese tuto e dire e conter,*
Le pene e le travaile qe m'è convenu durer,
345 En un mois ne vos poria derasner.
Unde nu se dovon en tute mois penser*
Como Dodo posemo amater,
E vençer la mort de Gujon mon per."
Dist Synibaldo, "Tu parli como ber."
350 E dist Bovo, "Ben ò veçu la via e li senter.
Quant fu en l'estor, en le grande torner,
Ferì quel Dodo si le fi trabuçer;
Si forte li navre qe vi li sangue rajer.
A gran pena le fi soa çente monter;*
355 El mandarà por mires par tot la river,
A burgi et a vile a çité *et* a docler,*   3ra
Por li milor q'elo porà trover.
Et (e)o a mo de mires me farò adober,*
E portarò unguenti de plusore mainer,
360 Si le farò croire a·l mondo non ò me per,
Ne qe mejo saça una plaga curer.

---

329 Reinhold, Rosellini: voit açenoler
330 MS.: alarmaier
336 Reinhold, Rosellini: volivi
349 Rosellini: Diust
350 Reinhold: voia e li senter
353 Rosellini: navré
355 Rosellini: En mandara (also corrected by Holden, "El")
356 MS.: 7 for *et*
357 Rosellini: ele
358 MS.: co a mo de; Rosellini: eo à mo de

Enfances Bovo

      Se en la çanbra eo porò entrer,
      Et eo avese qualche amigo e frer
      Qe me doust secorer *et* aider,
365 De tal medesine li averia porter
      Qe in soa vita no li averoit salder."
      Dist Synibaldo, "Ben est da otrier."

Rubric 6
Coment Sig(in)baldo amunisoit Bovo / Comant doit e(n)trare in Antone.*
Laisse 7

      "Bel filz," dist Synibaldo, "entendì mun talant;
      Quant ton pere fu morto eri petit enfant,
370 Asa à tu en Antona amisi e benvojant,*
      Por amor de ton per qe amò dolçemant.*
      Daqe te plas fare ceste convant,*
      El se vole faire saviamant.
      Quant serà en Antona non demorarà niant;*
375 A un albergo descendì, meravilos e grant;
      Ilec troverà un oster molto saçant:
      Uberto da la Cros si se voit anomant,*
      Q'el amò plu ton pere de nul hon vivant,
      Plu qe non fasoit nesun so parant.
380 A colu te palenta seguramant,
      E prendi son conseil e fà·l çelcemant,*
      Qe plu no·l saça nesun homo vivant;
      Qe da traitor ne se poit cir guardant."
      Lor dist Bovo, "Tropo sto longemant."
385 Adonc se parile de cele robe grant;
      Teris vait avec lu, qe fature saçant;
      Oit cançé e le visaço davant.*
      Ensent de·l çastel, e si s'en vont erant

---

  364 Reinhold: doust; Rosellini: doust; MS.: 7 for *et*
  Rubric 6 (after 367) MS.: signibaldo; MS.: Comāt doit etrare; Keller: bouo. Co-/mant doit etrare
    370 Reinhold: Asà' a' tu
    371 Reinhold, Rosellini: amo
    372 Reinhold, Rosellini: Da qe
    374 Reinhold: sera' . . . demorara'
    376 Reinhold: trovera'. Cf. 374.
    381 Reinhold, Rosellini: çeleemant
    387 Rosellini: Oit cançer

Tantq'i fu ad Antone, a la porta davant.
390 Et ilec davanti si desant;
Li portoner li apelle, si li dist en ojant:
"Qe querés, segnors, qe aleç demandant?"
Bovo li responde, qe fo plus en avant,
"Nu semo mires, li miler qe fu anc;
395 Por guarir sen venu Does amantenant."*
Dist li porter, "Or m'atendés atant,
Qe nostra dama saçe li convenant.
Nesun lì po entrer sença li so comant,
Por la guere c'oit dure e pesant,
400 La qual li fait un çastel qui davant."
E dist Bovo, "Serà a li Deo comant."*
Li porter se partì, vait a·l palés co(r)ant;*
O vi la dame, a derasner la prant:*   3rb
"Dama," dist il, "saçés a esiant,*
405 A la porta son venu dos mires molto grant;
Dient qe in tot li mondo de le segle vivant
No sonto dos milor ne qe aça plu siant."
Dist Blondoja, "Vegna seguramant,
Ma si li diés qe me vegna davant."
410 E quant li porter vait arer tornant,
Qui entra en Antona, a l'albergo desant,
D'Uberto da la Cros, li saço e li valant.
Ses palafroi fa ostaler mantenant,
Pois vont a li palés a la sale pl*us* grant
415 Por veoir Dodo, e sa plaie de·l flanc;
Et entrent en la çanbre, trova la dame plurant.
"Dama," dist Bovo, "no aça spavimant,
Qe deman, avanti none, se Jesu li consant,

---

394 Reinhold, Rosellini: milor

395 Reinhold: a ma(n)tenant; Reinhold: does (= "two"?); Roques: lire "does" (commenting on Rosellini)

396 Reinhold: a tant

401 Reinhold: Soia a li Deo; Rosellini: Soia à li Deo

402 MS.: coiant; Reinhold: çoiant (with the cedilla in square brackets). Rosellini: çoiant, emendation.

403 Reinhold, Rosellini: à derasner

409 Reinhold: diés (p. 512)

412 Reinhold: li saçe

414 Reinhold: sala

417 Rosellini: ne aça

Entro ses plaie meteron tel unguant*
420 Qe tosto li guarirà; farò·lo sano e manant."*
Pois à cerché la plaie darer e davant
I dient a la dama, "Questo si è niant.
Meno n'est a guarir qe un trepaso de vant."
La dama quant l'intent, si li fa bel senblant,
425 E dist, "Signur mires, vu si starì çadant."*
"Nen faron," dist Bovo, "mille marçé vos rant.
El ne conven aler a far nostri onguant;
Nu avemo veçu ço qe mester li atant."
Dist la dame, "Aleç a Deo comant;*
430 E si vos pre qe vos venés por tanp."
E Bovo li responde, "A l'aube parisant
Seremo revenu cun tot nostri onguant,
Si le faron e sano e çojant."
I se partent, nen demorò niant;
435 A so oster retornent erant.
E Uberto li reçeve molto alegramant,
Si le apareille ben e cortoismant.*
Quanto ont mançé si fu de bon talant,
Bovo en una canbre entrò çelcemant
440 Et apella son osto; por me la man li prent.
En la çanbra li mene cun Teris ensemant,
E quant fu dedens, si li dis li convenant,
Con il fo filz de Gui, li bon conbatant
Et oit nome Bovo en la bataile de canp.
445 A cort endure tant pene e tormant,*
E çerche li mondo darer e davant.*
Quant Uberto l'intent, a li pe li desant,
Si legro non fo unqua a son vivant.*
El s'ençenocle, ma Bovo no li consant

---

419 Rosellini: Entre
425 Reinhold, Rosellini: ça dant
429 Reinhold. à Deo [vos] comant
430 Reinhold: prè
434 Reinhold: I sa partent
437 Reinhold: cortois[e]mant
439 Reinhold, Rosellini: çeleemant
441 Rajna (*Ricerche intorno ai Reali*, 198): mené
442 Rajna (*Ricerche intorno ai Reali*, 198): dis[t]
445 Rosellini, Reinhold: Qe oit enduré
446 Reinold, Rosellini: çerché

450   E si li fe lever suso en estant,
E pois li parle, si le diste bellemant,*
Q'elo vada a querir amisi e parant,   3va
Qe a·l matin a l'aube parisant
Sia a li palés cu*n* tot son guarnimant;
455   E porti soto le cape li bon brandi trençant.
E quando i oldirà lo corno de l'olifant,
Si le secora ne no se faça lant.
E dist Uberto, "No*n* parlés plus avant;
Qe plus de doa milia saverà li co*n*vant,*
460   Qe tot sont amisi e benvojant
E qe amava vestre pere lojalmant.
Volunter li vençaroit a li brandi tre*n*çant
Ver li traitor culverti seduant,
Qi le venent oncire a tradiment;
465   E quel fo Do le segnor de Maganc."
El se depart, nen demore niant,
Ne non mena scuero ni sarçant.
Tota la noit li voit apelant,
E çercha la tere darer e davant.
470   Quando qui le soit, sen molto çojant;
Çascun parele tuto son guarnimant.
Atant s'en va la noit, vene li jor aparisant;
Bovo e Teris se levarent por tanp
Por aler a·l palés a porter son unguant.
475   Dist Uberto, "Alé seguremant,
E farés quelo qe aveç en talant;
Quant sonarés li corno de l'olifant,
Vu averés secorso bell e jant,
Qe ça sont a·l palés plu de mile sesant;
480   Qe çascun oit li bon brant trençant."

---

451 MS.: diste; Reinhold, Rosellini: dist bellemant; Rajna (*Ricerche intorno ai Reali*, 199): parlé . . . dist
     453 Rajna (*Ricerche intorno ai Reali*, 199): al matin
     454 Rajna (*Ricerche intorno ai Reali*, 199): à li palés
     459 Reinhold: s'averà
     463 Rosellini: traiter
     465 Reinhold: Magança (with the cedilla in square brackets)
     469 Rajna (*Ricerche intorno ai Reali*, 199): cercha
     470 Rajna (*Ricerche intorno ai Reali*, 199): çoiant
     472 Rajna (*Ricerche intorno ai Reali*, 199): A tant se 'n . . . le ior
     474 Reinhold: aporter (see note, 377)

      E qui s'en voit droit a li pavimant,
      Ben resenbloit mires a li vestimant.
      A(n)cor non estoit levé de Do la soa jant,
      Mais de qui de Bovo li estoit ben tant
485 Qe preso avoit li palés tot quant,
      Qe toti stava atenti d'oldir li olifant.

Rubric 7
Coment Bovo e Teris retornent / A·l palés e recovrerent la cité.*
Laisse 8

      Ora fu Bovo en la çanbra entré;
      Dama Blondoja li est encontra alé
      E si li dist, "Bei mires, benvené."
490 "Dama," dist Bovo, "nu n'avon a planté.*
      Ora ne dites coment il est esté."
      Dist la dama, "Molto s'è travalé;
      Petit avoit en questa noit polsé
      Por la gran plaga c'oit en le costé."
495 E Teris non oit mie l'ovra oblié;
      L'uso de la çanbre oit ben seré,
      Porqe la dama ne s'en fose scanpé.
      Aprés li leto fu Boves apoçé;
      Enverso sa mere oit dito e parlé:*   3vb
500 "Dama," fait il, "e vojo qe vu saçé,
      Ma non fu mires, Deo soit la verité,*
      Nean nesun de le mun parenté.
      E son ben mires a çostrar en un pre,
      E si vos di, par droita verité,
505 Qe a Dodo donè la plaga de·l costé.*
      Colu qe son dirò en verité:*
      Or vos remenbri li or e·l tenporé, *
      Quant en la çanbra vu m'avisi seré,

---

    482 Rosellini: ben
    483 MS.: Acor; Reinhold, Rosellini: A[n]cor, emendation
    Rubric 7 (after 486) Reinhold: Boro; Rosellini: Bovo; line 2: Keller: al . . . recouerent
    489 Reinhold, Rosellini: ben vené
    493 questa: the final 'a' is darker ink, almost black.
    502 Reinhold: Ne an
    505 Reinhold: Q'e'; Rosellini: Q'e à Dodo doné
    506 Reinhold: q'e' son; Rosellini: q'e son
    507 Rosellini: 'l jor e 'l tenporé; Reinhold: li or' el . . .

	Si me mandasi la pavon tosegé?
510	Vos estes ma mer, e çeler no·l poé;
	Mais nule mere non fi tel crudelté.
	E cun cestu, qi est qui amalé
	Qe in cesto leito si case ennavré,
	Ordenasi li tradimento e la falsité,*
515	Donde me per fu morto e le vi(n)te donçé.*
	Saçés li ben, no li ò oblié,
	La pena e li tormant qe por quel ò duré.
	Par tot li mondo, e d'inverno e d'esté,
	Et en preson lungo tenpo pené."
520	La dama l'olde, tuto fo spavente;
	Volunter s'en foçist de la canbra pavé.
	Quant Teris oit ben li uso seré,
	E si li dist, "Dama, tra vos aré!
	Filz son Sinibaldo, qe tant aveç guerojé;
525	Segondo le servisio vu serés merité.
	E ben guardés qe moto non soné,
	Se non voleç estre por la gorça schané."
	Adonc la dama de dolor fu pasmé,*
	E Bovo oit l'olifant soné
530	Quant qui defors, qe erent parilé,
	Li oldirent si ont trato lor spe,
	Por li palés son coru *et* alé,
	Uberto davanti qe li oit escrié,
	"Mora li traitor, presa è la cité!
535	Bovo est venu, qe l'oit co(n)qui(s)té,*
	Le nostro segnor, qe Deo l'oit mandé,
	Qe lungo tempo avemo aspeté."
	Por li palés sonto corant alé,
	E por le çanbre e davant e daré.
540	Quant i n'oit ne veçu ni trové,
	De qui de Dodo ni de son parenté,
	Tot furent morti, a martirio livré.
	Quant per la tera fu la novela alé,
	Ad arme corent tot qui de la cité,
545	Ne non remist nesun, ni bon ni re,

---

513 Rosellini: çase (emendation)
515 MS.: vite donçe
531 Rajna (*Ricerche intorno ai Reali*, 197): spé
532 Rajna (*Ricerche intorno ai Reali*, 197): palés . . . coru e alé
535 MS.: coquite; Reinhold, Rosellini: conqui[s]té
540 Reinhold, Rosellini: quanti n'oit

	De qui de Dodo qe s'en furent scanpé;	
	Ont quel çorno molto ben aovré.	
	Or entendés de Bovo gran lialté;	4ʳᵃ
	Non volse ocire Dodo, porq'era navré;	
550	Qe en soa vita en seroit avilé,	
	Et el meesmo en seroit blasmé,	
	Q'el aust son per vençé	
	Desovra un hon qe estoit navré.	
	Bovo prist Dodo, cun ses man l'oit levé,	
555	E si l'oit ben e vest(i) e calçé,*	
	E ses plage stroitamente ligé.	
	Entro ses braçe qelo l'oit engonbré,	
	Çoso de·l palés elo l'oit aporté;	
	Desor un palafroi l'oit via mandé,	
560	E dist, "Amigo, ora si vos alé,	
	E quant vu serì e guari e sané,	
	Et eo ve trovi, ve serà calonçé.*	
	La mort mon per, e di .XX. donçé,	
	Qe a tradiment vos furent envojé	
565	Defor Antone por caçer a li pre;	
	Quela qe vi traì ne serà ben pajé,*	
	Avantqe da moi ela soja desevré."	
	E quel s'en voit, ben fu aconpagné,	
	Q'el non fust da nul hon engonbré.	
570	E quant i l'ont a salvamento mené,	
	Da lu se sevrent, sont arer torné.	
	S'el non fust qe Bovo li oit comandé,	
	Mais a Magançe el non fuse alé.	
	Adonc Bovo oit sa mer pié;	
575	De le oncir si li parse peçé,*	
	E da la jent el seroit blasmé,	
	Porqe l'avit in son corpo porté.	
	Ma segondo quel qe le fo conselé,	
	Ne l'ancis; mais anci, l'oit aseré*	
580	Entro dos mura elo l'oit muré.	
	Por una fenestra qe era ben seré	

---

552 Reinhold: aüst
555 MS.: vest ecalçe; Reinhold, Rosellini: vest[i] (emend)
556 Reinhold: stroitamente; Rosellini: stroitamente
566 Reinhold, Rosellini: Quela qe m[e] (emend)
576 Reinhold: de la
579 Reinhold, Rosellini: ancis mais, anci

Vedea li cor Jesu quant estoit levé
Da una çapela qe era ilec fermé.
Et en quela preson stete en soa viveté;
585 Ben se pote amendar de li ses gran peçé.
Da boir e da mançer avea a gran planté,
E quela donçela Bovo li oit delivré,
Qe li servia d'inverno e d'esté,
Qe li aportò li paon atosegé
590 Quando in la çanbra il estoit seré.

Rubric 8

Coment Bovo oit recovré sa cité; e de Drixiana / Ni de ses filz non save niant; e coment / Braidamont li mandoit mesaçer.
Laisse 9

Bovo fu en Antona, li pro e·l conbatant,
E Teris avec lui, si li vene ses parant,
E Synibaldo, e Latro, son enfant.*
Grant fu la cort e darer e davant *   4ʳᵇ
595 La novela fu alea por li mondo en avant,
Por vile et por cité e por li çasté grant,
Jusqua a Sydonia, la porta li merchadant.*
Braidamont l'oì, fa·se legra e çojant,*
Porçoq'ela·l scanpò da li stacon pendant,*
600 E de la tore o fi li sagramant.
Son per estoit morto, non avea hon vivant
Qe a la corone pertinist de niant.
Asa era rois prinçes et amirant,
Qe prender la voloie; m'ela no li consant,

---

585 Reinhold: sos gran peçe
Rubric 8 (after 590) Reinhold, Rosellini: Drixiana. Keller: recoure... e de / drixiana... sauo
591 Reinhold, Rosellini: li pro
592 MS.: E Teris aveç...; Rosellini: avec
594 Reinhold, Rosellini: çoie; MS. cort? Reinhold, Rosellini: Gran fu
596 Reinhold, Rosellini: et por cite e por li...
597 Reinhold, Rosellini: l'aporta li merchadant
598 Rosellini: fase. But cf. his 617, *fe se.*
599 Reinhold: Por ço q'ela-l; Rosellini: Por ço q'ela'l
602 Reinhold, Rosellini: pertinist
603 Reinhold: Rois
604 Rosellini: me 'la

605	Qe in Bovo avoit metu tut son entant:
	Plus l'amava de nesun ho*n* vivant.
	Ora s'en voit ces roman enforçant;*
	Si cu*n* questa Braidamo*n*t fu saça e valant,
	Mandò por Bovo e letere e senblant,
610	Q'el se remenbri quant fi li sagramant.
	De Druxiana ancor non è dito niant;
	Como ela s'en fo(c)ì cu*n* anbes ses enfant,
	De la gran selve, qua*n*t morto fu Pulicant,
	Cum li lion o el estoit co*n*batant.*
615	Asa durò Druxiana e pena e tormant,
	Çercando la çasté, cité, vile e pendant.
	E fe·se çugoladra, si aloit sonant
	Un arpa onde n'inparò tant*
	Qe molto ela plaxea a petit e a grant,
620	Si·n guadagnava robe *et* ar coit et arçant*
	Donde oit nori ses dos petit enfant,
	E si le fe bateçer ad un bon çapelant.
	L'uno oit nome Synibaldo a li bateçamant,*
	E l'altro Gujon, qe molto fu saçant.
625	Quant l'infant fo cresu q'el soit parler niant
	Ela li fe enparer de romant,*
	E de çanter dolçi versi e çant,
	Si le foit baler e salter en avant.
	Tant fu alea por le mondo en avant
630	Q'ela vene ad Arminie, et ilec la desant.*
	Son per no la conoit, ne nesun so parant,
	Ne qui qe l'avoit noria primemant.
	Tante so dolç i versi e·l çanter d·i enfant,*
	Qe li rois Armenion si le amava tant;
635	Non era ren e·l mondo se ella li demant,*
	Qe ne li sia doné alo demantenant.
	E si grant amor prist ad ambesdos li enfant,*

---

608 Reinhold: saçe
612 MS · fori; Reinhold: foçì (emend); Rosellini, foçì (emend)
618 Reinhold, Rosellini: Un'arpa (cf. Modern Standard Italian)
624 Reinhold: Guioa
630 Reinhold: là
633 MS.: Tant eso dolçi . . . ; Reinhold: tant son dolc'i . . . di enfant; Rosellini: Tant eno dolç i . . . di enfant
635 Reinhold: Nen . . . el mondo; Rosellini: Nen era ren
637 Reinhold: prist ad ambes dos; Rosellini: prist

        Non poit mançer, si no era davant.
        Ora lason de Druxiana qe sta a bon convant;
640   De dama Braidamont ben est qe je vos çant,
        Cum per Bovo mandò et il lì aloit atant.
        Bovo cuitoit morti fust ses enfant,
        E Druxiana la bella a li cor franc.   4va

Rubric 9

Coment Braidamont dapoische son / Pere fo morto, mandò por Bovo mesaçer.
Laisse 10

        Braidamont la polçele nen volse demorer,
645   Quant el la vi qe morto era son per;
        E de Bovo oit ben mesaçer,
        Q'el oit sa tere prise sença engonbrer,
        Morti ses enemis et in preson sa mer.
        Druxiana morta plu de sete ani enter,
650   De·l sagramento s'en prist a remenbrer,
        Q'elo li fe a li son desevrer,
        Dedens la tor o oit tant engonbrer,
        O il oncist li serpant malfer,
        E li malvés qe li voloit liger,
655   A li soldan e condur e mener,
        Et a·l stacon li volea apiçer.
        Ela sa qe il est li milor çivaler
        Qe se poust en tot li mondo trover.
        Poisqe il oit morto Luchafer son frer,
660   Nen volse pais lungament entarder.
        D·i meltri de son reame li mandò mesaçer,
        Q'el vegna a le a tor·la por muler.
        Richa corona d'or li farà in çevo porter;
        Rico reame averà governer,
665   E s'el venist, non volese otrier,[*]
        De li stacon li devés remenbrer,

---

   640 MS.: è; Reinhold: è qe
   641 7 for *et*
   Rubric 9 (after 43) Keller: da pois che; Reinhold: dapois che
   645 Reinhold, Rosellini: ella vi
   657 Reinhold: sà
   658 Reinhold: poüst
   661 Reinhold, Rosellini: Di meltri
   665 MS.: E sel venist; Reinhold: venir non volese; Rosellini: <<E s'el venir non volese . . . >>

	Quant ne·l fi e partir e sevrer.
	Li mesaçer ne se volse entarder;
	Tant alirent de noit e de jorner,
670	Venent a 'Ntone, (s)i se font ostaler,
	Pois vont a li palés a Bovo parler.
	S'anbasea le dient con homes pros e ber,
	"Ai, sire Bovo, nu semo mesaçer,
	D'una rayne qe molto se fait priser.
675	Non è plu bella trosqu'a Mont d'Oliver,
	Nian plu saçe por rason ascolter:
	Braidamont oit nome, fila fu l'amirer.
	Son per è morto, ne s'en po governer,
	Ni son reame tenir ni guarder.
680	Por vos nos manda, qe la veneç aider,
	E si la prenderés a per e a muler.*
	Rica corona vos farà in çevo porter,
	E rico reame avereç a governer;
	Negan de qui non demanda ni quer;*
685	Por vostro amor se farà bateçer,
	Macon et Apolin averà renojer,
	Si averà Jesu aorer."
	"Segnur," ço dist Bovo, "laseç moi conseler."
	E cil li respondent, "Ben est da otrier."
690	Bovo ven a Synibaldo, si·l prist a demander:* 4ᵛᵇ
	"Synibaldo," dist il, "veés ces mesaçer,
	Qe m'aporta novelle da loer,
	D'una rayne, fila d'un amirer,
	Qe me fe de Syndonia de la preson scanper,
695	E da·l stacon si me scanpò en primer,
	Dont malamant me volea apiçer.
	Et eo si le çure a le retorner,*

---

670 MS.: fise; Reinhold: Venent [à] Antone si (emend); Rosellini: Venent Antone si se . . .

673 Reinhold, Rosellini: Misire Bovo

676 Reinhold: Ni an

681 Rosellini: la renderés

684 Reinhold, Rosellini: Negun

685 Rajna (*Ricerche intorno ai Reali*, 147): fara

686 Rajna (*Ricerche intorno ai Reali*, 147): e Apolin avera

687 Rajna (*Ricerche intorno ai Reali*, 147): avera Iesu

690 Reinhold: si-l; Rosellini: si'l prist

694 Reinhold: Sydonia

697 Reinhold: çurè; Rosellini: çuré

Se Druxiana fust morta, de tor·la por muler.
Son per è morto, manda·me mesaçer,*
700 Q'ela se vole bateçar e laver,
E vada a Syndonia mon sagramento a 'quiter;
Unde a vos eo le digo en primer,
Qe de ço me diça conseler;
Qe in vos ò tuta moja fe e ma sper.
705 Ço qe dirés, averò otrier."
Dist Synibaldo, "Non è da intarder;
Questa venture qe Deo vos vol mander,
Se vos averés riame a governer,
Poco porés vos enemis doter;*
710 Par tot tere li farì descaçer.
A li anbasaor tosto respondì arer,
Qe vu sì prestes senpre de l'otrier.
Trosqu'a un mois vos diça aspeter,
Qe vos farés ves arms pariler,*
715 Qe aler li voli a mo de çivaler,
Siqe quela poeç honorer,
E son riame e tenir e guarder."
Bovo ven a li mesages, si le prist gracier,
E grant onor le fi, si le foit aconvojer;
720 E si le donò a çascun un destrer,
De riche robes si li fe adober.
"Segnur," dist Bovo, "ça çeler nen vos quer;
A·l retornar quan tornareç arer,
Salués ma dame, si le dites sens nojer,*
725 Trosqua a un mois se diça pariler
De tute quele colse qe li oit mester,
Qe si altament l'intendo ad honorer,
Como r(ai)ne qe se poust trover."*
E qui li dient, "Ben est da otrier;
730 Vestra anbasea ben averon finer."
Conçé li demandent, si s'en retorna arer,
E si menent qui coranti destrer.
Molto prendent Bovo a loer,
De cortesie e d'altro berner.*

---

701 Reinhold, Rosellini: E vada . . . aquiter
709 Reinhold, Rosellini: ves enemis
714 Reinhold: arm[e]s, emendation; Rosellini: arnis
724 Reinhold: Salvés; Rosellini: Salués
728 MS.: riame; Reinhold, Rosellini: raine

Enfances Bovo

Rubric 10
Coment li anbasaor de Braidamont / Parlerent com Bovo.
Laisse 11

735	Li mesaçer ne son pais demoré;
	Da Bovo se partent, conçé ont demandé,
	Por la bona anbasea gran çoja ont demené. 5ra
	Por le çamin tanto sonto eré,
	E pasent qui po e valé
740	E qui gran porti de la mer salé,
	Qe a Syndonie i furent torné.
	A la rayna la novella conté,
	E quant li soit, molto li fu a gre;
	Doncha oit mandé par tota sa contré
745	A ses barons, princes e casé,
	E a totes autres çivaler aprisé.
	De vitualia fu molto ben parilé;
	Plu de mile robes son coxi e (talé),*
	De richi pani de samite e de çendé.
750	Avantiqe Bovo fust a Syndonia alé
	Era ça la corte e bania e crié,
	Par tot part environ e da le,
	Quela novella si le fu aporté.
	Mile çubler furent aparilé,
755	Qe vont a la cort como est usé;
	Altri sonent enstormant *et* altri ont çanté,*
	Por tel mester ont robe guaagné.
	Druxiana fo in Arminia, la saça e la doté;
	Quella novella oit ben ascolté.
760	Quando la soit, molto li fo a gre;
	A li rois d'Arminie conçé oit demandé,
	Por aler a la cort, por eser anomé,
	E por veoir li baron de celle contré.
	"Nient valt avoir ne dignité,
765	Qi de·l mondo non avoit cerché;
	Le ben e·l mal s'atrova en le cité,

    Rubric 10 (after 734): Keller, Reinhold: com Bovo; Rosellini: con Bovo
    748 MS.: tâle; Reinhold, Rosellini: tailé
    752 Reinhold, Rosellini: da lé
    756 Reinhold, Rosellini: en stormant
    764 Rosellini: avor

E vi le cort d·i baron alosé;*
Por boir ni por mançé ne seroit desevré,*
Qi m'en donés asa a gran planté."
770 Dist li rois, "Se croire me volé,
No lì alirés, ne le meterì pe.*
Non avés ben ço qe vos est a gre,
Robe e avoir e diner moené?*
"Si, ò, " dist Druxiana, "mille marçé n'açé.*
775 E no li vo por robe; anci, n'averò doné,*
E vo por veoir cella nobilité
De cella rayne, d'oltra la mer salé,
Qe dient qe avoit cotanto de belté
E de la cort como serà finé.
780 Mes enfant la verà, qe serà plus doté,
E si serà plu saçi e maistré."*
Dist li rois, "Li seno m'avés cançé;
Ora alés e pasé, non tardé,*
E quant la cort seroit delivré,   5ʳᵇ
785 Por Deo vos pre, qe tosto torneç aré."
Dist Druxiana, "Ben serà otrié."
E Druxiana nen fu pais oblié;
De robe fi far plu de quaranta sé,
E d'arnise oit un somer carçé.
790 A palafro è la dama monté,
Et avec le, anbesdos ses rité.
Deverso Syndonia oit le çamin pié,
Tant oit la dama alé e çaminé,*
Pasa qui porti in nave *et* en galé,
795 E monti e plan oit asa pasé,
Molto gran poine ela li oit enduré,
Avantiq'ela fust in Syndonia intré.
Era ça Bovo a la corte alé
A do cento homes, çivaler coroé;
800 No lì è quelo de menor parenté,
Non abia robe devisé

---

767 Reinhold, Rosellini: E in le cort; Reinhold, Rosellini: di baron
768 MS.: seroit; Reinhold, Rosellini: seroie (emend); Holden: seroit
771 Rosellini: mentiri pé
773 Reinhold: moënè
781 Reinhold: maïstré; Rosellini: plusaçi
783 Reinhold, Rosellini: e[n] pase
791 Reinhold: anbes dos (as always; last time noted)
794 MS.: 7 for *et*

Nen una sola, mais n'oit plu de le.*
Avantiqe Druxiana fust ostalé,
Si era la dama cun qui de la cité
805 En santo fonte lavé e bateçé;
E qui qe no volse croire in Dé,
Ni Macometo avoir arenojé,
Furent morti et inpresoné.
A gran mervele fo Bovo doté,
810 E quela Braidamont molt l'avoit amé;
Le primer çorno q'ela le vi en primé,
Oit en lu son amor apojé.
Una corona d'oro li avoit aparilé,*
Donde le peres qe lì sont sajelé,*
815 Valent d'avoir molto gran riçeté.
Grant fu la cort par tota la cité,
E desor li palés en la sala pavé,
Bovo cun Braidamont asa s'avont parlé;
E de çoie et amor parlé e conselé.
820 E ordenent li terme qe doit eser sposé,
E in leito anbesdos colçé.
Si cun li termen se fu aprosemé
Q'elo no lì era s(e) no una jorné,*
E Druxiana fu en Syndonia entré,
825 Ad <un> grant oster ela fu desmonté,*
Et oit ses robe e mué e cançé.
E quando ella oit e bevu e mangé,
A li palasio vent cun anbes ses rité,*
E so arpa aporta, ne l'oit pais oblié,
830 E quando la sona li (ç)u(bl)er aprisé,*
Se le arotent e venent apreso le.
Et ela fu cortois si le ont honoré
E si le dona robe e manté aflubé.* 5va
Dist l'un a l'altro, "Cun questa à ben soné!
835 E qui çubler qe va por le contré,

---

802 Reinhold, Rosellini: plu de sé; Reinhold, Rosellini: Non
819 Reinhold: e d'amor
822 Reinhold, Rosellini: terme
823 MS.: so; Reinhold, Rosellini: so no . . .
825 Reinhold, Rosellini: un grant oster
828 Rosellini: vait
830 MS., Reinhold, Rosellini: bulçer (see note). Reinhold, Rosellini: quando 'la sona
832 Rosellini: E cla
833 Reinhold, Rosellini: afuibé

	Si va por robe, e questa ne le à doné.
	Or soit ella beneoita da Dé;
	Nen poroit estre por tot l'or de Dé,
	Q'ela non fust de çentil parenté."
840	No li fo çivaler conte ni amiré,
	Qe a Druxiana no le sia daré.
	Metesmo Bovo l'avoit aconvojé,
	A mançer a sa table l'avoit aseté.
	E quando ela avoit e bevu e mançé,
845	En pe se driça, sa arpa oit pié
	E si la sonè, un verso oit çanté,*
	E ses enfanti ont e balé e dansé.
	Tota la cort s'en fu alegré,
	E la cançon q'i ont çanté,
850	Dient en l'arpa e menu e soé,
	"A, Bovo, Bovo, molto son mervelé,
	Qe no conosi Druxiana e vestre dos rité,
	Qe pitete fu de la boscho sevré,
	Quant Pulican fo morto e delivré
855	Da li lion en la selva ramé.
	E m'en partì cun l'ovra fu finé,
	Por venir enver la mer salé.
	Ma in le boscho e fu aradegé,*
	Por altra via eo fu açaminé.
860	Asa son por li mondo pené e travelé,
	Tantqe nu semo en sta cort arivé."
	Quant Druxiana çanta li fanti restont aré,*
	Ne le fu en la cort nesun si ben doté
	Qe la cançon aust anoté,
865	Porqe li enfant l'avoit si ben çanté.
	Ma Bovo no l'à mia de nient oblié,
	E quant ela oit asa e soné e çanté,
	E qui enfant e balé e dansé,
	Donde la cort fu tota resvigoré,*
870	Bovo s'aprosme l'arpa oit pié,
	Ver Druxiana estoit acosté,
	E si l'apelle si la oit arasné,

---

846 Reinhold, Rosellini: l'a soné
851 Reinhold: Bove, Bovo
854 Rosellini: quant
859 Reinhold, Rosellini: voia
862 Reinhold, Rosellini: respont

"Ora me dites, dama, la verité;
Quella cançon qe vos avés çanté,
875 Donde l'avés vos, qi vos l'oit ensegné?
Ne la oldì çanter .vii. ani son pasé."
Dist Druxiana, "Daqe savoir le volé,
Ça vos serà tot l'afar conté."

Rubric 11
Coment Bovo demande la dama de la cançon / Et ela li contò tot ço qe li ert avenu.
Laisse 12

"Bovo," dist Druxiana, "e no ve·l vojo çeler;
880 Questa cançon eo inparè primer,*   5ᵛᵇ
En una stalle da un cortois palmer,
Qe me facea croire q'è un bon scuer
Quan Machabrun si s'en foçì arer,*
D'una poso(n) ben me pois menbrer;*
885 E de Rondel, li corant destrer,
D'una fontane no me poso oblier.
Non veés vos quest dos baçaler,
Qe si ben soit e baler e çanter?
A quella fontane li avè ençendrer,
890 E si le fi bateçer e laver.
L'uno à nome Synibaldo, e l'altro, Gujon son frer;
De Pulican e vos vojo conter,
Plus lojal homo mais no nasi de mer.
Quando le vi con li lion (ç)ostrer,*
895 E m'en foçì verso le li de mer;
Le mun segnor e cuitava trover.
El me falò la via e li senter,
Tant sont alé por tera e por mer,
Ça son venua por la cançon çanter."
900 Quando Bovo l'oldì si nomer,*

---

876 Reinhold: .VII.ani (noted also by Plouzeau, missing space)
880 Reinhold: e' ò inparé; Rosellini: e ò inparé
882 Reinhold, Rosellini: q'è un
884 MS.: poso; Reinhold: poso(n); Rosellini: poson
887 Reinhold, Rosellini: queste; Reinhold: des baçaler
889 Rosellini: are
891 MS.: guion
894 MS.: costrer; Reinhold: çostrer (with the cedilla in square brackets, emend);
Rosellini: çostrer (emend for costrer)
900 Rosellini: oldí

    Tute le cose cosi por orden aler,
    El prist Druxiana a mervele guarder.
    Par nul ren ne la poit aviser,
    Q'ela avoit lo viso tuto groso e lainer,
905 Qe soloit estre e lusant e cler.*
    Mais Druxiana se le voit segurer;
    En una çanbra ela voit a intrer,
    E si se fait de cler aigua aporter,*
    E le vis ela se pris laver
910 N'ese for de la çanbre cun le visaçe cler.
    Tota la sala ela fe enluminer;
    Bovo la guarde, si la prist a 'viser,
    Qe li aust doné e França e Baiver,*
    E tot li mondo e davant e darer,
915 Una parola averoit posu parler.*
    E quant il parla, prist Deo a 'dorer,*
    "Ai, sire Deo, bel per e spirter,
    Ben me donés, quant domando e quer."
    Non volse por la çente far nosa ni treper;*
920 Mais qi(r)eist li dos enfant baser,
    Estoitament tenir e acoler*
    De quelo la çente no savea merveler;*
    I cuitava q'elo·l fese por ses dolçe çanter.
    "Dama," ço dist Bovo, "non vos diça nojer;
925 Sofrés en pais sens nosa e tençer,
    Apreso de Teris q'è nostro frer.
    E lasés moi a Braidamont parler;
    Cortesement ne conven desevrer."
    E quela li dist, "De greç e volunter."   6ra
930 Adoncha Bovo no se volse entarder;
    Ven en la çanbre o la poit atrover,
    Desor un banco s'asise a parler.
    "Dama," dist il, "n'en vos aça merveler,

---

905 Reinhold: MS., et ler; e cler (emend)
912 Reinhold, Rosellini: aviser
916 Reinhold: aorer; Rosellini: ad orer
917 Reinhold, Rosellini: bel Per e Spirter; Rosellini: Sire Deo
920 MS.: qileist?; Reinhold: q[u]i seist . . . baser; Rosellini: qi veist . . . baser
921 Reinhold, Rosellini: E st[r]oitament
922 Reinhold, Rosellini: no s'avea
929 Rosellini: de greçe e
933 Reinhold: "nen vos aça . . ."

         D'una venture vos en vojo conter,*
935   Qe vi in Syndonie por vos cors honorer
         Et a prender vos a per et a muler.
         Ma ben saçés el ne fala li penser;
         Venu è Druxiana qe çurè en primer,
         E lojalment s'eo me vojo salver
940   Qe ça por le nul autre poso cançer.
         De ço q'è fato, preso sui de l'amender."*
         Braidamont l'olde, molto li parse nojer;
         "A, Bovo, sire, como me dovés laser?
         Por vostro amor eo me fi bateçer;
945   Or vos prego eo, por quel justisier
         Qe se lasò sor la cros encloder,
         Qe vos no ve deça da moi desevrer,
         Dapoqe in vos e non ò nulle sper,
         Qe me donés a un altro çivaler,
950   Qe aça mun regno e tenir e guarder."
         "Dama," dist Bovo, "s'el no ve fose nojer,
         A un tel vos doneria qi est pro e ber;
         Ço est Teris, qe tegno si cun frer."
         Dist Braidamont, "Et eo milor no·l quer.
955   Faites·le venir, q'e lo laça creenter."*
         Bovo respont, "Ben est da otrier."

Rubric 12
Coment Bovo conoit Drusiane e ses enfa(ns)* / E coment parloit a Braidamont.
Laisse 13

         Bovo for de la çanbre vent erant;
         Trova Druxiana e Teris ensemant,
         Et aprés eus anbedos li enfant.
960   "Teris," dist Bovo, "el n'è mué convant.*
         Questa è Druxiana, qe eo amava tant,
         E quisti son me filz anbes comunelmant.

---

   934 Reinhold, Rosellini: D'una venture vos
   935 Reinhold, Rosellini: vi[n] in (emend)
   948 Reinhold: Da po qe
   954 Rosellini: Braidamont'
   955 Reinhold, Rosellini: q'elo l'aça
   Rubric 12 (after 956) MS.: enfai (?); Keller: en- /faz; Reinhold: enfa(n)z; Rosellini: enfanz
      960 Reinhold, Rosellini: el ne mue [li]

Cun Braidamont fato ò cardamant;
Se vu l'otriés, serì rico e manant;
965 En çevo portarés corona d'or lusant;
Por muler prendés Braidamont a·l cor çant."
Dist Teris, "Le dites en gabant."
"Nenil," fait il, "fato n'ò li convant.*
Veneç avec moi, si·n farì sagramant,
970 E si la çurarés a lo de nostre jant."
Teris l'olde, ma non fu si çojant;
Quando vi ben no·l dise por gabant,
Donde se partent totes comunelmant,
E menent avec loro Druxiana a·l cor franc,
975 Et ensement anbesdos l'infant.
Avec lor s'arotent çivaler plus de çant   6rb
Braidamont vi Druxiana, se levò en estant,
Contra li vait por la man si la prant,
Si se mostrò bel viso e bel senblant.
980 "Dama," dist Braidamont, "non me vo mervelant,
Se Bovo enver de vos porta lialtà tant;
P(l)us aveç belté qe la luna lusant.*
Eo le vi ça en un perfondamant,
A gran perigolo de morte e de tormant;
985 E s'e non fose estea, el avea mal convant;
Morto seroit, e apendu a·l vant
Ne le sapi tant projere ne far bel senblant,
Q'ele poese far muer de talant.
Ben le deveç amer; el v'ama lialmant."
990 Bovo l'intende, si s'en rise belemant.
"Teris," fait il, "or vos farez avant,
Si çurarés la dama, farì li sagramant,
A nostra lo e a quela d·i Franc."
E Teris la çurò, veçando tuta çant.
995 Grant fu la cort e darer e davant;
En celle noit se voit acolçant.
E Druxiana cun Bovo se stete ensemant;
Quando fi li jorno e l'aube parisant,

---

969 Reinhold: si-n; Rosellini: si'n
979 Reinhold: Si le (emend); Rosellini: Si le, emend for MS.: *Se le*
982 MS., Reinhold, Rosellini: Pus
988 Reinhold: Qe le
989 Rosellini: doveç amer
993 Reinhold, Rosellini: di Franc
998 Rosellini: fu

	Le tronbe fu sonée e levé tota çant
1000	Dama Braidamont se levò molto çojant;
	Ses baron apelle, "Segnur, veneç avant;
	Çurés la fedelté a Teris mantenant,
	E si l'incoronés ensi cun se convant."
	E qui le font tosto et isnelamant,
1005	No le fo nul ni çoveno ni ferant,
	Qe li onsast contradir de niant.
	Grant fu la çoie e li torniemant;
	Ilec demorò Bovo un mois tot grant.
	Quando Synibaldo soit por mesi e por senblant
1010	Qe son fil è coroné de corona d'or lusant,
	En soa vite el non fu si çojant,
	E Bovo pris conçé, si s'en tornò erant,
	E menò Druxiane et anbidos li enfant,
	Qe pois furent çivaler valant.
1015	Braidamont e Teris a Deo li comant;
	Bovo ven a Antone, son riçe casamant,
	E mena ses baron e ses peti enfant,
	Synibaldo e Gujon, e sa mer ensemant.
	Gran çoja fu e darer e davant,
1020	Par tot Antone va le cloche sonant;
	Grandi fu li bagordi e li torniemant
	Le dame e le polçele se vont carojant,
	Por amor Druxiane se sont molto çojant.

Rubric 13

Olldu avés cum Teris oit pris Bradamont* (6ᵛᵃ) / Por mulier e coment Bovo fu retornés a 'Ntone, / E menoit Druxiane e ses enfans; or se començe comant fu grant la guere.

Laisse 14

	Segnor baron, e vojo qe vu saçé,
1025	Gran pena durò Bovo en tuto son aé.
	Or q'el est en sa tere torné,
	E q'el cuitoit stare a sal(vi)té,*

1005 Rosellini: Non

1023 Reinhold, Rosellini: se font

Rubric 13 (after 1023) Keller: Oldu . . . an/tone; Reinhold: [à] Antone. enfans or se començe, comant fu/ grant/la guere.; Rosellini: [à] Antone

1027 MS., Rosellini: salulte; Reinhold: salvité

         Ancora no est sa ventura finé.
         Quando Do de Magançe fu da Bovo sevré,
1030   Deliberé l'oit por soa gran bonté.
         E quando fu en Maga(n)ça reparié,
         E de ses plaie e guari e sané,
         A li rois Pipin el se fu acosté,
         Tanto li oit de·l so qe promis qe doné,
1035   Qe avec lui estoi(t) si acordé,*
         Qe il oit mandé por França li regné,
         E fe bandir oste e davant e daré
         Por aler a Antone e prender la cité.
         Mes avantqe cesto fose, (s)i cun vos oldiré,
1040   Li rois Pepin li oit mesaçer mandé,
         A savoir qe Bovo oit en pensé,
         S'el cre tenir Antona, ni est tanto olsé,
         Contra Pepin li rois de la Crestenté,
         Et a Do de Magançe, qi tant est honoré,
1045   En tota França e davant e daré,
         Non est homo de major parenté.
         Se Bovo vole vivere en tant eré,
         Renda Blondoie e lasi sa cité;
         Colsa como no, el serà sbanojé
1050   De la corone e de tot li regné.

Rubric 14
Coma*n*t li rois Pepin envoie in Anto*n*e / A Bovo dos mesacer lui menaçando.
Laisse 15

         Li dos mesages ne volent demorer,
         Ad Antona venent, demandò li porter:
         "Ami," font il, "laseç nos entrer!
         De·l rois de France nu semo mesaçer,
1055   Qe li venon una rason nonçer."
         Dist li porter, "Laseç moi aler

1028 Reinhold: no[n]
1029 Reinhold: Maga[n]çe
1031 MS.: magaça; Reinhold: Magança; Rosellini: Maga[n]ça
1035 MS.: estoi; Reinhold, Rosellini: estoi[t] (emend)
1036 Rosellini: li oit
1039 MS.: fi cu; Reinhold, Rosellini: cesto fose, si cun
Rubric 14 (after 1050) Keller: enuoie
1052 Rosellini: Antone

Enfances Bovo

   A li dux Bovo et a Synibaldo parler;
   Se le otria, farò·lo volun̄ter.
   Colsa como no, vu tornareç arer."
1060 L'un li dist, "Or m'entendì, bel frer,
   A Bovo me dirà qe sonto Garner,
   E dama Blondoja certo si è ma mer;
   E da la soa parta, e(l)o è mun frer
   E da l'altra part si è Dodo mun̄ per,
1065 Q'e no li ama valisan\<t\> d'un diner.*
   E vegno a lui por dir e por rasner
   Quant questa guera se poust afiner,*
   E le dalmaço laser e oblier.   6vb
   Plu le amaria qe non̄ faroit mun̄ per."
1070 Le porter se departe, nen volse demorer;*
   E ven a li palés, a la sala plener,
   E trova Synibaldo cun̄ Bovo con̄seler.
   De Teris oit recevu mesaçer,
   Qe a lu ven cun̄ .X. mil çivaler,
1075 A bone arme et a corant destrer:
   Tot le milor qe il pote trover,
   De quela menent gran treper.*
   Atanto, ecote venir li porter:*
   "Segnur," fait il, "saçés sença boser,
1080 A·l rois de France vos (manda) mesaçer.
   L'un si dist filz est de vestra mer,
   E Do de Magança certo si è son per;
   E dist qe de Bovo por voir est son frer."
   Bovo le dist, "Or le laseç entrer."
1085 E li porter si li dist, "Volun̄ter."
   Da lor se departe, si s'en torna arer;
   Avre la porta, li ponte fa decliner.
   Dist li porter, "Ben li poeç entrer."

 1058 Reinhold: farò lo; Rosellini: farolo
 1061 Reinhold, Rosellini: dira'
 1063 MS.: eo e mun; Reinhold, Rosellini: el è mun frer (emend); Cf Reinhold's note (512) corrected from *mùn*
 1065 Reinhold, Rosellini: Qe . . . valisant; MS.: valisano
 1067 Reinhold: poüst
 1068 Rosellini: e de dalmaço
 1074 Rosellini: .X.mil
 1077 Reinhold: quela [colsa] (emend)
 1078 Reinhold, Rosellini: ecote venu
 1080 MS.: vos mesaçer; Reinhold, Rosellini: vos [manda] mesaçer

E qui lì entrent sença nul entarder,
1090 Qe no aient da nul homo engonbrer.
Por me Antone prendent a çivalcer;
Tota la jent li prendent a guarder.
Dist l'un a l'altro, "Qui sont mesaçer
De·l rois de França, qe voxe çercher
1095 Bovo cun Dodo e far·li apaxer,
Siqe p(l)u non sia guera ni tençer."*
A·l palés desendent li dos mesaçer,
Pois montent en palés sença nul entarder.

Rubric 15
Coment li rois Pepin, qi rois estoit de France / Envoja à Bovo dos anbasator Por demander Antone e Blondoja sa mere.
Laisse 16

Va s'en li mesajes, nen demorent niant;
1100 A la plaça venent, si descendent atant.
Nen oit avec soi escuer ni sarçant;
Montent sor li palés de la sala plus grant.
Guarner oit guardé da un çanton davant,*
Et oit veçu sa mere in cotanto tormant,
1105 Como eser murea dentro dos mur grant.
L'infant quant la vi, plura tenderemant,
Siqe de larmes bagna son guarnimant.
Una parola le dist a·l geto en suspirant:
"Mere," dist il, "nen vos doté niant,
1110 Qe tosto ensirés de pene e de tormant.
Li rois de França cun tota soa çant,
Si vegnirà ça defors a·l canp.
E nu sen venu por faire li convant,
Por força o por amor averon li casamant." 7ra
1115 La dama l'olde, plura tenderamant;

1089 Rosellini: quili
1091 Rosellini: Pro me
1093 Rosellini: l'un à l'altro
1096 MS., Reinhold, Rosellini: pu
1097 Reinhold, Rosellini: palas
Rubric 15 (after 1098) Keller: enuoia . . . ambasator; Reinhold: Çoment; Rosellini: Envoia à
1099 Rosellini: Vasen
1103 Reinhold: Guarner; Rosellini: Guerner. MS.: çanton; Plouzeau: canton

Ela maldist e li jor e·l tanp
Quant unchamais pensò nul tradimant.
Ela dist a son filz, "Va·ne, a De comant!"
E qui sont parti, e vont pur avant.
1120 Quant i furent a Bovo, si le fa bel senblant.
"Segnur," ço dist Bovo, "dites li ves talant,
E nu vos responderon posa in avant.
E dites segurament, nen vos doté niant."

Rubric 16
Coment li dos messajes entrarent en Antone
E coment dient a Bovo soa anbasea e coment li respo(n)dì.
Laisse 17

Li dos mesajes furent pros e valant,
1125 E dient a Bovo ben e saçamant,
"Li rois Pepin, a chi França apant,
Salu vos manda tot in primeremant;
Qe le rendés Antona amantenant,
E demanes veneç a son comant.
1130 E laseç ma mer, Blondoja a li cor franc,
Colsa como no, por Deo onipotant,
Verso li rois non averì defendimant:
Morti serés, delivré a tormant."
Bovo, quando l'intent, si le dist en riant:
1135 "Frere," fait il, "poco ais esiant.
Ta mere m'à eté d(a)to quando eri enfant;*
Tu è un çovençel, baçaler en jovant.*
Li rois Pepin, (a) qe França apant,*
Me deust envojer mesaçer plus saçant.
1140 Sì vu ça venir por dir·me ste convant?
Poco v'amò, qi vos dè li persant,*
Por celle Deo qe naque en Beniant.

1118 Rosellini: Vane
Rubric 16 (after 1123) MS.: respodi; Keller: ambasea . . . respodi; Reinhold, Rosellini: respo[n]di (emend)
1128 Reinhold: Amtona à mantenant
1136 MS., Reinhold, Rosellini: doto
1138 Reinhold: [à] qe (emend); Rosellini: qe [à] França
1139 Reinhold: deüst
1140 Rosellini: dirme
1141 Reinhold, Rosellini: v'amò . . . li persant

        Par un petit qe je nen vos apant,
        Tu è mun frer, ne no t'amo niant
1145 Quando çendrés fusi da un traito puant!
        Tosto ensì de ma cort e de me casamant,
        E dirés a li rois a qi Françe apant,
        Avanti octo jorni li serà aparisant,
        Ben me porà·l veoir a·l pre verdojant.
1150 Et a ton pere dirà seguramant,*
        Qe ò aparilé un molto bon unguant,
        Qe li vorò doner a li torniemant,
        Milor qe no li dè a li jor en avant."
        Adoncha se partent tosto et isnelamant,
1155 E plus non parlent a nul homo vivant.
        E content la novella a li rois primemant;
        E li rois quant li soit cela por niant,*
        E fe sa jent aler plus avant.
        Quilois lairon de li rois de li Franc,
1160 E de Bovo lase mant ensemant,*
        Qe mili contarè asa plus ça davant.*   7rb
        De li rois Pepin nu diron primemant,
        Con ten sa cort meravilosa e grant.

1145 Reinhold: traïto
1150 Reinhold: dira'
1157 Reinhold, Rosellini: te[n] la por niant
1160 Reinhold: lasen ensemant (emend); Rosellini: lasem ensemant (emend)
1161 Reinhold, Rosellini: Qe nu li

7.2 Berta da li pe grant

Rubric 17
Oldu avés de Bovo e coment avoit fine e como* / El oit Drusiane recovré et Antone. En ceste / Punto de lui avrò lasere e de li rois Pepin. / Buens est qe vu saçé con primamant fo marié.

Laisse 18

   Li rois Pepin avec ses baron*
1165 Tenoit gran cort a Paris sa mason,
   E fu a Pentecoste, dopos l'Asension;
   Çente li fu de mante legion:*
   Aquilon de Baiver li adota e semon,* (5)
   Et avec lu Bernarde de Clermon,
1170 Rayner li pros, e li conte Grifon.
   Gran fu la cort, major non la vi hon;
   Çivalçent e bagordent, donent robe a foson.*
   Dist l'un a l'altro, "Porqe le çelaron?*(10)
   La cort de li rois no valt un boton,*
1175 Quando non oit une dame a·l galon,*
   Dont il aust o fiol o guarçon,*
   Qe apreso de sa morte e de sa decesion*
   Qe fust nostre rois, cun esere dovon,* (15)
   E mantenist en pase soe rion;*
1180 E par lu aumes guarison."*
   Grant fu la cort entorno e inviron;*
   Quando li rois vol montar en arçon,
   Avec lui en monta plus de mil baron, (20)
   Tuti filz de çivaler de dux o de con.
1185 Mais seguente li rois ne le fo nesun hon,*
   Qe tanto fust avanti como fu Aquilon,

  Rubric 17 (after 1163) Plouzeau (commenting on Rosellini) "*avés*, non *aves*"; Rosellini: en Antone (corrected Morini, review); Keller: /e como e loit ... auron la sere buem ... com; Guessard: lascié; Mussafia: e como el oit; Rosellini: avion lasere (corrected Morini, review); Rosellini: Buem cot; 7 for *et*
  1173 Mussafia, Cremonesi: por qe
  1174 Mussafia: vale
  1175 Mussafia, Cremonesi, Rosellini: al galon
  1176 Mussafia, Cremonesi: aüst; Rosellini: li aust (corrected Morini, review)
  1178 Mussafia, Cremonesi, Rosellini: cum. Mussafia: notre rois
  1180 Mussafia: aümes
  1181 MS.: e inviron; Cremonesi: MS.: emviron
  1184 Rosellini: de duxo o de ... (corrected Morini, review)

              Qe dux è de Baivere, de celle region,
              En tota le Magne non oit conpagnon.* (25)
              Et avec lui si fu Bernardo de Clermon,
1190   E Morande de Rivere e le dux Salamon.
              Or stetes en pais, si oldirés sta cançon,
              De diverse colse qe nu vos contaron.
              Tal tradimenti, qe mais ne le oldì hon, (30)
              E por una dame, el crese tel tençon,*
1195   Donde ne morì plus de .X. mil baron,
              E França tota fu en tel tençon,
              Nen fust Deo qe le fe reençon,
              Le Batesmo fust a destruçion; (35)
              Trosqua a Rome fo la persecucion.

Rubric 18
Coment fo la corte grande de li rois Pipin;*
E li rois e baroz, qi la guioient e d·i çubler.*
Laisse 19

1200   Grant fu la cort, meravilosa e plener,
              Qe li rois Pepin oit fato asenbler.*
              Asa lì sont baron e çivaler;
              Mandé avoit par tot la river. (40)
              Asa li son venu bufaor e çubler,*   7ᵛᵃ
1205   E altra jent, peon e baçaler,
              Por veoir celle cort e por le tornojer,
              E por veoir baler e danser.
              Lì son venu plu de .X. miler, (45)

   1187 Mussafia: è de Baviere
   1188 Mussafia, Cremonesi, Rosellini: tot Alemagne; Cremonesi: no oit; Rosellini: compagnon (corrected Morini, review)
   1189 Mussafia: Bernard
   1193 Mussafia: oldi; Cremonesi: li oldì
   1194 Cremonesi: cresé; Mussafia, Rosellini: cresè
   1195 Mussafia: mori
   1197 Cremonesi: fé
   1198 MS.: batesmo ẛᵗᵘ fust
   Rubric 18 (after 1199) MS.: de li rois . . . di çubler; Keller: e du çubler; Cremonesi, Rosellini: del rois (corrected Morini, review) Pipin . . . du çubler
   1201 Mussafia: asembler
   1202 Mussafia, Cremonesi: Asa'; Mussafia, Rosellini: li sont; Cremonesi: li sont [venu]
   1205 Mussafia, Cremonesi, Rosellini: zent (cf. Morini, review)

       Qe tot avoient da boir e da mançer.
1210   Ne le fo nul qi fu li plu lainer,*
       Qe le fose dito qe se trese arer.*
       Li çivaler bagorda por li verçer,
       E por amor de dame çostrent a tornojer. (50)
       Doncha verisi mante robe mostrer,*
1215   De diversi color de palii e de çender,
       Qe pois li ont doné a li çubler,
       Por far se anomer por l'estrançe river.
       Ma un çubler lì fu qi fu li plu alter, (55)
       E qe era adobé a lo de çivaler,
1220   Et estoit plu anomés en cort de prinçer,
       Qe nul autres qe faça qel mester.*
       Ben savoit tornojer e bagorder
       E ben parler, e molto ben derasner; (60)
       El no è cort de là ne de ça da mer,
1225   Qe s'el g'è volu aler et erer,*
       Qe in tot cort no sia ançoner;*
       Si dona le robe a qi le vol doner.*
       Lengue el soit de plesore mainer; (65)
       En Ongarie avoit eu gran mester,
1230   E celle rois qe l'oit a governer
       A gran mervele l'amoit e tenoit çer.
       D'Ongarie soit e l'insir e l'intrer,
       Si conose de li rois e li filz e li frer, (70)
       E ensement Belisant, sa muler.*
1235   Et oit veçu sa file, qe molto se fait loer;
       Bella e cortois cun le çio de·l verçer;*
       Tant è sa belté qe nul homo la poit blasmer.
       Ma una colsa oit qe la fa anomer: (75)
       "Berta da li pe grandi" si se fa apeler.
1240   De finq'era petita, si la clamò sa mer.
       E qui vorà ste roman ascolter,

1208 Mussafia, Rosellini: Li son; Cremonesi: li son; Mussafia: plus de

1210 Mussafia: Ne le fu (emend for MS. *Ne le fè*); Cremonesi: Ne le fo; Rosellini: Ne le fo

1218 Mussafia, Cremonesi, Rosellini: li fu

1224 Mussafia: cort de la ne de ça; Cremonesi: è cort de là

1225 Cremonesi: ge

1226 Mussafia, Cremonesi: ançoner; Rosellini: ançorer; Holden re Rosellini: ançorer; lire *ançoner*; Roques: *anconer*; cf. Morini, review, *ançoner*

1229 Cremonesi: eü

1236 Mussafia, Cremonesi, Rosellini: cum le çio del; Cremonesi: belle e

1240 Mussafia: clama

E por rason le vorà adoter,*
Porà oldire de qi la fo mer: (80)
De le nasi Karlo li enperer,
1245 Qe po fu rois de tot li Batister.
Mes avantiq'elo aust eu a governer,*
Petito fantin s'en convene scanper.
El no fo tera qe l'olsase bailer;* (85)
A Saragoça cun Turchi et Escler
1250 Li convene se stare e demorer.
Son per si li fo morto, e Berta soa mer,
Qe du son frer le fe atoseger.
Mais el ge fo un valant çivaler, (90)   7vb
Qe mais no·l volse deliquir ni laser;*
1255 E quello fu Morando de River.
E li rois Galafrio si le fe alever;
Avec Marsilio li fasoit mançer.
Ne vos pois tot li plais aquiter, (95)
Coment el s'en foçì cojament a·l çeler,
1260 Si le conduse Morando de River,
Por la paure de qui malvasi Escler
Qe li voloit oncir e detrencer.
Por sorte i pooit e veoir e trover,* (100)
Qe costu dovoit regnar toto l'inperer,
1265 Et eser rois de tuto li Batister,
Trosque a Rome a l'altare de san Per.
Li amenò Morando de River,*
E vi ec li rois qi perde sa mer,* (105)
Li vene en secorso cun .X. mil çivaler.
1270 E Lanfré e Landros, qe erent anbidos frer,
De li reame li farent descaçer,

1244 Cremonesi: d'ele nasì; Rosellini: D'ele nasì
1246 Mussafia: qe lo aüst eü
1247 Mussafia: ssen convene
1249 MS.: saragoça; Cremonesi, Rosellini: MS.: Saragoca; Saragoça (emend)
1252 Cremonesi: fé
1252 Cremonesi: fé
1256 Cremonesi: fé
1259 Cremonesi: celer
1261 Mussafia, Cremonesi: qui' malvasi
1264 Mussafia: costu devoit
1268 Mussafia: Eviec [?] . . . qi [fu] per . . . ; Cremonesi: eviec . . . rois qi [fu] per de; Rosellini: Aviec (for 'avec') . . . qi [fu] per de; cf. Morini, review
1269 Rosellini: socorso; cf. Morini, review

```
              Dont furent morti, cun vos oldirés conter;
              E cun Damenedé, li voir justisier, (110)
              Mandò ses angle, c'un clama Gabrier,*
1275     Qe coronò Karlo maino en primer
              De la corone de lo santo enperer;
              Porço devés vonter sta cançon ascolter.*
```

Rubric 19

Coment li çubler parlò a li rois Pepin
E si li conte la belté de dama Berte e de son per.
Laisse 20

```
              Grant mervelle fu celle (çubl)er valant,* (115)
              Saço e cortois e ben aparisant,
1280     E soit ben parler en lengua de Romant.*
              De tot le cort el soit le convant,
              E de l'afaire el soit li fondamant.
              El ven davant li rois, si li dist en riant: (120)
              "Ai, sire rois de França, molto estes manant,*
1285     La vestre cort è bella e avenant;
              Non è major en le bateçamant.
              Si ò çerché jusqua in Jerusalant,*
              Non trovo nula c'aça baron tant. (125)
              Ma non vos poés apriser la monte d'un besant,
1290     Quando dama non avés a li vestre comant,
              Donde vu avisi e fio e infant
              Qe pois la vestre morte mantenist li reant.
              E quando a vos el vos fust a talant,* (130)
              Una vos contaria cortois et avenant,
1295     Et è filla de rois cun vu sì ensemant;*
              Plu bella dame non è in Oriant,
              Nian plu saçe se la mer no me mant.
```

1274 Mussafia: angle c'um clama
1275 Mussafia: enprimer; Rosellini: Karlomaino
1277 Mussafia, Cremonesi, Rosellini: Por ço
Rubric 19 (after 1277) Cremonesi, Rosellini: al rois (cf. Morini, review); Keller, Cremonesi, Rosellini: e si li conte
1278 MS.: bulçer
1280 Mussafia, Cremonesi, Rosellini: romant
1285 Cremonesi: corte è
1287 Cremonesi, Rosellini: s'io çerche . . .
1293 Mussafia: a vos [plaist] et
1295 Mussafia: sì; Cremonesi: si'

        Una colsa oit qe tegno por niant: (135)
        Ela oit li pe asa plus grant
1300 Qe nulle autre dame qe soit de son co*n*vant;   8ra
        "Bertal' a li pe grant" si l'apella la jant.
        E soa mer oit nome Belisant;
        Plu francha rayne no è a li segle vivant; (140)
        Son per estoit rois d'Ongarie la grant."*
1305 Li rois l'intent, si s'en rise bellemant;
        E a·l çubler el mostrò bel senblant
        Por cella parole, el non perdè niant:
        Doner li fe robe e guarnimant, (145)
        Et in apreso un palafroi anblant.

Rubric 20
Come*n*t li rois Pepin fi gra*n* çoja por la parole
Qi li dixe li cubler, e si apelò sa jent.*
Laisse 21

1310 Quando li rois Pepin oit la parole oie,
        Qe cil çubler li oit arasn(i)e*
        A gran mervelle le plase e agrie,
        E conose benq'el no*n* dise stultie. (150)
        De la parole oit son cor abrasie,*
1315 Tantoto cu*n* il oit la parola finie.*
        Le rois Pepin ne la oblia mie;
        El se comanda a Deo, le filz Marie.
        A le çubler fi far gran cortesie; (155)
        De riche robes de palio e de samie,
1320 Un palafroi li done, a la sella dorie.
        Li rois li oit la soa fo plovie,
        Qe s'el avent qe cel sia conplie

    1297 Mussafia: Ni an . . . se la mer
    1301 MS.: berta lali pe; Cremonesi: Berta da li pè; Mussafia, Rosellini: Berta da li pe grant
    1306 Mussafia: semblant
    1307 Cremonesi: perdé; cella parola
    Rubric 20 (after 1309) MS.: cubler; Cremonesi: çubler (emendation); Rosellini: çubler (corrected Morini, review)
    1310 Cremonesi: oïe
    1311 Mussafia: Que cel. . . . MS.: arasne; Mussafia, Cremonesi, Rosellini: arasn[i]e
    1312 Mussafia: et agrie; Rosellini: gan (corrected Morini, review)
    1315 Mussafia, Cremonesi, Rosellini: tanto[s]to (emend)

	(Qe cella dame el aça por amie (160)
	E por muler elo l'aça sposie)
1325	Tant li donerà avoir e manentie,
	Asa n'averà tot li te*n*po de sa vie,
	Mais no li farà mester fare çugolarie.
	E le çubler molto ben le mercie. (165)
	Li rois Pipin non se·nne tardò mie,*
1330	Ne n'oit metu la colsa en oblie.
	El fa apeler la soa baronie,
	Et avec lor la soa çivalerie:
	Aquilon de Baivere, o cotanto se fie, (170)
	E Bernard de Clermont, a la çera ardie,
1335	Morando de Rivere, e li cont de san Çie;*
	Plus de cento baron el n'oie:
	"Segnur," fait il, "ne lairò nen vos die;
	Conseil vos demando, d'avoir co*n*pagnie, (175)
	De una dama qe estoit d'Ongarie.
1340	Fila est li rois, e saça e dotie;
	Se me doneç dama, vu farì cortesie*
	Forsi le voroit le fil sante Marie,
	Qe de le averoie o fiolo o fie (180)
	Qe guarderà ste regno qua*n*do serò fenie."

Rubric 21
*[Come*n*t li dux Aq(u)iluz de Baiver fo li primer / qi dona li co*n*seil / a Pepin.]**
Laisse 22

1345	Li primer qe parlò fu li dux Aquilon,	8rb
	Qe ten la tere entor e inviron;	
	E quel fu pere de le dux Naimon.	

1329 MS.: no sen netardo; Mussafia: no se nne; Cremonesi: no se ne tardò mie; Rosellini: se nne tardò

1333 Mussafia, Cremonesi: o'cotanto

1334 Mussafia: Bernardo

1336 Mussafia, Cremonesi: oïe

1342 Cremonesi: Sante Marie

1343 Mussafia, Cremonesi: Qe d'ele

1344 Rosellini: sarò fenie (corrected Morini, review)

Rubric 21 (originally after 1371) MS.: aqiluz; Keller: aqiluz . . . pepim; Cremonesi: donò . . . conseil / a Pepin; Rosellini: Coment li dux Aquiluz de Baiver fo li primer qi dona li conseil à Pepin.

        En estant fu, s'apoja a un baston, (185)
        Davant Pepin el dist una rason:
1350   "Çentile rois, porqe vos çelaron?
        Grant è vostra tere e grande region;
        Anomé estes plu de nul rois de·l mon.*
        Asa avés çivaler e baron; (190)
        Se vu morise sença filz o guarcon,
1355   Entro nos seroit e nosa e tençon.*
        Qui de Magançe, e qui de Besençon,
        E qui d'Austrie, cun quille de Clermon;
        Çascun de lor demandaroit la coron. (195)
        Ma s'erese avés a ves decesion,*
1360   Questo non po avenire por nesune cason.
        Ora prendés le conseil qe vos don,
        E non creés a dito de bricon;
        Prendés una dame de qualche region, (200)
        Qe filla estoit de rois o de con.
1365   E non è nulla, jusqua li Carfaraon,*
        Se la vorés qe i no ve la don,
        Cun grant avoir e cun grande machon."
        E dist li rois, "Ben vos entendo, Aquilon. (205)
        Li ves conseil senpre ò trovà bon;
1370   Ma no me diisi colsa de traison,*
        Ne qe a nul fese altro qe ben non."

Rubric 22
[Coment parlò Bernardo de Clermont.]
Laisse 23

        Bernardo de Clermont si fu en pe levé,
        Saçes homo fu, si fu ben adoté; (210)
        Pere si fu Milon, si como vu savé,

    1348 Cremonesi: apoià; Rosellini: apoia
    1350 Mussafia, Cremonesi, Rosellini: Gentile
    1352 Cremonesi: mil rois
    1354 Mussafia (no note), Cremonesi, Rosellini: guarçon (emendation).
    1357 Cremonesi: cum
    1356–57 Mussafia, Cremonesi: qui' . . . qui'/ qui'
    1364 Mussafia: Qe fila
    1365 Mussafia: jusqu'a li car Faraon; Cremonesi: jusqu'a
    1370 Mussafia: Ma'
    1372 Cremonesi: pè

1375 E quel Milon fu per Rolando l'avoé;
     Si oit par muler Berta la insené.
     Quando de la cort elo fo sbanoé,
     De le naque Rolando si con vos oldiré (215)
     Avantqe ces roman soja toto finé.
1380 E Bernardo parlò cun sajes e doté:
     "Çentile rois, saçés por verité,
     E no so pais qe vos en demandé;
     Aquilon v'oit un tel conseil doné, (220)
     Qe ça par moi, nen serà amendé.
1385 Quel qe volés faire, si le faites en bre,
     De prender dama, e saça e doté,
     Ora ne dites, se n'aveç rasné*
     De nula qe soit en la Cresteneté." (225)
     "Si ò," dist li rois, "s'el vos vent a gre,
1390 Fia d'un rois e de gran parenté,
     De Ongarie è, de quel regné.*
     S'el ne la done seron çojant e lé;
     Qe un çubler qe è qui arivé, (230)
     Por veoir questa cort e la nobilité,
1395 Tuto li son afaire el m'à dito e conté:
     Qe in la dama no è nul falsité,
     Salvoq'ela oit un poco grande li pe.
     Nian porço non vole qe stagé:* (235)
     Qi la po avoir qe no la demandé."
1400 Li baron s'en rist, si s'en oit gabé.*
     Dist li rois, "Ne·l teneç a vilté;
     Se Deo me dona gracia, no m'aça refué*
     Porqe eo sui petit e desformé; (240)
     Altament eo serò marié."

8ᵛᵃ

    1377 Mussafia: çorte elo
    1378 Mussafia, Cremonesi, Rosellini: d'ele
    1382 Cremonesi: e' no so pais
    1387 MS.: diteis? Mussafia, Cremonesi, Rosellini: dites se
    1391 Mussafia, Rosellini: e de quel . . .
    1392 MS.: ne la; Cremonesi, Rosellini: . . . el me la done
    1398 Mussafia: vo' je qe; Cremonesi, Rosellini: voie; Mussafia, Cremonesi, Rosellini: por ço
    1399 Mussafia: q'i; Rosellini: Qila
    1401 Cremonesi: nel teneç
    1402 Cremonesi: no m'aç'a refué; Rosellini: no m'aç à refué

Rubric 23
[Coment Morando de River / Donò li conseil.]
Laisse 24

1405 En son estant Morando se levà,*
      Quel de Rivere, qe gran segnoria à,
      Meltre de lui non è en Crestentà.
      Dist a li rois, "Mun sire, entendés ça; (245)
      Veeç Aquilon, qe v'à li conseil dona.
1410 En Crestentés non è milor, ne unques non serà;
      Qui mesaçer prendés, qe se convegnerà;
      Mandés en Ongaria, la dama querirà
      A quello rois qe la ençendrà. (250)
      Qe l'oit norie, e qe in cura la à.
1415 S'el vos la done, i vos la menarà;
      Colsa como no, arer tornerà."
      Dist li rois, "Qi envojer l(ì) porà,
      E qi de ço li conseil me dondrà?" (255)
      Dist Aquilon, "Pensé ò e l'ò ça;*
1420 Siqe nesun no le stratornerà,
      Colu vojo eser qe li pla moverà.*
      Bernar de Clermonte avec moi verà,*
      E Morando de Rivere qe nos convojerà, (260)
      E Grifon d'Altafoile, qe li rois tant anamé à."*
1425 Doçe furent qe Aquilon oit nombra,
      Tot li milor qe in la corte à;
      No le fu nul li qual s'en escusa.
      Çascun lì vait de bona voluntà; (265)
      Mal aça quel qe projer se lasa.
1430 De riçe robes çascun si s'adoba,
      E son pooir çascuno si mostra.*

1411 Cremonesi: Qui'
1417 Mussafia, Rosellini: li pora; Cremonesi: là porà
1419 Mussafia, Cremonesi: penseo e' l'o ça; Rosellini: Penseo e l'ò ça
1422 Mussafia: Bernar[d] (emendation)
1423 Cremonesi, Rosellini: Morande
1424 Mussafia, Rosellini: anama; Cremonesi: anamà
1425 Cremonesi: nonbrà
1427 Mussafia: Ne le fo
1428 Mussafia, Cremonesi, Rosellini: li vait
1431 Cremonesi, Rosellini: poeir; Rosellini: çascun

Rubric 24
[Coment fo aleu li anbaseor qi devent / Aler en Ungarie por la file li rois.]*
Laisse 25

        Aquilon de Baiver e li altri anbasaor
        Por conplasir a li rois q'i tenent a signor, (270)
        Se font far robes de diversi color,*
1435   A li palafroi le selle pint\<e\> a flor*
        Tute endorés de oro le milor.
        Çamais tel anbasea \<non se vite anc\>or:*
        De doçe baron colu q\<e i è\> le menor* (275)
        Avoit a guarder richo çastel e tor,   8ᵛᵇ
1440   E richa cité por li ses antesor,
        Qe ma(i)s non querent labor,*
        Da Deo e da Pepin qe tinent por segnor.*
        Li rois lor dist dolçement por amor, (280)
        "Entendés moi, li me anbasaor,
1445   E vos vojo projer, por Deo li Criator,
        E si cun a ves en cal de mun amor,*
        Qe a li rois d'Ongrie non sia mentior.
        Le vor diés, non sia boseor, (285)
        De ma fature, e de mes cor ancor.
1450   S'el vos dona sa file, me ne sia a onor;*
        Colsa como no, tosto faites retor,
        Qe d'altra dama nu pensaron ancor."

    Rubric 24 (originally after 1454): Keller: abeu; Cremonesi, Rosellini: aleu. MS.: aleri? aleu? unclear.
    1433 Mussafia, Cremonesi, Rosellini: qi tenent
    1435 Mussafia, Cremonesi, Rosellini: pinte
    1437 Cremonesi, Rosellini: anbasea no se vit ancor; Mussafia: non se vite ancor
    1438 Cremonesi, Rosellini: qe i è . . . ; Mussafia: qe i e
    1440 Mussafia, Cremonesi: ancesor
    1441 MS., Mussafia, Cremonesi, Rosellini: mas
    1442 MS.: qi tinenent; Mussafia, Cremonesi, Rosellini: , , . qi tinent por segnor
    1444 Rosellini: anbasador
    1445 Mussafia: E' vos . . . ; Cremonesi: e' vos . . . criator
    1446 Mussafia: E[n]si cun a vos . . . ; Cremonesi: e si cun a vos; Rosellini: E si cun à vos en cal
    1447 Mussafia, Cremonesi: sia'; Mussafia: Ongarie; Rosellini: mentitor
    1448 Mussafia, Cremonesi: sia'
    1449 Rosellini: de ma fature
    1450 Cremonesi, Rosellini: mené sia

Dist Aquilon, "No ve metés en iror, (290)
Tosto conpliron ceste nostre labor."

Rubric 25
[Coment li mesacer s'aparilent de·l tot quele / coses que mestere li avoit.]
Laisse 26

1455 Li mesaçer nen son pais demoré;
A son oster se son reparié,
Et a li rois conçé oit demandé,
Et el li oit doné e otrié. (295)
De riçe robes fo ben çaschun coroé,
1460 E palafroi richament açesmé;
Plus de trenta somer ont d'arnise carçé.
E quant de tot i furent aparilé,
Avantqe de Parise i fosen desevré (300)
Li fo la mesa dita e l'oficio çanté,
1465 E tuti doçe furent comuné,*
De·l cor Jesu benei e sagré.
E quando i venent a prender li conçé,
Li rois meesme fu a çival monté; (305)
Cun plus de mil de li son parenté,
1470 Avec lor i sont çivalçé
Plu de dos legue fora de la cité.
Pois s'en tornent, a Deo li ont comandé
E qui s'en vont baldi, çojant e lé. (310)
Nen son pais mie por Alemagna alé
1475 Cun i farent quant furent retorné;
Por la Provençe i sont oltrapasé,

Rubric 25 (originally after 1494) Keller: mesacer saparilent del . . . Cremonesi, Rosellini: mesacçer
1459 Mussafia, Cremonesi, Rosellini: fo ben
1461 Mussafia: carcé
1465 Mussafia, Cremonesi, Rosellini: cominié
1466 Cremonesi: Jesù beneì
1467 Mussafia: concé
1470 Mussafia, Rosellini: çivalcé
1472 MS.: Qois?
1474 Mussafia: N'en; Rajna (*Ricerche intorno ai Reali*, 321): Nen . . . l'Alemagna
1476 Rajna (*Ricerche intorno ai Reali*, 321), Cremonesi: Provence; Rajna (*Ricerche intorno ai Reali*, 321): oltra pasé

	E Lon(bar)die cun est lunga e le.
	E a Venecie i furent in nef entré, (315)
	Qe in Sclavanie i (s)ont arivé.*
1480	Qui n'ese in tere e sunt açaminé;
	Tant alirent nen furent seçorné,
	Li rois trovent a una soa cité
	O il avoit lungo tempo esté. (320)
	Li anbasaor (s)i se sunt ostalé*
1485	A li milor albergo qe soit en la cité.*
	E quant i oit e bevu e mançé,
	Li son oster oit a li rois mandé,
	Qe anbasaor sont de França li regné; (325)
	A lu li oit li rois Pepin mandé,
1490	Si le porta novela de gran nobilité,
	Dont el serà molto çojant e lé.
	E li oster fu saço e doté,
	Ne non oit mia la ovra oblié; (330)
	Vent a li rois si ge l'oit conté.*

9ra

Rubric 26
[Coment li anbasaor entrent / En Ongarie e parlerent a li rois.]
Laisse 27

1495	"Mon sir," dist l'oster, "e no ve·l vojo nojer;*
	Descendu sont anco a mon oster.
	Dise qe son de França, vegnu qui vos a parler,
	Da parte li son rois, qi est de gran berner; (335)
	E novelle v'aporta, dont le devreç agraer.
1500	Quant el vos plait, vos virà a parler."
	Quando li rois oit oldu li oster,
	E la novele q'el dis d·i mesaçer,
	El promis a Deo, li voir justisier, (340)
	Qe no li envojarà nesuno mesaçer,*

1477 MS.: londie; Mussafia, Cremonesi, Rosellini: Lon[bar]die; Rajna (*Ricerche intorno ai Reali*, 321): e lé
1478 Cremonesi: en
1479 MS.: font; Mussafia: font; Cremonesi: sont. Rosellini: sont arivé (no note)
1484 MS.: fi se; Mussafia, Cremonesi: si se
1496 Cremonesi: anco'
1497 Rosellini: vegnú
1502 Mussafia, Cremonesi, Rosellini: di mesaçer
1504 Mussafia, Cremonesi, Rosellini: no li

1505 Ma il meesme li alirà a mener.
Nen volse pais longament entarder;
De ses baron quant i ne pote trover,
Tuti li foit a uno amaser, (345)
Cun le çentil homes, li milor de son terer.
1510 Vont arer li cortois hoster;
Quant a sa mason venent a 'prosmer,
Li oster fu sajes, si savoit desevrer;*
Avant vait corando a nonçer, (350)
A li anbasatori dire e conter
1515 Qe li venent veoir e convojer.
E ci non volent mie tant aspeter,
Qe li rois doust in l'albergo entrer;
Defor ensent por li rois honorer. (355)
A l'incontrer l'un l'autro s'en vont a cliner,
1520 E dolçement l'un l'autro saluer.
Por man se prendent, se metent a erer
Tros li palés sor la sale plener.

Rubric 27

[Coment li rois d'Ongarie aloit encontre li anbasaor / Li rois de Françe e coment se parlerent, / E dient l'ambasea li rois, som signore.]
Laisse 28

Li rois d'Ongarie si fu saço e manant, (360)
Cortois e pros e ben aparisant;
1525 A qui anbasarir en mostrò bel senblant,*
Si le demande e ben e dolçemant,
"Qe est de mun segnor, le riche rois de Franc?"
E cil li dient, "El è sano e çojant, (365)
E si vo ame de cor lialmant."
1530 Dist li rois, "Soja a li Deo comant." 9rb

1505 Mussafia, Cremonesi, Rosellini: meesme li; Mussafia, Cremonesi: amener
1507 Mussafia: baron, e. Mussafia, Cremonesi, Rosellini: quanti
1511 Mussafia, Cremonesi, Rosellini: venent aprosmer
1512 Cremonesi, Rosellini: s'avoit
1513 Mussafia, Cremonesi, Rosellini: vait corando anonçer
1516 Mussafia: E ei non . . .
1517 Mussafia, Cremonesi: doüst
Rubric 27 (originally after 1566) Keller: lambasea
1525 Mussafia: anbasaür; Cremonesi, Rosellini: anbasaur

	Molto se mervele li rois e soa çant;
	Nen cuitoit pais tant fust la colsa avant.
	Li rois si fu cortois e valant; (370)
	Le primer jorno, ne le dise niant.
1535	Me l'altro jorno elo·l fi saçemant;
	El fe convojer d·i meltri de sa jant,
	Tantq'il n'avoit plus de cento sesant.
	Un disner el fi fare molto richo e grant; (375)
	E qui mesajes si li fu a·l presant.
1540	Honoré fu de molto riche provant,
	Siqe molto le loent li anbasaor de Franc.
	Ma una colsa lì fu qe despresiò vilmant,*
	Qe no se mançava sor disches ni sor banc: (380)
	Le tables furent mises desor li pavimant.
1545	Quando ci le veent si s'en voit gabant;
	Aquilon estoit pres li rois en seant,
	Si le parle belemant en riant,*
	"Ai, sire rois, vos estes si manant, (385)
	Aveç tel carestie de dische e de banc?
1550	En nostra tere si manue li truant,
	E la jent povre e la menue jant,
	Qe non oit da spendere or coito ni arçant.
	Mais se·l vo, se·l no vos vait nojant,* (390)
	Deman faron parler altremant."
1555	Dist li rois, "Soja a li ves comant."
	Dont farent parler disches e banc;
	Quant le rois le oì, si le diste belemant,*
	"Faites cosi en le tere de Franc?" (395)
	"Oïl, voir, sire, le petit e li grant,
1560	Li çivaler, e tot li mercaant."
	E l'altro jorno qe fu ilec seguant,
	Li rois con li mesajes si fu a·l parlamant;

1535 Cremonesi: ma l'altro
1536 Mussafia, Cremonesi: di meltri
1537 Cremonesi, Rosellini: centosesant
1542 Mussafia, Cremonesi, Rosellini: li fu; Mussafia: despressiò
1547 Mussafia, Cremonesi, Rosellini: belement
1551 Mussafia: poure
1553 Mussafia: s'el vos [plaist, s'] el (emend); Cremonesi: Mais s'el vos el . . .
1554 Rosellini: pariles
1557 Mussafia, Cremonesi, Rosellini: le vi, si le . . . .
1559 Mussafia: Oil, uoir; Cremonesi: Oïl
1560 Mussafia: mercant; Cremonesi: civaler

           Afor li rois ne le fo homo vivant. (400)
           En una çanbre fure*n*t cojemant,
1565   E Aquilon si parlò primemant,
           Si le dist l'anbasea dont li rois fu çojant.

Rubric 28
*[Com*en*t Aquilon de Baivere dise a li rois / p*rimema*nt l'a*n*ba/sea de li rois de F*ra*nçe e con*m*ent li rois en fi gra*n *çoja.]**
Laisse 29

           "Bon rois d'Ongrie, e vojo qe vu saçé,
           Celi qe a vos nos ont envojé (405)
           Est rois de Fra*n*çe, d'un molto bon regné;
1570   De Crestentés est li plus doté,
           E en le cuitrés est plus honoré.*
           El n'oit a ves tramis et envojé*
           Por grant amor e por nobilité; (410)
           Avec vos voria parenté
1575   Se eser poust e(n) voluntà de Dé,*
           De una vestra file qe molto li è loé;   9ᵛᵃ
           El non à feme de ch'el aça rité.
           Se le volés dare vestra file a sposé, (415)
           Elo la prenderà volu*n*ter e de gre,
1580   Et avec vos si farà parenté.
           Ma d'una colse no vos serà çelé:
           Açoqe anqes non fomes blasmé,*
           De soa fature vos dirò verité. (420)
           Petit homo est, mais groso e*st* e quaré;*
1585   E de ses menbres est ben aformé.
           Questa anbasea el vos oit mandé
           E da sa parte vos l'aven nonció."*

    Rubric 28 (originally after 1609) Keller: bauiere lanbasea coment . . . grant. line 2: Rosellini: proiamant. line 3: Cremonesi, Rosellini: coment.
        1568 Mussafia, Rosellini: Celu
        1572 MS.: tramis e/n/ et; Mussafia, Cremonesi, Rosellini: a vos tramis
        1575 MS.: e; Cremonesi: poüst e[n] voluntà; Mussafia: poüst en; Rosellini: en voluntà
        1576 Mussafia: vestre file
        1579 Mussafia: El la prendera
        1582 Mussafia, Cremonesi: A ço qe. Mussafia: unques; Cremonesi, Rosellini: unqes
        1584 Mussafia: est e quaré; Cremonesi: groso e enquaré; Rosellini: è e quaré
        1587 Mussafia, Cremonesi, Rosellini: vos l'avon

| | Dist li rois, "Vu siés ben trové!
| | Dites vos questo, por droita verité
| 1590 | È mon segnor tant ver de moi decliné,*
| | Qe avec moi vol fare parenté,
| | E qe ma file soja soa sposé?"
| | "Oil," font il, "porço n'oit envojé. (430)
| | Dist li rois, "E vojo qe vu saçé;
| 1595 | La fatura de li rois vos m'avés conté,
| | Et eo de ma file vos dirò verité:
| | Asa estoit bella e adorné,
| | Ma una colsa oit qe no v'ert çelé; (435)
| | Major d'altre dame oit grande li pe.
| 1600 | Mais una colsa vojo qe vu saçé:
| | Tanto e ò mia fila amé,
| | E ma muler qe l'avoit alevé,
| | Qe (se a) li plase est otrié et graé,* (440)
| | Colsa como no, nient aveç ovré.
| 1605 | No le daria a homo, s'el no g'è ben a gre."
| | Dist Aquilon, "Dito avon l'anbasé;
| | A la demant, quant l'alba est levé,
| | Si (v)os pregon qe vos ne respondé."* (445)
| | Dist li rois, "Voluntera e de gre."

Rubric 29

[Coment li mesaçer contoit la novele a li rois / D'Ongarie e con/ment li rois de France en fi çoya.]*
Laisse 30

| 1610 | Li rois d'Ongarie si fu legro e çojant;
| | De l'anbasé el foit saçemant.
| | Li mesaçer honorò riçemant,
| | A lor delivre ço qe quer e demant, (450)
| | E si le foit hostaler riçemant.

1590 Rosellini: monsegnor
1593 Mussafia, Cremonesi, Rosellini: por ço
1594 Rosellini: voio que vu
1597 Mussafia: bela e adornè
1603 MS. : Qe ase li plase; Mussafia: Qe se a li plase, est otrié e graé; Cremonesi: qe se a li plase est ostrié et graé; Rosellini: Que se à li plase est otrié e graé (emend)
1608 Mussafia, Cremonesi, Rosellini: Si vos
Rubric 29 (originally after 1677) Cremonesi: e coment li rois. Keller: dongarie . . . coment

1615 De tote quele colse qe a çenti hon apant.
Le çentil rois non s'areste niant;
Entra en sa çanbre, si trovò Belisant
Soa çentil muler, cun Berta a parlamant. (455)
Quando li rois le vi, si li dist en ojant:
1620 "Dame," fait il, "honor vos crese grant.
Se vu li otriés, nu avon bon parant,
Qe li rois a chi França apant
M'oit envojé anbasaor de sa çant* (460)   9vb
Por querir ma file Berte da li pe grant;
1625 Por muler la demande, s'ela li consant.*
Mes avantqe l'ovre vait plus avant,
De sa fature e vos dirò alquant:
El est petit e non guare mie grant; (465)
Desformé est da tote l'autre jant,
1630 Si est groser in menbres et in flanc.
Ma noportant ben sest en auferant,
Si è p(ro)don en bataile de canp.*
Rois è de France, corona d'or portant; (470)
Non è nul rois en le segle vivant
1635 Qe nobilité s'oit a lu parisant."*
Quant la parole oit oldu Belisant,
Sa filla guarde, si li dist en riant,
"Filla," fait il, "a v(o)s ven ste convant;* (475)
Vostro per vos à dito tot li convenant,
1640 De sa fature e de le so senblant;
S'elo vos plait, dites seguremant;
Colsa como no, no s'en farà niant.
Asa avon de l'or e de l'arçant; (480)
Ben vos poon ancora guarder longo tanp,
1645 E pois vos donaron a un altro amirant
Qe forsi a vos serà plus en talant
Qe cil no è, qe par petit enfant."

1615 Rosellini: çentihon
1620 MS.: Dame ⱡø fait.
1625 Mussafia: le demande . . . li consant
1627 Mussafia: diré
1632 MS.: pordon; Mussafia, Cremonesi, Rosellini: p[ro]don (emend)
1633 Rosellini: coron d'or
1635 Mussafia, Cremonesi, Rosellini: qe [de] nobilité soit
1638 Mussafia, Cremonesi, Rosellini: a vos ven; Rosellini: fait ila (emend)
1646 Rosellini: ves

Berta oldì si parler Belisant,* (485)
Soa çentil mer qe la perama tant;*
1650 E de son pere oldì li convenant.
Ça oldiré parler Berta da li pe grant,
E coment a li per parlò saçant;*
Ne la poroit reprender hon qe soja <viv>ant. (490)
E la raine c'*oit* nome Belisant,
1655 Ancor a sa file parlò en ojant:
"Filla," fait ila, "entendì saçamant;
Ancor non savés qe soja hon niant;
Ne prender celui qe no le sia a talant,* (495)
E qe de lui ben no sè contant.
1660 Colu qe prenderés, o petit o grant,
Viver devés con lui a tuto ves vivant;
Non fi doné la dame par un di e un ant.*
Ma se dapois no li plas, daq'è fato li convant, (500)
E quela faça colsa qe non sia avenant,*
1665 A son segnor porta tel penetant,
Brusea fi, çité la polvere a·l vant.
Senpre n'oit vergogne tot li ses parant,
Dolente ne sont a tute son vivant. (505)
Questo te diç'(e)o ben si por tanp,*
1670 Qe jo non poria pois avoir blasmo da la jant;
S'el ben te plas, dì·lo siguremant,
E no te dotar de hon qe soja vivant,   10ra

1648, 1650 Mussafia: oldi
1649 Cremonesi: q'ela per ama; Rosellini: q'ela
1650 Mussafia: son per
1652 Mussafia: saç[em]ant
1653 Mussafia, Cremonesi, Rosellini: qe soia vivant
1654 Mussafia, Cremonesi, Rosellini: oi
1658 Mussafia: prendez . . . no ve sia
1659 Mussafia: sì contant (emend)
1661 Mussafia: touto
1664 Mussafia, Cremonesi, Rosellini: qu'ela faça
1666 Cremonesi: cité
1668 Cremonesi: ne sout a tute; Mussafia: Dolent (emend)
1669 MS.: diç co; Mussafia: diç eo; Cremonesi: te diç eo ben si portanp; Rosellini: diç eo (emend for *diçco*); Morini: digo
1670 MS.: poria; Mussafia, Cremonesi: voria pois (emend); Cremonesi: de la. Mussafia, Rosellini: Qe io; Cremonesi: qc io.
1671 Mussafia, Cremonesi, Rosellini: dilo

	Cha por çel Deo qi naque in Oriant, (510)
	Qe dapoisqe serés alea a son comant,
1675	E vilanie li fais de niant
	E non staroge par tot l'or qe fu anc,*
	Qe de vu non venisse a far li çuçemant."

Rubric 30
[Coment li ro(is) e sa ragina parlarent (10rb) / a sa fille, si le dient la fature de li rois.]
Laisse 31

	"Filla," dist la raine, "e vos vojo en projer, (515)
	Qe primament vos diça porpenser,
1680	S'elo vos plas, cel petit çivaler,
	Qe est rois de Françe e de Baiver.
	Veeç qui avec (n)os (v)os per,*
	Qe contra vos voloir ne vos le vole doner. (520)
	Cortesement a quilli mesaçer
1685	De l'anbasea li responderà arer,
	Siqe nu no seren pais mie da blasmer."
	Quant la polçele olde sa mer parler,
	Et avec le la vede son per, (525)
	Un poco porpense si le respont arer:
1690	"Pere," fait ella, "e vos qe sì ma mer,
	Si me devés droitament conseler.
	El est venu de França mesaçer,
	Qe molto sonto da loer e priser. (530)
	Li rois de França si me vol por muler,
1695	E cun raine far moi encoroner
	E no so pais ne dire por rasner:
	Coment me porisi plu altament marier?
	Se dites qe çelle rois cun altro çivaler (535)

1675 Mussafia, Cremonesi: faïs

Rubric 30 (originally after 1717) MS., Keller: rose; Cremonesi, Rosellini: rois (emend); Keller: e sa ragina; Cremonesi, Rosellini: e la ragina

1678 Cremonesi, Rosellini: enproier

1681 Cremonesi: France

1682 Mussafia: avec vos vos; Cremonesi, Rosellini: avec nos vos

1686 Rosellini: balsmer

1690 Mussafia, Rosellini: sì; Cremonesi: si' (as always)

1694 Mussafia, Cremonesi: Françe

1695 Cremonesi: cum (as always; will not be commented again)

	Non è pais si grande ni plener,
1700	Nian porço no li vojo refuser
	Qe de petito albore, bon fruto se po mançer*
	E quel de·l grant si non val un diner.
	Questa ventura qe Deo vos vol doner, (540)
	Si la prendés de greç e volunter;
1705	Et eo si vos l'otrio, e le vojo volunter,
	Et a vos, raine, qe estes mia mer,
	De moi non aça unchamés reo penser,
	Qe de moi oldés ne dire ni conter (545)
	Nulla colse qe vos diça nojer;
1710	Mon segnor amarò de greç e volunter."
	Li rois l'intent, si la vait a 'coller,
	E por la façe droitament a baser.
	Quant el olde sa file li pla acreenter,* (550)
	S'el oit çoie non è da demander.
1715	Por man el pris soa çentil muler,
	Sor le palés venent a li mesaçer
	E lasa sa file entro la çanbra polser.*

Rubric 31
[Coment la raina d'Ongarie fu saçe / E ço q'ella dist a sa fille Berte.]
Laisse 32

	Li rois d'Ongarie, c'oit none Alfaris, (555)
	A gran mervile estoit de gran pris.
1720	E sa muler oit si le cor ardis,
	Non è çivaler en toto quel pais,
	Conte ni dux, principo ni marchis,
	Qe la olsast guarder por me le vis. (560)

1698 Rosellini: Si dites
1700 Mussafia, Cremonesi, Rosellini: por ço
1702 Rajna (*Ricerche intorno ai Reali*, 238): del grant
1707 Mussafia, Cremonesi: uncha mes
1711 Mussafia, Cremonesi, Rosellini: acoller
1712 MS.: ƀ a baser
1717 Mussafia, Cremonesi, Rosellini: çambra
Rubric 31 (originally after 1736) Keller: dongarie . . . qella
1718 Mussafia, Cremonesi, Rosellini: nome (emend)
1719 Rosellini: grant mervile
1721 Cremonesi: païs (as always)

Quant vide li mesaçi de·l rois da san Donis,*
1725 E vide qe tot sont çivaler de gran pris,
Ela voit a celu qe li par plu altis;
Çe furent Aquilon de Baivera, marchis.*
Por la man li prent, si le fait bel vis (565)
E dolçement ela li parla e dis:
1730 "De vestra venue, segnur, gran marcis.
Da parte li vestre rois, qe oit nome Pepis,*
Si vos avés tel colsa requis
Qe vos si n'avrés toto li vos servis, (570)
Qe mia file si n'è ben talentis.
1735 Dont çojant tornarés en le vestre pais,
Si menarés ma file qe oit cler le vis."

Rubric 32
[Coment Aquilon de Baviere parlò / A la raine por veoire soa fille Berte.]
Laisse 33

Aquilon de Baiver si fu en pe levés;
A gram mervile fu saçes e dotés, (575)
Si fo vesti d'un palio rosés;*
1740 (G)rant oit l'inforchaure e por le spale les.*
Quella raine el oit merciés:
"Dama," fait il, "nen vos serà çelés;
Nu semo doçe, tal dux, tal amirés. (580)
De nostre rois nu semo tuti casés,
1745 E li menor oit çasté e cités.
E si vos poso ben çurer por lialtés,
Qe in toto li mondo de la Crestentés,

1724 Cremonesi, Rosellini: de san Donis
1727 Mussafia, Cremonesi, Rosellini: Ce
1730 Cremonesi: mercis
1731 MS.: pepis; Mussafia, Cremonesi, Rosellini: Pepis
1732 Mussafia: nos avés
1733 Mussafia: aurés
Rubric 32 (originally after 1772) MS., Keller: bauiere
1738 Mussafia: gran mervile; Cremonesi: gram mervile; Rosellini: gran merveile
1739 Mussafia: vestu
1740 MS.: Orant? Qrant?; Mussafia, Cremonesi, Rosellini: Grant
1742 Mussafia: fait il, «il nen vos . . .
1744 MS.: nostres
1745 Mussafia: çaste[ls]

	El non è rois, prinçes ni amirés (585)
	Qe de li rois de Française s'el te\<ni\>s por viltés*
1750	(D)e avec lui avoire parentés.*
	Quando nu averon vestra file amenés,
	E qe raina serà encoronés,
	Ela serà de France raina clamés; (590)
	A gran mervile n'en porì eser lés.*
1755	Se li rois è petito, Deo si l'oit formés;*
	Ma noportanto, saça por verités:*
	Prodomo ert a çostrer en tornés.
	El non è çivaler quel qe è li plu menbrés, (595)
	Cun q'il non çostri a lança et a spés."
1760	La dama s'en rist bellament e soés;
	E dist ad Aquilon, "Dites moi verités:
	Estes vos sire, conte ni amirés,
	\<Ami a·l\> roi, ni drudo ni pr(i)vés?" (600)
	"Si, son, madame, en mia lialtés. 10ᵛᵃ
1765	Se li rois non fust en nos tot fiés,
	El no n'averoit quialois envojés."*
	Dist la dame, "Ben senblant n'avés;
	A ves voloir et a ves voluntés (605)
	Ve soit mia file de·l tot delivrés,
1770	A celle rois, qe vu si l'amenés,
	Q'elo ne façe la soa voluntés."
	Dist Aquilon, "Mille marçé n'ajés."

1749 Mussafia: Qe . . . sel tenis . . . vilté; Cremonesi: qe de li . . . sel tenis; Rosellini: Qe de li rois . . . se'l tenis

1750 MS.: Qe; Mussafia, Rosellini: De . . . ; Cremonesi: de . . .

1753 Mussafia: E la sera de França raine . . .

1754 Mussafia, Rosellini: nen

1756 Mussafia, Cremonesi: Ma no por tanto

1757 MS.: ert; Cremonesi: est (emend)

1758 Mussafia: est li plus; Cremonesi: è li plu menbés; Rosellini: est li plu menbrés

1759 7 for *et*; Cremonesi: e a spés

1760 Mussafia: rise

1763 MS.: prves; Cremonesi: [e a li]; Mussafia: [Ami au] roi; Rosellini: [Al] roi ni drudo; Mussafia, Cremonesi, Rosellini: privés

1764 Mussafia, Cremonesi, Rosellini: ma dame

1772 MS.: mille; Mussafia: marçè

Rubric 33
[Coment la raina mena Aquilon / Por veoir soa fille nue.]
Laisse 34

        "Çentil raine, nen vos doit nojer, (610)
        Se vestra file vu ne volés doner.
1775 Nu la prenderon de greç e volunter,
        E por li rois nu l'averon sposer,
        E pois avec nos nu l'averon mener.
        Mais d'una ren nen vos vojo enganer: (615)
        Quando li rois de Françe ven a prender muler,
1780 Avantqe cun le dame el se diça acolçer,
        Se fait la dame tuta nua despoler,
        E fi ben guardea e davant e darer.
        S'el aust altro q'ela non par mostrer,* (620)
        Lo mariaço se tornaria arer."*
1785 Dist la raine, "Non aça quel penser;
        Qe la ma file vos farò despoiler,
        Si la porés tot por menu çercher.
        Se vu no la trovés tuta sana e senç'er, (625)
        Afors li pe d'altro no me porés blasmer."
1790 Dist Aquilon, "De qui no ve requer;*
        Ma se me volés, sor vostra fois creenter,
        Q'el è ço voir qe vos oldo conter,
        Ben me averò en vos afiançer." (630)
        Dist la raine, "Entendés, çivaler,
1795 Nen vojo qe unchamés vu m'en diça blasmer;
        Entro ma çanbre venerés a·l çeler,
        E vos farò ma file despoler.
        Tota nue la porés veer."* (635)
        Qe vos doie li plais plus alonçer?*

    Rubric 33 (originally after 1822)
    1774 Rosellini: file ne vu ne volés . . .
    1780 Mussafia: la dame; Cremonesi, Rosellini: le dame
    1782 Mussafia: fi . . . davante e
    1783 Mussafia, Cremonesi: aüst (as always; not commented again)
    1784 Mussafia: Le mariaço se; Cremonesi: lo mariaço se; Rosellini: Lo mariaçco se . . .
    1788 Mussafia, Cremonesi, Rosellini: sençer
    1795 Cremonesi: uncha mes
    1798 Cremonesi: tota nua; Rosellini: Tota nua
    1799 Mussafia: do je

1800 Quella raine prist d·i çivaler,*
Dux Aquilon e Morando de R(i)ver;*
Cun ceste dos vait en la çanbra entrer,
E soa file oit fata despoler. (640)
A cele dos la mostra, e davant e darer,
1805 Qui s'en contente, si s'en retorna arer.
Qi donc veist *tot* li mesaçer,
Avec li rois la gran çoja mener.
Li rois nen volse la ovra oblier: (645)
El fa sa jent e baron asenbler,
1810 Tot li milor qi fu de son terer,
Por venir a sa file q'elo vol nucier.   10vb
Gran corte fo, e davant e darer,
Donda verisi çivaler tornier (650)
E celle dames baler e carojer,
1815 Por amor de Berte le veisés danser.
Quella corte durò quinçe jor to(t) enter,*
Quant Aquilon vait a li rois parler,
Por domander conçé si s'en volent aler; (655)
E a la raine dolçement projer,
1820 Qe soa file li diça delivrer.
Dist la raine, "De greç e volunter;
Or me laseç ma fille adorner."

Rubric 34

[*Coment la rayne semonisoit sa fille / tuto ço qe faire devoit; e·n tot li otria.*]
Laisse 35

Cella raine si fu saça e valent, (660)
A gran mervele oit li cor molt çent.
1825 A soa file parloe dolçement:
"Filla," fait ella, "li penser vos soment.*
E vos ai mariea molto onorablement,

1800 Mussafia, Cremonesi, Rosellini: di çivaler
1801 MS.: derver; Mussafia, Rosellini: de R(i)ver (emend); Cremonesi: de R[i]ver
1804 Mussafia: davante e
1806 Mussafia, Cremonesi: donc veïst tot (as always)
1815 Mussafia, Cremonesi: veïses (as always)
1816 MS.: tor enter?; Mussafia: tos enter; Cremonesi, Rosellini: toz enter
1818 Mussafia: demander
Rubric 34 (originally after 1844) line 2: Keller, Cremonesi, Rosellini: en tot; MS.: Rayne. Cremonesi: otrià
    1824 Cremonesi: molto çent

Donde portarés corona d'or lusent; (665)
E si vos ai deliverea a una strania gent.
1830 Mener vos doverà a son comandament;
Asa vos donarò e or coito e arçent,
Siés cortese e ben aparisent,*
Q'i no vos tenise raina da nient; (670)
A lor donés robe e vestiment.
1835 Sor tute ren de li monde vivent,*
Vestre segnor amerés lojalment,
Si le farés toto li son talent.
Serés cortois a tote l'autre jent, (675)
A çascun servés lojal e droitament;
1840 Faites qe de vos no se blasmi escuer ni sarçent."
Dist la dama, "E l'ò ben en talent;
Lojal e tegno vestro castigament,
Et eo lo tirò a tuto mon vivent; (680)
E de questo states segurament."

Rubric 35
[Coment Aquilon parole a la (raine) / e demandente sa fille.]
Laisse 36

1845 Dux Aquilon, li bon conseleor,
Unques a·l segle n'en estoit un milor,
Ne qe a li rois faist major honor,
Per fu de Naimes qe sor tot fu la flor, (685)
Dist a li rois dolçement por amor:
1850 "Ai, sire rois, par Deo le Criator,
Poisqe nu avon aconpli nos labor,
Car ne faites bailer de Pipin sa usor,
Qe torner volen en le tere major; (690)
E vestra file mener a grant honor."
1855 Dist li rois, "Volunter, sens busor."

1829 Mussafia, Cremonesi: ai delivrea a una strania gent; Rosellini: delivrea à . . .
1835 Mussafia, Cremonesi, Rosellini: mondo
1836 Cremonesi: Vostro
1843 MS.: mon t̸a̸l̸e̸ vivent
Rubric 35 (originally after 1855) MS.: Aquilon . . . la iie; Keller: laue e demandete; Cremonesi, Rosellini: a l[i rois] e demandete; Rosellini: Keller, parole alaue e demādēte; original position, new fol. begins here, at first line: 11ra
1845 Mussafia: fu bon
1847 Mussafia, Cremonesi: faïst maior

Rubric 36
[Coment li rois apella sa muler / e coment li fu la dame delivriée.]
Laisse 37

	Li rois d'Ongarie nen volse demorer;	(11 ra)
	El apelò Belisant sa muler:	
	"Dama," fait il, "veeç li mesaçer, (695)	
	Li qual ne vole vestra fila amener.	
1860	Car ge la bailés, se l'avés fata adorner	
	De tot quelle colse qe li oit mester,	
	Qe no li manchi ren che se posa penser."	
	Dist la raine, "Laseç quel pla ester; (700)	
	Si grandemente nu l'averon mander,	
1865	Ne li faliria solo a li soler.	
	Tot ses arnise ò fato renoveler."	
	Adoncha fait venir li mesaçer;	
	Da l'autra parte Berta li fait erer. (705)	
	"Segnur," fait ella, "ne vos doja nojer;	
1870	Prendés la dama a ves justisier.	
	E sana e salva vu la diça mener,	
	A son segnor qe l'oit a desier."*	
	Qui li dient, "De greç e volunter." (710)	
	Un palafroi fait la raina coroer,	
1875	Qi sol la sela volese bragagner	
	Par mille livre ne la poroit eslojer.	
	Gran fu la çoja quant vene a·l delivrer;	
	Grande fu quando vene a·l desevrer. (715)	
	Qi donc veist la raine soa fia baser,	
1880	Da l'autra part, li rois qi è son per.	
	E la raine fait carçer .XV. somer	
	D'or e d'avoir, d'or coito e de diner,	
	E altretanti de robe da doner, (720)	
	Qe tuti erent de palii e de çender.	
1885	Quando s'en prendent a 'ler li mesaçer,	
	Qe soa file se deveroit desevrer,	
	Li rois e la raine començe a larmojer;	
	E pois prendent a cival monter, (725)	

Rubric 36 (orginally after 1918) Cremonesi: apellà
1872 Mussafia: adesier
1879 Mussafia, Cremonesi: veïst . . . raïne (as always)
1885 Mussafia, Cremonesi, Rosellini: aler
1887 Mussafia: comence
1888 Mussafia: [a] monter

A plus de mille nobli çivaler.
1890 Sa filla convoie plus de dos legue enter;
A·l departir ila no vont a acorler.*
Li rois e la raine començe a larmojer;
I s'en torne e lasa qui aler. (730)
I non soit mie li grande engonbrer!
1895 Par Ongarie çivalçent trois jorni tot enter,
Qe de·l so non spendent valisant un diner.
Nen volse pais por Lonbardia torner;
Por Alemagne se prendent a erer, (735)
Quant i çonçent a castel o docler,*
1900 Et elo sia ora de l'alberçer,
I no vol mais in hoster alberçer;*
A cha de cont o de gran çivaler,
Quella dame i font desmonter, (740)   11rb
E richament la font hostaler.
1905 No le fo dux, conte ni princer,
Qe por amor li rois qe França oit a bailer,
Ne la recoit e vega·la volunter.*
E la raina tant fu cortois e ber; (745)
S'ela trovava donçela da marier,
1910 Fila de qui qe l'avoit hostaler,
Por cortesia, li vait a demander,
Si le promete altament marier;
Se i le done, mena sego vonter.* (750)
Tant çivalçent por via e por senter,
1915 Qe una soir a l'ora de·l vesprer
En Magançe venent a alberçer,
A cha d'un conte qe oit nome Belençer,
Qe de qui de Magançe a cil tenps fu li plu alter. (755)

1891 Cremonesi: I la ne vont; Mussafia, Rosellini: i la vont (emend for MS. *ila nouont acorler*); Mussafia, Cremonesi, Rosellini: acoler (emend)

1898 Mussafia: Alamagne

1899 Cremonesi, Rosellini: çastel

1901 Mussafia: no vol pais (ms: vol vais); Rosellini: MS. = i no uol uais; Cremonesi: mais (ms: vol pais)

1906 Mussafia: rois que

1907 Mussafia, Cremonesi, Rosellini: vegala. Mussafia, Cremonesi, Rosellini: reçoit

Rubric 37
[Coment li mesaçer f(u o)stalé in Magançe / e coment la raine porist amor a la donçelle.]*
Laisse 38

	Li mesaçer sont en Magança entré,
1920	A cha de Belençer i sont alberçé.
	E quel si le receve, volunter e de gre,
	Por amor li rois li oit molto honoré.
	Quel oit una file, plu bela nen veré,* (760)
	Qe a la raine fu si asomilé,
1925	E l'una e l'autre qua*n*t fusen asenblé,*
	L'una da l'autre nen seroit desomilé.
	A la raine venoit si a gre,
	A·l boir e a·l mançer ela li seoit a pe, (765)
	E in un leto anbesdoe colçé.
1930	Terço çorno furent ilec seçorné,
	Avantiq'ela fost partia ni sevré,
	A son per l'oit queria e demandé,
	Q'ela in França si vaga avec le, (770)
	E li sea altament marié.
1935	Tanto l'avoit Aquilone projé,
	E la raine q'el li oit delivré,
	E altament el li oit mandé,
	Un d·i milor de la soa contré, (775)
	Li qual si fu de le so parenté,
1940	Por so bailo li avoit envojé;
	E qe li doni ço qe le fust a gre.
	Li mesaçer sont a çival monté;
	Quando a Paris i furent aprosmé, (780)
	Mesaçer ont a li rois envojé
1945	Qe la raine vent cu*n* sa nobilité,
	Si altament con raina encoroné.*

Rubric 37 (orginally after 1959) fo h[o]stalé: MS.: fouctale; Keller: fou stale . . . porist; Cremonesi, Rosellini: fou stalé . . . prist; Guessard: prist; MS.: Raine
1923 Mussafia: plus
1925 Mussafia: Que l'una . . . , emendation
Rosellini: de l'autre
1929 Mussafia: ambesdoe
1938 Mussafia, Cremonesi, Rosellini: un di milor
1941 MS.: doni ɖ ço
1942 Mussafia, Rosellini: cival
1946 MS.: encorone; Mussafia: raïne

De quela colsa li rois si fu çojant e lé;
El oit mandé par toto son regné, (785)
E fa venir li conte e li casé,
1950 Por aler encontre, fu a çival monté   11ᵛᵃ
Plus de mile de çivaler prisé.
Quan(d)o furent pres Paris a meno de dos le,*
E Berta fu lasés, e tuta travalé, (790)
Porq'ela oit cotanto çivalçé,
1955 A la donçela oit dito e parlé:
"Çentil co*n*pagna, coven qe me servé
D'una colsa donde n'averò gra*n* gre."*
Dist la donçela, "Dites e comandé; (795)
Ço qe vos plait serà ben otrié."

Rubric 38
[Coment la raine proja la donçelle qe / pro le in celle noit se deus apresenter a li rois *in le leit, magis non far so*n *voloir.]**
Laisse 39

1960 "Çentil polçele," dist Berte en ojant,*
"Toto me dole le costes e li flanc,
Por lo çivalçer sonto de maltalant.
Plus me co*n*fio en vos q'a in persona vivant; (800)
Porço vos di mon cor e mo*n* talant.
1965 Se me devés unqamais servire de nojant,
En ceste noit farés li mon comant.
Si cu*n* raine vos fareç en avant,
E intrarés in le çanbre ardiamant; (805)
Et eo serò darere, starò me planamant.

1950 Cremonesi: cival
1952 MS., Mussafia: Quanto; Cremonesi, Rosellini: Quando . . . ; Mussafia: près
1956 Rajna (*Ricerche intorno ai Reali*, 232): compagna, co[n]ven . . .
1957 Mussafia, Rajna (*Ricerche intorno ai Reali*, 232), Cremonesi, Rosellini: v'averò
1959 Rajna (*Ricerche intorno ai Reali*, 232): sera
Rubric 38 (originally after 1984) Keller: proia; Cremonesi: proià; 2nd line: Cremonesi: por le deü . . . ; Rosellini: Por le . . . ; Keller: a presente; Cremonesi: por le deüs; 3rd line: Keller: uoloir; Cremonesi: al rois . . . voloir; Rosellini: Al rois . . . voloir
1963 Mussafia: qa in
1964 Mussafia, Rosellini: Por ço; Cremonesi: por ço
1965 Cremonesi: unqa mais
1966 Mussafia: li me comant
1969 Mussafia, Cremonesi, Rosellini: starome

1970 Cun li rois alirés in le leto solamant;
S'el vos volese toçer, ni a vos dir niant,
Si le projés e ben e dolçemant,
Nen vos diça toçer trosq'a un jor pasant, (810)
Qe por le çivalçer tuta sì fata lant;
1975 A l'altro jorno farì li son comant."
Dist la donçele, "De ço non dotés niant;
E farò ben ço qe a l'ovra apant."
Atant ven li rois con tota soa jant, (815)
Cun gran bagordi e desduti en avant.
1980 Le dame menarent molto honorebelmant;
A l'entrer de la çanbra, la donçela ne se fa lant;
En le leto entrò quant li rois li comant.
E Berta sta darere, qe non fi esiant;* (820)
Mais en sa vite nen fo cusi dolant.

Rubric 39
[Coment la doncelle par le volore de Berte / intra in lo leito cum li rois e ben fi son voloir; si oldirés qe avene de Berte e coment fu traie.]*
Laisse 40

1985 Quella donçelle non fu pais lainer;
Entro le leto ela se voit colçer,
Nen fu hon ni feme qi li alast contraster;
Si grande era la corte, nul hon à quel penser. (825)
E Aquilon e li altri mesaçer
1990 Erent torné, alé a son hoster,
E dama Berta si stoit pur darer.
Tal oit la vergogna, no olsa moto soner;
E li rois se vait in son leito colçer,* (830)   11vb
E quella dame strençer e toçer.
1995 Quando ven a ço qe la volse solaçer,

1974 Mussafia: tota
1977 Mussafia: ço che
1978 Mussafia, Cremonesi: A tant
Rubric 39 (originally after 2026) 1st line: Keller: uoloire; Rosellini: le volere. 2nd line: Keller: li rois . . . uoloir; Cremonesi: entrà .lo leto . . . voloir . . . ; Rosellini: lo leto . . . voloir. 3rd line: Keller: si oldrois; Guessard: oldires; Cremonesi: traïe
1987 Mussafia: home ni feme; Cremonesi: hom ni feme
1988 Rosellini: nul hom
1993 Mussafia, Rosellini: leto

La donçella fu cortois, no se trase arer;
En cella noit cun ella fu enter,
Ne fi li rois tuto li son voler. (835)
Ben la çercò tuta quanta por enter;
2000 Li pe trovò petit, dont s'en pris merveler,
Por la parola qe li dise le çubler.
E pois se prist entro soi penser,
"Li çublers si li dist por far moi irer." (840)
Tanto n'à son voloir, nen cura de nojer;
2005 El prist li avoir, l'or coito e li diner,
E le arnise de palii e de çender,
E si le done a qui cortisi çubler.
Li rois no se pensava de sa dama mal penser; (845)
Cuitoit ben q'ela fust sa muler droiturer,
2010 Cum Aquilon, le segnor de Bavier,
En Ongarie l'avoit sposea primer.
Pasoit quel çorno e tuto l'altro enter,
Tantqe Berta le dist qe tropo poria demorer; (850)
Qe entro sa çanbra volea pur entrer.
2015 Dist la donçela, "Ben lo vojo otrier.
A çesta noit vos diça pariler;
A le matin, quant el averà soner,
E eo me levarò si como a orier.* (855)
Enlora, porés en le leito entrer."
2020 E dist Berta, "Ben est da otrier."
Ela no sa mie qe le doit encontrer,
Qe quela malvés, qe Deo dona engonbrer,
Fi li son bailo querir e demander, (860)
Qe son per li donò qe la doust guarder.
2025 A colu ela prist tuto l'afar conter;
Quant cel l'intent molt s'en pris merveler.

2000 Rosellini: s'en prist
2001 Rosellini: le dise
2008 Rosellini: ne se pensava
2010 Mussafia, Cremonesi, Rosellini: Baiver
2015 Cremonesi: doncela
2016 Mussafia, Rosellini: Cesta noit
2018 Mussafia: ori[n]er (emend)
2022 Cremonesi, Rosellini: doni
2024 Mussafia, Cremonesi: doüst
2026 Rosellini: molto s'enpris

Rubric 40
[*Coment cille false feme stablì a sum / Baillis qa* Berte *(fu) amenée in le bois a is(ill)ere.*]*
Laisse 41

        "Bailo," dist la malvés, "entendés ma rason:
        Quando eo me sevrè de la moja mason, (865)
        Mon per me ve donò por frer e conpagnon,
2030 Qe far deustes mon voloir e mon bon.*
        Quella Berte qe ça nos conduson,
        Tot primament me donò·la li don
        De colçer moi avec li rois enson;* (870)
        Mais toçer no me lasase por nesuna cason.
2035 Quella promese non valse un boton—
        Qe li rois si m'avoit o e volese o non.
        Se tu fa ço qe nu vos contaron,
        Eo serò raine de França e da Lion,* (875)   12ra
        E de toi farò si gran baron,
2040 Major de toi non serà en tota Legnon."*
        Dist li bailo, "Dites, no li faron.
        Deo me confonde, qe sofrì pasion,
        Se mais por moi le saverà nul on." (880)

Rubric 41
[*Coment la malvvasia donçelle prima/ment li dist ço que faire devoit de Berte.*]
Laisse 42

        Quella malvés qe le diable oit tanté,
2045 A cil son baille oit li afar mostré:

    Rubric 40 (originally after 2043) MS.: fuil; . . . boise; Keller: alle . . . ferme/qua .B. ful . . . boise aisillere; Guessard: cille feme; Mussafia: cille false feme, Cremonesi: Coment Aliç false feme stablì a sum/bailis qe .B. fut amenee . . . ; Rosellini: Coment Aliç etablì . . . / . . . qe B[erta]
    2028 Mussafia: sevré da la . . . ; Cremonesi, Rosellini: sevré
    2030 Mussafia, Cremonesi: deüstes
    2032 Mussafia, Cremonesi: donò-la li; Rosellini: donò 'la
    2033 Mussafia: en son; Cremonesi, Rosellini: enson ("together")
    2038 MS.: dalion
    2040 Mussafia, Cremonesi, Rosellini: Le[ma]gnon (emend)
    2042 Mussafia, Rosellini: sofri; Cremonesi: sofrì
    Rubric 41 (originally after 2095) Keller: maluuasia; Cremonesi, Rosellini: malvuasia

	"Bailo," dist ela, "savés qe vos faré?
	En cesta soire, quant serà ascuré,
	Vu la prenderés oltra sa volunté, (885)
	E si le averés la bocha si esbaeré,
2050	S'ela criast, qe non soja ascolté.
	Pois la menés en un boscho ramé,
	E illec soja morta e delivré;
	En un fose vu si la seteré, (890)
	Qe de le mais no se saça novella ni anbasé."
2055	E quel le dist, "Jamés plus non parlé.
	Mejo faroie qe non l'avés devisé."
	"Alé," dist ella, "e tosto tornaré!"
	E quel s'en est da la dama sevré; (895)
	Avec lui avoi dos autres demandé,*
2060	Li qual furent de la soe contré.
	Quant vene la noit, qe li jor fu pasé,
	A l'ora qe la malvés li avoit ordené
	Qe la raine cuitoit conplir sa volunté, (900)
	Et avec li rois in leito eser entré,
2065	E cil malvés la ont e presa e ligé;
	E por la boçe la ont esbaré.
	Via la portent, oltra sa volunté,
	E si isent de Paris la cité. (905)
	Nen demoren tros li boschi ramé,
2070	E pois la ont desbaré e deslié.
	Oncir la volent; quela quer piaté,
	Da(va)nti lor se fu ençenoilé,
	"A, segnur," fait ella, "merçé, por l'amor Dé, (910)
	No me onciés, qe farisi gran peçé.
2075	Se vu la vite por Deo me lasé,
	En tal logo andarò, mais novella non oldiré."
	Quant qui la intende, si le parse piaté;
	L'un si oit li altro regardé, (915)
	E si dient, "Questo è gran peçé;

2049 Mussafia: esbaré (emend)
2053 Mussafia: un[e] fose (emend)
2054 Mussafia, Cremonesi, Rosellini: Qe d'ele; Cremonesi: faça
2055 Mussafia, Cremonesi: Jamés; Mussafia: n'en parlé
2059 Mussafia, Cremonesi, Rosellini: avoi[t] (emend)
2062 Mussafia: A l'ora que
2069 Rajna (*Ricerche intorno ai Reali*, 232): Non
2072 MS.: Danti; Mussafia, Rosellini: Da[va]nti; Cremonesi: da[va]nti (emendation, which I accept)

2080	Çamai major no*n* fu par homo pensé."	
	Li cor li est da Deo omilié;	
	I dist, "Dama, de vos ne ven peçé.	
	Ora ne çurarés qe mais no*n* reverteré (920)	
	En questa tere e in questa contré."	
2085	Et ella li foit volunter e de gre,	12rb
	E sor li santi si avoit çuré,	
	Qe mais no la verà in soa viveté.	
	Qui se partent, arer si son torné; (925)	
	Et ella remist en la selva ramé.	
2090	E quela malvés qe li oit aspeté,	
	Quant i furent arer repairé,*	
	Ela li dema*n*de come*n*t i ont ovré;	
	"Pur ben, madame, de le estes deliberé;* (930)	
	Morta l'aumes, si l'aon seteré,	
2095	En le gran boscho entro da un fosé."	

Rubric 42

[Qui se conte de cella malvés femena / e de le filç q'ela avoit de le rois Pepin.]
Laisse 43

      Or laseron de la malvés, qe estoit en gra*n* sejor;
      De nula ren plus no*n* oit paor.
      E li rois la ten lojal cun sa usor; (935)
      Nen savoit mie come*n*t fust li eror.
2100 Ne l'aust mie tenue a tal valor,*
      Anci averoit eu onta e desenor,
      S'el aust ben saplu trestoto ad estor*
      Quel qe ont fato li malvés liceor. (940)
      Qe por quelle dame crese si gran eror*
2105 Dont ne morì plus de mile peçor,
      Qe mais no*n* vede ne files ne seror.
      Cun li rois stoit si cu*n* por soa usor,

    2092 Mussafia: Come[n]t (emend; resolutions not normally noted by M.; cf. 917)
    2093 Mussafia, Cremonesi, Rosellini: Pur ben, ma dame . . . ; Mussafia, Cremonesi, Rosellini: d'ele
    2094 Mussafia, Cremonesi: aümes (as always)
    Rubric 42 (originally after 2112) Keller: qe la avoit
    2100 Mussafia, Cremonesi: aüst (as always)
    2101 Rosellini: desonor
    2104 Mussafia, Rosellini: cresè; Cremonesi: cresé
    2105 Rosellini: mille; Mussafia: mori

Por fila li rois d'Ongarie ela avoit clamor. (945)
De li rois avot tros filz, si cu*n* dis l'autor:*
2110 Lanfroi e Land(r)ix, Berta fu la menor,
Qe mere fu Rolando, li nobel pugneor,
E de Milon si cu*n* oldirés anco(r).*

Rubric 43
[Coment Berte remisis en li bois / e coment Synibaldo la trova.]
Laisse 44

Ora fu Berte en le boscho remés;* (950)
S'ela oit paure, or ne*n* vos mervelés.
2115 Si come feme qi fu abandonés,
Si plure e plançe molto s'è lame*n*tés.*
Non poit veoir se ne arbori ramés,
O li boschaje, qe est longo e les.* (955)
Por la paure de le bestie enverés,*
2120 Ver Demenedé se clama ben co*n*fés:
"A, Verçen polçele, raine encoronés,
De cesta peçable vos vegna piatés.
Anco de ceste jor, qe vu me cu*n*dués (960)
En celle lois o je fose albergés.*
2125 Nen morise qui in cotanta viltés!
A, malvas feme, cu*n* tu m'ais enganés!
Nen cuitoie mie de ceste fa(l)sités;*
Por grant amor eo t'aví amenés, (965)
Plu t'onorava qe tu fusi mego ençendrés.
2130 A, raina d'Ongarie, questo vu non savés,   12ᵛᵃ
De sta grant poine, o je sonto entrés.*
Jamais de moi non saverì meso ni anbasés;

2110 MS.: Landix; Mussafia, Cremonesi, Rosellini: Land[r]ix (emend)

2112 MS.: de *l* Milon . . . ancon; Mussafia, Cremonesi, Rosellini: ancor (emend)

Rubric 43 (originally after 2157) MS.: Remisis; Keller: synibaldo; Cremonesi: Sinibaldo la trovà

2113 Rosellini: ne le; Roques: en? (for Rosellini's *ne*)

2116 Mussafia: plura . . . se lamentés; Cremonesi, Rosellini: s'è lamentés

2117 Mussafia, Cremonesi, Rosellini: se no

2118 Mussafia, Cremonesi, Rosellini: E li . . .

2127 MS.: fasites; Mussafia: fa[l]sité (emend); Cremonesi, Rosellini: fasités

2128 Mussafia, Rosellini: avi

2131 Mussafia: D'esta. Mussafia, Cremonesi, Rosellini: o je sonto

2132 Rosellini: saverì (as always)

	Ma ventura m'est contraria alés!"* (970)
	Quant asa ela s'oit lamentés,
2135	Et asa oit e planto e plurés,
	Le viso se segne, a Deo fu comandés.
	En le gran boscho ela s'est afiçés,
	De ramo en ramo tanto est alés, (975)
	Cum Damenedeo si l'avoit amenés.
2140	N'esì de·l bois e voit en un bel pres
	Davant da soi ella oit reguardés,
	Un çivaler voit venir, tot lasés.
	E quant celu la vi, molt s'è mervelés. (980)
	En cella part ello est alés,
2145	Quant li aprosme, si la oit arasnés:
	"Dama," fait il, "qi vos oit ça menés,
	Por la gran selve e li boscho ramés?
	Vu me parì tuta espaventés." (985)
	"Mon sire," dist Berte, "or nen vos mervelés,
2150	Qe un mon segnor m'è morto da malfés,
	Si aust fato de moi si m'aust bailés.
	Ai, çentil homo, por santa caritès,
	Vos vojo projer qe vu si m'amenés, (990)
	In qualqe logo o eo fose albergés."
2155	"Par foi," dist il, "ben serì ostalés.
	A mon çastel vu serì amenés;
	Ilec seçornarì a vestra voluntés."

Rubric 44
[*Coment le fille Sinibaldo alent incontre / Berte e demandent son per qe illa est.*]
Laisse 45

	Quel çastelan si fo pro e valant, (995)
	Et oit nome Sinibaldo, se la istolia no mant.
2160	A son çastel mene Berte, tote plurant;
	Et oit dos filles, belle et avenant.
	Quant virent son pere cun la dame erant,
	Encontra voit a demander li prant: (1000)

2133 Mussafia, Cremonesi, Rosellini: Ma ventura
2139 Rosellini: Demenedeo
2143 Mussafia: se mervelés
2148 Mussafia: tota
Rubric 44 (originally after 2179) Keller: in contre; Cremonesi: ale[re]nt (emend)
2158 Mussafia: valan

"Qe femene è queste, qe ven cosi dolant?"
2165 Et ello li dise toto li convenant,
Cun son mari fo morto, qe era un mercaant;
E de le aust fato altretant,*
Quant ella s'en foçì cojamant. (1005)
"Scanpé s'en est par celle selve grant;*
2170 Damenedé l'à mené a salvamant,
Et è venua a li vostro comant.
Unde e vos prego, se vos m'amés niant,
No le mostrés s(e n)on bel viso e riant."* (1010)
E celle le dient, "Volunter por talant."
2175 E celle damesele furent molto saçant;
Contra li vent e por la man la prant,
E si la vont dolçement confortant.   12vb
En sa çanbre la mene cojamant, (1015)
Si la onore cum fust soa parant.

Rubric 45
*[Coment le fille Synibaldo farent / Grant (çoie) a la raine Berte.]**
Laisse 46

2180 Dist le polçele, "Dama, vestre venue*
A gram mervile ne delete et argue.*
A bon oster estes rechaue;
Por nostra mer vos tiron, ben serés proveue. (1020)
Dache nostra mer nos est deschaue,
2185 Avec nos serés e calçé e vestue.
Nen mançaron valsant une latue,
Si cun nos no vos sia partue."
Quant dama Berta le oit entendue, (1025)
Molto le mercie e a lor s'è rendue,
2190 Si como femena, la qual era perdue.
E Damenedé si le fo en ajue;

2167 Mussafia, Cremonesi, Rosellini: d'ele
2168 Mussafia: ela
2173 MS.: son bel; Mussafia: se no bel . . . ; Cremonesi, Rosellini: s[e n]on
Rubric 45 (originally after 2196) Keller: grant / a la . . . ; Cremonesi, Rosellini: grant [onor] (emend)
2180 MS.: Distę le; Mussafia: Diste la; Cremonesi, Rosellini: Dist la
2181 Rosellini: agrue (emend); Holden: keep MS. reading (cf. 3655)
2182 Mussafia: rechaüe

	Por çest çastelan ela fo revertue.
	De Pepin prima fo soa drue, (1030)
	E po si fo raine quant sa mer fo venue,
2195	E la malvés qe l'oit si deçeue
	A mala mort ella fo confondue.

Rubric 46

[*De la venturie qe avene a Berte e comente / li rois Pepin envoja a Synibaldo Oysac.*]*
Laisse 47

	Oeç, segnor, s'el vos plas ascolter,
	Nul hon se doit da Deo desperer, (1035)
	Qe sa venture ne li poit faler.
2200	Nul hon poit unquamais porpenser,
	Ço qe li poit venir ne incontrer.
	Berte la raine, qe devoit enperer,
	Or li convent li altru pan mançer;* (1040)
	Ne no sa pais o ela diça aler.
2205	Mais celle polçele la tenia si çer,
	Non parea mie femena strainer.
	Avec lor stasoit a boir e a mançer;
	Mais nonportant tant avea li cor lainer, (1045)
	Qe die e note no stava de·l plurer.
2210	Con çelle çastelan dont m'oldeç çanter,
	E cun ses file qe tant avoit çer,
	Demorò Berte plus d'un an enter.
	Berta fu si mastre de tot li mester,* (1050)
	Nulla milor no se poroit trover.
2215	Ben savoit e cosir e tailer,
	E si fo mastra sor tot li friser.*
	A celle dameselle prist si dotriner
	Qe plus l'amava, qe s'ela fose sa mer. (1055)

2192 Mussafia: fo rrevertue
2195 Mussafia: deçeüe
2196 Mussafia: ela
Rubric 46 (originally after 2225) Keller: lauenture . . . / . . . mersanc; Guessard (re Keller): lisez *mesacer* pour *messager*; Cremonesi: aventuire . . . envoia a Synibaldo. . . . (blank at line end); Rosellini: aventuire/ à Synibaldo . . . (no final word)
2200 Cremonesi: unqua mais
2208 Mussafia: no por tant (as always)

```
                A celle tenp donde me oldés conter,
2220    Pepin voloit aler por caçer.
                A Synibaldo envoie qe le diça apariler
                De vitualia e de ço qe li è mester;*                    13^(ra)
                A li çastel vol venir alberçer, (1060)
                Et illec terço çorno seçorner;
2225    E Synibaldo li foit de greç e volunter.
```

Rubric 47
[Coment li rois Pepin voit a chaçer / a (l)i çastel de Synibaldo e avec li ses baron.]
Laisse 48

```
                Or vait li rois a soa chaçason,
                Et oit avec lui ses conte e ses baron.
                Altri portent sparver et altri porten falcon; (1065)
                Brachi e livrer mene*n*t a foson,
2230    A·l çastel Synibaldo venen a·l dojon.
                Et ilec alberçent çivaler e peon,
                Pois vont a chaçer qua*n*t vent la sason.
                E Pepi mist Sinibaldo por rason, (1070)
                De ses bestie e d'altre reençon.*
2235    Quant i ont asa rasné, vont por li dojon,
                Veçando li çastel entorno et inviron.
                Li rois regarde, qe non fi se ben non,
                E vide le polçele stare a li balcon. (1075)
                Quando le vi, molt s'amervelon,*
2240    Qe mais no*n* vi Berte entro quella mason.
```

2221 Mussafia: Sygnibaldo
2225 Mussafia, Cremonesi, Rosellini: de grés
Rubric 47 (originally after 2240) MS.: a si castel; Keller: a/ si; Cremonesi, Rosellini: a li . . .
2228 7 for *et*; Rosellini: portent
2229 Cremonesi: i menent
2230 Mussafia: venent
2236 7 for *et*
2239 Cremonesi, Rosellini: molto
2240 Cremonesi: no vi

Rubric 48
[*Coment Pepin vide Berte e si la covota / e si la demonda a Synibaldo.*]*
Laisse 49

   Pepin li rois oit Synibaldo apelé:
   "Ora me dites, si dites verité,
   Una dame ai veue, molto ben açesmé; (1080)
   Molto me par aver de gran belté."
2245 Dist Synibaldo, "Ben vos serà conté;
   E la trovè en la selva ramé,
   Ben est li termen d'un a(n) pasé.
   Si l'ò tenua e molto ben guardé; (1085)
   Cun me enfant q'el à si maistré,
2250 Çascuna est bona mastra proé."
   Dist li rois, "Ora si vos alé,
   E fais qe in çesta noit n'aça ma volunté;
   Colsa como no, vu avì malovré." (1090)
   Dist Sinibaldo, "De niente en parlé!
2255 Zamais por moi cil non serà otrié;
   Avant me lasaria esere sbanojé,
   E pasaroie oltra la mer salé,
   Qe in ma mason fose de ren violé, (1095)
   S'elo no fose ben por soa volunté."
2260 Dist li rois, "Vu avì ben parlé;
   Aleç a le, e si la demandé,*
   Se consentir me vol cun soa volunté."
   Dist Sinibaldo, "Ora si m'aspecté, (1100)
   Tanto qe eo soja a vos retorné."
2265 Li roi remist, e cil se n'est alé;*
   Ven a la çanbra o avoit Berta trové.
   Elo l'apella, si l'oit demandé: 13rb
   "Dama," fait il, "nu avon malovré.* (1105)

 Rubric 48 (originally after 2286) Keller: demonda; Cremonesi: si la covotà / si la demandà; Rosellini: demanda
  2245 Mussafia, Rosellini: sera
  2246 Mussafia, Cremonesi, Rosellini: trové
  2247 MS.: d un a pase
  2250 Rosellini: Çascuna
  2253 Mussafia, Cremonesi, Roselllini: mal ovré (cf. line 2268)
  2261 Cremonesi: aléç a lé
  2265 Mussafia: rois; Mussafia, Cremonesi. Rosellini: cil s'en est
  2268 Mussafia, Cremonesi, Rosellini: mal ovré

	Aler me convent in estrançe contré;
2270	Li rois si oit e plevi e çuré,
	Se il no v'oit a soa volunté,
	Ne me laserà tera un sol pe mesuré.
	Et eo vojo esere inançi deserté, (1110)
	Qe colsa aça qe no vos sia a gre."
2275	Berta, quan l'olde, oit un riso çité;
	E dist a Synibaldo, "De ço no ve doté.
	Tanto m'avés servi e honoré,
	E si m'avés pasua e nurié (1115)
	Cun vestre file, e vestua e calçé,
2280	Unqua par moi non serés destorbé;
	Presta sui de faire la soa volunté."
	Quant Synibaldo l'olde, si l'oit mercié;
	S'elo n'à çoie, ora non domandé;* (1120)
	Tel no l'avoit en soa vi(vi)té.*
2285	Ven a li rois, si ge l'oit conté;
	Li rois n'en fu tuto çojant e lé.

Rubric 49

[Quant Synibaldo oit parlé a dama Berte et / Coment ela otria de fair la volunté de li rois; / e li rois li ordena di far li leto sor un char.]*
Laisse 50

	Li rois estoit sor la sala pavée,
	E Synibaldo fo a lu retornée; (1125)
	E la novella li oit dito e contée,
2290	Qe la dama si est aparilée
	De voloir fare tuta sa voluntée.
	Li rois n'en fu molt çojant e lee,
	E dist a Synibaldo, "Vu avés ben ovrée. (1130)
	Por li calor (qe fu da meça stée),*
2295	En celle corte sor un caro roée

2269 Cremonesi: en estrançe
2270 Cremonesi: plevì
2273 Rosellini: inanci
2277 Rosellini: servi
2284 MS.: vite; Mussafia: vi[vi]té; Cremonesi, Rosellini: vité
2286 Mussafia: fut tuto
Rubric 49 (originally after 2317) Keller: de fair; Cremonesi: otrià . . . ordenà
2292 MS.: nen fu; Mussafia: ne fu (emend); Cremonesi: n'en . . . molto leé; Rosellini: n'en fu molt . . . lée

	Faites qe un gran leito si li sia ben conçée,
	De richi palii soja ben açesmée.
	Suso me vorò colçer con eso ma sposée, (1135)
	E far de le la moja vuluntée."*
2300	Elo·l dise por gabes, m'el fu ben averée;*
	Li jor s'en voit, la noit fu aprosmée,
	E cil car si fu ben parilée.
	Li rois li fu cun Berta su montée; (1140)
	Avantqe de le faese sa voluntée,
2305	Çerchò la dame por flanc e por costée.
	Nul manchamento oit en le trovée,
	Aforsqe li pe trovò grant e desmesurée.
	Nian porço non ait li rois lasée; (1145)
	De le ne prist amor e amistée
2310	Tota la noit, como la fu longa e lee.
	E Damenedé li dè tal destinée,
	En cella noit oit si ben ovrée,
	Encinta fu d'una molt bella ritée:* (1150) 13va
	E cil fu Karlo li maine incoronée,
2315	E fu da Deo benei e sagrée.
	Major rois de lui nen fu en Crestentée,
	Ne plu dotés da la jent desfaée.

2296 Cremonesi: conrée
2297 Mussafia, Rosellini: palii; Cremonesi: acesmée
2299 Mussafia, Cremonesi: d'ele la . . . ; Rosellini: d'ele la moira voluntée
2300 Mussafia: me'l
2304 Mussafia, Cremonesi, Rosellini: Avant qe d'ele
2307 Mussafia, Rosellini: desmesuré
2308 Mussafia, Cremonesi, Rosellini: por ço
2309 Mussafia, Cremonesi, Rosellini: D'ele
2311 Mussafia, Cremonesi: dé; Rosellini: dè
2313 MS.: duna molt bellaritee; Mussafia, Cremonesi, Rosellini: bella rité
2314 Rosellini: icoroneé
2315 Mussafia: beneï; Cremonesi: beneì

Rubric 50
[Coment li rois Pepint quant il avoit f(a)to* / de Berte son voloir s'en retornò a Paris <ciuta>.]
Laisse 51

	Quando Pepin oit fato son talant (1155)
	De dama Berte a la cera riant,*
2320	Da le se departì e legro e çojant;
	Non oit eu nul mal entindimant.
	A Sinibaldo la dà e la comant,
	Qe de le façe mejo qe non fasoit davant. (1160)
	E se nulla ren ella quer e demant,
2325	Conpli le sia alo demantenant;
	E Synibaldo otria son comant.
	A Paris retorne li rois e soa çant,
	Cun quela malvés raine stasoit a bon convant. (1165)
	Obeir la fasoit a petit e a grant;
2330	Coronea era de·l reame de Frant.
	E Berta fu encinte nove mesi pasant;
	En cha de Synibaldo avoit un bel enfant.
	De ço fo Synibaldo e legro e çojant; (1170)
	El meesmo montò a·l palafroi anblant,
2335	La novela a li rois portò amantenant.
	E li rois le dist, "Farés li mon talant:
	Batiçer farés primerano l'infant.
	Karlo li metés nome, qe eo li comant." (1175)
	Et i le font ne nesu li contant;
2340	E Synibaldo fu e saço e valant;
	A çella dame fait toto li so comant.
	Qui laseron de le da ste jur en avant;
	De la raine d'Ongarie li roman se comant. (1180)

Rubric 50 (originally after 2343) MS.: Rois; Keller: futo . . . paris e la cant; Guessard: fato; Cremonesi: Pepin quant il avoit . . . fato/ a Pa[r]is [la] cité (ms: *Pepint . . . avoit fauto . . . a pais ciut*); Rosellini: Pepin . . . fauto . . . / . . . retornò à Pa[r]is. (MS.: *pepint . . . fauto . . . pains/ . . . cluo*)

2320 Mussafia, Rosellini: departi
2321 Mussafia, Cremonesi: entindimant; Rosellini: entidimant
2323 Mussafia, Cremonesi, Rosellini: d'ele
2325 Mussafia: alo'; Cremonesi: conplì le sia a lo' demantenant
2326 Cremonesi: otrià
2339 Mussafia: nesu[n] (emend)
2342 Mussafia, Cremonesi, Rosellini: d'ele

Rubric 51
[Coment la raine d'Ongarie in(v)oja in Fra(n)çe / mesaçer pro savoir novelle de sa fille.]*
Laisse 52

	De la raine d'Ongarie e vos vojo conter,
2345	Dapoisqe sa file s'avè da le desevrer,
	Nesun mesaje pote de le ascolter.*
	E quant a le envoja mesaçer,
	Neson la pooit veoir ni esguarder. (1185)
	Como ela savea qe in França dovea entrer,
2350	In leto se metea si se fasea voluper,*
	Et a qui mesaçer fasea robe doner,
	E de diner por avor da spenser.
	Letere e brevi fasea sajeler, (1190)
	Si cum a sa mer le fasea aporter.
2355	E quant li mesaçi s'en retornava arer,
	La raina li prende a querir e demander 13vb
	De soa fila, s'ella aust (eu ri)ter,*
	Si l'ont veue in via ni en senter, (1195)
	Ne in nulla çanbre, ni en sala plener.
2360	E li mesaçer le dient, "Nu no veren bosier;
	Ne la poumes veoir ni esguarder.
	Senpre malea nu la poon trover;
	Ela ne fa doner e or coito e diner, (1200)
	Si ne fa fare letere, e brevi sajeler,
2365	E pois ne fa li conçeo doner;
	O no vojamo o no, ne conven retorner."
	La dama l'olde, cuita li sen cançer;
	Ven a li rois, si le prist parler: (1205)

Rubric 51 (originally after 2378) MS.: innoia; Keller: dongarie inuoia in / fraçe . . . / pro . . . ; Cremonesi: invoià . . . Fra[n]çe/ . . . por savoir; Rosellini: Fra[n]çe/ . . . por savoir

2345 Rosellini: s'ave le

2346 Mussafia, Rosellini: potè d'ele; Cremonesi: poté d'ele

2347 Cremonesi: envoià

2348 Mussafia: Nesun la poit

2356 Mussafia, Cremonesi, Rosellini: prendea querir

2357 MS.: curiter; Mussafia: s'ella aüst eu riter; Cremonesi: aüst eü riter; Rosellini: s'ella aust eu riter. Mussafia: fille

2358 Mussafia: S'i l'ont veue

2360 Mussafia, Cremonesi, Rosellini: voren bosier. (Mussafia, emendation)

2363 Mussafia, Cremonesi: fa; Rosellini: fi

2368 Mussafia: si le prist [a] parler; Cremonesi: si li prist

"Mon sir," fait ela, "molt me poso merviler,
2370 A ma fila ò envojé plus de .XX. mesaçer;
Nesun me sa de le nula novela nonçer,
Qe l'aça veue in çanbra ni en soler.
Molto me redoto q'ela no aça engonbrer; (1210)
Se no la veço, jamés viver non quer.
2375 S'elo ve plas, e m'ame de ves amer,*
Laseç me aler a ma file parler.
E quant eo averò saplu de son ovrer,
Demantenant eo tornerò arer." (1215)

Rubric 52
[Coment la raine d'Ongarie parloit a li rois / si lle demanda parole d'aler in Fra(nc)e.]
Laisse 53

La raina d'Ongarie oit gran segnorie;
2380 A gran mervele oit la çera ardie.
Ela dist a li rois, "Donés moi conpagnie;
Aler m'en vojo en França la guara(ni)e,*
Veoir quel rois e soa baronie, (1220)
E cun è ben porté de Berte mie fie."
2385 Dist li rois, "Vos querés la folie!
Longo è li çamin, e dubiosa la vie;
Vestra file sta ben, *et* à gran segnorie,*
Et oit de li rois e fioli e fie; (1225)
E questo so por vor, por misi e por spie."*
2390 La dama, quando l'olde, in ojando desie:*
"Çativo rois, tu no vale un alie!
Se conçé no me donì, por Deo, le fi Marie,
A tot to malgré, me meterò en vie; (1230)
Sola lì alirò, sença nul conpagnie,

2371 Mussafia, Cremonesi, Rosellini: d'ele
2375 Mussafia, Cremonesi, Rosellini: m'ame devés amer
Rubric 52 (originally after 2438) MS., Keller: fraire; Keller: dongarie / sil le remanda . . . daler in fraire; Guessard: lisez "in France"; Cremonesi: demandà
2382 MS.: guaraiiie; Mussafia, Cremonesi, Rosellini: guarnie
2384 Cremonesi: Berta
2385 Mussafia: le rois
2387 7 for *et*
2391 Mussafia, Cremonesi: un' alie. Cremonesi: ne vale
2392 Cremonesi: doni
2394 Mussafia, Cremonesi, Rosellini: li alirò

2395	E tal colsa farò, sempre serà honie."
	E li rois quant l'intent, tuto fo spave*n*tie;
	Por sa paure, el no sa q'elo die.
	Dever de le tuto se homilie; (1235)
	Plu la dota de nula ren qe sie.
2400	"Dama," dist il, "e v'ò tropo ben oie;
	Vestre voloir vos soja otrie."

Rubric 53
[Coment li rois d'Ongarie aconplì li voloir / de la raine, si·lle donò parole de aler in France.]*
Laisse 54*

	Quando li rois olde soa dama parler,	14ra
	E qe pur vole a Paris aler, (1240)	
	Veoir sa file o la porà trover,	
2405	O voja o no le conven otrier.	
	"Dama," fait, "no me devés por nojen nojer;*	
	Ne por cesta ovra no me devés blas(m)er.*	
	E v'amo tanto, no se poria conter, (1245)	
	Perço no me voria da vos deslonçer.	
2410	Se vos en França en deverés aler,	
	Mille an*n*i me parerà qe retornez arer;	
	Nen porò pais ni boir ni mançer,	
	Ne in leito dormire ni polser; (1250)	
	Senpre de vos m'averà reme*n*brer.	
2415	Ma daqe vos plais e volés pur aler,	
	Aleç, si non aça reproçer.	
	Asa portés or coito e diner,	
	Qe por çamin aça ben da spenser. (1255)	
	Si vos co*n*ven amenar çivaler,	
2420	A l'aler e a venir vos diça aco*n*pagner.	

2398 Mussafia, Cremonesi, Rosellini: d'ele

2400 Cremonesi: oïe

Rubric 53 (originally after 2473) MS.: Rois ... fãnçer. Keller: dongarie aconpli/ sil le ... frãnçer; Cremonesi: aconplì ... / ... in Françes; Rosellini: aconpli ... Françes. No rubric in this position in MS., top of 14^r.

2404 Mussafia: o'lo; Cremonesi: o' lo

2406 Mussafia, Cremonesi, Rosellini: fait [il] (emend). Mussafia: no ve

2407 MS.: blaser; Mussafia, Cremonesi, Rosellini: blas[m]er

2409 Mussafia, Rosellini: Per ço; Cremonesi: per ço

>
> Quant li rois e li baron vos verà si aler,
> Plu serà vestra file digna da honorer;
> E metesmo li rois la tegnirà plu çer, (1260)
> Si s'en tirà plus grant e plus alter."
> 2425 Dist la raine, "Mo v'oe oldu parler;
> Questo devi vu dir anco en primer,
> E no far moi per nient coroçer.
> Non vojo de·l vostro espenser un diner; (1265)
> Asa oe da spender e da doner.*
> 2430 Non virà cun moi nesuno çivaler,
> Qe de le mon avoir non aça asolder."
> La çentil dame prist li rois gracier;
> Ela non volse de nient entarder. (1270)
> E richament se foit coroer,
> 2435 De drapi de soja, de porpore e de çender,
> E li çivaler qe la devoit conpagner,
> Si altament li fait adorner
> Çaschun menoit palafro e destrer. (1275)

Rubric 54
[Coment la raine d'Ongarie s'aparelle / d'aler in France por conçé li rois.]
Laisse 55

>
> Quant la raine en fu aparilé,
> 2440 E son segnor l'oit ben agraé,
> Do xento çivaler fu por le coroé.
> E la raine pais si fu atorné,*
> Trenta somer d'avoir oit carçé, (1280)
> Ça por aler e por tornar aré
> 2445 Asa averà da spender e doné,
> Par le e por qui qi li voit daré.
> Segurament ben porà çivalçé; 14rb
> Qe da nul homo no averà reproçé. (1285)

2421 Mussafia: vostra
2426 Mussafia: devivu; Cremonesi: devì vu
2427 Cremonesi: por nient
Rubric 54 (originally after 2489) MS.: Raine ... Rois. Keller: dongarie saparelle da-/ ler
2441 Rosellini: çivalier
2442 MS.: pais; Mussafia: puis (emend); Cremonesi, Rosellini: pois
2446 Cremonesi: par lé (as always; cf. 2458, etc.)

Quant la raine se ven a desevré,
2450 E quella volle li conçé demandé,*
Li rois la vait tros fois a basé,
E si la prist dolçement a projé,
Qe a·l plu tosto q'ela poit ela diça torné. (1290)
E quela dist, "Non ò altro pensé.
2455 Quando eo porò plu tosto desevré,
A vos averò retornar aré."
Monta a çival, nen volse plu entardé;
Et avec le, li soi çivalé, (1295)
E li rois vait a çival monté,
2460 Cum tuta sa baronie por le aconpagné
For de la tere peon e çivalé.
La convoient plus de .X. legue enté
A Deo li comandent, e retornent aré. (1300)
A·l departir li rois en prist a larmojé;
2465 Mal volunter lì la lasò alé.*
Mais tanto la dotava, porq'ela era si fe*
No la olsava por le viso nul hon guardé.
Par toto li regno se fasea si doté, (1305)
No la olsava nul hon de nient contrasté.
2470 Ela s'en vait, e li rois torna aré;
E tal la vide de·l reame sevré,
Qe prega Deo li voir justisié,
Qe unchamés nen posa retorné. (1310)

2450 Mussafia: qu'ella; Cremonesi, Rosellini: volse
2457 Cremonesi: Montà
2459 Mussafia: cival
2462 Plouzeau: Rosellini .X.legue (add blank)
2465 Mussafia, Cremonesi, Rosellini: il la
2466 Mussafia: Mai tanto; Rajna (*Ricerche intorno ai Reali*, 229): por q' ela . . . fé
2467 Rajna (*Ricerche intorno ai Reali*, 229): nul hom
2473 Cremonesi: uncha mes; Mussafia, Rosellini: non posa

Rubric 55

[Coment s'en vait la raine qe pris conçé / Da son segnor e coment çi(v)alçe a (o)nor.]
Laisse 56

        Va s'en la raine, a çoja e a baldor;
2475   Quant oit eu conçé da˙l son segnor,
        Ela regracie Deo le Creator,
        Q'ela voit cun tot li son amor.*
        En sa conpagnie oit manti contor; (1315)
        Do xento furent totes a (m)ilsoldor.
2480   Unques raine non veistes ancor
        Qe de çoie portaste plu bel lusor,*
        Ne no fu en sa conpagne ni grande ni menor,
        Qe non çivalçast palafro anblaor. (1320)
        E qui destrer corant e milsoldor*
2485   Se font mener avant per plu honor;
        Non vait mie corando ad estor.
        Petite jornée vait çascun jor;
        Jamais en France non fu raine ancor (1325)
        Qe da la jent recevese tel honor.

Rubric 56

[Coment s'en vait la Raine a do xento / Çivaler e si civ(a)lçoit por Alemagne].
Laisse 57

2490   Va s'en la raine a la clere façon;
        En sa conpagne do xento conpagnon,
        Li meltri d'Ongrie de celle region.   14va
        Çaschun oit palafroi e destrer aragon, (1330)
        Çaschun oit bon hauberg flamiron,
2495   Elmi a or e bon brandi a˙l galon.

    Rubric 55 (originally after 2515) line 1: Keller: sen; Cremonesi: que pris. line 2: MS.: çiaalçe anor; Keller: çiarcilçe anor (*ciualce* at page bottom); Cremonesi: çivalçe a [o]nor; Rosellini: çivalçe à [o]nor
    2474 Cremonesi, Rosellini: Vasen; Rosellini: balor (Holden: "lire *baldor*")
    2479 MS.: nulsoldor? Cf. 2484
    2481 Mussafia, Rosellini: portase; Cremonesi: portasse (emend for *portasce*)
    2489 Cremonesi: recevesse
    Rubric 56 (originally after 2546) MS.: Raine . . . ciulçoit; Keller: sen . . . / ciulçoit; Cremonesi: . . . civ[a]lcoit..; Rosellini: çiv[a]lçoit
    2490 Cremonesi, Rosellini: Vasen
    2492 Rosellini: Ongarie

```
              Ensegne portent, e indoré penon;
              No le fo nul qe somer non conduson.
              Si grande fu <la frote> la jent s'en mervelon;*    (1335)
              Qui d'Alemagne donde i çivalçon.
       2500   I no arivent a çastel ni dojon
              Ne a çités qe fust de çenti hom,
              Qe no la ostalés con tot ses conpagnon,
              E por amor li rois ne le faist don.    (1340)
              E quella raine fu de grande renon;
       2505   A qui çivaler qe avec lei son,
              E qe in France por amor l'aconpagnon,
              A lor donava et or coito e macon
              E diner a si grande foson,    (1345)
              Ne spendea de·l so valisant un speron.
       2510   Dient entro soi çascuno d·i baron:
              "Nostra raine si è de gran renon;
              Non lasa spender de·l nostro un boton."*
              Tant çivalçent, e por poi e por mon,    (1350)
              Nen fu si tosto cun dist li sermon,
       2515   Qe en France s'aprosma la region.
```

Rubric 57

[Coment la raine civalçe ve(r) Paris / e invoja a li rois qe li alast encontre.]
Laisse 58

```
              La raine çivalçe, qe oit gran segnorie;
              Raina estoit de·l reame d'Ongarie.
              E costoient d'Alemagne une partie;    (1355)
              Ses çivaler la conduit e la guie.
       2520   Et ella fu cortois, enver de lor se plie;
              De li so li done avoir e manentie;
              N'i lasa spender valisant un alie;
```

2498 Mussafia: la frote la jen
2501 Mussafia: çités
2502 Rosellini: compagnon
2503 Mussafia, Cremonesi: faïst
2504 Mussafia: renom
2506 Rosellini: l'acompagnon
2512 Mussafia: No-n
Rubric 57 (originally after 2578) MS.: ve; Keller: ue Paris . . . in / uoia; Cremonesi, Rosellini: ve[r]
2522 Mussafia, Cremonesi: un'alie

E i de ço humelment la mercie. (1360)
Tant çivalçò la dama e por noit e por die,
2525 Q'ela aprosma a Paris a dos jornée e dimie,
Donde prende mesajes con le rame florie,
Qe a li rois qe oit Fra(n)ça en bailie
Li porta la novelle, dont molto s'en joie: (1365)
Por lui veoir la ven la raine d'Ongrie.*
2530 Li rois, quando li soit, de çoja el ne rie;
Donde oit mandé por soa baronie,
Por honorer la dama q'el non vede en sa vie.
Mais cella dame q'el oit en sa baillie,* (1370)
Qe a dama Berta fe cotanta stoltie,
2535 Quant la novella elle oit oldrie,*
El à tal dol par poi ne forsonie.
Ela ne sa q'ela faça ne die;
Ela vi ben sa fin est conplie,* (1375)
Qe la raine qe vent d'Ongarie,   14vb
2540 Ben conoserà nen serà soa file.
S'el à paure, non vos mervelés mie,
Q'ela soit ben com ella oit oie,*
E si l'avoit e por mesi e por spie,* (1380)
Qe in Crestenté nianche in Paganie,
2545 Nen fu ma dama qe fust si ardie,
Ne qe aust eu si tanta stoltie.

2526 Cremonesi: la rame
2527 MS.: fraça; Mussafia: que
2528 Mussafia: s'enjoïe; Cremonesi: s'en joïe; Rosellini: s'enjoie
2531 Rosellini: par
2533 Mussafia: dama qu'el
2534 Cremonesi: fe'
2535 Mussafia, Cremonesi, Rosellini: oit oldie; Cremonesi, emend for MS. *oldue*
2538 Mussafia, Rosellini: complie
2539 Rosellini: venti d'O . . . ; Cremonesi: que
2540 MS.: file; Cremonesi: fie (emend)
2541 Mussafia: S'el'a; Cremonesi: S'el'à; Rosellini: S'el'a
2543 Mussafia: e si savoit (emend for *si l'avoit*)
2544 Mussafia, Cremonesi, Rosellini: ni anche
2545 Mussafia: que; Mussafia, Cremonesi: ma' dame
2546 Mussafia: qe aüst cusì tanta stultie; Cremonesi: qe aüst ensi tanta; Rosellini: cusi tanta

Rubric 58
[*Coment la raine entroit en Paris / e montoit a li palés e li rois la convojò.*]
Laisse 59

	La raina d'Ongarie çivalça con soa jent,
	A do cento çivaler saçi e conosent; (1385)
	Ne le fo çil n'aça bon guarniment,
2550	E bon destrer e isnel e corent.
	Et i çivalçe li palafroi anblent;
	Ne le fu çil qe fust le plus lent,
	Non aça armaure a oro e arçent. (1390)
	Por Alamagne aloit a salvament;
2555	Quan a Paris ili si s'aprosment,*
	A .X. legues li mesaçes erent
	Qe la novelle portoit novellement.
	Li rois e li barons toti s'aparilent (1395)
	De le recevere si honorablement,
2560	Como raine de segle vivent.*
	Ma cella dama qe fe li tradiment,
	Ela pensoit de fare altrament;
	Ma la soa ovra no li valse nient. (1400)
	Malea se foit en le leito se stent,*
2565	E a son bailo fe li comandament
	Qe in la çanbra no lasi entrer nula persona vivent.
	E le fenestre e li usi ensement
	Fait aserer fortement, (1405)
	Qe in la çanbra ni darer ni davent
2570	Ne se pooit veoir lume de nient.
	Atant ven la raine, qe a Paris s'aprosment;
	Li rois li vait encontre con tute l'autre jent.*

Rubric 58 (originally after 2648) Keller: entroit en paris; Rosellini: entrò en. line 2: MS.: Rois . . . convoio

2549 Mussafia: cil

2553 MS.: armaure; Mussafia: armaure a or e arçent

2558 Mussafia: aparillent

2559 Mussafia, Cremonesi, Rosellini: D'ele

2561 Cremonesi: fe'

2564 Mussafia: s'estent

2565 Cremonesi: fe'

2566 MS.: p̄vivēt (abbreviation over the *p* followed by a small space); Mussafia, Cremonesi, Rosellini: persona

2571 Mussafia, Cremonesi: A tant

La raine vi li rois, in ses braçe li prent, (1410)
Por amor de sa file l'acolla dolçement.
2575 Quant furent a la plaça, monta a li paviment,*
Mais de sa fille ella non vi nient,
Donde s'en mervelle de le grandement;
Nen pote muer q'ela no se spavent. (1415)

Rubric 59
[Coment la Raine d'Ongarie quant fu monté / Sor li palés e par tot reguardoit e no (vi) sa file / e coment aloit a le leto o ella malvasia estoit.]*
Laisse 60

Quant la raine fu sor li palés monté,
2580 Qe li rois e li baron l'avoit convojé,
Ele reguarde e davant e daré.
Non vi sa fille, molt se n'è mervellé;   15ra
Adoncha oit li rois aderasné, (1420)
"De mia fille, qe n'est encontré?
2585 Ben è septe ani e conpli e pasé
Qe no la vi e pero son sevré
De Ongarie, una longa contré."
Dist li rois, "Or nen vos mervelé; (1425)
Vestra fila est in leto amalé.
2590 Terço çorno est, q'ela no s'è levé."
La dama l'olde, tuta fu spaventé;
Ven a l'uso de la çanbre, si la trovò seré;
E celle bailo si fu davant alé; (1430)
Dist, "Madame, por Deo vos sofré,*
2595 Qe le mires si n'oit comandé:
Qe no le sia nula persona entré.
Un petit s'est la dama adormençé."
La dama l'olde, si fu tuta abusmé, (1435)
E ver de cil ella fu coruçé.
2600 Ela le prent por mala volunté,

2577 Mussafia, Cremonesi, Rosellini: d'ele
Rubric 59 (originally after 2698) MS.: Raine ... non ī (for *no (v)i*); Keller: dongarie / enon in sa ... ; Guessard: e non vi sa fille; Cremonesi: non (v)i; Rosellini: non [v]i
2580 Mussafia: barons
2581 Cremonesi: ela
2582 Mussafia: se ne mervellé; Cremonesi, Rosellini: s'en è
2590 Mussafia, Cremonesi, Rosellini: s'è levé
2594 Mussafia, Cremonesi, Rosellini: Ma dame

| | Dà·le una trata, e si le tira aré.*
| | Ven a l'uso de la çanbra, si l'oit desfermé;
| | Dedens entra contra sa volunté.* (1440)
| | E quant fu en la çanbra vide tel oscurité,
| 2605 | Ela ven a una fenestra si l'oit despasé.
| | Quando lume avoit, a li leto fu alé,
| | O quella dame estoit envolupé.
| | E la raine si l'oit demandé, (1445)
| | "Filla," fait ela, "com estes amalé?
| 2610 | Quando d'Ongaria son partia e sevré,
| | Per vos amor me son travalé."*
| | E quella dama qe in malora fu né,*
| | Pur pla(na)ment cum femena amalé (1450)
| | A la raina ela responde en dre,
| 2615 | "Mere," fait ila, "ora me perdoné,
| | Qe grement eo me sonto amalé."
| | E la raine si fu saça e doté,
| | A carne nue ella l'oit toçé, (1455)
| | E si la çerca por flanchi e por costé,
| 2620 | E por le piç e davant e daré.
| | Pois vene a li pe, qe non oit oblié;
| | Trove·l petit, e non cosi formé
| | Como avoit Berta soa nobel rité. (1460)
| | Quando ço vide, tuta fu spaventé,
| 2625 | E dist, "Malvés, vu m'avì engané!"
| | Non oit la raine avec le tençé;
| | Por le çavi ela l'oit pié.
| | La raina fu de grande poesté; (1465)
| | Contra son voloir e soa volunté,
| 2630 | Fora de li leto ela l'oit tiré.
| | Sor li palés par força l'oit mené,*   15rb

2601 Mussafia: Da-le; Rajna (*Ricerche intorno ai Reali*, 233), Cremonesi, Rosellini: Dale

2603 Rajna (*Ricerche intorno ai Reali*, 233): De dens

2607 Cremonesi: o'

2612 Mussafia: mal ora; Rosellini: quella dame

2613 MS.: plament; Mussafia, Cremonesi, Rosellini: pla[na]ment

2614 Mussafia: en dre; Cremonesi, Rosellini: endré

2618 Mussafia: ela

2620 Cremonesi: davanti

2622 Mussafia, Cremonesi, Rosellini: Trovel

2627 Mussafia: le çavi'

Por le çavi donando gran collé.*
A le corent totes, e bon e re, (1470)
Meesmo li rois li vait tot eslasé,*
2635 Si dist, "Madame, avés li sen cançé?
Qe v'à fato vestre file qe avés cosi tiré?"
La dama, o li rois vi, cella dama oit lasé,
E prende li rois si l'oit çoso afolé; (1475)
E si le dist, "Fel traito renojé,
2640 O est ma file? Tosto me rendé,
Colsa como no, en malora fusi né!"
Tuta la baronia li fu corant alé;
Ne li valea amor ni amisté, (1480)
Qe a li rois aust pieté;
2645 Si le feria cun man e cun pe,
Par un petit ne l'oit acreventé.
E quella dama s'en fust via alé,
Quant qui de la raine ne la oit lasé. (1485)

Rubric 60
[Coment la raine d'Ongarie tenoit li rois par / forçe e si le demanda so fille e s'el non fust li ba(r)on . . .]*
Laisse 61

O è la raine non querì conseler,*
2650 Par nul ren nen voloit li rois laser.
Nen valea li baron dire ne en projer,
"Dama, porqe faites vos a li rois ste nojer?"
E ella le dist, "Non v'aça merveler, (1490)
Por mia file qe non poso trover."
2655 Adoncha li rois se prist porpenser*
De çella dame c'avoit a·l çasteler;
Quant sor li caro elo la vit primer,

2632 Rajna (*Ricerche intorno ai Reali*, 229): li çavi'
2635 cf. 2594. Cremonesi, Rosellini: Ma dame
2637 Mussafia: cela dama
2643 Cremonesi: no li
Rubric 60 (originally after 2714) MS.: Raine . . . Rois/ . . . li basō; Keller: dongarie / . . . sel non fust li bair; Cremonesi: demandà so[a] . . . lì baso; Rosellini: lí baso
2649 Mussafia: Quela raina; Cremonesi, Rosellini: Qela
2650 Rosellini: non
2651 Mussafia, Cremonesi, Rosellini: enproier
2652 Mussafia, Cremonesi, Rosellini: por qe

Li pe li trovò grandi como dise sa mer.* (1495)
El dist, "Madame, or vos trai arer;
2660 Bona novela e vos averò conter.
Ma primament ne conven çivalcer
Trosqua a un çastel apreso d'un verçer.
Eo creço par voir e si ò quella sper, (1500)
Qe vestra fille avereç illec trover."
2665 Dist la raine, "Ne se vol entarder;
Ma una ren saçés sença boser:
Qe vos da moi no v'en averì sevrer,
Se moja file no m'aça a presenter." (1505)
Adoncha li rois si montò a destrer,
2670 E la raine cun li ses çivaler,
E de qui de li rois lì andò plus d'un miler.
A Sinibaldo aloit avanti mesaçer,
Q'elo se diça de tot apariler, (1510)
Qe li rois vent por soi esbanojer.
2675 E la raine ne le volt oblier,
Qe d'Ongarie se sevroit l'autrer.   15ᵛᵃ
Qi donc veist Synibaldo li castel adorner,
De richi palii, de porpore, de cender. (1515)
E quando li rois se le vait a 'prosmer,
2680 E Synibaldo li voit a l'incontrer,
Ça avea Karleto tros ani tot enter;
Si grant estoit, ben pooit aler.
Corando vait por veoir son per, (1520)
E la raine la prist a demander,
2685 "Questo fantim molto me pare ançoner;
A sa fature pare e pro e ber."
E la raine si le fait baler,*
E dolçement si le prist a baser. (1525)
Atanto i desendent entro li çasteler;
2690 Li rois si prist Sinibaldo a 'peler:
"Faites a nos cela dama parler,

2659 Mussafia, Cremonesi: trai, Rosellini: traí
2667 Rosellini: averi
2668 Mussafia: apresenter
2670 Rosellini: Adonca
2671 Mussafia, Cremonesi, Rosellini: li rois li
2678 Mussafia: palii
2679 Mussafia, Cremonesi, Rosellini: aprosmer
2685 Rosellini: fantin
2687 MS.: baler; Mussafia, Cremonesi, Rosellini: ba(i)ler (emend)

Qe vu savés qe vos fi acoma*n*der."
Dist Sinibaldo, "De greç e volunter." (1530)
Entra en le çanbre, si la fait adorner;
2695 "Dama," fait il, "el vos ven a parler
Li rois de France, qe tant fait a loer,
E la raina d'Ongarie vos vent a visiter."
E dist Berta, "Questo vojo vonter." (1535)

Rubric 61
[*Quant la raine d'Ongarie vide sa fille si / la conoit ama*n*tenant e si menoit gram (çoja)*].*
Laisse 62

Quando Berte oì quella novelle,
2700 De soa mer, tot li cor li saltelle.
El apelò le autre damoselle,
"Venés cu*n* moi davant a li çastele,
Por veoir la raine qe ven de longa tere."* (1540)
E celle le font qe nesuna revelle;*
2705 Quant fo çoso li palés en la praelle,
E la raine, qe tant estoit belle,
Quant ela voit tot trois le polçelle
Venir ensenbre fora par una vançele,* (1545)
Ela reguarda sa file en la gonele.
2710 Ben la conoit a li pe e a la favelle;
Quant la conoit no l'apella de novele,
De le veoir tot li cor li saltele.*
Plu çojant nen fu qe l'onor de Tudele;* (1550)
Sovent li basa le viso e la maselle.

2689 Mussafia, Cremonesi: A tanto
2690 Mussafia, Cremonesi, Rosellini: apeler
2694 Cremonesi, Rosellini: la çanbre
Rubric 61 (originally after 2751) MS.: Raine. Keller: Quant la raine dongarie . . . / gram; Cremonesi: Quant la . . . ; Rosellini: Quant la . . . gram . . . (line not completed)
2704 Mussafia: ce font
2708 Mussafia, Cremonesi: vauçele
2712 Mussafia: D'ele; Cremonesi, Rosellini: d'ele
2713 Mussafia: fu[st] de l'onor (emend)

Rubric 62
[Coment Berte parloit a sa mer la raine / e si li contò tot ço qe li avent e con fu tramé.]
Laisse 63

2715	Li rois Pepin nen fu mais si çojant,	
	Quant il conoit par voir e certamant	
	Qe questa è Berte qe oit li pe grant,	
	Qe fu sposea de li rois primemant. (1555)	
	Nen fu si legro unques a son vivant;	
2720	Ver la raine Berte parla en ojant,	15vb
	"Mere," fait ela, "entendés voiremant;	
	De questa ovre e de questo senblant	
	Le mon segnor non calonçé de niant; (1560)	
	S'e ò eu mal e inojamant,	
2725	Moja fu la colpa a lo començamant.	
	Quella donçelle qe menè de Magant,	
	En le me fiava de cor e lialmant;	
	Et ela de moi si fe li tradimant. (1565)	
	Ne·l fi tal Jude a Deo onipotant.	
2730	Menea fu entro un boscho grant,	
	Par moi oncire par li ses comant.	
	Tanto querì piaté e marçé grant,*	
	Qe i me perdonò la ire e·l maltalant; (1570)	
	E si me fi çurer sor Deo e li sant	
2735	No ma venir en ceste partimant.	
	Tant me penè per celle boscho grant,	
	Q'eo n'esì fors e vini a guarant.*	
	Synibaldo me trovè qe venia çivalçant;* (1575)	
	Menò·me a ste castel, si m'à fato honor tant*	
2740	Como fose sa fille e sa sor ensemant;	

Rubric 62 (originally after 2766) Keller: com fu . . . traine; Guessard: *traine*, lisez *trahie*; Rosellini: com. Position originally at beginning of 16ra.
2726 Mussafia, Cremonesi, Rosellini: mene
2727 Cremonesi. lé (cf. 2754, etc.)
2728 Cremonesi: fé
2729 Cremonesi: nel; Mussafia, Cremonesi, Rosellini: Jude
2732 Mussafia, Rosellini: marcé
2736 Mussafia, Cremonesi, Rosellini: pené
2737 Mussafia: Q'eo n'esi; Cremonesi: q'eo n'esì
2738 Mussafia: trovè; Cremonesi, Rosellini: trové
2739 Mussafia: Menò-me; Cremonesi: menome; Rosellini: Menòme. Mussafia, Rosellini: çastel

Dont e·ma vie serò sa benvojant.*
A li rois me co*n*sentì, do*n*de n'avì st'infant;
S'el averà vite serà pro e valant." (1580)
E la raine nen foit arestamant;
2745 Li rois apele, si le dist en ojant:
"Deo vos oit secoru, e la majesté sant,
Car por cel Deo, qe naque en Oriant,
Se mia filla tornea nen aumes a·l pr*e*sant,* (1585)
Morto v'averoie a un coltel tre*n*çant;
2750 Ne da le mi man nen ausés guarant."
Li rois l'olde, s'en rise bellemant.

Rubric 63
[Coment la Raine parolò a Pepin e pois / se partent ensenble e venoit a Paris.]
Laisse 64

Gran çoja oit li rois Pepin eu,
Quant dama Berta oit reconou, (1590)
Et oit da le par voir tot entendu:
2755 Tot l'afaire qe le fu avenu
E cu*n* quella malvés la oit deceu.
Se la fe mener, qe era son dru,
Par le oncire en le boscho folu. (1595)
Li rois çura Damenedé e Jesu,
2760 Qe quella malvés qe l'avoit co*n*sentu,
Como meltris en un foço metu.*
Li rois de Frànçe ne*n* fu demoré plu;
Con la raine qe d'Ongarie fu, (1600)
E cum Berte, qe Deo oit secoru,

2741 Mussafia, Cremonesi, Rosellini: e[n] (emend)
2742 Mussafia: consenti
2743 Rosellini: valat
2746 MS.: maieste; Mussafia, Rosellini: Maesté
2748 MS.: tornea? Mussafia, Cremonesi: tornea; Rosellini: trovea (emend for MS. *tornea*)
Rubric 63 (originally after 2822)
2756 Cremonesi: cum
2757 Mussafia: que; Cremonesi: fé
2759 Rosellini: Demenedé
2761 Cremonesi, Holden: [serà] en un; Rosellini: meltris [sia] en un; Mussafia, Rosellini: fogo
2764 Rosellini: E cum Berte qe oit secoru (missing *Deo*)

2765 De le çastel i se sonto partu,
      Et a Paris i sonto revenu.

Rubric 64
[*Qui conte la novelle comente la dame / qe fi li tradiment fu arse e bruxée.*]*

[16va]

Laisse 65

      Quant li rois fu a Paris retorné,   (16ra)
      Quella raine qe tanto fu renomé (1605)
      Avec soi ello l'oit amené;
2770 E dama Berte nen fu pais oblié,
      E avec lor Karleto oit mené.
      Gran fu la çoie par tot la cité;
      Grant fu la cort e davant e daré. (1610)
      Li tradiment çascun oit blasmé,
2775 E la malvés si fo presa e ligé.
      Avantqe la raine fust partua ni sevré,
      Fo çella dame en un fogo brusé.
      Por le nen fu asa li rois projé (1615)
      Da li barons de li son parenté,
2780 Metesma Berte por soa gran bonté,
      L'avoit en don a li rois domandé.
      Mais no le valse una poma poré,*
      Qe la raine d'Ongarie n'estoit si abus<m>é,* (1620)
      Ne la lasaroit scanper par l'or de Crestenté.
2785 E cele dame qe in malor fu né,
      Avantq'ela fust en le fogo bruxé,
      Ella se fu molto ben confesé
      A tota jent dise li so peçé. (1625)
      A Berta oit li perdon domandé,
2790 Et ella li oit lojalment doné.
      Qe vos dè eser li pla plus alonçé,

2766 Mussafia, Rosellini: Et a; Cremonesi: et a Paris
Rubric 64 (originally after 2859) Keller: comende, Guessard: comente; Cremonesi, Rosellini: arse e bruxée. Original position, the second line of the rubric is the first line on folio 16va.
2767 Rosellini: Qant. Foglio begins with rubric, here replaced by Rubric 64.
2776 Mussafia: Avant que; Cremonesi, Rosellini: Avant qe
2782 Mussafia: no le valse una poma poré; Cremonesi, Rosellini: no le valse una poma poré
2783 Mussafia, Cremonesi, Rosellini: abusmé
2786 Mussafia: Avant q'ela

Cella dama fu en un fois bruxé.
Una colsa fi Berta donde fu ben loé: (1630)
Tantosto com ela fu de le mondo finé,
2795 For de le fois ella si fu tiré.
A san Donis, o est li grant abé,
A grant honor ela fu seteré.
Dos enfant de le s'en remist daré: (1635)
Lanfroi e La(n)dris, ensi fu apelé,
2800 E una fille petite, Berta fu anomé;
Quella si fu mere Rolando li avoé.
Oldés, segnur, de Berta gran lialté,
Qe qui enfanti qe remist daré, (1640)
Si cun Karleto li avoit alevé.
2805 Ne sa pais mie ço qe le fo encontré,
Quando le dos enfant furent tant alevé,
Qe pais poent avoir arme baillé.*
Cun li baron prendent tel amisté, (1645)
E por la força de li ses parenté,
2810 Tant oit li traiti con eso lor ovré
Qe Pepin e Berte furent envenée;
Donde cuitent avoir sa mer vençé.
(B)en averoit Karleto morto e delivré,* (1650)
Nen fust Morando qe l'oit via mené;   16rb
2815 Nen pote star in la Crestenté,
En Spagna fu avec lui alé,
A li rois Galafrio elo fu presenté,
Qe le norì si l'avoit alevé; (1655)
E soa filla en lu fu marié.*
2820 Nen serà pais ste roman finé,
Qe oldirés cun fu la colsa alé;
Mais de Bovo d'Antone oldirés asé.

2797 Cremonesi: setiré
2798 Mussafia, Rajna (*Ricerche intorno ai Reali*, 230), Cremonesi, Rosellini: d'ele. Rajna (*Ricerche intorno ai Reali*, 230): son remist
    2799 MS.: ladris; Mussafia, Cremonesi, Rosellini: La[n]dris (emend)
    2800 Rajna (*Ricerche intorno ai Reali*, 230): file
    2801 Rajna (*Ricerche intorno ai Reali*, 230): Rolando li ancé
    2807 Mussafia: puis; Cremonesi, Rosellini: pois (emend)
    2810 Mussafia: traite
    2811 Mussafia: envene[n]é
    2813 MS.: Ven?; Mussafia, Cremonesi, Rosellini: Ben

Rubric 65
[Dapoisqe la dame qe de Berte fi li tradimant / Fo çuçté, se departe la raine, e si aloit en Ungarie.]*
Laisse 66

        Oeç, segnur, e saçé, quant*
        de cele dame fu fato li çu(ç)emant,* (1660)
        Qe de dama Berte fist li tradimant,
2825 Ilec demorò la raine trois mois en avant.
        E quant oit metu sa file a le convenant,
        Non volse ilec demorer longo tanp, (1665)
        Q'ela se porpense li çorno en avant,
        Quando da li rois en fi desevremant,
2830 De·l retorner la projò dolçemant.
        A li rois Pepin e a sa file ensemant,
        Conçé demanda e ben e dolçemant. (1670)
        E quando de la raine <i vi> li so comant,*
        E ço qe a le plais e oit en talant,
2835 Si le consente con li vene a talant.
        Adonc Pepin se levò en estant,
        E ses baron avec lu ensemant. (1675)
        Por convejer la raine, montent en auferant.
        Berta vi sa mere, larmoja tenderamant,
2840 Et ella la basa, si le dist dolçemant,
        "Fila," dist ela, "a Jesu te comant,
        La merçé de Deo, li pere onipotant, (1680)
        Vu sì scanpea de cosi gran tormant.
        Sor tot ren de le segle vivant,
2845 Vestre segnor vos amarés avant;
        Faites vos ben voloir a petit e a grant."
        "Mere," dist ella, "e l'ò ben en talant. (1685)

    Rubric 65 (originally after 2895) Keller: Da pois qe/ çuçce ... departo ... roine; Cremonesi: Da pois qe; Rosellini: Dapois qe; Cremonesi, Rosellini: çuçée
    2823 Mussafia, Cremonesi, Rosellini: çuçemant
    2823–24 Mussafia: e sace; Quant ...
    2832 Mussafia: Concé; Rosellini: Çoncé; Cremonesi: conçé
    2833 MS.: quado de la raine vir (?) li som comat; Mussafia: E qua(n)do ... i vi ... li so ... (emend); Cremonesi: e qua[n]do de la raine i vi li som ...; Rosellini: i vi li so comant (no note)
    2834 Mussafia: qe'a le
    2839 Cremonesi: larmoià
    2840 Cremonesi: basà

| | Ço qe vos die, ben serà otrié tot qua*n*t;*
| | E mo*n* per da mia part salué dolçema*n*t.
| 2850 | Mais d'una re*n* vos sia reme*n*bré ata*n*t:
| | Non tornés mie por le çami*n* era*n*t
| | Qe vos faistes l'autre jor en avant, (1690)
| | Por la paure d·i baron de Magant,
| | Qe sont alti homes e ont ta*n*ti para*n*t.
| 2855 | Torbea en poreç estre e vos e vestre çant,
| | De ço cuitoit vençer quella da·l tradima*n*t."
| | Quela le respondì, "Farò li to*n* comant. (1695)
| | Pasarò por Lonbardie in (m') anant,*
| | Pois pasarò en nef et en calant."

Rubric 66
[Coment la raine d'Engarie se departì di / li rois Pepin e da sa fille, e si s'en aloit en sa terre.]
Laisse 67

| 2860 | Quant la raine desis de la sala pavée,   (16va)
| | Tota la jent fu par le relevée,
| | Et ella oit tota jent saluée. (1700)
| | Soa filla oit basé e acolée;
| | De pietés çascuna oit plurée,*
| 2865 | E mante larme el ont butée.
| | La raine, qe tant avoit beltée,
| | Soa fille oit a Deo comandée, (1705)
| | Et ella e Karleto, ella oit segnée.
| | A palafroi quant ella fu montée
| 2870 | Li rois Pepin monta da l'altro lee,
| | A plus de mil baron l'avoit co*n*vojée;
| | E qui çivaler qe d'O*n*garia fu née (1710)
| | Se sonto ben guarni e parilée,

2848 Mussafia, Cremonesi: dié
2852 Cremonesi: faïstes
2857 Mussafia: Quella le respondì:« Farò li to comant . . .
2858 MS.: in in; Mussafia: in avant (for MS. *in inauant*); Cremonesi: in m'anant (for MS. *mmanant*); Rosellini: inmanant
Rubric 66 (originally after 2917) MS.: tre, with an abbreviation line above the whole word, ends the line; Keller: dengarie sen naloit . . . terre; Cremonesi: Ongarie . . . / departì de . . . tere; Rosellini: Ongarie . . . /tere; Rosellini: raina (cf. Morini, review)
2860 First line after rubric on 16^v. (Rubric here replaced.)
2870 Cremonesi: montà

	Par soi defendre si trovase meslée.*
2875	Va s'en la raine, qe ben fu convojée;
	A li rois oit sa fila comandée.
	Non sa pais mie con fu la colsa alée, (1715)
	Ço qe a le en furent destinée.
	Mais no la vide en soa vivetée
2880	Li rois la mena fora de la citée;*
	Plus de quatro legues la oit aconpagnée.
	La raina s'en voit, e cil (est) arer tornée, (1720)
	E da cel çorno avanti, Berta la ensenée
	Si fu par tot raina de France clamée.
2885	Et ella fu de si grande bontée,
	Qe la petita Berte oit tanto amée
	Como ela aust en son corpo portée. (1725)
	E si l'oit si ben noria e maistrée,
	Cum fust ma dama qe fose plu maistrée.*
2890	E la raina d'Ongarie fu tanto apenée,
	Entrò en nef si fo oltrapasée,*
	En Ongarie quando fu arivée, (1730)
	Li rois le fu encontra lui alée;
	Gran çoja fu par tot part menée,
2895	De la raine qe arer fu tornée.

Rubric 67
[Coment la Raina d'Ongarie fu repariée / en sa tere, et a li rois contoit la novelle.] *
Laisse 68

	Or fu la dama de França repariés,
	Gran çoja mena tot qui de la contrés. (1735)
	Li ro(is) vi la raine si l'oit arasnés,*
	E si le oit de novelle demandés,
2900	De·l rois Pepin, como la oit honorés.
	E quella li oit tot l'afar contés,

2874 Cremonesi: s'i trovase
2875 Cremonesi, Rosellini: Vasen
2880 Mussafia, Rosellini: l'amena; Cremonesi: l'amenà
2882 MS.: est est
2884 Mussafia: França
2889 Mussafia, Cremonesi: ma' dama
2891 Mussafia, Cremonesi, Rosellini: oltra pasée
Rubric 67 (originally after 2942) Keller: dongarie . . . terre
2888 MS.: ro ỿí la; Mussafia, Cremonesi, Rosellini: li ro[is] vi la . . .

Como sa fille fu trasfigurés (1740)
Da una mavés traita *et* enganés.
"Saçés, bon rois, se no le fose alés,
2905 Senpre seroit vestre fie soa orfanés;*
Jamés de França ne fosse encoronés.   16vb
La mercé de Deo, de la moja bontés, (1745)
Tanto e ò fato et auvrés,*
Q'ela est raina de tota França clamés."
2910 Li rois l'intent, si l'oit merciés;
Por la venue l'oit trois fois basés.
Gran çoja n'oit anbidos amenés.* (1750)
Da qui avanti fu li çanter enforçés;* (1165)
Lasaron de li rois, qe fu çojant e lés.
2915 A Bovo d'Antone nu seron retornés,
Cun por Pepin el fu asediés
Contra li voloir de ses richo bernés.

2903 7 for *et*
2905 Cremonesi: sea orfanés
2908 Mussafia: tant'o eo; Cremonesi: Tanto e' ò; Rosellini: Tant ò eo
2912 Cremonesi: ambidos. End of Mussafia's and Cremonesi's editions.
2917 Cremonesi: riche barnés (117, note to *Berta*)

7.3 Chevalerie Bovo
Rubric 68
[Coment li rois Pepin por g(r)ant avoir qe / li dona Do de Magançe (f)i bandir sa oste et/ Civalçoit ad Antone desor Bovo.]*
Laisse 69

	Pla vos oldir une nove çanson? (1170)
	Nen fu milor oldie pois li tenp Sanson,
2920	De stormeno e de bataile e de gran capleson.
	Oldi avés cum fu morto Gujon
	A tradimento de le dux Duon,
	Cil de Magance, qe oit malecion, (1175)
	E de dama Blondoja qe è en la preson;
2925	E cun Bovo tanto à peneson,
	Q'el oit Druxiana da la belle façon.
	Asa durò par le pene et aflicion,*
	Ma mo q'elo cuitoit stare en sa rason, (1180)
	E seçornar cum ses dui garçon,
2930	Sovra li vene grande aflicion,
	Qe le malvés de le dux Duon
	Alò a Pepin por mala entencion.
	Tant li donò et or coito e macon (1185)
	Q'el fe bandir oste en Françe *et* a Lion;*
2935	E questo fe·lo por soa malecion, *
	Contra li voloir de le dux Aquilon,
	(Morando) de Rivere e (Bernardo) de Clermon.*
	Li rois n'avoit ço qe li convenon, (1190)
	E si fo morto quelo dux Duon,

Rubric 68 (originally after 3005) MS.: Rois . . . porgant; Keller: porgant; Reinhold: Rois Pepin; Reinhold, Rosellini: g[r]ant (emend); line 2: MS.: si bandir; Keller: fi; Reinhart: *fi bandir (emend); Rosellini: fi bandit. line 3: Keller: de sor

2920 Rosellini: stormento (corrected by Morini, review)
2923 Reinhold, Rosellini: Magançe; Rosellini: e oit
2924 MS.: qe è en la . . . ; Reinhold: q'è en . . . ; Rosellini: q'é en (cf. Morini, review)
2927 Reinhold: Asa' (as always)
2928: Reinhold: mo' (as always)
2934 7 for *et*
2937 MS.: Bernardo de rivere e morando de clermon; Reinhold, Rosellini: Morando de . . . e Bernardo (emend)
2938 Reinhold: MS. reads *nanoit*

2940 So frer don Albrigo, cun plus de mil baron.
Da qui avanti se començe la cançon,
Si la oldirés tota quanta por rason.

Rubric 69
[Qui se començe li roman coment li rois Pepin / Contra li volir de li ses baron por grant avoire...]*
Laisse 70

    Do de Magançe, quando el fu sané (1195)
    De ses plaie qe Bovo li oit doné,
2945 E Antona perdue, la cité
    Qe il avoit prise a grande falsité,*
    E sa muler estoit enpresoné,   17ra
    Entro dos muri e clusa e seré (1200)
    El oit ben, e soit por verité,
2950 Qe son daumaje nen serà mais stauré,
    Se por Pepin el non ert vençé.
    Conseil demande a li ses plus privé:
    Coment il poroit avoir cella ovra ovré. (1205)
    E cel li dient, "Nu l'avon ben pensé;
2955 Andemo a li rois; tanto li soit doné
    O(r e)t avoir e diner moené,*
    Qe nu l'açamo de son seno cançé.
    Se poon faire qe il soja airé (1210)
    Encontre Bovo, nu averon ben ovré;
2960 Qe a Antone el meterà l'asé.*
    Nu averon Blondoie cun tota la cité;
    Por mal Bovo unchamais fu né."*
    E dist Doo, "Eo l'avea ben pensé;* (1215)
    Et eo le farò, dache me l'otrié.*
2965 Za por avoir non serà stratorné."
    Savés qe fi celle traitor proé?*
    El voit a la cort cun li ses parenté;

    2942 MS.: sll; Reinhold: MS. reads *Slla*; Rosellini: Si la (no note)
    Rubric 69 (originally after 3028) line 1: MS., Reinhold: Roman... Rois; line 2: Keller: por-/gant; Reinhold: vol[o]ir (emend)... g[r]ant; Rosellini: voloir... jant avoire
    2949 Reinhold: oït ("heard")
    2956 MS., Reinhold: O ert; Rosellini: Vert avoir (emend)
    2958 Reinhold: aïré
    2962 Reinhold: uncha mais (as always)
    2964 Reinhold, Rosellini: da che (as always)

	Avec lui, e dux e casé. (1220)
	Saçés par voir, e quest'è verité,
2970	Qe la cha de Magançe fu la plu honoré,
	E la plu riçe e mejo enparenté*
	De nulla qe fust en la Crestenté.
	Ma una colsa avoit donde furent blasmé: (1225)
	Q'i no portent ni fe ni lialté,
2975	Ne non ament qi l'avoit usé.
	Doo fu a la cort con li ses parenté;
	Conti lì furent plu de quaranta sé.*
	Avantqe a li rois ausent de ren parlé, (1230)
	De cope d'oro e d'altri vasé
2980	N'oit a li rois asa doné,
	Qe por mile marches non seroit conpré.
	Quant a li rois furent ben aconté,
	E qui li ont asa doné e livré,* (1235)
	Davanti li rois en fu Doo alé,
2985	E si le quer merçé e piaté:
	"Merçé, bon rois, por la vestre bonté;
	Vos me devés faire rason e lialté
	De un traites qe m'oit desoré. (1240)
	Ma muler prisa, e tolta ma çité;
2990	E mo ferì e durament navré.
	Non ò fiançe d'omo de mere né,
	Q'el de lu me posa avoir vençé,
	Se vu non estes, çentil rois coroné." (1245)
	E dist li rois, "No l'ò pais oblié;
2995	Tosto en serì de quella onta vençé."
	Et Aquilon estoit ilec aseté,
	Et oit oldu cun Doo oit parlé,
	E com li rois se n'est aconversé* (1250)
	De far a Doo la soa volunté.
3000	El dist a li rois, "Guarda qe vu façé;
	Bovo è prodon, e de bon parenté.
	Son per li fo morto, e presa sa çité;

17rb

2970 Reinhold: cha'
2971 Reinhold, Rosellini: en parenté
2978 Reinhold, Rosellini: Avant qe (as always)
2983 Rosellini: quili ont
2990 Reinhold, Rosellini: feri
2998 Reinhold, Rosellini: s'en est
3000 Reinhold: Guardà

              S'e l'oit recovra, non dè esere blasmé.* (1255)
              Par mon conseil vu no lì aliré,
3005   N'e(n) cel ovra ne vos trometeré."*

Rubric 70
[Coment Aquilon e li altri baron donarent / a li rois li conseil de non çivalçer a Antone;
E (de çes) li rois non volse quel conseil.]*
Laisse 71

              Aquilon parloe a li rois en ojant:
              "Çentil rois de França, non creés por niant,
              Ne far asenbler ves homes ni vestre jant (1260)
              Par lo voloir d·i segnor de Maganç.
3010   S'el g'è forfaito, i ne prenda vençamant;
              A lor parten, a vu no dè niant."*
              E dist li rois, "Farò li mon talant.
              S'el no me rende Antone primemant, (1265)
              Ma non averà cun moi pax ni acordamant."
3015   E dist le dux, "Non farés a siant;
              E se le faites e nesun mal ve prant,
              Dirà la jent qe seno avì d'infant,
              Quant prendés guere la qual no vos aprant."* (1270)
              Quant li rois l'olde e le intant,*
3020   El dist ad Aquilon, "Vu parlé de niant.
              Doncha no sont e rois, ni corona portant,*
              Se non fi obei da una cotal çant?
              Eo lì alirò malgra qi li contant; (1275)
              E se prendo Bovo, farò·ne tel çuçemant

     3003 Reinhold: Se l'oit . . . dè esere; Rosellini: Se l'oit . . . balsmé (cf. Morini, review)
     3004 Reinhold: alirè
     3005 MS.: Ne; Reinhold: N'e[n]; Rosellini: Ne'[n] (emend)
     Rubric 70 (originally after 3095) Reinhold: MS. reads *a Quilon*; Reinhold: conseil (emend for his MS. reading *conseu*, in lines 2 and 3); Rosellini: conseu. Reinhold: Rois; Reinhold, Rosellini: A li rois (line 2); MS.: E li Rois de çes li Rois . . .
     3006 Reinhold, Rosellini: oiant (as always)
     3008 Rosellini: jant
     3009 Reinhold, Rosellini: di segnor (as always)
     3018 Reinhold: laqual . . . ap(r)ant; Rosellini: laqual apant (emend)
     3019 Reinhold: . . . e le vi tant; Rosellini: l'olde eser à tant (cf. Morini, review)
     3021 Reinhold: e' rois . . .
     3022 Reinhold: obeï
     3024 Reinhold: farò ne; Rosellini: farone

3025   Como traites, culverto seduant."*
        Dist Aquilon, "Non farì a siant.
        Ora nen faites a li vestre talant,
        Qe de questa colsa ne vo dir plus avant." (1280)

Rubric 71
[Coment li rois Pepin fi bandir soa oste / Par tota Fra(n)çe por aler ad Antone.]
Laisse 72

        Li rois Pepin nen volse demorer,
3030   Ni d'Aquilon li son consel otrier;
        Ni de Bernardo, ni de Morando de River.
        Non fe qe sajes, cun oldirés conter;*
        El fe ses brevi e letre sajeler; (1285)
        Mandò por França la novela nonçer,
3035   E par tot e bandir e crier,
        Q'el s'apareil peon e çivaler
        De venir a Paris con tot son coruer.
        Avant un mois, fi sa jent asenbler: (1290)
        Vinti milia furent a corant destrer;
3040   E qui de Magançe n'avoit .XX. miler.   17ᵛᵃ
        E quando Bovo oldì quella novella nonçer,*
        Demantenant fa breve sajeler,
        Et a Syndonia envojò mesaçer (1295)
        A·l rois Teris, e dire e conter,*
3045   Qe li rois de França e de Baiver
        Oit fato sa oste e bandir e crier.
        "Tanto li oit Doo dona de ses diner,
        A 'Ntona vol venir par moi desariter. (1300)
        El se dè ben celle jor remenbrer,

    3025 Rosellini: saduant
    3028 Reinhold: vo' dir
    Rubric 71 (after 3028), was originally after 3129.
    3033 Rosellini: brei (for *brevi*) (cf. Morini, review)
    3035 Reinhold, Rosellini: partot
    3041 Reinhold, Rosellini: noncer (cf. Morini, review); Rosellini: oldì
    3043 Reinhold: envoiò
    3044 Reinhold, Rosellini: Al.. (as always)
    3048 Reinhold, Rosellini: Antona
    3049 Reinhold: dè; Rosellini: dé (for MSI *deve*); Rosellini: remembrer (cf. Morini, review)

3050 Qe de Sydonia le fi coroner.
S'elo m'ama, ni Synibaldo son per,
Si nos vegna secorer et aider."
Adoncha se parte, va s'en li mesaçer; (1305)
Trosqu'a Syndonia ne volent seçorner.
3055 Teris trovò avec soa muler;
Quando vi li mesaçi, si le vait a 'coler,
Si le oit dito, "Benvenés, mesaçer.
Qe est de Bovo, mon segnor droiturer?" (1310)
E cil li dient, "Vu le porés saçer,
3060 Qe queste letre vos dirà le çerter."
Teris le prende, si va la çira oster; *
Vide l'afaire, prist Deo a 'orer,
E posa dist enverso sa muler, (1315)
"Li mon segnor oit de secorso mester,
3065 Car li rois de France con li ses guer *
Ont çuré de lu desariter."
Dist Braidamont, "Quant da·l staçon e·l fi desevrer,
E de la tore l'insegna de scanper, (1320)
Neanche mo ne le vojo abandoner.*
3070 Par mon conseil e vos vojo en projer,*
Qe vu li diça secorer et aider.
De nostra jent mena .XX. miler,
E vos meesmes le diça çivalçer, (1325)
E se cun quisti ne poi si ben ovrer,
3075 Et eo de vos veese mesaçer
E vos averò secorer con plus de .XXX. miler."
Quando Teris l'à oldu si parler,
A soa dame vait le viso baser, (1330)
Et in apreso dolçement merçier.

3050 Reinhold: fi'
3053 Rosellini: vasen
3054 Reinhold, Rosellini: Trosqua
3057 Reinhold, Rosellini: Ben venés
3060 Reinhold, Rosellini: dira le çerter
3062 Reinhold, Rosellini: aorer
3067 Reinhold: e'-l fi'; Rosellini: e'l fi
3069 Reinhold: Ne anche mo'
3070 Reinhold: vos voio; Rosellini: enproier.
3073 Reinhold: diçà
3074 Reinhold: poisì; Rosellini: no poisi ben
3076 Reinhold: E' = "eo" (as always; no longer commented)
3079 Reinhold, Rosellini: mercier (cf. Morini, review)

3080	Dont oit fato soa jent asenbler;	
	Vinte milia furent a coranti destrer,	
	Tot li milor q'il pote trover.	
	Quant à ço fato, si dist a li mesaçer, (1335)	
	Qe demanes diça tornar arer,	
3085	E dir a Bovo, no se diça doter;	
	Secorso averà de .XX. mil çivaler,	
	A bone arme et a corant destrer.	
	E qui s'en torne, tant vont por la river (1340)	17vb
	Venent a Antone, o Bovo po trover.	
3090	Quando çi le prendent la novella nonçer,*	
	S'el oit çoja, non è da demander.	
	Li rois non dota plus valisant un diner,	
	Ne qui de Magançe una poma porer. (1345)	
	Ora devon a li rois reparier,	
3095	Qe oit fato sa oste e bandir e crier.	

Rubrics 72–73

[Coment li rois çivalçò cum sa oste ad Antone / e coment Bovo mandò a Sydonie e T(e)ris li dona . . .]*

[Coment Dursiana parole a Bovo por far savoir / a li rois d'Armune qe Bovo si è revonu et oit pris . . .]*

Laisse 73

Li rois de França, qe Pepin oit non,
Por grant avoir qe li donò Duon
Fi asenbler de França li baron (1350)
Por aler ad Antone desovra li cont Bovon,
3100 E questo fe contra li voloir de le dux Aq(ui)lon.
Li rois çivalçe a cuita de speron,

3085 Rosellini: Bovo o se diça (cf. Morini, review)
3086 Reinhold: avera
3089 Reinhold: o' Bovo pò . . .
3090 Reinhold, Rosellini: çıle
3091 Reinhold: çoia
3092 Rosellini: no dota
Rubric 72 (originally after 3146) MS., Reinhold: Rois; Keller: sydonie / etous; Mussafia: e toris (for *Teris*); Reinhold: *Teris (for MS. *Toris*); Reinhold, Rosellini: [secorso] (to finish the rubric)
Rubric 73 (originally after line 3197) MS.: darmune; Reinhold, Rosellini: d'Armune
3100 MS.: aqlon; Reinhold: Aquilon; Rosellini: Aquilon (for MS. *aqlon*)
3101 Reinhold, Rosellini: d'esperon

Con sa grant oste, çivaler e peon.
Tant çivalçent a soe guarison, (1355)
Et avec lui la soe legion,
3105 Vene*n*t ad Antone ava*n*ti l'Asension.
Apreso Antone, a·l trato d'un bolçon*
L'etendirent tende e pavilon;
L'oriaflama levare*n*t contramon. (1360)
Bovo le vi, qe estoit a li balcon;
3110 O el vi Druxiane, si la mist por rason:
"Dama," fait il, "el nos crese tençon.
Dodo è venu a prender nos dojon;
Pepin oit (m)ené por avoir guarison, (1365)
Qe rois est de França e de Lion.
3115 Veeç l'oriaflame desplojea co*n*tremon,
E tant ensegne e indoré penon?
Li rois oit eu co*n*sejo de guarçon,
Se Teris ven, cu*n* per letere avon, (1370)
Partir nu li faron a paso e a·l tron!"*
3120 Dist Druxiana, "Deo gracia nos le don!
Or le saust mon per Arminion,*
Qe vu scanpé sì de morte e de preson,*
Qe donea fose a cosi nobel hon. (1375)
E fose quella qe in la soa mason,
3125 Avea li dos petiti garçon,
Qe li çantava li versi e le cançon.
S'elo·l saust, par nul ren de·l mon,
Ne s'en aliroit li rois sença destrucion."* (1380)

3102 Reinhold, Rosellini: civaler
3107 Reinhold, Rosellini: Le tendirent
3108 Reinhold, Rosellini: contra mon
3113 MS. : inene (for *mene*); Reinhold: mené (note, p. 14: Hs. *ineue*)
3115 Reinhold, Rosellini: contre mon (as always; cf. 3108); Reinhold, Rosellini: desploiea
3121 Reinhold: saüst
3122 Reinhold, Rosellini: scanpesi
3124 Reinhold: soe mason
3127 Reinhold: S'elo-l saüst; Rosellini: S'elo 'l

Rubric 74

[Coment Teris vene en secorso de Bovo a 'Ntone / Cun .XX. mil çivaler, e si le salue da part la dame.]
Laisse 74

   Segnur baron, Deo vos soit en aie,
3130 Le glorios, le filç sante Marie!   18ra
   Grant fu l'oste e grande (la) baronie*
   Qe li rois Pepin avoit establie;*
   Atorno Antone fu la çivalerie. (1385)
   Bovo s'estoit con Druxiana, sa mie;
3135 Atant ven Teris con soa conpagnie,
   Vinte mil homes avoit a bataile remie.*
   Non poit remandre qe bataila non sie
   Quant en Antone entrent celle baronie. (1390)
   Bovo le vi, à sa çoja conplie,*
3140 El acolla Teris, por amor le disie:
   "Teris," fait il, "de la vestra sperançe non m'à vos falì mie.*
   Çeste filz d'Ançelo, qe le cor Deo maldie,
   Por grant avor m'à tolu en aie;* (1395)
   Con qui de Magançe à fato conpanie.
3145 Non lasaroie par nul ren qe sie
   Qe eo non vada defor a la meslie."

Laisse 75*

   "Bovo," dist Teris, "e no vos quer çeler;
   Da part de Braidamont e vos don saluer. (1400)
   Ela vos manda .XX. mil çivaler,
3150 Si n'oit fato .XXX. mil pariler,
   Qe vos manderà, se vos farà mester."
   E dist Bovo, "Molto la poso gracier.

 Rubric 74 (originally after line 3223) line 1· Keller: bouo/antone; Reinhold, Rosellini: [d'] Antone (emendation); line 2: Reinhold: salve da
 3129 Reinhold: en aïe; Rosellini: en aie
 3131 MS. : grande baronie; Reinhold, Rosellini: grande [la] baronie (emend)
 3132 Rosellini: avoir establie
 3134 Reinhold, Rosellini: se stoit; Rosellini: s'amie
 3141 Reinhold: non m'a' vos fali; Rosellini: non ma vos fali
 3145 Reinhold: lasarò je; Rosellini: lasaroie
 3146 Reinhold: meslée
 3148 Reinhold: e' vos dò saluer; Rosellini: Braidanont

Ben poso par voir e dir e conter, (1405)
Quando me poso de le aremenbrer;
3155 Quant a·l stacon ela me vi en primer,
De la schala me fe çoso desmonter,
Pois me menò davanti da son per.
Se fose ste cativo e lainer, (1410)
Za Druxiana non aust soa sper,
3160 Qe la dama averia tolta a muler;*
En mia vita l'averò regracier.*
Sire Teris, e no ve·l quer nojer;
E so par voir qe por oro e por diner (1415)
Li rois Pepin m'è venu a guerojer.
3165 Jamais li rois Angelo, li qual si fu son ser,*
Si como e poso oldir e desrasner,
Ne li plaqe mais traimento user,
Ne guera prendre con li ses çivaler. (1420)
Ançi, le deveroit, se le fose mester
3170 Par tot tenpo secorer et aider.
Avantqe a li canp voja aler a çostrer*
Avec li rois e voria parler;
Se por amor el s'en volese aler, (1425)
Lasar la guera a qi qe l'oit mester,
3175 E qi qe cuitent soa muler vençer;
E se le rois no le vol otrier, *   18ʳᵇ
Da lor avanti se mal le po encontrer,
Jamais non do eser plu da (blasmer)." (1430)
Dist Teris, "Vu parlés como ber.
3180 Or le mandés a lui un mesaçer,
E se li plais e li vol otrier,
Avec lui (v)orisi parler,*
En celle pre avec cil verçer. (1435)
E no serà con vos se no dos çivaler,

3154 Reinhold: areme[m]brer (emendation!); Rosellini: aremenbrer
3158 Reinhold: sté
3160 MS.: aveva?; Reinhold, Rosellini: averia
3164 Reinhold, Rosellini: gueroier
3165 Reinhold, Rosellini: per (emend); cf. Rajna
3167 Reinhold: traïmento
3171 Reinhold: Avant q'e' à . . . voia; Rosellini: Avant q'è à li canp . . .
3177 Reinhold: le pò; Rosellini: le po econtrer
3178 MS.: blalmer; Reinhold, Rosellini: blasmer (emend); Reinhold: dò eser
3182 MS., Rosellini: vu orisi; Reinhold: vu [v]orisi
3183 Rosellini: pre ave[n]t cil verçer

3185	Et aça avec lui Aquilon de Baiver,
	Et ensement Morando de River.
	De qui de Maganç, non demando ni quer."*
	Adoncha Bovo no se volse entarder; (1440)
	El l'invoì Bernardo da Mondiser,
3190	Qe a mervile savoit ben parler,
	E de rason dir e conter.
	Un palafroi el se fe coroer;
	Elo li monte si s'en vait sens tarder. (1445)
	Quant Bovo li oit dito ço q'elo doit crer,*
3195	Via s'en vait Bernardo da Mondiser;
	En men el porta un ramo d'oliver:
	Quel senefie q'el est mesaçer.

Rubric 75
[Coment s'en vait Bernardo, qe porta / a li rois Pepin la novelle].
Laisse 76

	Bernardo çivalçe, qe cor oit de lion; (1450)
	Saçes homo ert, si soit ben rason.
3200	Quant de Pepin el fu a·l pavilon,
	Dodo de Magançe e le dux Aquilon,
	Et avec lor Bernardo de Clermon,
	Morando de River e le dux Sanson. (1455)
	Le mesaçer desis de·l muleto aragon,
3205	E ven davant li rois, si le dist sa rason:
	"Salu vos mande Bovo, le filz Gujon;
	Parler ve voroie, a vos *et* a 'Quilon,*
	E a Morando e a Bernardo de Clermon. (1460)
	Ne vol qe avec vos aça plus conpagnon;
3210	Et el averà avec lui Teris, rois de Sindon
	E de Baldras — de tot la legion,*
	E Synibaldo, qe bailo fu Bovon."

3187 Rosellini: MS. maccanç
3188 Rosellini: Adonca
3189 Reinhold: invoi[a]; Rosellini: l'invoi
Rubric 75 (originally after 3256) Keller: sen uait . . . nouelle
3199 Rosellini: Seçes homo
3203 MS.: sanlon; Reinhold, Rosellini: Sanson (emendation)
3205 Reinhold: li dist
3207 ȝ for *et*; Reinhold, Rosellini: [à] Aquilon; Reinhold: veroie
3209 Reinhold: açà
3212 Rosellini: e Synibaldo

　　　　Li rois l'inte*n*de, s'infronçì li gregnon; (1465)
　　　　E çura Deo, qe sofrì pasion,
3215　"S'el no me rende d'Antona li dojon,*
　　　　E sa muler el no*n* rende a Doon,
　　　　Et el non ven a ma subecion,
　　　　Apendu ert cu*n* pesimo lairon! (1470)
　　　　Tota sa jent meterò a co*n*fosion,
3220　Nen scanperà ni veilardo ni garçon."
　　　　Dist Bernardo, "Perqe vos çelaron?
　　　　Ne son qui venu por far vosco tençon.　　　　18ᵛᵃ
　　　　Dites le moi, se le verés o non." (1475)

Rubric 76
[Coment Aquilon parlò a Pepin/Por li (mesacer).]*
Laisse 77

　　　　"Bon rois," dist Aquilon, "ben aveç ascolté;
3225　Li mesaçer v'à dito sa anbasé.
　　　　A lu non dè eser nula ranpogna doné,
　　　　Ne nul mesaço non dè eser destorbé.
　　　　Honor e bel senblant li doit eser mostré (1480)
　　　　Davanti çelu q'il oit qui envojé;
3230　Le devés dire la vestre volunté."
　　　　Dist le rois, "El est un malfé.
　　　　Aleç, mesaço, e plus no*n* entardé,
　　　　E si le dites qe son aparilé. (1485)
　　　　Vegna a moi defors en cele pre,
3235　Ne non aporte arme, fors li brant amolé."*
　　　　Quel responde, "Ben serà otrié."
　　　　El se depart, si s'en fu alé,
　　　　Ven a Antone, nen fu pais demoré. (1490)
　　　　Bovo le vi, si li est encontra alé;
3240　E cil li oit li mesaço no*n*çé.

　　3213 Reinhold: si-n froncì; Rosellini: si'n fronçí
　　3214 Rosellini: sofrí
　　3217 Reinhold: mia
　　3220 Reinhold, Rosellini: N'en (*Nen* and *N'en* are difficult to distinguish, as noted elsewhere)
　　Rubric 76 (originally after 3281) line 2: MS., Keller, Reinhold: mesancer; Rosellini: mesacer
　　3227 Rosellini: dé (as always)
　　3229 Reinhold, Rosellini: envoié (as always)

Chevalerie Bovo 423

      Quan Bovo li soit, si·n fu çojant e lé
      Por dir a li roi la soa volunté.
      E li rois Pepin non oit l'ovre oblié; (1495)
      Dux Aquilon oit a soi apelé,
3245 Et avec lu fu Morando de Rivé,
      E Bernardo de Clermon nen fu plus demandé.
      A palafroi i furent monté;
      Deveir Antone i furent açaminé.* (1500)
      E Bovo estoit a·l balcon apoçé;
3250 El vi li rois, Teris oit apelé;*
      A Sinibaldo oit li rois mostré:
      Non oit pais li rois mie oblié;
      "Or tosto enscamo de la cité, (1505)
      Qe tel dos homes oit avec lui mené,
3255 Qe sont amisi de le nos parenté."
      Dist Sinibaldo, "Eo le conosco asé."

Rubric 77
[Coment s'en vait Bovo a p(a)rl(e)r a li rois / et avoit avec lui Synibaldo e Teris.]*
Laisse 78

      Bovo desis de palés eramant;
      Sinibaldo e Teris font lo somiant; (1510)
      En palafro entrent isnelemant,
3260 D'Antone ensirent por la porte davant.
      Bovo, quant vi li rois, tosto a tere desant,
      E Sinibaldo ne le parse mie lant.
      Teris, avec loro, mais Bovo va davant; (1515)
      Bovo si s'ençenoge davant li rois de Frant.
3265 Et Aquilon por me la man li prant,
      E Bovo le salute, da Deo onipotant.
      Dist li rois, "Qe quer e qe demant?"   18vb
      E Bovo li responde, "Pax et acordamant. (1520)

    3241 Reinhold: si-n fu; Rosellini: si'n fu
    3245 Reinhold, Rosellini: River; Reinold, Rosellini: E ave . . .
    3248 Reinhold, Rosellini: Dever (as always); MS.: deveR (or) deveir
    3253 Reinhold, Rosellini: enseamo
    Rubric 77 (originally after 3305) line 1: MS.: Rois . . . por lor . . . boua; Keller: sen uait bouo a . . . por lor; Guessard: à parler (correction of Keller); Reinhold: Bovo . . . parler (emendation for *por lor*); Rois. line 2: Keller: symbalto; Mussafia: symbaldo (correction of Keller); Rosellini: Et

A, çentil rois, qe tant sì mana*n*t,
3270 De una ren molto me vo mervelant,
Quant por co*n*seil de li segnor de Magant,
Con l'oriaflame sì venu tant avant,
E no*n* fais pais se no de niant; (1525)
E non savés come*n*t l'ovra apant,
3275 E qe avenir poit da ste jor en avant.
En Antona ert tel .XX. mil co*n*batant,
Qe no*n* vos renderà la tere si por niant.
Çentil rois, sire, faites·le saçamant; (1530)
Torneç en França co*n* tota vestre jant,
3280 Da mo a Dodo partirò li co*n*vant."
Li rois l'intent, si·l tene por niant.

Rubric 78
[Coment Aquilon parole a le duse Bovo / dapoiske li rois Pepin li avoit parlé.]*
Laisse 79

Aquilon parloe a le dux Bovon:
"Bovo," fait il, "entendé sta rason; (1535)
Fa un convento, e nu li otrion.
3285 A Dodo rendi Blondoja a li çevo blon;
El è ta mere, si la ten en preson;
Por amor li rois, ora si le perdon,
Ten toa tere, cun fi ton per Gujon.* (1540)
Ben doit le filz avoir la reençon,
3290 Burgi e çasté, e çité e dojon;
Tu si fa ço, nu si s'en aliron
Cun nostra jent, se Dodo vol o non."
Dist li rois, "E nu li otrion, (1545)
Tot enseme*n*t cum dist Aquilon."
3295 E dist Bovo, "Vu parleç a perdon;

3269 Reinhold: sì; Rosellini: sì
3270 Reinhold: vò
3272 Reinhold: sì venu (as always); Rosellini: sí
3281 Reinhold: si·l; Rosellini: si'l
Rubric 78 (originally after 3347) MS.: Rois; Keller: ale . . . boua; da pois ke; Reinhold: . . . duse *Bovo [for MS. *boua*], / dapois ke li Rois li avoit parlé; Rosellini: Dapois Ke li rois li avoit parlé [both omit Pepin]
3286 Reinhold: El' è (= "Elle est")
3287 Reinhold: Par

Quant me (reme*n*bra) de la gra*n* traison,*
Qe ma mer fe a mon per Gujon
Por lui trair a li conte Doon, (1550)
Se le tramis fora por venason,
3300 Creeç, rois, qe soja si garçon,
Qe no me reme*n*bri de la mortel preson,
E quando m'e*n*vojè la tosegé paon,
E de quella ovra no*n* porti pasion? (1555)
Qi me donast tot l'or de·l mon,
3305 Un sol çorno no la daria a Duon."

Rubric 79

[Coment Bovo parole a li rois de França / e coment li rois li respundì].
Laisse 80

Quando li rois olde Bovo parler,
El vede ben q'el no li val projer.
El dist a Bovo, "Cu*n* te cri defenser? (1560)
Encontra moi virà tu por çostrer?
3310 De la corona te farò sbanojer,
De tota França e davant e darer."
E dist Bovo, "Deo est mia sper.   19ra
Quant me voleç le droit calonçer, (1565)
Nen vojo plus avec vos tençer.
3315 Quando vos plais, v'en poeç aler,
Daqe me devés de França sbanojer;
Da Clarença ma spea vos co*n*vent guarder,
Qe me çinse Druxiana quant me fe çivaler; (1570)
Jamais nula spea no*n* fu meltre d'açer."
3320 "Bon filz," dist Aquilon, "or no te coruçer.
Molto fu pro li dux Gujon ton per;
Jamais cu*n* li rois el no*n* volse te*n*çer.
Ço qe te di, eo te vojo projer, (1575)

3296 MS.: me reb remēbra; Reinhold: traïson
3300 Reinhold, Rosellini: soia (as always)
3302 Reinhold: m'e*n*voiè; Rosellini: m'envoié; Reinhold, Rosellini: l'atosegé
Rubric 79 (originally after 3377) MS.: Rois . . . Respundi.; Keller: respundi; Reinhold: Rois . . . Rois . . . Respundì.; Rosellini: E . . . respondi.
3308 Reinhold: cri'
3309 Reinhold: vira'
3310 Rosellini: sbanoier (as always; cf. 3316)
3323 Reinhold: di'

          Qe por amor de li rois, tu lasi ta mer,
3325 E cun Dodo te deçi apaser.
          E cest pla è ben droit a demander;
          Ton per Gui oncis de Do son per.
          Se la vença non è (pais) da blasmer;* (1580)
          E de ta mer, oit filo q'è ton frer,
3330 Qe de rason, tu le di ben amer;
          E in ta tera tu le di governer,
          Qe a le besogne te poit avoir mester."
          E dist Bovo, "De tel frer non quer. (1585)
          Or vos alés, et eo vojo retorner;
3335 Prender mes armes, e montar en destrer,
          E defender ma tere, qi la vol calonçer,
          Açoqe nul m'en poust blasmer.
          A vos, bon rois, e vos vojo nonçer, (1590)
          Et avec vos Aquilon de Baiver,
3340 A Bernardo de Clermonte e Morando de River,
          Por cortesia, vos en deça aler,
          E laseç Dodo avec moi tençer,
          Se vos le faites, fareç como ber. (1595)
          E se no le faite, mal (v)os po encontrer;*
3345 E non serò da nul homo da blasmer."
          Adoncha Bovo se pris a li strever;
          Monta en palafroi, si s'en retorna arer.

    3324 Rajna (1888:499): Ke por
    3326 Rosellini: è droit ademander
    3328 MS.: plais da . . . ; Reinhold: p(l)ais; Rosellini: Se l'à vençà . . . pais da
    3330 Reinhold: tu le dì (also in 3331)
    3337 Reinhold, Rosellini: A ço qe
    3341 Reinhold: deçà
    3344 MS.: fait emal nos po; Reinhold: faite[s] . . . vos pò; Rosellini: faite, . . . vos po

Rubric 80
[Coment se partì li parlamento e Bovo / s'en retorna arere in Antone.]
Laisse 81

    Bovo s'en vait, e Teris ensemant, (1600)
    E Synibaldo, li saço e li valent;
3350 E li rois Pepin nen demorò nient.
    Aquilon de Baivere e li altri erament
    A·l pavilon tornent ireement;
    Da Bovo non poit avoir nesun bon convent. (1605)
    Ilec trovent dux Dodo qe li atent,
3355 Si le demande tot primerement
    S'el averà sa muler e li son casament.
    Dist li rois, "El non à quel talent;*
    Nen vol laser sa tere por nient. (1610)
    De soa mere vos dirò brevement: 19rb
3360 No la laseria par tot l'or d'Orient;
    Morir la farà a dol e a torment."
    Dodo, quando l'oldò, li cor toto li soprent;
    Ben aleria l'on li trato d'un arpent* (1615)
    Avantiqe un moto parlese de nient.
3365 Dist Aquilon, "Saçì ad esient:
    Se vo avoir nesun restorement,
    Avoir tel conven a li torniement.
    Saçì por voir Bovo ni soa çent (1620)
    No t'ama ren un diner valisent.
3370 Bovo s'aparecle, alò demantenent
    Por defender sa tere e casament;
    Le porà veoir a li pre verdojent.
    Saçés, serà qi, averà bon guarniment." (1625)
    Çil Aquilon parlò si altament

  Rubric 80 (originally after 3420) Reinhold, Rosellini: s'en retorna . . . ; Rosellini: parti . . avere in Antone
  3353 MS.: bo[n] ⱷ; Reinhold: *bon ɫɫ*; Rosellini: bon ⱷ
  3357 Reinhold: *quel* talent; Rosellini: quil talent
  3358 Reinhold: *tere*
  3362 Reinhold: l'olde (emendation)
  3363 Rosellini: lon li trato
  3368 Rosellini: bovo; Cf. Plouzeau.
  3373 Reinhold: guarnimant
  3374 Rosellini: aquilon; cf. Plouzeau

3375 Q'el mise Doo in si gran spavent;
Par un petit q'elo no l'atent,
En gran paure furent tota la je*n*t.*

Rubric 81
[Coment Bovo retorna in Antone; / Coment Drusiana le mie por rason.]
Laisse 82

Ora fu Bovo in Antona tornée; (1630)
Dama Druxiana li fu encontra alée
3380 E si le oit por rason demandée,
"Qe dist li rois? Qe oit il en pensée?"*
"Dama," fait il, "el oit li sen cançée.
El me demanda Antona, ma çitée, (1635)
E mia mer, qe soja delivrée,
3385 E a·l dux Duo ela soja presentée.
Qe dites vos? Serà·lo otriée?
De questa onte, qe co*n*seil me donée?"
Dist Druxiana, "Se ben vos porpensée (1640)
Zo qe avés soferto et endurée,
3390 Et avant *et* arer por le stran co*n*trée,
Avantqe por lor recreant vos clamée,*
En devés estre pené e travailée.*
E se por arme defendre no la volée, (1645)
Rendés a moi, qe ben serà guardée,
3395 E çorno e noit serò sor le fosée."
Bovo, quant l'olde, oit un riso çitée;
Trois fois basa la dama por amistée.*
"Dama," fait il, "ben serà defensée." (1650)
El non oit mie pais l'ovra obliée;
3400 El oit sa jent e partie e sevrée,
A Teris n'oit doné una mitée.
E li altri se retent cu*n* çivaler me*n*brée;
A Sinibaldo n'oit mile donée, (1655)
Por ben guarder Antona sa çitée.
3405 Bovo s'adobe, oit l'auberg endosée;*

Rubric 81 (originally after 3493) line 2: MS., Rosellini: mie; Reinhold: mis
3382 Reinhold: cançé
3386 Reinhold: sera lo; Rosellini: seralo
3392 Rosellini: MS. deveo estre
3398 Rosellini: «Dama,» fait . . .
3405 Rosellini: aubers

        E Druxiana li oit la ventaja *fermé*e.*   19va
        Alaça l'elmo, si oit la spea cinté;
        Le ganbere calça, e li speron dorée. (1660)
        Rondel li fu davant amenée;
3410   E cil li monta, qe non bailì strevée;
        D'altra parte Teris fu montée.
        "Teris," dist Bovo, "le honor vu averée,
        Porqe vu estes rois, vos soja otriée,* (1665)
        X. mil homes avec vos menée.
3415   Et avec vos eo vegnirò darée."
        Dist Teris, "Mille marçé n'açée."
        A çival monte, est a Deo comandée;
        La porta fu averta, e li pont abasée. (1670)
        Fora ensent, le fren abandonée;
3420   Nen poit remandre ne le sia mes(l)ée.*

Rubric 82
*[Coment Bovo donò a Terise li primer / Colpo de la bataille a .x. mil (cival)er.]**
Laisse 83

        Teris çivalçe li nobel guerer;
        En sa conpagna, .X. mil çivaler.
        L'oste asalta a costé una river;* (1675)
        Tende e pavilon fait a tera verser,
3425   Homes e çivals cair e trabuçer.
        Li rois de Françe, quant oì li noser,
        Demantenant fa sa çent monter.
        Guarner l'infant se pris son corer; (1680)
        Fil estoit de Dodo e de Blondoja a·l vis cler;
3430   En sa conpagna oit .XX. mil çivaler.

    3406 Reinhold, Rosellini: fermée
    3407 Reinhold, Rosellini: çinte
    3409 Reinhold: fa davant
    3420 MS.: messee; Reinhold, Rosellini: meslée (emendation); Reinhold, Rosellini: poit remandre . . . meslée
    Rubric 82 (originally after 3518) Keller: dona a terise; Reinhold: *Teris [emend for MS. *Terise*]; Rosellini: dona à Terise
    3423 Rosellini: a coste
    3425 Reinhold: caïr (as always)
    3426 Reinhold, Rosellini: França; Rosellini: oí
    3428 Reinhold: l'infant (emend for *linfunt*); Rosellini: l'infant (emend for MS. *l'infunt*) . . . sen corer

Grant fu la bataile a celle començer;
Li pro Teris molto se fait apriser;
A·l primeran vait tel colpo doner, (1685)
Ne le valse arme valisant un diner;
3435 Morto l'abate de·l corant destrer.
Atanto ecote vos pungant Guarner,
Frer de Bovo e fio de sa mer.
Mais no l'ama mie la monta d'un diner; (1690)
Vait a ferir Teris sor li scu a quarter.
3440 Li scu li speçe, mais non pote endaner
Li blanc auberg, nian maja falser.
L'asta fu fraita, fa li torson voler;
E Teris trait li brant forbi d'açer* (1695)
Qe li donò Braidamont sa muler.
3445 Guarner ferì desor l'eumo verçer,
E quel fu bon e d'un bon açer;
Trençer nen poit valisant un diner.
La spea torne, sor le scu ad or cler, (1700)
La guinca fait a·l preo voler.*
3450 Trença de l'auberg le guiron tot enter;*
Le çevo trença a·l corant destrer,
E cil caì in l'erba verdojer.
Quant fu a tera, n'ait qe coruçer; (1705)
Tosto se driçe, si trait li brant d'açer;
3455 Se il porà, el se vorà vençer.
La spea trait, c'oit li pomo dorer;
A Teris vait un gran colpo doner
Desor son heume o reluse l'açer. (1710)
De quelo trençe quant ne poit bailer;
3460 Deo le guardi, quant fi li brant torner

19ᵛᵇ

3433 Rosellini: primeram
3435 Rosellini: de corant
3436 Reinhold: pugant
3440 Rosellini: endamer (emend for MS. *endanier*)
3441 Reinhold: ni an (as always)
3445 Rosellini: ferí
3446 Reinhold, Rosellini: e fu d'un bon açer
3447 Reinhold, Rosellini: n'en poit
3448 Reinhold: à d'or
3449 Rosellini: fair al
3451 Rosellini: detrer
3452 Rosellini: caí
3455 Reinhold: pora . . . vora; Rosellini: Se li pora . . . vora

La spea avala sor li col de·l destrer.
Li çevo li trençe, si fait Teris trabuçer;
Avantqe Teris se poust rediçer, (1715)
Çelu se fait avant par lui contrarier.
3465 Ben li aust eu por presoner
Quant li secorse plus de mil çivaler;
Par liura força le font su lever;*
I·le amenent un corant destrer (1720)
E cil le salta, qe non bailì striver.*
3470 Avantiqe Guarner poust reparier,
Teris le fert ancora con li brando d'açer;
Por si gran force li vait un colpo doner
Trença li eume cun tot li çapeler.* (1725)
La blança cofie ne li valt un diner;
3475 Trosqua in le dente fait la spea coler;
Morto li fait a tera trabuçer.
E pois escria, "Monçoja, çivaler!
Fereç ben, qe Deo ne vol aider." (1730)
E cil le font de greç e volunter;
3480 Li .XX. mil qe furent de Guarner
Le virent ancir e mal bailer,
E qui gran colpi doner et enplojer;
Lasent li canpo a li .X. miler. (1735)
Li rois le vi, cuita li sen cançer;
3485 Dist ad Aquilon, "Nostra jent par scanper."
Dist Aquilon, "Ben vos disi l'autrer,
Qe mal fames altru guera pier.*
S'el est morto le filz, or ne demandec li per,* (1740)
Qe a lu perten de son filz vençer,
3490 E par lu vent tot ste guerojer."
"Dodo," dist li rois, "or vos aleç armer;
Qe lo otria Aquilon de Baiver."
E dist Dodo, "De greç e volunter." *(1745)

3462 Reinhold, Rosellini: trençe
3463 Reinhold: Avant que
3467 Reinhold, Rosellini: Par lura [= emend] força . . . sulever
3469 Reinhold: qe non bailì; Rosellini: qe non bailí
3470 Rosellini: post
3477 Reinhold: civaler
3486 Reinhold, Rosellini: autrer
3488 Reinhold: demandeç, with the cedilla in square brackets.
3490 Rosellini: e par lu (no capitals)
3493 Rosellini: freç for "greç" (Cf. Holden, Plouzeau)

Rubric 83
[Coment li rois por li conseli d'Aquilon / Comanda a Dodo de Maga(n)çe qe se deust . . .]
Laisse 84

        Dodo s'adobe a lois de conbatant;
3495   Veste l'aubers a la maje lusant,
        Alaça l'eume e cintò li brant.
        Monta a cival isnelo e corant;*
        A col la tarçe tenis d'un olifant; (1750)
        Fa soner ses grailes e darer e davant,   20ra
3500   XX. mil furent a verdi helmi lusant.
        Lora vont a ferir tot comunelmant;
        De ben çostrer i font le senblant.
        Do de Magançe tent una lança trençant; (1755)
        Vait a ferir un çivaler davant.
3505   Le scu li speçe, e l'auberg ensemant;
        Morto l'abate enverso le canp,
        E pois escrie, "Ferés ben mie çant!"
        Teris l'oldì, molto li vait reguardant; (1760)
        Ben le conoit a li son guarnimant;
3510   Ver lu s'en vait cun sa spea trençant.
        Feri l'averoit, mes altri li sorvant;
        A lui non poit aler ni mostrer son talant,
        Por la gran presie quant vene çele jant. (1765)
        E qui le fer e menu e sovant,
3515   Siqe qui d'Antone nen pote durer a·l canp.
        Ça fusent metue en fue tuti quant,
        Quando Bovo le secore con l'altra soa çant,
        Ça oldirés bataile meravilosa e grant.* (1770)

    Rubric 83 (originally after 3540) Reinhold: Rois . . . co[n]seli . . . deüst [armer]. Rosellini: se deust [armer].
    3496 Reinhold, Rosellini: cinto
    3497 Reinhold: MS. cillal; cival (emendation); Rosellini: *cival, comments on *ll* in the middle
    3504 Rosellini: civaler
    3508 Rosellini: oldí
    3511 Rosellini: Feri l'everoit
    3514 Reinhold, Rosellini: fer e menu . . .
    3515 Reinhold: si que qui (as always; not further commented)

Rubric 84
[Coment fu grant la bataille quando Bovo / entra en l'estor, e da l'autre parte (venin)ete Do.]*
Laisse 85

          La gent d'Antone nen potent plus sofrir;
3520   Veent lor gent detrençer e morir,
          E qui de France in la canpagne courir.
          Teris vide qe no li poit resortir;
          O voja o no, coven li canp gerpir. (1775)
          Ben vos poso dir senca nesun mentir,
3525   Nen fust Bovo qe le fait retenir,
          E dolçement li comença a dir,
          "Segnur," fait il, "no me devés falir;
          Se a Deo plais, vos donarò ben air; (1780)
          Torneç cun moi e non diça foir."
3530   E cil le font; quando le vi venir
          Do de Magançe, le vait a envoir.*
          Qi donc veist tanti colpi ferir,
          L'un morto sor l'autro trabuçer e cair. (1785)
          Tot li plus meltre n'ait talento de joir,
3535   Qi de quel canpo pote li jor ensir;
          En soa vite ben li doit sovenir,
          E Bovo fer un çivaler por grant ir;
          Morto l'abate, si·l fait a·l canpo cair; (1790)
          Donc por cil colpo fait una presia sclarir,*
3540   Do(n)de nen foit sete morir.

    Rubric 84 (originally after 3553) line 2: MS.: viernete do?; Reinhold: *i vene *Dodo (for *l . . . dedò*); Rosellini: porte i veniete Do (for MS. *Dode*)
    3520 Reinhold: Veut lor gent . . .
    3521 Reinhold: covrir
    3523 MS., Reinhold: coven; Rosellini: conven
    3524 Reinhold, Rosellini: sença (emendation)
    3525 Reinhold: rentenir
    3528 Reinhold: aïr
    3529 Reinhold: diça foïr
    3538 Reinhold: si-l . . . caïr; Rosellini: si'l fait
    3539 Reinhold, Rosellini: Dont
    3540 MS.: Dode; Reinhold: Donde; Rosellini: Do[n]de (emendation)

Rubric 85
[Coment Dodo de Magançe conoit Bovo a l'armaire / et a li grant colpi de lançe, e forment se dota.]
Laisse 86

        Quant qui de Françe ont Bovo veuç,
        Li plus ardi est coardo devenuç;
        E li plus sajes est par fol tenuç. (1795)   20[rb]
        Do de Magançe nen fu pais esperduç;
3545 Una (spea) tent dont li fer fu aguç.
        Le destrer ponçe qe ra*n*dona menuç;
        Apreso Bovo oit un d·i so feruç,
        Li qual estoit son amigo e son druç. (1800)
        Ne li valse auberg ni escuç;
3550 En me li ca*n*po li çetò morto e sperduç.
        Bovo le vi, tot en fu irascuç;
        Ben li conoit a l'arme de le scuç;
        Punçe Rondel, sovra li fo coruç. (1805)

Rubric 86
*[Coment Bovo a(v)oit gran dol de son çivale(r)s / Qe Dodo avoit morto e come*nte *le voit ferit.]**
Laisse 87

        A gran mervele fu Bovo orgolos,
3555 Fort et ardi e de mal sofraitos.
        En bataile fu a mervele ençegnos;
        Vide son çivaler morir tot a estors,
        De dol q'el oit, deventa tot ros. (1810)
        Quant vide Dodo, tuto fu doloros.
3560 Quant Teris le dist, "Qe faites vos?
        Secorés nostra jent qe sont en gra*n* pavos,

    Rubric 85 (originally after 3564)
    3541 Rosellini: Quant qi
    3545 Reinhold, Rosellini: Una [spea] tent (emendation)
    3546 Reinhold: ra[n]dona; Rosellini: randona
    3547 Reinhold: un di so'
    3550 Reinhold, Rosellini: esperduç (one word)
    Rubric 86 (originally after 3601) line 1: MS.: anoit; Keller: auoit grando / . . . çivaler qe; Reinhold: avoit . . . çivale[r]s. Line 2: MS.: ferit; Reinhold, Rosellini: ferir (emend for MS. *ferit*)

Ça plus de cento ne sonto de le çevo blos."
E Bovo adoncha punç le milsoldors (1815)
Entro lor fer como fust un dra(g)oç.*

Rubric 87
[Coment fu grande quella bataille; e coment / Teris oncise don Albrigo, qe frer estoit Doon.]*
Laisse 88

3565 A grant mervelle si fu Bovo valant;
      Ni ait nul si argolos ni valant
      Q'elo li fer cun Clarençe li brant,
      Qe en soa vite el vada vantant (1820)
      Q'el no le çeti morto o recreant.
3570 Nean Teris ne fu pais enfant;
      Le rege cercha e darer e davant.
      Grande fu la bataile, mervelosa e pesant;
      Teris reguarde una arçea davant,* (1825)
      E voit don Albrigo venir speronant.
3575 Quando le vi, no l'apella de nojant;
      A ferir le voit con la spea trençant
      Desor li eume, qe tot li p(e)rfant.*
      No li valse la cofie un diner valisant; (1830)
      Morto l'abate in me logo de·l canp,
3580 Q'el non parlò, ni non dise niant.
      Quando Dodo le vi, nen fo mais si dolant;
      El vide ben sa morte li vait aproçant,
      Quant vi son frer cair de l'auferant. (1835)
      Voluntera guinchese, mais li cor no li consant;
3585 E quando el vait Bovo reconoscant,
      E vi Clarençe tuta tinta de sang,
      S'elo se smaie, ne vos çi mervelant.
      Por gran paure, se vait guiscant, (1840)

3564 Reinhold, Rosellini: dragos
3567 Rosellini: Clarançe
3570 Reinhold: Ne an (as always)
3573 Reinhold: reguardò una arçea; Rosellini: reguarde un arçea
3577 Reinhold, Rosellini: perfant
3579 Reinhold: me' logo
3580 Rosellini: Q'el parlò
3583 Reinhold: caïr (as always)
3587 Rosellini: se smanie

	E ven a·l pavilon, vi le rois enseant.*
3590	Elo li parloe, si le dist altemant:
	"Ai, rois de France, el vos va malamant;
	De nostra jent son morti mille sesant,
	E a gran perigolo stoit li remanant. (1845)
	Morto est mon frere, qe je amava tant."
3595	Li rois l'intende, por pois d'ire non fant;
	En pe se drice por ire e maltalant,
	E fa soner ses graile en ojant.
	L'oriaflame fa desplojer a·l vant; (1850)
	Li rois meesme prise son guarnimant,
3600	E Aquilon e li conte Morant,
	A çival montent, li petit e li grant.

Rubric 88

[Coment li rois con tota sa baronie montarent; / e coment fu grande quella bataille in le canp.]

Laisse 89

	Va s'en li rois, non ait qe coruçer;
	Quant en l'estor elo vait a intrer, (1855)
	Ses graile fa soner e davant e darer.
3605	Qi donc veist grant stormen comencer,
	Tant pe, tant pugni, e tant teste couper;
	Grand è el dalmaço, ne se poroit staurer.
	Li rois de France fu orgolos e fer;* (1860)
	Brandist un aste, dove li fer fu d'açer,*
3610	Por maltalent ne vait un a çoster;
	Morto l'abate, q'elo vede un (miler);*
	Bovo le vi, molto li parse nojer.*
	Ben li conoit, e le çerchò d(a)rer.* (1865)

3591 Rosellini: el nos va
3592 Reinhold: mille e
3593 Rosellini: remant
3602 Rosellini: Vasen (as always)
Rubric 88 (originally after 3652)
3602 Rosellini: Vasen (as always)
3609 Reinhold: branndist un'aste
3610 Reinhold: ne vait un à çost[r]er (emendation)
3611 MS.: du (?) ler; Reinhold: *miler (for *du (?) ler*); Rosellini: qe le ve de un miler
3612 Reinhold: *vi*; Rosellini: MS. Bour (for *Bovo*)
3613 MS.: dorer; Reinhold: Ben *li* conoit e . . . *darer (emend for *dorer*); Rosellini: Bon . . . dorer

Encontra lui stratorna son destrer;
3615 En me la voja encontra Morando de River.*
No li conoit, mais gran colpo li fer,*
Qe a la tere li fait trabuçer.
O voja o no, li oit por presoner; (1870)
A soa çent li doit a guarder,
3620 Dedens Antone li fait amener.
Li rois le vi, cuita li seno cançer;
Volunter ferist Bovo, quando se trait arer.

Rubric 89

*[Coment Bovo d'Antone abatì Aquilon de·l çival, / e si l'oit por proesoner, si l'invoja en Antone avec . . .]**
Laisse 90

Por me li canpo si se vait Bovon; (1875)
Ben fu armés desor son aragon.
3625 El prist un aste qe furent d'un peon,
E vait a ferir sor le scu Aquilon.
Le scu li spece mais l'auberg fu bon;
L'asta fu roide ne s'en fi pais tronchon.* (1880)
El çivaler est de gran renon;*
3630 O voja o no, l'abatì a·l sablon;*
O voja o no, si l'oit por preson;   20ᵛᵇ
En Antona l'invoja, o il volist o non.
Quant en Antona fu mena Aquilon, (1885)
Quant Synibaldo le vi, ne le dist se ben non;
3635 El e Bernardo, le segnor de Clermon,
A Druxiana (l)i dà en sa prison.*
E ela fu saça e de bona rason,
Dist a Synibaldo, "Qi son quisti baron?" (1890)
Et elo l(e) dist, "L'uno è·l dux Aquilon,*
3640 E li altro est Bernardo de Clermon.*
En tota Françe et in la legion,*

3616 Reinhold: mais, gran . . .
Rubric 89 (originally after 3663) line 1: Keller: dantone . . . del / çival; Line 2: Keller: esi loit . . . si linuoia . . . auee; Reinhold: *presoner . . . avec . . . , (left incomplete; emended from *proe soner*); Rosellini: proesoner . . . avec . . . (left incomplete).
3625 Reinhold: un' aste (as always)
3627 Reinhold, Rosellini: speçe
3636 MS.: si da; Reinhold, Rosellini: li dà
3639 Rosellini: è 'l dux
3640 Rosellini: MS. lodist (unclear)

Dos major baron atrover no*n* poron;
E de li rois i sont conpagnon.* (1895)
Li rois no*n* prende co*n*seil se çestor no li don."
3645 Dist Druxiana, "E nu li guardaron;
Tel preson li daron cu*n* a lor co*n*veron."
La çentil dame, qe fu de gran renon,*
Por man ela prist anbesdos li baron (1900)
E si le parle si le mis por rason:
3650 "Segnur," fait ella, "e vos do la preson,
Tota sta sala, li palés e·l dojon;
Por amor de Bovo, e vos faço ste don."

Rubric 90
*[Coment li presu*n*és fu doné a Druxiane, / e cella li mis por rason de son afaire.]*
Laisse 91

"Segnur," dist Druxiane, "de la vestra venue (1905)
A gran mervelle me delete *et* a<r>gue.*
3655 De Bovo son sa muler e sa drue,
E son cella dama q'el avoja perdue.
De mala preson vu sì ben asolue,
Quant li traitor seroit co*n*fondue (1910)
E nostra jent seroit revenue,
3660 De vos ert molto bona proveue."
Quant li baron oit la dama ente*n*due,
Nen le fu cil q'en fust irascue;
I la mercia, dolçement la salue. (1915)

3648 Reinhold: anbes dos (as always)
3650 Rosellini: » fait ella, e vos . . .
Rubric 90 (originally after 3684) MS.: presūes; Keller: presunes; Reinhold: presu*n*és; Rosellini: presunés
3654 Reinhold, Rosellini: argue
3657 Reinhold: sì; Rosellini: sí
3660 Reinhold: De vos ert . . . proveüe
3661 Rosellini: ot (for *oit*)

Rubric 91
[Coment Drusiana fait grant / onor a li baron de France.]
Laisse 92

        Quant li baron oit la dama oie,
3665 Q'ela li fa cotanta cortesie,
        Çascun de lor dolçement la mercie
        De le parole l'oit molto agraie.
        "Segnur," fait ela, "tuto ço qe vos delie, (1920)
        Diés·le moi, qe tot serà conplie."
3670 "Dama," dist Aquilon, "ça por nostra stoltie,
        Ne qe por nos fust otrié ni graie.*
        Non venimes ça en cesta oste banie,*
        Ançi fo par nos tota fois contralie. (1925)
        Mais li rois de France, par soa leçerie,*
3675 Consentì a Dodo de venir en sta vie.
        Volunter aumes refusé sa conpagnie,   21ʳᵃ
        E de ço ben soit Deo, le filz sante Marie,
        Qe asa contradise de questa gran folie.* (1930)
        Mais li rois de França, por la gran manentie,
3680 Qe li donò li traito, qe Damenedé maldie,
        Qe li rois n'avoit si le cor enbrasie,
        Qe nul conseil no le valse a una alie
        Qe lu poust retrar de soa vie." (1935)
        Dist Druxiana, "Ço fu gran briconie."*

Rubric 92
[Coment Druxiana faxoit grant honor a qui çivaler / qe Bovo ma(n)doit por pris e si diron de la bataille.]*
Laisse 93

3685 Lasen de Druxiana, e d·i dos çivaler;
        Tel preson oit, cun i demanda e quer,*
        Asa atoit mejo qe eser a·l torner;*

    Rubric 91 (originally after 3711) Keller: grand . . . France.
    3667 Reinhold: agraié
    3671 Rosellini: per nos
    3672 Reinhold, Rosellini: çesta oste
    3679 Rosellini: grn (Cf. Plouzeau, Martin)
    Rubric 92 (originally after 3735) MS., Keller: çivaler . . . madoit
    3685 Reinhold, Rosellini: di dos (as always)
    3687 Reinhold: stoit meio; Reinhold, Rosellini: altonier

>   I no sa ren querir ni demander* (1940)
>   Qe Druxiana ne li faça aporter;
> 3690   Si çoga sego a schachi e a tabler.
>   E Bovo fu en le stormeno plener,
>   E ten Clarençe, qe li dè sa muler.
>   Tanti non fer cun li brant forbi d'açer, (1945)
>   Qe in soa vie jamais non quer mançer.
> 3695   E Teris non fu mie lainer;
>   I cercha Dodo, e davant e darer;
>   Quando no·l trova, cuita li seno cançer.
>   De çella jent de França e de Baiver, (1950)
>   Plus de cento n'oit por personer,*
> 3700   Qe tuti font en Antona mander,
>   A Druxiana toti apresenter.
>   Grande fu la bataila, e li stormeno capler;
>   Tanti pe, tant pugni e teste da coper, (1955)
>   E tant çival, voide sele, scanper.*
> 3705   Li rois le vi, non po star de plurer;*
>   El maldist Dodo e sa muler.*
>   Mais no li valt la monta d'un diner,*
>   Qe Bovo non spar(m)ia ni amigo ni frer.* (1960)
>   Mejo fust a·l rois, an saça primer*
> 3710   Coment l'ovra deust afiner,*
>   Qe metere a mort tant bon çivaler.

3691 Rosellini: le stormeo
3693 Rosellini: tanti (not capitalized); cf. Plouzeau. Rosellini: nen fer
3697 Reinhold: no-l; Rosellini: no'l
3699 Reinhold, Rosellini: presoner (emendation for MS. *personer*)
3704 Reinhold: çival [à] voide . . . (emendation); Rosellini: [à] voide
3708 Reinhold: sparmia; Rosellini: sparmia
3709 Reinhold: à saç . . . primer; Rosellini: ausaçir. Rosellini, note: "per assaçir?"
3710 Reinhold: de*ust af*iner
3711 Reinhold: *à* mort

Rubric 93
[Coment fu grande quella bataille, e coment / Bovo va cerchando Do de Magançe par tot li canp, / Q'el i \<trova\> e si le oncis e fu vençé son per.]*
Laisse 94

	Bovo çivalçe qe oit gran dolor,*
	Quant il no poit atrover li traitor (1965)
	Qe oncis son per vignando da estor.*
3715	El oit guardé a l'onbra d'un arbor;
	El vide Dodo ilec a seçor.
	Quando Bovo oit veçu quel contor,
	S'el oit çoie, ne l'oit unqe gregnor; (1970)
	El ne regracie Jesu le Criator.
3720	E Dodo reguarde, si n'oit gran paor; 21rb
	Qe por paure, nen pote star non plor;
	Voluntera en faist retor.
	Quando Bovo punçe le milsoldor, (1975)
	Si le iscrie, "Non alirés, traitor!
3725	Mal veisés Blondoja, ta usor!"
	El ten Clarençe, li brando de color,
	E si le vait a ferir por tel valor
	Desor li eume qe estoit pinto a flor. (1980)
	Cusi li trençe, cum una ramo d'arbor;
3730	Trosqua in le spale li trença tot a estor.
	Morto l'abate de·l destrer milsoldor;
	"Via," (f)ait il, "malvasio traitor!
	Doné vos ai l'onguento de l'altro jor." (1985)
	Li rois le vi, el n'oit si gran paor,
3735	En soa vite no l'oit unqa major.

    Rubric 93 (originally after 3767) Keller: camp   qe li troua (always uses *u* for *v*; no longer noted); Reinhold: oncls (emend), Rosellini: oncis (for *ocincis*)
    3712 Reinhold: *gran dolor*
    3714 Rosellini: vignado (cf. Plouzeau)
    3715 Rosellini: d'u arbor (noted also by Holden, "lire *un*")
    3716 Rosellini: el vide (Initial minuscule for majuscule)
    3728 Reinhold: eumo
    3729 Reinhold: un (a)ramo
    3732 MS.: vait; Reinhold, Rosellini: fait (emendation)
    3735 Rosellini: en soa vite o l'oit (for *no l'oit* . . . ; Cf. Plouzeau)

Rubric 94

*[Oi avés co*n *Bovo oit morto Dodo de Ma/gançe, e vençé la morte de so*n *per. Or oldirés . . .]**
Laisse 95

        Or oit Bovo son pere ben vençé;
        Damenedé si l'oit molto amé,
        En tote colse servi et honoré. (1990)
        El vi li rois toto quanto spaventé;
3740 Voluntera s'en fust via alé.
        Mais Bovo oit infra de soi rasné,
        "A, rois de Françe, pa(r) toi son travalé;
        Nen vos vantarés a Paris la cité (1995)
        Qe vos m'aça qilois asedié;
3745 Mais no ve ofendì in moja viveté."
        Una aste demande, tosto li fu aporté.
        Non volse ocir li rois, qe li parse peçé,*
        E q'el ne seroit durament blasmé.* (2000)
        Li fer davanti; el se mise daré,*
3750 Com li restojo, tel colpo li oit doné,*
        Qe a la tere li oit trabuçé.
        Avantqe il fust en estant levé,*
        Bovo li fu sovre cun Clarença sa spe; (2005)
        E li rois li quer merçé e piaté:
3755 "No m'oncir, Bovo, qe t'en prego por Dé!"
        E Bovo fu cortois, si li tole la spe;
        En braçe li prent, belament e soé.
        A çival le mis, Teris oit apelé, (2010)
        "Mena li rois in la nostra çité;
3760 A Druxiana el soja apresenté,
        E si le dites qe ben en soja guardé,
        Tantqe eo averai li canpo delivré.
        De mon per ai ben vengança pié; (2015)

    Rubric 94 (originally after 3787) Keller: Ol alies; Guessard: oï avés; Mussafia: Oi aves; Reinhold: Oï avés; Rosellini: Oi avés
    3736 Rosellini: vençe
    3738 Reinhold, Rosellini: servi et
    3742 MS.: pa toi; Reinhold, Rosellini: pa[r] (emendation)
    3744 Reinhold: açà
    3745 Reinhold: ofendì . . . moia; Rosellini: ofendi . . . moia
    3750 Reinhold, Rosellini: restoio
    3753 Rosellini: bovo li fu (cf. Plouzeau.)
    3759 Reinhold: Menà; Reinhold, Rosellini: çité

        Morto ai Dodo a·l trençar de ma spe;
3765 Ormais averon paxe e t<ra*n*q>uilité,*   21va
        Si seçornaron d'inverno e d'esté."
        E cil responde, "Ben serà otrié."

Rubric 95
*[Coment T(e)ris mena li rois Pepin / e(n) Antone e si·lle presenta a Drusiane; e como Aquilon ne menoit gra*n* çoie.]*
Laisse 96

        Via va Teris qe li rois convoja; (2020)
        Cento çivaler avec lui mena.
3770 Ven a 'Ntone, la porta trapasa;
        E Druxiana encontra li ala,
        E si le dist, e si demanda,
        "Qi est de Bovo? Dites, come*n*t il sta?" (2025)
        "Por ma fois, dama, ge*n*tilme*n*t nos va.
3775 Vinto è li canpo, mais ne*n* no serà;*
        Dodo è morto, qe tant pené nos (à);
        L'osto de França jamais no restorerà.*
        Veés li rois, qe ça lì amena?* (2030)
        Bovo vos manda, se de ren vu l'ama,
3780 Qe lo guardés tantq'elo revirà."
        E Druxiana por la man le pia,
        Avec li altri ela si l'amena.
        Aquilon, quant le vi, gra*n* çoja en mena; (2035)
        De lui s'en rise e si se ne gaba.
3785 E Druxiana paxe no l'oblia;
        Grant honor le fi, cu*n* a rois enclina;
        E·l pro Teris a li canpo torna.

    3765 Reinhold, Rosellini: Oimais; MS.: tr . . . uilite; Reinhold: tra[n]quilité; Rosellini: tranquilité (emendation)

    Rubric 95 (originally after 3829) line 1: MS.: Tiris . . . Rois; Keller: tiris . . . en an-/tone; Reinhold: Tiris

    line 2: MS.: e vantone; Keller: sil le; Reinhold: *En (emend) Antone . . . si lle, Rosellini: si lle

    3770 MS.: Ven antone; Reinhold: Ven [à] Antone (emend); Rosellini: Ven Antone
    3772 Rosellini: E si dist e si . . .
    3776 MS.: pene nos.; Reinhold, Rosellini: pené nos [a]
    3777 Reinhold, Rosellini: L'oste
    3778 Reinhold: li a' menà; Rosellini: li a mena
    3780 Reinhold, Rosellini: revira
    3787 Reinhold, Rosellini: E 'l pro . . .

Rubric 96
[Coment fu fenia la bataille dapois/qe Doo fu morto e li rois Pepin pris.]
Laisse 97

	Quant Bovo oit ben aco*n*pli son talant, (2040)
	Et oit morto Dodo de Magan*ç*,
3790	E preso li rois e d·i altri ben tant,
	Com a lui vene en voja e in talant,
	Vinto e sco*n*fito el avoit li canp.
	Recolse la proie e l'ar coit e l'arçant, (2045)
	Tende e pavilon se fait porter avant.*
3795	Vent a Antone gran çoie demenant;
	Ne le f<o> nul ni petito ni grant,*
	N·en menì destrer o palafro anblant,
	Quant in Antone i intra *pr*imemant. (2050)
	Contra li vent Druxiana en riant,*
3800	E Synibaldo avec lei ensemant.
	Druxiana l'apele, dolçeme*n*t en ojant,
	"Bovo," (f)ait elle, "co*n* vos ert co*n*venant?"*
	"Molto ben, madame, mercé Deo e sant. (2055)
	Vençé ai mu*n* pere ver li traiti de Maganc,
3805	Morto e ò Doon a·l trençer de mu*n* brant,
	E Teris son frer, e son filz ensemant.
	A vos envojè un tesor ben si grant,
	Qe plus valt qe l'onor de Brusbant, (2060)
	Qe vos avés Pepin, li rois de Frant, 21vb
3810	E de sa cort li çivaler plus grant."
	Dist la dama, "Mile marcé vos rant."

Rubric 96 (originally after 3852) line 1: Keller: da pois qe; Reinhold: da pois/Q(u)e; Rosellini: do pais/ Que Dodo. Line 2: MS.: Rois.

3788 Rosellini: bovo (cf. Plouzeau)

3790 Reinhold, Rosellini: di altri (as always)

3791 Rosellini: e i talant

3796 Reinhold, Rosellini: Ne le fo

3797 Reinhold, Rosellini: Nen meni . . . o palafro

3798 Reinhold: *pr*imemant

3802 MS.: vait; Reinhold, Rosellini: fait elle (emend); Cf. 3732. Reinhold, Rosellini: cun

3804 MS.: Maganc; Reinhold: traïti de Magan*ç* (emend; cedilla within square brackets); Rosellini: Magan*ç* (emend)

3805 Reinhold: e' ò

3807 Rosellini: envoie

3811 MS.: marce; Reinhold, Rosellini: marcé

| | E Druxiana nen demorò niant;
| | Por la man prist Bovo li conbatant; (2065)
| | Desor la sale le menò en riant.
| 3815 | Ilec trovò li presoner seant —
| | Çogent a schachi et a tables lì alquant.
| | Quant virent Bovo, se levent en estant;
| | E Bovo dolçement li demant: (2070)
| | "Çugés, segnur, fa vos legri e çojant,
| 3820 | Qe en petit d'or(e) vos (mua)rò convant.*
| | Metere vos farò en le perfondamant
| | D'una gran tor o è oscure tant.
| | Mais non verés li sol ni la luna lusant; (2075)
| | Ilec murirés a dol e a tormant."
| 3825 | Li rois quando l'oldì, oit paura si grant,
| | Ne l'oit tel unques a son vivant.
| | E Druxiana s'en rise bellemant;
| | E dist a Bovo, "Vu nen farì niant; (2080)
| | Delivré m·i avés, fa\<rò\> li me talant."*

Rubric 97
[Coment li rois de France avoit gram paure / Quando Bovo li menaçoit de metere i(n) la tor, / e ço qe Drusiane li fist, qe molto fu saçe.]*
Laisse 98

| 3830 | Quant li rois de França oit la parole oie,
| | Saçés por voir, non à talent qe rie;
| | De gran paor elo se omelie.
| | E Druxiana ver de Bovo desie,* (2085)
| | "Le mon segnor, questo non farés mie;
| 3835 | Doné me li avés in la moja bailie,
| | Non averà da nos altro qe cortesie."
| | Dist Aquilon, "Vu farì gran stoltie;
| | Ben devemo morir et en carçer perie. (2090)
| | Avantiqe de França nu fosemo partie,

3816 7 for *et*
3819 Reinhold, Rosellini: fa vos
3820 Reinhold: d'ore (for MS. *doro*), Rosellini: d'or (for MS. *doro*); MS.: uos inuaro; Reinhold, Rosellini: vos invarò
3829 Reinhold, Rosellini: m'i avés
Rubric 97 (after 3883) line 1: MS.: Rois; Rosellini: gran; line 2: Keller: in la tor; Reinhold: metere i*n*
3830 Reinhold: li parole
3835 Rosellini: baille

3840 Ben disi a·l rois qe questo era folie,
De prender guera s'ela no li soplie.
E ben li remenbre tota l'ançesorie,
Qi fo Gujon e sa sclata antie; (2095)
Jamais da li rois non farent partie,
3845 E senpre tenent la soa conpagnie.
Li rois de ço ne me volse croir mie;
Qi de Magançe el volse por amie,*
Qe ont França morta e perie. (2100)
Ça ste dalmaço non serà restaurie;
3850 Se vu n'apendés vu farì cortesie.
De mia vite non darie una alie,
Poisqe li rois avés in la vestra bailie."

Rubric 98
[Comente Aquilon de Bavire parlò a Bovo; / Coment Bovo li respose, e Durisiane.]
Laisse 99

    In estant fu leveç Aquilon; (2105)   22ra
    El dist a Bovo, "Ja ne vos çelaron;
3855 Ne eo ni Morando, ni Bernardo de Clermon,
Non receumes da D(o)o reençon.*
Pepin le fi entro lui e Duon;
Ben le contradise, planament a laron;* (2110)
Mais no me valse valisant un boton.
3860 Li rois ovra, ne no fe cun saç hon,
Quant fi asenbler de França e de Lion
La çivalerie e tot li baron,
Por venir a Antone, a mover tençon; (2115)
Mal voluntera e fo so conpagnon,
3865 Mais de la colse ne disi ne si ne non;
Obeir me convene si cun fare devon."
Li rois l'oì, si fronçì li gregnon;

    3842 Reinhold: remenbrè
    3847 Reinhold: Q(u)i (emend)
    Rubric 98 (originally after 3912) line 2: MS.: Durisiane; Rosellini: Coment Bovo respose à Drusiane
    3854 Reinhold, Rosellini: celaron
    3856 MS.: deo; Reinhold: receümes . . . Doo (emend for *deo*); Rosellini: da Doo (emend)
    3857 Reinhold: lui en Duon
    3866 Reinhold: Obeïr

	De gran paure ven roso cun un carbon; (2[1]20)
	Ne le voria eser par tot l'or de·l mon.
3870	E dist Bovo, "Entendés, Aquilon,
	Ben vos conosco e qi de vos son;
	Dolente sui de vos e de li conpagnon,
	Quant por folie estes en sta preson; (2125)
	E por altru ovre portarés pasion.
3875	Ad apender li rois ben seroit rason;
	Ben me cu(i)toit metere a destruction,*
	Quando cun Doo el se fe conpagnon,
	Por venir a 'Ntone a mover tençon, (2130)
	Zuzé serà si cun li converon."
3880	Li rois si trenble de paura qe il on,
	E Druxiana si s'en rise a foson,
	E dist a li rois, "Laseç dire Bovon;
	Ço q'elo dist no monta un speron." (2135)

Rubric 99

[Coment Bovo fi grant honor a li rois, / e si aparilent li (tables) et alent a mancare,
E poi(s)q'(i) ont mançé tratarent de la pax.]*
Laisse 100

	Druxiana, la dama, nen volse demor(er);*
3885	O vide Synibaldo, si le prist a 'peler,*
	Si fe le tables guarnir e pariler.
	E Druxiana, qe tant fait a loer,
	Li rois Pepin vait por (m)an cobrer: (2140)
	"Venés," fait ela, "aliron a mançer."
3890	E cil le fait, de greç e volunter.
	E Bovo prist Aquilon de Baiver,
	E Teris prist Morando de River,
	E dan Sinibaldo nen fu pais darer; (2145)
	Avec Bernardo se vont aseter.

3868 Reinhold: 2020 (error in line number; should be 2120)
3876 MS.: cutoit; Reinhold, Rosellini: cuitoit
3878 Reinhold: [à] Antone (emend); Rosellini: venir Antone.
3879 Rosellini: Zusé
Rubric 99 (originally after 3950) line 2: MS.: tabloes; Keller: tabloes poit qe; Reinhold: tables mançare (emend); Rosellini: li tables mançare. line 3: MS.: poit qr; Reinhold: pois qe (emend for *poit qr*); Rosellini: pois qe ont
3884 MS.: demor; Reinhold, Rosellini demor[er]
3885 Reinhold, Rosellini: prist apeler
3888 MS.: por nian; Reinhold, Rosellini: por man

3895	E Druxana tant se fe aloer,
	Qe cun li rois ela fu a taler.*
	Mais li rois fu a li çevo primer;
	De gran dolor non pooit mançer. (2150)
	Mais Druxiane le prist a conforter, 22rb
3900	Q'el no se diça de nula ren doter,
	Qe cum Bovo li farà acorder.
	E Aquilon prist Bovo a 'rasner
	De molte colse dir e diviser, (2155)
	E cum quella colse en poroit aler,
3905	Qe cun li rois se poust acorder;
	Qe amisi fosen como erent en primer.
	E dist Bovo qe apreso mançer,
	Con Sinibaldo se vorà conseler. (2160)
	Dist Aquilon, "De ço est agraer."
3910	Quant ont mançé, font le table lever,
	E li baron si se vont a laver;
	Por li palés se vont a deporter.

Rubric 100
[Coment li rois alirent por li palés deportant / E virent in le mur serée dame Blondoie et ella . . .]
Laisse 101

	Si cum li baron furent por li palais alé, (2165)
	En un canton de la sala pa(vé),
3915	Vide Blondoja en le mur aseré.
	Quant la virent son a le aprosmé,
	E si la conoit si l'oit aderasné:*
	"Dama," font il, "coment vos esté?" (2170)
	"Pur mal, segnur, si con vos veé;
3920	Qui fo pene(te)ncie de tot li me peçé.*

3895 Reinhold: Druxiana
3902 Reinhold, Rosellini: à rasner
3903 Reinhold, Rosellini: dire e diviser
3905 Reinhold: peüst
3907 Reinhold: apreso [li] mançer (emend)
Rubric 100 (orginally after 3986) line 1: MS., Reinhold: Rois; MS., Guessard: E uirent; Keller: de/portant fuirent in lermur. line 2: MS., Guessard: in le; Mussafia, MS. = in lo; Rosellini: lo mur . . . Blandoie
3914 MS.: paire; Reinhold, Rosellini: pavé (emend for *paire*)
3920 Reinhold: pene[te]ncie; Rosellini: pene [te]ncie [sic] (emend)

| | Mon fio Bovo m'oit qilo seré.
| | Qi estes vos, segnor? No me·l çelé."
| | "Dame, de França, de·l major parenté;* (2175)
| | E cestu ert li nostro rois clamé.
| 3925 | Bovo n'avoit qi por presener mené."
| | Dist la dama, "Dites moi verité;
| | Qe est de Doo? Est il arer torné?"
| | "Nenil, madame, el oit malovré; (2180)
| | Bovo s'est ben de lui delivré.
| 3930 | Dodo est morto cun una sa rité."
| | La dama l'olde, par poi n'oit li seno cançé;
| | De gran dolor la dama fu pasmé.
| | Or ve·la ben, qe est abandoné; (2185)
| | Ela li quer merçé e piaté:
| 3935 | "Segnur," fait ela, "e vos prego por Dé,
| | Qe a mon fio vu si me recordé,
| | Dapoisqe il oit li son per vençé,
| | De moi el faça la soa volunté. (2190)
| | Mejo me seroit eser en un fois brusé,*
| 3940 | Qe en ceste mur stare quilo seré."
| | "Dama," dist li rois, "vu aveç ben parlé.
| | Vu non savés mie como nu avon ovré;*
| | Si durament Bovo n'à menaçé, (2195)
| | De nu apendre por la vestre bonté.
| 3945 | Se avec lui nu seren acordé,   22ᵛᵃ
| | De vu, madame, li serà ben rasné."
| | Dist la dama, "Mile ma(r)çé n'açé."
| | E Bovo n'oit mie la ovra oblié, (2200)
| | Qe Aquilon li oit dito e conté;
| 3950 | A Sinibaldo el s'est aconselé.

3922 Reinhold: me-l; Rosellini: me'l
3923 Reinhold, Rosellini Dame[l]; Morini: Dame
3924 Reinhold, Rosellini: nosto rois
3925 Reinhold: q[u]i (emend); MS.: mene; Reinhold: mener; Rosellini: . . . mené (emend)
3928 Reinhold, Rosellini: mal ovré
3933 Reinhold: vè 'la; Rosellini: ve 'la
3940 Reinhold: quilo'
3947 MS.: maçe; Reinhold, Rosellini: ma[r]çé (emend)
3950 Rosellini: il s'est aconselè

Rubric 101

[Coment Bovo se consela a Synibaldo e a Teris, / e a dama (D)rusiane de ço que Aquilon li avoit / a la tabra deras(n)é, e prist son conseil.]*

Laisse 102

        Bovo se parte de la sala pavée;*
        Por me la man oit Sinibaldo piée.
        Rois, Teris, Druxiana la ensenée (2205)
        En una çanbra entrent a la celée;
3955   Desor un banc furent asetée.
        "Segnur," dist Bovo, "ben est nos encontrée,
        Quant en ma vie e sui tanto penée.
        Ora m'à Deo quel dono donée,* (2210)
        Qe senpre li ò queri e demandée,
3960   Qe tanto poust viver in atée,
        Qe eo aust li mon pere vençée;*
        Et eo de ço en sui ben delivrée:
        Vençé li ò a·l trençar de mia spee. (2215)
        Preso nu avon de França li regnée,
3965   Tota flor qe po eser trovée,
        Si avon li rois e(n) nostra poestée.
        Car or me soja li mon consejo donée,
        De lor tenir o eser delivrée." (2220)
        Quant qui l'intent, çascun fu porpensée,
3970   Mais Druxiana oit primeram parlée,*
        Si como dama saça e ben dotée.
        "Bovo," fait ela, "se ben vos remenbrée,
        Ço qe vos est venu e incontrée, (2225)
        De tante pene cun aveç endurée
3975   Par tot li mondo e davant e darée,

    Rubric 101 (orginally after 4025) line 2: MS.: brusiane; Keller: brusiane; Reinhold, Rosellini: Drusiane (emend). line 3: Keller: derasue . . . prise; Guessard: cabra . . . prist; Reinhold: derasne (emend for MS.: *derasue*); Rosellini: canbra (emend) . . . derasné
    3953 Reinhold, Rosellini: Rois Teris . . .
    3954 Reinhold, Rosellini: celée
    3956 Rosellini: 'Segnur>>, dist Bovo (cf. Plouzeau)
    3959 Reinhold: demandé
    3963 Reinhold: el trençar
    3966 MS.: e; Reinhold, Rosellini: e[n] (emend)
    3967 Reinhold: (mon)
    3969 Rosellini: Quat (noted also by Holden: "lire *Quant*")
    3970 MS., Reinhold: primeram; Rosellini: primeran

         E in preson è a morte çuçée,
         Or vos oit Deo a tal porto menée
         Qe retorné estes in la vestra citée,* (2230)
         E da vestri enemisi vos estes delivrée;*
3980   E vestre per vu avés ben vençée.*
         Or non avés plu de querir meslée*
         Vu avés qui de França li bernée;*
         Li rois meesmo aveç qui amenée.* (2235)
         Çascun en soja tant honorée,
3985   Como çascun v'avese ençendrée.
         Se i vol pax, par Deo, no la vée."

Rubric 102
[Coment a Drusiane parle Synibaldo / e si·lli dona li lojal conseil e li bon.]
Laisse 103

         Sinibaldo parloe, qe oit li cor çojant,
         "Bovo," fait (il), "tu consejo demant.* (2240)
         Druxiane vos dona si bono e saçant,   22vb
3990   Ne son celu qe die plu avant,
         Mais una colsa faroie por eser plus manant:*
         A cil baron de·l reame de Franc,
         Si vol avec vos pax e acordamant, (2245)
         Ne li laseç aler si por niant,
3995   Se da lor non avés ostajes de ses enfant,
         De non far·ve guere ni bubant,*
         En soa vie da ste jor en avant."
         Dist Bovo, "Ces consei est avinant; (2250)
         Non est sajes qe questo ne contant."
4000   De la çanbra ensirent, Bovo vene avant;
         O vi li rois, por me la man li prant,
         Et Aquilon el prist ensemant;

  3981 Reinhold: meslée
  3982 MS.: Vu aves; Rosellini: MS. reads vu aveo; Plouzeau: Rosellini has no accent on *aves* (not his usual policy)
  3988 MS.: fait tu; Reinhold, Rosellini: fait [il], "tu
  3992 Rosellini: riame
  3995 Rosellini: Ne da lor
  3996 Reinhold: far-ve; Rosellini: farve
  3997 Rosellini: hor
  3998 Reinhold: consei[l]

E Sinibaldo si oit pris Morant. (2255)
A un canton se trait a parlamant;
4005 "Bon rois de France," dist Bovo en ojant,
"E vojo ben qe saçés a siant,
Quant nos fuimes a li torniemant,
Ben vos poeria oncire a·l trençer de mon brant,* (2260)
Da la lança da li fer trençant,
4010 Quando cun le restojo vos abatì a·l canp.*
E vojo avec vos pax e acordamant;
Ma vojo aver da vos ostajes bon e çant.*
Çascun de vos me donì ses enfant; (2265)
Avec moi le tirò a mon talant.
4015 Et ensi vos alirés baldi, legri e çojant."
Dist Aquilon, "Et altro non demant;
Lì me farò venir tot primeremant."
E dist li rois, "Et eo ensemant. (2270)
Lì farò venir Karleto, mon enfant."
4020 E dist Bovo, "Milor non demant."
"Qi lì alirà?" dist Bovo en ojant;
"Morando de Rivere, se vos li consant."
E dist Bovo, "Va aseguremant. (2275)
Meni li enfant avec lui ensemant."
4025 E cil responde, "Ben farò li convant."

Rubric 103
[*Coment li rois parole a Morando de Rivere / Q'elo die a la raine Berte q'ele envoi son fil.*]*
Laisse 104

"Morando," dist li rois, "e vos vojo projer,
Se unchamés vu me deveç amer,
Qe vos diça a nos tosto reparier. (2280)
Direç a Berte, moja çentil muler,
4030 Q'ela me diça ses filo envojer,
Qe se eo vojo en França reparier,
El me lo conven por ostajes laser

4008 Reinhold, Rosellini: poeva
4022 Reinhold: Morande
4023 Reinhold: Vaa seguremant
4025 Rosellini: »Ben farò (cf. Plouzeau)
Rubric 103 (originally after 4062) line 1: MS., Reinhold: Rois; Reinhold, Rosellini: Morande. line 2: Keller: de lo die ... qe le en/uoi; Mussafia: q'elo (emend); Guessard: "lisez *qe lo die*"

	A Bovo d'Antone, li cortos e li ber; (2285)
	E de nula ren no se diça doter,
4035	El non averà onta ni engonbrer; 23^(ra)
	Tosto averà a (n)os reparier."*
	E dist Morando, "Alirò sens tarder."
	Bovo li fait son çival delivrer, (2290)
	E in apreso li arme e li corer.
4040	Un altra colsa fi Bovo da loer:*
	Qe tot les autres qe erent presoner,
	Toti li fait de preson delivrer,
	Si le fa donar le arme e li destrer, (2295)
	Q'i aportent quando vene a çostrer,
4045	Purq'i le posa conoser ni trover.

Rubric 104
[Coment s'en vait Morando de Rivere e li altri / Qe a l'istor furent pris si arent gran çoie.]*
Laisse 105

	Via çivalçe Morando sença dotançe,
	Avec lui avoit li presoner de France.
	Par tota France aloit la nomenançe, (2300)
	Qe preso estoit li rois, qe tot li autri avançe.
4050	Por Doo fu gran dol en Magançe;
	Va s'en lo meso, qe non fe demorançe;
	A l'intrer de Paris fu gran piatançe;
	Le bele dame avoit gran pesançe, (2305)
	Por ses mari sont en gran dotançe.
4055	Avantqe Morando alase a sa abitançe,
	Ne qe il veist sa feme ne ses enfançe,
	El misi çoso el scu e la lançe,
	E si desis de li palafroi blançe. (2310)
	Monta a·l palés sença nulla tardançe;
4060	Ilec trovò la raina de France.
	Quando ela·l vi, si ne fu en gran balançe,
	Por oldir novelle tot les autri avançe.

4036: MS.: uos; Reinhold, Rosellini: nos reparier (emend)

4040 Reinhold, Rosellini: Un'altra (as always)

Rubric 104 (originally after 4088) line 2: Keller: qe a l'istor ... pois; Reinhold, Rosellini: li stor

4052 MS.: Piantançe (the first *n* is expunctuated)

4056 Reinhold: veïst (as always)

4061 Reinhold: ela-l; Rosellini: ela 'l

Rubric 105
[Coment Morand(o) entrò en Paris, e desis / a·l palés et aloit parler a la raine.]
Laisse 106

          Davant la raine fu Morando en estant, (2315)
          O il parole altament en ojant:
4065   "Çentil raine, entendés mun talant;
          Li rois Pepin a chi França apant
          Par moi vos mande, qe le sieç guarant.
          En preson l'oit Bovo li conbatant, (2325)
          E Aquilon e Bernardo ensemant.
4070   Par moi vos mande, se l'amés de nojant,
          Qe l'invojés Karleto vos enfant.
          Por ostajes serà en Antona là dant;
          Tant cun a Bovo vegnirà por talant. (2325)
          Ne vos dotés q'el aça enojamant,
4075   Qe Druxiane si est tant avenant,
          Ela·l tirà avec ses enfant."
          Dist la raine, "Vu parlé de nojant;
          E li envojaria s'en aust ben çant. (2330)
          Or li prendés, faites li ves talant."
4080   E cil le fait, alo demantenant;   23rb
          Nen demorò e·l palés longemant,
          Si cun da li rois avoit li comant.
          El prise Karleto et un altro enfant, (2335)
          Filz Aquilon, ben fu reconosant:
4085   Naimes avoit nome, si l'apela la jant;
          Cosi petit avoit seno tant,
          No le savoit conter nul hon qe soja vivant. *
          Via le mene cun gra(n)z çoie façant. (2340) *

    Rubric 105 (originally after 4108) MS.: moriande; Keller: moriando ... al ... ; Reinhold: Mor(i)ando; Rosellini: Morando; line 2: Reinhold: Raine
    4072 Reinhold, Rosellini: là dant
    4076 Reinhold: Ela-l; Rosellini: Ela 'l
    4078 Reinhold: se-n aüst; Rosellini: se'n aust
    4081 Reinhold, Rosellini: el pales
    4086 MS.: avoit; Rosellini: MS. avaoit
    4088 MS.: graz; Reinhold, Rosellini: gra[n]z (emend)

Rubric 106
[*Coment Mora*n*do de Rivere enmena li / (e)n/fant Ka(r)leto e Naimon e retorna a 'Ntone.*]*
Laisse 107

         Via s'en vait Morando de River,
4090   Avec lui anbes li baçaler.
         El non finò de broçer e d'aler,
         Tantqe Antone se prist a 'prosmer.
         Contra li vait peon e çivaler; (2345)
         Karleto vi son pere, si le corse a 'braçer;
4095   E Naimes, Aquilon son per.
         Gran fu la çoie de qui du baçaler;
         Dos plu be enfanti ne se poroit trover.
         Gujon e Synibaldo le corse a'mbraçer, (2350)
         E qi son filz de Bovo e de sa muler.
4100   Druxiana le vi, si·n prist a larmojer;
         Ela se pense de li te*n*po primer,
         Quant li co*n*vene por li bosco porter.
         Lor dist a li rois, "Non aça re penser; (2355) *
         Avec moi averà demorer,
4105   E si cu*n* filz e tenir e guarder."
         Li rois l'oldì, pris la mercier;
         "Segnur," dist Bovo, "or no vos dè nojer;
         A vos plasir soja li star e de aler." (2360)

   Rubric 106 (originally atter 4143) line 1: Reinhold, Rosellini: enmena li en (Reinhold: for *eu*)
     line 2: MS.: Fant, Keller: lien-/lant kaleto . . . antone; Reinhold: *fant (emend); Reinhold, Rosellini: [à] Antone. Reinhold: Naimon (emend for MS. *uaimon*)
   4092 Reinhold: [à] Antone, aprosmer; Rosellini: aprosmer (as always)
   4094 Reinhold, Rosellini: corse abraçer
   4097 Reinhold: be'
   4098 Reinhold, Rosellini: corse ambraçer
   4100 Reinhold: si-n; Rosellini: si'n
   4103 Reinhold: açà (cf. 4138, "açà") re penser
   4107 Reinhold: dè; Rosellini: de'

Rubric 107
[Coment Drusiane parole a li rois et a li atris* / Baron e coment li on\<o\>ra e si le fi vestir e li rois . . .]
Laisse 108

	Druxiana fu saça e de grande renon;
4110	Meltre dama trover no*n* poroit hon:
	Molto fu saça, e de bona rason
	Avantqe se partise de ilec i baron,
	Vestir le fait d'un vermi siglaton. (2365)
	Dist a li rois, "No*n* ajés dotason,
4115	De ves enfanti ne de vestri garçon;
	En breve te*n*po nu vos envojaron.
	E die e noit avec moi seron;
	Cosi li tirò cu*n* Sinibaldo e Gujon; (2370)
	Jamais da Bovo ne*n* averà si ben non."
4120	Dist li rois, "A Deo benecion;
	E li coma*n*do en vest(r)a sobecion."
	Dist Druxiana, "E cosi li tolon;
	A Deo, e a vos, nu si li comandon." (2375)
	Li rois de França non fi demorason;
4125	O el vi Bovo, si le dist son sermon: 23va
	"Bovo," fait il, "si cu*n* vestre preson,
	Me delivrés, moe *et* Aquilon, *
	Morando de River, e Bernardo de Clermon, (2380)
	Delivrés nos, qe aler s'en poson."
4130	E Bovo dist, "A Deo benecion."
	Bo\<v\>o li done palafroi e re*n*çon,*
	E por çascun bon destrer aragon.
	Quant li rois e le dux Aquilon (2385)
	S'en volent aler, veent ses garçon;
4135	I le segne*n*t de le benecion:
	A Deo li comanden, e a son santo non.
	Bovo s'en rise, cojame*n*t a laron; *

Rubric 107 (originally after 4188) line 1: MS., Reinhold: Rois; Mussafia, Reinhold: atri(s); Rosellini: altris. line 2: MS., Reinhold: Rois; Keller: onora e sil e fi/u estu; Mussafia: e si le fi uestir; Guessard: . . . vestir; Reinhold, Rosellini: onora e si . . .

4121 MS.: vesta; Reinhold, Rosellini: vestra
4131 Reinhold, Rosellini: Bovo
4132 Reinhold: ben destrer
4136 Reinhold, Rosellini: e à son santo non.
4137 Reinhold, Rosellini: à laron

             E dist a li rois, "No*n* aça dotason, (2390)
             Q*e* vestre filz no*n* reman en prison.
4140   En breve te*n*po nu vos l'invojaron;
             (V)e filz serà cu*n* Sinibaldo e Gujon."
             Li rois e le dux Aquilon
             Si le mercie quant il poit e·l mon. (2395)

Rubric 108
[Coment (Pepin) avantqe s'en volust aler / Recomanda Karleto, son fiu, a Drusiana.]
Laisse 109

             Li rois Pepin ne*n* volse demorer;
4145   El dist a Bovo, "Ne vos (vojo) nojer; *
             Senpre vos do servir *et* honorer.
             De una ren vos voria projer,
             Se ma pregere en poust çoer; (2400)
             Q*e* vos reme*n*bré de cele vestre mer,
4150   Q*e* tanta pena li faites endurer.
             No la lasés en cele mur ester!
             Dach'è morto Dodo, vestre guerer,
             En cui la dama avea soa sper, (2405)
             Or la farés guarder un monester,
4155   O ela posa Damenedé projer,
             De ses peçé se posa ame*n*der;
             Ancor se poit la soa arma saluer.
             Vestra mer est, ces no*n* poés çeler." (2410)
             E dist Bovo, "Tuto ço laseç ester,
4160   Qe por so ovra fo morto mu*n* per.
             Quant me porpe*n*so q'ela, me fasoit raçer.
             E de mançer no me volea doner;
             Plus de tros çorni me fasea ester. (2415)

4141 MS.: Me filz; Reinhold, Rosellini: Ve filz (emend)

Rubric 108 (originally 110 after 1213) line 1; MS.: Bovo; Keller: avant qe sen; Reinhold, Rosellini: Pepin (emend for Bovo); line 2: Keller: soa sur a; Mussafia: son fiu; Reinhold: fiu (emend for "fun"); Rosellini: fiu

4145 Reinhold, Rosellini: vos [voio] noier (emend)

4146 Reinhold: dò

4149 Reinhold, Rosellini: reme*n*bre; Rosellini: . . . cele cestre mer (cf. Holden, Martin, Plouzeau)

4155 Rosellini: Demenedé

4157 Reinhold, Rosellini: salver

E quant por pietà eo le querì da mançer,
4165 Cun un paon me volse envenener;
Dont me convene ad inçegne sçanper,
E çorno e noit me fa star en penser.
E de le me prega Druxiana ma muler. (2420)
De le farò ço q'e ò in penser;*
4170 Mais qe a le deust ben guarder—*
Ad albespine la deveroit far bruser."
E Druxiana prist li rois a guarder;   23vb
Segno le fait, nen diça plu parler. (2425)
Le rois de France nen se volse entarder;
4175 Por man el prist Aquilon de Baiver;
Desis de le palés, ven a çival monter.
A Druxiane pris conçé demander,
Li dos enfanti li lasò a bailer, (2430)
Et ella le prist de greç e volunter.
4180 Li rois se monte por volor soi aler,*
Et avec lui Aquilon de Baiver,
E Bernardo, e Morando de River;
Mais Bovo ne volse l'ovra oblier; (2435)
A çival monte, cun Teris e Rainer,
4185 Et avec lui plus de mil çivaler.
Li rois convoja plus de dos leges enter;
Quant à ço fato, q'i volent retorner,
A Deo li comande, si le lasa aler. (2440)

Rubric 109

[Comente li rois de Françe s'en tornarent / E(n) Françe, et avec lui Aquilon de Baviere.]
Laisse 110

Va s'en li rois, qe conçé oit pié;
4190 S'el oit çoja, or non demandé,
Qe de la morte molto fu spaventé.
Sor tote ren oit Bovo laudé,

4169 Reinhold, Rosellini: ço qe ò
4171 Reinhold: albe spine
4181 Rosellini: et avec lui (minuscule initial)
4182 Rosellini: Morado
Rubric 109 (orig. 111, after 4242) line 1: Keller: Coment... sen tornarent; Reinhold: Coment(e); Rosellini: Coment. line 2: Keller: e françe; Reinhold, Rosellini, Cremonesi: E[n] (emend)
4189 Rosellini: Vasen.. coçé

	E Druxiane, la saça e l'ensené. (2445)
	Tant est a(l)é por vie e por stre,*
4195	Ven a Paris, soa nobel çité.
	Quando la vi, n'oit Deo aoré;
	Ven a·l palés, monta sor li degré,
	E la raine li est encontra alé. (2450)
	La prime colse donde l'oit demandé
4200	Fu de Karleto, soa nobel rité.
	"Dama," fait il, "de lu ne vos doté;
	A bon hoster nu l'avemo ostalé,
	E per e mer el oit trové. (2455)
	Dama Druxiana li ten por soa rité;
4205	Davanti le senpre i stont en pe,
	Cum du ses filz li oit aconpagné."
	Dist la raine, "Ela fa gran bonté;
	Ela ne sia da Deo merité." (2460)
	"Çentil raine, ora ne vos doté;
4210	Quando d'Antona eo me fu sevré,
	I m'en promise por la soa lialté
	Qe in breve termen, ne seroit envojé."
	La dama l'olde, si n'oit larmojé. (2465)

Rubric 110
[Coment ancor parloit li rois a la raine, / Si li conta tuto l'afar de Bovo.]*
Laisse 111

	"Çentil raine," dist li rois en ojant,	
4215	"De cele Bovo e vos dirò alquant;	
	Qi cerchase li mondo, tuto d'in cant en cant,	
	Non trovaria un milor conbatant.	24ra
	A li ses colpi non dura hon vivant. (2470)	
	Veor·le çostrer est un ençantamant,	
4220	Q'el i atent un colpo de li brant,*	
	Mais en sa vie el non serà çojant.	
	De soa mei vos dirò li senblant;	

4194 MS.: Tant est are; Reinhold, Rosellini: Tant est aré
4197 Rosellini: morta sor (cf. Holden, Martin, Plouzeau)
4200 Rosellini: fu (minuscule initial)
4207 Rosellini: gra bonté
4210 Reinhold: fu'
Rubric 110 (originally 112, after 4272) line 1: MS., Reinhold: Rois; line 2: Keller: si le . . . la fin de; Guessard, Mussafia: l'afar
4219 Reinhold, Rosellini: Veor le çostrer

Sor li palés en la sala plus grant, (2475)
L'oit serea en un muro davant,
4225 Porçoqe de son pere ela fi tradimant.
Una dama oit, qe est si saçant,
Qe çerchese ben li mondo tot quant,
Non trovaroit una soa parisant. (2480)
Tanto n'oit fato e darer e davant,
4230 Qe senpre serò ses benvojant.
Davanti nos el lasò nostra çant;
A tuti donò arme e guarnimant,
E nu si fe vestir cun est aparisant, (2485)
Si ne donò destrer e palafroi anblant;
4235 Pois si ne convojò dos legues en avant."
Dist la dama, "Laudés Deo e sant,
Qe sì scanpé da morte e da tormant.
Ma noportant conseil avisi d'infant, (2490)
Quant por le dito de Dodo de Maganç,
4240 Volivi prendre li altru casamant.
Se ben vos è venu, e si vos faites çojant,
De tel folie ma non ajeç talant."

Rubric 111
[Coment Terise se departe da Bovo / e prist conçé e aloit en son r(iam)e.]
Laisse 112

Quant li rois fu sor la sala pavé, (2495)
S'el oit çoja or ne m'en demandé.
4245 Or lasen de li rois, qe est çojant e lé;
Quant i se partì d'Antone, avoit ben ovré.
Conter vos vojo de Bovo l'aduré,
E de Druxiana, la saça e l'insené, (2500)
E de Teris, li bon rois coroné,
4250 Qe de Baldras el fo signor clamé;
E de Sindonie, e de longo e de lé.
Tant estoit en Antone como li vene a gre,

4224 Rosellini: sera
4225 Reinhold, Rosellini: Por ço qe (as always)
4241 Reinhold: venu, si
Rubric 111 (originally 113, after 4322) line 1: Reinhold: Teris(e). line 2: MS.: raine; Reinhold: R[i]ame (emend); Rosellini: riame (emend)
4246 Reinhold: Quant(i); Rosellini: Quant se (emend)
4251 Rosellini: Sidonie

	E quando a lu plait, el domandò conçé; (2505)
	E Bovo si le done, qe molto l'oit agreé.
4255	Adoncha entrent e(n) nef et en galée,*
	E si s'en voit por me la mer salé,
	Tantqe il fu a Baldras arivé.
	E Braidamont li fu encontra alé; (2510)
	De sa venue i se font molt lé.
4260	E Braidamont si le oit demandé,
	De Bovo e de Druxiana, coment sont esté.
	"Dama," dist il, "nu avon ben ovré.
	Morto avon li traitor renojé, (2515)
	Qe tanto n'oit pené e travalé.
4265	E Bovo e Druxiana si son cojant e lé;
	Nen furent si en soa viveté.
	Li rois prendimes, e d·i altri asé;
	Donde Bovo è si aseguré, (2520)
	Nen averà plu guera in son aé."
4270	Dist Braidamont, "Deo ne soit aoré."
	E Teris, poisq'el fu retorné,
	Se seçornent en soa viveté.

24rb

Rubric 112
*[Coment Bovo por li conseil de Druxane e de Synibaldo / envoja a li rois Pepin et a Aquilon de Baviere ses / enfant; e pois (co*ntaron*) de Bovo ço qe li avenì in / Engeltere, o il aloit por veor ses oncle li rois Gui.]**
Laisse 113

	Segnor baron, plaça vos d'ascolter, (2525)
	Questo roman non est da oblier;
4275	Oir porés colse molto strainer,
	Dont v'en porés de l'oir merveler.
	Ancor non est li plais adefiner,
	Nian de Bovo fenio li çanter; (2530)

4256 Reinhold: me'
4265 Reinhold, Rosellini: çoiant (emend)
Rubric 112 (originally 114, after 4369) line 1: Keller: Symbaldo; Rosellini: Druxiane. line 2: MS.: a Quilon. Reinhold, Rosellini: Baivere. line 3: MS.: cōtraron; Keller: con-/traron; Reinhold: cont(r)aron; Rosellini: contaron . . . averi. line 4: MS.: en Geltere; Reinhold, Rosellini: Engeltere; Reinhold, Rosellini: po veor. MS.: Gui; Keller: grael; Reinhold: Grae[l]? Rosellini: Gui (?)
4275 Reinhold: Oïr, also 4276
4278 Reinhold: Ni an de Bovo feniò; Rosellini: Nian de Bovo feni ò

　　　　　Mais tot por ordene vos li averò conter.
4280　Dapoisqe li rois Pepin s'en retornò arer,
　　　　　E Aquilon son mastro conseler,
　　　　　Avantqe da Bovo se poust sevrer,
　　　　　Elo le fe e ple(v)ir e çurer (2535)
　　　　　Qe en soa vie ne le faria engonbrer,
4285　Si le lasent ses filz por mejo asegurer.
　　　　　Ma Druxiane tant li pote projer,
　　　　　Pasa li mois, elo li mandò arer.
　　　　　Ne l'invojò mie a mo de paltroner; (2540)
　　　　　Molto ben le fi vestir e adorner.
4290　E Sinibaldo fi a çival monter,
　　　　　Avec lui ben cento çivaler;
　　　　　Trosqua a Paris nen vorent seçorner.
　　　　　Quando li rois vide li baçaler, (2545)
　　　　　De quella colse molto le pris merveler,
4295　E Bovo desor tuti lolder,
　　　　　E Sinibaldo altament gracier.
　　　　　Grant fu la çoie qe font li civaler,
　　　　　Mais desor tot Aquilon de Bavier. (2550)
　　　　　El dist a·l rois, "Entendés moi, meser,
4300　Çamais cil Bovo no devon oblier.
　　　　　Se par nul tenpo li aust mester,
　　　　　Nu le devon secorer et aider,
　　　　　E l'oriaflame en li canpo porter." (2555)
　　　　　Dist li rois, "E l'ò ben en penser."
4305　A Sinibaldo, qe fu li mesaçer,
　　　　　Elo le dist, "Entendés, amigo çer,
　　　　　A Bovo d'Antone vu me deverés conter,
　　　　　Qe li rois de Françe est ses presoner. (2560)
　　　　　En soa vite no li stoit doter;　　　　　　　　　　　　　24va
4310　Se par nul ren li aust mester,
　　　　　Eo le secoreria a cento mil çivaler.*
　　　　　Et eo meesmo, sor mon corant destrer."
　　　　　E Sinibaldo, quant l'oldì si parler, (2565)
　　　　　Altament le pris a gracier.
4315　Sinibaldo nen vos plu lì ester;

4283 MS.: plenir; Reinhold, Rosellini: plevir
4288 Reinhold: a mo'
4292 Rosellini: seçoner (cf. Martin, Plouzeau)
4294 Reinhold: se (emend for le)
4304 Reinhold: E' l'ò ben

Conçé demanda, q'el s'en volea aler;
E li rois li dona palafroi e destrer,
Et a Bovo mandò doni molto strainer, (2570)
Por l'amistà tenir e conserver;
4320 E fi far letre, e brevi sajeler,*
Q'el l'invojò por celle mesaçer
A mostrar ben q'el no·l vol oblier.

Rubric 113
[Coment Sinibaldo s'en torne a 'Ntone et aporte / a Bovo l'a(n)basée, e li don qe li rois l'i(n)vo(j)a.]
Laisse 114

Sinibaldo s'en torne por le çamin feré; (2575)
A Bovo oit retorné soa anbasé,
4325 Ço qe li rois li avoit envojé,
E como fu servi et honoré.
Da tota jent molto fu agraé,
E queli brevi (qe) li ont bailé;* (2580)
Cil françe la çira, si oit dentro guardé.*
4330 Savés, qe li rois li avoit mandé*
Qe l'oriaflame estoit aparé,
E cil meesme si le vent a gre?
Se Bovo à çoie, or no m'en demandé; (2585)
El dist a Druxiane, "Bona fu la mandé,*
4335 Quando li rois de France tant s'è decliné
Q'el m'oit letre e brevi envojé,
Qe l'oriaflame si m'est abandoné,*
E il meesme s'el m'est a gre."* (2590)
Dist la dama, "Questo è voloir de Dé;
4340 Daqe vos estes ensi asegur(é),*
Or secornon a nostra volunté."

4321 Rosellini: Q'el li 'novoio
Rubric 113 (originally 115, after 4396) line 1: Keller: sen torne antone; Reinhold, Rosellini: [à] Antone. line 2: MS.: liuona; Keller: la basee . . . lui ona; Reinhold: l'a[n]basée. . . . Rois *li *' [n]voia (for MS. *liuona*); Rosellini: anbasée.. li [n]voia
4328 Reinhold, Rosellini: brevi [qe] (emend); Rosellini: bailè
4329 Reinhold: Cil (France) la çira [osta] si oit; Rosellini: Cil france
4332 MS.: Et cil meesme; Reinhold: Et il (emend); Rosellini: E il (emend)
4333 Reinhold, Rosellini: m'en
4340 MS.: asegurier; Reinhold: asegure(r); Rosellini: aseguré (emend)
4341 Reinhold, Rosellini: seçornon (the cedilla in square brackets for Reinhold) (emend)

E dist Bovo, "E l'ò ben en pensé;
Ormais non dote plus d'omo qe soja né,* (2595)
Daqe mon per e ò molt ben vençé,*
4345 E li traitur morti et afolé,*
E moja mer e ò enpresoné,*
Qe por le fu tant pené e travalé."
Dist Druxiana, "Ben aveç parlé; (2600)
Dapoisqe Deo v'à celle don doné,
4350 Non devés mie vilan eser clamé;
Vu avés vestre mer, qe in ses ventre ve portè.*
S'ela de ves pere (ela) fi li peçé,*
E de vos, ora, li perdoné, (2605)
Q'ela non soja en celle mur muré.
4355 Se me la donés, e me la delivré,
En un monster e la meterò seré. 24ᵛᵇ
Ilec farà penetencie, e serà confesé
De ses peçé quant n'avoit ovré,* (2610)
Qe vos dè eser li pla plus alonçé."
4360 Tanto l'oit Druxiana e die e noit projé,*
Q'elo la oit enfine delivré.
E Druxiana non à l'ovra oblié;
Par son amor defor da la cité, (2615)
Ela avoit un monester fondé;
4365 E si ge l'oit metua e conversé.
Par son amor li fu cento entré,
Qe cella dame à con tot conpagné.
E Druxiana spese fois la visitè,* (2620)
E si li fa donar ço qe li vent a gre.*

Laisse 115

4370 Bovo seçorne e legro e çojant;
Plu no se dote de nul homo vivant.
Gran çoja oit d'anbidos ses enfant,
E de Druxiane dont durò penetant (2625)

4343 Reinhart, Rosellini: Oimais . . . dote
4344 Reinhold, Rosellini: molto ben
4352 MS.: ela fi; Reinhold: [ela] fi; Rosellini: ela fi
4359 Rosellini: de eser
4360 Reinhold: dit e n'oit proié (emend)
4361 Reinhold, Rosellini: en fine
4368 Reinhold, Rosellini: l'a visité
4373 Reinhold, Rosellini: pene tant

	Plus de sete ani tot enter pasant.
4375	Atant ecote vos un mesaçer erant*
	Ven a Antone, monta a li pavimant.
	O el vi Bovo, si le dist en ojant:
	"Li rois d'E(n)geltere, qe est vestre parant, (2630)
	A vos envoie, se l'amés de niant,
4380	Veneç a lu alo demantenant,
	Por honorer sa cort e sa çant;
	Qe muler, fila d'un amirant,
	El oit doné a son enfant." (2635)
	E dist Bovo, "De ço sonto çojant.
4385	Direç a mon u(n)cle qe farò son comant;
	A lui virò ben e cortesemant."
	S'el saust Bovo la pene e li tormant
	Qe li avene por li so auferant,* (2640)
	No le seria alé por mil marche d'arçant.
4390	Bovo si fo pro, saço e avenant;
	Quela anbasea no misi por niant.
	El s'aparele e ben e çentilmant,*
	De bele arme e de be guarnimant, (2645)
	E de celle colse qe a cort apant.
4395	Mostrer vorà li ses grant ardimant,
	En totes autres eser reconosant.

Laisse 116

	Bovo çivalçe a la çera ardie;
	A gram mervele oit gran segnorie;* (2650)
	De tote colse el fu ben guarnie. 25ra
4400	Tre sento çivaler oit en sa conpagnie;*
	Zascun avoit richa roba fusie.*
	Se il porà el non serà scrinie*
	Qe nesun die qe non vaga un alie. (2655)
	Quando çunse a la cort, molto fo honorie;
4405	Sor tot les autres el fu ben hostalie,
	Da tota gente honoré e servie.

4378 MS.: de Geltere; Reinhold: d'E[n]gleterre (emend); Rosellini: d'Engeltere
4385 MS.: uucle; Reinhold: uncle (emend); Rosellini: uncle
4389 Reinhold: marche
4392 MS.: Elasa parele
4393 Reinhold: be' quarnimant
4400 Reinhold: Tre sento; Rosellini: Tresento
4403 Reinhold: un'alie; cf. 4412

Li rois Guielme no l'obliò ne mie;
Senpre li tenoit en sa conpagnie, (2660)
E de la cort li onor otrie,
4410 Q'elo ne faça la soa comandie.
Bovo menò Rondel, qe li altri castie
A·l bagorder li altri no val un alie,
Por corer ni salir una poma porie; (2665)
Le filz li rois molto l'aco(v)otie.

Rubric 116
Coment Bovo fi far mervelle a·lli camp / de Ru(n)del son destrer; e coment le filz li / Rois li con(v)ota, si le demanda a Bovo.*
Laisse 117

4415 A gran mervele fu Bovo da loer;
Qi le veist sor Rondel son destrer,
Et avant e arer aler e tornojer,
Sor tot les autres el se fait apriser. (2670)
Le filz li rois qi doit avoir muler
4420 Quelo çival prist a covoter.
El dist a Bovo, "Bel cosin, dolçe frer,
Un don, cosin, e vos vojo demander,
Qe a moi deça donar quel destrer." (2675)
"Cosin," dist Bovo, "el vos fala li penser,
4425 Qe mon çival eo aça ben si çer
Qe no lo donaria por or ni por diner.*
E d'autra part ne vos vojo enganer:
El no se lasa a nesun homo toçer, (2680)
Nian strejar ne sor lui monter;
4430 El à ça morto plu de .XX. scuer."
Dist l'infant, "Tuto ço laseç ester;
Ben averò le çival acostumer."
"Cosin," dist Bovo, "asa se poroit parler, (2685)

4409 Reinhold: li onor [li] otrie (emend)
4414 MS.: aconotie; Reinhold, Rosellini: acovotie
Rubric 116 (after 4414) line 1: Keller: fifar; Reinhold, Rosellini: à lli; line 2: MS.: Rudel; Reinhold, Rosellini: Ru[n]del, (emend); line 3: MS.: conota?; Reinhold, Rosellini: con(v)ota (emend)
4423 Reinhold: deçà
4426 Rosellini: pr or (for *por or*; cf. Plouzeau, Martin)
4430 Reinhold, Rosellini: El a ça

	Qe le çival nen vos poria doner,
4435	Se Druxiana no·l savese in primer;
	Qe le norì tros ani tot anter,
	Quando a Syndonia eo era presoner.
	S'ela l'otria, no ve l'averò veer." (2690)
	Quant voit l'infant no li valoit projer*
4440	Qe le çival el li voja doner,
	Entro son cor el pensò mal penser:
	Qe quando Bovo seroit a·l mançer,
	El alirà li çival a furer, (2695)
	En altre parte e condur e mener.
4445	Mal fi le penseir, si le conprarà çer, 25ʳᵇ
	Qe quela cort farà tota destorber.

Rubric 117
Coment le filz li rois, poisqe il voit qe / Bovo no li voit (doner) son destré, se porpensa / De lui furé; e quant lì aloit por prendre le / Çival, li oncis; fu de lu fato gram dol.*

Laisse 118

	Li damisel, qi oit nome Folcon,
	Quant il oit ben saçu da Bovon (2700)
	No le donerà son destrer aragon,
4450	Ne no lo daria par or ni por macon,
	Gran felonie vene en cor a·l garçon;
	Qe quel çival, qe tant li paroit bon,
	De lui furer por mal entencion.* (2705)
	Dont apelò a si dos conpagnon
4455	A celle ore qe le tables ponon.
	A mançer sest civaler e baron,

4435 Reinhold: no-l; Rosellini: no'l savese
4438 Reinhold: no ve-l; Rosellini: no ve'l avero'
4439 Reinhold: n'oït l'infant
4440 MS., Reinhold, Rosellini: el li voia doner; Reinhold: Qe lo çival
4443 Reinhold: cival afurer
4444 Reinhold: altre parte parte
4446 Reinhold: Qe qaela
Rubric 117 (after 4446) line 1: Keller: pois qe; Reinhold: Rois. line 2: Keller: no li voit son . . . ; Reinhold: destré [doner] . . . porpensa; Rosellini: destrer [doner] . . . se porpesa (emend). line 3: MS.: fure . . . Rois; Keller: fare; Reinhold, Rosellini: De lui fure. line 4: Keller: cival

4456 Reinhold, Rosellini: çivaler

	E avec lor si estoit Bovon.
	Savés qe fi le damisel Folcon? (2710)
	Entro le stalle el entrò a laron,
4460	E avec lui celle dui co*n*pagnon;
	L'infant no*n* fu sajes, andò a l'aragon,
	Si·l volse pre*n*dere por la caveça enson.
	Rondel le guarda, qe no*n* era Bovon; (2715)
	Elo porp*r*ende atraverso li gropon.
4465	Stre*n*çe·l par forçe, si l'abate enson
	Tant li dona di pe e por testa e por fron,
	Qe ocli e çervele fi cair lì enson;
	Morto le çete, sença redencion. (2720)
	Quando le vi li ses dos co*n*pagnon,
4470	Via s'en fuit, criando ad alto ton,
	"A, çe*n*til rois," ço dient li garçon,*
	"Un çival, qe est de Bovon,
	Si oit morto vestre fio Folcon." (2725)
	Li rois l'intent, ven tinto cu*n* un carbon;
4475	Da tables se levent li cont e li baron,
	En le stale corent çivaler e peon,
	Altri cum stange et altri cu*n* baston;
	Bovo le vi ne le sait pais bon. (2730)

Rubric 118

Coment tota la cor tornent en dolor l'i*n*fant, / Si corerent en le stalle par lui aider; ma nul / Non fu qi li olsast apro(s)mer, se no Bovo.*
Laisse 119

	Ora fu Bovo tuto enpris de dotançe;
4480	De son çival oit gran dubitançe,
	Q'i no l'oncia et a spea et a lançe.
	De cil enfant avoit gran pesançe;*

4461 Reinhold, Rosellini: al aragon
4462 Reinhold: Si-l . . . en son; Rosellini: Si'l volse . . . enson
4464 Reinhold: Elo-[l] (emend) . . . à traverso. Rosellini: E lo . . . à traverso
4465 Reinhold: Stre*n*çe-l . . . en son; Rosellini: Strengel
4466 Reinhold: li pe
4470 Reinhold: fuït
4471 Reinhold: centil
Rubric 118 (after 4478) line 1: Keller: linfant. line 2: Keller: lestalle. line 3: MS., Keller: aprormer . . . bouo; Reinhold: aprosmer (emend for *aprormer*); Rosellini: aprosmer
4482 Rosellini: De ci l'enfant

           Tota la cort fo metu en tristançe, (2735)
           Qe venua estoit a la cort so amançe;
4485   Morto est il in quo avoit fiançe.
           L'infant prende*n*t sença nul demorançe;
           A un monster li portent sens tardançe.   25ᵛᵃ
           Ilec fu seveli a dol e a tristançe. (2740)
           Por Rondel fu Bovo en gra*n* balançe;
4490   Volunter fust e·l riame de France,
           O a 'Vignon o a la tera de Valançe.*

Rubric 119
Coment fu gram dol de le filz li rois, e come*n*te / Le sevelirent a un monster a gra*n* dol; *et* come(n)t / Le plure li rois e li baro(n), e sor tot Bovo.*
Laisse 120

           Grant fu li dol mené por cele enfant;
           De lui plure*n*t le petit e li grant. (2745)
           Mais desor tot Bovo li fait avant;*
4495   De son çival se dota duremant,
           Qe par lu ert morto cel enfant.
           Quant l'infant fu seveli, la cort fu en ojant;
           Dist l'un a l'altro, "Droit est li çuçemant; (2750)
           Si est droit e rason li comant,
4500   Qi fa li peçé, porte la penetanç;
           Morir doit le çival droitmant,"
           A li rois (le dient) le petit e li grant;*
           Dist li rois, "Et eo si li comant, (2755)
           Quando (s)i le çuçés li petit e li grant."*
4505   Quando Bovo l'olde dire, non à talant
           Qe plu ama le çival qe ren qe fust vivant,
           Enfra de soi el dist planamant,

4485 Reinhold: quo'
4487 Reinholdi: tardençe
4491 Reinhold, Rosellini. O [à] (emend)
Rubric 119 (after 4491) line 1: MS.: Rois; Keller: comente; Reinhold: coment(c); Rosellini: coment; line 2: 7 for *et*; Keller: seuelirent ... gran ... coment; Reinhold, Rosellini: come[n]t; line 3: MS.: baror; Reinhold: baron (emend for *baror*); Rosellini: baron ... sortot
4494 Reinhold, Rosellini: de sortot
4498 Rosellini: est çuçemant
4502 Reinhold, Rosellini: A li rois [le dicnt] (emend)
4504 MS.: fi le; Reinhold, Rosellini: si le çuces

        "Ai, (bon) Rondel, cum tu me fa dolant,* (2760)
        Par toi e vojo morir da une mior parant,*
4510 Quando non varà merçé ni pietanç."*

Rubric 120
Coment li çival fu çuçé a morir, e Bovo le / Plure e pur lui demande gran piaté a li rois.*
Laisse 121

        Se Bovo oit dol non è da merveler,
        Quant son çival vi a morte çuçer,
        Qe tot li volent ferir et inavrer. (2765)
        Mais li bon çival non fu si da toçer;
4515 Qe li veist ver de lor adriçer,
        E cun pe e cun boçe traire e amener,
        Qe tot li fa e foir e scanper.
        Bovo le vi, n'ait en lu qe irer; (2770)
        Ven a·l çival, si le va disliger;
4520 Quand cil li verent qe sovra li poit aler,
        No le fo nul tanto ardi ni fer
        Qe no s'en fuça por paura de·l destrer.
        Segnur, saçés, grande fu li noser (2775)
        Por li palés e davant e darer.*
4525 Si gran fu li dol de·l baçaler,
        Ne vos poroie par nul ren conter.
        Quand a la dama q'il devoit nocier . . .*
        Qui qe l'amenent là, volse arer torner; (2780)
        Qe ben verent en lui no è nula sper.
4530 Adoncha veisés li dol a inforçer,
        Tant palme batre e de çavi tirer.   25vb
        Bo(v)o si stoit como un hon strainer;
        Tal oit li dol, ben ne cuitò raçer. (2785)

    4508 MS.: ai bon*t*; Reinhold: fa' dolant
    4509 Reinhold: morir da un(e) mior parant
    Rubric 120 (after 4510) line 1: Keller: çuçe . . . bouo; line 2: MS.: Rois; Keller: par . . . gran; Reinhold, Rosellini: par
    4513 7 for *et*
    4526 Reinhold: Ne ves poroie
    4527 Reinhold: nocier . . . ; Reinhold, note: Quanda
    4528 Reinhold: l'amenent la volse
    4531 Reinhold: çavì; Rosellini: cavi
    4532 MS.: Bono?; Reinhold, Rosellini: Bovo

Chevalerie Bovo

	A sevelir l'infant sor lu veisés son per,
4535	Plançer e plurer e sovent pasmer.
	"Fillo," fait il, "qi me doit eriter,
	Aprés ma mort ma corona porter,
	E ceste pople avoir a (ju)stier,* (2790)
	Si altament v'avea dona muler
4540	Con se poroit ne dir ni penser;
	Dont estes mort par un destrer;
	No so cun de vos me diça vençer."
	Quant li baron l'oldent si plurer, (2795)
	Çascun prende(n)t Bovo a regarder,
4545	E a di *et* a palmes l'un l'altro mostrer.*
	Bovo le vi, n'ait en lui qe irer.

Rubric 121
Coment li rois pluroit son fil, *et* coment / Por li barom (ç)uçé fu le çival a morir.
Laisse 122

	Por celle enfant fu grande li dolor;
	Desovra lui en pasment plusor. (2800)
	Qui çivaler, li dux e li contor,
4550	Guardent Bovo por ira e por foror.
	Si s'el mostrent por li palés entor,
	Bovo le vi si n'oit ben paor,
	Porqe la mort Rondel son milsoldor (2805)
	Sovente fois el mua son color;
4555	E·l maleist cel di e(t) çel jor*
	Qe unqesmais el vene (a la) cor.
	Cuitoit fair a li rois grant honor;

4538 MS.: uistier; Reinhold: justi[s]ier (emend); Rosellini: justi[s]er
4542 Reinhold: cò; Rosellini: de vos diça (*me* missing)
4544 MS.: prendet; Rosellini: prendet; Reinhold: prende[n]t
4545 7 for *et*
Rubric 121 (after 4547) line 1: MS., Reinhold: Rois; 7 for *et*. line 2: MS.: çuçe; Keller: alçe suleçival; Mussafia: çuce fu le çival . . . ; Reinhold, emendation: çuçé (the first cedilla in square brackets); Rosellini: Por li baron çuçé
4551 Reinhold: se-l; Rosellini: se'l
4553 Reinhold: Por q'el amoit (emend for *qe la mort*); Rosellini: Por qela mort (cf. Martin)
4555 Reinhold, Rosellini: El; MS.: el çel ior; Reinhold, Rosellini: et çel (emend)
4556 Reinhold, Rosellini: [à la] cor (emend); Reinhold: unques mais

Ora g'oit fato onta e desenor (2810)
Major qe austes unqes ses antesor.
4560 Bovo (ç)ura a Deo, li maine Criator,*
Avantqe mora Rondel son milsoldor
Ne qe lu aça onta ni desenor,
"El ne conven morir de lor plusor,* (2815)
Qe se tira plus grandi e major."

Rubric 122
Coment li rois demanda conseil / a li barons por far la justi(si)e, et ille
Donente d'oncir li çival; e Bovo li contra . . .*
Laisse 123

4565 Quant l'infant furent seteré,
Li rois e li baron furent arer torné;
Gran fu li dol quant sont reparié.
Adonqa li rois, quant se fu repolsé, (2820)
Ses saçes apela, si le oit demandé:
4570 "Segnur," fait il, "qe conseil me doné?"
E cil le dient, "Porqe le demandé?
Rason si volt e si est ordené,
Qe cil porti la pena qe oit fato li peçé. (2825)
Par droit çuçen, sença nul falsité,
4575 Qe cil çival soja preso e ligé,   26ra
Cum malfator soja justisié;
Li çevo li sia da li bust colpé
Desor la plaçe en le major merçé, (2830)
Qe veoir le pose tot qui de la cité."
4580 E dist li rois, "Daqe li otrié,
Si soja fato coment vos li çuçé."
Bovo l'oldì, qe estoit lì asenblé,
Par un petit nen trase soa spe (2835)
Sovra colu c'oit li conseil doné.
4585 Mais gran mesure li oit atenperé;
Davant li rois el fu ençenolé,

4559 Reinhold: aüst(es)
4560 MS., Reinhold: cura; Rosellini: çura (emend)
Rubric 122 (after 4564) line 1: MS., Reinhold: Rois. line 2: Keller: iustisie et ille; Reinhold: iustisie et ille; Rosellini: justisie et ille. line 3: Keller: ille douente concir li quale bouo li contra; Mussafia: il le donente (donnent conseil) d'oncir li cival; Guessard: d'oncir li civale; Reinhold: ordonent (emend for *Donente*)
4566 MS.: e li . . . ; Reinhold: i li baron

E dolçement li oit dito e parlé:
"Merçé, bon roi, por la vestra bonté, (2840)
Quest qi v'ont li consejo doné,
4590 E qe a morir ont mon çival çuçé,
No v'ont pais dita la verité.
E vos dirò cun la colsa est alé;
Se vestre filz est morto, ben l'oit merité, (2845)
Quant por furer fist tel folité.
4595 Prender le volse contra sa volunté;
Ben ge lo disi, non è tros çorni pasé,
Quant me l'avoit en don ademandé,
No le doneroie a hon de mer né, (2850)
Ne por avor, ne por nul riçeté,
4600 Qe mun çival si estoit costumé
Ne se lasa toçer a hon qe soit né.
Se il est mort, qi n'à doncha li peçé?
Quant nu foimes a·l mançer aseté, (2855)
Prender el volse le çival aduré
4605 Contra mon voloir, l'averoit via mené.
Le çival fe quel q'el oit acostumé:
Morti n'oit ça plu de quaranta sé,
Questo no savivi vu qe fi li çuçé." (2860)
Quant qi l'intent qi l'ont çuçé,
4610 A gran mervele furent spaventé.
Bovo virent de mala volunté;
Ben conosent son cors e sa ferté.
Tutor ten la man sor le tenir de la spe; (2865)
Li plus ardi voroit eser enteré.
4615 Ni ben ni mal i no ont parlé.*

4592 Rosellini: alée
4603 Reinhold: foïmes
4608 Reinhold, Rosellini: qe si li çuçé
4609 Reinhold: q[u] l'intent; Reinhold, Rosellini: qi l'ont
4613 Reinhold: tutor'

Rubric 123

Coment Bovo mostrò por rason qe son / Çival non devoit morir; pois apreso si le querì en don por humilité.*
Laisse 124

       Gran dol oit Bovo, mervelos e pesant;
       Por son çival el fu en gran tormant.
       Si dolente non fu unqa a son vivant; (2870)
       El maldist cel jor e cil tanp,
4620 Qe a la cort menò quel auferant.
       Davant li rois en çenoclon s'estant;   26rb
       "Mercé, bon rois, par Deo onipotant,*
       Se mon çival v'à forfato de niant,* (2875)
       Morto ves filz dont sui tant dolant,
4625 Come poroie l'eser par nul convenant?*
       S'el oit fato li peçé, farò la penetant;
       Quando vos plait, e vos ven por talant,
       Parilé sui aler en Jerusalant, (2880)
       A le sepolcro servire lojalmant,*
4630 Por arma de l'infant dè servir ge quatro ant;*
       A mon avoir, cun quatrocento conbatant
       A bone arme e a destrer corant;
       Questo si çoarà a l'arma de l'infant. (2885)
       Por ancir le çival seroit gran viltanç,*
4635 Qe bestia non soit rason de nojant."
       Quant cil l'intendent qe fi le çuçemant,
       Dient a li rois, "Quest'è bon convant!
       Mal à quel qi melor li demant." (2890)
       Tuti li baron dient comunelmant,
4640 "Otrié·li, rois," ces loen tuti quant.*
       E dist li rois, "Ne eo no li contant;
       A (m)un Bovo, l'otrio son comant."*

    Rubric 123 (after 4615) line 1: MS.: Rason; Keller: mostro; Reinhold: Bovo Mostrò por Rason. line 3: Reinhold, Rosellini: queri
        4618 Rosellini: no fu
        4622 Reinhold, Rosellini: Merçé
        4625 MS.: Come; Reinhold, Rosellini: Con je poroie eser
        4629 Reinhold: servir; Reinhold 1912: servire
        4630 Reinhold: infint; Rosellini: de servir ge
        4634 Reinhold: viltant; Rosellini: viltant
        4640 Reinhold: Otrie-li . . . loen; Rosellini: Otrieli, rois ces loen tuti quant
        4642 MS.: inū (for (m)un); Reinhold: A mun Bovo l'otrio; Rosellini: A mun Bovo l'otrio

	Me no sa Bovo la pena e li tormant, (2895)
	Qe il durò por cele auferant
4645	Oltra la mer cun la pa(i)ne jant*
	Quant il oncis le mervelos serpant,
	Et in apreso lo me(r)veloso çigant
	Qe a lu non dura nesun hon vivant. (2900)

Rubric 124
Coment Bovo por scanper son cival da mort / Promis a li rois de aler oltra (mer) a li sepolcre.*
Laisse 125

	Quant Bovo oit son çival delivrés
4650	Qe a morir el estoit çuçés,
	De tel colse oit çoja menés;
	Donde pois nen fu e gramo e irés.
	A gran mervele fu Bovo ben dotés; (2905)
	Li rois oit altament merciés,
4655	E in apreso toto quanto li bernaés.
	A demorer ilec molto fose ranpognés
	Por son çival, qe oit fato la folités.
	Doncha oit il li conçé demandés, (2910)
	E li rois li oit mantenant donés:
4660	"Ne vo vos . . . , si v'en alés;*
	Por arma de mon filz farì la carités.
	Vu savi ben qe promeso m'avés."*
	E dist Bovo, "De ço ne vos dotés. (2915)
	E farò ben la vestra voluntés
4665	A vos e vini e çojant e lés;
	Arer m'en torno e gramo e irés.
	E d'una colsa e vojo qe vu saçés:
	Se nesun hon aust fato tel folités (2920)*	26ᵛᵃ
	Cum fi mon çival, qe non est ensenés,
4670	Eo n'averò ge la vengança pres;

4643 Reinhold: sà
4645 MS.: parne; Reinhold: par(v)e; Rosellini: paine
4647 MS.: meveloso; Reinhold, Rosellini: merveloso
Rubric 124 (after 4648) MS., Keller: miser; Keller: a li sepolcre; Reinhold: *mer à li sepolcro (emend for *miser*); Rosellini: oltre mer . . . sepolcro.
4651 Reinhold: cel (emend for *tel*)
4660 Reinhold, Rosellini: vos [arester] si v'en . . . (emend from Reinhold)
4661 Rosellini: mom filz fari
4670 Reinhold: averò ge . . . piés; Rosellini: averoge

Par soa mort zamais non serò lés."
Li rois li oit de ço amerciés;
Li conçé li donè, e cil s'en est alés. (2925)
Ses civaler sont a çival montés,*
4675 Qe tot li av<o>ient por amor convojés.*
A l'aler qi il n'oit, mil li ont reguardés,*
Por le çival q'el oit via menés.
Dist l'un a l'altro, "Cil oit ben ovrés; (2930)
Mal ait li rois, nen valt un pel pelés,
4680 Quant sor cestu non è son filz vençés."
E Bovo çivalçe cun sa bela masnés,
Do sento çivaler molto ben coroés.

Rubric 125
Coment Bovo prist conçé da li rois / e da li barons e se s'en torne ad Antone Sa cité; e contoit a Druxiane ço qe li ert / avenu e ço que far devoit, donde ne fi gra(n)z dol.*
Laisse 126

Bovo s'en vait, li cortois çivaler, (2935)
Con sa masnea qe sont e pros e ber;*
4685 Qui qi le convoient, qe furent un miler,
Qe tot li ament por amor de son per;
A Deo li rende, pois retornent arer.
Tanto çivalça Bovo, ne se volse arester; (2940)
Ven a Antone (son) mastro terer.*
4690 E Druxiana quant le voit reparier,
S'el oit çoja non è da demander.
Contre le vait por la man asaçer,
Ela le guarde si·l vi de mal penser;* (2945)

4672 Reinhold, Rosellini: amerçiés
4673 Reinhold, Rosellini: li done
4674 Reinhold, Rosellini: çivaler
4675 Reinhold, Rosellini: avoie[n]t
4676 Reinhold: Al aler . . . voit (emend for *noit*)
Rubric 125 (after 4682) line 1: MS., Reinhold: Rois. line 2: Keller: da li . . . se sentorne; Reinhold: e (se) s'en torne; Rosellini: e se s'en torne. line 4: MS.: graz; Keller: granz; Reinhold, Rosellini: gra[n]z
4689 MS.: se ne mastro; Reinhold: s'en è (not *é* as Rosellini quotes); Rosellini: son mastro (emend)
4691 Rosellini: denander (cf. Holden)
4693 Reinhold: si-l; Rosellini: si'l de mal penser

Ne no le vi ni rir ne treper,
4695 Ne cun le ne rir ne çuger,
Cum autre fois era usa de fer.*
Ela le prist por rason demander:*
"Ai, sire Bovo, coment vos veço ester? (2950)
V'ait nu hon fato nul enojer?"*
4700 "Nenil, madame, me son en gran penser
Por Rondel, nos corant destrer.
Le ver diable si me·l fe amener;
El no è bestia, anç è·l li vor malfer. (2955)
A la cort alè por mon oncha onorer;*
4705 Saveç vos qe me fi li destrer?
Quando estoie asis a·l mançer
Le filz li rois, qe oit mena muler,
Me le querì qe li dovese doner. (2960)
Et eo le disi no se deust pener,
4710 No le donaria par or ni por diner.
Quando el vi non valoit projer,
El alò a·l çival, si le voloit furer.
E quando volse le civalo asaçer (2965)
Le çivalo le pris por li flanco darer.
4715 No li lasò si l'avè a strangoler;*
Dont çuçarent p(e)on e çivaler
Por far justisie si cun rason requer,
La testa far trençer a li destrer. (2970)
S'eo avea doja, non è da demander;
4720 Non era in la cort nul hon si lainer
Non me guardast como fose un çubler.*
Plesor fois i me fe remenbrer
De trar Clarençe, li bon brando d'açer;* (2975)
Mais astinencie si me fe repolser,
4725 Porqe me voie contre tant averser.*
Se fose esté defors a li verçer

26^(vb)

4696 Reinhold: autres
4697 Reinhold: permander
4699 MS.: nu ho (titulus above o); Reinhold: nu[l] hon; Rosellini: nu hon
4700 Rosellini: Neil
4702 Reinhold: me-l; Rosellini: me'l
4703 Reinhold, Rosellini: è 'l
4704 MS., Rosellini: oncha; Reinhold: oncle (emend)
4709 Reinhold: deüst (as always)
4715 Reinhold, Rosellini: ave astrangoler
4716 MS., Rosellini: poon; Reinhold: peon (emend)

Tel me tenoit vil qe m'averoit tenu çer.
A molto gran pene potì le çival scaper;* (2980)
Avantqe le poust de tot delivrer,
4730 Me le convene e plevir e çurer
Qe eo pasaroie oltra l'aigua de·l mer
Ander en Jerusalen cun quatrocento çivaler,
Servir a li sepolcro quatro ani tot enter." (2985)
Druxiana l'olde, n'oit qe coruçer;
4735 A gran mervele el li parse nojer.
Mais son segnor ne volt contraster,
Qe son voloir conoit tot enter.

Rubric 126
Coment Bovo ancor parloit a la dame; / e coment Drusiana li respondì.*
Laisse 127

Bovo parole a la dame in ojant, (2990)
"Dama," fait il, "come eo son dolant,
4740 Quant me vos convent laser si por niant,*
E li me filz, qe je amo cotant;
Mal acontè Rondel l'auferant."*
Dist Druxiana, "El no vos val niant.* (2995)
Dapoisqe vos faistes li sagramant,
4745 Ça non pois tradir li convenant.
Se vos aleç oltra Jerusalant,
De ves peçé farì la penetant;
A·l revenir vu serì tuto sant. (3000)
Ben guardarò anbidos vestri enfant,
4750 E la çité e darer e davant."
Molto li vait Druxiana confortant,
Açoqe de l'ovre no s'en vada nojant.
"Bovo," dist Druxiane, "un don e vos demant; (3005)
Quant vos serés en çele tere sant,

4728 Reinhold: sca[n]per
4735 Rosellini: parse oier
Rubric 126 (after 4737) MS., Reinhold: Respondi
4739 Rosellini: fait il, »come eo . . .
4742 Reinhold, Rosellini: Mal a conté
4747 Rosellini: farí
4751 Rosellini: cofortant
4752 Reinhold, Rosellini: A co qe de
4753 Rosellini: dist Druxiane, »un . . .

4755 De moi e de ves filz vos sovegna sovant,
　　　 Si me aportarés de le requilie sant*
　　　 Qe trovarés là en Jerusalant."
　　　 "Dama," fait il, "farò li ves talant. (3010)
　　　 Tosto a vos farò retornamant."
4760 Un mois seçorne por far son guarnimant;　　　　　　　　27ra
　　　 E si fe pariler ses homes e sa çant.
　　　 De li milor e de li plus valant
　　　 Avec lui n'oit pris quatro çant, (3015)
　　　 Qe çascun li vait volunter por talant,
4765 A bone arme e a destrer corant.
　　　 E çascun de lor porta de l'avoi(r) tant
　　　 Cun spender poit por cele tot tanp.

Rubric 127

Coment Bovo s'apareille *et* lui e soa çant / Por paser mer et aler en Jerusalant.*
Laisse 128

　　　 Bovo d'Antone li ardi e li pros, (3020)
　　　 Nen fu uncha hon si perigolos,
4770 Ne tante pene durese pauros.
　　　 Mais Damenedé, li per glorios,
　　　 Senpre en sa vite si le donò secors;
　　　 Mais non teme ni amiré ni ros.* (3025)
　　　 D'estar en pais senpre fo desidros,
4775 E de mal faire senpre fo vergognos.
　　　 Mais non amò coardo ni traitors;
　　　 Senpre el fu dolçe e piatos,
　　　 Contra li malvés felon *et* orgolos. (3030)
　　　 En soa tere molto fu poderos;
4780 Dever li povre nen fu voluntaros
　　　 De questa vie molto fo ocios,
　　　 E çorno e noit el n'estoit ir(o)s.*

　　　 4756 Reinhold, Rosellini: reliquie (emend)
　　　 4757 Reinhold, Rosellini: là
　　　 4763 Reinhold, Rosellini: quatro çant
　　　 4766 MS.: la voit; Reinhold, Rosellini: l'avoir (emend for *lavoit*)
　　　 Rubric 127 (after 4767) line 1: 7 for *et*; Keller: sapareille
　　　 4769 Reinhold: Non
　　　 4770 Reinhold: paüros
　　　 4774 Reinhold, Rosellini: De star
　　　 4782 MS.: ires; Reinhold: irés (!) [sic]; Rosellini: iros

Druxiana li conforte, q'el sia sofraitos, (3035)
E si se reputì a hon pecaors.*
4785 De ses peçé se clamì doloros,
"Ma senpre mais sireç desiros*
De retorner, bel nos amigo dos."

Rubric 128
Coment Bovo fu parilés, e lui e soa jent; / E si parloit a Synibaldo si le reconmande Sa feme e ses enfant e soa çité aprés . . .*
Laisse 129

Quant Bovo fu de tot aparilé, (3040)
Sinibaldo apele, si l'oit aderasné:
4790 "Sinibaldo," fait il, "molto vos ò amé,
E vos estes par moi pené e travailé;
Ne vos ai mie de nojant oblié.
Aler me convent oltra la mer salé; (3045)
Prendés ma tere e mes anbes rité,
4795 E ma muler qe tant avì amé,
Par cui eo sonto tanto tenpo pené,*
Si le guardés a vestre volunté."
Dist Sinibaldo, "Si con vos comandé; (3050)
Mais d'una ren e vos prego por Dé,
4800 Qe tosto a nos vu sia retorné."
Responde Bovo, "De ço ne vos doté."
Adonqa Bovo nen oit plus parlé;
Muli e somer, cento n'oit encarçé, (3055)
De vitualie, d'arnois, e de coré.   27rb
4805 Tanta enportent defor de la cité,
Qe por gran tenpo, ela no le fu manché.
Quant oit ço fato, q'elo fu parilé,
A Druxiana el demanda li conçé. (3060)
Qi donc veist coment sont acolé,
4810 E l'un l'autro e strençu e basé,
E cum larmoient cun li ocli de·l çe;

4784 Reinhold, Rosellini: reputi
4785 Reinhold, Rosellini: clami
Rubric 128 (after 4787) line 2: Keller, Rosellini: recommande. line 3: Reinhold, Rosellini: soa çité aprés
4800 Reinhold: sià
4805 Reinhold, Rosellini: en portent
4811 Reinhold, Rosellini: çé

| | Nen est homo nen prendist piaté.
| | Druxiana l'oit a Deo comandé, (3065)
| | E Sinibaldo fo a çival monté.
| 4815 | Avec lui tuti qui de la cité,
| | Tant li convoient cun li vene a gre.
| | Bovo s'en vait e qui retorna aré,
| | Por le çamin e por la strea feré. (3070)
| | Cil le condue qi de la Vergene fu né,
| 4820 | Qe a gran travaile elo fu envojé.

Rubric 129
Coment Bovo s'en vait por le çamin, / e lui e soa çant; e pasarent la mer,
Si s'en voit a li seporcre en Jerusalant.*
Laisse 130

| | Or s'en vait Bovo por aler oltra mer;
| | A Sinibaldo el lasò sa muler,
| | E ses enfanti e sa tera guarder. (3075)
| | Tanto s'en vait, q'el fu (ç)onto a la mer;*
| 4825 | Ilec se fi en nef et en dormon lever;
| | E Damendé si dè bon orer.
| | Tant naçarent q'i venent a river,
| | Verso Alexandre de cella part de mer. (3080)
| | Droit en Jerusalen venent ad alberçer;
| 4830 | Pois alent a·l sepolcro por dever visiter.
| | Ilec trovent un mortel engonbrer,*
| | Qe da Baldras estoit venu un Sarasin, Corcher,
| | Com trea mile de cela jent averser, (3085)
| | Por le sepolcro veoir e guarder,
| 4835 | E qe Cristian no le venist a rober,
| | E le reliquie tore et anbler.
| | Quant virent qe venu sont qui çivaler
| | Si le volent de·l tot contraster, (3090)
| | Qe non devent in le sepolcro entrer
| 4840 | Adoncha Bovo fe soa çent armer

Rubric 129 (after 4820) line 1: Keller: sen . . . e lui. line 3: MS.: si senvoit; Keller: sen
4824 MS.: coto; Reinhold: conto; Rosellini: çonto
4825 Rosellini: se fi e nef
4826 Reinhold: dè; Rosellini: dé
4835 Reinhold: cristian . . . venist arober
4839 Reinhold: Que

| | Quatro cento sont, qui son trea miler.*
| | Mal fi Bovo li sacramento çurer;
| | Devoit paser oltra l'aigua de·l mer, (3095)
| | Cum si petita conpagna de çivaler.
| 4845 | Se Deo non pense, li vor jus(t)isier,
| | Ça averà Bovo un si fer engonbrer
| | Qe çero averà Rondelo son destrer.

Rubric 130
Coment Corché cum li paim venent / a li sepolcro e atrovarent Bovo.
Laisse 131

| | Bovo d'Antone non senblò pais enfant; (3100)*   27ᵛᵃ
| | Quando el voit venir qui mescreant,
| 4850 | Davanti lor Corcher, qe estoit un çigant,
| | Con trea mile Serasin e Persant.
| | Saçés de quel Corcher, il estoit si grant,
| | Qe tot les spales e lo çevo en avant (3105)
| | Major estoit de nul altro conbatant.
| 4855 | Quando Bovo le vi venir cosi avant,
| | S'elo se smaie, no ve ci mervelant.*
| | Dist a ses homes, "Nos sumes a·l presant,
| | Por Damenedé sostenir gran tormant. (3110)
| | Mais d'une colse nos sumes ben certant;
| 4860 | Qi morirà en porà eser çojant,
| | En Paradiso averò corona d'or lusant."*
| | Quant cil l'entendent, sença demoramant
| | Çascun se segne, fait soi la cros davant. (3115)
| | E dist Bovo, "Vos faites saçemant;
| 4865 | Ne vos movés, se je ne vos comant.

    4841 Reinhold: Quatro cento, Rosellini: Quatrocento; Rosellini: qui trea miler (cf. Martin)
    4843 Reinhold: Qe voit (emend)
    4845 MS.: jusisier; Reinhold: jus[t]isier; Rosellini: jusisier
    Rubric 130 (after 4847) line 1: Reinhold: Corché . . . païm; Rosellini: Corché cum li paim. line 2: MS.: atro varent; Keller: a trovarent
    4848 Rosellini: on senblò (cf. Holden, Plouzeau)
    4856 Rosellini: s'esmaie
    4861 Reinhold, Rosellini: avera (emend for MS. *avero*)
    4863 Rosellini: cros davat

	Avantqe feré de lança ni brant,

        Avantqe feré de lança ni brant,
        Ve vo parler a quel qi ven davant;*
        A moi resenble qe soja un çigant." (3120)
        Qui li dient, "Soja a li Dé comant."
4870 Arester le foit en un pre verdojant;
        Da lor se parte tuto quant en ojant,
        E si s'en vait ver celle amirant.
        E quel Corcher si fu reconosant, (3125)
        Quant solo le vi sença hon vivant.
4875 Dist a sa jent, "Non venés plus avant;
        Quel me resenble de Cristiane jant.
        A moi vol parlé, como mostra senblant."*
        E cil le font, daqe i·le comant. (3130)

Rubric 131
Coment Bovo aloit verso li Sa(ra)sin, / E si pa(r)lò a Corcher, qe çigant estoit.*
Laisse 132

        Le Sarasin non fu pais garçon;
4880 Punçe son çival, si vent ves Bovon.
        E si le dist, "Qi est cil baron?
        Cristian me resenbli, qe as la cros e·l fron;
        Ben es armé, si à bon aragon. (3135)
        Porqe pasè a ta confosion,*
4885 De toa vite non daria un boton,
        Se no è venu por adorer Macon,
        E Apolin, e nos deo Balatron."
        "Par fois," dist Bovo, "ja no vos çelaron; (3140)
        E son ben Cristian, ne non croi altro non,
4890 S(e) no en quel Deo qe sofrì pasion,*
        En su la cros si cun por vor saçon.
        Pasé ò la mer en neve et en dormon,
        Por servir le sepolcro qe ilec veon. (3145)

    4867 Reinhold, Rosellini: Je vo (emend)
    4876 Reinhold, Rosellini: cristiane jant
    4877 Reinhold: parle(r) (emend); Rosellini: parle[r] (emend)
    Rubric 131 (after 4878) line 1: MS.: sairiſui?; line 2: MS.: palo a; Keller: palo acorcher; Reinhold, Rosellini: pa[r]lò à
    4884 Reinhold: pasé [a'] à ta; Rosellini: pasè [as] à ta
    4886 Rosellini: Mancon
    4887 Reinhold, Rosellini: Apolin e nos
    4890 MS., Reinhold, Rosellini: So

	Çentil ho*n*, sire, qe me parés si (b)on,*	
4895	Por cortesie e vos demando un don,	27vb
	Qe no*n* faça nula engonbrason.	
	Lasa a nos recever li perdon	
	Qe avon por pene*t*e*n*cie e por co*n*fesion, (3150)	
	Et avec moi quisti me co*n*pagnon;	
4900	Colsa como no, ça ne vos çelaron,	
	Deo par nos sostene pasion	
	E nu par lui sostenir la volon."	
	Dist li pain, "Tu parli a bandon; (3155)	
	Parole di qe resenbla a garçon.	
4905	Nu si savon et è droit e rason,*	
	Qe vestra loi no*n* val un speron.	
	Saçì por voir, se no*n* aorì Macon	
	Nu vos donaron una tel benecion, (3160)	
	Qe mais no*n* tornaresi en la vestre mason."	
4910	Bovo l'oldì, ven tinto cun un carbon;	
	Le pain g(u)a(r)de da li pe jusqua enson;*	
	A gram mervele elo li parse felon,	
	E si le parse homo de gran renon; (3165)	
	S'(e)lo li dote, no se mervil nul hon.	

Rubric 132

Coment Bovo parle a li Sarasin, / li Sarasin parole a lui.*
Laisse 133

4915	"Sarasin, frere," (dist) Bovo enn ojan,*
	E vos prego, nen siés pais vilan;
	Pasé avon mer en neve *et* en çalan,
	Por fare qui la nostre penetan. (3170)

4894 MS.: lon; Reinhold, Rosellini: bon
4896 Reinhold: façà
4897 Reinhold: Lasà
4903 Reinhold: païn (as always)
4904 Reinhold: di'
4905 MS., Rosellini: et e droit; Reinhold: et à droit et à rason
4907 Reinhold, Rosellini: Saçi . . . aori
4911 MS.: grande; Reinhold, Rosellini: guarde (emend); Reinhold: jusqua en son
4914 MS.: Solo; Reinhold, Rosellini: S'elo (emend)
Rubric 132 (after 4914) line 1: Keller: e li sa/rasin parole . . .
4915 MS.: disto; Reinhold: dist(o); Rosellini: dist (emend)
4917 7 for *et*. Reinhold: nave

| | Non seria cortexie torber nos de nian;
| 4920 | Nu avon soferto gran poine e torman.
| | E quando el non poroit aler altreman,
| | Morir volun por Deo onipotan,
| | Defenderen nos a (n)ostre spee trençan; (3175)
| | Encontra vos se fustes doa tan,
| 4925 | Deo averon por nostre capetan.
| | Et avec lui serà tot li san."
| | Dist li pain, "Or m'entendì, Cristian;
| | De cele gent, è tu li plu manan?" (3180)
| | E dist Bovo, "I son a me coman;
| 4930 | E de lor e sonto li plus gran."
| | Dist le pein, "Tu è a grant achan;*
| | Avec moi tu resenbli un enfan.
| | Or a me dì, no me·l çeler nojan:* (3185)
| | En toa tere è tu conte ni amiran?*
| 4935 | Se tu fusi çentil, con tu à li senblan,
| | Avec moi sença hon vivan
| | A un a un conbateria a li can.
| | Se conquerer me poisi a la spea trençan, (3190)
| | Segnur po star pois en Jerusalan,
| 4940 | E guarder li sepolcro a tuto li to coman."
| | Bovo l'oldì, si s'en mostrò çojan.

Rubric 133

Coment Bovo oldì parler quel Sarasin, (28ra) / Que a mervelle estoit grant, que li demande / de far sego la bataille; e coment Bovo li respondì.*
Laisse 134

| | "Sarasin, sire," dist Bovo en ojant,
| | "Tu me domandi bataile et eo si la consant. (3195)
| | Ben me senblés de moi asa plus grant;
| 4945 | Ora me dites, meterì vu li convant:*
| | Se vos conquer a·l trençer de mon brant,
| | A li sepolcro starò e pois seguremant."

4923 MS.: vostre; Reinhold, Rosellini: nostre (emend)
4931 MS.: pein; Reinhold: peïn; Rosellini: pein
4933 Reinhold: Or à me dì, no me-l . . . ; Rosellini: Ora me di, no me'l çeler
4934 Reinhold: conto
Rubric 133 (after 4941) line 1: Keller: ovoi; Mussafia, Guessard: oldi
4945 Rosellini: meterí
4947 Reinhold: starò e' pois; Rosellini: starò e pois

        "Oïl voir, sir," ço dist li mescreant; (3200)
        "E s'eo conquer toi, farò cortesia tant
4950   Qe toa çent qe son a·l to comant
        Eo li lasarò aler a salvamant."
        E dist Bovo, "Et altro (non) demant."
        "Ora tornés," ço dist li mescreant, (3205)
        "A vestra jent; fa vos legro e çojant,
4955   Trosqu'a deman, a l'aube aparisant,*
        Et eo farò tot li somiant.*
        Deman seremo anbidos a li canp;
        Qi vinçerà serà richo e manant; (3210)
        Qi perderà serà tristo e dolant."
4960   "Par foi," dist Bovo, "e questo non contant."
        Corcher s'en vait, qe non dota hon vivant;
        E Bovo d'Antone retorne a sa jant.
        La novela li conte dont forte se spavant, (3215)
        Qe i verent le pain cosi grant.

Rubric 134

Coment Bovo parole a sa jent / de la bataille qe far devoit.*
Laisse 135

4965   "Segnur," (dist) Bovo, "e no vos quer çeler;
        Con quel pain el me conven çostrer.
        Cum tal cove(n)to cun vos averò deviser,
        Se le porò vincer ni afoler, (3220)
        Nu poren pois le sepolcro guarder,
4970   A nos voloir stare e seçorner,
        Qe de pain non estoit plus doter;
        Q'elo est sire de tota sta river.
        E s'el conquer moi, vos porés retorner (3225)
        A salvamento, sença nul engonbrer;
4975   E vojo ançi morir qe vos desariter.

    4948 Reinhold: Oïl (as always)
    4952 Reinhold: [non] demant (emend); Rosellini: [nen] (emend)
    4955 Reinhold, Rosellini: Trosqua
    4957 Reinhold: anbi dos (as always)
    4960 Rosellini: 'Par foi»,
    Rubric 134 (after 4964) Reinhold: fer devoit (emend for *devoit*)
    4965 MS.: disti; Reinhold: dist(i); Rosellini: dist (emend)
    4967 MS.: coueto; Reinhold: convento; Rosellini: convento

Ma arma serà salva, de ço non ò pe*n*ser.
E vos comando Druxiana ma muler,
E mes enfanti vos diça co*n*server, (3230)
Et anbidos como moi reguarder."
4980 Quando cil le olde*n*t si parler,
Tuti ensenble començe*n*t a plurer,
"O, çentil dux, ne ves (volon) si laser!*
Se vos morés, mais no*n* volu*n* torner; (3235)
Avec nos mais no*n* queron sper."*
4985 En cella noit, trosqua a l'alba cler
Elo se fi una mesa çanter,   28ʳᵇ
Et apreso se fi comuner*
De·l corp Jesu, por soa arma salver. (3240)
Quant à ço fato, no*n* fu longo entarder,
4990 Elo demande le arme e li corer;
E cil le aporte qe le ont a guarder.
Bovo s'adobe a lois de çivaler;
Veste l'aube*r*s e calça le ganber, (3245)
Alaça l'eume, çinse li brant d'açer.
4995 Fa s'amener Rondel, son destrer;
E cil li monte, qe no*n* bailì striver.
Pois pris conçé da li ses çivaler,
Ver la bataile prist a çaminer. (3250)
Quando l'oit veçu venir Corcher,
5000 Qi le veist de ses arme adober,
E monter a çivale corser,
Dever de Bovo vait como corser;
Ça serà la bataile meravilosa e fer. (3255)
Quando Bovo se vait a 'prosmer a·l corser,
5005 Elo l'apele, "Benvenés, çivaler!
A Deo plasese li vor justisier
Sença bataile s'aumes acorder."
Dist le pain, "E le vojo otrier, (3260)
Se vos volés Damenedeo renojer,
5010 Croir en Macon e lasai li Batister."

4978 Reinhold: diçà
4982 Reinhold, Rosellini: ne ves [volon] (emend)
4984 Rosellini: mais queron sper
4987 Reinhold: comun[i]er; Morini: cominier
5001 Reinhold: cival e corser; Rosellini: ciavale corser
5004 Reinhold, Rosellini: vait aprosmer
5005 Reinhold, Rosellini: Ben venés

E dist Bovo, "De ço n'estoit parler;
Ançi me lasaria tot li me*n*bre coper,
Q*e* colu renojase qi me doit justisier. (3265)
Vegna de moi, qe ne po encontrer;
5015 Daqe altrame*n*t la no poit aler.
E vos desfi, ben vos stoit guarder."
Dist le pain, "Et eo vos sens tarder."

Rubric 135
Coment començe*n*te la bataille e fer(i)re*n*t / L'um l'autre des lançes gram colpi.
Laisse 136

A gran mervele fu li baron orgolos, (3270)
Fort et ardi como lion e ors.
5020 L'un contre l'autre punçe le milseldors;
Brandist le lançe a li fer perigolos.*
Gram colpi se fer sor li scu de colors;
Le scu se speçe, tros a li aube(r)s blos; (3275)
Le aste se frosent, via vole*n*t li tors.*
5025 Ne l'un ni l'autre ne*n* fu si vigoros,
Q*e* de la sella se plegase en jos.

Rubric 136
Coment dapoisqe le a(s)te(s) furent fraites / Se fe*r*irent de le spee l'um l'a(u)tre
mervelos / colpi, e tren(ç)ent tot ses armes.*
Laisse 137

Tot primeran a la prima envaée,
Bovo d'Antone si oit trato sa spee, (3280)
Ço fu Clarençe, c'oit li pomo endorée.
5030 Fer le pain desor l'eume gemée;   28ᵛᵃ
Tanto le trova e duro e serée,

5011 Reinhold, Rosellini: ne stoit

Rubric 135 (after 5017) line 1: MS.: ferrent; MS., Keller: començente.. feri-/rent lun lautre; Reinhold: fer[i]rent (emend); Rosellini: ferirent. Reinhold: començe*n*t(e) (emend); Rosellini: començent

5023 MS.: aubes; Reinhold, Rosellini: aube[r]s (emend)

Rubric 136 (after 5026) line 1: MS.: atre... ferent (*ri* is written above the line); Keller: da pois qe le astes. line 2: Keller: ferirent de lespee luus latre; Reinhold: fe*r*irent... l'atre mervelos; Rosellini: ferirent l'um l'atre. line 3: MS.: trentent; Keller: etrentent; Reinhold, Rosellini: trencent (emend)

           Nen po trençer valant una derée.
           La spea torna, qe le scu oit frapée; (3285)
           Cum tota la guincha li çeta a le pree,
5035   E de l'aubers tota (la) ghironée;
           Mais en la carne ne l'oit pais toçée.*
           Dist le pain, "De nient m'amée!
           A gran mervelle trença ben quella spee; (3290)
           Ancora non avés de la moja cerchée."
5040   Li Sarasin fu forte *et* adurée
           E a mervelle fu grande e desmesurée;
           La spea trait, a Bovo l'oit presentée
           Desor li elme gran colpo li oit donée.* (3295)
           Bon fu li elme, tel li oit donée,
5045   Nen fu un milor in la Crestenetés;*
           Ver Luchafer l'avoit conquistée,
           Quando l'oncis soto Arminia a·l pree.
           Por celle heume Bovo fu guarentée; (3300)
           Nen po trençer valant una derée.
5050   Si grande fu li colpo qe li dè quel malfé,
           Qe sor l'arçon li oit enbronçée;
           Par un petit ne le çeta a li pree.

Rubric 137

Coment fu grant la bataille de celle dos / Baron, e coment se ferirent de le spede.

Laisse 138

           Quant le pain oit Bovo veu, (3305)
           Ne l'oit mie de·l çival abatu;
5055   Nen oit son heume peçoré un festu.
           El dist a Bovo, "Ben vos est avenu;
           Nen cuitoie mie qe austes tel vertu,
           Mais a la fin, se non lasi Jesu, (3310)
           E non croi in Macometo e Cau,
5060   Tu serà morto e confondu."

   5035 Reinhold, Rosellini: tota [la] (emend)
   5040 7 for *et*
   5043 Reinhold: li elme gran colpo; Rosellini: li elme gra colpo
   5045 Rosellini: Crestenetée
   5059 Reinhold: Caü
   5060 Reinhold: sera'

E dist Bovo, "Deo me seroit en aju;
Cil me secoré, qe de Verçene né fu."
Bovo ten Clarençe, sovra li è coru. (3315)
Gran colpo li fer desor l'eume agu;
5065 De quel non trençe valisant un festu.
A li desendere, c'oit li brando desendu,
De l'auberg trençe quant n'oit conseu.
E in le flanco si durament feru (3320)
Qe a li canpo el l'oit abatu,
5070 Et a·l çival oit li çevo tolu.
Quando Bovo vi qe ço ert avenu,
Demantenant fo de·l çival desendu.
A·l Sarasin averoit li çevo tolu, (3325)
Mais cel li quer e marçé e salu:*
5075 "Ai, çivaler, por amor de Jesu,
No me onciré, qe me son proveu
Qe Macometo no à força ni vertu." 28vb

Rubric 138
Coment Bovo ferì le pain *et* durament / li navra se le çitò da çival.
Laisse 139

Quando Bovo oit cella parola oie, (3330)
A gram mervelle li delecte *et* agrie.
5080 El dist a le pain, "Nen vos dotés ne mie;
Se orer voleç le filz sante Marie,
E laser Macon, qe non val una alie,
Avec li santi averés conpagnie." (3335)
Dist le pain, "Questo non contralie;
5085 De servir Deo ò li cor abrasie,
E ceste lois, o el fu sevelie."
Bovo li prent, en estant li metie;
A ses pavilon elo lo condusie. (3340)

5061 Reinhold: aiü
5068 Rosellini: duranent
5076 Reinhold: 'proveü
Rubric 138 (after 5077) line 1: 7 for *et*. line 2: Keller: naura si le . . . ; Reinhold: da[l] çival (emend)
5079 7 for *et*

Rubric 139
Coment Corchers re(n)egò Machon / E si prist bateseme.
Laisse 140

	Quant Bovo fu a·l pavilon torné,
5090	Le Sarasin oit vinto et amaté.
	De totes oit li pain desarmé;*
	Ses mires oit queri e demandé,
	Qe avec soi el avoit amené, (3345)
	Si fa çercher le plaie e davant e daré,
5095	E si la oit e streta e ligé;
	De bon unguant li oit metesiné.
	E quant à ço fato, si cun oit demandé
	Elo fu lavé e bateçé. (3350)
	E dis Corcher, "Bovo, or m'entendé;
5100	E vos demando qe conçé me doné,
	Tantoqe aça a ma çente parlé,
	E qe soja torna en ma çité.
	Si non farà la moja volunté, (3355)
	Par vos envojarò qe secorso me doné;
5105	Quanti non serà de fonte ençendré,
	En serà tot a mala mort çuçé."
	E dist Bovo, "El vos soja otrié."
	Bovo li oit un palafroi doné, (3360)
	E cil li monte, c'oit preso conçé,
5110	Ven a sa jent, o erent asenblé.
	"Segnur," fait il, "nu avon ben esploité.
	Tot tenpo sumes pené e travalé,
	Tanto aumes Macometo projé, (3365)
	Qe ver de nos el est coruçé.
5115	El non val plus una poma poré;
	Men esiant, e vojo qe vu saçé,
	Qe li rois d·i Franchi no è endormençé,
	E qi li serve si fait gran bonté, (3370)
	Qe a le besogne li serve ben a gre.
5120	Par son amor eo sui bateçé,
	E lui servirò en moja viveté."

Rubric 139 (after 5088) MS.: Revego; Keller: reuego; Guessard: renego; Reinhold: Renegò (emend); Rosellini: renegò

5101 Reinhold, Rosellini: Tanto qe aça

5107 MS.: vois (*i* expunctuated)

5120 Rosellini: beteçé

	Quant cil l'intendent, toti son spave*n*té;	29ʳᵃ
	Mal ait quel de lor, ni bon ni re, (3375)	
	Qe po paure aça li çevo levé;*	
5125	Ne un sol moto ver lui aça parlé.	

Rubric 140
Coment la gent Corcher se farent / bateçer *et* homes *et* femes.
Laisse 141

	Corcher parole irés come lion,
	"Segnur," fait il, "saçés qe nu faron?
	Çascun de nos aça bona entencion, (3380)
	De delinquir Trivigant e Macon,
5130	E servir Deo qe sofrì pasion
	En su la cros par nostra redencion.
	Qi prenderà batesmo, serà me co*n*pagnon;
	E qi far no li vorà no*n* averà de·l perdon. (3385)
	Morti serà como engresun felon."*
5135	Quant cil l'intendent, crient a alto ton:
	"Zo qe vos plais, nu si li otrion."
	Adoncha Corcher si mandò per Bovon,
	E cil li vent qe non fi arestason; (3390)
	Avec lui quatro cento co*n*pagnon.
5140	A Baldras alirent, qi ne pi si o non;*
	Bovo apelle ses presti e clerençon,
	De un flume el oit fato un fon;
	E si le dè la soa benecion. (3395)
	Olio e cresme li çetò a foson,
5145	Salmi le dist, e mante leçion.
	Doncha veisés veilard e g(arç)on,*
	Homes e femes, e petit valaston,
	Por amor Deo çetar·se in le fon. (3400)
	Pois alirent e trovare*n*t Macon;
5150	Tot li ont brisé la teste e li gropon.

5124 Reinhold: po[r] paüre (emend); Rosellini: po[r] paure
Rubric 140 (after 5125) Keller: gorcher; 7 for *et* (twice)
5138 MS., Rosellini: fi; Reinhold: fi (emend)
5139 Reinhold: quatro cento
5140 Reinhold, Rosellini: pisi o non
5143 Rosellini: dé
5146 MS., Reinhold, Rosellini: veilard e gon
5148 Reinhold: çetar-se; Rosellini: çetarse

Bovo le voit, si s'en rise a foson;
Corches apela Bovo, si le mis por rason,
"Çivaler, sire, ça no vos çelaron; (3405)
Preso ò li batesmo, la Deo salvacion;
5155 Par tot teres alirà questo non.
Jusqua in Persie si l'aportarà l'on,
E in Alexandre entorno et inviron.
Quant li soldan li saverà per non (3410)
A nu non falla ni nosa ni tençon."

Rubric 141
Coment Corcher se convertì / E si parlò a Bovo de la fe.
Laisse 142

5160 "Corchés," dist Bovo, "e no ve·l quer çeler;
Quando eo pase da cesta part de mer,
Ne le veni mie por çanter ni danser.
Ançi, le vini por mia arma salver, (3415)
E por Deo conbatre e çostrer,
5165 Contra color qe volust li sepolcro violer.
Vegna qi volé, si fust cento miler,
Tuti no li doto la monta d'un diner.   29ʳᵇ
Savés porqoi eo me faço si fer? (3420)
Qe so par voir, e no creço eser mençoner,
5170 Qe çascun qi ven da questa part de mer,
Por le sepolcro servir et honorer,
Se il more, lì no est da parler;*
Avec li santi li fa Deo coroner; (3425)
Unde nu no doten morte ni engonbrer."
5175 Dist Corcher, "Vu avì bona sper;
Serà si de nos, qe aumes pris batister?"
"Oil," dist Bovo, "ne vos estoit doter.
Corona d'or vos farà Deo porter." (3430)
Quella parole li fait si conforter,
5180 Qe plus non dota de la çent averser.

Rubric 141 (after 5159) Keller: conuerti
5161 Reinhold: e' ò pasé; Rosellini: e ò pasé
5166 MS.: fust en cento (*en* expunctuated and crossed out)
5168 Reinhold, Rosellini: por qoi
5169 Reinhold: sò

Rubric 142
Coment Corchés fu batiçé *et* pois / alioit a convertir soa çant.
Laisse 143

	Quant Corchés oit pris bateçamant,
	E de sa tere li petit e li grant,
	La novelle se porte darer e davant. (3435)
	Quando li soldan li soit, ne*n* fu pais çojant;
5185	Qe quel Corchés era le plus manant,
	Qe trover se poust en tot Jerusalant.
	Adonc apelle Baldichin, son enfant,
	"Filo," fait il, "prendés, e vos comant,* (3440)
	Çinqua*n*ta mil d·i meltri de nos çant.
5190	Aleç a Corchés, dites qe je li mant,
	Qe demanes vegna a li mo*n* comant."
	S'el no·l vol fare, morto sia eramant;
	Ne ge lasés tera ni casamant. (3445)
	Si le prendés, si me·l mené davant."
5195	E cil le dist, "Faron li ves talant."
	Quel Baldichin si fo pro e valant;
	Filz li soldan, si l'amoit dolçemant;*
	Ancora estoit çovençel et enfant. (3450)
	El fa soner ses grailes en ojant,
5200	Dont s'armare*n*t çele jent mescreant.
	Çinqua*n*ta mille mo*n*tent en auferant;
	Tant çivalcent e darer e davant,
	Vene*n*t a Baldras una dema*n* por ta*n*p. (3455)
	Corcher se leve a l'aube parisant;
5205	Qua*n*do vi quelle ensegne, si le va reconosant,
	O el vi Bovo, si le dist en ojant,
	"Çivaler Deo, el vos va malamant;
	Venu è li soldan, cu*n* una çente grant; (3460)
	Par voir saçés, averon torniema*n*t."
5210	Bovo responde, "E altro no*n* demant,
	Qe de ma vie nen curo plus niant.
	Qe çest mo*n*do ert cu*n* un trepas de vant;

Rubric 142 (after 5180) line 1: 7 for *et*; Rosellini: Chorchés. line 2: Reinhold: Al(i) oit; Rosellini: Alioit à convertir soa . . .

5188 Reinhold: en [v]os (for *enos*, his MS. reading); Rosellini: e vos (emend)
5190 Rosellini: Chorchés
5192 Reinhold: no-l vol . . . sia eramant . . . ; Rosellini: S'el no'l vol . . . sia . . .
5194 Reinhold: me-l; Rosellini: me'l
5205 Reinhold, Rosellini: qaelle

	Qi en lui s'en fie, si vene a niant; (3465)	
	Deo soit ben qi ait bon talant,*	29ᵛᵃ
5215	E qi lu serve n'oit guerdon tant.	
	Nen saust dire hon qe soit vivant,	
	Tant cuito ferir de·l trençer de mun brant.	
	Sor celle jent qi venent d'Oriant (3470)	
	Qe ma venue conprarà si çeramant	
5220	Qe no l'oit si unques nul merçaant."	
	A le parole qe çesti vont disant, . . .*	
	E Baldichin, qe filz est li soldant,	
	Si oit pris tuto son guarnimant, (3475)	
	E fu monté sor un çival ferant.	
5225	Ven a la tere da la porta davant;	
	Ad alta vos el criò altamant,	
	"Corchés," dist il, "fates vos qi davant;	
	Parler vos vojo e dir de mon talant, (3480)	
	Ço qe vos manda mon per li s(o)ldant."*	
5230	E quel le dist qe se fait en avant,	
	"Veeç moi? E son qi a·l presant."	

Rubric 143

Coment Baldachi, qe filz estoit li soldan, / Alloit a la tere por pa(r)ler a Corcher.*

Laisse 144

	Baldichin parole quant oit Corcher veu:*
	"Dì mo, Corcher, parquoi es recreu? (3485)
	Ça à arenojé Macometo e Cau,
5235	E cri en Deo, qe fo preso e (v)endu,
	E da li Çudé en su la cros metu?"
	Dist Corcher, "È tu parço venu?
	Saçì par voire, eo creço ben in Jesu." (3490)

5221 Reinhold: disant . . . [sic]

5227 Reinhold: q[u]i (emend)

5229 MS.: saldant; Reinhold, Rosellini: soldant

5231 see 5227, Reinhold, emendation, q[u]i

Rubric 143 (after 5231) line 1: Reinhold: Baldachi[n] (emend); MS.: lis olda; Keller: estoit lis olday; Mussafia: li solday. line 2: MS.: alatere; MS., Keller: paler; Reinhold, Rosellini: pa[r]ler (emend)

5233 Reinhold, Rosellini: par quoi

5234 Reinhold: Ça a' renoié; Rosellini: Ça a renoié

5235 MS.: nendu. Reinhold: cri' . . . vendu (emend for *ne ndu*); Rosellini: vendu

5237 Reinhold, Rosellini: par ço

Dist Baldichin, "Tu ne serà deçeu;
5240　Qe por la gorçe en serì apendu."
　　　Dist Corcher, "Ne te doto un festu;
　　　E e defenderò a lança *et* a scu,
　　　La fe de Deo e la soa salu; (3495)
　　　Qe Machometo e li (s)o Deo Cau
5245　Nen valt mie la monte d'un fu."*
　　　E si le dist, "Ça sereç asalu,*
　　　Si parerà com el averà vertu."

Rubric 144
Coment Baldechin retorne a sa jent, / Si·lli foit armer *et* allent a·lla bataille.
Laisse 145

　　　A soa çent fu Baldichin torner,* (3500)
　　　De graille fa soner plus de quaranta ser.
5250　Pain s'adobe, quella jent renojer;
　　　Cinquanta mile sunt a çival monter
　　　Por asalir la tere, se sonto aprosmer.
　　　Bovo oldì la nose, le cri et la uer, (3505)
　　　Dist a Corcher, "El nos conven armer;
5255　Alen defors cun qui a tornojer,
　　　Se nu muron nu averon bon loer;*
　　　Mejo vojo morir, qe star qi presoner."
　　　"Por la ma fois," ço le dist Corcher, (3510)
　　　"Questa parole ben est d'agraer."　　　　　　　　29^(vb)
5260　Or doncha veisés qui çivaler
　　　Le arme prendre, e salir a destrer.
　　　Bovo si fi soa çent armer,
　　　E si le fait çascun de lor croxer,* (3515)

5239 Reinhold: sera' deçeü
5244 MS.: li fo; Reinhold: li fo deo Caü; Rosellini: li so deo Cau
5245 MS., Reinhold, Rosellini: fu
5246 Reinhold: E cil le dist.. (emend)
5247 Rosellini: parerea
Rubric 144 (after 5247) 7 for *et*. MS., Reinhold: Retorne; Keller: sil / li . . . alla
5253 Reinhold: et la ver; Rosellini: e la uer
5257 Reinhold: q[u]i (emend)
5259 Rosellini: da graer
5260 Reinhold: Or . . . veïst (emend for MS. *veises*); Rosellini: Qi doncha veises
5263 MS.: croxer; Reinhold: coroer (emend for *cioxer*?); Rosellini: aoxer

	Davant le piç por mejo reguarder.
5265	Quant fu armé, no se volse entarder;
	La porta fa avrir e li pont abaser.
	Fora ensirent, sens nosa e tençer
	Bovo davanti, sor Rondel son destrer. (3520)
	A·l primer colpo ne fait un trabuçer;
5270	Pois fer un altro, si ne fe a·l tel ter*
	Avantqe l'aste el poust briser,
	Nen fait .vii. si vilment aler,
	Qe de soa vite non ert nula sper. (3525)
	Pois tra Clarençe, qe trença volunter,
5275	A qi un colpo el ne poit doner,
	De soa vite non ait nulle penser.
	Aprés de lui si se vait Corcher;
	Da l'altra part, fu Baldichin li Escler. (3530)
	Doncha veisés un gran stor començer,
5280	Tant pe, tant pugni por la plaça voler,
	E tante testes veisés colper,
	A voide selle foir tanti destrer,
	Qe de·l veoir s'en poroit l'on merveler. (3535)
	En me la voie atraverso un senter,
5285	Bovo e Baldichin se voit a incontrer;
	L'un contra l'altro lasa aler le destrer;
	Ça olderì bataila meravilosa e fer.

Rubric 145
Coment Bovo e Baldechin s'encontrent / a li canpo e Bovo li oncis a la spee.*
Laisse 146

	Quant en le canpo s'encontrent li baron, (3540)
	Bovo e Baldichin ensenbre se çostron.
5290	Baldechin guarde e si vide Bovon,
	Qe davant soi avoit la cros enson;
	Dont conòlt ben qe non era Sclavon,*

5264 Rosellini: Devant
5270 Rosellini: alteler
5272 Reinhold: ·VII·; Rosellini: .VII.
5277 Rosellini: Aprés
5279 Reinhold: veïsés, also 5281
5282 Reinhold: foïr
5284 Reinhold: me'
Rubric 145 (after 5287) Keller: sencontrerent
5291, 5295 Reinhold: en son

Ne no*n* estoit de celle legion (3545)
De qui qe adore*nt* Trivига*nt* e Macon.
5295 Ferir le vait desor l'elmo enson;*
Nen poit trençer la mo*n*ta d'un boton.
E Bovo fer lui, se(n)ça nul question;
Desor li eume a l'ovre Salamon. (3550)
Cosi li tre*n*çe, co*n* faroit un baston,
5300 Ni por la cofie non oit guarison.
Cosi la trençe, como un pano d'aquiton;*
Tota la teste por mité li deron
Si le trençò li peito e li gropon, (3555)
Tros in la selle, no*n* fi arestason.
5305 En do mité li mis tros li arçon.
Quant Sarasin vi cair quel baron,   30ra
Dist l'un a l'altro, "Porqe le çelaron?
A gran mervelle celu est prodon; (3560)
A quelo colpo no resenbla garçon.
5310 Qi l'atenderà non averà guarison."
En fua torne e par poi e par mon.*

Rubric 146
Coment (pain) furent morti e scunfiti / Par la mort de Baldechin.*
Laisse 147

Quant qui pain de la lo mescreant
Vi son segnor aler si malamant, (3565)
Tot li plus meltre avoit tel spavant,
5315 Ne l'atenderoit par tot l'or d'Oriant.
En fua torne a miler e a çant;
E Bovo si le incalçe cu*n* Clarença ses brant.
Tanto l'oit porté Rondel son auferant, (3570)
Q'el oit pasé un pois e un pendant;
5320 L'oste se lasa darer dos legue grant.
A·l paser de cel pois, el s'oit guardé davant;
El vi da una chaverne ensir un mal se*r*pant.

5294 Rosellini: adoret
5297 MS.: seça; Reinhold: se(n)ça (emend); Rosellini: se[n]ça (emend)
5306 Reinhold: caïr
5308 Rosellini: mervele
Rubric 146 (after 5311) line 1: MS.: pepin; Keller: pepin . . . escunfiti; Mussafia, Guessard: e scunfiti; Reinhold: païn (emend) . . . Morti; Rosellini: pain
5322 MS.: ſpant

Plus estoit il noire, no*n* est ag(r)amant;* (3575)
Par boce bute e fois e vanp.*
5325 Bovo le vi, de rir non à talant;
Volunter retornase l'auferant.
Quant cil s*er*pe*nt* li vait tutor davant,
E·l bon Rondel li vait guischisant,* (3580)
Ne se le lasa aprosmer de niant.
5330 Bovo mena la spee, e menu e sovant,
Se il se smaie, ne vos çi mervelant;
Deo reclame e la majesté sant.

Rubric 147

Coment Bovo por la paure de quel s*er*pant / dist la oracion, e fi a Deo la pregere.
Laisse 148

Bovo fu en cel po molto doloros e (las),* (3585)
E vide li s*er*pant qe senbla Satanas;
5335 Reclama Deo e·l baron san Nicholas:*
"Ai, sire Deo, qe tot li mo*n*do f(o)rmas,*
Adam li primer ho*n* de tes dos man crias,
De limon de la tere si cu*n* tu comandas, (3590)
Et Eva sa muler de sa costa gitas,
5340 Paradis perdirent en esilio li ma*n*das;
E vivere*nt* a po(in)e e vestire*nt* dras
Porçoqe co*n*tra fe, ço qe tu comandas
E lu e lor legnages en Enferno ma*n*das, (3595)

5323 MS.: agamant; Reinhold: noire, no*n* est agamant; Rosellini: noire non est agramant
5324 Reinhold, Rosellini: boce . . . fois. . . .
5327 MS.: spēt
5331 Rosellini: s'esmaie
5332 Reinhold, Rosellini: Majesté
Rubric 147 (after 5332) line 1: MS.: ſpēt; Keller: ser-/pant. line 2: Keller: fi a deo
5333 MS.: lais; Reinhold, Rosellini: las (emend)
5334 Reinhold: E[l] (emend)
5336 MS.: fermas; Reinhold, Rosellini: formas (emend)
5338 Reinhold: De li mon; Rosellini: De limon de la tere . . .
5341 MS.: porme; Reinhold: poine (emend); Rosellini: poine (emend for MS.: *paime*)
5342 Reinhold, Rosellini: Por ço qe
5343 Reinhold: enfer (no) ma*n*das (emendation); Rosellini: en enferno . . .

	Ilec starent tantqe le visitas.
5345	De çelo venisi en tera, par nu qe ta(n)t amas;*
	San Gabriel angle a la Verçen mandas,
	Q'ela te reçevese, e pois si l'eno*n*bras.
	En Belieme nasisi, qua*n*do la stela mostras;* (3600)
	Li trois rois te quirire*nt*, Merchior e Jaspas;
5350	Oro et encenso *et* mira portare*nt* in lor bras.
	Son oferta prendisi, pais ne la refuas; 30rb
	Trenta trois an*n*i in çesto mo*n*do duras,
	Pois vos vendè li traitor de Judas.* (3605)
	Trenta diner vos vendè cil malvas;
5355	Metu fosi en cros en meço de dos las.
	A·l terço çorno, susitasi Deo veras,
	En l'Asension de sovra celo montas,
	E·l jorno de Pasche le Spirto santo envojas,* (3610)
	A li Apostole qe vu tant amas;
5360	Si cu*n* è voir qe Laçaro susitas
	Si me guardé, e moi e mo*n* çivals,
	Da questa bestie qe senbla Satanas;
	Qe tel paure no*n* avì unqa jamas."* (3615)

Rubric 148

Coment Bovo por paure de cil (serpant) . . . / soa orason; e quando l'oit dite, si vait vi/gorosemant co*n* li serpant, et si le oncis.
Laisse 149

	Quant Bovo oit fenia soa orason,
5365	Dont fo plu fer qe no(n) ert un lion,
	El ten la spee, don a or è li pon;
	Por maltalant vait sovra li dragon,

5345 MS.: tat; Reinhold, Rosellini: ta[n]t, emend
5348 Reinhold, Rosellini: nasisi
5350 7 for *et*
5352 Reinhold, Rosellini: Trenta trois
5357 Reinhold, Rosellini: desovra (one word)
5358 Reinhold: E i*n* jorno; Rosellini: El jorno
5362 Reinhold: bestia
Rubric 148 (after 5363) line 1: MS.: sperpant; Keller: cil serpant soa orason; Reinhold: *serpant [dit] (emend); Rosellini: serpant [dist] (emend). line 2: Keller: /oit viro / rose mant com
5365 MS.: nou; Reinhold: non (emend); Rosellini: non

	E cil a lui qe pais ne le doton, (3620)
	Bovo li fer desovra li gropon.
5370	Nen po tre*n*çer valisant un boton;
	Tros colpi li fer desovra enson.
	Non po trençer, tanto dur son,
	E quela serpe de malvasa rason, (3625)
	Morto l'aust, nen fust l'aragon*
5375	Qe si li fer de li pe environ,
	Q'elo li fait cair a·l sablon.
	Bovo le vi, si·l ferì en ponçon;
	Por me li vent(r)e do*nt* non oit guarison. (3630)
	Elo li trençe le figa e·l polmon;*
5380	Morto li verse aprés un çexon.*
	Quant Bovo le vi morto a li peron,
	Nen seria si çojant par tot l'or de·l mon.
	Ormais se te*nt* il a guarison; (3653)
	Da lu se parte, ponçe son aragon,
5385	Et oit pasé e li po e li mon.
	Davanti soi el vide li dojon,
	E de Baldras le gran tore enson.
	A(n)cora d·i pain vide a gran foson, (3640)
	Qe s'en fuçent entorno et environ.
5390	Tanto l'oit travalé çelle malvas dragon,
	Q'elo no*n* cure qi s'en fuça o non.

5370, 5372 Reinhold: pò
5371, 5387 Reinhold, Rosellini: en son
5377 Reinhold: si-l; Rosellini: si'l
5378 MS.: vente; Reinhold, Rosellini: vent[r]e (emend)
5379 Reinhold: figà e 'l polmon; Rosellini: e 'l
5380 Reinhold, Rosellini: aprés
5383 Reinhold, Rosellini: Oimais
5385 Reinhold: po'
5388 MS.: Acora; Reinhold, Rosellini: A[n]cora (emend)

Rubric 149

Coment Bovo quant oit morto li serpante, / si s'en retorna ver li campo tuto lasés, e dist / A Corchés la novelle, dond(e) s'en merveilla.

Laisse 150

        Quant Bovo fu arer retorné,
        A Corchés oit la novella nonçé, (3645)
        Ço qe li ert venu et incontré.   30va
5395 Corchés l'oì, toto fu spaventé;
        "Bovo," fait il, "vu avés ben ovré.
        Daqe Deo v'oit da·l se*r*pant delivré,
        A gran mervele Deo si v'oit amé. (3650)
        Tanto estoit cil serpant doté,
5400 Nul homo olsava stare in sta contré;
        Ça n'oit morto plus de quaranta sé."
        E dist Bovo, "Molto m'à travalé;
        Nen fust Ro*n*del qi m'oi ben aidé,* (3655)
        Qe le ferì co*n* boçe e cum pe."*
5405 Dist Corchés, "Poisqe estes scanpé,
        Deo e santi ne soja adoré.
        Nu si avon cest canp afiné,
        Deo e santi ne soja adoré." (3660)
        Tota la proja, q'i trovent pro li pre,*
5410 Tota la ont e covi e levé.
        A Bovo fu la proja delivré;
        Muli e çival, palafroi enfeltré,
        Non retene Bovo un diner moené. (3665)
        A soa çent et a qui de la çité,
5415 Tota n'ont partia e doné;
        E vo, segnurs, par voir qe vu saçé,
        Tanto stete Bovo oltra la mer salé,
        Qe li termen fu venu et apros(m)é,* (3670)

    Rubric 149 (after 5391) line 1: MS., Reinhold: Morto; Keller: tous; Guessard: Bovo; Mussafia: bouo. line 2: Keller: sen; Reinhold: lasés; Rosellini: Si s'en … lasés. line 3: Keller: sen; Reinhold, Rosellini: Corchés; MS.: dondo; Reinhold, Rosellini: donde
    5392 Rosellini: retornè
    5395 Reinhold: oï (dieresis and grave accent)
    5403 Reinhold, Rosellini: moi
    5405 Rosellini: Pos qe
    5409 MS.: Pro; Rosellini: Por
    5412 Reinhold: en feltré; Rosellini: enfeltré
    5413 Reinhold: moëné; Rosellini: moemé (cf. Holden)
    5416 Reinhold: E' vo', …
    5418 MS., Rosellini: aprosé; Reinhold: apros[m]é

De li quatro ani e conpli e pasé.
5420 Molto i oit ben sa ovra devisé,
E le sepolcro servi et honoré.
Quant à ço fato, elo prist conçé
Por retorné se fu aparilé; (3675)*
Avec lui, ses çivaler prisé.
5425 Ven a Corchés, si le oit arasné:
"Corchés," fait il, "eo sui porpensé;
Conpli ai tota ma volunté.
Da moi avanti e vojo tornar aré." (3680)

Rubric 150
Coment Bovo dapoisqe il oit conpli / li terme q'el avoit in promesis a li rois d'Ingeltere prist çonçé a Corcher *et* a soa / Gent, si s'en torna ad Antone.*
Laisse 151

Bovo d'Antone nen volse plus demorer;
5430 Quant li termen li vent a 'prosmer,
Qe a·l sepolcre devoit servir et honorer,
Adoncha prist conçeo da Corcher.
"Corcher," fait il, "el me conven aler, (3685)
En mia tere a veor ma muler,*
5435 E mes enfant qe sont baçaler.
Se le volés avec moi herer,
Nen vojo avoir valisant un diner,
Qe con eso moi non sia parçoner."* (3690)
Corcher, quan l'olde, si prist a larmojer;   30vb
5440 Ben alase l'on li trato d'un arçer
Avantiqe il posa un sol moto parler.
"Bovo," fait il, "doncha me volés laser.
Daqe vos plais de l'aler, (3695)
A Deo vos vojo et a santi comander.
5445 Mais d'una ren e vos vojo en projer:

5423 MS.: retorne; Reinhold: retorne[r] (emend); Rosellini: retorne
Rubric 150 (after 5428) line 1: Keller: da pois qe i loit conpli. line 2: Keller: MS.: Rois; li terme qe lavoit inpromesis . . . dingel-/tere; Reinhold: Li . . . inprom(es)is . . . Rois; Rosellini: Li terme . . . inpromesis. line 3: 7 for *et*; Keller: il oit sentorna; Reinhold: çonçé (first cedilla is in square brackets)
5430 Reinhold, Rosellini: vent aprosmer
5433 Rosellini: eo me conven . . .
5434 MS.: muleR.
5445 Reinhold: en proïer; Rosellini: enproier

	Se ma de ça venise mesaçer,
	De vos afaire me manda a conter.
	Si vonter li oldirò como d'un me frer." (3700)
	Responde Bovo, "Ben est da otrier;
5450	Et eo si le farò de greç e volunter."*
	Quando l'un da l'altro se ven a desevrer,
	Çascun prendent des oil a larmojer.
	Bovo s'en vait a un dormun entrer, (3705)
	Avec lui furent ses çivaler.
5455	Cola le vele et vait por l'alto mer;*
	Tant naçarent por vento e por orer,
	E por la tere par mont e par river,
	Trosqu'a Antone nen volse seçorner. (3710)
	Quando Druxiana le vi reparier,
5460	S'ela oit çoja, non è da demander;*
	Anbi se vont a 'coler e baser.

Rubric 151

Coment Bovo fu d'oltra mer reparié et vent / A 'Ntone, et il le trova Drusiana sa mu(i)ler et / A(vec) le Sinibaldo et si li contò novelle.*
Laisse 152

	Quando Druxiana oit Bovo veu,*
	Unqua jamés si çojant nen fu, (3715)
	Qe de sa promese el ert asolu.
5465	E Druxiana l'oit por rason metu,
	Qe tere son qu'el oit veu.*
	"Dama," fait il, "e ò ben veu
	Celle lois o Deo fo metu; (3720)
	La tera santa çercha tot por menu,*

5446 Reinhold: Se ma'
5447 Reinhold: mandà; Reinhold, Rosellini: aconter
5448 Rosellini: oldirò omo (cf. Martin)
5451 Rosellini: l'u da l'altro (cf. Holden)
5455 Reinhold: cola le vele
5461 Reinhold, Rosellini: vont acoler
Rubric 151 (after 5461) line 1: 7 for et; Keller: uent doltra. line 2: MS.: murer?; Keller: antone . . . mulier; Reinhold: [A] Antone . . . ille[c] . . . muiler (emend); Rosellini: Antone et ille[c] . . . muiler. line 3: MS.: Alliec (?); Keller: alliec le conto; Mussafia: aviec; Reinhold: Avec (emend); Rosellini: Aviec
5466 Reinhold: q(u)' el oit veü (emend)
5469 Reinhold: Tera . . . çercha'; Rosellini: Tera

5470	E gran bataile e fate e vençu,
	Dont a li batesmo ne son plus de .X. mil venu,*
	Li qual creent Macometo e Cau."
	Dist Druxiana, "Beneto soja Jesu, (3725)
	Qe sano e salvo vos estes revenu."

Rubric 152

Coment Bovo ancora parole a Drusiane / Si li conte de li serpant q'el i oncise.*
Laisse 153

5475	"Dama," dist Bovo, "entendés mun talant,*
	Nen savés mie la pena et li tormant,
	Qe e ò enduré contra un mal serpant.
	Morto m'aust nen (fust) me auferant, (3730)
	Qe li ferì si forte e duremant,
5480	Q'elo·l çetò roverso en le canp,
	E pois l'ancisi a ma spea trençant.
	Por cella bestie tant proi e Deo e sant,*
	Qe ver de le i me farent guarant." (3735)
	Dist Druxiana, "Non siés plus enfant." 31ʳᵃ
5485	Da qui avanti vait li çanter enforçant;
	Nu lasaren de Bovo da ste çorno en avant;
	Asa durò e pene e tormant.
	De li rois Pepin ben est qe je vos çant, (3740)
	E de dama Berte, qe avoit li pe grant,
5490	Ço qe li vene en un petit tanp.*

5471 Reinhold, Rosellini: batesme
Rubric 152 (after 5474) line 1: Keller: encora. line 2: Keller: qe li; MS.: qe liocise; Rosellini: qe li oncise
5475 Reinhold, Rosellini: entendé
5477 Keller: eo endure
5478 MS · fufust; Keller: maust nen fu fust; Reinhold: nen fust me . . .
5480 Keller: Qe lol çeto; Mussafia: q'elo-l; Reinhold: Q'elo·l çetò; Rosellini: Q'elo'l çetò
5481 Keller: lancisi ama
5482 Keller: proie; Reinhold: proiè Deo; Rosellini: proié
5483 Keller: Qe uer de le mie; Mussafia: ime = i me; Reinhold: de le i me
5485 Rosellini: avanti vai li . . .
5486 Keller: laseren . . . daste; Mussafia: MS. = lasaren; da ste
5487 Keller: A sa; Mussafia: Asa
5489 Keller: dame; Mussafia: MS. = dame
5490 Keller: Eo qe . . .

7.4 Karleto
Rubric 153
Oldu avés de Bovo d'Antone, coment pasò la mare / E servì a·lli sepolcro quatro an(n)i, e si è arer venu. / Or se comence de li rois Pepin e dama Berte.*
Laisse 154

        Segnur, pla vos oir une noble cançon,*
        De stormeno e de bataile e de gra*n* caplexo*n*,
        E in apreso de grande traixon?*
        De tel mervile uncha no oldì hon.*
5495   Oi aveç de le dux Bovon, (5)
        E de Druxiane a la clere façon;
        Como l'uno e l'autre durò gran passion,
        Cerchò li mondo entorno et inviron.
        Or lairon de lui a soe guarison;
5500   Meltre çivaler de lui atrover nen poron; (10)
        E ses dos filz furent de gran renon.
        De li rois Pepin or nu vos çantaron,
        E de dos ses filz qe li cor Deo mal don,
        Qe de son pere farent gran traison,
5505   E de dama Berte a la clere façon; (15)
        L'un oit nome (Lanfroi) par non,*
        L'altro Landris, ensi cun nu trovon.

    Rubric 153 (after line 5490) line 1: Keller: ol du . . . dantone; Mussafia: oldu. Chichmaref, Rosellini: avés. line 2: MS.: anui; Keller: senu alli . . . anni/ esten; Guessard: e si est; Mussafia: MS. = esie; Reinhold, Chichmaref: servi; Reinhold, review of Chichmaref, MS. seiui; Chichmaref: alli . . . anni; Mussafia: MS. = servi; Guessard: servi; Rosellini: a li sepolcro. line 3: MS., Reinhold: Rois Pepin
    5491 Chichmaref, Reinhold: oïr (as always)
    5493 Keller: An apreso; Mussafia et al.: E in; Chichmaref, Reinhold: traïxon (as always). Cf. l. 5504.
    5494 Keller, Chichmaref, Reinhold, Rosellini: uncha; Chichmaref: oldi
    5495 Chichmaref, Reinhold: Oï (as always; cf. 5509, 5514, etc.); Rosellini: Oi (as always)
    5497 Keller: luno e lautre
    5498 Keller: en torno et in uiron
    5500 Keller: a trover; Mussafia: atrover
    5503 Keller: maldon; Chichmaref: fils; Frati, Reinhold [review of Chichmaref]: filz
    5504 Keller, Chichmaref: grant traïson; MS., Frati, Reinhold [review of Chichmaref]: gran
    5506 MS.: Çifroi; Reinhold, Rosellini: Lanfroi (emend for *Çifroi* [cf. Reinhold, lines 122, 124])
    5507 Keller: Laltro . . . en si . . .

Rubric 154
Coment dama Berte, la reine de France, / Norì Bertelle et Lanfroi e Landris.
Laisse 155

	Or entendés, segnors, qe Jesu beneie,*
	Le glorios, le filz sante Marie;
5510	Questa cançon non è de triçarie. (20)
	Oi avés quando Berta vene d'Ongarie,
	Con quela dame qe la pres en conpagnie.*
	De le en fi si grande felonie
	Qe jamés non fu una major oie;
5515	De le remis dos filz e una fille. (25)
	Mais cella dama Berte, par soa cortexie,
	Cosi la onora con Karleto son fie.*
	Quela Bertela non obliò pais mie,*
	Con eso Karleto la tenoit en conpagnie.
5520	De quella Bertella s'el serà qi vos die, (30)
	Vos oldirés como fi gran stoltie,
	Quant a Milon se dè par soa amie.
	Via la menò in estranie partie;
	De le naque Rolando li ardie,
5525	Qe in çeste mondo avè gran segnorie. (35)
	Mais qui de sa mer ne fi pois felonie,* 31rb
	Qe le traì a li rois Marsie,
	Por grant avoir e por gran manentie.*

Rubric 154 (after 5507) Keller: raine; Chichmaref: raïne; Reinhold, Rosellini: reine (corrected Morini 1992)
5508 Chichmaref, Reinhold: beneïe (as always)
5510 Keller: none de; Mussafia: non e
5511 MS.: quando; Keller: dongarie
5512 Chichmaref, Reinhold, Rosellini: q'ela pres
5514 Chichmaref: iamés . . . maior
5517 Chichmaref: Cosí (always; it will not be noted again)
5518 Keller: pus
5519 Keller: coneso; Mussafia et al.: con eso
5520 Keller: sel; Chichmaref: sera (always, not noted again)
5523 Reinhold: estranje; Rosellini: estraine (corrected Morini 1992)
5525 Chichmaref: ave gran . . .
5526 Chichmaref, Reinhold: qui'. MS.: ne; Reinhold, Rosellini: ni fi
5527 Reinhold: traï (as always)
5528 Chichmaref: grant manentie; Frati: gran (correction of Chichmaref; cf. Reinhold, review of Chichmaref); Rosellini: mantenie (corrected Morini 1992)

Rubric 155
Coment cresent Lanfroi e Landris / E Bertelle, soa sor, qe filz estoit de celle dame ch'estoit da Magançe.*
Laisse 156

          Segnur baron, plaroit vos ascolter?
5530   De li rois Pepin començà li çanter, (40)
          E d'Aquilon, li segnor de Baiver,
          E de Bernardo, e Morando de River;
          Quisti furent de Pepin conseler.
          Mais li rois oit dos filz, qe molto fait asalter;
5535   E da li baron li fait servir et onorer, (45)
          E por sa mer molto se font doter,
          Qe qui de Magançe non estoit si lainer,*
          Qe de sa jent nen fust quarant çivaler.
          Ben veoit Aquilon ço qe poroit encontrer;
5540   Mais por Lanfroi qe se fasoit plus alter,* (50)
          E por li rois qe tanto li tenoit çer,
          El no onsoit un sol moto parler.*
          Mais qui enfant prendent si a monter
          Qe en la corte non avoient son per.
5545   E cil Lanfroi fato era si fronter,* (55)
          Et a mervile era bon çivaler;
          Non era meltre quant se fasoit torner,*
          Por tanto son per li tenoit plus çer;
          Nen fasoit ren ne le fust agraer.*

    Rubric 155 (after 5528) line 2: Reinhold, Rosellini: file (emend for *filz*). line 3: Keller: chestoit; Rosellini: che estoit (Morini 1992 corrects to *che stoit*)
    5529 Rosellini: Segnur Baron
    5530 Keller: commença
    5531 Keller: daquilon
    5533 Rosellini: Questi (corrected Morini 1992)
    5534 Keller: a salter; Mussafia: asalter, "exhausser"
    5537 Keller: lamer; Mussafia et al.: lainer; Chichmaref, Reinhold: qui' (always for demonstrative pronoun or adjective. It will not be noted again.) Keller, Reinhold: Mangançe
    5538 Keller: ient
    5539 Keller: Sen ueoit; Mussafia et al.: Ben
    5540 Chichmaref: qe fasoit; MS., Frati: qe se fasoit (cf. Reinhold, review of Chichmaref)
    5543 Keller: amonter
    5548 Rosellini: tenoir (corrected Morini 1992)
    5549 Reinhold, Rosellini: à graer

5550 Mais çel enfant ne se volse contenter, (60)
Qe tradimento pensarent de son per:
De lui e de dama Berte voloir atoseger.
M'i non soit mie ço qi li doit encontrer;*
Ancor por altro tenpo i·l conpra çer.*

Rubric 156
Coment Lanfroi e Landris tenoit / Parlamento con qui de Magançe.
Laisse 157

5555 Grant fu la cort, meravilosa e grant, (65)
Qe Pepin tent de conti e d'amirant;
Si le fo Aquilon e Çofré e Morant.
Mais desor tot se farent plus avant
Landris e Lanfroi con eso ses parant.
5560 A Karleto petito no atendoit homo vivant, (70)
S'el non estoit de River Morant;
E quel le tenoit si con per son enfant.
Mais li dos traites, qe n'avoit mal entant,
Cun ses paranti farent un parlamant.
5565 En una çanbre se metent çeleemant; (75)
Landris parloe, qe li cor Deo crevant:
"Segnur," fait il, "senpre serò dolant,
Quando ma mer fo morta si vilmant.
Se a mon conseil volez eser creant,
5570 Nu seren rois de France e de Normant. (80)   31va
Tant cuito faire par me ençantamant,
Mon per e Berte anbes comunelmant

5553 Keller: Mi; Chichmaref: ço q'i; Chichmaref, Reinhold, Rosellini: M'i; Reinhold: ço qi li

5554 Keller, Chichmaref: il conpra; Reinhold, review of Chichmaref: i-l conpra; Rosellini: i 'l

5555 Rosellini: mervelosa (corrected Morini 1992)

5556 Keller: damirant

5558 Keller: de sor

5559 Keller: coneso (cf. Mussafia, p. 308)

5561 Keller: Sel

5563 Keller: navoit; Reinhold: traïtes (as always)

5566 Reinhold, Rosellini: Lanfroi (emend)

5571 Keller: auto; Mussafia et al.: cuito; Chichmaref: me' (from MEDIU[M]), his standard punctuation

5572 Keller: aubes; Mussafia et al.: anbes

       Seront morti a dol et a tormant."
       Quant cil oent parler cosi l'infant,
5575   Dist l'un a l'atro, "Questo è bon co*n*venant."* (85)
       Nen fu de lor ni petito ni grant,
       Qe no le die, "Fà·lo seguremant;
       Çascun de nos te serà en guarant,
       E si·n seremo e legri e çojant."

Rubric 157
Coment Landris cuitoit la novelle / A celes autres de Magançe.*
Laisse 158

5580   Quando Landris avoit dito soa rason, (90)
       A qui traites savoit molto bon.*
       Mais (Lanfroi), q'era menor garçon,*
       A lui non plasoit de cele traison.
       Elo le dist, "Entendés moi, baron:
5585   Nu semo tot d'una legion. (95)
       Se nostra mer fe quella mespreson
       Contra quella dame, qe tanto li fe don,
       Se pene ne portò, questo blasemo non son.
       E cela dame, qe Berte avoit non,
5590   Estoit ben de si bona rason,* (100)
       Jamais a nos no mostrò mal gujerdon.
       Cosi ne ten con fumes ses feon;

    5574 Keller: cent . . . linfant; Mussafia et. al: oent . . . l'infant
    5575 Chichmaref: a l'altro (correction also made by Frati and Reinhold); Rosellini: altro convenant» (corrected by Morini 1992)
    5576 Keller: petits; Mussafia et al.: petito
    5577 Reinhold: Fa-lo seguremant; Rosellini: Falo
    5579 Keller: sin . . . çoiant; Chichmaref, Reinhold: si-n; Rosellini: si'n
    Rubric 157 (after 5579) Keller: autoit; MS., Mussafia, Reinhold, Rosellini: cuitoit; Guessard 1857: cuntoit
    5580 Reinhold, Rosellini: Lanfroi (emend for *Landris*)
    5582 Keller: qera; Reinhold, Rosellini: Landris (emend for *Çofro*). Chichmaref: Çofro c'era (error noted also by Frati, Reinhold [review of Chichmaref])
    5583 Keller: Alui
    5584 Keller: E lo le; Mussafia et al.: Elo le
    5585 Keller: duna; Chichmaref: legïon
    5586, 5587 Chichmaref: fè (as always)
    5591 Keller: Ja mais

```
             Bertela, nostra sor, de ses filz è conpagnon,
             Com ela fust de soa norison;
    5595     Ne nostro per no ne ten por bricon. (105)
             De tota la cort aven li major non;
             Ben poon çivalçer palafroi e ronçon,
             Robe avon e destrer aragon.
             Ancir nos per nu no g'aven rason;
    5600     En cesta cort est molti alti baron, (110)
             Qe de Bavier lì est Aquilon,*
             E si lì est Bernardo de Clermon,
             Morando de River e le dux Sanson.
             Quisti ament Pepin par bona entencion;
    5605     Se vos pensés qe avenir poron (115)
             Por altro tenpo, o por altra sason,
             Non pensarés a queste traison."
             Quant cil entendent, s'inf(ron)çì li grenon,*
             Si li dient q'el estoit un bricon;
    5610     Ço q'elo dist non monta un boton,* (120)
             I lo farà, o el voja o non.
```

5593 Keller: Berta, la nostra sor, . . . compagnon; Chichmaref: Berte la nostra sor . . . compagnon

5594 Keller: come la

5596 Keller, Chichmaref: maior (as always)

5599 Keller: gauen rason

5600 Rosellini: certa cort (corrected Morini 1992)

5601 Keller: bauier; Rosellini: MS. reads "biaver"; Reinhold: Baiver. Keller: Chichmaref, Reinhold, Rosellini: li est (li always unaccented; cf. 5602 etc. Not further noted)

5602 Keller: bernard de; Chichmaref: Bernard de (corrected by Reinhold, review of Chichmaref, wrong line #: 111, not 112)

5604 Chichmaref: entencïon

5607 Reinhold: traïson (as for all forms- traïto etc. It will not be noted again.)

5608 MS.: inforçi; Keller: sinforçi (misquoted by Rosellini); Chichmaref, Reinhold: si' nforçì; Rosellini: si'nforcì

5609 Keller: qe le stoit; Guessard: q'el estoit

5610 Keller: qe lo; Guessard, Mussafia: q'elo

5611 Keller: Ilo fara . . . oel (misquoted by Rosellini); Guessard: I lo . . . o el

Rubric 158
Coment Lanfroi parloe contre / son frer e con\<trar\>ia son dito.*
Laisse 159

        Quando Lanfroi olde son frer parler,*
        Elo li parle cun homes forsoner:*
        "Ai, Landris, no te ven porpenser,*
5615 A quela mort qe morì toa mer? (125)   31vb
        E tu di no voler·la vençer,*
        Contra color qe la farent finer?
        Por celle Deo qi se lasò pener,
        Se unchamais e ve n'oldo parler,
5620 A le mes man tu non porà scanper, (130)
        Qe no t'oncie a mon brando d'açer.
        Doncha, volés senpre eser scuer,*
        Quant poés estre e rois, çivaler?*
        Lanfroi li fait si forte spaventer,
5625 Da ora avanti no olsò plus parler. (135)
        Mais saça par voir, no le fe volunter;
        Mes quando vi li voloir de son frer,
        E de li altri parenti de sa mer,
        Ço qe li plas li vait a otrier.
5630 Nen soit pais Lanfroi ço qe le doit encontrer, (140)

    Rubric 158 (after 5611) Chichmaref: Landfroi... contra (cf. Frati, Reinhold [review of Chichmaref]; line 2: Keller: contrana son dud; Guessard 1857: contraria son dito; Mussafia, "Handschriftlich Studien II": contrana son dito
    5613 Keller: E lo par le... cum... forsonez; Guessard 1857, Mussafia, "Handschriftliche Studien II": Elo... parle; Guessard: forsonez; Chichmaref: cum... forsoner
    5614 Keller, Chichmaref: por penser
    5615 Chichmaref: Aquela... mort que... (corrected Reinhold [review of Chichmaref] qe); Guessard: Aquela que
    5616 Reinhold: dì no voler-la; Guessard: voler la; Chichmaref, Rosellini: volerla
    5619 Chichmaref: uncha mais; Chichmaref: se uncha mais e' ve-n; Guessard: nen oldo; Mussafia: uen
    5622 Rosellini: eser scuser (corrected Morini 1992)
    5623 Chichmaref, Guessard, Reinhold, Rosellini: rois [e]. Chichmaref: çivalers; Frati: ciualer; Guessard: tois [e] çivalers; Frati, Reinhold [review of Chichmaref] çivaler
    5624 MS.: Çofroi; Reinhold, Rosellini: Lanfroi (emend)
    5625 Guessard, Chichmaref: non olso; Reinhold [review of Chichmaref]: no olso
    5629 Guessard: Co
    5630 Chichmaref, Guessard: pas Lanfroi ço q'el; Frati, Mussafia, "Handschriftliche Studien II": pais L. co qe le...; Reinhold, review of Chichmaref: ço qe le

        Poisqe il oit morta Berte e Pepin son per,
        Remis Karleto, le petit baçaler,
        Qe in Spagne se aloit ad alever;
        E li rois Galafrio li avoit si çer
5635 Qe li dè Belisant, sa file, par muler. (145)
        Et elo vene un si bon çivaler,
        Braibant oncis a li brant forbi d'açer;
        E pois cil Karleto f(u) leva enperer;*
        Meesmo l'angle li vene encoroner.
5640 Mervelle oldirés in ceste roman con*n*ter, (150)
        Se vos starés en pais ad scolter.*

Rubric 159
Coment La(n)froi e(t) La*n*dris e li altri ses pa(r)enti
Oncirent li rois Pepin e Berte a venen.*
Laisse 160

        Li rois Pepin, qe sire est de Fra*n*çe,
        Qe tenoit la tere jusquame*n*t in Valançe,
        A gran mervile avoit gran posançe.
5645 En ses dos filz avoit gran fiançe; (155)
        Prodomo estoit *et* a brando *et* a lançe,
        Ver pover jent avoit gran pietançe;
        D·i pover çivaler avoit gran pesançe.
        Par tot part de lui aloit la nomena*n*çe,

    5631 Guessard, Reinhold: Pois qe (as always; not annotated any further); Chichmaref: Pois que . . . et; Reinhold, review of Chichmaref: qe
    5634 Chichmaref: le rois (corrected also by Frati, Reinhold [review of Chichmaref])
    5635 Guessard: dé; Reinhold: li dè; Rosellini: dè
    5638 Reinhold, Rosellini: fu levà enperer (emend; Rosellini: MS. = *fil leva*); Guessard: fil le va; Chichmaref: si s[e] leva . . . ; Reinhold, review of Chichmaref: fu levà e (emend)
    5639 Guessard: en coroner
    5641 Chichmaref, Guessard: ad ascolter (G. misquoted by Rosellini); MS., Reinhold: ad [a]scolter (emend); Reinhold, review of Chichmaref: ad scolter; Mussafia, "Handschriftliche Studien II": MS. reads *scolter*
    Rubric 159 (after 5641) line 1: MS.: Lafroi el Ladris . . . altri parlenti; Keller: ellandris . . . par lenti; Mussafia, "Handschriftliche Studien II": parlenti = parenti (parienti?); Reinhold, Frati, Rosellini: altri parenti. Reinhold, Rosellini: La[n]froi et; Rosellini: MS. = *etLandris*; line 2: MS., Reinhold: Rois; Keller: auenen
    5646 7 for *et* (twice)
    5648 Reinhold, Rosellini: Di pover (as always)

5650 Soa segnoria tot le autre avançe. (160)*
Mais çil (Lan)froi, qe in Deo non oit fiançe,
Ne le portoit ne amor ne liançe;
Par lui oncir sempre stoit en balançe;
Si pris conseil a le segnur de Magançe.
5655 De lui oncir non fi longa tardançe; (165)
De cil penser n'avoit pois tristançe,
Qe in bataile ne portò pesançe.

Rubric 160
Coment (Lanfroi) e Landris tratarent la mort / De son per e de dama Berte, filla li rois de / Ongarie, et anbidos oçirent a venen.*
Laisse 161

Grant fu la cort a Paris la cité,
Par tot França e davant e daré;   32ra
5660 La baronia lì furent asenblé, (170)
Cento civale(r)s fo la jor cor(o)é.
Li rois Pepin a tot oit doné
Robe e destrer, palafro sejorné.
Quant a·l mançer i furent aseté,
5665 Davant Pepin tottora serve en pe (175)
Son filz (Lanfroi), qe mal oit porpensé.
E davant la raine, cun avoit ordené,
Servoit Landris cun les autres donçé.
Çascun avoit tosego e venen destenpré,
5670 Tot li pejor qe il ont trové; (180)
En le vivande, quant furent aporté
De(n)s demetent planament e soé.
Li rois si ne manue, qe ne se n'oit guardé,
E la raine le fist da l'autre le.
5675 E quant ont mançé li dolor li est monté; (185)
Li rois Pepin oit son filz reguardé,

5651 Reinhold, Rosellini: Lanfroi (emend for Çifrei)
Rubric 160 (after 5657) line 1: Reinhold, Rosellini: Lanfroi (emend); line 2: MS., Reinhold: Rois; line 3: Keller: anbi dos . . . auenen; Guessard, Mussafia, "Handschriftliche Studien II": a venen; Reinhold: anbi dos (as always) ocirent; Rosellini: ocirent
5661 MS.: civales; Reinhold, Rosellini: civale[r]s (emend); MS.: corore; Reinhold: coro[r]é; Rosellini: coroé (as always)
5665 MS.: tot tora; Rosellini: tottora
5666 MS.: Çofroi; Reinhold, Rosellini: Lanfroi (emend)
5672 MS.: Deus demetent; Reinhold, Rosellini: Dens demetent

| | "Bel filz," fait il, "(in) malora fus tu ne,*
| | Maleta l'ora qe tu fustiençendré.
| | E sento ben qe m'à envenené.*
| 5680 | Segnur, car li bailés ste traito renojé." (190)
| | Ben fust Lanfroi malamente bailé;
| | Quant ses parenti furent aparilé,
| | Qui de Magançe, cun avoit ordené,
| | Çascun de lor oit trata la spe;
| 5685 | Sor li palés comencent la meslé. (195)
| | Aquilon de Baivere e Morando de Rivé,
| | Bernardo de Clermont tosto se fu levé.
| | Quando virent la corte sbaraté,
| | De le palés furent devalé;
| 5690 | Çascun s'en vait ver la soa contré. (200)

Rubric 161
Coment Landris e Lanfroi onçirent / li rois e dama Berte a venen.
Laisse 162

| | Grant fu la nosa sor la sala pavée,
| | E por Paris fu la novela alée,
| | Coment li rois estoit envenenée,
| | Et avec lui Berte, la ensenée.
| 5695 | Çascun de ceus qe le avont amée (205)
| | Si s'en fuçirent por rivé e por stree.
| | E Landris e Lanfroi, quant i ont guardée,*
| | Qe li rois e la raine sunt morti versée,
| | Demantenant desendent a·l degrée.
| 5700 | Monta a çival e furent ben armée, (210)
| | Con tot celor qe l'ont con lor pensée.
| | Corerent la tere e tota la contrée;
| | Ne le fu homo de tanta renomée,

5677 MS.: fait il malora; (in): my emendation; Reinhold: mal ora . . . ; Rosellini: malora . . .
5678 Rosellini: eçendré (corrected Morini 1992)
5679 Rosellini: que (corrected Morini 1992)
Rubric 161 (after 5690) Keller: auenen; Mussafia, "Handschriftliche Studien II," Guessard: a venen
5691 Rosellini: pavéee
5692 Rosellini: aléee
5697 Reinhold, Rosellini: gardée
5699 Reinhold: De mantenant (misquoted by Rosellini)

	Qe contra lor olsast prender spee.
5705	Quando de la tere furent asegurée, (215)
	A le palés furent retornée. 32ʳᵇ
	Una colsa farent, par non eser blasmée:
	Li rois e la raine ont aseterée
	Si altament cun pote eser devisée,
5710	Por li conseil de li son parentée. (220)
	Açoqe entro lor non cresese meslée,
	Çascun de lor si fu rois coronée.
	Mais Lanfroi si fu li plus dotée;
	E Landris estoit plus ensenée.
5715	Por mal aient cella ovra porpensée, (225)
	Qe Damenedé n'i oit plus obliée.
	A çascun donò coment ont ovrée,
	Nen porent avoir fato major peçée.
	Con dist Salamon, qe fo li plus dotée,
5720	Apreso Adam qe in ste mondo fu née, (230)
	E Jesu (qe) de Verçene fu née:*
	"Qi ofent a li per, mal avoit esploitée;*
	Nen poit falir ne l'aça çer conprée."

Rubric 162
Coment parole Salamon, "qi ofent / A li per avoit mal g(uj)erdon."
Laisse 163

	Segnur baron, de ço siés çertan:
5725	Qi ofent a li per a torto *et* a ingan, (235)
	Non po paser lungo tenpo nian
	Qe por son per non duri grant achan.
	Landris e Lanfroi furent dos tyran;
	Quant onçient son per a torto *et* a ingan,
5730	De cesta colsa aloit si grant enfan* (240)
	Partot se dient en tere de Cristian,

5711 Reinhold: A ço qe
5712 Rajna: coronee
5715 Reinhold, Rosellini: aient (as always)
5721 MS.: Jesu de; Reinhold, Rosellini: Jesu [qe] de (emend)
Rubric 162 (after 5723) line 2: Reinhold: A li (emend for MS. *All*); Rosellini: All per . . . . MS.: gi uerdon
5725 7 for *et*
5726 Reinhold: pò (as always)
5729 7 for *et*

| | E in Paganie, en tere d·i pagan;
| | Tot li blasment, li petit e li gran,
| | E çivaler, burgois e vilan.
| 5735 | De ces dient tros en Jerusalan; (245)
| | Pur de l'oldir n'oit la jent spavan.
| | Li rois Galafrio, qi no l'amoit un pan,
| | Li desplasoit quel ovre e quel engan.
| | Dist l'un a l'altro, "De ço siés certan;
| 5740 | Qe por ces ovre non virà longo tan. (250)
| | Si ont malovré, i non serà çojan;*
| | Morir convirà a dol et a torman:
| | Qe de le rois Pepin remist un enfan,*
| | Karleto, le petit çovençel de pois an;
| 5745 | Filz fu de Pepin e de Berte enseman." (255)
| | Mais celle frer no l'ament nian;
| | Ne·l vose oncir; tent el con ses fan,*
| | Lasa·l aler et arer et avan.

Rubric 163
Coment Karleto dure gram sofraite / In la cort de son frer *et* de Galafrie li rois.*
Laisse 164

| | Oeç, segnor, e siez entendant,
| 5750 | Li du malvés qe li cor Deo crevant, (260)
| | Qe son per oit morto a mortel traimant, *   32va
| | E la raine avec lui ensemant,*
| | Karleto le petit baçaler de jojant*
| | En la cusina . . . cum fait li sarçant.*
| 5755 | E qui so(i) frer li tenia por niant (265)
| | Si se fasoit doter qe nesun homo vivant
| | Ne le pooit contradir de niant.*

5735 MS.: De de ces; Reinhold, Rosellini: De ces dient . . . (emend)

5741 Reinhold, Rosellini: mal ovré (as always). Reinhold, Rosellini: çoiant

5747 MS.: ten tel cō ses fan; Reinhold: Ne-l . . . con un [in]fan (emend); Rosellini: Ne'l vose . . . , tent el con ses fan

5748 Reinhold: Lasa-l; Rosellini: Lasal

Rubric 163 (after 5748) line 2: 7 for *et*. Keller: jn la . . . de gala fru . . . ; Mussafia, "Handschriftliche Studien II": Galafre, "Charles Beschützer"; Reinhold: Galafrio (emend for *Gala fue*); Rosellini: Galafrie

5752 Reinhold, Rosellini: raina

5755 MS.: sor frer; Keller: so(i); Reinhold, Rosellini: soi frer (emend for *sor*)

5757 Reinhold: poit

	Qui de Magançe, qi estoit ses parant,
	Fasoit de la cort tot le so comant.
5760	Aquilon de Bavier e des autres ben çant (270)
	Ne l'olsent aparer da celle jor avant,
	Qe morto fo Pepin e Berte ensemant.
	Ma Morando de River tant amoit l'infant,
	Qe por paure ni autre destorbamant,
5765	Karleto no anbandonò finq'el fo vivant. (275)
	Mais por paure de celle male jant,
	Ne se olsoit descovrir de niant.
	Volez oir, segnor, un grant inçantamant,
	De li rois Galafrio, de la paine jant?
5770	Novella oit oldu de França e de Normant, (280)
	Si fait çiter ses sorte e ses encantamant.
	Li saçi qe le butent trovent noiremant*
	Qe un Karleto q'estoit petit enfant
	Deveroit eser enperer droitmant,
5775	Et avoir la corona trosqua in Jerusalant. (285)
	Mes avantqe cil soie, durerà pene tant
	Ne le saveroit dir nesun homo vivant;
	Deschaçé seroit de le son casamant,
	Por altru tere aliroit mendigant.
5780	Unde Galafrio par tot son tenimant (290)
	Si fe bandir et arer et avant,*
	Qe paser non posa ne petit ni grant*
	Se primement ne li è mené davant.
	E questo fe li rois a esiant,
5785	Par savoir se par nula ren vivant, (295)
	Elo poust avoir celle infant.

5760 Reinhold, Rosellini: Baiver
5761 MS.: Nel colsent; Reinhold: Ne le olsent (emend for *Nel colse*); Rosellini: Ne l'olsent
5765 Reinhold, Rosellini: fin q' (as always); Rosellini: no abandonò
5767 Reinhold: descovrir
5768 Reinhold: oïr (as always)
5769 Reinhold: païne (as always)
5772 Reinhold, Rosellini: voiremant
5776 Reinhold, Rosellini: avant qe (as always)
5778 Reinhold: Deschacé
5782 Reinhold: pesa
5786 Reinhold: poüst (as always)

Rubric 164
Coment Ka(r)leto ferì son frer / Cum un spe de la cosine.*
Laisse 165

	Segnur baron plaroit vos ascolter,
	Ço qe fe Karleto le petit baçaler,
	Qe de rois estoit fato cusiner?
5790	En la cusine estoit a·l spi mener; (300)
	Non olsoit a·l palés ne a la sala monter,
	Si gran paura avoit de ses frer,
	Qe de lui non faissent ço ch'arent de·l per.*
	Tant stoit l'infant ne pote plus endurer;
5795	Una gran feste, el guardoit sor li soler; (305)
	Landris el voit illec traverser.
	L'infant le vi, cuita de·l dol raçer,
	Quant se pense de·l per e de la mer, 32vb
	Cum qui le farent a mala mort finer.
5800	Davant soi el prist a guarder; (310)
	Un spe el prist de arse de aroster.*
	Por ira e maltalant, el va contra son frer;*
	Por me le viso elo li vait doner.
	Ma le enfant estoit petit baçaler;
5805	Ne le pote ben de·l tot enperer,* (315)
	Mais si le fait de·l vis le sangue rajer.
	Morto aust l'infant, mais Morando de River
	Si se sasi, s'il vait a co<v>oter,*
	Siche no li poent ni prender ni bailer.*
5810	Via l'en mene, qi ne doja nojer. (320)

Rubric 164 (after 5786) line 1: MS., Keller: Kaleto; Reinhold, Rosellini: Ka[r]leto
5790 Reinhold, Rosellini: al spi (as always)
5793 Reinhold: faïssent
5795 Rosellini: guadoit (cf. Martin)
5798 Reinhold, Rosellini: pense del per
5801 Reinhold: (de) arsé de aroster; Rosellini: de arsa de aroster
5803 Rosellini: lo viso
5805 Rosellini: enprier (for *enperer*)
5806 Reinhold, Rosellini: del vis le sangue
5807 Rosellini: linfant
5808 MS.: Si se sasi; Reinhold: Si le sasì si-l (emend for *se*); Rosellini: Si le saisi si 'l vait à cujoter ... (emend)
5810 Rosellini: l'enmene

E d'Aviçon, lì fu Rainero li çivaler;
For de Paris l<e> mena en un verçer,
Et illec le tenent tres jor tot enter.
Porço le fi Morando de River,
5815 Por li malvés qi le fasoit spier, (325)
Par tot parte lu çercher par trover;
Voluntera l'aust <fato> finer.*
Or se comença de Karleto li çanter,
Cum li menò Morando de River.
5820 Nen pote pais en França demorer; (330)
En Sarasinia le conven amener.*

Rubric 165
Coment Morando de Rivere en menò / Karleto li enfant en Saraçoçe, et coment fu apresenté davanti li rois Galafrio.
Laisse 166

Morando de Rivere si oit grant atent;
Plus aime Karleto de nesu hon vivent.*
Por amor de son per, li amoit lojalment,
5825 E de lu estoit plus dolent, (335)
De homo qe fust a li mondo vivent.
Por son amor el se mis en torment;
En tel tera lo menò dont avè gran spavent.
Trosqua a Saragoça nen foit arestament;
5830 Cuitoit cel infant mener çeleement, (340)
Mais no li valse un diner valisent,
Qe li oster oit por comandament
De lor apresenter sença demorament.
Or entendés, segnur e bona jent,
5835 Quant Morant de Rivere l'infant menarent (345)
Quanti el çerchò e 'mis e parent,*

5814 Reinhold, Rosellini: Por ço
5818 Reinhold: K[arleto]
5820 Rosellini: emorer (cf. Martin)
5821 MS.: conve; Reinhold: conve[n], emend; Rosellini: convè
Rubric 165 (after 5821) line 1: Reinhold, Rosellini: enmenò; Rosellini: Saragoçe; line 2: 7 for et, MS.: lie nfant; line 3: Keller: a presente
5823 Reinhold: nesu[n] (emend)
5828 Rosellini: ave
5832 Rosellini: comandement
5836 Reinhold, Rosellini: Quanti el cerchò e [a]mis e ...

	Tot prime*n*ent por lo men esie*n*t,*
	Ad Aquilon l'infant condudent.
	E cil de lui molto en fo dolent,
5840	E ben li fe ço qe a lui apent; (350)
	De lui servire nen fu pais mie lent,
	Si le donò ço qe li fu a talent.
	"Bel filz," fait il, "nu semo a nient;*
	Landris e (Lanfroi) cum altri ses parent 33^(ra)
5845	Si ont si pris le tere e i teniment,* (355)
	Qe n'i poremes contrastar de nient.
	A nos convent aspeter altro tenp;*
	Qe pois faron, se Deo plas altrament."
	E cil le dient, "A ves comandament."*

Rubric 166
Coment Aquilon de Baivere / Parole a Morant de Rivere.
Laisse 167

5850	"Segnur," dist Aquilon, "ne vos doja nojer;* (360)
	Questi dos frer, qe Deo posa creventer,*
	Ont si pris le tere e le river,
	Si fait a la jent a soi decliner,*
	Qe no li porumes de nojant <con>traster.
5855	E ò un filz qe tanto è saço e <ber>; (365)
	En tot le mondo el non oi<t son p>er,
	Qu'el vos saverà de·l tot co<nseiler>,*
	Cum vos devés e fare e o<vrer>."
	Doncha farent Naimeto apeler;
5860	L'infant vi Karleto, si le corse enbraçer, (370)
	E si le dist, "Benvenez, meser;*
	Li mon conseil e vos vojo doner:
	Qe non deça qui de lo seçorner.*

    5837 Reinhold, Rosellini: por lo men
    5839 Reinhold: dolant
    5844 MS.: Çofroi; Reinhold, Rosellini: Lanfroi (emend for *Çofrei*)
    5849 Reinhold, Rosellini: Avés comandament (cf. Martin: "lire *A ves*")
Rubric 166 (after 5849) Keller: bauiere
    5853 Reinhold, Rosellini: Si fait à la jent
    5854 Reinhold: *con*traster
    5857 Reinhold, Rosellini: Quel vos
    5861 Reinhold, Rosellini: Ben venez
    5863 Reinhold, Rosellini: Qe non deça; Rosellini: de lo' seurner

En autre part vos conven\<t\> erer,
5865 Por li amisi querir e demander. (375)
Mo no è tenpo de guera comen\<çer\>,*
Qe li traites qe \<oncirent so*n* per\>,*
De tota França sont fato coroner;
A lor atent peon e çivaler.
5870 Ma d'una ren e no vos quer nojer; (380)
Vu, mon segnor, estes un baçaler;
Ne mo ne vos nen porumes bailer
Nulle arme por ferir e çostrer.
Quan tel seron, qe nos poron aider,
5875 Mal aça quel qe s'en trarà arer, (385)
De qui traites confondre e mater."*
Quando Karleto li oldì si parler,
Elo li vait a li col abracer,
E anbedos acoler e baser.
5880 I demorent ilec un mois tot enter; (390)
Pois prendent conçé, pensent de·l çivalçer.
A Bernardo de Clermont i vont a parler,
E prendent son co*n*seil d'en altro regno aler;*
E i le font sença nesun tarder.
5885 Ora s'en vait Morando de River, (395)
E mena Karleto, le petit baçaler.
E Rainer d'Aviçon ne le volse abandoner;
Tant alirent cun Deo li volse mener,
Qe i çonçent a un malvais oster,
5890 Qe estoit preso una selva meravilosa e fer, (400)
O starent li larons; nul homo po paser   33rb
Qe i non faça oncire e rober,
E quant avoir i poent guaagner,
Tot le darent a celle son oster;
5895 El fu de França, e lu e son per. (405)
Quant morto fu Pepin, el se co*n*vene aler,
Qe avec lor non pote converser.
Quando çelor se farent ostaler,
L'oster conoit Morando de River,

5866 Reinhold, Rosellini: Non c'è (emend for *Mon*)
5869 Reinhold: civaler
5872 Reinhold: mo' (as always)
5879 Reinhold: anbe dos (as always)
5881 Reinhold: de çivalçer
5898 Reinhold, Rosellini: estaler (usual *e/o* confusion)

5900 Karleto l'infant el prist ad aviser. (410)
Doncha le prist por rason demander,
"Segnur," fait il, "ne vos estoit doter,
Ne contra moi de vos devés celer.
Ben vos conosco, vu, Morando de River,
5905 E vos, Bernardo, qe estes pro e ber, (415)
Questo è Karleto, mon segnor droiturer."

Rubric 167
Coment arrivarent a la mason / de li hoster qe li dona li avoir.*
Laisse 168

Quando Morant oit cella parola oie,*
Ver li oster ne se çelò pais mie.
Quando el vi qe si le conovie,
5910 E li oster si fu tot plen de cortexie, (420)
Molto riçament li oit hostalie;
Da boir e da mançer li dona a gran plantie;
Ilec demorent, terço jorno conplie.
Quant s'en volent aler, a li osto disie*
5915 Qe conçé li donast par soa cortexie. (425)
Dist li oster, "Daq'el vos delie,*
E vos comant a·l filz sante Marie.
Ma non alirés si poverament mie;
De mon avoir portarés a gran manentie."
5920 XX. somer d'avoir ben carcie (430)
Li ont doné; pois l'ont convoie*
Por celle bois e por celle male vie,
O estoit li larons, qe Jesu mal en die.
Quant li larons voit celle somarie,
5925 S'i ont çoja, no m'en demandés mie; (435)
M'i ont guardé for por la praerie,
Voit li oster sego en conpagnie.
Quant le verent, se tenent scernie;
Lasa·li aler droitament en sa vie.
5930 E li oster, qe Jesu benedie, (440)
Dist a Karleto, "Ne vos dotés mie.

Rubric 167 (after 5906) line 1: Keller: ariuarent; Reinhold, Rosellini: arivarent
5909 Reinhold: qe si li convie
5913 Rosellini: domorent
5925 Reinhold, Rosellini: Si ont . . .
5929 Rosellini: Lasali

Asa avon avoir e manentie;
Toto li conservo a vestra segnorie,*
Quant vos serés in etae conplie."
5935 Unde Karleto e Morando le mercie; (445)
Da lor se part quant fu asegurie.
A li oster çunçent donde e vos lasie,*
Qe in Saragoça furent alberçie.* 33ᵛᵃ
E quel fu saço, por bando de la crie,
5940 Davant Galafrio, tot tros li convie. (450)

Rubric 168
Coment furent representé davant / Li rois Galafrio, et il li parole.
Laisse 169

Davant Galafrio si fu l'osto alé,
Li qual s'estoit molto cojant e lé.
E la raine estoit a son costé;
Una fila avoit, petit en eté,
5945 Una plu bella non fu unqua trové; (455)
Li rois la tent apreso son costé.
Quant voit li rois, si le ont demandé,
Qe çent sont et dont furent né.
Li rois le guarda, si s'en fu mervilé,
5950 E dist, "Segnur, dites mo verité." (460)
Morando parole, qe ben fu adoné,*
"Merçeant sumes, alon por li me(r)çé."
Dist Galafrio, "Ces croir non pos e;*
À li merçé qe vendés e conpré?"
5955 "Çival, bel sire, palafroi e destré." (465)
E dist li rois, "Vos dites falsité."

5932 Rosellini: mantenie
5937 Reinhold, Rosellini: l'afie (emend for *lasie*); Capusso: e vos l'asie
Rubric 168 (after 5940) MS., Reinhold: Represente . . . Rois.
5942 Reinhold: çoiant, with the cedilla in square brackets.; Rosellini, çoiant (emend for MS. *coiant*)
5949 Reinhold: fù
5950 Reinhold: dites mo'
5951 Capusso: cf. adoté
5952 me(r)çé: MS.: merçe; Reinhold, Rosellini: me[r]çé
5953 Reinhold: pos' e'; Rosellini: pos é
5956 Reinhold, Rosellini: Vu dites

Saçés, segnors, como estont coroé?*
Çascun avoit capuç, çapiron daré.
En meço de lor dos estoit Karleto acovoté,*
5960 E li rois Galafrio li oit aregardé. (470)
A la fature qe a lu fu conté,
Entro son cor avoit devisé,
"Questo è Karleto, q'i frer ont deschaçé."*
Alor dist a Morando, "Pas ne vos doté,
5965 Vos e q(ui) altre qe vos sont daré; (475)
Aço longo tenpo querì e demandé.
Vu sì de França nasu et ençendré,
E quel petit, qe vos tenés daré,
Estoit Karleto, e questo çelar non poé."
5970 Morando l'oldò, molto fo spaventé; (480)
Ben croit qe Galafrio li aust atué,
Por la vegnançe de son frer l'amiré*
Qe Pepin oncist en bataja de pre,
Quando li rois li ont aseguré.
5975 "Mon sir," dist il, "ben dites verité." (485)
Adoncha li rois oit Karleto apelé,
"Bel filz," fait il, "la capa vos osté."*
E cil le foit, poisqe l'oit comandé;
En un blial de soja fu remé.*
5980 Qi doncha veist de Karleto la belté: (490)
Plus est il blanco qe neve glaçelé,
Li ocli var como falcon mué,
Li çavi oit blondi reçerçené,
E plu lusenti de l'or smiré;
5985 Plus fer oit li guardo qe lion encaené. (495)   33vb
Sa fia Belisant molto l'oit reguardé,
E li rois le dist, belament e soé,
"Bel filz Karleto, e vo ca marié*
En mia fila, se prender la volé."

5957 Plouzeau: Rosellini should read *Saçés* (not *saçes*)
5959 Reinhold: lor des estoit
5963 Reinhold, Rosellini: deschacé
5965 MS.: qiu; Reinhold: qui' altri; Rosellini: qui altre
5970 Reinhold: *l'olde (emend for *loldo*)
5972 Reinhold: ve[n]gnançe
5988 Reinhold: e' v'oe à (emend for *evoca* [?]); Rosellini: e v'ò ça marié (for *evoca*)

Rubric 169
Coment li rois apelle Karleto / Li enfant se le fait grant ho(n)or.*
Laisse 170

5990 Li rois apela Karleto en ojant; (500)
      "Bel filz," fait il, "or vos faites avant.
      S'elo vos plas, e vos do Belisant,
      Ma bela file, qe je poramo tant." ((155))
      E dist Karleto, "Et eo no la contant."
5995 Anche petit fust, el parlò saçemant: (505)
      "Bon rois," fait il, "je sui a·l ves comant.*
      Se ço qe dites, la raina li consant,
      E questa polçeleta, qe vos est davant, ((160))
      Eo la prenderò per un tel convenant,
6000 Q'ela prenda la loe o je sui creant; (510)
      Ço est Crestentés, e li batecamant."
      Dist la raine, "Et eo si le consant."
      Doncha verisés baldor e çoja grant; ((165))
      Ilec fu Falsiron e Marsilio e Balugant.
6005 Gran çoja menent le petit e li grant; (515)
      Li rois l'ama cosi como un de ses enfant.
      Un gran palés li dona a son comant;
      Savés coment s'en aovrò Morant? ((170))
      Por oldir mese e li Deo sagramant,
6010 Gran cort mantenent K*arleto* l'infant.* (520)
      Tant l'amoit Galafrio cum Balugant,
      Marsilio avec lui ensemant.
      Nian K*arleto* no era pais si lant ((175))

Rubric 169 (after 5989) line 1: MS., Reinhold: Rois; line 2: MS.: homor; Chichmaref: honior; Reinhold: si . . . honor (emend); Rosellini: honior
  5990 Chichmaref, Reinhold: en oiant (as always)
  5993 Chichmaref, Reinhold: por amo
  5996 Chichmaref: ie . . . al ves
  5998 Rosellini: quest polçeleta
  6000 Reinhold: la loe, o' je sui . . . ; Chichmaref: la loe, o' ie sui . . .
  6001 Reinhold: bateçamant (emend; cedilla in square brackets); Chichmaref, Rosellini (emend): bateçamant; Reinhold's review, col 247.
  6008 Chichmaref, Reinhold, Rosellini: no punctuation at the end, making the question two lines long.
  6010 Chichmaref resolves 'K' as 'Karleto' always, here also.
  6011 Rosellini: cun Balugant
  6013 Chichmaref, Guessard, Reinhold: Ni an (as always); Chichmaref: Ni an non era (error also noted by Frati, Reinhold [review of Chichmaref])

```
              Q'el non donast robe e palafroi anblant,
       6015   Falcon e sparaveri tenoit plus de çant;         (525)
              De lu se parloit tros in Jerusalant.*
              Braibant l'olde dire, un rois oltreposant,
              Qe li rois Galafrio, e lui e sa jant,
              Tant honoroit la Cristiane jant,                ((180))
       6020   En son palés fasoit orer li sant,               (530)
              E çanter mese e li Deo sagramant.
              Tal oit li dol par poi d'ire non fant;
              Dist a sa jent, "Ben do eser dolant,            ((185))
              Quando Galafrio è fato recreant;
       6025   Renojé oit Macon e Trevigant."                  (535)
              Dist Danabrin, "Vu no valì niant.
              Envojez a lui tosto, demantenant;
              Sença demore, ve mandi cele enfant,             ((190))
              E cele autres qe son en Deo creant.
       6030   S'elo·l vol faire, reçevés cun parant;*         (540)
              E soa fille qe oit nome Belisant,*
              La donarés a ves fil Bruant.                                 34ra
              S'el no·l vol faire, morto sia eramant;*        ((195))
              Desovra lui menarì tant çant,
       6035   Non se porà nonbrer li miler ne li çant;        (545)
              No li lasaron tera ni casamant."
              Dist Braibant, "Par mon deo Trevigant.
```

6014 Guessard: Quel

6016 Guessard: Falcon, esparaveri (Mussafia, "Handschriftliche Studien II": e sparaveri)

6017 Reinhold: oltre posant

6018 Rosellini: Galfrio

6020 Guessard: lisant (Mussafia, "Handschriftliche Studien II": li sant)

6023 Reinhold: do eser oblant; Guessard: Ben de (Mussafia, "Handschriftliche Studien II": Ben do)

6026 Chichmaref, Reinhold: valì; Guessard: un no vali (Mussafia, "Handschriftliche Studien II": vu)

6027 Guessard, Chichmaref, Reinhold: de mantenant (as always; not noted further)

6030 Chichmaref: S'elo-l vol . . . , com (noted also by Frati, Reinhold [review of Chichmaref]); Reinhold: S'elo-l vol; Guessard: S'elol; Rosellini: S'elo 'l

6032 Chichmaref: a vos fil (error; cf. Reinhold, review of Chichmaref); Guessard: a vos fil

6033 Reinhold, Chichmaref: S'el no-l . . . eramant; Guessard: S'el nol vol faire; Rosellini: S'el no'l

6037 Guessard: mon Deo

Milor co*n*seil no quero ni no demant." ((200))
Quatro pain d·i meltri de sa çant
6040   Fi pariler alo demantenant. (550)

Rubric 170
Coment Braibant en(v)oja li mesancer / A li rois Galafrio por Karleto.*
Laisse 171

Rois Braibant nen volse demorer;
Quatro mesajes el foit pariler.
"Segnur," dist Braibant, "el vos co*n*vent aler ((205))
Enç en Spagne a Galafrio parler;
6045   Da la ma part vu li dovés nonçer, (555)
Qe de lu me poso durament merviler,
Quando s'oit lasé si vilment ençegner,
Qe in Deo croi, qe fu un paltroner. ((210))
Se demanes no m'invoja li baçaler,*
6050   Li qual se fait K*arleto* apeler (560)
(Filz fu Pepin, un rois d'oltra mer),
El me verà sor lu çivalçer,
Cun tant de jent cu*n* porò asenbler. ((215))
E se le porò prendre, si le farò çuçer (565)
6055   Como laron, qi est repris d'anbler."*
Dist li mesaçi, "Non stoit plus doter;
Ben faron l'anbasée, se le poron trover,
Mejo qe non savés ne dir ni diviser." ((220))
Li quatro mesajes, sença plus demorer
6060   Conçé prendent, se vont a 'pariler (570)

6039 Guessard, Chichmaref, Reinhold, Rosellini: di meltri

Rubric 170 (after 6040) line 1: MS.: ennoia; Keller: enuoia li mesancer; Chichmaref: envoia; Guessard: envoia (no note); Reinhold: envoia (emendation for *en noia*); Chichmaref, Reinhold: mesa(n)çer (= "n" unnecessary), Reinhold puts the cedilla in square brackets. Cf. Reinhold, review of Chichmaref re Chichmaref's reading. Rosellini: envoia li mesaçer; MS.: en voia. line 2: MS., Reinhold: Rois.

6044 Chichmaref: En çen (cf. Reinhold [review of Chichmaref]); Reinhold: Enç en (emend for MS. *En çeu*); Rosellini: Enç en (emend for *En ceu*)

6052 Chichmaref: vera

6053 Rosellini: esenbler; Chichmaref: cum porò

6055 Rosellini: repris (emend for *ropris*)

6056 Chichmaref: No-n stoit

6060 Chichmaref, Reinhold, Rosellini: a pariler

	De celle colse qe li ont mester;
	Pois se metent por le çamin herer.
	Tant alirent e por tera e por mer, ((225))
	D'un çorno e d'altro, como dist li çanter,
6065	Vent a Saragoçe in l'ora de·l disner. (575)
	Ad un oster se von ad alberçer,
	E si mançent qe li oit gran mester.
	E quant ont ma(n)çé, se vont a coroer ((230))
	De riçe robe, de porpre e de çender,
6070	Por honorançe de Braibant, son ser. (580)

Rubric 171
Coment li mesançer de Braibant / aloit davanti Galafrio.*
Laisse 172

	Li mesaçer nen fu pais esperdu;
	Molto riçament son calçé e vestu.
	Ven a la cort e ben son conou; ((235))
	Plus de mil çivaler i·le ont veu,*
6075	Qe tot creent Macometo e Cau. (585)
	Si le fu Karleto e Morando son dru,*
	E Balugant e son frer anbidu. 34rb
	E quant Galafrio s'en est aperceu, ((240))
	Contra le vait, si le oit a le man prendu.
6080	Pois si le dist, "Vu siés benvenu. (590)
	Unde estes vos; qi vos oit trametu?"*

6061 Reinhold: mestfer
6064 Reinhold: canter
6065 Reinhold: Kent à (for Vent a) . . . l'ora. Chichmaref: del disner (as always)
6068 MS.: maçe; Chichmaref, Reinhold, Rosellini: ma[n]çé (emend)
6070 Chichmaref: Por honorançe re Braibant (cf. also Frati, Reinhold [review of Chichmaref])

Rubric 171 (after 6070) line 1: MS.: mesançer; Chichmaref, Reinhold: mesa(n)çer (which means, as in 170, "n" unnecessary); Rosellini: mesaçer

6073 Chichmaref, Reinhold: o' ben. Chichmaref: conoü (same for the whole laisse where two vowels form the rhyme, thus ll. 6074, 6075, 6077, 6078, 6088).
6074 Chichmaref, Reinhold: veü (as always); Chichmaref: ile[c] ont . . .
6075 Chichmaref, Reinhold: Caü (as always; cf. 6088, etc.)
6077 Chichmaref, Reinhold: son frer, Anbroü; Rosellini: anbidu
6078 Reinhold: aperceü
6080 Chichmaref, Reinhold, Rosellini: ben venu
6081 Reinhold: trametü

Un de lor parole, qi fu li plus menbru:*
"Mesaçer sumes Braibant li çanu;* ((245))
A vos el n'oit por mesaz trametu;
6085 El no vos manda amisté ni salu. (595)
Savés porquoi il est irascu?
Qe por mesaçi el oit entendu
Qe non creés Machometo ni Cau; ((250))
Faites orer la loi de Jesu
6090 Par un damisel, qe filz Pepin fu. (600)
Elo ves mande, se volez salu,
Qe quel K*arleto* vu l'invojez a lu.
Colsa como no, vos è mal avenu; ((255))
Nen vos valerà valisant un festu;
6095 Vu serés morto, con laron apendu." (605)
K*arleto* fu apreso qe l'oit ben entendu;
Za li aust por li çevo feru,
Quant li rois li oit retenu. ((260))

Rubric 172

Quando Karleto olde li rois menaçer, / a mervelle fu dollant, si volse ferir li me/sajes, quando li rois le pristi . . .*
Laisse 173

Gran dol oit K*arleto*, ne l'oit onqa major,
6100 Quant il oldì menaçer l'almansor,* (610)
Q'il tenoit a per et a segnor.
Galafrio parole verso li anbasaor:

6086 Chichmaref, Reinhold, Rosellini: por quoi il . . .

6087 Chichmaref: por mesaçe (error also noted by Frati, Reinhold [review of Chichmaref])

6091 Chichmaref, Reinhold, Rosellini: vos mande

6093 MS.: è; Reinhold: vos e*n* [ert] mal (emends); Chichmaref: vos en [sera] mal avenu; Rosellini: vos est mal . . . (lists Reinhold's reading incorrectly also)

Rubric 172 (after 6098) Line 1: Chichmaref: Coment Karleto . . . (cf. Frati and Reinhold, review of Chichmaref); MS., Reinhold: Rois; line 2: Keller: feru li; line 3: Reinhold: mesajes . . . prist(i); Chichmaref: prist(i). Rosellini: prist; MS., Reinhold: Rois

6099 Chichmaref: n'el oit

6100 MS.: alimansor (i expuncutated); Keller: al(i)mansor; Reinhold: l'Alimansor; Chichmaref: menaçer almansor (cf. Reinhold, review of Chichmaref); Rosellini: menaçer l'Alimansor

6101 Chichmaref: et a signor (error noted also by Frati, Reinhold [review of Chichmaref])

| | "Segnur," fait il, "no*n* parlez por iror, ((265))
| | Qe por Macon, qi est mon defensor,
| 6105 | Uncha n'à mais li mon antesor* (615)
| | Nen oldì mais un tel desenor,
| | De mo apendre a guisa de traitor.
| | Nen fose por tanto qe estes anbasaor, ((270))
| | Asa vos faroie pena major;
| 6110 | Arder vos faroie en fois et en ardor, (620)
| | E questo vos faroie por li vestro segnor.
| | Demantenant tornarés sens demor,
| | Si le dirés qe no·l doto una flor; ((275))
| | E ò tros filz, a·l mondo non è milor;
| 6115 | A Karleto ò doné ma fila por amor; (625)
| | Tanto amo lui como eo faço lor.
| | S'el pasa mer, el non farà retor*
| | Qe non remagna de li so(n) milor,* ((280))
| | Si·n tornerà cun onta e desenor.
| 6120 | Si me le dì, e no*n* aver paor, (630)
| | Ben po savoir se son gran segnor,
| | Qe dos Domenedé eo aço por defensor:
| | Tot primament, Macometo li major, ((285))   34va
| | E pois cil Deo qe clama li peçaor,
| 6125 | Li qual qe soja me farà vinçeor." (635)
| | Quant cil l'intendent, par poi nen mor d'iror;
| | Cosi starent coi cu*n* fait l'avoltor.*

6105 MS · Unchana; Reinhold: Uncha no mais (emend for *na*); Chichmaref: Unchana mais li mon ancesor (corrected by Reinhold, review of Chichmaref also); Rosellini: Uncha no mais (emend for *Unchana*)

6106 Chichmaref: Nen oldì un tel resenor (error noted by Frati, Reinhold [review of Chichmaref])

6112 Chichmaref, Reinhold: De mantenant (as always)

6113 Chichmaref, Reinhold: no-l; Rosellini: no'l

6118 MS.: sor; Chichmaref: so(i); Reinhold, Rosellini: soi

6119 Chichmaref, Reinhold: Si-n; Rosellini: Si' n

6120 Reinhold: li dì . . .

6122 Rosellini: Domenedée eo

6126 Reinhold: n'en

Rubric 173
Coment Karleto parole a li mesaçer / De quo li rois n'oit çoie.
Laisse 174

	Quant li rois oit dito soa volunté ((290))
	Verso color qe l'avoit menaçé,
6130	Si gran dol n'oit, par pois n'en son raçé.* (640)
	Mal aça quelo qe aça moto parlé,
	Quando K*arleto* li oit aderasné:*
	"Segnur," fait il, "dites moi verité; ((295))
	Perqe oit Braibant par moi envojé?
6135	E son celu qe vos en demandé." (645)
	E li mesaçi ont K*arleto* guardé,
	E si le virent si bel e informé:
	Li ocli var con falcon mué, ((300))
	Le braço groso, e le pugni enquaré. (650)
6140	Dist l'un a l'altro, "Questo è d·i bateçé,
	Si è colu par cui nu semo envojé.
	A gran mervile avoit gra*n* belté;
	De lu oncire seroit gran peçé." ((305))
	E dist K*arleto*, "De qe vos conselé?"
6145	E celle le dient, "Ne vos serà çellé; (655)
	Nu sì conten de la vestra belté.
	Se mon segnor v'aust en poesté,
	Ne vos donroie por grande riçité, ((310))
	Quando renojesi celu qe aoré;
6150	Colsa como no, serise a morte çuçé." (660)
	Lor dist K*arleto*, "Da ma part li conté,
	Qe richamente eo sonto marié,
	Qe li rois Galafrio m'à sa fia doné, ((315))
	Ço est Belisant, la saça e la doté.
6155	Par moi amor ela s'è bateçé; (665)
	Delinqui oit Macon e si croit en Dé,

Rubric 173 (after 6127) MS., Reinhold: Rois; Keller: noit çoie
6129 Rosellini: menacé
6130 Reinhold, Rosellini: n'en son
6132 Reinhold: li at
6134 Chichmaref, Reinhold, Rosellini: Per qe (as always)
6139 Rosellini: Le braço e le pugni
6140 Chichmaref, Reinhold, Rosellini: di bateçé (as always)
6145 Chichmaref: cellé (error noted by Frati, Reinhold [review of Chichmaref])
6155 Chichmaref: moi'; Rosellini: s'é

   Çelui qe fu sor la cros enclodé.
   Ben la defenderò a·l trençar de ma spe
   Dever Braibant, qe l'oit demandé." ((320))
6160 Galafrio l'olde, un riso n'oit çité; (670)
   Elo l'acolle por grande amisté;
   E Balugant l'oit por la man pié,
   En autre part el l'oit mené.

Rubric 174
Coment li mesaçer s'en alent / e retornarent a son segnor.*
Laisse 175

   Li mesaçer ne volent demorer; ((325))
6165 Prendent conçé, se metent ad aler. (675)
   Tant alirent, ne volent demorer,
   E pasarent e por tera e por mer,
   A son segnor venent a repairer. ((330))   34ᵛᵇ
   La novela li conte qe li foit airer;
6170 "Mon sir," dist li mesajes, "nu vos devon conter; (680)
   Li rois Galafrio non v'ama un diner.
   A quel damisel qe è de·l Batister
   Oit doné sa fila por muler. ((335))
   Plu ama lui, ne vos poria conter;
6175 Si cun son fil elo le fa clamer." (685)
   Quando li rois li olde si parler,
   S'el oit dol, non è da demander.
   Dist li mesajes, "Fol est quel baçaler; ((345))
   Feru n'averoit, sença altro menaçer,
6180 Quando Galafrio si le prist darer."* (690)

  Rubric 174 (after 6163) Keller: sen alent
  6169 Chichmaref, Reinhold: aïrer (as always)
  6171 Chichmaref: non va[l] ma'; Reinhold [review of Chichmaref]: emendation unnecessary
  6172 Chichmaref, Reinhold, Rosellini: del batister (as always)

Rubric 175
Coment li mesaçer parole a Braibant.
Laisse 176

        Li mesaçer nen demorent mie;
        Dist a li rois, "Macon vos benedie;
        Li damisel non oit barba ne mie.
        Çovençel est, si oit gran segnorie; ((345))
6185 Forment l'ama Galafrio, si le oit doné sa fie: (695)
        Por muler l'oit presa, si l'oit bateçie,
        Si croit en Deo, le filz sante Marie.*
        Cil damisel oit si la çera ardie, ((350))
        Qe de·l veoi(r) la çent è spaventie.*
6190 Molto vos menaça a la spea forbie,* (700)
        Et avec lui tota sa conpagnie."
        Dist Braibant, "Ces non obliarò mie;
        Si e lo trovo in canpo ni en vie, ((355))
        Per Macometo, o je sui avoie,*
6195 Se trovo Galafrio non portarà la vie; (705)
        Morte serà, lui e sa baronie."*

Rubric 176
Coment Braibant demanda conseli a ses barons.
Laisse 177

        Li rois Braibant nen fu pais demoré;
        Adonc apelle ses rois e ses amiré, ((360))
        A un conseil n'oit quarante sé,
6200 Tot d·i milor e d·i plus honoré, (710)

    6187 MS.:s̄t̄ē; Chichmaref, Rosellini: sante Marie
    6189 MS.: del veoit; Reinhold: de-l veoir (emend for *veoit*); Chichmaref: veoir . . . çent espanventi (corrected Reinhold, review of Chichmaref); Rosellini, MS.: veoir
    6190 Chichmaref: Molto nos
    6191 Chichmaref: la conpagnie (error also noted by Frati, Reinhold [review of Chichmaref])
    6192 Rosellini: on obliarò (typo; noted also by Holden, "lire *non*")
    6193 Reinhold: Se (emend); Chichmaref: S[e] ie
    6194 Reinhold: Por Macometo, o' je sui avoïe; Rosellini: Per Macometo, o je sui avoïe. Chichmaref: Por Macometo, o ie . . .
    6196 Chichmaref, Reinhold, Rosellini: Morto
    6200 Rosellini: li milor

Karleto 535

        Qe il avoit dentro da son regné.
        En una çanbre li mena a la çelé;
        "Segnur," fait il, "mal avon esploité,* ((365))
        Quando Galafrio estoit arenojé.*
6205 Renojé oit Macon, e si croit en Dé, (715)
        Cil Crucifixo qi prendent li Çué,
        Par un damisel, de França la loé,
        Qe filz fo Pepin, qe son filz oit atosegé; ((370))
        Et oit nome K*arleto*, cosi est apelé.
6210 E so par voir, e i n'à sorte çité, (720)
        Se cil enfant po vivere in eté,
        Segnor serà de tota Crestenté,
        E sovra tot enperaor clamé. ((375))
        E porço Galafrio qe à questo trové*
6215 (Qe a Roma doit esere coroné), (725)   35ra
        Li oit sa filla por mojer doné.
        Sor son palés en la sala pavé,
        Oit una glese et un altar sagré, ((380))
        E fa çanter mese, e l'oficio de Dé;
6220 E Macometo si li è oblié. (730)
        De questa onte par poi non son raçé;
        Conselés moi a foi et a lialté,
        A ves conseil, si con vos me diré;* ((385))
        Eo me serò a ves conseil ovré."

    6203 Chichmaref, Reinhold, Rosellini: mal (final *l* faded)

    6204 Reinhold: à renoié; Chichmaref: a renoié. Rosellini: Galfrio

    6206 Chichmaref: crucifiso (error also noted by Frati, Reinhold [review of Chichmaref])

    6207 Chichmaref: l'a loé, Reinhold, [review of Chichmaref]: la loé OR l'aloé; Rosellini: l'aloé

    6210 Chichmaref: e ma sorte (corrected by Reinhold, review of Chichmaref)

    6212 Chichmaref: de tote (also corrected by Frati, Reinhold [review of Chichmaref])

    6214 Chichmaref, Reinhold, Rosellini: por ço

    6218 Chichmaref, Rosellini: una glese

    6221 Chichmaref: Da questa (corrected also by Frati)

Rubric 177
Coment Cornuç parole a li rois.
Laisse 178

6225 Quant li baron oldent et intendent,* (735)
      Rois ni baron no lì forent solament.
      Un rois parole d'oltre Jerusalent;
      Cil oit nome Cornuç, se la istolie no ment. ((390))
      Davant Braibant parla ireament,
6230 "Ai, sire rois, vu no valì nient, (740)
      Quando vos faites tant demorament;
      Ad asenbler ves omes e vestra gent,
      XL. rois avés a ves comandament; ((395))
      A le menor riche reame apent.
6235 Se far le volés, de ces non doto nient,* (745)
      Qe li rois Galafrio, vu lo farì dolent,
      Si le torì tere e casament,
      E quello Karleto condurì vilanement. ((400))
      Morto serà, delivré a torment,
6240 Qe tot son arte ne le varà nient. (750)
      Jamais contra vos, ni la vestra jent,
      El non prenderà arme ni guarniment."
      Li rois l'intent, si s'en rise belament; ((405))
      Por la parole mile marçé li rent.
6245 E si le dist, e ben e lojalment, (755)
      "Cornuz," fait il, "e vos tegno a parent.
      Quant averò asenblé mes homes e ma çent,
      Mon astendardo serà a ves comandament." ((410))

Rubric 177 (after 6224) MS., Reinhold: Rois
  6232 Chichmaref: Adasenblez (error also noted by Frati, Reinhold [review of Chichmaref])
  6236 Rosellini: vu la fari
  6244 Chichmaref: marçe; Reinhold [review of Chichmaref]: marçé
  6246 Reinhold, Rosellini: Cornuç

Rubric 178
Coment Braibant parole a li rois.*
Laisse 179

   Un autre rois, c'oit nome Balatron,
6250 Quel ten la tere qe fu rois Salamon, (760)
   A gran mervile oit li cor felon;
   Non è si fol pain tros li Carfaraon.
   Davant li rois departì la tençon: ((415))
   "Bon rois," fait il, "porquoi vos çeleron?
6255 Ne vos dirò mençogna de bricon; (765)
   Tanti avés Sarasin e Sclavon,
   Se far le volés cun vestra legion,
   A vos non durerà ne çité ne dojon. ((420))
   Con vestra jent prenderì tot li mon;
6260 Li rois Galafrio, ne le petit garçon, (770)
   Encontra vos non averà guarison.   35rb
   Se pason mer en nef et en dormon,
   Nu li ape(n)deron davanti un stacon, ((425))
   Ça ver de nos non averà guarison.*
6265 Pois aliron en França et a Lion, (775)
   Si conquiron tota la legion;
   Trosqua a Rome nu vos coronaron;
   Li son san Pero fora nu li traron, ((430))
   Si le meteron Trivigant e Macon."
6270 Dist Braibant, "E nu questo otrion; (780)
   A gran mervile quest'è bona rason.
   Milor consejo no*n* quero en ceste mon;
   E mo e vos, nu seren conpagnon." ((435))

 Rubric 178 (after 6248) Guessard, Reinhold, Rosellini: Balatron (emend); MS., Reinhold: Rois
 6251 Reinhold: mermile
 6252 Chichmaref, Reinhold: car Faraon (see Glossary)
 6253 Rosellini: departi
 6254 Chichmaref: vos celaron (missing cedilla) (Frati, Reinhold [review of Chichmaref] also correct to *uos çelaron*)
 6259 Chichmaref: prendron (corrected also by Reinhold [review of Chichmaref])
 6260 Rosellini: ne li
 6263 MS.: apederon; Reinhold, Chichmaref, Rosellini: ape[n]deron (emend)
 6266 Chichmaref: region (corrected by Reinhold [review of Chichmaref] also)
 6269 Reinhold: Trevigant

Rubric 179
Coment li rois Damabruz . . . *
Laisse 180

	Rois Danabruns si fu en pe levé;
6275	Saçes omo ert, e molto ben doté, (785)
	E in sa loi estoit molto amé.
	"Bon rois," fait il, "e vo qe vu saçé,
	En tot li mondo, e de longo e de le, ((440))
	Meltre de vos nen soroit trové.*
6280	Se mon conseil prender volé, (790)
	Vu mandarés par tot le contré,
	A bors a ville a cité et a çasté.
	Asenblarés vestra jent, e rois et amiré,* ((445))
	Tanti n'averés quando forent asenblé
6285	Qe ça li nonbre n'en seroit conté. (795)
	Pasaron mer en nef et en galé,
	Spagna prenderon; Galafrio l'amiré,
	Morto serà tote tros so rité, ((450))
	Falsiron e Marsilio, q'el celi en tel herté,*
6290	E Balugant, li menor in eté. (800)
	E dapoisqe de çestor nu seron delivré;
	Quel Karleto non doto una poma poré."
	Dist li rois, "Vu avì ben parlé; ((455))
	Eo farò ben la vestra volunté."
6295	Li rois Braibant nen oit demoré; (805)
	Letere oit fato, e brevi sajelé,
	Et oit mandé par tot le contré,
	Por le reami e davant e daré. ((460))
	E celle rois qe le ont en poesté
6300	Ont sa çent requesta e demandé. (810)
	Quando tota çent furent asenblé,
	Tanti furent a verdi helmi çemé,

Rubric 179 (after 6273) Guessard, Reinhold, Rosellini: Damabruz [parole] (emend). MS., Reinhold: Rois

6279 Reinhold: seroit

6283 MS.: et amire; Chichmaref: et amirè; Reinhold [review of Chichmaref]: e amiré; Reinhold, Rosellini: e amiré

6287 Reinhold, Rosellini: [e] Galafrio (emend)

6289 Reinhold: ten (emend for *teli*); Rosellini: q'el teni; Chichmaref: q'el te[n] li en

6291 Reinhold: seren delivré. Chichmaref: dapois qe

    A nove tarçe, a lançe et a spe, ((465))
    Quatro cento mille furent adesmé.
6305 Si le furent trenta rois coroné; (815)
    De çivaler lì fu a gran planté.

Rubric 180
Coment li rois Braibant (f)i asenbler / Sa jent por aler a Saragoçe.
Laisse 181

    Li rois Braibant nen volse demorer;
    El fi ses rois e sa jent asenbler. ((470))   35ᵛᵃ
    Quatro cento mille se poent esmer,
6310 A bone arme a corant destrer. (820)
    Li rois Braibant tanto se fait priser,
    En soa loi n'à milor çivaler.
    Le arme qe il porte no se po rojer,* ((475))
    Por grant avoir qi le deust conprer.
6315 Durendarda porte qe tant fait loer; (825)
    De l'elmo qe il porte tanto fu dur l'açer,
    E si avoit si bon li tenper,
    Jamais de lui ne se pote trençer. ((480))
    De le aubergo no vos vojo conter,
6320 Ne teme qe par lui se poust endaner.* (830)
    Qe vos doie li plais plus alonçer?*
    Se il creist a li voir justisier,
    Milor de lui ne se poroit trover. ((485))
    E quando cun Karleto el vene a çostrer,
6325 Ben li mostrò s'elo era lainer. (835)
    Donc fait il soa jent asenbler,
    E pasarent oltra l'aigua de·l mer.
    Ençe en Espagne venent ad ariver;* ((490))

Rubric 180 (after 6306) line 1: MS.: si; Keller: fi; Keller: fi, Reinhold: (f)i (emend);
Chichmaref: fi asenbler; Rosellini: fi esenbler; MS., Reinhold: Rois
    6316 Chichmaref: Del elmo
    6320 Chichmaref: temé; Reinhold: temè
    6321 Reinhold: dò; Chichmaref: do ie
    6322 MS.: Selilcreist; Reinhold: Se(l) il (i.e., *l* is not necessary); Rosellini: Se il; Chichmaref: S'el i[l] creïst
    6324 Chichmaref: cum Karleto
    6325 Chichmaref: lanier
    6328 Chichmaref: En çen . . .

Apreso Saragoça s'alirent a loçer;
6330 Tendent tendes en pre et in verçer. (840)
Galafrio le vi, n'ait en lu qe irer;
El vide ben qe li estoit mester
De soi defendre, o far·se vergonçer. ((495))
O vi K*arleto* le prist a demander:
6335 "Bel filz," fait il, "par vos ai ste nojer. (845)
Veeç pain e davant e darer?
Ça son venu par moi desariter,
E vos prendre s'i ve poront bailer." ((500))
Dist K*arleto*, "Avì altro penser.
6340 S'i son venu par vos desariter, (850)
Por mal lì vene*n*t, se poso arme bailer;
Tosto li averò li afar calonçer.
Jamais mon Deo non averò renojer, ((505))
En lo qual e ò tota quanta ma sper.
6345 Bon m'averà il da lor defenser." (855)
Li rois l'intent, si le vait acoler.

Rubric 181
Coment s'aloçent a Saragoçe.
Laisse 182

Davanti Saragoçe in le pre verdojant,
S'aloçarent Sarasin e Persant. ((510))
E furent tanti a verdi helmi lusant,
6350 Conter ne se poroit le milor ne li çant. (860)
Li rois Braibant si se fait en avant,
E si apelle ses rois, ses amirant;*
Davant lu n'avoit plus de çant. ((515))
"Segnur," dist il, "ben est aparisant,
6355 Qe Galafrio si me ten a niant, (865)
Quando demanes, sença termen prendant,*   35vb
Elo no m'oit envojé celle enfant.
Cornuz, bel frer, monteç en auferant,* ((520))

6329 Reinhold: aloçer
6333 Reinhold: far-se; Chichmaref, Rosellini: farse
6334 Chichmaref: Qui Karleto (corrected by Reinhold, review of Chichmaref)
6345 Rosellini: ben m'avera [sic]
Rubric 181 (after 6346) Keller: saloçent
6352 Chichmaref: amirant; Reinhold: amirant (emend for MS. *amriant*); Rosellini: amiriant
6358 Reinhold: Cornuç; Rosellini: euferant

	Aleç a Saragoça, si le dites en ojant,
6360	Se demanes ne m'envoja l'infant (870)
	A cui oit doné sa file Belisant,
	Cosi farò de lui ensemant
	Com de çelu q'è apendu a·l vant." ((525))
	Dist Cornuç, "Por mon Deo Trevigant,
6365	Eo le dirò plu dur et aspremant." (875)
	Li rois Cornuç nen fait arestamant;
	Ven a sa tende, pris son guarnimant.
	Veste l'aubers, alaça l'elmo lusant; ((530))
	Çinse la spea, monta en auferant.
6370	Brandist un asta a li fer trençant, (880)
	Davant da soi, tarça de olifant.*
	Ven a Saragoça, da la porta davant,
	Ad alta vos el criò altamant: ((535))
	"A, rois Galafrio, el vos va malamant;
6375	Savés parcoi vu ne demorés tant? (885)
	Qe a mon segnor, li forte rois Braibant,
	No le envojés Karleto li enfant,
	Qe vu tenés en ves sale plus grant, ((540))
	O fa çanter mese e li Deo sagramant.
6380	Doné li avì vestra filla Belisant. (890)
	Tosto me·l bailés a moi en cest canp,
	Qe je le moine a mon sir l'amirant.
	Se vu no·l faites, saçés a esiant, ((545))
	En vostre vite nen daroie un guant.
6385	Apendu serés con lairon puant, (895)
	<O> arse en fois, çité la polvere a·l vant."*
	Li rois l'intent, si·l ten por niant;
	Karleto estoit ilec de presant, ((550))
	De le parole estoit ben atant.

6370 Chichmaref, Reinhold, Rosellini: un' asta (as always for feminine article + vowel)

6371 Chichmaref: soa tarça (corrected in his notes to soi tarça)

6380 Chichmaref, Reinhold, Rosellini: Doné; Chichmaref, Reinhold: li avì vestra filla . . .

6381 Chichmaref, Reinhold: me-l; Rosellini: me'l

6382 Chichmaref: mon fiz l'amirant (corrected by Reinhold [review of Chichmaref] also)

6383 Chichmaref, Reinhold: no-l; Rosellini: no'l

6386 Chichmaref, Rosellini: arse; Reinhold: arsé (Reinhold [review of Chichmaref] corrects Chichmaref also to *arsé*, from an Old French *arser*); Chichmaref, Reinhold, Rosellini: O

6387 Chichmaref, Reinhold: si-l; Rosellini: si'l

6390 Za dirà il un pois de son talant:* (900)
"Bon rois," fait il, "se vos m'amés niant,
Doneç a moi le arme e·l guarnimant.
A quel pain dites·le segurmant, ((555))
Qe un petit atende en avant,
6395 Qe demanes l'invojarì l'infant." (905)
Dist Galafrio, "Ces non farò niant;
Vu sì un damisel, baçaler de jojant,
E cil est un rois a mervile posant. ((560))
Encontra lui non varisi niant;
6400 No le durarise a spea ni a lanç." (910)
Dist Karleto, "Se vu non faites nojant,
Nen serò jamais ves benvojant,
Ne mais non prenderò vestra fila Belisant." ((565))
Quando li rois olde pur son talant,
6405 O voja o no, elo li consant. (915)*   36ra
A li balcon de celle pavimant,
Dist a·l pain qe defora l'atant:
"Or vos sofrerés en pais bellemant, ((570))
A li rois Braibant vojo envojer l'infant."
6410 Dist Cornuç, "Vu farì saçemant." (920)

Rubric 182
Coment Ka(r)leto s'adobe, e Morant / li fait çivaler; et il aloit defors et oncis li pain, de quo fu grant çoie.
Laisse 183

Li rois Galafrio, qe tant fait a loer,
A Karleto fait riçe arme porter,
E si le vol far çivaler. ((575))

6390 Chichmaref: S' adira (Reinhold, review of Chichmaref corrects also)
6392 Chichmaref: e-l guarniment (error which Frati, Reinhold [review of Chichmaref] also note); Reinhold, Rosellini: e 'l
6393 Reinhold, Chichmaref, Rosellini: dites le
6395 Reinhold: li 'nvoiarì; Chichmaref, Rosellini: l' invoiari
6397 Chichmaref: baçaler deloiant (Reinhold [review of Chichmaref] corrects also; cf. Bovo v. 1137); Reinhold, Rosellini: de joiant
6402 Reinhold: ben-voiant; Chichmaref: ben voiant
6409 MS.: lirois
Rubric 182 (after 6410) line 1: MS.: kaleto (no abbreviation line present); Keller: kaleto sadobe; Reinhold, Rosellini: Ka[r]leto; Chichmaref: Karleto (Frati, Reinhold [review of Chichmaref] also note his error); line 2: Keller: de . . . fors
6411 MS.: Galafrio; Reinhold: Galafroi

	Dist Karleto, "Non aça quel penser;
6415	Ç(i)valer non serò da le man de Escler." (925)
	Civaler se fi faire a Morando de River;*
	El veste l'aubers e calça le ganber;
	Morando le çinse le brando forbi d'açer, ((580))
	Le speron li calçoit li altro civaler.
6420	Li rois Galafrio li donò un bon destrer, (930)
	E cil meesme li vait l'eume a laçer.
	E la raine li vait a baser:
	"Bel filz," fait ela, "se ve lasés mener, ((585))
	En mia vite mais viver non quer."
6425	E Belisant nen stoit de plurer; (935)
	Quando Karleto la voit a baser,
	Si la conforte: no se doja nojer,
	Qe en petit d'ore el tornerà arer.* ((590))
	Adoncha Karleto tosto monta a destrer;
6430	Una grosa aste q'estoit d'un pomer, (940)
	Si le bailì Morando de River;
	E una tarçe depinta molto cler.
	E quel pain no fait se no uçer: ((595))
	"Galafrio, sire, tropo po entarder,
6435	Quando me fa quilois tan demorer." (945)
	Dist li rois, "E·l faço apariler;
	En petit d'ore ne le porés mener."
	E quando Karleto fo monté a destrer, ((600))
	Nen volse pais longament entarder.
6440	El fi la porta e li pont abaser; (950)
	A l'ensir fors, manti ne fe plurer.
	Molto le plure Morando de River,
	Desor tot Belisant, sa muler. ((605))
	E la raine vait Macon orer,
6445	Qe guardi son enfant da mortel engonbrer. (955)

6415 MS.: Çualer; Reinhold, Rosellini: Ç[i]valer; Chichmaref: Çivaler (Frati, Reinhold [review of Chichmaref] also note the error)

6416 Chichmaref: Çivaler (error also noted by Frati (who misquotes as çivoler) Reinhold, review of Chichmaref)

6419 Chichmaref, Reinhold, Rosellini: l'esperon. Chichmaref: çivaler (error also noted by Frati, Reinhold [review of Chichmaref])

6422 Reinhold: abaser

6426 Reinhold: abaser

6435 Chichmaref, Reinhold: qui lois (as always)

6436 Chichmaref, Reinhold: E'-l; Rosellini: E 'l

6441 Chichmaref: fè

	A le fenestre de le palas plener,*	
	Li rois Galafrio e Morando de River	
	S'apoçarent por l'infant guarder.* ((610))	
	No remis en la tere peon ni çivaler	
6450	Qe a le murs ne se voit a 'pojer, (960)	
	Por veoir cel voslato çostrer.*	36rb

Rubric 183
Coment Karleto ensì (d)e Saragoçe / e vait enverso le pain.*
Laisse 184

	Quando Karleto fu de Saragoça ensu,
	Par lui veoir corent li grant e li menu. ((615))
	Li Sarasin li voit, est a lu venu,
6455	Si le escrie, "Vu siés malvenu. (965)
	Sì vu celu qe aora Jesu?
	Par vu avoir tel oste è removu,*
	Nen fu major esguardé ni veu. ((620))
	Alez avanti, for por ces pre herbu,
6460	A li rois Braibant qe vos oit atendu; (970)
	Vu ne serés por la gorça apendu."
	Dist Karleto, "No son parço venu;
	Tant ai parlé, tu ne serà mu. ((625))
	Se me volés amener a ves dru,*
6465	Ne le virò se no son abatu (975)
	De mon çival, e a tera cau."
	Dist le pain, "Vu siés malvenu;
	Doncha cuités avoir contra de mo vertu? ((630))

6446 Chichmaref, Reinhold, Rosellini: palas

6450 Chichmaref, Reinhold, Rosellini: voit apoier

6451 Chichmaref: veoir celu o slato (see note)

Rubric 183 (after 6451) line 1: MS., Keller: ensile; Reinhold: ensì de (emend for *ensile*); Mussafia, "Handschriftliche Studien II": ensi le; Chichmaref, Rosellini: ensi de (Chichmaref, at end, corrects to *ensi le*)

6455 Reinhold, Rosellini: mal venu

6458 Reinhold, Chichmaref: veü; Reinhold: esgardé (not Chichmaref, as noted by Rosellini!)

6462 Chichmaref, Reinhold, Rosellini: par ço

6464 Chichmaref, Reinhold, Rosellini: volés

6465 Chichmaref: se non son abatu (error also noted by Frati, Reinhold [review of Chichmaref])

6466 Chichmaref, Reinhold: caü

	Plu de trenta anni ai porté mon escu,
6470	E tu è un damisel qe non è conou. (980)
	Tosto me donés li brant d'açer molu,
	Si metés jos la lançe e li escu."*
	Dist Karleto, "No te doto un festu; ((635))
	Por mal ancoi da li altri movu;*
6475	Serà pro bon ora fusi nasu." (985)

Rubric 184
Coment se parlarent ensenbre.
Laisse 185

	Li pro Karleto si·l mist por rason:*
	"Sarasin, sire, qe aorì Macon,
	Et eo creço en Deo et in ses non, ((640))
	Ça è venu por mal entencion,
6480	Por mener moi en durisima preson?" (990)
	Dist le pain, "Tu parle cun bricon;
	No te voroie oncir, par l'onor de Sanson.
	Se davant Braibant <v>i<v>o no ve menon,* ((645))
	Ço q'e ò fato non varoit un speron."
6485	Dist Karleto, "Porqe tanto tençon? (995)
	De ta venue, te darò gujerdon."*
	Lor se fait arer li trato d'un bolçon;*
	Ça oldirés bataile d'anbesdos li baron. ((650))
	Li destrer broçe de li doré speron;
6490	Brandist le aste o li fer trençant son.* (1000)
	Por tel esforço (in)porta li aragon,
	La tera trenble entorno et inviron.

6469 Chichmaref: Plus de (error also noted by Frati, Reinhold [review of Chichmaref])

6470 Chichmaref, Reinhold: conoü

6472 Reinhold: Rimetés; Chichmaref: Si metes ios (Reinhold [review of Chichmaref] also notes); Rosellini: Si metés joʒ

6475 Reinhold, Rosellini: bon' ora; Chichmaref: sera pro, bon'ora

6476 Reinhold, Chichmaref: si-l; Rosellini: si'l

6478 Chichmaref: en De et . . . (error noted also by Frati, but not *De'*, as he misquotes)

6484 Reinhold, Rosellini: Ço qe ò fato; Chichmaref: Ço qe o fato

6488 Chichmaref, Reinhold: anbes dos (as always)

6491 MS.: niporta; Reinhold: n'i porta; Frati, MS.: ni porta; Chichmaref, Rosellini: vi porta (Frati: ni porta, Reinhold [review of Chichmaref]: n'i porta)

Rubric 185
Coment se (v)ont a ferir anbidos / li baron mes Ka(r)leto l'abatì.*
Laisse 186

     Li du baron se sont desfié; ((655))
     Li Sarasin molto fu redoté,
6495 Qe no l'oncie a li fero quaré; (1005)   36va
     E li fer davanti, elo se mis daré.
     Quando K*arleto* le oit reguardé,
     De cella colsa el se est amervelé. ((660))
     Dist enfra soi, "E seroie blasmé,
6500 Se insement eo non fais de·l me." (1010)
     De le restoi anbedos s'adonè;
     L'asta de·l pain fo in troncon volé,
     E quella de K*arleto* nen fo pais frosé. ((665))
     Si grande colpo elo li oit enplojé,
6505 Qe cun tot le çival le çitò a·l pre. (1015)
     Galafrio le vi, n'oit un riso çité;
     Qui qe a le mur estoien apojé,
     N'oit gran çoja por çel colpo mené. ((670))
     Le Sarasin fo en pe levé;
6510 S'el oit dol de ço, non demandé. (1020)
     Or voit il ben qe il estoit vergogné,
     Quant por un enfant estoit deroçé.
     La spea trait, como homo ben menbré; ((675))
     O vi son çival, quella part est alé;*
6515 Monté le fust, quant le fu calonçé. (1025)
     K*arleto* li pros non oit l'ovra oblié;

    Rubric 185 (after 6492) line 1: MS.: se nont; Keller: se uont . . . anbi dos; Reinhold: se vont (emend for MS. *senont)*; Rosellini: se vont (ms); Chichmaref: se vont . . . anbi dos; line 2: MS.: Mes kaleto (no abbreviation line); Keller: kaleto labati; Chichmaref: Karleto (error also noted by Frati); Reinhold, Rosellini: Ka[r]leto

    6495 Chichmaref: l' oncis

    6500 Chichmaref, Reinhold: del me; Rosellini: del mé

    6501 Chichmaref, Reinhold, Rosellini: s'a doné. Chichmaref: resto i anbe dos . . . (Reinhold, review of Chichmaref also corrects to *de le restoi*, cf. Bovo 2002); Rosellini: rostoi (typo; cf. Plouzeau)

    6502 Chichmaref: fu in troncon (corrected Frati and Reinhold [review of Chichmaref])

    6514 MS.: vi ɋ son

    6515 Rosellini: Moté le . . . (cf. Plouzeau "lire *monté?*"). Chichmaref: Monte le . . . calonçé (corrected Reinhold [review of Chichmaref]); Frati, MS.: cabençé

Tent la spee a li pomo doré,
Ver lui s'en vait, li fren abandoné. ((680))
E le çival s'en fuit, si le oit lasé
6520 Deverso l'oste Braibant l'amiré. (1030)

Rubric 186
Coment se ferirent de li brandi / e li çival s'en fuit ver l'oste.
Laisse 187

Grande fu la bataile d'anbes li çivaler;
Le Sarasin fu orgoloso e fer.
Quant el veoit qe s'en vait son destrer, ((685))
Tel dol en oit, ben cuita raçer.
6525 La spea trait, c'oit li pomo d'or cler; (1035)
A Karleto vait un gran colpo doner
Desor li eume, qe tot li fait fraper.
Nen fust Deo, li voir justisier, ((690))
Qe le guarì e fe la spea torner,
6530 Fendu l'averoit trosqu'a li dent cler. (1040)
La spea torna, qe fe le scu fraper,
Con tot la guincha a li canpo voler.
Se il aust conseu li destrer, ((695))
Karleto en fust avec lui peoner.
6535 M'el se manten con valant e ber; (1045)
Le pain fer de la spea d'açer;
Un si gran colpo elo li vait doner,
L'elmo li trençe con tot li çapeler.* ((700))
Ne le valt la cofie valisant un diner;
6540 Trosqua in le dente elo la fa caller; (1050)
Roversa li colpò, morto li fait verser.*

6518 Chichmaref: Per lui

Rubric 186 (after 6520) line 1: Reinhold, Rosellini: Brandi (corrected by Plouzeau also); line 2: Keller: sen . , . uer loste

6530 Reinhold: trosqua li . . .

6531 Chichmaref: qe fè le sai fraper l'escu . . . ; (also noted by Frati, Reinhold [review of Chichmaref], misnumbered (683 for 693); cf his 818, below, also noted by Frati; Reinhold, Rosellini: le scu

6532 Chichmaref: Con tot[a] la

6535 Chichmaref: M'el . . . com; Reinhold, Rosellini: Me'l

6541 Chichmaref: Reversa (emend; Corrected Reinhold [review of Chichmaref]) . . . li colpo . . . cf. 6543, sperono

                    Quant à ço fato, nen volse tornar arer;   36^(vb)
                    Anci speronò verso l'oste d·i Escler; ((705))
                    Davant Braibant elo fait un torner,
      6545   Qe le virent plus de cento miler. (1055)
                    A alta vos començoit uçer,
                    "Ai, Braibant, eo sui li baçaler,*
                    Porqe vu sì pasé oltra la mer, ((710))
                    Par moi meesme querir e demander."
      6550   Quant à ço dito, si s'en torna arer; (1060)
                    Avantqe pain poust arme bailer,
                    Entra in Saragoça sença nul engonbrer.

Rubric 187
Coment Karleto aloit a l'oste de (Braibant) / E si li menaçoit e pois retornoit a Saragoçe; / E Sarasin si s'armarent por conbatre.*
Laisse 188

                    Quant Braibant oit veçu li vasal, ((715))
                    Qe né fu en França la lojal,
      6555   Qe croit en Deo, li per e li spirtal, (1065)
                    A gran mervile e·lo tent por mal.*
                    Quant oit morto Cornuç l'amiral,
                    Dist a so jent, "Quel è homo natural; ((720))
                    S'el non creist en cele loi mortal,
      6560   Meltre çivaler non vide hon carnal." (1070)
                    Un ses nevo apelle, c'oit non Florial,*
                    "Florial," dist il, "tosto monteç a çival,
                    Avec vos e Baldino e Moral, ((725))

6543 Chichmaref: sperono (corrected Reinhold [review of Chichmaref] also)

Rubric 187 (after 6552) MS.: balugat; Keller: loste . . . balugat; Reinhold, Rosellini: Braibant (emend); Chichmaref: Baluga[n]t; line 2: MS., Reinhold: Retornoit; line 3: Keller: si sarmarent

6554 Chichmaref, Reinhold, Rosellini: ne fu

6555 MS.: sprirtal; Reinhold: Spirtal; Rosellini: Sprirtal; Chichmaref: li per (el) ispirital (Frati corrects *e li sprirtal*); Reinhold [review of Chichmaref]: li per e li Spirtal (cf. Bovo 918)

6556 Chichmaref, Reinhold, Rosellini: elo [li] tent

6558 Chichmaref: Dist a saient (corrected by Frati and Reinhold [review of Chichmaref])

6559 MS.: mortal; Chichmaref: mortal(e) (noted also by Frati; Reinhold [review of Chichmaref]); Rosellini misquotes as *nortal(e)*

6562 Reinhold: cival

        E Danabrin li pros e lo lojal;
6565 Trosqua a Saragoça no*n* fareç estal. (1075)
        Cinquanta mille de mon ancional,*
        Q*i* non ament ni desduto ni bal
        Seront avec vos a·l canpo comunal. ((730))
        Alez a Saragoça, si le donaz l'asal;
6570 Se la poez prendre, nen vojo plu ostal.* (1080)
        Galafrio serà apendu cu*n* traito deslojal;
        A quel K*arleto* eo farò tanto mal,
        Ne saveroit co*n*ter nesun homo mortal." ((735))

Rubric 188
Coment Florial, Baldoin, e Morial, et avec
Lor Damabrum cu*n* .l. mill homes s'armarent.*
Laisse 189

        Florial çivalçe, e lui e sa co*n*pagnie;
6575 Cinqua*n*ta mille oit en sa conestablie. (1085)
        Baldin e Danabrin li cançele e le guie,*
        E Moradal a la barba florie.
        Meltre çivaler non è en co*n*pagnie, ((740))
        Ne qe mejo fera de la spea forbie.
6580 Quando da Braibant i se sont partie, (1090)
        Trosque a Saragoçe nen demorent mie;
        Davant la porte font une remie.*
        Galafrio le voit, non à talent qe rie; ((745))
        Par un pitet qe non ese de vie.
6585 Quant cil K*arleto* li conforta e prie, (1095)
        Qe de nul ren no se dot il mie;   37ra
        Qe mo parerà qi averà coardie.
        Adonc apella Falsiron e Marsie, ((750))
        E Balugant a la cera ardie;
6590 Morando de River, e Guarner li ardie. (1100)
        "Segnur," fait il, "qi averà coardie,*

    6571 Reinhold: Galafroi
    Rubric 188 (after 6573) line 1: Reinhold: Baldoïn; line 2: Keller: damabrun; MS., Chichmaref: Damabrum; Reinhold: *Danabrun (emend); Rosellini: Danabrun; MS.: sar marent
    6576 Chichmaref, Reinhold, Rosellini: Danabrin
    6580 Rosellini: e se sont
    6583 Rosellini: telent
    6586 Chichmaref: non se

Da soa amia ben serà escernie;
Mais en sa vie non serà anomie." ((755))
Quant cil l'intent, çascun li disie,
6595 "Frer K*arleto*, ne vos dotés ne mie; (1105)
Ben seron nos tot, e bona aie."*

Rubric 189
Coment Karleto parloite a li infant / E si li amunisent de conbatere.
Laisse 190

Quando K*arleto* oit parlé a li guarçon,
Qe unchamés no*n* prist guarnison, ((760))
Ne mais non ensirent fora de sa mason;
6600 Quando il oldirent cosi parler Karlon, (1110)
Çascun venoit fero cu*n* un lion.
Dist K*arleto*, "Porqe vos çeleron?
Ne le oit mester arco ni bolçon; ((765))
Auberg et eumes e spee da galon,
6605 Quelle seroit nostra defension. (1115)
Veez pain qe venent de randon,
Coverto n'est li poi e li mon?
Ben ne cuitent prender cum bricon. ((770))
Mais, s'a Deo plas, e son santisime non,
6610 Ancois li averon tot quant en preson; (1120)
Tot seront mis a destrucion."
Quant cil entendent si parler li guarçon,
Tot li plus lent devent prodon; ((775))
Dont s'armarent, sença nosa e tençon.

6596 Chichmaref, Reinhold: vos tot . . . e[n] (emend; Chichmaref corrected by Reinhold [review of Chichmaref]); Rosellini: nos . . . e[n]
 Rubric 189 (after 6596) MS., Keller: parloite; Rosellini: parloit; Chichmaref, Reinhold: parloit(e)
 6597 Reinhold: garçon
 6598 Chichmaref: Qe uncha més; Reinhold: Qe uncha mes (as always)
 6602 Chichmaref: celeron (error also noted by Frati, Reinhold [review of Chichmaref]); Reinhold, Rosellini: çeleron
 6605 Chichmaref: nostre defensïon (noted also by Frati, Reinhold [review of Chichmaref]) (as always)
 6608 Chichmaref: Ben ve cuitent (error noted by Reinhold [review of Chichmaref] also)
 6609 Chichmaref: a Deo plais (noted also by Frati, Reinhold [review of Chichmaref]); Rosellini: s'à Dei plas

6615 A Karleto s'acostent, cum bona entencion; (1125)
E Sarasin civalçe a cuita de speron;
Trosque Saragoçe vent Floramon.

Rubric 190
Coment Karleto parlò a li rois.
Laisse 191

Quando Karleto oit veçu qui Escler, ((780))
Cinquant mille a verdi eumi d'açer
6620 A nove targies, a corant destrer, (1130)
Davant la porte corer e stratorner,*
Floriamont e Danabrun li fer,
Balduin li pros e Morial li Escler, ((785))
Entro soi se prendent conseler,
6625 De conbatre la tere e l'asalto doner. (1135)
Mais ço q'i croit, si le fale li penser,
Qe qui dedens no sont si lanier
Qe i se lasì si vilment mener; ((790))
Enanci le seroit qe ferir e çostrer.*
6630 Karleto l'infant nen pote plu demorer; (1140)
O el vi Galafrio, si·l prist a derasner:
"Ai, çentil rois, e vos vojo en projer   37ʳᵇ
Qe le conçé vos me diça doner. ((795))
E vojo aler defors a tornojer
6635 Encontra ceus qe la veço ester, (1145)
Qe son venu da la porta primer.
Çaminerés ensi desbarater,
Qe non saveront o i se diça aler." ((800))

6616 Chichmaref: d'esperon; Reinhold, Rosellini: çivalçe ... d'esperon
6617 Chichmaref: Trosque [a]
6622 Rosellini: Flariamont
6624 Reinhold: [à] conseler (emend); Chichmaref: prendent [a] conseler
6626 Chichmaref: ço qi croit (emend also by Reinhold [review of Chichmaref])
6627 Chichmaref: lanier
6629 Chichmaref: e çost[r]er (error noted also by Frati, Reinhold [review of Chichmaref]); Reinhold: En anci
6631 Chichmaref: si-l prist a derasner; Reinhold: si-l prist à derasner; Rosellini: si 'l prist à derasner
6632 Chichmaref, Reinhold, Rosellini: enproier
6635 Chichmaref, Reinhold, Rosellini: qe là veço
6637 MS.: neres; Chichmaref, Reinhold, Rosellini: Ça m'i verés ... desbareter

　　　　　Dist li rois, "Et eo li vojo otrier;
6640　Dex mil omes averés de çivaler,* (1150)
　　　　　E quando serés defora a li torner,
　　　　　E vos secorerò, s'el vos averà mester."
　　　　　Dist Karleto, "et altro non recher." ((805))

Rubric 191
Coment Karleto aloit a·lla bataile.
Laisse 192

　　　　　Karleto s'arme sença demoramant,
6645　E Falsiron avec lui ensemant. (1155)
　　　　　X. mil furent a verdi eumi lusant;
　　　　　E montent a cival e isné e corant.*
　　　　　Ensent de Saragoçe, da la porte davant; ((810))
　　　　　Ver li pain se vait por maltalant.
6650　Quant le vi Florial, si·n apella Moral: (1160)
　　　　　"Moral," fait il, "eco li conbatant;
　　　　　Batailla averon meravilosa e grant."
　　　　　Atant ven Karleto ponçando l'auferant, ((815))
　　　　　Davant autres li trato d'un arpant.
6655　Fer un pain qe il trova davant; (1165)
　　　　　Ne le scu ni l'aubers ne le fu en guarant.*
　　　　　Morto l'abate in l'erbe verdojant,
　　　　　E pois escrie, "Monçoie, l'amirant!* ((820))
　　　　　Ferez ben, me çivaler valant,
6660　Si defendon la tere e Belisant, (1170)
　　　　　Q'elo no l'aça l'amiré Braibant."
　　　　　E cil le font voluntera por talant;
　　　　　Qi donc veist Guarner e Morant, ((825))
　　　　　E Falsiron, Marsilio e Balugant;*

　　6643 ꝫ for *et*
　　Rubric 191 (after 6643) Keller, Chichmaref, Reinhold, Rosellini: alla bataile
　　6647 MS.: isne e corant; Chichmaref: çival e ... isne (error also noted by Frati, Reinhold [review of Chichmaref]); Reinhold, Rosellini: isné
　　　　6649 Chichmaref, Reinhold: mal talant (as always)
　　　　6650 Chichmaref, Reinhold: si-n; Rosellini: si 'n
　　　　6653 Chichmaref, Reinhold: A tant (as always)
　　　　6656 Chichmaref: Ne le sai ... (noted also by Frati, Reinhold [review of Chichmaref]); cf. line 6531
　　　　　6658 Reinhold: Monçoi
　　　　　6659 Reinhold: civaler

6665 Çascun abate le soe morto e sanglant. (1175)
Quant le aste son frate, ont trato li brant,
Donc veisés, è li esto(r)men si grant:
Tant pe, tant pugni, voler por me li canp. ((830))
Li pro Karleto fo da·l cevo davant;
6670 A qi un colpo el dona de li brant, (1180)
Morto lo çeta, o lue o l'auferant.*
Da l'altra part si ven Floriant,
E Danabrin, Balduyn e Morant. ((835))
Quisti pain ne fue mie lant;
6675 Çascun è pro e de grant ardimant; (1185)
De qui de Saragoçe fait dalmaço grant.
Quando Karleto s'en vait aperceant
En celle part ponçe l'auferant, ((840))
E ten la spea a li pomo d'or lusant,*
6680 Morial ferì a loi de conbatant. (1190)   37ᵛᵃ
Gran colpo li done sor l'eume flanbojant;
Trença li eume e la cofia ensemant.
Trosqu'a le spales, li ait colé li brant; ((845))
Morto l'abate sença nosa e bubant.
6685 Quant Danabrin l'oit veçu morto a·l canp, (1195)
A gram mervile oit loé l'infant.
Elo parlò enverso Floriant:
"Par cestu prender n'oit mandé Braibant, ((850))
Me·l no sa mie come trençe son brant.
6690 Moral è morto de cu e son dolant; (1200)

6665 Chichmaref: abatu le fo e morto (emend for *abate*); corrected Reinhold, review of Chichmaref (cf. *Enf. Ogier* 400)

6666 Chichmaref, Reinhold, Rosellini: frate

6667 MS.: eli estomen; Chichmaref, Reinhold, Rosellini: e[n] li esto[r]men (emend)

6669 Chichmaref: çevo davant (error also noted by Frati, Reinhold [review of Chichmaref])

6672 Chichmaref: Da l' autra (also noted by Frati, Reinhold [review of Chichmaref])

6675 MS.: grant; Chichmaref: de gran ardimant (noted also by Frati, Reinhold [review of Chichmaref])

6683 Chichmaref: Trosqu'a; Reinhold: Trosqua; Rosellini: Trosqu'à (this word division will not be remarked again)

6686 Reinhold, Rosellini: ait loé

6688 Reinhold, Rosellini: çestu

6689 Chichmaref: M' el; Reinhold, Rosellini: Me'l

6690 Reinhold: é son; Chichmaref: de cu è; Rosellini: de cu e

De nu farà tot le sumiant.*
Çama non vi nesun homo vivant,
Qe si resenble ad ardi conbatant." ((855))
Dist Floriant, "Ben est aparisant;
6695   El non fer tanti q'el nen çeti sanglant." (1205)

Rubric 192
Coment Karleto entrò en le stor.
Laisse 193

Quando Karleto entrò dedens li stor,
Lor oldirés soner tanti tanbor.
Gran fu la nose, ne le oisés gregnor; ((860))
E li daumajes e de nos e de lor. (1210)
6700   Karleto l'infant qe porta l'orieflor;
Meltre çivaler non veisés ancor;
Davant li autres fer un amansor,
Qe estoit de Braibant filz de sa seror. ((865))
Trosqu'a li dent mis li brant de color;
6705   Morto l'abate sença nosa ni plor. (1215)
Dist Danabrun diverso li contor,
"Florial, sire, nu averon li pejor;
Por mal fuimes anco si coreor. ((870))
Mal fait celu qi croit a traitor;
6710   Li rois Braibant se stava a gran sejor. (1220)
En tot Egipto non era un major,
Por ces damisel qe est de gran valor;*
Ne s'en poon aler sença desenor, ((870))
Tanti n'à morti! Quando faren retor*
6715   De lor se farà gran dol e gran plor." (1225)

6691 Reinhold: sumiant; Chichmaref, Rosellini: simiiant. Frati- MS.: le sumiant (correction of Chichmaref); Chichmaref: De vu fara

Rubric 192 (after 6695) Keller: K lestor . . .

6696 Chichmaref, Reinhold, Rosellini: li stor (cf. 6720)

6701 Chichmaref: Meltro

6703 Chichmaref: de la seror (corrected also by Frati, Reinhold [review of Chichmaref])

6710 Reinhold: grant

6713 Rosellini: desonor

6714 Reinhold- MS.: faron

Rubric 193
Coment Florian oncist le çival K*arleto*.
Laisse 194

        A gran merville fu K*arleto* valent;
        Fort e ardi e ben reconosent.
        En tota Spagne çivaler non furent ((880))
        Qe ver de lui en fust aparisent.
6720 Por li stor fer e menu e sovent; (1230)
        Tanti no*n* fer q'el non çeti sanglent.
        Rois Danabrun si fu saç e valent;*
        Enver K*arleto* el mis son entent. ((885))
        Ne le vol mie aprosmer de nient;
6725 Por me li canpo li voit guischisent. (1235)
        Mais Florian no fe lo sumient;
        An, le çe a ferir de la spea trençent.*   37ᵛᵇ
        Desor li elme si gran colpo li rent, ((890))
        Nen fust Deo qe li fu en guarent,
6730 Morto l'aust e fato recreent. (1240)
        Mais celle spee atraverso li prent;*
        Qe de le auberg trença de maje çent.
        Et a·l cival por la schina li fent; ((895))
        Le cival caì morto en l'erba verdojent.*
6735 E K*arleto* fu a li pre ensement;* (1245)
        De·l relever nen fi demorament.
        E tra la spea a li pomo lusent,

    Rubric 193 (after 6715) Keller, MS.: .k.
    6726 Reinhold: lo sumient; Chichmaref, Rosellini: simiient. Cf. 6691. Frati, Reinhold [review of Chichmaref] (cf. 853) correct Chichmaref to *lo sumient*
    6727 Chichmaref: An, le çè; Reinhold: An le çè; Rosellini: An le çe
    6728 Reinhold: Desor (emend for MS. *De soi*)
    6731 Chichmaref: a traverso; Rosellini: à traverso
    6732 Chichmaref: de li auberg (error also noted by Frati, Reinhold [review of Chichmaref])
    6733 Chichmaref: al çival (corrected Frati, Reinhold [review of Chichmaref]); Reinhold, Rosellini: al cival
    6734 Chichmaref: Le çival. (also corrected by Frati, Reinhold [review of Chichmaref]); Reinhold: cai' (dieresis and grave accent; cf. 6749)
    6735 Chichmaref: a li pié ensemant (error also corrected by Frati, Reinhold [review of Chichmaref])
    6737 Chichmaref: trà

                    Vençer vorà sa ire e maltalent. ((900))
                    Ver Florian vene por maltalent;*
6740   Quant cel le vi venir ireement,* (1250)
                    Ver lu guenchist li trato d'un arpent;
                    No l'atenderoit par tot l'or d'Orient.*

Rubric 194

Coment K*arleto* fo a li pre e morto son çival.

Laisse 195

                    Quando K*arleto* se oit veçu a·l pre, ((905))
                    S'el oit dol or, ne vos mervilé;*
6745   De son çival el estoit delivré. (1255)
                    Morando le voit ne fu ma si iré;
                    Isnelamant li oit secorso doné.
                    Fer un pain, druo de l'amiré; ((910))
                    Morto li çete, ni braì ne crié.*
6750   Prent le çival por la rena doré; (1260)
                    Ven a K*arleto*, si li oit delivré.
                    E cil le monte, nen oit streve bailé.*
                    De son çival, q'elo vi a li pre, ((915))
                    A gran mervile elo l'oit pluré.
6755   Galafrio li avoit doné por amisté. (1265)
                    Vi Floriant, qe estoit aresté;
                    Avec pain e stroit e seré;
                    E Danabrun estoit da l'altro le. ((920))
                    Quando K*arleto* li oit ben avisé,*
6760   Qi li donast l'onor d'una çité, (1270)
                    Nen remaneroit ne le dese meslé
                    E son çival non fust par lui vençé.

    6738 Chichmaref: mal talent (as always; cf. 6739); misquoted by Rosellini, p. 415 as *mal talant*
    6740 Chichmaref: ce[l] le vi
    Rubric 194 (after 6742) MS., Keller: .k.
    6744 Chichmaref: dolor
    6747 Reinhold: Isnelament
    6752 Chichmaref: oit strene (see note); Reinhold: n'en oit
    6757 Chichmaref: estroit e seré
    6761 Chichmaref: N'en (corrected by Reinhold [review of Chichmaref])
    6762 Chichmaref: non fist (error corrected also by Frati, Reinhold [review of Chichmaref])
    6763 Chichmaref: Per Florian (corrected Reinhold [review of Chichmaref]; cf. 6739)

| | Ver Florian son çival oit lasé, ((925))
| | E ten la spea a li pomo doré.
| 6765 | A Florian el donò tel colé (1275)
| | Desor li elme, tel colpo li à doné,
| | Qe un quarter el n'oit detrençé;
| | Le destro braço e le pugno e la spe, ((930))
| | Reondament li oit avalé.
| 6770 | Mort aust le çival quant cil l'oit speroné, (1280)
| | Verso la tende de Braibant est alé.
| | Karleto le vi, un riso n'à çité;
| | Dist a Morando, "Quel porta l'anbasé ((935))
| | A son segnor, por eser plu doté."*
| 6775 | Dist Morant, "El à mal bragagné;* (1285)   38ra
| | El n'à lasa lo braço e la spe;
| | Por mal ancoi el fu qui asenblé."
| | Danabrun le vi, si ne fu spaventé; ((940))
| | Nen fo ma si en soa viveté.
| 6780 | Li Sarasin de la lo desfaé, (1290)
| | Si comencent le cri e la ué;
| | Por Floria(n) sont en fua torné.*

Rubric 195

Coment Floriam s'en fuit ver l'oste, / E (Karleto) li oit trençé li braço cun li spee.
Laisse 196

| | Via s'en vait fuçando Floriant; ((945))
| | A·l canpo lase li braço e li brant.
| 6785 | Quando le vi revenire Braibant, (1295)
| | Tuto sanglent lui e l'auferant,
| | Ne le ve mie la spea en sa mant.*

6765 Chichmaref: Floriant (error corrected also by Frati, Reinhold [review of Chichmaref] [off by one line])

6766 Reinhold: elmo; Chichmaref: De sor (as always)

6778 Chichmaref: fu espaventé (Frati and Reinhold correct)

6779 Reinhold: vivité

6782 MS.: floriau; Reinhold: Florian (emend for MS.: floriau); Chichmaref, Rosellini: Florian

Rubric 195 (after 6782) line 1: Keller: sen . . . loste; line 2: MS.: karlo.eto; Keller: karloeto . . . cum; Rosellini: Karloeto; Chichmaref, Reinhold: Karl(o)eto; Chichmaref: cum

6787 Chichmaref, Reinhold: ensamant; Rosellini: ensemant. Chichmaref: Ne leve (corrected Reinhold [review of Chichmaref]); Reinhold: Ne le ve; Rosellini: ne leve

	Elo l'apelle, si le dist enn ojant: ((950))
	"Florian, sire, qe est de l'infant?
6790	E no ve·l veço ni darer ni davant." (1300)
	Dist Florian, "El est da luntant;
	Quant anco ferì primerant,
	Elo v'à morto un rois e du soldant.* ((955))
	Et eo apreso, non ve(i o era) de niant;*
6795	Por mal venistes prender le Cristiant.* (1305)
	Le meltri de nos el tent por niant,
	Morto oit Moral q'e·l vi cair da luntant." 38rb

Rubric 196
Coment s'arma B(rai)bant.
Laisse 197

	Quando Braibant olde Florian parler, ((960))
	Como elo li conte son mortel engonbrer,
6800	De Florian vi le sangle rajer; (1310)
	Tel dol en oit q'elo cuita raçer.
	El dist a Florian, "Or v'alez a polser;
	Et eo alirò par vostro cor vençer." ((965))
	A ste parole, li rois prist a guarder
6805	Por la carer, por vie e por senter. (1315)
	Vide sa çent e foir e scanper,
	Qe ça le fio non atendoit li per.
	Karleto li encalçe, e Morando de River, ((970))
	E Falsiron con anbidos ses frer.
6810	Li .X. mile molto se font apriser; (1320)
	Arer li vent cun fait li sparaver*
	A la quaje, quant le va pier.

6788 Chichmaref: en voiant (corrected Reinhold [review of Chichmaref])

6789 Chichmaref: Fiorian (corrected Reinhold [review of Chichmaref])

6790 Reinhold: E' no ve-l; Chichmaref: E' non el veço ni da(ra)rer.. (corrected Reinhold [review of Chichmaref]: E' ne ve-l veço ni darer ni d.).; Rosellini: E no ve 'l

6794 MS.: vero eras; Reinhold: non verò elas (emend for MS. *cras*); Chichmaref: non verò e[n] tal demant; corrected by Frati: non verò etas [sic] demant; Rosellini: non vei o era demant (emend for MS. *non veio eras (ocras)* [sic] *demant*)

6797 Chichmaref, Reinhold: q' e'-l; Rosellini: q'e 'l vi

Rubric 196 (after 6797) MS.: b'aribant; Keller: sarma baribant; Reinhold: *Braibant (emend for MS. *baribant*); Chichmaref: Braibant (emend Reinhold [review of Chichmaref]), Rosellini: Braibant

6806 Reinhold: foïr (as always)

| | Braibant le vi, no cura de tençer; ((975))
| | Demantenant sença nul entarder
| 6815 | El oit pris le arme e li corer. (1325)
| | Doncha verisés tota l'oste monter;
| | Tanti furent, ne se porent esmer.
| | Quando Karleto oldì le graille soner, ((980))
| | Da tot part montar le çivaler,*
| 6820 | El fi qe sajes quant retornò arer,* (1330)   38ᵛᵃ
| | E soa çent el fi reparier,
| | Preso di Saragoça li trato d'un arçer.
| | Mais en la tere el no volse entrer; ((985))
| | E quando Braibant fu monta a destrer,
| 6825 | Arme oit bone, ne se poroit esmer, (1335)
| | E tel osbergo e tel elmo d'açer,
| | Ne se poroit por diner esloger.*
| | Durendarda oit, qe trença volunter; ((990))
| | Plu val la spea, qe l'onor de Baiver.
| 6830 | Helmont dapois un tenpo darer (1340)
| | Si l'avoit par un so çubler,*
| | Qe la furò si cun traitor lainer.
| | Dapois l'avè Rolando l'avoer, ((995))
| | En Ronçival quant fu morto li doce per.
| 6835 | Da lor avanti ne se oldì plu parler,* (1345)
| | Mais non fu homo qi la olsase bailer.
| | Braibant civalçe, qe in le oit gran sper;
| | Par celle spee se fa si fort e fer, ((1000))

6813 Chichmaref: non cura (error also corrected by Frati, Reinhold [review of Chichmaref])

6814 Chichmaref, Reinhold: De mantenant

6821 Chichmaref: E soa cent (error also corrected by Frati, Reinhold [review of Chichmaref])

6827 Reinhold: esroger, Chichmaref: esloyer; Frati: esloger (wrong line—off by two); Chichmaref, note at the end of text: esroyer; Reinhold [review of Chichmaref]. esroger

6830 Chichmaref: Nel mond da pois . . . (as always); Frati: Nel mont (correcting Chichmaref); Reinhold [review of Chichmaref]: Helmont

6832 Reinhold, Rosellini: furò (for furtò); Chichmaref: furo (Reinhold [review of Chichmaref], corrected)

6833 Reinhold, Rosellini: l'ave; Chichmaref: Da pois l' ave

6835 Rosellini: D'alor

6837 Chichmaref: çivalçe (error also corrected by Frati, Rosellini 1912, misquoted Rosellini [çivalce])

	Qe sir estoit d'oltra l'aigua de·l mer.
6840	Par tot tere, e davant e darer, (1350)
	Davant les autres li trato d'un arçer,
	Vait a ferir un de qui çivaler.
	Morto l'abate, sença nosa e tençer;* ((1005))
	Ne le valse arme valisant un diner.
6845	Pois abatì Morando de River; (1355)
	De l'auferant le fe ços devaler;
	Vii. n'abate Braibant li Escler.
	Karleto le voit, n'ait en lu qe irer; ((1010))
	Feru l'averoit con li brant d'açer,
6850	Quant son çival si le fe stratorner. (1360)
	E li rois Braibant fu retornez arer;
	Ad alta vos començoit uçer:
	"Ferez ben, me baron çivaler, ((1015))
	Qe qui no*n* posa ni fuir ni aler."
6855	Doncha verisés li stormeno come*n*çer, (1365)
	Tanti scu fendre, ta(n)ti osberg desmajer,
	Tan pe, tan pugni, tant teste couper,
	A voide selle foir tant destrer,* ((1020))
	Qi le veroit s'en poroit merveler.
6860	Li rois Braibant cu*n* li ses çivaler* (1370)
	Fe qui de Saragoça si forte spaventer
	O voja o no, conven li canpo laser.
	Ver Saragoça prendent li senter; ((1025))
	Galafrio le vi arer torner,
6865	Or vede·l ben, secorso li oit mester. (1375)

38vb

6839 Chichmaref: estoit d'aigua del mer (word omitted); Reinhold [review of Chichmaref] notes also

6847 Chichmaref: VII; Reinhold, Rosellini: .VII.

6849 Chichmaref: Del auferant

6851 Chichmaref: fu retorné(r) arer (Frati, Reinhold [review of Chichmaref] note error also)

6852 Chichmaref: comencoit (error also noted by Frati, Reinhold [review of Chichmaref])

6856 MS.: tati; Reinhold, Rosellini: ta[n]ti; Chichmaref: tanti osberg (error corrected by Frati, Reinhold [review of Chichmaref])

6861 Chichmaref: si forte spavente[r] (Frati, Reinhold [review of Chichmaref]), too note that the *r* is there)

6862 Chichmaref: Q[e], voia o no (error also noted by Frati, Reinhold [review of Chichmaref])

6863 Chichmaref: Per (error also noted by Frati, Reinhold [review of Chichmaref])

6865 Chichmaref: ved' el; Reinhold: vede 'l; Rosellini: ved el

Karleto

      Fe ses graile e bosine soner,
      Arme prendent, quant ne poit bailer;*
      Ne remis en Saragoçe peon ne çivaler, ((1030))   39ra
      N'en esise defors a tornojer.*
6870 Quando Galafrio fo monté a destrer, (1380)
      Ben .XXX. mille i se poent esmer.
      La porta font avrir e li pont abaser,
      Fora ensirent sença nesun tençer. ((1035))
      Ça olderì bataila començer;
6875 Mais de major non oldisi parler.* (1385)

Rubric 197
Coment s'en vait Karleto.
Laisse 198

      Quella bataille fu grant e aduré,
      Tot quel çorno qe l'alba fu duré;
      De anbes part si durò la meslé. ((1040))
      Karleto l'infant non tornò mie aré;
6880 Avant civalçe cun tuta nua sa spe; (1390)
      Trapase l'oste plus d'una le.
      Rois Malatras, un grant amiré,
      Par lui oncire si le vait daré. ((1045))
      Karleto çivalçe, qe fiançe oit en Dé;
6885 Entro doe montagne, grant e desmesuré, (1395)
      L'oit son çival e conduto e mené.
      Ne savoit pais o el soja arivé;*
      De anbes part estoit enseré, ((1050))
      De dos montagne avoit da çascun le.
6890 "Deo," dist Karleto, "bel sir Damenedé,* (1400)

    6869 Reinhold: N'en esise; Chichmaref, Rosellini: Nen esise (C. misquoted by Rosellini as Reinhold)

    6870 Rosellini: fo montè

    6874 Chichmaref: comencer (error also corrected by Frati, Reinhold [review of Chichmaref])

    Rubric 197 (after 6875) Keller: sen uait

    6880 Chichmaref: Avant çivalçe (error also corrected by Frati, Reinhold [review of Chichmaref])

    6882 Chichmaref: Pois Malatras, . . . gran amiré (second error is noted by Frati, Reinhold [review of Chichmaref]; the first not)

    6884 Chichmaref: qe fiance (Frati, Reinhold [review of Chichmaref] also note)

    6887 Chichmaref, Reinhold: o' el

    Cun in malora eo fu ençendré!
    Mon çival m'à trai e ingané,
    Ne so aler avanti ne tornar aré. ((1055))
    Deo me consoli, qe mal sont hostalé."
6895 Si cun il s'oit a Deo comandé, (1405)
    Davant s'è guardé for por la caré;*
    Vi Malatras, qe le venoit daré;
    Non ert cun lui homo qe soit né.* ((1060))
    Quando le vi, no l'oit pais redoté.
6900 Quant Malatras fo a lu aprosmé, (1410)
    Cortoisment el oit derasné.
    "Çivaler, sire, estoit vos le bateçé,*
    Parcoi nos sumes pené e travalé? ((1065))
    Por vos avoir avon la mer pasé,
6905 Con tant çent, nen po eser esmé. (1415)
    Doncha cuités eser e foi e scanpé;*
    Men esiant, li penser v'è fallé,
    Parçoqe estes de pitet eté. ((1070))
    Ne vos ofenderoie par li olz de mun çe;
6910 Eo ne seroie da la çent blasmé; (1420)
    Si me·l tiroit li baron a vilté.
    Par cortesia, me dona quella spe*
    E quel aubergo, a la maja seré; ((1075))
    Aleç avant, davant moi aroté,
6915 Trosqu'a Braibant vu serì amené;* (1425)
    De vu farà la soa volunté.   39rb
    Se quello Deo qe vui aoré,
    Por Macometo renegar le voré, ((1080))

  6891 Reinhold, Chichmaref: mal ora (as always; no longer commented)

  6893 Reinhold: sò (as always; cf. 6926, etc.)

  6898 Chichmaref: cum lui homo o qe soit né (error also corrected by Frati, Reinhold [review of Chichmaref])

  6901 Chichmaref, Reinhold, Rosellini: el [l'] oit (emend); Chichmaref: Cortoisement (error also corrected by Frati, Reinhold [review of Chichmaref])

  6902 Reinhold: estes (emend for MS. *estoit*); Rosellini: estes vos

  6903 Chichmaref, Reinhold, Rosellini: Par coi

  6906 Reinhold: foï; Chichmaref: eser en foi escanpé (error also corrected by Frati, Reinhold [review of Chichmaref]). Reinhold, Rosellini: cuités

  6908 Chichmaref, Reinhold, Rosellini: Par ço qe (as always)

  6909 Chichmaref: di mun çé (error also corrected by Frati, Reinhold [review of Chichmaref])

  6911 Chichmaref, Reinhold: me-l; Rosellini: me'l

  6912 Reinhold: donà

	Ancor porez viver en eté.
6920	Colsa como no si serez encloé, (1430)
	Con fo çelu qe fo crocifié."
	K*arleto* l'olde si le à regardé;
	Un poco sorist, si n'oit un riso çité. ((1085))
	Adoncha parole cun omo ensené:
6925	"Sarasin, sire, vu avì li seno cançé, (1435)
	Ne so s'avés cun vu plu amené
	Mais a vu solo non daria mia spe,
	Ne mes armes un sol pelo pelé. ((1090))
	E dirò plus, ne so se le creé,
6930	Ne le daria, se fustes trenta sé."* (1440)

Rubric 198
Coment Maradras li parole.
Laisse 199

	Maradas parole quant oldì li guarçon:
	"Damisel, sire, tu parli cun bricon;
	Cuiti tu contra moi mantenir en arçon? ((1095))
	No te vorave oncir, par nesune cason,
6935	Blasemo n'averoie en moja region. (1445)
	Por cortesia, descendì a·l sablon;
	Ven a Braibant e aora Macon."
	Dist K*arleto*, "Vu parlez a perdon, ((1100))
	Ç'a Deo no*n* plaça e son santisimo non,
6940	Qe per un homo descenda a sablon. (1450)
	Or laseron ester questa tençon;
	Nen poez aler par nesuna cason*

6921 Chichmaref: fo celu qe fo croicifié (noted also by Frati, Reinhold [review of Chichmaref])

6925 Chichmaref: çançé (corrected Frati, Reinhold [review of Chichmaref])

6926 Chichmaref. Neзo cavés cun un pluame né (Cf. Reinhold [review of Chichmaref])

6929 Reinhold: E'. Chichmaref: neso se le creé . . . (corrected Reinhold [review of Chichmaref])

6930 Reinhold: trenta sé

6931 Reinhold: garçon

6936 Reinhold: desendi

6937 Chichmaref: c' aora Macon

6939 Rosellini, Chichmaref: Ça (cf. Reinhold [review of Chichmaref])

6942 Chichmaref, Reinhold, Rosellini: N'en

  Sença bataile o venir en preson."* ((1110 [sic]))
  Dist le pain, "Malvasio garçon,
6945 Cuiti tu avoir contra moi guarison?" (1455)
  Dist K*arleto*, "Quando a ço nu seron,
  Lor parerà qi serà canpion.
  Ma je da vos, e vojo aver un don.* ((1115))
  Se demo co*n*batre sença nul co*n*pagnon,*
6950 Qe entro nos no sia traison." (1460)
  Dist le pain, "E nu le otrion."*

Laisse 200*

  "Damisel, sire," ço dist li Escler,
  "Por tel co*n*ve*n*to nu averon çostrer: ((1120))
  Qe da mo a vos no se parçoner."
6955 Dist K*arleto*, "E·l vojo volunter." (1465)
  De·l canpo se donent le trato d'un arçer;*
  A ferir se venent anbes le çivaler.
  Por si gran força (in)porta li destrer,* ((1125))
  La tera treme e davant e darer.
6960 Si gran colpi i se vont a doner,* (1470)
  Le scu se speçe tros li auber dopler;
  E qui son bon, non po maja falser.*
  Por gran força inporta li destrer,* ((1130))   39ᵛᵃ
  Qe anbidos se conven ençenocler.
6965 A·l relevar, fa le aste briser; (1475)
  Ne l'un ne l'autro no s(e) plega en strever.*
  Tosto se volçent, si tra li brant d'açer;

  6944 Chichmaref: guarçon (Cf. Frati, Reinhold [review of Chichmaref])
  6945 Chichmaref: contro moi
  6948 Reinhold: e[n] voio (Cf. Reinhold [review of Chichmaref])
  6949 Chichmaref: compagnon
  6954 Reinhold: no sè (Cf. Reinhold [review of Chichmaref], comment on Chichmaref); Rosellini: s'è
  6955 Chichmaref, Reinhold: E'·l; Rosellini: E 'l
  6958 MS.: ni porta; Chichmaref, Reinhold, Rosellini: n'i porta
  6960 Chichmaref, Reinhold, Rosellini: vont adoner
  6961 Chichmaref: L'escu
  6962 Chichmaref: falcer (Frati, Reinhold [review of Chichmaref]—corrects from *falçer*. There is no cedilla in the MS. or Chichmaref)
  6963 Chichmaref, Reinhold, Rosellini: n'i porta
  6966 MS.: no so plega; Chichmaref, Rosellini: no se plega; Reinhold: no se plega, emend for *uo se*
  6967 Chichmaref, Reinhold: trà. Cf. 7005 (his 1515)

| | Gran colpi se done sor li elmi verçer, ((1135))
| | Qe i ne fait flama e fois voler.
| 6970 | E de le scu trencent li quarter,* (1480)
| | E d·i aubers fa le maje coler.
| | Deo pensi de Karleto li baçaler;
| | Gran pena averà a·l pain conquister. ((1140))
| | Or laseron de lor un petit parler;
| 6975 | En petit d'ore, nu li averon torner.* (1485)
| | De le rois Galafrio e vos vojo conter;*
| | Quando el vene a li stor por çostrer,
| | De Karleto demandò Morando de River, ((1145))
| | E Falsiron et anbidos ses frer.
| 6980 | Dist Balugant, "Da nu s'avè sevrer;* (1490)
| | No saven de lui ne vi ne senter;
| | Tant se fa fer a ferir et a çostrer,
| | Nesun a lu po en canpo durer. ((1150))
| | Avanti çivalçe quant nu se tremo arer."*
| 6985 | Dist Galafrio, "Malvasii liçer, (1495)
| | Por Macometo qe je do aorer,
| | Se demanes no le poés trover,
| | Si <li dir>és q'el me vegna a parler,* ((1155))
| | E se vos no l'aça reçater,
| 6990 | Tuti vos fa<rò> por la gorça apiçer."* (1500)
| | Quant cili intendent li rois cosi parler,
| | Molto durament se prende a spaventer.
| | Da li rois se partent, no li olsent plu ester; ((1160))

6970 Chichmaref: L'escu trençent (Cf. Frati)
6972 Reinhold, Rosellini: baçeler
6973 Chichmaref, Reinhold: avera al païn; Rosellini: al pain
6976 Rosellini: paler
6980 Chichmaref, Reinhold, Rosellini: s'ave
6981 Chichmaref, Reinhold: vi'
6984 Chichmaref: nu serremo arrer (cf. Reinhold [review of Chichmaref])
6985 MS.: Malvaslj; Reinhold, Rosellini: Malvasii; Chichmaref: Malvasiz (Cf. Reinhold, review of Chichmaref)
6986 Reinhold: dò (as always)
6987 Chichmaref: demanes vo le poés . . . (Reinhold [review of Chichmaref]: demanés, cf. 211); Reinhold: Si *li dir*és; Rosellini: Si li dirés
6988 Chichmaref: l*[i]* d*[i]r*és; Reinhold: Si *li dir*és; Rosellini: Si li dirés
6989 Reinhold: *se vos* no l' açà; Chichmaref: no lo ça [poés] reçater
6990 Reinhold: *Tuti vos* farò
6991 Reinhold: *cili int*endent
6992 Reinhold: *dura*ment

	Ver la bataile começa a çivalçer.
6995	Si la pasent por estrança ri(v)er; (1505)
	Pasent li pre, li broili e li verçer;
	Desor li pois i prist a monter.
	Quant fo desus, prendent a regarder; ((1165))
	Vi la bataile d'anbes li çivaler.
7000	Quant cil la vi, volent adevaler; (1510)
	Mais le pain se n'acorse en primer.*
	Dist a Karleto, "Vu no sì droiturer;
	Veez vestra jent qe vos ven por aider." ((1170))
	Dist Karleto, "De ço no aça penser."
7005	Cria a sa jent, "Tosto ve tra arer. (1515)
	Se devalés, mal vos po encontrer;
	Da moi a lui e non vojo parçoner."
	Quant qui l'intendent, si lasò li tençer, ((1175))
	E guardent la bataile como averà finer.

Rubric 200
Coment fu grande quella bataille.*
Laisse 201

7010	Grande fu la bataile, meravilosa e pesant,* (1520)
	La qual farent anbi li conbatant.* 39vb
	Detrençé s'oit le arme e le guarnimant;
	Par li aubers apar la carne blanc. ((1180))
	Karleto ten la spea a li pomo d'or lusant;
7015	Desor li eume el ferì le Persant (1525)
	Un si gran colpo si duro e pesant,
	Qe la spea vole in du troncon a·l canp.
	Quando Karleto la vi, si n'oit spavant; ((1185))
	Or vede·l ben qe le va malemant.
7020	Morando e les autres reclama Deo e sant, (1530)

6995 MS.: rier; Reinhold, Chichmaref, Rosellini: ri[v]er
7000 Rosellini: volen
7001 Chichmaref, Reinhold, Rosellini: s'en acorse; Chichmaref: li païn (Cf. Frati, Reinhold [review of Chichmaref])
7004 Chichmaref: non aça'; Reinhold: acà
7005 Reinhold: trà; Chichmaref: tra'
7008 Chichmaref: qui' (as always for MSI *quelli*)
7011 Rosellini: Laqual
7019 Reinhold: vede 'l; Chichmaref: ved' el; Rosellini: ved el

	E la Verçen polcele, qe le soja secorant.
	Dist le pain, "Damisel," a l'infant,
	"Or venerés a le rois Braibant; ((1190))
	Se non aorés Macon e Trevigant,
7025	Vu serì arso e apendu a·l vant."* (1535)
	Dist Karleto, "Ben ne serò dolant."
	Karleto regarde e darer e davant;*
	No vide lançe ni espée ni brant. ((1195))
	Apreso un broilo, d'una çesa avant,
7030	Vi un palon meraviloso e grant, (1540)
	Groso et agu da la ponte davant.
	Quant le vi, celle part va corant,
	Tosto le prist, si le va palmojant.* ((1200))
	Dist le pain, "Cuités qe sia enfant?
7035	Tosto murirés a ma spea trençant." (1545)
	Le Sarasin, le culverto mescreant,
	La spea tent, don si trença li brant.*
	Se ja cil colpo aust conseu l'infant,* ((1205))
	Morto l'aust sença retinemant.
7040	Quando Karleto se fa un pe avant, (1550)
	De le palon, qe fu groso e tenant,
	Si como quel pain li vol ferir de li brant,
	Quel le fer de·l palon sor le braço davant. ((1210))
	Si gran fo li colpo qe li dà quel enfant,
7045	Li braço le detrençe quant qe il ne prant; (1555)
	La spea li fait voler a li canp.
	Quant le pain fo delivré de·l brant,
	La soa força si vait menuant, ((1215))
	Qe plus non valt un diner valisant.*

7022 Reinhold: Dist li pain damisel à l'infant (Reinhold [review of Chichmaref])
7025 Chichmaref: arso o apendu
7028 Chichmaref: ni spee (noted also by Frati, Reinhold [review of Chichmaref])
7031 Chichmaref: de la pointe (Reinhold [review of Chichmaref])
7033 Chichmaref: si leva (corrected Reinhold [review of Chichmaref])
7034 Chichmaref: Cuites; Reinhold, Reinhold, review of Chichmaref; Rosellini: Cuités
7038 Chichmaref, Reinhold: aüst conseü
7047 Chichmaref: Quant li pain (error also noted by Frati, Reinhold [review of Chichmaref])
7048 Chichmaref: la soa força (error also noted by Frati, Reinhold [review of Chichmaref])
7049 Rosellini: no; Chichmaref: no valt

7050 E·l pro K*arleto* no fo pais mie lant; (1560)
La spea prent, quant de·l çival desant;*
Ver le pain vait por maltalant;
La testa li trençe, si le versò a·l canp. ((1220))
Quant celi le verent, qe son sor li pendant,
7055 En soa vite nen furent si çojant, (1565)
Quando a lu est venu Morant,
E Falsiron, Marsilio, e Balugant,
Si le dient, "Or retornez atant; ((1225))
Par vu sen menaçé d'eser apis a·l vant.*
7060 Li rois Galafrio de vu fo in spavant; (1570)   40ra
S'el no vos ve, no serà mais çojant."
Dist K*arleto*, "Soja a li Deo comant."

Rubric 201
Coment K*arleto* tornò a tere qu'istoit morto le pain.*
Laisse 202

Quando K*arleto* fu da le pain delivré, ((1230))
Qe durament li avoit menaçé,
7065 Sa spea fraite, quella oit lasé;* (1575)
E quella de·l pain se çinse a li costé.
Con ses conpagni fu retorna aré,
Ver la bataille o est l'amiré.* ((1235))
Tant alirent e por vie e por stre,*

7050 Chichmaref: E-l; Reinhold, Rosellini: E'l
7051 Reinhold, Rosellini: cival
7053 Chichmaref: trença (error also corrected by Frati)
7055 Chichmaref: non furent (cf. Reinhold [review of Chichmaref])
7058 Reinhold: à tant
7060 Chichmaref: Galafrio [par] vu fo; Frati: de uu fo (correction; Reinhold [review of Chichmaref])
7061 Reinhold: vè
Rubric 201 (after 7062) MS., Keller: quist oit; Chichmaref: li païn (error also noted by Frati, Reinhold [review of Chichmaref])
7063 Chichmaref: li païn (error also noted by Frati, Reinhold [review of Chichmaref])
7066 Chichmaref: se cinse (error also noted by Frati, Reinhold [review of Chichmaref])
7067 Chichmaref: retorna arer (error also noted by Frati, Reinhold [review of Chichmaref])
7068 Chichmaref: Per la . . . (noted by also Reinhold [review of Chichmaref])

7070	Qe li rois Galafrio i ont atrové. (1580)	
	Quando le rois le vi, ne fo çojant e lé;	
	E cil li ont la ventura conté:*	
	Ço qe li ert venu et incontré, ((1240))	
	Como sa spea fu frata e brisé,	
7075	E com o un palon qe il oit trové* (1585)	
	Da quel pain el se fu delivré.	
	Galafrio l'olde, molto l'oit lodé;	40rb
	Par lui n'oi Macometo aoré.* ((1245))	
	Alor se comencent le cri e la ué,	
7080	Espesament venent a la meslé.* (1590)	
	Li rois Braibant no à l'ovra oblié;	
	A gran mervile fu pro e doté.	
	Durendart oit, dont si trença la spe; ((1250))	
	A le non val arme una poma poré.	
7085	Grande fu la bataile, si fort et aduré (1595)	
	Par nesun homo non fu tel esguardé.	
	Qi doncha veist Karleto li alosé,	
	Por me li pre, e davant e daré, ((1255))	
	Ferir e capler a soa volunté.	
7090	Un rois à morto, nevo de l'amiré, (1600)	
	E un altro rois el oit si amaté,	
	Roverso l'oit çiteo a li pre.*	
	Danabrun quan le vi, molto l'oit loé; ((1260))	
	Enfra de soi oit dito e parlé,*	
7095	"Questo damisel si è pro e doté;* (1605)	40va
	S'el oit vite longament en eté,	
	Hector de Troie, qe sor tot fu prisé,	
	Nen valse a lui una poma poré. ((1265))	
	Macon volist par soa pieté,*	
7100	Qe (l)e fose amigo e privé." (1610)	
	Volez oir de·l pain sa bonté?	

7071 Chichmaref: le roi le vi (error also corrected by Frati, Reinhold [review of Chichmaref]); Chichmaref: fu çoiant (noted by Reinhold [review of Chichmaref])

7072 Chichmaref, Reinhold, Rosellini: l'aventura

7075 Chichmaref: E como [cun] un . . . .

7078 Reinhold, Rosellini: n'oi[t]. Chichmaref: Par lui voi Macometo aorer (Frati, Reinhold [review of Chichmaref] also corrects)

7092 MS.: pre; Chichmaref: Po' verso . . . pré (Frati corrects to *pié*, saying it is the MS. reading); Reinhold: pré, emend for *pie*

7095 Rosellini: demisel

7100 MS.: defose; Chichmaref, Reinhold, Rosellini: Qe de [lu] fose (emend)

>   En Paganie, oltra la mer salé,
>   Meltre de lui non seroit trové; ((1270))
>   Tel spea avoit çinta a son baudré,*
> 7105   Qe ben valoit l'onor d'una çité. (1615)
>   Çojosa fu cella spea apellé;
>   For Durendarda meltre non fu proé.*
>   Quello pain si fo de gran berné: ((1275))
>   O vi Karleto, cella part est alé,*
> 7110   Karleto le vi, cella part est alé (1620)
>   Feru l'averoit quant cil li oit scrié:
>   "No me tocer, qe me son porpensé*
>   Qe tu è li meltre homo qe soit e·l mondo né. ((1280))   40ᵛᵇ
>   A ti me rendo de bona volunté,
> 7115   Si te donarò Çojosa mia spe, (1625)
>   Si vojo eser ves dru e ves privé;
>   Jamais da moi non serez engonbré."
>   Dist Karleto, "Quest'ò ben a graé; ((1285))
>   Ço qe vos plais a moi comandé."

Rubric 202

Coment Danabron donò sa spee a Ka(r)leto,
e pois li am(o)nisoit con fare devoit en bataille.*
Laisse 203

> 7120   Rois Danabrun fu orgolos e fer; (1603)
>   Dist a Karleto, "E no ve·l vojo çeler;
>   En vu ò meso tuta quanta ma sper.
>   De una ren e vos vojo en projer; ((1290))

7104 Chichmaref: bandré; Reinhold [review of Chichmaref]: corrected to *baudré*

7112 Rosellini: torcer

7113 Chichmaref, Reinhold, Rosellini: el mondo (continuing their policy of combining preposition and article combined in a single lexeme; will not be not be noted further)

7118 Chichmaref, Reinhold: ben agraé

7119 Chichmaref: Ço que (error also corrected by Frati, Reinhold [review of Chichmaref] [with wrong line no.: 1256 for 1286])

Rubric 202 (after 7119) line 1: MS.: kaleto; Keller: karleto; Reinhold, Chichmaref, Rosellini: Kar[l]eto; line 2: Keller, Chichmaref, Reinhold: amonisoit; Chichmaref: com fare

7121 Chichmaref, Reinhold: E' no ve-l; Rosellini: E no ve'l . . .

7123 Chichmaref, Reinhold, Rosellini: enproier

	Qe da Braibant vu ne deça guarder.*
7125	Tel spea oit ne se poroit lojer, (1635)
	Qi le deust un riame doner,
	Plus trençaroit e fero e açer,
	Qe nul falçe herbe por seger.* ((1295))
	Durendarda oit nome, si la fait nomer; 41^(ra)
7130	E ò una spea qi trença volunter; (1640)
	Por druerie e vos la vojo doner."
	Dist Karleto, "Ço me venent a graer."
	La spea prent de grez e volunter, ((1300))
	E a·l pain dè la soa por cançer.
7135	Dist le pain, "Entendés, çivaler, (1645)
	Non creés mie qe fose mençoner;
	Blasemo averoie se venise a çostrer
	Por mon segnor qe in mi avea sa sper. ((1305))
	De la bataile eo me farò arer,
7140	E si verò como l'averà finer. (1650)
	Se da Braibant ve poisi delivrer,
	Vinto seroit li canpo tot enter."
	Dist Karleto, "Vu parla como ber; ((1310))
	De quella colse non serés da blasmer."*
7145	Adoncha Danabrun si se retra arer, (1655)
	E Karleto vait en le stor a capler,
	E ten Çojosa, si la vol asaçer;
	S'el è si bona con le dist li Ascler, ((1315))
	A un pain la voit a presenter.
7150	Desor li eume si gran colpo li fer, (1660)
	L'eumo li trençe cun tot li capler.
	Avantqe li brant pout arester,
	Tros a li dent elo l'à fait aler, ((1320))
	Versa li colpo, morto li fa verser.*
7155	Dist Karleto, "Ben dise voir li Escler; (1665)
	Jamais ne vos vojo par nul autre cançer."

7124 MS.: vu ne; Chichmaref, Rosellini: vu ve deça (Reinhold [review of Chichmaref]: deçà); Reinhold: vu ve deçà

7132 Rosellini: k[arleto]

7143 Chichmaref: parla (corrected, Reinhold [review of Chichmaref]: parlà); Reinhold: parlà

7144 Chichmaref: colsa

7148 Chichmaref, Reinhold: S'el' è; Rosellini: S'el è

7149 Chichmaref, Reinhold, Rosellini: la voit apresenter; Rosellini, MS.: lanoit; la voit apresenter (emend)

Rubric 203
Coment Braibant ferì li rois Galafrio, / e si le abatì a tere de·l çival.
Laisse 204

        Quando pain oit K*arleto* veu,
        Qe quel pain oit tel colpo feru, ((1325))
        Li plus valant oit gran paura eu.
7160   Davant lui fuçent li grant e li menu; (1670)
        E K*arleto* le encalçe a·l brant d'acer molu.
        Qui Sarasin sont en fua metu;
        Quando Braibant le voit si li à secoru, ((1330))
        Ten Durendarda quel q'el à co*n*seu;
7165   Jamais por lui non fo colpo feru. (1675)
        E quel Braibant fo de si gran vertu,
        Tanti non fer non aça confondu.
        Tot li plus meltre fo si fort esperdu, ((1335))
        Li canpo li lasent tot nu.
7170   Li rois Braibant ten li brant molu; (1680)
        O vi Galafrio, cella part è venu,
        Desor li eume li oit aconseu.
        Quanto ne prent, n'oit a tera abatu;* ((1340))
        Se un petit l'aust plu prendu,*
7175   Morto l'aust tros li dent fendu. (1685)
        A·l çival trençe li çevo davant li bu,   41rb
        E Galafrio fu a la tera cau.
        Karleto le vi, tuto fo esperdu; ((1345))
        Vencer li vole, se li consent Jesu.
7180   E ten Çojosa qe li dè Danabru, (1690)
        Dever Braibant ven a salti menu.

    Rubric 203 (after 7156) line 1: MS.: B'raibant . . . . Rois; Keller, Reinhold: Rois
    7161 Chichmaref: d'açer molu (error also corrected by Frati, Reinhold [review of Chichmaref])
    7173 Chichmaref, Reinhold: Quando
    7178 Chichmaref: fu esperdu (error also corrected by Frati, Reinhold [review of Chichmaref])
    7179 Chichmaref: Vençer (error also corrected by Frati, Reinhold [review of Chichmaref])
    7180 Chichmaref, Reinhold: dè; Rosellini: dé
    7181 Chichmaref: De ver

Rubric 204
Coment Braibant ferì Galafrie gran colpo / De D(ur)endarde, e ancise le çival e l'in abatì a·l / campo e Karleto aloit par lui vençer.*
Laisse 205

	Quando Karleto vi Galafrio a li canp,
	En soa vite el non fo si dolant. ((1350))
	A Braibant vi Durendarda li brant,
7185	Cum le non fer ni petit ni grant, (1695)
	Qe el non çeti o morto o sanglant;
	Non è mervile se de lui oit spavant.
	Çascun le guichist como fust un serpant, ((1355))
	Lasa·l aler et arer et avant.
7190	Karleto le vi, no s'apresia niant; (1700)
	Ver lui s'en vait por ire e maltalant.
	Feru l'averoit, nen fust un mescreant,
	Quel fo Baldi(n), qe se mis en avant.* ((1360))
	E Karleto le fer un colpo si pesant,
7195	Tot li trençe trois en le feutrement. (1705)
	Quando le voit li fort rois Braibant,
	Saçés par voir, de rire no à talant.
	El se percoit a·l trençer de li brant,* ((1365))
	Et a·l senblant de le son guarnimant,
7200	Q'elo estoit ni Turcho ni Persant. (1710)
	A lu resenble quel damisel enfant,
	A cui Galafrio oit doné Belisant;
	Voluntera le ferist de Durendarda li brant. ((1370))
	Quant Karleto l'aloit guischisant,
7205	Segondo cun Danabru le dise en avant, (1715)

Rubric 204 (after 7181) line 1: Keller: galafrie a gran . . . ; Chichmaref: Galafrio (emendation for Galafrie)

line 2: MS.: diRendarde. Keller: direndarde e ancise . . . el in bati al; Chichmaref, Reinhold: li n' abati al; Rosellini: li n'abati al; Chichmaref, Reinhold: Durendarde (emendation for DiRendarde)

7183 Rosellini: el no fo si . . .

7189 Reinhold: Lasa-l; Rosellini: Lasal aler; Chichmaref: L' asaler [?] [sic!] (Frati also corrects Chichmaref, saying the MS. reads "Lasal aler . . . "; Reinhold [review of Chichmaref]: Lasa-l aler . . .)

7193 MS., Chichmaref: Baldi. qe; Reinhold, Rosellini: Baldi[n]

7197 Chichmaref: non a talant (error also corrected by Frati, Reinhold [review of Chichmaref])

7198 Chichmaref: se perçoit (emend for se percoit)

Quando de lui li aloit muniscant,
Q'el se guardase da Durendarda li brant,
Qe meltre spee no è a·l mondo vivant; ((1375))
Plu val la spea qe oro ni arçant.

Rubric 205
Coment K*arleto* oncis le pain e vent / a Ga(la)frio, si le donò le cival.*
Laisse 206

7210 Grant fu la bataile e fo ben manten(u)e; (1720)
      K*arleto* l'infant qe forment san(gu)e,*
      Le çival de Baldin oit por la rena prendue,*
      E si ven a Galafrio si le oit rendue; ((1380))
      E cil le monte, qe paure oit eue.*
7215 Li pros K*arleto* nen fu pais esperdue; (1725)
      Un rois oit morto e un altro ferue.
      Pain no·l ve, ni veilart ni canue,
      Qe no*n* maldist li jor q'el fo nasue, ((1385))
      Si le guienchist cu*n* sparver fa la grue;*
7220 Mal aça quel qi li oit atendue. (1730)   41^(va)
      Ve·le Braibant, tot li sangue li remue;
      S'el no le po ferir, no s'apresia una latue.

7206 Rosellini: aloir (typo; noted also by Holden, "lire *aloit*," Plouzeau, *aloit* non *aloir*; Martin: *aloir*, lire *aloit*)

Rubric 205 (after 7209) line 1: MS., Keller: .k.; line 2: MS.: Gafrio; Keller: ga- /frio si se dono; Chichmaref: Galafrio . . . le çival (both errors also corrected by Frati, Reinhold [review of Chichmaref]); Reinhold, Rosellini: Ga[la]frio

7210 MS.: mantenne; Chichmaref, Reinhold, Rosellini: mantenue

7211 MS.: sangner; Chichmaref, Reinhold: sangue(r); Rosellini: sangue (emend for *sanguer*)

7212 MS.: ɸoit por; Rosellini: por la ren prendue

7214 Rosellini: oit aue

7217 Chichmaref, Reinhold: no-l ve; Rosellini: no 'l ve

7218 Rosellini: do nasue

7219 Reinhold, Rosellini: Si li guienchist

7221 Chichmaref, Reinhold, Rosellini: Ve le

Rubric 206

Coment Braibant fu forte e fer, e coment / Abatì Morando de Rivere, et apreso lui dos / Autres çivaler; e de ço K*arleto* oit gran dol.
Laisse 207

	Li rois Braibant oit cor de lion; ((1390))
	Meltre çivaler atrover non poron,
7225	Qi ben cerchase entorno et inviron. (1735)
	Dorindarda tent dont a or è li pon;
	Cu il consegue, no g'à redencion,
	Qe morto no·l çeti lui o l'aragon. ((1395))
	Morando de River abatì a·l sablon;
7230	Ancis son destrer, lu ferì a·l menton, (1740)
	Siqe le sangue li alò a·l talon.
	E pois oncis un nevo Clarion,
	Qe de Galafrio era, de sa mason. ((1400))
	Et in apreso ferì un altro Sclavon,
7235	Siqe l'oncis sença redencion. (1745)
	"Deo," dist K*arleto*, "qe sofrì passion
	Desor la cros par nos rendençion,
	Se d'este pain delivrer ne se poson, ((1405))
	Jamais de·l canpo victoria no averon."
7240	O vi Galafrio, si l'oit mis por rason; (1750)
	"O çentil rois, dites, con la faron?
	Questo pain se ne ten por bricon;*
	Tot nostra jent mete a destrucion." ((1410))
	Atant Danabrun si le vene a esperon;
7245	"Damisel," fait il, "e vos digo e semon, (1755)
	No v'aprosmés a Braibant par nesuna cason.
	Si vos dirò e po*r*qe e comon:*
	Durindarda oit qe fu rois Faraon, ((1415))
	Meltre espée no è in tot li mon.
7250	A chi un colpo el ne dà de randon, (1760)
	Arma no li val la monta d'un boton.

Rubric 206 (after 7222) line 3: Keller: deço .k . . . .
7228 Chichmaref: no-l-çeti; Reinhold: no-l çeti; Rosellini: no'l çeti
7229 Chichmaref: a¹ sablon
7235 Chichmaref: redençïon (cf. Reinhold [review of Chichmaref])
7237 Chichmaref: redençïon (corrected Reinhold [review of Chichmaref])
7238 Chichmaref, Reinhold, Rosellini: Se de ste
7242 Reinhold: si ne (emend for MS. *se ne*); Rosellini: si ne (no note)
7243 Chichmaref: vostra ient (cf. Reinhold [review of Chichmaref])
7251 Chichmaref: non li val (cf. Reinhold [review of Chichmaref])

Tel arme avoit, uberg e çapiron,*
No teme spea valisant un speron; ((1420))
Por quelle arme el se fa un lion."*

Rubric 207

Coment Danabrum (conseille) K*arleto* çe / qe faire devoit, se conquister vol Brai/bant; si li co*n*te la fature de ses arme(s).*
Laisse 208

7255 "Karleto," dist Danabrun, "eo te vojo conseler; (1765)
 Se a mon conseil vos volez ovrer,
 Da·l rois Braibant el vos estoit guarder.
 E quando venisi sego a çostrer, ((1425))
 No·l ferir mie desor l'elmo d'açer;
7260 Qe non porisi detrençer un diner, (1770)
 Qe cento fois e l'ò fato proer.
 Ni de l'auberge non porisi endaner;*
 Dentro l'elmo e le spale tu le poisi saçer; ((1430))   41ᵛᵇ
 A celle colpo no le seroit nule sper."
7265 Dist K*arleto*, "Vu sì e pro e ber; (1775)
 Ormai so e ben como e do aovrer;*
 Vu me savés ben a droit conseler.
 Se in eta poso longo durer, ((1435))
 Ben vos averò de ço gujerdoner."
7270 Danabrun lase, e Galafrio ester;* (1780)
 En le gran stor el se vait a fiçer.
 Qe plus de .XXX. ne fa deçivalçer:
 Falsiron e Marsilio, e Balugant son frer, ((1440))
 Apreso lui se vont a 'roter.

7252 Chichmaref: usberg (cf. Frati and Reinhold [review of Chichmaref])

7253 Chichmaref: Non teme (cf. Frati and Reinhold [review of Chichmaref])

Rubric 207 (after 7254) MS.: conseiller; Rosellini: Danabrun; line 3: MS., Keller: armeo; Chichmaref (emend), Reinhold (emend), Rosellini (no note): armes

7259 Chichmaref, Reinhold: No-l; Rosellini: No 'l

7261 Chichmaref: e' l' o; Reinhold: e' l'ò fato

7263 Reinhold: Me 'ntro (note: "Dentro (?)"); cf. Reinhold [review of Chichmaref]: "Es ist eher *M'entro l'elmo* etc. zu lesen" (249).

7266 Reinhold, Rosellini: Oimai; Chichmaref: *O*imai. Reinhold: sò e' ben, como e' dò

7267 Chichmaref, Reinhold: adroit

7269 Chichmaref: vo saverò (cf. Reinhold [review of Chichmaref])

7271 Reinhold, Rosellini: afiçer

7274 Chichmaref, Reinhold, Rosellini: vont aroter

Karleto

7275 Çascun redote Braibant por li brant d'açer; (1785)
　　　Meesmo K*arleto* ne fu en gran penser.
　　　Grande fu la bataile, e li stormen capler;*
　　　Adoncha verisi pe, pugni coper, ((1445))
　　　Çival foir, e le rene rainer,*
7280 Qi por rason ne volese deviser* (1790)
　　　De quella bataille como fo dura e fer,
　　　Vu creeresi q'el fose mençoner.

Rubric 208
Coment quella bataille fu grant e fort / de anbes part de li baron.
Laisse 209

　　　Grant fu la bataile d'anbes part comunelment; ((1450))
　　　Li rois Braibant ne fu pais mie lent.
7285 A gran mervile oit de bone jent, (1795)
　　　Bon çivaler, saçi e conosent.
　　　E li rois Galafrio n'oit asi ensement;
　　　Una colsa oit, qe lui plus defent: ((1455))
　　　Con lui oit K*arleto*, qi est en Deo cre(e)nt.*
7290 Jesu e Macometo el ten por son guarent;* (1800)
　　　Quant Macometo li fala, Jesu si le defent;
　　　Doncha poit il çostrer segurament.
　　　Li rois Braibant, a chi Egito apent, ((1460))
　　　Tanti quello çorno oncise de quella jent,
7295 Qe plus de cento el ne lasa sanglent, (1805)
　　　Qe mais non vi amigo ni parent.
　　　Aconter vos l'ò fato brevement;
　　　Meltre çivaler no è a·l mondo vivent: ((1465))
　　　Aprisier le fa le arme e li guarniment;
7300 Por Durendarda no dota homo vivent. (1810)
　　　Por celle spee plu le teme la jent,
　　　Q'i no faroit dragon ni serpent.
　　　Nen fust Danabrun, qe de municiment, ((1470))

　　7276 Rosellini: Meesmo K[arleto] e fu
　　7278 Reinhold: pé [e] pugni (emend)
　　7279 Reinhold: Çival foïr . . . rainer; Chichmaref: Çival foir e le rene rainer (see endnote); Rosellini: Çival foir . . . rainer
　　7280 Reinhold, Rosellini: ve volese
　　7287 Chichmaref: n'oit asi (= "assez"?); Rosellini: n'oit à si
　　7289 MS.: crent; Chichmaref, Reinhold, Rosellini: cre[e]nt (emend)
　　7302 Chichmaref: non faroit

E li conseil a K*arleto* l'infent,
7305 De lu ferir e por qual convent, (1815)
Morto fust Galafrio, e livré a torment,
Qe contra lui no*n* aust defendiment;
Morto en fust con tuta soa jent. ((1475))

Rubric 209
Coment (Braibant) se inco*n*tra cun K*arleto*, / e si le parloit e·nn'oit lui a vilté; e molto (42^(ra)) / li menaçoit avantq'i s'alast a ferir.*
Laisse 210

Karleto l'infant, qe a merville fo ardis,
7310 Molto fo amé da Deo de·l Paradis. (1820)
En lui se fie, e·l baron san Donis,*
Lui e Morando, e Guarner li marchis
E Balugant, q'el no l'ama a envis, ((1480))
Falsiron e Marsilio, li ardis:
7315 I verent Braibant cun li brant forbis, (1825)
Qe un de lor oit morto e conquis,
Qe de Saragoçe estoit li plu altis.*
Quando le vi K*arleto* le petis, ((1485))
Ses co*n*pagnon el oit requis:
7320 "Segnur," fait il, "par poi no*n* raço tot vis. (1830)
Par un sol ome tot sumes smaris;
Non è (u)n de vos non soja spaventis.
E vos voi ben a·l senblant el m'est vis; ((1490))
E non staroie por eser oncis,
7325 Qe de bataile par moi no*n* sia requis. (1835)

Rubric 209 (after 7308) line 1: MS.: Branibant; Keller: branibant... cun .k.; Reinhold: *Braibant[= emend for MS. *Branibant*] ... cun K*arleto*; Chichmaref: Bra(n)ibant... cun Karleto; Rosellini: Braibant ... cun Karleto; line 2: Keller: en noit lui avint e molto; Reinhold: e nn'oit ... [e] molto; Chichmaref: e nnoit lui avie(t) e molto; Rosellini: e nn'oit lui à vilté molto; line 3: Keller: avant qi salast ...

7310 Chichmaref, Reinhold: paradis
7311 Chichmaref: En lui se fi' e el baron ...
7317 Chichmaref: estoit li plu astis (cf. Reinhold [review of Chichmaref]); Reinhold: plus astis (not Chichmaref, as Rosellini notes)
7322 MS.: Nonen de; Chichmaref: è-n ... no soia Chichmaref: no soia (cf. Reinhold [review of Chichmaref]); Reinhold, Rosellini: è u[n] (emend)
7325 Chichmaref: por moi (error corrected also by Frati, Reinhold [review of Chichmaref])

```
              Tanto me fio en Deo de·l Paradis,
              Qe l'onçirò a·l brando forbis."
              Dist Morando, "Bel frer e dolçe amis, ((1495))
              Lasés·l aler, da Deo soja maleis;
       7330   A son talant fora por le loris,* (1840)
              E nu staron en sto preo floris."
              Dist Karleto, "Mal m'avez servis;
              Questo non faroie par hon qe soja vis.* ((1500))
              E vos pre, se estes me amis,
       7335   E(n) questo lois vu serez asis; (1845)
              Ne vos movés se je ne vos requis."
```

Rubric 210

Coment Karleto se p(a)rte da sa conpagne / e si vait enverso Braibant.*
Laisse 211

```
              Quando Karleto se partì da çestor,
              Qe de paure remis de·l mal color, ((1505))
              Gran paura oit de lor li plusor,
       7340   Ma sor tot Morando si fu en gran tremor. (1850)
              Ma li damisel, qe pois fu enperaor,
              Por maltalant lasa le milsoldor.
              La spea en pugno, cum hon de gran vigor, ((1510))
              Ver Braibant s'en vait sença nulle paor;
       7345   Braibant le vi si·l ten por un pastor. (1855)
              Enver de lui elo fait clamor:*
              "No venir plu avanti, dolent peçaor,
              Qe por Macon, qe tegno por segnor, ((1515))
              De toi oncire n'averoie desenor;
       7350   A moi resenbli qe es petit ancor. (1860)
```

7329 Chichmaref, Reinhold, Rosellini: Lasés l'aler

7330 Reinhold, Rosellini: larls (emend for *loris*); Chichmaref: le laris (no note)

7333 Rosellini: Quaesto; Chichmaref. por hon (error corrected by Frati, Reinhold [review of Chichmaref] also)

7334 Chichmaref: pre'; Reinhold: prè

7335 MS.: E; Chichmaref, Reinhold, Rosellini: E[n] (emend)

7336 Chichmaref: [se] ie ne (cf. Reinhold [review of Chichmaref])

Rubric 210 (after 7336) MS.: prte; Keller: .k. se parte . . . ; Reinhold: p[a]rte; Chichmaref: se parte (cf. Reinhold [review of Chichmaref]); Rosellini: se parte

7342 Chichmaref: mil soldor (cf. Reinhold [review of Chichmaref])

7344 Chichmaref: nul[le] paor (questioned by Frati, Reinhold [review of Chichmaref] also)

7345 Chichmaref, Reinhold: si-l; Rosellini: si 'l

	Se vo venir eser me coreor,	
	Eo te farò e presio e onor;	
	Tanto nen oit unqua tes antesor." ((1520))	
	Dist Karleto, "No me conosi ancor.	42rb
7355	Ne son pais mie de vilan da labor; (1865)	
	Fis fu d'un rois de France li pastor,	
	Da moi conbatre non averà desenor."	
	Dist Braibant, "È tu quel liçeor, ((1525))	
	Qi cri en Deo, li ma(i)no Criator,*	
7360	Qe in ste mondo si fo un (b)oseor?"* (1870)	
	Dist Karleto, "De ço sì mentior;	
	Pa(r) lui vos oncirò a li brant de color."*	
	Dist li pain, "Tu n'averà li pejor." ((1530))	

Rubric 211

Coment Karleto e Braibant se conbatent / ensenbre e Karleto li onçis e conquist la spee, / e l'eume, e l'uberg, e pain furent s(c)onfiti / e morti; e Karleto conquis tot li ca(n)po *et* tot li (nave).

Laisse 212

	Quando Karleto oit Braibant derasnés,
7365	Avec lui non oit plu tençés; (1875)
	Enver Deo oit sa colpa clamés,
	De ses peçé el se clama confés.
	Çojosa trait a li pomo dorés, ((1535))
	E Durendarda tent Braibant l'amirés.
7370	L'un ven ver l'altro, li fren abandonés; (1880)

7353 Rosellini: non oit

7356 Reinhold: fu' d'un

7357 Reinhold: avera'; cf. 7363

7359 MS.: malno; Reinhold: malv[asi]o criator; Rosellini: malvo criator; Chichmaref: Deo li mal, no criator

7360 MS.: loseor?; Reinhold, Rosellini: boseor; Chichmaref: si fu un boseor (corrected by Frati to *si fo*)

7362 MS.: Pa lui (no abbreviation); Reinhold, Chichmaref: Pa[r]

Rubric 211 (after 7363) line 1: MS., Keller: .k.; Keller: se combatent en- /senbre; line 2: MS., Keller: .k.; line 3: MS.: sonfiti; Keller: e leume e luberg . . . furent son fin (Corrected by Mussafia, "Handschriftliche Studien II": sonfiti, further corrected by Guessard: sonfiti for sconfiti); Chichmaref: sconfiti (emend for MS.: son fiti); Reinhold, Rosellini: s[c]onfiti; line 4: MS., Keller: capo; MS., Keller: .k.; Reinhold, Rosellini: ca[n]po; Chichmaref: ca[m]po. MS.: naule; Chichmaref: nav[i]le; Reinhold: *et* tot li nave (emend); Rosellini: et tot li nav[i]le

Karleto   581

           Le Sarasin, qe fu maltalentés,
           Promerament oit K*arleto* asoltés.
           De Durendarda tel colpo li à donés, ((1540))
           De l'elmo trençe quant n'oit piés.
7375   Nen fust Deo e soa santa bontés, (1885)
           A celle colpo morto l'aust çités.
           Quando la spea fo e*n* le pugno tornés,
           De(·l) scu li oit un quarter trençés, ((1545))
           E de l'auberg trençò da un d·i les;
7380   Trosqua in tera fo la spea avalés. (1890)
           Se K*arlo* oit paure, or no m'en domandés;
           En soa vite, non fu si spaventés.
           "Deo," reclama, "la vo(ir)a majestés;* ((1550))
           Santa Maria, or me secorés
7385   Qe je non soja morto ni afolés." (1895)

Rubric 212
Coment Braibant ferì K*arleto* gram colpo de la / Spee; e Ka(r)leto pois ferì lui de Çoi(o)se, mes / avanti se parlarent e(n)senbre.*
Laisse 213

           Quando K*arleto* sent le colpo de Braibant,
           S'el oit paure ne vos çi mervilant.
           Elo reclame Damenedé e sant: ((1555))
           "Sante Marie, roine roimant,*

    7371 Chichmaref, Reinhold, Rosellini: mal talentés
    7373 Chichmaref: tal colpo (error also corrected by Frati, Reinhold [review of Chichmaref [with wrong line no: 1549 for 1540]])
    7374 Chichmaref: Del elmo
    7378 MS., Chichmaref: De scu; Reinhold, Rosellini: De[l]
    7381 Rosellini: D[arleto] ... demandés; cf. Plouzeau
    7382 Reinhold: nen; Chichmaref, Rosellini: non
    7383 MS.: voria; Reinhold: la voira (emend for MS. *voiia*); Rosellini: la voira Majestés (for MS. *voira*); Chichmaref: la voira (emend for MS. *la voiia* [237])
    Rubric 212 (after 7385) line 1: MS., Keller: .k.; Reinhold: *la (emend for *lo*); line 2: MS., Keller: kaleto ... çoise; Chichmaref, Reinhold: Ka(r)leto ... Çoi[o]se (cedilla in square brackets); Rosellini: Ka[r]leto ... Çoi[o]se; line 3: MS.: esenbre (no titulus); Keller, Chichmaref: esenbre; Reinhold, Rosellini: e[n]senbre (emend)
    7388 Chichmaref: çi'; Reinhold: çì; Rosellini: çi
    7389 Chichmaref: roiniant (emend for *roimant*; corrected Reinhold [review of Chichmaref])

7390	Ancois me siés da la mort en guarant,* (1900)	
	Questo gran colpo no resenbla d'infant."	
	El ten Çojose a·l pomo d'or lusant;	
	Non po trençer un diner valisant. ((1560))	
	La spea salte quan ren ella no*n* prant;	
7395	Desor l'auber ella va glatisant, (1905)	
	N'en po trençer de·l noir ni de·l blanc.*	42va
	Dist Braibant, "El vos va malemant,	
	Se non aorés Macon e Trevigant ((1565))	
	E ne daria en vestra vite un besant.*	
7400	Ma quando tu vo, po aver bon convant, (1910)	
	Se tu no renojer Damenedé e sant.	
	Plu te donarò or coito et arçant;	
	Tant non oit unqua vestri parant. ((1570))	
	Lasez ester Galafrio e Belisant;	
7405	Muiler vos donarò plu bela doa tant."* (1915)	
	Dist K*arleto*, "Le penser vos semant;*	
	No la poria laser ne no l'ò por talant;	
	Por moi amor preso oit bateçamant." ((1575))	
	Dist Braibant, "Eo t'en farò dolant;	
7410	Morir conven a Durendarda li brant." (1920)	

Rubric 213
Coment Braibant ferì <K*arleto*> co(n) la spee, / e si ancis son çival.*
Laisse 214

	"Sarasin, sire, ja ne vos çelaron;	
	Nos Cristian tel usança tenon,	42vb
	Dapoisc'ont pris muler e oit benecion, ((1580))	

7390 Chichmaref: de la . . . guarant" [sic] (error also corrected by Frati, Reinhold [review of Chichmaref])
7392 Rosellini: Çoise
7399 Reinhold: E' no. Chichmaref: ne daria en vostra vita; Reinhold, Rosellini: ne daria . . . vestra vite
7401 Chichmaref: tu vo' renoier; Reinhold: Se tu vo'; Rosellini: Se tu vo
7405 Chichmaref: Muiler, . . . *d*oa
7406 Chichmaref, Rosellini: vos se mant (Reinhold [review of Chichmaref] corrects)
7408 Rosellini: bateçamant'
Rubric 213 (after 7410) line 1: Chichmaref, Keller: de la spee (corrected by Frati, Reinhold [review of Chichmaref] to *con la spee*); Reinhold: B*raibant* . . . *con*; Rosellini: [Karleto con]; line 2: Reinhold: *e* anc*i*s
7413 Chichmaref: Da pois c'ont

	Mais en sa vie, tant cun vivo son,
7415	Par nul autre cançer ne la poron." (1925)
	Dist le pain, "Vu parlés cun bricon.
	Tu moriras, e Belisant averon;
	A li rois Galafrio la pase nos i faron." ((1585))
	Dist Karleto, "A Deo benecion!
7420	Poisqe eo serò trapasé d'este mon, (1930)
	De le non averò blasmo ne reprension.
	Mes ancor non sui e morto ni abatu d'arçon."
	Dist le pain, "Tosto vos conquiron!" ((1590))
	Ten Durendarda a l'indoreo pon,
7425	Ferir le vait, mais cil non fu bricon; (1935)
	Quant se stratorne davanti a l'aragon,
	Siqe Braibant no le consegue, se no de dre l'arçon,
	Dos mité oit fato cel auferant Guascon.* ((1595))
	E Karleto fo cau a li sablon;*
7430	Ben le vi Morando, lui e li conpagnon; (1940)
	S'i ont paure, ne s'en merveli l'on.
	E Karleto se leve en estant contremon;
	Reclama Deo e son santissimo non. ((1600))
	Dist le pain, "Vo tu orar Macon?
7435	Ben po veoir, se tu no è bricon, (1945)
	Qe li ton Deo non val un boton;
	Per peço te tegno qe no faço un molton."

43ra

Rubric 214

Coment Karleto, dapoisqe fu morto son çival / Se leva sus; e le pain li contrarie, et il aloit / A(·llue), si le ferì coment Danabron li avoit / Conselé, e si le ocise a cil co(l)p.*

Laisse 215

	Quando Karleto vi morto son destrer, ((1605))
	Sentì li colpo qe li donò l'Ascler;
7440	S'el oit paure, non è da merviler; (1950)

7414, 7416 Chichmaref: cum

7420 Chichmaref, Reinhold, Rosellini: de ste mon

7428 MS.: cel; Chichmaref, Reinhold: de l'auferant (emend for MS. *cel*); Rosellini: de l'uferant guascon

Rubric 214 (after 7437) line 1: Chichmaref: da pois qe; Reinhold, Rosellini: dapois qe; line 2: 7 for *et*; Rosellini: cotrarie; line 3: MS.: une; Keller: aune; Reinhold: A *llue (emend, MS. reads *une*); Chichmaref: a llue; Rosellini: A llue; line 4: MS., Keller: cop; Chichmaref, Rosellini: a cil cop; Reinhold: co[l]p

	Deo reclame, e·l baron sa*n* Riçer.
	"Santa Marie," dist K*arleto* a·l vis fer,
	"Ancoi me guardés da mortel engonbrer. ((1610))
	Ben me dist voir Danabrun d'oltra mer,
7445	Qe de le arme de Braibant ne poria endaner. (1955)
	Li consejo de lui no vojo trapaser;
	Plu è·l lojal d'altro çivaler."
	El ten Çojosa a li pomo dorer, ((1615))
	Ben l'avisò o el dovoit doner.
7450	Ne se soit Braibant tant covrir ni guarder; (1960)
	Entro l'elmo e le spale li vait li brant fiçer.
	Çojosa fo de un dolçe tailer,
	Si reondament li fait la testa trençer, ((1620))
	Qe in le canpo je la fe voler;*
7455	Morto li fait de·l çival trabuçer. (1965)
	Quando le vi Morando de River,
	Et avec lui li altri çivaler,
	Qe a Braibant no se olsava aprosmer, ((1625))
	I le loent sor autri çivaler.

Rubric 215
Coment K*arleto* oncist Braibant / A la spee, donda li ca*n*po fo deli(v)ré.
Laisse 216

7460	Quando K*arleto* oit Braibant delivré (1970)
	A gran mervile ne fu çojant e lé,
	Ven a Braibant, si l'oit desarmé;
	Tot primament elo li tole la spe; ((1630))
	A Morando l'oit en sa guarda doné.
7465	L'elmo li oste, qe avit en çevo laçé, (1975)
	E pois li trase li aubergo safré.
	Avantqe de ilec fust K*arleto* alé,
	S'oit de l'aubergo vesti e coroé, ((1635))
	Qe mais ne le cançò en sa viveté.

7441 Chichmaref: e-l baron; Reinhold, Rosellini: e 'l

7447 Chichmaref: è-l loial; Reinhold, Rosellini: è 'l

7449 Chichmaref: dov' oit doner (corrected Reinhold [review of Chichmaref])

7454 Chichmaref: in le canpo le fa fè; Reinhold: ie la; Rosellini: in le canpo iela fe

7459 Chichmaref: altri (error corrected also by Frati, Reinhold [review of Chichmaref])

Rubric 215 (after 7459) line 2: MS.: delinre; Keller: campo . . . deliure; Chichmaref, Reinhold, Rosellini: delivré

7465 Chichmaref, Reinhold: avoit (Frati corrects Chichmaref also)

7468 Chichmaref: del aubergo

7470	Nean li elmo el no à oblié; (1980)	
	Qe da nul arma mais no fu endané.	
	Pois prende le çival, fo en sela monté,*	
	Quant a Galafrio fu la novella nonçé, ((1640))	43rb
	Qe Balugant ge l'avoit aporté,	
7475	Qe Karleto cun li brant amolé (1985)	
	Oit a Braibant li çevo da·l bug sevré,	
	A grant mervile ne fu çojant e lé;	
	Macometo n'oit aoré e projé. ((1645))	
	Dist a sa jent, "E vojo qe vu saçé:	
7480	Saçés porquoi li ò mia fia doné? (1990)	
	Qe custu doit estre enperaor clamé,	
	De Crestentés, de la jent bateçé.	
	Desovra tot el serà coroné; ((1650))	
	Par lu seron temu e redoté,	
7485	Cun lui averon pax e bona volunté." (1995)	
	Qui le dient, "Nu avon ben ovré."	
	Li rois Galafrio ne fu pais demoré;	
	Cum cilla jent qe il avoit asenblé, ((1655))	
	Tanto aloit pungando por li pre	
7490	Qe a Karleto se fu aprosemé (2000)	
	O il estoit sor Braibant aresté.	
	Quando le vi, si le oit enbraçé,	
	"Bel filz," fait il, "ben sì li plu alosé ((1660))	
	Qe se trovase en tot li mondo né.	
7495	Braibant estoit uno d·i plu doté, (2005)	
	Qe en Paganie fust reçaté."	
	Dist Karleto, "Nu avon sa spe,	
	E li son eume, e l'aubergo safré." ((1665))	
	Dist Galafrio, "Vu (sì) molt ben armé.	
7500	Tel arme avés, saça por verité, (2010)	
	Qe non po eser ni dané ni falsé,	
	Ne quella spea por mior cançé."	

7470 Chichmaref, Reinhold: Ne an (as always)

7473 Chichmaref: fo la novela (error corrected also by Frati, Reinhold [review of Chichmaref])

7483 Chichmaref: De sovra

7488 Chichmaref: asenblé(r) (why parentheses? Corrected Reinhold [review of Chichmaref] also)

7492 Reinhold: se le oit . . .

7493 Rosellini: si li plus alosé

7496 Rosellini: paganie (but 7482: Crestentés)

7499 Chichmaref, Reinhold: Vu [sì]; Rosellini: Vu [si] (emend)

7500 Reinhold: saçà; Chichmaref: saça'

Rubric 216
Coment K*arleto* oncis Braibant / donde li canpo fo sconfito.
Laisse 217

    Quando pain ont son segnor veuz, ((1670))
    Qe K*arleto* li oit li çevo da·l bu toluz,
7505 Tot li plus meutre en fo fort esperduz. (2015)
    Mal aça quel, ni çoven ni canuz,
    Qe in le canpo aça colpo feruz;
    Qe tot sont en gran fue metuz. ((1675))
    E qui l'incalçe, con li brandi moluz; (2020)
7510 E si le trençe, por test e por buz.
    Via s'en vait fuçando li mescreuz,
    Por le laris e por li po aguz.

Rubric 217
Coment pain s'en vait fujant.
Laisse 218

    Pain se vont, li culverti mescreant, ((1680))
    Dist l'un a l'autre, "Mort è nos amirant;
7515 Plus no valen la monte d'un besant." (2025)
    Dist li plusor, "Macon e Trevigant,"
    Ver li son deo, "Nu*n* estes regreant;*
    A lui non valés un diner valisant." ((1685))
    En fua torne tot li plu valant;*   43ᵛᵃ
7520 Colu darer vorave eser davant. (2030)
    E K*arleto* li encalçe, et avec lui Morant,
    E li rois Galafrio e ses filz ensemant.
    En celle jor i oit ben fato tant, ((1690))
    Qe de lor se dirà tros a li çuçemant.

  7508 Rosellini: metus
  7510 Chichmaref, Reinhold: test' e
  Rubric 217 (after 7512) Keller: sen uait furant; Guessard: s'en vont fuiant; Reinhold: fuïant
  7513 Reinhold, Rosellini: s'e[n] vont; Chichmaref: Païen s'en vont (corrected in Reinhold [review of Chichmaref] also; wrong line no., 1689 for 1680)
  7516 Reinhold, Rosellini: et Trevigant
  7517 Chichmaref, Reinhold, Rosellini: vu estes regreant
  7519 Chichmaref: En fu atorné (corrected Reinhold [review of Chichmaref]); Rosellini: torne li plu valant (*tot* missing)

7525	Tant li alont K*arleto* encalçant,* (2035)
	Trosqu'a la mer elo li mena batant;
	Si le tolent le nef e le chalant.
	Qui Sarasin qi s'en aloit fujant,* ((1695))
	Se a(ll)oir ne poit molto ne fu çojant;*
7530	E qui qe perirent, en fu grami e dolant; (2040)
	Oncis furent, e a dol e·n tormant.*
	L'onor avoit K*arleto* de li canp,
	E si co*n*quis Durendarda li brant, ((1700))
	E l'elmo e l'aubers de li rois Braibant.
7535	Pois si avè Çojose, donde ne fu çojant; (2045)
	E quella non cançò en tuto son vivant.*

Rubric 218
Coment li canpo fo delivré, et li baron / tornent arere, et pain s'en fuit.
Laisse 219

	Arer torne li valant çivaler;
	Conquis avoit li canpo, e morti so*n* li Escler;*
	Por mal Braibant en pasò oltra mer.
7540	<K*arleto*> l'oncis a·l brant forbi d'açer,* (2050)
	<Si cun> Danabrun li doit li maistrer.
	<Ben> le doit il amer e tenir çer;
	En <so>a vita ne le doit oblier.
	<La> proja reculent sarçant e scuer;
7545	Çascun n'oit plus qe non poent porter. (2055)
	Quando venent en Saragoça entrer,
	I vont menant si gran nosa e treper,*
	Ne vos poria ne dir ne conter.
	E la raine va K*arleto* acoler;
7550	Ne Belisant no*n* fu mie darer; (2060)
	Gran çoja mena peon e çivaler.
	Se li rois Galafrio li amoit en primer,
	Or oit en lu metu tuta sa sper;

7525 Reinhold: alent (footnote "alont?"); Chichmaref: aloit; Reinhold [review of Chichmaref]: MS. reads *alent*

7528 Chichmaref, Reinhold, Rosellini: fuiant

7529 MS.: aſioir; Chichmaref, Rosellini: se alloir (Chichmaref, note: *Se avon* oppure *avoir*); Reinhold: avoir (Reinhold [review of Chichmaref]: MS. reads *auoir*)

7531 Chichmaref, Reinhold, Rosellini: e 'n tormant

Rubric 218 (after 7536) Keller: sen fuit

7541 Reinhold, Rosellini: doit amaistrer* (emend for *doit li maistrer*)

No è ren a·l mondo qe se poust porcaçer,
7555 Se Karleto la volea querir ni demander, (2065)
Qe li rois Galafrio no li fese bailer.
Da qui avanti se començа li çanter;
Mais de milor non oisés conter.
Je vos dirò, se vorés ascolter,
7560 Coment Falsiron e Marsilio, son frer, (2070)
E Balugant s'aloit a conseler
De Karleto oncir e detrençer,
Porq'i veent qe son per li avoit tanto çer.
Non pooit ni boir ni mançer,*
7565 Se avec lui non era en primer; (2075)
Et ensement li fasoit sa mer,
E soa sor qe il oit a muler,*
En una çanbre se me(te)nt a·l çeler;
Dist Falsiron, "Or m'entendés, me frer;
7570 De una ren ben me poso merviler. (2080)
Cun le poés sofrir e indurer,
Qe un Cristian ne diça segnor eçer?*
Plu è ama da per e da mer
Qe nu no sen; e plus l'oit a graer.*
7575 Por Macometo, el è bon de trençer, (2085)
Siqe de lui s'açamo delivrer."
Dist Balugant, "Tropo serì da blasmer,
Por nostra sor qe il oit a muler;
E po por armes el est si pro e ber,
7580 Qe da Braibant el n'à fato delivrer. (2090)
Se l'oncion, qe porà dir nos per?
El ne farà de tot desariter,
E for de Spagne caçer e sbanojer."
Dist Marsilio, "Ne le daria un diner;
7585 Qe non poria pasar li anno enter, (2095)
Qe nu s'averon cun nos per acorder.*
O voja o no, Balugant, li conven otrier,

43ᵛᵇ

7561 Reinhold: aconseler; Rosellini: à conseler
7564 Reinhold: poit
7568 MS.: ment; Reinhold, Rosellini: me[te]nt (emend)
7572 Reinhold, Rosellini: e çer
7573 Reinhold, Rosellini: è amà
7581 Rosellini: qe por dir
7586 Rosellini: cn nos
7587 Reinhold, Rosellini: O voia o no Balugant, li . . .

De K*arleto* a mala mort finer."
Adoncha se sevrent, e lasa li parler;
7590 Mes avantqe se volust sevrer, (2100)
I ordenent d'aler a caçer,
E a la caçe onçir e detrençer.

Rubric 219
Coment orde(n)ent d'oncir K*arleto*.*
Laisse 220

De le conseil quant furent parti,*
La mort de K*arleto* avont stabeli,
7595 E Balugant no mis l'ovra en obli; (2105)
Ven a sa mer e sa sor ausi.
"Mer," fait il, "nen poso star nen vos di;
Mon frer ont malement ordi.
De oncir K*arleto* avoient stabeli;
7600 Secretament sonto da lor parti; (2110)
Oncir le doit a li brandi forbi."
La raina l'olde, tuta vene enteri;
Cosi amoit K*arleto* como fust son fi,
Por soa file qe l'oit a mari.
7605 "A, Balugant," el(a) dist, "gran merci."* (2115)
Da Balugant mantenant se partì;*
Un damisel qe illec ella vi,
Por K*arleto* ela li tramet ì.
E quel si vene a le, qe no le contradì.

Rubric 220
Coment li conte la raine.
Laisse 221

7610 Quant la raine oit veçu l'infant,* (2120)
Ela li parla e ben e dolçemant:
"Bel filz," fait ella, "el nos va malemant,

Rubric 219 (after 7592) MS.: ordevent; Keller: or deuent doncir; Mussafia, "Handschriftliche Studien II": ordenent*; Guessard: ordenent; Reinhold: orde[n]ent (emend for MS. *or devent*); Rosellini: ordenent
7602 Reinhold, Rosellini: enteri
7605 MS.: el dist; Reinhold, Rosellini: el[a] dist (emend)
7609 Reinhold: contradì; Rosellini: contradi
Rubric 220 (after 7609) MS., Reinhold: Raine; Keller: raina

	Quando mun fil oit fato parlamant	44ʳᵃ
	De vu oncire a dol e a tormant.	
7615	No so porpensé qe le avì servi tant."* (2125)	
	"Cun savi questo?" dist Karleto en ojant;	
	"Ne·l poria croir par nul ren vivant."	
	Dist la raine, "A moi le dist Balugant,	
	Qe avec lor el fo a·l parlamant."	
7620	Dist Karleto, "Doncha è·l ben verisant?" (2130)	
	"Si è, bel filz, por Macon (e) Trevigant.*	
	Conseler vos vojo e ben e lojalmant,	
	Qe non demorés par nul ren vivant.	
	Daqe mon filz ont quel maltalant,	
7625	Con lor contendre non seroit siant. (2135)	
	Morir porisi, dont ne seria dolant;	
	En cesta noit farà desevramant,	
	Et avec toi si mena Belisant."	
	Dist Karleto, "E l'ò ben en talant."	
7630	Da la raine se partì mantenant, (2140)	
	Et oit demandé Bernard e Morant.	
	La novela li conte, dont fo in gran spavant.*	
	Conseilo li done de fair le desevremant,	
	E non demorer plu cun quel jant.	
7635	Quant vene la soir, qe l'alba fu colçant, (2145)	
	I vene a la raine, qe in la çanbra li atant;	
	La raina le vi, si·n plura tendramant;	
	Plu amava Karleto d'omo qe fust vivant.	
	"Bel filz," fait il(a), "a cil Deo te comant	
7640	In le quale tu è voire creant; (2150)	
	Recomandé te soja ma fila, Belisant.	
	Tu t'en anderà durando pene e tormant;	

7615 MS.: No so; Reinhold, Rosellini: No s'è porpensé (emend for *so*) . . . servi
7617 Reinhold: Ne-l; Rosellini: Ne'l
7620 Rosellini: è 'l..ben
7621 MS.: macon trevigant; Reinhold, Rosellini: Macon [e] Trevigant (emend)
7622 Rosellini: e be e
7627 Reinhold: fara'
7628 Reinhold: menà
7630 Rosellini: parti
7637 Reinhold: si-n; Rosellini: si'n
7639 MS.: fait ila cil; Reinhold, Rosellini: fait ela (emend)
7640 Reinhold: voir e creant
7642 Reinhold: andera'

	Me ancor por tenpo serà rico e manant.
	De toa loi serà sor tot jant,
7645	E questo (s)i s'è trova par nos ençantamant." (2155)
	Dist Karleto, "Soja a li Deo comant."
	Adoncha Karleto fait çercher (l)i brant,
	Qe il conquis quant il oncis Braibant.
	No trovò Durendarde, donde ne fo dolant;*
7650	Çojosa prist, q'el trovò a un pendant. (2160)
	Demantenant el se la çinse a·l flanc,
	Si fo ben guarni de arme de Braibant.
	Et in apreso tole son auferant;
	Belisant leve sor un palafroi anblant;
7655	Conçé demande da la raine in plurant.* (2165)
	"Bel filz," fait ila, "cil Deo te comant,
	Qe de la Verçene naque en Beniant."
	Çama nul dame nen demenò dol si grant,
	Como ela fi de sa fila Belisant.
7660	E cil s'en voit cun Bernard e Morant; (2170)
	De Saragoçe ensì planetemant.
	Ne le soit pais Galafrio l'amirant, 44rb
	Nian son filz, s'el non fu Balugant,
	Qe a la raine le dist secretamant.
7665	E Karleto s'en vait por le çamin erant; (2175)
	Deo le condue, qe formò Moisant,*
	Qe por son freri durò pena e tormant.

7643 Reinhold: sera' (as always for *tu /vous*; not commented any longer)
7645 MS.: fi; Reinhold, Rosellini: questo si (emend)
7647 MS.: di brant; Reinhold: li brant (emend); Rosellini: li brant
7648 Reinhold: li oncis
7655 Reinhold, Rosellini: inplurant
7656 MS.: fait il; Reinhold, Rosellini: fait ela (emend)
7658 Reinhold: Çama'
7659 Rosellini: sa Belisant (missing *fila*)
7661 Rosellini: ensi

Rubric 221
Coment s'en vait K*arleto*.
Laisse 222

    Quando de Saragoçe fu K*arleto* desevré,
    En la noit s'en voit cojament a çelé.
7670 Dever de Rome el fu açaminé; (2180)
    Q'el le condue, qe de la Verçene fu né.*
    Quando Galafrio (soit) de lui la verité,*
    Qe la raine li oit dito e conté,
    De·l tradimento, como estoit ordené,
7675 De lui oncire, s'el non s'en fust alé, (2185)
    Cun Balugant li oit dito e conté.
    Quant li roi le soit, gran dol n'à demené;
    Son filz el n'oit de Spagna sbanojé;
    Ne le tornent si fo l'ano pasé.
7680 Ça estoit K*arleto* de França coroné, (2190)
    E son freri estoit delivré;
    L'un fu morto, e l'altro fu apiçé,
    Cun oirés quant seroit finé
    Cest romans, qe est d'antiquité.
7685 E K*arleto* s'en vait, qe non fu seçorné; (2195)
    Avec lui Morando de Rivé.
    A l'ensir de Spagne oit una tor trové
    E un palés cun una rocha da le.
    Cento rainons l'oit fata e fondé;*
7690 No po paser nul homo por la contré, (2200)
    Q'elo non sia morto e derobé.
    Tota la tor è tota d'or gobré;*
    Çascun de ceus ont dama pié,
    S'el no*n* fo l'un qe ancor n'en oit trové.
7695 Quant quella dama vi qe K*arleto* oit mené, (2205)
    De (c)ella dame ont gran çoja mené.
    Dist l'un a l'altro, "Nu avon ben ovré;

  Rubric 221 (after 7667) Keller: sen uait .k.; Guessard: coment s'en vait Karleto
  7671 MS.: Qel se?; Reinhold: Q[u]el le (emend); Rosellini: Qel le condue
  7672 MS.: Galafrio de lui; Reinhold, Rosellini: [soit] de (emend)
  7674 Reinhold, Rosellini: ordoné
  7687 Rosellini: l'esir
  7689 MS., Reinhold, Rosellini: rainons
  7692 MS.: gobre (no abbreviation); Reinhold, Rosellini: go[n]bré
  7696 MS.: della dame; Reinhold, Rosellini: cella dame (emend)

Qe li nostro co*n*pagno seroit marié."
Dever K*arleto* i se sont adriçé;
7700 La dama volse prender oltra volunté, (2210)
E de l'avoir i fosen derobé,
Quando K*arleto* si oit trato la spe.
Tot le primer qe il oit encontré,
Tel colpo li donè qe le çevo li oit colpé;*
7705 E pois apreso nen oit sparmié,* (2215)
Qe un altro oit morto çité.*
Quant li altri le virent, sont in la mason entré,
Si prendent arme e lançe et spe.
Sovra K*arleto* corent de randoné,
7710 Si le ferirent e davant e daré; (2220) 44va
Ne le nosì una poma poré,
Qe de bone arme estoit ben armé.
Or le secora la voira majesté;
Quando (Bernardo) e (Morando) de Rivé
7715 Ont veçu l'ovra si atorné, (2225)
Demantinent çascun trait la spe;
Entro lor fer a força e a duré.
E K*arleto* tent Çojosa soa spe;
Tel colpo dona a uno sor li çe,
7720 Qe tros en tera lo fende in do mité. (2230)
Quando li altri le vi cosi versé,
En fua torne, ont la tor lasé,
Cun tot le dame e l'avoir amasé.
Mais noportant diando la verité,
7725 Plus de .XXX. de lor le remis detrençé. (2235)

7704 Reinhold, Rosellini: li done
7705 Reinhold, Rosellini: sparimé
7714 MS.: morando e bernardo de rive; Reinhold, Rosellini: Bernardo e Morando (emend) (cf. line 7921)
7716 Reinhold: De mantinent

Rubric 222
Coment K*arleto* vençì la tor.
Laisse 223

        Quant K*arleto* voit çelor via scanper,
        Deo e li santi prist a regracier.
        Qi donc (oldist) quelle dame plurer;*
        Ben cuitoit qe K*arleto* le deust atuer.
7730   Dist K*arleto*, "Ne vos estoit doter. (2240)
        Ne vos farò onta ni engonbrer."
        Adonc vait en la tor entrer,
        E ses conpagni, e sa çentil muler;
        Du çorni ilec s'estoit a seçorner.
7735   De quel avoi(r) qe le pote trover, (2245)
        Elo ne fait .V. somer carçer,
        Siq'el posa ben avoir da spenser.
        Quant à ço fato, se mist ad herer,
        E lasoit la tor e le dame ester.
7740   Por çamin se mis a çaminer; (2250)
        Por le çités por burs e por docler.
        Asa durò pena et inojer;
        Trosque a Rome nen volse demorer,
        E si desis en un molto bon oster.
7745   Molt richament se fait hostaler, (2255)
        Qe asa avoit da spender e da doner.
        E quel oster avoit una çentil muler,
        E un son fil qe era pro e ber
        Qe retrasoit a fil de çivaler,*
7750   E cun K*arleto* se vait si aconter, (2260)
        Qe avec lui aloit *et* avant *et* arer.
        Or lason de K*arleto* qe estoit a bon oster;
        De l'Apostoile e vos vojo conter,*
        Qe de qui de Magançe si fo lu e son per.

    Rubric 222 (after 7725) Keller: venci
    7728 MS.: oldiste; Reinhold: oldist(e); Rosellini: oldist (emend)
    7734 Reinhold, Rosellini: aseçorner; Rosellini: s'estoir (cf. Martin: *s'estoir*, lire *s'estoit*
(ed. v. 12122))
    7735 MS.: avoit; Reinhold: avoir (emend); Rosellini: MS. reads *avoir*
    7746 Rajna: asa'avoit
    7747 Rosellini: oster avoir
    7751 7 for *et*; 7 for *et*
    7753 Reinhold, Rosellini: l'apostoile (and so for the entire section)
    7754 Guessard: Magance

7755 Par tot Rome fe banir e crier: (2265)
     "Çascun qe le poust Karleto presenter,
     Qe mil marche li faroit doner*
     De·l milor or qe se poust trover."   44vb

Rubric 223
Coment Karleto albrega.
Laisse 224

     Cel Apostoile fu de male rason,
7760 Si fo de·l parenté de qui de Gainelon. (2270)
     Mesaçer mande entorno et inviron,
     A principi e a dux, a marchisi et a con,
     Et a li rois e altri baron,
     Qe a Rome vegna sença demorason,
7765 Qe de l'inperer vol fair la lecion.* (2275)
     Ben cuita faire un de soa mason;*
     Ma ço q'el pense, li penser li semon,*
     Qe li rois Brunor, qe d'Ongaria son,
     Qe per estoit de Berte, et avo de Karlon,
7770 Venoit a Rome por fair quela lecion; (2280)
     En sa conpagne, .X. mil conpagnon,
     A bone arme et a destrer Guascun.*
     Si s'ostalent en un gran mason;
     Plu fu onorés qe nul altro baron.
7775 A lu atendoit François e Bergognon, (2285)
     E Loerens, Manselés e Berton.*
     Se l'Apostoile non fust de si male mason,*
     Çeste Brunor aust eu la lecion.
     Ma Damenedé e son sa(n)tisimo non

    7755 Guessard: tote Rome
    7756 Guessard: poüst (always; not further noted)
    7759 Guessard: Del (always; not further noted)
    7760 Guessard: Si fu del . . .
    7761 Guessard: intorno
    7762 7 for et
    7765 Rosellini: l'alecion
    7769 7 for et
    7770 Rosellini: quel alecion (cf. 7765)
    7772 7 for et; Reinhold: guascun; Rosellini: guascon
    7776 Reinhold: Manselés; Rosellini: Menselés
    7778 Rosellini: l'alecion
      7779 MS.: satisimo (no abbreviation); Reinhold, Rosellini: sa[n]tisimo (emend); Rosellini: Demenedé

7780 Tel l'invoirà dont gran çoja en seron; (2290)
Cun oldirés a la fin de·l sermon.
Karleto stoit a son oster, ne dist ne si ne non;
De quela corore non fa nul mencion.*
Da spenser e da doner n'oit a gran foson,
7785 E por avoir non lasa venason. (2295)
Le çentil homes qe son preso sa mason,
L'oro convoie, e pois li fa li don;*
E a li povres qe sonto da viron,*
Boir e mançer li dona a foson.
7790 De lu parole çivaler e peon; (2300)
Avec lui avoit Bernardo de Clermon,
Qe de quel ovre li castiga e semon.

Rubric 224
Coment li hoster parole (c)u(n) sa (m)uiler.*
Laisse 225

Quant cel oster oit veçu cel infant,
Qe a lu resenble a çivaler valant,*
7795 Ne no resenble a filz de merçadant, (2305)
A çentil ome el par a li senblant:
A·l donojer, et a le cortesie grant;
De sa nature non po savoir niant.
Savés qe fist ste malvés seduant?
7800 El vent a sa mule(r)s si le dist planamant:* (2310)
"Dama," fait il, "e vos pre e comant,
Se vu ren m'amez de niant,
Quant vu serés cun cele dame a parlamant,
Qe muler estoit de cele nostre enfant,
7805 Qe de donojer è si largo e manant, (2315)   45ra
Vu la domandarés e ben e dolçemant,
Dont est li son segnor, e de qual pertinimant."
Dist la dame, "Non parlé plu niant;*
Ben li saverò tuto certanamant."

7780 Reinhold, Rosellini: li'nvoira
7787 Reinhold, Rosellini: Loro
7788 Reinhold, Rosellini: d'aviron
Rubric 224 (after 7792) MS.: u sa Muiler; Keller: u sa muiler; Reinhold: à sa (emend) Muiler; Rosellini: à sa muiler (no note)
7794 Reinhold: Je à lu . . .
7800 MS.: Mules; Reinhold, Rosellini: muler (emend)

7810	E quela dame, qe oit mal entant, (2320)
	Se departì da celle parlamant.
	Ven in la çanbre o trova Belisant;
	Por man la prist, si le fe bel senblant.
	Anbedos s'asist sor un banc;
7815	De plesor colse se dient en ojant, (2325)
	E quela ostera la quer e la demant,
	"Çentil madames, qe ajés cortesie tant,
	Avì vu mer ni per qe soja vivant?
	E cest vestre segnor è de grande esiant;
7820	Plus est il largo qe non fu Alexant. (2330)
	De cortesia el pasa tota jant;
	È·l çentil homo o est me(r)çaant?"*
	Dist Belisant, qe non à mal entant,
	"Dama," fait ela, "li penser vos somant.*
7825	E vos dirò de moi primemant: (2335)
	Filla sui d'un roi de la paine jant,
	Li rois Galafrio qe la Spagna destrançç*
	Est mun per, se ma mer no me mant.
	Si ò tros frere qe sonto molto valant;
7830	Ço est Falsiron, Marsilio e Balugant. (2340)
	E questo mon segnor, qe par si avenant,
	Mon per l'avoit nori de petit mis en grant;
	Caçé fo de sa tere quant era petit enfant."

Rubric 225
Coment Belisant parole a cella dame.*
Laisse 226

	"Dama," dist Belisant, "ne vos serà çelé;
7835	Ces mon segnor, c'oit tant bonté, (2345)
	Meltre çivaler non è a·l mondo né.
	E si fo filz d'un rois de la Cristeneté,
	Qe de França estoit rois coroné,
	De un Pepin, qe tant fu alosé,*
7840	Qé da dos ses filz el fo atosegé, (2350)
	E questo mon segnor en fo via mené,

7818 Reinhold: Avì vu; Rosellini: Avi vu

7822 Reinhold, Rosellini: È 'l; MS.: meçaant; Reinhold, Rosellini: me[r]çaant (emend)

7824 Cf. Plouzeau re 7767–68.

7827 Rosellini: Glafrio

7839 Rosellini: slosé (cf. Martin)

	Da cest dos qe vu con lu (v)eé.*
	Mon per li oit nori et alevé;*
	K*arleto* oit nome e fi si apelé;*
7845	Meltre çivaler nen seroit trové. (2355)
	Braibant oncis a·l trençar de sa spe;
	Por sa proeze mon per me li donè.
	Mais li mon frere ne l'avoit ren amé;
	Anci(r) le volse quant semo sevré.
7850	Avoir avremo a molto gran planté,* (2360)
	Qe a una tor l'avoit guaagné."
	Quant Belisant li avoit dito e conté,
	Qe de cella dame non avoit mal pensé, 45rb
	S'ela aust sau con la colsa fose alé,
7855	Ne l'averoit quela novela nonçé (2365)
	Por grant avoir qe li aust doné.
	E quella ostera, como fo dotriné,
	Plutosto q'ela poit da le sevré,*
	E ven a son segnor, si le oit nonçé
7860	Cun custu è K*arleto* li qual è sbanojé. (2370)

Rubric 226
Coment li hoster parole a l'Apostoille.
Laisse 227

	Quant li oster olde soa dama parler,
	S'el oit çoja, non è da demander;
	Ben croit da lo papa grant avoir guaagner.
	Demantenent se prist a erer,
7865	Ne no demanda sarçante ni scuer. (2375)
	Por la malvés de cela sa muler,
	Qe a Belisant se fe tot nonçer

7842 MS.: vu . . . vuee; Reinhold, Rosellini: vu con lu veé (emend)

7844 Reinhold, Rosellini: si fi

7849 MS.: Ancit (noted by Reinhold and Rosellini); Reinhold, Rosellini: Ancir (emend)

7851 Reinhold: tor 'l avoit

7854 Reinhold: aüst saü

7657 Reinhold: quela

7858 Reinhold: Plu tosto . . . da le [se] sevré (emend); Rosellini: Plu tosto . . . da le [s'é] sevré (emend)

Rubric 226 (after 7860) Keller: a lapostoille

Li tradime*n*to de li ses malvasii frer.
A l'Apostolio elo ven a parler;
7870 Con un Cardinal li trovò co*n*seler, (2380)
Le qual estoit parent d·i segnor de Baiver.
Li oster l'apele si·l prist a derasner:
"Sire," fait il, "se me volés doner
Quel avoir qe faisi banojer,
7875 E vos farò K*arleto* delivrer, (2385)
Qe in mon oster è venu alberçer.
Avec lui el oit una sa muler,
Qe fila estoit d'un Sarasin Escler."
Dist l'Apostolio, "Ne se vol demorer;
7880 Prendés l'avoir, e tornez arer, (2390)
Q'elo no poust ni foir ni scanper."
Son canbarlengo elo fe demander
Tot l'avoir elo fe nonbrer;
En soa ga(r)da le mist, si le ne vol porter;*
7885 Via s'en vait, qe a poina li po porter. (2395)
Maleta l'ora q'el naque de mer;
De·l tradime*n*to el n'averà son loer.
Si como volse arer reparier,*
Desor la plaça apreso son oster,
7890 K*arleto* e son filz estoit a deporter; (2400)
Da l'altra part estoit Bernardo e Rainer.
Quando l'infant vide venir son per,
Cuitoit qe fose fruite q'el venist da co*n*prer.*
Contra li vait, lasa K*arleto* ester;
7895 Quando se le aprosme, si·l prist a derasner: (2405)
"Pere," fait il, "qe fruite averés porter?"
E cil le dist, "I son toti diner
Qe l'Apostolio me li à da por loer.
E quisti e altri si nos averà mester,

7868 MS.: malvasij; Reinhold, Rosellini: malvasii
7872 Reinhold: si-l prist a derasner; Rosellini· si'l ,, . à derasner. cf. 7895 and 7912.
7874 Reinhold: faïsi
7878 Reinhold, Rosellini: escler
7881 Reinhold: foïr (as always)
7884 MS.: gada; Reinhold, Rosellini: gada
7888 MS.: nolse; Reinhold, Rosellini: volse
7895 Reinhold: si-l; Rosellini: si'l
7896 Rosellini: «Pere«, fait il ...

7900 Qe eo li vegno e dire e nonçer (2410)
     Qe questo damisel, c'avemo fato ostaler,   45ᵛᵃ
     Estoit quel Karleto q'è fato sbanojer."
     L'infant l'olde, cuita li sen cançer;
     "Pere," fait il, "murirì de tal mester;*
7905 De tradimento me farì repro(ç)er? * (2415)
     Si m'ai Deo, li voir jus(t)isier,*
     Da mo avanti no ve n'averés vanter."
     De un co(l)tel el ferì si le per,*
     Qe elo lo fi illec morto verser;
7910 E pois por la plaça el çitò li diner. (2420)
     Voi·le Karleto, si le parse nojer;
     A lui s'en vait, si·l prist a derasner,
     Por qual cason el oit morto li per.
     Dist l'infant, "Nu averon destorber.
7915 Mon per vos ven cun traitor losençer (2425)
     Da l'Apostolie, da vos acuser,
     Dir qe estes Karleto q'è fato sbanojer,
     E porço oit il aporta sti diner."
     Karleto l'olde, nen oit qe airer;
7920 Plutosto qe il poit, entra en le oster, (2430)
     El e (Bernardo) e (Morando) de River,
     E si prendent ses arme e ses corer,
     Si s'aparele de soi ben defenser.

7904 MS.: muririi; Reinhold: murirì; Rosellini: muriri
7905 MS.: reproer; Reinhold, Rosellini: reproer
7906 MS.: iusisier; Reinhold, Rosellini: jus[t]isier (emend)
7908 MS.: cotel; Reinhold, Rosellini: co(l)tel (emend)
7911 Rosellini: Voile
7912 Reinhold: si-l; Rosellini: si'l
7918 Reinhold, Rosellini: por ço . . . aportà
7919 Reinhold: n'en . . . aïrer
7921 MS.: morando e bernardo; Reinhold, Rosellini: Bernardo e Morando de River (emend) (cf. line 7714)

Rubric 227
Coment l'Apostoille fi pariler sa jent.*
Laisse 228

   Quant l'Apostolie olde la contenançe,*
7925 Le Cardinal apele sença nul demorançe. (2435)
   "Tosto," fait il, "et a scu et a lançe,
   X. mil omes prendés de ma posançe,
   Alez a l'albergo, ne non farez senblançe,
   E prendés K*arleto*, qe fo neo de Françe,
7930 Si me·l menez, sença nul fiançe." (2440)
   "Volunter, sire," ço dist le Cardinal Blançe.

Rubric 228
Coment li (C)arde(n)al mandoit a li rois.*
Laisse 229

   Quant li Cardinal oit la parole oie,
   Saçes homo fu, de ren no li contralie;
   Plu amava K*arleto* de nula ren qe sie.
7935 Un mesaçer apelle, en cui forment se fie; (2445)
   "Va·t'en," fait il, "ne non demorar mie,
   E si me dì a li rois d'Ongarie,*
   Qe l'Apostolio oit saçu por spie,
   Qe K*arleto*, le filz de sa fie,
7940 Est in Roma preso santa Sofie. (2450)
   Li Apostolio li oit tant en aie,

  Rubric 227 (after 7923) Keller: lapostoille si; Mussafia, "Handschriftliche Studien II", MS. reads *fi*
  7925 Guessard: demorance; Reinhold, Rosellini: cardinal (and so always)
  7926 Guessard: lance
  7927 Guessard: posance
  7928 Guessard: senblance
  7929 Guessard: France
  7930 Guessard: mel; Reinhold: me-l; Rosellini: me'l
  7931 Reinhold: "Volunter, Sire, ço dist li cardinal Blance."; Rosellini: cardenal Blançe
  Rubric 228 (after 7931) MS.: Gardeval Mandoit . . . Rois; Keller: gaiteual; Guessard: cardenal; Reinhold: Cardenal . . . Rois; Rosellini: Cardenal
  7932 Reinhold: oïe
  7936 Reinhold: Va t'en; Rosellini: Vaten
  7941 Reinhold: aïe; Rosellini: aie

Qe da tot parte li oit sbanie.*
Se tosto no·l secoré, el perderà la vie,
Qe .X. mil omes, toti de sa masnie,
7945 Con tot armes sont a çival salie. (2455)
S'el no·l secoré, e le cuita sa vie."*
Dist li mesaço, qe fu de bona vie,*   45vb
"Molto vontera farò questa anbasie."*
Le mesaçer nen demorò pas mie;
7950 Ven a li rois Brunor, qe rois est d'Ongarie; (2460)
A mançer estoit asis con soa baronie,
De questa colsa ne savoit ne mie.

Rubric 229
Coment li rois d'Ongrie s'aparele.
Laisse 230

Le mesaçer si fo saço e valent;
Ven a li rois, por davanti se rent.
7955 "Bon rois," fait il, "el vos va malement; (2465)
Li Cardenal Blanco, q'è tan pro e valent,
A vos m'envoie secretement
Qe Karleto è in Rome, venu çeleement.
Un malvasio oster o el si desent
7960 L'à palenté por oro e por arçent, (2470)
Et è apreso santa Sofie, li trato d'un arpent.
X. mil çivaler ont pris guarniment,
Par lui oncire s'el no è qe le defent."
Li rois l'oì, si ne fo en gran spavent;
7965 Tosto se leve, nen fe demorament (2475)
Ne le fo aporté plu ni vino ni plument;*
El fa soner ses graile et arer et avent,
X. mil çivaler monta en auferent.
Li rois meesme si aloit davent,
7970 E la çent de l'Apostoile çivalçò a·l present, (2480)
A li oster o Karleto li atent.

7942 Reinhold, Rosellini: tot part li*
7943 Reinhold: no-l; Rosellini: no'l
7946 Reinhold: S'el no-l; Rosellini: S'el no'l . . . el è fuita (emend) sa vie
7947 Reinhold (emend), Rosellini: bon avie
Rubric 229 (after 7952) Keller: dongrie saparela; Guessard: d'Ongrie s'aparela
7953 Reinhold: mesacer (missing cedilla)
7955 Rosellini: fait il »el vos . . .
7969 Rosellini: si aloir

Rubric 230
Coment fu grant la bataielle.*
Laisse 231

      Quant Karleto fu armé e monta en destrer,
      Avec lui Bernardo e Morando de River,
      E le filz de l'osto, qe fo e pro e ber,
7975 Qe por Karleto avoit morto son per. (2485)
      Atant ecote vos qui malvas çivaler,
      Qe l'Apostoile li oit fato envoier;
      Li Cardinal li oit a guider.
      Quant il s'aprosma apreso li oster,
7980 Elo reguarde, vide qui çivaler (2490)
      Qe de foir non fait nul penser.
      Li Cardinal fu saçes, qe se retrase arer;
      E quela jent lasa avant aler.
      E prega Deo, li vor justisier,
7985 Qe guardi Karleto da mortel engonbrer. (2495)
      Quando Karleto li voit a 'prosmer,
      Davanti se fait, si le va contraster;
      Le primer fer davanti a l'incontrer,
      Li scu li speçe, l'aubergo li fa falser.
7990 Ple(g)a sa lançe, morto li fait trabuçer;* (2500)
      E un altro ferì Morando de River.
      Çascun de ceus fe li so deroçer;
      Valent fu li fiol de l'oster,
      Mais li pro Karleto si fo plu pro e ber;   46ra
7995 En tot le mondo non è milor çivaler. (2505)
      Quant l'asta fu fraita, el tra li brant d'açer;
      Qi le veist por la presia aler,
      E qui gran colpi donar e inplojer,
      Contra Çojosa ne valea arma un diner.
8000 Ma qui le corent sovre, a cento e a miler; (2510)
      Morto en fust sença nul recovrer.
      Contre cotanti no li averoit durer;
      A gran mervile fose esté l'ingonbrer.
      Quando de·l rois d'Ongarie vene li çivaler,

    Rubric 230 (after 7971) MS., Keller, Reinhold, Rosellini: bataielle; Guessard: bataille (401)
    7986 Reinhold, Rosellini: voit aprosmer
    7990 MS.: Plena; Reinhold, Rosellini: Plega (emend)
    7997 Reinhold: veïst (as always)
    8000 Rosellini: a certo e a miler

8005 Por K*arleto* secorer et aider, (2515)
Ne le fo parole dite ne nul tençer;*
Entro lor fer de grez e volunter.
Gran fu la nose quant vene a·l començer;
Doncha veisés mante selle voider,
8010 E manti çivaler cair e trabuçer. (2520)
Qui de l'Apostolie ne le porent durer;*
En fua torne por via e senter,
Non atendoit le fiolo li per.

Rubric 231
Coment fu grant la bataille quant / Li rois Brunor entra en le stor, e celle Gent de l'Apostoielle s'en fuit.*
Laisse 232

Quando li rois Brunor fu en le stor entré,
8015 A gram mervile fu grant la meslé; (2525)
Testes trençé e spales decopé,*
Tant çival foir por me li pre.*
Qui de l'Apostolio avoient malovré;
Tot s'en fuçent e por vie e por stre,
8020 La major part fo morti e detrençé. (2530)
Le Cardenal, quant vi l'ovra atorné,
A gram mervile el fo ben dotriné;
Nen est pais ne foi ne scanpé.
O vi K*arleto*, cella part est alé,
8025 E li rois Brunor si le fu aprosmé, (2535)
Quant vi K*arleto* si l'oit asiguré
A la guardaure q'el oit de sa mulé.
A lui s'aprosme si l'oit acolé:
"Bel filz," fait il, "perche tan demoré,
8030 Qe da moi tu è ste çelé? (2540)

8005 Rosellini: K[arleto]
Rubric 231 (after line 8013) line 2: MS., Reinhold: Rois. Reinhold, Rosellini: entra; Keller: entra e lestor; line 3: Keller: de lapostoielle sen fuit
8016 Reinhold: trençé
8017 MS.: Tant çival foir por me li pre; Reinhold: Tant . . . foïr; Rosellini: Tant . . . foir
8026 Rosellini: aisiguré
8027 Reinhold: guardaüre
8029 Reinhold: per che
8030 Reinhold: sté; Rosellini: ste

>   Ben sapi qe tu estoie e foi e scanpé*
>   Quando ton per si fo atosegé,
>   E toa mer qe tanto avoit bonté."
>   Dist Karleto, "De ço ne vos mervilé;
> 8035 Quando me frer m'avoit sbanojé, (2545)
>   Ne ause alberçer en la Cristeneté;*
>   En Paganie e sonto alevé,
>   Cun li rois Galafrio qe tant m'à honoré
>   Qe soa fila m'oit per moler doné.
> 8040 Da lor e son parti cojament a çelé, (2550)   46ʳᵇ
>   E ma muler avec moi mené."
>   (Dist) li Cardenal, "Vu avì ben ovré;*
>   Mo no è tenpo de querir parenté,*
>   Se a mon conseil croir voré,
> 8045 Vu serés rois et enperer clamé. (2555)
>   Ma non farés tropo longa demoré;
>   Alez a l'Apostolio tuti si coroé,
>   Avantiqe il soja ne foi ne scanpé;
>   Morto el soja, a martirio livré,
> 8050 Qe il estoit de quel mal parenté (2560)
>   Qe vos oit caçé e sbanojé."
>   (Dist) li rois, "Vu avì ben parlé;
>   Se Deo ne dona, por soa santité,
>   Qe da lui siamo delivré,
> 8055 Vu ne serì Apostolio clamé." (2565)
>   Dist li Cardenal, "Mil marçé n'açé."
>   Adonc Karleto nen fu pais demoré;
>   Por li conseil qe cil li oit doné,
>   Si çivalçent li fren abandoné.
> 8060 Ça oldirés coment averont ovré; (2570)
>   Qe l'Apostolie estoit ben adoté,
>   Qe de sa jent e de son parenté,
>   Plus de .X. mil lì furent asenblé;
>   Nen poit aler ne le sia gran meslé.

8036 Reinhold, Rosellini: ausé
8042 MS.: Disti li; Reinhold, Rosellini: Dis li
8043 MS.: Mo; Reinhold: Me (emend for "Mo"); Rosellini: Ma (emend)
8046 Reinhold, Rosellini: fares
8052 MS.: Disti li; Reinhold, Rosellini: Dist li
8058 Rosellini: qe cil oit doné (*li* missing)

Rubric 232
Coment asallirent l'Apostoille.
Laisse 233

8065 Va s'en K*arleto*, li pros e li valant; (2575)
E li rois d'Ongarie avec lor ensemant.
E aprés lor, e Bernardo e Morant,
Tantqe a l'Apostoile se vait aprosmant,
Davant le palés en la plaça q'è grant,
8070 Furent armé .X. mil co*n*batant. (2580)
Çascun avoit lançe e spea trençant,
E bon çival isnele e remuant.
K*arleto* fu avant, sor un çival ferant;
Una grosa lançe li bailì un sarçant,
8075 E cil la tent, si la va palmojant; (2585)
Fer le primer q'el voit encontrant.
Morto l'abate entro lor plus de çant;
E pois escrie, "Ferés, me co*n*batant."
E cil le foit, qe nesun li contant;
8080 Li rois d'Ongarie, quando vi son enfant, (2590)
Si pro e fer e de tant ardimant,
Se il oit çoie, nesun no m'en demant;
De lui secorere no*n* fait arestamant.
Qi donc le veist ferir en le canp,
8085 Cun ses çivaler ardi e co*n*batant. (2595)
Grant fu la nose, meravilosa e gran;*
Qi donc veist K*arleto* li enfant,
Cum Çojose, sa bona spea trençant,   46ᵛᵃ
Menar colpi et arer et avant.
8090 A lu no*n* val arme un diner valisant! (2600)
El no*n* fer tanti q'el no*n* faça sanglant;
Çascun li fai rue, si le fuçe davant;*
Davant lui fuçì le petit e li grant;
E·l Cardenal se stava en estant;
8095 Prega Deo, li pere onipotant, (2605)

 Rubric 232 (after 8064) Keller: lapostoille
 8065 Reinhold: Va s'en; Rosellini: Vasen
 8068 Reinhold, Rosellini: Tant qe (as always)
 8074 Rosellini: baili
 8086 Reinhold, Rosellini: gran(t) (emend)
 8092 Reinhold: fai[t] rue; Rosellini: fairue
 8094 Reinhold, Rosellini: E 'l cardenal

Qe guardi Karleto da mort e da tormant,
Qe vos doie li plais plus çir avant?
Da la terçe trosqu'a li sol colçant
Durò quella bataila meravilosa e grant.

Rubric 233
Coment fu grant la bataille.
Laisse 234

8100 Grant fu la bataile e mervilos li stor; (2610)
　　　Qui de li rois fo bon çostreor;
　　　Desor tuti fu Karleto le milor.
　　　Çojosa tent, dont recoit honor;
　　　Tanti non fer q'el non çeti a l'arbor.*
8105 Qui de l'Apostolio ne fo en gran paor; (2615)
　　　Qe tanti ne vi cair morti de lor.
　　　Non è mervile, se i n'avoit paor;
　　　Deo reclame, e li soe pastor.
　　　E Karleto li fer a força et a vigor;
8110 O voient o no, s'en fuçent a estor; (2620)
　　　Non atendoit li grande li menor.*
　　　E l'Apostolie montò sor une tor,
　　　Por guarder la bataile, qe seroit vençeor.
　　　Quando la vi, mais non oit tel paor;
8115 El vide ben qe il estoit perdeor. (2625)
　　　Elo reguarde environ et entor;
　　　Par s(e) foir, mais no le vi retor,
　　　Qe davant e darer son la jent Francor.

Rubric 234
De li rois d'Ongarie.
Laisse 235

　　　Li rois d'Ongarie, li pros e lo loyal,
8120 Entro li altri rois el est natural; (2630)
　　　Plus ama Karleto de nesun omo carnal.*

　　8097 Reinhold: dò je
　　8111 Reinhold, Rosellini: li grand e li menor
　　8103 Rosellini: reçoit (emend)
　　8117 MS.: so; Reinhold, Rosellini: Par se (emend)
　　Rubric 234 (after 8118) MS., Reinhold: Rois; Keller: dongarie
　　8121 MS.: k. de l/ nesun

Par lu defendre e da mort e da mal,
Contre les autres el se mis comunal.
De l'Apostolie ferì li maraschal*
8124 (So nevo ert e so parent carnal). (2635)
Morto l'abate, no le fi altro mal;
E li ses çivaler tuti ferirent por ogual.
Qui de l'Apostolio metent a dol et a mal;
O voja o no, s'en fuçent por un val.
8130 E qui le encalçe cun le spee pugnal,* (2640)
Qe plus de mil ne mis en un canal.

Rubric 235
Coment cil furent vençu.*
Laisse 236

Quant Karleto oit çelor vençu,
Qe tot furent morti e confondu,
Li Apostoile fo preso e retenu;   46vb
8135 Demantenent despolé tot nu. (2645)
E li Cardenal si fo a lor venu;*
"Segnur," fait il, "qe avez atendu
Por ste malvés traito e recreu,*
Si sta banojé, è de ves reame ensu,*
8140 Li conseil dona qe fustes deçeu; (2650)
Quella meesme farez de lu."
Quant qui l'intent li grant e li menu,
Por maltalant li son sovracoru,
Cun dardi e cun brandi e cun spee agu,
8145 Si le donent por teste e por bu. (2655)
Quel fo plu çojant qi l'oit mejo feru;*
E de sa çarne n'avoit plu prendu.
A mala mort i l'ont confondu,
E tot sa jent vinta e recreu.

8124 Rosellini: feri li
8135 Reinhold: De mantenent (as always). Rosellini: desplé
8136 Reinhold, Rosellini: alor
8138 Reinhold: recreü (as always)
8139 Reinhold, Rosellini: Si sta banoié e de ves . . .
8143 Reinhold, Rosellini: sovra coru
8147 Rosellini: E de a çarne

Rubric 236
Co qe fi K*arleto* en Rome.
Laisse 237

8150	A gran mervile fu K*arleto* valent, (2660)
	Fort et ardi e ben reconosent.
	Quel Apostoile non amò de nient,
	Ne non amò ses amis e parent.
	O vi li Cardinal, por me la ma*n*s li prent;*
8155	"Fa vos avant, vu sì de nostra jent; (2665)
	Vu serì Apostolio da ste ora en avent;
	Morto serà qi de ren vos content."
	Dist li rois d'Ongarie, "Vu parlé saçement;*
	Par vos scanper da mort e da torment,
8160	Un mesaçer el me mandò erent, (2670)
	Qe a moi conta tot li convenent.
	Qi fa tel ovre, bon gujerdon atent."
	Dist K*arleto*, "Et eo si le guarent;
	Ço qe vos plais, e fo lo sumient."*
8165	Ne le fo Cardinal qe de ren guischisent;* (2675)
	Çascu de ço en fu legro e çojent;
	E l'Apostoilo por me la man li prent.
	"K*arleto*," fait il, "de una ren ne vos ment;
	En Roma son venu baron jusqua d'Orient,
8170	Por clamer enper qe sia pro e valent.* (2680)
	Non è milor de vos en le segle vivent;
	Vu serì enperé fato novelament."*
	Dist K*arleto*, "Non refu li present;
	Mais d'una ren e vos digo en guarent.
8175	Nen prenderò corone qe sia d'or lusent, (2685)
	Se França no co*n*quer tot en primement,
	E qui mon freri q'è traiti seduent,
	Qe son per oncis a mortel tradiment,
	E la ma mer dont a·l cor sui dolent,
8180	Se no la venço e no averò nient."* (2690)
	Dist li rois d'O*n*garie, "Vu parlé saçement;

Rubric 236 (after line 8149) Reinhold: Ço (emend for *Co*); Rosellini: Ço (emend)
8156 Guessard: d'aste ora; Rosellini: vu seri (as always with futures)
8166 Rosellini: Çascun
8170 Reinhold: enper[er] (emend)
8172 Guessard: enperere; Reinhold: enpere[r] (emend)
8180 Rosellini: non; Reinhold: e' no*n* averò nient

XX. mil omes vos donarò de ma jent,
Et eo meesme lì serò a·l present,
Por mia file ma pase no li rent."*

47^(ra)

Rubric 237
Coment l'Apostolie parole.
Laisse 238

8185   Li Apostoile si fo saço e valant; (2695)
       Elo parole altement en ojant:
       "*Karleto*," fait il, "vu parlé saçemant;*
       Nen cuitoie mie qe austes seno tant.
       Per vos amor e vos farò tant;
8190   Avec vos virò, chi pluri ne chi cant. (2700)
       Le perdon li darò, a petit e a grant,
       Qe a çest ponto vos serà secorant."
       Karleto l'olde, mil marçé li rant;
       Grant fu la çoja por *Karleto* l'infant,
8195   Qe livré est da cil malvasio tirant, (2705)
       Qe parent estoit d·i traitor de Magamç.
       Li rois d'Ongarie si vent a Belisant,
       Si la demande, "Cun vos ert li convant?"
       "Pur ben, bel sire, e son legra e çojant,
8200   Quant mon segnor vos ait a pertinant." (2710)
       E cil le dist, "Non virà longo tanp,
       Corona en çevo averés d'or lusant;
       Raina serés desor tot la jant."
       La dama l'olde, si le fa bel senblant;
8205   Ela·l mercie e ben e dolçemant. (2715)

Rubric 238
Coment li rois d'Ongarie parole a (*Karleto*).*
Laisse 239

       Li rois d'Ongarie, qe tant è pro e ber,
       Karleto apele, si·l prist a derasner:

    8184 Reinhold: ma' pase
    Rubric 237 (after 8184) Keller: lapostolie
    8205 Reinhold: Ela-l; Rosellini: Ela 'l
    Rubric 238 (after 8205) Keller: kongarie parole a b.; MS., Reinhold, Rosellini: parole ab.; Reinhold: *Karleto; Rosellini: K[arleto] (emend)
    8207 Reinhold: si-l; Rosellini: si'l

	"Bel filz," fait il, "eo te vojo conseler,
	Qe tu te dici guarnir e pariler,
8210	E par tot part mandar li mesaçer, (2720)
	A qui qe estoit amisi de ton per,*
	Qe i te vegna secorer et aider,
	Qe ton reame tu posi conquister."
	Dist Karleto, "E l'ò ben en penser."
8215	Adonc apella Morando de River; (2725)
	"Sire," fait il, "el vos convent aler
	Trosqua a Baiver, Aquilon a parler,
	E da ma part e dir e nonçer
	Qe li remenbri de la mort de mon per,
8220	E de ma mer q(e) avoit li cor fer."* (2730)
	E cil le dist, "Ne vos estoit doter;
	Ben li ò dir e tot l'afar conter."*
	El se part si se mis ad erer;
	Or vos vojo d'un çivaler conter,
8225	Rainero d'Aviçon el se fait anomer. (2735)
	Lanfroi e Landris l'oit fato sbanojer,
	Dapoisqe Pepin fu morto, ne li olsò demorer;
	De tot ses tere i le fe deschaçer,
	E cil s'en alò, si pasò oltra mer.
8230	Meltre çivaler ne se poroit trover; (2740)
	Çercando vait Karleto de là e de ça da mer.
	En Paganie tant se fi anomer,
	Mant cità prist a·l brant forbi d'açer,
	Encontra lui nul homo poit durer.
8235	En Babilo(in)e conquis un çivaler,* (2745)
	Qe meltre de lu ne se poroit trover;
	Par son amor, el se fe bateçer.
	Cil oit nome Sansoneto; filz fu d'un amirer.*
	Tant estoit et ardio e fer,
8240	A·l brant d'açer trova pochi çivaler (2750)
	Qe in canpo posa ver lu durer.

47ʳᵇ

8220 MS.: qa avoit; Reinhold: qe (emend); Rosellini: q'avoit (emend)
8223 Rosellini: ad arer
8227 Reinhold, Rosellini: Dapois qe
8231 Reinhold: Çerchando . . . de la e de ça; Rosellini: Çercando . . . de là e de ça
8235 MS.: babilome?; Reinhold, Rosellini: Babiloine

Rubric 239
Coment a Karleto venoit gram jent.
Laisse 240

      Or entendés, segnur, por Deo de majesté,
      Milor cançon jamés non oiré.
      Questo civaler si fo pro e doté;
8245 Por amor de Karleto tant pene oit duré, (2755)
      Ne ve poroit eser ne dite ni conté;
      De Crestentés elo fo sbanojé.
      Landris e Lanfroi, qe estoit rois clamé,
      De tota França li avoit sbanojé,
8250 Prese son tere e arse e brusé,* (2760)
      Et il s'en alò oltra la mer salé,
      Çerchando Karleto et avant et aré.
      E Damenedé por la soa bonté,
      Tant l'avoit (l)oué *et* prisé,*
8255 Preso avoit plu de .vii. cité; (2765)
      È questo Sansoneto, qe era un rois clamé.*
      Rainer d'Aviçon costu est anomé;
      Novel oldì ançiq'el fust trapasé,
      Qe l'Apostoile avoit convojé
8260 Tot li baron de la Cristeneté, (2770)
      Enperer vo levar de·l son parenté.*
      Quando Rainer oit la novela ascolté,
      Sansoneto apele, si le oit arasné,
      Qe venir voloie a Rome la çité
8265 Por contraster a cil q'el non sia levé. (2775)
      A Sansoneto li vene molto a gre;
      Cun lui el vene, si con vos oldiré,
      Cento mil pain oit cun lu mené.
      A Roma vent e ben fu ostalé,
8270 Si le estoit venu quela çorné, (2780)
      Quando l'Apostoile fu morto e livré,
      E le papa Milon en seça repolsé.
      Quando Karleto oit qilo trové,
      Se il oit çoie, or ne me demandé;

Rubric 239 (after 8241) Keller: a k.
8250 Reinhold: arsé
8254 7 for *et*. MS.: houe; Reinhold, Rosellini: loué
8256 Rosellini: E (conjunction)
8258 Reinhold: Novel'
8261 Reinhold, Rosellini: vo[l] levar (emend)

8275	A lui s'en vait, si le fu aconté. (2785)
	Quant se conoit tel çoja oit demené,
	Major non fu veua ni guardé. 47ᵛᵃ
	"Mon segnor," dist il, "or vos ai trové,*
	Qe tant por vos son pené e travalé,
8280	Par tot li mondo e davant e daré; (2790)
	Ne ve dotés qe ben sui parelé,
	De civalçer guarni e coroé.
	Cento mil omes e vos ò amené,
	E de l'avoir e ò a gran planté."
8285	Karleto l'olde, si l'oit abraçé; (2795)
	De ço q'el dist molt l'oit agraé,*
	De la parole si l'oit amercié;
	Gran fu la çoja en Roma la cité
	Por Rainer d'Aviçon q'è reparié,
8290	E por l'Apostoile le qual si fu clamé. (2800)
	Li bon Milon, qe fu saço e doté,
	Qe par tot part oit bani e crié:*
	Çascun de ceus qe le virà daré,*
	Tut ses peçé li serà perdoné.
8295	E qi no le virà, si serà condané (2805)
	Cun pataroi, eretego clamé.*
	Grande fu l'oste in Roma asenblé;
	Li rois d'Ongaria no à l'ovra oblié;
	Son guarniment avoit aparilé.
8300	A çamin se metent quant fu ordené; (2810)
	Por Lonbardie i sont acaminé,
	E la Toscane i ont trapasé.

Rubric 240
Coment la novelle aloit par tot part.
Laisse 241

	Quant la novele porta li coreor,
	Par tot part environ et entor,
8305	Por le çité a conti et a valvasor, (2815)
	Et a Paris a quelli dos traitor,
	Qe son per e sa mer oncient a dolor,
	Saçés por voir q'i fo en gran paor.
	Por celle jent tant qe li ven a tor,*

    8278 Rosellini: Non segnor (cf. Plouzeau and Martin)
    8296 Reinhold: pataroi; Rosellini: patoroi (cf. Martin)
    8298 Rosellini: d'Ongaria o a

8310 Nen voloit pais fare longo sejor. (2820)
Por qui çivaler avoit fato onor;
Per lor mandò, qe le vegna en secor,*
E si fa co*n*vojer tuto so(n) parentor.*
Gran çent asenblent, e pri*n*ces e co*n*tor,
8315 E si le fu de valant pugneor, (2825)
Dont gran bataile fu e gran stor,
De le major qe ausés ancor.

Rubric 241
Coment aloit li mesacer a Girard Aufraite.*
Laisse 242

Lanfroi e Landris ne volsen demorer;
A Girardo Aufraite i mandent mesaçer,*
8320 Qe i le vegna a secorer et aider. (2830)
Li mesaçer qe le vont a nonçer,
A Viene le poront trover.*
Quant li mesaçer li vait li brevi bailer,
Girardo e Milo, li qual estoit son frer,   47vb
8325 I le trovent anbidos conseler. (2835)
Davant Girardo s'en vait a çenoler,
"Mon sir," fait il, "nu semo mesaçer
De Landris e de Lanfroi, qe anbidos son frer,
Rois son de Fra*n*çe, si manten li terer.
8330 I ont novelle por li ses spioner, (2840)
E por ses mesi e por li ses corer,
Qe quel K*arleto* q'i farent sbanojer
Sovra li vent cu*n* oste de çivaler.
I le vos mande qe le venez aider,*
8335 Si come celu in chi ont gran sper." (2845)
Dist Girardo, "Faròꞏlo volunter."
Millon apelle, siꞏl prist a derasner:
"Frere," fait il, "alez vos coroer.

    8313 MS.: so parentor; Reinhold: so*n* parentor; Rosellini: son parentor
    8317 Reinhold, Rosellini: ausés
    Rubric 241 (after 8317) MS.: aufraite; *te* is written above the line; Keller: au /fraite; Reinhold, Rosellini: Aufraite. Rosellini: mesaçer
    8321 Reinhold, Rosellini: vont anonçer
    8326 Reinhold, Rosellini: vait açenoler
    8336 Reinhold, "Farò lo . . . ; Rosellini: Faròlo . . .
    8337 Reinhold: si-l . . . à derasner; Rosellini: si'l

          X. mil omes vu averés mener,
8340 A bone arme et a corant destrer." (2850)
          "Frer," fait il, "qe vos ò oldu parler?
          Donc me volés a qui traiti envojer,
          Qe a tradiment onciént son per,
          E quella dame, q'i tenoit por mer?
8345 I son strepon, e malvasii e lainer* (2855)
          E quel Karleto, qe est droiturer,
          Si deveroit la corona mantenir e guarder,
          Qi vait contra rason si doit mal ariver."*
          Girardo l'olde, cuita li seno cançer;
8350 El oit çuré li voir justisier, (2860)
          O voja o no, li conven aler.
          Quando Milon l'oldì si parler,
          Ben le conoit, no le olsa contraster;
          O voja o no, li convent otrier.*
8355 E·l dux Girardo si dist a·l mesaçer: (2865)
          "Ami," fait il, "or vos tornez arer;
          A Lanfroi e Landrix si li avrì nonçer,
          De nula ren se diça smajer;
          Secorso li darò de .X. mil çivaler;
8360 Milon mon frer li farò envojer. (2870)
          Segurament ben porà guerojer."
          Le mesaçer le prist a mercier;
          Arer tornent a son segnor conter
          Questa novela (qe ben fo d'agraer);
8365 S'i ont çoja non è da demander. (2875)
          E Milon fait sa çent apariler;
          X. mil furent a coranti destrer.
          El no sa mie ço qe le doit encontrer,*
          Qe de la bataile mais el no tornò arer.
8370 Sansoneto l'oncis a·l brant forbi d'açer,* (2880)
          Como vu porés oldir et asculter.*
          E quel Milon non fu pais da blasmer,
          Qe a Paris vait mal volunter.   48ra

8348 Reinhold, Rosellini: li doit (emend)
8352 Rosellini: oldi
8355 Reinhold, Rosellini: E 'l
8361 MS.: seguramet (titulus over the final e); Reinhold: Segurament; Rosellini: Segurament
8364 Rosellini: da graer
8368 Reinhold: El ne sà
8370 MS.: albrant (see endnote)

       Le voloir de son frer non olsò co*n*traster;
8375   Monta a çival, briga de çivalçer; (2885)
       Ven a Paris, ben se fe ostaler;
       Grant onor le fait anbidos li frer.

Rubric 242
Coment çivalça K*arleto*.
Laisse 243

       Karleto çivalçe, c'oit cor de lion;
       E li rois d'Ongarie a .XX. mil co*n*pagnon,
8380   E si le fu Rainero d'Aviçon, (2890)
       Et avec lui li riant Sanson.
       Cento mil ont de la loi de Macon,
       E l'Apostoile c'oit nome Milon.
       En sa co*n*pagne fo manti clereçon,
8385   E tanto altro povolo per la benecion, (2895)
       Qe le miler conter n'en poroit l'on.*
       Donqua verisés tanti be co*n*falon,
       E tant ensegne e indoré penon,
       Qe tot n'en flonboie e li po e li mon.*
8390   I civalçent a cuite de speron;* (2900)
       Pasent Lonbardie e Proença enson.*
       Dever Paris çivalçe qui baron;
       Da l'altra part si venia Aquilon,
       E mena son fil c'oit nome Naymon;*
8395   E si le fu Bernardo de Clermon. (2905)
       Quant a Paris ili si s'aprosmon,
       Davant li Roine metent li co*n*falon,
       Si le tendent tende e pavilon.
       Da l'altra part de·l Roine si estoit Milon,
8400   Qe frer estoit Girard li Bergognon;* (2910)
       Si le fu qui de Magançe, tot quant par non;
       Lanfroi e Landrix, cu*n* conti e baron,

Rubric 242 (after 8377) MS., Keller: çivalça .k.
8386 Rosellini: nen
8389 Reinhold, Rosellini: nen flonboie
8390 Reinhold, Rosellini: d'esperon
8391 Reinhold, Rosellini: en son
8397 Rosellini: li Roine li confalon (missing verb)
8400 Reinhold, Rosellini: Girardo

　　　　　Qe furent de France e de la legion,
　　　　　Qe le obedisent, o volist o non,
8405　　　Cun qui de Paris a tende e a pavilon. (2915)

Rubric 243
Coment fu grande l'oste.
Laisse 244

　　　　　Grande fu le oste, mervelos e grant;
　　　　　D'anbedos part furent çivaler tant,
　　　　　Ne vos poroit conter nesun ho*n* vivant.
　　　　　Aquilon de Baiver si fo bo*n* co*n*batant,
8410　　　A gran mervile el fo pro e valant.* (2920)
　　　　　L'aigue pasò une dema*n* por tanp,*
　　　　　Cun .X. mil de çivaler valant.
　　　　　L'oste asalì qi estoit d·i Franc;
　　　　　Avantqe celle jent mo*n*tase en auferant,
8415　　　Tende e pavilon ne trençò plu de çant, (2925)
　　　　　E plus de mil omes oncis a·l fer tre*n*çant.
　　　　　Grant fu la nose qe levarent qi Franc;
　　　　　A çival monte, a miler et a çant;
　　　　　E Aquilon s'en torne legro e çojant.
8420　　　Quant K*arleto* le soit, si le voit a graant; (2930)　　　48rb
　　　　　El voit ben qe le ama dolçemant.
　　　　　Dist Aquilon a K*arleto* en ojant,
　　　　　"Bel filz," fait il, "ben saçì ad esiant,
　　　　　Se volés vinçer li malvasi seduant,
8425　　　Ne vos reçés a li seno d'infant.* (2935)
　　　　　Seno e proeçe li volt, et ardimant,
　　　　　Quel vos farà quant querì e demant."

Rubric 243 (after 8405) Keller: loste
8411 Rosellini: pro tanp (for *por tanp*)
8413 Rosellini: asali
8417 Reinhold: q[u]i' Franc
8425 Reinhold, Rosellini: reçés

Rubric 244
Coment Aquilon pasò l'aigue.
Laisse 245

        Quant Aquilon fu arer torné,
        K*arleto* l'oit gran çoja demené.
8430 L'altra deman, quant l'aube fu levé, (2940)
        E Lanfroi fu a çival monté
        Da quella part o Aquilon avoit pasé,
        Pasoit Lanfroi molto ben coroé.
        L'eve pasent por gran nobilité;
8435 L'oste asalì o plus estoit seré; (2945)
        Grande fu la nose e li remor levé,
        Qe Aquilon fo a çival monté,
        E Sansoneto, qe tant fu alosé,
        Proer el volt ver lor soa ferté.
8440 Lora verisés come*n*çar gran meslé; (2950)
        Testes trençer, e spales e costé,
        Tanti çival foir gole baé,
        Dont le segnor en son deçivalçé.
        E cil Lanfroi fo pro e dotriné,
8445 E de bataile molto ben adoté. (2955)
        Le primer colpo qe il oit doné
        Un çivaler oit morto versé,
        Et in apreso un altro atué.
        Si grant fu la nosa e la meslé,
8450 Qe par nul omo poroit eser co*n*té. (2960)
        Celle Lanfroi fu fort *et* aduré;
        La spea tent a li pomo d'or entalé.
        En me la voie oit Aquilon enco*n*tré;
        Gran colpo li done desor l'eume çemé*
8455 O son le pere, c'oit gran clarité. (2965)
        Nen poit trençer valant una deré;*
        La spea torne davant li costé,
        La tarça trençe e l'aubergo safré.
        Por me li cors el li mis la spe;
8460 Cor e coraies li trençò por mité. (2970)

    Rubric 244 (after 8427) Keller: laigue
    8435 Rosellini: asali
    8437 Reinhold, Rosellini: fo
    8451 7 for *et*
    8454 Reinhold, Rosellini: li done . . . euma

A celle colpo, l'oit morto çité.
Quant à ço fato, si s'en retorna aré.

Rubric 245
Coment fu gran dol d'Aquilon.
Laisse 246

      Gran dol fo por Aquilon demenés;
      Li rois l'oit planto e␣regretés,
8465 Ma desor tot Naimon, soa rités. (2975)
      E Lanfroi oit oltra l'aigua pasés;
      Quando fo oltre si fo çojant e lés.   48va
      O vi son frer si li avoit contés,
      "Frer," fait il, "e vos ò delivrés
8470 De celu qe n'oit tanto pené e travalés, (2980)
      Cil Aquilon, qe in Baiver fu nés."
      Dist Landrix, "Deo ne soja aorés;
      Oimai da lui seremo delivrés."
      E Rainer d'Aviçon fu a *K*arleto alés:*
8475 "Mon sir," fait il, "mal avon esploités; (2985)
      Perdu avon li meltre de nos masnés,
      Colu qe estoit plu saçe e dotés
      De nesun homo de la Cristenetés;
      Por Deo vos pre q'elo soja vençés."
8480 Dist *K*arleto, "E l'ò ben en pensés; (2990)
      La deman quan l'aube ert levés,
      Tot mon graile en seroit sonés.
      L'aigua pasaron a força *et* a durés,
      De ça no remarà ho*n* qe soja nés;
8485 Preso de Paris seremo a la meslés." (2995)
      Dist Sansoneto, qe fu ilec pres,
      "Questa novella si m'est molto a graés."
      E li rois d'Ongarie li oit acreentés,
      E Naimes l'intant par pol ne des(vi)éo,*
8490 Quando son per lasa morto a·l pres. (3000)

  Rubric 245 (after 8462) Keller: daquilon
  8471 Rosellini: Aquion
  8479 Reinhold: prè
  8483 7 for *et*
  8484 Reinhold, Rosellini: remara
  8486 Rosellini: qe fu lec prés
  8489 MS.: desures; Reinhold: desviés (emend); Rosellini: desvrés

Rubric 246
Coment fu morto Aquilon.
Laisse 247

       Por Aquilon çascun si fo dolent,
       Qe asa avoit amisi e parent.
       Seveli l'oit e ben e çentilment;
       La noit repolse trois l'aube aparisent.
8495 A la jornée i le fe altrement; (3005)
       De graile fait soner plus de çent.
       Çascun s'adobe e prende guarniment;
       K*arleto* l'infant nen fait arestament.
       Le arme prent, e ben e lialment;
8500 E Rainer d'Aviçon e Sansoneto l'infent, (3010)
       E li rois d'Ongarie co*n* tot soa jent,
       A çival montent tost et isnelament;
       L'aigue pasent a grant enforçament.
       Quant Lanfroi e Landrix le vide ad esient,*
8505 De lor veoir ont gran spavent, (3015)
       Ma noportant i son pro e valent,
       Ne de foir non fait nul senblent;
       Mais por co*n*batere prende*nt* guarniment.
       Ça oldirés començer tel tençonent,*
8510 Dont manti çivaler en remaneroit sanglent. (3020)

Rubric 247
Coment K*arleto* pasò l'aigue.
Laisse 248

       Quando K*arleto* fo oltra l'aigua pasé,*
       Avec lui, ses çivaler prisé,
       Adoncha començent una grande meslé.   48vb
       (Lanfroi) e Landrix, quant furent armé,
8515 E·l dux Milon, qe tant fu redoté, (3025)
       Cun quili de Bergogne s'alirent a·l pre;*
       Grande fu la meslée qua*n*t fu començé.

8493 Reinhold, Rosellini: Seveli
8505 Rosellini: ont spavent (*gran* missing)
Rubric 247 (after 8510) Keller: laigue
8514 MS.: Çofroi; Reinhold, Rosellini: Lanfroi (emend for *Çofroi*)
8515 Reinhold, Rosellini: E 'l
8516 Reinhold, Rosellini: salirent

Adonc ont levé la grant orié;*
Celu fo fole, qe non trait la spe.
8520 Quando Karleto fo en le stor entré, (3030)
E ten Çojosa sa trencant espé,
A qi un colpo el n'oit doné,
Morto o navrés, li çeta a li pre.
E Sansoneto no à l'ovra oblié;
8525 Meltre çivaler nen seroit trové. (3035)
Qi ben çercase tros a la mer bité.*
E Rainer d'Aviçon si fo pro e doté;
Entro lor ferirent si fort et aduré,
Qe de çival n'ont mil ateré.
8530 Landrix e Lanfroi con qui de la cité (3040)
Si ferirent e menu e soé.

Rubric 248
Coment asa(l)irent l'oste.
Laisse 249

D'anbes parties fu grande li remor;*
Unqua bataila non oisés major.
De cele spee ferirent de tel vigor,
8535 Qi non fo pro si n'oit gran dolor. (3045)
Manti prodomes en caent a l'albor,*
Qe mais no le vi ne fio ne uxor.
Qi de le canpo averoit l'onor;
Laudar porà Deo le Creator,*
8540 Qe mais de tel non avè tel paor. (3050)
Par me li canp ven pugnando un contor
(Milon l'apelle celle jent Francor).
Por grande esforço punçe le milsoldor,
E va a ferir Guarner da Monteflor.
8545 Tel colpo li done, q'elo l'abate a l'arbor; (3055)
Voit·le Sansoneto, si n'avoit gran paor,
Qe morto non fust ilec ad estor;
Ne vos mervolés s'el oit dolor.

8521 Reinhold, Rosellini: trençant (emend for trencant)
Rubric 248 (after 8531) MS.: asairent; Keller: asairent loste; Reinhold: asaïrent l'oste; Rosellini: asairent
8534 Reinhold: De cel espée; Rosellini: De cele spée
8539 Reinhold, Rosellini: poia

Rubric 249
Coment Sansoneto oncis Milon.*
Laisse 250

       Quando Sansoneto oit Milon veu,*
8550 Qe Guarner oit a la tera abatu, (3060)
       Molto fo pro e de molt gran vertu.
       S'el no le vençe, no s'apresia un festu;
       Por grande esforço li è sovrasalu.
       Gran colpo li done desor l'eumes agu;
8555 Nian por cil el no fo defendu. (3065)
       Trença li eume e la cofia por menu;
       Trosqu'a li denti li oit la spea metu,
       E versa li colpo si l'oit morto abatu.*
       Quant celi veent, ma si dolent nen fu.   49ra
8560 E Sansoneto fo arer revenu; (3070)
       Karleto le vi, cela part fo venu,
       Si le apela por amigo e dru.

Rubric 250
Coment Karleto pasò l'aigue.
Laisse 251

       Quando Karleto oit l'aigua pasé,*
       E li rois d'Ongarie li saçes e li doté,
8565 Li stormeno fo grant e desmesuré; (3075)
       Major non fo veçu ni esguardé;
       De le spee donent gran colé.
       Qi donc veist qui çivaler prisé,
       Qe Karleto avoit aconvojé.
8570 Karleto reguarda for por me la stre, (3080)
       E vide Lanfroi venir por me un pre.
       Entro son pugno tent nua la spe.
       Ben le conoit, si l'oit derasné:
       "Çivaler, sire, a cele arme doré,
8575 Come estes vos clamé et apelé?" (3085)
       E cil le dist: "Ne vos serà çelé
       Rois son de Française, e de Paris la cité;

Rubric 249 (after 8548) MS.: milion, with the second *i* expunctuated
8553 Reinhold, Rosellini: sovra salu
Rubric 250 (after 8562) Keller: .k. . . . laigue
8570 Reinhold: por me' la stré; Rosellini: stré

E si fu filz Pepin, li maine coroné
Qe se trovast trosqu'a la mer bité.
8580 E vos, qi estes, qe m'avés demandé? (3090)
A gran mervile en estes ben armé;
Le vestre arme en çeta gran clarté.
Como avés nome en la vestra contré?"
Responde Karleto, "Ben vos seria conté;
8585 Se m'avesés de vu dito la verité, (3095)
Vos si me dites qe estes rois clamé,
E fusi fil Pepin li maine encoroné,
Nen desdi mie nen soja verité.
Ma filz non fustes de sa muler sposé;*
8590 Da una meltrix vos fustes ençendré, (3100)
Unde est bastardo e peço apelé.*
E la rason l'oit dito e comandé
Qe non poez avoir nula dignité;
Et in apreso vu avì major peçé
8595 Qe ma posa eser ne dito ni pensé. (3105)
Ancir li per ni la mer si estoit comandé
Por la Scritura q'elo soja dané.
Malvasio traites, fole e renojé
E son colu qi li averò vencé!
8600 E fu filz Pepin, le vestro sbanojé (3110)
Qe par tot li mondo vu m'avez caçé.
Ora sui e a ma mason retorné."
Quant cil l'intent, ferament l'oit reguardé;
S'el oit paure, or ne m'en demandé,
8605 Qe in soa man elo vide la spe (3115)
Tuta sanglent de colpi c'oit doné.
"Frer," dist Karleto, "ora ne vos doté;
Nen vojo qe par moi en seez destorbé."
Da lu se part e si l'oit lasé
8610 En le gran stor elo fo afiçé, (3120)
E va a ferir et avant et aré.

49ʳᵇ

8579 Reinhold, Rosellini: mere bité
8591 MS.: est; Reinhold, Rosellini: est[es] (emend)
8597 MS. scritura
8598 Reinhold: fol e renoie (emend)

Rubric 251
Coment fo pris La(n)froi.
Laisse 252

        Grant fu quela bataile, mervelos e pesant;
        Ben le ferì Karleto l'infant,
        E Guarner d'Aviçon avec lui ensemant,
8615   E Morando de River, li ardi conbatant. (3125)
        Bernardo de Clermo(n)t a la çere riant,
        E Sansoneto li pro e li valant,
        E li rois d'Ongarie cun tota soa çant.
        Si le fu Naimes, le petit enfant,
8620   Qe de son pere estoit molto dolant. (3130)
        Da l'altra part estoit tot qui de Maganç,
        E qui de Paris a spee et a lanç,
        E la jent de Girardo Aufrate li posant;
        Son segnor estoit morto, dont fo li dol grant.
8625   Quela aja durò de ilec a longo tanp;* (3135)
        Qe no s'en fe pais ni acordamant.
        Por me li canpo vait Sansoneto pongant;
        Tent una lançe a li fer trençant.
        En me la voie vait Lanfroi encontrant,
8630   Qe frer estoit de Karleto l'infant. (3140)
        Ne le parole ne le fe bel senblant,
        Ferir le vait por si fer maltalant.
        Le scu le speçe e la pene davant;*
        Fort fu l'auberg, qe maja non destant;
8635   E l'asta fu grosa e ben tenant; (3145)
        E cil la pinse por si fer maltalant,
        Q'elo l'abate roverso a li canp.
        Lever se volse, quant cil no li consant;
        Avec lui s'arotent ses çivaler valant,
8640   Guarner d'Aviçon e li cont Morant. (3150)
        Preso li oit, oltra son maltalant;
        Por maltalento li oit tolto li brant.
        Aprés lor vent Naimes li enfant;
        Morto l'aust a la spea trençant,
8645   Quant Karleto li vent esperonant. (3155)
        Si no li à consentu de nojant,
        Qe il fust morto ilec a·l presant.

    Rubric 251 (after 8611) MS.: laufroi; Keller: lanfroi; Reinhold: Lanfroi (emend); Rosellini: Lanfroi
    8616 MS.: clermot; Reinhold, Rosellini: Clermo[n]t (emend)

Rubric 252
Quanto durò quella bataille.
Laisse 253

      Tuto quel çorno durò quela meslé;
      Tera delivré ne le seroit trové*
8650 O non fust hon mort o armes o espé. (3160)
      Lanfroi fo pris et arere mené;
      Karleto li oit doné a li ses plu privé,
      Qe ben li oit tenu e guardé.
      Ancora fo li stor si grant e aduré,   49va
8655 D'anbesdos part qe major ne·l veré.* (3165)
      Quant Landrix vi qe son frer n'est amené,
      Gran dol n'oit, por poi ne des(v)é.
      La spea tent a·l pomo d'or entailé;
      O vi Morando, cela part est alé;
8660 Gran colpo li done desor l'eume çemé. (3170)
      Quant el ne prent, el çitò a·l pre;
      Deo le guardi, q'el ne l'oit pase pié.*
      La spea torne sor la tarça roé;
      La guinche con le scu el çitò a·l pre.
8665 E de l'aubers, cento maile trençè; (3175)
      De l'auberg çetò a·l pre la ghironé.
      Et a·l çival oit li çevo copé;
      Cil caì morto e quel fo roversé,
      Siqe li eume ficò en la pon dre.*
8670 Gran fo li colpo qe cil li oit doné; (3180)
      Preso l'aust oltra sa volunté,
      E in Paris conduto e mené,
      Quando Sansoneto li ven de randoné;
      E Guarner d'Aviçon, qe no l'à oblié,
8675 O voja o no, el l'oit lasé, (3185)
      Dever Paris el fo açaminé
      (Q)e sa qe çivaler, s'el aust lialté,*
      Quant son per oncis, el no fo plu privé;

Rubric 252 (after 8647) Rosellini: Coment durò
8655 Reinhold: ne-l veré; Rosellini: ne'l veré
8657 MS.: desne; Reinhold, Rosellini: desve
8662 Reinhold: Deo le guar(d)ì . . . pas(e) (misquoted by Rosellini)
8665 Reinhold, Rosellini: trençé
8669 MS.: en la pon dre; Reinhold, Rosellini: en la poudré
8670 Rosellini: cil oit done (*li* missing)
8677 MS., Reinhold, Rosellini: Desa qe

Da tota jent el fo avilé.
8680 Si gra*n*t fu la bataile, ne*n* fo major guardé, (3190)
D'anbesdos part e de lançe e de spe.
Tant çivaler çase, gola baé,
Qe de·l veoir en seroit peçé,
Porqe i son Cristian batezé.
8685 Trosqua a li vespro durò quela meslé; (3195)
Sor totes autres fo Sansoneto doté.

Rubric 253
Coment K*arle*to çivalçe a li stor.
Laisse 254

Karleto çivalçe, li ardi e li fer,
For por li stor, irés como un çengler,
E ten Çojose, so bon brando d'açer
8690 Qi li donò Danabrun li Escler. (3200)
A qi ne dà un colpo, ne li à plu mester;
Morir li convent sença nul demorer.
Qui de Paris se vide mal bailer;
Oncis se vide a cento et a miler,
8695 Si s'en fuçent par poi e por river. (3205)
Qui qi poent en Paris entrer,
Devent ben Damenedé orer.
Si grant fu la bataile no se poroit co*n*ter;*
Landrix s'en vait por davant un senter.
8700 Ben se cuitoit a salvament aler, (3210)
Quando le çivalçe Morando de River,
Quel d'Aviçon, li valant Guarner,
E Sansoneto, li ardi e li fer.
Quando vi Landrix, q'el no s'en po aler,
8705 E qe de foir el no li fa mester, (3215)
La spea tent, e volse li destrer.
A gran mervile el fo bon çivaler;*
Ça nul milor no se poroit trover.
Sansoneto fer davanti a l'incontrer;
8710 Tel colpo li done desor l'eume verçer, (3220)
De quel no*n* trençe, ma si le foit enbronçer.
Desor l'arçon de·l corant destrer
Par un petit ne le fe trabuçer.
Quant Sansoneto se vi si mal bailer,

49vb

8705 Rosellini: foir no li fa . . . (*el* missing)

8715	S'el oit dol, non è da merveler. (3225)
	La spea tent par soi defenser,
	E fer Landrix si gran colpo plener,
	Qe cil no li poit sofrir ni endurer.
	Par soi guarir, se lasò trabuçer
8720	En celle pre, e si fo peoner. (3230)
	La spea tent, ne la volse oblier;
	Si se defende a loi de çivaler.
	Qi la veist mener e inplojer,
	E menar colpi et avant et arer,*
8725	Si durament fa celo spaventer. (3235)
	O voja o no, i se traent arer;
	Plus d'un arpant le foit reculer.
	Mais no li valt la monta d'un diner,
	Qe in tal fuga fo li ses çivaler,
8730	Qe nesun no li vent secorer ni aider. (3240)
	Quando elo vi no li à nula sper,
	Monta a çival, ben se cuitoit aler*
	Dedens Paris, a salvamento torner.
	Ma ço q'il croit, si le fala li penser, (3245)
8735	Qe quili son e davent e darer,
	E tota l'oste si le pris a 'roter.
	Dardi e lançe si le prendent a lançer,
	Deso lui oncis son destrer.
	Quando vi ben defendre, ni oit mester,
8740	Qe in fua vi tuti ses çivaler, (3250)
	Elo se rende e si fo presoner.
	E qui lo prent, si le fe desarmer,
	E si le tole li brant forbi d'açer.
	Pois le menent apreso de son frer,
8745	E ben le foit e tenir e guarder, (3255)
	Qe i no posa ni foir ni scanper;
	Quant à ço fato, ritorna a li torner.

8723 Reinhold, Rosellini: Qi le (emend)
8735 Reinhold: qui' li
8736 Reinhold, Rosellini: vont aroter

Rubric 254
Coment K*arleto* parole a Sanso(ne)to.*
Laisse 255

        Dont oit K*arleto* Sansoneto apelés,
        Morando li pros, e d·i altri asés;
8750 "Segnur," fait il, "ben avon esploités, (3260)   50ra
        Quant cest canpo avon desbaratés.
        Veez cun s'en vait fuçando por li pres?
        Çama por loro no seremo engo*n*brés.
        Prisi son coloro qe tenia li regnés,
8755 E qe de tot m'avoit desarités. (3265)
        Avantqe da moi i soja desevrés,
        De le servisio ben serà merités.
        Nesun de vos ne sia alentés;
        Ardiament ançemo a la çités,
8760 Qe de la tera so ben la verités, (3270)
        Qe tanti li averò amisi e parentés.
        Daqe çesti dos avemo enpresonés,
        Qe da lor no*n* serà ren dotés;
        Qe voluntera me darà la çités."
8765 Çeli li dient, "Vu avì ben parlés." (3275)
        Comunelment i sont arotés.
        E qui s'en fuit, li fren abandonés;
        En Paris entrent, si ont le porte serés,
        E le gran ponti ont amont levés;
8770 E tot li canpo en fu desbaratés. (3280)

    Rubric 254 (after 8747) MS.: sansouto; Keller: sausouto; Mussafia, "Handschriftliche Studien II": sanson[e]to (307, emend for *sausouto*); Reinhold: Sanson[e]to; Rosellini: Sanson[e]to (emend for MS. *sausouto*)
    8758 Reinhold: soia alentés; Rosellini: sia alentés
    8759 Rosellini: li çités

Rubric 255
Coment fo pris li do frer.*
Laisse 256

        Or oit Karleto preso li dos felon,
        Lanfroi e Landris, c'oit benecion,*
        Qe son per oncis a mortel traison.
        De quel ovre n'averà gujerdon;
8775 Apisi serà como incresun felon. (3285)
        E·l bon Karleto, e li valant Sanson,
        E l'Apostoile, c'oit nome Milon,
        Davant la porte fe tendre li pavilon.
        Prendent la plaçe entorno et inviron,
8780 Qi dedens se tenent por bricon. (3290)
        Quant vi guaster ses broili e ses mason,
        Dist l'un ver l'altro, "Ora qe demandon?
        Nostri segnor son metu en preson,
        Siqe da lor no averon plu reençon.
8785 Nu semo foli quant tant demoron, (3295)
        Quant a Karleto no demo sa mason,
        Qe ben è soa par droita nasion.
        El fo lojal, e quisti era strepon;
        Son per oncis a mortel traison."
8790 Or entendés coment la fe Karlon; (3300)
        A si apele li damisel Naimon,
        Li rois d'Ongarie, e li prode Sanson,
        E Morant de River, qe le fu conpagnon,
        E l'Apostoile c'oit nome Milon.
8795 "Segnur," fait il, "Coment la faron?" (3305)
        Dist Naimes, "Porqe vos çelaron?
        Nu la faron a seno de saço hon.
        Ora prendés l'Apostoile Milon,   50rb
        En Paris l'invojés par (u)n tel cason,

    Rubric 255 (after line 8770) MS.: prisi; the final *i* is expunctuated, Keller: fo pris li do frer; Guessard: fo pris li dos frer (402); Reinhold, Rosellini: prisi li do frer
    8771 Rosellini: Or oir (cf. Plouzeau, Martin)
    8772 Rosellini: be[r]necion (= "signoria")
    8776 Reinhold, Rosellini: E 'l
    8780 Reinhold: Q[u]i'
    8790 Reinhold: Karlon; Rosellini: K[arleton]
    8799 MS.: ui tel; Reinhold, Rosellini: un tel

8800   Qe la pax façe si li die li perdon." (3310)
       E cili dient, "Ben parla ces Naimon;
       El no resenble q'elo sia garçon."

Rubric 256
Coment Naimes parole a K*arleto.*
Laisse 257

       Quant Naimes oit li conseil doné,
       E l'Apostoile si fo aparilé,
8805   De prist oit avec lui asé.* (3315)
       Ven a la porte de la bone cité,
       E altament li oit escrié:
       "Avrés la porte e li pont avalé!
       Parler vos vojo da la part de Dé;
8810   E son li Apostoilo qe da Deo fui sagré, (3320)
       Si vegno por pax, se aver la voré;
       E li perdon vos darò d·i peçé."
       Quant cil l'intent, gra*n* çoja n'à mené;
       Porqe la pax li venoit ben a gre.
8815   La porta li ont mantenant desfermé, (3325)
       E si le ont li pont devalé.
       E l'Apostoile entrò en la cité;
       Quant fu dedens q'i l'ont a(s)iguré,*
       E bon e re se arotent aré,
8820   Qe tot ont quella pax crié: (3330)
       "Vegna nostro segnor, qe avon desiré."
       Dist l'Apostoile, "Deo sia aoré;
       De ço qe dites, farez gran bonté."
       Tros a la plaçe elo li oit amené;
8825   Quant fo ilec, si li oit prediché; (3335)
       Le voir le dist, ne no pais falsité.
       "Segnur," fait il, "ben avez esploité;*
       Vestre segnor vos est aprosmé,
       Qe tant pene avoit par vu duré.
8830   Por strançe tere durè de gran ferté; (3340)

   Rubric 256 (after 8802) Keller, MS.: .k.
   8810 Reinhold, Rosellini: sui
   8816 Rosellini: E si le ont pont (*li* missing)
   8818 MS.: afigure; Reinhold: q'i l'ont afiguré; Rosellini: qi l'ont asiguré
   8830 Reinhold, Rosellini: duré

Ora l'oit Deo a vos envojé.
Par moi vos mande, qe vos le recevé,
Por segnor le tenés con tenir le devé."
Quant cil l'intendent, tuti ont escrié
8835 Qe seguramen*t* entri en la cité.* (3345)
Ne le fo nul, ne çoven ni barbé,
Qe cel consel avoient contrasté.
Mais li traitor avoient malovré;
Qe estoient de li so parenté,
8840 Via s'en fuçent fora de la cité (3350)
Par soi guarir, si s'en son via alé.
E l'Apostoile no à l'ovra oblié;
Con tot li pople el fo defor alé.
Ven a Karleto, si le oit apresenté:
8845 "Mon segnor," fait il, "e vo qe vu saçé: (3355)
Veez li pople de la bona cité,   50ᵛᵃ
Veez le clave q'i v'ont aporté.
Tota la tere i v'ont abandoné; (3360)
Or la prendés, se prender la volé,
8850 Qe i vos la dà volunter e de gre."
Dist li rois, "Deo ne sia adoré."

Rubric 257
Coment l'Apostoi(le) parole a Karleto.
Laisse 258

Li Apostoile si oit pris a parler;
"Karleto," fait il, "e no vos quer nojer;
Questo pople qe veez qui erer,
8855 Quant en Paris eo entra in primer, (3365)
E bon e re, me venerent arer.
Tuti vos clame por segnor droiturer;*
Ne le vi un qe le volese contraster.
Çascun le otrió, de griez e volunter.
8860 Or le poés seguramen*t* entrer, (3370)
Sor vos palés v'averés ostaler.
E po farés ves baron asenbler,

Rubric 257 (after 8851) MS.: apostoiel; Keller: lapostoiel; Reinhold: apostoile (not emend); Rosellini: apostoile (emend p. 773, *l'apostoile*)
8855 Reinhold: entra'
8857 Reinhold, Rosellini: clamé
8858 Rosellini: qe volese (*le* missing)

Si vos faron de l'inper coroner."
E dist Karleto, "Vu parlés como ber.
8865 Ço qe vos plas, nen vojo contraster." (3375)
Adonc fait tronbe e tanbur soner;
E tote ses baron elo fa pariler,
E li traites anbidos amener.
En Paris entrent peon e çivaler;
8870 Quant a·l palés vene a desmonter, (3380)
Sa sor li (v)ene incontre, si li corse enbraçer.
"Frer," fait il(a), "or ai mon desier;
Ne vos cuitoie mais veoir ni guarder."
Dist Karleto, "Deo ne poso gracier,
8875 Qe son venu a vençer mon per, (3385)
Qe vestre frer en fi atoseger."
La dama l'olde, si se trase arer;
Ni ben ni mal plu no li volse parler;
Sor li palés montò, si se vait ostaler.
8880 Gran çoja mena peon e çivaler; (3390)
Atant eco vos Naimon de Baiver:
"Sire," fait il, "non devez oblier
La mort qe fist Pepin, li ves per.
De Aquilon ne vos vojo remenbrer,
8885 Qe in ves servisio menò tant çivaler? (3395)
Or me l'à morto, li malvas losenger.
Se eo de loro e no me voi vençer*
Par vos servire mais non prenderò corer."
Li rois l'intent, pris le viso enbronçer;
8890 Ni ben ni mal no li responde arer; (3400)
Mal voluntera onceja ses frer.

Rubric 258
Coment parole Naimes de Baiver.
Laisse 259

Naimes l'infant, qe fu filz Aquilon,
E avec lui fo Guarner d'Aviçon, 50ᵛᵇ
E l'Apostoile, c'oit nome Milon,
8895 E Morant e Bernardo de Clermon, (3405)

8863 Reinhold: inper[io] (emend)
8871 MS.: nene; Reinhold: vene (emend for MS. *nene*); Rosellini: vene
8872 MS.: fait il; Reinhold, Rosellini: fait ela (emend for *il*)
8879 Reinhold, Rosellini: si s'en vait
8887 Reinhold, Rosellini: Se [tos]to

	E si le fu li valent Sanson,
	Davant Karleto dient une rason.
	"Çentil sire rois, parqe vos çelaron?
	Doné nos li conçé, qe aler s'en volon;
8900	Ne ma da (v)os no volun reençon, (3410)
	Se no çuçés anbidos qui felon,
	Qe ancis ton per a mortel traison."
	Dist l'Apostoile, "Non prenderés coron;*
	Nian por moi non averés benecion,
8905	Se no le voi anbidos li felon, (3415)
	Como traites apendu a·l stacon."
	Karleto li oldì, nen dist ne si ne non;
	O li otrie, o il volist o non.
	Mal volunter le fi la delivreson,
8910	M'a gran mervile estoit qui baron,* (3420)
	Qe comunalment li demandent in don,
	Por vençer Pepin e li dux Aquilon
	Qe morto fo a mortel traison.
	Ma i fo saçes par non far turbason,
8915	I volse far encoroner Karlon, (3425)
	Par lui traire de la sospicion.
	Doncha l'Apostoile nen fe demorason;
	Quant li traites fo delivré a li baron,
	A san Donis i amenent Karlon;
8920	Ilec li ont doné benecion, (3430)
	De tota França li donò la coron,
	E de l'inperio, entorno et inviron,
	E l'inperes si se clamò a mon.
	Quant l'Apostoile li dè benecion,
8925	Elo s'encline par droita devocion; (3435)
	Elo mercie çivaler e peon.

8900 MS.: nos; Reinhold, Rosellini: vos; Rosellini: da vos volun (*no* missing)
8910 MS.: Ma gran; Reinhold, Rosellini: [à] gran (emend)
8915 Rosellini: K[arleton]
8919 Reinhold: A San-Donis ja menent . . . ; Rosellini: A San Doris ja menent K[arleton] (cf. Martin)
8923 Reinhold: inpere[r]s . . . amon (emend); Rosellini: a[l] mon

Rubric 259
Coment K*arleto* fu encoronés.
Laisse 260

       Quando K*arleto* fo encoronés,
       De tot li mondo el fo sire clamés.
       Tot li baron li oit amerciés,
8930 Dapoisqe i ont toto ço adovrés, (3440)
       A le palés i le ont amenés.
       Gran çoja fo par tota la çités;
       Ma li baron no à l'ovra obliés.
       De dos traites qe furent çuçés,
8935 D'eser apendu con traitor renojés, (3445)
       Davant K*arleto* li avont amenés.
       Li rois li vi, si le avoit plurés;
       "Freri," fait il, "mal avì aovrés;
       Vestre per onceist a grande falsités,
8940 E moi avì caçé por le strançe contrés. (3450)   51ra
       Asa ò dura pena e gran fertés;
       La mercé de Deo e de soa bontés,
       Retorné sui ilec o e fu nés;
       Conquisté ai mon regno e ma cités.
8945 Se eo vos çuço, non do eser blasmés, (3455)
       Q'eo li faço contra ma voluntés;
       Unde vos pre, qe vu me perdonés."
       Dist Lanfroi, "Deo vos saçé malgrés,
       Mais d'una ren ne vos serà çelés;
8950 Qe se fose de quiloga sevrés, (3460)
       E vos tenisse en la mia poestés,
       Ça par moi non serisi tant aderasnés;
       Tosto en sirisi a dos fors apiçés,
       Ne no le seront nesun termen piés."
8955 Dist K*arleto*, "Mal fusi conselés; (3465)
       Quando mon per austes atosegés,
       E mo qe vos veés qiloga çuçés,
       Nen estes pais de ren umiliés,

Rubric 259 (after 8926) MS., Keller: .k. fu . . .
8939 Reinhold: onceïst
8940 Reinhold, Rosellini: l'estrançe
8941 Reinhold: dura
8943 Reinhold: ò' e' fu' nés
8948 Reinhold, Rosellini: saçe
8958 Reinhold: umilés

        Ne no me querì merçé ni pietés;
8960 E tota fois vu m'avì menaçés. (3470)
        E cre qe estes diables encantés;
        Men esiant vos estes desvés."

Rubric 260
Coment K*arleto* çuçò li frer.*
Laisse 261

        "Frer," dist K*arleto*, "e no vos poso aider,*
        Q'elo vos çuça peon e çivaler.
8965 Ora pensez de ves arme salver, (3475)
        Qe questo mondo si è falso e lainer.
        Se questa morte poez en pax durer,   51rb
        Davant a Deo vue averés aler,
        Là o porés co*n* li santi converser."
8970 Dist Lanfroi, "Ben savés predicher; (3480)
        Bon mastro avisi a inparer.
        S'eo fose desligé, qe me poust aider,
        Tel oferta vos averia doner,
        Qe tel non oit prest de monester."
8975 Dist K*arleto*, "El vos fala li penser." (3485)
        Atanto Berta venoit por li soler,
        O vi son frer si le vait a 'braçer.
        Qi donc veist quela dame plurer,
        Ses man debatre, e ses çavi tirer,
8980 Molti baron ela fa si larmoger. (3490)
        "Sore," dist K*arleto*, "ne vos estoit doter;
        Ne vos averò delenquir ni laser.
        Questi traites, lasés·le via mener;
        I son çuçé q'i oncis li per,
8985 Et in apreso i ancise ma mer." (3495)
        Dist li rois d'O*n*garie, "Qua*n*t me poso reme*n*brer
        De·l tradime*n*to li qual fe ca mer—
        Quele mando a li bois a tuer   *
        Mais Deo no·l volse quela ovra endurer.

        Rubric 260 (after 8962) Keller: çuço; Reinhold: Çuçò
        8969 Reinhold: Là, o' porés; Rosellini: Là o porés
        8977 Reinhold: abraçer; Rosellini: vait à braçer
        8983 Reinhold: lasés-le; Rosellini: lasés le via
        8988 Reinhold, Rosellini: Quele mandò . . .
        8989 Reinhold: no-l; Rosellini: no'l

8990	Se mantenant ne le faites apiçer, (3500)
	Çamai in moi non averés nul sper."
	Adoncha fait la dama via aler,
	E li dos frer el fa via amener.
	A Naimes li oit dà a bailer,* 51^(va)
8995	E a quel d'Aviçon, c'oit nome Guarner,* (3505)
	E cil le menerent, qe le font stroit liger.*
	Davant les oile le font inbinder,
	Con se fait a cil qe font tel mester.
	Çama traites non dè asormonter:
9000	Çascun le doit ancir e detrencer;* (3510)
	Qe vos doie li plais plus alonçer?
	Ad un stacon i le f(o)nt amener,
	E a le fors i le font apiçer;
	Ne li ostò ne arme ni corer;
9005	Apiçé fu a lo de çivaler. (3515)
	Adonqua Karleto petit li lasa ester,
	Qe de le fors o le fa devaler,
	E ben le fi vestir e adorner,
	De riche robes de palio e de cender.
9010	E a li major baron de tot li terer, (3520)
	Elo li fait a·l monister porter,
	E altament li oficio çanter.
	En un sarcoil le font enterer,
	E pois tornent arer, lasent li dol ester.
9015	Dolent en fu de lor Karleto a le vis fer; (3525)
	Or se començe li çanter enforçer,
	Coment Karleto tenoit corte plener.
	A la corte fu Morando de River,
	Guarner d'Aviçon, qi tant fo pro e ber,
9020	Qe tant pene durò por Karleto son ser, (3530)
	Ne vos poria dir ni conter. 51^(vb)
	Tel cose oldirés da qui avant parler,
	Qe vu meesme v'en avrì merviler;
	Li rois d'Ongarie si s'en tornò arer,
9025	Et avec lui menò ses çivaler; (3530)
	E lasa Karleto a Paris ester.*

9001 Reinhold: dò je
9002 MS.: fant; Reinhold, Rosellini: font (emend for MS. *fant*)
9013 Reinhold: E un
9026 MS.: E lasa; Reinhold, Rosellini: Et lasa

7.5 Berta e Milone

Rubric 261
Coment K*arlo* tenoit grant corte a Paris.*
Laisse 262

    Karlo manten gran cort a Paris sa mason;
    Asa lì sont dux, conti e baron.
    E si le fu Bernardo de Clermon,
9030 Avec lui un son filz Milon:
    Plu bel damisel non è calça speron,*
    Nian plu saçes e de bona rason.
    Sa justisia fe li rois de ces dos mal felon,
    De lor parlent Francés e Bergognon
9035 E Normant e Mansel e Berton.*
    Entro la cort si fo le dux Naimon,
    Conseler est de l'inperer K*arlon*.
    Gran çoja fo entorno et environ;
    Soa sor ten K*arlo* como tenir devon.
9040 Ne le fo tera, ni a po ni a mon,
    Qe a l'inperer non faça reençon.
    E l'Apostoile si retornò a Ron;
    Sor tot ren elo loe K*arlon*.
    Son seschalco estoit Milon,
9045 Qe filz estoit Bernardo de Clermon.
    Ancor estoit baçaler çovençon;
    E quela Berta, c'oit clera façon,   52ra
    En lu ela mis tot sa entençion.
    Se atenderés tantqe feniron,
9050 Questo roman contar vos faron,
    De le cont Rolant tota sa nasion;

Rubric 261 (after 9026) MS., Keller: .k.
 9028 Rosellini: Asa li son dux, amiré, baron . . . , (cf. Morini) (*li* always without accent in Mussafia, Cremonesi, Rosellini; not further noted—Cf. Mussafia, Cremonesi 9056: Asa' li fo)
 9031 Rosellini: non çalca (emend for *none calça*)
 9033 Rosellini: Se (cf. Morini)
 9034 Rosellini: Francés
 9038 Rosellini: çoia (as always; not remarked further here)
 9046 Rosellini: çovençon (cf. Morini)
 9048 Rosellini: En lui . . . entencion (cf. Morini)
 9049 Rosellini: tant qe (as always)

Con sa mer e so per s'en foì a laron*
Por stranie tere a tapin por li mon;
Sbanojé fo de tot la coron.

Rubric 262
Coment K*arlo* tenoit grant corti, / e tot asenble tota soa baronie.*
Laisse 263

9055 Grant cort manten K*arlo* l'inperaor;*
      Asa lì fo dux, princes e contor.
      De tote France li fo li almansor;
      Naimes le dux si fu ses co*n*seleor;
      Bernardo de Clermont, ne le fo nul milor, (5)
9060 Davanti li rois porte l'orieflor.
      V. filz oit, Milon fo li menor,*
      A l'inperer servoit e de noit e de jor.
      Molto fi amés da li baron de la cor;
      Dame e polçele si le ten a baldor,* (10)
9065 Meesma Berta, seror l'inperaor.
      En lu oit mis toto li so amor;*
      Nen poit boir ni ma*n*çer ta*n*t li tent in savor.*
      E la raine c'oit fresco li color,
      Amoit Berte por fe e por amor.* (15)

Rubric 263
Coment fo grande la cort.
Laisse 264

9070 Grant fu la cort a Paris la cité,
      Qe tent K*arlo* li maine encoroné.
      Bernardo de Clermont oit son fil mené;
      Ces fu Milon, li saço e li doté,
      E quel serve a K*arlo* volu*n*ter e de gre. (20)
9075 Tant avoit Milon en soi gra*n* belté,

9052 Rosellini: s'en foi à
Rubric 262 (after 9054): Keller: .k.... et ot; Mussafia: K. (as always; never resolved); Rosellini: sa baronie (cf. Morini)
9056 Mussafia, Cremonesi: Asa'; cf. 9028
9063 Mussafia, Cremonesi, Rosellini: amés
9066 Mussafia: mis oit (cf. Holtus 1975)
9069 MS.: por fe; Mussafia: por fe (emend for MS. *por se*)

```
        Desor tot ren Berta li oit amé.
        Si malament ne fo enamoré,
        Mançer ni boir non poit a planté,
        Qe in son cor ne le sia sajelé.* (25)
9080    Tant fo li fato avant alé,
        Qe cun quela dame el avoit peçé;
        De le en prist amor e amisté.
        Ne s'en percoit homo de mer né,
        Ne Belisant qe l'avoit en poesté. (30)
9085    Se li rois l'amoit or ne m'en demandé;
        De le cuitoit far un gran parenté,
        Doner·la a rois a cons o amiré.
        Contra de le non avoit mal pensé;
        Mais li amor tanto oit ovré (35)
9090    Qe anbidos oit fraito castité.
        Se li rois li aust ni saplu ni esmé,*
        Milon fust a dos fors apiçé,
        Et ella fust e arsa e brusé.                     52ʳᵇ
        Tant fu la colsa de jor en jor alé, (40)
9095    Qe cella dame si fo engravidé.
        Quant se sent ençinta, tanto fo adolosé,
        Nen poroit eser plus en soa vivité.
        Ela se clama, "Çativa, maluguré,*
        Cun in malora eo fu ençendré! (45)
9100    Ma mer me fu et arsa e bruxé;
        E dos me frer en furent apiçé.
        Or sonto eo ençinta de filz e de rité;
        Se li rois li soit cun averò malovré,
        Por li grant amor qe me frer m'à mostré,* (50)
9105    Da tota jent eo ne serò laideçé,
        E si ne serò onia e vergogné."
        Nen sa qe faire, tanta fo adolé;
        Plu dolant dame non è a·l mondo né.
```

9076 Rosellini: K[arlo]
9082 Mussafia, Cremonesi, Rosellini: D'ele
9083 Rosellini: perçoit (emend)
9086 Mussafia, Cremonesi, Rosellini: D'ele
9087 Mussafia, Cremonesi: Doner la; Rosellini: Donerla
9091 Cremonesi: aüst (as always)
9099 Mussafia: mal ora.. fu'
9103 Mussafia: cum averò mal ovré!; Cremonesi, Rosellini: mal ovré (as always)
9104 Mussafia: que me frer
9105 MS., Rosellini: laideçe; Mussafia, Cremonesi: laide[n]çé

Rubric 264
Coment Berta se sente graveda.
Laisse 265

	Quant Berta se sent ençinta de l'infant, (55)
9110	En soa vite la no fo plu dolant.
	O vi Milon, si le dis planemant:
	"Milon," fait il(a), "el nos va malemant;
	Eo conpli tot li ves talant,*
	E vu de mi avés fato altretant. (60)
9115	Se avemo eu çoie, or ne reven in plant;
	E son ençinta de filla o de infant.
	Se li rois li soit, toti vestri parant
	Ne vos varoit un diner valisant,
	Qe non siés meso ad un stacon pendant; (65)
9120	Et eo brusea a li fogo ardant.
	E queste è una colsa si aparisant,
	No se poit çeler por or ni por arçant.
	E con vait la colsa plu avant,
	Tanto est la colsa plu aparisant. (70)
9125	E se par nul ren s'en percoit Belisant,
	A l'inperer le dirà mantenant.
	Or qe farà la çativa dolant,
	Qe atendea d'avor honor cotant?
	Dexorea serò entro tota la jant, (75)
9130	De moi se scrinirà le petit e li grant.
	E questo saçì ben, Milon, ad esiant;
	Questo serà in molto breve tanp."
	Milon, quan l'olde, nen fo ma si dolant;
	Par un petit nen mor de maltalant. (80)

9111 Mussafia, Cremonesi: O' vi (apostrophe use not further noted; always for O', "where")

9112 MS., Mussafia, Cremonesi: fait il; Rosellini: fait ela (emend)

9113 Mussafia: Eo conpli; Cremonesi: E' ò; Rosellini: E ò compli

9115 Cremonesi: eü (as always)

9116 Mussafia, Cremonesi: E' (apostrophe no longer noted; always for e', "I")

9119 Mussafia, Rosellini: siés; Cremonesi: sies

9125 Rosellini: s'en perçoit (emend)

9126 Mussafia: imperer

9131 Mussafia, Cremonesi: saçì; Rosellini: saçi

9133 Mussafia, Cremonesi: ma' (as always for "but")

9134 Mussafia: mal talant

Rubric 265

Coment la dame se sent ençinta / e si parole a Million e si li dist li vor.*
Laisse 266

9135	Quant quela dame oit oldu Milon,*	
	S'el oit dol no s'en mervilì nu hon,*	
	Por le mesfato q'el oit fato a Karlon,	
	Qe plu l'amava qe nul altro baron;	
	Ne se fioit en altri se en lui non; (85)	52va
9140	Segnor estoit de tota sa mason.	
	El plura e plançe sa man a ses menton,	
	Qe de le larmes (bagne) li aquinton.*	
	Dever la dame el dist sa rason:	
	"Dama," dist il, "dites cun la faron. (90)	
9145	Leçu m'avés malvasia lecion,	
	Donde me voi en gran confosion,	
	Plus qe ma fo veilart ni garçon;	
	Or voie ben la nostra destrucion.*	
	Se de la mort voren redencion, (95)	
9150	Aler nos convirà tapiner por li mon,*	
	E Deo sa ben se nu li scanparon;	
	El no è tera ni castel ni dojon,	
	Qe non soit sota li rois *Karlon*; *	
	E çascun reame qe de Cristian son, (100)	
9155	Si l'obedise por honor de la coron	
	Qe il oit da l'inperio de Ron.	
	Nu semo morti, qual part qe nu alon."	

Rubric 265 (after 9134) MS.: Million . . . vor; Keller: million . . . noir; Rosellini: Million . . . voii
9135 Mussafia, Cremonesi: oldù
9136 Mussafia, Cremonesi, Rosellini: mervili nu[l] (emend)
9138 Cremonesi, Rosellini: Ke (cf. Morini)
9142 MS.: de lelarmes li aquinton; Cremonesi: [bagne] li . . . (emend); Mussafia, Rosellini: [moile] li . . . (emend)
9145 Mussafia, Cremonesi: Leçù; Rosellini: Leçú
9148 Mussafia: vo je; Cremonesi, Rosellini: voie
9150 Mussafia: convira (as always for the future, no written accent)
9156 Rosellini: oit la l' (cf. Morini)

Rubric 266
Coment Milliuz parole a la dame.*
Laisse 267

	"Dama," dist Milon, "non val nostro plurer,
	Qe in dol faire ne se po guaagner. (105)
9160	Dolent e peçable quando naque de mer,*
	Qe je cuitoie honor porcaçer,
	E porço a la corte (s)i me menò mon per;
	Porqe a foi servise l'inperer.*
	Et eo li ò fato li major vituper (110)
9165	Qe se posa ne dir ne penser.
	Degno son de morte dura e fer,
	Plu de nul homo qe ma nasese de mer.
	Se avese mesfato ad un sol çivaler,
	Encontra lui poria arme bailer. (115)
9170	Ma questo è tale qe no lì (è) da parler;*
	Qesto è sire de la tera e de·l mer,*
	En tote tere o e porò aler,
	El me farà prender e liger,
	Si cun traites el me farà çuçer." (120)
9175	Dist la dama, "Non è pais da blasmer,
	Qel homo qe poit soa vita alonçer.
	E vos vojo por amor Deo projer,
	Qe questo dol vu lasez ester,
	Si se porpensen de la corte sevrer, (125)
9180	E le çamin qe nu deveron pier.
	Forsi da Deo averen quaqe sper,
	Qe n'averà droitament conseler.
	Se nu no poron en cité alberçer,
	A le forest averemo ostaler, (130)

Rubric 266 (after 9157) MS.: Milliuz; Mussafia: Milliun; Rosellini: Milliun (emend for MS. *milliuz*)
9160 Cremonesi: Dolente pecable . . .
9162 Mussafia, Cremonesi, Rosellini: por ço; MS.: fi me
9163 Mussafia, Rosellini: Porqe; Cremonesi: Por qe
9167 Rosellini: Plus (cf. Morini)
9170 MS.: li da; Mussafia, Cremonesi, Rosellini: no li [è] . . .
9171 Rosellini: Questo (Cf. Morini)
9172 Cremonesi: o' e' (as always: "ove eo")
9174 Mussafia: cum (as always)
9179 Rosellini: propensen (cf. Morini)
9181 MS.: quaqe; Mussafia, Cremonesi, Rosellini: qua[l]qe (emend)

9185   E in le bois cun le bestie cunverser;
         No creço pais là ne vegna a trover."*
         "Deo," dist Milon, "cun ben savés parler.   52vb
         Li ves conseil non è da oblier;*
         Ancor por tenpo, se Deo ne vol aider, (135)
9190   Ben e onor nu poron reçater."

Rubric 267
Coment Millon parole a Berte.*
Laisse 268

         "Dama," dist Milon, "ne lairò ne vos die;*
         Molto è guari, qe in Deo se fie.
         El estoit plen de tote cortexie;
         Non avez oldu qe dist la proficie, (140)
9195   Ço qe fe la Verçen Marie,
         Qe por paura de Herodes ela foçì vie?
         Portò son fil, q'el avoit norie.
         Se s'en alon, averon qualche remie,
         En quaqe bois o en selva ram(i)e."* (145)
9200   Dist la dama, "Ne se vol tarder mie,
         Qe in breve tenpo è nostra desertie."*
         Lor ordonent li termen e la die.*
         Quando un mois fu pasé e conplie,*

    9186 Rosellini: creco (cf. Morini); Mussafia: atrover; Cremonesi: vegna a trover; Rosellini: vegna à trover
    9188 Rosellini: no è (cf. Morini and endnote)
    9189 MS., Mussafia, Rosellini: tenpo; Cremonesi: tempo
    Rubric 267 (after 9190) Keller: millon . . . berte.
    9192 Mussafia, Cremonesi, Rosellini: guari; Bartoli: deo
    9194 Mussafia, Cremonesi: oldù; Rosellini: oldú (cf. Plouzeau: should not have accent); Bartoli: estoie
    9195 Bartoli: verçen (cf. line 9211)
    9196 Mussafia, Rosellini: foçi
    9197 Mussafia, Cremonesi, Rosellini: q'el'avoit . . .
    9198 Bartoli: se se n'alon averon . . . reinie
    9199 MS.: quaqe . . . ramue?; Mussafia, Cremonesi, Rosellini: qua[l]qe . . . ramie; Bartoli: qualche . . . ramue (sic)
    9200 Bartoli: vol far dormie
    9201 MS.: deṗtie; Bartoli: Qe'm . . . tempo . . . departie; Mussafia, Cremonesi, Rosellini: nostra desertie
    9202 Bartoli: ordenent
    9203 Bartoli: complie

                Berta e Milon si se sont guarnie. (150)
9205   Prendent de cil avoir q'i ont en bailie;
                Non portent pani qe fust de gran delie.*
                E una soir fo de Paris partie,*
                Via s'en vait por landa hermie.
                Tota la noit tros l'auba sclarie, (155)
9210   Le çamin pris dever Lonbardie.
                Deo li condue, e la Verçene Marie,*
                Qe i s'en posa aler a salvetie.

Rubric 268
Coment s'en vait Milon e Berte.
Laisse 269

                Va s'en Milon e Berta l'insené;
                Son çamin oit ver Lonbardia pié. (160)
9215   La noit çamine, e li jor oit polsé,
                Entro li bois e le selve ramé.
                De ço q'i ont, ont bevu e mançé.
                Non oit palafroi ne destrer seçorné;
                A pe s'en vait, durando gran ferté. (165)
9220   Lason de lor, qe mal ont ovré;
                De l'inperer e vojo qe vu saçé,
                Quant la novela li estoit aporté,
                Cun Milon n'oit via Berta mené,
                Molto ferament s'en fo amervelé, (170)
9225   Como il avoit fato tel falsité.
                En soa çanbra era li plu privé

9205 Bartoli: qi ont . . . ; cf. 9217
9206 Holtus 1975: delïe, not delié
9207 Bartoli: una fou fo
9208 Bartoli: sen vait (as always: cf. Rubric 268; 9219; 9224; 9258)
9210 Bartoli: Lombardie
9212 Bartoli: se posa
Rubric 268 (after 9212) Keller: sen uait milon a berte; Bartoli: sen . . .
9213 Bartoli: Vasen . . . li 'nsene; Rosellini: Vasen
9214 Bartoli: Lombardie
9215 Bartoli: ior
9217 Bartoli: qi ont
9219 Cremonesi: pè
9220 Bartoli: Ja son . . . oure
9221 Bartoli: inperer; . . . .
9226 Bartoli: canbra

        De nul autre de la soa masné.
        S'el oit dol, ora non demandé;
        Belisant oit queri e demandé*
9230 Se de quela colse jamés s'en fose adé.* (175)
        Dist la dama, "No, por ma lialté,
        Jamais cun le no·l vi a la çelé."
        Adoncha li rois en fo si abosmé,
        Toto quel çorno non à moto parlé. (180)   53ra
9235 Mais le dux Naimes si l'à reconforté;
        Adoncha li rois à por tot part mandé,
        A burs et a vile, a çasté e a doclé;
        Par lor avoir non ait ren lasé.
        Quando no li trova si li oit sbanojé, (185)
9240 E un tel bando mandò por le contré:
        Çascun de ceus qe li avoit trové,
        Davant Karlo li aust apresenté,*
        Qe grant avoir le seroit doné.
        Sovra son per fust li rois alé, (190)
9245 Quando dux Naimes li avoit deveé:
        "Bon rois," fait il, "tant ne vos deroé,*
        Qe Bernardo de Clermont è de gran parenté;
        Non è in França ni dux ni casé,
        Qe non soja ses amigo e privé. (195)
9250 De ço ch'à fato son fil, el n'è gramo et iré;
        Se·l fante n'ait vestra sor amené,*
        Nen poit ester en la Cresteneté,
        Qe non saça coment averont ovré."
        A molto gran poine li ont reconforté.* (200)

    9228 Bartoli: dolor a
    9230 Bartoli: . . . sen fo seade; Mussafia, Cremonesi, Rosellini: s'en fose adé
    9232 Bartoli: Iamals cun le nolui el'a . . . , Mussafia: no l; Cremonesi, Rosellini: nol vi; Cremonesi: celé; Mussafia, Rosellini: çelé
    9237 Mussafia: caste[l] (emend); Cremonesi, Rosellini: çasté
    9239 Bartoli: sbanoie
    9241 Mussafia: au[r]oit (emend)
    9242 Bartoli: K . . . a presente; Cremonesi: Karle li aüst; Rosellini: K[arle]
    9244 Bartoli: soura
    9246 MS.: deroe; Mussafia, Cremonesi: dervé (emend); Rosellini: deroé
    9249 Rosellini: soia amigo (missing ses; cf. Morini)
    9251 Bartoli: Sel; Mussafia: Se-l fante; Cremonesi, Rosellini: Se'l
    9252 Bartoli: crestenete

Rubric 269
Coment K*arlo* fi s(b)anojer Milon / e Berte de tota França.*
Laisse 270

9255	Lason de K*arlo*, qi est gramo e dolant;
	Nen fo ma si a tuto son vivant,
	Et avec lui estoit Belisant.
	E Milon s'en vait por le camin erant;*
	De noit çamine a la luna lusant, (205)
9260	E tot le çorno se stoit planemant*
	Entro le bois e le selve pendant.
	La dama estoit ençinta, petit vait avant;
	Non estoit usé de durer tel achant.*
	Ela duroit gran poine e tormant; (210)
9265	Por me ces bois aloit mendigant.
	Non albergoit a oster, no*n* gustoit provant;
	Pane et eve manuò solemant,
	En tera çasoit sor l'erba verdojant.
	Ele se plure e si se clama dolant: (215)
9270	"A, lasa," fait ela, "porqe viv'e cotant,
	Qe de raine e son fata ser(v)ant?"
	Dist Milon, "Non parlé tant avant;
	Li ben e·l mal si est d'un senblant;
	Nen poit l'omo aver li son talant. (220)
9275	E ben e mal li stoit avoir sovant;*
	Nul homo po viver in ste mo*n*do dolant

Rubric 269 (after 9254) MS.: so anoier; Keller: so anoier milon e berte /; Mussafia 1863: sbanoier (for *soanoier)*; Cremonesi, Rosellini: sbanoier Milon; Bartoli: K . . . ; line 2: Keller: france; Mussafia: tote F . . .

9255 Bartoli, Mussafia: K.; Cremonesi: Karle; Rosellini: K[arlo]
9256 Bartoli, Mussafia, Cremonesi: ma' si
9259 Bartoli: camine
9260 Cremonesi: se stoit; Mussafia: s'estoit. Bartoli: tot lo
9263 Mussafia, Cremonesi, Rosellini: use
9265 Bartoli, Mussafia, Cremonesi: me'
9268 Bartoli: verdoiant
9270 Mussafia, Cremonesi, Rosellini: A lasa. Mussafia: por qe viv'e' . . . ; Bartoli, Cremonesi: por qe vive cotant; Rosellini: porqe vive cotant
9271 MS., Bartoli: serpant; Mussafia, Cremonesi, Rosellini: servant (emend). Mussafia, Cremonesi: e'
9273 Mussafia: e-l mal; Cremonesi, Rosellini: e 'l
9274 Rosellini: pot l'omo

	Sença poine e gran tormant.	
	Se mo avemo dol, ancor seron çojant."	
	Et ensi la voit dolçement confortant. (225)	
9280	Ma quel conforto si torne a niant,	
	Qe tanto estoit de l'altro enojamant.	53ʳᵇ
	Ne boie ni mançe qe le soja a talant,	
	E de quel oit molto poveremant.	
	A l'ensir de Provençe en une selve grant, (230)	
9285	De robaor li trovò plus de trant,	
	Qe robent le çamin dont va li merçaant;	
	Tol·ge l'avoir, li diner e li besant,*	
	Pois li oncient se li ven por talant.	
	Quando virent Milon cun la dama solemant, (235)	
9290	(Non avoit arme fora le vestimant)	
	E virent la dama tant bela et avenant,	
	Par lor rober i se fait avant.	
	Quando Milon le voit, si le dist en ojant:	
	"Segnur," fait il, "nu no sen merçaant, (240)	
9295	Ne no portemo ar coit ni besant.*	
	Lasé·n aler, por Deo e por li sant."*	
	E cil le dient, "Vos estes un truant!	
	Menés sta dame oltra so maltalant;	
	Doner·la vorì por or e por arçant."* (245)	

9278 Bartoli: çoiant
9281 Bartoli: del . . . enoiamant
9282 Bartoli: soia
9283 Bartoli: vit molto . . .
9284 Bartoli: al . . .
9286 Bartoli: merçaant
9287 Bartoli, Cremonesi, Rosellini: Tolge; Mussafia: Tol-ge
9288 Rosellini: pro talant
9293 Bartoli: enoiant
9295 MS.: ar coit; Bartoli: arcoit; Mussafia: or coito (emend for *ar coito*); Cremonesi: or coit (emend); Rosellini: ar coito (cf. 621, 3794)
9296 Bartoli: Lasen . . . deo . . . ; Mussafia, Cremonesi: Lasé-n' aler; Rosellini: Lasé n'aler
9299 Bartoli: Doner la . . . arçant?; Mussafia, Cremonesi: Doner la vorì; Rosellini: Done la vori

Rubric 270
Coment Milon oncis qui robaor / Qi li volent tor la dame.
Laisse 271

9300   "Segnurs," dist Milon, "por Deo vos vojo projer,
        Qe a mon çamin ne lasez aler.
        E no son pais truant ni paumer,*
        E no darò sta dama por or ni por diner.
        Qi contra mon voloir me la vorà bailer, (250)
9305   Avec lui m'averò coruçer."
        E qui le dient, "Ne la porés mener;
        Avec nos el averà converser."*
        Un de color qe fu li plu liçer,*
        Avant se fait, qe la voloit saçer,* (255)
9310   E por la man la voloit pier.
        Quando Milon le vi, non ait qe airer;
        Un baston tent, qe estoit d'un pomer,
        Qe in le bois se fi por apojer.
        Celu ferì un si gran colpo plener, (260)
9315   Por me li çevo si gran colpo li fer,
        Ocli e cervele le fait de·l çevo voler.
        "Oltra," fait il, "malvasio liçer,
        Ne ve senblarò qe soja paltoner?
        Por mal pensasi de ma dama toçer." (265)
9320   Quando li altri le vi si malovrer,
        Sovra li corers qe li voloit bailer,*
        Morto l'aust quando se trase arer.
        Le baston ten par soi defenser,
        E si le moine et avant et arer.* (270)
9325   A manti oit fato li sang d·i çevi rager;
        Quant le baston fo fraito, el tra li brant d'açer,*

   Rubric 270 (after 9299) line 1: MS.: Robaor; Keller: milon; line 2: Keller: uolent
   9302 Mussafia, Cremonesi: E' no son
   9304 Mussafia, Rosellini: me la vora . . .
   9306 Mussafia: qui'
   9307 Mussafia, Cremonesi: el'averà
   9314 Mussafia, Rosellini: feri (cf. 9331)
   9315 Mussafia, Cremonesi: me' (as always)
   9319 MS., Mussafia: dama; Cremonesi, Rosellini: dame (cf. Holtus 1975)
   9320 Mussafia, Cremonesi, Rosellini: mal ovrer
   9322 Cremonesi: aüst (as always)
   9324 Mussafia: si le; Cremonesi, Rosellini: si lo
   9326 Cremonesi: d'acer (cf. Holtus 1975)

	E vait a ferir colu q'era le primer,
	Qe a lui plu s'avoit a 'prosmer.
	Tel colpo li dona sença nul menaçer, (275)
9330	Q'elo·l porfendò, tros a·l (n)o de·l baldrer;*
	E pois ferì l'altro, si le vait li çevo voler.
	Quando li altri le vi si duro e fer,
	Mal ait quel qi li voja aspeter.
	En fua torne quant s'en poit aler, (280)
9335	E mant s'alent in le bois a covoter.
	Voi·le Milon, ne se volse sego tençer;
	Por le çamin el se mis ad erer.
	E lasa·ne de morti plu de .X. a·l verçer.*
	Va s'en Milon, li cortois çivaler, (285)
9340	La dama en moina, qi s'en doja nojer.
	Ven a Papie, no li volse dentro entrer;
	Defor Papie desis a un oster.
	Ilec manue, si se fe ostaler,
	A la deman pois se mist ad aler, (290)
9345	Dever Ravene planeto por li senter.*

53va

Rubric 271
Coment s'en vait ver (R)avene / e mena sa dame a gram dolo.*
Laisse 272

	Va s'en Milon, coroços e pensiç,
	Quant sconfito oit qui qi l'oit asaliz.
	Quant à ço fait, si fo da lor grepiz,
	Tanto çamine por poi e por lariz, (295)
9350	Pasa li plan, li val e li lariz;
	Deo li condue, li rois de Paradiz,

9327 Mussafia: colu' q'era . . .
9328 Mussafia, Cremonesi, Rosellini: aprosmer
9330 Mussafia: Q'elo-l porfende (emend); Cremonesi, Rosellini: Q'elo 'l porfende. MS.: al vo del; Mussafia, Cremonesi, Rosellini: al no del . . . (emend)
9335 Mussafia, Cremonesi, Rosellini: s'alent in le bois acovoter
9336 Mussafia, Cremonesi: Voi le; Rosellini: Voile
9338 Mussafia, Cremonesi: lasa-ne; Rosellini: lasane
9339 Cremonesi, Rosellini: Vasen (as always)
9343 Cremonesi: si se fe'
Rubric 271 (after 9345) line 1: MS., Mussafia: Vavene; Cremonesi, Rosellini: Ravene (emend). Mussafia: Coment [Milon]; Keller: sen uait uer uauene (Note: l. rauene)
9347 Mussafia: qui' qi

E soa mer, la Verçene genitriz.
S(a) dama moine dont fu sbanoiz*
De França bele e de la çité de Pariz. (300)
9355 Quant fu a Ravene si lì stete tros diz,
Posa pasè oltre, qe da nul fo requiz.*

Rubric 272
Coment s'en vait Milon.
Laisse 273

Va s'en Milon dever le li de·l mer;
E vi la torbea e le onde lever.
Nen volse pais oltra la mer paser,* (305)
9360 Porqe a la dame non faist nojer.
Non alò avanti, ançi tornò arer;
Dever Romagne prist a çaminer.
La dame è si grose qe (a) pene poit aler;*
Apreso de Ymole a une fontane cler, (310)
9365 Qe ilec estoit fora por la river,
Ilec partorì li son fio primer;
Ço fu Rolando, li meltre çivaler
Qe se poust a so tenpo trover,
Nian dapois de cento anni enter.* (315)
9370 Or non poit Berte plu avanti aler,
Quant Rolant partorì ne fo en gran penser.
Nian Milon no se soit conseler;
Petit dame avit a le son relever.

9352 Cremonesi: E soa mer le Verçene . . . (cf. Holtus 1975)
9353 MS.: Se dama
9354 Mussafia: et de la
9356 Mussafia: Posa pase . . . ; Cremonesi: Pos à pasé; Rosellini: Pos a pasé
Rubric 272 (after 9356) Keller: sen uait milon
9359 Cremonesi: passer
9360 Cremonesi: Por qe (as always) . . . faïst
9363 MS.: qe pene; Mussafia, Cremonesi: [a] pene (emend); Rosellini: [a]pene
9364 Rosellini: una fontane
9366 Mussafia, Rosellini: partori
9368 Cremonesi: poüst (as always) . . . tempo
9369 Mussafia: Ni an (as always); Cremonesi, Rosellini: Nian da pois
9371 MS.: R. (cf. Holtus 1975); Mussafia: partori . . . grant penser; Cremonesi: Roland partorì; Rosellini: R[oland] partori
9373 Mussafia, Cremonesi: av[o]it (emend); Rosellini: à le so relever

	Quant quele qe le furent va l'infante saçer, (320)	53ᵛᵇ
9375	A gran mervile li parse aviser,	
	Qe de l'infant li parse strainer;	
	Q'el ge par q'el aust plus de dos an enter.	
	E quant fu né, le pris a reguarder,	
	Nen fe mie cun li altri baçaler, (325)	
9380	Quando nasent començent a plurer.	
	Ele·l bagnent, si·l prist a laver;	
	A molt gran poine ele·l poont faser;	
	Ne se lasoit li pe ni le man liger.	
	Dist l'una a l'autre, "Questo serà hon fer." (330)	

Rubric 273
Coment (n)ase Ro*lant*.
Laisse 274

9385	Là o R*olant* fo né, no le fo pavilon,*
	Ni çanbra depinte, ni palés ni mason,
	Ni leito grande como a lui convenon;
	Coltra ni lenço ni altra guarison.
	Se nu de lu volen ben far rason, (335)
9390	A Jesu *Christo* nu li asomilon,*
	Qe naque en un presepio, cun dist li sermon;
	En una stable cun bois e con molton:
	Ensement fist R*olandin* filz Milon;*
	Non fo mervile s'el oit benecion. (340)
9395	E dama Berte, c'oit la pasion,
	Non plaça Deo ne li so santo non,
	Q'ela aust galina ni gapon,*

9379 Cremonesi: fe' (as always)
9381 Mussafia: Ele-l . . . si'l; Cremonesi: Ele 'l . . . si 'l; Rosellini: Ele 'l . . . si'l
9382 Mussafia: ele-l; Cremonesi, Rosellini: ele 'l
9384 Mussafia: hom fer
Rubric 273 (after 9384) MS.: vase Ro.; Keller: ua se ro (cf. Mussafia 1863, *nase*); Mussafia: uase Ro. (note: *nase*); Cremonesi, Rosellini: nase (emend); Holtus 1975: MS. reads .Ro.; Rosellini: R[oland]
9385 Mussafia: Là o' R.; Cremonesi: Là o'; Rosellini: Là o' R[oland]
9388 Rosellini: guar[n]ison (emend); Mussafia, Cremonesi: lenço'
9390 MS.: χρο (with a line above); Mussafia, Rosellini: Christo; Cremonesi: Jesù Christo
9391 Cremonesi: cum dist
9393 MS., Mussafia: R. (cf. Holtus 1975); Cremonesi: Rolandin; Rosellini: R*olandin*

       Cun le altre dame qe foit quela rason.
       En pase le s(os)tent sença tençon;* (345)
9400   Molto la plure li son segnor Milon,
       Quant le conforte la seror de Karlon.
       "Mon segnor," fait ela, "non farés plurason;
       Qe en cesta noit vide una envision,
       Qe por ces enfant ancor retornaron (350)
9405   En nos pais a grande guarison.
       Sor totes autres costu serà prodon;
       Se mo avon qualche aflecion,
       Questo n'è avenu por peçé qe nu avon.
       Se questa colsa en pas sostinon,* (355)
9410   Nu n'atendon da Deo gujerdon."
       Milon la intende, tuto se conforton.

Rubric 274
Coment Milon parole a Berte.
Laisse 275

       "Dama," dist Milon, "de vos e son dolant,
       Quan je vos vi in pena et in tormant."
       Dist la dama, "Non parlés plus avant; (360)
9415   Daq'eo pur partorì mon enfant,
       Non ò nul mal e nul enojamant."
       Saçés, segnur, e saçés a siant,
       Petite dame fu in le segle vivant,
       Qe plus de Berte avoit esiant. (365)
9420   Quel enfant norì e ben e dolçemant,*   54ra
       Si le fe batiçer e dar·le li olio sant.
       Quant fo li termen le .XV. jor pasant,
       Quele qe le portent a li bateçamant,
       Ne le portoit mie a·u monester grant, (370)

9399 MS.: stotent; Mussafia, Cremonesi, Rosellini: sostent (emend)
9401 MS.: K. (cf. Holtus 1975)
9405 Cremonesi: païs
9406 Mussafia: costu' sera; Rosellini: sera
Rubric 274 (after 9411) Keller: milon . . . berte
9412 Mussafia, Cremonesi: e' son
9415 Mussafia, Rosellini: Da q'eo . . . partori; Cremonesi: Da q'eo . . .
9420 Cremonesi: dolcemant; Mussafia, Rosellini: nori
9421 Cremonesi, Rosellini: darle; Mussafia: dar-le
9422 MS.: xv. (cf. Holtus 1975)

9425	Mais a une çapele qe estoit lì davant;
	Ma totefois Milon li fo ensemant.
	A·l batezer le mis nome Rolant;*
	Donde li prest s'en vait mervelant,
	Qe no li mis nome ni Pero ni Çoant. (375)
9430	Quant à ço fato, s'en retorna çojant;
	A soa mer donò le petit enfant.
	E quela l'alatò, si le tene tant,
	Qe un petit se levava in estant.
	En celle lois o e fo nasu Rolant,* (380)
9435	Ne le demorò mie longamant;
	Un mois aprés i alirent avant.
	Nen avoit qe porter se no cel enfant;
	Non portoit valis con fa li merçaant,
	Nian somer carçé d'or e d'arçant; (385)
9440	Ne non avoit palafroi ne muleto anblant.
	Por tera alent durando tel tormant,
	Ne vos saveria conter par nula ren vivant.
	De çorno en çorno tant vait erant,
	Qe a Sutrio vent et ilec desant. (390)
9445	Si se mis ad ester en un desertamant,
	O no estoit homo de mer vivant.
	E questo fait qe la paura oit grant,
	De Karlo (m)ai(n)e, le riçe sorpojant;
	L'enfant norì e ben e planemant. (395)

9425 MS., Cremonesi, Rosellini: li; Mussafia: li
9429 Rosellini: nome Pero ni Çoant (missing *ni*)
9434 Mussafia, Cremonesi, Rosellini: oe fu; Rosellini: nasú
9436 Mussafia, Rosellini: aprés; Cremonesi: après (cf. Holtus 1975)
9446 Mussafia, Cremonesi: O' (cf. 9475, 9481)
9448 MS.: .K. naime; Mussafia: K. maine (emend); Cremonesi: Karle maine (emend); Rosellini: K[arle]maine
9449 Mussafia, Rosellini: norì

Rubric 275
De la po(in)e qe durò Milon.
Laisse 276

9450   De Milon, saçés por verité,
       Qe in quela selve el durò gran ferté,
       E grande poine e d'inverno e d'esté.
       Quant l'infant avoit li quatro ani pasé,
       A la cité l'oit a la scola mandé; (400)
9455   Çamais non fo nul hon in ste mondo né,
       S'el non fo le filz de Damenedé
       Qe a inparer en fust tanto doté.
       Plus enparoit en un jor qe altri non fasoit in sé;
       Don le maistro l'en avoit en aé,* (405)
9460   E si disoit, "Se costu ven en eté,
       El me torà la moja dignité."
       Non è hon in ste mondo si saçes ni doté,
       Quando Rolant en fo en soa até,
       De seno e de scriture l'aust trapasé. (410)
9465   Son per li alevò en grande poverté,
       Tantqe il avoit .VII. ani pasé.
       Mal fo vesti e mal acoroé,
       E mal fo pasu e seçorné.
       E quel Milon si fo forte et aduré; (415)   54rb
9470   De çivaler el devene boscher.

    Rubric 275 (after 9449) MS.: ponie? pome?; Mussafia: duro; Keller: milon
    9455 Mussafia, Cremonesi, Rosellini: hom (cf. 9462)
    9458 Rajna: un ior; Cremonesi: in se' (cf. Holtus 1975)
    9460 Rajna: sì; Mussafia: costu'
    9461 Rajna, Rosellini: tora
    9464 Rosellini: auste
    9466 Mussafia, Cremonesi: Tantqe (as always)

Rubric 276
Coment Million aloit a li bois.*
Laisse 277

	Entendés moi, segnur e bona jent,
	Celle Milon ne fo pais mie lent.
	Çascun jor a l'aube aparisent,
	Si se levoit, nen foit arestament; (420)
9475	A le bois vait, o durò gran torment.
	Si fasoit legne, si le aloit vendent,
	Si le donoit por diner d'argent.
	E de qui diner el conproit la plument*
	Donde vivoit e ben e poverment. (425)
9480	Mais Rolandin, porq'era si saçent,
	Celle enfant o el era acontent,*
	De·l pan e de la çarne i·le dava sovent;
	Siqe de çorno en çorno el aloit en avent.
	Or laseron de Milon li valent, (430)
9485	E de dama Berte, qi fo in gran spavent.
	Gran poina durò en cele bois longament,
	Finqe Damenedé li dè restorament,
	Q'ela ensì de tanto ennojament,*
	Con vos oldirés, se serés atendent. (435)
9490	Nen fust Rolant a tuto son vivent,
	Nen fust ensu de poine e de torment,
	Ne mais aust eu acordament,
	A Karlo maine le riçe sorpojent,
	Ne mais en Française aust eu teniment, (440)
9495	Ne anomé da nesun so parent.*

Rubric 276 (after 9470) Keller: million; Mussafia, Cremonesi: au bois, MS., Keller, Rosellini: a li
9475 Mussafia, Cremonesi: o'; cf. 9481
9478 Mussafia, Cremonesi: qui' diner ... comproit
9480 Cremonesi: Rolandin; Rosellini: Rolandin
9487 Mussafia, Rosellini: li de; Cremonesi: li de'
9488 Mussafia, Rosellini: ensi
9490 Cremonesi: Roland
9492 Cremonesi: aüst eü (as always)
9493 Cremonesi, Rosellini: Karle

7.6 Enfances Ogier le Danois
Rubric 277
Or se conmença de li soldan.*
Laisse 278

   Or laseron de le dux Milon,
   E de dama Berte a la clere façon,
   E de Rolant son petit garçon,
   Qe gran poine el durò en ste mon, (445)*
9500 Petit enfant e veilart e garçon. ((5))
   Mais a la fin si con por voir saçon,*
   Quant le traì le conte Gainelon,*
   Donde fo morto con tot ses conpagnon
   Da li malvés, li rois Marsilion, (450)
9505 Da Deo n'oit si gran benecion, ((10))
   Qe il fo santo, si porte li confalon,
   De tot li martires qe in celo se trovon;*
   Porço è bon oldir questa cançon.
   De le soldan de Persia contaron,*
9510 Qe cun grande oste el vene a Ron; (15)*
   Prese la tere entorno et environ,*
   Si ne caçò l'Apostoilo Milon.*

 Rubric 277 (after 9495) Keller, Guessard: commença; Subak: se comença; Frati: se commença; Cremonesi: s'encomença; Rosellini: se comença
 9497 Guessard, Rosellini: à la clere façon (as always)
 9498 MS.: R. (as always where abbreviation is written out; not commented again); Subak: Rolant; Mussafia, Cremonesi: Rolant; Rosellini: Rolant
 9499 Subak, Rosellini: Que (as always for Subak)
 9501 Subak: com (as always; not commented further)
 9502 Subak: traï; Cremonesi: traï (diereses no longer commented). Rosellini: conte (no note of resolution as always; no longer noted)
 9503 Subak: fò (no longer noted)
 9504 Subak: malvès; Cremonesi, Rosellini: malvés (as always; no longer noted)
 9506 Subak, Rosellini: portò (Frati: corrects Subak to porte). Subak, Rosellini: Que
 9507 Subak, Cremonesi, Rosellini: que (cf. Morini re Rosellini: que]qe)
 9508 Subak, Cremonesi, Rosellini: Por ço (as always; will not be noted further)
 9509 Subak: Pèrsia; cf. 9521: Pèrsie (as always; will not be noted further)
 9510 Guessard: cum . . . à; Mussafia: cum grande . . . ; Rosellini: Que
 9511 Guessard: entorne
 9512 Guessard: caço l'apostoilo . . . ; Subak, Cremonesi, Rosellini: l'apostoilo (never capitalized; not noted again)

```
            Su l'alter san Pero, san Polo e san Simon,
            Fe adorer Trevigant e Macon,
    9515    Donde le Cristian no li oit reençon. (20)
            Morti furent quant i s'en tornon,*                       54ᵛᵃ
            Se non fust Deo qe mandò a Karlon,
            Par li son angle a far nonciason,
            Qe a Roma alast con li ses confalon,
    9520    Çamais a Rome ne le fose perdon. (25)
```

Rubric 278
Coment li soldan fe sa oste.*
Laisse 279

```
            Li soldan de Persie si fo orgolos e fer;
            El fe sa oste e banir e crier.
            Por Paganie mandò ses mesaçer,*
            Ne lasò ni cità ni ville ni docler,*
    9525    Q'el non faist venir çivaler. (30)
            Si le avoit de rois e d'amirer,
            Qe a gran mervile furent da priser
            Entro li qual, dos se poroit nomer,
            Qe non fu mie en li altri plu lainer:
    9530    L'un si fo Karoal, li Escler, (35)
            E l'altro Sidonio, in bataja capler.*
            En quisti dos li soldan oit tuta sa sper;
            De tota l'oste elo li fe ançoner.*
            Quant il oit fato sa oste asenbler
    9535    (Do cento mile se poent esmer), (40)
            En nef entrent si pasarent la mer,*
            E vent a Rome, ilec ad alberçer.
```

9513 Subak: Sul alter
9514 Subak: Fè, Cremonesi. Fe' (as always; not noted further)
9515 Subak, Cremonesi: le cristian
9516 Subak, Cremonesi, Rosellini: quanti s'en
9517 MS.: K. (as always for resolved abbreviations; not noted further)
Rubric 278 (after 9520) Keller: fes a
9521 Cremonesi: Soldan
9524 Subak: in cità, in ville, in docler; Cremonesi: ni . . . ni (emend for MS. in . . . in)
9525 Subak, Cremonesi: faïst (not commented further)
9529 Subak: fù (as always; not noted further)
9530 Subak: fò . . . escler; Cremonesi: escler; Cremonesi, Rosellini: fo
9531 Subak: El altro (corrected also by Reinhold, review Subak, column 20)

Quant l'Apostoilo li veoit, cuita de·l dol raçer;
De soi defendre no fait nul penser.
9540 El non à jent ver de lor canporer, (45)
Nean q'el posa la tera defenser.*
O voja o no, el s'en convene aler;
E lasò la tere a onta et a vituper;
De Cristian, se no se voient renojer*
9545 Petita gent li porisés trover,* (50)
Tuti s'en vont cun filz e con muler,
E si lasent son avoir e son diner.
Quant Sarasin li venent a intrer,
Asa li trovoit da boir e da mançer;
9550 Deo li confonda, li vor justisier! (55)
Qe Macometo li metent sor li alter,*
E si le font a cil pain orer.
E le penture qe le poent trover,
Via le fait tore e spegaçer,*
9555 E si le foit onta e vituper, (60)
E posa vont corando por la river.*
Ne li lasoit depreso .XX. lege enter,
Qe i no faça et arder e bruxer;
Tot la rivere i ont fato rober.

Rubric 279
Qui se conte de Rom(e).*
Laisse 280

9560 Dedens de Roma e for por li pendant, (65)
Si le estoit e dol e t(or)mant;*
E n'en (v)i ma tel in le bateçamant.*
Quan la cité de Roma, con tot li sant,   54vb
Si è poblea de Turs e de Persant.
9565 Desor l'auter san Pero e san Jovan* (70)

9545 Subak: porisés (always on *-es* endings; not noted further)
9547 Guesssard: à la
9549 Subak: Asà (as always; not noted further)
9550 Subak: voir iustisier, emendation of MS. *vor*
Rubric 279 (after 9559) MS. Romœ; Keller: roma; Subak: Roma; Cremonesi: Rome; Rosellini: Romae
9561 MS.: tromant; Subak, Cremonesi, Rosellini: tromant
9562 Subak: E' n' en vì ma . . . ; Cremonesi: E' n'en vi ma' . . .
9565 Cremonesi: Jovan; Rosellini: Iovan

	Ont polsé Macon e Trevigant,

                Ont polsé Macon e Trevigant,
                Si le aore cele jent mescreant.
                De Cristian n'in à lasé ni çoveno ni ferant,*
                Ne sia morto a·l trencer de li brant.
9570   E l'Apostoile caçè vilanemant,* (75)
                Et avec lui, amisi e parant.
                Qui Sarasin qi no son in Deo creant,
                Font de Rome tot li son talant.
                Questo non soit Francés et Alamant,
9575   Ni Karlo el maine, le riçe sorpojant. (80)
                Mais a Damenedé, li rois q'è sorpojant,*
                Nen pote sofrir cotant enojamant,*
                Qe Sarasin alase tant avant,
                Qe i prendese tot li batezamant.
9580   Quant a Karlo l'inperer poisant (85)
                Oit tramis son angle en dormant,
                Qe tot li conte de Rome li convant,
                Cun prisa estoit Roma sença colpo de brant,
                E l'Apostoile caçé vilanemant,
9585   Morta sa çente a miler et a çant. (90)

9566 Subak: polsè

9568 Subak: n'i n'a lasè . . . ni çòveno; Cremonesi: n'i n'à lasé; Rosellini: n'i n'à lasé . . .

9570 Cremonesi, Rosellini: caçé. Subak: uilanemant; Reinhold, review Subak, column 23: vilanement (noting Subak's error)

9572 Subak: qui (as always; not commented further)

9573 Rosellini: lo son talant (corrected Morini, lo] li)

9574 Subak: Frances (Reinhold, review Subak, column 23, Francès should be Subak's reading for consistency)

9576 Subak: Damenedè (Frati corrects to "Damenedé"); Cremonesi: Damenedé; Rosellini: Damanedé (Morini re Rosellini: Damanadé] damenede)

9577 Subak: potè; Cremonesi, Rosellini: pote

9580 MS.: K; Cremonesi: Karle, as always (not noted any further); Rosellini: K[arlo]

9584 Rosellini: l'postoile; Morini: l'postoile] l'apostoile (cf. Martin)

Rubric 280
Coment l'angle vene a K*arlo*.
Laisse 281

        En una noit quant K*arlo* fu endormençé*
        E Damenedé, qe ame Cristenté,
        A K*arlo* oit son angle envojé
        (San Gabriel qe molto avoit amé)
9590   A K*arlo* el maine la noit a la çelé,* (95)
        Qe li co*n*tò tota la verité:
        Coment li Saldan cu*n* la jent desfaé*
        Ont prisa Roma la cité,
        E l'Apostoile è foi e scanpé,*
9595   E li Cristian qe lì furent trové (100)
        È gran partie morti e detrençé.*
        Li angle fu en la çanbra entré;
        Davant li leto el se fu apojé.
        O il vi K*arlo* si l'oit aresveilé:
9600   "Enperer, sire, vu dormés a segurté; (105)
        Nen savés mie ço qe est encontré,
        E li dalmaço grande e desmesuré.
        (Sarasin) son ençe Roma entré,*
        E si ne oit l'Apostoilo caçé.
9605   Desor li altari qe da Deo son sagré, (110)
        Lì ont son dei metu e repolsé,
        Si le adorent celle jent renojé;
        Si cuitoit prendre tota la Crestenté.

    Rubric 280 (after 9585) Keller: langle
    9586 Subak: endormençè (grave accent for entire laisse rhyme)
    9589 Rosellini: Sa Gabriel; cf. Morini
    9590 Subak: Subak: K*arlon* . . . la noit alà çelè; Cremonesi: noit alà çelé; Rosellini: la noit ala çelé
    9592 Subak, Cremonesi, Rosellini: Coment li soldan
    9594 Subak: e[n] foi escanpè; Cremonesi: foì
    9595 Subak, Cremonesi, Rosellini: li furent (never stress on *li*; not noted again)
    9596 MS.: E gran; Subak, Cremonesi, Rosellini: E[n] (emend)
    9598 Subak: apoiè; Rosellini: apoié
    9599 Cremonesi: O' (as always; not noted further)
    9601 Subak: sarès
    9603 MS.: Sasarasin. Subak, Cremonesi, Rosellini: Sarasin; Subak, Cremonesi: enç e[n] (emend); Rosellini: son ençe . . .

	Perdua est in tot, se no da Deo la defensé;	
9610	Deo a vos si m'avoit mandé, (115)	
	Por anonçer questa grant anbasé;*	55ra
	Non so cun major ve poust eser conté."	
	Li rois s'esvelle, qe fu de·l sono gravé;*	
	A le sant angle elo responde aré:	
9615	"Dì mo, ami, como è tu ça entré,* (120)	
	Quando le uso è cluso e seré?	
	È tu fantasma, o spirto ençanté,	
	Qe mon polser m'avez contrarié?"	
	E cil le dist, "Vu avì ben falé.	
9620	Ne son fantasma, ni bestia ençanté. (125)	
	Angle sui de Deo de majesté;*	
	A vos el m'oit tramis et envojé,	
	Qe vos die une grant anbasé:	
	Qe li soldan c'oit nome Ysoré	
9625	Avoit pasé oltra la mer salé, (130)	
	E si oit pris Roma la cité,	
	Dont l'Apostoile se n'è fujando torné.	
	Le Cristian qe le furent trové,	
	Tuti furent morti, a martirio livré.	
9630	Sor li altar li qual sonto sagré, (135)	
	Macon et Apolin i le ont polsé,	
	Si le adorent quela jent desfaé,	
	Si menaçent la santa Crestenté,	
	Q'i la destrueroit se no le fi veé."*	
9635	Li rois l'intent, tuto fo abosmé; (140)	
	Gran dol en oit, par poi n'est desvé.	
	Adonc l'angle, quando se fu sevré,	
	El dist a Karlo, "E vos comando a Dé;	

9609 Subak: Perdüa . . . seno da Deo; Frati: se no da Deo . . .

9612 Subak, Cremonesi: poüst (as always)

9613 Subak, Rosellini: s'esveile

9615 Subak: Dì mo, ami . . . ; Cremonesi: "Di' mo', ami, como e' tu . . . ; Rosellini: «Dì mo, ami, . . . e tu . . .

9617 Rosellini: spirito (corrected Morini)

9619 Cremonesi: Vu aví

9620 Subak: bèstia

9621 Cremonesi: maiesté

9622 7 for et; Subak: tramìs

9629 Subak: martìrio

9634 Subak: Qu'i la . . . se no le fì veè; Rosellini: Q'i la . . . li fi (Morini: le]li)

A vos m'envojò, et eo ve l'ò nonçé;
9640 Guardez ben, q'el non soja oblié." (145)
A·l departir çitoit tel clarité, 55ʳᵇ
Qe tota la çanbra en fo aluminé.

Rubric 281
Coment angle (parole) a Karlo.
Laisse 282

Quant l'angle fu retornez arer,
Karlo se leve sença nul entarder.
9645 Si oit envojé por Naimes de Baiver, (150)
Et ensement por Morando de River,
Por Çofré de Paris, et Aleris li ber,*
E Bernardo de Clermont, e le dux Guarner,
E·l Dainese, q'el ama e ten çer,
9650 E Karloto son filz, qi estoit baçaler. (155)
"Segnur," fait il, "e vos so ben nonçer,
Qe l'angle de Deo m'è venu a parler.
Tel consa m'à dito donde son en penser;*
Qe un soldan, qe oit nome Ysorer,
9655 Cun una grant oste oit pasé la mer. (160)
Roma oit prisa, qe no i è nul sper;
Caçé l'Apostoilo cun tot li terer.*
Desor l'auter major de san Per,
Macometo lì oit fato polser.
9660 Tot le reliquie en oit fato oster; (165)
Là le orarent Sarasin et Escler,
E(n) quela lois qe Deo non oit çer,*

9639 Rosellini: eo l'ò (Morini: eo ve l'ò)
Rubric 281 (after line 9642) MS., Keller: paroler .ak.; Subak, Cremonesi, Rosellini: parole (emend for *paroler*)
9643 Subak: Qᵛant (as always in first line of laisse; *Qvant* at beginning of line; not commented further)
9646 Rosellini: esement (Morini corrects also)
9649 Subak, Cremonesi, Rosellini: E 'l Dainese
9651 Subak: sò (as always; not noted again)
9653 MS., Subak, Cremonesi: consa; Rosellini: colsa (emend for MS. *consa*)
9658 MS., Subak, Cremonesi: maior
9659 Subak, Cremonesi, Rosellini: li oit . . .
9661 7 for *et*; Cremonesi, Rosellini: Là le . . .
9662 MS., Subak, Cremonesi, Rosellini: E quela

E si dient q'i no l'avoit a defenser;*
La Crestenetà virà a deserter.
9665 Conselés moi, e vos vojo en projer, (170)*
Qe le mior nu p(o)samo pier."*
Dist dux Naimes de·l ducha de Bavier,
"O çentil rois, qe voli vu demander?*
Non è nul hon qe n'olsase parler,
9670 Contra colu qi mandò li mesaçer, (175)   55ᵛᵃ
Qe Roma diça secorer et aider.
Unde vos pre, qe non diça tarder;
Far vestra jent venir *et* amaser,
E si gran oste e banir e crier,
9675 Qe segurment vu posa çivalçer, (180)
Trosqua a Roma secorer et aider.
E qi de ço vos vole contraster,
Ne vos ama mie la monta d'un diner,
E si vol Deo en toto contrarier."
9680 Dist li rois, "Vu parlés como ber." (185)

Rubric 282
Coment Karlo demanda conseil.*
Laisse 283

Karlo li rois, qe filz fo de Pepin,
A gran mervile fo hon de gran lin.
Por li conseil de cil baron d'alto brin
Fe scrivere letre in carte de bergamin;
9685 Si l'envojò a tere et a çamin (190)
Par tot cil qe li sonto vesin.
E fa fair bander de palio e de lin

9663 Subak: qui no la voit; Cremonesi: qi no l'avoit; Rosellini: qi no la voit
9665 Cremonesi, Rosellini: enproier (Subak: en proier). Subak: e' vos . . .
9666 Subak: posamo pïer; Cremonesi, Rosellini: posamo pier
9667 Subak, Rosellini: duchà; Cremonesi: ducha'
9668 Subak, Cremonesi: volì
9669 Subak: hom; Reinhold, review Subak, column 23, correct to hon
9671 Cremonesi: diça' . . .
9672 Subak: Vnde vos prè; Cremonesi: pre' . . . diça'
9673 7 for *et*
9675 Subak: posà; Cremonesi: posa'
9677 Rosellini: Q qi (corrected Holden, Morini)
9684 Subak: scrìvere
9687 Rosellini: fa far (Morini: far] fair)

E l'oriaflama d'un palio astorin.
Plus de cento mil homes a bo*n* bra*n*t açarin,
9690 A bone targes, aubers doplantin, (195)
Fait asenbler K*arlo*, le filz Pepin.

Rubric 283
Coment K*arlo* asenbla sa jent.
Laisse 284

Karlo maine fait asenbler sa jant,
Par tot tere le petit e li grant.
Ne lì lasò conte ni amirant,
9695 Q'el no lì vegne co*n* tot son guarnimant. (200)
Çascun lì vent, legro e çojant;
Tuto son avoir i le mete in presant.
Naymes lì fu, e Çofré e Morant;
E Sansoneto, qe ça fu mescreant;
9700 E li Danois, e Çarloto l'infant— (205)
Nen è ancor guaire q'el oit p*ri*s guarnima*n*t,*
Filo est li rois, si l'ama dolçemant—
Cento mil sont a verdi heumi lusant.*
Adonc verisés ensegne de mant se*n*blant,
9705 E mant destrer isné e remuant. (210)
En questa oste no*n* fo homo vivant,
Non ame li rois de cor e de talant;
Par lui servire li dona son arçant.
Grande fu l'oste, meravelosa e grant.

Rubric 283 (after 9691): MS., Keller, Subak: ient
9692 Rosellini: fai asenbler (cf. Morini)
9694 Subak, Cremonesi, Rosellini: li (cf. 9695; 9696, 9698)
9695 Rosellini: so guarnimant (cf. Morini)
9703 Subak, Cremonesi: aver di; Reinhold, review Subak, column 21, Rosellini: a verdi . . . (cf. 3500; 6302; 6349; 619; 6646; etc.)

Rubric 284
Coment li rois fo en Paris.
Laisse 285

9710 Or fu li rois en Paris sens dotançe, (215)
       Sor li palés sença nul demorançe.
       Molto fo ben coneu de la çente de Françe;
       Par tot part alò la nomenançe,
       De l'oste de Karlo e de sa gran posançe.
9715 Par lui servir li vent trois en Valançe;* (220)
       Çascun li vent cun bona entendançe,   55vb
       Cun bon çival e con scu e con lançe;
       Li rois le vi, en lor oit sa fiançe.
       L'oriaflame qe fu de gran valançe,
9720 Ad Aleris la donò por bona mançe, (225)
       E cil la prent, qe se mis en balançe;*
       Si le çurò de no far·li falançe.

Rubric 285
Coment li rois dona l'oriaflame.
Laisse 286

       Quant li rois oit l'oriaflama doné,
       Ad Aleris qe de Puilla fu né,
9725 E quel s'ençenoile, si le oit li pe basé, (230)
       Vojant li barons li à plevi e çuré
       De no stratornar·la par hon qe soja né.
       Adonc li rois no fo pais entardé;

    Rubric 284 (after 9709) MS., Subak: Rois (Keller: rois)
    9710 Rosellini: li rois Paris (cf. Holden, Morini, Martin)
    9712 Subak: coneü . . çente de fiançe (also noted by Frati); Cremonesi: coneü . . . de la çente (corrected by Holtus, review Cremonesi, 444)
    9715 Subak, Cremonesi, Rosellini: en valançe; Reinhold, review Subak, column 21, Cerf: trois en Valançe
    9718 Subak: vì (as always)
    9722 Subak: far-li; Cremonesi: farli; Rosellini: farli; Cf. 9727, etc.
    Rubric 285 (after 9722) Keller: rois . . . loriaflame
    9725 Cremonesi: pè (as always)
    9726 Subak, Cremonesi: plevì
    9727 Subak, Cremonesi, Rosellini: stratornarla (inconsistent orthography); Rosellini: que soia. Rosellini: hom (Rosellini usually resolves the nasal abbreviation a 'n,' but differs here.)

Quant tota sa jent furent aparilé,
9730 Tota sa jent el oit devisé, (235)
E so bandere doné et otrié,
Et ordenent coment aler devé;*
L'oriaflame ad Aleris donè,*
Una deman quant fu l'aube levé,
9735 L'oste s'en voit por lo çamin feré. (240)
Pur bellament nen fo pais desroé
Qe .X. leues i vont por çorné.*
Por Lonbardie i se sont pasé,
E a Toschane i ont acostojé;
9740 Tanto se sonto de jorno en jorno alé, (245)
Qe a Rome i forent aprosmé.
Quando i forent apreso la cité,
Preso una leue i furent aloçé;*
Li rois comande sa çent soja armé.
9745 Quant li mesajes fu en Roma entré, (250)
A li rois soldan li oit anoncié;
A gran mervile el ne fo abosmé.
Rois Karaolo oit a soi apelé,*
E Sindonio e li rois Galatré;*
9750 "Segnur," fait il, "nu avon malovré; (255)
Pre de nos è venu li maine encoroné,
Qe soit de França e de la Cresteneté.
Bataila averon, se avoir la voré."
Dist Karaolo, "Eo ne son çojant e lé,
9755 S'i ven a canpo, e no serò daré: (260)
Le primeran eo serò armé,
Sor mon çival corant et abri(v)é.*
Ensirò de Rome, çirò a la meslé;
Con qui Francés proarò ma bonté."
9760 Dist li soldan, "De ço vos so bon gre." (265)

9732 Subak: doné (emend for MS. deue); Frati: aler devè; Reinhold, review Subak, column 21: devé (correction of Subak); Rosellini: dové

9733 Cremonesi, Rosellini: doné

9737 Cremonesi: leves

9745 Subak: Quando (corrected Reinhold, review Subak, column 21)

9749 Subak: Balatrè; Cremonesi, Rosellini: Balatré

9750 Subak: mal ovrè; Cremonesi, Rosellini: mal ovré . . .

9755 Subak: e' no serò

9757 7 for et. MS.: abrine; Subak: abriné; Cremonesi: abrivé (emend for abriné); Rosellini: abrivé (emend); Cerf also, abrivè, not abrinè.

9759 Subak: Françès; Cremonesi: Francés; Rosellini: Francés

Rubric 286
Coment K*arlo* çivalçe.
Laisse 287

	Karlo li rois fi sa çent çivalçer,	
	Par li co*n*seil dux Naimon de Baiver.*	
	Aprés de Rome s'en vait ad aloçer;	56ra
	Posa comande soa çent a monter,	
9765	Si devisò le schere e le bander. (270)	
	L'oriaflama fe davant fiçer;	
	"Aleris," fait il, "vu sì co*n*faloner;*	
	L'oriaflame vu avez a gujer.	
	Guarda·la ben, je vos vojo en projer,*	
9770	Qe por paure ne la diça stratorner." (275)	
	E cil le dist, "No aça quel penser,	
	Qe por morir no me farò lainer."	
	Adoncha li rois no se volse entarder;	
	La prime schile qe il volse ordener:	
9775	A Çofroi de Paris donò .X. mil çivaler, (280)	
	Et a Teris altri .X. miler,	
	E a Morando, li segnor de River,	
	E a celu ne dè .XX. miler.	
	E a·l dux N*aimes*, q'era so co*n*seler,*	
9780	Cun Bernardo de Clermo*n*t elo lasò darer, (285)	
	Con tot les autres par son cors guarder.	
	A·l Daynesin, q'estoit baçaler,	
	Segnor le fe de tot li scuer,	
	Si le donò in guarda mener.	
9785	E li rois comande qui davant mo*n*ter, (290)	
	E l'oriaflame avanti aporter;	
	E cil le fait de grez e volunter.	
	Adoncha Çofré si pris son corer;	

9761 Subak: fi (as always)
9762 Rosellini: fux (for *dux*)
9763 Subak: Après (as always); Cremonesi: Apres
9768 Subak: oriflame; Reinhold, review Subak, column 21, Frati also correct.
9769 Subak: Guardà-la ... en proier; Cremonesi: Guarda'-la ... enproier (as always); Rosellini: Guardala ... je vos voio enproier (and misquotes Cremonesi's reading in note)
9770 Subak: paüre (as always) ... diçà
9778 Cremonesi: dé
9779 Rosellini: E el dux (emend for MS. *E al dux*)
9788 Subak: Çofrè (as always)

Monta a çival a .X. mil çivaler.
9790 Dever de Rome prendent a çivalçer, (295)
Pres de la porta li trato d'un arçer.
Quant li soldan li voit a 'prosmer,
Demantenant fe Karaolo monter
A .XX. mile de celle jent Escler.
9795 La porta trapase, fa li pont devaler, (300)
Ver celle jent vait a tornojer.
Ça oldirés bataila començer,
Qe torner doi a molt gran destorber.

Rubric 287
Coment Çofré de Paris fo pris.
Laisse 288

Quant Karaolo ensì fora a li canp,*
9800 Dever Çofré ponçe son auferant. (305)
Grande fu la bataile a quel començamant;
Donc verisés mant çivaler sanglant,
E manti çivaler caire a li canp.*
La çent de Karles furent pro e valant;
9805 Ver Sarasin mostra grande ardimant. (310)
E Çofroi de Paris ten la spea trençant.
Co il conseit soa vita è niant.*
Da l'altra part fu Karaolo li posant;
A gran mervile fo ardi e valant;
9810 Non fer Francés q'el non çeti a li canp.* (315)
Li .X. mil de la François çant,   56rb
Contra le .XX. mil i fose ste perdant,
Quando Teris fa monter l'altre jant;*

9792 Subak, Cremonesi, Rosellini: voit aprosmer
9794 Subak, Cremonesi, Rosellini: escler (as always)
9798 Subak: doi' a (emend); Rosellini: doi[t]
Rubric 287 (after 9798) Keller: çofre . . . paris
9803 Subak: caü (emend for 'caue'); Cremonesi: caüe; Rosellini: cau (emend for MS. *caue*)
9809 Subak: ardì
9810 Cremonesi: ceti (Holtus, review Cremonesi, 444, corrects also)
9811 Subak, Cremonesi, Rosellini: françois (no capitalization)
9812 Subak: stè; Cremonesi: sté
9813 Rosellini: altra

	E furent .X. mil a verdi helmi lusant.
9815	Grande fu la bataile d'anbes comunelma*n*t. (320)
	Qi donc veist gra*n*di colpi de brant!
	A gran mervile fu Karaolo vailant;
	Por me la presie ven menu e sova*n*t,
	Donando colpi e darer e davant,
9820	Cu il co*n*seit soa vite è nojant. (325)
	E quant Çofroi li vai reconosant,
	Qe de sa jent fa li dalmaço grant,
	Enver de lui ponçe li auferant,
	E tent la spee a li pomo lusant.
9825	Gran colpo li done desor l'eumo lusant; (330)
	N'en po trençer un diner valisant,
	Ma de le scu la guincha el porprant,
	Cu*n* de l'auberg e de le maje ben çant.
	E l'oit çité en l'erba verdojant;
9830	Par un petit ne le fe recreant. (335)

Rubric 288
Coment Karaolo ferì.
Laisse 289

	Quant Karaolo sentì li colpo de baron,
	El ten la spee c'oit endoré li pon;
	Dever Çofroi punçe le aragon;
	Gra*n* colpo li done desor l'elmo enson.
9835	Q'elo·l fe enbro*n*çer desor da l'arçon. (340)
	S'el no*n* fust devalé, morto fust li baron;*
	Fendu l'averoit trosqa en le menton.

9814 Subak, Cremonesi: aver di helmi. Cf. l. 9703 above.
9816 Subak, Cremonesi: veïst (as always)
9818 Subak: Pormè la presie . . . ; Cremonesi: Por me'
9824 Rosellini: ten la spée
9825 Rosellini: desot
9826 Subak: pò (as always)
9827 Subak, Cremonesi, Rosellini: l'escu
9829 Subak: çitè (as always with final stresses; cf. 9832, *endorè*, etc.)
Rubric 288 (after 9830) MS., Keller: karaolo
9831 Rosellini: senti
9834 Subak: colpo . . . en son
9835 Subak: Qu' elo 'l fè; Cremonesi: Q'elo 'l fe' . . . ; Rosellini: Q'elo 'l fe . . .
9836 Subak: Se non . . . devalè

A·l cival trençe li çevo tot reon;
Çofré de Paris caì a·l sablon.
9840 Sovra li core Sarasin e Sclavon; (345)
O voja o no, i l'ont por preson;
En Roma le conduit, o el volist o non.*
Le .X. mil qe fu ses conpagnon
Par lui furent en grant aflecion.
9845 Morti fuissent sença redencion, (350)
Nen fust scanpé veilard ni garçon,
Quando Teris ven cun ses conpagnon.
E furent .X. mil sota ses confalon;
Si grant fu la nosa e la tençon,
9850 Mant çivaler en caent a·l sablon. (355)
Qui de Karaolo, o i volist o non,*
Le canpo gerpisent un arpant tot lon.
Quando Sindonio montò en arçon,
A .XXX. mile de Turs e de Sclavon,*
9855 E quando cestor ensirent de Ron, (360)
Gran fu la nose de graile qe son.
Se (a) Deo no pe(n)se, por so santisimo non,*
La çente de France mal esploité averon,*
Qe contra ces non averà guarison.   56ᵛᵃ

9838 Subak, Cremonesi, Rosellini: Al cival (as always); Subak: li cevo (corrected Frati)

9839 Subak: caì̈ (with dieresis and grave accent, as always); Cremonesi: caï (as always)

9841 Rosellini: O via o no

9842 Subak, Rosellini: cel volist. Reinhold, review Subak, column 21 corrects Subak: o el volist; Cremonesi: o el volist

9843 Subak: compagnon (as always; cf. 9847, etc.)

9857 MS.: pese; Subak, Cremonesi: pense; Rosellini: Se Deo no pense. Subak: santìsimo

9858 Subak, Rosellini: esploite; Cerf: read *esploitè*

Rubric 289
Coment Sandonio ferì.
Laisse 290

9860 A gran mervile fo Sandonio orgolos, (365)
      Fort *et* ardi e de mal en(a)r(t)os.*
      En Paganie environ et intors
      Pochi poisés atrover de milors.
      Bon çivaler est, ardi e virtuos;
9865 Dist a sa jent, "No*n* siés spavoros; (370)
      Çascun de vos ben ferà ad estors,
      Qe questa jent nu façan dolors."*
      E qi le font, qe no*n* farent sejors;
      Quant i ferirent, ferire*n*t de tel vigors,*
9870 Ne le durava nul arma pinta a flors. (375)
      Lora veisés tanti colpi doloros,
      Tant çivaler eser de·l çevo blos;
      L'erba verde devenoit tota ros;
      Mille çivaler çasoit a l'arbors,*
9875 Qe ma no le vede ne fio ne uxors; (380)
      O voja o no, Fra*n*çeis s'en tornoit a estors.*

Rubric 290
Coment Sandonio entra en l'estor.
Laisse 291

      Quando Sandonio va in l'estor entrer,
      Qe .XXX. mile avit de çivaler,*
      Quant el ferì en le stormeno primer,
9880 Si grande fo la nose ne se poroit co*n*ter. (385)

Rubric 289 (after 9859) MS.: sandonio
9861 7 for *et*. MS., Subak, Cremonesi: mal enorcos; Rosellini: mal inartos
9863 Cremonesi: poïses (as always)
9865 Rosellini: spaveros
9866 Subak: Cascun (cf. Frati)
9869 Subak, Rosellini: Quanti
9876 Subak: Fra*n*ceis (Reinhold, review Subak, column 23, Frati also note); Rosellini: Franceis
Rubric 290 (after 9876) MS.: sandonio; Keller: lestor
9877 Subak: và
9879 Subak: l'estòrmeno; but cf. his line 418 (9913), "li stor"! Holtus, review Cremonesi, 447: le stormeno

> A colpi ferir nen valt arme un diner;
> Sovra Franceis vene tot l'ingo*n*brer.
> O voja o no, co*n*ven li canpo laser,
> Qe no li poent sofrir ni endurer.*
9885 E qui l'encalçe por (v)ie e por senter,* (390)
> Quant se prendent a l'oste aprosmer.
> E la novele voit a l'inperer;
> Quan cil le soit, fa sa çent monter.
> Ço fo dux Naymes, de·l ducha de Baiver,*
9890 A plus de .XXX. mile fo mo*n*ta a destrer. (395)
> Quant ensirent, q'i vene*n*t a çostrer,*
> Ses grailes fait en ojando soner.
> Qi donc veist de Fra*n*ça li çivaler,*
> Cun le lançe ferir li colpi primer.
9895 Çascun abate li so a li vercer,* (400)
> Donc veisés qui Sarasin verser,
> Morti a la tera cair e trabuçer.
> Quando Sindonio le vi si mal aler,
> El li escrie, "Ne vos aça doter,
9900 Qe questa jent qe son de l'inperer, (405)
> Encontra nos petit averà durer!"
> Grande fu la bataile e li stormeno plener;
> Adonc verisés tant çivaler verser,
> E a la tera cair e trabuçer.
9905 Qi qi caì mal se poit relever,* (410)
> Tal estoit la presie d·i corant destrer.   56^(vb)
> Li rois Sandonio molt se fait priser;
> Con eso la spea si durame*n*t fer,
> Qe nule arme nen po a lui durer.

9881 Subak: vale
9882 Subak, Rosellini: Françeis; Subak: ingo*m*brer (as always before labial)
9885 MS.: me? (for *vie*); Subak, Cremonesi, Rosellini: vie
9888 MS.: sa çent; Subak, Rosellini: la çent (Frati corrects Subak's reading)
9889 Subak, Rosellini: duchà; Cremonesi: ducha'
9890 Rosellini: monta
9895 Subak, Cremonesi, Rosellini: alivercer (corrected Reinhold, review Subak, column 21, Morini)
9901 Rosellini: aver durer
9902 Subak: stòrmeno
9905 Subak: Qui qui; Cremonesi, Rosellini: Qi q'i
9906 Subak: prèsie
9908 Subak: Con-eso

9910   Quant Karaolo se le vait a 'prosmer,* (415)
        De cest dos non fa nula projer;*
        Çascun de lor estoit pro çivaler.

Rubric 291
Coment Naimes ferì in le canpo.
Laisse 292

        Por me li stor, eco vos Naimes pugnant;
        Sa grosa lançe el vait palmojant.
9915   Le primer q'el ferì fo un nevo l'amirant; (420)
        Le scu li speçe e l'auberg li destant.
        Par me li cors le mis le fer trençant;
        Morto l'abate, qi s'en rit ni s'en chant,
        E pois escrie, "Ferés, me conbatant!
9920   Qe çesta lois qe no son in Deo creant, (425)
        Enver de nos i serà recreant."
        Quant cil l'entendent, fait li so talant;
        Çascun li fer de cors e de talant.
        Grant fu la bataile e la nosa grant;
9925   Par me li stor ven Sandonio pungant. (430)
        O vi dux Naimes, li est venu davant;
        Elo l'apelle, si le dise en ojant:
        "Çivaler, sire, qe parés si manant,
        A gran mervile avés bel guarnimant;
9930   En la cort li rois sì vu reconosant,* (435)
        Estes vos çivaler o de menua çant?"
        E cil le dist, "A conter mon talant
        Encontra vos, no me varia niant.
        Com o le espée faron li parlamant!"*

    9910 Subak, Cremonesi, Rosellini: se le vait aprosmer
    9911 Cremonesi: nul aproier; Rosellini: nul aprover (emend for proier)
    Rubric 291 (after 9912) MS.: .N.; Rosellini: ferì (cf. 9915 etc.)
    9913 Cremonesi: Por me' li stor . . . eco-vos; Subak: Pormè li stor; Rosellini: li stor
    9915 Subak: nevò; Cremonesi: nevo'
    9916 Subak: L'escu
    9917 Subak: Parme
    9925 Subak: Parmè li stor; Cremonesi: Par me' li stor; Rosellini: Par me li stor . . . .
MS.: pūgant; Subak, Cremonesi: pugnant; Rosellini: pugnant (emend for MS. pungnant);
cf. l. 9913
        9931 Subak: menüa
        9934 Subak, Cremonesi: Como; Rosellini: Com o

9935   Adonc N*aimes* si le ferì de·l brant; (440)
       Desor li eume un tel colpo li rant,
       Fendu l'averoit tros in le feltramant.*
       Quando la spee le ferì in schivant,
       L'auberg li trençe e la tarça davant;
9940   E a·l çival por la schina el fant. (445)
       Morto li çete, e quel caì a·l canp;
       Ma el se driçe tosto et isnelmant.
       La spea trait si se mis en avant;
       Dever dux N*aimes* un gran salto el prant.
9945   Za l'aust morto son auferant, (450)
       Quant Sansoneto le colpo no li co*n*sant.*

Rubric 292
Coment Sandonio fo abatu.
Laisse 293

       Quando Sandonio se vi a tera abatu,*
       E son çival en le pre erbu,
       El se redriçe e ten la spea nu.
9950   Enver de N*aimes* est a salti metu; (455)
       Feru l'averoit desor l'eumes agu,
       Quant Sansoneto li oit secoru.*
       E cil le fert par si fera vertu,   57ʳᵃ
       Qe a la tera l'oit abatu,
9955   E prent le çival o cil ert cau. (460)
       Elo li salte, qe streve n'oit prendu;
       Atant ecote vos (un) rois c'oit nome Valbrun,*
       Sor Sansoneto corent por vertu.
       O voja o no, i l'ont prendu;
9960   A ses pain i l'ont rendu. (465)
       En Roma li oit a li soldan rendu,
       Avec Çofré li oit in preson metu.
       Naimes le vi, forment fo irascu.
       Grant fu la nose, si fo leva li u;
9965   Sarasin son for de Roma ensu, (470)
       Plu de cento mile a lançe et a scu.
       Qua*n*do Francés ont cosi veu,

   9951 Subak: averoie (corrected Frati, Reinhold [review Subak, column 21])
   9957 Subak: ècote vos; Cremonesi: ecote-vos; Rosellini: ecote vos. MS.: une rois; Subak, Cremonesi, Rosellini: un rois (emend for *une*)

Tot le milor fo en fua metu.
Ad Aleris fo la stendart abatu;
9970 E cil s'en va fuant si se·l tira rer lu; (475)
Grande fu el damaço, s'el no è secoru.

Rubric 293
Coment Aleris portoit l'oriaflame.*
Laisse 294

Va s'en Aleris, nen ait qe coruçer;
L'oriaflame el se tira darer.
E le dux N*aimes* è desendu a ter;
9975 O vi le rois, si·l prist a derasner: (480)
"Enperer, sire, e vos so ben nonçer,
Qe ò veçu l'oriaflame verser;*
Quel qe l'avoit se l'à tira darer.*
Grande è·l dalmaço de li ves çivaler,
9980 Qe s'en fuçen a cento e a miler." (485)
E li Daines estoit preso d'un boscher,
Qe sire estoit de tot li scuer.
Davant da soi elo prist a guarder;
Vi Aleris l'oriaflame trainer.
9985 "Segnur," fait il, "se me volés aider,* (490)
Colu qe l'oriaflame se vait traina*n*do rer,
Eo ge l'averò de ses man saçer."
E cil si li dient, "Ne vos estoit doter;
Viron cu*n* vos, et avant et arer."
9990 E cil le dist, "Tant ò in Dé bona sper,* (495)

9968 Subak: füa (as always)
9970 Subak, Cremonesi: Si se 'l; Rosellini: Si se'l
Rubric 293 (after 9971) Keller: a leris . . . loriaflame
9972 Subak: Ua (for *Va*); Rosellini: Vassen
9975 Subak, Cremonesi: si 'l prist; Rosellini: ci'l prist à derasner; Subak: ad erasner; Cremonesi: a derasner
9977 Subak: Qu'e'ò; Cremonesi: Q'e' ò veçu . . . ; Rosellini: Qe ò veçu . . .
9978 Subak, Cremonesi, Rosellini: se la tira
9979 Subak, Cremonesi, Rosellini: è 'l
9981 Subak: Dainès; Cremonesi: Dainés; Rosellini: Daines
9984 Subak: traïner
9987 Rosellini: El l'averò (missing *ge*)
9990 Subak: oi'nde (Reinhold, review of Subak, column 21, better, ò in Dè); Cerf: Tant à in Dè; Cremonesi: Tant ò in De' . . . ; Rosellini: Tant ò in De . . .

Qe toti vos eo farò çivaler."
Donc li Dainos prist un baston de pomer,
E grant e groso, merveloso e plener;
O el vi Aleris, ven davanti a l'inco*n*trer
9995 Elo li scrie, "Estes malvasio liçer! (500)
Como cuité vos si l'oriaflama porter?
Tosto desendés, si ne dà li destrer,
E l'oriaflama cu*n* tot li corer."
E cil le fait, no li olsò co*n*traster.
10000 E·l Daineseto s'armò tot en primer; (505)
Pris l'oriaflame, si la fa redriçer;   57rb
Ver qui pain se voit a 'fiçer.
Tanti no*n* fer, nen faça trabuçer,
E lì apreso furent li scuer*
10005 Qe li tolent le arme e li destrer. (510)
Quant a çival poent toti monter,
Çascun de lor senblava a çivaler.
Qi donc le veist por li estor aler,
E qui gran colpi donar e inplojer.
10010 Çascun de lor avoit una bander, (515)
Qe i avont fato sor pertege lever.
Ne son pais mie de palio ni de çender,
Ma de ses camises, q'i s'oit fato despoiler,
E de le peçé dont forbe li destrer.*
10015 En si gran fuga el mete qui Ascler, (520)
Qe le plu saço n'è sensa co*n*seler.*
Arer s'en fuçe, si se lasa li senter;
K*arlo* le voit, si le prist a guarder,
Et oit dito a le dux N*aimes* de Baiver:
10020 "Vu me deisì de·l mo*n* co*n*faloner* (525)
Qe l'oriaflame el se tirava arer?
Men esiant, mal n'oit li penser;

9994 Subak: al'incontrer
9995 Subak: malvàsio
10000 Subak, Rosellini: El Daineseto; Cremonesi: E 'l Daineseto
10002 Subak: a fiçer; Cremonesi: afiçer; Rosellini: à fiçer
10003 Subak, Rosellini: trebuçer (cf. Frati for correction also)
10011 Subak: pèrtege
10013 Subak: qu' i s' oit; Cremonesi: q'i s'oit . . . ; Rosellini: qi s'oit . . .
10014 Subak, Cremonesi, Rosellini: peçe
10016 Reinhold (review of Subak, column 21): ne s'en sà conseler
10020 Subak: deisì (Reinhold, review of Subak, column 23, deisi; Cerf deisi); Cremonesi: deïsi; Rosellini: deisi

```
              A li colpi q'e li veço doner,*
              No li val arme la monta d'un diner."
    10025  Dist Naimes, "El vos fala li penser; (530)
              Q'el est li Dainos, con tot li scuer."*
```

Rubric 294
Coment Naimes pa(r)ole a Karle, / Si li conta le nevelle de li D(a)n(o)is.
Laisse 295

```
              "Mon sire," dist Naimes, "entendés voiremant;
              Quel non è mie Aleris li valant,
              Qe l'oriaflame portò en primemant.
    10030  Le Daineseto è cil qe à tel ardimant, (535)
              Qe porta l'oriaflame et arer et avant.
              Scuer sont cil q'elo si destrançç;*
              A gran mervile el fer ben de cil brant."
              Li rois l'intende, si s'en va mervelant;
    10035  E si çurò sor li cor san Viçanç,* (540)
              Qe çivaler li farà novellemant;
              Por son amor elo n'adobarà çant.
              Dist Naimes, "Vu farì s(aç)emant."*
              Adonc li Dainois s'en retornò atant,
    10040  Qe li Sarasin e Turches e Persant (545)
              En Roma entrent dolant;
              Qe plus de mil en lasoit a·l canp.
```

Rubric 295
Coment l'oste s'en tornarent arer.
Laisse 296

```
              Li bon Dainois fu por li canpo alé,
              E li ses scuer avec lui sont alé,
    10045  Ferant qui Sarasin e davant e daré. (550)
```

10023 Subak: que li veço; Cremonesi, Rosellini: qe li veço

10026 Subak: Quel est; Rosellini: Qel est

Rubric 294 (after 10026) line 1: MS., Keller: parlole . . . karle. line 2: MS., Keller: neuelle . . . donais

10035 Cremonesi: sur li cor

10036 Subak: civaler (cf. Frati)

10038 Subak, Cremonesi, Rosellini: s[aç]emant

10039 Subak: a tant; Rosellini: Danois

Rubric 295 (after 10042) Keller: loste sen

Qe quant en fu en via trové,
Tot i furent morti, a martirio livré.* 57ᵛᵃ
Qui qi forent en orenga entré,
E questa fu Roma, la mirabel çité,
10050 A la tenda li rois i sonto desmonté. (555)
Li rois li guarda, oit Naimes apelé;
"Naimes," fait il, "dites moi verité:
Questa masnea q'è si ben coroé,
L'oriaflama i m'ont aporté.
10055 Qe vos deisés qe estoit sbaraté? (560)
Quel qi la porte me senbla de gran berné."
Dist dux Naimes, "Donc no le conosé?
Non è pais Aleris a qi la fu doné;
Anch'è·lo li Dainois, è li vestre scué,*
10060 Qe a 'Leris l'avoit de man saçé* (565)
Porq'elo la portava trainando soi daré;
Çestu oit le canpo vinto et aquité."
Dist li rois, "El oit ben ovré."
E li Dainois quando fu desmonté,
10065 Davant li rois estoit apresenté; (570)
Quant davant lui elo fo arosté,*
Avantqe moto el aust parlé
Elo se fu davant lui ençenolé,
E altament li oit salué:
10070 "Çentil rois, sire, vestra oriaflame prendé, (575)
Qe ves scuer si l'oit recovré.
Un autre fois a tel si la doné*

10046 MS., Subak, Rosellini: via; Cremonesi: via (emend for MS. *nia*)

10047 Subak, Cremonesi, Rosellini: Toti

10049 Subak: miràbel citè (cf. Frati)

10058 Subak: qui 'la

10059 Subak: Anch elo (Cerf: Anch è 'lo li Danois e li vestre scuè; Reinhold, review of Subak, column 21, Anch'è 'lo li Dainois . . . [or] Anche li Danois è li vestre scué); Cremonesi: Anch'elo li; Rosellini: Anch'elo li Dainois è li vestre

10060 MS.: Qe aleris; Subak: Que a Aleris (cf. Reinhold, review of Subak, column 21); Cremonesi: Qe Aleris; Rosellini: Qe [à] Aleris

10061 Subak: traïnando

10066 Subak: devant . . . fò apostè (Reinhold, review of Subak, column 22, MS. = aroste; emend = aresté); Frati, Cremonesi: davant . . . arosté; Rosellini: elo fo aresté (emend for *arosté*)

10069 Subak: salüe

10071 Subak: Vn (as always at the beginning of a line; commented no further)

10072 Cremonesi: Un'autre

Qe no sia coardo ne qe fuça aré,
Perdua estoit quando l'ò reçaté."
10075 Dist li rois, "Vu avì ben ovré. (580)
Dache l'avés in le canpo conquisté,
Da ora avanti ve soja otrié,
Qe por un altro vu non serì cançé.
A ves voloir la condué e mené."
10080 E quel le dist, "Mile marçé n'açé." (585)
E Naimes le dist, "Ben l'avés esploité;
Poisqe l'avés donea e delivré,
L'oriaflame non doit eser avilé.
Colu qe la doit porter doit eser adobé,
10085 E çivaler adobé e coroé." (590)
Dist li rois, "El me ven ben a gre;
Tot les autres qe son d(e) sa masné,*
Por son amor seran tot adobé."
Quant li Dainois li oit asculté,
10090 Plu fo·lo çojoso cha se le fust doné (595)
Toto l'onor d'una bona çité;
Por ses conpagni plu qe de lu asé.

Rubric 296
Coment s(e) conta de Karlo.*
Laisse 297

De una ren, segnur, siés certan,
Qe Karlo el maine uncha no fo vilan;
10095 Ne mais no servì ad omo a ingan. (600)   57vb
A li prodomes no fu mie da luitan,*
A li povres çivaler qe estoit en achan,*
Doner li fasoit e de·l vin e de·l pan,
Siq'elo li fasoit toti quant çojan.

10076 Cremonesi: Da che (as always)
10079 Subak; condüe; Rosellini: mené» (no period at end of line)
10081 Rosellini: espolité (corrected Plouzeau: read *esploité*)
10087 MS.: son dae sa; Subak: da sa; Frati: de; Cremonesi, Rosellini: de sa
10089 Rosellini: Danois
10090 Subak: fò 'lo; Cremonesi: fo-lo; Rosellini: fo 'lo
10091 Subak: citè
Rubric 296 (after line 10092) MS.: soeconta? ; Subak: sò dontà; Cremonesi: se conta (emend for *so)*; Keller, Rosellini: se conta
10096 MS., Cremonesi, Rosellini: da luitan; Subak: dà luitan

10100 Li ses nemisi q'era mal Cristian (605)
Elo metea en dolo et en torman;
Tanto li dotava Sarasin e Persan
Como fasoit ne lion ni serpan.
A li Dainese donò arme e guarniman
10105 Por son amor ne fe adober çan; (610)
Qe çascun avoit çinto li bran,
Qe scuer furent apelé de ilec in avan.*
Qe dapois çascun fo si valan,
Q'i no dotava ni rois ni amiran.

Rubric 297
Coment (K)*arlo* fi le Danois çivaler, / E tot (li) altri scuer.*
Laisse 298

10110 Quant Karlo oit fato qui çivaler (615)
Por le conseil dux Naimes de Baiver,
Çascun de ceus c'oit pris corer,
A gran mervile dapois se fe priser;
En tota l'oste n'estoit milor çivaler.
10115 Gran dolo oit Karlo maino l'inperer, (620)
Por Çofré de Paris e por li altri çivaler.
Qe estoient amena presoner.
Se li rois oit dol, non è da merviler.
Or laseron de Karlo, si vos averon conter,
10120 Coment Karaolo se retornò arer. (625)
Avec lui Sandonio, qi est pro e ber;
En Paganie ne sonto milor çivaler.
Li soldan le prist a desrasner,
Coment ont fato là defor a·l çostrer. (630)
10125 E cil le dient, "Françés son pro e fer;
Meltri çivaler ne se poroit trover;
Molto n'oit ad aste a ferir et a capler,
Si m'ont mort mon corant destrer.

10101 Subak: e en torman (corrected Reinhold, review of Subak, column 22 [under l. 606], Frati)
10109 Rosellini: Qi no
Rubric 297 (after verse 10109) line 1: MS.: k.; Keller: çiualer. line 2: MS., Keller: tot .k.; Subak: tot *cento*; Cremonesi: tot çento; Rosellini: tot cento
10113 Cremonesi: da pois
10123 Subak: ad esrasner; Cremonesi: a derasner; Rosellini: à derasner (cf. 10132)
10124 Subak: la defor; Cremonesi, Rosellini: là defor

Enfances Ogier le Danois

```
             A molto gran poine da lor me potì sevrer."
   10130    Dist li soldan, "Nu avon presoner." (635)
             Adonc se le fait avanti lui amener;
             Quando le vi le prist a derasner,
             "Segnur," fait il, "estes vos çivaler,
             O d'altra jent qe soja soldaer?"*
   10135    Çofré le dist, qe parlò en primer, (640)
             "Sarasin, sire, ne vos le do nojer;
             En l'ost Karlo, qi est enperer,
             No se poroit trover nul soldaer.
             Çascun serve li rois de grez e volunter,
   10140    A son espese cun arme e destrer; (645)
             Qi mejo po se fait plus priser."
             Dist li rois, "Quest'è ben da graer                   58ra
             Oltra la mer entro Turs et Ascler,
             Molto l'ò oldu loer et apriser;
   10145    Et avec lui tuti so çivaler. (650)
             Gran peçé fait quant se lasa ençegner,
             Croir celu qe no li po aider."
             Dist Çofré, "Vu avì mala sper;
             No val Macon la monta d'un diner,
   10150    Se no por l'oro dont le faites acesmer." (655)
```

Rubric 298
Coment li Soldam parlò.*
Laisse 299

```
             Li rois soldan si le mist por rason:
             "Cristian, sire, tu me par ben saçes hon;
             Karlo, ton sir, el è de gran renon."*
             "Oil voir, sire, nul meltre no saçon;
   10155    Bon çivaler est, un d·i milor de·l mon. (660)
```

10132 cf. 10123
10134 Subak, Cremonesi, Rosellini: Od altra
10136 Subak: dò noier
10137 Subak, Rosellini: qui est
10142 Subak: Quest'è ben d'agraer; Cremonesi, Rosellini: Quest' è ben da graer
10150 Subak: por loro
Rubric 298 (after 10150) MS.: soldam; Subak, Cremonesi, Rosellini: Soldam (cf. Plouzeau)
10154 Subak: O il voir (Reinhold, review of Subak, column 22, also corrects); Cremonesi: Oïl (as always)

           Si oit en sa masné de molto çe*n*til hon
           Qe a lui serve por soa reençon,
           Qe volu*n*tera voit a risa et a te*n*çon
           Ver Sarasin de la loi de Macon.
10160   E quisti son Françés e Bergognon, (665)
           Qe tent l'autre jent tota qua*n*t a bricon."*
           Dist li soldan, "E nu questo savron:*
           Qe un mesaço l'invojarò de randon,
           Savoir se in sa cort aust du de·l renon
10165   Qe co*n*batre volust cu*n* du me canpion (670)
           Por tal co*n*vento cu*n* nu vos co*n*taron:
           S'i me serà vençu, nu Roma lasaron;
           Si pasaren oltra mer sens tençon.
           E se li so è vi*n*ti, nu altro no*n* queron,
10170   Q'el torni arer, lui e ses baron. (675)
           El è ben mejo qe dos parta sta tençon
           Cha el ge mora tanti çentil hon."
           Dist Çofré, "Quest'è droita rason;
           S'e fose fora de la vestra preson,
10175   Eo voria eser un de qui ca*n*pion." (680)

Rubric 299
Coment Soldam mandò a K*arlo* li me(s)açer.*
Laisse 300

           Li rois soldan non demorò nojant;
           Por li co*n*seil de le ses amirant,
           Un mesaçer oit apelé erant:
           "Va·t'en," fait il, "a li rois de li Franc.
10180   Di·li da ma part, q'eo si le mant, (685)

10161 Subak, Rosellini: quanta bricon
10163 Subak: li' nvoiarò
10167 Cremonesi: S'i me' (as always for MSI *miei*, masc. pl. possessive; cf. du me', l. 10165; not noted again)
10171 Subak: E l' è ben; Reinhold, review of Subak, col. 22, El è b. m., Cerf: El è
10174 Subak: S' e'
10175 Subak: èser
Rubric 299 (after 10175) MS.: mers'aç (abbreviation line above the final *ac*); Subak: mensaç*er* (Reinhold, review Subak, column 22, mesaçer); Cremonesi: mensaçer; Rosellini: mesaçer. MS., Subak, Cremonesi, Rosellini: soldam (cf. Plouzeau re consistency of capitalization)
10179 Subak: Và-t' en; Cremonesi: Va-t-en; Rosellini: Vaten
10180 Subak: Dì-li; Cremonesi: Di'-li; Rosellini: Dili

　　　　Se çest pla vol definir a·l presant,
　　　　Qe elo prenda du de ses co*n*batant,
　　　　De le milor e de le plus valant.
　　　　Et eo si averò du d·i me ensemant;
10185　Du contra dos çostrerà a li canp. (690)
　　　　S'i me serà vi*n*ti ni recreant,
　　　　Roma laserò sença . . . de brant,*
　　　　Si m'en andarò oltra en Jerusalant.
　　　　E s'i so è vi(n)çu, el farà altretant:*　　　　　　　　58ʳᵇ
10190　Si tornerà en França et en Proanç.* (695)
　　　　Et in tal mo faremo acordamant;
　　　　Nen io ne lu no le perderen nojant."
　　　　Dist li mesajes, "Farò li ves comant;
　　　　Ben le dirò ço qe a l'ovra apant."
10195　E cil mesaçer fu saçes e valant; (700)
　　　　Nen volse pais demorer tant ni quant.
　　　　Desor un palafroi el mo*n*ta erant;
　　　　Ne finò pais enfina a l'oste d·i Franc.
　　　　O·l trove li rois, ilec el desant.
10200　Un damisel pris li mulet anblant; (705)
　　　　E le dux N*aimes* por me la man li prant.
　　　　Davant li rois el si le present;
　　　　Li rois le vi, si l'apele primemant,
　　　　S'il est mesaçer, o ho*n* d'altro co*n*vant.
10205　E cil le dist, "Ne vos çelo niant; (710)
　　　　Mesaçer sui de le riçe rois soldant,
　　　　Li meltre rois qe soja en Oriant.
　　　　Soa anbasea e ço qe li apant,*
　　　　E vos dirò ben e lojalmant;
10210　Ne vo·l falderò par nul ren vivant." (715)
　　　　Dist li rois, "Vu farì gran siant,
　　　　Qe mesaçer po ben dir son talant."

　　　10184 Subak, Rosellini: du di me; Cremonesi: du di me'
　　　10187 Subak, Rosellini: sença [colp] de brant; Cremonesi: sença de brant
　　　10189 MS.: viçu; Subak, Cremonesi: vi[n]çu (emend), Rosellini: E s'i so è viçu
　　　10198 Cremonesi: en fina
　　　10199 Subak, Rosellini: O 'l; Cremonesi: O ' l
　　　10201 Subak: Pormè; Cremonesi: por me'
　　　10204 Rosellini: s'i, with an inverted apostrophe. Subak: ho*m* (Reinhold, review Subak, column 23, correction); Rosellini: hom
　　　10208 Subak: è ço; Reinhold, review Subak, column 22 and Cerf: e ço (and no period at the end of verse); Cremonesi: e co. Rosellini: li arpant
　　　10210 Subak, Cremonesi: vo 'l; Rosellini: vo'l

Rubric 300
Coment parole li mesaçer.*
Laisse 301

     Dist il, li mesaço, "E no vos quer nojer.*
     De li rois soldan eo son mesaçer;
10215 Elo vos mande, e no vos do nojer, (720)
     Se in vestra oste fose du çivaler,
     Qe por arme se volese far priser,
     Contra du d·i so volist en canpo çostrer.
     Dos contra dos, questo pla adefiner,*
10220 Por tel convento con vos saverò deviser. (725)
     Se li so en vinti, el s'en vol aler,*
     Con soa jent pasar oltra mer,
     Si v'avrà Roma tot in aquito laser;
     Ne no lì remarà Sarasin ni Escler.
10225 E se li ves è vi(n)ti, vu averés retorner (730)
     En dolçe França cun li ves çivaler.
     Mei è qe du cun dos deça ste pla adefiner,
     Qe meter a morir cento mil çivaler."
     Li rois l'oì, si le parse strainer,
10230 Quela ovre si de leve acreenter,* (735)
     Qe se li so perdese gran seroit li danger;
     Se Roma deust eser senpre d·i Escler.
     Quant Naimes oì quel mesaçer,
     El dist a·l roi, "Ben est da 'creenter!
10235 Milor novela no demando ni quer; (740)

    Rubric 300 (after 10212) Cremonesi: parole (emend for MS. *paroie*)
    10213 Subak: DIs cil, „Li mesaço . . . ; Cremonesi: Dist il: "Li mesaço . . . ; Rosellini: Dist il: «Li mesaço e . . . '
    10214 Rosellini: eo so
    10215 Cremonesi: e' no . . . (as always for *eo*)
    10219 MS., Subak, Cremonesi: pla a definer; Reinhold, review Subak, column 22, pla definer (emend); Rosellini: pla definer
    10225 MS. viti; Subak, Cremonesi, Rosellini: è vi[n]ti (cf. l. 10189)
    10227 Subak: Mei' è . . . adefiner (no note)
    10228 Subak: mèter
    10229 Subak: oï; Cremonesi: oï (as always; not noted again for either)
    10230 Rosellini: si le deve (emend)
    10232 Subak: deüst èser
    10234 Subak: d'acreenter (but cf. l. 10230); Cremonesi, Rosellini: da creenter

Mei è q'el mora dos sol çivaler,
Qe cento mile metere a justisier. 58ᵛᵃ
Otrié·li, rois, ço q'el demanda e quer,*
Et eo serò un de qui çivaler."
10240 "Non serì," dist li rois, "par tot l'or de Baiver." (745)
A ste parole, eco dos baçaler,
Qe de novelo preso ont li corer:
Ço fo le Dainese, qe s'apela Uçer,
E l'altro fo Çarloto, qe estoit pro e ber,
10245 E si fo filz de K*arlo* de sa prima muler.* (750)
Quisti dient a·l roi qe in don i requer
Questa bataila fare e definer,
Contra li dos de la loi averser.
Dist li rois, "De l'un vojo otrier;
10250 Ma vu Çarloto, alez vos repolser, (755)
Tropo estes vos çovençel, aler a tornojer;*
E guardés ben, ne ve olda plu parler."
Çarloto l'olde, cuita li seno cançer.
"Pere," fait il, "donc me tenés lainer?
10255 Plu de·l Dainois me faites aviler. (760)
Ma d'una ren nen serò mençoner;
Qe demanes prenderò mo*n* corer,
En Roma alirò a li soldan parler.
E s'el vorà a mon co*n*sei(l) ovrer,*
10260 El me farà un de qui dos çivaler (765)
Qe avec li vos vignirà a çostrer."
Li rois l'olde, pris le vis enbronçer;
Ni ben ni mal no li respo*n*de arer.
Naimes l'olde, si le prist a guarder;
10265 Dist a li rois, "Quest'è grant destorber; (770)
Quest'è ben colse da dever otrier."

10236 Cremonesi: qe 'l mora
10237 Subak: mètere
10238 Subak: Otrie li; Cremonesi: Otrie-li; Rosellini: Otrie li rois ço . . .
10242 Rosellini: preso ot
10251 Subak: aler atornoier; Rosellini: çonvençel
10256 Rosellini: mançoner
10259 Subak: E se 'l . . . ; Cremonesi, Rosellini: E s'el. MS.: cōseit; Subak, Cremonesi, Rosellini: conseil

Rubric 301
Coment N*aimes* parole.*
Laisse 302

  Quant N*aimes* oit entendu l'infant,
  Tot airés e plen de maltalant,
  Elo parole, dist a li rois posant,
10270 "Çentil rois, sire, veez li ves enfant, (775)
  Qe vos demanda la bataile p*ri*memant,*
  Con li Dainois eser a·l torniemant
  Verso qui dos pain de la lo mescreant?*
  Se vu li otriés, elo s'en fa çojant,
10275 Colsa como no, dise apertemant (780)
  Qe in Roma alirà a l'amirant,
  Da la part serà de Turs e de Persant.
  Nen vos plaça mie de perder ves enfant,
  Qe ço q'elo dist, tuto l'oit en talant."
10280 Li rois l'oldì; par poi d'ire no*n* fant. (785)
  Por li conseil N*aimes*, li guanto li rant,
  De la bataile qe ben le virent çant*
  Li qual ne furent grami e dolant,
  Qe se dotent de lui porqe estoit si enfant.
10285 Se Çarloto oit çoie, nesuno non demant; (790)   58vb
  En soa vite el no fo si çojant.
  E li rois parole a·l mesaçer en ojant:
  "Va·t'en ami, non demorer nojant,
  E dì a ton sir q'eo si le mant,
10290 E si le otriò tuto li son comant. (795)
  Du contra dos, sença altro ho*n* vivant,
  Por lialté, sença nul tradimant."

  10268 Subak: aïrès
  10272 Subak: èser
  10273 Subak: la lo[i]; Cerf, Cremonesi: la lo'
  10275 Subak: c'omo no (corrected Cerf: colsa como no); cf. Cremonesi, Rosellini: Colsa como no
  10276 Subak: a l'almirant (corrected Reinhold, review Subak, column 22, Frati: a l'amirant (emend)); Rosellini: à l'almirant
  10278 Subak: pèrder
  10284 Subak: porquè; Cremonesi, Rosellini: por qe (as always; not commented further)
  10288 Subak: „Va-t'en . . . ; Cremonesi: Va-t-en; Rosellini: Vaten
  10291 Guessard: hom

```
              Dist li mesaço, "Vu parlé saçemant.
              Només li terme quando serà a·l canp."
    10295     Dist li rois, "Deman a l'aube aparisant."* (800)
              Li mesaçer non demanda plu nojant;
              Arer s'en torne e legro e çojant.
              El entre en Rome, a li palés desant;
              O vi li rois, por rason li demant.
    10300     Tuto li conte, ço qe a l'ovra apant. (805)
```

Rubric 302
Coment li mesoço retorne.
Laisse 303

```
              "Çentil rois, sire, saça por verité,
              Qe li François son çente ben adoté.
              Vestre mesaço ont molto agraé,
              Si como jent ben saça e dotriné.
    10305     La bataila ert, si ert ben acreenté; (810)
              Dos damisé de novelo adobé,
              Qe a moi apare eser de gran berné
              De la bataile ont li guanto pié.
              Deman a l'aube seran adobé,
    10310     A li pre serà sença nul falsité." (815)
              Dist li soldan, "Questo m'è ben a gre.
              Qi prenderà sta bataile contra li batezé?"
              Dist Karaolo, "E son aparilé."
              Da l'altra part fu Sa(n)donio levé;
    10315     Quisti dos ont quel ovra otrié, (820)
              E de far la bataile ont li guant pié.
              En Paganie ni oltra la mer salé,
              Dos milor nen seroit reçaté,*
              Ne de bataile fust plu adoté.
    10320     Le enperer de Françe mal se fu conselé (825)
```

10295 Subak: al'aube; Reinhold, review Subak, column 22: a l'aube (correction)
10298 Subak: Rome e a (cf. Frati); Rosellini: Rome e à . . .
Rubric 302 (after 10300) MS., Keller: mesoço; Subak, Cremonesi, Rosellini: mesaço (emend for *mesaço*)
10314 MS.: Sadonio; Subak: Sa[n]donio (emend); Cremonesi: Sadonio; Rosellini: Sandonio
10315 Subak, Cremonesi: quel' ovra
10316 Rosellini: guat; cf. Plouzeau. Subak: pïè
10318 Cremonesi: seroie

Quant a son fil elo oit otrié
De far quela bataile contra tel amiré.
Ma li rois li otrie, veçando sa volunté,
Qe dapoi en fu dolant *et* abosmé.
10325 Nen fust N*aimes* qe l'oit conselé, (830)
Par nul ren no li fust li guanto doné;
Daq'el è fato, non serà st(r)atorné.*
Tuto quel çorno i ont seçorné,
E tuta la noit como fu longa e le.
10330 A la deman quan l'aube fu levé, (835)
Li Dainois no à l'ovra oblié.
Nian Çarloto non remist daré;
Çascun si s'arme e prende ses coré.   59ra

Rubric 303
Coment s'ar(maient) (çivaler).
Laisse 304

Li dos damisé prendent ses corer;
10335 N*aimes*, le dux de·l ducha de Baiver, (840)
Ad arme prendere d'anbi li baçaler.
Le muniscoit coment deveroit ovrer,
Quando seront a·l ferir e çostrer.
Dist li Danois, "Quel pla lasez ester."
10340 Adoncha montent anbidos a destrer; (845)
Li rois li otria a li canpo aler;
E cil le font, sença nul entarder.
E Karaolo e Sandonio li Ascler,
D'arme prendre se vont a 'pariler.
10345 Çascun veste l'aubers e calça le ganber; (850)
Alaça li elmi, çinse li brandi d'açer;

10321 Rosellini: elo otrie (missing *oit*)
10323 Subak: ueçando (cf. Reinhold, review Subak, column 23)
10324 7 for *et*
10327 MS.: statorne; Subak: stratornè (emend); Reinhold, review Subak, column 22: st[r]atornè, Cremonesi, Rosellini: st[r]atorné (emend)
Rubric 303 (after 10333) MS., Keller: sarimaient; Subak, Cremonesi: s'armaient (emend); Rosellini: s'armaient. MS.: çivavler; Keller: çiualer; Subak, Cremonesi: çivaler (emend); Rosellini: çivalar
10336 Subak: prèndere
10340 Subak: anbi dos (as always)
10344 Subak, Cremonesi, Rosellini: vont apariler

	Posa montent sor li corant destrer.
	E li soldan li voit a*n*vojer,
	Trois a li canpo o dovent çostrer.
10350	Dist Karaolo, "E vos vojo nonçer,* (855)
	Se ne veisés oncir e desmenbrer,
	No ne venés secorer ni aider."
	Dist li soldan, "Ne vos estoit doter."
	Arere torne, si le lasa ester.
10355	Karaolo fu molto sajes in la lo averser; (860)
	O vi li Danois si·l prist ad apeler:
	"Çivaler, sire, dites moi veriter;
	En la cort K*arlo* avez nul mester?"
	Dist li Danois, "Eo fu so scuer,*
10360	Ma por sa cortexia fato m'à çivaler, (865)
	Si m'à doné soa ensegna a porter.
	E questo altro, qe veez qui ester,
	Filz est li rois de·l maino enperer;
	Non è a·l mondo ren q'elo aça plu çer."
10365	"Por la ma foi," ço dist Karoer, (870)
	"Quest'è una colsa q'è molto da graer!
	Quando son fil manda a nos çostrer,
	No ne ten mie coardi ni lainer.
	Nu saveron in tel modo deviser,*
10370	Enver de moi vu averì capler, (875)
	E quel enfant co*n* l'altro çivaler."
	Dist li Danois, "Ben est da otrier."
	Nen volse plus ni plaider ni tençer;
	De le canpo se done li trato d'un arçer.
10375	L'un contra l'altro lasent li destrer,* (880)
	E fait ses lances brandir e palmojer.
	Grant colpi se fer a·l primer encontrer,
	Qe le tarçe font fe(n)dere e peçojer.
	Fort fu li aubers, ne le pote desmajer;
10380	Tot le aste fait in troncon voler, (885)

10355 Subak: lo[i]; Cremonesi: lo'; Rosellini: lo. Cf. 10273 above.
10356 Rosellini: prist apeler. Subak, Cremonesi: si 'l
10366 Subak: d'agraer
10369 Subak, Cremonesi, Rosellini: Nu s'averon
10378 MS.: federe; Cremonesi, Rosellini: fe[n]dere (emend); Subak: fè[n]dere (emend)
10379 Subak: potè
10380 Subak: tronçon (emend)

Ne l'un por l'autre no se pl(o)ja en destrer.* 59rb
Quant le aste son fraite, i tra li bra*n*t d'açer;
L'un contra l'autre ven fort cun cengler.

Rubric 304
Coment fu grant la bataille.*
Laisse 305

      Defor de Rome en le pre verdojant
10385 Fo la bataile mervilosa e grant. (890)
      Rois Karaolo si oit traito li brant;
      Fer li Dainois desor l'elmo lusant.
      Quanto ne prende, elo·l çeta a·l canp;
      Deo le guarì, quant in carne no li prant.*
10390 Gran fo li colpo, merviloso e pesant; (895)
      E de maile trença plus de çant.
      Trois in l'erbeta est avalé li brant;
      Ne li Danois no se smaja niant.
      El ten la spea a·l pomo d'or lusant;
10395 Fer Karaolo un colpo si pesant, (900)
      De l'elmo no trençe la monta d'un besa(n)t.*
      Ma li colpo fo merveliso e grant,
      Q'elo·l fe enbronçer sor li col de l'aufera*n*t;
      Par un petit ne li çitò a·l canp.*
10400 D'altra part fu Sandonio li posant, (905)
      Con Çarloto a le spee trençant.
      L'un ferì l'altro e menu e sovant;
      Le armaure se trençoit tot davant.
      Li un por l'altro no s'apresia un guant;
10405 Ma Sindonio si era plu manant; (910)
      Par un petit ne·l fasea recreant.
      Quant li Danois s'en vait apercevant,
      E vi Çarloto en pena et in tormant,

    10381 MS.: pleia; Subak, Cremonesi, Rosellini: se ploia
    10382 Subak: trà
    10388 Subak, Cremonesi, Rosellini: elo 'l (cf. 10398)
    10389 Subak, Cremonesi: guarì; Rosellini: guari
    10393 Rosellini: no 's'esmaia
    10396 MS.: besat; Subak, Cremonesi, Rosellini: besa[n]t (emend)
    10398 Subak, Cremonesi, Rosellini: elo 'l
    10401 Subak, Cremonesi, Rosellini: l'espee
    10404 Subak: aprèsia

Enfances Ogier le Danois

```
          E cil Sandonio l'andava si adestant,*
10410  Qe enver de lui n'aust de mort guarant. (915)
          Quant li Danois le voit, paure oit de l'infant;
          El lasava Karaolo, a Sandonio vait corant,
          E si le feria e menu e sovant,
          Qe a Çarloto dava res(t)oramant.*
10415  Qe a celle fois se fasea en rer alquant.* (920)
          Quella bataile era si dura e pesant;
          Ne·l poria conter nesun hon vivant.
          Or entendés de li mal amirant,
          Ço fo li soldan malvasio recreant.
10420  Quando (vi) la bataile durer si longemant,* (925)
          De li ses çivaler se dotò feremant.
          Demantinent el pensò tradimant;
          Mille çivaler fa monter en auferant,
          Si le comande de aler a li canp
10425  Por prender li Francés o mener·se davant. (930)
          E qui li otrient, oltra son maltalant;*
          Quant se partent, q'i vont a li canp,*
          E li Dainois s'en vait aperçevant;
          Dist a Karaolo, "Fraita è vestra fianç;                59ᵛᵃ
10430  La foi de Turs non val mie un besant." (935)
          Karaolo, quant le vi, no fo ma si dolant.
```

  10409 Subak: Sandoio (corrected Frati); Subak, Cremonesi, Rosellini: si adestant
  10411 Cremonesi: paure (without her usual dieresis)
  10413 Subak: feri (emend) (corrected Reinhold [review Subak, column 22]: feria)
  10414 MS., Subak, Rosellini: resoramant; Cremonesi: res[t]orament (emend). Martin, correction to Rosellini: res[t]oramant
  10415 Subak: Que acelle
  10419 Subak: malvàsio
  10420 MS.: bataile durer; Subak, Rosellini: bataile dura (emend); Reinhold [review Subak, column 22]: [vi] la bataile . . . ; Cremonesi: bataile [vi] durer (emend)
  10425 Subak, Cremonesi, Rosellini: menerse
  10426 Subak, Rosellini: E quili (corrected Holtus [review Cremonesi, 444], and Martin: qui li)
  10427 Subak: qui vont; Rosellini: qi vont
  10430 Cremonesi: no val mie (corrected Holtus [review Cremonesi, 444])

Rubric 305
Coment Karoer vi venir la jent.*
Laisse 306

    Quant Karaolo vi venir q(ue)la je*n*t deslojal,*
    Li qual erent de li son general,*
    A gran mervile elo li ten por mal.
10435 Dist a Sandonio, "Li soldan à fato mal;* (940)
    En la bataile erames tot ogual,
    Quant le venimes anco en ste jornal.
    Mais li soldan si est deslojal;
    Ço q'el promis no*n* oit tenu a estal.*
10440 Mais en ma vite e no·l tirò lojal."* (945)

Rubric 306
Coment ensent de Rome li çivaler.
Laisse 307

    Le mil çivaler son de Roma ensu,
    A li dos çivaler sont sovracoru.
    E i le ont molto ben recevu;
    A·l primer colpo ont si ben feru
10445 Qe li Danois fo a tera abatu; (950)
    Qe son çival soto li fo cau;
    I le oncient i·me li pre erbu.
    Ma li Danois no fo mie esperdu;
    El ten la spea a·l pomo d'or batu.

    Rubric 305 (after 10431) Cremonesi: karoer. Keller: inuenir (for *vi venir*) (corrected Mussafia, "Handschriftliche Studien II": ui uenir); Reinhold (review Subak, column 22): veniz

    10432 MS.: venir qla; Subak: qu*e*la ie*n*t

    10435 Rosellini: «li soldan . . .

    10436 Subak: èrames

    10439 Rosellini: promis on oit (cf. Holden, "lire <u>non</u>")

    10440 Subak: e' n' olcirò loial (note: e' no 'l tirò loial (?)); Reinhold [review Subak, column 22]: correct to footnote reading; Cremonesi: e' no 'l tirò; Rosellini: no'l tirò

    Rubric 306 (after 10440) Keller: çiualer

    10442 Subak, Cremonesi, Rosellini: sovra coru

    10446 Subak, Cremonesi: caü

    10447 MS.: i me (no titulus); Subak: imè (Reinhold [review Subak, column 22]: i[n] mè); Cremonesi: i[n] mé (emend); Rosellini: i me

10450 Tot li primer qe il oit conseu, (955)
       Trois en l'arçon elo l'oit fendu.
       E fer un altro, si le oit li çevo tolu;*
       E qui li lançent li gran dard amolu;
       O voja o no i l'ont prendu.
10455 Quando Çarloto vi ço qe ert avenu, (960)
       E vide ben q'el no è secoru,
       De soi defendre n'oit penser metu.
       Via s'en fuit a força et a vertu,
       Trosqua a l'oste no à rena tenu.
10460 Karlo le vi, a rason l'oit metu: (965)
       "De le Danois, qe est adevenu?"
       E cil le dist, "Nu l'avemo perdu;
       Qe da mile pain nos fumes asalu.
       Encontra lor non aumes vertu;
10465 Li Danois si fo preso e retenu. (970)
       Et eo perço si m'en sonto venu,
       Qe dever qui pain e no fu secoru."
       Dist li rois, "Se ma creça en Jesu,
       Vu ne serés por la gorça apendu."

Rubric 307
(Ç)o qe fi Kar(o)er.*
Laisse 308

10470 A gran mervile fo prodomo Karoer; (975)
       Quant li Danois vi prender e liger,
       Contra son gre en Roma mener,
       Tel dol n'oit cuita li seno cançer.
       Sa lieltà el non volse falser;
10475 Nen dist mie de retornar arer, (980)   59vb
       Ançi, civalça droito por li senter,
       A l'oste Karlo e Naimes de Baiver.
       Davant Karlo se vait presenter:

10450 Subak, Cremonesi: conseü
10466 Subak: perçò; Cremonesi, Rosellini: per ço
10468 Subak: creçà
10469 Rosellini: ependu
Rubric 307 (after 10469) MS., Keller: Co . . . karer; Subak: Ço . . . Karer (emend);
Cremonesi: Ço . . . Kar[o]er (emend for *Co . . . Karer*); Rosellini: Ço . . . Karer
10471 Subak: prènder

"Bon rois," fait il, "je son ves presoner.
10480 Dapoiqe li soldan non est droiturer, (985)
A vos me rendo cun arme e destrer,
Qe quelo qe li soldan faroit de li ves presoner,
Facés de moi, e vos vojo en projer."
Li rois l'intent, molto le prist a loer;
10485 A·l pavilon li fait desendre e desmonter, (990)
A le dux Naimes le fait aconvojer,
Qe altament le prist ad honorer.
E li rois Karlo, tant fu de mal penser,*
Qe no li valt ni amor ni projer;
10490 Q'elo vol Zarloto far apiçer. (995)
E ça l'avoit fato prender e liger,
Davant la façe li ocli enbinder.
Ne le valea projer ni losenger,
Qe de son cor le poust remuer.
10495 Quant Naimes si n'oit prega Karoer, (1000)
Q'elo le diça a li rois demander,
Qe in don elo le diça doner,
Karoer responde, "De greç e volunter."
Davant li rois se vait ençenoler:
10500 "Ai, çentil rois, eo son ves presoner, (1005)
E si son rois clama amirer,
De un reame d'oltra l'aigua de mer.
E vos vojo un don ademander,
Qe vu Çarloto me diça doner,
10505 Qe davanti vos ben le poso escuser. (1010)
S'elo s'avè de li canpo desevrer*
E·l vojo çuçer q'el fe si cun ber,
Qe li soldan si cun malvasio lainer
La lialtà el vos avè falser."*

10480 Cremonesi, Rosellini: Da poi qe; Subak: Dapoi que
10483 Cremonesi, Rosellini: enproier
10486 Subak: a convoier
10488 Subak, Rosellini: malpenser
10491 MS.: çalanott; Subak, Cremonesi, Rosellini: E ça l'avoit
10504 Subak: diçà
10506, 10509 Subak, Cremonesi, Rosellini: s'ave
10507 Cremonesi: E' 'l
10508 Subak: malvàsio
10509 Subak, Rosellini: el vos; Reinhold [review Subak, column 22], Cremonesi: el nos

10510 Li rois reguarde ferament Karoer, (1015)
E si le dist, "Ben li val vestra projer.
Non è hon in France ni Puile ni Baiver,*
Qe de ste don poust vanter,*
Or le prendés, si le faites deslojer;
10515 Ma ben se guardi plu de far tel mester, (1020)
Anci se lasi tot le menbre couper,
Q'elo s'en fuça par un sol çivaler."

Rubric 308
Coment Çarloto fo çuçés.
Laisse 309

Çarloto fu delivrés da li stacon pendant;
Nen fust Karoer, par tot l'or de Brusbant
10520 Nen fust scanpé, nen fust apendu a·l vant. (1025)
Ma la marçé Deo, li per roimant,
El est delivré da mort e da tormant.
Dist Karoer, "Bon roi, ora m'entant
Qe un mesaçer me faites venir davant;
10525 Mandar dir vojo a·l soldan un poi de mon talant." (1030)
Dist li rois, "Vu parlé saçemant."
Adonc un mesajes li fo mené a·l presant;
Karoer quant le vi, si le dist en ojant:
"Mesaçer, frer, eo si te comant,
10530 Qe tu entri en Rome demanes a·l presant. (1035)
A li soldan dirà certanemant,
Se demane sença termen prendant,*
El no m'envoie li presoner tot quant,
Eo renegaroie Macon e Trevigant;
10535 Crerò en Deo, prenderò bateçamant: (1040)
Mai en ma vite ne le serò so benvojant;
E si le dì, no li çeler de nojant,
Qe presoner sui de l'inperer d·i Franc."*
Dist li mesaço, "No ne doté niant;*
10540 L'anbasea farò e ben e lojalmant." (1045)

60ra

10512 Subak, Cremonesi: Baiver; Rosellini: ò hon . . . Baiver
10513 Subak, Rosellini: d'este
10521 Subak: roïmant
10532 Subak: damane (for MS. *doemane*); Rosellini: damane (emend for MS. *daimane*); Cremonesi: demane (emend for MS. *daemane*)
10533 Rosellini: envoioe

Rubric 309
Coment s'en vait li mesaçer.
Laisse 310

       Li mesaçer no fo pais demoré;*
       Da Karoer oit conçé demandé.
       El ven a Rome, entrò en la çité;
       A li palés oit li soldan trové,
10545 Qe li preson li estoit davant mené. (1050)
       Si durament li avoit menaçé,
       S'i no renojese la loi de le son Dé,
       Apendu seroit, et a forçes levé.
       Quant li mesaço li fu davant alé,
10550 Tot primement li oit salué;* (1055)
       E pois le dist, "Bon rois, or m'e(n)tendé;
       Mesaçer sui, a vos son envojé
       Da part Karaolo, qe rois est coroné.
       Elo vos mande, ne vos serà çelé,
10555 Qe li rois Karlo si l'oit enpresoné, (1060)
       Par son voloir e por sa volunté.
       Elo ve fa asavoir, se vu no le envojé*
       Li presoner qe v'è sta amené
       Elo renegarà Macometo son dé.
10560 En Deo crerà se serà batezé; (1065)
       Nen serà ma ves dru ni ves privé."
       Li soldan quan l'olde, tuto fo trapensé;
       Dist Sandonio, "Bon rois, torto avé.*
       Non est mervele se il est airé,
10565 Quant contra nos faistes deslialté. (1070)
       Men esiant, ela fo falsité*

    Rubric 309 (after 10540) Keller: senuait
    10542 Cremonesi: domandé (cf. Holtus [rev. Cremonesi])
    10543 Cremonesi: entro
    10547 Subak, Rosellini: Si no . . .
    10550 Subak: salüè
    10551 MS.: etende; Subak: entendè; Frati, Cremonesi: e[n]tendé (emend); Rosellini: entendé
    10557 Subak, Cremonesi: a savoir; Rosellini: asavoir
    10558 Subak: ve stà; Cremonesi: v'è sta'
    10563 Subak, Cremonesi: Dist li Sandonio
    10564 Subak: aïrè
    10565 Rosellini: faites
    10566 MS.: ela fo falsite; Subak: è la to falsité (Reinhold [review Subak, column 22]: fo falsité); Rosellini: è la to falsité; Cremonesi: ela fo falsité (misquoted by Rosellini, "elo")

          Qe in nostra vite nu seren avilé;
          Ora en faites la soa volunté."
          Dist li rois, "Dapoiq'el vos agré,
10570 Eo ne farò la vostra volunté." (1075)
          E li soldan si fo saço e doté;*   60rb
          Avantiqe li presoner li fust envojé,
          Molto richament furent coroé,
          De riche robe, de manté aflubé.
10575 Tot ses arme li furent delivré, (1080)
          E bon destrer corant (e) abravé.*
          E quant de Roma i furent desevré,
          Sandonio fo a palafroi monté;
          A plus de mil li ont aconvojé;
10580 Trosqua a l'oste non à rena tiré.* (1085)
          Li rois le vi, molto s'en fu mervelé;
          Tot li baron qe erent asenblé,
          Contra li vont tot çojant e lé.
          Ma no fo çoja veua ni esguardé,
10585 Como s'ont fato quant se sont encontré; (1090)
          Ma desor tuti fu Sandonio honoré.

Rubric 310
Coment retornent in Rome.
Laisse 311

          Grant fu la çoja, mervilosa e plener,
          Quando Françeis vede li presoner.
          E Karoer si dist a l'inperer,
10590 "Çentil rois, sire, de vos me poso lolder; (1095)
          Ben dist voir li Turchi e li Ascler,
          Qe vos estes li meltro rois qe se posa trover.
          Se non creist la mia lois falser,
          Eo me faroie bateçer e laver.
10595 Eo m'en andarò a mon segnor parler; (1100)
          A la deman, quan l'aube serà cler,
          Vu farés ves çivaler monter;
          Et eo averò prender mon corer,

    10569 Subak: Dapoi qu'el; Cremonesi, Rosellini: Da poi q'el
    10571 Subak, Rosellini: saçe
    10574 Subak: mante; Cremonesi: mante'
    10576 MS.: a cabrave; Subak: acabravè (Reinhold [review Subak, column 22]: e abravé, emend); Cremonesi, Rosellini: cabravé
    10584 Subak: vëua; Cremonesi: veüa
    10593 Subak, Cremonesi: creïst

Cun Sandonio seremo a li çostrer."
10600 Dist li rois, "Et eo li vojo otrier. (1105)
Ma d'una ren e vos vojo en projer;
Qe a·l soldan deça dir e nonçer,
Q'elo lasi plu de far quel mester,
Q'elo no se perten a rois ni amirer:
10605 Par nul ençegno traimento mener." (1110)
Dist Karaolo, "E l'ò ben en penser."
Conçé el prist, si se m<is> ad aler;*
Avec lui . . . li altri çivaler,*
Qe con Sandonio era venu a convojer
10610 Li Danois e li altri presoner. (1115)
Quant fu en Rome se vait ad hostaler,
E posa vait a li palés monter.
Li soldan vi Karaolo, prist so a vergogner,
E Karaolo si le prist a parler:
10615 "O çentil rois, qe tant estes pro e ber, (1120)
En vestra vite perdu avés ves loer,
Qe homo traites non è pais da priser.
E son esté en l'oste l'inperer;
De vos oldì boni e re parler,   60ᵛᵃ
10620 Li rois meesme (s)i ve n'avè blasmer,* (1125)
Et ensement dux Naimes de Baiver,
Le milor dux qe se poust trover.
Ne vos poria ne dir ni conter
Como i me ont fato servir et honorer.
10625 Da part de Karlo, e vos do en projer, (1130)
Qe de trair vu lasa li mester;
Lasa 'n avanti tot le menbre couper,*

10600 Subak: Otrïer (as always)
10601 Subak: en proier; Cremonesi, Rosellini: enproier
10605 Subak, Cremonesi: Traïmento
10606 Subak, Cremonesi: E' l' ò
10607 Subak, Cremonesi, Rosellini: si se mis
10609 Subak, Cremonesi: venu aconvoier; Rosellini: à convoier
10610 Rosellini: Donois
10613 Subak, Cremonesi: so[i] (emend)
10618 Rosellini: estè
10620 MS.: fi ve nave; Subak: fì ve 'n anc; Cremonesi: fi ve n'ave; Rosellini: si ve n'ave (misquotes Subak, "fi ve n'ave balsmer")
10624 7 for et
10625 Subak: e' vos do' en proier; Cremonesi, Rosellini: enproier
10627 Subak: Lasà-v'avanti (misquoted by Rosellini); Cremonesi: Lasa'-n'avanti (misquoted by Rosellini to 'Lasà-n' avanti'); Rosellini: Lasav'avanti

            Qe n'invoja secorso por aider.
            A la deman, quando serà l'auba cler,
10630   Nu den tornar ancora a li çostrer." (1135)
            Dist li soldan, "Et eo li vojo otrier;
            Ma d'una ren e vos vojo nonçer:
            El vos estoit ben eser bon çivaler,
            Qe dever moi non aça nulla sper."
10635   Dist Karaolo, "Vu farì como ber, (1140)
            Qe altro non demando ni quer."

Rubric 311
Coment s'(a)rmaient.
Laisse 312

            A la deman, a l'aube aparisant,
            Rois Karaolo pris son guarnimant,
            Et avec lui Sandonio ensemant.
10640   Quant sont armé, montent en auferant; (1145)
            Lançe oit grose, e li feri trençant.*
            Karaolo oit çinta Curtana, li bon brant,
            Pois quirirent conçé a l'amirant,
            E cil li oit comandé a Trevigant.
10645   E qui ensent de Rome sença termen prendant; (1150)
            Trosqua a li canpo non vait rena tirant.
            Li Danois, quant le voit, demanda ses guarnimant;
            Nian Çarloto no se fe pais lant.
            Quant furent armé e monté en auferant,
10650   Karlo li proie e ben e dolçemant, (1155)
            Qe i soie e pro e valant.
            "Anda," fait il, "a Jesu vos comant."
            E cil s'en vont ad esperon bronçant,
            Tantq'i forent là o çelor li atant.
10655   Karaolo, quant le vi, si le dist en ojant, (1160)
            "Ben soja venu li nostri conbatant;
            Cosi vada l'ovra como andò en avant."
            Dist li Danois, "Et eo si le contant."

    10628 Cremonesi: n'invoia'
    Rubric 311 (after 10636) MS., Keller: sormaient; Subak: s'armoient; Cremonesi: s'armaient (emend for *sormaient*); Rosellini: s'armaient
    10641 MS.: Lāçe; Subak: La[n]çe; Cremonesi, Rosellini: Lançe
    10645 Subak: tèrmen
    10647 Subak: demanda (misquoted by Rosellini, "demandà")
    10654 Subak: Tant qu'i . . . la, o; Cremonesi, Rosellini: Tant q'i . . . là o

Lor se donent de li canpo un arpant;
10660 L'un dever l'altro ponçe l'auferant. (1165)
Bra*n*dist le aste là ò est li feri tre*n*çant,*
Si se ven a ferir totes comunelmant.
Si gra*n*t colpi se done qe çival auferant
Ne le pote sofrir: ançi s'ençenocla a li canp.
10665 Ma li baro*n* le pu*n*çì por si fer maltalant, (1170)
A·l relever le aste vola avant.
Quant à ço fato si ont trato li brant,
E Çarloto cu*n* Sandonio se ferì ensemant.
Anbi s'abatent a tera d·i auferant,
10670 M'i se redriçe tosto et isnelemant, (1175)
Prende son çivali n·i alò deslojant;*
A cival monte, qe strivere no*n* prant*
Quant à ço fato, si oit trato li brant;
La bataila come*n*çent mervilosa e grant.

60vb

Rubric 312
Coment fo pro li baron.
Laisse 313

10675 Grande fu la bataile de qui quatro baron; (1180)
Çascun è pro (s)i oit cor de lion.*
Karaolo ten Curtane dont a or è li pon;
Fer li Danois desor l'elmo enson.
Quant ne prende, fa cair a·l sablon;
10680 E tota l'armaure de·l hermin sigloton,* (1185)
Cun la ghironée de l'auberg framiron,*
Si l'oit trençé cu*n* pano d'aquinton.*
Deo le guardi por soa redencion,
Qe in carne no le fe engonbrason.
10685 E le Danois fer lui si fort enson, (1190)
De l'elmo no trençe la mo*n*ta d'u*n* boton.

10661 Subak: la, o est; Cremonesi: là o' est; Rosellini: là o est
10665 Subak: pu*n*çi
10670 Subak: M'i
10671 Cremonesi: n'i alò; Rosellini: ni alò
10676 MS.: fi oit; Subak, Cremonesi, Rosellini: si oit
10678 Subak: en son; Cremonesi, Rosellini: enson
10680 Subak: del hermin; Cremonesi, Rosellini: de l'hermin
10682 Subak: da quinton; Reinhold [review Subak, columns 22–23], Cerf also correct, *d'aquinton*. Holtus, rev. Cremonesi: da quinton
10685 Subak, Rosellini: en son; Cremonesi: enson

>   Ma rer la grope conseguì l'aragon;
>   Do mité oit fato de l'auferant Guascon,
>   E Karaolo remist a li sablon.
> 10690 Dentro Sandonio e·l damisel Çarlon (1195)
>   Si començoit grande la capleson;
>   Gran colpi se done desor li elmi reon.
>   I se trençent quant i ne prendon,*
>   E d·i aubergi trençent li ghiron.
> 10695 A gran mervile fu Sandonio prodon; (1200)
>   Morto aust Çarloto sença redencion,
>   Quant li Danois li fu bon conpagnon.
>   Quant feru avoit Karaolo, po fa retornason;
>   A quel Sandonio un altro colpo li donon.
> 10700 Grant fu la bataile, conter ne la poroit hon; (1205)
>   Karaolo vi li Danois si le mis por rason:
>   "Çivaler, sire, morto ai mon aragon;
>   Le vostro non vojo oncir, qe blasmo me seron.
>   Desendés avec moi, seremo anbi peon,
> 10705 E questo serà cortexia, se me perdoni Macon." (1210)
>   Dist li Danois, "Vu avez rason."
>   Demantenant desis de l'aragon;
>   Or son i anbi comunal a·l sablon.
>   Con le spee se fa gran capleson;
> 10710 Çarloto e Sandonio anbidos descendon, (1215)
>   Plu d·i altri nen volse avoir reençon.

Rubric 313
Coment fu grant la bataille.
Laisse 314

>   Defor de Rome en le pre verdojent,
>   Grande fu la bataile e dura e pesent.
>   Da la deman a l'aube aparisent   61ra
> 10715 Durò entro lor grande torniament. (1220)
>   Çascun s'oit doné d·i colpi plus de cent;

  10687 Subak: conseguí
  10688 Subak, Cremonesi, Rosellini: guascon (no capital, as always)
  10690 Subak, Cremonesi: e·l damisel; Rosellini: e 'l demisel
  10693 Subak, Cremonesi, Rosellini: Il se (Reinhold [review Subak, column 23]: I se; / interpunctuated)
  10707 Subak: desìs
  Rubric 313 (after 10711) Guessard includes this rubric, p. 404.

            Trençé s'avoient tot li guarniment,
            Si son lasé de poine e de torment
            Qe çascun se fa indré un arpent,
10720   Por dar a soi un poi de s(t)orament.* (1225)
            Por li gran colpi q'i s'ont doné sovent,
            Quant son polsé i vont ardiement,
            L'un contra l'autre con le spee trençent.
            Gran dol oit li Danois, par poi d'ire non fent;*
10725   Quant la bataile dura si longament, (1230)
            E Karaolo non fo mie recreent,
            El ten Curtane a·l pomo lusent;
            A li Danois un si gran colpo li rent,
            Par un petit a tera no se destent.
10730   Dist le pain, "El vos va malement; (1235)
            E vos conseilo, se avez esient,
            Qe contra moi vos clama recreent;
            A li rois soldan vos darò por present.
            Nen vos farà nesun ennojament;
10735   Ançi vos farà richo e manent, (1240)
            Se adorarés la loi qe a noi apent."
            Dist li Danois, "Tu parli folement;
            E no t'apresio un diner valisent!
            E veço ben, tu me ten por nient.
10740   Avantiqe da moi faça desevrament, (1245)
            Vu senterì de ma spea trençent."
            Sovra li cor por ire e maltalent;
            Gran colpo li done desor l'elmo lusent;
            Ne l'inpira, ma la spea desent
10745   Par me l'auber, qe li trença e fent. (1250)
            Navré l'oit un petit, qe li sangue li desent,
            Dont Karaolo par poi d'ire non fent.
            Et apreso cest colpo, li Danois se fa en avent;
            Un altro en done a Sandonio ensement,
10750   Qe a la tera elo·l çeta sanglent. (1255)

        10717 Rosellini: Trençe
        10720 MS.: sorament; Subak, Cremonesi, Rosellini: sorament
        10732 Subak: clamà
        10738 Subak: t'aprèsio
        10740 Subak: façà
        10741 Subak, note: Un sen terì (?)
        10744 Subak, Cremonesi: inpirà

Rubric 314
Coment fu mort Karoer.
Laisse 315

       Gran dol oit Karoer, no l'oit unqua major;
       Le sangue se vi rajer environ et entor.
       Nul se mervile se il oit gran dolor;
       Elo reclama Macometo son segnor.
10755 Dist a·l Danois, "Vu sì bon çostreor! (1260)
       Mais en ma vie e non vi un milor.
       Navré m'avés, mais ne le daria un flor;
       Ma çer la conprarés en petit de or."
       La spea tent cun homo de gran vigor;
10760 Fer li Danois sor l'eume pint a flor; (1265)
       De l'elmo trençe e de la cofia ancor.
       Si grande fo cil colpo q'el valant pugneor 61rb
       Ne·l pote sostenir, ançi caì a l'arbor.
       Ma tosto se redriçe, cun homo de gran vigor;
10765 La spea tent, ne la mis en sejor. (1270)
       Ver Karoer s'en vent por grant iror;
       No·l volse ferir sor l'e(u)mo pinto a flor.*
       Un colpo li done a la guisa Francor;
       Entro l'elmo e le spales le mis li brant de color.
10770 La testa li trençe, sença nesun restor; (1275)
       Voler la fait en me lois de l'erbor.*
       Quant à ço fato, nen volse far nul demor;
       El pris Curtane da le rubio color.*
       Quando la tent, ne fe çoja e baldor,
10775 Dever Sandonie s'en vait a gran vigor. (1280)

    Rubric 314 (after 10750) Keller: kaioer (corrected Mussafia, "Handschriftliche Studien II": karoer)
    10753 Subak: s'emervile
    10761 Subak: còfia
    10762 Subak: que 'l; Cremonesi, Rosellini: qe 'l
    10763 Rosellini: poté
    10767 MS., Subak, Rosellini: emo; Cremonesi: e[l]mo (emend)
    10770 Subak, Rosellini: teste (cf. Frati)
    10771 Subak: enmè
    10773 MS.: rubio; Subak: rùbio; Cremonesi, Rosellini: rubro

Rubric 315
Coment fu mort Sidonio.*
Laisse 316

      Quando Sandonio vi q'è mort Karoer,
      S'el oit dol non è da merviler.
      Dever Çarloto el se·l cuita vençer;
      Contra lui vent cun li brando d'açer.
10780 Un si gran colpo elo li va doner, (1285)
      Qe de l'elmo trençe un gran quarter.
      Pres la orele fait li brant aler;
      Un petit l'à navrés aprés la çerveler.
      Si le stornì a tera, li fa verser;
10785 Morto l'aust o au presoner, (1290)
      Quan s'en percoit li bon Danois Uçer,*
      E vi le sang de la testa rajer,
      E a li canpo elo lo vide verser.
      Or vede·l ben, secorso li ait mester;
10790 En quella part vene sença entarder, (1295)
      E ten Curtana qe fo de Karoer
      (Ne quella spea no volse unqua cançer).
      Tel colpo li dona desor l'elmo verçer,
      Tuto li trença, nen lasa qe couper.
10795 Trosqu'a le spales elo la fa aler, (1300)
      E pois escria, "Monçoja, çivaler!*
      Por Karlo el maine vinto avon li torner!"
      Adonc li rois e Naimes de Baiver,
      Teris d'Ardene e Morando de River,
10800 Bernardo de Clermont *et* le dux Belençer, (1305)
      E des autres, plus de .X. miler,
      Li corent por lor esguarder.
      Quando li soit li soldan Ysorer,
      De gran dolor cuita li seno cançer.
10805 Dist a sa jent, "Qui avon mal converser.* (1310)
      Dapoisq'è morti Sandonio e Karoer,
      De tot les autres nen daria un diner.
      Se qui avon longament demorer,
      E i ne poust ni prender ni bailer,

    10786 MS.: percoit; Subak: perçoit; Rosellini: perçoit (emend)
    10796 Subak: Mon çoia
    10800 7 for *et*
    10809 Subak: prènder

10810 Tot l'or de·l mondo non aust mester (1315)　　　61ᵛᵃ
　　　 Qe no·n faist a mala mort finer."*
　　　 Adonc farent ses arms torser*
　　　 E si prendent ses muli e ses destrer.
　　　 Avantqe de Rome se volist sevrer,
10815 A l'inperer son venu a parler, (1320)
　　　 E si le prist conçé a demander.
　　　 "E inperer, sire," ço dist Ysoler,
　　　 "Dapoiq'è morto Sandonio e Karoer,
　　　 E no intendo contra vos tençer.
10820 Ço qe fo fato e no vojo stratorner, (1325)
　　　 Mais ben vos poso desor Macon jurer,
　　　 Q'el est morto li milor çivaler
　　　 Qe se poust trovar da çela part de mer.
　　　 De una ren e vos vojo en projer:
10825 Qe vu le façés altamant enterer." (1330)
　　　 Dist li rois, "Quel pla lasez ester,
　　　 Qe si cun rois dux e amirer
　　　 E li farò altament seveler,
　　　 E a li major de ma çent aporter."

Rubric 316
Coment s'en vait li soldan.
Laisse 317

10830 Quant li soldan fu da Karlo sevré, (1325)
　　　 Tot en quito li lasò Roma la cité.
　　　 Cun soa jent elo fo açaminé
　　　 E si pasò oltra la mer salé.
　　　 E lasò morto li fort rois Karoé,
10835 Et avec lui Sandonio l'amiré. (1340)
　　　 Gran dol en fait e Turchi et Asclé;
　　　 Ne vos poroit nul hon dire ni conté.
　　　 E l'inperer fo saço e doté;
　　　 Avantiqe in Roma elo fose intré,
10840 Li dos pain fo molto ben enteré, (1345)
　　　 E a li major de ca jent aporté;

　　　 10811 Subak, Cremonesi: no 'n faïst; Rosellini: no 'n faist
　　　 10812 Subak, Rosellini: arms; Cremonesi: arnis
　　　 10824 Subak: en proier; Cremonesi, Rosellini: enproier
　　　 Rubric 316 (after 10829) Keller: sen
　　　 10836 Subak: e Turchi e asclè; Cremonesi: et Asclé; Rosellini: Turchi e Asclé

E richament fo vesti e coroé,
En un sarcol furent repolsé;
Non pais mie in logo qe fust sagré,*
10845 Porq'i no furent batezé e lavé. (1350)
Quant à ço fato, qe pain fo sevré,
Adonc li rois con tot li berné
En furent entra in la çité.
Quele maconarie q'i le ont trové*
10850 Tot en furent e arse e brusé. (1355)
Gran çoja fo da tot part mené;
Por l'Apostoile i ont envojé.
E cil le vene voluntera e de gre;
Grande honor li fe Karlo l'inperé;
10855 E l'Apostoilo no à l'ovra oblié. (1360)
Çascun de ceus qe li forent trové
Tuti li ses pezé li furent perdoné.
Gran çoja n'oit çes Françés amené,   61vb
Bia colu qe là fo envojé,*
10860 Qe in sa vite avoit li gran peçé. (1365)

Rubric 317
Coment l'Apostoille . . .
Laisse 318

Gran çoja oit l'Apostoile Milon:
Deliberé fu da Turs e da Sclavon
La merçé de Deo e l'inperer Karlon,
E de·l Dainois e de le dux Naimon,
10865 E de Çarloto, li novel canpion. (1370)
"Segnur," dist l'Apostoilo, "porqe vos çelaron?
Caçé fu de Rome por Turchi e Sclavon,
Qe in Roma orent Trevigant e Macon,
Et Apolin e ses deo Balatron.
10870 Çascun de ceus q'è venu a perdon, (1375)

10846 Subak: païen; Cremonesi: païn; Rosellini: paien
10852 Subak, Cremonesi, Rosellini: apostoile (always lower case)
10857 MS.: Tuti li ses; Subak: Tuti le ses (Reinhold [review Subak, column 23]: Tuti li . . .); Cremonesi: Tuti li ses; Rosellini: Tuti le ses
10859 Subak, Cremonesi: Bià
Rubric 317 (after 10860) MS., Keller: lapostoille; Cremonesi: apostoile (Holtus [rev. Cremonesi], corrected)

Eo li do cotal remision,
Qe tot li peçé q'oit fato n·iste mon,*
No le seria reme*n*bré unqua in l'altro mon.
Ma una colse primiran nu faron:
10875 Avantiqe vos ve departa de Ron, (1380)
Par tot la tera entorno et environ,
Nu aliron co·la precesion,*
E de novo tuti li sagraron."
Dist li rois, "A Deo benecion!"
10880 Lor se levò l'Apostoilo Milon, (1385)
Cun veschivi, arçiveschivi, prete e clereçon;
Tuti li altari quanti trovent in Ron
Tuti quanti de novo li sagraron;
Quando à ço fato, dè la benecion.*
10885 Çascun s'en vait a le soe mason, (1390)
E l'inperer e le dux Naimon,
XV. jorni i demorò en Ron,
Po pris co*n*çé co*n* tot li ses baron.
Gran çoja en fait Ma*n*seli e Berton,*
10890 E li Françeis, Normandi, e Guascon. (1395)
A le çamin se metent, arer s'en tornon;
E l'Apostoiles co*n* tot li clericon,
Le co*n*voient trois defor de Ron.
K*arlo* s'en vait, a Deo benecion,
10895 E l'Apostoile remist a Deo non. (1400)

10872 MS.: niste; Subak, Cremonesl, Rosellini. in stc
10875 Subak: departà; Cremonesi: departa'
10876 Subak: Partot . . . e environ; Cremonesi: Par tot . . . et environ; Rosellini: Par tot . . . etorno e environ
10877 Cremonesi: co[n] (emend)
10881 Subak: vèschivi, arçivèschivi
10884 Subak, Cremonesi, Rosellini: de; MS.: beñecion?
10887 Rosellini: .X.iorni
10889 MS.: māseli; Subak: Ma*r*sel[es]i (emend); Reinhold [review Subak, column 23], correction: Ma(n)seli; Cremonesi, Rosellini: Marseli

7.7 Orlandino

Rubric 318
Qui conta de K*arlo*.*
Laisse 319

  Segnur baron, de ço siés certan,
  Le milor rois de França e de Norman,
  Colu si fu l'inperer K*arlo* el man.
  E colu qe plu durò e pena e torman,
10900 Trosqua el fo petit enfan, (1405)
  Si fo caçé for de son rian
  E si fu alevés cu*n* Turs e co*n* Persan.
  E quant cuitoit avoir i*n* çoja tuta quan,
  Si le fo morto Oliver e Rolan,
10905 Por G(ain)elun qi fe li traiman.* (1410)   62ra
  Gran fu la çoja qe fait li Norman,*
  E l'inperer çiva(l)ça ardieman*
  Con ses çivaler e petit e gran.
  A·l Bachanel pasent q'è li camin sovran;
10910 Trosque a Sotrio no*n* fe arestaman;
  E ilec fo ostalé .XV. jor en avan, (5)
  Por li ses çivaler c'oit duré grant achan.
  Por aler e venir no furent ben san;
  Ilec seçornent qe non vait plus avan.
10915 E l'inperer li maino K*arlo* el man*

  Rubric 318 (after 10895) Keller: .k.; Subak: K*arlon*; Cremonesi: Karle; Rosellini: K[arlo]
  10898 Subak: fù; cf. 10906
  10900 Subak: fò; cf. 10904; Subak, Cremonesi, Rosellini: Trosqua
  10901 Subak: caçè . . . rïan; Cremonesi, Rosellini: caçé
  10902 Subak: fù alevès; Cremonesi, Rosellini: alevés
  10903 Subak, Cremonesi, Rosellini: çoia; cf. 10906
  10904: Subak, Rosellini: Olivier
  10905 Subak: qui fè . . . ; Rosellini: qui fe; MS., Subak: Gainrelun; Cremonesi: Gainelun; Rosellini: Garnielun
  10906 Subak: que fait; Cremonesi: qi fe' li traïman
  10907 MS., Cremonesi, Rosellini: çivaça
  10910 Lazzeri: fé; Cremonesi: fe' (as always; not noted further)
  10913 Lazzeri, Monaci: non furent
  10914 Mussafia, Monaci: que non . . . .
  10915 Mussafia: K. (as always); Lazzeri, Monaci, Cremonesi, Rosellini: Karle; Mussafia, Lazzeri, Cremonesi, Rosellini: li maino

Par tot Sotrio fe criar un ban (10)
Q'el non romagna burgois ni castelan,
Vada a veoir la cort de li rois Karlo el man,*
Qe asa averont pan, vino e provan;
10920 Çascun li vait, a cui li atalan.
Rolandin l'olde dire, qe estoit cun altri enfan; (15)
Quant li oldì, no·l tene a nian;
En conpagnie se leve cun plus de tran;*
A la cort s'en vait, tuti legri e çojan.
10925 Ma Rolandin senpre andava avan,
Come el fust un soe capitan; (20)
Non finent pais trois a li palés gran.*

Rubric 319
Coment Rolant monta a·l palés.
Laisse 320

Rolandin fu a·l palés cun altri baçaler;
Nesun no olsa davanti Rolandin aler.*
10930 Rolandin guarde et avant et arer,*
Da tot part vide li çivaler (25)
Qe sont asis a tables a mançer.
Rolandin guarde e vide l'inperer,
Qe major de li altri avoit li taler.*
10935 Rolandin, quant le vi, priste le a covoter;*
El no volse mie longament demorer; (30)
Dever li rois el se mis ad aler.   62ʳᵇ
Quant qui serventi li vait a incontrer*

10917 Lazzeri: né; Monaci: nè
10919 Mussafia, Monaci, Lazzeri, Cremonesi: asa' (as always)
10922 Mussafia: oldi, no-l; Lazzeri: oldì, nol; Monaci: oldì nol tene; Cremonesi: oldi nol; Rosellini: oldi no'l
10923 Cremonesi: compagnie (always *m* before labial; no longer commented)
10924 Mussafia, Lazzeri, Cremonesi, Rosellini: çoian (as always; not noted further); Monaci: çojan (as always)
19925 MS., Mussafia: R.; Lazzeri, Cremonesi, Rosellini: Rolandin (as always)
10927 Mussafia, Lazzeri, Cremonesi, Rosellini: palés
Rubric 319 (after 10927) MS., Keller: .ro.; Mussafia: .Ro.; Cremonesi, Rosellini: Ro[landin]; Lazzeri: montá al
10929 Cremonesi: Rolandin; Rosellini: Rolandin; cf. 10930, 10933, 10935, etc.
10934 Mussafia, Monaci: altre; Lazzeri: maior . . . altre
10937 Mussafia, Monaci: le rois
10938 Mussafia: qui' (as always for plural demonstrative)

            E si le volse far indreo çeser.*
10940 Quan Rolandin se fa si dur e fer,
       Q'el ne fe un a tera trabuçer. (35)
       Li rois le vi, si s'en prist a gaber,
       E si oit dito contra Naimes de Bavier,
       "Qi vide mai un si pro baçaler?"
10945 E pois si dist a li serventi uçer,*
       "Lasés·le venir, no le fate engonbrer." (40)
       E cil le font, quant li rois li requer.
       E Rolandin si fo molto liçer;*
       El non va mie a li altri tajer,*
10950 Se no a quelo de Karlo l'inperer,
       Qe de çarne le vi tuto plener. (45)
       Quando le fu q'el se le pote aprosmer,
       Jamais non fu ni bracho ni levrer
       Cun Rolandin pris la carne a mançer;
10955 Molto li guarda dux Naimes de Baiver.
       Qe vos deie li plais alonçer?* (50)
       No se poroit un arpant aler,
       Qe Rolandin oit livro quel tajer.*
       Quant li rois le vide si mançer,
10960 Una carega el ge fe aporter;
       Si fe l'infante ilec aseter. (55)
       E quando fo livro tuto quel tajer,
       Li rois le fi un altro aporter.
       E li baron le prendent a guarder,
10965 Qe se prendea de lui a merviler.

       10940 Mussafia: Quand; MS., Monaci, Cremonesi, Rosellini: Quan
       10941 Monaci: ne fa
       10944 Lazzeri: sí (as always; only remarked when missing after this line)
       10945 Mussafia, Cremonesi, Rosellini: serventi uçer; Lazzeri: sí . . . uçer
       10946 Mussafia, Cremonesi, Rosellini: Lasés le; Lazzeri: Lases le
       10949 Cremonesi: taier
       10950 Cremonesi, Rosellini: Karle
       10951 Monaci: Que de
       10953 Lazzeri: fi . . . brancho
       10954 Cremonesi, Rosellini: Rolandin; cf. 10958, etc.
       10955 Mussafia, Lazzeri: N.; Cremonesi, Rosellini: Naime
       10956 Mussafia: de je; Lazzeri: dé je; Cremonesi, Rosellini: deie
       10958 Mussafia: oit livro; Lazzeri: R. livro . . . taier (cf. 10962); Cremonesi: taier; Holtus, rev. Cremonesi: tajer (ms. reading)
       10960 Lazzeri: fé

Ma R*olandin* non avea quel penser, (60)
Ne se guardava avanti ni arer,
Ma senprefois el guardoit li tajer.
Quando fo ben pasu, qe plus no*n* poit ma*n*çer,*
10970 De quela carne qe li parse avançer,   62^(va)
El s'à pris en seno a covoter;* (65)
E de·l pan q'el poit anbler.
K*arlo* le vi si·l prist a reguarder,
E pois le prist por rason demander,
10975 "Dì mo, damisel, guarda, no me·l çeler,
No à tu au asa da boir e da mançer?* (70)
Que vo·tu far de quel qe tu voi furer?*
La çarne e li pan e te voi acovoter."
Dist R*olandin*, "No v'aça merveler;
10980 Qe eo la togo por portar a ma mer,*
Et avec le un qe est mo*n* per." (75)
Li rois l'oì, demanda son canbrer;
Una toagia blanca el (f)e aporter,*
De carne e de pan la fa tota raser,
10985 E pois a li col li fait avoluper.
E dist, "Bel filz, questo averì porter (80)

10969 Lazzeri: pasú; Monaci; pasù
10971 Mussafia, Monaci, Lazzeri, Cremonesi, Rosellini: pris en seno acovoter
10972 Lazzeri: del pan (as Mussafia, Cremonesi, Rosellini; not further remarked)
10973 Mussafia: si-l; Monaci: sì l prist; Lazzeri: sí'l; Cremonesi: si 'l; Rosellini: si'l
10975 Mussafia: Di' mo, dàmisel, . . . no mel çeler; Monaci: Dì mo, . . . no me l çeler; Lazzeri: me 'l; Cremonesi: Di' mo . . . mel; Rosellini: me'l
10976 Lazzeri: aú; Mussafia: a' tu; Monaci: No à tu asa' (*asa'* as always); Cremonesi: a' tu aü da..
10977 Mussafia: Qe vo' tu (emend for MS. *Qe te voi*); Monaci: Qe vo' tu; Lazzeri: vo' tu; Cremonesi: Que vo' tu; Rosellini: Que vo tu . . . tu voi furer
10978 Lazzeri: e' te; Monaci: e' te
10979 Mussafia, Monaci: v'açà; Lazzeri: Rolandin.. n'açá; Cremonesi: Rolandin . . . v'aça
10981 Mussafia: le [a] un (misquoted by Rosellini); Lazzeri, Monaci: le a un
10982 Lazzeri: l'oi, demandá; Mussafia, Monaci, Cremonesi, Rosellini: l'oi, demanda
10983 MS.: se aporter; Mussafia, Rosellini: el fe aporter (emend for MS.: *se*); Lazzeri: fé; Cremonesi: el fe' aporter (emend for MS. *el se aposter*); Morini: se
10984 Lazzeri: çarne
10986 Lazzeri: fils . . . averí; Mussafia, Cremonesi: averì: Monaci: bel fils . . . averì . . . ; Rosellini: averi

A vestre pere et a la vestra mer;
E si vos di, si vos vojo comander,
Qe deman venés ça a mançer."
10990 Dist Rolandin, "De grez e volunter."
Cosi cun Rolandin s'en voloit aler, (85)
E l'inperer prist dos donçé a 'peler:
"Segnur," dist il, "or li alez arer,
E si saçés qi è·l pere e la mer."*
10995 E cil le dist, "De grez e volunter."

Rubric 320
Coment Rolant s'en retorne.*
Laisse 321

Va s'en Rolandin, non fo ma si çojant; (90)
Quant el fu ços de·l palés, el se mis en avant;
No l'atenderoit un levrer ben corant;*
El sa le r(u)e, le petit e li grant.
11000 Non est alé delunçi dos arpant,
A qui qi le voit darer, li è desparu davant;* (95)
Non poit veoir de lui ni ovra ni senblant.
I torna a Karlo, si le dist comant
Li damisel li è de(s)paru davant.
11005 Dist li rois, "Malvasii seduant!
Par un petit qe je ne vos apant. (100)

10991 Lazzeri: Cosí cun Rolandin . . . ; Cremonesi: Così
10992 Mussafia, Lazzeri, Cremonesi, Rosellini: donçé apeler; Monaci: l'imperer . . . donçé apeler
10994 Lazzeri: sí . . . è 'l; Mussafia: è-l; Monaci: qui è l pere . . . ; Cremonesi, Rosellini: è 'l
Rubric 320 (after 10995) Keller: .ro. sen retorne; Lazzeri: Ro.; Holtus, rev. Cremonesi: .Ro.
10996 Cremonesi, Rosellini: Vasen (as always; not be remarked any longer)
10998 Lazzzeri: atendroit
10999 MS.: salerne le; Mussafia, Monaci, Lazzeri, Cremonesi, Rosellini: rue
11000 Mussafia, Monaci, Lazzeri, Cremonesi, Rosellini: de lunçi
11001 Mussafia: d'avant; Lazzeri, Monaci: desparú d'avant
11002 Lazzeri: semblant (as always before labial); Monaci: nì..nì (as always)
11003 Lazzeri: torná a Karle sí . . .
11004 MS.: deparu; Mussafia, Cremonesi, Rosellini: de[s]paru (emend); Monaci: desparù davant; Mussafia: d'avant; Lazzeri: desparú
11005 MS.: malvasij; Mussafia, Cremonesi, Rosellini: Malvasii

Ma deman, se non virà l'infant
A la cort non mançarà ne petit ni grant."
E R*olandin* s'en va, legro e çojant;*
11010 Por le çamin el s'en vait çantant;
Non fo si legro en tuto son vivant. (105)
Quant vi sa mer, q'elo li fo davant,
Elo li dona li pan e la provant.
Quant ela·l vi, molto ne fo dolant,
11015 E dist, "Bel filz, qi vos dè sta provant?"*
"Mere," fait il, "un signor bel e çant, (110)
Si m'à da da mançer a tot li me comant."
Donde la dame si se va porpensant: 62^(vb)
"Quest'è mon frer donde me ven li present."
11020 E R*olandin* si le dist en riant,
"Mançé, mere, fa·ve legra e çojant! (115)
Deman nu n'averon altretant.
Quel segnor me·l dise, qe me dè la provant."*
Atanto ecote vos Milon erant;
11025 Quando vi quela colse, molto se fe çojant,
Qe uso non ert de mançer tel provant. (120)
"Bel filz," dist Berte, "farì li mon comant.
No le alé plu par nule ren vivant."
Dist R*olandin*, "Farò li ves comant."
11030 Elo le dise cun boche, mais no l'à en talant.*

11007 Lazzeri: virá; Mussafia, Monaci, Cremonesi: virà; Rosellini: vira

11008 Mussafia, Cremonesi: mançara; Lazzeri: mançará né . . .

11009 Lazzeri: Rolandin; Monaci: çoiant (not usual *çojant*)

11013 Lazzeri: doná

11014 Mussafia: ela-l; Monaci: ela l vi; Lazzeri, Cremonesi, Rosellini: ela 'l

11015 Mussafia, Cremonesi: de'; Monaci: "bel filz . . . " (as always, lower case with continuing quote)

11017 Mussafia, Cremonesi, Rosellini: dà da . . . ; Lazzeri. da' da; Monaci: m'à da' da . . .

11018 Mussafia, Monaci: dama

11019 Lazzeri, Monaci: Quest è

11020 Lazzeri: Rolandin sí

11021 Mussafia: fa-ve; Lazzeri, Monaci, Rosellini: fave; Cremonesi: fa' ve

11023 Mussafia: me-l . . . de'; Lazzeri: me 'l . . . dé; Monaci: me l dise; Cremonesi: mel..de'; Rosellini: me'l..dè

11026 Lazzeri: qé; Monaci: Qé

11027 Lazzeri: farí; Rosellini: fari

11030 Mussafia: le dist

E Berta parle a Milon planemant: (125)
"Milon," fait ella, "el nos va malemant.
Quest'è mon frer onde en ven R*olant*;*
A la toaile conosco li senblant.
11035 Non è sença cason quant li dà la provant;
Si ne po aconoscere, tot l'or qe fu anc* (130)
Nen scanparoit mort non fumes entranb;*
Vu apendu a le forches pendant,
Et eo arse a li fogo ardant."
11040 Milon, quan l'olde, si fo de maltalant;*
Anbidos plurent, planeto tendremant. (135)
Tot quel çorno stete Milon manant,*
Qe da mançer oit a·l convenant.
De R*olandin* el non cura niant,
11045 Ma la dame si le fa altramant:
De son frer conoit sa ire e maltalant. (140)
A l'altro çorno ela retene l'infant;*
No le lasa aler arer ni avant,
Si fo l'ora trapasé tuta quant
11050 Qe la cort sole mançer en avant.
E R*olandin* aloit pur guischisant, (145)
Tantqe a sa mere el desparì davant.
Qui da la cort stava tuti en ojant;
No le fo nul, ne petit ni grant,
11055 Qe olsase mançer se no venia l'infant.
Quando le vi venir, tuti se fa çojant; (150)
I se lavent si se vont asetant.

11033 Lazzeri: Quest è ... Rolant; Mussafia: frere; Rosellini: R[oland]

11035 Lazzeri: dá

11037 Mussafia: Ne-n scamparoit ... entranb; Lazzeri: scamparoit ... entranb; Monaci: Nen scamparoit

11040 Lazzeri, Monaci, Mussafia: mal talant (as always; cf. lines 11046, etc.; will not be noted further)

11041 Lazzeri: lasá

11045 Lazzeri: sí (as always; only the absence of accent will only be noted in the future)

11047 Rosellini: E l'altro çorno el retene; Morini: A ... ela (correcting Rosellini); Lazzeri: retené

11052 Mussafia: d'avant; Lazzeri: tant qe ... disparí d'avant; Mussafia, Monaci, Cremonesi, Rosellini: Tant qe

11053 Mussafia, Cremonesi, Rosellini: oiant (as always)

E saçés por voir, pres era nona pasant,
Avantqe fust venu quel enfant.
11060 Asa li po sa mer querir darer e davant,*
Qe a la cort est a mançer primemant.* (155)

Rubric 321
Coment Ro*lant* vene a la cort.
Laisse 322

Quant R*olandin* fo a la cort venu,
Gran çoja en fait li gra*n*di e li menu,
Por li bando qi estoit metu.
11065 Davant K*arlo* senpre R*olandin* fu;
Ilec manue a força e a vertu.* (160)   63ra
Naimes apelle, dan K*arlo* li menbru;
"Enperer, sire, ne sì vu aperçeu,*
Quest'è miracolo de li rois Jesu,
11070 Ça ces enfant no è de vilan nasu.
A·l reguarder el par de fera vertu; (165)
E creço q'el est filz d'un qualqe deçeu,
D'un çivaler q'è in poverté cau."

11058 Lazzeri, Monaci: posant; Rosellini: prés
11059 Lazzari: avant qe; Mussafia, Cremonesi, Rosellini: Avant qe (as always)
11060 Lazzeri: Asá; Monaci: Asà; MS.: Asa li poỷ
11061 Lazzeri: esta a
Rubric 321 (after 11061) MS.: Ro.; Holtus, rev. Cremonesi: .Ro.; Keller: .ro. uene a . . .
11062 Lazzeri: venú; Monaci: venù
11063 Lazzeri: menú; Monaci: çoia . . . menù
11064 Lazzeri: metú; Monaci: metù; Rosellini: K[arle]
11065 MS., Mussafia, Rosellini: senpre; Cremonesi: sempre (cf. Holtus, rev. Cremonesi)
11066 Lazzeri: vertú; Monaci: vertù
11067 Lazzeri: mentrú; Monaci: menbrù; Cremonesi: Karle; Rosellini: K[arle]
11068 Mussafia: ne si' vu aperçu; Lazzeri: si' . . . aperçeú, Monaci: ne si' vu aperçeù; Cremonesi, Holtus, rev. Cremonesi: ve si'; Rosellini: ve si vu
11069 Lazzeri: Iesú; Monaci: Jesù; Cremonesi: Jesù
11070 Lazzeri: no e . . . nasú; Monaci: nasù
11071 Lazzeri: al regarder . . . vertú; Monaci: Al regarder . . . vertù
11072 Lazzeri: e' . . . deçéú; Monaci: E' . . . deçeù
11073 Cremonesi: civaler . . . povertè (Cf. Holtus, rev. Cremonesi); Lazzeri: caú; Monaci: caù

        Ancora li rois comandò a qui du
11075 Qe a·l departir lo fant soja persegu,
        De·l per e de la mer soja li vor sau. (170)
        E qui le dient, "Or non parlez plu.
        Arer li aliron, no*n* serà pais foçu."

Rubric 322
Coment Ro*lant* fo davant K*arlo*.*
Laisse 323

        Davant K*arlo* s'estoit Rolandin,
11080 O il manue cu*n* faroit un mastin.
        Avant ni arer no*n* guarda le fantin, (175)
        Se no a la çarne et a·(l) pan et a·l vin.*
        Gran çoja n'oit qui q'erent vesin;
        Naimes parole ver K*arlo*, filz Pepin,
11085 "Costu no*n* est filz de barbarin:
        Pur il est filz d'omo d'alto lin, (180)
        De qualqe çivaler, conte o palatin.
        Veez como est belo? La fame li fa hain.*
        A·l reguarder q'el fait, e ne sonto devin.
11090 S'el ait vite ançiq'el prenda la fin,
        Dolent farà pais pajan e Sarasin. (185)
        Questo qe digo, no digo ad inçin;

    11074 Lazzeri: comandó
    11075 Lazzeri: persegú; Monaci: persegù
    11076 Lazzeri: saú; Monaci: saù
    11078 Lazzeri: sera . . . foçú; Monaci: serà . . . foçù; Mussafia, Rosellini: sera
    Rubric 322 (after 11078) Keller: .ro. fo dauant .k.; Holtus: .R.; Lazzeri: Ro. . . . k.; Rosellini: Ro*landin* . . . K[arlo]
    11079 Cremonesi: Karle; Rosellini: K[arle]
    11080 Lazzeri: é (for *O*); Mussafia, Holtus, rev. Cremonesi: cum; Monaci: ó
    11082 MS.: a pan; Mussafia, Cremonesi, Rosellini: a[l] pan (emend); Lazzeri, Monaci: al pan
    11083 Mussafia: qui' qu'erent; Monaci: qui qu'erent
    11084 Cremonesi: Karle; Rosellin: K[arle]
    11085 Mussafia: Barbarin; Lazzeri: Costú; Monaci: Costù; Mussafia: Costu'
    11089 Lazzeri, Monaci: e' ne
    11090 Lazzeri, Monaci, Mussafia, Cremonesi, Rosellini: ançi q'el; Rosellini: Se'l
    11091 Lazzeri: farà; MS., Mussafia, Cremonesi: paian; Cremonesi: païs . . . sarasin; Rosellini: sarasin

Le cor me·l manefesta a·l guarder de·l fantin.
Non veés vos cun ten li ocli enchin?
11095 Ma quant leva la teste se le serés vesin,
Un lion senble o dragon marin, (190)
O un falcon qe soja pelegrin."

Rubric 323
Coment N*aimes* parle a K*arlo*.*
Laisse 324

"Bon rois," dist N*aimes*, "entendés ma rason;
Questo damisel, q'est petit guarçon,
11100 A moi no*n* resenble eser filz de poltron.
Le reguarder oit como un lion; (195)
Faites·li ben qe n'avrés gujerdon,*
Quant vu savrì de soa nasion.
Se son per è povero et elo nos le don,
11105 Avec nos li menés a Lion.
En vestra cort non aça si ben non; (200)
S'el averà da mançer, serà un canpion."
Dist li rois, "E nu ben li faron."
E R*olandin* manue avec li rois Karlon;
11110 Quant oit mançé, no*n* dist ne si ne non.
La toaile fu parilée, cu*n* le enbandison, (205)
Cun pan e carne e groso capon,
E questo fe fare li bon dux Naimon.   63ʳᵇ
La tojala li baile, via va li garçon
11115 E darer li va li du conpagnon.

11093 Mussafia: me-l; Lazzeri: me 'l; Monaci: me l; Cremonesi: mel manifesta; Rosellini: me'l

11094 Mussafia, Cremonesi, Rosellini: veés vos; Monaci: No vees vos

Rubric 323 (after 11097) MS.: ak.; Monaci: parle a R., Cremonesi: parle a Karle; Rosellini: à K[arlo]

11102 Mussafia: Faites li . . . aurés; Lazzeri: faites li . . . aures; Monaci: Faite li . . . aures; Cremonesi, Rosellini: Faites li . . . avrés

11103 Lazzeri: savrí; Rosellini: savri

11107 Lazzeri: averá . . . será; Monaci: serà

11109 Morini: E (correcting Rosellini's *R*); Rosellini: R R*olandin*

11110 Lazzeri: né sí né . . . ; Monaci: mançé non dist nè sì nè non

11111 Monaci: parilee (no accent)

11112 Lazzeri: çarne

Mo no li vale la monta d'un boton, (210)
Qe ili posa savoir o il vada o non.*
Tel dol li rois oit, par poi q'il non fon;
"Mo ben çuré l'ò a Deo, qe sofrì pasion,*
11120 Non mançarà la cort s'el no*n* ven li garçon!"
"Bon rois," dist N*aimes*, "nu altrament faron. (215)
De cil enfant lasés moi la rason;
Eo e Teris rer lui aliron,
A palafroi o a bon ronçon.
11125 El no*n* porà scanper par nul ren de·l mon,
Qe nu no·l seguamo trosqu'a soa mason." (220)
Dist li rois, "A Deo beneçion."
E R*olandin* s'en vait, çantando una cançon;
"Nen plançi, mere, e·vos du bon capon,*
11130 E de·l pan blanço, no de quel qe uson,
Q'est noiro com est li carbon." (225)
La dama plure, ma no pais Millon,
Qe volunter manue de celle enbandison.

11117 Mussafia, Cremonesi: o' il vada; Lazzeri: ó il va; Monaci: ó il; Cremonesi: Que ili

11119 Mussafia, Cremonesi: Mo ben çur'elo a . . . ; Lazzeri: mo . . . çur'elo; Monaci: Mo ben çur'elo a De qe sofrì; Rosellini: Mo ben çur elo . . . sofri

11120 Mussafia, Lazzeri: mançara; Rosellini: No mançarà (cf. Morini); Monaci: no end quote

11122 Mussafia: lasés moi; Lazzeri: lases moi; Monaci: lases moi; Cremonesi, Rosellini: lasés moi . . .

11125 Lazzeri: porá

11126 Mussafia: no-l; Lazzeri: no 'l; Monaci: no l seguamo; Cremonesi: nol; Rosellini: no'l

11127 Cremonesi, Rosellini: benecion (cf. Holtus, rev. Cremonesi)

11128 Mussafia, Lazzeri, Monaci: cantando; Mussafia: plançi; Lazzeri: plançí . . . e'

11129 Lazzeri, Rosellini: e vos; Mussafia, Monaci, Cremonesi: e' vos

11132 Rosellini: plure (cf. Plouzeau)

Rubric 324
Coment Berta parole a Ro*lant*.
Laisse 325

      Berta vi R*olandin*, si oit pris a plurer;
11135 En braçe el prist, si·l comença a baser.
      "Bel filz," fait ela, "eo te vojo en projer, (230)
      Qe a quela cort no*n* diçi plu aler."
      "Mere," fait il, "porqe vos ert enojer?*
      No ve aporte asai da mançer?
11140 Mal verò l'ore q'i s'en avrà sevrer;
      S'el non fose por vos, eo li aleria rer. (235)
      Da mançer me dà de grez e volu*n*ter;
      Quant è livro un tajer, l'altro fa aporter,
      E de tel colse non potì ma mançer.
11145 E prego Deo, qe me faites orer,
      Qe mai no se diça de quilo sevrer." (240)
      "Bel filz," dist ela, "vu me l'avrì çurer,
      Qe a quela cort non averì plu aler."
      Dist R*olandin*, anch'el fust baçaler,
11150 "Mere," fait il, "dur è li otrier;
      Colsa qi no me poit valoir ni çoer. (245)
      Vu me faites in çes bois converser.

    Rubric 324 (after 11133) Keller: .ro.; Holtus, rev. Cremonesi: .aRo.; Lazzeri, Monaci: Berte . . . R.
    11135 Mussafia: si-l comença; Lazzeri: si 'l començá; Monaci: sì l; Cremonesi, Rosellini: si'l
    11136 Mussafia, Lazzeri, Monaci, Cremonesi, Rosellini: enproier
    11138 Mussafia, Monaci, Lazzeri: por qe (as always); Cremonesi: <<Mere, fait, por qe . . .
    11139 Lazzeri: aporté
    11140 Mussafia: aura; Lazzeri: q'i s'en aurá; Monaci: s'en aurà; Holtus, rev. Cremonesi: aura
    11141 Lazzeri: eu li; Monaci: per vos, cu
    11142 Lazzeri: da de . . .
    11144 Mussafia: cose; Lazzeri: ma'; Mussafia, Cremonesi: poti ma' . . . ; Monaci, Rosellini: poti
    11145 Monaci: E' (as always)
    11146 Lazzeri, Monaci: quiló; Cremonesi: quilo'
    11147 Lazzeri: l'avrí
    11150 Lazzeri: fiat il
    11151 Cremonesi: qui no (cf. Holtus, rev. Cremonesi)

E a quel palés si sta plu çivaler,
E vu me faites qui de fame raçer.
11155 Daqe vos plas, là no ò plu aler;
Ma por nul ren no ve l'averò çurer." (250)
Adoncha Berte si le lasa aler;
Ma tutafois ela li sta darer,
Q'elo non posa ni fuir ni scanper,
11160 Ne por nul ren a la cort aler.
Tantqe a none se parse aprosmer, (255)   63va
Quant R*olandin* vi li termen paser
Q'elo soloit a la cort aler,
Ne·l sape sa mer si setilme*n*t guarder
11165 Q'elo no s'en fuçe fora por un senter.
Quant a la cort se vait a 'prosmer (260)
Çascun escrie, "Eco li baçaler!"
Adoncha li baron fu asis a·l mancer;
E Rolandin no·l mis en oblier.
11170 Cosi manue como fi da primer;
Quant oit mançé, q'il s'en voit aler,* (265)
Li rois le fi la toaila aporter,
E de pane e de çarne tot quanta raser.
Avantqe de·l palés aust a desmonter,
11175 Naimes e Teris montò sens entarder;
Quant li fant va avanti, et i le vont arer. (270)

 11155 Mussafia: Da qe; Lazzeri: Da qe . . . lá non ò; Monaci: Da qe . . . là non ò; Cremonesi: Da qe vos . . . là no ò; Rosellini: Da qe . . . là no ò

 11160 Lazzeri: né (as always; no further remarked)

 11164 Mussafia: Ne-l; Lazzeri: ne 'l . . . sí; Monaci: Ne l sape; Cremonesi: Nel; Rosellini: Ne'l

 11165 Lazzeri, Monaci: per un

 11166 Mussafia, Lazzeri, Monaci, Cremonesi, Rosellini: vait aprosmer

 11168 Monaci: mançer

 11169 Mussafia: no-l; Lazzeri: no 'l; Monaci: no l; Cremonesi: nol; Rosellini: no'l

 11170 Lazzeri: cosí; Monaci: così

 11173 Lazzeri: reser

 11174 Cremonesi: aüst (as always); Avant qu del . . .

 11176 Mussafia, Lazzeri, Monaci: e i le

Rubric 325
Coment N*aimes* va rer Rolan(din).*
Laisse 326

       Via va R*olandin*, por le çamin erant,
       N*aimes* e Teris vait rer lui planemant.
       Quant s'aprosme*n*t a la cha de l'infant,
11180 Sa mer li ven enco*n*tra, tenerame*n*t plurant,
       Atant ecote N*aimes* e Teris ensemant; (275)
       En la mason vi la dama avant.
       Quando Berta le vi, si ne fo molto dolant;
       De paura q'el oit, tuta vait tre*n*blant.
11185 E si le dist, "Segnur, qe alez demandant?
       E no son quella qe vos alez querant." (280)
       E N*aimes* la reguarda, tot li color li soprant;*
       Figuré l'oit a·l viso et a le senblant.
       I s'ençenocle davant lei a·l presant;
11190 "Dama," fait il, "ne vos doté niant;
       Vu no*n* poez avoir nesun enojamant." (285)
       R*olandin* quan le vi, una stanga il prant;
       Feru n'averoit N*aimes*, por li çevo davant,
       Quant soa mer de nient no li co*n*sant.
11195 Atant ecote Milon da celle boscho grant,
       Cun una torse de legne molto pesant. (290)
       Quant vi çele jent, oit paure grant;
       A tera la bute, por si fer maltalant,
       La tera treme e darere e davant;

    Rubric 325 (after 11176) MS.: Rolandoin; Keller: .n. ua rer rolandin; Mussafia, Monaci, Lazzeri, Cremonesi, Rosellini: Rolandin
    11181, 11195, etc. Mussafia, Monaci, Lazzeri: A tant (as always)
    11184 Mussafia, Monaci: q'el' oit; Lazzeri: q' el' oit; Cremonesi, Rosellini: q'el'oit
    11187 Mussafia: so[r]prant; Lazzeri: reguardá . . . si sorprant; Monaci: sorprant; Rosellini: regurda
    11189 Lazzeri: ençenoclé
    11192 Mussafia, Monaci: quand
    11193 Lazzeri: ferú . . . N.; Monaci: Ferù; Cremonesi: Naime; Rosellini: N[aime]
    11194 Cremonesi: ne li (cf. Holtus, rev. Cremonesi)
    11197 Mussafia, Lazzeri, Monaci: cele
    11198 Mussafia, Lazzeri: mal talent (as always [cf. 11203, etc.]); Lazzeri: buté . . . sí . . .

11200 Quant à ço fato, si se mis en fujant,
Quant le dux N*aimes* pais no li co*n*sant. (295)
Elo li escrie, "No aler plu avant!"
Torner le fa oltra so maltalant.

Rubric 326
Coment N*aimes* parole.

Laisse 327

Naimes parole, qe fo saço e doté,
11205 "Segnur," fait il, "pais ne vos doté;
De nula ren nen serez engonbré. (300)
E vu, Teris, demanes vos alé,
Demantenant dentro de la cité   63vb
E faites faire robe como el se co*n*vé,
11210 A raine e a conte privé;
E a questo damisel, un vesti a quarté."* (305)
Dist Teris, "Ben serà otrié."
Elo s'en vait dentro da la cité;
Tuti li sarti qe il oit trové,
11215 A cosir quel robe li oit otrié;
Si le oit pagé a soa volunté; (310)
Quando fo fati, si s'en retorna aré.
Quant fu a Naimes si le oit delivré,
Milon e Berta fo vesti e cançé.
11220 E Rolandin non fo pais oblié;
Soa vestitura si fo fata et ovré* (315)
Ad un quarter q'elo fo destiné,
Qe quela ensegne portò en soa vivité.
Quant R*olandin* se vi si parilé,
11225 Gran çoja elo n'oit amené.
Comunalment i sonto aroté; (320)
Tuti ensenbre enverso la cité.*

11206 Cremonesi, Rosellini: non (cf. Holtus, rev. Cremonesi); Rosellini: egonbré
11211 Mussafia: aquarté; Lazzeri: vestí; Monaci: vestì
11217 Lazzeri: sí ... retorná; Monaci: arè
11219 Lazzeri: vestí; Monaci: vestì
11221 Rajna: li fo fata
11223 Rajna: porti; Lazzeri: portó e soa ... ; Monaci: portò e soa; Rosellini: esegne
11227 Mussafia, Monaci: ensembre en verso; Lazzeri: ensembre en verso

Avantq'i fose a li palés monté,
E li dux Naimes si fu davant alé,
11230 Davant a Karlo si fu apresenté.
Li rois le vi, si l'oit ademandé: (325)
"De le enfant, como avez ovré?"
E cil le dist, "Vu le savrì asé;*
Vu si m'avrez un don otrié,*
11235 A me voloir et a ma volunté."
Dist li rois, "De ço è verité." (330)
E Naimes dist, "Ora si le veé;
Quest'è li don qe vos è demandé:*
Milon e Berta, qe avés sbanojé."
11240 Adoncha li furent davant lui presenté.
Li rois le vi, tuto fo trapensé; (335)
En man el tent un coltel amolé;
Ça li aust por li çevo buté,
Quant Rolandin fu avant alé.
11245 Por me la man elo l'oit gobré,*
Una tel streta li oit en la man doné,* (340)
Qe por le ongues ne fo le sangue volé.
Li rois le vi; qi le aust doné
Tot li mondo davant e daré,
11250 El non seroit si çojant ne lé.
Enfra de soi oit dito e devisé, (345)
"Costu serà li falcon de la Crestenté."
Enlora dist a Naimes, "Li don vos ert doné.
Por amor de cest enfant, li est perdoné

11228 Mussafia, Monaci, Rosellini: Avant q'i
11230 Lazzeri: a R.; Cremonesi, Rosellini: a Karle
11234 Mussafia: si m'aurez; Lazzeri: sí m'aurez; Monaci: sì m'aurez
11235 Lazzeri: volonté
11237 MS · naimes; Mussafia: N, Lazzeri· N , .. sí
11238 Mussafia, Rosellini: Quest'è; Monaci: Quest e ... vos e; Cremonesi: Quest'é (cf. Holtus, rev. Cremonesi). Mussafia, Lazzeri, Cremonesi: vos è
11239 Mussafia, Lazzeri, Monaci: Berte
11240 Monaci, Lazzeri: presanté
11245 MS.: gobre; Mussafia: go[m]bré; Lazzeri, Monaci: gombré; Cremonesi, gobré; Rosellini: le man ... gonbré. Mussafia, Cremonesi: Lazzeri: me' (cf. 11314)
11250 Lazzeri: né le; Monaci: nè lé
11252 Guessard: Costu sera ... crestenté; Lazzeri: costú será; Monaci: Costù serà
11253 Mussafia, Monaci: En l'ora ... M. (cf. Holtus, rev. Cremonesi); Lazzeri: En l'ora ... Milon; Cremonesi: Enlora ... Naime; Rosellini: Enlora ... N[aime]

11255 L'ira e li voloir e la mala volunté."
       Adoncha Milon se fo ençenoclé, (350)
       Et ensement Berta da l'altro le;*   64ra
       E R*olandin* por la sala oit guardé,
       Se il veoit le table aparilé.

Rubric 327
Coment N*aimes* parole a K*arlo*.
Laisse 328

11260 Davant K*arlo* estoit le dux Milon,
       E dama Berta a la clera façon. (355)
       A li rois demandent e merçé e perdon;
       Li rois li oldì, si f(ron)çì li gregnon;*
       Ni ben ni mal elo no li respon.
11265 Ma Damenedé, por soa redencion,*
       Donò a R*olandin*, q'era petit garçon, (360)
       Entro son cor tant descrecion: . . .*
       "Vu, çentil homo, qe me donesi li capon,
       Se a mo*n* per ni ma mer faites nul mespreson,
11270 Tel vos donarò de·l pugno por li menton, (365)
       Qe mal me veistes unqa nasu a·l mon."*
       Quant quela parola oit oldu Naimon,
       Elo dist en riando a Karlon,
       "Guardé·ve ben da ste petit guarçon,

11257 Monaci: lé
11259 Monaci: la table
Rubric 327 (after 11259) MS.: .ak.; Cremonesi, Rosellini: Karle
11260 Cremonesi, Rosellini: Karle
11262 MS.: merçe; Lazzeri, Cremonesi: mercé (cf. Holtus, rev. Cremonesi)
11263 MS.: forçi; Mussafia: fronci; Lazzeri: oldi . . . si fronçí; Cremonesi: fronçì (emend); Monaci: fronçì; Rosellini: fronçi
11264 Lazzeri: ni be . . .
11265 Lazzeri: per soa; Monaci: Damenedè per . . . ; Rosellini: Damanedé
11267 Rosellini: Etro; Monaci: . . . . after 11267
11268 Cremonesi: centil (cf. Holtus, rev. Cremonesi)
11269 Rosellini: ni à ma mer
11271 Mussafia: unqua nasu (emend for natu; cf. Holtus, rev. Cremonesi); Lazzeri: nasu; Monaci: nasù; Cremonesi: veïstes
11272 Lazzeri: oldú; Monaci: oldù
11273 Lazzeri, Monaci: Elo dit
11274 Mussafia: Guardé-ve (misquoted by Holtus, rev. Cremonesi); Monaci, Cremonesi: Guardeve; Lazzeri, Rosellini: Guardave

11275 Qe a sa mer non faça se ben non." (370)
       Li rois le prist atraverso li galon;
       El ge basa (l)a bocha, le viso e la fron;
       E si ge·l dist, "Bel filz, e no ve·l çelaron;*
       Por filo vos tirò como faço Çarlon."
11280 Molto li agrea a le dux Milon, (375)
       Et ensement a·l duc Naimon.
       "Mon segnor," dist N*aimes*, "porqe le çelaron?
       Dapoqe vu avés doneo li perdon,
       Faites·li far une colse qi savrà a ogn'o*n* bon:*
11285 Faites qe Berte si prenda li fançon,* (380)
       E entro ses braçes tanto le tenon,
       Qe davanti vos si la sposi Milon
       Siqe la veça çivaler e peon."
       E dist K*arlo*, "Questo conseil è bon,
11290 Qe ma l'enfant no*n* olda si ben non." (385)
       E dist N*aimes*, "No*n* farés se ben non;
       Vu n'averés lojal gujerdon."
       Oez, mon sire, un petit ma rason,
       Ço qe le dist li vailan Milon,
11295 "Vestra marçi, doné m'avì perdon; (390)
       Ma e vos dirò de ma entention.
       Non est homo ni veilart ni garçon

11275 Lazzeri, Monaci: faça'

11276 Mussafia, Lazzeri, Monaci, Cremonesi: a traverso; Rosellini: à traverso

11277 MS.: ba bocha; Mussafia, Lazzeri, Monaci, Cremonesi, Rosellini: la bocha. Lazzeri: basá

11278 Mussafia, Monaci, Cremonesi, Rosellini: gel; Lazzeri: sí gel . . . e' no ve 'l; Mussafia: ve-l; Monaci, Cremonesi: vel; Rosellini: ve'l

11280 Lazzeri: agreá

11282 Mussafia, Monaci, Cremonesi, Rosellini: Por qe (as always)

11283 Mussafia: Dapo' que; Lazzeri, Monaci: Dapò que; Cremonesi: Da po' qe; Rosellini: Da po qe

11284 Mussafia: saura. Mussafia, Cremonesi, Rosellini. Faites li; Lazzeri: faites li . . . saurá; Monaci: Faites li . . . saura a ogn'on

11285 Mussafia: l'i[n]fançon; Lazzeri: l'infançon; Monaci: l'ifançon; Rosellini: li façon (but cf. l. 11176)

11288 Mussafia: civaler; Monaci: Sì qe . . . civeler

11290 Lazzeri: ma' . . . se . . . ; Monaci: se ben non

11294 Mussafia, Lazzeri, Monaci: vailant

11295 Lazzeri: merçi, duné m'aví . . .

11296 Rosellini: entencion

Qe poust dir in verso ni cançon,
La gran poine q'e ò sotenu e·l mon
11300 Por alever ste petit garçon. (395)
De çivaler eo deveni poltron,
E aler a li boscho a durer pasion."*

Rubric 328
Coment Milon parole a·l rois.
Laisse 329

"Entendés moi, çentil enperer,
Dapoisqe de França eo m'avì sevrer,   64rb
11305 E son esté en le bois converser, (400)
A tajer legne e gran torse porter,
Por no(r)ir cest enfant e ma çentil muler.*
E cun tuto ço e no vos quer nojer,
A gran poine ò au da mançer.
11310 Vestra merçi, si como eo sper,* (405)
Vu m'avrés trato de quel penser.*
Omais me conven penser d'altro mester,
Dever pain conbatre e çostrer."*
Adonc Berta vait son filz a gobrer,*

11298 Cremonesi: poüst (as always)
11299 Mussafia, Lazzeri, Monaci, Cremonesi, Rosellini: el mon. Monaci: q'e' ò; Mussafia, Lazzeri, Cremonesi: q'e' ò
Rubric 328 (after 11302) Keller: parolo al; Mussafia ("Handschriftliche Studien II," 309): parole; MS., Cremonesi, Rois
11303 Mussafia, Lazzeri, Monaci, Cremonesi, Rosellini: Entendés moi; Cremonesi, Rosellini: no quote marks
11304 Mussafia, Lazzeri, Monaci: Dapois que; Lazzeri: m'avi
11305 Mussafia, Monaci: E'; Lazzeri: e'
11306 Cremonesi: taier
11307 MS.: noir; Mussafia, Lazzeri, Cremonesi, Rosellini: no[r]ir (emend); Monaci: norir
11309 Lazzeri: aú; Cremonesi: aü (as always); Monaci: aù
11310 Mussafia, Monaci: come. Mussafia, Lazzeri, Cremonesi: e' ò sper; Lazzeri: merçi sí come e' ò . . . ; Rosellini: e ò sper
11311 Mussafia: aurés; Lazzeri, Monaci: aures
11313 Mussafia, Lazzeri, Monaci, Cremonesi: Pain; Holtus, review Cremonesi, 204: Cremonesi should read *Païn* to be consistent
11314 Mussafia: a go[m]brer; Lazzeri, Monaci: a gombrer; Cremonesi: a gobrer; Rosellini: à gobrer

11315 Entro ses braçe R*olandin* lever. (410)
A l'onor Deo, li vor justisier,
De dos ané qe li donò l'inperer,*
Milon vait la dama a sposer,
Veçando la cort e tot li berner.
11320 Gran corte fo e davant e darer, (415)
E l'inperer, qe tant se fi loer,
Quella ovre non volse oblier;
Segondo li conseil de N*aimes* de Baiver,
Elo fe Milon çivaler
11325 E de les autres qi volse arme bailer. (420)
Qi donc veist R*olandin* aler
Por me la sale *et* avant et arer.
Vestu estoit d'un pano a quarter;
Çascun qe le voit, le prent a loer:
11330 "Costu serà li meltre çivaler (425)
Qe se trovase en tot le Batister.
Por mal l'à vezu nasere Sarasin *et* Escler.
El serà colu qe serà avoer,
De tota Françe e serà guerojer,
11335 Contra Pain e Turs et Escler."* (430)

11315 Cremonesi: brace (cf. Holtus, review Cremonesi, 204)
11317 Mussafia: ané . . . dono; Monaci: ané . . . que
11323 Cremonesi: Naime; Rosellini: N[aime]
11326 Cremonesi: veïst (as always)
11327 7 for *et*; Monaci: Por me'
11328 Lazzeri: Vestú; Monaci: Vestù
11330 Lazzeri: Costú será; Monaci: Costù serà
11331 Mussafia, Lazzeri, Monaci, Cremonesi, Rosellini: batister
11332 7 for *et*. Mussafia, Rosellini: l'a vezu; Lazzeri: l'à vezú; Monaci: l'à vezù; Cremonesi: l'à vezu
11333 Mussafia: sera colu'; Lazzeri: será colú; Monaci: serà colù
11334 Lazzeri: será; Monaci: serà